McDougal Littell

THE LANGUAGE OF
LITERATURE

Teacher's Edition

Grade 6

McDougal Littell
A HOUGHTON MIFFLIN COMPANY
Evanston, Illinois • Boston • Dallas

ISBN 0-395-93183-5

2 3 4 5 6 7 8 9 – DWO – 06 05 04 03 02 01 00

Question

Visualize

Evaluate

A passion for reading and skills for success

Good readers are not born—they're made. ***The Language of Literature*** provides students with the tools they need to become thoughtful, active readers.

- **Active reading strategies** before, during, and after the selections teach students how to think as they read and to connect the printed word to their own experiences.
- **An engaging selection of literature**, including classic and contemporary fiction and nonfiction, motivates students to compare selections, authors, and cultures.
- **Comprehensive skills instruction** in reading, writing, critical thinking, and other skills naturally flows from the literature. Assessment instruction and practice prepare students to use those skills on standardized tests.

By teaching students the skills they need to become active readers, ***The Language of Literature*** helps them become successful students.

Predict

Connect

THE LANGUAGE OF LITERATURE

A Passion for Reading
Skills for Success

clarify

Active Readers

Predict

Evaluate

Connect

Reading support from start to finish

The Language of Literature integrates literary skills and active reading skills at the beginning of every selection. When students finish reading, follow-up activities address those same skills.

PREPARING to Read

"I had to leave Brooklyn, on my own, for the first time in my life."

Scout's Honor

Short Story by AVI

Connect to Your Life

Tough Enough? Have you ever been faced with a difficult situation and felt you "chickened out"? Did other people seem braver than you? With a partner, discuss a situation like that from your own life. What lessons might be learned from your experience?

Build Background

CONNECT TO HISTORY Did you know that there are more than 16 million Boy Scouts around the world today? "Scout's Honor" tells about three friends who go camping in an effort to meet a Boy Scout requirement. The first camping group of Boy Scouts was organized in Great Britain in 1907 by a former soldier.

To become Scouts, boys must swear to live by the Scout Oath. In doing so they promise to give their best effort in everything they do. They promise to respect God and their country, including its laws and natural resources. They promise to help others, and to be honest and fair. They promise to care for their bodies and their minds. They also promise to obey the rules of the Scout Law and to honor the Scout Motto—Be Prepared.

WORDS TO KNOW
Vocabulary Preview

bellow	retort	suspicion
envious	rival	vent
immense	smugly	
pummel	straddle	

Focus Your Reading

LITERARY ANALYSIS SETTING The **setting** of a story (or poem or play) is the time and place of the action. The time may be past, present, or future. The place may be real or imaginary. Sometimes setting is very important in a story. It may shape the characters, or even create a conflict. For example, in "Scout's Honor," the main character must prove his camping abilities even though he lives in the heart of the city.

ACTIVE READING VISUALIZING When you form a picture in your mind based on what you are reading, you are **visualizing**. To visualize, pay attention to descriptions of the setting as well as details about what the characters see, hear, and do.

READER'S NOTEBOOK

As you read this story, jot down the details that help you visualize each scene. Next to these details, list which of the five senses they relate to—sight, smell, hearing, taste, or touch. Then describe the picture you visualize. Start with a chart like the one shown here.

Details	Senses
asphalt	touch
tall buildings	sight
roaring cars	hearing

See the Skills Trace at the beginning of the unit for information on TEKS covered in this lesson.

52 UNIT ONE PART 1: THE COURAGE TO BE ME

Thinking about LITERATURE

Connect to the Literature

1. **What Do You Think?** What was your reaction to this story?

Comprehension Check
- How do the **main character** and his friends prepare for their camping trip?
- Name three difficulties they encounter.
- What do the boys agree about at the end of their trip?

Think Critically

2. Why do you think the main character doesn't want to be the first person to suggest going home? Do you think his friends feel the same way? Give examples from the story to support your answer.

3. Do you think the main character will think differently about being "tough enough" after his adventure in Palisades Park?

THINK ABOUT
- the main character's conversation with Max and Horse about the planned trip
- his thoughts just before crossing the bridge
- his friends' reaction when he suggests going home

4. **ACTIVE READING VISUALIZING** How clear were the mental pictures you described in your **READER'S NOTEBOOK**? Discuss with a partner the **details** from your notebook and how they helped you to **visualize**.

Extend Interpretations

5. **COMPARING TEXTS** Scout Law requires the boys in this story to be "loyal, helpful, friendly, courteous, kind, obedient, cheerful, thrifty, brave, clean, and reverent." Evaluate the characters in this story and in "President Cleveland, Where Are You?" Which traits apply to each character? Explain.

6. **Connect to Life** At the end of the story, Max says he wants to quit but isn't tough enough to do it. Do you agree that sometimes it is harder to quit than to keep going? Explain.

Literary Analysis

SETTING The time and place of a story is called the **setting**. Along with facts about time and place, a setting includes **sensory details** that describe sights, sounds, and smells.

There was a small fire, but more light came from our flickering flashlight.

Sensory details affect the moods of the characters. They can have a powerful effect on how the characters grow and change.

Paired Activity Make a chart like the one shown below. Working with a partner, look back through the story and find details that suggest the story's setting. When your chart is complete, discuss your findings with another pair in the class. Consider:

- Which details tell you the most about the story's time and place?
- What parts of the setting are most important to the action of the story?
- How do details about the setting make the story come alive?

Place	Details
Brooklyn	Ebbets Field

Time	Details
1946	

64 UNIT ONE PART 1: THE COURAGE TO BE ME

THE LANGUAGE OF LITERATURE

THE InterActive READER

McDougal Littell

More reading support

The *InterActive Reader*™ is an interactive worktext that coaches students to become better readers. Students can underline, annotate, and mark up featured selections reprinted from *The Language of Literature*.

T4

Question *visualize* *clarify*

comprehensive assessment to help students succeed

The Language of Literature offers a full range of assessment options to meet your needs, including:

- standardized test practice
- reading skills assessment
- portfolio assessment

Assessment Resources

Teacher's Edition
Includes Formal and Informal Assessment Mini-Lessons and project assessments in the Speaking and Listening Projects.

Pupil's Edition
Features assessment practice in the Writing Workshops, Reading and Writing for Assessment, Vocabulary in Action: Assessment Practice, and Comparing Literature: Assessment Practice.

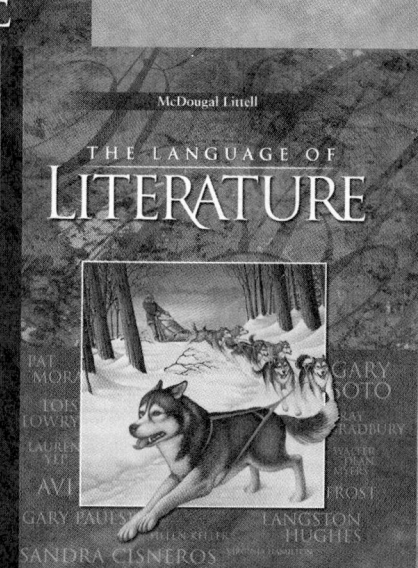

Unit Resource Books
Contain Selection Quizzes.

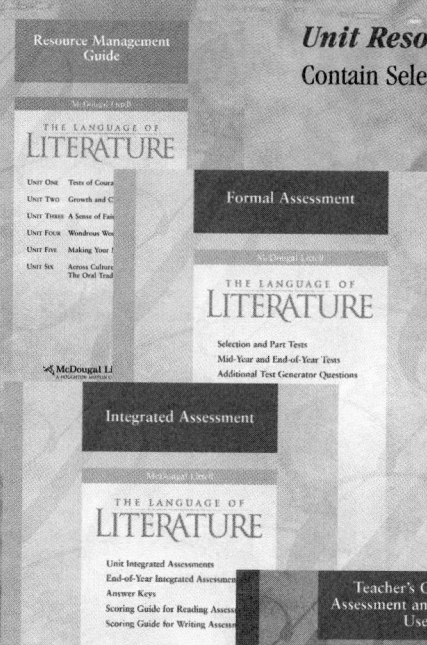

Formal Assessment
Features Selection Tests, Standardized Test Practice, Writing Prompts, and Scoring Rubrics.

Integrated Assessment
Includes Unit Integrated Assessments and an End-of-Year Integrated Assessment.

Test Generator CD-ROM
Provides over 1500 test items and the option to edit or create your own questions and tests.

Teacher's Guide to Assessment and Portfolio Use
Contains portfolio assessment, writing rubrics, and other forms of open-ended assessment.

Predict

Evaluate

Connect

There are three sides to
with The Lang

questioning

researching

comparing

analyzing style

critical thinking

viewing and
representing

writing

evaluating

communicating

Author Study **GARY PAULSEN**

A Writer of Adventure

"If I can write a story, it's because of actually going, being there, and doing those things. It's more than 'Write what you know.' It's kind of like: Write what you are!"

born 1939

CONTENTS

Meet the Author 150
Older Run — ESSAY 154
A Life in the Day of
Gary Paulsen — INTERVIEW ... 163
from Woodsong
— MEMOIR 165
The Author's Style 172
Author Study Project 173
Other Works by
Gary Paulsen 174

LOST AND FOUND

Born into a military family in Minneapolis in 1939, Paulsen was raised by his aunts and grandmother and was shuffled around from school to school. Never a dedicated student, and without a permanent home or friends, young Paulsen found few opportunities in school and couldn't manage to fit in. Luckily, he reached a turning point in his early teens that

changed his life. On a cold winter night he went into a library just to warm up. There a librarian offered him a library card, a book, and a chance to get as many books as he wanted, as long as he brought them back. As Paulsen tells it, "It was as though I had been dying of thirst and the librarian handed me a five-gallon bucket of water."

ALWAYS AN EXPLORER

Through his reading Paulsen developed a taste for action and adventure. In his teens, he worked on a farm, hunted and tracked animals, and even joined a carnival. Not surprisingly, his eagerness to experience new things stayed with him in the years ahead. As an adult, Paulsen held jobs as a teacher, engineer, soldier, actor, rancher, truck driver, professional archer, singer, and sailor. All the while he continued reading and exploring the world through stories. And with each new book and new adventure, Paulsen's desire to tell his own stories grew.

Did You Know?

- Gary Paulsen has written more than 130 books.
- He has raced in the Iditarod twice.
- His wife, Ruth, has illustrated some of his books.
- He once rode his motorcycle from New Mexico to Alaska.
- He travels around the world on his sailboat.
- He has covered 22,000 miles by sled.

His **LIFE** and **TIMES**

| 1939 Born May 17 in Minneapolis, Minnesota | 1953 Receives first library card | 1955 Joins a carnival | 1957 Graduates from high school | 1966 Moves to Hollywood | 1968 Completes first novel, *Some Birds Don't Fly* | 1978 Marries artist Ruth Wright | 1983 Races in his first Iditarod | 1986 *Dogsong* is named a Newbery Honor Book. | 1999 Lives and works mostly on board his sailboat |

| 1940 | 1950 | 1960 | 1970 | 1980 | 1990 | 2000 |

| 1941–1945 United States in World War II | 1951 *Rock-and-roll* is first used as a term to describe music. | 1955 Bus boycott begins in Montgomery, Alabama. | 1965–1973 U.S. ground troops in Vietnam War | 1979 Hostage crisis begins in Iran. | 1987 AIDS quilt is displayed to raise awareness. | 1993 Internet becomes widely available. | 1998 President Clinton is impeached. |

150

GARY PAULSEN 151

T6

Question *Visualize* *Clarify*

every story
uage of Literature!

LITERATURE IN PERFORMANCE

The Language of Literature connects print, audio/video, and computer resources to help students see the full picture of literature. Skills instruction and teaching resources work together to give students a passion for reading and skills for success!

Tools to teach

Literature in Performance Videos

NetActivities CD-ROM

ClassZone website

Audio Library cassettes and CDs

Transparencies and Copymasters

Formal Assessment

Informal Assessment

LaserLinks

The InterActive Reader™

THE LANGUAGE OF LITERATURE
A Passion for Reading
Skills for Success

T7

Predict

 Evaluate

Connect

Resources that put

When you spend your time hunting for teaching resources, you lose precious time for actual teaching. ***The Language of Literature*** gives you some important resources that help make preparing your lessons easier.

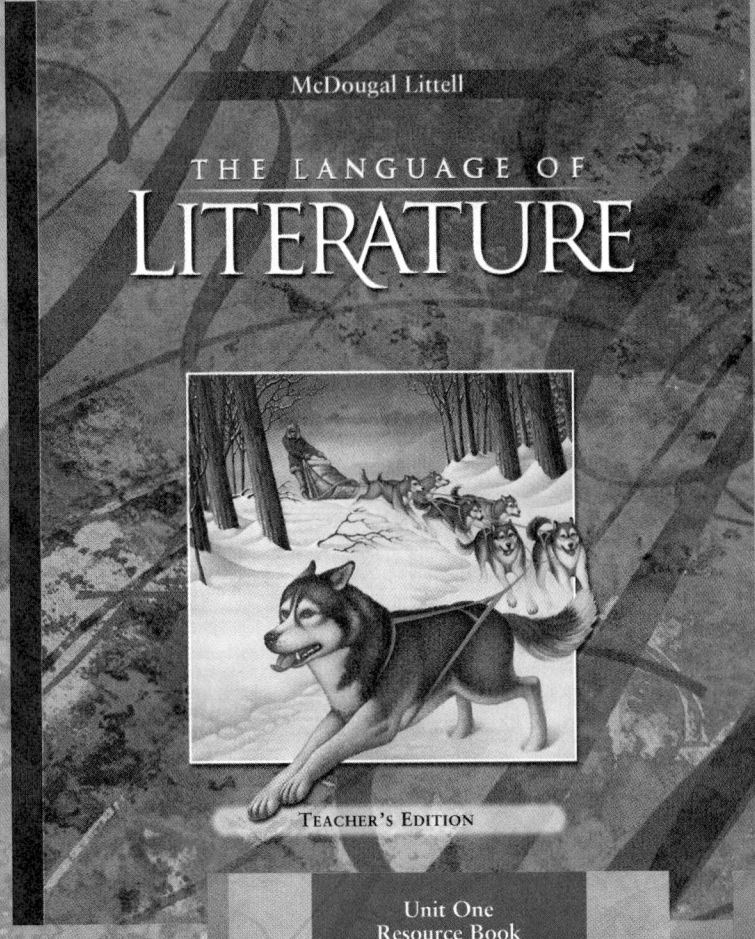

McDougal Littell

THE LANGUAGE OF

LITERATURE

TEACHER'S EDITION

The ***Annotated Teacher's Edition*** is your complete reference manual for *The Language of Literature*. Each page contains teaching strategies, background information, references to ancillary materials, and a wealth of other information right at your fingertips.

The ***Unit Resource Books, Resource Management Guide*** and ***Lesson Plans*** offer teaching support in convenient, portable booklets. The Unit Resource Books, one per unit, provide additional skills work, activities, and exercises. The Resource Management Guide matches the appropriate ancillary materials for every selection. The Lesson Plans outline instructional opportunities from the student and teacher texts, with associated activities available in key ancillary components.

Unit One Resource Book

McDougal Littell

THE LANGUAGE OF

LITERATURE

Family and Community Involvement
Selection Summary
Active Reading SkillBuilder
Literary Analysis SkillBuilder
Words to Know SkillBuilder
Grammar SkillBuilder
Spelling SkillBuilder
Selection Quiz
Building Vocabulary SkillBuilder
Writing Workshop
Rubric for Evaluation
Reflect and Assess
Answer Keys

Resource Management Guide

McDougal Littell

THE LANGUAGE OF

LITERATURE

McDougal Littell
A HOUGHTON MIFFLIN COMPANY
Evanston, Illinois   Boston   Dallas

Question Visualize clarify

teaching first

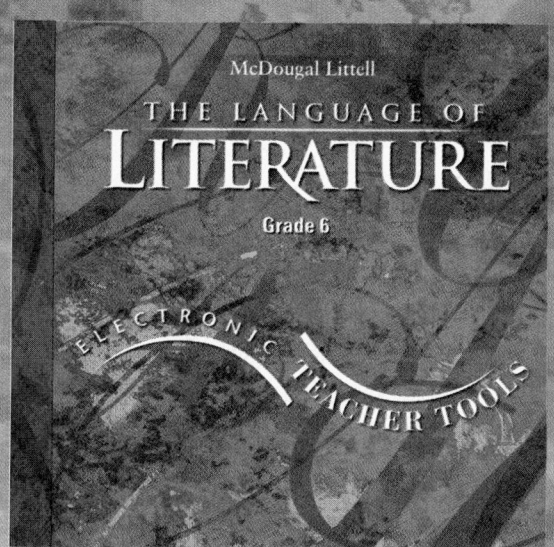

The **Electronic Teacher Tools** CD-ROM puts many of the teaching resources available for *The Language of Literature* on one convenient disc that you can use in class or from the comfort of your own home. Search for documents by resource, chapter, or keyword, and print them for use in your classroom.

The Internet-based **Online Lesson Planner** makes it easy to plan or check your lessons anytime, anywhere. Choose your ancillaries, your class times, and other options to customize your lesson plans to meet your needs.

THE LANGUAGE OF LITERATURE

A passion for Reading

skills for success

complete Program Components

Core Components

Pupil's Edition
Teacher's Edition

Teaching Resources

Reaching Middle School Readers
Resource Management Guide
Organizational guide for each level that matches ancillary materials for each selection

Unit Resource Books
Complete resources for each selection, including reading, vocabulary, grammar, spelling, writing, and literature support plus annotated models and rubrics for evaluation

Lesson Planning Guides

Students Acquiring English
Teacher's Sourcebook for Language Development

Spanish Study Guide
Selection summaries in Spanish, ESL Strategies

Assessment
Teacher's Guide to Assessment and Portfolio Use
Portfolio Assessment, Writing Rubrics, and other open-ended forms of assessment

Formal Assessment
Selection Tests, Standardized Test Practice, Writing Prompts, Scoring Rubrics

Integrated Assessment

Skills Transparencies and Copymasters
- Writing
- Grammar
- Vocabulary (includes spelling practice)
- Communications (includes transparencies for Speaking, Listening, and for Viewing Fine Art)
- Literary Analysis
- Reading and Critical Thinking

The InterActive Reader™
An interactive worktext that builds reading comprehension

Technology Resources

Literature in Performance
Video Series
Help students compare written selections to adaptations of great literature.

Contents include:
- **Amelia Earhart,** documentary
- **All Summer in a Day,** adaptation of Bradbury's story
- **Pool Party,** adaptation of Soto's story
- **Words on a Page,** adaptation of Leckie's drama
- **The Icarus Myth,** 3 versions
- **The Cow-Tail Switch,** storytelling

Website: www.mcdougallittell.com
A treasury of online resources, including selection support, links, activities, and more

NetActivities (CD-ROM) Helps students extend learning and explore favorite authors in greater depth through interactive activities and links to the Internet

Audio Library (audio CD and cassette)
ClassZone (website)
LaserLinks (videodisc)
Writing Coach (CD-ROM)
Electronic Teacher Tools (CD-ROM)
Test Generator (CD-ROM)
Power Presentations (CD-ROM)
Online Lesson Planner (website)

THE LANGUAGE OF LITERATURE
A Passion for Reading
skills for success

McDougal Littell

THE LANGUAGE OF
LITERATURE

Senior Consultants

Arthur N. Applebee

Andrea B. Bermúdez

Sheridan Blau

Rebekah Caplan

Peter Elbow

Susan Hynds

Judith A. Langer

James Marshall

McDougal Littell

A HOUGHTON MIFFLIN COMPANY

Evanston, Illinois • Boston • Dallas

Acknowledgments

Lensey Namioka: "The All-American Slurp" by Lensey Namioka, from *Visions,* edited by Donald R. Gallo. Copyright © 1987 by Lensey Namioka. Reprinted by permission of Lensey Namioka. All rights are reserved by the author.

Excerpt from "The All-American Slurp" by Lensey Namioka, from *Visions,* edited by Donald R. Gallo. Copyright © 1987 by Lensey Namioka. Reprinted by permission of Lensey Namioka. All rights are reserved by the author.

Unit One

Susan Bergholz Literary Services: "Eleven," from *Woman Hollering Creek and Other Stories* by Sandra Cisneros, published by Vintage Books, a division of Random House, Inc., and originally in hardcover by Random House, Inc. Copyright © 1991 by Sandra Cisneros. Reprinted by permission of Susan Bergholz Literary Services, New York. All rights reserved.

Highlights for Children: "Who's the New Kid?" by Lois Lowry, *Highlights for Children,* January 1994. Copyright © 1994 by Highlights for Children, Inc., Columbus, Ohio. Reprinted by permission.

Pantheon Books: "President Cleveland, Where Are You?," from *Eight Plus One* by Robert Cormier. Copyright © 1980 by Robert Cormier. Reprinted by permission of Pantheon Books, a division of Random House, Inc.

Jay D. Johnson: "Trading Card Talk" by Jay Johnson, *Boys' Life,* May 1994, published by the Boy Scouts of America. Reprinted by permission of Jay D. Johnson.

McIntosh and Otis: "Scout's Honor" by Avi, from *When I Was Your Age,* edited by Amy Ehrlich, published by Candlewick Press. Copyright © 1996 by Avi. Reprinted by permission of McIntosh and Otis, Inc.

Excerpt from "Scout's Honor" by Avi, from *When I Was Your Age,* edited by Amy Ehrlich, published by Candlewick Press. Copyright © 1996 by Avi. Reprinted by permission of McIntosh and Otis, Inc.

Continued on page R129

ISBN 0-395-93169-X

2 3 4 5 6 7 8 9 – DWO – 05 04 03 02 01 00

Senior Consultants

The senior consultants guided the conceptual development for *The Language of Literature* series. They participated actively in shaping prototype materials for major components, and they reviewed completed prototypes and/or completed units to ensure consistency with current research and the philosophy of the series.

Arthur N. Applebee Professor of Education, State University of New York at Albany; Director, Center for the Learning and Teaching of Literature; Senior Fellow, Center for Writing and Literacy

Andrea B. Bermúdez Professor of Studies in Language and Culture; Director, Research Center for Language and Culture; Chair, Foundations and Professional Studies, University of Houston–Clear Lake

Sheridan Blau Senior Lecturer in English and Education and former Director of Composition, University of California at Santa Barbara; Director, South Coast Writing Project; Director, Literature Institute for Teachers; Vice President, National Council of Teachers of English

Rebekah Caplan High School and Middle Grades English/Language Arts Specialist for the New Standards Project, National Center on Education and the Economy, Washington, D.C.; served on the California State English Assessment Development Team for Language Arts.

Peter Elbow Professor of English, University of Massachusetts at Amherst; Fellow, Bard Center for Writing and Thinking

Susan Hynds Professor and Director of English Education, Syracuse University, Syracuse, New York

Judith A. Langer Professor of Education, State University of New York at Albany; Co-director, Center for the Learning and Teaching of Literature; Senior Fellow, Center for Writing and Literacy

James Marshall Professor of English and English Education, University of Iowa, Iowa City

Contributing Consultants

Jeffrey N. Golub Assistant Professor of English Education, University of South Florida, Tampa

William L. McBride Reading and Curriculum Specialist; former middle and high school English instructor

Sharon Sicinski-Skeans, Ph.D. Assistant Professor of Reading, University of Houston–Clear Lake

Multicultural Advisory Board

The multicultural advisors reviewed literature selections for appropriate content and made suggestions for teaching lessons in a multicultural classroom.

Dr. Joyce M. Bell Chairperson, English Department, Townview Magnet Center, Dallas, Texas

Dr. Eugenia W. Collier author; lecturer; Chairperson, Department of English and Language Arts; teacher of Creative Writing and American Literature, Morgan State University, Maryland

Kathleen S. Fowler President, Palm Beach County Council of Teachers of English, Boca Raton Middle School, Boca Raton, Florida

Noreen M. Rodriguez Trainer for Hillsborough County School District's Staff Development Division, independent consultant, Gaither High School, Tampa, Florida

Michelle Dixon Thompson Seabreeze High School, Daytona Beach, Florida

Teacher Review Panels

The following educators provided ongoing review during the development of the tables of contents, lesson design, and key components of the program.

TEXAS

Gloria Anderson Language Arts Department Chairperson, Campbell Middle School, Cypress Fairbanks Independent School District

Gwen Ferguson Assistant Principal, Northwood Middle School, North Forest Independent School District

Rebecca Hadavi Parkland Middle School, Ysleta Independent School District

Patricia Jackson Pearce Middle School, Austin Independent School District

Sandy Mattox Coppell Middle School North, Coppell Independent School District

Adrienne C. Myers Foster Middle School, Longview Independent School District

Pam Potts Clute Intermediate School, Brazosport Independent School District

Frank Westermann Jackson Middle School, North East Independent School District

Bessie B. Wilson W. E. Greiner Middle School, Dallas Independent School District

continued on page R144

Manuscript Reviewers

The following educators reviewed prototype lessons and tables of contents during the development of The Language of Literature program.

William A. Battaglia Herman Intermediate School, San Jose, California

Hugh Delle Broadway McCullough High School, The Woodlands, Texas

Robert M. Bucan National Mine Middle School, Ishpeming, Michigan

Ann E. Clayton Department Chair for Language Arts, Rockway Middle School, Miami, Florida

Linda C. Dahl National Mine Middle School, Ishpeming, Michigan

Shirley Herzog Reading Department Coordinator, Fairfield Middle School, Fairfield, Ohio

continued on page R145

Student Panel

LITERATURE REVIEWERS

The following students read and evaluated selections to assess their appeal for the sixth-grade.

Ted Burke East Aurora Middle School, East Aurora, New York

Ian Graham Churchill Road Elementary School, McLean, Virginia

Melissa Hall Frenship Intermediate School, Wolfforth, Texas

Stephanie Liberati Hampton Middle School, Allison Park, Pennsylvania

Bridget McGuire St. John of the Cross, Western Springs, Illinois

Eileen Pablos-Velez Henry H. Filer Middle School, Hialeah, Florida

Nicole Putnam Rockway Middle School, Miami, Florida

Eli Shlaes Davidson Middle School, San Rafael, California

Theresa Sullivan St. Ann's School, Wilmington, Delaware

Christine Tran Foothill Middle School, Walnut Creek, California

Alexis Wong Foothill Middle School, Walnut Creek, California

ACTIVE READERS

The following students participated in the development of The Active Reader: Skills and Strategies pages in this book:

Tiffany Providence

Jay Pepitone

Ryane Griffis

Sean Mtunis

Carine Miranda

Michael Beaupre

Ricky Wong

Jillian DeBaie

Orlando Castillo

Brittany Regan

Talisa Murray

Chris McGarry

STUDENT MODEL WRITERS

The following students wrote the student models for Writing Workshop pages that appear in this book:

Valenne Ogden

Samantha Piwinski

Carolyn Nash

Tiffany George

M. McGoff

Weston Sager

Ben Wright

Jared Taitel

Katherine Helming

Yoshio Adach

THE *Language* OF LITERATURE

❯ O V E R V I E W

UNIT SIX Across Cultures: The Oral Tradition

STUDENT   **Glossary of Literary and Reading Terms**
RESOURCE   **Writing Handbook**
BANK   **Grammar Handbook**
       Spelling Handbook
       Communication Handbook

Literature Connections

Each of the books in the *Literature Connections* series combines a novel or play with related readings —poems, stories, plays, personal essays, articles—that add new perspectives on the theme or subject matter of the longer work.

The House of Dies Drear
BY VIRGINIA HAMILTON

WITH THESE RELATED READINGS

Valerie Worth	**Haunted House**
Walter B. Gibson	**The House on the Island**
Jim Haskins	*from* **Get on Board: The Story of the Underground Railroad**
Alice Childress	**When the Rattlesnake Sounds**
Robert Hayden	**Runagate Runagate**
William M. Dorr	**The Secret Room**
Laura P. McCarty	**Bound for Freedom**

Listed below are some of the most popular choices to accompany the Grade 6 anthology:

Number the Stars
BY LOIS LOWRY

Taking Sides
BY GARY SOTO

Dogsong
BY GARY PAULSEN

The Glory Field
BY WALTER DEAN MYERS

Tuck Everlasting*
BY NATALIE BABBITT

Maniac Magee
BY JERRY SPINELLI

The Cay
BY THEODORE TAYLOR

The Call of the Wild*
BY JACK LONDON

Dragonwings
BY LAURENCE YEP

Homecoming
BY CYNTHIA VOIGHT

Roll of Thunder, Hear My Cry*
BY MILDRED D. TAYLOR

*A Spanish version is also available.

UNIT ONE
PAGE 18

Tests of Courage

UNIT TWO
PAGE 186

Growth and Change

UNIT THREE
PAGE 314

A Sense of Fairness

UNIT FOUR
PAGE 440

Wondrous Worlds

CONTENTS **xvii**

ACROSS CULTURES: THE ORAL TRADITION
For more stories related to the unit theme, see page 844.

UNIT SIX
PAGE 764

Across Cultures:
THE ORAL TRADITION

Student *Resource Bank*

Selections by Genre

Poetry

Song

Drama

Classical Myths

Oral Tradition

Special Features in This Book

Author Studies

Learning the Language of Literature

The Active Reader: Skills and Strategies

Comparing Literature

Real World Links

Writing Workshops

Communication Workshops

Building Vocabulary

Assessment Pages

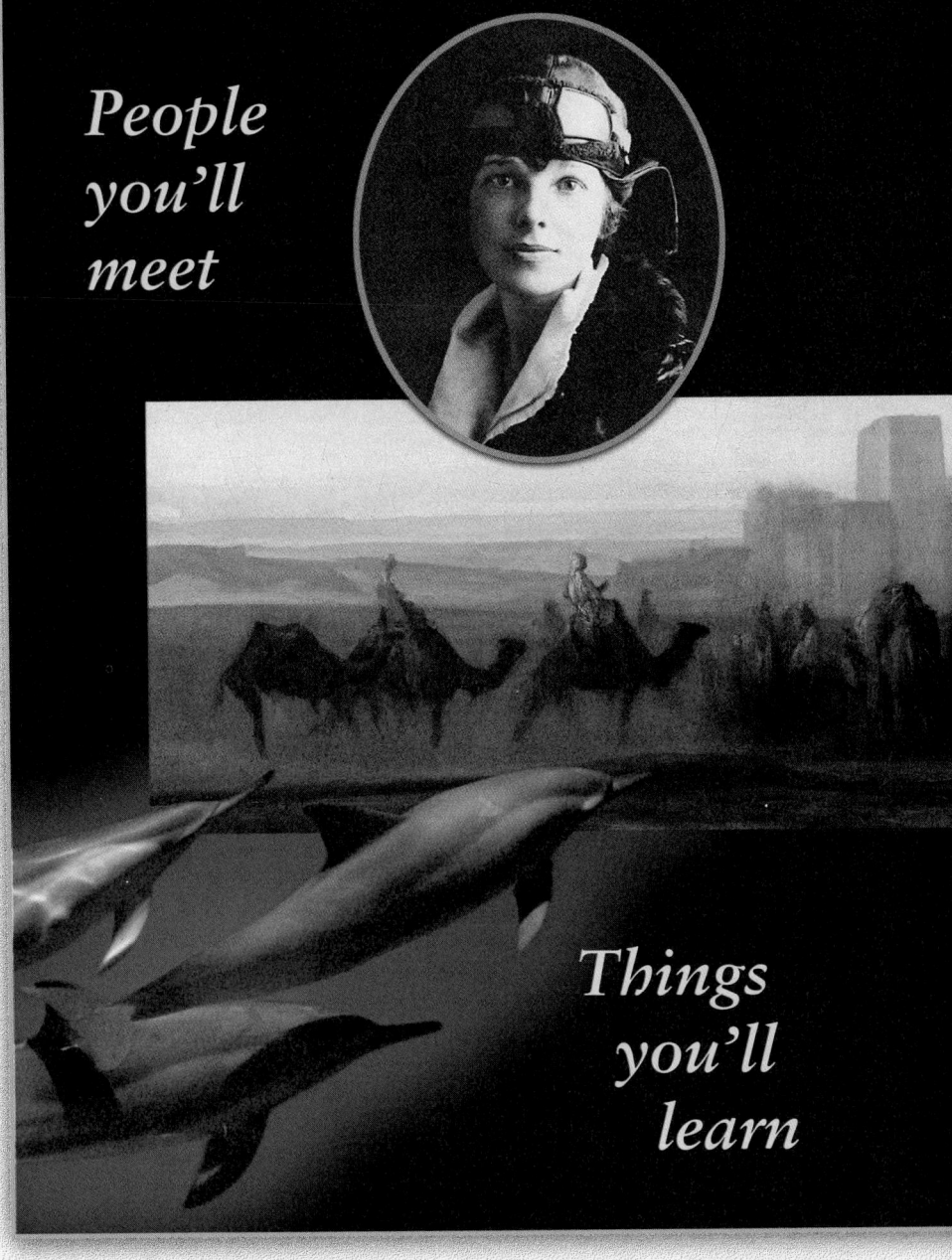

Becoming AN ACTIVE READER

People you'll meet

Things you'll learn

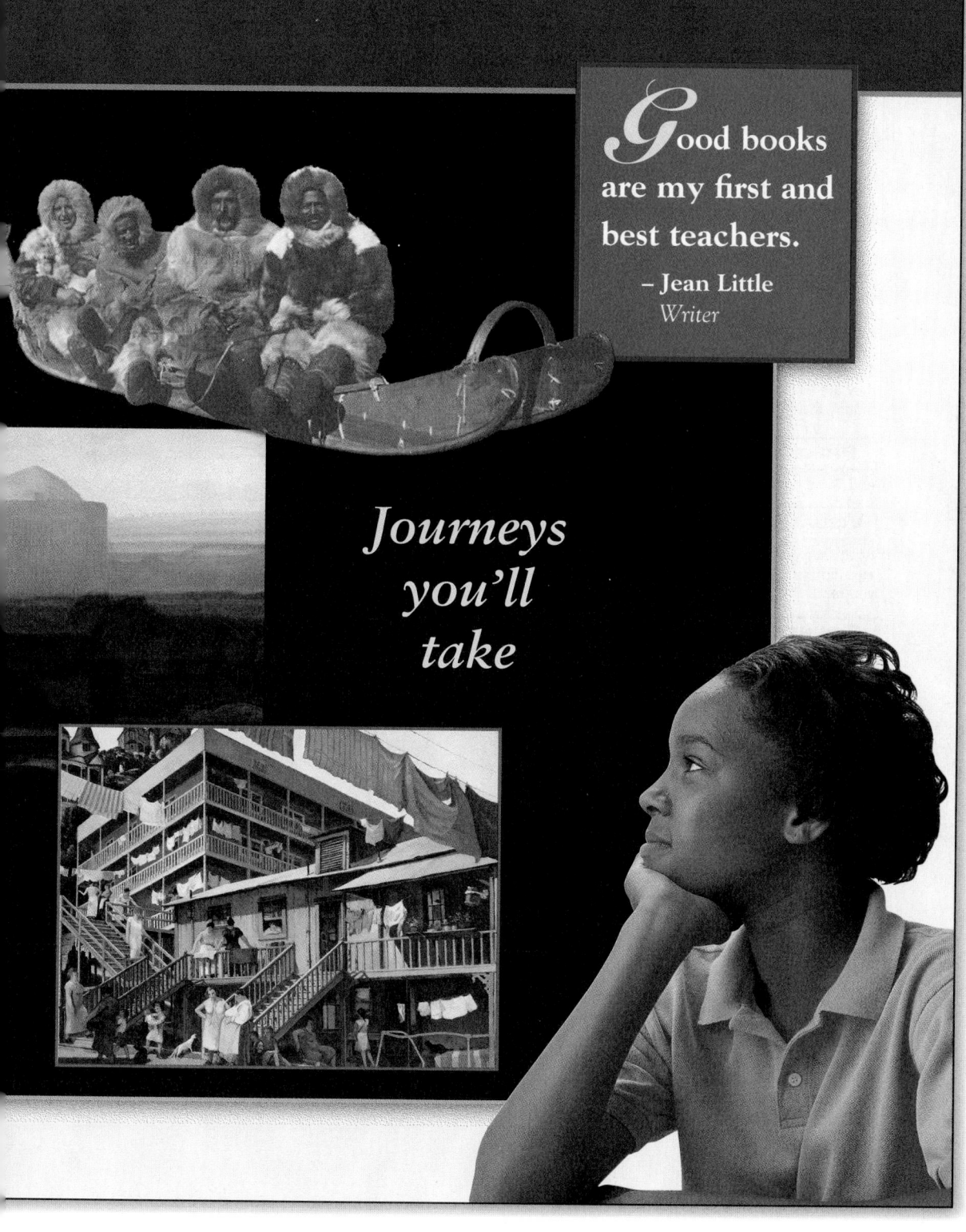

*G*ood books
are my first and
best teachers.

– **Jean Little**
Writer

*Journeys
you'll
take*

Strategies FOR READING

Becoming an Active Reader involves more than just enjoying the power of storytelling. To understand and appreciate the literature in this book, you'll need to learn and apply the reading strategies listed here. As you begin to learn the strategies and how to use them, stop from time to time to **monitor** how well they are working for you. If it helps your reading, modify the strategies as necessary to suit your needs.

PREDICT — Try to figure out what will happen next and how the selection might end. Read on to see how accurate your guesses were.

VISUALIZE — Visualize characters, events, and setting to help you understand what's happening. When you read nonfiction, pay attention to the images that form in your mind as you read.

CONNECT — Connect personally with what you're reading. Think of similarities between the descriptions in the selection and what you have personally experienced, heard about, and read about.

QUESTION — Question what happens while you read. Searching for reasons behind events and characters' feelings can help you feel closer to what you are reading.

CLARIFY — Stop occasionally to review what you understand, and expect to have your understanding change and develop as you read on. Use resources to help you clarify your understanding. Reread when necessary.

EVALUATE — Form opinions about what you read, both while you're reading and after you've finished. Develop your own ideas about characters and events.

On the next page, you will see how two readers applied these strategies to the story "The All-American Slurp."

Introducing the READING MODEL

Alongside "The All-American Slurp" are the comments of two sixth-grade students, **Tiffany Providence** and **Jay Pepitone**. Their comments reflect the kind of thinking that active readers do as they read. You'll notice that both Tiffany and Jay quite naturally used the reading strategies introduced on this page.

To get the most from this model, read the story first, jotting down your own responses on a piece of paper. (Cover up the side comments with a sheet of paper if you're tempted to peek.) Then read Tiffany's and Jay's responses and compare them with your own.

The All-American SLURP

by Lensey Namioka

The first time our family was invited out to dinner in America, we disgraced ourselves while eating celery. We had emigrated to this country from China, and during our early days here we had a hard time with American table manners.

In China we never ate celery raw, or any other kind of vegetable raw. We always had to disinfect the vegetables in boiling water first. When we were presented with our first relish tray, the raw celery caught us unprepared.

We had been invited to dinner by our neighbors, the Gleasons. After arriving at the house, we shook hands with our hosts and packed ourselves into a sofa. As our family of four sat stiffly in a row, my younger brother and I stole glances at our parents for a clue as to what to do next.

Tiffany: "Stole glances"? I guess that means they looked at each other when the others weren't looking.
CLARIFYING

Mrs. Gleason offered the relish tray to Mother. The tray looked pretty, with its tiny red radishes, curly sticks of carrots, and long, slender stalks of pale green celery. "Do try some of the celery, Mrs. Lin," she said. "It's from a local farmer, and it's sweet."

Mother picked up one of the green stalks, and Father followed suit. Then I picked up a stalk, and my brother did too. So there we sat, each with a stalk of celery in our right hand.

Jay: This doesn't make sense to me: "Father followed suit." How does that fit in?
QUESTIONING

Mrs. Gleason kept smiling. "Would you like to try some of the dip, Mrs. Lin? It's my own recipe: sour cream and onion flakes, with a dash of Tabasco sauce."

Most Chinese don't care for dairy products, and in those days I wasn't even ready to drink fresh milk. Sour cream sounded perfectly revolting. Our family shook our heads in unison.

Jay: Don't know what unison means. I think it means … like … "together" because it says "Our family…."
CLARIFYING

Mrs. Gleason went off with the relish tray to the other guests, and we carefully watched to see what they did. Everyone seemed to eat the raw vegetables quite happily.

Mother took a bite of her celery. *Crunch.* "It's not bad!" she whispered.

Father took a bite of his celery. *Crunch.* "Yes, it is good," he said, looking surprised.

Tiffany: How come they didn't eat raw vegetables?
QUESTIONING

I took a bite, and then my brother. *Crunch, crunch.* It was more than good; it was delicious. Raw celery has a slight sparkle, a zingy taste that you don't get in cooked celery. When Mrs. Gleason came around with the relish tray, we each took another stalk of celery, except my brother. He took two.

There was only one problem: long strings ran through the length of the stalk, and they got caught in my teeth. When I help my mother in the kitchen, I always pull the strings out before slicing celery.

I pulled the strings out of my stalk. *Z-z-zip, z-z-zip.* My brother followed suit. *Z-z-zip, z-z-zip, z-z-zip.* To my left, my parents were taking care of their own stalks. *Z-z-zip, z-z-zip, z-z-zip.*

Suddenly I realized that there was dead silence except for our zipping. Looking up, I saw that the eyes of everyone in the room were on our family. Mr. and Mrs. Gleason, their daughter Meg, who was my friend, and their neighbors the Badels—they were all staring at us as we busily pulled the strings of our celery.

That wasn't the end of it. Mrs. Gleason announced that dinner was served and invited us to the dining table. It was lavishly covered with platters of food, but we couldn't see any chairs around the table. So we helpfully carried over some dining chairs and sat down. All the other guests just stood there.

Mrs. Gleason bent down and whispered to us, "This is a buffet dinner. You help yourselves to some food and eat it in the living room."

Our family beat a retreat back to the sofa as if chased by enemy soldiers. For the rest of the evening, too mortified to go back to the dining table, I nursed a bit of potato salad on my plate.

Next day Meg and I got on the school bus together. I wasn't sure how she would feel about me after the spectacle our family made at the party. But she was just the same as usual, and the only reference she made to the party was, "Hope you and your folks got enough to eat last night. You certainly didn't take very much. Mom never tries to figure out how much food to prepare. She just puts everything on the table and hopes for the best."

I began to relax. The Gleasons' dinner party wasn't so different from a Chinese meal after all. My mother also puts everything on the table and hopes for the best.

Meg was the first friend I had made after we came to America. I eventually got acquainted with a few other kids in school, but Meg was still the only real friend I had.

My brother didn't have any problems making friends. He spent all his time with some boys who were teaching him baseball, and in no time he could speak English much faster than I could—not better, but faster.

I worried more about making mistakes, and I spoke carefully, making sure I could say everything right before opening my mouth. At least I had a better accent than my parents, who never really got rid of their Chinese accent, even years later. My parents had both studied English in school before coming to America, but what they had studied was mostly written English, not spoken.

Father's approach to English was a scientific one. Since Chinese verbs have no tense, he was fascinated by the way English verbs changed form according to whether they were in the present, past imperfect, perfect, pluperfect, future, or future perfect tense. He was always making diagrams of verbs and their inflections, and he

Tiffany: Why would they pull out the little strings in the celery?
QUESTIONING

Jay: Whenever I eat at anybody else's house, I eat slower than I usually do. That way, I can make sure nothing flies out of my mouth and I don't make any noise while I'm chewing.
CONNECTING

Tiffany: Was the brother's name mentioned before?
CLARIFYING

Jay: I wonder why he didn't learn to play baseball in China. I wonder if they don't have it there.
QUESTIONING

THE ALL-AMERICAN SLURP   **7**

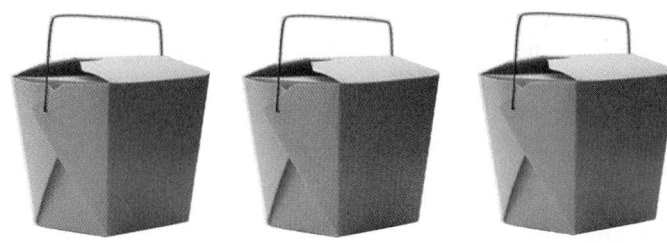

looked for opportunities to show off his mastery of the pluperfect and future perfect tenses, his two favorites. "I shall have finished my project by Monday," he would say smugly.

Mother's approach was to memorize lists of polite phrases that would cover all possible social situations. She was constantly muttering things like "I'm fine, thank you. And you?" Once she accidentally stepped on someone's foot and hurriedly blurted, "Oh, that's quite all right!" Embarrassed by her slip, she resolved to do better next time. So when someone stepped on her foot, she cried, "You're welcome!"

Jay: This is kind of funny—that she stepped on someone's foot and said "That's quite all right!" Same with saying "You're welcome!"
EVALUATING

In our own different ways, we made progress in learning English. But I had another worry, and that was my appearance. My brother didn't have to worry, since Mother bought him blue jeans for school, and he dressed like all the other boys. But she insisted that girls had to wear skirts. By the time she saw that Meg and the other girls were wearing jeans, it was too late. My school clothes were bought already, and we didn't have money left to buy new outfits for me. We had too many other things to buy first, like furniture, pots, and pans.

The first time I visited Meg's house, she took me upstairs to her room, and I wound up trying on her clothes. We were pretty much the same size, since Meg was shorter and thinner than average. Maybe that's how we became friends in the first place. Wearing Meg's jeans and T-shirt, I looked at myself in the mirror. I could almost pass for an American—from the back, anyway. At least the kids in school wouldn't stop and stare at me in the hallways, which was what they did when they saw me in my white blouse and navy blue skirt that went a couple of inches below the knees.

When Meg came to my house, I invited her to try on my Chinese dresses, the ones with a high collar and slits up the sides. Meg's eyes were bright as she looked at herself in the mirror. She struck several sultry poses, and we nearly fell over laughing.

The dinner party at the Gleasons' didn't stop my growing friendship with Meg. Things were getting better for me in other ways too. Mother finally bought me some jeans at the end of the month, when Father got his paycheck. She wasn't in any hurry about buying them at first, until I worked on her. This is what I did. Since we didn't have a car in those days, I often ran down to the neighborhood store to pick up things for her. The groceries cost less at a big supermarket, but the closest one was many blocks away. One day, when she ran out of flour, I offered to borrow a bike from our neighbor's son and buy a ten-pound bag of flour at the big supermarket. I mounted the boy's bike and waved to Mother. "I'll be back in five minutes!"

Before I started pedaling, I heard her voice behind me. "You can't go out in public like that! People can see all the way up to your thighs!"

"I'm sorry," I said innocently. "I thought you were in a hurry to get the flour." For dinner we were going to have pot-stickers (fried Chinese dumplings), and we needed a lot of flour.

"Couldn't you borrow a girl's bicycle?" complained Mother. "That way your skirt won't be pushed up."

"There aren't too many of those around," I said. "Almost all the girls wear jeans while riding a bike, so they don't see any point buying a girl's bike."

Jay: The setting ... the time must be pretty far back from when I was born because they didn't have a car.
EVALUATING

Tiffany: Was she wearing a dress while riding a bike?
QUESTIONING

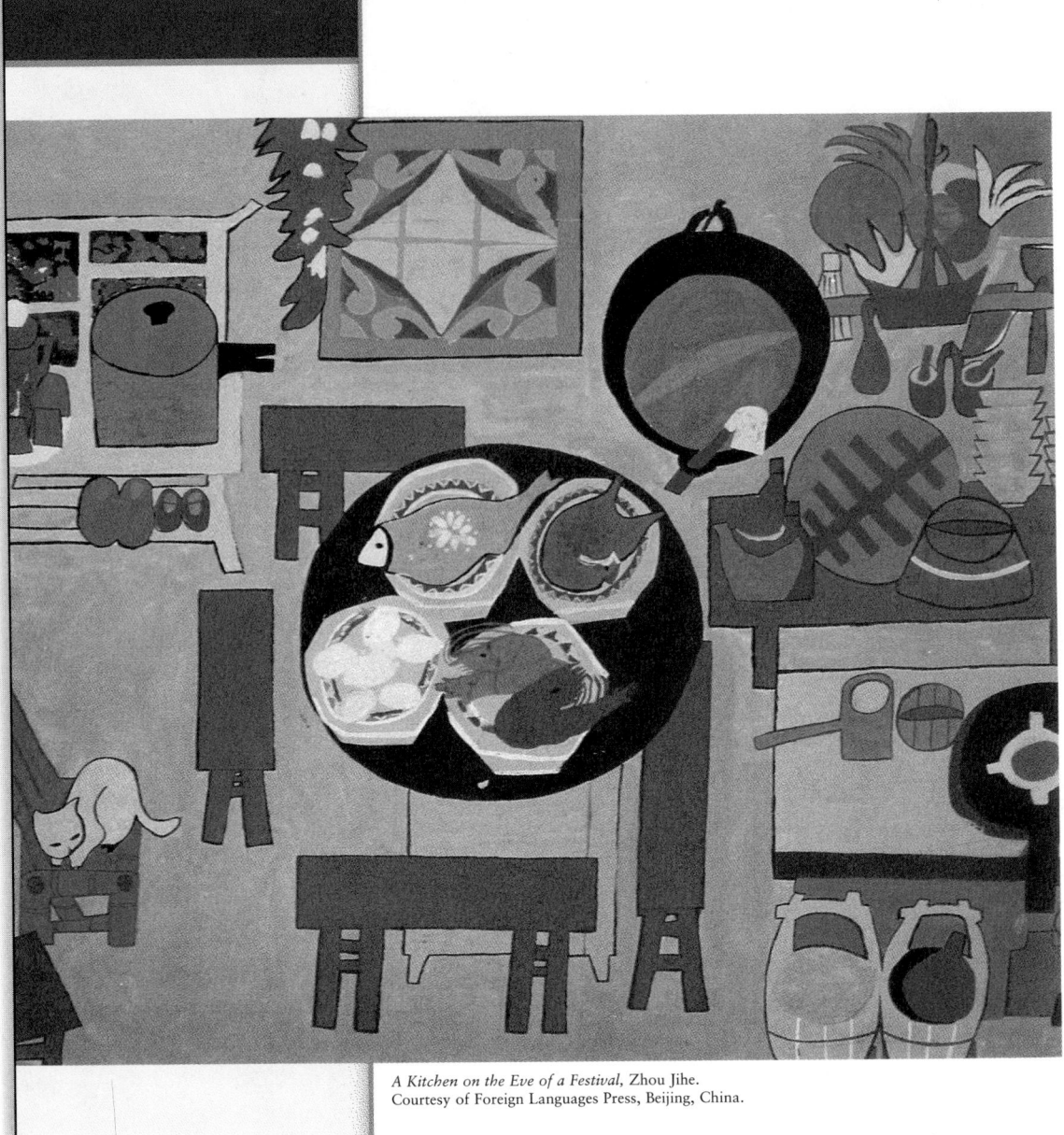

A Kitchen on the Eve of a Festival, Zhou Jihe.
Courtesy of Foreign Languages Press, Beijing, China.

We didn't eat pot-stickers that evening, and Mother was thoughtful. Next day we took the bus downtown, and she bought me a pair of jeans. In the same week, my brother made the baseball team of his junior high school, Father started taking driving lessons, and Mother discovered rummage sales. We soon got all the furniture we needed, plus a dart board and a 1,000-piece jigsaw puzzle (fourteen hours later, we discovered that it was a 999-piece jigsaw puzzle). There was hope that the Lins might become a normal American family after all.

Then came our dinner at the Lakeview Restaurant.

The Lakeview was an expensive restaurant, one of those places where a headwaiter dressed in tails conducted you to your seat, and the only light came from candles and flaming desserts. In one corner of the room a lady harpist played tinkling melodies.

Father wanted to celebrate, because he had just been promoted. He worked for an electronics company, and after his English started improving, his superiors decided to appoint him to a position more suited to his training. The promotion not only brought a higher salary but was also a tremendous boost to his pride.

Up to then we had eaten only in Chinese restaurants. Although my brother and I were becoming fond of hamburgers, my parents didn't care much for Western food, other than chow mein.

But this was a special occasion, and Father asked his coworkers to recommend a really elegant restaurant. So there we were at the Lakeview, stumbling after the headwaiter in the murky dining room.

At our table we were handed our menus, and they were so big that to read mine I almost had to stand up again. But why bother? It was mostly in French, anyway.

Father, being an engineer, was always systematic. He took out a pocket French dictionary. "They told me that most of the items would be in French, so I came prepared." He even had a pocket flashlight, the size of a marking pen. While Mother held the flashlight over the menu, he looked up the items that were in French.

"*Pâté en croûte*," he muttered. "Let's see . . . *pâté* is paste . . . *croûte* is crust . . . hmm . . . a paste in crust."

The waiter stood looking patient. I squirmed and died at least fifty times.

Tiffany: *Her mother finally got her a pair of jeans!*
EVALUATING

Jay: *Father started taking driving lessons, so I guess that means they'll get a car.*
CLARIFYING

Jay: *Maybe they live in the city, because they're going to a big, expensive restaurant with all the waiters dressed in suits.*
EVALUATING

Jay: *Systematic—here's another word I don't know.*
QUESTIONING

At long last Father gave up. "Why don't we just order four complete dinners at random?" he suggested.

"Isn't that risky?" asked Mother. "The French eat some rather peculiar things, I've heard."

"A Chinese can eat anything a Frenchman can eat," Father declared.

The soup arrived in a plate. How do you get soup up from a plate? I glanced at the other diners, but the ones at the nearby tables were not on their soup course, while the more distant ones were invisible in the darkness.

Tiffany: Her parents studied Western what? **CLARIFYING**

Fortunately my parents had studied books on Western etiquette before they came to America. "Tilt your plate," whispered my mother. "It's easier to spoon the soup up that way."

Jay: Here's another word I don't know—etiquette—but I think it means "manners" because they're telling her it's easier to spoon the soup that way. **CLARIFYING**

She was right. Tilting the plate did the trick. But the etiquette book didn't say anything about what you did after the soup reached your lips. As any respectable Chinese knows, the correct way to eat your soup is to slurp. This helps to cool the liquid and prevent you from burning your lips. It also shows your appreciation.

We showed our appreciation. *Shloop,* went my father. *Shloop,* went my mother. *Shloop, shloop,* went my brother, who was the hungriest.

The lady harpist stopped playing to take a rest. And in the silence, our family's consumption of soup suddenly seemed unnaturally loud. You know how it sounds on a rocky beach when the tide goes out and the water drains from all those little pools? They go *shloop, shloop, shloop.* That was the Lin family, eating soup.

Jay: They're all going to start slurping the soup, and everyone's going to stop eating and look at them. **PREDICTING**

At the next table a waiter was pouring wine. When a large

shloop reached him, he froze. The bottle continued to pour, and red wine flooded the tabletop and into the lap of a customer. Even the customer didn't notice anything at first, being also hypnotized by the *shloop, shloop, shloop.*

It was too much. "I need to go to the toilet," I mumbled, jumping to my feet. A waiter, sensing my urgency, quickly directed me to the ladies' room.

I splashed cold water on my burning face, and as I dried myself with a paper towel, I stared into the mirror. In this perfumed ladies' room, with its pink-and-silver wallpaper and marbled sinks, I looked completely out of place. What was I doing here? What was our family doing in the Lakeview Restaurant? In America?

The door to the ladies' room opened. A woman came in and glanced curiously at me. I retreated into one of the toilet cubicles and latched the door.

Time passed—maybe half an hour, maybe an hour. Then I heard the door open again, and my mother's voice. "Are you in there? You're not sick, are you?"

There was real concern in her voice. A girl can't leave her family just because they slurp their soup. Besides, the toilet cubicle had a few drawbacks as a permanent residence. "I'm all right," I said, undoing the latch.

Mother didn't tell me how the rest of the dinner went, and I didn't want to know. In the weeks following, I managed to push the whole thing into the back of my mind, where it jumped out at me only a few times a day. Even now, I turn hot all over when I think of the Lakeview Restaurant.

Jay: *That's what I would do!*
CONNECTING

Tiffany: *The narrator stayed in the bathroom all through dinnertime!*
CLARIFYING

Jay: *I don't think I'd be able to really forget about something like that.*
CONNECTING/EVALUATING

But by the time we had been in this country for three months, our family was definitely making progress toward becoming Americanized. I remember my parents' first PTA meeting. Father wore a neat suit and tie, and Mother put on her first pair of high heels. She stumbled only once. They met my homeroom teacher and beamed as she told them that I would make honor roll soon at the rate I was going. Of course Chinese etiquette forced Father to say that I was a very stupid girl and Mother to protest that the teacher was showing favoritism toward me. But I could tell they were both very proud.

The day came when my parents announced that they wanted to give a dinner party. We had invited Chinese friends to eat with us before, but this dinner was going to be different. In addition to a Chinese-American family, we were going to invite the Gleasons.

"Gee, I can hardly wait to have dinner at your house," Meg said to me. "I just *love* Chinese food."

That was a relief. Mother was a good cook, but I wasn't sure if people who ate sour cream would also eat chicken gizzards stewed in soy sauce.

Mother decided not to take a chance with chicken gizzards. Since we had Western guests, she set the table with large dinner plates, which we never used in Chinese meals. In fact we didn't use individual plates at all but picked up food from the platters in the middle of the table and brought it directly to our rice bowls. Following the practice of Chinese-American restaurants, Mother also placed large serving spoons on the platters.

The dinner started well. Mrs. Gleason exclaimed at the beautifully arranged dishes of food: the colorful candied fruit in the sweet-and-sour pork dish, the noodle-thin shreds of chicken meat stir-fried with tiny peas, and the glistening pink prawns in a ginger sauce.

At first I was too busy enjoying my food to notice how the guests were doing. But soon I remembered my duties. Sometimes guests were too polite to help themselves, and you had to serve them with more food.

I glanced at Meg, to see if she needed more food, and my eyes nearly popped out at the sight of her plate. It was piled with food: the sweet-and-sour meat pushed right against the chicken shreds, and the chicken sauce ran into the prawns. She had been taking food from a second dish before she finished eating her helping from the first!

Horrified, I turned to look at Mrs. Gleason. She was dumping rice out of her bowl and putting it on her dinner plate. Then she ladled prawns and gravy on top of the rice and mixed everything together, the way you mix sand, gravel, and cement to make concrete.

I couldn't bear to look any longer, and I turned to Mr. Gleason. He was chasing a pea around his plate. Several times he got it to the edge, but when he tried to pick it up with his chopsticks, it rolled back toward the center of the plate again. Finally he put down his chopsticks and picked up the pea with his fingers. He really did! A grown man!

All of us, our family and the Chinese guests, stopped eating to watch the activities of the Gleasons. I wanted to giggle. Then I caught my mother's eyes on me. She frowned and shook her head slightly, and I understood the message: the Gleasons were not used to Chinese ways, and they were just coping the best they could. For some reason I thought of celery strings.

When the main courses were finished, Mother brought out a platter of fruit. "I hope you weren't expecting a sweet dessert," she said. "Since the Chinese don't eat dessert, I didn't think to prepare any."

"Oh, I couldn't possibly eat dessert!" cried Mrs. Gleason. "I'm simply stuffed!"

Meg had different ideas. When the table was cleared, she announced that she and I were going for a walk. "I don't know about you, but I feel like dessert," she told me, when we were outside. "Come on; there's a Dairy Queen down the street. I could use a big chocolate milk shake!"

Although I didn't really want anything more to eat, I insisted on paying for the milk shakes. After all, I was still hostess.

Meg got her large chocolate milk shake, and I had a small one. Even so, she was finishing hers while I was only half done. Toward the end she pulled hard on her straws and went *shloop, shloop*.

"Do you always slurp when you eat a milk shake?" I asked, before I could stop myself.

Meg grinned. "Sure. All Americans slurp." ❖

Tiffany: The Gleasons eat a lot!
EVALUATING

Jay: The same things are happening to the Gleasons that happened to the Lins. Meg probably wanted to laugh at the girl just like she wants to laugh at Meg now.
EVALUATING

Tiffany: So the Chinese and the Americans have something in common—slurping.
EVALUATING

Jay: I like this. It was pretty funny in some parts.
EVALUATING

THE ALL-AMERICAN SLURP   **15**

Creating a READER'S NOTEBOOK

Your Reader's Notebook

You can use almost any kind of notebook to help you interact with literature. Use a notebook of your choice to create your own Reader's Notebook. Then use your notebook to keep track of your thoughts as you read. Here are three ways to interact with the literature in this anthology.

The All-American Slurp
by Lensey Namioka

(page 9) She says they disgraced themselves while eating celery. How could they do that?

1 Record Your Thoughts

In your 📖 **READER'S NOTEBOOK**, log in ideas, responses, connections, and questions **before**, **during**, and **after** you read a selection. (See "Strategies for Reading," page 4.) Summarize important passages, and include sketches and charts, too, if they will help. If you wish, compare your ideas with those of a classmate.

I could write my own story about a dinner in my family.

2 Collect Ideas for Writing

Be aware of interesting themes, passages, and thoughts of your own as you read or complete follow-up activities. In a special section of your 📖 **READER'S NOTEBOOK**, jot down anything that may later be a springboard to your own writing.

Eleven
by Sandra Cisneros

RACHEL'S BIRTHDAY

	MY MEMORIES
Wakes up feeling like she is still ten	Lying in bed waiting for my birthday to begin
She feels too young. Wishes she were 102 years old	

PREPARING to Read

"You open your eyes and everything's just like yesterday, only it's today."

Eleven
Short Story by SANDRA CISNEROS

Connect to Your Life

Celebration Days As you may have guessed from the title, this story's main character has just turned 11 years old. What was turning 11 like for you? Or, what will turning 11 be like for you? On a sheet of paper, copy the diagram shown. Then record words and phrases that you associate with being 11 years old. Share your diagram with a partner.

Build Background

The Child Inside When she was interviewed about this story in 1986, Sandra Cisneros commented that she sometimes feels 11 years old inside, even as an adult: "When I think how I see myself, I would have to be at age eleven. I know I'm thirty-two on the outside, but inside I'm eleven. I'm the girl in the picture with skinny arms and a crumpled shirt and crooked hair. I didn't like school because all they saw was the outside me."

LaserLinks: Background for Reading
Author Background

WORDS TO KNOW Vocabulary Preview
except   invisible
expect   sudden

Focus Your Reading

LITERARY ANALYSIS CHARACTER Every person, animal, or imaginary creature in a story is a **character**. Usually one or two characters are the most important; they are called **main characters**. Less important characters are called **minor characters**. As you read this story, think about the **traits**, or qualities, of the main character.

ACTIVE READING CONNECTING When reading a story makes you think about things you already know or have experienced, you are **connecting**. Characters, settings, and events in a story may remind you of

• people you know
• feelings you've had
• other stories you've read

READER'S NOTEBOOK Make a chart like this one. As you read, jot down details about Rachel's 11th birthday in one column. In the other, jot down things—either in your own life or in other stories—that those details bring to mind. Try to focus on thoughts and feelings, such as Rach...

26 UNIT

③ Improve Your Reading Skills

Complete the specific 📖 READER'S NOTEBOOK activity on the **Preparing to Read** page of each literature lesson. This activity will help you apply an important skill as you read the selection.

Your Working Portfolio

Artists and writers keep portfolios in which they store works in progress. Your portfolio can be a folder, a box, or a notebook. Add drafts of your writing experiments, summaries of your projects, and your goals and progress as a reader and writer.

📓 Creating a Personal WORDList

Vocabulary As you read the selections in this book you will learn many new words. You can add these words to a special list called a personal word list—a list of words you want to use. Words for your list can come from:

• selections in this book
• stories and poems you write
• newspapers and magazines
• the Internet

Spelling There will be times when you misspell a word or need to write a word that you have not yet learned to spell. Add these words to a separate spelling list. To build your personal vocabulary and spelling lists, add a section for new words to your 📖 READER'S NOTEBOOK.

Go Beyond the Text

Your involvement doesn't stop with the last line of the text. Use these technology products to further your study and understanding:

• **Literature In Performance videos**
• **NetActivities CD-ROM**
• **Writing Coach CD-ROM**
• **McDougal Littell's companion Web site at www.mcdougallittell.com**

Tests of Courage

There are many kinds of courage: for instance, physical courage, inner strength, and the courage it takes just to live every day. In Unit One, students will read about people who face various challenges—some internal, some external. This unit contains two parts, both of which contribute to the unit theme by examining the tests of courage people face, and particularly, their reactions to those tests.

———— Part 1 ————

The Courage to Be Me In this part, young people face one of life's greatest tests—knowing who you are and what is important to you. For example, in "Nadia the Willful," a young girl learns about the importance of custom, law, and family. In doing so, she teaches others what real strength is.

———— Part 2 ————

Courage in Action Another kind of courage is highlighted in the nonfiction, fiction, and poetry of this section. Feats of daring and danger challenge and bring out the best in the people and characters students will read about. For example, in "Matthew Henson at the Top of the World," a man risks everything in his quest for the North Pole.

UNIT ONE

Tests of Courage

All serious daring starts from within.

Eudora Welty
AMERICAN WRITER

© Reggie Holladay/SIS.

18

 Viewing and Representing

Untitled **by Reggie Holladay/SIS**

ART APPRECIATION
Instruction Explain that this illustration has some of the qualities of a photograph—its immediacy and realism—and some of the qualities of a painting. The artist has mixed realistic elements—the skateboarders and the wave itself—with imagination, so the boys on wheels appear to ride the waves.

Ask: Why do you think the artist shows skateboarders riding a wave instead of on a sidewalk?
Possible Response: Not only does it take physical courage to do the kinds of flips and tricks both skateboarders and surfers do, but also it takes courage to do things a little differently than most people do them. By putting the skateboarders in the setting of a large wave, the artist emphasizes the challenge facing them.

R. HOLLADAY '95

To help students explore the connections between the art, the quotation, and the unit theme, have them consider the following questions:

Ask: Who is the most courageous person you know or have read about? Why?
Students' responses will vary, but should provide reasons why they think the person they have chosen is courageous.

Ask: How would you paraphrase the quotation by Eudora Welty on page 18?
Possible Response: It's what's inside people that enables them to face challenges.

Ask: What kind of courage do you think the painting relates to?
Possible Response: The people in the painting must have physical courage and daring to perform the gravity-defying feats they do.

Ask: What kinds of stories and experiences might you expect to read about in this unit?
Possible Response: ones with strong people facing real or fictional challenges, some with action and physical danger

Features and Selections	Literary Analysis	Reading and Critical Thinking	Writing Opportunities		
Tests of Courage **The Courage to Be Me**					
Learning the Language of Literature Fiction	Fiction, 21				
The Active Reader Skills and Strategies		Reading Fiction, 25			
SHORT STORY Eleven **Difficulty Level: Easy** **Literary Link** Who's the New Kid?	Character, 26, 28, 31	Connecting, 26, 28, 30, 31 Connect to Your Life, 26 Comparing Texts, 31 Standardized Test Practice, 30	Recollection Diary, 32 Greeting Card, 32		
SHORT STORY President Cleveland, Where Are You? **Difficulty Level: Average**	Plot, 34, 36, 38, 42, 45 Review: Character, 45	Sequence of Events, 34, 36, 38, 40, 42, 44, 45 Standardized Test Practice, 44	Character Comparison, 46 Decisive Narrative, 46		
Real World Link Trading Card Talk		Paraphrasing, 49			
SHORT STORY Scout's Honor **Difficulty Level: Easy**	Setting, 52, 54, 56, 58, 60, 64	Visualizing, 52, 54, 56, 58, 62, 64 Comparing Texts, 64 Standardized Test Practice, 63	Persuasive Essay, 65 Adventure Guide, 65		
SHORT STORY Nadia the Willful **Difficulty Level: Average** **Literary Link** Life Doesn't Frighten Me **Building Vocabulary**	Theme, 67, 68, 72, 76 Review: Plot, 76	Recognizing Cause and Effect, 67, 68, 70, 72, 76 Comparing Texts, 76 Standardized Test Practice, 73	Descriptive Poem, 77 Personal Profile, 77 Spatial Order Description, 77		
Writing Workshop: Responding to Literature **Assessment Practice**		Analyzing a Student Model, 90	Writing Your Response to Literature, 92 Supporting Your Response, 93		

	Literary Analysis	Reading and Critical Thinking	Writing Opportunities		
Courage in Action					
Learning the Language of Literature Nonfiction	Nonfiction, 96				
The Active Reader Skills and Strategies		Reading Nonfiction, 100			
BIOGRAPHY Matthew Henson at the Top of the World **Difficulty Level: Average** **Literary Link: Into Lucid Air**	Biography, 101, 102, 104, 106, 111	Identifying Main Idea and Details, 101, 102, 110, 111 Comparing Texts, 111 Standardized Test Practice, 110	Log Entry, 112 Acceptance Speech, 112 Mood Diary, 112		

Features and Selections	Literary Analysis	Reading and Critical Thinking	Writing Opportunities		
INFORMATIVE NONFICTION Summer of Fire **Difficulty Level:** *Average*	Informative Nonfiction, 114, 116, 118, 121	Chronological Order, 114, 116, 118, 120, 121 Connect to Your Life, 114 Standardized Test Practice, 122	Cause-and-Effect Essay, 122 Park Pamphlet, 122		
SHORT STORY Ghost of the Lagoon **Difficulty Level:** *Average*	Conflict, 124, 126, 130, 132 Review: Plot, 132	Predicting, 124, 126, 128, 130, 132	Royal Tribute, 133 Battle Narrative, 133 Informal Assessment, 131		
AUTOBIOGRAPHY *from* The Fun of It **Difficulty Level:** *Challenging*	Autobiography, 135, 136, 138, 140, 142	Identifying the Author's Purpose, 135, 136, 138, 142 Standardized Test Practice, 143	Newspaper Interview, 143 Personality Profile, 143		
Real World Link Daring to Dream **Building Vocabulary**		Using Text Organizers, 146			

Features and Selections	Literary Analysis	Reading and Critical Thinking	Writing Opportunities		
ESSAY Older Run **Difficulty Level:** *Average* A Life in the Day of Gary Paulsen	Anecdote, 154, 156, 158, 161	Identifying Effects of Author's Perspective, 154, 156, 161 Comparing Texts, 161 Drawing Conclusions, 163, 164	Informal Assessment, 160		
MEMOIR *from* Woodsong **Difficulty Level:** *Average*	Memoir, 165, 166, 170	Questioning, 165, 166, 170 Standardized Test Practice, 169			
The Author's Style Author Study Project	Analysis of Style, 172	Active Reading, 172	Writing, 172 Book Review, 173 Pen Pal Letters, 173		
Writing Workshop: Personal Experience Essay **Assessment Practice**		Analyzing a Student Model, 177 Necessary Details, 180	Writing Your Personal Experience Essay, 179		
Reflect and Assess	Reviewing Literary Concepts, 183	Noting the Newsworthy, 182 Evaluating Reading Experiences, 182	Building Your Portfolio, 183		

Additional Support

	Unit Resource Book	Assessment	Integrated Technology and Media	Literary Analysis Transparencies
Eleven *pp. 26–33*	• Summary p. 7 • Active Reading p. 8 • Literary Analysis p. 9 • Words to Know p. 10 • Grammar p. 11 • Spelling p. 12 • Selection Quiz p. 13	• Selection Test, Formal Assessment pp. 5–6 Test Generator	Audio Library LaserLinks, Teacher's SourceBook p. 6	• Analyzing Character T3
President Cleveland, Where Are You? *pp. 34–47*	• Summary p. 14 • Active Reading p. 15 • Literary Analysis p. 16 • Words to Know p. 17 • Grammar p. 18 • Spelling p. 19 • Selection Quiz p. 20	• Selection Test, Formal Assessment pp. 7–8 Test Generator	Audio Library	• Plot T5 • Analyzing Character T3 • Setting T6 • Conflict T8
Scout's Honor *pp. 52–66*	• Summary p. 21 • Active Reading p. 22 • Literary Analysis p. 23 • Words to Know p. 24 • Grammar p. 25 • Spelling p. 26 • Selection Quiz p. 27	• Selection Test, Formal Assessment pp. 9–10 Test Generator	Audio Library Research Starter www.mcdougallittell.com	• Setting T6 • Irony T27
Nadia the Willful *pp. 67–78*	• Summary p. 28 • Active Reading p. 29 • Literary Analysis p. 30 • Words to Know p. 31 • Grammar p. 32 • Spelling p. 33 • Selection Quiz p. 34	• Selection Test, Formal Assessment pp. 11–12 Test Generator	Audio Library LaserLinks, Teacher's SourceBook p. 7 Research Starter www.mcdougallittell.com	• Theme T7

Writing Workshop: Response to Literature

Unit Assessment

Unit Technology

Unit One Resource Book
• Prewriting p. 36
• Drafting and Elaboration p. 37
• Peer Response Guide pp. 38–39
• Revising, Editing, and Proofreading p. 40
• Student Models pp. 41–43
• Rubric for Evaluation p. 44

Writing Coach

Writing Transparencies T1–4, T13, T26

Reading and Critical Thinking Transparencies T40

Teacher's Guide to Assessment and Portfolio Use

• Unit One, Part 1 Test, Formal Assessment pp. 13–14
Test Generator
• Unit One Integrated Test, Integrated Assessment pp. 1–6

ClassZone www.mcdougallittell.com
Electronic Teacher Tools

Reading and Critical Thinking Transparencies	Grammar Transparencies and Copymasters	Vocabulary Transparencies and Copymasters	Writing Transparencies	Communications Transparencies and Copymasters
• Connecting T2 • Strategies for Reading T1	• Daily Language SkillBuilder T1 • Correcting Sentence Fragments C58	• Analyzing Word Parts C18		• Reading Aloud T11
• Sequencing T3 • Venn diagram T35	• Daily Language SkillBuilder T1 • Exclamatory Sentences C52 • Punctuating Four Types of Sentences C119	• Using Context Clues C19	• Organizing Your Writing T11 • Locating Material in the Library T41	• Impromptu Speaking: Dialogue, Role-Play T13
• Visualizing T4	• Daily Language SkillBuilder T2 • Identifying Simple Subjects and Verbs C53 • Verb Phrases: Main and Helping Verbs C77	• Context Clues: Compare/Contrast C20 • Context Clues: Restatement C21	• Structuring the Essay T6 • Using an Outline T54	• Interviewing T9
• Cause and Effect T5 • Sequence Chain T39	• Daily Language SkillBuilder T2 • Identifying Direct Objects C54 • Indirect Objects C55	• Using a Dictionary C22	• Topic Sentences and Thesis Statements T7 • Organizing Your Writing T11	• Reading Aloud T11 • Dramatic Reading T12

STUDENTS ACQUIRING ENGLISH

The **Spanish Study Guide,** pp. 1–15, includes language support for the following pages:
• Family and Community Involvement (per unit)

• Selection Summaries and Vocabulary
• Active Reading
• Literary Analysis

UNIT ONE
RESOURCE MANAGEMENT GUIDE
PART 2

To introduce the theme of this unit, use Fine Art Transparencies T19–21 in the Communications Transparencies and Copymasters.

Additional Support

	Unit Resource Book	Assessment	Integrated Technology and Media	Literary Analysis Transparencies
Matthew Henson at the Top of the World *pp. 101–113*	• Summary p. 45 • Active Reading p. 46 • Literary Analysis p. 47 • Words to Know p. 48 • Grammar p. 49 • Spelling p. 50 • Selection Quiz p. 51	• Selection Test, Formal Assessment pp. 15–16 ◉ Test Generator	◯ Audio Library ◉ LaserLinks, Teacher's SourceBook pp. 9 ↝ Research Starter www.mcdougallittell.com	• Biography T10
Summer of Fire *pp. 114–123*	• Summary p. 52 • Active Reading p. 53 • Literary Analysis p. 54 • Words to Know p. 55 • Grammar p. 56 • Spelling p. 57 • Selection Quiz p. 58	• Selection Test, Formal Assessment pp. 17–18 ◉ Test Generator	◯ Audio Library ↝ Research Starter www.mcdougallittell.com	• Text Structure T12
Ghost of the Lagoon *pp. 124–134*	• Summary p. 59 • Active Reading p. 60 • Literary Analysis p. 61 • Words to Know p. 62 • Grammar p. 63 • Spelling p. 64 • Selection Quiz p. 65	• Selection Test, Formal Assessment pp. 19–20 ◉ Test Generator	◯ Audio Library ◉ LaserLinks, Teacher's SourceBook p. 11 ↝ Research Starter www.mcdougallittell.com	• Conflict T8 • Plot T5
from **The Fun of It** *pp. 135–144*	• Summary p. 66 • Active Reading p. 67 • Literary Analysis p. 68 • Words to Know p. 69 • Grammar p. 70 • Spelling p. 71 • Selection Quiz p. 72	• Selection Test, Formal Assessment pp. 21–22 ◉ Test Generator	◯ Audio Library ▬ Video: Literature in Performance, Video Resource Book pp. 3–9	• Autobiography T11
Older Run *pp. 154–162*	• Summary p. 74 • Active Reading p. 75 • Literary Analysis p. 76 • Words to Know p. 77 • Grammar p. 78 • Spelling p. 79 • Selection Quiz p. 80	• Selection Test, Formal Assessment pp. 23–24 ◉ Test Generator	◯ Audio Library ◉ NetActivities	• Autobiography T11 • Flashback T29
from **Woodsong** *pp. 165–171*	• Summary p. 81 • Active Reading p. 82 • Literary Analysis p. 83 • Words to Know p. 84 • Grammar p. 85 • Spelling p. 86 • Selection Quiz p. 87	• Selection Test, Formal Assessment pp. 25–26 ◉ Test Generator	◯ Audio Library ◉ LaserLinks, Teacher's SourceBook p. 13 ↝ Research Starter www.mcdougallittell.com ◉ NetActivities	• Autobiography T11 • Author's Purpose T16

Writing Workshop: Personal Experience Essay

Unit One Resource Book
• Prewriting p. 88
• Drafting and Elaboration p. 89
• Peer Response Guide pp. 90–91
• Revising, Editing, and Proofreading p. 92
• Student Models pp. 93–95
• Rubric for Evaluation p. 96

◉ **Writing Coach**

Writing Transparencies T1–4, T13, T25

Teacher's Guide to Assessment and Portfolio Use

Unit Assessment

• Unit One, Part 2 Test, Formal Assessment pp. 27–28
◉ Test Generator
• Unit One Integrated Test, Integrated Assessment pp. 1–6

Unit Technology

↝ ClassZone www.mcdougallittell.com
◉ Electronic Teacher Tools

Reading and Critical Thinking Transparencies	Grammar Transparencies and Copymasters	Vocabulary Transparencies and Copymasters	Writing Transparencies	Communications Transparencies and Copymasters
• Main Ideas and Supporting Details T25	• Daily Language SkillBuilder T3 • Agreement with a Compound Subject C117	• Using a Dictionary C23 • Using Root Words C24	• Note Taking T49 • How to Paraphrase T50 • How to Summarize T51 • Paraphrasing and Summarizing T52	• Evaluating Roles in Groups T8 • Impromptu Speaking: Dialogue, Role-Play T13
• Chronological Order T6	• Daily Language SkillBuilder T3 • Action and State-of-Being Verbs C79 • Active and Passive Voice C134	• Using a Pronunciation Key C25 • Specialized Vocabulary C26	• Cause and Effect T36 • How to Summarize T51	• The Active Listener T1 • Persuasive Techniques T3
• Predicting T7	• Daily Language SkillBuilder T4 • Punctuating Dialogue C120 • Predicate Nouns and Predicate Adjectives C88	• Context Clues: Example C27		• The Active Listener T1 • Interviewing T9 • Impromptu Speaking: Dialogue, Role-Play T13
• Author's Purpose and Audience T8	• Daily Language SkillBuilder T4 • Using Commas to Prevent Misreading C122 • Subjects in Questions, Exclamations, and Commands C57	• Synonyms C28 • Root Words C29	• Note Taking T49	• Interviewing T9 • Verbal Strategies T14 • Nonverbal Strategies T15
• Author's Bias T28	• Daily Language SkillBuilder T5 • Varying Sentence Length and Type C135 • Subject-Verb Agreement T113	• Context Clues: Example C30	• Effective Language T15	• Dramatic Reading T12
• Questioning T9	• Daily Language SkillBuilder T5 • Correcting Run-on Sentences C61	• Context Clues: Example C31	• Locating Information Using the Internet T47–48	• Evaluating Roles in Groups T8

STUDENTS ACQUIRING ENGLISH

The **Spanish Study Guide,** pp. 16–33, includes language support for the following pages:
• Family and Community Involvement (per unit)
• Selection Summaries and Vocabulary
• Active Reading
• Literary Analysis

Selection	SkillBuilder Sentences	Suggested Answers
Eleven	1. Don't you think it was unfair for Mrs. Price to make Rachel where the sweater? 2. The day might have been worse if Rachel had throne the sweater away at lunch time.	1. Don't you think it was unfair for Mrs. Price to make Rachel **wear** the sweater? 2. The day might have been worse if Rachel had **thrown** the sweater away at lunch time.
President Cleveland, Where Are You?	1. Boys went to the movies and trade cowboy cards for fun during the Depression. 2. All the boys wanted to be the first to completed their set.	1. Boys went to the movies and **traded** cowboy cards for fun during the Depression. 2. All the boys wanted to be the first to **complete** their set.
Scout's Honor	1. Before him and his friends went camping, they should have made a plan. 2. Their mothers helped they get ready.	1. Before **he** and his friends went camping, they should have made a plan. 2. Their mothers helped **them** get ready.
Nadia the Willful	1. Nadia was given the nickname "nadia the willful" because she was stubborn and had a quick temper. 2. when Nadia grew angry, only her brother hamed could calm her down.	1. Nadia was given the nickname "**Nadia** the **Willful**" because she was stubborn and had a quick temper. 2. **When** Nadia grew angry, only her brother **Hamed** could calm her down.

Selection	SkillBuilder Sentences	Suggested Answers
Matthew Henson at the Top of the World	1. Matthew Hensons first adventure was on a ship called the *Katie Hines*. 2. Their leaving for the North Pole tomorrow.	1. Matthew **Henson's** first adventure was on a ship called the *Katie Hines*. 2. **They're** leaving for the North Pole tomorrow.
Summer of Fire	1. The fire fighters did'nt think they could put out the fire at Yellowstone. 2. The fire finally went out after burning for month's.	1. The fire fighters **didn't** think they could put out the fire at Yellowstone. 2. The fire finally went out after burning for **months.**
Ghost of the Lagoon	1. Mako's mother said "Hush! Would you bring trouble on us all?" 2. Did the ghost see Mako and Afa	1. Mako's mother said, "Hush! Would you bring trouble on us all?" 2. Did the ghost see Mako and Afa**?**
from The Fun of It	1. amelia earhart was the first women to fly across the atlantic ocean. 2. she had some problems with her plane before landing in ireland.	1. **Amelia Earhart** was the first **woman** to fly across the **Atlantic Ocean.** 2. **She** had some problems with her plane before landing in **Ireland.**

Selection	SkillBuilder Sentences	Suggested Answers
Older Run	1. While Paulsen was rubbing one dog's ears, another trotting up. 2. People still used the tracks though they were abandon.	1. While Paulsen was rubbing one dog's ears, another **trotted** up. 2. People still used the tracks though they were **abandoned.**
from Woodsong	1. In the reegen ware Paulsen lives, there are lots of pine trees. 2. Bare hunting is aloud, but Paulsen does not hurt the bares.	1. In the **region where** Paulsen lives, there are lots of pine trees. 2. **Bear** hunting is **allowed,** but Paulsen does not hurt the **bears.**

Grammar Focus by Unit	Unit One	Unit Two	Unit Three	Unit Four	Unit Five	Unit Six
	The Sentence and Its Parts	Nouns, Pronouns, and Verbs	Modifiers	Phrases	Compound and Complex Sentences	Review

The Language of Literature offers several options for integrating grammar instruction and literature.

- Each unit has a specific grammar focus. The grammar focus for this unit is highlighted on the planning chart. Categories of grammar skills for this unit are shown in red.
- The Pupil's Edition includes instructive features entitled *Grammar in Context*. The instruction in these features arises from the selections and relates to the grammar focus for each unit.
- The Writing Workshops in the Pupil's Edition include grammar tips that help the students produce error-free drafts.
- Mini Lessons in the Teacher's Edition complement the instruction in the *Grammar in Context* features. Additional Mini Lessons relate to the grammar focus for each unit as well as to the literature.
- Daily Language SkillBuilders in the Teacher's Edition provide students with ongoing proofreading practice and reinforce punctuation, spelling, grammar and usage, and capitalization.
- Grammar Copymasters and Transparencies, which may be used independently or in conjunction with the Mini Lessons in the Teacher's Edition, present grammar in a traditional, systematic sequence.

PE instruction shown in black
TE Mini Lessons shown in green

Part 1

THE SENTENCE AND ITS PARTS
Sentence Fragments
"Eleven," p. 33
Correcting Sentence Fragments
"Eleven," p. 33
Exclamatory Sentences
"President Cleveland, Where Are You?",
p. 42

Four Kinds of Sentences
"President Cleveland, Where Are You?",
p. 47
Identifying Simple Subjects and Verbs
"Scout's Honor," p. 61

Subjects and Verbs
"Scout's Honor," p. 66
Identifying Direct Objects
"Nadia the Willful," p. 72

Direct Objects
"Nadia the Willful," p. 78
Indirect Objects
"Nadia the Willful," p. 78

VERBS
Verb Phrases: Main and Helping Verbs
"Scout's Honor," p. 66

SUBJECT-VERB AGREEMENT
Subject-Verb Agreement
Writing Workshop, p. 93
Subject-Verb Agreement
Assessment Practice, p. 94

PUNCTUATION
Punctuating Four Types of Sentences
"President Cleveland, Where Are You?",
p. 47

Part 2

THE SENTENCE AND ITS PARTS
Compound Subjects and Predicates
"Matthew Henson," p. 113

Subjects in Unusual Order
"The Fun of It," p. 144
Subjects in Questions, Exclamations,
and Commands
"The Fun of It," p. 144
Correcting Run-on Sentences
"Woodsong," p. 171

PRONOUNS
Subject and Object Pronouns
Writing Workshop, p. 180
Correct Use of Pronouns
Assessment Practice, p. 181

VERBS
Action and State-of-Being Verbs
"Summer of Fire," p. 118

ADJECTIVES AND ADVERBS
Predicate Nouns and Adjectives
"Ghost of the Lagoon," p. 134
Predicate Nouns and Adjectives
"Ghost of the Lagoon," p. 134

SUBJECT-VERB AGREEMENT
Agreement with a Compound Subject
"Matthew Henson," p. 113

Subject-Verb Agreement
"Older Run," p. 162
Subject-Verb Agreement with Pronouns
"Older Run," p. 162

PUNCTUATION
Punctuating Dialogue
"Ghost of the Lagoon," p. 128
Using Commas to Prevent Misreading
"The Fun of It," p. 140

STYLE
Active and Passive Voice
"Summer of Fire," p. 123
Active and Passive Voice
"Summer of Fire," p. 123
Varying Sentence Length and Type
"Older Run," p. 158

Varying Sentence Length
"Woodsong," p. 171

OVERVIEW

Students work in small groups to produce a news program featuring characters from the unit who took risks or made tough choices when faced with a challenge. Students collect characters' stories and compile them for a national evening newsmagazine broadcast.

Project at a glance The selections in Unit One feature characters who confront a challenge by taking a risk or making a tough choice. For this project, some students will assume the roles of characters in the stories and other students will interview them. Students will present the stories in a *60 Minutes*-type video newsmagazine format. Members of each group will share responsibilities for researching the topic, writing the script, narrating, conducting interviews, and taping their segment. Each topic should be well thought out with a focus on the challenge in the story, the events that led up to it, and the resulting choice made or risk taken. If your school has access to a video camera, the program might be videotaped for presentation. If not, staging will work just as well.

SCHEDULING

Individual segments should take no more than ten minutes. The entire "program" should run about 60 minutes. You may want to schedule the presentations over the course of 2–3 class periods. This project may take place over the course of the unit or at the end of the unit, depending on your scheduling purposes.

PROJECT OBJECTIVES

- To demonstrate the speaking and listening skills introduced in the activity
- To identify what a character learned by making a tough choice or taking a risk
- To conduct in-depth interviews with students playing character roles
- To write an original script synthesizing the events in a story
- To combine the story with those of other groups into a full-length newsmagazine

SUGGESTED GROUP SIZE
4–5 students per group

Video Newsmagazine

1 ▶ Getting Started

Explain that students will be working in small groups to plan and produce a video newsmagazine along the lines of *60 Minutes, Dateline,* and *20/20.* Each group will produce an interview segment with a character from a story in the unit. Characters will reveal what they learned by taking a risk or making a tough choice in the face of a difficult situation.

Have students watch one of the television shows mentioned above and note some key elements: background information, interviews, transitional statements made by the anchors, and introductory and concluding statements made by the reporters. Remind students that a real television show has the luxury of high-tech editing.

If video equipment is available, have someone videotape each of the segments when they are all ready. Students who cannot videotape can present their findings as if on live television.

Interviews should be well rehearsed. If you are using video equipment, arrange for interviewees to come to one taping at a specific time. Allow for extra time to complete the project.

Writing Workshop Connection

As a springboard, students may use the Writing Workshop assignment **Response to Literature,** p. 94, or **Personal Experience Essay,** p. 174, which they will complete in this unit.

2 ▶ Directing the Project

Preparing *(1 class period)* Divide students into groups of four to five. Have students choose their favorite stories from the unit. List main characters from the stories and the difficult choices or risks they took in the face of a challenge. Ask groups to write a brief description of the character, the choice or risk taken, and the resulting insight.

Assigning Roles

- Select two students to act as anchors.
- Assign one main character from a story, as well as minor characters for each group.
- Choose reporters to interview the main characters and writers to help the reporters prepare questions as well as an introduction and a concluding thought for the piece.
- Assign a "tech team" to work the video camera, build sets, and make cue cards.

▶ Have students brainstorm a list of interview questions for the main character. Meet with each group to help refine the script. Group members should "prep" the main character by asking him or her questions. Have students review their notes. They'll feel more comfortable knowing they have more than enough material to present. Review with students the Speaking and Listening Skills listed on the next page, as well as the interview tips found on page R106 of the Communication Handbook at the back of the pupil edition.

▶ Students should be aware of the guidelines for working in a group, found on page R106 in the Communication Handbook.

Practicing *(2 class periods)* Allow time for students to coordinate their interview and to rehearse. Tell students that giving and receiving feedback during the rehearsal stage is crucial. Refer to the tips in the Feedback Center.

▶ Anchors should briefly meet with groups to "prescreen" each interview so that they can write transitional statements, as well as an introduction and a conclusion.

Presenting *(2–3 class periods)* This project could culminate in a screening for the entire student body or just for your class.

▶ To begin, have students take a few deep breaths and focus on what they want to communicate. Anchors should look directly into the camera during the introduction, transitional statements, and conclusion of each piece. They should appear natural, using gestures and facial expressions that fit the content. Characters should use appropriate verbal and nonverbal cues that reflect the tone of their stories. Reporters should appear interested but neutral.

Teaching the Speaking and Listening Skills

The student is expected to:

Demonstrate effective communication skills that reflect such demands as interviewing, reporting, and requesting and providing information

Teaching Suggestions: Have students review the interview guidelines on page R106. Remind them that often an interviewer has to ask the same question in different ways to get the necessary information. Also tell students to take clear notes or tape the interview sessions to get a better idea of their subject's style and main points. Discuss the idea of the "objective reporter." In other words, reporters should present their findings in a balanced manner. They should also make sure that all main points are supported with evidence and examples from the stories.

Use appropriate rate, volume, pitch, and tone for the audience and the setting

Teaching Suggestions: Tell students to rehearse their parts several times in front of a mirror. They should speak at a comfortable pitch, placing emphasis on important words. Coach them on making their delivery fit their message, audience, and setting.

Understand the major ideas and supporting evidence in spoken messages

Teaching Suggestions: After the presentation, have the class reflect on the coherence of each piece. Did it make sense? Were major ideas supported by examples from the text? Were their insights and conclusions logical? Were the characters convincing? To check for understanding, have audience members identify the important event in the life of each featured character and summarize the character's discovery and insight.

Feedback Center

Students can use the following guidelines when giving and receiving feedback during this project:

Giving Feedback

▶ Ask questions concerning content, delivery, purpose, and point of view (for instance, is tone appropriate to purpose?)

▶ Provide feedback about the coherence and logic of the content, delivery, and overall impact on the listener.

▶ Comment on the verbal and nonverbal delivery (pitch, pace, volume, body language) and its impact on the listener.

▶ Respond to persuasive messages with questions, challenges, or affirmations.

▶ Question the evidence to support the speaker's claims and conclusions.

Receiving Feedback

▶ Listen to constructive criticism with an open mind.

▶ Use audience feedback and modify the presentation to clarify meaning or organization.

 ## Assessing the Project

The following rubric can be used for group or individual assessment.

3 *Full Accomplishment*

The group produced a news segment that shows what a character learned by taking a risk or making a difficult choice in the face of a challenging situation. Students worked effectively in a group and demonstrated all three of the Speaking and Listening Skills listed, including effective communication skills, appropriate delivery of information, and a logical presentation of the points.

2 *Substantial Accomplishment*

The students produced a newsmagazine segment, but it lacks some key information or clarity of subject matter. Students worked in a group with adequate communication in organizing and fulfilling individual roles. Two out of three of the Speaking and Listening Skills were demonstrated.

1 *Little Accomplishment*

The students' segment is incomplete or does not fulfill the requirements of the assignment. Organization of the presentation was unclear, and students did not fulfill group roles. Students demonstrated only one of the Speaking and Listening Skills.

PART 1   The Courage to Be Me

Reflecting on the Theme In Part One of this unit, characters struggle with making decisions that could have long-lasting effects. Tough choices take courage. The decisions a person makes can say a lot about who he or she really is. Is she bold or shy? Does he think about other people, or only himself? Sometimes, nothing takes more courage than staying true to yourself.

ACTIVITY

With a group of classmates, brainstorm some kinds of problems and obstacles that young people face every day. Then create a board game called "What's My Next Move?" Be sure that the game represents daily problems and offers options for solutions.

Obstacle:
Spelling test
Options:
• good night's sleep
• study with a friend

Fiction

> *Wherever [people] have lived there is a story to be told . . .*
> —Henry David Thoreau, writer

A good story is a work of art. Like a beautiful painting, it springs from the imagination. It can be sparked by a memory, an experience, or even a dream. Many people say that the best stories find us. They seem to appear when we're not looking. Once here, they demand to be told.

Stories that come from a writer's imagination are called **fiction.** Two types of fiction are **short stories** and **novels.** Both contain the main elements of **plot, character, setting,** and **theme.**

Key Types of Fiction

short story
- usually revolves around a single idea
- is short enough to be read at one sitting

novel
- a longer work
- involves a more complicated plot

21

Objectives
- understand the following literary terms:

fiction	conflict
short story	exposition
novel	rising action
plot	climax
character	falling action
setting	(resolution)
theme	

- understand and appreciate fiction
- recognize the distinguishing features of fiction

Teaching the Lesson

This lesson analyzes the types and the elements of fiction and demonstrates how each of the elements contributes to the fictional work as a whole.

Introducing the Concepts
Have students think of an especially memorable film or television program they have seen recently that is fictional. Ask them to explain how this work would change if one of its most pivotal events had not happened, if the work had been set in a different time and place, or if one of the minor characters became the main character.

Use **Literary Analysis Transparencies,** pp. 1, 3, 5–7 for additional support.

Presenting the Concepts
Plot
Point out to students that writers make plans for the framework of their story. This framework, called a plot, has a beginning, middle, and end.

YOUR TURN
Possible Response: The conflict is that, because of their unfamiliarity with American customs, the family acts differently from the rest of the guests at the dinner party.

Plot

The **plot** of a story is made up of a sequence of events. It is the writer's blueprint for what happens, when it happens, and to whom it happens. One event causes another, which causes another, and so on until the end of the story. Generally, a plot is built around a central **conflict**—a problem or struggle that drives the story. A conflict might be a life-or-death battle, or it might be just a disagreement between friends.

> **PLOT**
>
> It [the dining table] was lavishly covered with platters of food, but we couldn't see any chairs around the table. So we helpfully carried over some dining chairs and sat down. All the other guests just stood there.
>
> —Lensey Namioka, "The All-American Slurp"

YOUR TURN The "we" in the passage at the right is a family that has recently emigrated from China. The family members are attending their first American dinner party. What conflict is introduced in the passage?

Most plots develop in four stages:

• **Exposition** First the stage is set and the background of the action is described. Then the conflict begins.

• **Rising Action** As the conflict grows, excitement and energy build.

• **Climax** Eventually the plot reaches a turning point. The outcome of the conflict is decided. Someone may make a discovery or take an important action. Often a change results.

• **Falling Action** The climax is usually followed by a falling action or resolution, in which loose ends are tied up before the story ends.

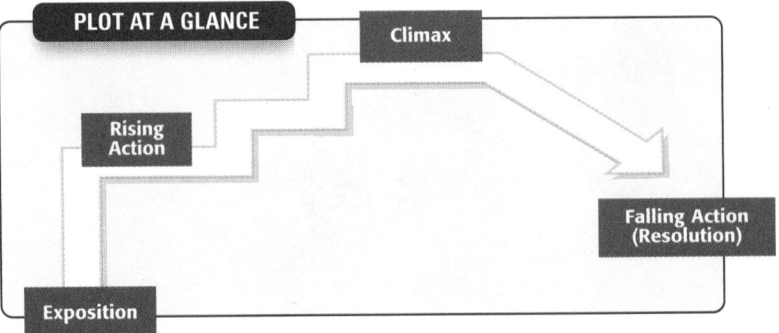

PLOT AT A GLANCE

Climax

Rising Action

Falling Action (Resolution)

Exposition

22   UNIT ONE   PART 1: THE COURAGE TO BE ME

Character

Characters are the people, animals, and imaginary creatures in stories. Generally, the action of a story centers on one **main character.** Usually, there are some **minor characters** who interact with the main character and with one another. Characters are revealed by their **traits,** or qualities. These include their physical characteristics; their speech, thoughts, feelings, and actions; the writer's direct statements about them; and the thoughts, speech, and actions of other characters.

YOUR TURN In the story "Nadia the Willful," the main character is a young Bedouin girl with a reputation for being strong-willed. What details in the passage at the right show this character trait?

CHARACTER

And the less she was listened to, the less she was able to recall Hamed's face and voice. And the less she recalled, the more her temper raged within her, destroying the peace she had found.

By evening, she could stand it no longer. She went to where her father sat, staring into the desert, and stood before him.

"You will not rob me of my brother Hamed!" she cried, stamping her foot. "I will not let you!"

—Sue Alexander, "Nadia the Willful"

"Margot stood alone. She was a very frail girl. . . ."
—Ray Bradbury, "All Summer in a Day"

". . . Mako's mother had food ready and waiting."
—Armstrong Sperry, "Ghost of the Lagoon"

"Aaron wasn't quite certain what his mother would say. . . ."
—Myron Levoy, "Aaron's Gift"

". . . I had begun to really look at myself, . . ."
—Elizabeth Ellis, "Flowers and Freckle Cream"

LEARNING THE LANGUAGE OF LITERATURE   **23**

Character

Invite the class to brainstorm a list of well-known fictional characters from novels, short stories, movies, and television. List all the characters on the chalkboard. Ask for volunteers to identify them as main characters or minor characters and to discuss some of their traits.

YOUR TURN

Possible Responses: Nadia is revealed as being strong-willed by the temper that rages in her, her need to confront her father, her words to her father, and her stamping of her foot.

Setting

Have students describe what they consider the most effective setting for a horror story and explain their choice.

YOUR TURN

Possible Response: The story takes place in Brooklyn in the 1940s. The setting is described using the words "slate pavements," "asphalt," "tall buildings," and "puny pin oak tree."

Theme

Ask students to share some important lessons they have learned about life, such as "Treat others as you wish to be treated" and "Honesty is the best policy." Explain that such messages are often what authors of fiction present in their stories as themes. Point out that the theme of a story can be understood by considering its characters, setting, and plot.

YOUR TURN

Possible Response: Possible themes for this work might be: the difficulties of fitting into a new place; how hard it is to be different; the courage it takes to face new and unfamiliar situations; the courage all new Americans have had to have in order to come to this country.

Setting

Does your favorite story take place today in New York City, or on the planet Venus a thousand years from now? The time and place in which a story unfolds is called the **setting.** The time may be in the past, the present, or the future; during the day or the night; in any season. The place, or scene, may be imaginary or real. Sometimes a story's setting is described directly. Sometimes it becomes clear through what the characters say and do.

YOUR TURN Look at the passage at the right. When and where does this story take place? What words or phrases describe the setting?

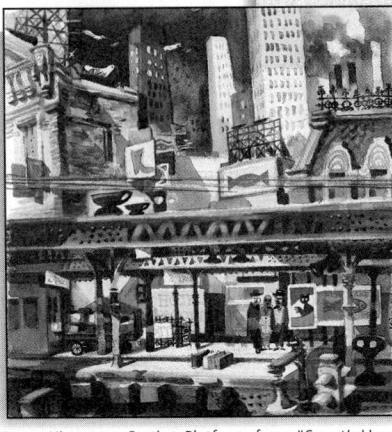

Dong Kingman, *Station Platform,* from "Scout's Honor"

SETTING

Since I grew up in Brooklyn in the 1940s, the only grass I knew was in Ebbets Field where the Dodgers played. Otherwise, my world was made of slate pavements, streets of asphalt (or cobblestone), and skies full of tall buildings. The only thing "country" was a puny pin oak tree at our curb, which was noticed, mostly, by dogs.

—Avi, "Scout's Honor"

Theme

Theme is a message about life or human nature that the writer delivers to the reader. A theme in a short story might be "Good friends stand by each other," or "The harder something is to get, the greater the reward." Most themes are not stated openly. They become apparent as stories unfold.

You can gather clues to a story's theme by thinking about:

• the title
• statements about big ideas, such as courage or freedom
• the ways characters change and the lessons they learn

YOUR TURN Read the passage at the right. What do you think one theme of the story might be?

THEME

I splashed cold water on my burning face, and as I dried myself with a paper towel, I stared into the mirror. In this perfumed ladies' room, with its pink-and-silver wallpaper and marbled sinks, I looked completely out of place. What was I doing here? What was our family doing in the Lakeview Restaurant? In America?

—Lensey Namioka, "The All-American Slurp"

24   UNIT ONE   PART 1: THE COURAGE TO BE ME

The world is full of stories that entertain and inform. Our favorite stories may be filled with interesting **characters,** far-away **places,** and exciting **events.** But all stories leave room for our imaginations. To get the most from every work of fiction you read, try using the strategies explained here.

Reading Fiction

How to Apply the Strategies

Preview the story and set a purpose for reading. Before you begin, look at the title and pictures. Skim through and read a few words on each page. Can you tell what the story is about?

CONNECT Do the characters share thoughts or experiences that you have had? Does the story remind you of an event or a person you've heard of or read about?

QUESTION Ask questions as the story unfolds. The events, characters, and ideas in the story should make sense to you.

PREDICT As you become more involved in the story, try to predict what will happen next. Look for clues that hint of events to come.

VISUALIZE As you read about a character, place, or event, pay attention to the descriptive details. Try to imagine how something might look, sound, feel, taste, or smell. Can you picture the setting in your mind? Is the action easy to imagine?

EVALUATE Think about the characters and their actions. What are your feelings toward them? Also evaluate how well the writer is telling the story.

CLARIFY Remember to pause now and then. Reread when necessary. You also can take notes or discuss the story with a friend.

Here's how Ryane uses the strategies:

*"When I read fiction, I like to sit in a quiet place. I try to **visualize** how a person or place looks. When I see these characters and the problems they face, I **connect** the story to my own life. At different points in the story, I stop to **predict** what is happening. Sometimes, I become so lost in the story that I forget about time."*

Need More Help?

Remember that active readers use the essential reading strategies explained on page 4: • visualize • predict • clarify • question • connect • evaluate • monitor.

THE ACTIVE READER **25**

OVERVIEW

Objectives
• understand and enjoy fiction by using strategies such as preview, connect, question, predict, visualize, evaluate, and clarify
• connect personal experiences to the experiences of characters in fiction

Teaching the Lesson

The strategies on this page will help students interpret fiction by focusing on useful strategies for understanding and connecting with what they read.

Presenting the Strategies
Point out that this page offers strategies for helping students get the most out of what they read.

Use **Reading and Critical Thinking Transparencies,** p. 1, for additional support.

PREVIEW
Allow students time to preview several stories in their books. What conclusions did they draw about the content of each story? What clues did they use to help them figure this out?

CONNECT
Ask students to think about "The All-American Slurp." With which incidents did they particularly connect and why? How does this help them understand how the Lins felt?

Possible Response: Students may mention times when they did something embarrassing because they did not know a custom or way of doing something in an unfamiliar setting. Remembering their own embarrassments helps them understand why the Lins acted the way they did.

QUESTION and PREDICT
Remind students to ask themselves questions as they read, then predict what the answers might be, given the characters' personalities and the events of the story so far.

VISUALIZE
Remind students that picturing in their minds what is happening will make the story seem more real to them. Ask them to describe what they see in their mind's eye when the four Lins are sitting on the couch eating celery.

EVALUATE
Remind students that their response to a story and its characters will be based on their own experiences, tastes, and interests.

CLARIFY
Discuss with students something they may have misread the first time they read a story. Ask how it affected their understanding of the story. If it didn't make sense, what did they do then?

OVERVIEW

 This selection is included in the **Grade 6 InterActive Reader.**

Objectives

1. understand and appreciate a **short story** (Literary Analysis)
2. identify qualities of a main **character** (Literary Analysis)
3. **connect** a story to prior knowledge and experiences (**Active Reading**)

Summary

Rachel wakes up on her eleventh birthday feeling as if she's still ten—and nine, and eight, and all the ages that came before. At school, what should be a happy day turns gloomy when the teacher insists that an ugly, unclaimed sweater belongs to Rachel. Mrs. Price puts the sweater in an embarrassing pile on Rachel's desk. Worse yet, she makes Rachel put the sweater on. It smells bad, it itches, it's full of germs—and Rachel, feeling all her years of childhood rattling around inside her, cries in front of the whole class. The classmate who is the real owner of the sweater finally claims it, while Rachel longs for the day to end.

Thematic Link

Rachel doesn't quite have the courage to stick up for herself regarding the sweater, but she is able to accept the younger self who cries in the face of injustice.

5-Minute Warm-Up

Daily Language SkillBuilder

Have students **proofread** the display sentences on page 19i and write them correctly. The sentences also appear on Transparency 1 of **Grammar Transparencies and Copymasters.**

Eleven

"You open your eyes and everything's just like yesterday, only it's today."

Short Story by SANDRA CISNEROS

Connect to Your Life

Celebration Days As you may have guessed from the title, this story's main character has just turned 11 years old. What was turning 11 like for you? Or, what will turning 11 be like? On a sheet of paper, copy the diagram shown. Then record words and phrases that you associate with being 11 years old. Share your diagram with a partner.

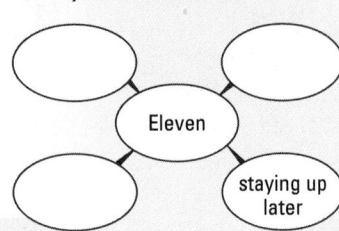

Build Background

The Child Inside When she was interviewed about this story in 1986, Sandra Cisneros commented that she sometimes feels 11 years old inside, even as an adult: "When I think how I see myself, I would have to be at age eleven. I know I'm thirty-two on the outside, but inside I'm eleven. I'm the girl in the picture with skinny arms and a crumpled shirt and crooked hair. I didn't like school because all they saw was the outside me."

 LaserLinks: Background for Reading
Author Background

WORDS TO KNOW
Vocabulary Preview
except	invisible
expect	sudden

Focus Your Reading

LITERARY ANALYSIS **CHARACTER** Every person, animal, or imaginary creature in a story is a **character.** Usually one or two characters are the most important; they are called **main characters.** Less important characters are called **minor characters.** As you read this story, think about the **traits,** or qualities, of the main character.

ACTIVE READING **CONNECTING** When reading a story makes you think about things you already know or have experienced, you are **connecting.** Characters, settings, and events in a story may remind you of

- people you know
- feelings you've had
- other stories you've read

READER'S NOTEBOOK Make a chart like this one. As you read, jot down details about Rachel's 11th birthday in one column. In the other, jot down things—either in your own life or in other stories—that those details bring to mind. Try to focus on thoughts and feelings, such as Rachel's disappointments.

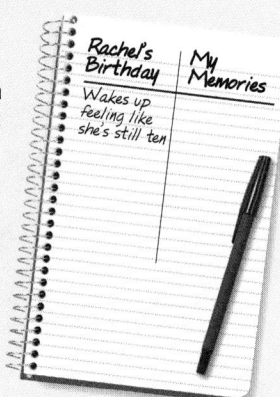

Rachel's Birthday | My Memories
Wakes up feeling like she's still ten |

LESSON RESOURCES

UNIT ONE RESOURCE BOOK, pp. 7–13

ASSESSMENT
Formal Assessment, pp. 5–6
Teacher's Guide to Assessment and Portfolio Use
Test Generator

SKILLS TRANSPARENCIES AND COPYMASTERS
Literary Analysis
• Analyzing Character, TR 3 (for Cooperative Activity, p. 31)
Reading and Critical Thinking
• Connecting, TR 2 (for Thinking Through the Literature, p. 31)

Grammar
• Correcting Sentence Fragments, CM 58 (for Mini Lesson, p. 33)
• Analyzing Word Parts, CM 18 (for Mini Lesson, p. 27)

INTEGRATED TECHNOLOGY
Audio Library
LaserLinks
• Author Background. See **Teacher's SourceBook,** p. 6

Visit our website:
www.mcdougallittell.com

ELEVEN

by Sandra Cisneros

What they don't understand about birthdays and what they never tell you is that when you're eleven, you're also ten, and nine, and eight, and seven, and six, and five, and four, and three, and two, and one. And when you wake up on your eleventh birthday you expect to feel eleven, but you don't. You open your eyes and everything's just like yesterday, only it's today. And you don't feel eleven at all. You feel like you're still ten. And you are—underneath the year that makes you eleven.

Like some days you might say something stupid, and that's the part of you that's still ten. Or maybe some days you might need to sit on your mama's lap because you're scared, and that's the part of you that's five. And maybe one day when you're all grown up maybe you will need to cry like if you're three, and that's okay. That's what I tell Mama when she's sad and needs to cry. Maybe she's feeling three.

Because the way you grow old is kind of like an onion or like the rings inside a tree trunk or like my little wooden dolls that fit one inside the other, each year inside the next one. That's how being eleven years old is.

You don't feel eleven. Not right away. It takes a few days, weeks even, sometimes even months before you say Eleven when they ask you. And you don't feel smart eleven, not until you're almost twelve. That's the way it is.

Only today I wish I didn't have only eleven years rattling inside me like pennies in a tin Band-Aid box. Today I wish I was one hundred

WORDS
TO
KNOW   **expect** (ĭk-spĕkt′) v. to look forward to something that is likely to occur

27

TEACHING THE LITERATURE
Customizing Instruction

Less Proficient Readers
Guide students to use the title and art to infer that the story is about an eleventh birthday.
Set a Purpose Have students read to find out what Rachel (the "birthday girl") thinks people don't understand about birthdays. Ask why she thinks this way.

Students Acquiring English
Make sure students understand the English idiom for stating one's age: *I am eleven* means "I am eleven years old" or "I have passed my eleventh birthday." Review the numbers from one to eleven and ask students to discuss how children act at each age.

Use **Spanish Study Guide,** pp. 4–6 for additional support.

Gifted and Talented
Have students consider the meaning of the saying "act your age." Ask students, as they read, to make observations about Rachel's behavior and what kind of behavior people expect from an eleven-year-old. Discuss whether or not the same behavior is expected of boys and girls. Ask students to list other expressions about age and behavior.
Possible Responses: "wasn't born yesterday," "as old as you feel"

Students Acquiring English
1 Make sure students understand that the subject pronoun *you* is used here to mean the narrator, the reader, and people in general.
2 Point out that the idiomatic phrase *kind of* is often used in informal English to mean "approximately" or "somewhat."

Mini Lesson Preteaching Vocabulary

ANALYZING WORD PARTS
Instruction One way to figure out the meaning of an unfamiliar word is to break it into its parts and think about what the parts mean. Prefixes are word parts added to the beginning of a base word or a root that change its meaning.
in + visible = invisible
in- ("not") is combined with the base word *visible* ("able to be seen"), so the meaning of *invisible* must be "not able to be seen."

Application Show students the two other words from the story, below. Have them break each word into a prefix and a base or root word. Then have them tell what the prefix means and use a dictionary to find the meaning of the word. Finally, have them use each word in a sentence.
except   expect

Use **Unit One Resource Book,** p. 10 for more practice. Use **Vocabulary Transparencies and Copymasters,** p. 18.

Sometimes a narrator will describe a character directly. At other times, readers can make inferences from what a character says, does, and thinks. Ask students to look for clues about Rachel. What do they know about her from her words, actions, and thoughts?

Possible Responses: She is thoughtful (she thinks about what birthdays mean); she is shy (she cannot speak up for herself); she is thin (she describes herself as "skinny").

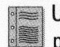 Use **Unit One Resource Book**, p. 9 for more practice.
Use **Literary Analysis Transparencies**, p. 3, for additional support.

Active Reading CONNECTING

Tell students that although they may not have had the same experiences as Rachel, they can still connect with many parts of this story. Use the following questions to help them make connections to their own experiences:

• How would you describe Mrs. Price and Sylvia Saldívar? Have you ever known people like them?

• How does Rachel feel when she cannot fight back against Mrs. Price? Have you ever felt this way?

 Use **Unit One Resource Book**, p. 8 for more practice.
Use **Reading and Critical Thinking Transparencies**, p. 2, for additional support.

ACTIVE READING

Ⓐ **CONNECT** Possible Response: her voice.
Ⓑ **CONNECT** Possible Response: Students may say that they've been embarrassed to cry in front of other people at one time or another.

---

and two instead of eleven because if I was one hundred and two I'd have known what to say when Mrs. Price put the red sweater on my desk. I would've known how to tell her it wasn't mine instead of just sitting there with that look on my face and nothing coming out of my mouth.

"Whose is this?" Mrs. Price says, and she holds the red sweater up in the air for all the class to see. "Whose? It's been sitting in the coatroom for a month."

"Not mine," says everybody. "Not me."

"It has to belong to somebody," Mrs. Price keeps saying, but nobody can remember. It's an ugly sweater with red plastic buttons and a collar and sleeves all stretched out like you could use it for a jump rope. It's maybe a thousand years old and even if it belonged to me I wouldn't say so.

Maybe because I'm skinny, maybe because she doesn't like me, that stupid Sylvia Saldívar says, "I think it belongs to Rachel." An ugly sweater like that, all raggedy and old, but Mrs. Price believes her. Mrs. Price takes the sweater and puts it right on my desk, but when I open my mouth nothing comes out.

"That's not, I don't, you're not . . . Not mine," I finally say in a little voice that was maybe me when I was four.

"Of course it's yours," Mrs. Price says. "I remember you wearing it once." Because she's older and the teacher, she's right and I'm not.

Not mine, not mine, not mine, but Mrs. Price is already turning to page thirty-two, and math problem number four. I don't know why but all of a sudden I'm feeling sick inside, like the part

Only today I wish I didn't have only eleven years rattling inside me.

of me that's three wants to come out of my eyes, only I squeeze them shut tight and bite down on my teeth real hard and try to remember today I am eleven, eleven. Mama is making a cake for me for tonight, and when Papa comes home everybody will sing Happy birthday, happy birthday to you.

But when the sick feeling goes away and I open my eyes, the red sweater's still sitting there like a big red mountain. I move the red sweater to the corner of my desk with my ruler. I move my pencil and books and eraser as far from it as possible. I even move my chair a little to the right. Not mine, not mine, not mine.

In my head I'm thinking how long till lunchtime, how long till I can take the red sweater and throw it over the schoolyard fence, or leave it hanging on a parking meter, or bunch it up into a little ball and toss it in the alley. Except when math period ends, Mrs. Price says loud and in front of everybody, "Now, Rachel, that's enough," because she sees I've shoved the red sweater to the tippy-tip corner of my desk and it's hanging all over the edge like a waterfall, but I don't care.

"Rachel," Mrs. Price says. She says it like she's getting mad. "You put that sweater on right now and no more nonsense."

"But it's not—"

"Now!" Mrs. Price says.

This is when I wish I wasn't eleven, because all the years inside of me—ten, nine, eight, seven, six, five, four, three, two, and one—are pushing at the back of my eyes when I put one arm through one sleeve of the sweater that smells like cottage cheese, and then the other arm through the other and stand there with my arms apart like if the sweater hurts

ACTIVE READING

Ⓐ **CONNECT** What is it about Rachel's thoughts and actions that reminds you of a four-year-old?

WORDS TO KNOW **except** (ĭk-sĕpt´) *prep.* other than; but

28

Teaching Options

Cake Window (Seven Cakes) (1970–1976), Wayne Thiebaud. Courtesy of Allan Stone Gallery, New York.

me and it does, all itchy and full of germs that aren't even mine.

That's when everything I've been holding in since this morning, since when Mrs. Price put the sweater on my desk, finally lets go, and all of a <u>sudden</u> I'm crying in front of everybody. I wish I was <u>invisible</u> but I'm not. I'm eleven and it's my birthday today and I'm crying like I'm three in front of everybody. I put my head down on the desk and bury my face in my stupid clown-sweater arms. My face all hot and spit coming out of my mouth because I can't stop the little animal noises from coming out of me, until there aren't any more tears left in my eyes, and it's just my body shaking like when you have the hiccups, and my whole head hurts like when you drink milk too fast.

ACTIVE READING

B **CONNECT** How does this description of crying relate to how you have experienced it?

But the worst part is right before the bell rings for lunch. That stupid Phyllis Lopez, who is even dumber than Sylvia Saldívar, says she remembers the red sweater is hers! I take it off right away and give it to her, only Mrs. Price pretends like everything's okay.

Today I'm eleven. There's a cake Mama's making for tonight, and when Papa comes home from work we'll eat it. There'll be candles and presents, and everybody will sing Happy birthday, happy birthday to you, Rachel, only it's too late.

I'm eleven today. I'm eleven, ten, nine, eight, seven, six, five, four, three, two, and one, but I wish I was one hundred and two. I wish I was anything but eleven, because I want today to be far away already, far away like a runaway balloon, like a tiny *o* in the sky, so tiny-tiny you have to close your eyes to see it. ❖

WORDS
TO
KNOW

sudden (sŭd′n) *adj.* happening without warning
invisible (ĭn-vĭz′ə-bəl) *adj.* impossible to see; not visible

29

Customizing Instruction

Students Acquiring English

1 Students should be able to infer the meaning of *tippy-tip* from context. Have a volunteer point to the "tippy-tip corner" of his or her desk.

Multiple Learning Styles
Interpersonal Learners

2 Have small groups discuss the physical reactions that Rachel has when she finally lets go. Ask them to talk about times when they have let go after holding a feeling in for a long time.

Less Proficient Readers

3 Ask students to paraphrase what Rachel thinks people don't understand about birthdays.
Possible Response: People can be many ages at the same time. Sometimes they feel vulnerable and younger than they are, as Rachel does.

Gifted and Talented
Remind students that the climax of a story is the most exciting or interesting moment. Ask them to identify the climax of this story and tell how the events leading up to it build suspense.
Possible Response: The climax is when Rachel breaks down and cries. When she wakes up on her birthday and does not feel any older, readers wonder whether she will have a reason to act younger. The interaction between Mrs. Price and Rachel builds tension as Rachel becomes more upset. When Rachel feels all her younger selves pushing against the back of her eyes, readers can predict that she is about to cry.

Viewing and Representing

Cake Window (Seven Cakes)
by Wayne Thiebaud

ART APPRECIATION Thiebaud (born 1920) says that reality, or realistic painting, is "just a method of interpreting our perceptions." As the cake frosting in this painting shows, Thiebaud conveys not only the visual but also the tactile qualities of objects that he paints. Discuss the painting and have students describe how the cakes are different and alike.
Application Ask students which cake they would prefer for their birthday and why. Ask them which

one they think Rachel would like and to explain why they think that.
Possible Responses: After her rough day at school, Rachel might like the one with the heart because it would symbolize her family's love. The cake with the layers could represent all the different ages Rachel feels, and the way she was "cut open" and exposed in front of her class. The thin yellow cake in the back row could represent how her birthday fell flat.

Active Reading CONNECTING

 A Ask: Have you ever worn clothing or a hair style that made you feel as if you were "not yourself"? Why are such things important to a person's identity?

Possible Response: Clothing and hair styles can make a statement about the kind of person we are or want to be. Although people should be judged on more than their appearance, it is hard to escape judgments based on looks.

Reading Skills and Strategies: COMPARE/CONTRAST

What are some similarities and differences between "Who's the New Kid?" and "Eleven"?

Possible Response: Both main characters are shy eleven-year-old girls. In both stories, the main character has a humiliating experience in school. Rachel's embarrassing experience revolves around a sweater, whereas the narrator in "Who's the New Kid?" is embarrassed because of a haircut. "Eleven" ends with Rachel wanting to escape, but "Who's the New Kid?" ends with a funny comment from the narrator's adult perspective.

Use **Reading and Critical Thinking Transparencies,** p. 40, for additional support.

Lois Lowry

Lois Lowry's father was an army dentist whose transfers kept her family on the move throughout her childhood. She was born in Hawaii and had lived in Pennsylvania and Tokyo by the time she started high school in New York. She went to college in Rhode Island before marrying a naval officer whose career again led her to move a lot. Later she graduated from the University of Southern Maine before beginning to write.

"WHO'S THE NEW KID?"

by Lois Lowry

Because of my father's job, my family moved a great deal. I was always (at least it felt like always!) the "new kid" in school.

I remember that when I was eleven years old, I was once again entering a brand-new school. And school had already begun. The kids had already gotten to know each other, had made friends, and had learned the teachers' names, the layout of the classrooms and the hallways, and the schedules.

A I arrived in the middle of the day, feeling very awkward and shy. I had had my hair cut the day before; it had been very long, and now it was very short, so I didn't even feel like myself. My mother took me to the school office, and they did the necessary paperwork to enroll me, and then she left me there. Someone took me to the classroom where I was supposed to be.

Everyone stared at me, of course, when I entered the room. One of the students—reacting to my very short hair, I suppose—called out, "Is it a boy or a girl?"

Do you know, that was *forty-four* years ago, that moment—yet I still remember how humiliating it felt.

But guess what. I still wear my hair very short. I think it's my way, now, of saying, "Nyah nyah. I don't care *what* you think."

Teaching Options

Mini Lesson Standardized Test Practice

DESCRIBING THE SETTING OF A STORY For some standardized tests, students will be expected to recognize or describe the setting of a selection. Write the following question on the board.
Which of these statements best describes the setting of "Eleven"?
A. Mrs. Price is Rachel's teacher.
B. It is Rachel's eleventh birthday.
C. Rachel is an eleven-year-old girl.
D. Rachel cries when she must put the sweater on.

Guide students to identify the correct answer. Remind them that setting is the time and/or place in which a story happens. B is the correct choice because it tells when "Eleven" takes place. A identifies one of the characters in the story, C describes the main character, and D describes the climactic event.

Connect to the Literature

1. What Do You Think?
Do you sympathize with Rachel's feelings? Why or why not?

Comprehension Check
- What does Rachel think about the sweater?
- What does Rachel do after she puts on the sweater?

Think Critically

2. **ACTIVE READING** **CONNECTING** Look at the notes you took in your **READER'S NOTEBOOK**. What **connections** did you make between Rachel's birthday and your own recollections?

3. Why do you think the incident with the sweater affects Rachel so powerfully?

THINK ABOUT
- Rachel's feelings about turning 11
- her description of the sweater
- Mrs. Price's responses to Rachel

4. Does Mrs. Price treat Rachel unfairly, or does she just make an honest mistake? Explain.

5. When Rachel cries, it seems that her 11th birthday is ruined. If you were a friend of Rachel's, what would you say or do to help her feel better?

Extend Interpretations

6. **COMPARING TEXTS** Read "Who's the New Kid?" on page 30. What comparisons can you make between Lois Lowry's experience and Rachel's?

7. Critic's Corner One critic has said that Sandra Cisneros "makes the invisible, visible." How does Cisneros make Rachel's feelings "visible" to readers?

8. Connect to Life Do you think people of all ages share Rachel's feelings about becoming a year older? Discuss with your classmates your own thoughts about growing up.

Literary Analysis

CHARACTER Each person (or animal or imaginary creature) that appears in a story is a **character**. In "Eleven," Rachel is the **main character** and the teacher and students are **minor characters**. A story usually focuses on events in the life of the main character. The minor characters serve mainly to help move along the action.

Cooperative Learning Activity
Get together with three classmates. Have two members of your group pretend to be Rachel and Mrs. Price, discussing why they acted as they did about the sweater. As they hold their discussion, the other two group members should take notes about what **traits,** or qualities, they see in the characters' behavior and language. Afterward, compare your group's observations with another group's.

Extend Interpretations

6. Comparing Texts Possible Response: Like Rachel, Lois Lowry felt misunderstood—in her case, when a student thought she might be a boy. Also like Rachel, she felt embarrassed and alone in front of the class when all the children stared at her.

7. Critic's Corner Possible Response: Rachel says that the sweater "hurts" her and describes it as "all itchy and full of germs that aren't even mine." When she cries, Cisneros describes how it feels to have one's body overcome by sobs.

8. Connect to Life Students may say that they expect to feel older and wiser each year, and that they hope that people will remember their birthdays and do things to make it a special day.

Connect to the Literature

What Do You Think?
1. Possible Response: It is understandable that Rachel is so upset because she has been singled out and her teacher will not believe what she says.

Comprehension Check
- Rachel thinks the sweater is ugly and embarrassing and smells bad.
- After Rachel puts on the sweater, she begins to cry.

Use Selection Quiz **Unit One Resource Book,** p. 13.

Think Critically

2. Possible Response: It is easy to relate to feeling unfairly treated and embarrassed. These feelings are worse when your classmates do not stick up for you.

Use **Reading and Critical Thinking Transparencies,** p. 2, for additional support.

3. Possible Response: Rachel felt younger than 11 years old when she awakened. Maybe she went to school feeling sensitive. Not only is the sweater not hers, but she feels singled out, publicly wronged, and humiliated.

4. Possible Responses: Mrs. Price treats Rachel unfairly. She should see that Rachel is telling the truth and that Rachel is upset. She should know that it's Rachel's birthday. Or, Mrs. Price makes a mistake because she is too busy to notice Rachel's reactions. She thinks Rachel is acting silly about the sweater.

5. Possible Response: I would tell Rachel that other people understand how she feels. Also, she can still have a good birthday celebration with her family tonight.

Literary Analysis

Character After the role-playing activity, groups may discuss whether the students who played the roles followed the story and acted in character for Mrs. Price and Rachel.

Use **Literary Analysis Transparencies,** p. 3, for additional support.

Writing Options

1. **Recollection Diary** Students can begin by listing things that contribute to a good birthday, such as being with friends and family, having a party, eating cake and ice cream, and getting cards and presents. Instead of focusing on their last birthday, they might write about the one that was the most memorable or the most surprising.

2. **Greeting Card** Have students think about the standard formats for greeting cards. Humorous ones have the beginning of a joke on the front and the punch line inside. More serious ones often have poems. Some have pop-up art on the inside. Encourage students to use one of these formats or invent one of their own.

Activities & Explorations

1. **Comic Strip** Students may use a computer to create the art for their comic strips. Successful strips should focus on the most important events in the plot and leave out less important details.

2. **Letter From Mrs. Price** Remind students to put themselves in Mrs. Price's place and to tell the story from her point of view this time.

Use **Communications Transparencies and Copymasters**, p. 11, for additional support.

Inquiry & Research

Celebrate! After all students have reported their findings, lead a class discussion on the similarities and differences in how birthdays are observed from family to family and country to country. Be sensitive to the fact that Jehovah's Witnesses do not celebrate birthdays, and allow any of these students to explain their beliefs.

Vocabulary and Spelling

Exercise A:
1. sudden
2. invisible
3. except
4. expect
Exercise B: Answers will vary.

Writing Options

1. **Recollection Diary** Think of your last birthday. Was it all that you expected? Better? Worse? Jot down notes about your birthday or about the birthday of a made-up character. Place the notes in your **Working Portfolio.**

2. **Greeting Card** Pretend that you are Rachel's best friend. Make a greeting card that you think would cheer her up on her 11th birthday.

Activities & Explorations

1. **Comic Strip** Draw a comic strip that shows the events of Rachel's 11th birthday. Pay attention to visual details, such as the appearance of the sweater, as well as to the interactions between characters. **~ ART**

2. **Letter from Mrs. Price** Mrs. Price has a difficult time dealing with Rachel and the fuss over the sweater. Pretend that you are Mrs. Price. Write a letter in which you tell a friend about your day. Read the letter to the class. **~ SPEAKING AND LISTENING**

Inquiry & Research

Celebrate! Birthday celebrations vary from family to family and from country to country. Interview someone about the birthday celebrations and traditions in his or her family. Find out whether the celebrations feature any particular songs, decorations, or foods. (Or, you might choose a country and find out how people typically celebrate birthdays in that country.) Report your findings to the class.

A piñata is a traditional birthday decoration and game.

Vocabulary and Spelling

EXERCISE A: RESTATEMENT CLUES On a sheet of paper, write the Word to Know that best completes each sentence.

1. With a _____ movement, Rachel pushed the sweater to the floor.

2. She could not read the letter because it was written with _____ ink.

3. No one _____ me knew that it was my birthday.

4. We _____ to have some chocolate cake at the party.

EXERCISE B: COMPOUND WORDS A compound word is a word that is made up of smaller words, called base words. These base words are joined together with no changes in spelling.

You can often figure out the meaning of a compound word from the meaning of its base words. Sometimes, however, putting the base words' meanings together does not give you the correct meaning. *Cowlick* does not refer to a lick from a cow; a cowlick is a piece of hair that stands up on its own.

Make a list of all the compound words you can find in "Eleven." Write down the base words that make up each one. Then use one of the base words to spell another compound word.

Example: waterfall = <u>water</u> + <u>fall</u>
                        downfall

Spelling Handbook p. R86

WORDS TO KNOW	except	expect	invisible	sudden

Teaching Options   Mini Lesson **Spelling**

POSSESSIVES AND CONTRACTIONS

Instruction Apostrophes are used with nouns to show possession. Generally, if the noun is singular, add an apostrophe plus an *s*. (Today is Rachel<u>'s</u> *birthday.*) For possessive plural nouns that end in *s*, simply add an apostrophe. (*Rachel hated her classmates<u>'</u> teasing.*)

Apostrophes are also used in contractions—joined words from which letters have been dropped. The apostrophe appears in place of the missing letters. (*Rachel was<u>n't</u> having fun.*)

Make sure students understand the difference between *whose* and *who's* and between *its* (possessive) and *it's* (contraction of *it is*).

Exercise Write the sentences on the board and have volunteers add apostrophes where they belong.

1. People just dont understand about birthdays. *(don't)*

2. The calendar says youre eleven. *(you're)*

3. I wouldnt wear a sweater if its sleeves were all stretched out. *(wouldn't)*

4. Its Phyllis Lopezs fault; she didnt remember! *(it's, Lopez's, didn't)*

 Use **Unit One Resource Book,** p. 12 for more practice.

Grammar in Context: Sentence Fragments

In "Eleven," Rachel becomes so frustrated that she speaks and thinks in broken pieces, or **fragments,** of a sentence.

> An ugly sweater like that, all raggedy and old. Mrs. Price puts it on my desk. "That's not, I don't, you're not . . . Not mine," I finally say in a little voice that was maybe me when I was four.

A sentence expresses a complete thought. A fragment is only a piece of a thought. Although fragments are rare in good writing, sometimes writers use them to communicate extreme emotion.

Usage Tip: The word *and, or, but,* or *like* at the beginning of a sentence may introduce a fragment. Try to avoid beginning a sentence with one of these words.

WRITING EXERCISE Rewrite each fragment as a complete sentence. You may add or delete words.

Example: *Original* Because nobody listened to me.

Rewritten Nobody listened to me.

1. Feels scared and small.
2. A little child.
3. Because nobody understands.
4. Tried to explain.

Connect to the Literature Reread the paragraph on page 28 that begins, "But when the sick feeling goes away . . ." Rewrite the paragraph so that it contains only complete sentences but remains packed with emotion.

Grammar Handbook Writing Complete Sentences, p. R59

"I'm trying to write the stories that haven't been written."

Sandra Cisneros
born 1954

Traveling Years Sandra Cisneros moved frequently as a child, particularly between Chicago, the city where she was born, and Mexico, the country her father came from. "I didn't like school because we moved so much, and I was always new and funny looking," she says. As a writer, Cisneros has drawn on her childhood memories of her Spanish-speaking neighborhood in Chicago, especially in her award-winning book *The House on Mango Street.*

A Quiet Observer Cisneros was shy in school. "I never opened my mouth," she remembers, "except when the teacher called on me, the first time I'd speak all day." Her out-of-class reading sparked her interest in writing. After studying literature in college, Cisneros earned a master's degree and began to publish poems, essays, and short stories. She has won praise both in this country and overseas for her writing about Mexican Americans.

AUTHOR ACTIVITY

The Lone Daughter As the only daughter in a family with seven children, Sandra Cisneros often felt overlooked and misunderstood. In your opinion, which details in "Eleven" express these feelings? Share your ideas with your classmates.

President Cleveland, Where Are You?

Short Story by ROBERT CORMIER

Objectives

1. understand and appreciate a **short story (Literary Analysis)**
2. understand the **plot** of a story **(Literary Analysis)**
3. understand the **sequence of events** in fiction **(Active Reading)**

Summary

Jerry and his friends are obsessed with cowboy cards. When Jerry's brother Armand asks him to chip in for a birthday gift for their father, Jerry holds back some money to spend on cards. But when Jerry gets to Lemire's store to buy them, he learns that the company is not making them anymore and is making president cards instead. Jerry races to catch his brother before he buys the birthday gift, so he can contribute more, but he is too late. He feels guilty. Later, when Jerry must again choose how to spend his money, he gives it to his brother, who needs money to attend a dance. Jerry deprives himself of being the first boy to collect a complete set of cards, thereby losing out on the grand prize of a baseball glove. But that's not the worst part. Now he must tell his best friend that he was responsible for the biggest braggart in town's winning the glove.

Thematic Link

After making a decision that benefits himself and regretting it, Jerry makes a courageous decision, and as a result, must face his friend's anger.

5-Minute Warm-Up

Daily Language SkillBuilder

Have students **proofread** the display sentences on page 19i and write them correctly. The sentences also appear on Transparency 1 of **Grammar Transparencies and Copymasters.**

"Weren't you supposed to feel good when you did something fine and noble?"

(**Connect to Your Life**)

Costly Choices Making your own choices takes courage. Think of a time when you chose to do something different from what someone else wanted or expected. Or think about someone in a book or movie who made a difficult choice. What was so difficult?

Build Background

CONNECT TO HISTORY "President Cleveland, Where Are You?" is set in the 1930s. In that decade, the United States suffered through the economic crisis now known as the Great Depression. Thousands of people lost their jobs, and banks and businesses closed all over the country.

Despite hard times, the 1930s was also a great decade for entertainment. Children enjoyed the Sunday "funny papers," four-hour movie matinees, and radio programs like *Little Orphan Annie* and *Dick Tracy*. Many children, like the boys in this story, collected trading cards that featured the heroes of movies and sports.

WORDS TO KNOW
Vocabulary Preview

allot	incredulous
betrayed	indignant
contempt	lethargy
divulge	obsess
dwindle	stalemate

Focus Your Reading

LITERARY ANALYSIS PLOT The series of events in a story is called the **plot.** A plot usually revolves around a **conflict,** or problem, faced by the main character. In the story you are about to read, the main character's brother helps create a conflict with these words:

"Ken Maynard!" he snorted. "Who's more important—him or your father?"

Usually, a plot builds with **rising action** toward a **climax,** or turning point. The **falling action** follows, as the characters deal with the problem's resolution, and the story ends. As you read, try to identify the main conflict and its resolution.

ACTIVE READING SEQUENCE OF EVENTS To understand a story, you must be able to follow the **sequence of events** in the plot. Look for events that help to move the plot along. Some may seem unimportant at first but turn out to be significant.

READER'S NOTEBOOK As you read, use a story wheel like the one at the right to keep track of six important events. The wheel will help you see how events move the plot forward.

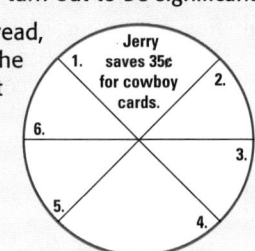

Jerry
1. saves 35¢ for cowboy cards.
2.
3.
4.
5.
6.

LESSON RESOURCES

UNIT ONE RESOURCE BOOK, pp. 14–20

ASSESSMENT
Formal Assessment, pp. 7–8
Teacher's Guide to Assessment and Portfolio Use
Test Generator

SKILLS TRANSPARENCIES AND COPYMASTERS
Literary Analysis
• Plot, TR 5 (for Paired Activity, p. 45)

Reading and Critical Thinking
• Sequencing, TR 3 (for Thinking Through the Literature, p. 45)
Grammar
• Exclamatory Sentences, CM 52 (for Mini Lesson, p. 42)
• Punctuating Four Types of Sentences, CM 119 (for Mini Lesson, p. 47)
Vocabulary
• Using Context Clues, CM 19 (for Mini Lesson, p. 35)

INTEGRATED TECHNOLOGY
Audio Library

Visit our website:
www.mcdougallittell.com

President Cleveland, WHERE ARE YOU?

BY ROBERT CORMIER

T HAT WAS THE AUTUMN OF THE COWBOY CARDS—
Buck Jones and Tom Tyler and Hoot Gibson and especially
Ken Maynard. The cards were available in those five-cent packages of
gum: pink sticks, three together, covered with a sweet white powder.
You couldn't blow bubbles with that particular gum, but it couldn't
have mattered less. The cowboy cards were important—the pictures
of those rock-faced men with eyes of blue steel.

On those wind-swept, leaf-tumbling afternoons, we gathered after
school on the sidewalk in front of Lemire's Drugstore, across from
St. Jude's Parochial School, and we swapped and bargained and
matched for the cards. Because a Ken Maynard serial[1] was playing
at the Globe every Saturday afternoon, he was the most popular
cowboy of all, and one of his cards was worth at least ten of any
other kind. Rollie Tremaine had a treasure of thirty or so, and he
guarded them jealously. He'd match you for the other cards, but he
risked his Ken Maynards only when the other kids threatened to
leave him out of the competition altogether.

---

1. **serial** (sîr′ē-əl): a movie appearing in weekly parts.

Literary Analysis: CONFLICT

A Ask students what conflict Jerry faces.
Possible Response: Jerry is torn between spending money on cowboy cards and being generous to his father.

Literary Analysis PLOT

B Remind students that the first part of a story usually introduces the characters and the setting. Ask students to summarize the plot thus far.
Possible Response: Jerry and the other boys are obsessed with cowboy cards. Jerry has some extra money which he plans to use to buy cards. He gives Armand some (but not all) of his money for a birthday gift for their father.

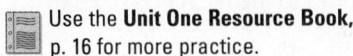 Use the **Unit One Resource Book**, p. 16 for more practice.

Active Reading
SEQUENCE OF EVENTS

Have students record the sequence of events on a story map like the one below. Ask them to add to it as they continue to read.

| First: Jerry got some extra money. |
| Then: Armand asked him for some money. |
| Next: |
| Next: |
| Finally: |

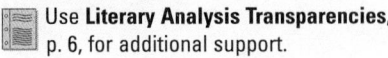 Use **Unit One Resource Book**, p. 15 for more practice.
Use **Literary Analysis Transparencies**, p. 3, for additional support.

Literary Analysis: SETTING

Remind students that the setting is the time and place in which a story takes place. The setting may also include the social environment—what people are like and what they expect. Ask what is known so far about the setting.
Possible Response: It is autumn during the Depression in a town where most of the people don't seem to have a lot of money to spend.

Use **Literary Analysis Transparencies**, p. 6, for additional support.

---

1 You could almost hate Rollie Tremaine. In the first place, he was the only son of Auguste Tremaine, who operated the Uptown Dry Goods Store, and he did not live in a tenement[2] but in a big white birthday cake of a house on Laurel Street. He was too fat to be effective in the football games between the Frenchtown Tigers and the North Side Knights, and he made us constantly aware of the jingle of coins in his pockets. He was able to stroll into Lemire's and casually select a quarter's worth of cowboy cards while the rest of us watched, aching with envy.

Once in a while I earned a nickel or dime by running errands or washing windows for blind old Mrs. Belander, or by finding pieces of copper, brass, and other valuable metals at the dump and selling them to the junkman. The coins clutched in my hand, I would race to Lemire's to buy a cowboy card or two, hoping that Ken Maynard would stare boldly out at me as I opened the pack. At one time, before a disastrous matching session with Roger Lussier (my best friend, except where the cards were involved), I owned five Ken Maynards and considered myself a millionaire, of sorts.

One week I was particularly lucky; I had spent two afternoons washing floors for Mrs. Belander and received a quarter. Because my father had worked a full week at the shop, where a rush order for fancy combs had been received, he allotted my brothers and sisters and me an extra dime along with the usual ten cents for the Saturday-afternoon movie. Setting aside the movie fare, I found myself with a bonus of thirty-five cents, and I then planned to put Rollie Tremaine to shame the following Monday afternoon.

---

2. **tenement** (tĕn′ə-mənt): a low-rent or rundown apartment building.

WORDS
TO
KNOW
allot (ə-lŏt′) v. to parcel out to; distribute to

Teaching Options

Monday was the best day to buy the cards because the candy man stopped at Lemire's every Monday morning to deliver the new assortments. There was nothing more exciting in the world than a fresh batch of card boxes. I rushed home from school that day and hurriedly changed my clothes, eager to set off for the store. As I burst through the doorway, letting the screen door slam behind me, my brother Armand blocked my way.

He was fourteen, three years older than I, and a freshman at Monument High School. He had recently become a stranger to me in many ways—indifferent to such matters as cowboy cards and the Frenchtown Tigers—and he carried himself with a mysterious dignity that was fractured now and then when his voice began shooting off in all directions like some kind of vocal fireworks.[3]

"Wait a minute, Jerry," he said. "I want to talk to you." He motioned me out of earshot of my mother, who was busy supervising the usual after-school skirmish[4] in the kitchen.

I sighed with impatience. In recent months Armand had become a figure of authority, siding with my father and mother occasionally. As the oldest son, he sometimes took advantage of his age and experience to issue rules and regulations.

"How much money have you got?" he whispered.

"You in some kind of trouble?" I asked, excitement rising in me as I remembered the blackmail plot of a movie at the Globe a month before.

He shook his head in annoyance. "Look," he said, "it's Pa's birthday tomorrow. I think we ought to chip in and buy him something. . . ."

I reached into my pocket and caressed the coins. "Here," I said carefully, pulling out a nickel. "If we all give a nickel, we should have enough to buy him something pretty nice."

He regarded me with contempt. "Rita already gave me fifteen cents, and I'm throwing in a quarter. Albert handed over a dime—all that's left of his birthday money. Is that all you can do—a nickel?"

"Aw, come on," I protested. "I haven't got a single Ken Maynard left, and I was going to buy some cards this afternoon."

"Ken Maynard!" he snorted. "Who's more important—him or your father?"

His question was unfair because he knew that there was no possible choice—"my father" had to be the only answer. My father was a huge man who believed in the things of the spirit. . . . He had worked at the Monument Comb Shop since the age of fourteen; his booming laugh—or grumble—greeted us each night when he returned from the factory. A steady worker when the shop had enough work, he quickened with gaiety on Friday nights and weekends, . . . and he was fond of making long speeches about the good things in life. In the middle of the Depression, for instance, he paid cash for a piano, of all things, and insisted that my twin sisters, Yolande and Yvette, take lessons once a week.

I took a dime from my pocket and handed it to Armand.

---

3. **vocal fireworks:** because Armand's voice is changing, its pitch varies unexpectedly from high to low.

4. **skirmish** (skûr′mĭsh): a minor battle or conflict.

WORDS TO KNOW **contempt** (kən-tĕmpt′) *n.* the feeling produced by something disgraceful or worthless; scorn

37

Reading Skills and Strategies: PREDICT

 Ask students to predict what Jerry will do now that he can't buy any cowboy cards.

Possible Response: He will give the money to Armand for the present for his father.

Active Reading

SEQUENCE OF EVENTS

Remind students that they can represent text information in different ways. Have them continue filling out their story maps with the events on this page.

Possible Responses: There are no more cowboy cards. Jerry hurries to give his brother more money. He is too late.

Literary Analysis   PLOT

 Remind students that the climax of a story is the point the action builds to—the most dramatic moment. Ask what has been the most dramatic moment so far.

Possible Response: Jerry's race to catch Armand

Use **Literary Analysis Transparencies,** p. 5, for additional support.

Literary Analysis: CONFLICT

Analyze and discuss Jerry's conflict with students. Is it an internal conflict or an external one?

Possible Response: It has elements of both. It begins with an external conflict when Armand asks him for money and argues about how much he gives, but the conflict continues for Jerry as he thinks over the decision he made.

Use **Literary Analysis Transparencies,** p. 8, for additional support.

Whelan's Drug Store, Berenice Abbott. Photography Collection, Miriam and Ira D. Wallach Division of Art, Prints and Photographs, The New York Public Library, Astor, Lenox and Tilden Foundations.

WHEN I ARRIVED AT LEMIRE'S, I SENSED DISASTER IN THE AIR.

38

Teaching Options

Mini Lesson — Viewing and Representing

Whelan's Drug Store,
by Berenice Abbott

ART APPRECIATION When Berenice Abbott came back to visit New York after eight years in Europe, the changes taking place in the city so interested her that she stayed and embarked on an extensive photographic exploration of the city.

Instruction Tell students that photographs like this one convey a lot of information about life at a particular time. Ask what time of year this photograph was taken. How can you tell?

Answer: It was probably taken just before Valentine's Day, because there are heart-shaped candy boxes for sale.

Application Ask students whether they think this photograph was well chosen for this selection. Why or why not?

Possible Response: Yes, it was well chosen. It shows what a drug store in the 1930s looked like. It's interesting to compare prices then and now.

"Thanks, Jerry," he said. "I hate to take your last cent."

"That's all right," I replied, turning away and consoling myself with the thought that twenty cents was better than nothing at all.

When I arrived at Lemire's, I sensed disaster in the air. Roger Lussier was kicking disconsolately at a tin can in the gutter, and Rollie Tremaine sat sullenly on the steps in front of the store.

"Save your money," Roger said. He had known about my plans to splurge on the cards.

"What's the matter?" I asked.

"There's no more cowboy cards," Rollie Tremaine said. "The company's not making them any more."

"They're going to have President cards," Roger said, his face twisting with disgust. He pointed to the store window. "Look!"

A placard in the window announced: "Attention, Boys. Watch for the New Series. Presidents of the United States. Free in Each 5-Cent Package of Caramel Chew."

"President cards?" I asked, dismayed.

I read on: "Collect a Complete Set and Receive an Official Imitation Major League Baseball Glove, Embossed with Lefty Grove's Autograph."

Glove or no glove, who could become excited about Presidents, of all things?

Rollie Tremaine stared at the sign. "Benjamin Harrison,[5] for crying out loud," he said. "Why would I want Benjamin Harrison when I've got twenty-two Ken Maynards?"

I felt the warmth of guilt creep over me. I jingled the coins in my pocket, but the sound was hollow. No more Ken Maynards to buy.

"I'm going to buy a Mr. Goodbar," Rollie Tremaine decided.

I was without appetite, indifferent even to a Baby Ruth, which was my favorite. I thought of how I had betrayed Armand and, worst of all, my father.

"I'll see you after supper," I called over my shoulder to Roger as I hurried away toward home. I took the shortcut behind the church, although it involved leaping over a tall wooden fence, and I zigzagged recklessly through Mr. Thibodeau's garden, trying to outrace my guilt. I pounded up the steps and into the house, only to learn that Armand had already taken Yolande and Yvette uptown to shop for the birthday present.

I pedaled my bike furiously through the streets, ignoring the indignant horns of automobiles as I sliced through the traffic. Finally I saw Armand and my sisters emerge from the Monument Men's Shop. My heart sank when I spied the long, slim package that Armand was holding.

"Did you buy the present yet?" I asked, although I knew it was too late.

"Just now. A blue tie," Armand said. "What's the matter?"

"Nothing," I replied, my chest hurting.

He looked at me for a long moment. At first his eyes were hard, but then they softened. He smiled at me, almost sadly, and touched my arm. I turned away from him because I felt naked and exposed.

"It's all right," he said gently. "Maybe you've learned something." The words were gentle, but they held a curious dignity, the dignity remaining even when his voice suddenly cracked on the last syllable.

I wondered what was happening to me, because I did not know whether to laugh or cry.

---

5. **Benjamin Harrison:** president of the United States from 1889 to 1893.

WORDS TO KNOW   **indignant** (ĭn-dĭg′nənt) *adj.* angry at something unjust, mean, or unworthy

39

Literary Analysis: HUMOR

 A Discuss the humorous tone the author has taken throughout this story. For example, he says, "We journeyed on our bicycles to the North Side, engaged three boys in a matching bout, and returned with five new presidents, including Chester Alan Arthur, who up to that time had been missing." Ask students if he really means the President himself had been missing. If not, what does he mean and why do they think he says it this way?

Possible Response: No, he means that President Arthur's *card* has not been seen around yet. It makes it funnier, though, to say it as if the president himself were missing.

Active Reading
SEQUENCE OF EVENTS

B Have students add the important information that Jerry learns about Armand on page 41 to their story maps.

Possible Response: Jerry learns that Armand is in love.

S ister Angela was amazed when, a week before Christmas vacation, everybody in the class submitted a history essay worthy of a high mark—in some cases as high as A minus. (Sister Angela did not believe that anyone in the world ever deserved an A.) She never learned—or at least she never let on that she knew—we all had become experts on the Presidents because of the cards we purchased at Lemire's. Each card contained a picture of a President and, on the reverse side, a summary of his career. We looked at those cards so often that the biographies imprinted themselves on our minds without effort. Even our street-corner conversations were filled with such information as the fact that James Madison was called "The Father of the Constitution," or that John Adams had intended to become a minister.

The President cards were a roaring success, and the cowboy cards were quickly forgotten. In the first place, we did not receive gum with the cards, but a kind of chewy caramel. The caramel could be tucked into a corner of your mouth, bulging your cheek in much the same manner as wads of tobacco bulged the mouths of baseball stars. In the second place, the competition for collecting the cards was fierce and frustrating—fierce because everyone was intent on being the first to send away for a baseball glove and frustrating because although there were only thirty-two Presidents, including Franklin Delano Roosevelt,[6] the variety at Lemire's was at a minimum. When the deliveryman left the boxes of cards at the store each Monday, we often discovered that one entire box was devoted to a single President—two weeks in a row the boxes contained nothing but Abraham Lincolns. One week Roger Lussier and I were the heroes of Frenchtown. We journeyed on our bicycles to

the North Side, engaged three boys in a matching bout, and returned with five new Presidents, including Chester Alan Arthur, who up to that time had been missing.

Perhaps to sharpen our desire, the card company sent a sample glove to Mr. Lemire, and it dangled, orange and sleek, in the window. I was half sick with longing, thinking of my old glove at home, which I had inherited from Armand. But Rollie Tremaine's desire for the glove outdistanced my own. He even got Mr. Lemire to agree to give the glove in the window to the first person to get a complete set of cards, so that precious time wouldn't be wasted waiting for the postman.

We were delighted at Rollie Tremaine's frustration, especially since he was only a substitute player for the Tigers. Once, after spending fifty cents on cards—all of which turned out to be Calvin Coolidge—he threw them to the ground, pulled some dollar bills out of his pocket, and said, "The heck with it. I'm going to buy a glove!"

"Not that glove," Roger Lussier said. "Not a glove with Lefty Grove's autograph. Look what it says at the bottom of the sign."

We all looked, although we knew the words by heart: "This Glove Is Not For Sale Anywhere."

Rollie Tremaine scrambled to pick up the cards from the sidewalk, pouting more than ever. After that he was quietly <u>obsessed</u> with the Presidents, hugging the cards close to his chest and refusing to tell us how many more he needed to complete his set.

I too was obsessed with the cards, because they had become things of comfort in a world

6. **Franklin Delano Roosevelt:** president of the United States from 1933 to 1945; president at the time of the story.

WORDS
TO
KNOW
   obsess (əb-sĕs′) *v.* to occupy the mind of; concern excessively

40

Teaching Options

Mini Lesson   Spelling

SUFFIXES: -ING
Instruction Explain that most words do not change their spelling when the suffix -ing is added, but some do:
- One-syllable words with a consonant, vowel, consonant (CVC) pattern double the final consonant: *rub, rubbing.* However, words ending in *w, x, y,* or *z* do not change: *bow, bowing*
- Two-syllable words with the stress on the second syllable also double the last consonant: *admit, admitting*
- Words ending in silent *e* drop it: *pile, piling*

Application Have students make a three-column chart labeled *No change, Drop* e, *Double Consonant.* Ask them to find all words ending in -ing on these two pages, and list each under the proper head.
Answers: (col. 1) *roaring, collecting, matching, missing, longing, thinking, spending, going, pouting, snooping, warning;* (col. 2) *bulging, frustrating, including, refusing, writing;* (col. 3) *hugging, shrugging, webbing, padding*

 Use **Unit One Resource Book**, p. 19 for practice.

[1] that had suddenly grown dismal. After Christmas, a layoff at the shop had thrown my father out of work. He received no paycheck for four weeks, and the only income we had was from Armand's after-school job at the Blue and White Grocery Store—a job he lost finally when business dwindled as the layoff continued.

[2] Although we had enough food and clothing—my father's credit had always been good, a matter of pride with him—the inactivity made my father restless and irritable. . . . The twins fell sick and went to the hospital to have their tonsils removed. My father was confident that he would return to work eventually and pay off his debts, but he seemed to age before our eyes.

[B] When orders again were received at the comb shop and he returned to work, another disaster occurred, although I was the only one aware of it. Armand fell in love.

I discovered his situation by accident, when I happened to pick up a piece of paper that had fallen to the floor in the bedroom he and I shared. I frowned at the paper, puzzled.

"Dear Sally, When I look into your eyes the world stands still . . ."

The letter was snatched from my hands before I finished reading it.

"What's the big idea, snooping around?" Armand asked, his face crimson. "Can't a guy have any privacy?"

He had never mentioned privacy before. "It was on the floor," I said. "I didn't know it was a letter. Who's Sally?"

[3] He flung himself across the bed. "You tell anybody and I'll muckalize you," he threatened. "Sally Knowlton."

Nobody in Frenchtown had a name like Knowlton.

"A girl from the North Side?" I asked, incredulous.

He rolled over and faced me, anger in his eyes, and a kind of despair, too.

"What's the matter with that? Think she's too good for me?" he asked. "I'm warning you, Jerry, if you tell anybody . . ."

"Don't worry," I said. Love had no particular place in my life; it seemed an unnecessary waste of time. And a girl from the North Side was so remote that for all practical purposes she did not exist. But I was curious. "What are you writing her a letter for? Did she leave town or something?"

"She hasn't left town," he answered. "I wasn't going to send it. I just felt like writing to her."

I was glad that I had never become involved with love—love that brought desperation to your eyes, that caused you to write letters you did not plan to send. Shrugging with indifference, I began to search in the closet for the old baseball glove. I found it on the shelf, under some old sneakers. The webbing was torn and the padding gone. I thought of the sting I would feel when a sharp grounder slapped into the glove, and I winced. [4]

"You tell anybody about me and Sally and I'll—"

"I know. You'll muckalize me."

I did not divulge his secret and often shared his agony, particularly when he sat at the supper table and left my mother's special butterscotch pie untouched. I had never realized before how terrible love could be. But my compassion was short-lived, because I had other things to worry about: report cards due at Eastertime; the loss of income from old Mrs. Belander, who had gone to live with a daughter in Boston; and, of course, the Presidents.

WORDS TO KNOW

dwindle (dwĭn'dl) v. to become less and less
incredulous (ĭn-krĕj'ə-ləs) adj. unbelieving
divulge (dĭ-vŭlj') v. to reveal, especially something private or secret

41

Cross Curricular Link Social Studies

FRENCH AMERICANS Explorers from France were not the first Europeans to reach the Americas, but they played a major role in the early exploration of what is now the United States and Canada. Some came to trade with Native Americans. Others came to fight on the American side in the Revolution. From the late 17th to mid-18th centuries, about 15,000 Huguenots (French Protestants) came to escape religious persecution. Political refugees came following the French Revolution. Many French Canadians began to move to the United States in the mid-1800s to find work in the mills and factories. Most of them settled in New England.

The impact of French Americans has been great. Paul Revere, Alexander Hamilton, Henry David Thoreau, Henry Wadsworth Longfellow, and Jacqueline Bouvier Kennedy Onassis are just a few of the people of French heritage who have had a profound effect on the cultural, political, scientific, and humanitarian life of the United States.

A Ask: What do you think Jerry will do once he has a Grover Cleveland card?

Possible Response: He will turn in his full set and win the baseball glove.

Reading Skills and Strategies:
MAKE INFERENCES

Ask what the thinking behind Jerry's decision may have been.

Possible Response: He was not happy with his decision about the gift money. He wanted to do something different this time.

Literary Analysis PLOT

Tell students that the climax of this story has passed, and the resolution (a fairly long one) is taking place. See if students can identify the key pieces of information on this page that are part of the resolution.

Possible Response: No one has a Grover Cleveland card. Rollie offers five dollars for one. Armand needs money to take Sally to a dance. Jerry finds out where he can get a Grover Cleveland card. He gets one. Armand goes to the dance.

Active Reading
SEQUENCE OF EVENTS

Have students continue to fill in their story maps.

Possible Response: Jerry gets a Grover Cleveland card.

Because a <u>stalemate</u> had been reached, the President cards were the dominant force in our lives—mine, Roger Lussier's, and Rollie Tremaine's. For three weeks, as the baseball season approached, each of us had a complete set—complete except for one President, Grover Cleveland. Each time a box of cards arrived at the store, we hurriedly bought them (as hurriedly as our funds allowed) and tore off the wrappers, only to be confronted by James Monroe or Martin Van Buren or someone else. But never Grover Cleveland, never the man who had been the twenty-second and the twenty-fourth President of the United States. We argued about Grover Cleveland. Should he be placed between Chester Alan Arthur and Benjamin Harrison as the twenty-second President, or did he belong between Benjamin Harrison and William McKinley as the twenty-fourth President? Was the card company playing fair? Roger Lussier brought up a horrifying possibility—did we need two Grover Clevelands to complete the set?

Indignant, we stormed Lemire's and protested to the harassed store owner, who had long since vowed never to stock a new series. Muttering angrily, he searched his bills and receipts for a list of rules.

"All right," he announced. "Says here you only need one Grover Cleveland to finish the set. Now get out, all of you, unless you've got money to spend."

Outside the store, Rollie Tremaine picked up an empty tobacco tin and scaled it across the street. "Boy," he said. "I'd give five dollars for a Grover Cleveland."

When I returned home, I found Armand sitting on the piazza[7] steps, his chin in his hands. His mood of dejection mirrored my own, and I sat down beside him. We did not say anything for a while.

"Want to throw the ball around?" I asked.

He sighed, not bothering to answer.

"You sick?" I asked.

He stood up and hitched up his trousers, pulled at his ear, and finally told me what the matter was—there was a big dance next week at the high school, the Spring Promenade, and Sally had asked him to be her escort.

I shook my head at the folly of love. "Well, what's so bad about that?"

"How can I take Sally to a fancy dance?" he asked desperately. "I'd have to buy her a corsage. . . . And my shoes are practically falling apart. Pa's got too many worries now to buy me new shoes or give me money for flowers for a girl."

I nodded in sympathy. "Yeah," I said. "Look at me. Baseball time is almost here, and all I've got is that old glove. And no Grover Cleveland card yet . . ."

"Grover Cleveland?" he asked. "They've got some of those up on the North Side. Some kid was telling me there's a store that's got them. He says they're looking for Warren G. Harding."

"Holy smoke!" I said. "I've got an extra Warren G. Harding!" Pure joy sang in my veins. I ran to my bicycle, swung into the seat—and found that the front tire was flat.

"I'll help you fix it," Armand said.

Within half an hour I was at the North Side Drugstore, where several boys were matching cards on the sidewalk. Silently but blissfully I shouted: President Grover Cleveland, here I come!

---

7. **piazza** (pē-ăz'ə): porch.

WORDS
TO
KNOW

stalemate (stāl'māt') *n.* a situation in which none of the people playing a game are able to win

42

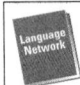 **Grammar**

Mini
Lesson

EXCLAMATORY SENTENCES

Instruction Remind students that they can use punctuation to clarify and enhance meaning. When they wish to emphasize a command or show excitement or another strong feeling, they may choose to use an exclamation point. Point out that these should be used sparingly so they won't lose their impact.
Note this passage:
"Holy smoke!" I said. "I've got an extra Warren G. Harding!"
The exclamation points show the speaker's excitement.

Exercises Ask students to decide whether each of the following sentences should have a period or an exclamation point at the end.

1. I can't believe I got a Grover Cleveland (!)
2. I'd almost given up (.)
3. Give me that Grover Cleveland card (!)
4. I'd like to help my brother (.)

📖 Use **Grammar Transparencies and Copymasters**, p. 52.

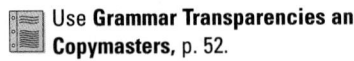 Use McDougal Littell's **Language Network**, Chapter 1, for more instruction and practice in exclamatory sentences.

Tenement Flats (Family Flats) (1934), Millard Sheets. National Museum of American Art, Washington, D.C./Art Resource, New York.

Less Proficient Readers

1 Ask students why the store owner is angry.

Possible Response: He is tired of all the bother caused by the cards. The boys have probably been pestering him about missing cards and other things connected to the contest.

Students Acquiring English

Help students use context to find the meanings of:

2 *scaled*—context clue: *picked up, across the street;* meaning: "threw"

3 *corsage*—context clue: *flowers for a girl;* meaning: "small bouquet of flowers worn at the shoulder, waist, or wrist"

Less Proficient Readers

Be sure students understand that time passes after Jerry tries to get a Grover Cleveland card and before Armand leaves for the dance.

Check to see that students are aware that Jerry gets a Grover Cleveland card, sells it to Rollie, and gives the money to Armand, who buys a corsage.

"HE SAYS
THEY'RE LOOKING FOR
WARREN G. HARDING."

43

Mini Lesson Viewing and Representing

Tenement Flats, by Millard Sheets

ART APPRECIATION Millard Sheets, born in California in 1907, was known not only as a painter and muralist, but also as an architect, teacher, art historian, and film production designer.

Instruction Point out the way the artist contrasts the angularity of the buildings and porch railings with the more flowing outlines of the people and the hanging laundry.

Application/Interpretation Ask students to describe the mood of this painting.

Possible Response: The mood is cheerful. The many people visiting with each other, the bright, clean laundry, the general feel of bustle, and the cats perched here and there all create a scene of warmth and human interaction.

• Ask how the scene below differs from what is visible in the upper left corner of the painting.

Possible Response: In the upper corner, only one person is visible. The houses are fancier, but that section looks almost deserted by comparison.

A After Armand had left for the dance, all dressed up as if it were Sunday, the small green box containing the corsage under his arm, I sat on the railing of the piazza, letting my feet dangle. The neighborhood was quiet because the Frenchtown Tigers were at Daggett's Field, practicing for the first baseball game of the season.

I thought of Armand and the ridiculous expression on his face when he'd stood before the mirror in the bedroom. I'd avoided looking at his new black shoes. "Love," I muttered.

Spring had arrived in a sudden stampede of apple blossoms and fragrant breezes. Windows had been thrown open and dust mops had banged on the sills all day long as the women busied themselves with housecleaning. I was puzzled by my lethargy. Wasn't spring supposed to make everything bright and gay?

I turned at the sound of footsteps on the stairs. Roger Lussier greeted me with a sour face.

"I thought you were practicing with the Tigers," I said.

"Rollie Tremaine," he said. "I just couldn't stand him." He slammed his fist against the railing. "Jeez, why did he have to be the one to get a Grover Cleveland? You should see him showing off. He won't let anybody even touch that glove. . . ."

B I felt like Benedict Arnold[8] and knew that I had to confess what I had done.

"Roger," I said, "I got a Grover Cleveland card up on the North Side. I sold it to Rollie Tremaine for five dollars."

"Are you crazy?" he asked.

"I needed that five dollars. It was an—an emergency."

"Boy!" he said, looking down at the ground and shaking his head. "What did you have to do a thing like that for?"

I watched him as he turned away and began walking down the stairs.

"Hey, Roger!" I called.

He squinted up at me as if I were a stranger, someone he'd never seen before.

"What?" he asked, his voice flat.

"I had to do it," I said. "Honest."

He didn't answer. He headed toward the fence, searching for the board we had loosened to give us a secret passage.

I thought of my father and Armand and Rollie Tremaine and Grover Cleveland and wished that I could go away someplace far away. But there was no place to go.

Roger found the loose slat in the fence and slipped through. I felt betrayed: Weren't you supposed to feel good when you did something fine and noble?

A moment later, two hands gripped the top of the fence and Roger's face appeared. "Was it a real emergency?" he yelled.

"A real one!" I called. "Something important!"

His face dropped from sight and his voice reached me across the yard: "All right."

"See you tomorrow!" I yelled.

I swung my legs over the railing again. The gathering dusk began to soften the sharp edges of the fence, the rooftops, the distant church steeple. I sat there a long time, waiting for the good feeling to come. ❖ **C**

---

8. **Benedict Arnold:** an American general who became a traitor to his country's cause during the Revolutionary War.

WORDS TO KNOW **lethargy** (lĕth′ər-jē) *n.* a lack of activity; sluggishness
betrayed (bĭ-trād′) *adj.* made a fool of; tricked **betray** *v.*

44

✓ Assessment **Standardized Test Practice**

Connect to the Literature

1. **What Do You Think?** What was your reaction to Jerry's decision to sell the Grover Cleveland card?

Comprehension Check
- Why do the other kids resent Rollie Tremaine?
- Why does Jerry want a full set of President cards?
- How does Jerry get the Grover Cleveland card?

Think Critically

2. How would you describe Jerry's feelings toward Armand? Support your answer with examples.

3. Why does Jerry say he felt "like Benedict Arnold" after Rollie got the new glove?

4. **ACTIVE READING** **SEQUENCE OF EVENTS** Look back over the story wheel you created in your **READER'S NOTEBOOK.** What events in Jerry's family life contribute to his decision to sell the card?

5. Why do you think the author chose to have the **main character** tell this story?

THINK ABOUT
- Jerry's desire for trading cards and a new baseball glove
- his observations of his father and brother
- his relationships with his friends

Extend Interpretations

6. **Different Perspectives** Imagine that the last scene of the story were told by Roger instead of Jerry. How would it be different? What might Roger say about his thoughts and feelings?

7. **Connect to Life** Near the end of the story, Jerry tells us, "I felt betrayed. Weren't you supposed to feel good when you did something fine and noble?" How would you answer this question? Explain your thinking.

Literary Analysis

PLOT The **plot** is the series of events in a story. Usually, the plot centers on a **conflict**—a problem faced by the main character. You can see Jerry begin to experience a conflict when he feels guilty about giving so little money for his father's birthday gift. The **rising action** of events leads to the story's **climax,** or turning point. Often, it occurs when the main character makes an important discovery or choice. The remaining events are **falling action,** as characters work on the **resolution** of the main problem or conflict.

Paired Activity Copy the chart shown below. With a partner, go back through the story to fill in the chart. In the first box, identify the conflict. In the second box, identify the climax of the story. In the third box, state how the conflict is resolved. Use examples to support your ideas.

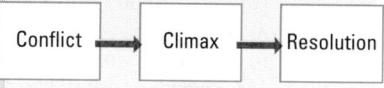

Conflict → Climax → Resolution

REVIEW **CHARACTER** Jerry is clearly the **main character** in this story. Who are the **minor characters,** and how is each important to the plot?

Extend Interpretations

6. **Different Perspectives** Students may say that Roger might talk about his appreciation for his brother and what he did.

7. **Connect to Life** Students may say that doing something "fine and noble" often involves sacrifice, risk, or discomfort. They might point to examples of firefighters, pioneers, missionaries, and other heroes who risk their lives, health, or personal comfort to help others. They may also know from experience that doing something right is not always easy or socially rewarding. Sometimes, the "good feeling" is a sense of integrity or satisfaction, rather than happiness; it has to come from within, and it comes at a cost.

GUIDING STUDENT RESPONSE

Connect to the Literature

1. **What Do You Think?** Students may be surprised that Jerry sold the card when he needed it to get the baseball glove. They may also admire his selflessness and generosity toward his brother Armand.

Comprehension Check
- His family has money. He can buy almost anything he wants, and he flaunts his good fortune.
- If Jerry is the first to collect a full set of President cards, he will win a new baseball glove to replace his old one.
- Armand tells Jerry that boys on the North Side have a Grover Cleveland card to trade.

Use Selection Quiz **Unit One Resource Book,** p. 20.

Think Critically

2. Possible Response: Jerry feels that Armand has changed, assuming an authority Jerry sometimes resents. Yet he also admires Armand's dignity and gentleness following the tie incident, and he feels sympathy when he learns Armand has fallen in love with a girl from the upscale North Side.

3. Possible Response: Rollie was the last person the other kids would want to have the glove, yet Jerry in effect gave it to him.

4. Possible Responses: Jerry's father and brother lose their jobs, so money is tight. Jerry is sorry he did not contribute more toward the gift. Also, Jerry learns that Armand has a girlfriend from a wealthy area.

Use **Reading and Critical Thinking Transparencies,** p. 3, for additional support.

5. Possible Response: This lets Cormier tell the story through the eyes of a boy, to whom cards and a new baseball glove are very important. We better understand Jerry's feelings and decisions.

Literary Analysis

Plot Students' charts should include: Conflict: how to spend his money; Climax: Jerry's chase to find Armand; Resolution: Jerry gives Armand the money he needs.

Use **Literary Analysis Transparencies,** p. 5, for additional support.

Writing Options

1. **Character Comparison** Students may say that Jerry and Armand both love their father. Jerry is interested in things like card collecting and baseball. Armand takes more responsibility and is interested in dating.

 Use **Reading and Critical Thinking Transparencies,** p. 35, for additional support.

2. **Decisive Narrative** To help students organize their thinking, tell them that after they choose a decision, they should state it simply and make two separate lists: one with the reasons for making one decision, one with the reasons for a different one. They may also want to think about whether there was one overriding factor that caused them to decide as they did. After they've written this, they can write up their stories.

 Use **Writing Transparencies,** p. 11, for additional support.

Activities & Explorations

1. **Dramatic Scene** Scenes will vary, but should get across the information that Jerry has gotten five dollars from the sale of the Grover Cleveland card, and that he wants Armand to have the money.

 Use **Communications Transparencies and Copymasters,** p. 13, for additional support.

2. **Collector's Card** Cards will vary, but should include both a likeness and information on the heroic figure.

Inquiry & Research

Talking Cards Students may need support figuring out where to find the information they need. Allow time for small groups to share their research.

 Use **Writing Transparencies,** p. 41, for additional support.

Writing Options

1. **Character Comparison**
In what ways are Jerry and Armand similar and different? Use a Venn diagram to record your thoughts. Then write a paragraph from the diagram.

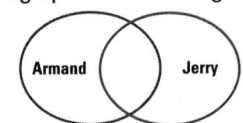

Place the comparison in your **Working Portfolio.**

Writing Handbook
See p. R35: Compare and Contrast.

2. **Decisive Narrative** Recall a time when you (or someone you know) had to make a difficult decision. What happened? Write a one-page story describing the decision.

Writing Handbook
See p. R33: Narrative Writing.

Activities & Explorations

1. **Dramatic Scene** Working with a partner, write a scene in which Jerry gives Armand the money from selling the card. Perform the scene for your class. ~ **PERFORMING**

2. **Collector's Card** Create a collectible card for a heroic figure. Show a picture on the front and write a summary of career highlights on the back. ~ **VIEWING AND REPRESENTING**

Inquiry & Research

Talking Cards In this story you read about a time when children "swapped and bargained and matched for" cards depicting cowboys and presidents. People still collect and trade cards. What types of cards are made today? Are they meant to be collected, or do they have a different purpose? Research the types of trading cards that are available. If possible, include information about their cost and the ways they are used, sold, and packaged.

 Real World Link Read the article on p. 48 before writing your response.

Vocabulary in Action

EXERCISE: ASSESSMENT PRACTICE Write the letter of the word or phrase that is closest in meaning to the boldfaced word.

1. The children's father would **allot** them extra money on the weekends.
   (a) give (b) show (c) find

2. Armand felt **betrayed** when Jerry offered to contribute only a nickel.
   (a) relieved (b) lonely (c) cheated

3. Jerry's offer was met with **contempt.**
   (a) pride (b) lack of respect (c) pleasure

4. Drivers honked their horns loudly at Jerry, **indignant** at his recklessness.
   (a) angry (b) afraid (c) confused

5. His new hobby came to **obsess** him.
   (a) disgust (b) unite (c) absorb

6. When business began to **dwindle,** Armand lost his job.
   (a) decrease (b) grow (c) pick up

7. Jerry's questions about Armand's girlfriend had an **incredulous** tone.
   (a) unreal (b) horrified (c) disbelieving

8. Jerry did not **divulge** his brother's secret.
   (a) keep (b) reveal (c) understand

9. The boys reached a **stalemate** when each needed the same card.
   (a) decision (b) standoff (c) conclusion

10. Since it was a sunny day, Jerry was surprised at his own **lethargy.**
    (a) inactivity (b) energy (c) ability

Building Vocabulary
For an in-depth study of context clues, see p. 79.

WORDS TO KNOW	allot	contempt	dwindle	indignant	obsess
	betrayed	divulge	incredulous	lethargy	stalemate

Vocabulary in Action

Exercise
1. a
2. c
3. b
4. a
5. c
6. a
7. c
8. b
9. b
10. a

Grammar in Context:
Four Kinds of Sentences

There are four basic types of sentences. Each serves a purpose.

A **declarative** sentence makes a statement.

An **imperative** sentence issues a request or a command.

An **exclamatory** sentence expresses strong emotion.

An **interrogative** sentence asks a question.

> "The company's not making any more." (declarative)
> "Look what it says at the bottom of the sign." (imperative)
> "There's no more cowboy cards!" (exclamatory)
> "What's the matter?" (interrogative)

Usage Tip: The subject of an imperative sentence is often the pronoun *you*. Usually it is not written but is implied or understood. For example, it is understood that "Wait a minute" really means "You wait a minute."

Apply to Your Writing: Exclamatory sentences "shout" at the reader. Use exclamatory sentences sparingly so that they will have more force.

WRITING EXERCISE Think about the short story "President Cleveland, Where Are You?" Write a paragraph about the Spring Promenade, to which Armand is going to escort Sally. In your paragraph, use one sentence of each of the four types.

Connect to the Literature Reread page 42. Find one complete sentence of each type—declarative, imperative, exclamatory, and interrogative.

Grammar Handbook Quick Reference: Punctuation, p. R56

"Even if I'd never been published, I would still be writing."

Robert Cormier
born 1925

Starting Out As a boy in Leominster, Massachusetts, Robert Cormier's favorite place was the library. He published his first short story while he was a college student, and began his career working for a radio station and newspapers. Still, he recalls, "I regarded myself as a novelist who was a reporter in order to support his family." After writing adult novels, Cormier published *The Chocolate War,* the first of his acclaimed novels for young adults.

Criticism and Praise Some reviewers criticize Cormier's books because they deal with controversial issues such as crime and death. At times, people have even demanded that Cormier's novels be taken off library bookshelves. Other critics praise Cormier's stories for their realistic style and gripping plots.

Author Activity

True to Life In his writing, Cormier often uses realistic details seen from a young person's point of view. For example, Jerry describes Rollie Tremaine's home as "a big white birthday cake of a house." Read some of Cormier's other stories and look for details that seem to capture exactly how a character sees something. Make a list of these descriptions, writing them down in Cormier's own words.

Grammar in Context

WRITING EXERCISE
Answers will vary but should reflect students' understanding of the story, for example, that Armand is the narrator's brother, that the Spring Promenade is a big dance at the high school, or that Sally is a girl from the other side of town. Students' writing should include one of each of the four sentence types.

CONNECT TO THE LITERATURE
Answers will vary, but each should be the correct type of sentence, chosen from the story.
Possible Responses:
Declarative: His mood of dejection mirrored my own, and I sat down beside him.
Imperative: Now get out, all of you, unless you've got money to spend.
Exclamatory: I've got an extra Warren G. Harding!
Interrogatory: How can I take Sally to a fancy dance?

Author Activity

True to Life Give students ample time to find the Cormier stories. Lists should focus on descriptive language.

Robert Cormier

Cormier has great respect for the young people he writes for. He says, "A lot of people underestimate that intelligent teenager out there. These kids today . . . are really far ahead of a lot of adults. They have been exposed to so much. Anybody who writes down to these people is making a mistake."

 Grammar
Mini Lesson

PUNCTUATING FOUR TYPES OF SENTENCES
Instruction Tell students that they need to use correct punctuation to make their writing clear. Remind them that every sentence must start with a capital letter and end with either a period, a question mark, or an exclamation point.
Exercises Read each sentence aloud. Have students decide which end punctuation would best complete the sentence. (Tell students that some sentences could use either a period or an exclamation point.)
1. Armand said, "Give me more money" (*!* or *.*)
2. I ran to Lemire's to buy more cards (*.*)

3. Did you give Armand five dollars (*?*)
4. You want to know what Rollie said when I gave him the money, don't you (*?*)
5. Get out of my way (*!*)

 Use **Unit One Resource Book**, p. 18.
Use **Grammar Transparencies and Copymasters**, p. 119.

Use McDougal Littell's *Language Network,* Chapter 9, for more instruction and practice in end punctuation.

Source: *Boys' Life*

Objectives
• read to be informed
• read and analyze a magazine article
• learn to paraphrase
• make an outline
• create a glossary

Connecting to the Literature
"Trading Card Talk" takes students into the world of card trading, which is central to "President Cleveland, Where Are You?" Since the time when that story took place, card trading has grown from a young person's hobby to a much more lucrative industry. Terminology and standards—and deception—have grown with it.

Trading Card Talk

by

Jay Johnson

★★★★★★★★★★★★★★★

To be a savvy card collector, you must know how to talk the talk.

Walking into a hobby card shop for the first time is like visiting another country. Everyone seems to be speaking a foreign language. But don't worry. You can learn card lingo right now. Once you do, chatting with another collector is easy.

Condition Is Critical

Before buying a card, you should find out what condition it's in. That goes for non-sports cards as well as for baseball and other types of sports cards.

A card in *mint* condition is perfect. It should look brand-new, no matter how old it is. Cards that are *near mint* have only one defect, or flaw. For instance, a worn corner or an off-center picture will knock a mint card down to near mint.

Most collectors don't want to buy cards newer than 10 years old unless they are mint or near mint. Older cards, printed before 1980 or so, can still be desirable even if they are in worse condition.

An *excellent* card may have several defects. It is worth about half as much as a mint version of the same card. For example, a card sometimes loses its gloss, or shine, as it gets older. Combine that problem with a couple of fuzzy, or frayed, corners, and you have a card that would rate an excellent grade. Many collectors who are on a budget prefer to collect excellent-grade cards. They are attractive, but cheaper.

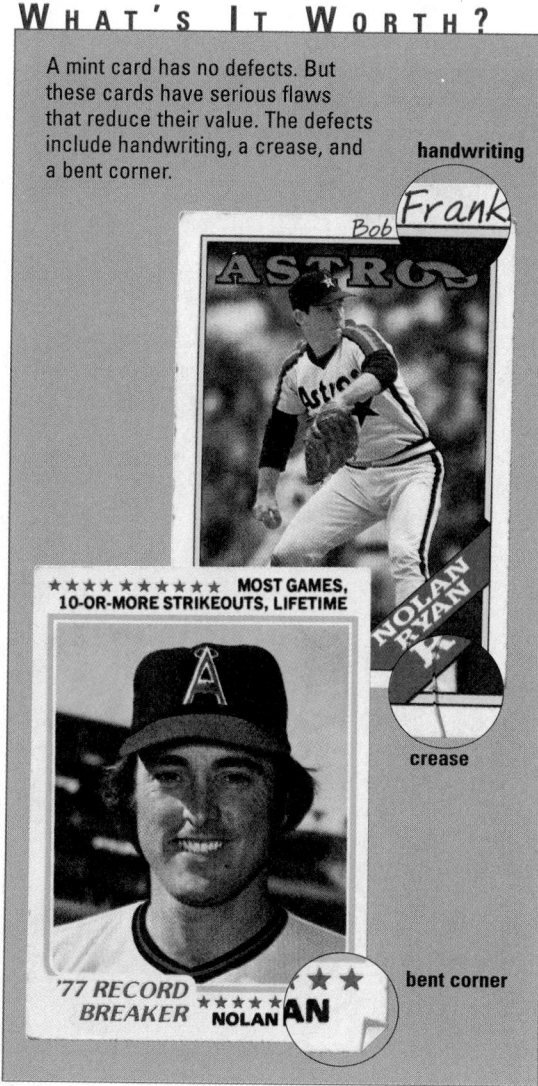

WHAT'S IT WORTH?

A mint card has no defects. But these cards have serious flaws that reduce their value. The defects include handwriting, a crease, and a bent corner.

handwriting

crease

bent corner

MOST GAMES, 10-OR-MORE STRIKEOUTS, LIFETIME

'77 RECORD BREAKER NOLAN RYAN

Reading for Information

Has your teacher ever cautioned you against plagiarism—presenting someone else's work as your own? To avoid plagiarism when writing a report, be sure to mention the sources of your information. Also, when you take notes from books or other resources, don't copy the information word for word. Instead, **paraphrase** it by restating the main points in your own words.

PARAPHRASING When you paraphrase, you put information in your own words. Paraphrasing is not only a good way to avoid copying; you can use it to make sense of complicated or confusing material. Rewriting a passage in your own words can help you understand and remember what you have read. Paraphrasing is also a way of organizing information. You can use it when you want to present ideas to readers in a fun or easy-to-read form.

YOUR TURN *Use the questions and activities below to help you learn how to paraphrase.*

1 Read this paragraph carefully and identify its **main idea.** Use **paraphrasing** to write one sentence describing the main idea. Write a sentence or two describing the main idea of the article.

2 Suppose that a friend asks you to explain what a mint card is. You probably wouldn't use the exact words that the writer of this article used. Write a sentence in which you define *mint card* in your own words.

Tell students that this article appeared in the magazine *Boys' Life.* Have students use the material in the right-hand column to help them learn to paraphrase. The following are possible responses to the questions and activities.

1 There is a special vocabulary for talking about trading cards that is easy to learn.

2 A mint card is one that looks just like it did when it came out of the factory.

Use **Reading and Critical Thinking Transparencies,** p. 19, for additional support.

WRAP IT UP!

The way trading cards are packaged also contributes to their value.

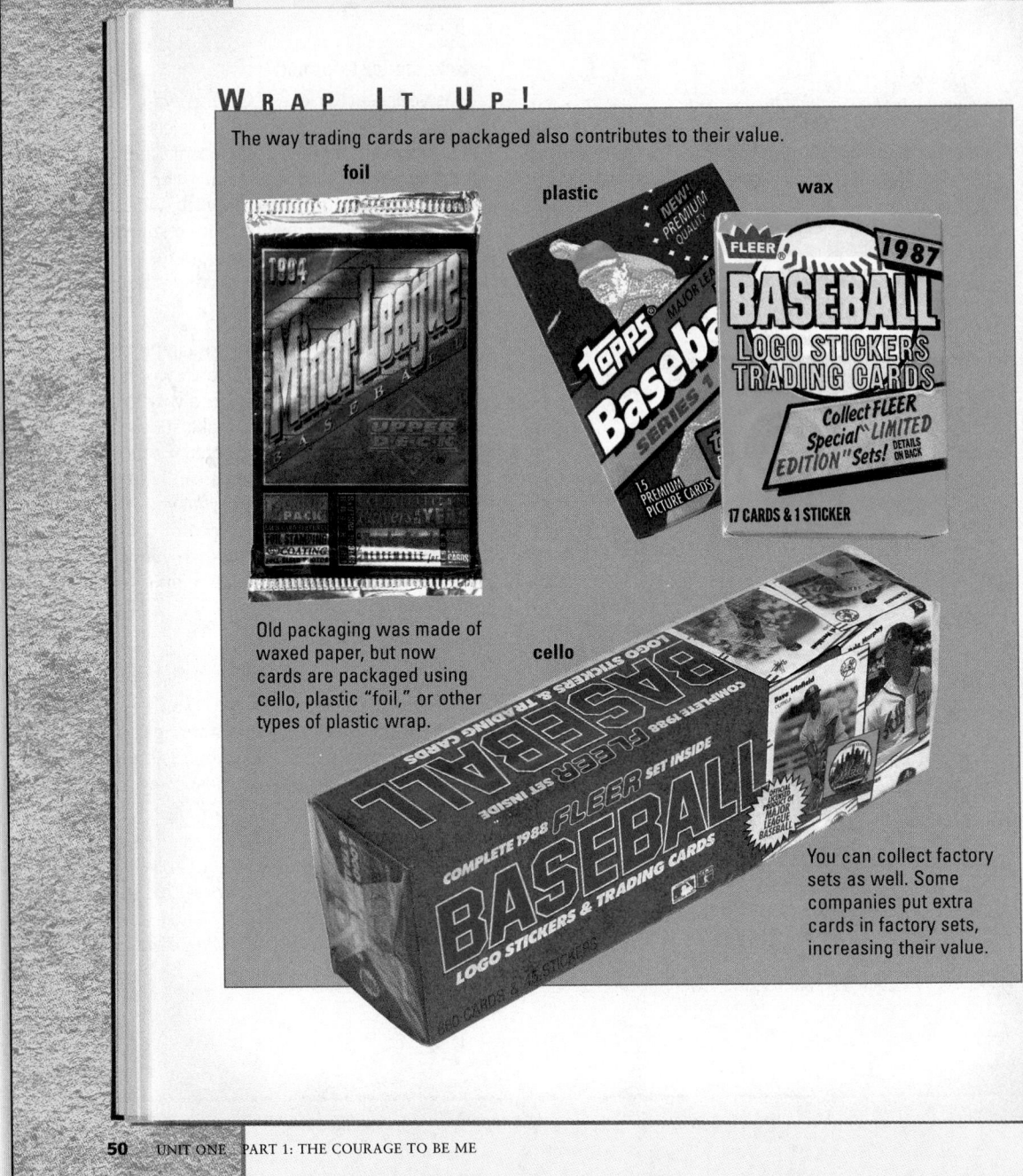

foil

plastic

wax

Old packaging was made of waxed paper, but now cards are packaged using cello, plastic "foil," or other types of plastic wrap.

cello

You can collect factory sets as well. Some companies put extra cards in factory sets, increasing their value.

Leader of the Packs

New cards should always be mint. Words used to describe new cards deal not with condition, but with how the cards are packaged.

Not long ago, almost everything was sold in *wax packs*. Thick waxed paper was wrapped around 10 or 15 cards. The pack sold for 50 cents to $1. Wax packs aren't as popular anymore. People often opened the pack and removed the good cards. Then they resealed it by running a warm iron over the waxed paper. To stop that, card companies began wrapping packs with *cello*, short for cellophane, a thin plastic.

A *foil pack* is the same as a cello pack, except the wrapping is made of a shiny plastic that looks like aluminum foil. Cello and foil packs cannot be resealed so easily.

Another common package is a *jumbo pack*. It contains 25 to 35 cards, depending on the brand. The price is usually $1 to $2.

Make a Box Set

Larger packages of cards have their own terms. Experienced collectors often buy an entire box of 20 or 30 cello packs. They take care that the box is still wrapped with the factory seal, which means no one has removed any packages. The collector opens all the packages in the box and tries to assemble all the cards, making a *set*. Once he has put every card in numerical order, he has created a *hand-collated set*. That means the set was put together by hand, one card at a time.

A *factory set* is similar, except it is assembled by machine at a card company. Like boxes, factory sets usually are sold with a seal. Some companies put extra cards in factory sets, which can make the sets more valuable.

Before you buy, sell or trade cards, learn trading card lingo. That knowledge will help you enjoy this wonderful hobby.

Reading for Information *continued*

3 Now that you have read the article, write a brief outline. You can use a title, headings, and paraphrasing to help you organize ideas. Use a format like the one shown below. Record this article's title and headings. Paraphrase the supporting details under each heading.

Trading Card Talk
I. Condition Is Critical
  A. Detail:
  B. Detail:
  C. Detail:
II. Leader of the Packs

Inquiry & Research

Activity Link: "President Cleveland, Where Are You?" p. 46. What new terms have you learned from reading "Trading Card Talk"? Locate nine special words or terms explained in the article. Then create a **glossary**, or dictionary, in which you define each term by paraphrasing information found in the article.

Reading for Information

3 Trading Card Talk

I. Condition Is Critical
  A. Trading cards are rated according to their condition.
  B. To be desirable to collectors, recent cards should be mint or near mint; older cards may keep their value even if their condition isn't as good.
  C. Collectors with less cash often choose cards in excellent condition.

II. Leader of the Packs
  A. Packaging, rather than condition, is most important with new cards.
  B. Manufacturers have replaced wax packaging with plastic to stop tampering.
  C. The more cards in a pack, the higher the price.

III. Make a Box Set
  A. Some collectors make their own sets from many packages of cards.
  B. Sometimes companies assemble sets.

 Use **Writing Transparencies,** p. 54, for additional support.

Mini Lesson Inquiry & Research

The Inquiry & Research activity on this page links with the Inquiry & Research section of Choices & Challenges that follows "President Cleveland, Where Are You?" on page 46.

Instruction: Show students the glossary of this book or of other books as a model. Encourage them to notice how a glossary entry differs from a dictionary entry.

Practice: Students should include 9 of the following words in a glossary for card collectors.

cello: thin plastic; short for cellophane
excellent: with several flaws
factory set: manufacturer-assembled complete set
foil pack: pack of cards wrapped in plastic made to look like foil
hand-collated set: collector-assembled complete set
jumbo pack: pack with 25 to 35 cards

mint: in perfect condition
near mint: with one flaw
set: all cards in a series
wax pack: pack of cards wrapped in wax paper

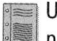 Use **Writing Transparencies,** p. 43, for additional support.

OVERVIEW

This selection appears in Spanish in the **Spanish Study Guide**.

Objectives
1. understand and appreciate a **short story (Literary Analysis)**
2. understand **setting** and its effect on characters and plot in a short story **(Literary Analysis)**
3. use the reading strategy of **visualizing** to help understand setting, characters, and action **(Active Reading)**

Summary
The story's narrator joins the Boy Scouts because he believes the organization will "make a man" of him. He learns that moving up the Boy Scout ranks requires an overnight hike in the country. Consequently, he and two fellow Scouts leave their Brooklyn neighborhood to "rough it" in the woods for a night. On the advice of their scoutmaster, the boys decide to cross the George Washington Bridge by foot and camp in New Jersey. Poor planning and bad weather turn the trip into a fiasco. The boys wish to return home, but nobody wants to be the one to give up first. Finally the narrator gathers the courage to suggest that they go home, and the others eagerly agree. All vow to keep the details of their experience secret.

Thematic Link
Three city boys know that leaving their neighborhood for their first camping trip takes courage. They learn that being honest and able to admit defeat can take even more courage.

5-Minute Warm-Up

Daily Language SkillBuilder

Have students **proofread** the display sentences on page 19i and write them correctly. The sentences also appear on Transparency 2 of **Grammar Transparencies and Copymasters.**

Mini Lesson **Preteaching Vocabulary**

If you would like to preteach the WORDS TO KNOW for this selection, use the Mini Lesson, TE p. 54.

52   UNIT ONE   PART 1

"*I had to leave Brooklyn, on my own, for the first time in my life.*"

Scout's Honor

Short Story by AVI

Connect to Your Life

Tough Enough? Have you ever been faced with a difficult situation and felt you "chickened out"? Did other people seem braver than you? With a partner, discuss a situation like that from your own life. What lessons might be learned from your experience?

Build Background

CONNECT TO HISTORY Did you know that there are more than 25 million Boy Scouts around the world today? "Scout's Honor" tells about three friends who go camping in an effort to meet a Boy Scout requirement. The first camping group of Boy Scouts was organized in Great Britain in 1908 by a soldier.

To become Scouts, boys must swear to live by the Scout Oath. In doing so they promise to give their best effort in everything they do. They promise to respect God and their country, including its laws and natural resources. They promise to help others, and to be honest and fair. They promise to care for their bodies and their minds. They also promise to obey the rules of the Scout Law and to honor the Scout Motto—Be Prepared.

WORDS TO KNOW
Vocabulary Preview

bellow	retort	suspicion
envious	rival	vent
immense	smugly	
pummel	straddle	

Focus Your Reading

LITERARY ANALYSIS **SETTING**   The **setting** of a story (or poem or play) is the time and place of the action. The time may be past, present, or future. The place may be real or imaginary. Sometimes setting is very important in a story. It may shape the characters, or even create a conflict. For example, in "Scout's Honor," the main character must prove his camping abilities even though he lives in the heart of the city.

ACTIVE READING **VISUALIZING**   When you form a picture in your mind based on what you are reading, you are **visualizing.** To visualize, pay attention to descriptions of the setting as well as details about what the characters see, hear, and do.

READER'S NOTEBOOK
As you read this story, jot down the details that help you visualize each scene. Next to these details, list which of the five senses they relate to—sight, smell, hearing, taste, or touch. Then describe the picture you visualize. Start with a chart like the one shown here.

Details	Senses
asphalt	touch
tall buildings	sight
roaring cars	hearing

LESSON RESOURCES

UNIT ONE RESOURCE BOOK, pp. 21–27
Formal Assessment, pp. 9–10
Teacher's Guide to Assessment and Portfolio Use
Test Generator

SKILLS TRANSPARENCIES AND COPYMASTERS
Literary Analysis
• Setting, TR 6 (for Paired Activity, p. 64)
Reading and Critical Thinking
• Visualizing, TR 4 (for Thinking Through the Literature, p. 64)

Grammar
• Identifying Simple Subjects and Verbs, CM 53 (for Mini Lesson, p. 61)
• Verb Phrases: Main and Helping Verbs, CM 77 (for Mini Lesson, p. 66)

Vocabulary
• Context Clues: Compare/Contrast, CM 20 (for Mini Lesson, p. 54)
• Context Clues: Restatement, CM 21 (for Mini Lesson, p. 60)

INTEGRATED TECHNOLOGY
Audio Library
Internet: Research Starter

Visit our website:
www.mcdougallittell.com

SCOUT'S HONOR

The Scouting Trail, Norman Rockwell.
Art from the Archives of Brown & Bigelow,
Inc. and with permission from The Boy
Scouts of America.

by Avi

Back in 1946, when I was nine, I worried that I wasn't tough enough. That's why I became a Boy Scout. Scouting, I thought, would make a man of me. **1**

53

TEACHING THE LITERATURE

Customizing Instruction

Less Proficient Readers
Have students keep these questions in mind as they begin to read:
• Why do the boys go camping?
• What do the boys try to prove to one another?
• What does their first camping trip teach them?

Set a Purpose Have students read to find out how well-prepared the boys are for their first camping trip.

Students Acquiring English
Explain that Brooklyn is a borough, or section, of New York City, the country's largest city. The George Washington Bridge crosses the Hudson River, which separates New York and New Jersey.

 Use **Spanish Study Guide,**
pp. 10–12 for additional support.

Gifted and Talented
Explain that *irony* is the difference between what is expected and what actually exists or happens. As they read, have students look for details and situations that are ironic. Suggest they look to the story's title and setting.
Possible Responses: A "hike in the country" includes a subway ride and a busy bridge; the boys use the phrase "Scout's Honor" when promising to hide their experience from the Scoutmaster.

Use **Literary Analysis Transparencies,**
p. 27, for additional support.

Students Acquiring English
1 Tell students that "make a man of me" is an expression meaning "make me stronger or tougher." It reflects the stereotypical idea that one must be physically and emotionally tough in order to be a "real" man.

Mini Lesson Viewing and Representing

The Scouting Trail
Illustration by Norman Rockwell

ART APPRECIATION The paintings and illustrations of Norman Rockwell (1894–1978) often give an idealized view of everyday American life. Rockwell created a number of paintings for the Boy Scouts.
Instruction Have students study the image of the Boy Scouts on the manual. What emotions do the faces of the boys seem to show?
Possible Response: pride, excitement, happiness

Application Why might an illustration like this attract young boys, like the narrator, to the Boy Scouts?
Possible Response: The illustration shows the boys in uniform, looking happy, strong, and active. This poster makes the organization seem fun, exciting, and important.

Reading and Analyzing

Reading Skills and Strategies: PREVIEW

Ask students to read the title of the story. What does this phrase mean to them? What do they think the story will be about? As they read, they can modify their ideas about the story and the meaning of the title.

Active Reading | VISUALIZING |

Avi describes each location and incident in vivid detail. These details help readers to appreciate the boys' experience. Tell students to pause from time to time as they read. Encourage them to close their eyes and try to see, hear, touch, taste and smell each scene. Invite volunteers to describe mental images the text descriptions evoke.

Use **Unit One Resource Book**, p. 22 for more practice.

Literary Analysis | SETTING |

Encourage students to recognize and analyze details of the story's setting as they read. Tell students that setting is an important element of the story. It has a strong effect on characters and events and provides part of the story's humor. Students can keep a record of details and their significance in a chart like the one below.

Setting	Details	Meaning to Story
subway		

Use **Unit One Resource Book**, p. 23 for more practice.

It didn't take long to reach Tenderfoot rank. You got that for joining. To move up to Second Class, however, you had to meet three requirements. Scout Spirit and Scout Participation had been cinchy. The third requirement, Scout Craft, meant I had to go on an overnight hike in the *country*. In other words, I had to leave Brooklyn, on my own, for the first time in my life.

Since I grew up in Brooklyn in the 1940s, the only grass I knew was in Ebbets Field where the Dodgers played. Otherwise, my world was made of slate pavements, streets of asphalt

Station Platform, Dong Kingman. Hirshhorn Museum and Sculpture Garden, Smithsonian Institution, gift of Joseph H. Hirshhorn, 1966. Photo: John Tennant.

(or cobblestone), and skies full of tall buildings. The only thing "country" was a puny pin oak tree at our curb, which was noticed, mostly, by dogs.

I asked Scoutmaster Brenkman where I could find some country. Now, whenever I saw Mr. Brenkman, who was a church pastor, he was dressed either in church black or Scout khaki. When he wore black, he'd warn us against hellfire. When he wore khaki, he'd teach us how to build fires.

"Country," Scoutmaster Brenkman said in answer to my question, "is anywhere that has lots of trees and is not in the city. Many boys camp in the Palisades."

Teaching Options

 Preteaching Vocabulary

CONTEXT CLUES: COMPARE/CONTRAST
Instruction Remind students that they may be able to figure out the meaning of an unfamiliar word by using context clues. Use the model sentence to show how they can clarify a word's meaning by finding a comparison or contrast to a familiar word. Tell them that comparisons are often signaled by words such as *like, as,* and *than* and contrasts by words like *although, but, yet, however,* and *on the other hand.*
Model Sentence
His *bellow* was louder <u>than thunder</u>.

Exercises Ask students to use comparison and contrast clues to define the underlined WORDS TO KNOW in the following sentences.
1. At first they were <u>rivals</u>, but then they worked together.
2. The bridge seemed as <u>immense</u> as a mountain range.
3. In the lean-to, they made a <u>vent</u> that worked like a chimney.
4. He felt <u>suspicion</u>, yet acted quite trusting.

Use **Unit One Resource Book**, p. 24.
Use **Vocabulary Transparencies and Copymasters**, p. 20, for additional support.

"Where's that?"

"Just north of the city. It's a park in Jersey."

"Isn't that a zillion miles from here?"

"Take the subway to the George Washington Bridge, then hike across."

I thought for a moment, then asked, "How do I prove I went?"

Mr. Brenkman looked deeply shocked. "You wouldn't *lie*, would you? What about Scout's honor?"

"Yes, sir," I replied meekly.[1]

My two best friends were Philip Hossfender, whom we nicknamed Horse, and Richard Macht, called Max because we were not great spellers. They were also Scouts, Tenderfoots like me.

Horse was a skinny little kid about half my size whose way of arguing was to ball up his fist and say, "Are you saying . . . ?" in a threatening tone.

Max was on the pudgy side, but he could talk his way out of a locked room. More importantly, he always seemed to have pocket money, which gave his talk real power.

I wasn't sure why, but being best friends meant we were <u>rivals</u> too. One of the reasons for my wanting to be tougher was a feeling that Horse was a lot tougher than I was, and that Max was a little tougher.

"I'm going camping in the Palisades next weekend," I casually informed them.

"How come?" Max challenged.

"Scout Craft," I replied.

"Oh, *that*," Horse said with a shrug.

"Look," I said, "I don't know about you, but I don't intend to be a Tenderfoot all my life. Anyway, doing stuff in the city is for sissies. Scouting is real camping. Besides, I like roughing it."

---

1. **meekly:** in a humble manner.

WORDS
TO
KNOW   **rival** (rī'vəl) *n.* one who tries to win over another; competitor

55

Customizing Instruction

Students Acquiring English

1 Tell students that *cinchy* is an informal word meaning "easy." It comes from the noun *cinch*—"something effortless."

2 Explain that the word *puny* means small and sickly.

3 Tell students that *khaki* is a light brown color. The word also describes a sturdy cloth of this color or a uniform made of the cloth.

Less Proficient Readers

4 Ask the following questions to help students understand the characters' traits and motivations.

• According to the narrator, what is interesting about each friend's personality?
Answer: Horse is small but tough. Max always has money and is a big talker.

• What does the narrator say about his relationship with Horse and Max?
Answer: They always compete.

• What is the main reason that the narrator wants to go camping?
Answer: He wants to prove that he is tough.

Students Acquiring English

5 Tell students that *sissies* is a label used to insult people who seem timid or cowardly. *Roughing it* is an expression meaning "to endure uncomfortable conditions."

Multiple Learning Styles
Intrapersonal Learners

Intrapersonal learners can use their own experiences to understand the feelings of the characters. Ask students to write about a time when they felt they had to prove themselves to friends or adults.

BLOCK SCHEDULING: MANAGING TIME

If your schedule requires that you cover the lesson objectives in a shorter time, use . . .
• Preparing to Read, p. 52
• Thinking Through the Literature, p. 64
• Vocabulary in Action, p. 65
• Grammar in Context, p. 66

If you want to take advantage of longer class time, use . . .
• TE Teaching Options: Viewing and Representing, pp. 53, 62; Preteaching Vocabulary, p. 54; Cross-Curricular Links, pp. 56, 59; Spelling, p. 57; Vocabulary Strategy, p. 60; Grammar, pp. 61, 66; Standardized Test Practice, p. 63
• Choices & Challenges and Author Activity, pp. 65–66

Literary Analysis: DIALOGUE

A This selection can help students to understand the important role dialogue can play in a story. Tell students that dialogue consists of the words characters speak aloud to one another. Explain that dialogue often reveals important information about characters and their relationships. Ask students what the characters are discussing in this paragraph and what their conversation reveals about their relationship.

Possible Response: They argue about who is tough enough to go camping. This passage shows that the characters are competitive and care about how they appear to one another.

Reading Skills and Strategies: QUESTION

Have students raise questions about the items the boys decide to bring. Do students believe the boys are well-prepared for a hike? Why, or why not?

Active Reading | VISUALIZING |

B Ask students to visualize the scene in which the boys become separated, first from the point of view of Max, then from the point of view of Horse and the narrator. What do they see? How do they feel?

| Use **Reading and Critical Thinking Transparencies**, p. 4, for additional support.

Literary Analysis | SETTING |

Ask students to analyze and discuss the subway as a setting. How does this setting affect the characters and the events of the story? Ask students to think about how this scene sets the mood of the story.

| Use **Literary Analysis Transparencies**, p. 6, for additional support.

"You saying I don't?" Horse snapped.

"I'm not saying nothing," I said.

They considered my idea. Finally, Horse said, "Yeah, well, I was going to do that, but I didn't think you guys were ready for it."

A "I've been ready for *years*," Max protested.

"Then we're going, right?" I said.

They looked around at me. "If you can do it, I can do it," Max said.

"Yeah," Horse said thoughtfully.

The way they agreed made me nervous. Now I really was going to have to be tough.

We informed our folks that we were going camping overnight (which was true) and that the Scoutmaster was going with us—which was a lie. We did remember what Mr. **1** Brenkman said about honesty, but we were baseball fans too, and since we were prepared to follow Scout law—being loyal, helpful, friendly, courteous, kind, obedient, cheerful, thrifty, brave, clean, *and* reverent—we figured a 900 batting average was not bad.

So Saturday morning we met at the High Street subway station. I got there first. Stuffed in my dad's army surplus knapsack was a blanket, a pillow, and a paper bag with three white-bread peanut-butter-and-jelly **2** sandwiches—that is, lunch, supper, and Sunday breakfast. My pockets were full of stick matches. I had an old flashlight, and since I lived by the Scout motto—Be Prepared—I had brought along an umbrella. Finally, being a serious reader, I had the latest Marvel Family comics.

Horse arrived next, his arms barely managing to hold on to a mattress that seemed twice his size. As for food, he had four cans of beans jammed into his pockets.

Max came last. He was lugging a new knapsack that contained a cast-iron frying pan, a packet of hot dogs, and a box of saltine crackers—plus two bottles. One bottle was mustard, the other, celery soda. He also had a bag of Tootsie Rolls and a shiny hatchet. "To build a lean-to,"[2] he explained.

Max's prize possession, however, was an official Scout compass. "It's really swell," he told us. "You can't ever get lost with it. Got it at the Scout store."

"I hate that place," Horse informed us. "It's all new. Nothing real."

"This compass is real," Max <u>retorted</u>. "Points north all the time. You can get cheaper ones, but they point all different directions."

"What's so great about the north?" Horse said.

"That's always the way to go," Max insisted.

"Says who?" I demanded.

"Mr. Brenkman, dummy," Horse cried. "Anyway, there's always an arrow on maps pointing the way north."

"Cowboys live out west," I reminded them. They didn't care.

On the subway platform, we realized we did not know which station we were heading **3** for. To find out, we studied the system map, which looked like a noodle factory hit by a

---

2. **lean-to:** a shelter with a flat, sloping roof.

WORDS
TO
KNOW   **retort** (rĭ-tôrt′) *v.* to reply, especially in a quick or unkind way

56

Cross Curricular Link **Geography: Map Reading**

MAPS AND COMPASSES Just as Horse says, maps do usually feature an arrow pointing north. For thousands of years, people trying to understand where they are have looked to the north. People lost in the woods at night could find Polaris, the North Star, and find their way north. Hikers lost during the daylight hours could poke a stick in the ground at noon. In the northern hemisphere, the stick's shadow will always point north as sun shines on it from the south. The arrow on a map usually points to the geographic North Pole, a spot in the

Arctic Ocean that marks the northern end of the earth's axis of rotation. The North Star is close to the north celestial pole, the highest point in the sky above the earthly North Pole.

The magnetic needle of a compass is attracted to the earth's magnetic poles—located near the geographic North and South Poles—where the earth's magnetic field is most intense. Most compasses are constructed of a circular dial that shows directions and a magnetized steel needle that always points north.

bomb. The place we wanted to go (north) was at the top of the map, so I had to hoist Horse onto my shoulders for a closer look. Since he refused to let go of his mattress—or the tin cans in his pockets—it wasn't easy. I asked him—in a kindly fashion—to put the mattress down.

No sooner did he find the station—168th Street—than our train arrived. We rushed on, only to have Horse scream, "My mattress!" He had left it on the platform. Just before the doors shut, he and I leaped off. Max, however, remained on the train. Helplessly, we watched as his horror-stricken face slid away from us. "Wait at the next station!" I <u>bellowed</u>. "Don't move!"

The next train took forever to come. Then it took even longer to get to the next stop. There was Max. All around him—like fake snow in a glass ball—were crumbs. He'd been so nervous he had eaten all his crackers.

"Didn't that make you thirsty?"

"I drank my soda."

I noticed streaks down his cheeks. Horse noticed them too. "You been crying?" he asked.

"Naw," Max said. "There was this water dripping from the tunnel roof. But, you said don't move, right? Well, I was just being obedient."

By the time we got on the next train—with all our possessions—we had been traveling for

THE BEST WAY
TO STOP ARGUMENTS
IS TO GET PEOPLE TO
EAT PEANUT BUTTER
SANDWICHES.
THEY CAN'T TALK.

an hour. But we had managed to go only one stop.

During the ride, I got hungry. I pulled out one of my sandwiches. With the jelly soaked through the bread, it looked like a limp scab.

Horse, <u>envious</u>, complained *he* was getting hungry.

"Eat some of your canned beans," I suggested.

He got out one can without ripping his pocket too badly. Then his face took on a mournful look.

"What's the matter?" I asked.

"Forgot to bring a can opener."

Max said, "In the old days, people opened cans with their teeth."

"You saying my teeth aren't strong?"

"I'm just talking about history!"

"You saying I don't know history?"

Always kind, I plopped half my sandwich into Horse's hand. He squashed it into his mouth and was quiet for the next fifteen minutes. It proved something I'd always believed: The best way to stop arguments is to get people to eat peanut butter sandwiches. They can't talk.

Then we became so absorbed in our Marvel Family comics we missed our station. We got to it only by coming back the other way. When we reached street level, the sky was dark.

"I knew it," Max announced. "It's going to rain."

"Don't worry," Horse said. "New Jersey is a

WORDS TO KNOW	**bellow** (bĕl′ō) *v.* to shout in a deep voice **envious** (ĕn′vē-əs) *adj.* jealous

57

Spelling

Mini Lesson

ADDING -ED:

Instruction Tell students that adding the suffix -*ed* changes the spelling of certain base words. If a word ends in silent *e*, the silent *e* is dropped. If a word ends in *y*, *y* is changed to *i*. If a one-syllable word or a word accented on the final syllable ends with a single vowel followed by a single consonant, the final consonant is doubled. Explain that adding -*ed* will usually not change the spelling of words that do not meet these conditions.

Give these examples: walk + ed = walked; use + ed = used; cry + ed = cried; grab + ed = grabbed; rain + ed = rained; pummel + ed = pummeled (ends in a single vowel and single consonant, but has two syllables and accent on the first syllable); retort + ed = retorted (ends in two consonants)

Exercise Ask students to add -*ed* to the following words: *create, supply, rob, fear, order, roll*, and use them in a sentence.

 Use **Unit One Resource Book,** p. 26, for more practice.

Reading Skills and Strategies:
PREDICT

Review with students what has happened on the trip so far. Ask them to predict what might happen as the boys continue on their journey. Students should be able to explain what details from the story help them to make their predictions.

Possible Response: Students might say that the trip will continue to be a disaster. The boys don't seem to know where they are going and they have already used up their food supplies.

Literary Analysis SETTING

A Ask students why Horse feels it might not be raining in New Jersey. What does his suggestion reveal about his understanding of his surroundings?

Possible Response: He feels that because New Jersey is "a whole other state," it might not be raining. In saying this, he reveals that he does not understand they are close to home, despite the fact they are about to enter a different state.

Active Reading VISUALIZING

B Ask students why the writer compares the boys to war refugees. What does this comparison help readers to visualize?

Possible Response: Like people fleeing their homes on short notice, the boys are burdened with too many belongings, and they don't seem to have a strong sense of where they are going.

Whitestone Bridge, Ralston Crawford (51.2). Memorial Art Gallery, University of Rochester, New York.

58 UNIT ONE PART 1: THE COURAGE TO BE ME

Teaching Options

whole other state. It probably won't be raining there."

"I brought an umbrella," I said <u>smugly</u>, though I wanted it to sound helpful.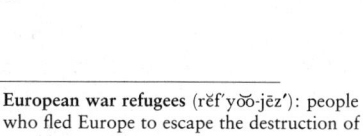

A

As we marched down 168th Street, heading for the George Washington Bridge, we looked like European war refugees.[3] Every few paces, Horse cried, "Hold it!" and adjusted his arms around his mattress. Each time we paused, Max pulled out his compass, peered at it, then announced, "Heading north!"

B

I said, "The bridge goes from east to west."

"Maybe the bridge does," Max insisted with a show of his compass, "but guaranteed, *we* are going north."

1

About then, the heel of my left foot, encased in a heavy rubber boot over an earth-crushing Buster Brown shoe, started to get sore. Things weren't going as I had hoped. Cheerfully, I tried to ignore the pain.

The closer we drew to the bridge, the more <u>immense</u> it seemed. And the clouds had become so thick, you couldn't see the top or the far side.

Max eyed the bridge with deep <u>suspicion</u>. "I'm not so sure we should go," he said.

"Why?"

"Maybe it doesn't have another side."

2

We looked at him.

"No, seriously," Max explained, "they could have taken the Jersey side away, you know, for repairs."

"Cars are going across," I pointed out.

---

3. **European war refugees** (rĕf′yo͞o-jēz′): people who fled Europe to escape the destruction of World War II (1939–1945).

WORDS TO KNOW	**smugly** (smŭg′lē) *adv.* in a very self-satisfied way **immense** (ĭ-mĕns′) *adj.* huge; enormous **suspicion** (sə-spĭsh′ən) *n.* a feeling of doubt or mistrust

---

Cross Curricular Link **Science**

SUSPENSION BRIDGES The George Washington Bridge, completed in 1931, is one of the largest suspension bridges in the country. This type of bridge features a roadway suspended by flexible but strong cables that are anchored at both ends. Modern suspension bridges are made up of three important parts: cables, towers, and anchorage. The cables are usually high-strength steel wires. They provide support for the bridge roadway. Each cable is fastened to evenly spaced bridge towers.

Most modern towers are made of steel, but some older suspension bridges have towers of concrete or stone. The ends of the cables are embedded in enormous blocks of concrete or bedrock for anchorage. Some suspension bridges also have braces beneath the roadway or diagonal cables stretching from the towers for additional support. Because of their unique system of supports, suspension bridges can span greater distances than can other bridge types.

A Ask students to question the narrator's hope that his friends have "chickened out," and why he feels better when he hears fear in Horse's voice.

Possible Response: Students might wonder if the narrator wants to quit, but does not want to be the first to suggest such a thing.

B Point out to students that Horse challenges one of his friends again with his favorite phrase: "You saying . . . ?" Ask what this response reveals about his character.

Possible Response: Students might wonder if it is a defensive response because he is really not as tough as he wants to appear.

Literary Analysis: HUMOR

C Sometimes a simple repeated detail can create humor in a story. Ask students: What is funny about Horse's mattress?

Possible Response: The mattress is big and awkward and a serious hiker would never have brought it.

Literary Analysis   SETTING

D Why, according to Max, is the area of their campsite "just like Brooklyn"?

Possible Response: The area is near lots of buildings and is littered with garbage.

• What were they expecting?
  Possible Response: "country"

• How does the campsite add to the humor of the story?
  Possible Response: It is humorous because it is so different from what the boys imagined.

"They could be dropping off," he suggested.

"You would hear them splash," Horse argued.

"I'm going," I said. Trying to look brave, I started off on my own. My bravery didn't last long. The walkway was narrow. When I looked down, I saw only fog. I could feel the bridge tremble and sway. It wasn't long before I was convinced the bridge was about to collapse. Then a ray of hope struck me: Maybe the other guys had chickened out. If they had, I could quit because of *them*. I glanced back. My heart sank. They were coming.

After they caught up, Horse looked me in the eye and said, "If this bridge falls, I'm going to kill you."

A quarter of a mile farther across, I gazed around. We were completely fogged in.

"I think we're lost," I announced.

"What do we do?" Horse whispered. His voice was jagged with panic. That made me feel better.

"Don't worry," Max said. "I've got my compass." He pulled it out. "North is that way," he said, pointing in the direction we had been going.

Horse said, "You sure?"

"A Scout compass never lies," Max insisted.

"*We* lied," I reminded him.

"Yeah, but this is an official Scout compass," Max returned loyally.

"Come on," Max said and marched forward. Horse and I followed. In moments, we crossed a metal bar on the walkway. On one side, a sign proclaimed: NEW YORK; on the other, it said: NEW JERSEY.

"Holy smoke," Horse said with reverence as he straddled the bar. "Talk about being tough. We're in two states at the same time."

It began to rain. Max said, "Maybe it'll keep us clean."

"You saying I'm not clean?" Horse shot back.

Ever friendly, I put up my umbrella.

We went on—Max on one side, Horse on the other, me in the middle—trying to avoid the growing puddles. After a while, Max said, "Would you move the umbrella? Rain is coming down my neck."

"We're supposed to be roughing it," I said.

"Being in the middle isn't roughing it," Horse reminded me.

I folded the umbrella up so we all could get soaked equally.

"Hey!" I cried. "Look!" Staring up ahead, I could make out tollbooths and the dim outlines of buildings.

"Last one off the bridge is a rotten egg!" Horse shouted and began to run. The next second, he tripped and took off like an F-36 fighter plane. Unfortunately, he landed like a Hell-cat dive-bomber as his mattress unspooled before him and then slammed into a big puddle.

Max and I ran to help. Horse was damp. His mattress was soaked. When he tried to roll it up, water cascaded like Niagara Falls.

"Better leave it," Max said.

"It's what I sleep on at home," Horse said as he slung the soaking, dripping mass over his shoulder.

When we got off the bridge, we were in a small plaza. To the left was the roadway, full of roaring cars. In front of us, aside from the highway, there was nothing but buildings. Only to the right were there trees.

"North is that way," Max said, pointing toward the trees. We set off.

"How come you're limping?" Horse asked

WORDS
TO
KNOW

straddle (străd′l) *v.* to stand with a leg on either side of

60

Mini Lesson   **Vocabulary Strategy**

CONTEXT CLUES: RESTATEMENT

Instruction Tell students that restatement clues are context clues that restate, or rephrase, a difficult word in easier language. Common signal words for restatement clues are *that is, in other words,* and *or.* Punctuation marks such as dashes and commas can also signal restatements.

Model Sentence

He smiled *smugly,* that is, in his usual *snobbish, self-important way.*

Exercises Allow students to work in pairs to underline the restatement clues and define the underlined words. Then ask them to write their own sentences with restatement clues for these words and two other WORDS TO KNOW.

1. We were surprised by his strong retort—a reply that was both quick and fierce.

2. The rain seemed to pummel, or thrash, the roof of the cabin.

Use **Vocabulary Transparencies and Copymasters,** p. 21.

me. My foot *was* killing me. All I said, though, was, "How come you keep rubbing your arm?"

"I'm keeping the blood moving."

We approached the grove of trees. "Wow," Horse exclaimed. "Country." But as we drew closer, what we found were discarded cans, bottles, and newspapers—plus an old mattress spring.

"Hey," Max cried, sounding relieved, "this is just like Brooklyn."

I said, "Let's find a decent place, make camp, and eat."

It was hard to find a campsite that didn't have junk. The growing dark didn't help. We had to settle for the place that had the least amount of garbage.

Max said, "If we build a lean-to, it'll keep us out of the rain." He and Horse went a short distance with the hatchet.

Seeing a tree they wanted, Max whacked at it. The hatchet bounced right out of his hand. There was not even a dent in the tree. Horse retrieved the hatchet and checked the blade. "Dull," he said.

"Think I'm going to carry something sharp and cut myself?" Max protested. They contented themselves with picking up branches.

I went in search of firewood, but everything was wet. When I finally gathered some twigs and tried to light them, the only thing that burned was my fingers.

Meanwhile, Horse and Max used their branches to build a lean-to directly over me. After many collapses—which didn't

help my work—they finally got the branches to stand in a shaky sort of way.

"Uh-oh," Horse said. "We forgot to bring something for a cover."

Max eyed me. "Didn't you say you brought a blanket?"

"No way!" I cried.

"All in favor of using the blanket!"

Horse and Max both cried, "Aye."

Only after I built up a mound of partially burned match sticks and lit *them*, did I get the fire going. It proved that where there's smoke there doesn't have to be much fire. The guys meanwhile draped my blanket over their branch construction. It collapsed twice.

About an hour after our arrival, the three of us were gathered inside the tiny space. There was a small fire, but more light came from my flickering flashlight.

"No more rain," Horse said with pride.

"Just smoke," I said, rubbing my stinging eyes.

"We need a <u>vent</u> hole," Horse pointed out.

"I could cut it with the hatchet," Max said.

"It's my mother's favorite blanket."

"And you took it?" Max said.

I nodded.

"You *are* tough," Horse said.

Besides having too much smoke in our eyes and being wet, tired, and in pain, we were starving. I almost said something about giving up, but as far as I could see, the other guys were still tough.

WORDS TO KNOW — **vent** (věnt) *n.* an opening that allows gas, liquid, or smoke to escape

61

Grammar
Mini Lesson

IDENTIFYING SIMPLE SUBJECTS AND VERBS
Instruction Tell students that the subject of a sentence tells *whom* or *what* the sentence is about. The predicate tells what the subject *does* or *is*. Explain that the key word in a subject is the simple subject. It is a noun or a pronoun. The key word in a predicate is the simple predicate. It is the verb. Display the following sentence, underlining the simple subject and simple predicate:

Application The fearful <u>boys</u> <u>hiked</u> on the trail.
Have students locate the simple subjects and verbs in the highlighted sentences on page 61.
Exercise Ask students to locate the verb and its simple subject in each of these sentences.
1. Many young men joined the Boy Scouts. (V—joined, S—men)
2. Cold rain hit the roof of the tent. (V—hit, S—rain)

3. The boys brought supplies from home. (V—brought, S—boys)
4. They went camping in the dark. (V—went, S—They)

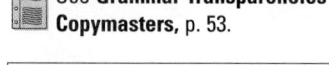 Use **Grammar Transparencies and Copymasters**, p. 53.

 Use McDougal Littell's **Language Network**, Chapter 1, for more instruction and practice in subjects and verbs.

(A) Have students visualize the campsite after the food fight. What details help them to imagine how the boys look and feel?

Possible Responses: details of the wet, dripping beans; the mud; the wet blanket; the image of the boys picking wet beans off of each other

(B) Ask students to visualize how the boys must look to others when they are standing on the subway. Why might people back away from them?

Possible Response: They must look dirty and wet. They might also look suspicious carrying all their dirty, wet belongings.

Reading Skills and Strategies:
CONNECT

(C) Ask students to think about how the boys' definition of *tough* has changed. How is this conversation both different from and similar to other conversations they have had on the subject of being tough? What has finally made the narrator the leader he wants to be?

Literary Analysis: CHARACTERS

(D) Discuss why the characters seem to feel a sense of relief at the end of the story, despite the fact that their trip was not what they wanted it to be. Was being good Boy Scouts what was most important to the boys?

Literary Analysis: HUMOR

Have students explain what elements create the most humor in the story. Do they believe it is the characters, the setting, the plot, or the writer's voice and style?

Number 8, 1949, Jackson Pollock. Neuberger Museum of Art, Purchase College, State University of New York, gift of Roy R. Neuberger. Photo: Jim Frank. Copyright © 2001 Pollock-Krasner Foundation/Artists Rights Society (ARS), New York.

Max put his frying pan atop my smoldering smoke. After dumping in the entire contents of his mustard bottle, he threw in the franks. Meanwhile, I bolted down my last sandwich.

"What am I going to eat?" Horse suddenly said.

"Your beans," I reminded him.

Max offered up his hatchet. "Here. Just chop off the top end of the can."

"Oh, right," Horse said. He selected a can, set it in front of him, levered himself onto his knees, then swung down—hard. There was an explosion. For a stunned moment, we just sat there, hands, face, and clothing dripping with beans.

(A) Suddenly Max shouted, "Food fight! Food fight!" and began to paw the stuff off and fling it around.

Having a food fight in a cafeteria is one thing. Having one in the middle of a soaking wet lean-to with cold beans during a dark, wet New Jersey night is another. In seconds, the lean-to was down, the fire kicked over, and Max's frankfurters dumped on the ground.

"The food!" Max screamed, and began to snatch up the franks. Coated with mustard, dirt, grass, and leaves, they looked positively prehistoric. Still, we wiped the franks clean on our pants then ate them—the franks, that is. Afterward, we picked beans off each other's clothes—the way monkeys help friends get rid of lice.

For dessert, Max shared some Tootsie Rolls. After Horse swallowed his sixteenth piece, he announced, "I don't feel so good."

The thought of his getting sick was too much. "Let's go home," I said, ashamed to look at the others. To my surprise—and relief—nobody objected.

Wet and cold, our way lit by my fast-fading flashlight, we gathered our belongings—most of them, anyway. As we made our way back

1

Teaching Options

 Mini Lesson **Viewing and Representing**

Number 8, 1949 (detail) **by Jackson Pollock**

ART APPRECIATION American painter Jackson Pollock (1912–1956) was a leader in an art movement known as Abstract Expressionism. Art in this style does not represent concrete, familiar images. It appears free and unplanned—using lines, shapes, or splashes of color to express ideas and feelings.
Instruction This abstract piece is created in the "drip and splash" style that Pollock began to develop in 1947. This style involved placing his canvas on the floor or the wall, pouring or drip-ping paint from a can or with a brush, and moving the paint around with sticks, knives, and other objects. Call students' attention to the colors and random patterns in the painting. What feeling does the piece give them?
Application Encourage students to connect the painting to a scene or moment in the story. They should explain why the painting reminds them of certain scenes.
Possible Responses: Students might suggest the food fight, the messy campground, or the confusing subway map.

over the bridge, gusts of wind-blown rain pummeled us until I felt like a used-up punching bag. By the time we got to the subway station, my legs were melting fast. The other guys looked bad too. Other riders moved away from us. One of them murmured, "Juvenile delinquents." To cheer us up, I got out my comic books, but they had congealed into a lump of red, white, and blue pulp.

With the subways running slow, it took hours to get home. When we emerged from the High Street station, it was close to midnight.

Before we split up to go to our own homes, we just stood there on a street corner, embarrassed, trying to figure out how to end the day gracefully. I was the one who said, "Okay, I admit it. I'm not as tough as you guys. I gave up first."

Max shook his head. "Naw. I wanted to quit, but I wasn't tough enough to do it." He looked to Horse.

Horse made a fist. "You saying I'm the one who's tough?" he demanded. "I hate roughing it!"

"Me too," I said quickly.

"Same for me," Max said.

Horse said, "Only thing is, we just have to promise not to tell Mr. Brenkman."

Grinning with relief, we simultaneously[4] clasped hands. "No matter what," Max reminded us.

To which I added, "Scout's Honor." ❖

---

4. **simultaneously** (sī′məl-ta′nē-əs-lē): at the same time.

WORDS
TO   **pummel** (pŭm′əl) *v.* to beat, as with the fists
KNOW

"I am a twin and that meant—and still means—sharing with my twin sister Emily. For example, usually it's me who tells the jokes while she laughs. Or, if we're at a party together, Emily does most of the talking, while I tend to be the listener.

When we were kids, one of her jobs was remembering. Thus, though we were in the same class from nursery school through seventh grade, Emily remembers our classmates' and teachers' names. I recall just my friends' names. In short, my memories of childhood are only of those things I did without her.

So, when asked to write a story about when I was young, I recalled the time I was trying to be a Boy Scout, my first attempt at an overnight camping trip. Emily wasn't there.

Keep in mind that 'Scout's Honor' is a piece of fiction. Though I can't recall the actual words we spoke, much less the moment to moment events, the broad outlines of that fiasco are true. What's more, I recall that, even then, we thought it was all pretty funny.

At the age when this story takes place—though I was a voracious reader—it had never occurred to me that I might become a writer. But I was an inventor of stories, which I—and my friends—acted out, much as described in my book Who Was That Masked Man, Anyway? Only during high school, when I was told I was a bad writer, did I decide to prove that I could write. As for my twin sister, she too is a writer. She writes poetry and nonfiction. So you see, we still divide things up."

Customizing Instruction

Less Proficient Readers

1 The narrator is surprised that nobody objects to his suggestions. Why? Ask students if they are surprised as well.

Possible Response: The narrator is surprised because he never thought for a moment his friends weren't "tough." Students might say they picked up on clues that the other boys wanted to go. Ask students to briefly summarize the events from when the characters step off the bridge to when they end up on street corners near their own homes.

Students Acquiring English

2 Be sure students understand why the writer repeats the phrase "Scout's Honor" at the end of the story. Ask them to flip back to page 55, when the Scoutmaster uses it. What meaning does it have there? What meaning does it have here, when the boys use it?

Gifted and Talented

Avi writes this story from the point of view of an adult looking back on a childhood experience. Suggest that growing older and more distanced from events gives the writer a clearer understanding of himself and his friends. Ask students to explain how the story would be different if it were written from a child's perspective on events as they were unfolding. Invite them to back up their statements with details from the text.

Possible Response: Students might say that the humor comes from the author's understanding of how foolish some of the boys' actions were. The writer seems to have understanding into why the boys behave in certain ways. A child talking about events as they unfold might not have this understanding.

✓ Assessment **Standardized Test Practice**

DESCRIBING THE SETTING OF A STORY For some standardized tests, students will be asked to choose a word or phrase that describes a story's setting. To give students practice recognizing details that describe setting, write the following on the board:

1. When the three main characters in "Scout's Honor" finally agree to go home, they are
   A. crossing the George Washington Bridge.
   B. standing in the rain, building their lean-to.
   C. lost in the busy subway station.
   D. sitting in their muddy campsite.

2. At what time of day do the final events of the story take place?
   A. late night
   B. daybreak
   C. late afternoon
   D. early evening

Point out that, according to details and facts in the story, D is the best choice for item 1 and A is the best choice for item 2.

GUIDING STUDENT RESPONSE

Connect to the Literature

1. What Do You Think?
Possible Response: Going home was a wise decision. The boys had already faced many challenges.

Comprehension Check
- They gather an assortment of ill-chosen items, such as cans without can openers, a mattress, a blanket, a hatchet, and a compass.
- Possible Responses: They get separated and lost on the subway; they run out of food; they get caught in the rain; they lack tools for creating warmth and shelter.
- They agree that they all really wanted to go home, but not all were tough enough to admit it; they agree that they won't tell Mr. Brenkman that they went home early.

 Use Selection Quiz
Unit One Resource Book, p. 27.

Think Critically

2. Possible Response: The main character doesn't want to be the first to suggest going home because he wants to appear tough in front of his friends. They probably feel the same way: though no one else suggests going home, no one protests when the narrator suggests leaving.

3. Possible Response: The main character may say later that admitting one's fears is tougher than just acting brave. Still, his wanting to keep his experience a secret shows that he hasn't completely changed his definition of toughness.

4. Responses should include specific details from the story. For example, the details about the familiar objects the boys carry with them should make it easy for students to visualize their belongings and the burdened, slow-moving way they begin their journey.

 Use **Reading and Critical Thinking Transparencies**, p. 4, for additional support.

Connect to the Literature

1. What Do You Think?
What was your reaction to this story?

Comprehension Check
- How do the **main character** and his friends prepare for their camping trip?
- Name three difficulties they encounter.
- What do the boys agree about at the end of their trip?

Think Critically

2. Why do you think the main character doesn't want to be the first person to suggest going home? Do you think his friends feel the same way? Give examples from the story to support your answer.

3. Do you think the main character will think differently about being "tough enough" after his adventure in Palisades Park?

 THINK ABOUT
- the main character's conversation with Max and Horse about the planned trip
- his thoughts just before crossing the bridge
- his friends' reaction when he suggests going home

4. **ACTIVE READING** **VISUALIZING** How clear were the mental pictures you described in your **READER'S NOTEBOOK**? Discuss with a partner the **details** from your notebook and how they helped you to **visualize**.

Extend Interpretations

5. **COMPARING TEXTS** Scout Law requires the boys in this story to be "loyal, helpful, friendly, courteous, kind, obedient, cheerful, thrifty, brave, clean, and reverent." Evaluate the characters in this story and in "President Cleveland, Where Are You?" on page 46. Which traits apply to each character? Explain.

6. Connect to Life At the end of the story, Max says he wants to quit but isn't tough enough to do it. Do you agree that sometimes it is harder to quit than to keep going? Explain.

Literary Analysis

SETTING The time and place of a story is called the **setting.** Along with facts about time and place, a setting includes **sensory details** that describe sights, sounds, and smells.

There was a small fire, but more light came from my flickering flashlight.

Sensory details affect the moods of the characters. They can have a powerful effect on how the characters grow and change.

Paired Activity Make a chart like the one shown below. Working with a partner, look back through the story and find details that suggest the story's setting. When your chart is complete, discuss your findings with another pair in the class. Consider:
- Which details tell you the most about the story's time and place?
- What parts of the setting are most important to the action of the story?
- How do details about the setting make the story come alive?

Place	Details
Brooklyn	Ebbets Field

Time	Details
1946	

Literary Analysis

Setting Students' charts should show an understanding of the most important elements of the story's setting. Students should describe how setting adds to the humor of the story.

 Use **Literary Analysis Transparencies**, p. 6, for additional support.

Extend Interpretations

5. Comparing Texts Students may respond that the three main characters in "Scout's Honor" possess all of these qualities, with the possible exceptions of obedient, clean, and reverent.

They are not quite honest in their actions, but they are loyal and helpful friends to each other. The boys in "President Cleveland, Where Are You?" with the exception of Rollie Tremaine, also possess most of these qualities. In fact, the narrator's loyalty and kindness to his brother causes him no end of problems.

6. Connect to Life Students may respond that quitting is sometimes harder than continuing, because you might be embarrassed in front of your friends or face negative consequences such as losing a race or failing a test.

Writing Options

1. Persuasive Essay Think about the challenges the boys faced in going camping. Then write a persuasive essay to convince Mr. Brenkman that the boys should be promoted to Second Class Scouts.

Writing Handbook
See p. R39: Persuasive Writing.

2. Adventure Guide What lessons might these Scouts have learned from their adventure? Write a page for an adventure guide with tips for tackling tough challenges. If you want, use the Scout Craft camping requirement as an example of a challenge, or choose a sport or activity from your own experience.

Activities & Explorations

Map and Directions Suppose the boys have to present a map and directions with their report of the camping trip. Create a map of their travels. Add directions based on the story. ~ **VIEWING AND REPRESENTING**

Inquiry & Research

How to Be Prepared What is Scouting like today? Talk with troop leaders and Scouts. How do today's Scouts follow the Oath? What goals must Tenderfoots achieve?

 More Online: Research Starter
www.mcdougallittell.com

Art Connection

Making a Splash Look again at the painting by Jackson Pollock on page 62. Pollock created paintings by dripping or pouring paint directly onto the canvas. What words would you use to describe this image?

Number 8, 1949 (detail), Jackson Pollock. Copyright © 2001 Pollock-Krasner Foundation/Artists Rights Society (ARS), New York.

Vocabulary in Action

EXERCISE: CONTEXT CLUES On a sheet of paper, write the vocabulary word that best completes each sentence.

1. I began to _____ loudly at my friends to meet me at the next train station.
2. When we camped, we cut a _____ in our lean-to so that smoke could escape.
3. Horse is my _____, and we compete in everything; but he is my best friend.
4. Horse had to _____ a metal bar on the sidewalk to have one foot in New York and one in New Jersey.
5. "I brought an umbrella," he said _____, seeing that we were getting soaked.
6. Horse was _____ of the food we brought, since all he had was canned beans.
7. The harsh wind and rain continued to _____ our little group.
8. We Scouts stared at the bridge, not believing its _____ size.
9. Max just had to _____ in his own defense when we doubted his skill.
10. As we walked through the fog, we viewed our surroundings with _____.

Building Vocabulary
For an in-depth lesson on context clues, see p. 79.

WORDS TO KNOW				
bellow	immense	retort	smugly	suspicion
envious	pummel	rival	straddle	vent

Writing Options

1. Persuasive Essay Students' essays should focus on specific qualities the boys exhibit as they deal with the hardships of their journey. Tell students that a good persuasive essay should support ideas and opinions with solid facts and details and should address any objections Mr. Brenkman might raise.

📄 Use **Writing Transparencies,** p. 6, for additional support.

2. Adventure Guide Suggest that students make an outline of the story. In their outline, they should record each incident that can be seen as a learning experience. Students who are basing their pages on personal experiences should also create outlines in which they record important and helpful details.

📄 Use **Writing Transparencies,** p. 54, for additional support.

Activities & Explorations

Map and Directions Students' maps should be accurate in their presentation of the area. They can also be creative in highlighting details and landmarks that are emphasized in the story. Maps should reflect an understanding of the area and an understanding of the story.

Inquiry & Research

How to Be Prepared Encourage students to prepare specific questions before they interview people. They should think about what information they need from each source.
To extend this activity, have students use their information to prepare a guide to Scouting that can be used by students considering joining the organization.

📄 Use **Communications Transparencies and Copymasters,** p. 9, for additional support.

Art Connection

Making a Splash Students' answers will vary, but should include words that indicate messiness and chaos.

Vocabulary in Action

1. bellow
2. vent
3. rival
4. straddle
5. smugly
6. envious
7. pummel
8. immense
9. retort
10. suspicion

Grammar in Context

WRITING EXERCISE

Answers will vary. Possible answers are shown.

1. My two best friends *went* camping with me in the park.
2. With the subways running slow, the trip home *took* hours.
3. Horses *are* very intelligent animals.
4. The bridge *spanned* the mighty river.

Author Activity

Past Times Students should review biographies, library catalogs, and online resources to locate information on Avi's other works. Students can look for quotes from Avi and information about Avi's life that give clues about his interests and the themes of his work. Have students analyze why certain historical periods might appeal to Avi.

 Use **Writing Transparencies,** p. 45–48, for additional support.

Choices & CHALLENGES

Grammar in Context: Subjects and Verbs

A complete sentence has two important parts: the **subject** and the **verb.** The subject "performs" the action of the verb. Verbs can express physical action, as in this example:

> I **pounded** up the steps into the house.

Verbs can also express a state of being:

> Scouting **is** real camping.

Usage Tip: Sometimes a sentence has a **verb phrase**—a **main verb** and one or more **helping verbs:**

> He <u>could talk</u> his way out of a locked room.

Apply to Your Writing Check your writing to be sure that your sentences are complete—that they contain both a subject and a verb.

WRITING EXERCISE Write a sentence using the subject provided. In each case, underline the subject and circle the verb.

Example: *Original* The overnight hike

Rewritten The overnight hike (turned) into a test of bravery.

1. My two best friends
2. The trip home
3. Horses
4. The bridge

Grammar Handbook Quick Reference: The Sentence and Its Parts, p. R55

"Everybody has ideas. The vital question is, what do you do with them?"

Avi
born 1937

Writing Relations Many of Avi's relatives, including both of his parents, were writers. Avi has said he learned more from reading books than from going to school. School was a struggle for Avi. Because of a learning problem, he had a hard time in class and once even flunked out. He found his first success as a writer during college, when one of his plays won a prize and was published.

Books and More Books Avi worked as a librarian for 25 years. Meanwhile, he made up

stories for his own children. These stories eventually became his first book, *Things That Sometimes Happen.* Since then, Avi has published dozens of books, including two Newbery Honor Books, *The True Confessions of Charlotte Doyle* and *Nothing but the Truth.* Although Avi has earned a reputation as a historical novelist, he also writes spooky stories, science fiction, and humorous novels.

AUTHOR ACTIVITY

Past Times Do research to find out about the settings of some of Avi's historical novels. Choose the one you find most interesting and write a short report about why you would like to read a story that takes place in that era. Share your report with the class.

Teaching Options

VERB PHRASES: MAIN AND HELPING VERBS

Instruction Tell students that many verbs are single words but sometimes a verb is made up of two or more words. The last word is the main verb; other words are helping verbs. Write the following examples on the board.

Helping Verb(s)	Main Verb	Verb
is	hiking	is hiking
has been	raining	has been raining
might have	made	might have made

Grammar
Mini Lesson

Tell students that forms of the verbs *be, have,* and *do* are the most commonly used helping verbs. Explain that forms of *be, have,* and *do* can also be used as main verbs.

Example He <u>is</u> hiking. (helping verb)
He <u>is</u> a hiker. (main verb)

Exercises Have students underline the main verb once and the helping verbs twice in each of the following sentences. Note: One sentence contains no helping verbs.

1. He <u>was</u> <u>hoping</u> for success.

2. The camping trip <u>might have</u> <u>been</u> a mistake.
3. They <u>should have</u> <u>prepared</u> for rain.
4. Avi <u>was</u> a Boy Scout.
5. He <u>has been</u> <u>remembering</u> his childhood.

 Use **Unit One Resource Book,** p. 25.
Use **Grammar Transparencies and Copymasters,** p. 77, for additional practice.

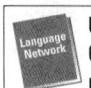 Use McDougal Littell's ***Language Network,*** Chapter 4, for more instruction and practice in main verbs and helping verbs.

PREPARING to *Read*

Nadia the Willful

Short Story by SUE ALEXANDER

ACROSS the CURRICULUM — GEOGRAPHY

Connect to Your Life

This story is set in the Sahara Desert. How does climate affect life in your region?

Build Background Despite its harsh climate, the Sahara—the largest desert in the world—supports some 2.5 million people, as well as many kinds of plant and animal life.

MOROCCO · TUNISIA · ALGERIA · LIBYA · EGYPT · WESTERN SAHARA · MAURITANIA · Sahara Desert · MALI · NIGER · CHAD · ERITREA · SUDAN

Bone-dry and scorched by the sun, the Sahara Desert covers about 3.5 million square miles—an area about as large as the United States. It is sometimes called "the sea without water."

The climate is severe and dangerous. Food is scarce, sandstorms are common, and temperatures can reach 130°F.

Because the Sahara is so dry, heat disappears quickly at night. Temperatures can drop as much as 100°F when the sun goes down.

Rare oases (places with water and pasture) provide relief for people and animals.

Focus Your Reading

LITERARY ANALYSIS **THEME** A **theme** is a message about life or human nature that a writer shares with the reader. A theme may be stated directly, but more often it is a message that the reader must figure out.

WORDS TO KNOW **Vocabulary Preview**
banish bazaar clan decree ponder

LaserLinks: Background for Reading
Cultural Connection
Visual Vocabulary

ACTIVE READING **RECOGNIZING CAUSE AND EFFECT** When one event brings about, or causes, another, the two events are related as **cause and effect.** The event that happens first is the cause; the one that follows is the effect. Looking for examples of cause and effect can help you understand why a story unfolds in a particular way. As you read this story, jot down notes in your **READER'S NOTEBOOK** about events that cause changes.

Objectives
1. understand and appreciate a **short story** (Literary Analysis)
2. understand the **theme** of a story (Literary Analysis)
3. understand how to **recognize cause and effect** in fiction (Active Reading)

Summary
A young Bedouin girl (the Bedouin are a nomadic people of North Africa and the Middle East) has earned the nickname Nadia the Willful because of her quick temper. Her brother, Hamed, is the only one who can tame her temper, and when he disappears and is presumed dead, she is sad and angry. Her father, Tarik, decrees that no one shall speak Hamed's name. Nadia finds herself struggling with the loss of Hamed, and the only way she can keep his memory alive is to talk about him. She makes the brave decision to willfully disobey her father. In the end, Nadia shows her father how he can keep Hamed's memory alive.

Thematic Link
Making difficult decisions takes courage. In honoring the memory of her brother, the inner peace Nadia's memories brought her outweighed the threat of punishment from her father. Nadia's decision was true to herself and consistent with her character.

5-Minute Warm-Up

Daily Language SkillBuilder

Have students **proofread** the display sentences on page 19i and write them correctly. The sentences also appear on Transparency 2 of **Grammar Transparencies and Copymasters.**

Mini Lesson **Preteaching Vocabulary**
If you would like to preteach the WORDS TO KNOW for this selection, use the Mini Lesson, p. 69.

LESSON RESOURCES

Reading and Analyzing

Literary Analysis [THEME]

The theme of this unit is "The Courage to Be Me." Ask students what they think it means and how it might be connected to a story called "Nadia the Willful." (Discuss what it means to be willful.)

Possible Response: The theme might mean that sometimes it takes courage to be yourself, to do what you think is right. A willful person is one who is determined to achieve his or her goals or unwilling to give in. It can also mean "stubborn," and there is a fine line between determination and stubborn-ness. "Nadia the Willful" sounds like a story about someone who is deter-mined to do things her way.

 Use **Unit One Resource Book,** p. 30 for more practice.

Active Reading [RECOGNIZING CAUSE AND EFFECT]

Ⓐ Why is Nadia called "willful"? Why is her father "praised in every tent"?

Possible Responses: Nadia is stub-born and has a temper; her father is kind and gracious.

 Use **Unit One Resource Book,** p. 29 for more practice.

Reading Skills and Strategies: PREDICT

Ask students to predict how Hamed is able to calm Nadia.

Possible Response: He is able to calm her with his sense of humor.

Bedouins (about 1905–1906), John Singer Sargent. Watercolor, 18″ × 12″, The Brooklyn Museum, New York. Purchased by special subscription (09.814).

Teaching Options

 Mini Lesson ## Viewing and Representing

Bedouins
by John Singer Sargent

ART APPRECIATION

Instruction John Singer Sargent (1856–1925) is chiefly known as a painter of high-society por-traits. He also traveled widely, however, and often recorded his experiences in his paintings. *Bedouins,* painted about 1905 or 1906, shows a Bedouin man and woman, members of one of the nomadic tribes of Arabs.

Application Ask students how the brush strokes and choice of colors help create a feeling for the Bedouins and their home.

Possible Responses: The rough, irregular strokes suggest a desert mirage. The blues and browns are the colors of the shimmering sky and the desert sands.

Nadia the Willful

by Sue Alexander

In the land of the drifting sands where the Bedouin move their tents to follow the fertile grasses, there lived a girl whose stubbornness and flashing temper caused her to be known throughout the desert as Nadia the Willful.

Nadia's father, the sheik Tarik, whose kindness and graciousness caused his name to be praised in every tent, did not know what to do with his willful daughter.

Only Hamed, the eldest of Nadia's six brothers and Tarik's favorite son, could calm Nadia's temper when it flashed.

Literary Analysis: SETTING

A Ask students to describe the desert setting of this story.

Possible Responses: There are some grassy areas surrounding the oases where the sheep graze. Pillars of wind and blowing sand separate the oases. Merchants travel by camel across the empty land.

Active Reading   RECOGNIZING CAUSE AND EFFECT

B Nadia and her father are struggling with intense feelings. What are those feelings, and what has caused them?

Possible Response: Nadia and her father are experiencing grief and sadness caused by the disappearance and presumed death of Hamed.

C What are some of the situations that cause Nadia to remember Hamed, and what effect does this have on Nadia?

Possible Response: Some of the things that cause Nadia to remember Hamed are the games that her brothers play, the women weaving by the tents, and the shepherds with their flocks. They cause Nadia to feel unhappy, angry, and lonely.

Reading Skills and Strategies: EVALUATE

D Have students evaluate Nadia's response to her brothers' game. Is speaking Hamed's name a wise thing for Nadia to do? Why or why not?

Possible Responses: Speaking Hamed's name might be good because Nadia needs to release her grief and frustration. It also helps her to remember him. It could also be bad because she is going against the wishes of her father.

"Oh, angry one," he would say, "shall we see how long you can stay that way?" And he would laugh and tease and pull at her dark hair until she laughed back. Then she would follow Hamed wherever he led.

One day before dawn, Hamed mounted his father's great white stallion and rode to the west to seek new grazing ground for the sheep. Nadia stood with her father at the edge of the oasis and watched him go.

Hamed did not return.

A Nadia rode behind her father as he traveled across the desert from oasis to oasis, seeking Hamed.

Shepherds told them of seeing a great white stallion fleeing before the pillars of wind that stirred the sand. And they said that the horse carried no rider.

Passing merchants, their camels laden with spices and sweets for the <u>bazaar</u>, told of the emptiness of the desert they had crossed.

1 Tribesmen, strangers, everyone whom Tarik asked, sighed and gazed into the desert, saying, "Such is the will of Allah."[1]

*A*t last Tarik knew in his heart that his favorite son, Hamed, had been claimed, as other Bedouin before him, by the drifting sands. And he told Nadia what he knew— that Hamed was dead.

Nadia screamed and wept and stamped the sand, crying, "Not even Allah will take Hamed from me!" until her father could bear no more and sternly bade her to silence.

B Nadia's grief knew no bounds. She walked blindly through the oasis, neither seeing nor hearing those who would console her. And Tarik was silent. For days he sat inside his tent, speaking not at all and barely tasting the meals set before him.

Then, on the seventh day, Tarik came out of his tent. He called all his people to him, and when they were assembled, he spoke. "From this day forward," he said, "let no one utter Hamed's name. Punishment shall be swift for those who would remind me of what I have lost."

Each memory brought Hamed's name to Nadia's lips.

Hamed's mother wept at the <u>decree</u>. The people of the <u>clan</u> looked at one another uneasily. All could see the hardness that had settled on the sheik's face and the coldness in his eyes, and so they said nothing. But they obeyed.

Nadia, too, did as her father decreed, though each day held something to remind her of Hamed. As she passed her brothers at play, she remembered games Hamed had taught her. As she walked by the women weaving patches for the tents and heard them talking and laughing, she remembered tales Hamed had told her and how they had made her laugh. And as she watched the shepherds with their flock, she remembered the little black lamb Hamed had loved.

C

---

1. **Allah** (ăl'ə): the name for God in the Islamic religion.

WORDS **bazaar** (bə-zär') *n.* in Middle Eastern countries, an outdoor market of small shops
TO   **decree** (dĭ-krē) *n.* an official order
KNOW   **clan** (clăn) *n.* a family group

70

BLOCK SCHEDULING: MANAGING TIME

If your schedule requires that you cover the lesson objectives in a shorter time, use . . .	**If you want to take advantage of longer class time, use . . .**
• Preparing to Read, p. 67 • Thinking Through the Literature, p. 76 • Vocabulary In Action, p. 77 • Grammar in Context, p. 78	• TE Teaching Options: Viewing and Representing, pp. 68, 75; Preteaching Vocabulary, p. 69; Cross-Curricular Link, p. 71; Grammar, pp. 72, 78; Standardized Test Practice, p. 73; Spelling, p. 74; Multicultural Link, p. 77 • Literary Link, p. 74 • Choices & Challenges, pp. 77–78

La caravane [The caravan] (1880), Alexandre-Gabriel Decamps. Louvre, Paris. Giraudon/Art Resource, New York.

Each memory brought Hamed's name to Nadia's lips, but she stilled the sound. And each time that she did so, her unhappiness grew until, finally, she could no longer contain it. She wept and raged at anyone and anything that crossed her path. Soon everyone at the oasis fled at her approach. And she was more lonely than she had ever been before.

One day, as Nadia passed the place where her brothers were playing, she stopped to watch them. They were playing one of the games that Hamed had taught her. But they were playing it wrong.

Without thinking, Nadia called out to them. "That is not the way! Hamed said that first you jump this way and then you jump back!"

Her brothers stopped their game and looked around in fear. Had Tarik heard Nadia say Hamed's name? But the sheik was nowhere to be seen.

"Teach us, Nadia, as our brother taught you," said her smallest brother.

And so she did. Then she told them of other games and how Hamed had taught her to play them. And as she spoke of Hamed, she felt an easing of the hurt within her.

Cross Curricular Link **Social Studies**

BEDOUINS The Bedouins are an Arab people of the Sahara and the desert lands of the Middle East. The leader of a Bedouin tribe or clan is called a sheik. Bedouins live as nomads, or wanderers, searching the desert for oases (places with water and pasture) where they can settle with their goats, sheep, camels, and horses. When water becomes scarce, the group moves on. Life in the desert is hard and dangerous. Food is scarce, sandstorms are common, and temperatures can reach up to 130 degrees Fahrenheit.

Traditionally, Bedouins live in tents. Their diet includes meat and dairy products produced from their livestock, as well as rice and dates. When Bedouins want to acquire manufactured goods, they often trade their meat and dairy products with people in villages. During the past fifty years or so, some Middle Eastern nations have encouraged many Bedouins to settle in designated places. This has led many of them to give up their nomadic lifestyle and live in one place, seeking jobs and sending their children to school.

Active Reading | RECOGNIZING CAUSE AND EFFECT

A What causes the conflict between Nadia and her mother and the other women in her clan?

Possible Response: Her mother and the other women are afraid to listen to Nadia talk about Hamed because of the sheik's decree. They fear Tarik's punishment.

B What effect does speaking about Hamed have on Nadia?

Possible Response: The more she talks about him, the clearer his memory becomes. Nadia becomes less angry and hurt, and finally comes to feel peace.

Literary Analysis | THEME

Authors often try to teach us something through their stories. By considering the plot, characters, and setting, readers can often determine the theme. What theme, or message, is the author of "Nadia the Willful" trying to get across to the reader?

Possible Response: Nadia has to make a difficult choice in this story. She has to disobey her father in order to come to grips with her own inner struggle over her brother's death. Making hard decisions takes courage, and Nadia has to do what she believes is right.

Literary Analysis: CONFLICT

C Ask students to describe the inner conflict Nadia is experiencing and how she resolves it.

Possible Response: Nadia is conflicted by her father's decree and her intense desire to talk about Hamed. She resolves the conflict by talking to her father about Hamed.

So she went on speaking of him.

She went to where the women sat at their loom and spoke of Hamed. She told them tales that Hamed had told her. And she told how he had made her laugh as he was telling them.

At first the women were afraid to listen to the willful girl and covered their ears, but after a time, they listened and laughed with her.

"Remember your father's promise of punishment!" Nadia's mother warned when she heard Nadia speaking of Hamed. "Cease, I implore you!"

A Nadia knew that her mother had reason to be afraid, for Tarik, in his grief and bitterness, had grown quick-tempered and sharp of tongue. But she did not know how to tell her mother that speaking of Hamed eased the pain she felt, and so she said only, "I will speak of my brother! I will!" And she ran away from the sound of her mother's voice.

She went to where the shepherds tended the flock and spoke of Hamed. The shepherds ran from her in fear and hid behind the sheep. But Nadia went on speaking. She told of Hamed's love for the little black lamb and how he had taught it to leap at his whistle. Soon the shepherds left off their hiding and came to listen. Then they told their own stories of Hamed and the little black lamb.

 he more Nadia spoke of Hamed, the clearer his face became in her mind. She could see his smile and the light in his eyes. She **B** could hear his voice. And the clearer Hamed's voice and face became, the less Nadia hurt inside and the less her temper flashed. At last, she was filled with peace.

But her mother was still afraid for her willful daughter. Again and again she sought to quiet Nadia so that Tarik's bitterness would not be turned against her. And again and again Nadia tossed her head and went on speaking of Hamed.

Soon, all who listened could see Hamed's face clearly before them.

"I have spoken!" roared the sheik. "It shall be done!"

One day, the youngest shepherd came to Nadia's tent, calling, "Come, Nadia! See Hamed's black lamb; it has grown so big and strong!"

But it was not Nadia who came out of the tent.

It was Tarik.

On the sheik's face was a look more fierce than that of a desert hawk, and when he spoke, his words were as sharp as a scimitar.[2]

"I have forbidden my son's name to be said. And I promised punishment to whoever disobeyed my command. So shall it be. Before the sun sets and the moon casts its first shadow on the sand, you will be gone from this oasis—never to return."

"No!" cried Nadia, hearing her father's words.

"I have spoken!" roared the sheik. "It shall be done!"

Trembling, the shepherd went to gather his possessions.

---

2. **scimitar** (sĭm′ĭ-tər): a curved sword.

Teaching Options

 Grammar

IDENTIFYING DIRECT OBJECTS Remind students that a direct object is the noun or pronoun that receives the action of a verb. Asking *whom* or *what* after the verb helps determine the direct object.

Instruction Write the following sentence on the board:

Hamed loved the little black lamb.

Ask students to identify the direct object in this sentence. *(lamb)*

Exercises Have students identify the direct object in each of the following sentences.

1. Nadia's mother missed her <u>son</u> a great deal.
2. Nadia tossed her <u>head</u> back and kept talking.
3. They feared the <u>banishment</u> by Tarik.
4. Nadia brought the <u>memories</u> of Hamed back to life for Tarik.

 Use **Grammar Transparencies and Copymasters**, p. 54.

Use McDougal Littell's *Language Network,* Chapter 1, for more instruction and practice in direct objects.

And the rest of the clan looked at one another uneasily and muttered among themselves.

In the hours that followed, fear of being <u>banished</u> to the desert made everyone turn away from Nadia as she tried to tell them of Hamed and the things he had done and said.

And the less she was listened to, the less she was able to recall Hamed's face and voice. And the less she recalled, the more her temper raged within her, destroying the peace she had found.

By evening, she could stand it no longer. She went to where her father sat, staring into the desert, and stood before him.

"You will not rob me of my brother Hamed!" she cried, stamping her foot. "I will not let you!"

Tarik looked at her, his eyes colder than the desert night.

But before he could utter a word, Nadia spoke again. "Can you recall Hamed's face? Can you still hear his voice?"

Tarik started in surprise, and his answer seemed to come unbidden to his lips. "No, I cannot! Day after day I have sat in this spot where I last saw Hamed, trying to remember the look, the sound, the happiness that was my beloved son—but I cannot."

And he wept.

Nadia's tone became gentle. "There is a way, honored father," she said. "Listen."

And she began to speak of Hamed. She told of walks she and Hamed had taken and of talks they had had. She told how he had taught her games, told her tales, and calmed her when she was angry. She told many things that she remembered, some happy and some sad.

And when she was done with the telling, she said gently, "Can you not recall him now, Father? Can you not see his face? Can you not hear his voice?"

Tarik nodded through his tears, and for the first time since Hamed had been gone, he smiled.

"Now you see," Nadia said, her tone more gentle than the softest of the desert breezes, "there is a way that Hamed can be with us still."

The sheik <u>pondered</u> what Nadia had said. After a long time, he spoke, and the sharpness was gone from his voice.

"You will not rob me of my brother Hamed!"

"Tell my people to come before me, Nadia," he said. "I have something to say to them."

When all were assembled, Tarik said, "From this day forward, let my daughter Nadia be known not as willful but as wise. And let her name be praised in every tent, for she has given me back my beloved son."

And so it was. The shepherd returned to his flock, kindness and graciousness returned to the oasis, and Nadia's name was praised in every tent. And Hamed lived again—in the hearts of all who remembered him. ❖

WORDS TO KNOW
banish (băn´ĭsh) *v.* to send away; exile
ponder (pŏn´dər) *v.* to think about carefully

73

Customizing Instruction

Students Acquiring English
1 Explain that the idiom *day after day* means "each day for many days."
2 Help students understand that Nadia is not speaking literally when she asks Tarik, "Can you not see his face? Can you not hear his voice?"

Less Proficient Readers
Have students summarize the events following Tarik's decree in their own words.
Possible Response: Nadia disobeys her father in order to remember Hamed. One of the shepherds uses Hamed's name when he thinks he's speaking to Nadia, but Tarik hears him and banishes him. This leads Nadia to confront her father. Tarik revokes the sentence when he understands that Nadia is right.

Gifted and Talented
Ask students if they believe that Nadia has become any less willful and to explain their answers.
Possible Responses: No, Nadia is still willful; her willfulness is what forced Tarik to reconsider his actions and to recognize her wisdom. Yes, she is now able to communicate her viewpoint to Tarik with gentle words.

Multiple Leaning Styles
Kinesthetic Learners
Have students act out the scene between Nadia and her father. Ask them to think about how each character feels and to portray those feelings in their reenactment. They can use their own words or the actual words from the story.

☑ **Assessment** **Standardized Test Practice**

UNDERSTANDING THE FEELINGS AND EMOTIONS OF CHARACTERS In some standardized tests, students are asked to identify how characters felt about certain events in the story. Ask students to think about how Hamed's family might have felt after Tarik conceded that the drifting sands of the desert had claimed Hamed.
A. confident
B. amused
C. devastated
D. embarrassed

Guide students through the process of selecting the correct answer. A: *confident* usually connotes a positive feeling; Hamed's family wasn't feeling positive. B: *amused* means happy or delighted: they were certainly not that. They may have been *embarrassed* (D) by showing their grief, but it is not the best answer. C: *devastated* is the best answer because the sadness caused by the death of a loved one can completely throw us off guard and cause us to lose hope.

Use the following questions to help students analyze and understand the poem.

- Think about the title of this poem and about a time when you had to overcome a fear. What qualities helped you succeed? What qualities do you need to succeed in life? Work with a group to generate a list.

Possible Responses: a kind heart, a good work ethic, self-confidence, faith, family, a good education

- Explain to students that a word, phrase, line, or group of lines repeated regularly in a poem is called a refrain. Ask them to identify this feature in this poem and to describe its effect.

Possible Response: "Life doesn't frighten me at all," with some variations, is the refrain. Each time the author mentions something that might be frightening, she repeats the refrain as if to convince herself that she is not scared.

- What mental image did you create as you read or heard this poem?

Possible Response: This poem creates a picture of a scared little girl in her room at night in the dark trying to be brave.

Maya Angelou

Born in 1928, Maya Angelou grew up in Stamps, Arkansas. She has worked as a dancer, singer, composer, writer, and teacher. She earned a National Book Award nomination for the first volume of her autobiography, *I Know Why the Caged Bird Sings,* and read an original poem at the inauguration of President Clinton in 1993.

Life
Doesn't
Frighten Me

by Maya Angelou

Shadows on the wall
Noises down the hall
Life doesn't frighten me at all
Bad dogs barking loud
5 Big ghosts in a cloud
Life doesn't frighten me at all.

Mean old Mother Goose
Lions on the loose
They don't frighten me at all
10 Dragons breathing flame
On my counterpane[1]
That doesn't frighten me at all,

I go boo
Make them shoo
15 I make fun
Way they run
I won't cry
So they fly
I just smile
20 They go wild
Life doesn't frighten me at all.

Tough guys in a fight
All alone at night
Life doesn't frighten me at all.

25 Panthers in the park
Strangers in the dark
No, they don't frighten me at all.

---

1. **counterpane** (koun'tər-pān'): bedspread.

Teaching Options

 Mini Lesson **Spelling**

THE SUFFIX -ABLE Remind students that the suffix *-able* is commonly added to words to form adjectives meaning "able to be." Note that when the base word ends with a silent *e,* the *e* is usually dropped before a suffix that begins with a vowel, such as *-able.*

Instruction

- Write this example on the board:
  value + able = valuable

- Ask students to work together to make new words by adding *-able* to these words from the selection:
  answer, approach, honor, bear, ponder, love

- Discuss the new words students have made.

Exercise Have students complete each analogy below, using words derived from the previous list.

1. comfort : comfortable :: desire : _____
   (*desirable*)

2. valuable : expensive :: _____ : worthy
   (*honorable*)

3. endurable : _____ :: unendurable : unbearable
   (*bearable*)

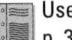 Use **Unit One Resource Book,**
p. 33 for more practice.

Boy and Dog in a Johnnypump (1982), Jean-Michel Basquiat. Galerie Bischofberger, Zurich, Switzerland. Copyright © 2001 Artists Rights Society (ARS), New York/ADAGP, Paris.

That new classroom where
Boys all pull my hair
30 (Kissy little girls
With their hair in curls)
They don't frighten me at all.

Don't show me frogs and snakes
And listen for my scream,
35 If I'm afraid at all
It's only in my dreams.

I've got a magic charm
That I keep up my sleeve,
I can walk the ocean floor
40 And never have to breathe.

Life doesn't frighten me at all
Not at all
Not at all.
Life doesn't frighten me at all.

Customizing Instruction

Gifted and Talented
Ask students to think about the tone of the poem and their own feelings about overcoming fear. Then have each student write a stanza about something that he or she thinks is frightening. Be sure students' stanzas reproduce the poem's defiant tone and its ". . . doesn't frighten me at all" refrain.

Less Proficient Readers
Set a Purpose As they read, ask students to identify the fears mentioned in "Life Doesn't Frighten Me" and the way the poet describes them.
1 To be sure students understand the poem, ask them how the poet deals with her fears.
Possible Response: She scares them away, laughs at them, and refuses to let them make her cry.

Students Acquiring English
Help students to appreciate the qualities of free verse. Free verse is written like conversation, without a regular pattern of rhyme, rhythm, or line length. The vocabulary in the poem is not particularly difficult, so students should enjoy the beauty and sound of the language.

Multiple Learning Styles
Auditory Learners
Listen to the natural rhythm of this poem. Choose one stanza and tap it out with your pencil or your foot. Students may want to extend this activity to the whole poem. They may also enjoy a variety of ways of marking the rhythm, such as clapping or snapping their fingers.

Mini Lesson Viewing and Representing

Boy and Dog in a Johnnypump
by Jean-Michel Basquiat

ART APPRECIATION The Caribbean-American artist Jean-Michel Basquiat (1960–1988) was one of the best-known artists of the 1980s. This painting is from his early period, during which he often depicted skeleton-like figures, reflecting his obsession with death.

Instruction Ask students to think about how this painting matches the mood or tone set in the poem. How does the style of the painting affect the mood?

Possible Response: The mood of the painting is scary because of the skeleton figures and the distorted features. The poem has a similar mood because it talks about magic charms, strangers in the dark, screams in the night, shadows and noises, dogs, and ghosts. Both make me think of something that could be frightening.

GUIDING STUDENT RESPONSE

Connect to the Literature

1. What Do You Think?
Possible Response: Nadia's disobedience of Tarik's decree is brave and admirable because she ends up helping so many people.

Comprehension Check
- When Nadia first hears of her brother's death, she screams and weeps and will not let anyone console her.
- Tarik orders his people to never again speak of Hamed.
- Nadia likes to talk about Hamed because keeping his memory alive makes her grief easier to bear.

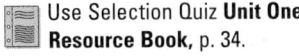 Use Selection Quiz **Unit One Resource Book,** p. 34.

Think Critically

2. Possible Responses: Nadia deserves to be called willful because she insists on saying and doing what she pleases. She is not willful; she is just honest about her feelings.

3. Possible Response: At first Nadia is very stubborn about her attitude. Over time, she learns to accept her brother's death and to confront Tarik in a calm and receptive way. In doing so, she becomes peaceful and wise.

4. Possible Responses: Nadia changes Tarik's mind because she is stubborn and refuses to back down. Nadia shows Tarik that silence does not erase grief and that remembering Hamed is both good and comforting.

 Use **Reading and Critical Thinking Transparencies,** p. 5, for additional support.

5. Possible Responses: Because Nadia is forbidden to speak of Hamed, she is frustrated and unhappy; because people are not allowed to speak of Hamed, they begin to forget him; because Nadia disobeys her father and begins to speak of Hamed, she begins to let go of her anger and grief.

Literary Analysis

Theme Students' lists should include some of the themes discussed throughout the story. Details and events listed should directly support each theme.

 Use **Literary Analysis Transparencies,** p. 7, for additional support.

76 UNIT ONE PART 1

Connect to the Literature

1. What Do You Think? What is your opinion of Nadia's behavior in the story?

Comprehension Check
- How does Nadia react at first to the news of Hamed's death?
- What order does Tarik give to his people?
- Why does Nadia like to talk about Hamed?

Think Critically

2. In your opinion, does Nadia deserve to be called willful? Why or why not?

3. How does Nadia change during the story? What causes the change?

4. Nadia's father promises to punish anyone who speaks Hamed's name. Why do you think Nadia is able to change her father's mind?

 THINK ABOUT
- Nadia's character
- her father's behavior after Hamed is lost
- the effect Nadia's words have on other characters

5. ACTIVE READING RECOGNIZING CAUSE AND EFFECT
Think about the **cause-and-effect** relationships you recorded in your READER'S NOTEBOOK. Compare your observations with those of a classmate.

Extend Interpretations

6. COMPARING TEXTS Read "Life Doesn't Frighten Me" by Maya Angelou on page 74. Compare it to "Nadia the Willful." What do these two selections say about the qualities a person needs to deal with challenges? Which one offers better ideas about overcoming fears? Explain.

VIDEODISC **LaserLinks: Background for Reading** Literary Connection

7. Connect to Life Nadia and Tarik have different ways of reacting to death. Do their differences bring to mind any differences between people that you know or have read about?

76 UNIT ONE PART 1: THE COURAGE TO BE ME

Literary Analysis

THEME A **theme** is a message that a reader finds in a work of literature. Most themes are lessons about life or human nature. In "Nadia the Willful," Nadia discovers that memories can help to ease the pain of losing someone close. This lesson is one of the story's themes.

Cooperative Learning Activity
What themes can you find in "Nadia the Willful"? With a small group of classmates, review the story's plot and discuss the changes that take place. On a piece of paper, write down the messages that the plot suggests. Under each theme list the details and events in the story that support it.

Theme: Memories can help ease the pain of losing someone close.

Nadia talks about the game Hamed taught her and feels "an easing of the hurt."

REVIEW PLOT The events that take place in a story make up its **plot.** The plot is the writer's plan for what happens, when it happens, and who is involved.

Extend Interpretations

6. Comparing Texts Both selections suggest that people need strength and the ability to let go of their fears if they are to deal with challenges effectively. Students may say that "Life Doesn't Frighten Me" gives more examples of fears that the writer needs to overcome.

7. Connect to Life Students may suggest that Tarik is like other people who think that not talking about sad feelings will make those feelings go away, while Nadia is like people who feel that talking about something is better than keeping it bottled up inside them.

Choices & CHALLENGES

Writing Options

1. Descriptive Poem Write a poem that conveys how Nadia feels in this story. (For a Writing Workshop on poetry, see page 236.)

2. Personal Profile A profile describes someone's qualities and achievements. Suppose Nadia were a real person. Write a profile describing her. Place the description in your **Working Portfolio.**

3. Spatial Order Description Write a paragraph describing the Bedouin camp. Include the details you might see if you were to look across the camp from left to right.

Writing Handbook
See p. R32: Spatial Order.

Activities & Explorations

1. Desert Diorama Make a "Nadia the Willful" diorama. Cut a small square opening in one side of a shoebox. Then use sandpaper, paint, and other materials to create the setting of the story. Make paper figures of the characters to position within the scene. ~ **ART**

2. Tarik's Proclamation Now that Tarik has changed his mind, write a new proclamation, or order, that he might issue. Read the proclamation aloud to the class. ~ **SPEAKING AND LISTENING**

Inquiry & Research

GEOGRAPHY DESERT LIFE
Find out what kinds of animals live in the Sahara and how they adapt to the environment. How do they protect themselves? How do they keep cool?

 More Online: Research Starter
www.mcdougallittell.com

Vocabulary in Action

EXERCISE A: MEANING CLUES On a sheet of paper, write the vocabulary word that is most clearly related to the idea in each sentence.

1. Angered by the theft of the horses, the sheik commanded that anyone found stealing a horse be punished.

2. The marketplace was packed with every imaginable item—blankets, saddles, robes of woven cloth, and even wooden toys for children.

3. Looking out at the horizon, Hamed sat and thought of the extraordinary size of the hot and silent desert.

4. When the families of the tribe camped at the oasis, they slept in tents and cooked their food over open fires.

5. Nadia could not survive in the desert alone, but she had to try because the members of the tribe would no longer let her live among them.

EXERCISE B: SYNONYMS On your paper, write the vocabulary word that is a synonym for each word. Then write a sentence using the word.

1. market   4. expel
2. order   5. think
3. tribe

Building Vocabulary
For an in-depth lesson on synonyms, see p. 230.

WORDS TO KNOW	banish	bazaar	clan	decree	ponder

Multicultural Link **Remembering the Dead**

Tell students that different cultures respond to death in different ways. In some cultures, before a person is buried, people hold a wake, a gathering of relatives and friends to honor the person who died. Jewish people observe *shiva,* a seven-day mourning period that follows a funeral. During shiva, the immediate family stays at the home of the deceased, sitting on low stools or on the floor.

They generally wear black clothes and refrain from normal activities, such as going to work or school. Friends and relatives visit, bringing food and keeping the mourners company. Ask students to think of other traditions and customs that various people have to remember the dead. They may want to think of books or movies that have depicted these customs.

Writing Options

1. Descriptive Poem Students may want to try their hand at free verse. See pp. 74–75 for Maya Angelou's "Life Doesn't Frighten Me" for an example of free verse.

2. Personal Profile Students may wish to compile a list of adjectives that describe Nadia to help get started.

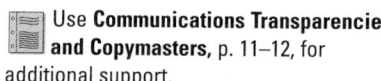 Use **Writing Transparencies,** p. 7, for additional support.

3. Spatial Order Description Students may want to refer back to their description of the setting from TE notes on page 70.

Use **Writing Transparencies,** p. 11, for additional support.

Activities & Explorations

1. Desert Diorama Encourage students to look back at the two paintings in the selection and to their own visualizations to help construct their dioramas.

2. Tarik's Proclamation Students should look back at Tarik's original decree on page 70 to help them with the language and style. Encourage students to use the style of language from the selection.

Use **Communications Transparencies and Copymasters,** p. 11–12, for additional support.

Inquiry & Research

Desert Life You may want to allow students time in the library to research the topic more fully.

Vocabulary in Action

EXERCISE A
1. decree
2. bazaar
3. ponder
4. clan
5. banish

EXERCISE B
1. bazaar
2. decree
3. clan
4. banish
5. ponder
Sentences will vary.

Grammar in Context: Direct Objects

In "Nadia the Willful," the author uses many **action verbs,** shown in red type below.

> She screamed. She wept. She stamped the sand.
> Nadia's grief knew no bounds.
> Nadia helped her father recall the face and voice of Hamed.

Sometimes an action verb also needs a **direct object** to "receive" its action. If a verb raises the question *what* or *whom,* a direct object may answer the question. Notice direct objects, shown in orange, below.

Incomplete	Hamed took. (Took what?)
Complete	Hamed took a horse.
Incomplete	Nadia loved. (Loved whom?)
Complete	Nadia loved her brother.

Usage Tip: Only an **action verb** can have a direct object.

WRITING EXERCISE Underline the verb. Ask *what* or *whom.* Then complete each sentence by writing a direct object.

Example: *Original* The clan said.

Rewritten The clan <u>said</u> nothing.

1. In the desert, Nadia saw.
2. The sheik Tarik learned.
3. Hamed had taught.
4. Nadia often lost.
5. Nadia disobeyed.

Connect to the Literature Look through the story to find three action verbs that raise the question *what* or *whom.* Then find the direct object of each of these verbs.

Grammar Handbook Quick Reference: The Sentence and Its Parts, p. R55

"I write for young people because they have imaginations that soar . . ."

Sue Alexander
born 1933

A Young Storyteller At the age of eight, Sue Alexander began writing stories for her friends. She says, "At that time I was small for my age (I still am) and very clumsy. So clumsy, in fact, that none of my classmates wanted me on their teams at recess time." One day Alexander spent recess time telling a made-up story to someone else who was not playing. Before her story was finished, the rest of the class had come to listen. This incident sparked her great love of storytelling.

Worlds of Imagination Alexander says she would not trade writing for any other profession because writing satisfies her sense of fun and her need to share. Her fantasy stories all begin the same way—with how she feels about something. Her best-loved works include *World Famous Muriel* and *Lila on the Landing.*

Award-Winning Work Alexander's short stories have been published in *Weekly Reader* and other magazines for young readers. The book publication of *Nadia the Willful* won many honors, including one from the American Library Association in 1983.

Grammar in Context
WRITING EXERCISE
Possible Responses:

1. In the desert, Nadia <u>saw</u> the black lamb.
2. The sheik Tarik <u>learned</u> a valuable lesson.
3. Hamed <u>had taught</u> them games.
4. Nadia often <u>lost</u> her temper.
5. Nadia <u>disobeyed</u> her father.

CONNECT TO THE LITERATURE
Possible Responses:

1. could calm <u>Nadia's temper</u>
2. called all <u>his people</u>
3. brought <u>Hamed's name</u>

Sue Alexander

In explaining why she writes for young people, Sue Alexander said, "because they have imaginations that soar, touched off by a word, a phrase, an image . . . a condition I share. To be able to provide a spark for this process gives me the greatest personal joy."

Teaching Options

 Grammar

INDIRECT OBJECTS Remind students that the indirect object of the verb usually tells to whom or for whom an action is done. Note that an indirect object never appears in any phrase beginning with the words *to* or *for.*
Instruction Write the following sentence on the board:

    Hamed taught <u>Nadia</u> something important.

Ask students to identify the indirect object in this sentence.
Exercises Have students identify the indirect object in each of the following sentences.

1. Merchants traveling to the bazaar told <u>Tarik</u> stories of an empty desert.
2. Hamed's death brought <u>his family</u> much grief.
3. Nadia showed <u>her father</u> her courage.
4. Tarik gave <u>Nadia</u> a new name to honor her.

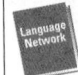 Use **Unit One Resource Book,** p. 32.
Use **Grammar Transparencies and Copymasters,** p. 55.

Use McDougal Littell's *Language Network,* Chapter 1, for more instruction and practice in indirect objects.

Clues to Meaning

How can you figure out the meaning of a word that is new to you? First think about the word's **context**—the other words around it. They can often be used as clues to help you understand what the word means.

> Max and I ran to help. Horse was damp. His mattress was soaked. When he tried to roll it up, water cascaded like Niagara Falls.
>
> —Avi, "Scout's Honor"

The meaning of **cascaded** is made clearer by the comparison to **Niagara Falls,** a huge and dramatic waterfall.

Strategies for Building Vocabulary

The clue in the example above is known as a **comparison clue.** The word's meaning is suggested by a comparison to something similar. Also helpful are **contrast clues,** places where writers point out differences between things or ideas. Contrast clues are often signaled by the words *although, but, however, unlike,* or *in contrast to.*

The following paragraphs explain some other types of context clues.

❶ **Definition and Restatement Clues** Often a tough word is followed by a definition or by a restatement of its meaning. Notice, for example, how the meaning of *banished* is restated in simpler language:

> Nadia knew that people feared being banished to the desert, sent away as outcasts.

The phrase "sent away as outcasts" suggests that to be banished is to be sent away.

❷ **Example Clues** Sometimes writers suggest the meanings of words with one or two examples. Notice how the meaning of *decree* is illustrated in the following sentence:

> People remembered some of Sheik Tarik's decrees, such as "From this day on, let my daughter be known as Nadia the Wise."

The example suggests that a decree is an official command.

❸ **Description Clues** When the meaning of a word is made clearer by descriptive details, you have a **description clue.** Look at the following passage.

> After that he was quietly obsessed with the Presidents, hugging the cards close to his chest . . .
>
> —Robert Cormier, "President Cleveland, Where Are You?"

The description suggests that *obsessed* means overly attached.

EXERCISE Use context clues to figure out the meanings of the underlined words. Identify each kind of context clue you used.

1. He had an attack of <u>lethargy</u>. In other words, he wasn't interested in anything.
2. The bridge was <u>immense</u>. Its top towered above the boys' heads.
3. At first, the boys looked at the bridge with <u>suspicion</u>, but later they decided to trust it.
4. They needed some kind of <u>vent</u>, such as a hole at the top of the tent, for the smoke.
5. Business began to <u>dwindle</u> like patches of snow melting in spring.

Building Vocabulary

Objectives
- use context to determine the meanings of words
- use a variety of types of context clues to determine the meanings of unfamiliar words

EXERCISE

1. feeling of dullness or tiredness; definition and restatement clue
2. enormous, vast; description clue
3. distrust, doubt; contrast clue
4. opening; example clue
5. shrink steadily; comparison clue

 Use **Unit One Resource Book,** p. 88, for more practice.
Use **Vocabulary Transparencies and Copymasters,** p. 3–4, for additional support.

Possible Objectives

You can use this selection to achieve one or more of the following objectives:

- enjoy silent sustained reading (Option One)
- read and analyze literature with a group (Option Two)
- use the Reader's Notebook to formulate questions about literature (Option Three)
- write in response to literature (Option Three)

Summary

June feels safe in her life with her loving mother until the Tuesday she starts a swimming class and meets a bully who is also named June. The Other June ridicules her and bruises her with punches and pinches, turning her weeks into miserable countdowns toward Tuesday, which she calls "Awfulday." After the last swimming class, June believes that she is finally free of the Other June's bullying and insults. But when June and her mother move to another part of town, she discovers that there is no escape, for the Other June is a neighbor and a classmate in her new school. Faced with being bullied every day, June desperately faces her attacker in class. "No. No. No. No more," she declares, taking the Other June by surprise. The Other June backs away, and June knows that her days as a victim are over.

Tuesday

of the Other

June

by Norma Fox Mazer

"Be good, be good, be good, be good, my Junie," my mother sang as she combed my hair; a song, a story, a croon, a plea. "It's just you and me, two women alone in the world, June darling of my heart; we have enough troubles getting by, we surely don't need a single one more, so you keep your sweet self out of fighting and all that bad stuff. People can be little-hearted, but turn the other cheek, smile at the world, and the world'll surely smile back."

We stood in front of the mirror as she combed my hair, combed and brushed and smoothed. Her head came just above mine; she said when I grew another inch, she'd stand on a stool to brush my hair. "I'm not giving up this pleasure!" And she laughed her long honey laugh.

My mother was April, my grandmother had been May, I was June. "And someday," said my mother, "you'll have a daughter of your own. What will you name her?"

"January!" I'd yell when I was little. "February! No, November!" My mother laughed her honey laugh. She had little emerald eyes that warmed me like the sun.

Every day when I went to school, she went to work. "Sometimes I stop what I'm doing," she said, "lay down my tools, and stop everything, because all I can think about is you. Wondering what you're doing and if you need me. Now, Junie, if anyone ever bothers you—"

"—I walk away, run away, come on home as fast as my feet will take me," I recited.

"Yes. You come to me. You just bring me

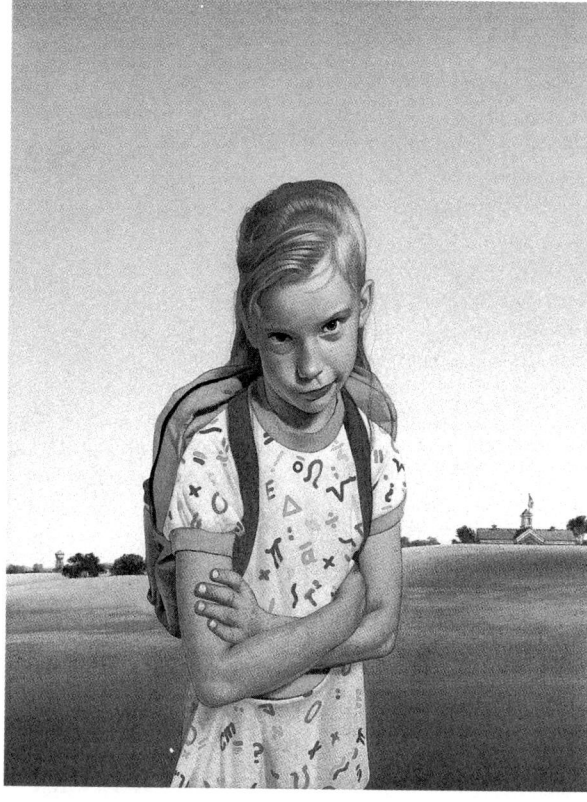

The Case for More School Days, C. F. Payne. First appeared in *The Atlantic Monthly*.

your trouble, because I'm here on this earth to love you and take care of you."

I was safe with her. Still, sometimes I woke up at night and heard footsteps slowly creeping up the stairs. It wasn't my mother, she was asleep in the bed across the room, so it was robbers, thieves, and murderers, creeping slowly . . . slowly . . . slowly toward my bed.

I stuffed my hand into my mouth. If I screamed and woke her, she'd be tired at work tomorrow. The robbers and thieves filled the warm darkness and slipped across the floor more quietly than cats. Rigid under the covers, I stared at the shifting dark and bit my knuckles and never knew when I fell asleep again.

In the morning we sang in the kitchen. "Bill Grogan's goat! Was feelin' fine! Ate three red shirts, right off the line!" I made sandwiches for our lunches, she made pancakes for breakfast, but all she ate was one pancake and a cup of coffee. "Gotta fly, can't be late."

I wanted to be rich and take care of her. She worked too hard; her pretty hair had gray in it

Option One
Silent Sustained Reading
You might set aside time each week for independent reading. During this time, you and all of your students would read for enjoyment. "Tuesday of the Other June" will appeal to many students and can be read independently in about fifteen minutes. If you want to encourage students to read for pleasure, you might forego any assignments related to this selection. Should you want to make assignments, Options Two and Three offer suggestions.

Option Two
Shared Reading Groups
You may assign students to groups or allow them to choose their own. Students can read the selection together, alternately reading sections aloud, or they can read independently and meet to cooperate in a project that portrays some element of the story.

Possible Projects
- Students can use information from the text to create portraits of the two Junes.
- Working in small groups, students can create a skit depicting June's first two days at her new school. This might include possible dialogue between the two Junes and should focus on June T.'s emotions and thoughts as implied by the author.
- Students can create a setting, such as a playground or a classroom, for a performance of the skit.

Art
Award-winning American illustrator C. F. Payne uses realism combined with distortion to make a point about the girl in this painting. The focus is on the expression on her face, seemingly a mixture of disgust and sarcasm.

that she joked about. "Someday," I said, "I'll buy you a real house, and you'll never work in a pot factory again."

"Such delicious plans," she said. She checked the windows to see if they were locked. "Do you have your key?"

I lifted it from the chain around my neck.

"And you'll come right home from school and—"

"—I won't light fires or let strangers into the house, and I won't tell anyone on the phone that I'm here alone," I finished for her.

"I know, I'm just your old worrywart mother." She kissed me twice, once on each cheek. "But you are my June, my only June, the only June."

She was wrong; there was another June. I met her when we stood next to each other at the edge of the pool the first day of swimming class in the Community Center.

"What's your name?" She had a deep growly voice.

"June. What's yours?"

She stared at me. "June."

"We have the same name."

"No we don't. June is my name, and I don't give you permission to use it. Your name is Fish Eyes." She pinched me hard. "Got it, Fish Eyes?"

The next Tuesday, the Other June again stood next to me at the edge of the pool. "What's your name?"

"June."

"Wrong. Your—name—is—Fish—Eyes."

"June."

"Fish Eyes, you are really stupid." She shoved me into the pool.

The swimming teacher looked up, frowning, from her chart. "No one in the water yet."

Later, in the locker room, I dressed quickly and wrapped my wet suit in the towel. The Other June pulled on her jeans. "You guys see that bathing suit Fish Eyes was wearing? Her mother found it in a trash can."

"She did not!"

The Other June grabbed my fingers and twisted. "Where'd she find your bathing suit?"

"She bought it, let me go."

"Poor little stupid Fish Eyes is crying. Oh, boo hoo hoo, poor little Fish Eyes."

"Your name is Fish Eyes." She pinched me hard.

After that, everyone called me Fish Eyes. And every Tuesday, wherever I was, there was also the Other June—at the edge of the pool, in the pool, in the locker room. In the water, she swam alongside me, blowing and huffing, knocking into me. In the locker room, she stepped on my feet, pinched my arms, hid my blouse, and knotted my braids together. She had large square teeth; she was shorter than I was, but heavier, with bigger bones and square hands. If I met her outside on the street, carrying her bathing suit and towel, she'd walk toward me, smiling a square, friendly smile. "Oh well, if it isn't Fish Eyes." Then she'd punch me, blam! her whole solid weight hitting me.

I didn't know what to do about her. She was training me like a dog. After a few weeks of this, she only had to look at me, only had to growl, "I'm going to get you, Fish Eyes," for my heart to slink like a whipped dog down into my stomach. My arms were covered with bruises. When my mother noticed, I made up a story about tripping on the sidewalk.

My weeks were no longer Tuesday, Wednesday, Thursday, and so on. Tuesday was

Awfulday. Wednesday was Badday. (The Tuesday bad feelings were still there.) Thursday was Betterday, and Friday was Safeday. Saturday was Goodday, but Sunday was Toosoonday, and Monday—Monday was nothing but the day before Awfulday.

I tried to slow down time. Especially on the weekends, I stayed close by my mother, doing everything with her, shopping, cooking, cleaning, going to the laundromat. "Aw, sweetie, go play with your friends."

"No, I'd rather be with you." I wouldn't look at the clock or listen to the radio (they were always telling you the date and the time). I did special magic things to keep the day from going away, rapping my knuckles six times on the bathroom door six times a day and never, ever touching the chipped place on my bureau. But always I woke up to the day before Tuesday, and always, no matter how many times I circled the worn spot in the living-room rug or counted twenty-five cracks in the ceiling, Monday disappeared and once again it was Tuesday.

The Other June got bored with calling me Fish Eyes. Buffalo Brain came next, but as soon as everyone knew that, she renamed me Turkey Nose.

Now at night it wasn't robbers creeping up the stairs, but the Other June, coming to torment me. When I finally fell asleep, I dreamed of kicking her, punching, biting, pinching. In the morning I remembered my dreams and felt brave and strong. And then I remembered all the things my mother had taught me and told me.

Be good, be good, be good; it's just us two women alone in the world. . . . Oh, but if it weren't, if my father wasn't long gone, if we'd had someone else to fall back on, if my mother's mother and daddy weren't dead all these years, if my father's daddy wanted to know us instead of being glad to forget us—oh, then I would have punched the Other June with a frisky heart, I would have grabbed her arm at poolside and bitten her like the dog she had made of me.

One night, when my mother came home from work, she said, "Junie, listen to this. We're moving!"

"Junie, listen to this. We're moving!"

Alaska, I thought. Florida. Arizona. Someplace far away and wonderful, someplace without the Other June.

"Wait till you hear this deal. We are going to be caretakers, trouble-shooters for an eight-family apartment building. Fifty-six Blue Hill Street. Not janitors; we don't do any of the heavy work. April and June, Trouble-shooters, Incorporated. If a tenant has a complaint or a problem, she comes to us and we either take care of it or call the janitor for service. And for that little bit of work, we get to live rent free!" She swept me around in a dance. "Okay? You like it? I do!"

So. Not anywhere else, really. All the same, maybe too far to go to swimming class? "Can we move right away? Today?"

"Gimme a break, sweetie. We've got to pack, do a thousand things. I've got to line up someone with a truck to help us. Six weeks, Saturday the fifteenth." She circled it on the calendar. It was the Saturday after the last day of swimming class.

Soon, we had boxes lying everywhere, filled with clothes and towels and glasses wrapped in newspaper. Bit by bit, we cleared the rooms,

Possible Activities
Independent Activities
- Have gifted students skim over the story, jotting down details about the relationship between June and her mother. Ask them to write in their Reader's Notebooks why they think the author emphasized the closeness of this relationship and what role this relationship played in the story as a whole.
- Have students review the Learning the Language of Literature and Active Reader pages 21–25. Ask them to note which skills and strategies they used while reading this selection.

Discussion Activities
- Use the questions formulated by the students as the start of a discussion about this story.
- Ask students how they felt about June T. finally standing up to the Other June. Do they feel that by doing so she let her mother down?

Assessment Opportunities
- You can assess student comprehension of the story by evaluating the questions they formulate in their Reader's Notebooks.
- You can use any of the discussion questions as essay questions.
- You can ask students to write an essay describing their interpretation of the story's central point.

leaving only what we needed right now. The dining-room table staggered on a bunched-up rug, our bureaus inched toward the front door like patient cows. On the calendar in the kitchen, my mother marked off the days until we moved, but the only days I thought about were Tuesdays—Awfuldays. Nothing else was real except the too fast passing of time, moving toward each Tuesday . . . away from Tuesday . . . toward Tuesday . . .

And it seemed to me that this would go on forever, that Tuesdays would come forever and I would be forever trapped by the side of the pool, the Other June whispering Buffalo Brain Fish Eyes Turkey Nose into my ear, while she ground her elbow into my side and smiled her square smile at the swimming teacher.

No more swimming class. No more Awfuldays. . . . No more Tuesdays.

And then it ended. It was the last day of swimming class. The last Tuesday. We had all passed our tests, and, as if in celebration, the Other June only pinched me twice. "And now," our swimming teacher said, "all of you are ready for the Advanced Class, which starts in just one month. I have a sign-up slip here. Please put your name down before you leave." Everyone but me crowded around. I went to the locker room and pulled on my clothes as fast as possible. The Other June burst through the door just as I was leaving. "Goodbye," I yelled, "good riddance to bad trash!" Before she could pinch me again, I ran past her and then ran all the way home, singing, "Goodbye . . . goodbye . . . goodbye, good riddance to bad trash!"

Later, my mother carefully untied the blue ribbon around my swimming class diploma. "Look at this! Well, isn't this wonderful! You are on your way, you might turn into an Olympic swimmer, you never know what life will bring."

"I don't want to take more lessons."

"Oh, sweetie, it's great to be a good swimmer." But then, looking into my face, she said, "No, no, no, don't worry, you don't have to."

The next morning, I woke up hungry for the first time in weeks. No more swimming class. No more Baddays and Awfuldays. No more Tuesdays of the Other June. In the kitchen, I made hot cocoa to go with my mother's corn muffins. "It's Wednesday, Mom," I said, stirring the cocoa. "My favorite day."

"Since when?"

"Since this morning." I turned on the radio so I could hear the announcer tell the time, the temperature, and the day.

Thursday for breakfast I made cinnamon toast, Friday my mother made pancakes, and on Saturday, before we moved, we ate the last slices of bread and cleaned out the peanut butter jar.

"Some breakfast," Tilly said. "Hello, you must be June." She shook my hand. She was a friend of my mother's from work; she wore big hoop earrings, sandals, and a skirt as dazzling as a rainbow. She came in a truck with John to help us move our things.

John shouted cheerfully at me, "So you're moving." An enormous man with a face covered with little brown bumps. Was he afraid his voice wouldn't travel the distance from his mouth to my ear? "You looking at my moles?" he shouted, and he heaved our big green flowered chair down the stairs. "Don't worry, they don't bite. Ha, ha, ha!" Behind him came my mother and Tilly balancing a bureau between them, and behind them I carried a lamp and the round, flowered Mexican tray that was my mother's favorite. She had found it at a garage sale and said it was as close to foreign travel as we would ever get.

The night before, we had loaded our car, stuffing in bags and boxes until there was barely room for the two of us. But it was only when we were in the car, when we drove past Abdo's Grocery, where they always gave us credit, when I turned for a last look at our street—it was only then that I understood we were truly going to live somewhere else, in another apartment, in another place mysteriously called Blue Hill Street.

Tilly's truck followed our car.

"Oh, I'm so excited," my mother said. She laughed. "You'd think we were going across the country."

Our old car wheezed up a long, steep hill. Blue Hill Street. I looked from one side to the other, trying to see everything.

My mother drove over the crest of the hill. "And now—ta da!—our new home."

"Which house? Which one?" I looked out the window and what I saw was the Other June. She was sprawled on the stoop of a pink house, lounging back on her elbows, legs outspread, her jaws working on a wad of gum. I slid down into the seat, but it was too late. I was sure she had seen me.

My mother turned into a driveway next to a big white building with a tiny porch. She leaned on the steering wheel. "See that window there, that's our living-room window . . . and that one over there, that's your bedroom . . . "

We went into the house, down a dim, cool hall. In our new apartment, the wooden floors clicked under our shoes, and my mother showed me everything. Her voice echoed in the empty rooms. I followed her around in a daze. Had I imagined seeing the Other June?

Maybe I'd seen another girl who looked like her. A double. That could happen.

"Ho yo, where do you want this chair?" John appeared in the doorway. We brought in boxes and bags and beds and stopped only to eat pizza and drink orange juice from the carton.

"June's so quiet, do you think she'll adjust all right?" I heard Tilly say to my mother.

"Oh, definitely. She'll make a wonderful adjustment. She's just getting used to things."

But I thought that if the Other June lived on the same street as I did, I would never get used to things.

That night I slept in my own bed, with my own pillow and blanket, but with floors that creaked in strange voices and walls with cracks I didn't recognize. I didn't feel either happy or unhappy. It was as if I were waiting for something.

Monday, when the principal of Blue Hill Street School left me in Mr. Morrisey's classroom, I knew what I'd been waiting for. In that room full of strange kids, there was one person I knew. She smiled her square smile, raised her hand, and said, "She can sit next to me, Mr. Morrisey."

"Very nice of you, June M. OK, June T., take your seat. I'll try not to get you two Junes mixed up."

I sat down next to her. She pinched my arm. "Good riddance to bad trash," she mocked.

I was back in the Tuesday swimming class, only now it was worse, because every day would be Awfulday. The pinching had already started. Soon, I knew, on the playground and in the halls, kids would pass me, grinning. "Hiya, Fish Eyes."

The Other June followed me around during recess that day, droning in my ear, "You are my slave, you must do everything I say, I am your master, say it, say, 'Yes, master, you are my master.'"

I pressed my lips together, clapped my hands over my ears, but without hope. Wasn't it only a matter of time before I said the hateful words?

"How was school?" my mother said that night.

"OK."

She put a pile of towels in a bureau drawer. "Try not to be sad about missing your old friends, sweetie; there'll be new ones."

The next morning, the Other June was waiting for me when I left the house. "Did your mother get you that blouse in the garbage dump?" She butted me, shoving me against a tree. "Don't you speak anymore, Fish Eyes?" Grabbing my chin in her hands, she pried open my mouth. "Oh, ha ha, I thought you lost your tongue."

"Oh, no! No. No. No. No more."

We went on to school. I sank down into my seat, my head on my arms. "June T., are you all right?" Mr. Morrisey asked. I nodded. My head was almost too heavy to lift.

The Other June went to the pencil sharpener. Round and round she whirled the handle. Walking back, looking at me, she held the three sharp pencils like three little knives.

Someone knocked on the door. Mr. Morrisey went out into the hall. Paper planes burst into the air, flying from desk to desk. Someone turned on a transistor radio. And the Other June, coming closer, smiled and licked her lips like a cat sleepily preparing to gulp down a mouse.

I remembered my dream of kicking her, punching, biting her like a dog.

Then my mother spoke quickly in my ear: Turn the other cheek, my Junie; smile at the world, and the world'll surely smile back.

But I had turned the other cheek and it was slapped. I had smiled and the world hadn't smiled back. I couldn't run home as fast as my feet would take me. I had to stay in school— and in school there was the Other June. Every morning, there would be the Other June, and every afternoon, and every day, all day, there would be the Other June.

She frisked down the aisle, stabbing the pencils in the air toward me. A boy stood up on his desk and bowed. "My fans," he said, "I greet you." My arm twitched and throbbed, as if the Other June's pencils had already poked through the skin. She came closer, smiling her Tuesday smile.

"No," I whispered, "no." The word took wings and flew me to my feet, in front of the Other June. "Noooooo." It flew out of my mouth into her surprised face.

The boy on the desk turned toward us. "You said something, my devoted fans?"

"No," I said to the Other June. "Oh, no! No. No. No. No more." I pushed away the hand that held the pencils.

The Other June's eyes opened, popped wide like the eyes of somebody in a cartoon. It made me laugh. The boy on the desk laughed, and then the other kids were laughing, too.

"No," I said again, because it felt so good to say it. "No, no, no, no." I leaned toward the Other June, put my finger against her chest. Her cheeks turned red, she squawked something—it sounded like "Eeeraaghyou!"— and she stepped back. She stepped away from me.

The door banged, the airplanes disappeared, and Mr. Morrisey walked to his desk. "OK. OK. Let's get back to work. Kevin Clark, how about it?" Kevin jumped off the desk, and

Mr. Morrisey picked up a piece of chalk. "All right, class—" He stopped and looked at me and the Other June. "You two Junes, what's going on there?"

I tried it again. My finger against her chest. Then the words. "No—more." And she stepped back another step. I sat down at my desk.

"June M.," Mr. Morrisey said.

She turned around, staring at him with that big-eyed cartoon look. After a moment she sat down at her desk with a loud slapping sound.

Even Mr. Morrisey laughed.

And sitting at my desk, twirling my braids, I knew this was the last Tuesday of the Other June. ❖

Primer Lesson
by Carl Sandburg

Look out how you use proud words.
When you let proud words go, it is
    not easy to call them back.
They wear long boots, hard boots; they
    walk off proud; they can't hear you
    calling—
Look out how you use proud words.

"I believe deeply and firmly that people should read what they want to read."

Norma Fox Mazer
born 1931

The Glories of Stories Norma Fox Mazer believes stories are a way to understand the world and the people in it. She says that readers of fiction "will find a world where people face troubles but act to help themselves."

Devoted to Her Craft Mazer's interest in writing started in high school when she was editor of her school paper and a correspondent for her town's newspaper. After a year at college, she married the novelist Harry Mazer. For ten years, she and her husband struggled to write while raising their four children. Today she is a widely recognized and prize-winning writer of fiction for young adults.

Keeping It Simple Mazer lives in New York but spends her summers in Canada, where she does without electricity, telephones, newspapers, radios, or indoor plumbing. About her writing, Mazer says, "I seem to deal in the ordinary, the everyday, the real. I should like in my writing to give meaning and emotion to ordinary moments. In my books and stories I want people to eat chocolate pudding, break a dish, yawn, look in a store window, wear socks with holes in them." Readers can encounter many of Mazer's true-to-life characters in works like *After the Rain,* a Newbery Honor Book.

Writing Workshop
Response to Literature

Writing what you feel...

From Reading to Writing Have you ever read a story and thought, "I admire the main character!" or "I had an embarrassing time like that once"? If so, you know that your own experiences often affect how you feel about a story. You might have been embarrassed for Rachel in the story "Eleven." As you read "Nadia the Willful," you might have felt proud of Nadia for speaking her mind. Writing a **response to literature** is one way to understand your reactions to a story. You can include your feelings about the plot, about a character, or about the author's technique.

See the Communication Handbook, p. R100 for speaking and presenting tips.

For Your Portfolio

WRITING PROMPT Write a personal response to a short work of literature.

Purpose: To share and explain your feelings about a work of literature
Audience: Others who have read the story and people who know you well

---

Basics in a Box

Response to Literature at a Glance

Introduction
Introduces the title, author, and a clear statement of your response

Body
Supports the response with evidence from the work

Evidence

examples from the story

quotations

specific reactions

Conclusion
Summarizes the response

RUBRIC STANDARDS FOR WRITING

A successful response to literature should

- include an introduction that names the literary work and clearly states your reponse to it
- tell enough about the work so that readers unfamiliar with it can understand your response
- contain clearly described, specific reactions and responses to the literary work
- support your statements with quotations and details
- summarize the response in the conclusion

WRITING WORKSHOP **89**

Objectives

- write a Response to Literature
- use a written text as a model for writing
- revise a draft to support response
- use correct possessive nouns and pronouns

Introducing the Workshop

Response to Literature Discuss with students what a response to literature is: a composition in which the writer shares personal feelings or experiences that relate to something he or she has read. Sometimes readers closely identify with something that they have read. Their memory is triggered and they think about a similar experience that they have undergone. Other times, readers have an emotional response to something even though they have not personally experienced something similar.

Ask students to think about a story or poem to which they had a strong response. Tell them to think about why they had particular feelings in response to the work.

Basics in a Box
Using the Graphic A personal response to literature begins with an introduction, which clearly expresses the writer's response. The body of the essay contains several examples, or evidence, from the poem or story to support the personal response. The conclusion summarizes or restates the response.

Presenting the Rubric To help students better understand the assignment, review the Standards for Writing a Successful Response to Literature. You may also want to share with them the complete rubric, which describes several levels of proficiency. Use the rubric to evaluate students' writing.

 Use McDougal Littell's *Language Network,* Chapters 10–17, for more instruction on essential writing skills.

 Power Presentation

To engage students visually, use **Power Presentation** 1, Response to Literature.

LESSON RESOURCES

USING PRINT RESOURCES
Unit One Resource Book
- Prewriting, p. 36
- Drafting and Elaboration, p. 37
- Peer Response, pp. 38–39
- Revising, Editing, and Proofreading, p. 40
- Student Models, pp. 41–43
- Rubric, p. 44

Writing Transparencies and Copymasters
- Writing Process Transparencies TR 1–TR 4
- Writing Structure Transparency: Elaboration, TR 13
- Writing Template Transparency: Response to Literature, TR 26

Reading and Critical Thinking
- Horizontal Category Chart, TR 40 (for Mini Lesson, p. 91)

INTEGRATED TECHNOLOGY
LaserLinks
Writing Springboards
See **Teacher's SourceBook** p. 56 for bar codes.

Writing Coach CD-ROM
Visit our website:
www.mcdougallittell.com

Analyzing the Model
"Nadia the Willful"

In the student model, the writer compares Nadia's experience with her own experience of losing her beloved Uncle Joe. The writer closely identifies with Nadia's feelings and explains how her own experience helped her to understand Nadia's situation.

Have students read the model and then discuss what makes it a successful personal response. Then discuss the Rubric in Action. Point out key words and phrases in the model that correspond to the elements mentioned in the Rubric in Action.

1. Ask why it is important to name the title and author in the introduction.
   Possible Response: By naming the title and author, the writer makes it clear what she's writing about.

2. Ask students why it is important for the writer to provide details about the story.
   Possible Response: The writer must provide details as evidence to support and justify his or her response.

3. Ask students to explain how the quotation from Nadia's father reveals something important about him.
   Possible Response: The quotation shows that Nadia's father was strict, controlling, and insensitive to other people's feelings.

4. Have students think about the reasons the writer gives. How does the story about yelling at her sister help you to understand the writer's response to "Nadia the Willful"?
   Possible Response: Like Nadia, the writer was upset and couldn't hold in her sadness. She expressed her anger by yelling at her sister.

Analyzing a Student Model

Valenne Ogden
Princess Anne Middle School

RUBRIC
IN ACTION

Responding to "Nadia the Willful"

When I read "Nadia the Willful" by Sue Alexander, I was surprised by how much I could relate to Nadia's situation of losing someone. Just like Nadia, I felt like I had to hold in my feelings one time, too.

Nadia is a person with strong feelings. In the story, she gets upset when she doesn't get her way. Her brother Hamed is the only one who can calm her down. One day Hamed rides off into the desert and doesn't come back. Everyone is grieving. Her father is so upset by Hamed's disappearance that he says, "From this day forward let no one utter Hamed's name. Punishment shall be swift for those who would remind me of what I have lost." His way of handling Hamed's death is to never speak of him again. Soon, Nadia realizes that this doesn't work. Her rebellious spirit comes out. She goes against her father's wishes as she says, "I will speak of my brother! I will!" The more she talks about Hamed, the better she feels.

The reason I say Nadia is so much like me is because I, too, thought I had to hold my feelings inside when someone close to me died. The person was my uncle. He was greatly loved by the family and everyone missed him after he was gone. Even though I felt upset, I didn't want to add to the sadness, and so I didn't cry. Holding it in made me angry at everybody just like Nadia when she yelled at people about things concerning Hamed. For example, when my little sister Codie burned herself on the heater, I yelled at her instead of patiently telling her to be more careful. I was really just angry at losing Uncle Joe.

❶ Names the title, author, and clearly expresses a response in the introduction

❷ This writer tells enough about the work so that readers unfamiliar with it can understand Nadia's reactions.

❸ Uses quotations from the story to show the father's personality

❹ Gives reasons that support the response

At the end of the story, Nadia realizes that talking about Hamed helps everyone. When she begins sharing her memories with others in the clan, and later with her father, she can see how much better everyone feels. <u>This touched my heart because I learned the same lesson.</u> At the end of my uncle's funeral, I started to talk about all the fun he and I had together, like when he would tell me jokes. As soon as I began telling my family about all the good memories, I started to feel a lot better. I was happy when my aunt came up and hugged me. Later she asked me to write down some of my uncle's jokes so she would never forget them. She said she felt much better.

I think that "Nadia the Willful" is an important story. It teaches people to talk about their memories. Like Nadia, I found that sharing stories from your past not only helps you, but helps everyone else as well.

> **❺** Includes a specific reaction to the work

> **❻** Draws a conclusion that brings out the theme of the story and the value of the story for others
> **Other Option:**
> • Summarize the response.

5. Ask students which sentence very clearly tells about the writer's response to "Nadia the Willful."
   Answer: "This touched my heart because I learned the same lesson."

6. Ask students to explain why the writer states a theme of the story in her conclusion.
   Possible Response: The writer's response to the story is consistent with the theme. The writer states the theme in order to compare it with her own experience.

 Mini Lesson # Viewing and Representing

PICTURING TEXT STRUCTURE

Instruction One way to structure a response to literature is to list several of the elements in the story or poem and then name your reaction to each element.

Activity Have students analyze the text of the student model by making a diagram that shows how the writer organized her essay in response to the story. In one column they should list elements of the story. In a second column they should list the writer's reactions to those elements. Here is a sample.

Circumstance in story	Reaction of writer
losing her brother	memory of losing uncle
refusal to remain quiet	becomes angry
talks about Hamed	talks about uncle
everyone feels better	feels much better

Tell students they can make a similar diagram to plan their compositions. You might suggest that they complete the diagram as they read the literature to which they are responding, or that they use a diagram to organize their notes.

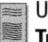 Use **Reading and Critical Thinking Transparencies**, p. 40, for additional support.

Prewriting

Choosing a Subject

If, after they have read the suggestions in the Idea Bank, students are still having difficulty choosing a story to respond to, offer the following suggestions:

- If you can't think of a character with whom you identify, think about a character whom you admire. It might be someone who possesses traits on which you would like to model yourself.
- Consider responding to a character whose actions you found somehow disturbing or unworthy of respect. Explain your response with examples of similar situations in which you behaved differently.

Planning Your Response to Literature

1. As students reread, have them ask themselves, "If I were a character in this story, who would I be and why?"
2. Tell students to jot down examples of situations that they have experienced that are somehow similar to those that the character in the story experienced.
3. Remind students that while they freewrite, they shouldn't be concerned with spelling. The purpose of this exercise is to get their feelings down on paper.
4. Help students by clarifying for them whether their intended audience should be peers, a teacher, or someone else.

Drafting

The student model represents just one effective way for students to organize their responses to literature. Suggest that students list several different examples of their personal responses to the story. Tell them to think about which examples have the strongest link to the story. Then tell them to choose the one that is most closely related to the story.

IDEABank

1. Your Working Portfolio
Look for ideas in the **Writing Options** that you completed earlier in this unit.
Recollection Diary, p. 32
Character Comparison, p. 46

2. Mirror Image
Choose the story in the unit that is the opposite of your life or portrays a character that is unlike you. Respond to the story or to the character.

3. Literary Journal
Keep a journal of your responses to literature that you read both in and out of school. Write about a story or poem to which you responded strongly.

Have a question?

See the **Writing Handbook.**
Using Peer Response, p. R25
Elaboration, p. R29

Writing Your Response to Literature

❶ Prewriting

The golden rule of writing is to write what you care about.
—Jerry Spinelli, author of *Maniac Magee*

In selecting a story for your response, recall the short stories you have read recently. Think about your favorite scenes. **Write** down the names of characters that are like you in some way. **List** similar situations you have experienced. See the Idea Bank in the margin for more suggestions. After you choose a story for your response, follow the steps below.

Planning Your Response to Literature

▶ 1. **Carefully reread the short story.** Notice the passages in the story that seem important, and that you can relate to. Jot down notes as you read.

▶ 2. **Make connections.** Ask: Which passages in the story reminded me of my own life? What did I think about the whole story? What affected me most? Why? Record your thoughts as you answer each question.

▶ 3. **Freewrite about your responses.** Try freewriting about the story to discover what you think. Remember, freewriting means writing down whatever thoughts you have. Don't decide until later whether your ideas are useful or not.

▶ 4. **Think about your audience.** Is your audience familiar with the work you are responding to? What will readers need to know in order to understand your response?

❷ Drafting

In a response to literature, there are no right or wrong responses. Do remember, however, that any essay has an introduction, a body, and a conclusion.

- Write an **introduction** that includes the title, the author, and your general response to the work.

Ask Your Peer Reader

What feelings came out the strongest in my essay?

Did I provide enough information about the story?

What details can I add to better support or explain my response?

What information is unclear?

- In the **body,** support your response with details from the story, such as specific examples or quotations. Relate these to examples from your own life.
- Summarize your response in the **conclusion.**

❸ Revising
TARGET SKILL ▶ SUPPORTING YOUR RESPONSE *"I think the main character is kind."* If you had written this response, your readers probably couldn't tell how or why you came to this conclusion. Adding quotations and details from the story can support your response statement.

> Soon, Nadia realizes that this doesn't work. Her
> rebellious spirit comes out. She goes against her father's
> wishes. / as she says, "I will speak of my brother! I will!"

❹ Editing and Proofreading
TARGET SKILL ▶ SUBJECT-VERB AGREEMENT In a sentence, verbs must agree with their subjects. A singular subject agrees with the singular form of a verb, and a plural subject agrees with the plural verb form. Compound subjects—two or more nouns or pronouns joined by *and*—require a plural verb form. When you proofread your response, check to make sure that all your subjects and verbs agree.

> When she beginˢ sharing her memories with others in
> the clan, and later with her father, she can sees/ how much
> better everyone feelˢ.

❺ Reflecting
FOR YOUR WORKING PORTFOLIO How did writing about the short story help you to understand it? Did your feelings about the story change as you wrote your essay? Attach your answers to your finished work. Save your response to literature in your **Working Portfolio.**

SPELLING From Writing
As you revise your work, look back at the words you misspelled and determine why you made the errors you did. For additional help, refer to the strategies and generalizations in the **Spelling Handbook** on page R86.

Need Revising Help?

Review the **Rubric,** p. 89

Consider **peer reader** comments

Check **Revision Guidelines,** p. R23

Puzzled about Agreement?

See the **Grammar Handbook,** Making Subjects and Verbs Agree, p. R60

Publishing IDEAS
- Set up a panel of students who wrote responses to the same short story. Videotape the panel discussion of students for classmates who did not write about that story.
- Sketch a scene from the story to accompany your response. Display your essay.

More Online: Publishing Options www.mcdougallittell.com

Revising
SUPPORTING YOUR RESPONSE
Ask volunteers to share a key sentence from their responses to literature. The sentence should express the writer's personal response. Then ask the class to make suggestions for more precise words that will make the response clearer and stronger. Remind students to back up their responses with examples from the story.

Editing and Proofreading
SUBJECT-VERB AGREEMENT
Go over the example with students, pointing out that the *s* at the end of the first verb, *begins,* means that it is a singular form and agrees with the singular subject, *she.*

The verb *feels* at the end of the sentence is also a singular verb. It agrees with the subject *everyone.* If this confuses students because *everyone* refers to more than one person, remind them that *everyone* is a collective pronoun. Collective nouns and pronouns, such as *class* or *everyone,* take a singular verb.

Reflecting
As students write their responses to literature, encourage them to consider what they learned about themselves by thinking about and comparing themselves to story characters.

Option
Teaching Tip
Suggest that students think of three examples that illustrate their response to the story they have chosen. Then have them show you the three examples and help them choose the one that is the strongest.

Assessment Practice

Have students read through the passage once before correcting the errors. Then show students how they can figure out the correct answer to Question 1 by reviewing the spellings of *except* and *accept*.

Answers:

1. D; 2. C; 3. B; 4. B; 5. A; 6. A

Read this passage from the first draft of a response to literature. The underlined sections may include the following kinds of errors:

- **verb tense errors**
- **spelling errors**
- **sentence fragments**
- **errors in subject-verb agreement**

For each underlined section, choose the revision that most improves the writing.

> In the beginning of the story, no one can control Nadia <u>except</u> her
> (1)
> brother Hamed. After his death, she really <u>missed</u> him. <u>Then she afraid</u>
> (2)   (3)
> <u>of losing her memories of him.</u> Nadia begins to disobey her father by
> speaking her brother's name and telling stories about him. When the
> shepherd is overheard saying Hamed's name, <u>Nadia showed courage</u> by
> (4)
> standing up to her father. Finally, <u>Nadia and her father agrees</u> that
> (5)
> talking about Hamed keeps his memory alive. <u>Nadia's stubborness</u>
> (6)
> <u>brings about good. By the end of the story.</u>

1. **A.** accept
   B. exept
   C. expect
   D. Correct as is

2. **A.** missing
   B. will miss
   C. misses
   D. Correct as is

3. **A.** She afraid, loses her memories of him.
   B. Then she becomes afraid of losing her memories of him.
   C. Then she becomes afraid. Loses her memories of him.
   D. Correct as is

4. **A.** show
   B. shows
   C. shown
   D. Correct as is

5. **A.** Nadia and her father agree
   B. Nadia's father agrees
   C. Nadia's father agree
   D. Correct as is

6. **A.** Nadia's stubborness brings about good by the end of the story.
   B. Nadia's stubborness brings. About good by the end of the story.
   C. Nadia's stubborness brings about. Good by the end of the story.
   D. Correct as is

Need extra help?

See the **Grammar Handbook.**

Writing Complete Sentences, p. R59

Using Verbs Correctly, p. R68

Teaching Options

 Mini Lesson Grammar

SUBJECT-VERB AGREEMENT

For use with Editing and Proofreading, page 93. Point out that singular subjects take singular verbs and plural subjects take plural verbs. Compound subjects require a plural verb, and collective nouns and pronouns require a singular verb.

Practice Have students read each of the following sentences and choose the correct verb form.

1. Nadia's relatives (<u>give</u>, gives) her a lot of support.
2. Hamed (<u>is</u>, are) the brother who (feel, <u>feels</u>) closest to Nadia.
3. The entire clan (<u>meets</u>, meet) to listen to Tarik.

4. Memories (is, <u>are</u>) important to the people who are left behind.
5. Tarik and Nadia (<u>love</u>, loves) their family.

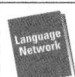 Use **Grammar Transparencies and Copymasters,** p. 113, for additional support.

Use McDougal Littell's *Language Network,* Chapter 7, for more instruction and practice in subject-verb agreement.

Reflecting on the Theme In Part Two of this unit, you will read about characters and real people who respond to a wide range of dangerous situations. All of these characters and people are risk-takers. Some of them go in search of particular challenges; others encounter danger on their quests for adventure. Often, they have to think "on their feet," making difficult choices in a moment's time. As you read about these challenges, ask yourself what you would have done if you had been there.

Objectives
- understand the following literary terms:
  - nonfiction
  - biography
  - autobiography
  - expository (formal) essay
  - personal (informal) essay
  - persuasive essay
  - informative article
  - interview
- understand and appreciate nonfiction
- understand literary forms by recognizing and distinguishing between biographies and autobiographies

Teaching the Lesson

This lesson defines nonfiction and analyzes five different types of nonfiction writing.

Introducing the Concepts
Have students think about a work of nonfiction they have recently read, such as a newspaper article, a true story about a famous person, or an article in a science magazine. Ask them to explain why they read it and what they got out of this work.

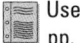 Use **Literary Analysis Transparencies,** pp. 10–11, 16, for additional support.

LEARNING the Language of Literature

Nonfiction

I write about anything that interests me—dogs, horses, forests, birds, mysteries, life in other countries. . . . The most important aspect is that [the subjects] interest me very much, because then I want to share them with other people.

—Patricia Lauber, writer

Chances are, you've read some nonfiction today. **Nonfiction** is writing that is about real people, places, and events. Unlike fiction, nonfiction is mostly based on facts. The nature magazine you may have on your desk or the school bulletin you may have in your backpack are both examples of nonfiction. Read any good magazine articles lately? What about movie reviews? These are examples of nonfiction, too. Nonfiction is everywhere—from the page you're reading now, to a weather report in the newspaper, to the history book you may have used yesterday to write a report on your home state.

> **Key Types of Nonfiction**
> - biography
> - autobiography
> - essay
> - informative article
> - interview

Biography

When someone writes the story of another person's life, the work is called a **biography.** Whenever possible, the writer, or **biographer,** interviews his or her subject. Biographers also learn a great deal through letters, books, diaries, and interviews with people who have known their subjects. A short biography of the African-American explorer Matthew Henson is included in this book. As you will see, biographies and autobiographies contain many of the same elements as fiction, such as **character, setting,** and **plot.**

YOUR TURN What details in the passage at the right tell you about Henson's life or the setting in which he lived?

BIOGRAPHY

Matthew Henson was born on August 8, 1866, in Charles County, Maryland, some forty-four miles south of Washington, D.C. His parents were poor, free tenant farmers who barely eked a living from the sandy soil. The Civil War had ended the year before Matthew was born, bringing with it a great deal of bitterness on the part of former slave-owners.

—Jim Haskins, "Matthew Henson at the Top of the World"

Autobiography

A person's account of his or her own life is called an **autobiography.** The roots of the word *autobiography* mean "self" (*auto-*), "life" (*bio-*), and "writing" (*graph*). Autobiographies can help you get to know people through their own words. They are almost always written from a **first-person point of view,** in which pronouns like *I* and *me* are used. Because autobiographies generally cover long periods of their writers' lives, most of them are book length. There are, however, shorter types of autobiographical writing, such as **journals, diaries, letters,** and **memoirs.**

YOUR TURN What words in the passage at the right let you know that it is from an autobiography rather than a biography?

AUTOBIOGRAPHY

I could not move, would not have time to react. I knew I had nothing to say about it. One blow would break my neck. Whether I lived or died depended on him, on his thinking, on his ideas about me—whether I was worth the bother or not.

—Gary Paulsen, *Woodsong*

Presenting the Concepts
Biography
Have students think about a famous person they would like to write about. Ask them to tell why this person interests them and what kinds of information they would want to include in a biography.

YOUR TURN
Possible Response: The author gives Henson's date of birth and describes in some detail the place of his birth. He also describes the situation of Henson's family and the cultural and social climate of the era.

Autobiography
Ask students if they have ever kept a journal or diary about the events in their own lives. Explain that this is a common form of autobiographical writing. Ask if students know of any personal diaries or journals that have become famous.

YOUR TURN
Possible Response: The author's use of the first-person pronoun "I," his use of the possessive pronoun "my," and the word "me"

Essay

Discuss with the class the different purposes an essay may have: to persuade, to entertain, to explain, to describe, to inform, or to express personal feelings.

Essay

An **essay** is a short work of nonfiction that deals with one subject. Essays are often found in newspapers and magazines. The writer of an essay might share an opinion, try to entertain the reader, or simply describe an incident that has special significance. Three common types of essays are **expository** (formal), **personal** (informal), and **persuasive.** Formal essays have a more scholarly and serious tone, while informal essays have a more conversational tone.

ESSAY

expository

- tightly structured
- impersonal style
- presents or explains information and ideas

The ancient Greeks were horrified by hydras, sea dragons with nine or more heads. As centuries passed, only seven-headed hydras were seen. The seventeenth-century naturalist Edward Topsell included a picture of a hydra in *The Historie of Serpents.*

—Rhoda Blumberg,
The Truth About Dragons

personal

- looser structure
- more personal style
- expresses writer's thoughts and feelings

My business is to make readers from non-readers, and if you think it's easy, then join me anytime and see how, where and why it's done. On the "where" front, I have slept on a lot of floors and couches, and on the "why" front I recall the kinder, gentler America that was proposed several years ago.

—Gary Soto,
"Who Are Your Readers?"

persuasive

- presents arguments
- tries to convince readers to adopt a certain viewpoint

If the white man wants to live in peace with the Indian, he can live in peace. There need be no trouble. Treat all men alike. Give them the same law. Give them all an even chance to live and grow.

All men are made by the same Great Spirit Chief. They are all brothers. The earth is the mother of all people, and all people should have equal rights upon it.

—Chief Joseph,
"Chief Joseph Speaks"

Informative Article

When people are looking for facts about particular subjects, they turn to **informative articles. Newspaper articles** and **feature stories** are examples of **informative nonfiction.** So are textbooks, encyclopedias, and informational books on subjects like car repair, ancient history, or juggling.

YOUR TURN What factual information does the passage at the right provide about forest fires in Yellowstone National Park?

INFORMATIVE ARTICLE

On June 23 lightning started a fire near Shoshone Lake in the southern part of the park. On June 25 another bolt of lightning started a fire in the northwest. These fires did not go out, and no one tried to put them out.

—Patricia Lauber, "Summer of Fire"

Interview

Have you ever interviewed anyone? If you have, you probably know how interesting and exciting an interview can be. An **interview** is a conversation in which one person questions another to get information. The interviewer takes notes or records the conversation on audiotape or videotape in order to write an accurate account of what was said.

An interview with the writer Gary Paulsen appears on page 153.

INTERVIEW

Q: You wrote your best-known works while you were running dogs. Where did you find the time?

A: With the dogs, you run them just four hours on, then four hours off. When they were sleeping those four hours, I'd sit by my campfire and write longhand.

Q: What is your favorite thing to write about?

A: Almost always, it's about making personal discoveries while struggling to survive in the great outdoors.

—"Talking with Gary Paulsen"

Informative Article
Ask students to think about why they would want to read informative nonfiction. Have them describe situations in which such works could be helpful.

YOUR TURN
Possible Responses: The passage tells the reader that forest fires can be started by lightning and that firefighters don't try to put out all the forest fires.

Interview
Ask students to think about one living person they would like to interview. Have them discuss what specific information they would want to get from the interview.

OVERVIEW

Objectives
- use a variety of strategies to read and appreciate nonfiction
- use graphic representations and cues to understand nonfiction

Teaching the Lesson

The strategies on this page will help students understand the upcoming nonfiction selections in this and other units.

Presenting the Strategies
Make sure students understand that there are different strategies for reading different kinds of nonfiction. For example, biography and autobiography are narrative forms of nonfiction and require strategies similar to those for reading fiction. Essays, informative articles, and interviews demand strategies geared more toward analyzing and evaluating a writer's reasoning and purpose.

Use **Reading and Critical Thinking Transparencies,** p. 1, for additional support.

PREVIEW
Remind students that the organization of a piece of nonfiction into sections with headings can provide an outline of the content. Words in boldface type often highlight the most important ideas presented in the article. Photographs, diagrams, and charts all give information at a glance.

FIGURE OUT THE ORGANIZATION
Tell students that before they read a piece of nonfiction, it is a good idea to figure out how it is presented: for instance, chronologically or by topic. In that way, they can better understand and evaluate the author's points.

The Active Reader: Skills and Strategies

Nonfiction writing informs us about real people, places, and events. **Autobiographies, biographies, essays, informative nonfiction,** and **interviews** provide answers to our questions and facts at our fingertips. The reading strategies explained here can help you to enjoy many types of nonfiction.

Reading Nonfiction

How to Apply the Strategies

Preview the selection. Look at the title, pictures or diagrams, and any subtitles or terms in boldface or italic type. As you read, stop now and then to predict what will come next. See if your ideas change as you build your understanding.

Figure out the organization. In a biography or an autobiography, the organization is probably chronological—events are presented in time order. Other selections may be organized around ideas the author wants to discuss. Dates and signal words, such as *before, after, next,* and *last,* may clarify the sequence of events.

Summarize the main idea. A **main idea** is the most important point about the topic. **Details** include words, phrases, or sentences that explain the main idea.

Distinguish facts from opinions. Facts are statements that can be proved, such as, "There are 24 hours in a day." Opinions are statements that cannot be proved. They simply express a person's beliefs. Writers of nonfiction sometimes present opinions as if they were facts. Be sure you recognize the difference.

Evaluate what you read. Evaluating means forming opinions about the people, events, and ideas. To evaluate, decide whether or not you like the way the piece was written. You can also evaluate the author's purpose. Ask yourself why you think the author wrote the piece. How can you tell?

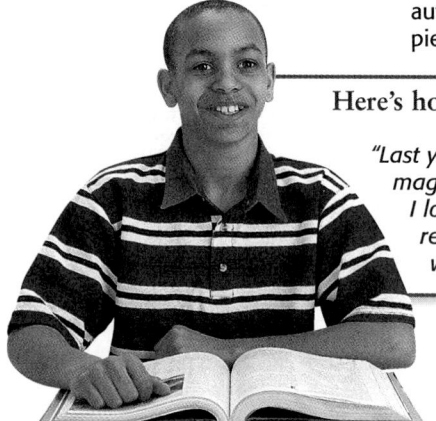

Here's how Sean uses the strategies:

*"Last year I wrote a report on horses. I had to read all sorts of magazines, books, and encyclopedias. As I skimmed the material, I looked for **main ideas** and **details. I evaluated** what I was reading by thinking about whether the author explained things well. After, I asked myself what I remembered most."*

Need More Help?
Remember that active readers use the essential reading strategies explained on page 4: • **visualize** • **predict** • **clarify** • **question** • **connect** • **evaluate** • **monitor.**

100   UNIT ONE   PART 2: COURAGE IN ACTION

SUMMARIZE THE MAIN IDEA
Tell students that once they know the main ideas of a selection, they can ask questions that will help them find the exact information about the topic they want and need.

DISTINGUISH FACTS FROM OPINIONS
Remind students that they will form a response to what is written. Are facts verified? Are opinions supported with good reasons? Reading should help students to form and evaluate their own opinions and to base them on good reasons.

EVALUATE WHAT YOU READ
Tell students to use all of the above strategies to help them make some judgments about what they read. Ask: What did you like or dislike about the article? Was the explanation clear and factual? Do you need to seek other sources of information?

Matthew Henson at the Top of the World

Biography by JIM HASKINS

ACROSS the CURRICULUM
SOCIAL STUDIES

Connect to Your Life

What images come to mind when you think of the word *explorer?*

Build Background In 1908, Matthew Henson joined Commander Robert E. Peary's expedition. Their goal was to be the first people in history to reach the North Pole. In their search, they were assisted by Eskimos known as Inuit.

The Asian ancestors of the Inuit followed the mammals they hunted into new lands.

Inuit are descendants of people who migrated to the Americas between 20,000 and 40,000 years ago.

Migration Routes, 40,000–10,000 B.C.

Arctic Ocean

ASIA

NORTH AMERICA

Bering Strait

Atlantic Ocean

Pacific Ocean

SOUTH AMERICA

■ Glacier ice, 12,000 B.C.
■ Connecting land mass
← Possible land migration routes
◄- Possible water migration routes

Focus Your Reading

LITERARY ANALYSIS **BIOGRAPHY** A biography is the story of a person's life, written by another person. In creating a biography, a writer may use interviews, diaries, and letters. As you read, think about sources the author might have used.

 LaserLinks: Background for Reading
Geographical Connection
Historical Connection
Visual Vocabulary

WORDS TO KNOW **Vocabulary Preview**

apt	menial	stamina	tyranny
ardent	proposition	surveyor	validate
deprivation	resentful		

ACTIVE READING **IDENTIFYING MAIN IDEA AND DETAILS** In most writing, it is possible to figure out the writer's most important points by identifying the **main idea,** or topic, of each paragraph. The main idea may be stated at any point in the paragraph, or it may be suggested by **details.** As you read, choose a few important paragraphs. In your **READER'S NOTEBOOK** jot down the main ideas of each paragraph. Below each main idea, note supporting details—such as facts or examples.

LESSON RESOURCES

UNIT ONE RESOURCE BOOK, pp. 45–51

ASSESSMENT
Formal Assessment, pp. 15–16
Teacher's Guide to Assessment and Portfolio Use
Test Generator

SKILLS TRANSPARENCIES AND COPYMASTERS
Literary Analysis
• Biography, TR 10 (for Activity, p. 111)

Reading and Critical Thinking
• Main Idea and Supporting Details, TR 25 (for Thinking Through the Literature, p. 111)
Grammar
• Agreement With a Compound Subject, CM 117 (for Mini Lesson, p. 113)
Vocabulary
• Using a Dictionary, CM 23 (for Mini Lesson, p. 102)
• Using Root Words, CM 24 (for Mini Lesson, p. 104)

Communications
• Evaluating Roles in Groups, TR8; Impromptu Speaking: Dialogue and Role-Play, TR13 (for Mini Lesson, p. 108)

INTEGRATED TECHNOLOGY
Audio Library
LaserLinks
• Historical Connection; Visual Vocabulary; Art Gallery; Geographical Connection. See **Teacher's SourceBook,** p. 9
• **Internet: Research Starter**

Visit our website:
www.mcdougallittell.com

 This selection is included in the **Grade 6 InterActive Reader.**

Objectives
1. understand and appreciate a **biography (Literary Analysis)**
2. identify **main ideas and details** and use them to locate and recall information **(Active Reading)**

Summary
Born in 1866, Matthew Henson grew up with a hunger for adventure. He had a hard childhood and went to school for only a few years. At the age of 14, he became a cabin boy on a ship and began exploring the world. In 1887, he signed on as the servant of Robert E. Peary, a naval officer and explorer. Four years later, Henson and Peary sailed off to the first of their five expeditions to the Arctic. The fifth expedition, in 1908, had as its goal the North Pole, which had never been reached before. Seven explorers and forty-one Eskimos began the grueling Arctic journey. Frostbite, exhaustion, and death reduced the party until only Peary, Henson, and four Eskimos remained. On April 6, 1908, Peary concluded that the group had reached the North Pole, and he asked Henson to place the U.S. flag on the spot. Upon his return to the United States, Peary became a hero for his achievement, but because Henson was African American, his own contribution was not honored until much later.

Thematic Link
Henson demonstrated great courage during his Arctic explorations and in his everyday life as an African American.

5-Minute Warm-Up

Daily Language SkillBuilder

Have students **proofread** the display sentences on page 19j and write them correctly. The sentences also appear on Transparency 3 of **Grammar Transparencies and Copymasters.**

Mini Lesson **Preteaching Vocabulary**

If you would like to preteach the WORDS TO KNOW for this selection, use the Mini Lesson, p. 102.

Literary Analysis | BIOGRAPHY |

Remind students that the writer of a biography gathers information from many sources. Some of this information is presented in the writer's own words. Other information is quoted directly from the source. Have students examine the text on page 102. What sources has Jim Haskins used for the information presented here?

Possible Responses: The writer has drawn on his own knowledge and research about explorers in the American West to make general statements and comparisons with Arctic exploration. He has quoted from the writing of Donald MacMillan, an Arctic explorer who knew Matthew Henson. He may have consulted birth records to find the date and place of Henson's birth, and a map to find the distance between Charles County and Washington, D.C.

 Use **Unit One Resource Book,** p. 47 for more practice.

Active Reading | IDENTIFYING MAIN IDEA AND DETAILS |

Ask students to identify the main idea of the opening paragraph. Then ask them to list several details that support the main idea.

Possible Response: Main idea—Matthew Henson had great stamina and courage. Details—Henson explored the North Pole with Robert Peary. In the Arctic, explorers could not count on finding water or game, and spring did not bring warmth; Donald MacMillan said that Henson was the most valuable member of Peary's expedition.

 Use **Unit One Resource Book,** p. 46 for more practice.

Teaching Options

MATTHEW HENSON AT THE
TOP OF THE WORLD

by Jim Haskins

W hile the explorers of the American West faced many dangers in their travels, at least game and water were usually plentiful; and if winter with its cold and snow overtook them, they could, in time, expect warmth and spring. For Matthew Henson, in his explorations with Robert Peary at the North Pole, this was hardly the case. In many ways, to forge ahead into the icy Arctic took far greater <u>stamina</u> and courage than did the earlier explorers' travels, and Henson possessed such hardiness. As Donald MacMillan, a member of the expedition [journey toward a goal], was later to write: "Peary knew Matt Henson's real worth. . . . Highly respected by the Eskimos,[1] he was easily the most popular man on board ship. . . . Henson . . . was of more real value to our Commander than [expedition members] Bartlett, Marvin, Borup, Goodsell and myself all put together. Matthew Henson went to the Pole with Peary because he was a better man than any one of us."

Matthew Henson was born on August 8, 1866, in Charles County, Maryland, some forty-four miles south of Washington, D.C. His parents were poor, free tenant

---

1. **Eskimos:** a term used throughout this account to refer to the native peoples of the Arctic; the Eskimos of Greenland, such as those who traveled on Peary's expeditions, call themselves Inuit, as do the Eskimos of Canada.

WORDS TO KNOW   **stamina** (stăm′ə-nə) *n.* the strength to withstand hardship

102

 Preaching Vocabulary

USING A DICTIONARY

Instruction If students can't find the meaning of an unfamiliar word from context, they can use a dictionary to look up the word. Many words will have more than one meaning listed. Students can use context clues to determine which is the correct meaning for that context.

Exercises Each of the sentences contains one of the WORDS TO KNOW for this selection. Have students look up each underlined word and use the context of the sentence to decide which dictionary meaning is appropriate.

1. Even at the age of five, Eileen was very <u>apt</u> at playing the violin.

2. Jon gets bored watching sports on television, but he is <u>ardent</u> about playing sports himself.

3. Most of our plants died of water <u>deprivation</u> while my family was on vacation.

4. What do you think of Aisha's <u>proposition</u> that we have pizza for lunch?

5. Joan claims she made 47 jump shots in a row, but she has no witness to <u>validate</u> her feat.

 Use **Unit One Resource Book,** p. 48 for more practice.
Use **Vocabulary Transparencies and Copymasters,** p. 23, for additional support.

Matthew Henson
in animal furs that
protected him from
the Arctic cold.

Less Proficient Readers
Engage students' interest in the selection by asking them to describe what they think the North Pole is like. Tell them that they are going to read about Matthew Henson, a member of the first group ever to reach the North Pole. Have them preview the photographs in the selection, which show Henson and Peary and some of the tools they used in their expedition.
Set a Purpose Have students read to find out about Henson's childhood.

Students Acquiring English
Students may benefit from background information about the history of the United States during the late 1800s. They may need help understanding references to slavery, the Ku Klux Klan, and Reconstruction. Use the historical note on page 105.

 Explain that *hardly* is a negative word meaning "not at all."

Use **Spanish Study Guide,** pp. 16–18 for additional support.

Gifted and Talented
Have students look for passages that describe hardships in Henson's life. Ask them to think about how Henson reacted to each hardship. Does his way of dealing with challenges and setbacks provide some insight into how he became one of the first people to reach the North Pole?

Multiple Learning Styles
Visual Learners
Have students study the photograph of Henson on this page. Ask them what impression they get from the photo. Does this impression match the description of Henson in the first paragraph?

BLOCK SCHEDULING: MANAGING TIME

If your schedule requires that you cover the lesson objectives in a shorter time, use . . .
• Preparing to Read, p. 101
• Thinking Through the Literature, p. 111
• Vocabulary in Action, p. 112
• Grammar in Context, p. 113

If you want to take advantage of longer class time, use . . .
• TE Teaching Options: Preteaching Vocabulary, p. 102; Vocabulary Strategy, p. 104; Cross-Curricular Links, pp. 105, 106; Spelling, p. 107; Speaking and Listening, p. 108; Viewing and Representing, p. 109; Standardized Test Practice, p. 110; Grammar, p. 113
• Literary Link, p. 110
• Choices & Challenges, pp. 112–113

A Ask students to monitor their own comprehension by clarifying why the Hensons moved to Washington, D.C.

Possible Response: The Hensons were tenant farmers in the South after the Civil War. Former slave owners resented the new independence of African Americans, and the Ku Klux Klan terrorized the former slaves. The Hensons moved north to avoid the Klan and to search for better opportunities.

Literary Analysis BIOGRAPHY

B Ask students what kind of source the author might have used to gather the information in this paragraph. Have them explain their answers.

Possible Response: The information probably came from Henson's own writings or memoirs. The paragraph discusses Henson's feelings about his situation as a teenager. It also describes experiences he had at the restaurant. This kind of information could only have come from Henson himself.

ACTIVE READING

C **QUESTION** **Possible Response:** Henson wanted adventure and decided to seek it at sea.

Literary Analysis: CHARACTER

D Ask students what details the author uses to characterize Matthew Henson in this paragraph.

Possible Response: Henson impressed his boss at the store, who recognized that he was "bright and hard working." Henson eagerly accepted Peary's offer despite the hazards involved; this shows that Henson was eager for adventure and was not afraid of challenges.

---

farmers[2] who barely eked a living from the sandy soil. The Civil War had ended the year before Matthew was born, bringing with it a great deal of bitterness on the part of former slave-owners. One manifestation of this hostility was the terrorist activity on the part of the Ku Klux Klan[3] in Maryland. Many free and newly freed blacks had suffered at the hands of this band of night riders.[4] Matthew's father, Lemuel Henson, felt it was only a matter of time before the Klan turned its vengeful eyes on his family. That, and the fact that by farming he was barely able to support them, caused him to decide to move north to Washington, D.C.

At first things went well for the Henson family, but then Matthew's mother died and his father found himself unable to care for Matthew. The seven-year-old boy was sent to live with his uncle, a kindly man who welcomed him and enrolled him in the N Street School. Six years later, however, another blow fell; his uncle himself fell upon hard times and could no longer support Matthew. The boy couldn't return to his father, because Lemuel had recently died. Alone, homeless, and penniless, Matthew was forced to fend for himself.

Matthew Henson was a bright boy and a hard worker, although he had only a sixth-grade education. Calling upon his own resourcefulness, he found a job as a dishwasher in a small restaurant owned by a woman named Janey Moore. When Janey discovered that Matthew had no place to stay, she fixed a cot for him in the kitchen; Matthew had found a home again.

Matthew Henson didn't want to spend his life waiting on people and washing dishes, however, no matter how kind Janey was. He had seen enough of the world through his schoolbooks to want more, to want adventure. This desire was reinforced by the men who frequented the restaurant—sailors from many ports, who spun tales of life on the ocean and of strange and wonderful places. As Henson listened, wide-eyed, to their stories, he decided, as had so many boys before him, that the life of a sailor with its adventures and dangers was for him. Having made up his mind, the fourteen-year-old packed up what little he owned, bade good-bye to Janey, and was off to Baltimore to find a ship.

ACTIVE READING

QUESTION What is the main idea of the paragraph you have just read?

Although Matthew Henson's early life seems harsh, in many ways he was very lucky. When he arrived in Baltimore, he signed on as a cabin boy on the *Katie Hines,* the master of which was a Captain Childs. For many sailors at that time, life at sea was brutal and filled with hard work, deprivation, and a "taste of the cat": whipping. The captains of many vessels were petty despots, ruling with an iron hand and having little regard for a seaman's health or safety. Matthew was fortunate to find just the opposite in Childs.

---

2. **tenant farmers:** people who farm land rented from others.
3. **Ku Klux Klan** (koōˊ klŭks klănˊ): a secret society, organized in the South after the Civil War, that used terrorism to reassert the power of whites.
4. **night riders:** mounted and usually masked white men who committed acts of terror against African Americans during the period following the Civil War.

WORDS
TO
KNOW **deprivation** (dĕpˊrə-vāˊshən) *n.* a lack of what is needed for survival or comfort

104

Teaching Options

Mini Lesson **Vocabulary Strategy**

USING ROOT WORDS

Instruction Remind students that many words in English have their roots in other languages, such as Greek and Latin. A complete dictionary will list the origin of each word. If you look up a word and see no information about its origins, try looking up its base word. For example, to find the root of *deprivation,* you would look up *deprive.* The origins of that word might appear at the beginning or end of the dictionary entry:
[Middle English *depriven,* from Old French *depriver,* from Middle Latin *deprivare* : Latin *de-,* + Latin

privare, to rob (from *privus,* alone, without)]
Once you know the root *privus,* you can recognize members of the same word family—such as *private, privation, privilege,* and *privy*—and understand how they are related.

Application Have students investigate the roots of the words *proposition, resentful, surveyor,* and *validate.* Ask them to list other words that have the same roots, where possible.

Use **Vocabulary Transparencies and Copymasters,** p. 24 for more practice.

Captain Childs took the boy under his wing. Although Matthew of course had to do the work he was assigned, Captain Childs took a fatherly interest in him. Having an excellent private library on the ship, the captain saw to Matthew's education, insisting that he read widely in geography, history, mathematics, and literature while they were at sea.

The years on the *Katie Hines* were good ones for Matthew Henson. During that time he saw China, Japan, the Philippines, France, Africa, and southern Russia; he sailed through the Arctic to Murmansk. But in 1885 it all ended; Captain Childs fell ill and died at sea. Unable to face staying on the *Katie Hines* under a new skipper, Matthew left the ship at Baltimore and found a place on a fishing schooner bound for Newfoundland.

Now, for the first time, Henson encountered the kind of unthinking cruelty and tyranny so often found on ships at that time. The ship was filthy, the crew surly and resentful of their black shipmate, and the captain a dictator. As soon as he was able, Matthew left the ship in Canada and made his way back to the United States, finally arriving in Washington, D.C., only to find that things there had changed during the years he had been at sea.

Opportunities for blacks had been limited when Henson had left Washington in 1871, but by the time he returned they were almost nonexistent. Post–Civil War reconstruction had failed, bringing with its failure a great deal of bitter resentment toward blacks. Jobs were scarce, and the few available were menial ones. Matthew finally found a job as a stock clerk in

A sextant (center) and other navigational instruments of Robert Peary. Victor R. Boswell, Jr.

a clothing and hat store, B. H. Steinmetz and Sons, bitterly wondering if this was how he was to spend the rest of his life. But his luck was still holding.

Steinmetz recognized that Matthew Henson was bright and hard working. One day Lieutenant Robert E. Peary, a young navy officer, walked into the store, looking for tropical hats. After being shown a number of hats, Peary unexpectedly offered Henson a job as his personal servant. Steinmetz had recommended him, Peary said, but the job wouldn't be easy. He was bound for Nicaragua to head an engineering survey team. Would Matthew be willing to put up with the discomforts and hazards of such a trip? Thinking of the adventure and opportunities offered, Henson eagerly said yes, little realizing that a partnership had just been formed that would span years and be filled with exploration, danger, and fame.

WORDS TO KNOW
tyranny (tĭr′ə-nē) *n.* an extremely harsh or unjust government or authority
resentful (rĭ-zĕnt′fəl) *adj.* angry due to a feeling of being treated unfairly
menial (mē′nē-əl) *adj.* fit for a servant

105

Customizing Instruction

Multiple Learning Styles
Interpersonal Learners
1 Invite students to discuss how Lemuel Henson might have felt when he had to send his son away.

Less Proficient Readers
Have students summarize the events of Henson's early childhood.
Possible Response: Henson was born in Maryland. When he was seven, his mother died, and his father, unable to support him, sent him to live with an uncle. Later, the uncle could no longer support him, so Henson went to work (and live) in a restaurant. He soon decided to become a sailor and left the restaurant to find work on a ship.
Ask the following questions to make sure that students understand the events that have taken place up to this point.
• What happened when Henson went to Baltimore to get a job on a ship?
  Answer: He found a job on the *Katie Hines.*
• Why did Henson leave the ship?
  Answer: Captain Childs died.
• For what job did Peary first hire Henson?
  Answer: Peary's personal servant
Set a Purpose Invite students to continue reading to find out what happens to Henson when he works with Peary.

Students Acquiring English
2 Show students that they can figure out the meanings of unfamiliar expressions from their context. Ask them to read this paragraph and then define the expression *took the boy under his wing.*
Possible Responses: "took care of the boy"; "acted as a father to the boy"

Cross Curricular Link History

THE CIVIL WAR AND RECONSTRUCTION The Civil War took place between 1861 and 1865. Northern states (the Union) fought to preserve the United States as one nation. Southern states (the Confederacy) fought for their right to leave the Union. Although the lightning-rod issue was slavery, the Civil War had deep-rooted political and economic causes. White Americans in both the industrial North and the rural South fought to preserve their economic systems and to protect their own political power. Reconstruction, which lasted from the end of the war through 1877, was the attempt to reintegrate the South back into the Union. It was a period marked by power struggles and violence. Many Northerners wanted to punish white Southerners by taking away their land and giving it to formerly enslaved African Americans. The Ku Klux Klan, formed in 1866, used terror to intimidate its political enemies as well as African Americans.

Robert E. Peary was born in Cresson, Pennsylvania, in 1856 but was raised in Maine, where his mother had returned after his father's death in 1859. After graduating from Bowdoin College, Peary worked as a <u>surveyor</u> for four years and in 1881 joined the navy's corps of civil engineers. One result of his travels for the navy and of his reading was an <u>ardent</u> desire for adventure. "I shall not be satisfied," Peary wrote to his mother, "until my name is known from one end of the earth to the other." This was a goal Matthew Henson could understand. As he later said, "I recognized in [Peary] the qualities that made me willing to engage myself in his service." In November 1887, Henson and Peary set sail for Nicaragua, along with forty-five other engineers and a hundred black Jamaicans.

Peary's job was to study the feasibility[5] of digging a canal across Nicaragua (that canal that would later be dug across the Isthmus of Panama).[6] The survey took until June of 1888, when the surveying party headed back to the United States. Henson knew he had done a good job for Peary, but even as they started north, Peary said nothing to him about

Arctic exploration would have been impossible without the use of snowshoes (above) and a compass (facing page).

continuing on as his servant. It was a great surprise, then, when one day Peary approached Henson with a <u>proposition</u>. He wanted to try to raise money for an expedition to the Arctic, and he wanted Henson to accompany him. Henson quickly accepted, saying he would go whether Peary could pay him or not.

"It was in June, 1891, that I started on my first trip to the Arctic regions, as a member of what was known as the 'North Greenland Expedition,'" Matthew Henson later wrote. So began the first of five expeditions on which Henson would accompany Peary.

ACTIVE READING

CLARIFY Does the main idea appear at the beginning, the middle, or the end of this paragraph?

During this first trip to Greenland, on a ship named *Kite*, Peary discovered how valuable Henson was to any expedition. He reported that Henson was able to establish "a friendly relationship with the Eskimos, who believed him to be somehow related to them because of his brown skin. . . ." Peary's expedition was also greatly aided by Henson's expert handling of the Eskimos, dogs, and equipment. Henson also hunted with the Eskimos for meat for the expedition and cooked under the supervision of Josephine Peary, Robert's wife. On the expedition's return to New York, September 24, 1892, Peary wrote, "Henson, my faithful colored boy, a hard worker and <u>apt</u> at anything, . . . showed himself . . . the equal of others in the party."

This first expedition to the Arctic led to several others, but it was with the 1905

---

5. **feasibility** (fē'zə-bĭl'ĭ-tē): possibility of being completed successfully.

6. **Isthmus** (ĭs'məs) **of Panama:** a narrow strip of land connecting the North and South American continents.

WORDS
TO
KNOW
surveyor (sər-vā'ər) *n.* a person who determines land boundaries by measuring angles and distances
ardent (är'dnt) *adj.* full of enthusiasm or devotion
proposition (prŏp'ə-zĭsh'ən) *n.* a plan offered for acceptance
apt (ăpt) *adj.* quick to learn or understand

106

Teaching Options

Cross Curricular Link Geography

THE PANAMA CANAL For centuries mariners dreamed of ways to eliminate the lengthy journey around Cape Horn. Ferdinand de Lesseps, the French engineer who connected the Mediterranean and Red Sea with the Suez Canal, planned to dig a canal across the Isthmus of Panama, which was then a part of Colombia. Work began in 1881, but tropical disease, engineering problems, and financial difficulties soon brought construction to a halt.

In 1903 President Theodore Roosevelt acquired the land and rights to the project for the United States. Between 1904 and 1914, thousands of workers cut a 50-mile swath across a continent, creating a series of locks that link the Atlantic and Pacific oceans via the Caribbean Sea in the northeast and the Bay of Panama in the south. The United States owned and operated the canal until 1978, when the Panama Canal Treaty was ratified. The canal reverted to Panamanian control at the end of 1999.

expedition that Peary first tried to find that mystical point, the North Pole, the sole goal of the 1908 expedition.

On July 6, 1908, the *Roosevelt* sailed from New York City. Aboard it were the supplies and men for an expedition to reach the North Pole. Accompanying Peary were Captain Robert Bartlett and Ross Marvin, who had been with Peary on earlier expeditions; George Borup, a young graduate from Yale and the youngest member of the group; Donald MacMillan, a teacher; and a doctor, J. W. Goodsell. And, of course, Matthew Henson. In Greenland the group was joined by forty-one Eskimos and 246 dogs, plus the supplies. "The ship," Henson wrote, "is now in a most perfect state of dirtiness." On September 5, the *Roosevelt* arrived at Cape Sheridan, and the group began preparing for their journey, moving supplies north to Cape Columbia by dog sled to establish a base camp. Peary named the camp Crane City in honor of Zenas Crane, who had contributed $10,000 to the expedition.

The plan was to have two men, Bartlett and Borup, go ahead of the rest of the group to cut a trail stretching from the base camp to the North Pole. On February 28, the two men set out, and on March 1, the remainder of the expedition started north, following the trail Bartlett and Borup had cut the day before. At first, trouble seemed to plague them. On the first day, three of the sledges[7] broke, Henson's among them. Fortunately, Henson was able to repair them, despite the fact that it was nearly 50 degrees below zero.

As the days passed, further trouble came the way of the expedition. Several times they encountered leads—open channels of water—and were forced to wait until the ice closed over before proceeding. On March 14, Peary decided to send Donald MacMillan and Dr. Goodsell back to the base camp.

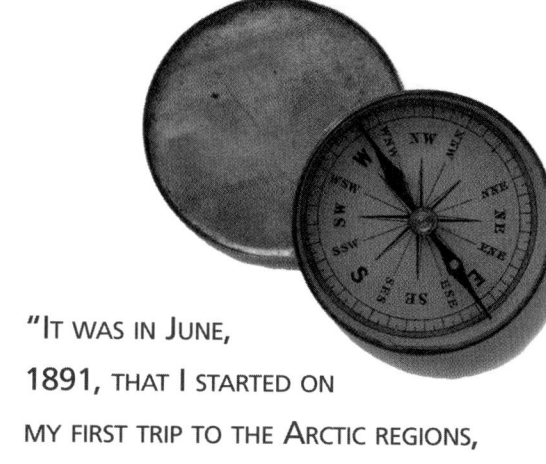

"IT WAS IN JUNE, 1891, THAT I STARTED ON MY FIRST TRIP TO THE ARCTIC REGIONS, AS A MEMBER OF WHAT WAS KNOWN AS THE 'NORTH GREENLAND EXPEDITION.'"

MacMillan could hardly walk, because he had frozen a heel when his foot had slipped into one of the leads. Dr. Goodsell was exhausted. As the expedition went on, more men were sent back due to exhaustion and frostbite. George Borup was sent back on March 20, and, on the 26th, so was Ross Marvin.

Although the expedition had encountered problems with subzero temperatures, with open water, and in handling the dogs, they had had no real injuries. On Ross Marvin's return trip to the base camp, however, he met with tragedy. On his journey, Marvin was accompanied by two Eskimos. He told them that he would go ahead to scout the trail. About an hour later, the Eskimos came upon a hole in the ice; floating in it was Marvin's coat. Marvin had gone through thin ice and, unable to save himself, had drowned or frozen. The Peary expedition had suffered its first—and fortunately its last—fatality.

---

7. **sledges:** sleds pulled by dogs.

Customizing Instruction

Students Acquiring English
1 You may want to point out that the term *colored* was used in the past to describe African Americans, but that it is now considered derogatory. Peary's use of the word *boy* to describe Henson, who was then twenty-six years old, is condescending and would be considered disrespectful today.

Less Proficient Readers
Ask students to summarize the relationship between Henson and Peary.
Possible Response: Henson starts out as Peary's personal servant. Peary then asks Henson to accompany him on an expedition to the Arctic. During this first expedition, Peary learns how valuable Henson is to him.
Set a Purpose Encourage students to continue reading to find out what happens during the 1908 expedition to the North Pole.

Multiple Learning Styles
Logical/Mathematical Learners
Ask volunteers to explain how snowshoes make it possible to walk across snow and ice without falling through, and how a compass works.

 Mini Lesson **Spelling**

SPELLING THE SOUND SHƏN
Instruction Explain to students that the sound *shən* is usually spelled *tion*. Write the following examples on the board and pronounce the words, pointing out the *tion* ending as you say each one.

deprivation   motivation   proposition
humiliation   expedition

Application Write the following words on the board. Have students write a paragraph about

Matthew Henson using at least six of them.
1. contribution   6. selection
2. observation   7. education
3. conjunction   8. reconstruction
4. violation   9. negotiation
5. connection   10. graduation

Use **Unit One Resource Book**, p. 50 for more practice.

Reading Skills and Strategies:
QUESTION

Take this opportunity to discuss questions or comments students have at this point. Have them add them to their notebooks with answers.

Reading Skills and Strategies:
ANALYZE

A Ask students to explain why Peary put part of an American flag and two letters in the jar that he left at the pole.

Possible Responses: Peary wanted to record the expedition's discovery; he wanted the world to know that his expedition had made it to the pole first; he wanted to claim any land at the pole for the United States.

Literary Analysis:
PRIMARY AND SECONDARY SOURCES

Primary sources, such as diaries and letters, convey first-hand knowledge of an event or a period. Secondary sources, such as biographies and textbooks, are removed from the events they describe. Point out the italicized passages in the text. Ask students to identify them as either primary or secondary sources.

Answer: primary sources

Ask students why they think Haskins and other writers might include quotations from primary sources in their work.

Possible Responses: Primary sources give readers a taste of the historical period; they bring characters to life because readers can "hear" their voices; they support the writer's own statements and conclusions.

Reading Skills and Strategies:
PREDICT

Ask students to predict what will happen once Peary's proofs about reaching the North Pole are validated.

 By April 1, Peary had sent back all of the original expedition except for four Eskimos and Matthew Henson. When Bartlett, the last man to be sent back, asked Peary why he didn't also send Henson, Peary replied, "I can't get along without him." The remnant of the original group pushed on.

We had been travelling eighteen to twenty hours out of every twenty-four. Man, that was killing work! Forced marches all the time. From all our other expeditions we had found out that we couldn't carry food for more than fifty days, fifty-five at a pinch. . . .

We used to travel by night and sleep in the warmest part of the day. I was ahead most of the time with two of the Eskimos.

So Matthew Henson described the grueling journey. Finally, on the morning of April 6, Peary called a halt. Henson wrote: "I was driving ahead and was swinging around to the right. . . . The Commander, who was about 50 feet behind me, called to me and said we would go into camp. . . ." In fact, both Henson and Peary felt they might have reached the Pole already. That day, Peary took readings with a sextant[8] and determined that they were within three miles of the Pole. Later he sledged ten miles north and found he was traveling south; to return to camp, Peary would have to return north and then head south in another direction—something that could only happen at the North Pole. To be absolutely sure, the next day Peary again took readings from solar observations. It was the North Pole, he was sure.

On that day Robert Peary had Matthew Henson plant the American flag at the North **A** Pole. Peary then cut a piece from the flag and placed it and two letters in a glass jar that he left at the Pole. The letters read:

90 N. Lat., North Pole
April 6, 1909

Arrived here today, 27 marches from C. Columbia.

I have with me 5 men, Matthew Henson, colored, Ootah, Egingwah, Seegloo, and Ooqueah, Eskimos; 5 sledges and 38 dogs. My ship, the S.S. Roosevelt, is in winter quarters at Cape Sheridan, 90 miles east of Columbia.

The expedition under my command which has succeeded in reaching the Pole is under the auspices of the Peary Arctic Club of New York City, and has been fitted out and sent north by members and friends of the Club for the purpose of securing this geographical prize, if possible, for the honor and prestige of the United States of America.

The officers of the Club are Thomas H. Hubbard of New York, President; Zenas Crane, of Mass., Vice-president; Herbert L. Bridgman, of New York, Secretary and Treasurer.

I start back for Cape Columbia tomorrow.
Robert E. Peary
United States Navy

90 N. Lat., North Pole
April 6, 1909

I have today hoisted the national ensign of the United States of America at this place, which my observations indicate to be the North Polar axis of the earth, and have formally taken possession of the entire region, and adjacent, for and in the name of the President of the United States of America.

---

8. **sextant:** an instrument used to measure the positions of heavenly bodies.

Teaching Options

Mini Lesson **Speaking and Listening**

PRESS CONFERENCE
Prepare Explain to students that a press conference is called when someone has an important announcement to make. Students have probably seen press conferences on television. Most press conferences include time for questions from reporters. Have students work in groups to plan a press conference in which Peary announces that he has reached the North Pole.

PRESENT
Have one group of students plan Peary's statement and elect a group member to portray Peary. The group may decide if other members of the expedition will speak. Another group of students should portray members of the press and plan questions to ask.

Use **Communications Transparencies and Copymasters,** pp. 8, 13, for additional support.

BLOCK SCHEDULING This activity is particularly well suited for longer class periods.

Robert Peary (second from right) and Henson (far right) on board ship with other members of an expedition, 1909.

I leave this record and United States flag in possession.

> Robert E. Peary
> United States Navy

Having accomplished their goal, the small group set out on the return journey. It was, Matthew Henson wrote, "17 days of haste, toil, and misery. . . . We crossed lead after lead, sometimes like a bareback rider in the circus, balancing on cake after cake of ice." Finally they reached the *Roosevelt*, where they could rest and eat well at last. The Pole had been conquered!

During the return trip to New York City, Henson became increasingly puzzled by Peary's behavior. "Not once in [three weeks]," Henson wrote, "did he speak a word to me. Then he . . .

ordered me to get to work. Not a word about the North Pole or anything connected with it." Even when the *Roosevelt* docked in New York in September of 1909, Peary remained withdrawn and silent, saying little to the press and quickly withdrawing to his home in Maine.

The ostensible[9] reason for his silence was that when the group returned to New York, they learned that Dr. Frederick A. Cook was claiming that *he* had gone to the North Pole—and done so before Peary reached it. Peary told his friends that he wished to wait for his own proofs to be <u>validated</u> by the scientific societies before he spoke. He felt sure that Cook would not be able to present the kinds of evidence that he could present, and so it proved.

---

9. **ostensible** (ŏ-stĕn′sə-bəl): claimed, but not necessarily true.

> WORDS TO KNOW **validate** (văl′ĭ-dāt′) *v.* to show to be correct

Customizing Instruction

Students Acquiring English

1 Explain that the idiom *get along* means "to succeed."

2 Peary's letters are written in very formal language. You may need to help students define the following words and expressions:

- *winter quarters*—the place where some person or thing stays during the winter
- *under the auspices of*—with the support of
- *fitted out*—outfitted, or given necessary supplies
- *hoisted the national ensign*—raised the national flag
- *adjacent*—surrounding, nearby

Less Proficient Readers
Ask students to explain what the expedition did once it reached the North Pole.

Answer: Henson planted the American flag. Then Peary left a glass jar containing part of the flag and two letters. The letters described the expedition and claimed the region for the United States.

Set a Purpose Have students read to find out what happens to Henson following the expedition.

Viewing and Representing

Robert Peary and Henson on board ship with other members of an expedition, 1909

Instruction Photographs are another type of primary source. Like diaries and letters, they convey direct information about historical events and periods. Ask students to examine the photo on this page and describe what it shows.

Possible Response: The photograph shows Peary, Henson, and two other explorers wearing fur parkas and boots. They are sitting on a dog sled on the deck of a ship. The ship is in port; buildings are visible in the background.

Application Ask students what this photograph conveys about the relationship between Peary and Henson. How does it jibe with the events that followed the expedition, as described in the selection?

Possible Response: In the photograph, Peary and Henson appear to be good friends and equals. They sit close together and appear relaxed with each other. Both look strong and confident. This picture of their relationship is in sharp contrast with Peary's abandonment and betrayal of Henson after the expedition.

Active Reading

IDENTIFYING MAIN IDEA AND DETAILS

A Ask students to state the main idea of this paragraph in their own words. Then have them list supporting details.

Possible Response: Main idea—Henson was not recognized for his contribution for many years. Details—He worked in a variety of unrelated jobs. His friends tried to get his work recognized. In 1937 he was invited to join the Explorers Club. In 1944 he received a medal from Congress.

Literary Analysis: SETTING

Ask students what the author's purpose for writing this biography was.

Possible Responses: to describe Henson's contributions; to right the wrong done to Henson when his contributions were ignored; to make sure that Henson is not forgotten

LITERARY LINK

Poet Walt Whitman (1819–1892) once said, "The United States themselves are essentially the greatest poem." He loved the vastness and variety of his country and its people. Whitman published his first and most famous collection of poems, *Leaves of Grass,* in 1855. During the Civil War he volunteered in an army hospital. His poems "When Lilacs Last in the Dooryard Bloom'd" and "O Captain! My Captain!" deal with the death of Lincoln.

Ask students to describe in their own words the feelings expressed in "Into Lucid Air." Would Matthew Henson have understood these feelings?

Possible Response: The poem expresses a love of wide-open spaces. Henson would have understood this love because he himself had a strong desire to explore the world around him.

Teaching Options

On December 15, Peary was declared the first to reach the North Pole; Cook could not present adequate evidence that he had made the discovery. Peary and Bartlett were awarded gold medals by the National Geographic Society; Henson was not. Because Henson was black, his contributions to the expedition were not recognized for many years.

A After 1909, Henson worked in a variety of jobs. For a while, he was a parking-garage attendant in Brooklyn, and at the age of forty-six, he became a clerk in the U.S. customshouse in Lower Manhattan. In the meantime, friends tried again and again to have his contributions to the expedition recognized. At last, in 1937, nearly thirty years after the expedition, he was invited to join the Explorers Club in New York, and in 1944, Congress authorized a medal for all of the men on the expedition, including Matthew Henson.

After his death in New York City on March 9, 1955, another lasting tribute was made to Henson's endeavors. In 1961, his home state of Maryland placed a bronze tablet in memory of him in the state house. It reads, in part:

MATTHEW ALEXANDER HENSON

Co-discoverer of the North Pole
with Admiral Robert Edwin Peary
April 6, 1909

Son of Maryland, exemplification of courage, fortitude, and patriotism, whose valiant deeds of noble devotion under the command of Admiral Robert Edwin Peary, in pioneer Arctic exploration and discovery, established everlasting prestige and glory for his state and country ❖

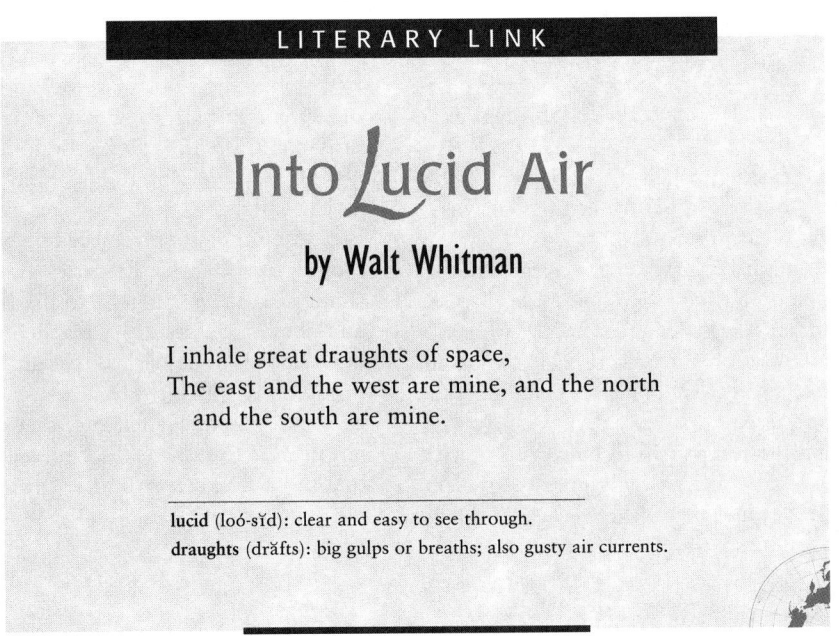

LITERARY LINK

Into Lucid Air

by Walt Whitman

I inhale great draughts of space,
The east and the west are mine, and the north
and the south are mine.

---

lucid (loó-sĭd): clear and easy to see through.
draughts (drăfts): big gulps or breaths; also gusty air currents.

✓ **Assessment Standardized Test Practice**

IDENTIFYING THE MAIN IDEA In some standardized tests, students are asked to select the best main idea statement for a passage they have read. Write the following question on the board or read it aloud.

Which statement best expresses the main idea of "Matthew Henson at the Top of the World"?

A. Matthew Henson loved adventure and decided to become a sailor.

B. Matthew Henson was awarded a Congressional medal in 1944 for exploring the North Pole.

C. Matthew Henson was a key member of the first expedition to reach the North Pole.

D. Robert Peary did not publicly acknowledge Matthew Henson's contribution after their expedition to the North Pole.

Guide students through the process of selecting the correct answer. A is not broad enough because it tells only about Henson's childhood dream. B tells what finally happened to Henson but is also too narrow. D focuses on Peary, whereas the selection is mostly about Henson. The best answer is C.

Connect to the Literature

1. What Do You Think?
In reading about Matthew Henson's life, what impressed you the most?

Comprehension Check
- Why did Henson leave his job at the restaurant?
- What was Henson's first job with Peary?
- Why wasn't Henson honored for his contributions to the North Pole expedition?

Think Critically

2. What words best describe Matthew Henson?

3. **ACTIVE READING** **IDENTIFYING MAIN IDEA AND DETAILS**
Look at the **main ideas** and supporting **details** you noted in your **READER'S NOTEBOOK**. How do the details support each main idea?

4. How would you describe the relationship between Peary and Henson?

> **THINK ABOUT**
> - what traits, or qualities, they had in common
> - their years of taking risks together
> - any descriptions of each other in their writings

5. If Robert Peary had asked Matthew Henson to accompany him on another expedition after 1909, do you think Henson would have? Why or why not?

Extend Interpretations

6. **COMPARING TEXTS** Compare the courage of Matthew Henson with the courage of the main character in "Nadia the Willful" on page 67. How are they similar and different?

7. **Connect to Life** How might Matthew Henson be a role model for people today? Explain your answer.

Literary Analysis

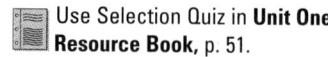 **BIOGRAPHY** A **biography** is an account of a person's life, written by another person, called a **biographer.** The biographer looks at all of the information available about the subject of the story and decides what facts to include. Then the biographer weaves the facts into a story, as Haskins did in this example:

His parents were poor, free tenant farmers who barely eked a living from the sandy soil.

Writing that tells a story is called a **narrative.** A narrative may be a work about real events, such as a biography. Or it may be a work of fiction, such as a novel.

Activity Look through the selection again. Choose three paragraphs that describe part of Henson's life that you found interesting. Then make a list of descriptive words and phrases that Haskins used to turn basic facts into a lively and interesting narrative.

"spun tales"
"wide-eyed"

Connect to the Literature

1. What Do You Think?
Possible Response: Henson risked his life to go where no one had gone before.

Comprehension Check
- He wanted to become a sailor and left to find work on a ship.
- He was Peary's personal servant during a trip to Nicaragua.
- He was not honored because of his race

 Use Selection Quiz in **Unit One Resource Book,** p. 51.

Think Critically

2. Possible Responses: brave, fearless, capable, curious, adventurous
3. Responses will vary, but details given should support the main idea.

Use **Reading and Critical Thinking Transparencies,** p. 25, for additional support.

4. Possible Responses: Henson and Peary had similar values and goals; because of this they respected each other. Peary's behavior after they reached the North Pole was insulting to Henson. The two could never be close because Henson was Peary's employee.
5. Possible Responses: Yes, because Henson wanted to go on expeditions for the adventure. No, since Henson was insulted by Peary, he would not risk his life again.

Literary Analysis

Biography Responses will vary, but should include adjectives, adverbs, and vivid verbs.

Use **Literary Analysis Transparencies,** p. 10, for additional support.

Extend Interpretations

6. Comparing Texts Both characters took risks to accomplish goals that were important to them. Henson risked his life to explore the harsh Arctic environment, and Nadia risked the wrath of her father in order to keep her brother's memory alive. Henson's courage was mainly physical in nature, while Nadia's was the courage of her moral convictions.

7. Connect to Life Henson could be a good role model because, despite many obstacles, he accomplished something no one else had done before. He was brave and had a sense of adventure.

Writing Options

1. **Log Entry** Students' log entries should be dated and should describe the thoughts and feelings of either Henson or Peary. To get students started on this assignment, have them recall a time in their own lives when they had a misunderstanding with someone who was important to them.

2. **Acceptance Speech** Students' speeches should reflect the events in the biography as well as Henson's character and personality. To get students started, suggest that they locate an acceptance speech in the library to use as a model.

3. **Mood Diary** Students may begin by brainstorming the feelings associated with trying something new, struggling with the task, and finally succeeding. **Visual learners** may create a drawing or painting that illustrates the experience.

Activities & Explorations

1. **Collage** Students may use the Internet to locate images for their collages. To use a search engine, they will need to type in key words that are likely to return relevant websites. Suggest that students work in pairs to brainstorm a list of key words.

2. **Mock Interviews** Students playing the roles of Henson and Peary should stay in character, and their answers should reflect information from the selection.

Use **Communications Transparencies and Copymasters**, p. 13, for additional support.

Inquiry & Research

Life on Ice To extend this activity, have students use the results of their research to create a website about the Inuit. Their site can include links to other, related sites that they discovered during their research.

Use **Writing Transparencies**, pp. 49–52, for additional support.

Writing Options

1. **Log Entry** Imagine that you are Henson or Peary. Write a log entry for one day of the three-week period after your arrival at the North Pole.

2. **Acceptance Speech** In 1937, Matthew Henson was invited to join the Explorers Club in New York. Write the acceptance speech he might have given to that group.

3. **Mood Diary** Think back to an incident in which you overcame your fear and did something you didn't think you could do. Write a diary entry that describes the change in feelings. Then put the entry into your **Working Portfolio.**

Activities & Explorations

1. **Collage** Make a collage of images that you think sum up the spirit of this selection. Consider the setting, the characters, and any vivid and memorable details. ~ **ART**

2. **Mock Interviews** In a small group, prepare interviews of Peary and Henson after the expedition's arrival in New York City in 1909. Share your interviews with the class. ~ **SPEAKING AND LISTENING**

Inquiry & Research

SOCIAL STUDIES **LIFE ON ICE**
Prepare a classroom display on the history and lifestyle of the Inuit. You can find information in nonfiction books or on the Internet. Offer brief descriptions of Inuit life and history, and include visual aids such as photos, copies of any interviews you find, and images of Inuit art.

 More Online: Research Starter www.mcdougallittell.com

 LaserLinks: Background for Reading Art Gallery

Vocabulary in Action

EXERCISE: SYNONYMS On a sheet of paper, write the Word to Know that can best replace the boldfaced word in each sentence.

1. For sailors in the 1800s, life at sea meant hard work and **shortages.**

2. The attention shown to Matthew Henson made some crew members **angry.**

3. Robert Peary worked as a **measurer** of boundaries.

4. After returning from the North Pole, Peary had to wait for scientific societies to **confirm** his discoveries.

5. After Henson's adventures, he found only **undesirable** jobs available.

6. Some of the crew feared the **cruelty** of their demanding captain.

7. Both Peary and Henson felt an **enthusiastic** desire for adventure.

8. Peary had a **plan** for an expedition to the Arctic.

9. Peary described Henson as a hard worker who was **quick-witted.**

10. The Inuit admired Henson's **endurance** in dealing with the Arctic weather.

Building Vocabulary
For an in-depth lesson on synonyms and antonyms, see p. 230.

WORDS TO KNOW	apt	deprivation	proposition	stamina	tyranny
	ardent	menial	resentful	surveyor	validate

Vocabulary in Action

1. deprivation
2. resentful
3. surveyor
4. validate
5. menial

6. tyranny
7. ardent
8. proposition
9. apt
10. stamina

Grammar in Context: Compound Subjects and Compound Predicates

Using a **compound subject** or a **compound predicate** can help a writer say more in fewer words. Instead of writing two separate sentences—one about Henson and one about Peary—Jim Haskins often combines the two subjects into one.

> In November 1887, Henson and Peary set sail for Nicaragua.

A **compound subject** has two or more **subjects.** A **compound predicate** has two or more **main verbs,** as shown below in green.

> Henson drove ahead and swung around to the right.

Usage Tip: The word *and, or,* or *but* is often used in a sentence to join compound elements, such as two subjects or two verbs.

WRITING EXERCISE Combine each pair of sentences by writing one complete sentence that has either a compound subject or a compound predicate.

Example: *Original* Bartlett went ahead of the rest of the group. Borup went ahead of the rest of the group, too.

Rewritten <u>Bartlett and Borup</u> went ahead of the rest of the group.

1. On February 28, the two men set out. They cut the trail for the others.
2. Donald MacMillan injured his foot. He returned to base camp.
3. Subzero temperatures caused problems. The dogs caused problems, too.

Grammar Handbook Making Subjects and Verbs Agree, p. R60

> *"It has always seemed to me that the truth is not just 'stranger than fiction,' but also more interesting."*

Jim Haskins
born 1941

True Tales Important African-American figures in history, politics, entertainment, and sports have been the subjects of Jim Haskins's books. All of his works are nonfiction because Haskins prefers true stories to made-up ones. He has said, "It seems to me that the more you know about the real world, the better off you are."

Writing with a Mission Although Haskins learned to read early in his childhood, the public library in his Alabama hometown did not welcome black children. He stayed home and learned to rely on his family's encyclopedia. Explaining why African Americans have usually been his subjects, he says, "I want children today, black and white, to be able to find books about black people and black history in case they want to read them." Haskins has written more than 100 books, which have received a number of citations and awards, including the Coretta Scott King Award.

AUTHOR ACTIVITY
Explorers Galore Read another short biography of an explorer in Jim Haskins's book *Against All Opposition: Black Explorers in America.* Compare traits of the main character with those of Matthew Henson. Create a poster telling about his or her most courageous actions.

 Grammar

AGREEMENT WITH A COMPOUND SUBJECT
Instruction Often two related sentences can be combined into one sentence with a compound subject. Compound subjects joined with the conjunction *and* are plural and take a plural verb. Write the following example on the chalkboard and point out to students how the verb changes in the revised sentence.
AWKWARD: Peary <u>was</u> honored by the National Geographic Society. Bartlett <u>was</u> also honored by the National Geographic Society.

REVISED: Peary <u>and</u> Bartlett <u>were</u> honored by the National Geographic Society.
Exercises Have students combine each set of sentences into one sentence with a compound subject.
1. Donald MacMillan was sent back to the base camp. Dr. Goodsell was sent back to the camp. George Borup was sent back, too.
2. I am interested in learning more about Matthew Henson. Geena is also interested in learning more about him.

3. Was Ootah a member of the first expedition to reach the North Pole? Was Egingwah a member of the expedition? Were Seegloo and Ooqueah members of the expedition?

Use **Unit One Resource Book,** p. 49.
Use **Grammar Transparencies and Copymasters,** p. 117, for additional practice.

 Use McDougal Littell's *Language Network,* Chapter 1, for more instruction and practice in compound subjects.

OVERVIEW

 This selection is included in the **Grade 6 InterActive Reader.**

Objectives
1. understand and appreciate **informative nonfiction (Literary Analysis)**
2. understand and identify **chronological order (Active Reading)**
3. use **visualizing** to help understand chronological order **(Reading Skills and Strategies)**

Active Reading Summary
In the summer of 1988, fires raged out of control in Yellowstone National Park. Initially, the fires were allowed to burn, but at a certain point, park officials began worrying about the scale of the destruction, and efforts were made to control the fires. Fire fighters could not stop or slow the fires, but were able to save the buildings around Old Faithful. Though it seemed like total devastation to outsiders, the fires only burned in one third of the park, and the new growth that resulted promoted the flourishing of certain birds, animals, and plants.

Thematic Link
The hundreds of fire fighters who worked to save Yellowstone exemplified courage in action by risking their lives as they tried to halt the destruction of the forest.

5-Minute Warm-Up

Daily Language SkillBuilder

Have students **proofread** the display sentences on page 19j and write them correctly. The sentences also appear on Transparency 3 of **Grammar Transparencies and Copymasters.**

PREPARING to *Read*

Summer of Fire

Informative Nonfiction by PATRICIA LAUBER

"Long before they could see the flames, fire fighters heard the fire's deep rumble . . ."

Connect to Your Life

Fighting Fires What do you know about wilderness fires? In a chart like the one below, record what you already know about wilderness fires, and what you want to learn.

What I Know	What I Want to Learn	What I Learned
1. Wilderness fires can spread quickly		

Build Background

CONNECT TO **BIOLOGY** In wilderness areas, fires can be started by lightning as well as by humans. Park managers must decide whether to let fires burn or put them out, because some fires are not necessarily harmful.

Burned plant material renews nutrients in the soil, and fire can clear away old branches so that sunlight may reach the ground. Although some animals die in small fires, most escape. Many animals, from ants to bears, find a new source of food in the plants that grow in the rich after-fire soil.

Large fires, however, can destroy huge areas of forest and threaten people who live or work nearby. That is what happened in Yellowstone National Park during the very dry summer of 1988. Despite the damage done in the fires, today Yellowstone is recovering well. Some species that had been rare before the fire are now thriving.

WORDS TO KNOW	**Vocabulary Preview**		
bear	geyser	threaten	veer
canopy	merge	tinder	withering
ember	oxygen		

Focus Your Reading

LITERARY ANALYSIS **INFORMATIVE NONFICTION**

Informative nonfiction is writing that provides factual information about real people, places, and events. Forms of informative nonfiction include newspaper and magazine articles, history and science books, and encyclopedias.

ACTIVE READING **CHRONOLOGICAL ORDER**

Chronological order, or time order, is a way of organizing a piece of writing. Stories or articles that are written in chronological order move forward in time from one event to another.

READER'S NOTEBOOK As you read "Summer of Fire," notice that many paragraphs mention dates. Use a chart like the one below to keep track of events. Make sure to include key **transition words** (*then, until, before, after,* and so on) or dates that help show chronological order.

summer of 1988 before the rains and snows of autumn	→		→	

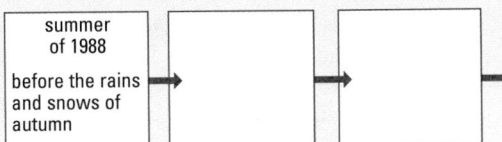

LESSON RESOURCES

UNIT ONE RESOURCE BOOK, pp. 52–58

ASSESSMENT
Formal Assessment, pp. 17–18
Teacher's Guide to Assessment and Portfolio Use
Test Generator

SKILLS TRANSPARENCIES AND COPYMASTERS
Literary Analysis
• Text Structure (Organization), TR 12 (for Activity, p. 121)
Reading and Critical Thinking
• Chronological Order, TR 6 (for Thinking Through the Literature, p. 121)

Grammar
• Action and State-of-Being Verbs, CM 79 (for Mini Lesson, p. 118)
• Active and Passive Voice, CM 134 (for Mini Lesson, p. 123)
Vocabulary
• Using a Pronunciation Key, CM 25 (for Mini Lesson, p. 115)
• Specialized Vocabulary, CM 26 (for Mini Lesson, p. 119)

Communications
• The Active Listener, TR 1; Persuasive Techniques, TR 3 (for Mini Lesson, p. 120)

INTEGRATED TECHNOLOGY
Audio Library
Internet: Research Starter

Visit our website:
www.mcdougallittell.com

SUMMER OF FIRE

by
Patricia
Lauber

The summer of 1988 was
hot and dry in much of
the United States.

115

TEACHING THE LITERATURE
Customizing Instruction

Students Acquiring English
Some students may not be aware of the extensive national park system of the United States. Point out Yellowstone National Park on a map, and explain that it was the world's first national park, established in 1872. Explain that the national parks are not playgrounds but areas with unique physical characteristics. Ask students to share their knowledge of parks.

 Use **Spanish Study Guide,** pp. 19–21 for additional support.

Less Proficient Readers
Explain that this is a true story of fires that burned in Yellowstone National Park in the summer of 1988.
Set a Purpose Ask students to read the first section of the story, through page 117, and summarize it.

Gifted and Talented
Ask students to pay attention to the assumptions people held about fires in Yellowstone and to park policy regarding fires, and to consider what the outcome might have been had there been different assumptions and policies.

Multiple Learning Styles
Visual Learners
Make copies of a map of the park on which students can track the paths of the fires.

Preteaching Vocabulary

Mini Lesson

USING A PRONUNCIATION KEY
Instruction Remind students that dictionaries have pronunciation keys to help in pronouncing words. Have them open their dictionaries and find a pronunciation key. Or you may copy and distribute one. Explain that after each letter and symbol, there is a common word that demonstrates how it should be pronounced. These letters and symbols are used in the phonetic respelling of every dictionary entry. Point out that each of the WORDS TO KNOW is followed in the dictionary by a respelling that shows how the word is pronounced. With

students, read aloud each letter and symbol in the pronunciation key.
Exercise Have students copy the phonetic respelling of each WORD TO KNOW from a dictionary. Working in pairs, have students take turns identifying the word from the respelling. They can use the key to sound out and pronounce each word.

Use **Unit One Resource Book** p. 55 for practice. Use **Vocabulary Transparencies and Copymasters,** p. 25, for additional support.

Reading and Analyzing

Reading Skills and Strategies:
PREVIEW

Ask students to read the title page and headlines and to look at the photographs, captions, and map. Ask what they think the selection is about.
Possible Response: It is about a large forest fire.

Active Reading
CHRONOLOGICAL ORDER

Ask students to begin their charts in their Reader's Notebooks. Their charts should include information such as the following:

 Use **Unit One Resource Book,** p. 53 for more practice.

Literary Analysis
INFORMATIVE NONFICTION

Explain that the author starts by giving an overview, then, on page 117, starts giving details. Ask: What caused the first fires of the summer?
Answer: lightning strikes

 Use **Unit One Resource Book,** p. 54 for more practice.

Literary Analysis: MAIN IDEA

A Ask students to determine the main idea of this paragraph and how that idea is supported with details.
Possible Response: Main Idea: It was a hot, dry time. Details: The sun blazed, fields baked and crops withered, water dried up, the earth cracked.

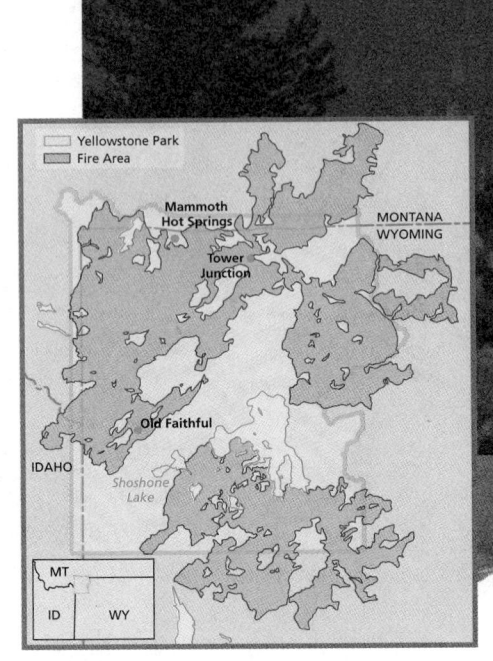

Yellowstone Park
Fire Area

Mammoth Hot Springs
MONTANA
WYOMING
Tower Junction
Old Faithful
IDAHO
Shoshone Lake

MT
ID   WY

During the summer of fire, about one half of the 3,400 square miles in Yellowstone National Park burned. Some 10,000 fire fighters battled the blazes.

A Above plains and prairies, the sun blazed out of an ever blue sky, baking fields and <u>withering</u> crops. Ponds and streams dried up. Rivers shrank. In places the very earth cracked open as underground water supplies dwindled away.

Farther west, forests were <u>tinder</u> dry. Sometimes skies grew dark with storm clouds. Thunder growled and lightning crackled, but little rain fell. Lightning strikes started forest fires that raged across the Rockies and other ranges with the roar of jumbo jets on take-off. Night skies turned red and yellow where flames soared 300 feet into the air. Smoke, carried on the winds, darkened skies as far away as Spokane and Minneapolis–St. Paul. Airline passengers, flying high above the fires, could smell the smoke. Before the rains and snows of autumn came, 2,600,000 acres had burned in the West and Alaska, an area twice the size of Delaware.

WORDS   **withering** (wĭth'ər-ĭng) *adj.* causing to dry out and shrivel up; wilting **wither** *v.*
TO   **tinder** (tĭn'dər) *n.* a material, such as dry twigs, that is used to start a fire because
KNOW   it burns easily

116

Teaching Options

Mini Lesson ### Viewing and Representing

MAP READING
Instruction Remind students that they can use maps to gather information and interpret important events. This map of Yellowstone has some important features. Point out the key in the top left corner. Using it, they can compare the size of the park with the amount of the park that had fires. The map shows important landmarks, state boundaries, lakes, and the park and fire areas. Confirm that students understand that this map— like most maps—shows north at the top of the map by asking: Is Montana north or south of Wyoming?
Answer: north
Application Ask students to compare the area of the park with the fire areas. What parts of the park were not part of the fire area?
Possible Response: A strip of land running diagonally across the middle of the park was not affected by the fire.

Many people
thought you couldn't
set fire to the
forest if you tried.

Violent winds and extreme heat made fire fighters' work exhausting.

Customizing Instruction

Multiple Learning Styles
Logical/Mathematical Learners
Have students use maps to determine the distances the text is referring to. Spokane is about 500 miles from Yellowstone, and Minneapolis-St. Paul is nearly 1000 miles away!

Less Proficient Readers
1 Suggest that the first part of the selection concludes here. Student summaries of the passage might mention the earth drying and cracking, the lightning, the smoke being carried far and wide, and the number of acres burned.
Set a Purpose Ask students to read on to learn how and why the fires spread.

Students Acquiring English
Check that students are familiar with these place names from the text: plains and prairies, Rockies, Spokane, Minneapolis-St. Paul, the West and Alaska.

In Yellowstone the fire season started on May 24, when lightning struck a tree in the northeastern part of the park. The fire stayed small. Rain fell later in the day and put it out. That was what usually happened. In Yellowstone, winters are long and cold, summers short and often rainy. Many people thought you couldn't set fire to the forest if you tried.

On June 23 lightning started a fire near Shoshone Lake in the southern part of the park. On June 25 another bolt of lightning started a fire in the northwest. These fires did not go out, and no one tried to put them out. Park policy was to let wildfires burn unless they <u>threatened</u> lives or property. Also, there seemed no reason to worry about the fires. Although winters in the 1980s had been dry, with little snow, summers had been unusually wet. The summer of 1988 was expected to be wet too. **1**

WORDS
TO   **threaten** (thrĕt'n) v. to be a danger to
KNOW

117

BLOCK SCHEDULING: MANAGING TIME

If your schedule requires that you cover the lesson objectives in a shorter time, use . . .
• Preparing to Read, p. 114
• Thinking Through the Literature, p. 121
• Vocabulary in Action, p. 122
• Grammar in Context, p. 123

If you want to take advantage of longer class time, use . . .
• TE Teaching Options: Preteaching Vocabulary, p. 115; Viewing and Representing, p. 116; Grammar, pp. 118, 123; Vocabulary Strategy, p. 119; Speaking and Listening, p. 120; Standardized Test Practice, p. 122
• Choices & Challenges and Author Activity, pp. 122–123

Active Reading
CHRONOLOGICAL ORDER

Ask students to update their charts with facts from these pages. They should include information like the following.

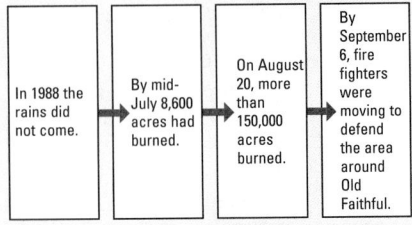

In 1988 the rains did not come.	By mid-July 8,600 acres had burned.	On August 20, more than 150,000 acres burned.	By September 6, fire fighters were moving to defend the area around Old Faithful.

Literary Analysis: SPATIAL ORDER

A Remind students that in a description, a thing or a place is described according to its layout, for example, from right to left, from north to south, or from top to bottom. Show a map of the region that includes the places mentioned in this selection. Have students describe the events of the fire in spatial order.

Reading Skills and Strategies: VISUALIZE

B Read aloud from the top of the column to this point and ask students to describe their own mental image of the fire.

Literary Analysis
INFORMATIVE NONFICTION

Ask students to describe what fire fighters did to protect the area around Old Faithful.

Possible Response: Planes dropped chemicals, and fire fighters on the ground wet down buildings.

But in 1988 the rains of summer did not come. The Shoshone and other fires blazed and spread. By mid-July, 8,600 acres had burned. Park officials decided that all fires should be put out, no matter whether they were wildfires or caused by human carelessness.

Fire fighters arrived by the hundreds to attack fires from the ground. Helicopters and airplanes attacked from above. But new fires started in the park. In 1988 Yellowstone had more than 50 lightning strikes, twice the normal number. Fires in neighboring national forests swept into the park. Old fires burned on. And still the rains did not come.

Cold fronts passed through, bringing winds of hurricane force with gusts of 60 to 80 miles an hour. Winds whipped and spread the fires and fed them <u>oxygen</u>, which fires must have to keep burning. Big fires met, <u>merged</u>, and became even bigger fires. In forests flames galloped through the tops, or crowns, of trees, through the <u>canopy</u>. Snags—dead trees that are still standing—burned like Roman candles.[1] Boulders exploded in the heat. Sheets of flame leaped forward. Gigantic clouds of smoke ringed the horizon, looking like thunderheads,[2] only bigger. There were days when the sun was no brighter than a full moon.

Fires jumped rivers, roads, canyons, parking lots. Glowing <u>embers</u>, some the size of a man's fist, shot a mile or more ahead, starting new fires. Flames were roaring through the park at

There were days when the sun was no brighter than a full moon.

By August, more than 50 individual fires had merged into eight huge ones.
(Right) Fire fighters drenched the historic Old Faithful Inn to protect it from advancing fires.

a rate of four or five miles a day. One fire ran 14 miles in only four hours. On August 20, a day known as Black Saturday, more than 150,000 acres burned inside the park and in neighboring forests. The 2,000 fire fighters could no more put out these fires than they could have stopped a hurricane. But what they

---

1. **Roman candles:** fireworks that shoot out showers of sparks and balls of fire.
2. **thunderheads:** the spreading upper parts of thunderclouds.

WORDS TO KNOW

oxygen (ŏk'sĭ-jən) *n.* one of the gases that make up air, needed for nearly all burning
merge (mûrj) *v.* to combine or unite
canopy (kăn'ə-pē) *n.* a rooflike cover; the covering formed by the branches and leaves of trees in a forest
ember (ĕm'bər) *n.* a small glowing bit of burning wood

118

Teaching Options

Mini Lesson **Grammar**

ACTION AND STATE-OF-BEING VERBS
Instruction Remind students that action verbs show action, which may or may not be visible. Some action verbs from this selection are *burn, spread,* and *decide.* State-of-being, or linking, verbs tell what something is or link the subject to a word or words in the predicate. Linking verbs include all forms of the verb *to be,* as well as words like *look, seem,* and *become.* Point out the highlighted passage, above. The first sentence has state-of-being verbs *were* and *was.* The second has the action verb *jumped.*

Exercises Circle the verb in each sentence. Write whether it shows action or state-of-being.
1. The sun blazed out of an ever blue sky. *(blazed, action)*
2. Farther west, forests were tinder dry. *(were, state-of-being)*
3. In Yellowstone, the fire season started on May 24. *(started, action)*

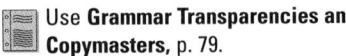
Use **Grammar Transparencies and Copymasters,** p. 79.

Use McDougal Littell's *Language Network,* Chapter 4, or more instruction and practice in verbs.

Called the North Fork fire, it had started in the Targhee National Forest on July 22, when a careless woodcutter threw away a lighted cigarette. Driven by shifting winds, the fire raced into Yellowstone, turned back into Targhee, neared the town of West Yellowstone, then <u>veered</u> back into the park. There it jumped roads and rivers, snarling its way through the crossroads at Madison on August 15. By the afternoon of September 7 it was approaching Old Faithful. Long before they could see the flames, fire fighters heard the fire's deep rumble and saw a churning wall of dark smoke towering skyward.

Planes dropped chemicals to damp down fires. On the ground weary fire fighters were wetting down buildings.

could do was defend the park communities—the information centers and the buildings where people slept, ate, and shopped.

By September 6 fire fighters were moving in to defend the area around the park's most famous <u>geyser</u>, Old Faithful. The geyser itself could not be harmed by fire, but the buildings around it could. One of them, the Old Faithful Inn, was the world's largest log building. Now one of the eight major fires in the park was <u>bearing</u> down on it.

The fire came on, a mass of red flames whipped by winds gusting up to 50 miles an hour. Sparks and embers were everywhere, flying over the inn, parking lots, and geyser, and setting fire to the woods beyond. At the last moment the wind shifted and the fire turned to the northeast, away from Old Faithful.

Saturday, September 10, began as another bad day. One arm of the North Fork fire was threatening park headquarters at Mammoth

A

B

WORDS TO KNOW	**geyser** (gī'zər) *n.* a natural hot spring that at times spouts water and steam into the air
	bear (bâr) *v.* to move forcefully; push
	veer (vîr) *v.* to turn aside; swerve

119

Customizing Instruction

Multiple Learning Styles
1 Logical/Mathematical Learners
Ask students how far a fire moving 14 miles in 4 hours travels in one hour.
Answer: 3.5 miles
How does that compare to the general rate of four or five miles per day mentioned in the text?
Possible Response: It is moving about 20 times as fast.

Less Proficient Readers
Ask students to review how and why the fires spread.
Possible Response: There were many lightning strikes. Park policy was to let the fires burn themselves out unless lives or property were in danger. Because recent summers had been wet, it was expected that this one would be, too, so there didn't seem to be much to worry about. By the time officials decided to put the fires out, it wasn't possible. High winds moved the fires along.
Set a Purpose Have students continue reading to find out who or what stopped the fires.

Gifted and Talented
Ask: What does Yellowstone National Park have more of than the rest of the world combined?
Answer: geysers and hot springs
Invite students to research the underground features that create geysers and hot springs.

 Vocabulary Strategy

SPECIALIZED VOCABULARY

Instruction Explain that this selection uses both weather- and forest-related terms. To understand a subject, it is often necessary to learn the specialized words that relate to it. Because specialized terms are not generally known, writers often provide definitions of specialized vocabulary they use. Point out the word *canopy* on page 118. It is a forest-related word defined in the selection.

Exercises Ask students to find the meaning of these words using a dictionary.

1. front (the boundary zone between two large masses of air with different temperatures)
2. hurricane (severe tropical cyclone)
3. force (*as in hurricane force*) (strength)
4. snag (dead tree that is still standing)
5. thunderhead (swollen upper portion of a thundercloud)
6. forecast (to predict weather)

 Use **Vocabulary Transparencies and Copymasters**, p. 26.

Have students complete the charts in their Reader's Notebooks.

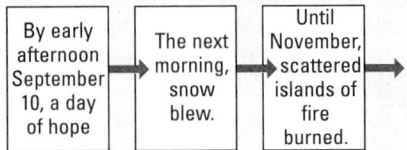

| By early afternoon September 10, a day of hope | → | The next morning, snow blew. | → | Until November, scattered islands of fire burned. | → |

Literary Analysis:
SUPPORTING DETAILS

 Ask students to determine the main idea of this paragraph and how that idea is supported with details.

Possible Response: Main Idea: It seemed like the park must lie in ruins, but that was not so. Details: Geysers, steam vents, and hot springs were unharmed, communities were saved, nearly two-thirds of the park was untouched by fire.

Reading Skills and Strategies:
MONITOR

Ask students to monitor their comprehension. If there was any part of the text they did not understand, encourage them to reread it aloud, use reference aids, search for clues, or ask questions.

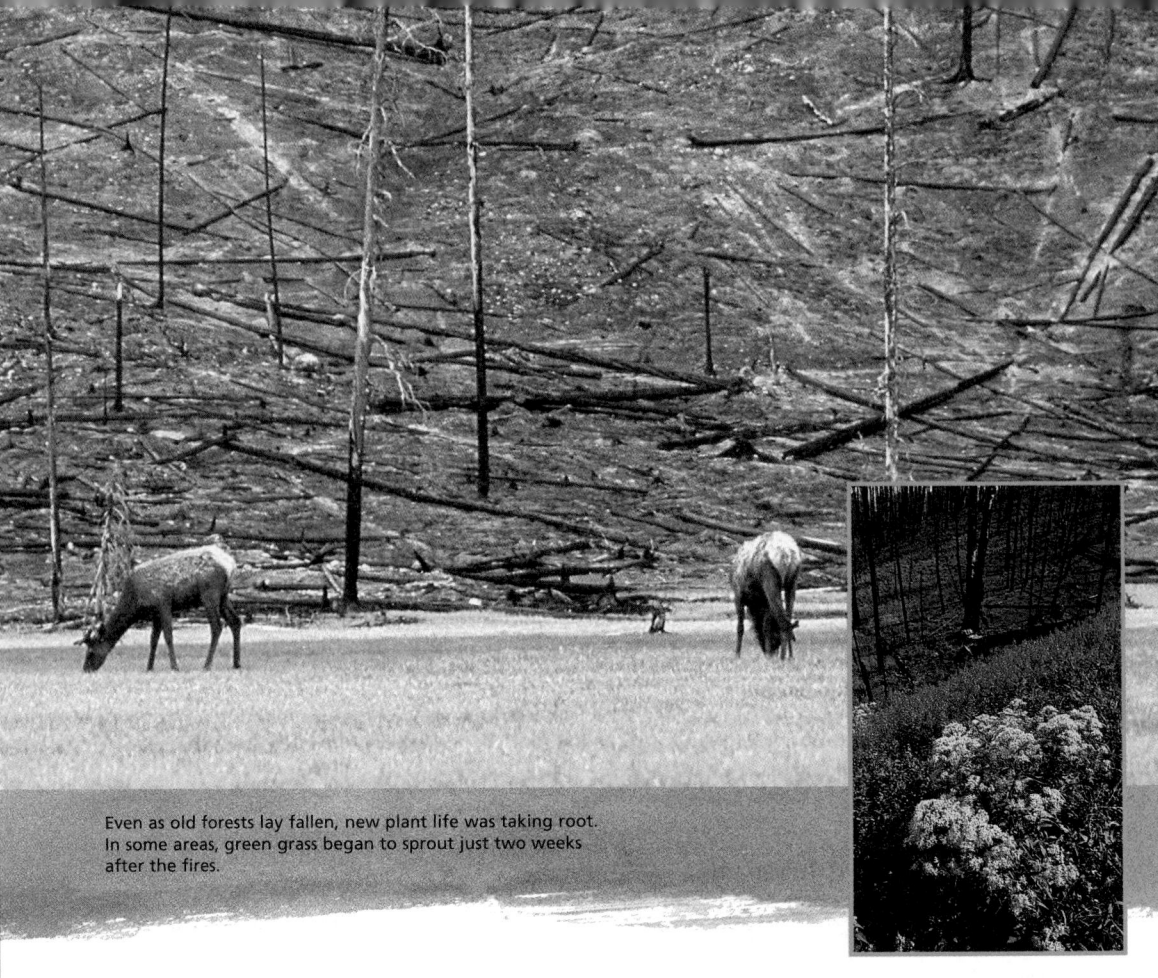

Even as old forests lay fallen, new plant life was taking root. In some areas, green grass began to sprout just two weeks after the fires.

Hot Springs, and another arm was a quarter of a mile from Tower Junction. The forecast was for winds of up to 60 miles an hour. But the sky was thick with clouds, and the temperature was falling.

By early afternoon, September 10 had turned into a day of hope. Rain was drenching the area around Old Faithful. The next morning snow blew along the streets of West Yellowstone. It sifted through blackened forests and dusted herds of bison and elk. Scattered islands of fire would burn until November blanketed them in snow. But the worst was over.

 At long last the summer of fire had ended. During it, eight major fires and many smaller ones had burned in Yellowstone. To people who had watched the fires on television news, it seemed the park must lie in ruins. But this was not so. The geysers, steam vents, and hot springs were unharmed. Park communities had been saved. Nearly two-thirds of the park had not even been touched by fire.

It was true that many once-green areas were now black and gray. Yet it was also true that they were not ruined. Instead, they were beginning again, starting over, as they had many times in the past. Fire has always been part of the Yellowstone region. Wildfire has shaped the landscape and renewed it. ❖

120   UNIT ONE   PART 2: COURAGE IN ACTION

Teaching Options

 Mini Lesson ## Speaking and Listening

DEBATE: LET THEM BURN vs. FIGHT, FIGHT, FIGHT
PREPARE Explain that controversial topics are often debated as a way of informing people and drawing them to one side or the other. A good debater will clarify and support spoken ideas with evidence, elaboration, and examples. He or she will study the subject thoroughly, gather facts that support the position, prepare clear arguments, anticipate points the

other side will make, and be prepared to rebut, or respond to, them. Listeners should understand the major ideas and supporting evidence, distinguish between the speaker's opinion and verifiable fact, and evaluate the spoken message in terms of its content, credibility, and delivery.
Present Choose teams to debate fighting forest fires vs. letting them burn. Students

should use the information in the selection to prepare their arguments. Each side should make an opening statement, rebut the other team's points, and make a closing statement. Listeners can offer opinions on which side was more convincing.

📄 Use **Communications Transparencies and Copymasters,** pp. 1, 3, for additional support.

Connect to the Literature

1. **What Do You Think?**
   What did you find most dramatic in this article?

   Comprehension Check
   - How did the 1988 fires in Yellowstone start?
   - Why were fire fighters unable to stop the fires?
   - How were the fires finally put out?

Think Critically

2. Why does Lauber say that Yellowstone was not ruined by the fires of 1988?

    THINK ABOUT
   - what was damaged
   - what was saved
   - what happened after the fires

3. Do you agree or disagree with the position that fire helps wilderness areas? Support your point of view.

4. **ACTIVE READING** **CHRONOLOGICAL ORDER** With a partner, take turns retelling the events of the selection in your own words. Use the chart you made in your **READER'S NOTEBOOK** to help you.

5. What skills and traits, or qualities, do you think a fire fighter needed in order to control the Yellowstone fires of 1988?

Extend Interpretations

6. **The Writer's Style** Lauber has said, "I believe that the best science books have a story line: that one thing leads to another . . ." Do you think that "Summer of Fire" has a story line? Explain.

7. **Connect to Life** In the last column of the chart you made for the Connect to Your Life activity on page 114, record any new information you learned about wilderness fires. What was most surprising to you? Explain.

Literary Analysis

INFORMATIVE NONFICTION

Informative nonfiction is writing that is meant to inform. It provides factual information, and may be organized in various ways. A writer might

- **compare and contrast**
- show **cause and effect**
- use **chronological order**
- present **main ideas** and **details**
- use **spatial order**

or use some combination of these methods.

One key step in understanding a work of nonfiction is to figure out how it is organized. Use these strategies to understand how a piece of writing is organized:

1. Take notes. You may find it helpful to use index cards, writing each main idea on a new card.

2. If the piece is written in chronological order, draw a time line to record events and dates.

3. Make a graphic organizer, such as an outline, to keep track of information.

Activity Make a time line like the one below. Go back through the selection and use the time line to record dates and events.

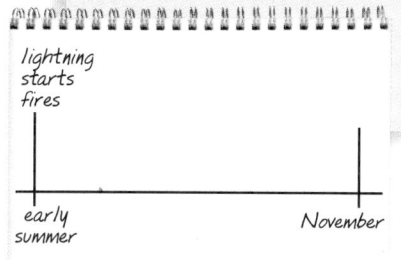

lightning starts fires

early summer   November

Extend Interpretations

6. **The Writer's Style** Possible Responses: Students may say that the article has a story line because one event leads to another, like events in a story's plot. As the fires spread, tension mounts as readers wonder how far the fires will burn, how much damage they will do, and how they will be stopped. On the other hand, students may argue that the article does not have characters other than the generic fire fighters.

7. **Connect to Life** Students should explain why their choices surprised them.

Connect to the Literature

1. **What Do You Think?**
   Possible Responses: Students might respond to the drama of the fire fighters battling the blazes, the fierce winds that whip flames through the park, or merging fires that set forests ablaze and cause rocks to explode.

Comprehension Check
- Most were started by lightning bolts. One big one was started when a woodcutter threw down a lit cigarette.
- Extremely dry conditions, twice the normal number of lightning strikes, and high winds made the fires impossible to stop.
- Rain and snow in September finally put out the fires in November.

 Use Selection Quiz
Unit One Resource Book, p. 58.

Think Critically

2. Although thousands of acres burned, almost two thirds of the park was untouched by fire. The fires did not damage the park's geysers, hot springs, or steam vents. All major park buildings were saved. After the fires, the forests and other areas began to regenerate.

3. Answers will vary. Students should support their opinions. They may agree that fire helps wilderness areas, saying that lightning is a natural force, and that after a forest burns, it regenerates. Or, they may argue that what burns cannot be quickly replaced.

4. Answers will vary. Refer to charts on pages 116–120 for information.

 Use **Reading and Critical Thinking Transparencies**, p. 6, for additional support.

5. Possible Response: The fire fighters needed courage, physical strength and stamina, good communication skills, and training in how to fight forest fires.

Literary Analysis

Informative Nonfiction Time lines should include the dates of major events over the course of the fire.

 Use **Literary Analysis Transparencies**, p. 12, for additional support.

Writing Options

1. Cause-and-Effect Essay Answers will vary, but should include facts from the selection, such as lightning strikes, human carelessness, drought, high winds, and park policy as causes, and widespread burning causing extreme alteration of habitat as effect.

 Use **Writing Transparencies**, p. 36, for additional support.

2. Park Pamphlet Students might wish to include sketches of the park before and after the fire (based on photos and information from the selection) in their pamphlets.

 Use **Writing Transparencies,** p. 51, for additional support.

Activities & Explorations

1. Policy Debate Refer to the Speaking and Listening Mini Lesson on page 120. Both sides should back their positions with facts from the selection.

2. Park Signboard If students are having difficulty thinking of rules, suggest that they consider rules to ensure personal safety, protect the park resources, and avoid disturbances.

Inquiry & Research

Forest Features If there is a forested area near the school or students' homes, students might enjoy studying it, rather than doing research in books or on the Internet. They should bring binoculars and field guides with them if available, and be prepared to make drawings or take photos of the plants and animals they find. They will need to spend time in quiet observation, and should be careful not to disturb the area.

Vocabulary in Action

1. oxygen   4. merge   7. veer
2. ember   5. bear   8. threaten
3. tinder   6. withering   9. canopy
                        10. geyser

Writing Options

1. Cause-and-Effect Essay
What have you learned about forest fires? Write a paragraph that describes some causes and possible effects of fires. To prepare for writing, make a chart or web of your thoughts.

Writing Handbook
See p. R36: Cause and Effect.

2. Park Pamphlet Summarize Lauber's article for a pamphlet that Yellowstone Park might distribute. The pamphlet should teach visitors about the fires of 1988 and their impact.

Activities & Explorations

1. Policy Debate Based on "Summer of Fire," debate the policy of "let natural fires burn." The class should divide into two groups. One group will write up arguments for the policy, while the other will argue against the policy. Next, the two groups should take turns presenting their arguments. ~ **SPEAKING AND LISTENING**

2. Park Signboard Make a list of ten rules visitors should follow to help protect a wilderness area. The list may be general, or it may be specific to an area near you. Create a park signboard to display the rules. ~ **ART**

Inquiry & Research

Forest Features Forests are complicated ecosystems made up of plants and animals of many kinds. Research the ecology of a forest and create a visual display showing the different parts of a forest community. Include a key that identifies each plant and animal.

 More Online: Research Starter www.mcdougallittell.com

Vocabulary in Action

EXERCISE: CONTEXT CLUES On a sheet of paper, write the vocabulary words that best complete the following sentences.

1. To burn, a fire needs both fuel and _____ from the air.
2. A glowing _____ can fly out of one fire and start another one nearby.
3. Small, dry branches burn quickly and are often used as _____ to get a fire started.
4. A group of small fires can _____ to become a large fire.
5. Forced onward by the wind, the fire seemed to _____ down on the building.
6. During one hot, dry summer, the sun shone with a _____ heat.
7. A change in the wind can cause a fire to _____ in a different direction.
8. Wildfires can _____ homes or other valuable property.
9. The branches of the treetops create a _____ over the forest floor.
10. A _____ like Old Faithful shoots out hot water and steam from deep inside the earth.

Building Vocabulary
For an in-depth lesson on context clues, see p. 79.

WORDS TO KNOW	bear	ember	merge	threaten	veer
	canopy	geyser	oxygen	tinder	withering

Teaching Options   ✓ Assessment   **Standardized Test Practice**

ARRANGING EVENTS IN SEQUENTIAL ORDER
Some standardized tests will require students to arrange events in the proper order. Ask students to decide which of these events occurred first.
A. The forest began regenerating.
B. On July 22, a woodcutter threw a lit cigarette away.
C. The fire veered away from Old Faithful, and the area around it was saved.
D. On June 23, lightning started a fire near Shoshone Lake.

Lead students through the process of choosing the earliest event. A could not be the correct answer, as the forest didn't regenerate until the fires were over. B started the fire near Old Faithful, so is earlier than C, but its date is later than D. C happened after B, so is not correct. D is the correct answer—nothing else listed happened prior to it.

Grammar in Context: Active Voice and Passive Voice

In **active-voice** sentences, the subject performs the action. In **passive-voice** sentences, the subject does not perform the action. Instead, the subject is acted upon by outside forces.

> The smoke blackened their faces. (active voice)
> Their faces were blackened by the smoke.
> (passive voice)

Notice the directness of the first sentence. In the second sentence the subject is merely acted upon by outside forces.

Apply to Your Writing: To strengthen your writing, rewrite passive-voice sentences in the active voice. Note the difference between these two sentences:

First draft The wildfires were put out.

Revision Exhausted fire fighters put out the wildfires.

WRITING EXERCISE Rewrite each sentence in the active voice.

Example: *Original* Millions of acres were burned by the fire.

Rewritten The fire raged over millions of acres.

1. Night skies were made red and yellow by the flames.
2. Forest fires are often caused by human carelessness.
3. The geyser could not be harmed by fire.

Connect to the Literature Reread page 118. Locate three powerful active-voice sentences. Notice how effectively the active voice communicates action. Then write five sentences about something dramatic or intense that happened to you. Use the active voice in your sentences.

Grammar Handbook Quick Reference: Parts of Speech, p. R54

"Some of my books are fiction, some are nonfiction, but all are based on what I've seen around me."

Patricia Lauber
born 1924

A Natural Writer Patricia Lauber has said, "I don't think that I 'became' a writer; I think I was born wanting to write." After graduating from Wellesley College, she became a writer and editor. Later she became a consultant to the science resource center of the Smithsonian Institution. Lauber has written more than 70 nonfiction books on topics ranging from the Ice Age to the Congo.

Endless Honors Lauber has won many awards for her writing. In 1983, she received the *Washington Post*/Children's Book Guild Award for her overall contribution to children's nonfiction literature. In 1987 she won a Newbery Honor Award for *Volcano: The Eruption and Healing of Mount St. Helens.*

AUTHOR ACTIVITY
Never a Dull Moment Lauber is often praised for her ability to make factual information dramatic and exciting. Read or look over some other nonfiction works by Patricia Lauber. How does she make science and history interesting? Share your thoughts with your classmates.

Grammar in Context
WRITING EXERCISE
Possible Responses
1. The flames turned the night skies red and yellow.
2. Human carelessness often causes fires.
3. Fire could not harm the geyser.

CONNECT TO THE LITERATURE
Answers will vary, but each of the five sentences should be written in the active voice.

Author Activity
Never a Dull Moment Students might point out that Lauber chooses interesting topics, includes real-life details, and writes as if she were telling a story.

Patricia Lauber
An author best known for her award-winning nonfiction, Patricia Lauber has also written fiction, including a series of books about a dog named Clarence, who likes to watch television, catch burglars, and drink cod-liver oil. The character of Clarence is based on her own dog. The first book of the series is *Clarence, the TV Dog.*

 Grammar
Mini Lesson

ACTIVE AND PASSIVE VOICE Remind students that sentences can be in either the active or passive voice.
Instruction Tell students that though the active voice is often preferable because it conveys action more directly and immediately, the passive voice is useful in the following cases:
• to avoid placing blame
   Passive: A mistake was made.
   Active: You made a mistake.
• to focus attention on the action rather than on the performer of the action

Passive: The fires were extinguished by the end of November.
Active: Snow extinguished the fires by the end of November.
• when the performer of the action is unknown
Passive: The fire was started on July 22.
Active: Someone started the fire on July 22.
Application Have students rewrite each of the following sentences in the active voice.
1. The flames were extinguished by fire fighters.

2. Great damage was inflicted by the fires.
3. Meadows were seen by rangers where there were once forests.
4. The story was written in an exciting way.

 Use **Unit One Resource Book,** p. 56.
Use **Grammar Transparencies and Copymasters,** p. 134.

OVERVIEW

 This selection is included in the **Grade 6 InterActive Reader.**

Objectives

1. understand and appreciate a **short story (Literary Analysis)**
2. understand and identify **conflict** in a short story **(Literary Analysis)**
3. **predicting** the action as the author describes it **(Active Reading)**

Summary

Mako grew up on the island of Bora Bora listening to his grandfather's stories about the shark Tupa—the "ghost of the lagoon." One of the most haunting stories tells how Tupa killed Mako's father. One day Mako hears that the king is offering a reward for Tupa's capture. Both for revenge and for the reward, he decides to kill Tupa. His mother begs him not to and reminds him of what happened to his father. One day while out gathering bananas, Mako and his dog Afa encounter the ghost. When Afa is threatened, Mako fights for him, and in the process, kills Tupa.

Thematic Link

Courage comes from deep inside us, and often is found when one least expects it. Mako shows a great deal of courage in this story as he fights for the life of his beloved dog, Afa. Through this event, he discovers the tremendous bravery and courage he never knew he had.

5-Minute Warm-Up

Daily Language SkillBuilder

Have students **proofread** the display sentences on page 19j and write them correctly. The sentences also appear on Transparency 4 of **Grammar Transparencies and Copymasters.**

"*Over the evening fires, old men told endless tales about the monster.*"

Ghost of the Lagoon

Short Story by ARMSTRONG SPERRY

Connect to Your Life

Brave Deeds Think of someone you know or have read about who has been courageous. What risks did he or she take? What dreams or ideas made this person take these risks?

Build Background

CONNECT TO GEOGRAPHY This story of danger and courage is set on Bora Bora, a small volcanic island in the southern Pacific Ocean. The Polynesians who live there grow coconuts, sugar cane, rice, and tropical fruits. Because it is faster to travel by canoe than it is to walk, the islanders often use canoes to travel from one part of the island to another.

Bora Bora is surrounded by coral reefs, underwater ridges made of a stony material. Coral reefs provide a home and food for many kinds of ocean life, including sharks. Sharks play an important role, eating small animals and plants, and leaving behind food scraps that nourish other reef life. Sharks are famous for their ability to eat almost anything. The largest sharks are at the top of the ocean's food chain, because few other species can survive a run-in with their sharp teeth.

WORDS TO KNOW Vocabulary Preview

expedition	lagoon	reef
harpoon	phosphorus	

Focus Your Reading

LITERARY ANALYSIS CONFLICT A **conflict** is a struggle, a problem, or a difficult decision. Almost every story or play is built around a conflict that the **main character** faces. A struggle between a character and an outside force, such as a dangerous animal, a storm, or another character, is an **external conflict.** A struggle within a character's mind is an **internal conflict.** A character may have an internal conflict when he or she has to make a difficult decision. As you read, pay attention to conflicts, and think about whether they are external or internal.

ACTIVE READING PREDICTING When you read a story and make guesses about what might happen next, you are **predicting.** Predicting means using what you already know to guess what might happen. You can look for clues, such as details about the characters, the setting, and any conflicts that occur, to help you make predictions. You can also use knowledge from your own experience.

READER'S NOTEBOOK As you read, jot down your predictions about what will happen next, and about how the story will end.

 LaserLinks: Background for Reading
Geographical Connection
Science Connection
Art Gallery

LESSON RESOURCES

UNIT ONE RESOURCE BOOK, pp. 59–65

ASSESSMENT
Formal Assessment, pp. 19–20
Teacher's Guide to Assessment and Portfolio Use
Test Generator

SKILLS TRANSPARENCIES AND COPYMASTERS
Literary Analysis
• Conflict, TR 8 (for Cooperative Activity, p. 132)
Reading and Critical Thinking
• Predicting, TR 7 (for Thinking Through Literature, p. 132)

Grammar
• Punctuating Dialogue, CM 120 (for Mini Lesson, p. 128)
• Predicate Nouns and Predicate Adjectives, CM 88 (for Mini Lesson, p. 134)
Vocabulary
• Context Clues: Example, CM 27 (for Mini Lesson, p. 125)

Communications
• The Active Listener, TR 1; Interviewing, TR 9 (for Mini Lesson, p. 129)

INTEGRATED TECHNOLOGY
Audio Library
LaserLinks
• Geographical Connection; Science Connection; Art Gallery. See **Teacher's SourceBook,** p. 11
Internet: Research Starter

Visit our website:
www.mcdougallittell.com

Ghost
of the
Lagoon

by Armstrong Sperry

The island of Bora Bora, where Mako lived, is far away in the South Pacific. It is not a large island—you can paddle around it in a single day—but the main body of it rises straight out of the sea, very high into the air, like a castle. Waterfalls trail down the faces of the cliffs. As you look upward, you see wild goats leaping from crag to crag.

© Cheryl Cooper, 1995.

125

TEACHING THE LITERATURE

Customizing Instruction

Less Proficient Readers
To help students understand the setting of this story, ask them to visualize the island as you read aloud page 125. Then have students look at the illustration on the page and discuss their mental images.

Set a Purpose Ask students to read on to find out more about Mako and his island.

Students Acquiring English
Ask students to share any stories or experiences about islands or the sea. Help them to think about how the culture on this island may be different from their own.

Use **Spanish Study Guide,** pp. 22–24 for additional support.

Gifted and Talented
Talk with students about legends and how oral retellings give us many legends. Have them predict how a legend may change with numerous retellings, and ask them to focus specifically on this legend, using the title and opening paragraph.

Multiple Learning Styles
Auditory Learners
Ask students to listen as you read from page 125. Have them list the sounds they might hear if they were on the island of Bora Bora. Students can share their lists by describing or imitating the sounds they listed.

 Preteaching Vocabulary

CONTEXT CLUES: EXAMPLE
Instruction Point out the list of WORDS TO KNOW. Remind students that they often use experience and the context to help them understand new words. Sometimes authors help readers understand new words by giving an example in the text.
• Read aloud this sentence from page 124: "Bora Bora is surrounded by coral reefs, underwater ridges made of a stony material."
• Ask students what a coral reef is, and how they knew.

• Discuss that the author used a comma to separate the unknown word and its meaning. Sometimes authors will use another sentence to give the meaning, or use key words that can signal an example clue *(especially, for example, like, for instance)*.
Application Ask students to locate the WORDS TO KNOW in the text and determine if the author has used example clues, and if so, what are they?

Use **Unit One Resource Book,** p. 62. Use **Vocabulary Transparencies and Copymasters,** p.27, for more practice.

Literary Analysis `CONFLICT`

Remind students that a conflict is a problem or struggle. What conflict are the people of Bora Bora facing?

Possible Response: The people face the terror of Tupa. He destroys their fishing nets and takes their gifts of food.

Often in short stories, the main character faces a personal conflict. It may be an external or an internal conflict. Ask what conflict(s) they think Mako will face in this story?

Possible Responses: Mako may have to fight Tupa. He may have to overcome his fear of Tupa.

Use **Unit One Resource Book,** p. 61 for more practice.

Active Reading `PREDICTING`

A Tupa is referred to as both a "ghost" and a "monster." Have students predict what they think Tupa really is.

Possible Responses: a ghost, a sea creature, a shark or whale

Ask students to predict what Mako will do. Remind them to use clues from the story.

Possible Response: Mako will find the ghost and capture it so he can collect the reward offered by the king.

Use **Unit One Resource Book,** p. 60 for more practice.

Reading Skills and Strategies: QUESTION

Ask students to think about the legends Mako has heard about Tupa. Have students raise a list of questions that Mako might have about Tupa.

Possible Responses: What is Tupa? Why is he killing people? Where does he live? Does he really exist? Can he really be captured if he is a ghost?

Mako had been born on the very edge of the sea, and most of his waking hours were spent in the waters of the <u>lagoon</u>, which was nearly enclosed by the two outstretched arms of the island. He was very clever with his hands; he had made a <u>harpoon</u> that was as straight as an arrow and tipped with five pointed iron spears. He had made a canoe, hollowing it out of a tree. It wasn't a very big canoe—only a little longer than his own height. It had an outrigger, a sort of balancing pole, fastened to one side to keep the boat from tipping over. The canoe was just large enough to hold Mako and his little dog, Afa. They were great companions, these two.

One evening Mako lay stretched at full length on the pandanus mats, listening to Grandfather's voice. Overhead, stars shone in the dark sky. From far off came the thunder of the surf on the <u>reef</u>.

The old man was speaking of Tupa, the ghost of the lagoon. Ever since the boy could remember, he had heard tales of this terrible monster. Frightened fishermen, returning from the reef at midnight, spoke of the ghost. Over the evening fires, old men told endless tales about the monster.

Tupa seemed to think the lagoon of Bora Bora belonged to him. The natives left presents of food for him out on the reef: a dead goat, a chicken, or a pig. The presents always disappeared mysteriously, but everyone felt sure that it was Tupa who carried them away. Still, in spite of all this food, the nets of the fishermen were torn during the night, the fish stolen. What an appetite Tupa seemed to have!

> "It is bad fortune even to speak of Tupa."

Not many people had ever seen the ghost of the lagoon. Grandfather was one of the few who had.

"What does he really look like, Grandfather?" the boy asked, for the hundredth time.

The old man shook his head solemnly. The light from the cook fire glistened on his white hair. "Tupa lives in the great caves of the reef. He is longer than this house. There is a sail on his back, not large but terrible to see, for it burns with a white fire. Once, when I was fishing beyond the reef at night, I saw him come up right under another canoe—"

"What happened then?" Mako asked. He half rose on one elbow. This was a story he had not heard before.

The old man's voice dropped to a whisper. "Tupa dragged the canoe right under the water—and the water boiled with white flame. The three fishermen in it were never seen again. Fine swimmers they were, too."

Grandfather shook his head. "It is bad fortune even to speak of Tupa. There is evil in his very name."

"But King Opu Nui has offered a reward for his capture," the boy pointed out.

"Thirty acres of fine coconut land, and a sailing canoe as well," said the old man. "But who ever heard of laying hands on a ghost?"

Mako's eyes glistened. "Thirty acres of land and a sailing canoe. How I should love to win that reward!"

Grandfather nodded, but Mako's mother scolded her son for such foolish talk. "Be quiet now, son, and go to sleep. Grandfather has

WORDS TO KNOW	**lagoon** (lə-gōōn′) *n.* a shallow body of water separated from a sea by sandbars or coral reefs
	harpoon (här-pōōn′) *n.* a spearlike weapon used to hunt large fish
	reef (rēf) *n.* a ridge of rocks, sand, or coral near the surface of water

126

Teaching Options

BLOCK SCHEDULING: MANAGING TIME

If your schedule requires that you cover the lesson objectives in a shorter time, use . . .
- Preparing to Read, p. 124
- Thinking Through the Literature, p. 132
- Vocabulary in Action, p. 133
- Grammar in Context, p. 134

If you want to take advantage of longer class time, use . . .
- TE Teaching Options: Preteaching Vocabulary, p. 125; Viewing and Representing, p. 127; Grammar, pp. 128, 134; Speaking and Listening, p. 129; Cross Curricular Link, p. 130; Informal Assessment, p. 131; Spelling, p. 133
- Choices & Challenges, pp. 133–134

Tahitian Woman and Boy (1889), Paul Gauguin. Oil on canvas, 37¼″ × 24¼″, Norton Simon Art Foundation, Pasadena, California. Gift of Mr. Norton Simon, 1976.

Multiple Learning Styles
Visual Learners

1 Have students create drawings of Mako's canoe based on the description in the story. Tell them that an outrigger is a bar that is parallel to and connected to one side of the boat. It helps support and balance the boat. They will want to include Mako and Afa in the boat to help with the scale.

Less Proficient Readers
To ensure that students understand the story, ask the following questions.

- Who is Tupa?
  Answer: He is the ghost, or monster, of the lagoon.
- Why are the people of Bora Bora afraid of Tupa?
  Possible Responses: Tupa tears the fishing nets, he eats animals and fish in the lagoon, and he has killed three fishermen.
- Has anyone ever seen Tupa?
  Answer: Mako's grandfather has.

Students Acquiring English
2 Students may question the inverted order in the sentence, "Fine swimmers they were, too." Explain that this type of construction is used to emphasize how dangerous Tupa is.

3 Point out that *very* is used before the noun *name* here for emphasis.

Gifted and Talented
Have students use the following questions to discuss the story grandfather told Mako about the three fishermen. Why do they think Mako had never heard this particular story before? Why might the author have grandfather tell this story now? How will this story affect Mako? Students may want to jot down responses in their Reader's Notebook prior to the discussion.

 Mini Lesson ## Viewing and Representing

Tahitian Woman and Boy
by Paul Gauguin

ART APPRECIATION
Instruction French artist Paul Gauguin (1848–1903) spent many years in Tahiti—pàrt of the same South Pacific island chain as Bora Bora. In its people, he saw communal values and a harmony with nature—which he felt European civilization lacked. Gauguin was particularly inspired by "primitive" art, with its non-naturalistic colors, flat planes, and strong shapes. He often used colors symbolically, rather than in a realistic way, to express feeling. He appreciated the simple, natural life he saw in the South Pacific and often painted its people as they went about their everyday lives.

Application Ask students how the colors and shapes in the painting make them feel.

Possible Responses: The colors are bright, yet peaceful and soft at the same time. They give a feeling of calm such as Gauguin probably felt when he was in the South Pacific. The shapes are strong and simple and give a feeling of solid relationships between the people in the painting.

Reading Skills and Strategies: CONNECT

Have students think about the relationship Mako has with Afa. Ask them to think of a pet, friend, or sibling with whom they share a similar relationship. Ask them to use their knowledge of this relationship to discuss how Mako feels about Afa.

Literary Analysis: PLOT

 Explain to students that the large initial letter marks a division in the organization of the story. Information given up to this point will lead to further action. Ask students to recall what has happened in the story so far.

Possible Response: The setting has been established, grandfather has told the legend of Mako's father, Mako has claimed he will seek revenge on Tupa.

Use **Literary Analysis Transparencies,** p. 5, for additional support.

Active Reading PREDICTING

Explain to students that good readers continue making and adjusting their predictions as they read. Ask students to adjust their previous predictions.

Possible Responses: Mako will meet up with Tupa. He will fight Tupa.

Use **Reading and Critical Thinking Transparencies,** p. 7, for additional support.

Reading Skills and Strategies: VISUALIZE

B Remind students that authors often use "sight" words to help the reader develop a mental image. Ask students to identify which detail words help them to visualize this scene.

Answers: broad green blades, golden ripe, nest of soft leaves, swift slash

Teaching Options

---

told you that it is bad fortune to speak of Tupa. Alas, how well we have learned that lesson! Your father—" She stopped herself.

"What of my father?" the boy asked quickly. And now he sat up straight on the mats.

"Tell him, Grandfather," his mother whispered.

The old man cleared his throat and poked at the fire. A little shower of sparks whirled up into the darkness.

"Your father," he explained gently, "was one of the three fishermen in the canoe that Tupa destroyed." His words fell upon the air like stones dropped into a deep well.

Mako shivered. He brushed back the hair from his damp forehead. Then he squared his shoulders and cried fiercely, "I shall slay Tupa and win the king's reward!" He rose to his knees, his slim body tense, his eyes flashing in the firelight.

"Hush!" his mother said. "Go to sleep now. Enough of such foolish talk. Would you bring trouble upon us all?"

Mako lay down again upon the mats. He rolled over on his side and closed his eyes, but sleep was long in coming.

The palm trees whispered above the dark lagoon, and far out on the reef the sea thundered.

The boy was slow to wake up the next morning. The ghost of Tupa had played through his dreams, making him restless. And so it was almost noon before Mako sat up on the mats and stretched himself. He called Afa, and the boy and his dog ran down to the lagoon for their morning swim.

Perhaps ghosts were only old men's stories, anyway!

When they returned to the house, wide-awake and hungry, Mako's mother had food ready and waiting.

"These are the last of our bananas," she told him. "I wish you would paddle out to the reef this afternoon and bring back a new bunch."

The boy agreed eagerly. Nothing pleased him more than such an errand, which would take him to a little island on the outer reef, half a mile from shore. It was one of Mako's favorite playgrounds, and there bananas and oranges grew in great plenty.

"Come, Afa," he called, gulping the last mouthful. "We're going on an expedition." He picked up his long-bladed knife and seized his spear. A minute later, he dashed across the white sand, where his canoe was drawn up beyond the water's reach.

Afa barked at his heels. He was all white except for a black spot over each eye. Wherever Mako went, there went Afa also. Now the little dog leaped into the bow of the canoe, his tail wagging with delight. The boy shoved the canoe into the water and climbed aboard. Then, picking up his paddle, he thrust it into the water. The canoe shot ahead. Its sharp bow cut through the green water of the lagoon like a knife through cheese. And so clear was the water that Mako could see the coral gardens, forty feet below him, growing in the sand. The shadow of the canoe moved over them.

A school of fish swept by like silver arrows. He saw scarlet rock cod with ruby eyes and the head of a conger eel peering out from a cavern in the coral. The boy thought suddenly of Tupa, ghost of the lagoon. On such a bright day it was hard to believe in ghosts of any

WORDS
TO
KNOW

expedition (ĕk′spĭ-dĭsh′ən) *n.* a journey with a goal or purpose

---

Mini Lesson Grammar

PUNCTUATING DIALOGUE
Remind students that dialogue must be punctuated with quotation marks. Commas, periods, exclamation points, and question marks separate explanatory words.

Instruction Point out the highlighted sentence on this page and the use of quotation marks and commas.

Exercises Have students rewrite these sentences adding quotation marks and other punctuation where necessary.

1. Mako exclaimed I'll defeat you one day Tupa
2. Afa Mako shouted Come here you silly dog

3. These bananas look good Mako announced I will take them home
4. This is a great net murmured Mako proudly

Use **Grammar Transparencies and Copymasters,** p. 120.

Use McDougal Littell's ***Language Network,*** Chapter 9, for more instruction and practice in punctuating dialogue.

sort. The fierce sunlight drove away all thought of them. Perhaps ghosts were only old men's stories, anyway!

Mako's eyes came to rest upon his spear—the spear that he had made with his own hands—the spear that was as straight and true as an arrow. He remembered his vow of the night before. Could a ghost be killed with a spear? Some night, when all the village was sleeping, Mako swore to himself that he would find out! He would paddle out to the reef and challenge Tupa! Perhaps tonight. Why not? He caught his breath at the thought. A shiver ran down his back. His hands were tense on the paddle.

As the canoe drew away from shore, the boy saw the coral reef that, above all others, had always interested him. It was of white coral—a long slim shape that rose slightly above the surface of the water. It looked very much like a shark. There was a ridge on the back that the boy could pretend was a dorsal fin, while up near one end were two dark holes that looked like eyes!

 Times without number the boy had practiced spearing this make-believe shark, aiming always for the eyes, the most vulnerable spot. So true and straight had his aim become that the spear would pass right into the eyeholes without even touching the sides of the coral. Mako had named the coral reef Tupa.

This morning, as he paddled past it, he shook his fist and called, "Ho, Mister Tupa! Just wait till I get my bananas. When I come back, I'll make short work of you!"

Afa followed his master's words with a sharp bark. He knew Mako was excited about something.

The bow of the canoe touched the sand of the little island where the bananas grew. Afa leaped ashore and ran barking into the jungle, now on this trail, now on that. Clouds of sea birds whirled from their nests into the air with angry cries.

Mako climbed into the shallow water, waded ashore, and pulled his canoe up on the beach. Then, picking up his banana knife, he followed Afa. In the jungle the light was so dense and green that the boy felt as if he were moving underwater. Ferns grew higher than his head. The branches of the trees formed a green roof over him. A flock of parakeets fled on swift wings. Somewhere a wild pig crashed through the undergrowth while Afa dashed away in pursuit. Mako paused anxiously. Armed only with his banana knife, he had no desire to meet the wild pig. The pig, it seemed, had no desire to meet him, either.

Then, ahead of him, the boy saw the broad green blades of a banana tree. A bunch of bananas, golden ripe, was growing out of the top.

At the foot of the tree he made a nest of soft leaves for the bunch to fall upon. In this way the fruit wouldn't be crushed. Then with a swift slash of his blade he cut the stem. The bananas fell to the earth with a dull thud. He found two more bunches.

Then he thought, "I might as well get some oranges while I'm here. Those little rusty ones are sweeter than any that grow on Bora Bora."

So he set about making a net out of palm leaves to carry the oranges. As he worked, his swift fingers moving in and out among the strong green leaves, he could hear Afa's excited barks off in the jungle. That was just like Afa, always barking at something: a bird, a fish, a wild pig. He never caught anything, either. Still, no boy ever had a finer companion.

The palm net took longer to make than Mako had realized. By the time it was finished

Students Acquiring English

1 Help students distinguish between the word *bow* (bow) meaning "the front of a boat," its homophone (to bend at the waist as a salute or show of respect), and its homograms (e.g., a weapon used to shoot arrows).

2 Ask students to try to figure out the meaning of "times without number." (too many times to count)

Less Proficient Readers

Ask students to describe what Mako learned from his grandfather's story and what he vowed on hearing it.

Answer: Mako's father was one of the three fishermen killed by Tupa. Mako vowed to kill Tupa.

Set a Purpose Tell students to look for a conflict as they read.

Multiple Learning Styles
Kinesthetic and Interpersonal Learners

Have students act out Mako pretending to spear the make-believe shark. They may want to discuss how they think Mako feels when he plays this game. Ask them to predict how this game may be helpful to Mako later.

Gifted and Talented

Have students look up the word *mako* in a dictionary. (It is a kind of shark, and the word comes from the Maori language.) Have them discuss why they think the author might have given the boy in this story the name *Mako.*

 Speaking and Listening

ORAL HISTORY

Explain to students that oral history is different from written history in that it is communicated through speaking rather than writing. Oral histories, such as the stories grandfather tells Mako, are an important part of the way people pass on knowledge and traditions from one generation to the next.

Prepare Ask students to interview an older family member. Have them prepare questions prior to the interview. Students may want to work in small groups to brainstorm and finalize the questions.

During the interview, students should listen carefully, taking notes if they choose.

Present After the interviews have been conducted, students will retell their elder's story to the class. Have them think about the mode of story telling as they present their story. They may want to look back at the way Mako's grandfather tells his stories.

Use **Communications Transparencies and Copymasters,** pp. 1, 9, for additional support.

 This activity is particularly well suited for longer class periods.

Active Reading | PREDICTING

Ask students to predict how the story will end.

Possible Responses: The great white shark will kill Afa; Mako will fight the shark and rescue Afa; Mako will kill Tupa.

Literary Analysis: CONFLICT

A Remind students that an internal conflict is a struggle within a character's mind.

What is the internal conflict Mako is facing?

Possible Response: Mako fears losing Afa and fears that Tupa will kill him. He has to decide if he is willing to risk his life to fight for Afa.

B Remind students that an external conflict is a struggle between a character and an outside force.

What is the external conflict Mako is facing?

Answer: Mako is fighting with the white shark, Tupa. He is fighting for his life and the life of his dog, Afa.

How does Mako resolve his conflicts, both internal and external, in this story?

Answers: Mako resolves the internal conflict by deciding to try to save Afa and fight Tupa. He resolves the external conflict by killing Tupa in the fight.

Reading Skills and Strategies: EVALUATE

Ask students to analyze Mako's decision. Do they agree with him? Why or why not? Have students write responses in their Reader's Notebooks. Students may meet in small groups to discuss their responses.

and filled with oranges, the jungle was dark and gloomy. Night comes quickly and without warning in the islands of the tropics.

Mako carried the fruit down to the shore and loaded it into the canoe. Then he whistled to Afa. The dog came bounding out of the bush, wagging his tail.

"Hurry!" Mako scolded. "We won't be home before the dark comes."

The little dog leaped into the bow of the canoe, and Mako came aboard. Night seemed to rise up from the surface of the water and swallow them. On the distant shore of Bora Bora, cook fires were being lighted. The first star twinkled just over the dark mountains. Mako dug his paddle into the water, and the canoe leaped ahead.

1 The dark water was alive with phosphorus. The bow of the canoe seemed to cut through a pale liquid fire. Each dip of the paddle trailed streamers of light. As the canoe approached the coral reef, the boy called, "Ho, Tupa! It's too late tonight to teach you your lesson. But I'll come back tomorrow." The coral shark glistened in the darkness.

And then, suddenly, Mako's breath caught in his throat. His hands felt weak. Just beyond the fin of the coral Tupa, there was another fin—a huge one. It had never been there before. And—could he believe his eyes? It was moving.

The boy stopped paddling. He dashed his hand across his eyes. Afa began to bark furiously. The great white fin, shaped like a small sail, glowed with phosphorescent light. Then Mako knew. Here was Tupa—the real Tupa—ghost of the lagoon!

2 His knees felt weak. He tried to cry out, but his voice died in his throat. The great shark

One flip of

that tail could overturn

the canoe.

was circling slowly around the canoe. With each circle, it moved closer and closer. Now the boy could see the phosphorescent glow of the great shark's sides. As it moved in closer, he saw the yellow eyes, the gill slits in its throat.

Afa leaped from one side of the canoe to the other. In sudden anger Mako leaned forward to grab the dog and shake him soundly. Afa wriggled out of his grasp as Mako tried to catch him, and the shift in weight tipped the canoe on one side. The outrigger rose from the water. In another second they would be overboard. The boy threw his weight over quickly to balance the canoe, but with a loud splash Afa fell over into the dark water.

Mako stared after him in dismay. The little dog, instead of swimming back to the canoe, had headed for the distant shore. And there was the great white shark—very near.

"Afa! Afa! Come back! Come quickly!" Mako shouted.

The little dog turned back toward the canoe. He was swimming with all his strength. Mako leaned forward. Could Afa make it? Swiftly the boy seized his spear. Bracing himself, he stood upright. There was no weakness in him now. His dog, his companion, was in danger of instant death.

Afa was swimming desperately to reach the canoe. The white shark had paused in his circling to gather speed for the attack. Mako raised his arm, took aim. In that instant the shark charged. Mako's arm flashed forward. All his strength was behind that thrust. The spear drove straight and true, right into the great shark's eye. Mad with pain and rage, Tupa whipped about, lashing the water in fury.

WORDS TO KNOW | **phosphorus** (fŏs'fər-əs) *n.* a substance that glows with a yellowish or white light

130

Cross Curricular Link **Science**

CORAL REEFS A coral reef is an underwater ridge of stone built up by the skeletons of many tiny sea animals. These reefs provide homes and food to many ocean creatures. These ridges form only in tropical or subtropical waters, where the surface waters are always warm.

There are three types of coral reefs: fringing reefs, which extend from the shore with little or no water between reef and shore; barrier reefs, which occur offshore, with a channel between reef and land; and atolls, which are typically a ring of coral islands around a shallow lagoon.

Bora Bora is a small island, covering less than 15 square miles (39 sq. km). It is in the South Pacific, and is surrounded by coral reefs.

The world's largest coral reef is the Great Barrier Reef, stretching for more than 1,250 miles (2,000 km) along Australia's northeastern coast. This reef is actually a chain of coral reefs in the Coral Sea. The reef is home to hundreds of species of coral in a beautiful range of colors and shapes. The reef also supports larger water animals, including about two thousand species of fish.

The canoe rocked back and forth. Mako struggled to keep his balance as he drew back the spear by the cord fastened to his wrist.

He bent over to seize Afa and drag him aboard. Then he stood up, not a moment too soon. Once again the shark charged. Once again Mako threw his spear, this time at the other eye. The spear found its mark. Blinded and weak from loss of blood, Tupa rolled to the surface, turned slightly on his side. Was he dead?

Mako knew how clever sharks could be, and he was taking no chances. Scarcely daring to breathe, he paddled toward the still body. He saw the faintest motion of the great tail. The shark was still alive. The boy knew that one flip of that tail could overturn the canoe and send him and Afa into the water, where Tupa could destroy them.

Swiftly, yet calmly, Mako stood upright and braced himself firmly. Then, murmuring a silent prayer to the shark god, he threw his spear for the last time. Downward, swift as sound, the spear plunged into a white shoulder.

Peering over the side of the canoe, Mako could see the great fish turn over far below the surface. Then slowly, slowly, the great shark rose to the surface of the lagoon. There he floated, half on one side.

Tupa was dead.

Mako flung back his head and shouted for joy. Hitching a strong line about the shark's tail,

Tahitian Landscape (1891), Paul Gauguin. The Minneapolis Institute of Arts.

the boy began to paddle toward the shore of Bora Bora. The dorsal fin, burning with the white fire of phosphorus, trailed after the canoe.

Men were running down the beaches of Bora Bora, shouting as they leaped into their canoes and put out across the lagoon. Their cries reached the boy's ears across the water.

"It is Tupa—ghost of the lagoon," he heard them shout. "Mako has killed him!"

That night, as the tired boy lay on the pandanus mats listening to the distant thunder of the sea, he heard Grandfather singing a new song. It was the song which would be sung the next day at the feast which King Opu Nui would give in Mako's honor. The boy saw his mother bending over the cook fire. The stars leaned close, winking like friendly eyes. Grandfather's voice reached him now from a great distance, "Thirty acres of land and a sailing canoe. . . ." ❖

Customizing Instruction

Less Proficient Readers
Make sure students understand Mako's conflicts and the ways in which they were resolved. Ask the following questions:
• Why did Mako attack Tupa?
  Answer: He decided to risk his life to save the life of his dog.
• What was the outcome of the fight?
  Answer: Mako kills Tupa, saves Afa, and returns home a hero.

Gifted and Talented
1 The word *phosphorus* comes from a Greek word meaning "bringer of light." Ask students to research and discuss phosphorescence and how it affected this story.
Possible Response: The element phosphorus is very flammable and can ignite spontaneously. Small sea creatures that give off light are described as phosphorescent. Sharks do not give off light. Tupa's fin was glowing, so he must have picked up the light from other sea life or reflected moonlight. It affects the story because the light is what allows Mako to see Tupa before he is close enough to surprise Mako. It gives Mako time to think about the encounter and to realize that Tupa is really a shark, not a ghost. The eerie, white glow is also probably why the shark is referred to as a ghost.

Students Acquiring English
2 Help students understand that "his voice died in his throat" is an example of personification, a figure of speech that assigns human traits to an object or idea. Make sure students understand that Mako is unable to cry out because he is so frightened.

Assessment **Informal Assessment**

WRITING A SUMMARY Students can use a variety of strategies to comprehend selections, such as paraphrasing and summarizing text to recall, inform, or organize ideas.
Ask students to recall the major events in this story. Write them on the board. Have students meet in small groups to organize these major events in sequential order. With a partner, have students orally retell the story using the group sequenced events. Ask students to individually write a summary of the story, using the oral retellings and the events generated as the basis for the summary.

RUBRICS
3 Full Accomplishment Response shows a full understanding of the story and its plot development.
2 Substantial Accomplishment Response states the central plot events but one or two events are given out of sequence.
1 Little or Partial Accomplishment Response omits major events in the story and does not relate events in sequential order.

Connect to the Literature

1. What Do You Think?
Possible Responses: It was exciting that Mako had a chance to kill Tupa. It was scary when Mako's dog, Afa, fell into the water.

Comprehension Check
• Mako lives on Bora Bora, an island in the South Pacific.
• When Mako returns from collecting bananas, he meets, fights, and kills Tupa.
• Mako is rewarded with thirty acres and a canoe.

 Use Selection Quiz
Unit One Resource Book, p. 65.

Think Critically

2. Possible Response: When Mako realized Tupa was swimming toward him, he probably felt scared. He was probably also excited at the chance to kill the shark.

3. Answers will vary.

 Use **Reading and Critical Thinking Transparencies,** p. 7, for additional support.

4. Possible Responses: Mako would still have tried to kill Tupa to avenge his father's death. Or, without the immediate threat to Afa, Mako would have been too frightened of Tupa to try to kill him.

5. Possible Responses: The desire to save Afa made Mako brave and strong. Mako had practiced spearing on the reef. Mako wanted to avenge his father's death.

Literary Analysis

Conflict Students' responses should reflect the conflicts evident in the story. Students should also be able to tell how each conflict fits in the plot of the story.

 Use **Literary Analysis Transparencies,** p. 8, for additional support.

Connect to the Literature

1. What Do You Think?
What was your reaction to Mako's fight with Tupa?

Comprehension Check
• Where does Mako live?
• What happens when Mako returns from collecting bananas?
• What is Mako's reward?

Think Critically

2. How do you think Mako felt when he realized that Tupa was swimming toward him?

3. **ACTIVE READING** **PREDICTING** Look at the predictions you wrote in your **READER'S NOTEBOOK.** How well do they match the actual events in the story?

4. What if Mako's dog were not in danger? Do you think Mako still would have tried to kill Tupa? Why or why not?

5. Why do you think Mako is able to defeat Tupa?

THINK ABOUT
• his reasons for fighting Tupa
• his abilities and experience
• the histories of both Tupa and Mako

Extend Interpretations

6. Critic's Corner Theresa Sullivan, a member of the student board that reviewed the stories in this book, says, "I liked how this story was scary and not scary at the same time." Do you agree with her comment? Explain.

7. Connect to Life Do you think that you could act as courageously as Mako does? In what kind of situation would you take such a great risk?

Literary Analysis

CONFLICT Generally, a story is built around a main **conflict,** a problem or struggle that involves two or more forces. A conflict may be external, taking place between a character and some outside force. Mako's fight with Tupa is an **external conflict.** A conflict may also be internal, taking place within a character's mind. Mako's decision about whether to face the shark or try to row quickly away is an **internal conflict.** A story may have a number of conflicts.

Cooperative Learning Activity
In a small group, look through "Ghost of the Lagoon" and jot down as many conflicts as you can find. Afterward, discuss how these conflicts helped the plot of the story move forward. Share your ideas with the class.

REVIEW **PLOT** The set of actions and events that make up a story is called the **plot.** Events in the plot are usually driven by a main conflict and the attempts to resolve it.

Extend Interpretations

6. Critic's Corner Possible Responses: Yes, it was scary when Mako and Tupa were attacking each other; but on the other hand it was not scary because you could guess Mako would be okay in the end. No, it was scary all the way through because you could never be sure that both Mako and Afa would be all right.

7. Connect to Life Anyone would hope that they could be as courageous as Mako is in this story. Someone might take such a great risk if a person or animal they loved was in danger.

Writing Options

1. Royal Tribute Write the tribute that King Opu Nui might give Mako at the feast. Which of Mako's accomplishments and traits will he mention?

2. Battle Narrative Imagine that Mako is now an old man. Write a narrative account, from Mako's point of view, relating the story of his battle with Tupa. Keep this account in your **Working Portfolio.**

Writing Handbook
See page R33: Narrative Writing.

Activities & Explorations

1. Travel Brochure Create a travel brochure advertising Bora Bora. Use details

from the story as well as information from a library to describe the island.
~ VIEWING AND REPRESENTING

2. Dramatic Scene In a group of three, assign the roles of Mako, his father, and his grandfather. Make up a scene in which they discuss how Tupa affected each of their lives. ~ **PERFORMING**

Inquiry & Research

Jaws People are fascinated— and frightened—by sharks. These mysterious animals have swum the ocean waters for hundreds of millions of years. Find out more about sharks, and share your information in an oral report.

More Online: Research Starter
www.mcdougallittell.com

Art Connection

Tropical Scenes French artist Paul Gauguin fell in love with Tahiti and spent his last years there. Look again at the painting *Tahitian Woman and Boy* on page 127. How well do you think the portrait fits the characters of Mako and his mother?

Vocabulary and Spelling

EXERCISE A: WORD MEANING Write the Word to Know that best fits each definition.

1. a ridge of rocks or coral
2. a glowing substance
3. a shallow body of water
4. a journey
5. a spearlike weapon

EXERCISE B: PROOFREADING PRACTICE The long vowel sound o͞o is most often spelled *oo*. Sometimes, however, it is spelled *ue, ew, ou,* or *oe.* Rewrite the following sentences using the correct spelling of each boldfaced word.

1. Would **yoo** like to swim in the **lagoun?**
2. When he **thrue** the **harpewn,** his aim was **troo.**
3. She **knou** how to guide the **canoo thrue** the reef.

Spelling Handbook p. R86

WORDS TO KNOW	expedition	harpoon	lagoon	phosphorus	reef

 Mini Lesson Spelling

THE LONG o͞o

Instruction Tell students that the vowel sound o͞o is most often spelled *oo* but is sometimes spelled other ways, including *ue* and *ew.*

- Demonstrate the sound with these examples from the selection: *lagoon, harpoon, food.*
- Point out to students that not all words with *oo* —for example, *look* and *stood*—are pronounced with the long vowel sound.

Exercise Ask students to think of other words with the long o͞o sound. Share words with oth-

ers in small groups, and add words to their personal word lists.

Exercise Ask students to write a description of Bora Bora using words from their lists.

 Use **Unit One Resource Book,** p. 64.

Writing Options

1. Royal Tribute Suggest that students reread the last few paragraphs of the story. You might want to discuss what usually goes into a tribute. Students should mention Mako's accomplishments, such as killing Tupa and saving the village from the terror, and the traits Mako exhibited, such as courage and determination.

2. Battle Narrative Remind students that in a narrative account they would pretend to be Mako and would tell the story in the first person. Students may want to reread pages 130–131 to recall the details of Mako's battle with Tupa.

Activities & Explorations

1. Travel Brochure Students might benefit from looking at actual travel brochures, which could serve as a model for format, style, and kinds of information to be included.

2. Dramatic Scene Students should reread the story to familiarize themselves with the character they have been assigned. Have them observe that character's point of view during the rereading. Allow students time to practice their scene prior to the performance.

Use **Communications Transparencies and Copymasters,** p. 13, for additional support.

Inquiry & Research

Jaws Students may need time and support in the library, online, or with a CD-ROM encyclopedia.

Art Connection

Tropical Scenes Students may think the characters in Gauguin's painting look a lot like Mako and his mother due to their physical attributes. Students may find their mental pictures of Mako and his mother do not look like the painting, and may choose to describe or draw their own visualizations of them.

Vocabulary and Spelling

EXERCISE A: 1. reef, **2.** phosphorus, **3.** lagoon, **4.** expedition, **5.** harpoon
EXERCISE B: 1. you, lagoon; **2.** threw, harpoon, true; **3.** knew, canoe, through

Grammar in Context

Author Activity

South Seas Sights Students will need to visit the school or public library to gather books written and illustrated by Armstrong Sperry.

Armstrong Sperry

Armstrong Sperry was educated at the Yale School of Fine Arts and the New York Art Students League before studying art in Paris. He started his career in publishing as an illustrator before combining his artistic talent with writing children's books. He has illustrated almost all of his numerous books and stories.

Grammar in Context: Predicate Nouns and Predicate Adjectives

Predicate nouns and predicate adjectives tell more about the subject. Sentences with predicate nouns and adjectives do not express action. Instead, a **predicate noun** follows a linking verb and renames the subject. A **predicate adjective** follows a **linking verb** and describes the subject. Notice the predicate noun, shown in red, and predicate adjective, in orange.

> In his imagination, the coral <u>became</u> a killer shark.
> His hands <u>were</u> tense on the paddle.

Here are some common linking verbs:
am, are, is, was, were, been, grow, become, remains, feels, tastes, smells, looks, sounds, seems, appears

WRITING EXERCISE Write each subject below. Add a linking verb and a predicate adjective that describes the subject.

Example: *Original* Little Afa

Rewritten Little Afa seems brave.

1. The oranges
2. Mako's grandfather

Write each subject below. Add a linking verb and a predicate noun that renames the subject.

Example: *Original* Fear

Rewritten Fear is an enemy.

3. The jungle
4. Opu Nui

"The world which belongs to the artist is a world to which few scientists possess the key."

Armstrong Sperry
1897–1976

A World Traveler Armstrong Sperry once said that a writer "should tell his story clearly, in a supple prose that leaves his reader—young or old—wondering 'What happens next?'" Sperry had an advantage in writing stories with exciting plots—he traveled widely in Europe, North America, and the West Indies. Inspired by his grandfather's stories of visits to the South Pacific, Sperry spent two years in French Polynesia. There he learned French and Tahitian and gathered information for many of his books.

Literary Adventures Sperry's talent for writing adventure stories set in exotic places led to the success of his book *Call It Courage*. This novel, based on a legend of the South Pacific, was awarded the Newbery Medal in 1941. Sperry's book *The Rain Forest* received the Boys' Clubs of America Junior Book Award in 1949.

AUTHOR ACTIVITY
South Seas Sights Armstrong Sperry was not only a writer but an artist. In fact, he illustrated nearly all of his many books and stories. Find one of Sperry's books that includes his own drawings of the South Pacific. How do these images compare with the setting he describes in "Ghost of the Lagoon"? Present your findings to the class.

Teaching Options

Mini Lesson **Grammar**

PREDICATE NOUNS AND PREDICATE ADJECTIVES Remind students that predicate nouns and predicate adjectives follow a verb and are part of the predicate. In sentences with predicate nouns or adjectives, the verb is a linking verb. The predicate noun or predicate adjective renames or describes the subject.
Instruction Write the following sentences on the chalkboard:
Mako felt courageous.
Afa was a little, white, dog.
Ask students to identify the predicate noun

and/or predicate adjective in each sentence. (*courageous, dog*)
Exercises Have students make three columns on their papers: Subject, Linking verb, and Predicate noun/adjective. Have them find these parts in each sentence below and write them in the proper columns. After the predicate word, write *n* or *adj* to indicate whether it is a noun or an adjective. Include helping verbs in the linking verb column.
1. Life on Bora Bora seems peaceful.
2. Mako's grandfather was a gentle old man.

3. Mako's expedition sounds like fun.
4. Tupa was a great white shark.
5. Mako became a hero.

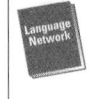 Use **Unit One Resource Book**, p. 63.
Use **Grammar Transparencies and Copymasters**, p. 88, for more practice.

Use McDougal Littell's ***Language Network,*** Chapter 5, for more instruction and practice in predicate nouns and predicate adjectives.

PREPARING to *Read*

from The Fun of It

Autobiography by AMELIA EARHART

"I was flying at about 12,000 feet. And then something happened . . ."

Connect to Your Life

Flying! What exciting goal would you like to accomplish in your lifetime? What would be good preparation for accomplishing this dream?

Build Background

CONNECT TO **HISTORY** Amelia Earhart was a pioneer in aviation, or flight. Wilbur and Orville Wright had made the first successful flight in 1903. In 1908, Earhart saw an airplane for the first time. She began watching military pilots practice flying. Later, she took flying lessons from Neta Snook. Earhart passed her pilot's test in 1922. Although Earhart had other jobs, she flew whenever possible. Soon she had set an unofficial record for women by flying to 14,000 feet—nearly three miles high.

In June 1928, Earhart became the first woman to fly across the Atlantic Ocean, as a passenger. Four years later she made her famous solo flight across the Atlantic Ocean. Earhart went on to make other flights that were firsts for both men and women.

In 1937, Earhart set a new goal: to become the first woman to fly around the world. During the flight, she, her plane, and her navigator disappeared. To this day, Earhart remains famous for her courage, her achievements, and the mystery surrounding her last flight.

WORDS TO KNOW **Vocabulary Preview**

accumulate	faculty	hospitality	sufficient
altitude	fleeting	margin	vessel
extent	fluctuation		

Focus Your Reading

LITERARY ANALYSIS **AUTOBIOGRAPHY**

An **autobiography** is the story of a person's life, told by that person. Listen for Earhart's voice:

And then something happened that has never occurred in my twelve years of flying. The altimeter . . . failed.

Only Earhart would know that her altimeter, a device that shows how high the plane is flying, had never failed before. As you read, notice other details that could only be told by someone with firsthand experience.

ACTIVE READING **IDENTIFYING THE AUTHOR'S PURPOSE**

An **author's purpose** is his or her reason for creating a particular work. The purpose may be to **entertain,** to **inform,** to **explain,** to **express an opinion,** or to **persuade** readers to do or believe something. An author may have more than one purpose, but usually one is the most important.

READER'S NOTEBOOK As you read, look for clues to Earhart's purpose for writing. Identify at least three sentences that show the author's purpose, and record them. Make sure to write down the purpose in each case.

OVERVIEW

Objectives
1. understand and appreciate an **autobiography (Literary Analysis)**
2. understand **author's purpose** in an autobiography **(Active Reading)**
3. use the reading strategy of **identifying** to help understand the author's purpose **(Active Reading)**

Summary
Amelia Earhart describes her solo flight across the Atlantic, beginning with her successful takeoff from the coast of Newfoundland and ending with her unplanned but safe landing in a pasture in Northern Ireland. During the long night, she must deal with broken instruments, ice on the plane's wings, storms, fog, and a fire in the exhaust system.

Thematic Link
Amelia Earhart embodies courage in action as she makes her solo flight across the Atlantic, putting thoughts of herself behind concern for her plane and her mission.

5-Minute Warm-Up

Daily Language SkillBuilder

Have students **proofread** the display sentences on page 19j and write them correctly. The sentences also appear on Transparency 4 of **Grammar Transparencies and Copymasters.**

Mini Lesson **Preteaching Vocabulary**

If you would like to preteach the WORDS TO KNOW for this selection, use the Mini Lesson, p. 136.

LESSON RESOURCES

Reading and Analyzing

Active Reading

IDENTIFYING AUTHOR'S PURPOSE

Let students know that being aware of the author's purpose helps them read more critically. Ask students to choose a sentence on this page that illustrates the author's purpose, and to write it and the purpose in their Reader's Notebooks.

Possible Response: "At twelve minutes after seven, I gave her the gun." The author's main purpose is to inform. Students may also say that her purpose is to entertain, because she has used action to get the reader's attention and interest.

 Use **Unit One Resource Book,** p.67 for more practice.

Literary Analysis AUTOBIOGRAPHY

Remind students that this is a factual account written by the narrator. Ask students why they think Earhart called her book *The Fun of It.*

Possible Response: She enjoyed flying.

 Use **Unit One Resource Book,** p.68 for more practice.

Literary Analysis: NARRATIVE NONFICTION

Let students know that narrative nonfiction deals with real people and events, but it is written to be read and experienced like fiction. Ask students to notice details on this page that make it seem like fiction.

Possible Responses: She jumps right into the events without preliminaries; she creates suspense when she says that something happened that had never happened before.

from

(Right) Amelia Earhart in the cockpit of her plane. (Above) Earhart made her historic solo flight across the Atlantic in this red Lockheed Vega.

136

Teaching Options

 Preteaching Vocabulary

SYNONYMS Remind students to draw on their knowledge of words to bring meaning to other words in context.

Instruction Tell students they will sometimes find a word's meaning by reading a synonym in the same sentence or one near it. For example: I was looking for a boat. I spotted one <u>vessel</u> in the distance.

You can figure out the meaning of the word *vessel* from knowing the word *boat.*

Exercises Have students write the sentences and circle the synonym of the underlined word.

1. My <u>course</u> put me on a route eastward across the Atlantic. (route)
2. I had a <u>fleeting</u> worry about the plane, but it was passing. (passing)
3. I needed to <u>accumulate</u>, or gather, plenty of money to finance the trip. (gather)
4. It was difficult to find a good <u>altitude</u>—each height had its own problems. (height)

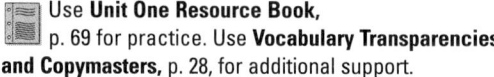 Use **Unit One Resource Book,** p. 69 for practice. Use **Vocabulary Transparencies and Copymasters,** p. 28, for additional support.

The FUN of It

by Amelia Earhart

The southwest wind was nearly right for the runway. At twelve minutes after seven, I gave her the gun. The plane gathered speed, and despite the heavy load rose easily.

A minute later I was headed out to sea.

For several hours there was fair weather with a lingering sunset. And then the moon came up over a low bank of clouds. For those first hours I was flying at about 12,000 feet. And then something happened that has never occurred in my twelve years of flying. The altimeter,[1] the instrument which records height above ground, failed. Suddenly the hands swung around the dial uselessly and I knew the instrument was out of commission for the rest of the flight.

---

1. altimeter (ăl-tĭm′ĭ-tər).

137

About 11:30, the moon disappeared behind some clouds, and I ran into rather a severe storm with lightning, and I was considerably buffeted about, and with difficulty held my course. In fact, I probably got off my course at this point to some <u>extent</u> because it was very rough. This lasted for at least an hour. Then I flew on in calmer weather though in the midst of clouds. Once I saw the moon for a <u>fleeting</u> instant and thought I could pull out on top of the clouds, so I climbed for half an hour when suddenly I realized I was picking up ice.

I knew by the climb of the ship which was not as fast as usual that it was <u>accumulating</u> a weight of ice. Then I saw slush on the windowpane. In addition, my tachometer,[2] the instrument which registers revolutions per minute of the motor, picked up ice and spun around the dial.

In such a situation one has to get into warmer air, so I went down hoping the ice would melt. I descended until I could see the waves breaking although I could not tell exactly how far I was above them. I kept flying here until fog came down so low that I dared not keep on at such an <u>altitude</u>. Instrument-flying[3] cannot be done safely very near the surface with the equipment we have today.

---

2. **tachometer** (tă-kŏm′ĭ-tər).

3. **instrument-flying** (ĭn′strə-mənt-flī′ĭng): piloting an airplane by relying on instrument readings rather than on one's view of the ground.

WORDS TO KNOW

extent (ĭk-stĕnt′) *n.* an amount or degree
fleeting (flē′tĭng) *adj.* passing quickly
accumulate (ə-kyōōm′yə-lāt′) *v.* to gather or pile up
altitude (ăl′tĭ-tōōd′) *n.* an object's height above a particular level, such as ground level or sea level

 Vocabulary Strategy
Mini Lesson

Her pilot's license showed Earhart wearing her leather flight helmet.

There was nothing left but to seek a middle ground, that is, to fly under the altitude at which I picked up ice and over the water by a <u>sufficient</u> <u>margin</u>. This would have been much easier to do had I been able to know my height

Later, I tried going up again with the same result. So I gave up, just plowing through the "soup" and not looking out of the cockpit again until morning came. I depended on the instruments there to tell me the position of the plane in space, as under these conditions human <u>faculties</u> fail. Had I not been equipped with the best I could never have succeeded. The gyro compass,[4] which is freest of all from <u>fluctuations</u>, was a real life-saver.

About four hours out of Newfoundland, I noticed that the flames were coming through a broken weld in the manifold ring.[5] I knew that it would grow worse as the night wore on. However, the metal was very heavy and I hoped it would last until I reached land. I was indeed sorry that I had looked at the break at all because the flames appeared so much worse at night than they did in the daytime.

As daylight dawned, I found myself between two layers of clouds, the first very high, probably 20,000 feet, the lower ones little fluffy white clouds near the water. This was the first sight of the sea in daylight.

I noticed from the blowing foam that there was a northwest wind. The little white clouds soon grew packed and resembled a vast snow field. I could see on the leading edge of my wings particles of ice which had not yet melted. Soon I went a little higher and ran into another bank of clouds. I was in these for at

---

4. **gyro** (jī'rō) **compass:** a compass that keeps its north-south alignment by means of a spinning disk instead of a magnetic needle.

5. **manifold** (măn'ə-fōld') **ring:** a seal in the engine's exhaust system.

WORDS
TO
KNOW

sufficient (sə-fĭsh'ənt) *adj.* being enough; adequate
margin (mär'jĭn) *n.* an amount or distance that allows for safety
faculty (făk'əl-tē) *n.* any of the powers of the mind
fluctuation (flŭk'chōō-ā'shən) *n.* an irregular movement or change

139

 Speaking and Listening

BEFORE AND AFTER INTERVIEW Students can use their communication skills for interviewing. They can listen to learn by taking notes, organizing, and summarizing them.
Prepare Tell students that conducting an interview requires preparation by the interviewer and careful thought by both parties. The interviewer should be well-informed on the topic so he or she can prepare questions to be answered.
When interviewing before and after an event, the interviewer would probably focus on background information in the initial interview and on how the event went in the second one. He or she could take notes or use a tape recorder. The interviewee should pay close attention to what is being asked and answer in a clear, concise manner.
Present Have students pair up and conduct before and after interviews. The person being interviewed should have an event like a test, sports event, or performance coming up. Interviews can take place on two separate days, before and after the event.

Use **Communications Transparencies and Copymasters**, p. 9, for additional support.

Literary Analysis: CHARACTER

(A) Ask students what this passage tells about Earhart's personality.

Possible Response: She is much more concerned about her plane and her mission than about herself.

Literary Analysis | AUTOBIOGRAPHY |

Ask students what details on this page could be known only by the author.

Possible Responses: The last two hours were the hardest; she decided to land as soon as possible; she thought she was south of her course; she was afraid of hitting mountains; and she hoped to find a city.

Ask students if they have changed their ideas about why Earhart called her book *The Fun of It.*

Possible Response: Despite the great dangers and challenges, the most important memory she has is of the fun of her flight.

Reading Skills and Strategies: CHRONOLOGICAL ORDER

Remind students that they can use the text's chronology to locate and recall information. Have them review the selection and make a time line of events, using times mentioned in the text.

Possible Response: She left Harbour Grace, Newfoundland, at 7:12; several hours of fair weather with sunset; about 11:15 noticed flames from manifold ring; about 11:30 severe storm for at least an hour; climbed for half an hour but picked up ice; same thing happened later; at daylight sea became visible; about 5, saw a boat; last two hours the hardest—manifold vibrating, reserve gas gauge leaking; landed in a pasture in Ireland.

Earhart ended her transatlantic flight in the green fields of Ireland.

least an hour and then came out in a clear space again over the white snow fields.

By this time, the upper layer was thin enough for the sun to come through, and it was as dazzling as on real snow. I had dark glasses but it was too much for me even so, and I came down through the lower layer to fly in the shade, as it were.

Anyway, ten hours had passed, and I wished to see the water lest[6] I was passing a boat. I had seen one <u>vessel</u> shortly after I left Harbour Grace. I blinked my navigation lights[7] but apparently no one saw me as I was flying high. Then I picked up either a fishing vessel or an oil tanker off the coast of Ireland, but those were the only two I saw until I met a fleet near the coast.

From then on I met sunshine and low hanging clouds, most of which I kept under even though they were very near the water.

 By the way, I didn't bother much about food for myself. The really important thing was fuel for the engine. It drank some 350 gallons of gasoline. My own trans-Atlantic rations

consisted of one can of tomato juice which I punctured and sipped through a straw.

Of course, the last two hours were the hardest. My exhaust manifold was vibrating very badly, and then I turned on the reserve tanks and found the gauge[8] leaking. I decided I should come down at the very nearest place, wherever it was. I had flown a set compass course all night. Now I changed to due east and decided to head for Ireland. I did not wish to miss the tip of Ireland and the weather was such I couldn't see very far. I thought I must be south of the course, for I had been told by the weather man in New York that I might find rain south of my course. There was a wind which might blow it on, so when I ran into the storm I thought that I was in this weather spoken of. Then when I saw the northwest wind, I was

---

6. **lest:** in case.

7. **navigation lights:** lights on the wings and tail of an airplane, which allow the plane to be seen in the dark.

8. **gauge** (gāj): an instrument for measuring or indicating an amount—in this case, the instrument that shows how much fuel is in the fuel tanks.

WORDS
TO   **vessel** (vĕs′əl) *n.* a boat or ship
KNOW

140

 Mini Lesson **Grammar**

USING COMMAS TO PREVENT MISREADING
Tell students they will need to punctuate correctly to clarify the meaning of what they write.
Instruction Point out the highlighted sentence in the text. Read it aloud twice, first without pausing at the comma, then as written. Help students understand that without the comma to set off the introductory words, the meaning of the sentence is not clear.
Exercises Ask students to add commas to the following sentences if they are needed for clarity. Some sentences may not require any.

1. Amelia Earhart the first woman to fly solo across the Atlantic never completed her round-the-world flight. (Earhart, the; Atlantic, never)
2. Although the trans-Atlantic flight lasted through the night she never even took a nap. (night, she)
3. She landed in a field in Ireland. (none)

 Use **Grammar Transparencies and Copymasters,** p. 122.

| Language Network | Use McDougal Littell's *Language Network,* Chapter 9, for more instruction and practice in the use of commas. |

sure I must be south. As it happened, I probably was exactly on my course, and I think I hit Ireland about the middle.

I started down the coast and found thunderstorms lower in the hills. Not having the altimeter and not knowing the country, I was afraid to plow through those lest I hit one of the mountains, so I turned north where the weather seemed to be better and soon came across a railroad which I followed hoping it would lead me to a city, where there might be an airport.

The first place I encountered was Londonderry, and I circled it hoping to locate a landing field but found lovely pastures instead. I succeeded in frightening all the cattle in the county, I think, as I came down low several times before finally landing in a long, sloping meadow. I couldn't have asked for better landing facilities, as far as that.

There ended the flight and my happy adventure. Beyond it lay further adventures of <u>hospitality</u> and kindness at the hands of my friends in England, France and America. ❖

An Irish farm family looked on as Earhart read messages of congratulations.

WORDS TO KNOW

hospitality (hŏs'pĭ-tăl'ĭ-tē) *n.* a friendly and generous attitude toward guests

141

Mini Lesson **Viewing and Representing**

ART APPRECIATION Students will have noticed that this selection is enhanced by numerous photographs—of Amelia Earhart, her plane, her destination, and her pilot's license.
Instruction Point out that photographs can make a time period come alive in a more immediate way than text. They present details that might be very tedious to read if written out.
Ask: Where can you find the year Earhart received her pilot's license?

Answer: in the photograph on page 139
Application Ask students to work in small groups. Have them describe how the photographs in the selection help to represent or extend the text's meanings. Have them list all the information they can discover in the photographs. Then have them cross out information that is also in the text. What is presented in the photos only? Groups can then compare their lists.

GUIDING STUDENT RESPONSE

Connect to the Literature

1. What Do You Think?
Possible Responses: Students may say they would have felt challenged by the problems and thrilled by the achievement. They might also say they would have been scared to be flying alone, without important instruments, through storms and ice.

Comprehension Check
- Earhart was flying across the Atlantic Ocean from Canada to Europe. She took off from Harbour Grace, in Newfoundland, and landed in Londonderry, Ireland (now in Northern Ireland).
- She took off at 7:12 P.M. and landed the next day.
- Without the altimeter, Earhart could not tell how high she was flying. She had to rely on her judgment to stay above the waves and beneath the level at which the plane picked up ice.

 Use Selection Quiz
Unit One Resource Book, p. 72.

Think Critically

2. Possible Response: Earhart knows about planes and engines, geography, and weather. She can also fly, navigate, and write. She is courageous, resourceful, flexible, outgoing, and appreciative of other people's hospitality. She seems to view life as a "happy adventure."

3. Possible Response: Earhart's main purpose was to inform readers about her flight.

Use **Reading and Critical Thinking Transparencies,** p. 8, for additional support.

4. Possible Response: The first-person point of view allows Earhart to speak directly to readers and tell her thoughts and impressions. For example, when she is landing she gives the reader a sense of the dangers she faced, and what it felt like to land in the countryside.

5. Possible Response: Because Amelia Earhart was a pioneer, it was important for her to share her stories. She was able to describe experiences that were unfamiliar to most people. It also gave her an opportunity to be a role model, especially for women.

Connect to the Literature

1. What Do You Think?
If you were in Earhart's place, how would you have felt?

Comprehension Check
- Where was Earhart flying?
- When did her flight begin and end?
- Why was the loss of the altimeter so significant?

Think Critically

2. Based on this story, what kind of person do you think Amelia Earhart was?

THINK ABOUT
- her personal **traits** and skills
- the way in which she tells a story
- how she responded to each problem on the flight

3. **ACTIVE READING** **IDENTIFYING THE AUTHOR'S PURPOSE**
What do you think was Earhart's main purpose for writing this story? To support your answer, refer to the notes you made in your **READER'S NOTEBOOK.**

4. How does hearing this story from Earhart herself make the story come alive? Look back through the selection to find **details** that support your answer.

5. Amelia Earhart wrote several books and articles, and toured giving lectures. Why do you think it was so important for her to tell others about her flying?

Extend Interpretations

6. What If? Imagine that Amelia Earhart had grown up later in the 20th century. What kinds of goals might she be dreaming about and accomplishing today?

7. Connect to Life Think about how you might write your own autobiography. What would be the most dramatic event to include? What would be your purpose?

Literary Analysis

AUTOBIOGRAPHY An **autobiography** is the story of a person's life, told by that person. Autobiography is usually written from the **first-person point of view,** meaning that the writer uses first-person pronouns to tell the story.

At twelve minutes after seven, I gave [the plane] the gun. . . . A minute later I was headed out to sea.

Since autobiographies are about real people and real events, they are a form of **nonfiction.** Forms of autobiography include **journals, travelogues, diaries,** and **memoirs.**

Paired Activity Working with a partner, go back through the story and create a flight log for Earhart's trip. A log is a set of entries that describe time, weather, position, routine events, unusual events, and problems during the course of a trip. The time might be general, for example, "dawn."

FLIGHT LOG: TRANSATLANTIC CROSSING.
A. Earhart.
7:12 P.M. Fair weather. Took off solo from Harbour Grace, Newfoundland. No problems. Headed out to sea.

Literary Analysis

Autobiography Logs should include details of take-off, landing, and problems encountered on the way. Where possible, times and positions should be included.

 Use **Literary Analysis Transparencies,** p. 11, for additional support.

Extend Interpretations

6. What If? Answers will vary widely but should reflect an understanding of Earhart's vision, competence, determination, and courage. Today Earhart might be an astronaut, for example, or someone who searches the rain forest for plants that will help make a cure for cancer.

7. Connect to Life Answers will vary. Students may say that they would like to share favorite stories, allow others to learn from their experiences, and introduce readers to people they would never otherwise meet.

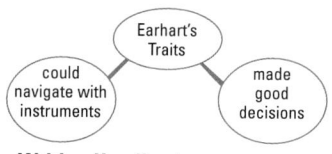

Choices & CHALLENGES

Writing Options

1. Newspaper Interview Make up questions a reporter might have asked Earhart. Next, write the answers you think Earhart might have given in response.

2. Personality Profile Write a description of Earhart's personality, using details from the selection. Use a web to organize your ideas.

Earhart's Traits
- could navigate with instruments
- made good decisions

Writing Handbook
See page R31: Descriptive Writing.

Activities & Explorations

1. Oral Report Find out about Earhart's last flight and her disappearance. Report your findings to the class.
~ SPEAKING AND LISTENING

2. Video Viewing View a video biography of Amelia Earhart. In a small group, discuss what seeing and hearing Earhart adds to your impressions of her character. Why do you think people continue to find her inspiring? ~ VIEWING AND REPRESENTING

 Literature in Performance

Inquiry & Research

Following Earhart's Lead In 1994 Vicki Van Meter became the youngest pilot to make a flight across the Atlantic Ocean. Find out about other record-breaking pilots. Make a chart showing the names of the pilots, the records they broke, and the dates of their accomplishments.

Real World Link
As part of your research, read the magazine article "Daring to Dream" on p. 145.

Vocabulary in Action

EXERCISE: RESTATEMENT CLUES On a sheet of paper, write the Word to Know that best completes each sentence. Then write a sentence of your own with that word.

1. The _____ of a flight is its length.

2. When you catch a _____ glimpse of the moon, you see it for a brief moment.

3. The plane began to _____ speed, going faster and faster.

4. The _____ of a plane is its flying height.

5. If the fuel in a plane's tank is _____, then the plane can land safely.

6. A plane that is above the ground by too small a _____ is flying too low.

7. A person who has lost the _____ of sight cannot see well.

8. Flying into the storm, the pilot noticed a _____, or change, in altitude.

9. A fishing _____ is a kind of boat.

10. Earhart's friends in England showed _____ by welcoming her.

Building Vocabulary
For an in-depth lesson on context clues, see p. 79.

WORDS TO KNOW				
accumulate altitude	extent faculty	fleeting fluctuation	hospitality margin	sufficient vessel

---

✓ **Assessment** **Standardized Test Practice**

USING CONTEXT CLUES Remind students that they can often find clues to the meaning of unfamiliar words in the surrounding words. They might find synonyms or examples to help them. Read this sentence aloud:
I blinked my navigation lights but apparently no one saw me, as I was flying high.
Ask which is the best meaning for *apparently*.
A. tiredly
B. surprisingly
C. happily
D. presumably

Talk through the process of choosing the correct answer. Point out that the words *as I was flying high* give the reason she could not be seen, and may be a clue to the meaning of *apparently*. A is not correct—it does not make sense. B is not correct, as it is not surprising that she couldn't be seen if she is flying high. C is also not correct—she has blinked her navigation lights in order to be seen, so she wouldn't be happy to remain invisible. D is the correct answer—she presumes that no one saw her because she was flying high.

Writing Options

1. **Newspaper Interview** A reporter would probably ask some factual questions concerning her departure, arrival, and events on the trip, and would likely also inquire as to how she felt during the trip and how it felt to be the first woman to fly across the Atlantic solo. Invented responses will vary, but should accord with information in the text where given.

2. **Personality Profile** Responses will vary but should include some of the following information: she was a skilled pilot, understood weather and its effect on the plane, had confidence in her abilities, put concern for her plane ahead of herself, enjoyed adventure, was both daring and careful.

 Use **Writing Transparencies**, p. 49, for additional support.

Activities & Explorations

1. **Oral Report** Students might want to highlight these areas: what she intended to do, how far she got, where she disappeared, efforts to find her, and events subsequent to her disappearance.

Use **Communications Transparencies and Copymasters**, pp. 14, 15.

2. **Video Viewing** Responses will vary, but should include that seeing her on video makes the viewer feel more connected to her.

Inquiry & Research

Following Earhart's Lead
Students might find this information in an almanac or book of records.

Use **Writing Transparencies**, pp. 44, 45 for additional support.

Vocabulary in Action

1. extent
2. fleeting
3. accumulate
4. altitude
5. sufficient
6. margin
7. faculty
8. fluctuation
9. vessel
10. hospitality

Grammar in Context

WRITING EXERCISE
Students' sentences will vary. Accept sentences that use subjects in unusual order.
CONNECT TO THE LITERATURE
The author uses the first and third methods.

Amelia Earhart

Because of her great achievements and the mystery surrounding her disappearance during her round-the-world trip, interest in Amelia Earhart has never waned. In 1997, a Texas woman named Linda Finch, using the same type of airplane as Earhart, completed the trip. It is believed that Earhart's plane went down near Howland Island in the Pacific, meaning Earhart had completed about three-fourths of her journey.

Grammar in Context: Subjects in Unusual Order

One way to make your writing more conversational—more like real speech—is to put the **subjects** of your sentences in different positions. There are many ways to do this. Here are four examples:

1. The word *there* or *here* at the beginning of a sentence usually means that the subject will follow the **verb.**

   > **There** ended my flight and happy adventure.

2. Sometimes the first words of a sentence are words of introduction, and the subject comes later.

   > **By the way,** I didn't bother much about food for myself.

3. Switching the usual subject-verb order, even without using *there* or *here*, is another way to add variety.

   > **Directly into the storm** flew the plane.

4. A question may not only switch the order of the subject and verb but may split up a verb phrase.

   > Statement: Amelia Earhart flew her plane over the Atlantic.
   > Question: Where did Amelia Earhart fly her plane?

WRITING EXERCISE Recall a time in your life when you acted bravely, or remember a story you have read about someone else's brave actions. Write five sentences about the experience, using the methods discussed above to add variety to the sentences.

Connect to the Literature Reread the first two paragraphs on page 139. Look for sentence subjects in different positions. Does the author use any of the methods discussed in the lesson?

Grammar Handbook Making Subject and Verbs Agree, p. R60

"Women must try to do things as men have tried."

Amelia Earhart
1897?–1937?

Breaking the Mold Amelia Earhart was born in Kansas. As children she and her sisters shocked their community by wearing pants and doing things usually done only by boys—things like hiking and sledding. Amelia even built a roller coaster in her backyard so that she could feel as if she were flying. As a young woman, she worked on airplane engines to pay for flying time. She also worked at several other jobs, but flying was always her passion.

Setting New Standards In accepting an award for her famous transatlantic solo flight, Earhart said, "I hope that the flight has meant something to women in aviation. If it has, I shall feel it was justified." Earhart published two memoirs in her lifetime, and some of her writings about her life and flying were published after her death. During her last flight—an attempt to fly around the world—she disappeared at sea.

144   UNIT ONE   PART 2: COURAGE IN ACTION

Teaching Options

 Mini Lesson

Grammar

SUBJECTS IN QUESTIONS, EXCLAMATIONS, AND COMMANDS
Instruction Tell students that to find the subject of an exclamation or a command, they can change the question or exclamation into a statement: *Was Amelia Earhart the first woman to fly across the Atlantic?* becomes *Amelia Earhart was the first woman to fly across the Atlantic. Amelia Earhart* is the subject of the verb *was.*
Wasn't she something! becomes *She wasn't something. She* is the subject of the verb *wasn't.*

For imperative sentences, explain that the word *you* is usually understood to be the subject, because the command is aimed at that person: *Get on the plane!* means *You get on the plane! You* is the subject of the verb *get.*
Exercises Ask students to circle the subject in each of the following sentences. If *you* is understood, they should write *you.*

1. Did Earhart fly with Lindbergh? (Earhart)
2. Be sure to notice where she landed. (you)
3. Was she a great pilot! (she)

4. Did you read about the ice on the wings? (you)

Use **Unit One Resource Book** p. 70.
Use **Grammar Transparencies and Copymasters,** p. 57, for more practice.

Use McDougal Littell's *Language Network,* Chapter 1, for more instruction and practice in finding the subject.

Daring to Dream

Adapted from *Taking Flight, My Story*

by **Vicki Van Meter** with **Dan Gutman**

Dreams can come true. Just ask Vicki Van Meter, 13, of Meadville, Pennsylvania. Vicki's amazing adventures began with a simple wish: to become an astronaut.

To encourage Vicki's soaring spirit, her father suggested that Vicki take flying lessons when she was ten years old. Less than two years later, Vicki became the youngest girl to pilot a plane across America!

The following summer, a new challenge called to Vicki: flying across the Atlantic Ocean. Vicki's sixth-grade graduation was on June 3, 1994, and the next day she took off to pilot a plane to Scotland. "I knew one thing for sure," Vicki says. "Writing an essay on my summer vacation would be a breeze!"

Since Vicki was too young to fly alone, an adult pilot accompanied her on the flight across America, and on the flight across the Atlantic. But Vicki did all the flying herself. What follows is Vicki's account of her incredible journey across the ocean.

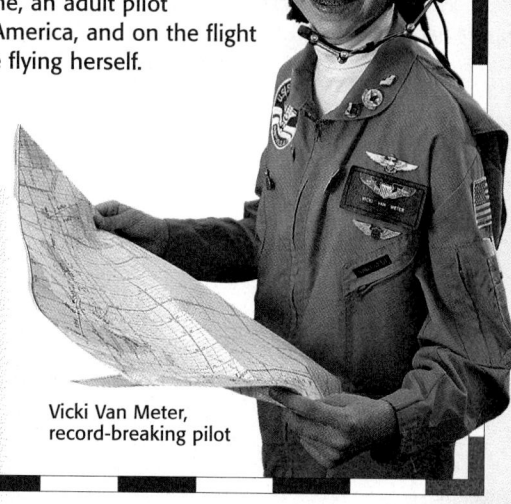

Vicki Van Meter, record-breaking pilot

Reading for Information

Writers often use pictures and other eye-catching features to clarify and explain ideas. **Graphics** such as maps, time lines, and photographs can organize information visually. Text organizers include tables of contents and **headings,** the large-type words that introduce sections of a work.

Objectives

- read for information
- read and analyze a magazine article
- understand and use text organizers
- use a time line to understand sequence of events

Connecting to the Literature

In Amelia Earhart's autobiography, students read about the first solo flight across the Atlantic by a woman. Vicki Van Meter was inspired by Amelia Earhart's achievements and decided to try the flight herself. She set a record as the youngest girl to fly across the Atlantic. Interested students may wish to read her book, which includes details on how to fly, as well as more information about the flight.

Reading for Information

Tell students that this article appeared in *American Girl* but was adapted from Vicki Van Meter's own autobiography *Taking Flight, My Story.* Have students use the material in the Reading for Information column to help them assimilate the information presented by the graphics and text organizers. The following pages contain possible responses to the questions and activities.

Use **Reading and Critical Thinking Transparencies,** p. 47, for additional support.

1 They tell you that the article is about a flight and show you the route taken. The headings show how many days the flight took as well as an important fact about that day. The photo caption gives information about Vicki. The final chart gives factual information about the trip.

2 There are photographs, a map, and a chart, which all present information in an organized way that is easy to scan. The photographs let you see what Vicki looks like, and information about her is given in the accompanying captions. The map shows the route. The chart gives important details about the trip.

3 Land is shaded green. The start and finish are marked by stars, the fuel stops by triangles, and each leg of the trip is a different color arrow.

Reading for Information continued

USING TEXT ORGANIZERS Organizers such as graphics and headings can add fun and drama to a writer's treatment of a topic. Graphics can also provide information that isn't in the text, such as related facts or personal details.

YOUR TURN Use the questions and activities below to help you get the most from the text organizers in this article.

1 Before you begin reading an article, scan the pages quickly. What do the headings and graphics in this article tell you?

2 What type of graphics are used in this article? How is each graphic helpful? What useful information does each graphic give?

3 Sometimes a graphic includes symbols. Here the blue represents water. What other symbols can you find? What do they represent?

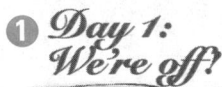

Day 1: We're off!

Along the way, I heard commercial pilots flying above us who were talking about me on the radio. They didn't know I was listening in on the same frequency.

"Hey, where's that little girl who's flying across the ocean?" they were saying.

I answered, "This is 127 Sierra, the girl who's flying across the ocean. Hi!"

Day 2: Trouble

We were a little over an hour into the flight when I noticed we were picking up some ice on the wings.

If we kept going like that, the ice would become so heavy that the plane wouldn't be able to fly.

"This is really starting to build up," I said to Curt. "Let's get on top of this stuff," he replied.

I pulled back on the yoke, but the nose of the plane didn't go up. Not a foot. We had waited too long.

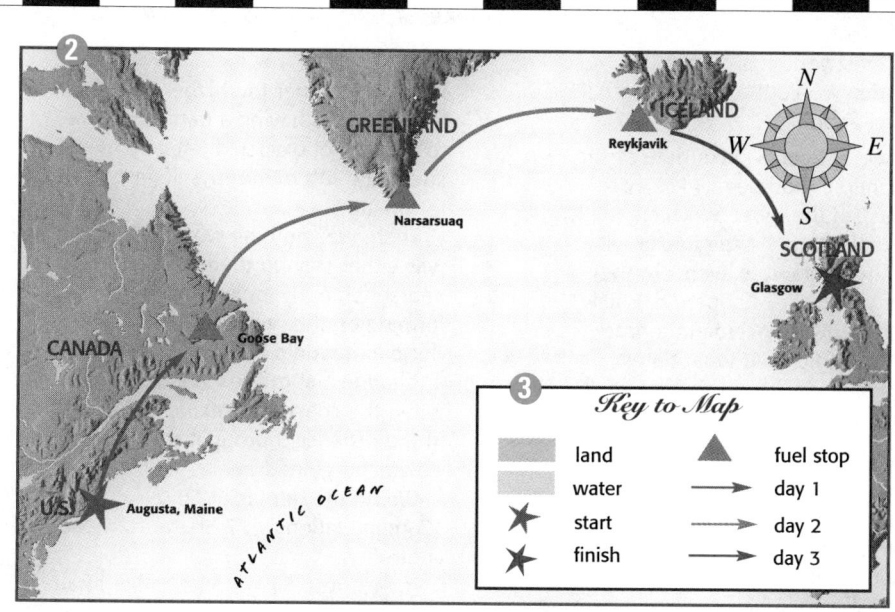

②

③

Key to Map

▬	land	▲	fuel stop
▬	water	→	day 1
✶	start	→	day 2
★	finish	→	day 3

There was no place to go but down. If we dropped below the clouds, the air would be warmer, and hopefully it would melt the ice.

I brought Harmony down to 7,000 feet, and then 5,000 feet, but the air was thick with clouds. I came down to 3,000 feet, then 2,000 feet, then 1,000 feet. Still there were clouds—and a real danger of crashing.

Finally, at 800 feet over the water, we broke out from the clouds. We kept going at 500 feet. Soon the ice was gone. The crisis was past.

Day 3: More trouble

The first hours were smooth, but then we found ourselves flying through clouds and I noticed ice forming on the wings. Not again!

I had to take Harmony all the way up to 13,500 feet before we popped out of the top of the clouds and the sun began to melt the ice.

Just as it's risky flying too low, it's also risky flying very high. The atmosphere surrounding the earth

4 Answers will vary, but students may mention the age limit on pilot licenses. The photograph shows what Vicki and her plane look like. It also shows her in her flying gear.

Sequence of Events Students might include her graduation, her take-off, each of her landings, the ice on the wings on days 2 and 3 and how she handled that, and the landing place and time. The time line would begin on June 3, 1994, and end on June 7, 1994.

Reading for Information *continued*

4 Often a caption or a sidebar gives you additional information. What details here interest you most? What information would the photo give if it had no caption?

Sequence of Events Take note of the date mentioned on page 145. Try to keep track of the order in which events took place. A time line is a graphic that organizes events in the order in which they happened. What events would you include in a time line for this article? At what dates would your time line begin and end?

Inquiry & Research

Activity Link: from *The Fun of It*, p. 143.
Using information found in this article and in the selection from *The Fun of It*, prepare two graphics—maps or time lines—that will help other students compare the two flights.

becomes thinner the higher you go. My body was having a hard time due to the lack of oxygen. I felt very tired suddenly, and found myself gasping for breath.

There was nothing we could do. It was either stay up there in the thin air and suffer, or fly lower and risk ice forming on the wings again. We decided it would be safer to suffer.

I had just about reached my limit when the coast of Scotland appeared in the distance. I brought the plane down and gulped air.

We hit the tarmac at 6:30 P.M. "Congratulations, 127 Sierra," said the controller.

It was over. Six months earlier I had set a goal to fly a plane across the Atlantic Ocean, and I had done it. It felt great. Better than great. It felt awesome.

Despite her experience, Vicki can't get her pilot's license until she's 17.

The Journey: Maine to Scotland

Distance: 3,105 miles over the freezing waters of the North Atlantic

Plane: A single-engine Cessna named Harmony. My call name was 127 Sierra.

Copilot: Curt Arnspiger, age 38

Important piece of emergency gear: Curt and I wore suits that were red and rubbery the entire trip. They were uncomfortable, but would keep us warm and afloat for 24 hours in case we had to land in water.

 Mini Lesson ## Inquiry & Research

The Inquiry & Research activity on this page links to the Inquiry & Research activity from the Choices & Challenges section following "*from The Fun of It*" on page 143.

Instruction As they do the Inquiry & Research activity, students may use print sources or CD-ROM encyclopedias. If your school computer is connected to the Internet, help students refine searches by noting specific keywords. For example, "pilot records" or "speed records" would be better search phrases than "pilots" or "aeronautics," both of which are too broad.

Application Have students take informal notes before they decide how to organize their charts. In that way, they will be better able to decide which kinds of information to include.

Use **Writing Transparencies,** pp. 45–48, for additional support.

Roots and Base Words

Did you know that when you speak English, you are also, in a way, speaking Greek, Latin, and other languages? Many English words have origins in these languages.

For example, the word hospitality is related to the Latin word *hospes*, meaning "guest."

Latin: **hospes** *(guest)*

English: hospitality
hospital
hospice
host

> There ended the flight and my happy adventure. Beyond it lay further adventures of hospitality and kindness at the hands of my friends in England, France and America.
>
> —Amelia Earhart,
> *The Fun of It*

Strategies for Building Vocabulary

A **root** is a word part from which various words can be formed. *Hospit,* the root of *hospitality,* is an example of a Latin root. If you know certain roots, or base words, you can figure out the meanings of new words.

❶ **Understanding Word Families** Words that have the same root make up a **word family**. Such words usually have related meanings. For example, the Greek root *graph,* meaning "writing," is found in the related words *autograph* (a person's signature or handwriting), *biography* (the written story of a person's life), and *graphite* (a mineral used in pencils).

❷ **Remembering Roots** Think of roots as clues that will lead you to the meanings of new words. The charts on this page show some common Greek and Latin roots. Notice how the meanings of the example words are related to the meanings of their roots.

Greek Root	Meaning	Word Family
aster, astr	star	asteroid (a small object in outer space) astronomy (the study of outer space)
geo	earth	geography (the study of earth's features) geode (a hollow, crystal-filled rock)
tele	far, distant	telephone (a device for transmitting sounds) television (a device for transmitting pictures)

Latin Root	Meaning	Word Family
mal	bad	malfunction (a failure to function) malady (an illness)
srib, script	write	scribble (to write hurriedly) description (a picture in words)
ten, tent	hold, keep	detention (a holding in custody) tenure (permanent holding of a job)

EXERCISE Identify a root in each word, and tell what the root means. Then use the word in a sentence. Use a dictionary if you need help.

1. prescription
2. malicious
3. tenacious
4. telecommunication
5. astronaut

Objectives
- understand how words are built from roots
- apply meanings of root words in order to comprehend

EXERCISE

Sentences given are examples.

1. script; write; A doctor writes many prescriptions in one day.
2. mal; bad; His actions were mean and malicious.
3. ten; hold; Melanie is the most tenacious player I have ever seen; she never gives up.
4. tele; far, distant; Telecommunication allows people all over the world to speak to each other.
5. aster, astr; star; The astronaut just returned after nine weeks at the space station.

Use **Unit Resource Book** p. 73. Use **Vocabulary Transparencies and Copymasters** p. 6 for additional support.

OVERVIEW

Objectives
• appreciate the works of a contemporary American writer for young adults
• analyze the effect of personal experiences on Paulsen's writing
• explore some of the works Paulsen has written during his career

The Author Study puts the focus on one particular writer, examining his life and works in detail. By using the Author Study, students can develop the ability to compare and contrast a writer's experience with his or her literary output.

Author Study **GARY PAULSEN**

A Writer of Adventure

"If I can write a story, it's because of actually going, being there, and doing those things. It's more than 'Write what you know.' It's kind of like: Write what you are!"

born 1939

CONTENTS

LOST AND FOUND

Born into a military family in Minneapolis in 1939, Paulsen was raised by his aunts and grandmother and was shuffled around from school to school. Never a dedicated student, and without a permanent home or friends, young Paulsen found few opportunities in school and couldn't manage to fit in. Luckily, he reached a turning point in his early teens that

His LIFE and TIMES

1939
Born May 17 in Minneapolis, Minnesota

1953
Receives first library card

1955
Joins a carnival

1957
Graduates from high school

1940   1950   1960

1941–1945
United States in World War II

1951
Rock-and-roll is first used as a term to describe music.

1955
Bus boycott begins in Montgomery, Alabama.

150

changed his life. On a cold winter night he went into a library just to warm up. There a librarian offered him a library card, a book, and a chance to **B** get as many books as he wanted, as long as he brought them back. As Paulsen tells it, "It was as though I had been dying of thirst and the librarian handed me a five-gallon bucket of water."

ALWAYS AN EXPLORER

Through his reading Paulsen developed a taste for action and adventure. In his teens, he worked on a farm, hunted and tracked animals, and even joined a carnival. Not surprisingly, his eagerness to experience new things stayed with him in the years ahead. As an adult, Paulsen held jobs as a teacher, engineer, soldier, actor, rancher, truck driver, professional archer, singer, and sailor. All the while he continued reading and exploring the world through stories. And with each new book and new adventure, Paulsen's desire to tell his own stories grew.

Did You Know?

- ◆ Gary Paulsen has written more than 130 books.
- ◆ He has raced in the Iditarod twice.
- ◆ His wife, Ruth, has illustrated some of his books.
- ◆ He once rode his motorcycle from New Mexico to Alaska.
- ◆ He travels around the world on his sailboat.
- ◆ He has covered 22,000 miles by sled.

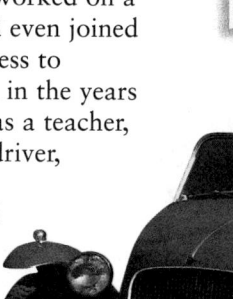

Childhood

A Paulsen's father was a Danish immigrant who served on General Patton's staff in Europe during World War II. His mother worked in a munitions plant in Chicago. In 1946, Paulsen and his mother traveled to the Philippines, where he met his father for the first time. In one interview, Paulsen noted, "I became a street kid in Manila when I was around seven." Elsewhere he comments: "After we returned to the States [in 1949], we moved around constantly. I lived in every state. The longest time I spent in one school was for about five months." He also says, "I grew up in a small Minnesota town. I was an 'at risk' kid, as they are called now, and a poor student. I actually flunked the ninth grade." In another interview he comments: "School was a nightmare because I was unbelievably shy, and terrible at sports. I had no friends, and teachers ridiculed me."

Reading

B Paulsen adds another comment to his story about starting to read: "Over the course of two years, [the librarian] got me reading. I can't even imagine what would have happened to me without her. First it was a book a month, then a book every three weeks. Eventually it was two books a week. I would get Zane Grey westerns or books by Edgar Rice Burroughs, and she would slip in a Melville or a Dickens, or something. When I brought them back, she would ask me what I thought. It was incredible."

1966 Moves to Hollywood	1968 Publishes first novel, *Some Birds Don't Fly*	1971 Marries artist Ruth Wright	1983 Races in his first Iditarod	1986 *Dogsong* is named a Newbery Honor Book.	1999 Lives and works mostly on board his sailboat

1970 **1980** **1990** **2000**

1965–1973 U.S. ground troops in Vietnam War	1979 Hostage crisis begins in Iran.	1987 AIDS quilt is displayed to raise awareness.	1995 Internet becomes widely available.	1998 President Clinton is impeached.

GARY PAULSEN **151**

Author Study GARY PAULSEN

Career

C Paulsen describes his first job in writing this way: "I wrote a totally fictitious resume, which landed me an associate editorship on a men's magazine in Hollywood, California. It took them about two days to find out that I knew nothing about publishing. I didn't know what a lay-out sheet was, let alone how to do one. My secretary—who was all of nineteen years old—edited my first three issues. They could see I was serious about wanting to learn, and they were willing to teach me. We published some excellent writers—Steinbeck, Bradbury, Ellison—which was great training and exposure for me."

Dogsled Racing

D Paulsen stopped writing shortly after the publication of his novel *Winterkill* in 1977, when he was sued for libel. He went back to living off a 60-mile trap line in the Minnesota wilderness. One day he was given four sled dogs so that he could work his line more easily. From then on, he was hooked on dogsled racing. At one point he took off for seven days on a completely free romp across northern Minnesota, with only a few beaver carcasses for food. Later, after he went on to run the Iditarod, he rediscovered the joy of writing and began producing books again.

Reverence for Life

E The Iditarod taught Paulsen a new reverence for life. In one interview he commented: "The Iditarod may sound like a macho thrill, but it's the opposite. You go where death goes, and death doesn't give a damn about macho. Besides, the last two races were won by women. Here's something that was brought home to me: macho is a lie. It's . . . garbage. Core toughness and compassion are the opposite of macho. The absence of fear comes with knowledge, not strength or bravura. More people should be telling this to young people, instead of 'climb the highest mountain and kill something.'"

A NEW CALLING

C To learn the art of writing, Paulsen decided he needed to be in Hollywood, if only to be near other writers. Once he arrived, he talked his way into a job with an ad agency and worked on his writing at night. At last he had found his true calling. His skills as a writer developed slowly, but with hard work and the advice of fellow writers, Paulsen developed his own voice and style.

INTO THE NORTH

D In order to write full-time, Paulsen returned to Minnesota, settled into an isolated cabin, and began living off the land. After one winter there, Paulsen had completed his first novel, *Some Birds Don't Fly.* He enjoyed living in the woods and hunting for food, but he decided to move farther north to train for the Iditarod, the famous trans-Alaska dogsled race. Even while training day and night in the cold, Paulsen continued writing. **E** He also grew to love and admire his sled dogs so much that he found he could never kill another animal. Today Paulsen is one of America's most prolific and popular writers. He and his wife, the illustrator Ruth Wright Paulsen, share a Southwestern ranch and a houseboat anchored off the coast of California.

Paulsen with Cookie, one of his favorite companions and lead sled dog.

TALKING WITH GARY PAULSEN

Gary Paulsen loves to respond to letters. Here's his response to some frequently asked questions.

Q: **What is your favorite thing to write about?**

A: Almost always, it's about making personal discoveries while struggling to survive in the great outdoors. When I go into the wilderness, I like to go it alone. That way, I can pay close attention to things around me, which helps make my writing more realistic. I become very wolflike. Wolves see and listen to every single thing.

Q: **Getting your first library card was your passport to becoming a reader. Do you still read as much as you did then?**

A: I read like a wolf eats. I read myself to sleep every night. And I don't think any of the good things that have happened to me would have been possible without that librarian and libraries in general.

Q: **Your childhood sounds hard, and you were a poor student, so how did you learn to write so well?**

A: Initially, I wasn't very good at it. But I was determined to get to the place where I could express my thoughts on paper—I had so many stories to tell! I had already tried a lot of jobs. Once I decided to be a writer,

I realized I had a lot to learn. I started to focus on writing with the same energies and efforts that I used training dogs. So we're talking 18- to 20-hour days, completely committed to work. I still work that way, and the end result is there's a lot of books out there.

Q: **Your adventurous life sounds like the plot of a Gary Paulsen novel. Is a lot of you in your stories?**

A: That's true of a lot of authors, you use what you are. Your life becomes your material.

Q: **You wrote your best-known works while you were still running dogs. Where did you find the time?**

A: With the dogs, you run them just four hours on, then four hours off. When they were sleeping those four hours, I'd sit by my campfire and write longhand.

Q: **Do you like writing better than the other jobs you tried?**

A: Absolutely. To be able to portray things I see and hear in writing is a privilege.

 More Online: Author Link
www.mcdougallittell.com

 NetActivities: Author Exploration

Audience

F Paulsen claims that he writes for young adults because they are the only ones who can still change the world for the better. He notes that it is "artistically fruitless to write for adults. Adults created the mess which we are struggling to outlive. Adults have their minds set. Art reaches out for newness, and adults aren't new. And adults aren't truthful. . . . I'm betting that young people have the answers."

Autobiography

G Paulsen has written an autobiographical book, *Eastern Sun, Winter Moon.* It recounts some of his horrifying experiences as a child, including seeing a plane crash in the Pacific Ocean and its screaming passengers torn to shreds by sharks. One reviewer called it "a raw portrayal of a child thrown into the horrors of war and the adult world."

Attitude

H Paulsen notes: "I write because it's all I can do. Every time I've tried to do something else I cannot, and have to come back to writing, though often I hate it—hate it and love it. It's much like being a slave, I suppose, and in slavery there is a kind of freedom that I find in writing: a perverse thing. I'm not 'motivated.' . . . Nor am I particularly driven. I write because it's all there is."

Objectives

1. understand and appreciate a **short story** (Literary Analysis)
2. understand **anecdote** in a short story (Literary Analysis)
3. use the reading strategy of **identifying effect of the author's perspective** (Active Reading)

Summary

While training his sled dogs, author Gary Paulsen gets into trouble. Caught in a precarious situation on a danger-ous railroad trestle, he is forced to free the dogs from their harness. He is sur-prised and disheartened to see them disappear promptly into the woods. Miles from home, he begins the long trudge back, feeling abandoned. The lead dog, however, brings back the oth-ers, as she had on a previous occasion, and Paulsen gains new respect for her.

Thematic Link

Paulsen shows courage in action as he deals with a difficult turn of events. Though he finds himself alone on a frigid night in the Minnesota woods, he refuses to panic, and his patience is soon rewarded.

5-Minute Warm-Up

Daily Language SkillBuilder

Have students **proofread** the display sentences on page 19K and write them correctly. The sentences also appear on Transparency 5 of **Grammar Transparencies and Copymasters.**

PREPARING to *Read*

Older Run

Essay by GARY PAULSEN

"You, her eyes said, *got us into this, and you'd better get us out."*

Connect to Your Life

Not Alone! Think about a time when you felt alone. Did someone come to help you? Describe the experience to a partner.

Build Background

CONNECT TO HISTORY

Mushing, or sled racing, is one of the oldest official sports in Canada. It was registered in 1908, even before hockey!

From the Chuchi of Siberia to the Inuit of Alaska, Greenland, and Canada, people in the north have traveled by dogsled for hundreds of years. European immigrants to Canada once used dogsleds to explore and chart the wilderness.

In recent years, long-distance racing and touring in the wilderness have become popular. "Sled" dogs are often hooked to skiers, bicycles, or four-wheelers.

> **WORDS TO KNOW**
> **Vocabulary Preview**
> anticipate   ricochet
> embankment   seasoned
> exceeding   spectator
> maneuver   transpire
> marvel   trestle

Focus Your Reading

LITERARY ANALYSIS ANECDOTE A short, amusing story or report about one event is an **anecdote.** The event and characters can be either real or fictional. The selection from *The Fun of It* tells of one event, so it is an anecdote. The biography of Matthew Henson tells all the major events in his life, so it is not an anecdote.

Paulsen's essay "Older Run" is an anecdote about a day in his life of training sled dogs. As you read, notice smaller anecdotes, or amusing events, within the larger one.

ACTIVE READING IDENTIFYING EFFECTS OF AUTHOR'S PERSPECTIVE

Every author has a different **perspective** or way of seeing the world. Think of a visit to the doctor. A parent and a child might describe the same visit using different **details** and a different **tone.** The doctor's perspective would be entirely different. Think of what you know about Paulsen. How might his experience, feelings, and beliefs affect the way he writes?

READER'S NOTEBOOK Begin a chart like the one shown below. First, list Paulsen's views about dogs, being outdoors alone, and adventure. As you read, fill in the chart with details from the story that show the effect of Paulsen's perspective.

	Paulsen's Views	Story Details
Dogs	cares about dogs	"running should, of all things, be fun for them."

LESSON RESOURCES

UNIT ONE RESOURCE BOOK, pp. 74–80

ASSESSMENT
Formal Assessment, pp. 23–24
Teacher's Guide to Assessment and Portfolio Use
Test Generator

SKILLS TRANSPARENCIES AND COPYMASTERS
Literary Analysis
• Autobiography, TR 11 (for Cooperative Activity, p. 161)
Reading and Critical Thinking
• Author's Bias, TR 28 (for Thinking Through the Literature, p. 161)

Grammar
• Subject-Verb Agreement, CM 116 (for Mini Lesson, p. 162)
• Varying Sentence Length and Type, CM 135 (for Mini Lesson, p. 158)
Vocabulary
• Context Clues: Example, CM 30 (for Mini Lesson, p. 155)
Writing
• Effective Language, TR 15 (for Mini Lesson, p. 159)

Communications
• Dramatic Reading, TR 12 (for Mini Lesson, p. 159)

INTEGRATED TECHNOLOGY
Audio Library

Visit our website:
www.mcdougallittell.com

Ider un

by **Gary Paulsen**

Illustrations by Ruth Wright Paulsen

"HELP."

It was, in an impossible situation on an impossible night in an impossible life, the only possible thing to say.

I had never been in such an untenable,[1] completely bizarre situation.

The night had started easy, ridiculously easy, and I should have taken warning from the ease. Generally, when running dogs and sleds, a good moment or two will be followed by eight or nine hours of panic and disaster.

---

1. **untenable** (ŭn-tĕn′ə-bəl): impossible to maintain or defend.

155

TEACHING THE LITERATURE
Customizing Instruction

Less Proficient Readers
Help students understand the action by mapping out the various times represented by parts of the text. For example, the story starts after Paulsen is abandoned; it then switches back to the beginning of his midnight adventure and follows it through to its conclusion, then jumps to the conversation he has with his wife about what happened.

Use **Literary Analysis Transparencies,** p. 29, for additional support.

Students Acquiring English

Use **Spanish Study Guide,** pp. 28–30 for additional support .

Gifted and Talented
Ask students to analyze characters in the selection. In particular, they should focus as they read on the relationship between Paulsen and his dogs. Are the dogs characters? When they have finished reading the selection they should write a paragraph explaining how this relationship differs from friendships between one human and another.

 Mini Lesson **Preteaching Vocabulary**

CONTEXT CLUES: EXAMPLE

Instruction Explain to students that sometimes they can determine the meaning of an unknown word by examining any examples that might be given in the text. If they saw the sentence, "The dog did many tricky maneuvers, such as leaping backwards, twisting her body, and ducking quickly," they would be able to guess that a maneuver is a movement or change in direction.

Exercises The following sentences use examples to explain some of the WORDS TO KNOW. Have students write a definition of each underlined word based on the examples given.

1. Spectators, whether they are football fans or innocent people at crime scenes, are often affected by what they see.
2. Embankments, such as those that protect castles, raise roadbeds, or cover underground houses, often change drainage patterns.
3. Trestles, whether they support railroad or highway bridges, require careful engineering.

 Use **Vocabulary Transparencies and Copymasters,** p. 30.

Reading and Analyzing

Reading Skills and Strategies: PREVIEW

Help students understand the story by drawing a rough diagram of the trestle. Use the diagram to show how the dogs run out on the trestle, how Paulsen falls off the sled, and how he releases the dogs one by one. Ask students to speculate on what might happen after the dogs are released.

Active Reading

IDENTIFYING EFFECTS OF AUTHOR'S PERSPECTIVE

Have students examine the paragraphs on this page for evidence of the effect the author's perspective has on the story.
Possible Response: The author's opinions and judgments on his role in training and running the dogs are evident throughout the story so far. He looks back on the dog run from the point of view of someone who is now older and wiser.

Use **Unit One Resource Book**, p. 75, for more practice.

Literary Analysis ANECDOTE

 Have students retell the passage about getting the dogs harnessed and starting off as a distinct anecdote. Point out that personal essays such as the selection they are reading are often composed of many shorter anecdotes.

Use **Unit One Resource Book**, p. 76, for more practice.

Reading Skills and Strategies: VISUALIZE

 Ask students to sit with their eyes closed and visualize the scene where the author takes the dogs into the forest while you read it to them. Then ask them to describe mental images that the text descriptions evoked.

Teaching Options

It was early on in training Cookie's pups. They were already trained, knew how to run, where to run, when to run and were having a ball. I was still in that phase of my life when I thought I had some semblance of control over the team, did not yet understand that the dogs ran the show—all of it—and, if I was extremely lucky and didn't hit a tree, I was allowed to hang on the back of the sled and be a <u>spectator</u>. The problem was that my education was coming so slowly that I had fallen behind the dogs—say a couple of years—and it was becoming difficult to keep up.

This night had begun cleanly, wonderfully. It was midwinter, clear, fifteen or twenty below, a full moon—absolutely beautiful. I put Cookie on the front end and took three of the <u>seasoned</u> dogs and six of the pups, a total of ten dogs, counting Cookie. <u>Exceeding</u> seven dogs was risky—more than seven dogs meant it would be difficult to stop them or control them, in fact it could not

WORDS
TO
KNOW

spectator (spĕk′tā′tər) *n.* someone who watches an event
seasoned (sē′zənd) *adj.* made skillful by practice; experienced **season** *v.*
exceeding (ĭk-sē′dĭng) *n.* having more than **exceed** *v.*

156

(Mini Lesson) Viewing and Representing

Illustration for "Older Run"
by Ruth Paulsen

ART APPRECIATION Ruth Paulsen, Gary Paulsen's wife, frequently contributes original artwork to his exciting adventure stories.
Instruction Tell students that sometimes what artists choose not to show is as important as what they do show. In this picture, shadow plays an essential role. Ask how the artist has used shadow to highlight the action on a moonlit night.

Possible Response: The form on the sled is dark and obscured, so the viewer's eye is caught by the dogs in front, which are the most active part of the illustration.
Application Ask students to explain how the picture would be different if it showed action taking place at noon.
Possible Response: It might include more detail—for example, the features of the man on the sled—and more color. It would not be so stark—that is, the extremes of light and shadow would not be so great.

be done unless they wanted to stop—but I knew that and loaded the sled heavily with gear and four fifty-pound sacks of dog meat to help me control them.

Cookie held the gang line[2] out while I harnessed the rest of them, the pups last because they were so excited they kept jumping over the gang line and getting tangled, and when I popped the quick-release holding the sled to a post near the kennel we snapped out in good order.

That's how I thought of it—almost in a stuffy English manner. *Ahh yes, we left the kennel in good order, everything quite, that is to say, quite properly lined up.*

The weight of the sled did not seem to bother them at all. This, of course, should have been a warning to me, a caution that I had exceeded my limits of ability and understanding, but it was a smashing night (still in the English mode), clear and quite, that is to say, quite beautiful, and I gave them their head (as if I had any choice).

We climbed the shallow hills out back of the kennel and moved into the forest. I had a plan to run a hundred miles—take twelve, fourteen hours with a rest stop—and see how the young dogs did with a slightly longer run. They had been to fifty twice and I didn't <u>anticipate</u> any difficulty. If they did get tired, I would just stop for a day and play—God knows I was carrying enough extra food.

I also decided to make it an "open" run and stay away from thick forests and winding trails. Young dogs tend to forget themselves in the excitement and sometimes run into trees on tight corners because they don't remember to swing out. It doesn't hurt them much, but it isn't pleasant and running should, of all things, be fun for them.

So I took the railroad grades. In northern Minnesota there used to be trains through the forests for hauling wood and supplies to the logging camps and to service the hundreds of small towns. Most of the towns are gone now, and much of the wood is hauled on trucks, but the railroad grades are still there.

In a decision so correct it seems impossible that government could have made it, they decided to pull the tracks and ties off the <u>embankments</u> and maintain them for wilderness trails. In the summer they use them for bicycles and hikers, in the winter for skiers and snowmobilers and now dogsledders.

The trails make for classic runs. It's possible to leave the kennel and run a week, hundreds and hundreds of miles, without seeing the same country twice.

The one problem is the <u>trestles</u>. Minnesota is a land of lakes and rivers and every eight or ten miles the trains would cross a river. They made wooden trestles for the tracks and the trestles are still there. They are open, some of them sixty or seventy feet high, and bare wood—although they took the tracks themselves off so it was possible to see down through the ties.

Because they were open they would not hold snow so the snowmobile clubs covered them with one-inch treated plywood to close them in and provide a base for the snow.

---

2. **gang line:** the rope by which a team of sled dogs are attached to a sled.

WORDS TO KNOW

anticipate (ăn-tĭs′ə-pāt′) *v.* to look forward to; foresee
embankment (ĕm-băngk′mənt) *n.* a long mound of earth or stone, sometimes built to raise a roadway or railroad above the surrounding land
trestle (trĕs′əl) *n.* a framework built to support a bridge

157

The first few times we crossed one, the dogs hesitated, especially on the higher ones, but I took it easy and the older dogs figured it out and passed confidence to the team and it worked all right.

We had by this time run the trestles many times, knew where each one was, and the dogs whizzed across when we came to them.

Until now.

A Twenty-five miles into the run, smoking through the moonlight, we came to a trestle over an open rushing river. I had turned my head lamp off to let them run in the moonlight, which they preferred, and was thinking ahead, way ahead of a place we were going to camp to rest the pups. It was one of the most beautiful places I had ever seen, a quiet brook kept open by small warm springs, winding through a stand of elegant spruce and tall Norway pines. It was a place to make you whisper and think of churches, and I liked to stop and sit by a fire, and I was thinking of how it would be to camp there and be peaceful when the dogs suddenly stopped.

Dead in the middle of the trestle.

I hit the brakes with my right foot and almost killed myself. Some maniac had come and stolen all the plywood from the trestle and when I jammed the two hardened steel teeth of the brake down instead of sliding on the plywood surface to a gradual stop, they caught on an open cross tie and stopped the sled instantly.

I, however, did not stop.

In a <u>maneuver</u> that would have looked right in an old Mack Sennett[3] comedy, I slammed **B** into the cross handlebar with my stomach, drove all the wind out of my lungs, flew up and over the sled in a cartwheel, hit to the right of the wheel dogs, bounced once on the iron-hard cross ties of the trestle, <u>ricocheted</u>

neatly into space, and dropped twenty feet into a snow bank next to the river, headfirst, driving in like a falling arrow.

All of this occurred so fast I couldn't mentally keep up with it and still somehow thought that I must be on the sled when I was upside down in the snow bank. As it was I had hit perfectly. Had I gone a few feet farther I would have landed in the river and probably have drowned or frozen, ten feet sooner and I would have missed the snow bank and hit the bare packed ice, which would have broken my neck. It was the only place for me to land and not kill myself, but at the moment I was having trouble feeling gratitude.

I pushed my way out of the snow, cleared my eyes—it had happened so fast I hadn't had time to close them and they were full of snow—and peered up at the underside of the trestle where I could look through the ties and see the team still standing there, the dogs balanced precariously, teetering over open space.

"Easy," I called up. "Just easy now. Easy, easy, easy . . ."

Cookie had hit the trestle without stopping and run out, thinking that's what I wanted, until the whole team was out on the open ties. What stopped her was the pups. Somehow the adult dogs had kept up, stepping on the ties as fast as possible to keep going, but the young dogs had less experience and had tripped and gone down. Thank heaven they weren't injured and Cookie stopped when she felt them fall.

But the problem was still there. The team was spread along the trestle, each dog on a tie, and it seemed an impossible situation. To swing a dog team around requires a great deal of space. If they are dragged back on top

---

3. **Mack Sennett:** an early director of silent movies, especially slapstick comedies.

> WORDS
> TO
> KNOW
>
> **maneuver** (mə-nōō′vər) *n.* a movement or change in direction
> **ricochet** (rĭk′ə-shā′) *v.* to bounce off a surface

158

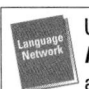

of each other they get dreadfully tangled and tend to fight, and I couldn't imagine a dogfight at night with ten dogs on a narrow railroad trestle twenty feet off the ground.

An answer did not come to me immediately. I climbed the bank back up onto the trestle. Cookie was frozen out in front of the team holding them, her back legs jammed against one cross tie and her front feet clawed on the one in front, and the snow hook had fallen in the impact of the stop and had set itself in the ties under the sled so the team was held in place while I decided what to do.

I couldn't turn them around.

I couldn't drive them over the trestle without injuring dogs.

"I can't do anything," I said aloud to Cookie, who was looking back at me waiting for me to solve the thing. "It's impossible . . ."

You, her eyes said, *got us into this, and you'd better get us out.*

Her message hung that way for half a minute, my thoughts whirling, and I finally decided the only way to do it was to release each dog, one at a time, and let them go forward or backward on their own. I thought briefly of carrying them out, one by one, but I had no extra rope to tie them (it was the last run I made without carrying the extra rope) when I got across the trestle.

I would have to let them go.

I started with the older dogs. I let them loose and set the ties and was amazed to see that each of them went on across the trestle— the longer way—rather than turn and go back. They didn't hesitate but set out, moving carefully from tie to tie until they were across. Whereupon they didn't stop and instead, as I

"Easy," I called up. "Just easy now. Easy, easy, easy . . ."

had feared, took off down the railroad grade. They had been here before and knew the way home. I let the young dogs go then and they were slower and more frightened, especially when they looked down, but as soon as they crossed they took off as well and vanished in the night as they tried to catch up with the rest of the dogs.

"Well," I said to Cookie. "It's you and me . . ."

I let her loose and was amazed to see her take off after the team. We were good friends, had been for years, and I was sure she would stay with me, but she was gone in an instant.

"Traitor." I said it with great feeling. The truth is she could not have pulled the sled anyway. It was too heavy for one dog. But it would have been nice to have company. I worried that they would have trouble, get injured somehow, run out on a highway and get hit by a car.

It was like watching my body leave me, my family, and I gathered up the gang line and unhooked the snow hook and dragged the sled across the trestle. Once I got it on the snow it slid a bit easier and I thought that it must be thirty, thirty-five miles to home the shortest way and it would take me three days—or three miserable days, as I considered it then. I had a thermos of tea on the sled and I took time to have a cup, feeling at intervals sorry for myself and hoping silently that I would someday meet up with the man who stole the plywood from the trestle.

It was putting the inevitable off and I finally accepted it and put away the thermos and moved to the front of the sled and put the gang line around my waist and started pulling.

Less Proficient Readers
Give students guidance and practice in paraphrasing and summarizing text to recall and organize ideas. Have them summarize the action that takes place after Paulsen has fallen from the bridge.

Possible Response: Paulsen determines that the only way to get out of the situation is to let the dogs loose from their harnesses so that each can get off the bridge individually. As he lets each go, it disappears into the night. Even his favorite dog, Cookie, runs after the others. He is disappointed and feels alone but drags the sled off the bridge and has a cup of tea while he thinks over his situation.

Students Acquiring English
1 Explain that the expression "with great feeling" means "with a lot of emotion."

Multiple Learning Styles
Kinesthetic Learners
Have students act out the action of the accident at the trestle. They can form a mimed dogteam, and one student can take the role of Paulsen. Then have them compare communication in the two different forms, the mime and the print version.

 Speaking and Listening

RETELLING

Prepare Explain to students that in retelling they should practice adapting spoken language through word choice, diction, and usage to their audience, purpose, and occasion. Suggest that while they retell a story, they think about how the audience will experience their telling, and use effective rate, volume, pitch, and tone.

Present Have students work in groups. Each student will retell the story of "Older Run" in his or her own words. The first retelling will be as if the story were being told as a bedtime story for a preschool child. The second retelling will be as if the story were being told as a speech on safety

given to a school class. Remind students to vary their retellings based on audience and purpose. For example, suggest that the retelling to the child should be slower, use simpler words, and leave out much of the details about the railroad trestle. As students work, monitor their progress by moving from group to group

Use **Writing Transparencies,** p. 15, for additional support. Use **Communications Transparencies and Copymasters,** p. 12 for additional support.

BLOCK SCHEDULING This activity is particularly well suited for longer class periods.

Literary Analysis: SUSPENSE

A Ask students to identify details that Paulsen uses to create suspense—that is, the things that slow the story down at this point.

Possible Response: He discusses the sled, having tea, how far away home is, his wish to meet the person who stole the plywood, and how he pulls the sled for a while along the railroad way.

Literary Analysis: SARCASM

B Explain that sarcasm is a type of humor that depends on biting wit directed against a particular individual. Ask students to examine the passage in which the dogs return to Paulsen to find examples of sarcasm.

Possible Response: Paulsen's questions "Get lonely?" and "What is this? Loyalty?" are sarcastic.

Reading Skills and Strategies: EVALUATE

C Have students evaluate the text to determine Paulsen's feelings when Cookie brings the team back to him.

Possible Response: He is very moved emotionally by Cookie's intelligence and loyalty to him; he says that he has a lump "the size of a football" in his throat.

Reading Skills and Strategies: PREDICT

Ask students to predict the changes Paulsen will make as he continues his training of dogs after the incident described in "Older Run."

Possible Response: He will have more faith in Cookie and he will carry an extra length of rope for emergencies.

A Once it broke free it slid well enough and I set a slow pace. I had thought of hiding the sled in some way and coming back for it later but it was coming on a weekend and the snowmobilers would be on the trails and there were hundreds of them. Surely, the sled— boiled white ash and oak with plastic runner shoes—would be too tempting.

I pulled half an hour on the embankment, trudging along—it seemed like a week—and I developed an updated gratitude for the dogs; their effortless strides covered miles so fast that I felt like with my own puny efforts I was on a treadmill. It seemed to take ten minutes to pass a tree.

Fifteen more minutes, I thought, *then I'll take a break*. I had also decided to throw out some of the dog food and let the wolves have it. It was commercial meat and had cost money but at the rate I was moving I wouldn't get it home until I was an old man anyway.

Ten minutes passed and I said to heck with it and sat down on the sled and was sitting there, sipping half a cup of tea, when I heard a sound and Minto, a large red dog who had a pointed face, came trotting up and sat down facing me.

"Hello," I said. "Get lonely?"

B He cocked his head and I petted him, and while rubbing his ears another dog, named Winston, trotted up.

"What is this?" I asked. "Loyalty?"

The truth is they shouldn't have been there. I had lost dogs several times and had them leave me and run home. Trapline teams,[4] or teams that are lived with and enjoyed recreationally, sometimes are trained to stay with the musher;[5] and indeed Cookie had brought a team to me when I was injured once while trapping. But that is rare. Mostly they go home. And race teams, trained for only one thing, to go and go and never stop, simply do not come back. These were not trapline dogs but race dogs, and while I sat marveling at them four more came back, then one more, then the last two pups and, finally, Cookie.

I stood and spread out the gang line and hooked up their harnesses, which were still on the dogs, putting Cookie in first and then the rest, and I wanted to say something and I finally did manage to get "thank you" out. But in truth I couldn't speak. I had a lump the size of a football in my throat. I stood on the back of the sled and they lined out and took off and I still wondered how it could be.

C I do not know what happened out there— although some of the dogs had slight wounds in the end of their ears clearly made by bites. I did not see nor could I even guess what had transpired.

I know how it looked. I had been alone, Cookie had run after them, and they had come back. All of them, some bleeding slightly from bitten ears. They all got in harness and we finished the run in good order and when I was sitting in the kitchen later, sipping a cup of hot soup and trying to explain it to Ruth, I shook my head.

"I know it sounds insane but it looked like Cookie went after them, caught them and sent them back to me. I've never heard of anything like it."

"Well, if it looks like a duck, quacks like a duck, and walks like a duck . . ."

I nodded. "I agree, but it's so incredible."

"I don't know about that, but I do know one thing."

"What's that?"

"You aren't paying her nearly enough . . ." ❖

---

4. **trapline teams:** teams of working sled dogs that provide transportation for animal trappers.

5. **musher:** a person who drives a dogsled.

WORDS TO KNOW

marvel (mär'vəl) *v.* to feel amazement or wonder at the sight of

transpire (trăn-spīr') *v.* to happen; occur

160

Teaching Options

✓ **Assessment** **Informal Assessment**

WRITING FOR A NEW AUDIENCE You can informally assess students' understanding of the selection by having them rewrite it for a new audience. Offer choices of different formats, including comic book and tall tale. Before doing their writing, they should analyze the characteristics of the text they have chosen and identify its purposes, such as whether it is intended to inform, influence, express, or entertain.

RUBRIC

3 Full Accomplishment Response reflects a full understanding of the events in the story and how addressing it to a new audience would alter the telling of those events.

2 Substantial Accomplishment Response shows some understanding of events but incomplete comprehension overall, or does not consistently reflect the needs of the intended audience.

1 Little or Partial Accomplishment Response shows little understanding of the events of the story or the needs of the audience.

Thinking through the **LITERATURE**

Connect to the Literature

1. **What Do You Think?** How did you feel when the dogs returned?

Comprehension Check
- What causes Paulsen's accident?
- Why does Paulsen let the dogs go?
- What does Paulsen say race teams are trained to do?

Think Critically

2. What does Paulsen mean when he says, "I was still in that phase of my life when I thought I had some semblance of control over the team, did not yet understand that the dogs ran the show . . ."?

3. **ACTIVE READING** **IDENTIFYING EFFECTS OF AUTHOR'S PERSPECTIVE** Look back at the chart you made in your **READER'S NOTEBOOK.** Compare notes with a classmate. Between the two of you, decide how Paulsen's perspective most strongly affects his storytelling.

4. How did reading Paulsen's story make you see the connection between dogs and people in a new way?

Extend Interpretations

5. **COMPARING TEXTS** In the story "Ghost of the Lagoon," on page 124, the main character faces danger together with a very loyal dog. How are the situations in that story and in "Older Run" similar or different?

6. **Different Perspectives** What do you think happened to the dogs when they ran away? What made them come back? Retell the scene after the accident from Cookie's point of view. Use details from the story and your own imagination.

7. **Connect to Life** Do you have qualities of an adventurer? Use examples from the story and from your own experience to explain your opinion.

Literary Analysis

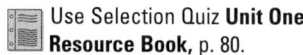

An **anecdote** is a short, entertaining story, either **fiction** or **nonfiction,** about a single event. Usually an anecdote is rich with small details.

Writers often use an anecdote to throw a spotlight on a character. For example, in "Older Run," Paulsen shows readers some traits of Cookie, his favorite dog. Notice what traits are shown in the following detail:

Cookie had hit the trestle without stopping and run out, thinking that's what I wanted, until the whole team was out on the open ties. What stopped her was the pups.

Cooperative Learning Activity

With a small group, brainstorm some traits of both Cookie and Gary Paulsen. Choose a group member to record your ideas in two webs. Then have the group's recorder add a detail from the anecdote that would help readers to see each trait.

OLDER RUN **161**

Extend Interpretations

5. **Comparing Texts** Responses should note similarities and differences between the two animal stories. **To make this activity more challenging,** ask students to write a new story in which the characters in the two stories meet, tell their tales, and compare and contrast their experiences.

6. **Different Perspectives** Responses should plausibly explain what the dogs were doing in the interval in which they were absent, focusing on Cookie's role in bringing them back.

To get students started on this activity, reread the end of the story aloud.

7. **Connect to Life** Responses should indicate what the qualities of an adventurer are and provide appropriate details from the story and from personal experience to support statements made. **To make this activity easier,** hold a discussion in which students explore what it takes to be an adventurer. Then suggest that students base their writing on some of the themes and ideas worked out in class.

GUIDING STUDENT RESPONSE

Connect to the Literature

What Do You Think?

1. Possible Responses: I felt relieved, surprised, justified in my confidence in dogs, and glad for Paulsen.

Comprehension Check
- Someone has stolen the plywood decking from the trestle.
- There is not enough room on the trestle to swing the team around.
- They are trained to keep going and not come back to the sled.

📃 Use Selection Quiz **Unit One Resource Book,** p. 80.

Think Critically

2. Possible Response: He means that he once believed that he could control the dogs, but he now knows that a sled driver has little if any real control over the dogs.

3. Possible Responses: Paulsen's perspective affects the story most in showing his acquired knowledge and wisdom about dogs, as well as his love for them.

📃 Use **Reading and Critical Thinking Transparencies,** p. 28, for additional support.

4. Possible Responses: It made me realize that dogs care about people in very intelligent and sophisticated ways, even though people sometimes underestimate them.

Literary Analysis

Anecdote Students' character webs should accurately and appropriately depict character traits of both Cookie and Paulsen. They should include details from the story that illustrate the given traits. Traits that might be mentioned include: Cookie: intelligence, loyalty, a can-do attitude; Paulsen: love of risk and adventure, coolness under stress, gratitude towards loyalty.

📃 Use **Literary Analysis Transparencies,** p. 11 for additional support.

Grammar in Context

WRITING EXERCISE Responses will vary. Possible responses are shown.
1. The trails lead to an open field.
2. The bear bothers the dogs.
3. The raven pecks the puppies away from the food pan.

CONNECT TO THE LITERATURE
Pairs include: It was, They were/knew/were having, I was, I thought, I had, I did (not yet) understand, dogs ran, I was, I didn't hit, I was allowed, problem was, education was coming, I had fallen, it was becoming.

Vocabulary in Action

EXERCISE A
1. d
2. c
3. b
4. c
5. d
6. c
7. d
8. a
9. c
10. b

EXERCISE B
Accept tips that make sense and use at least five of the WORDS TO KNOW.

Grammar in Context: Subject-Verb Agreement

If a subject is singular, its verb must also be singular. If a subject is plural, its verb must also be plural. This is what is meant by **subject-verb agreement.**

> **Singular: One dog jumps ahead.**
> **Plural: Two dogs jump ahead.**

Notice that adding an *s* makes a subject plural: "one dog," but "two dogs." Notice that adding an *s* makes a verb singular: "one dog jumps," but "two dogs jump." Some common verbs, like *to be, to go,* and *to have,* follow their own rules for changing number.

Usage Tip: The verb should always agree in number with the subject. Don't be confused by the position of the subject or the verb, or by the words that fall between them:

> **There were still problems.**
> **(Think "Problems were still there.")**

WRITING EXERCISE Rewrite each sentence. Change each singular subject to plural, and each plural subject to singular. Then make the verb agree with the changed subject.

Example: *Original* The dog seems nervous.

Rewritten The dogs seem nervous.

1. The trail leads to an open field.
2. The bears bother the dogs.
3. The ravens peck the puppies away from the food pan.

Connect to the Literature Read the first paragraph on page 156 of the story. Notice the agreement between subjects and verbs in the paragraph. Then list all of the agreeing pairs.

Grammar Handbook Making Subjects and Verbs Agree, p. R60

Vocabulary in Action

EXERCISE A: ASSESSMENT PRACTICE On your paper, write the letter of the word that does not belong with the other words in each set. Use a dictionary if you need help.

1. (a) embankment (b) dam (c) levee (d) bridge
2. (a) spectator (b) onlooker (c) player (d) witness
3. (a) motion (b) crash (c) maneuver (d) action
4. (a) trestle (b) support (c) guide (d) structure
5. (a) accustomed (b) seasoned (c) skillful (d) new

6. (a) surpassing (b) excelling (c) satisfying (d) exceeding
7. (a) anticipate (b) expect (c) foresee (d) ignore
8. (a) land (b) rebound (c) ricochet (d) bounce
9. (a) happen (b) occur (c) miss (d) transpire
10. (a) marvel (b) thin (c) ponder (d) muse

EXERCISE B Write some tips for sports safety. Use at least five of the Words to Know.

Building Vocabulary

For an in-depth lesson on synonyms and antonyms, see page 230.

WORDS TO KNOW					
	anticipate	exceeding	marvel	seasoned	transpire
	embankment	maneuver	ricochet	spectator	trestle

Teaching Options

SUBJECT-VERB AGREEMENT

Instruction Remind students that a pronoun is a word used *in place of* (Latin *pro*) a noun. The singular pronouns used as subjects are *I; you; he; she; it.* The plural pronouns used as subjects are *we; you; they.* Pronouns, like all subjects, take a verb that agrees with them. That is, if the pronoun is singular, the verb must also be singular. Write the following examples on the chalkboard.
SINGULAR I am a dog.
PLURAL We are dogs.

Mini Lesson Grammar

SINGULAR You are a dog.
PLURAL You are dogs.
SINGULAR He/She is a dog.
PLURAL They are dogs.
Point out to students that in some cases, the verb is the same in both singular and plural.

Exercises Have students change singular pronouns to plural and plural to singular, and then make the verb agree with the changed subject.
1. They love to run more than anything. (*She/He loves*)

2. I was ready to go anywhere on that sled. (*We were*)
3. We bounce off the trestle and fall in a snowbank. (*I bounce*)
4. You are the best dog in the world. (*You are*)
5. She was more loyal than Paulsen thought. (*They were*)

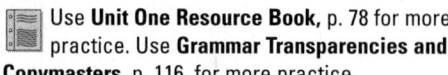 Use **Unit One Resource Book,** p. 78 for more practice. Use **Grammar Transparencies and Copymasters,** p. 116, for more practice.

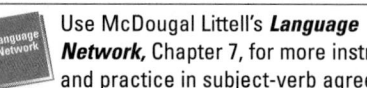 Use McDougal Littell's *Language Network,* Chapter 7, for more instruction and practice in subject-verb agreement.

LIFE IN THE DAY OF GARY PAULSEN

Preparing to Read

Focus Your Reading

ACTIVE READING | **DRAWING CONCLUSIONS**

One way of making inferences is by drawing conclusions. You use all the knowledge you have gained through reading about a subject. Then you can decide, or **conclude**: What are the most important things you learned? What are your strongest impressions?

When you read several pieces, or **sources,** about one subject, you get a variety of views, or **perspectives.** The piece you are about to read tells about a recent typical day for Gary Paulsen aboard his sailboat.

📖 READER'S NOTEBOOK

As you read Paulsen's words, try to recall what you already know about him. Jot down your conclusions about the following:
- his personality traits
- things he cares most about
- things about his life that you find exciting

At 5:30 A.M. I have a bowl of oatmeal, then I go to work. First up, I stow all the gear away. Then I take the covers off the sails and fire the engine up to get out of the harbor. I hate the motor—once it's off, there's silence. I have a steering vane so I can go below and cook or sit and write. Sailing is an inherently beautiful thing. To me it's like dancing with the wind and the water; it's like running with wolves—a perfect meeting of man and nature.

We all have the capability to work out of our minds, and I think we obstruct that constantly. So much of my life, and perhaps everybody's life, is television and traffic jams and trivia. A hundred yards into the woods on the back of a dog team, or the moment you clear the breakwaters in the harbors, all that is gone: my head clears and I feel calm. I have a radio but I frequently turn the darn thing off for a couple of days.

On the boat there is nothing, and I know I work better that way. I think that the writer in the city, with the traffic and the parties and the theater, is at a disadvantage, because the distractions are so enormous. I work in the city when I have to, but I find it really hard. I don't need much. The way I live is nobody's idea of luxury, but that's the way I like it. I use a battery to charge my laptop and I just head out to sea. Sometimes I go 150 miles out and 150 miles back; sometimes I head out and keep right on going.

I live on a diet of gruel because of my heart condition: no meat, no cheese, no fish; just beans and rice and marshmallows for treats, because they're fat free. I eat two meals a day and drink decaffeinated coffee—my cholesterol level has dropped to near normal.

I write all morning, then I have a two-hour break to answer mail. I get around 400 letters a day from children and I have a secretary in New York who helps me answer them all. I owe a great deal to dogs and a

Teaching the Literature

DRAWING CONCLUSIONS

Point out to students that people do not always say exactly what they mean in a piece of writing, or that sometimes what they mean is so complicated that it takes some hard thinking to understand it. For both of these reasons, it is often necessary to analyze a piece of writing in order to draw conclusions about the author's intent.

Students can analyze "A Life in the Day of Gary Paulsen" to draw conclusions about what kind of person the author is. To direct them in this process, ask the following questions:

- What does Paulsen mean when he says, "A lot of what I do is extreme"?

Possible Response: He means that he does dangerous things in lonely places where most other people would not want to go.

- What clues about the reasons behind his writing does Paulsen give?

Possible Response: He says that sometimes he writes to reach out and make things right for others through his writing, and he says that he is sharing his life with others through his writing so that he doesn't feel lonely.

- What is the most important thing in the world for Gary Paulsen?

Possible Response: The most important thing is having moments when he experiences something wonderful in nature.

📋 Use **Reading and Critical Thinking Transparencies,** p. 18, for additional support.

1. **Possible Response:** It is a life of danger, loneliness, freedom, and closeness to nature.

2. **Possible Response:** Students may have drawn the conclusion that Paulsen is independent because he does not need others with him on his boat. He cares most about writing, dogs, children, and nature, as is clear from the way he describes each of these.

3. **Possible Responses:** He eats gruel, just beans and rice, whereas it seems he once was a hunter and ate meat. He takes time to answer mail sent to him by his fans. He once needed company to keep him from getting lonely, but now he does not. He no longer pursues awards and money.

great deal to children, and I try to help both of those species. A lot of what I write is fiction based on my life. I spent my whole childhood running away. A lot of kids know this through my books, so I look for mail from kids in the same situation. It helps them to know you care. I'll try and get in touch with their school to let them know this child is in trouble. I'm aware I might be the only person they've told. I got a letter once from a girl who said, "My only friends in the world are your books."

Recently I was sailing down the Baja strip of Mexico from California. It's about 900 miles, with no anchorage, and it's very rough. I got caught in a storm and two other boats were lost. I talked to them over the radio before they went down. There was no way I could physically help them. Sometimes writing is that way. You want to reach out and make things right.

I'm not interested in money. I don't even know what I make. I give it all to my wife and she's very happy. I have all I want. Once a year I buy three new pairs of jeans and three denim shirts. I do have a jacket and tie for occasions, but I still got kicked out of the Savoy in London once.

I don't get lonely. There was a time when I lusted over having somebody who I could turn to and say, "Look at that!" I'd be leaning over the bow strip to touch the dolphins swimming alongside the boat. One time, three of them somersaulted in the air and crashed into the water, which was golden with the sinking sun. It was the most beautiful thing, and I felt so happy I just wanted to tell someone. But I realized that I'm telling it through my writing the whole time.

Occasionally I've tried to get people to go with me, but rarely do they understand. A lot of what I do is extreme. Sometimes Ruth meets me. She likes to fly to the pretty places and miss the slog [long, hard work]; for me, the slog is the beauty. I have no goal, no destination. I used to think I should be fulfilled by awards or by earning a million dollars, but with age has come some kind of self-knowledge. My rewards are less tangible: they're the killer whales who reared up out of the water to look at me. Or a 15-knot wind across my beam. Those are my moments of pure joy. ❖

Thinking Through the Literature

1. What is your impression of life on a sailboat?

2. **ACTIVE READING** **DRAWING CONCLUSIONS** With a partner, share some of the ideas you wrote in your 📖 **READER'S NOTEBOOK**. Discuss details from the sources in the author study that support your ideas.

3. Aside from living on a sailboat, what lifestyle changes do you see in Paulsen from the time he began writing to the time described in this article?

PREPARING to *Read*

"I did not move, did not breathe, did not think or do anything."

from **Woodsong**

Memoir by GARY PAULSEN

(Connect to Your Life)

In the Wild In the wilderness of Minnesota, wild animals, such as bears, were a part of Gary Paulsen's everyday life. With a small group of classmates, discuss what wild animals live in your region.

Build Background

CONNECT TO GEOGRAPHY Thick forests once covered 70 percent of Minnesota. Today, forests cover only about 35 percent of the state. Minnesota's most spectacular woods can be found in the 3-million-acre Superior National Forest, north of Lake Superior. The northern and northeastern sections of the state are the most rugged. In this region, people are scarce, but wild animals are plentiful. One of the few states where timber wolves still roam free, Minnesota is also home to white-tailed deer, beavers, and black bears.

Minnesota Population Density Map

Number of persons per square mile

More than 100
50 to 100
25 to 50
Less than 25

LaserLinks: Background for Reading
Geographical Connection
Science Connection

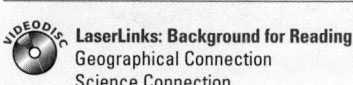
WORDS TO KNOW **Vocabulary Preview**
menace novelty predator rummaging scavenging

Focus Your Reading

LITERARY ANALYSIS MEMOIR A **memoir** is a writer's description of his or her own memories. It is a type of **autobiography**, or self-told life story. Because a memoir is written about real people and real events, it is considered to be **nonfiction**. But because a memoir relies so heavily on memory, it can sometimes read very much like fiction. As you read this selection from *Woodsong*, look for language that reminds you of a fictional adventure story.

ACTIVE READING QUESTIONING Good readers ask questions like these: Why did things happen the way they did? How did people feel? What is the writer's opinion about the subject? Questions can help you have a two-way conversation with the author.

READER'S NOTEBOOK As you read the story, jot down a few questions you have. Also, find statements that show the author's opinion. Decide whether you share the author's opinion.

WOODSONG **165**

LESSON RESOURCES

UNIT ONE RESOURCE BOOK, pp. 81–87

ASSESSMENT
Formal Assessment, pp. 25–26
Teacher's Guide to Assessment and Portfolio Use
Test Generator

SKILLS TRANSPARENCIES AND COPYMASTERS
Literary Analysis
• Autobiography, TR 11 (for Paired Activity, p. 170)

Reading and Critical Thinking
• Questioning, TR 9 (for Thinking Through the Literature, p. 170)
Grammar
• Correcting Run-on Sentences, CM 61 (for Mini Lesson, p. 171)
Vocabulary
• Context Clues: Example, CM 31 (for Mini Lesson, p. 167)

INTEGRATED TECHNOLOGY
Audio Library
LaserLinks
• See **Teacher's SourceBook,** p. 13
Internet: Research Starter

Visit our website:
www.mcdougallittell.com

This selection is included in the **Grade 6 InterActive Reader.**

Objectives
1. understand and appreciate a **memoir (Literary Analysis)**
2. use the reading strategy of **questioning** to understand and analyze characters **(Active Reading)**

Summary
So many bears search for food outside Gary Paulsen's Minnesota cabin that he gives them nicknames and treats them like pets. One day, as Paulsen is burning trash that includes food scraps, the smell attracts a male bear nicknamed Scarhead. In his eagerness to get at the food, Scarhead rips up the enclosure where the trash is burned. When Paulsen angrily and unthinkingly tosses a stick at Scarhead, the bear turns on him. Paulsen, knowing that the creature can kill him with one blow, waits helplessly while Scarhead decides his fate. The bear chooses not to attack, and Paulsen hurries to get his rifle. He is about to shoot Scarhead—and then he realizes that the bear not only has spared his life but has reminded him to respect his fellow animals. Humbled and wiser, Paulsen puts the gun away.

Thematic Link
Paulsen once again demonstrates the ability to keep cool under stress—or at least to get a grip on himself before he commits an angry act he would regret. This is a form of courage in action.

5-Minute Warm-Up

Daily Language SkillBuilder

Have students **proofread** the display sentences on page 19k and write them correctly. The sentences also appear on Transparency 5 of **Grammar Transparencies and Copymasters.**

Mini Lesson **Preteaching Vocabulary**

If you would like to preteach the WORDS TO KNOW for this selection, use the Mini Lesson, p. 167.

Literary Analysis MEMOIR

The Focus Your Reading section asked students to look for language in "Woodsong" that reminds them of fiction or ordinary storytelling rather than non-fiction, such as essays or news reports. Ask them to look for examples of a story-telling style on the first page. How are these examples different from what one might expect in a newspaper report?

Possible Response: Examples of story-telling style include: "We have bear trouble"; "Spring, when the bears come, is the worst"; "they are hungry beyond caution." The examples use more colorful, dramatic language than newspaper reports might.

 Use **Unit One Resource Book,** p. 83 for more practice.

Active Reading QUESTIONING

Ask students to form and revise questions arising from reading the material on the first page of the selection and to discuss them.

Possible Response: Why doesn't Paulsen build a strong enclosure to keep out the bears? How did his wife feel about being chased by a bear? What do the bears do when they annoy the dogs?

 Use **Unit One Resource Book,** p. 82 for more practice.

Literary Analysis: SENSORY DETAILS

Point out that a key part of Paulsen's story is the attraction that the smell of meat has for animals. Ask students to watch for details about smells as they read the story.

FROM WOODSONG

BY GARY PAULSEN

Wabana-Wagamuman [Bear in the forest] (1989), Tom Uttech. Oil on canvas, courtesy of Struve Gallery, Chicago.

Teaching Options

Mini Lesson **Viewing and Representing**

Wabana-Wagamuman
by Tom Uttech

ART APPRECIATION Tom Uttech's haunting wood-land paintings are inspired by the wilderness regions of North America. The title of this painting is in the Chippewa (or Ojibwa) language.
Instruction Have students describe how the illustrator's choice of elements helps to represent and extend the meaning of the text. As an example, point out that the painter has chosen to show the bear as a small part of the picture. Ask what effect this has on the viewer.

Possible Response: It makes the viewer appreciate that the bear is just part of a larger natural world.
Application Ask students to make a prediction about the message of the story based on the message of the picture.
Possible Response: Both the picture and the story are about animals as part of a larger world. In the story, humans are included with the animals in that world.

In Woodsong *Gary Paulsen describes his life as a trapper in the woods of northern Minnesota. He lived with his wife, Ruth, and his son, James, in a small cabin that did not have plumbing or electricity. At the time, Paulsen was not writing stories but simply learning the ways of the woods. This episode describes one of the lessons he learned.*

We have bear trouble. Because we feed processed meat to the dogs, there is always the smell of meat over the kennel. In the summer it can be a bit high[1] because the dogs like to "save" their food sometimes for a day or two or four—burying it to dig up later. We live on the edge of wilderness, and consequently the meat smell brings any number of visitors from the woods.

Skunks abound, and foxes and coyotes and wolves and weasels—all predators. We once had an eagle live over the kennel for more than a week, scavenging from the dogs, and a crazy group of ravens has pretty much taken over the puppy pen. Ravens are protected by the state, and they seem to know it. When I walk toward the puppy pen with the buckets of meat, it's a tossup to see who gets it—the pups or the birds. They have actually pecked the puppies away from the food pans until they have gone through and taken what they want.

Spring, when the bears come, is the worst. They have been in hibernation through the winter, and they are hungry beyond caution. The meat smell draws them like flies, and we frequently have two or three around the kennel at the same time. Typically they do not bother us much—although my wife had a bear chase her from the garden to the house one morning— but they do bother the dogs.

---

1. **it can be a bit high:** the smell can be rather strong.

| WORDS TO KNOW | **predator** (prĕd′ə-tər) *n.* an animal that hunts other animals for food |
| | **scavenging** (skăv′ən-jĭng) *adj.* searching for discarded scraps **scavenge** *v.* |

167

Customizing Instruction

Less Proficient Readers
Ask student to compare text events with their own experiences by having them write briefly about situations that they feel taught them valuable lessons and relate their experiences to Paulsen's experience. Tell them to jot down similarities they find between Paulsen's story and their own experiences as they read. Remind students to support their responses by referring to relevant aspects of the text and their own experiences.

Set a Purpose Have students think as they read about how Paulsen's life in the woods is different from or similar to their own. Ask them to consider if they have the same kinds of opportunity to learn the lessons Paulsen learns.

Students Acquiring English
Use **Spanish Study Guide,** pp. 31–33 for additional support.

Gifted and Talented
Have students look for phrases set off by dashes in the selection. Ask them to explain why Paulsen includes each phrase.
Possible Responses:
Page 169: "I fired it off and went back into the house for a moment—not more than two minutes." Paulsen is clarifying and emphasizing that the interval of time he is talking about is very short;
". . . and without thinking—because I was so used to him—I picked up a stick . . ." In describing an action, Paulsen inserts a clause that explains the reason for the action.

Multiple Learning Styles
Visual Learners
Have students draw or paint some of the details of the setting described in the selection, or depict a moment of the action that most impresses them.

Preteaching Vocabulary

Mini Lesson

CONTEXT CLUES: EXAMPLE
Instruction Point out to students that examples in texts sometimes give valuable clues to the meaning of an unknown word. From the sentence, "Skunks abound, and foxes and coyotes and wolves and weasels—all predators," they might be able to figure out from the examples given that a predator is an animal that hunts other animals.

Exercises The following sentences use examples to explain some of the WORDS TO KNOW. Have students write a definition of each underlined word based on the examples given.

1. A thunderstorm, an ant nest, or a hungry bear can be a menace to a picnic.
2. Paulsen is fascinated by novelty—new places, books he has never read, or sights he has never seen.
3. Bears are known for rummaging behavior, including digging through trash cans and poking into other forbidden sources of food.
4. Ravens live by scavenging, taking the food gathered by people, predators, or other birds.

Use **Unit One Resource Book,** p. 84.
Use **Vocabulary Transparencies and Copymasters,** p. 31, for additional support.

A Remind students that as they read, good readers gather information and combine it with what they know from their own experience to predict. Ask them to predict what might happen next.

Possible Response: The bear may injure Paulsen (he has described how a bear already killed two dogs).

Literary Analysis: CHARACTER

Instruct students in analyzing characters, including their traits. Ask what they can conclude about Paulsen from these actions: (1) He throws a stick at the bear; (2) he wants to kill the bear; (3) he decides not to kill the bear.

Possible Responses: (1) He is impulsive; (2) he responds with anger when challenged; (3) he has a merciful, thoughtful side to his personality.

Reading Skills and Strategies:
AUTHOR'S PURPOSE

Guide students to identify effects of the author's purpose. On the board, draw a circle with four circles clustered around it. In the center circle write "Author's Purpose." In the circles around it, write: "To Entertain," "To Inform," "To Express an Opinion," and "To Persuade." Explain that the outer circles represent purposes that an author may have in writing a work, though often writers have more than one purpose. Ask what purposes they believe Paulsen had in writing the selection.

Possible Response: Paulsen wrote to entertain readers, to inform them about a way of life different from their own, and to express his opinion about the place of humans in nature.

Use **Literary Analysis Transparencies,** p. 16, for additional support.

They are so big and strong that the dogs fear them, and the bears trade on this fear to get their food. It's common to see them scare a dog into his house and take his food. Twice we have had dogs killed by rough bear swats that broke their necks—and the bears took their food.

We have evolved[2] an uneasy peace with them, but there is the problem of familiarity. The first time you see a bear in the kennel it is a <u>novelty</u>, but when the same ones are there day after day, you wind up naming some of them (old Notch-Ear, Billy-Jo, etc.). There gets to be a too-relaxed attitude. We started to treat them like pets.

1 A major mistake.

There was a large male around the kennel for a week or so. He had a white streak across his head, which I guessed was a wound scar from some hunter—bear hunting is allowed here. He wasn't all that bad, so we didn't mind him. He would frighten the dogs and take their hidden stashes now and then, but he didn't harm them, and we became accustomed to him hanging around. We called him Scarhead, and now and again we would joke about him as if he were one of the yard animals.

At this time we had three cats, forty-two dogs, fifteen or twenty chickens, eight ducks, nineteen large white geese, a few banty hens, ten fryers which we'd raised from chicks and **2** couldn't (as my wife put it) "snuff and eat," and six woods-wise goats.

The bears, strangely, didn't bother any of the yard animals. There must have been a rule, or some order to the way they lived, because they would hit the kennel and steal from the dogs but leave the chickens and goats and other yard stock completely alone—although you would have had a hard time convincing the goats of this fact. The goats spent a great deal of time with their back hair up, whuffing

and blowing snot at the bears—and at the dogs, who would *gladly* have eaten them. The goats never really believed in the truce.

There is not a dump or landfill to take our trash to, and so we separate it—organic, inorganic[3]—and deal with it ourselves. We burn the paper in a screened enclosure, and it is fairly efficient; but it's impossible to get all the food particles off wrapping paper, so when it's burned, the food particles burn with it.

And give off a burnt food smell.

And nothing draws bears like burning food. It must be that they have learned to understand human dumps—where they spend a great deal of time foraging. And they learn amazingly fast. In Alaska, for instance, the bears already know that the sound of a moose hunter's hunt means there will be a fresh gut pile when the hunter cleans the moose. They come at a run when they hear the shot. It's often a close race to see if the hunter will get to the moose before the bears take it away. . . .

Because we're on the south edge of the wilderness area, we try to wait until there is a northerly breeze before we burn, so the food smell will carry south, but it doesn't always help. Sometimes bears, wolves, and other predators are already south, working the sheep farms down where it is more settled—they take a terrible toll[4] of sheep—and we catch them on the way back through.

That's what happened one July morning.

---

2. **evolved** (ĭ-vŏlvd′): developed by a series of small changes.

3. **organic** (ôr-găn′ĭk), **inorganic** (ĭn′ôr-găn′ĭk): on the one hand, things made of plant or animal material; and on the other, things made of material that has never been alive.

4. **take a terrible toll:** destroy a large number.

WORDS TO KNOW   **novelty** (nŏv′əl-tē) *n.* something new and unusual

BLOCK SCHEDULING: MANAGING TIME

If your schedule requires that you cover the lesson objectives in shorter time, use . . .
- Preparing to Read, p. 165
- Thinking Through the Literature, p. 170
- Grammar in Context, p. 171
- Vocabulary in Action, p. 171

If you want to take advantage of longer class time, use . . .
- TE Teaching Options: Viewing and Representing, p. 166; Preteaching Vocabulary, p. 167; Standardized Test Practice, p. 169; Grammar, p. 171
- Choices & Challenges, p. 171

Scarhead had been gone for two or three days, and the breeze was right, so I went to burn the trash. I fired it off and went back into the house for a moment—not more than two minutes. When I came back out, Scarhead was in the burn area. His tracks (directly through the tomatoes in the garden) showed he'd come from the south.

He was having a grand time. The fire didn't bother him. He was trying to reach a paw in around the edges of flame to get at whatever smelled so good. He had torn things apart quite a bit—ripped one side off the burn enclosure—and I was having a bad day, and it made me mad.

I was standing across the burning fire from him, and without thinking—because I was so used to him—I picked up a stick, threw it at him, and yelled, "Get out of here."

A

I have made many mistakes in my life, and will probably make many more, but I hope never to throw a stick at a bear again.

In one rolling motion—the muscles seemed to move within the skin so fast that I couldn't take half a breath—he turned and came for me. Close. I could smell his breath and see the red around the sides of his eyes. Close on me he stopped and raised on his back legs and hung over me, his forelegs and paws hanging down, weaving back and forth gently as he took his time and decided whether or not to tear my head off.

I could not move, would not have time to react. I knew I had nothing to say about it. One blow would break my neck. Whether I lived or died depended on him, on his thinking, on his ideas about me—whether I was worth the bother or not.

I did not think then.

Looking back on it, I don't remember having one coherent[5] thought when it was happening. All I knew was terrible <u>menace</u>. His eyes looked very small as he studied me. He looked down on me for what seemed hours. I did not move, did not breathe, did not think or do anything.

And he lowered.

Perhaps I was not worth the trouble. He lowered slowly and turned back to the trash, and I walked backward halfway to the house and then ran—anger growing now—and took the rifle from the gun rack by the door and came back out.

He was still there, <u>rummaging</u> through the trash. I worked the bolt and fed a cartridge in and aimed at the place where you kill bears and began to squeeze. In raw anger, I began to take up the four pounds of pull necessary to send death into him.

And stopped.

Kill him for what?

That thought crept in.

Kill him for what?

For not killing me? For letting me know it is wrong to throw sticks at four-hundred-pound bears? For not hurting me, for not killing me, I should kill him? I lowered the rifle and ejected the shell and put the gun away. I hope Scarhead is still alive. For what he taught me, I hope he lives long and is very happy, because I learned then—looking up at him while he made up his mind whether or not to end me—that when it is all boiled down, I am nothing more and nothing less than any other animal in the woods. ❖

---

5. **coherent** (kō-hîr′ənt): clear; logical.

WORDS
TO
KNOW

menace (mĕn′ĭs) *n.* a possible danger; threat
rummaging (rŭm′ĭ-jĭng) *adj.* searching thoroughly **rummage** *v.*

169

Connect to the Literature

1. What Do You Think?
Possible responses include: suspenseful, surprising, interesting, merciful, entertaining.

Comprehension Check
- He began naming them.
- He threw a stick at him.
- Scarhead ran over to him and almost killed him.

 Use Selection Quiz
Unit One Resource Book, p. 87.

Think Critically

2. **Possible Responses:** Paulsen thinks that animals are just as good as people, no better and no worse. I think he is basically right, because people are very similar to animals in many ways.

 Use **Reading and Critical Thinking Transparencies,** p. 9, for additional support.

3. **Possible Responses:** He could have built a strong enclosure around the property, lured the bears away somewhere else by putting food out, or discouraged them with an electric fence.

4. Most students will say that they learned that the risks of interactions with wild animals make living in the wilderness dangerous and that wild animals need to be left alone as much as possible.

Literary Analysis

Memoir Responses should list appropriate details and demonstrate an understanding of their importance to the story. To get students started on this activity, list a few details, such as the smell of the meat the dogs bury, the reaction of the goats to the bears, and the smell of the bear's breath.

 Use **Literary Analysis Transparencies,** p. 11, for additional support.

Connect to the Literature

1. What Do You Think?
Close your eyes for a moment, and think of five words that describe the selection. Compare your list with those of other classmates.

Comprehension Check
- What does Paulsen say he did that showed "a too-relaxed attitude" toward the bears?
- What mistake did Paulsen make when he saw Scarhead sniffing the burning trash?
- What happened when Paulsen confronted Scarhead?

Think Critically

2. **ACTIVE READING** **QUESTIONING** Look back at questions you wrote in your **READER'S NOTEBOOK.** What are some of Gary Paulsen's opinions about wild animals? Explain why you agree or disagree.

3. Faced with the problem of bears hanging around his home, what might Paulsen have done differently?

4. How did reading Paulsen's account affect your impression of living in the wilderness?

Extend Interpretations

5. **Different Perspectives** The story from _Woodsong_ takes place at an earlier time than "Older Run." How do Paulsen's views of animal behavior differ between the two stories? How do you think his opinion may have been affected by dogsled racing?

6. **Connect to Life** Animals such as skunks, insects, raccoons, and crows are sometimes called "pests" because they interfere with humans. Discuss some problems you know about that come from human and wildlife interaction. What might be done to help solve these problems?

Literary Analysis

MEMOIR A **memoir** is a writer's account of memories, of true events in his or her own life. It does not always tell about a person's entire life, but includes one or more life-changing events. These stories are usually told in the **first person,** using the pronouns _I, we, me,_ and _us. Woodsong_ is a memoir about one period in Gary Paulsen's life. Because a memoir is written about real people and real events, it falls in the larger genre of **nonfiction.**

Paired Activity With a partner, look through the piece from _Woodsong._ Work together to list details that could only be told by someone who experienced them. Try retelling the story to each other without these details. What happened to the memoir in your retelling? Together, write a paragraph telling why the details you chose are so important to the story.

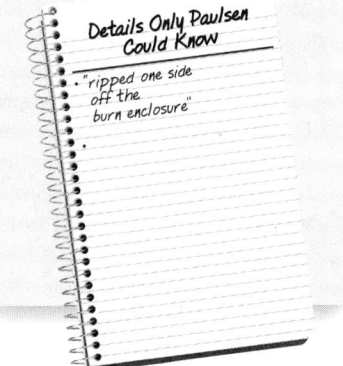

Details Only Paulsen
Could Know

"ripped one side
off the
burn enclosure"

Extend Interpretations

5. **Different Perspectives** Students may say that Paulsen seems to have gained much more respect for animals and for their intelligence at the end of "Older Run." In the earlier story he is more focused on his own needs as a human being and is not thinking as much about what animals need and want as he is by the end of the later story.

6. **Connect to Life** Wild animals sometimes attack people, pets, and farm animals; eat crops; destroy property; and spread disease. People can build fences, set humane traps, and learn ways of adjusting to the presence of animals.

Choices & CHALLENGES

Grammar in Context: Varying Sentence Length

Read the following passage from *Woodsong*. Pay attention to the length of the sentences—very long, short, short, and, at the end, a short **fragment.**

> The first time you see a bear in the kennel it is a novelty, but when the same ones are there day after day, you wind up naming some of them (Old Notch-Ear, Billy-Jo, etc.). There gets to be a too-relaxed attitude. We started to treat them like pets. A major mistake.

Paulsen creates drama not only with word choice but also with sentence length. He allows tension to build as sentences run long. Then he stops short, creating a dramatic pause, and ends with a broken thought.

When you write, be sure to use a variety of short and long sentences. Listen to their rhythm. As you revise, look for places to let your reader's imagination run with a long sentence. Also find places to pause.

Usage Tip: As you create variety, remember to watch out for sentence fragments and for run-on sentences. Fragments are not complete thoughts. They can be used sparingly to create emphasis. Run-on sentences will confuse your readers. Complete sentences, with proper punctuation, will give your writing the most clarity.

WRITING EXERCISE Rewrite the following paragraph so that it contains just five correctly punctuated sentences of varying length. Change words and punctuation as necessary.

> We once had an eagle. The eagle lived near our house. The eagle flew over our yard. The cats were afraid of the eagle. The eagle was afraid of nothing. That's what we thought. Crows lived nearby. Crows flew around the eagle. They cawed at it. They yelled at it. They teased it. The crows were smaller than the eagle. They chased the eagle away.

Grammar Handbook Writing Complete Sentences, p. R59

Vocabulary in Action

EXERCISE A: ASSESSMENT PRACTICE On your paper, write the word or phrase that best completes each sentence.

1. A **predator** is an animal that eats _____.
   (a) grass and fruits (b) vegetables
   (c) other animals

2. You can see bears **scavenging** in _____.
   (a) garbage piles (b) streams (c) caves

3. An animal that is a **menace** is _____.
   (a) harmless (b) dangerous (c) helpful

4. A polar bear is a **novelty** in _____.
   (a) Alaska (b) a zoo (c) Africa

5. A **rummaging** bear will _____.
   (a) make a mess (b) leave quickly
   (c) disappear without a trace

EXERCISE B Copy and fill in the chart below to analyze the word *predator*. Do the same with *menace* and *novelty*.

Definition of *Predator*	Examples of Predators	Use of *Predator* in Selection	Synonym of *Predator*

Building Vocabulary

For an in-depth lesson on learning and remembering new words, see p. 491.

 Grammar

CORRECTING RUN-ON SENTENCES

Instruction Explain that there are several ways to correct run-on sentences. Three good ways are: adding a comma and the word *and;* making two or more sentences out of one run-on sentence; or dividing the run-on sentence with a semicolon. To demonstrate these methods, write the following on the board:

RUN-ON SENTENCE
They have been in hibernation the meat smell draws them like flies.

USE A COMMA AND *AND*
They have been in hibernation, and the meat smell draws them like flies.

MAKE TWO SENTENCES
They have been in hibernation. The meat smell draws them like flies.

USE A SEMICOLON
They have been in hibernation; the meat smell draws them like flies.

Exercises Have students correct the following run-on sentences using each of the three methods suggested.

1. They are big and strong the dogs fear them.

2. He had a scar we called him Scarhead we would joke about him he was like one of the yard animals.

3. I was standing across the burning fire from him without thinking I picked up a stick I threw it I was too used to him.

Use **Unit One Resource Book**, p. 85.
Use **Grammar Transparencies and Copymasters**, p. 61.

 Use McDougal Littell's ***Language Network*** Chapter 1, for more instruction and practice in correcting run-on sentences.

Grammar in Context

Vocabulary in Action

EXERCISE A
1. c
2. a
3. b
4. c
5. a

EXERCISE B
Definition of *Predator:*
An animal that hunts other animals for food
Examples of Predators:
skunks, foxes, coyotes, wolves, weasels
Use of *Predator* in Selection:
"Skunks abound, and foxes and coyotes and wolves and weasels—all predators."
Synonym of *Predator:*
hunter

The Author's Style

Students will be made aware of Paulsen's style through the Key Style Points and will find examples in the author study.

Key Style Points

Possible Responses:

Sensory Details. Paulsen sees the way the muscles ripple under the bear's skin and the red around its eyes; he can smell its breath.

Vivid Verbs. slammed, drove, flew, hit, bounced

Precise Nouns. brook, springs, spruce, Norway pines

Applications

1. Active Reading Examples should represent sensory details, vivid verbs, and precise nouns. If necessary, begin the activity by helping students to choose one example of each type as a class activity.

2. Writing Students should prewrite a short summary of the experience they want to describe. They should build on their prewriting exercise by adding sensory details, vivid verbs, and precise nouns.

3. Speaking and Listening If necessary, demonstrate the rewriting students are being asked to do by rewriting the paragraph given as an example of vivid verbs, above. Students should demonstrate appropriate speaking and listening skills in this activity.

THE AUTHOR'S STYLE

Paulsen's Precise Language

Paulsen has said he searches for "that particular word, that phrase that would describe that particular light in the North Country." Like the focus device on a camera, precise language helps a writer create a sharp image. Notice how Paulsen's precise language brings each scene to life.

Key Style Points

Sensory Details Paulsen makes readers feel, see, hear, smell, and even taste a scene. What sensations do these words from *Woodsong* create?

Vivid Verbs To make the action in a story more exciting, writers like Paulsen use vivid verbs. Vivid verbs are precise instead of vague, active rather than passive, and fresh instead of dull or overly used. What powerful verbs do you notice in this description from "Older Run"?

Precise Nouns Because of Paulsen's expert knowledge of the outdoors, he chooses the precise nouns that make a setting real. In this scene from "Older Run," what precise names of things does Paulsen use?

Sensory Details

In one rolling motion—the muscles seemed to move within the skin so fast that I couldn't take half a breath—he turned and came for me. Close. I could smell his breath and see the red around the sides of his eyes.

—*Woodsong*

Vivid Verbs

. . . I slammed into the cross handlebar with my stomach, drove all the wind out of my lungs, flew up and over the sled in a cartwheel, hit to the right of the wheel dogs, bounced once on the iron-hard cross ties of the trestle . . .

—"Older Run"

Precise Nouns

. . . a quiet brook kept open by small warm springs, winding through a stand of elegant spruce and tall Norway pines.

—"Older Run"

Applications

1. Active Reading Look back at the selections in this author study. Find two examples for each of the three types of precise language.

2. Writing Think of an exciting or scary experience you have had. Write about the experience using three types of precise language. Underline details that appeal to the five senses.

3. Speaking and Listening Choose a paragraph from a Paulsen work that has plenty of strong, active verbs. Read it aloud. Now rewrite the paragraph using weak or over-used verbs. Try an oral reading of the new paragraph. How has the feeling changed?

Writing Options

1. Book Review Write a review of a Paulsen novel. What you say will make the difference between someone reading the book or not. Use details, but don't give the story away. Save the book review in your **Working Portfolio.**

2. Pen Pal Letters Read a Paulsen novel, such as *Hatchet,* from start to finish. As you finish each chapter, write short letters to a partner. Discuss how the main character changes. Ask questions and make predictions.

Activities & Explorations

1. Adventure Map Prepare a poster-sized map of North America. Attach index cards to locate settings of Paulsen books. Include information on each region's geography. **~ MAP READING**

2. Five Senses Poster Create an interactive poster. Label the five senses on 5-by-7-inch flaps. Tape the flaps onto the poster. Copy examples of Paulsen's descriptive writing under each flap. **~ PRESENTING**

Inquiry & Research

Become an Expert Use non-fiction books, the Internet, and other media to help you write a report on one of the following:

- search-and-rescue work
- sailing
- the Iditarod

More Online: Research Starter www.mcdougallittell.com

LaserLinks: Background for Reading Science Connection

Author Study Project
Survival Kit

What basic things do humans need to survive? Create a kit that could help a human being survive harsh conditions.

❶ Brainstorm a List In a group of three or four students, brainstorm a list of items to include in a survival kit. Start with 20 items, then cut the list to 12. How will you decide which are most important?

Survival Kit
compass
food
water

❷ Assemble the Kit Create the kit by collecting actual items, finding magazine pictures, or making drawings. Include cards that tell the use or importance of each item.

Kit Item:
compass: tells directions,
helps orient toward
familiar path

❸ Write a Report Create a written report that includes a summary of your favorite Gary Paulsen survival story and a description of the survival challenges in Paulsen's own life.

❹ Present the Kit Display your kit where class members can view it. Give a group presentation, or post your writing and images onto a Web page or electronic slide-show.

GARY PAULSEN **173**

Writing Options

1. Book Review Student reviews should indicate in-depth knowledge of the book and develop conclusive statements about it. To get students started on this activity, have them choose a book to read from pages 174–175.

2. Pen Pal Letters Students should turn in to you their "correspondence" after exchanging it with their partners. **To make this activity easier**, have students read and respond only to the first three chapters of the book.

Activities & Explorations

1. Adventure Map Students can draw a map of North America on poster board or use an opaque projector or other device to enlarge an existing map. Appropriate sources of information include encyclopedias and geography textbooks.

2. Five Senses Poster Students should correctly correlate examples from the writing with each of the five senses.

Inquiry & Research

Become an Expert Students may wish to work in pairs or small groups on one of the topics. Other sources of information include sailing, sporting, and popular news magazines. Allow plenty of time for research and provide support for online research.

Use **Writing Transparencies,** pp. 47–48, for additional support.

Author Study Project

SURVIVAL KIT
Before students begin, discuss the kind of challenges people face under harsh conditions. Begin with the basic need for food, water, clothing, and shelter. Then add the need for medical supplies, communication equipment, and various tools. Written reports should correlate various items in the kit with survival challenges in the Paulsen story.

Use **Communications Transparencies and Copymasters,** p. 8 for additional support.

Putting characters in difficult situations is what author Gary Paulsen does best. Drawing from his own experiences living in the wilderness, Paulsen writes novels of human survival. His is a world in which determination triumphs over hostile forces, both in nature and in society. Readers love his characters' narrow escapes and grueling tests of endurance.

Hatchet 1987
Newbery Honor Book

In *Hatchet*, Paulsen tells the story of 13-year-old Brian Robeson, the sole survivor of a plane crash. Brian must use his wits to survive in the Canadian wilderness. Paulsen says the idea for *Hatchet* came from a time when he almost crashed in a small plane. He also wanted to write about a young person taking care of himself. "I decided to take a city boy, put him in a wild environment, and then see what happened."

Dogsong 1985
Newbery Honor Book

Motivated by vivid dreams, 14-year-old Russel Susskit attempts to escape the modern ways of his Eskimo village in order to discover his own path. A dogsled trek across the frozen Alaska wilderness becomes a journey of the spirit as he struggles to confront himself and the forces of nature around him.

The Winter Room 1989

Newbery Honor Book

Set in the 1930s, this novel tells the story of Eldon, a young boy growing up on a remote Minnesota farm. On cold nights, Eldon, his brother Wayne, and the rest of the family gather in the winter room to listen to their Uncle David's stories of superheroes. One night Uncle David tells the story "The Woodcutter." The boys soon discover the truth about their elderly uncle and his tales.

The Voyage of the Frog 1989

Fourteen-year-old David Alspeth wants only to scatter the ashes of his recently deceased uncle over the sea when he sets out in his sailboat. But when a storm hits, David is stranded. With little water and just seven cans of food, David must survive many days on his own as he learns to understand himself and his uncle.

Soldier's Heart 1998

Paulsen based this historical novel on the real life of Charley Goddard, a 15-year-old farm boy who faked his age in order to join the First Minnesota Volunteers and fight in the Civil War. Only after Charley's first battle does he realize the horror of combat. By then, it is too late to turn back, and he can only hope to get out alive. Paulsen fills the book with true accounts of Civil War battles. He shows readers the gore and panic that produce "soldier's heart," an 1800s term used to describe the lasting mental and emotional damages of war.

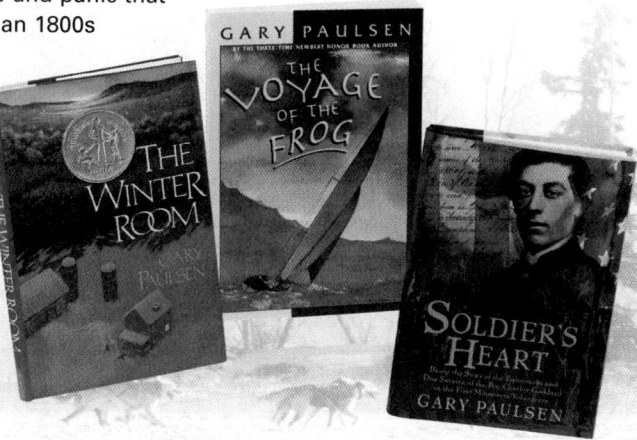

Objectives
- write a personal experience essay
- use a written text as a model for writing
- revise a draft to add details
- use correct subject and object pronouns

Introducing the Workshop

Personal Experience Essay Discuss with students what a personal experience essay is—a composition in which the writer describes something that he or she has done. Tell students that the personal experience they write about should have some significance in their life. It could be something that taught them an important lesson about themselves or about someone who plays a key role in their life.

Basics in a Box
Using the Graphic A personal experience essay should begin with an introduction that clearly states the experience and grabs the reader's attention. In the middle part, the writer should use vivid details and dialogue to bring the experience to life. This part is also where the writer should explain the importance of the experience. In the end, the writer should describe the outcome of the experience and express his or her feelings about it.

Presenting the Rubric To help students better understand the assignment, review the Standards for Writing a Successful Personal Experience Essay. You may also want to share with them the complete rubric, which describes several levels of proficiency.

 Use McDougal Littell's **Language Network,** Chapters 10–17, for more instruction in essential writing skills.

 Power Presentation

To engage students visually, use **Power Presentation**, 2, Personal Experience Essay

---

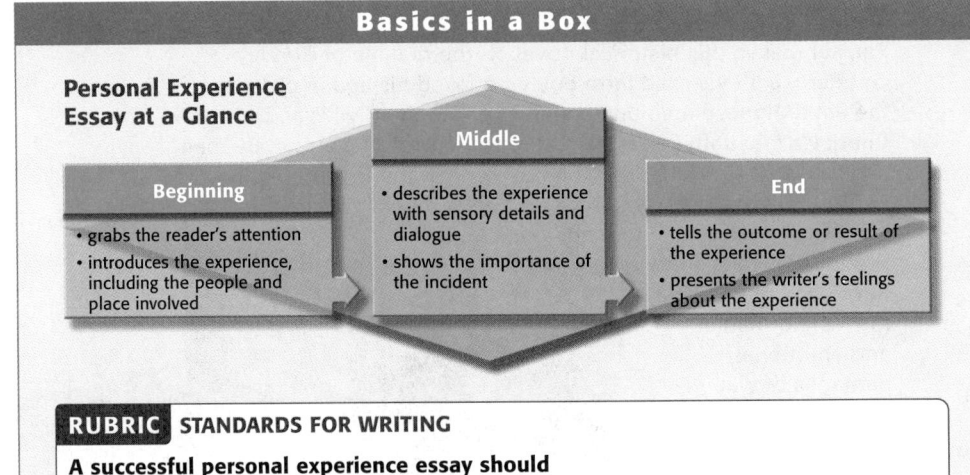

Writing Workshop — Personal Experience Essay

Telling your story . . .

From Reading to Writing In *Woodsong,* Gary Paulsen tells us that he never felt quite the same after he came face to face with a grizzly bear. He learned a lot about himself from this one experience. Maybe you haven't met a bear in your backyard, but other incidents have probably affected you. Writing a **personal experience essay** can help you see how your experiences have shaped the way you think and feel.

For Your Portfolio

WRITING PROMPT Write an essay about a personal experience that was important to you.

Purpose: To share and explain an experience from your life

Audience: Your family members, classmates, and friends

Basics in a Box

Personal Experience Essay at a Glance

Beginning
- grabs the reader's attention
- introduces the experience, including the people and place involved

Middle
- describes the experience with sensory details and dialogue
- shows the importance of the incident

End
- tells the outcome or result of the experience
- presents the writer's feelings about the experience

RUBRIC **STANDARDS FOR WRITING**

A successful personal experience essay should

- focus on one experience and why it is important to the writer
- grab the reader's attention at the beginning
- provide background information as needed
- make the order of events clear
- have a strong conclusion that summarizes the importance of the incident
- give a sense of time, place, and character through sensory details, precise descriptions, and dialogue

---

LESSON RESOURCES

USING PRINT RESOURCES
Unit One Resource Book
- Prewriting, p. 88
- Drafting and Elaboration, p. 89
- Peer Response, pp. 90–91
- Revising, Editing, and Proofreading, p. 92
- Student Models, p. 93–95
- Rubric, p. 96

Writing Transparencies and Copymasters
- Writing Process Transparencies TR1–TR4
- Writing Structure Transparency: Elaboration, TR13
- Writing Template Transparency: Personal Experience Essay, TR25

INTEGRATED TECHNOLOGY
LaserLinks
Writing Springboards
See **Teacher's SourceBook** p. 56 for bar codes.

Writing Coach CD-ROM
Visit our website:
www.mcdougallittell.com

Analyzing a Student Model

SPEAKING See the Communication Handbook, p. R100 for speaking and presenting tips. **OPPORTUNITY**

**Samantha Piwinski
Somerville Charter School**

Courage in the Water

"Remember to respect the ocean. It's a little cranky this year!" Uncle Ray said. "So you've got to be careful and watch to see what color flag the lifeguards raise!"

It was August of 1991 and my family was getting ready to take its yearly summer vacation at my uncle's beach house in York Beach, Maine. My brother, Curtis, held the phone as we listened to Uncle Ray's warning about the flag system. If there is an undertow, a red flag is raised from the beach. If the water is rough, there is a yellow flag, and if the water is calm, then the flag is blue. That's how you know it is safe. We knew this by heart.

We promised Uncle Ray we'd watch for the flag.

On our first morning, we awoke early. Gulls cried overhead as we drank orange juice on the porch and stared out at the glimmering horizon. Uncle Ray had already packed our sandwiches. "Now remember the flag," he ordered. I nodded. Curtis was busy packing his CDs into his favorite purple knapsack.

When we arrived at the beach, the sun blazed down on our cheeks as our feet melted into the hot sand. I helped my mother unpack my supplies. I looked around for Curtis, but he was already racing toward the water. "Be careful!" my father called after him.

Curtis dove into the water first. I followed. The cold water pierced my skin. Seaweed tangled in between my toes. I tried to call Curtis, but he was far away, laughing, riding the waves. I could see the beautiful, warm, sandy shore in the distance. I struggled to find the ocean floor. My feet reached for ground but it seemed to fall away as soon as I touched it. Then all of the sudden I remembered the flag. My eyes scanned the beach. The flag hadn't been raised yet. We had no way of knowing what the undertow was like.

"Curtis, the flag!" I yelled.

He didn't hear me. "The waves are awesome!" Curtis yelled. "C'mon!"

I told myself to calm down and went into the water. Soon, we were up to our knees riding the waves, when a really big wave rushed over us, knocking us headfirst into the salty water. For a

RUBRIC IN ACTION

❶ Begins with dialogue to draw readers in

Other option:
• Use questions.

❷ Writer establishes place and time of year.

❸ Background details provide necessary information for readers to understand story.

❹ Transitional phrases help readers follow order of events.

❺ Vivid verbs describe setting and show the danger in the situation.

Teaching the Lesson

Analyzing a Student Model

"Courage in the Water"

In the student model, the writer tells about the time when she and her brother were rescued after getting caught in a strong undertow while swimming in the ocean. After students read the model, discuss what makes this essay compelling. Then discuss the Rubric in Action.

1 Ask why dialogue is an effective way to begin a personal experience essay.

   Possible Response: Dialogue draws you right in because it puts you smack in the middle of the action.

2 Ask students why it's important to establish the setting early on.

   Possible Response: These important facts help readers visualize what they are reading.

3 Background information is critical here because readers need to know the system of different colored flags in order to understand what happens later.

4 Ask students how transitional phrases help readers follow the order of events.

   Possible Response: Transitional phrases clarify the placement in time of key events.

5 Have students look for other vivid verbs in the student model. Encourage students to talk about the impact of vivid verbs and to think about how they paint a detailed picture that engages readers.

   Possible Response: Other vivid verbs include *rushed, knocked, smothered, pounded,* and *struggled.*

Mini Lesson: Viewing and Representing

PICTURING TEXT STRUCTURE

Instruction Like the writer of the student model, some writers start a personal experience essay with a key piece of dialogue. Other writers begin by describing the first event and telling what hap-pened in chronological order. The writer of the student model uses both techniques.

Activity Have students analyze the text structure of the student model by making a diagram showing how the writer organized her essay.

 Use **Reading and Critical Thinking Transparencies,** p. 6 for additional support.

| Curtis gets warning from uncle over phone. | → | At beach, uncle repeats warning. | → | Writer and brother head for beach. | → | They get knocked down by waves. | → | They yell for help. |

| They are rescued by man and lifeguard. | → | Family greets writer and brother. | → | Curtis says ocean could take someone's life away. | → | Writer and brother take rescue classes. | → | They befriend man who rescued them. |

6 Ask students to tell which details create suspense and fear.

Possible Response: The phrase "... being smothered by a thick black blanket" creates suspense. The phrase "... only silence surrounded me" gives me a clear idea of how alone and scared the writer must have felt.

7 Have students discuss how staying focused on the rescue keeps the reader's attention.

Possible Response: By describing the rescue step-by-step, the writer almost recreates the feeling of being there watching them being rescued.

8 Ask students to tell why it's important for the writer to explain the significance of the experience.

Possible Response: By restating Curtis' comment about the power of the ocean, the writer explains why she chose to write about this event and why it is meaningful to her in a deeper way.

9 A conclusion that echoes what was said in the beginning can be especially effective. Ask students to think about why this technique works so well in the student model.

Possible Response: The opening paragraph includes the quotation from Uncle Joey about respecting the ocean. The conclusion refers to Uncle Joey's comment by paraphrasing his thoughts on the ocean's moods. This repetition emphasizes the message of this essay—that people must respect the power of the ocean.

moment, I couldn't see anything. I felt as though I were being smothered by a thick black blanket. A whoosh of water pounded in my ears. I could feel myself being pulled backward by the powerful undertow. When I surfaced, only silence surrounded me. Finally, I spotted Curtis floating far away.

"Swim in!" I yelled.

"Help! I can't!" he called back. "The undertow's too strong!" He began yelling for help. Eventually, I started to yell, too. Curtis was right. The ocean was too powerful. I struggled, and began to swallow water.

From out of nowhere, a man was swimming toward us. I could see he had white hair and he was wearing his glasses! He reached out to save me first. We fought our way through the steep waves toward Curtis. Then I saw a lifeguard running toward us from the beach. The old man held me and I grabbed hold of Curtis's arm. Before I knew it, the lifeguard threw in a yellow buoy. Curtis, the old man, and I shared it until another lifeguard arrived on a boat. He told Curtis to hold on to a blue buoy.

As the lifeguards pulled us in, I remember them telling me to hold on tight. When a big wave came, they pulled me out of the water so my head wouldn't go under.

Eventually, we arrived on the shore. My whole family surrounded us. Curtis's lips were blue. He said that the ocean was strong enough to take a life away. I agreed.

We stayed at the beach until we caught our breath. Afterward, we went back to Uncle Ray's cottage. Even Ed, the old man, came with us. He told us that he had been a champion swimmer when he was a boy. He also admitted that he had just lost his glasses. Later, my parents sent him a check for the glasses. They felt they needed to do something for him because of what he did for us.

When I think back to that day, it makes me feel good to know that a stranger would risk his life to try and save my brother and me. Curtis and I still love to swim, and we still go to York Beach. But now, things are a little different. We both have taken swimming rescue classes and we always pay attention to the flag. Just as Uncle Ray said, the ocean has moods—sometimes it's calm, other times it's angry. As for Ed, he has become a special person to our family. When we visit him each summer, we reminisce about the day when he became a champion swimmer again and saved a couple of kids.

6 Vivid details and sensory language create a feeling of suspense and fear.

7 The narrative stays focused on the rescue. No unnecessary details are included.

8 Clearly explains the importance of the experience

9 Has a strong conclusion; leaves no questions unanswered

Writing Your Personal Experience Essay

❶ Prewriting

You can only learn to be a better writer by actually writing.
—Doris Lessing, novelist and short story writer

Begin by thinking about major experiences in your life. **Brainstorm** a list of events from your past that were happy, sad, frightening, or humorous. Look through your photo album or talk to older family members to help you. See the **Idea Bank** in the margin for more suggestions. After you have chosen an incident, follow the steps below.

Planning Your Personal Experience Essay

▶ **1. Freewrite about the essay.** Write down your memories about the experience. Why is it important? Will you be comfortable sharing it?

▶ **2. Gather details.** Try to remember the details of your experience and your feelings at the time. Who was there? Was the weather important? What was on your mind?

▶ **3. Explore its importance.** What is the main point of the experience? Why was it important in your life? Did you learn a lesson? Did you realize something about yourself or someone else?

▶ **4. Tell your story aloud.** Describe the incident to friends before you write it down. They may have questions about details that are important to the story. Take notes about their reactions.

❷ Drafting

Once you start writing, don't worry about making your essay look or sound perfect. You can fix it later. Just get your ideas written down. Include details as they come to you.

- Use some or all of the story elements—**plot, character,** and **setting.**

- Use **dialogue, figurative language,** words that appeal to the senses, and **vivid verbs.** For example, instead of using the verb *drink,* think of a verb that describes the action more exactly, such as *sip, guzzle, gulp,* or *slurp.*

- Organize your essay. Usually, **chronological order** is the clearest method of organization.

IDEA Bank

1. Your Working Portfolio
Look for ideas in the **Writing Options** you completed earlier in this unit.
- **Mood Diary,** p. 112
- **Battle Narrative,** p. 133

2. Time Travel
Find your class photograph from an earlier grade. With a friend or alone, try to name each person in the group. This will lead you to think of what happened that year in school and out of school. Choose one event to write about.

3. Memory Lane
Watch home movies or look through old family photographs for reminders of significant events in your past. Then decide which one would make a good story to share with others.

Have a question?

See the **Writing Handbook.**
Elaboration, p. R29
Chronological Order, p. R34

Ask Your Peer Reader

- How could I make the beginning of my essay more interesting?
- Why do you think this experience was important to me?
- Which parts of my essay are confusing?
- How could I improve the ending?
- What was your favorite part? Why?

Guiding Student Writing

Prewriting

Choosing an Event
If students are having difficulty choosing an event after they have read the suggestions in the Idea Bank, make the following suggestions:

- Think of something that you wanted to learn how to do but were afraid to try. What happened when you actually learned? What did you learn about yourself? How was this event important to you in a deeper way?

- Look through your souvenirs at home. Think about family trips or outings that were especially meaningful. How does the souvenir remind you of this experience? Why did you save it?

Planning the Personal Experience Essay

1. As students write down their memories, have them think about why this memory stands out and why the event has had a lasting effect.

2. As students gather details, tell them to use vivid verbs and precise nouns that capture the experience.

3. While thinking about the importance of the experience, students might consider the element of surprise associated with learning something new about themselves.

4. Tell listeners to hold their questions until the storyteller is finished telling the story.

Drafting

Suggest that students use either a graphic organizer or an outline to plan their essay. Tell them to place the events in chronological order within the diagram or on the outline.

Revising
NECESSARY DETAILS

Invite volunteers to choose a paragraph from their personal experience essay that contains details. Tell them to read it aloud. Ask listeners to give positive feedback, naming details that helped them understand the experience. Then ask listeners to identify any unnecessary details.

Editing and Proofreading
SUBJECT AND OBJECT PRONOUNS

Remind students that when a sentence contains a compound subject, one way to figure out the correct pronoun is to omit one part of the subject.
For example, *[Susan and] I went ice skating last Tuesday.*
Jesse passed the dessert tray to [Darrell and] me.

Reflecting

Encourage students to remember why they chose to write about this particular experience, and not some others. Tell them to think about what this experience revealed about themselves.

Option
Teaching Tip

Suggest that partners read each other's essays. Tell students that when they finish reading the essay, they will write down the significance of the event or experience that they have just read about. Then have partners discuss whether the intended message of the essay was made clear.

Need revising help?

Review the Rubric, p. 176

Consider **peer reader** comments

Check **Revision Guidelines,** p. R23

SPELLING From Writing

As you revise your work, look back at the words you misspelled and determine why you made the errors you did. For additional help, refer to the strategies and generalizations in the **Spelling Handbook** on page R86.

Pronoun problems?

See the **Grammar Handbook,** Pronoun Case, p. R65

Publishing IDEAS

- Transform your personal experience essay into a comic strip that combines words and pictures to tell the story.

- With a few of your classmates, create a multimedia presentation to share your personal experience essays. You might tape your stories to go along with a slide show as a

❸ Revising

TARGET SKILL ▶ NECESSARY DETAILS Your essay must include details that make your reader understand what happened and why it is important. Details that are not important can confuse or bore your reader. If a detail does not add necessary information, leave it out. For example, if you are telling about something that happened at the fair one Saturday afternoon, it is probably not necessary to include information about someone who called later that day just to chat.

> As the lifeguards pulled us in, I remember them telling me to hold on tight. When a big wave came, they pulled me out of the water so my head wouldn't go under. ~~Still, my hair got soaked, and it made me mad because salt water is hard to wash out.~~

❹ Editing and Proofreading

TARGET SKILL ▶ SUBJECT AND OBJECT PRONOUNS It is easy to misuse pronouns. In conversation, you might say, *Me and my friend went downtown,* instead of *My friend and I went downtown.* However, in your writing it is important to use the following pronouns as subjects of sentences: *I, we, you, he, she, it, they.* Use the following as object pronouns: *me, us, you, him, her, it, them.*

> Curtis, the old man, and ~~me~~ I shared it until another lifeguard arrived on a boat.

❺ Reflecting

FOR YOUR WORKING PORTFOLIO How did writing about the experience help you to see the event more clearly? Why is telling about a personal experience a good way to make a point? Attach your answers to your finished essay. Save your personal experience essay in your **Working Portfolio.**

Teaching Options

Read this passage from the first draft of an essay describing a personal experience. The underlined sections may include the following kinds of errors:

- **incorrect use of pronouns**
- **spelling errors**
- **incorrect verb tense**
- **capitalization errors**

For each underlined section, choose the revision that most improves the writing.

> Last January 4th, I sat in the doctor's waiting room waiting for the news. When my parents and the doctor came back into the room, I could tell by <u>there</u> expressions that the news <u>weren't</u> too bad. Finally, <u>they gave I</u> all the information that I had been asking for. When I understood my condition, I felt as if a <u>wait</u> had been lifted off my shoulders. My parents suggested <u>us</u> stop by my grandparents' house on the way home and tell them the news. I had caught impetigo, which is serious, but can be treated with medicine. Thank goodness <u>dr. perez</u> has so much experience!
>
> (1) there   (2) weren't   (3) they gave I   (4) wait   (5) us   (6) dr. perez

1. **A.** they're
   B. their
   C. they are
   D. Correct as is

2. **A.** were not
   B. wasnt
   C. wasn't
   D. Correct as is

3. **A.** they gave me
   B. them gave me
   C. them gave I
   D. Correct as is

4. **A.** waight
   B. weight
   C. wieght
   D. Correct as is

5. **A.** them and me
   B. we
   C. they and I
   D. Correct as is

6. **A.** dr. Perez
   B. doctor Perez
   C. Dr. Perez
   D. Correct as is

Need extra help?

See the **Grammar Handbook.**

Using Nouns and Pronouns, p. R63

Using Verbs Correctly, p. R68

Quick Reference: Capitalization, p. R58

Assessment Practice

Demonstrate how students can eliminate incorrect choices for the first question.

A. This choice is incorrect because *they're* is a contraction for *they are* which doesn't make sense in the sentence.

B. This is the correct choice because *their* is a possessive pronoun referring to the writer's parents and the doctor.

C. This choice is incorrect because what is needed here is a possessive pronoun, not a pronoun and a verb.

D. The sentence is not correct as is. The writer needs to be more careful in using *there* and *their*. *There* refers to a place; *their* is a possessive pronoun.

Answers:
1. B; 2. C; 3. A; 4. B; 5. B; 6. C

 Mini Lesson Grammar

CORRECT USE OF PRONOUNS

For use with Editing and Proofreading, page 180.

Point out correct use of object pronouns—*me, you, her, him, us,* and *them.* For example, *Pass the chicken to Maria and me.*

Last summer my camp gave her a blue ribbon for swimming.

Practice Have students read each of the following sentences and correct the pronouns.

1. The mail carrier delivered a package to I.
2. My parents asked we to make dinner tonight for the whole family.
3. Because we've been walking their dog, the neighbors invited Juanita and I to a barbecue.
4. Tim and me took the bus to the baseball stadium.
5. Our soccer coach told he and I to skip tomorrow's practice session since we did such a good job today.

 Use **Grammar Transparencies and Copymasters,** p. 74 for additional support.

 Use McDougal Littell's *Language Network,* Chapter 3, for more instruction and practice in the correct use of pronouns.

Objectives

- reflect on unit themes and use personal knowledge and experience to comprehend
- review literary analysis skills used in the unit
- represent text information in different ways, such as in a graphic organizer
- assess and build portfolios

Reflecting on the Theme

OPTION 1

A successful response will

- rank a set of five characters in the selection according to the given criteria
- make an effective nomination of one of the characters on the list as number one
- present good reasons for the choice of the nominated individual
- clarify and support spoken ideas with evidence, elaborations, and examples

OPTION 2

A successful response will

- summarize in headlines the examples of courage demonstrated by characters in the unit
- use descriptive language in retelling the selected incidents
- demonstrate overall understanding of the effect of courage in various situations

OPTION 3

Have students prepare for the discussion by writing quick answers to the questions asked. They should jot down a few examples with which they can illustrate their answers when they discuss them with other class members. In the discussions, students should connect their own experiences, information, insights, and ideas with the experiences of others.

Self Assessment

Students' writing should take a stand one way or the other and support the position with appropriate examples. To get students started on this activity, have them discuss the meaning of the phrase "from within."

Tests of Courage

In the stories in this unit, characters show courage by speaking out, by facing unexpected challenges, and by struggling with forces of nature. What did you learn from their experiences? What kinds of adventures do you like to read about? Explore these questions by completing one or more of the options in each of the following sections.

© Reggie Holladay/SIS.

Reflecting on the Theme

OPTION 1

Comparing the Daring Many of the characters in Unit One face difficult—and sometimes dangerous—conflicts. Which five characters or real-life people do you think were the most daring? Rank them in order, from 1 (most daring) to 5. Write a brief speech to nominate your number one choice for the title Most Daring. Give supporting reasons why.

OPTION 2

Noting the Newsworthy A young girl disobeys her father's orders. In so doing, she helps both herself and an entire clan. Firefighters battle blazes that threaten the country's oldest national park. The characters and people in this unit take risks and make difficult choices. Write a one-page newsletter about four or five challenges portrayed in Unit One. Use headlines that tell how the characters or real people showed courage. Tell what happened as a result of their courageous acts. Display or distribute your newsletter for the class.

OPTION 3

Evaluating Reading Experiences Discuss the following questions with your classmates: Which selections in this unit did you like best? Why did you like those the best? Which pieces of literature convey a message or lesson that you can relate to your own life? Support your opinions with examples.

Self ASSESSMENT

READER'S NOTEBOOK

Consider the quotation at the beginning of the unit: "All serious daring starts from within." Write a few paragraphs in response. Support your ideas with examples from the selections in the unit.

REVIEWING YOUR PERSONAL
WORDList

Vocabulary Review the new words you learned in this unit. If necessary, use a dictionary to check the meaning of each word.

Spelling Review your list of spelling words. If you're not sure of the correct spelling, use a dictionary or refer to the **Spelling Handbook** on page R86.

Reviewing Literary Concepts

OPTION 1

Discussing Setting The Unit One selections are set in different time periods and in places all over the world. Choose five selections and make a set of ten cards. Write each title on a different card. Next, write each setting on a different card. With a partner, match the titles with their settings, and discuss how setting affects action in each selection. Which settings present characters with the most exciting risks? Then move the cards to mix titles and settings. Discuss how the selections' events might be different in the new settings.

OPTION 2

Looking at Character Make character webs for three selections in Unit One. In each web, show the main character surrounded by minor characters. Then, in a group, discuss the relationships between the characters. How do the decisions made by the main characters affect their relationships with the minor characters?

Building Your Portfolio

- **Writing Options** Several of the Writing Options in this unit asked you to present descriptions of characters. Choose the one that you think best captures the spirit of the character you described. Attach a cover note explaining the reasons for your choice, and place it in your **Presentation Portfolio.**

- **Writing Workshops** In this unit you wrote a Response to Literature. You also wrote a Personal Experience Essay. Reread these two pieces and decide which one better shows your strengths as a writer. Explain your choice in a cover note, attach it to the piece, and place it in your **Presentation Portfolio.**

- **Additional Activities** Think back to any of the assignments you completed for **Activities & Explorations** and **Inquiry & Research.** Keep a record in your portfolio of any assignments that you especially enjoyed, found helpful, or would like to do further work on.

Self ASSESSMENT

READER'S NOTEBOOK

On a sheet of paper, copy the following literary terms introduced in this unit. Next to each term, jot down a brief definition. If you don't understand a particular term very well, look it up in the **Glossary of Literary and Reading Terms** on page R6.

character	informative
plot	nonfiction
setting	biography
theme	autobiography
exposition	essay
conflict	anecdote
climax	memoir
resolution	primary source
rising action	interview
falling action	

Self ASSESSMENT

At this point, you may be just beginning your **Presentation Portfolio.** Are the pieces you have chosen ones you think you'll keep, or do you think you'll be replacing them as the year goes on?

Setting GOALS

As you worked through the reading and writing activities in this unit, you probably identified certain skills you would like to develop. Make a list of skills and concepts you'd like to work on in the next unit.

OPTION 1

Photocopy Unit One Resource Book, page 98, to provide students a graphic organizer for analyzing and comparing selection settings.

OPTION 2

A successful response will
- correctly identify main and minor characters in three or four unit selections.
- accurately indicate in a web the relationships between main and minor characters.
- serve as the basis for discussion in the group about the decisions made by main characters.

Building Your Portfolio

Students should evaluate the items in their Working Portfolios and choose pieces that represent their highest quality work for their Presentation Portfolios.

For more information on using Portfolios, use *Teacher's Guide to Assessment and Portfolio Use,* beginning on p. 53.

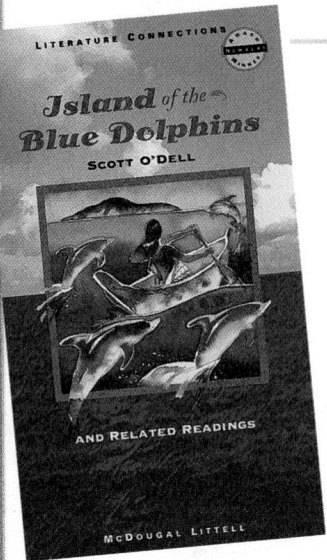

LITERATURE CONNECTIONS
Island of the Blue Dolphins

BY SCOTT O'DELL

In this novel, Karana, a Native American teenage girl, survives 18 years alone on an island off the Southern California coast. Loosely based on a true incident of the 1800s, the story comes alive with details about coastal wildlife, survival skills, and Chumash culture. Karana's courage carries her through danger to a better understanding of herself. Rich description and high drama won this novel a Newbery Medal among its many awards.

These thematically related readings are provided along with *Island of the Blue Dolphins*:

The Dolphin Walking Stick
BY GEORGIANA VALOYCE-SANCHEZ

from **The World of the Sea Otter**
BY STEFANI PAINE

The Ice-Hearts
BY JOSEPH BRUCHAC

Courage
BY DUDLEY RANDALL

from **The Girl with the White Flag**
BY TOMIKO HIGA

Staying Alive
BY DAVID WAGONER

Change
BY CHARLOTTE ZOLOTOW

And Even *More* . . .

Call It Courage

BY ARMSTRONG SPERRY

Of all Sperry's South Seas adventure stories, this is his best known. Based on a Polynesian legend, the story follows a shy young man who is labeled a coward by his peers. In order to prove his courage he sets out to sea, facing loneliness, his fear of the ocean, and many dangers.

Books
Heads or Tails: Stories from the Sixth Grade
BY JACK GANTOS
Young Jack faces backyard alligators, a mean sister, a pesky brother, and a secret crush.

My Side of the Mountain
BY JEAN CRAIGHEAD GEORGE
A teenage hero survives the wilderness.

Fire in Their Eyes
BY KAREN MAGNUSON BEIL
Wildfires and people who fight them

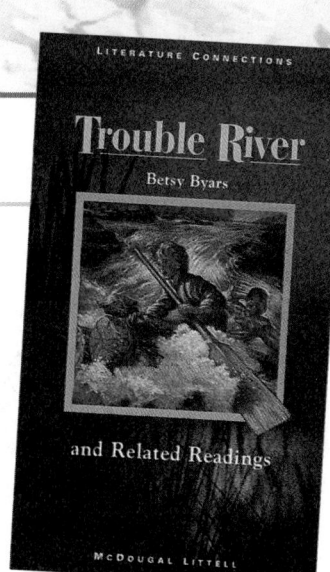

LITERATURE CONNECTIONS
Trouble River

By Betsy Byars

Dewey Martin, a 12-year-old boy living in the 1800s, is left behind to tend the family farm while his parents go to Hunter City. Fearing a Comanche raid, Dewey, his grandmother, and their dog Charlie set off on a small raft. Akin to Huckleberry Finn and company, the trio face a river of difficulties in their struggle to reunite with Dewey's parents. Byars's ability to create believable young characters makes this an exciting read.

These thematically related readings are provided along with _Trouble River:_

from **Buffalo Gals: Women of the Old West**
By Brandon Marie Miller

from **On the Way Home**
By Laura Ingalls Wilder

Favorite Frontier Songs
Traditional

Old Sly Eye
By Russell Gordon Carter

Points of View
By Ishmael Reed

Song for Smooth Waters
Native American song

Granny Squannit and the Bad Young Man
By Joseph Bruchac

Lost Star
By Patricia Lauber
Amelia Earhart's dreams, daring deeds, and disappearance

Taking Flight: My Story
By Vicki Van Meter
The youngest pilot to cross the Atlantic

Black Eagles: African Americans in Aviation
By Jim Haskins
Soaring bios include legendary barnstormer Bessie Coleman.

Other Media
Dogsong
Gary Paulsen's saga of an Inuit boy on a dogsled trek
Random House Video
(VIDEOCASSETTE)

Amelia Earhart
A tribute to Earhart's courage includes rare film footage, interviews, and insights.
PBS Video
(VIDEOCASSETTE)

Call It Courage
Lou Diamond Phillips narrates Sperry's classic adventure.
Bantam Doubleday Dell
(AUDIOCASSETTE)

Swiss Family Robinson
Interactive animated pages bring a Robert Louis Stevenson survival story to life.
Orange Cherry
(CD-ROM)

Sahara Travel Display

OVERVIEW

The largest desert in the world, the Sahara is nearly the size of the United States. Although best known for its seemingly endless sand, it comprises a varied terrain that includes such features as rivers, lakes, mountains, dunes, and oases. The Sahara also supports a population of about one person per square mile, as well as many kinds of flora and fauna.

Research Questions

• What geographical features does the Sahara include?

• Who and what resides there?

• How do they survive the extreme conditions?

Investigation The class will act as a team to produce a display, suitable for travelers visiting the Sahara. The display should include information that persons planning a trip to the area would find helpful. Students will work together to make a detailed map of the desert; learn about the people of the Sahara as well as flora and fauna; research what travelers to the region should bring; and assemble the display in a useful fashion.

Wrap-up Students can act as guides or travel agents hosting visiting classes or other guests, walking them through the display and taking questions. Guides may wish to dress as characters from "Nadia the Willful" or in clothing appropriate to Sahara tourists. If possible, invite a travel agent or tour guide to speak to the class about how to design materials, and about what information is most useful to tourists.

Links and Extended Reading
www.mcdougallittell.com

**LaserLinks: Background
Cultural Connection
Visual Vocabulary**

OBJECTIVES

❏ identify and represent geographical features of the Sahara

❏ research and write about the wildlife of the region

❏ describe the lives of desert nomads

❏ chart variations in climate

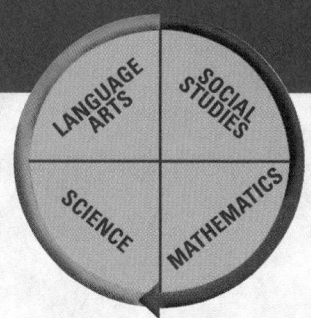

Team Teaching Assignments

CONNECT TO **LANGUAGE ARTS** Who might a traveler to the Sahara be likely to meet? Students should use reference books to learn about the lifestyle and culture of the people who make their home in this desert. Students should consider how these people adapt to the severe environment, and how it influences their housing, diet, clothing, and patterns of daily life. When did they begin to live in the desert? Working in pairs, students should read what they can find about one aspect of lifestyle or culture in this region. Next, they should make a poster about their area of research, writing paragraph-length captions for images and adding interesting quotations or fun facts. Students might include phrases in French or Arabic that a visitor to the region would find helpful. *(2–3 class periods)*

YOU WILL NEED:
- Web access (optional)
- reference books
- posterboard
- colored pens or pencils

CONNECT TO **SOCIAL STUDIES** The Sahara is a vast and surprisingly diverse landscape, covering much of the upper part of the African continent. Working in small groups, students should research land forms, geographical features, and countries and capitals located within the desert's reach. Lake Chad, the Atlas Mountains, and the Niger and Nile rivers are among the features of this extraordinary terrain. Next, students should create a large map that details these features. They may wish to first make a sketch on graph paper for greater accuracy. Students should carefully label features and make a key. Label major airports and possible routes of travel for persons planning to cross the desert. *(2–3 class periods)*

YOU WILL NEED:
- current atlas
- colored pencils or markers
- drawing paper or graph paper

CONNECT TO **SCIENCE** Various plants and animals have found a niche in the Sahara's harsh climate. Desert plants, for instance, have developed many ways of surviving in this hot, dry environment. In addition, students may be suprised to learn that the animals of the Sahara are not very different from animals in wetter climates; they have simply learned how to live in a desert environment. Gerbils, hyenas, baboons, and a variety of birds and reptiles have found a home in the Sahara. Working in two teams—for flora and for fauna—students should prepare pamphlets about the plants and animals that might be seen by visitors to the Sahara. Include sketches, descriptions, and fun facts. The pamphlets should be posted as part of the display, but photocopies should be available for visitors to take home. *(2–3 class periods)*

YOU WILL NEED:
- Web access (optional)
- reference books
- plain paper
- photocopier

CONNECT TO **MATHEMATICS** Temperatures in the Sahara can vary greatly in a single day, and rain can be so scarce as to seem nonexistent. Students should research the average daytime and nighttime temperatures per month in the Sahara, as well as the average monthly rainfall. Students can present their findings in a chart that includes bar graphs. They may wish to illustrate the charts with pictures of garments that travelers would need for day and night in that climate. Students should also find out how much water per day a traveler should expect to drink in this extreme heat, and display this amount in bottles or jars as a visual aid. *(2–3 class periods)*

YOU WILL NEED:
- reference books, especially almanacs
- graph paper or plain paper
- rulers and calculators
- bottles or jars

Polar Exploration Slide Show

OVERVIEW

The geographic North Pole lies in the Arctic Ocean at the northern end of the axis on which the earth revolves. There is no land at the North Pole, but for most of the year the ocean is frozen solid, providing a surface for travel. Across this harsh landscape, Robert E. Peary and the members of his expedition traveled by dogsled. On the last leg of the journey, Peary sent back all the members of the expedition except Matthew Henson and four Inuit.

Research Questions

● What challenges did explorers face in the early 20th century?

● Why was an expedition to the North Pole important?

● How was Peary's expedition accomplished?

Investigation Working in small groups, students will create audio-visual presentations about Henson's and Peary's 1908 expedition. They will plan a combination of text, visuals, and sounds, and present the show to classmates, families, and community members. If necessary, visuals could be displayed by using overhead transparencies as "slides".

Wrap-up When the presentations are complete, have students create a flyer or invitations specifying when and where other students, parents, and community members can view them. Distribute questionnaires to the viewers before the presentations. After the presentations, discuss the audience's answers.

Links and Extended Reading
www.mcdougallittell.com

LaserLinks: Background
Historical Connection
Visual Vocabulary
Art Gallery

OBJECTIVES

❏ read primary and secondary source accounts and record oral readings of Peary's 1908–1909 expedition

❏ research and report on Inuit culture and the contributions of Inuits to the expedition

❏ research the ecology of the Arctic Circle and represent flora and fauna on a map

❏ present and evaluate statistics about the expedition

Team Teaching Assignments

CONNECT TO **LANGUAGE ARTS** Many explorers kept journals to record and document their accomplishments. Direct students to find and read journal entries and other primary accounts from the North Greenland expedition. Have students record readings from these primary sources. The books *Robert E. Peary and the Rush to the North Pole* by Fred L. Israel and *Dark Companion: The Story of Matthew Henson* by Bradley Robinson may be helpful resources. (Students can also use the excerpts from Henson's journal that are quoted in the selection.) The readings can play in the background while students present visuals. Students can also select appropriate music to play during parts of the presentation. You may also wish to have students complete the interdisciplinary assignments below as they create their presentations. *(3 class periods)*

YOU WILL NEED:
- Web access (optional)
- reference works on the North Greenland expedition
- audio recording equipment

CONNECT TO **SOCIAL STUDIES** Matthew Henson learned many valuable skills from the Inuit, such as how to load a sled, manage a food supply, and treat frostbite. Suggest that students devote part of their presentations to Inuits. Topics might include the following: origins of the Inuit peoples, Inuit culture then and now, and contributions of Inuit members of the North Greenland expedition. Based on their research on the expedition and on Inuit culture, students may wish to write a journal entry from the point of view of one of the Inuit members of the expedition. Caution students that, in their presentation, they must make clear to the audience that the journal entry is a work of fiction, although based on factual accounts of the expedition. Students' research could be photocopied onto an overhead transparency. *(3–4 class periods)*

YOU WILL NEED:
- Web access (optional)
- current reference books

CONNECT TO **SCIENCE** At times during the expedition, Robert Peary and his men encountered temperatures of 50 degrees below zero. Direct students to research the ecology of the Arctic circle. What plants and animals live in such an inhospitable environment? Encourage students to create a map showing the countries of the Arctic Circle and to find or create pictures of Arctic landscapes, flora, and fauna. The map could be displayed on an overhead transparency. *(3 class periods)*

YOU WILL NEED:
- Web access (optional)
- current reference books on Arctic countries
- atlas
- graphics software or art materials

CONNECT TO **MATHEMATICS** Direct students to generate statistics about the expedition. These "Fast Facts" could be displayed on an overhead transparency or incorporated into the text of the presentation. For example, Matthew Henson wrote in his journal, ". . . we couldn't carry food for more than fifty days. . . ." Help students to estimate the amount of food that the expedition needed for 50 days, and about how much the food supplies weighed. Henson wrote that during one part of the expedition, they traveled 18 to 20 hours each day. Ask students to calculate what percentage of each day the explorers traveled. The expedition set sail from New York City. Have students use an atlas and estimate how many miles the group traveled to reach the North Pole. Then tell students that the entire expedition took 275 days. Suggest that they calculate the average number of miles that the expedition covered per day. *(1–2 class periods)*

YOU WILL NEED:
- calculator
- atlas

Growth and Change

One thing is certain: nothing remains the same. By the time you read this, things will have changed in the world from the way they were a minute ago. That is a fact of existence. It's how we respond to growth and change that counts. Is it a threat to be feared or a challenge to be welcomed? This unit contains two parts, both of which highlight not only where we come from, but also where we are going as we grow and change.

—— Part 1 ——

The Need to Belong Being part of something—a family, a group, a culture—buffers the pain of growth and change that all must face. Misery may love company, as the old saying goes, but so does joy. In "Chinatown," a young man tries to find just where he fits in as he approaches his young adulthood. This answer will give him the roots he needs in order to grow strong.

—— Part 2 ——

Home and Heritage We all come from somewhere as we begin life's journey, and this heritage is one of the things that makes us who we are. The characters in these selections come from many different "homes," be they physical or spiritual. In "The Circuit," a young boy's frequent moves make it difficult for him to have a sense of "home."

UNIT TWO

GROWTH

You start out with one thing, end

up with another, and nothing's

like it used to be, not even the future.

Rita Dove
American poet

David Peikon, *Spring Fair, Old Westbury Gardens*
30" x 40", Acrylic on canvas ©1998.
Courtesy of the Mark Humphrey Gallery,
Southampton, New York.

186

 ## Viewing and Representing

Spring Fair, Old Westbury Gardens,
David Peikon

ART APPRECIATION

Instruction The two teenagers in the foreground are watching something. Are they on the outside looking in or do they belong? One of the goals of the art that accompanies these selections is to get you to think. This picture might represent any number of different things.

Application What might the teenagers be looking at? Why?

Possible Response: The title of the painting is *Spring Fair,* so they might be watching the crowds of people attending the fair.

• How do you think the teenagers feel? Explain your answer.

Possible Response: From the way they are sitting, they seem relaxed and happy to be outside on a nice spring day.

• Why do you think this illustration was used for the theme of "Growth and Change"?

Possible Response: It may have been used because it shows young people at a point in their lives when they are growing and changing.

AND CHANGE

187

Making Connections

To help students explore the connections between the art, the quotation, and the unit theme, have them consider the following questions:

Ask: Think about a change in your life. How did it help you to grow?
Possible Response: Students' responses will vary, but should connect to the positive aspects of change.

Ask: How would you respond to Rita Dove's quotation about change?
Possible Response: Students may say they would agree with her statement, because change is constantly going on and always will, even in the future.

Ask: What aspect of growth and change do you think the painting portrays?
Possible Response: The young people in the painting may be friends attending an event in their community. Our friends and communities often shape the way we grow and change.

Ask: What kinds of stories and experiences might you expect to read about in this unit?
Possible Response: stories about people who learn important lessons about living as they grow and change

Features and Selections	Literary Analysis	Reading and Critical Thinking	Writing Opportunities	
Growth and Change **The Need to Belong**			Art Appreciation, 186	
Learning the Language of Literature Poetry	Poetry, 189			
The Active Reader Skills and Strategies		Reading Poetry, 193		
POETRY I'm Nobody! Who Are You? It Seems I Test People Growing Pains **Difficulty Level:** *Average*	Figurative Language, 194, 196, 198 Free Verse, 198	Making Inferences, 194, 196, 198	Advice Column, 199 Letter to the Poet, 199 Free Verse, 199 Informal Assessment, 199	
Real World Link Calling All "Nobodies"		Elaborating, 201		
POETRY Three Haiku **Difficulty Level:** *Easy*	Haiku, 205, 206, 207	Noting Sensory Details, 205, 206, 207 Informal Assessment, 208	Opinion Statement, 208 Your Own Haiku, 208	
SHORT STORY All Summer in a Day **Difficulty Level:** *Easy* **Literary Link** Change	Science Fiction, 209, 210, 214, 216 Review: Figurative Language, 216	Evaluating, 209, 210, 214, 216 Comparing Texts, 216 Standardized Test Practice, 215	Character Contrasts, 217 Final Scene, 217	
MEMOIR Chinatown, *from* The Lost Garden **Difficulty Level:** *Average* **Building Vocabulary** **Literary Link** Same Song/La misma canción	Primary Source, 219, 220, 226, 227	Distinguishing Fact from Opinion, 219, 220, 222, 226, 227 Comparing Texts, 227 Standardized Test Practice, 226	Imaginary Dialogue, 228 Role Web, 228	
Writing Workshop: Original Poem **Assessment Practice**		Analyzing Published Student Models, 237 Using Sound Devices, 240	Writing Your Poem, 239	

LEGEND   DLS – Daily Language SkillBuilder   Green type – Teacher's Edition

Speaking and Listening Viewing and Representing	Inquiry and Research	Grammar, Usage, and Mechanics	Vocabulary	
Paired Activity, 198 Poetry in Music, 199 Portrait, 199 Role-play, 199 Art Appreciation, 196 Presenting a Poem Orally, 197	Rhyme Time, 199 Outsiders, 200	DLS, 194 Identifying Nouns and Pronouns, 200		
	Activity Link: "I'm Nobody! Who Are You?" "It Seems I Test People," "Growing Pains," 204 Inquiry and Research, 204			
Paired Activity, 207 Recycled Haiku, 208	Pioneering Poets, 208	DLS, 205		
Cooperative Learning Activity, 216 Plot Comparison, 217 Art Connection, 217 Art Appreciation, 210, 212	Earth vs. Venus, 217 Changes, 218	Replacing Nouns with Pronouns, 218 DLS, 209 Plural and Collective Nouns and Pronouns, 214 Using the Right Pronoun Case, 218	Context Clues, 217 Using Context Clues, 211	
Paired Activity, 227 Heritage Collage, 228 Games Chart, 228 Art Appreciation, 221	Immigrant Communities, 228 Common Theme, 229	Proper Nouns, 229 DLS, 219 Collective Nouns, 224 Precise Nouns: Concrete and Abstract, 229	Antonyms, 228 Spelling sh, 228 Using Synonyms and Antonyms, 230 Using a Word Web, 220 Compound Words, 223 Spelling sh/, 228	
Picturing Text Structure, 237		Consistent Verb Tense, 240 Revising and Editing, 241 Consistent Verb Tense, 241		

Features and Selections	Literary Analysis	Reading and Critical Thinking	Writing Opportunities	
Growth and Change **Home and Heritage**				
Learning the Language of Literature Character and Setting	Character and Setting, 243			
The Active Reader Skills and Strategies		Predicting, 247		
SHORT STORY Aaron's Gift **Difficulty Level: _Challenging_**	Characterization, 248, 250, 252, 257	Predicting, 248, 250, 252, 254, 256, 257 Comparing Texts, 257 Standardized Test Practice, 256	Story Summary, 258 Diary Entry, 258	
Real World Link Your Family's History Will Come Alive		Using Multiple Sources, 261		
SHORT STORY The Circuit **Difficulty Level: _Average_** **Literary Link** the 1st	Description, 264, 266, 272	Making Inferences, 264, 266, 268, 270, 272 Informal Assessment, 273	A Story Retold, 273 Letter to Mr. Lema, 273 Predicting the Future, 273	
MEMOIR Oh Broom, Get to Work **Difficulty Level: _Easy_**	Point of View, 275, 276, 280, 281	Connecting, 275, 276, 280, 281 Standardized Test Practice, 280	Guest Rules, 282 Personality Profile, 282	
POETRY Western Wagons Night Journey **Difficulty Level: _Average_** **Building Vocabulary** **Literary Link** Saguaro	Sound Devices, 284, 286, 287	Reading Aloud, 284, 286, 287 Comparing Texts, 287 Informal Assessment, 286	Travel Narrative, 288 Travel Poem, 288	
Writing Workshop: Character Sketch **Assessment Practice**		Analyzing a Student Model, 299	Planning Your Character Sketch, 301 Adding Dialogue, 302	
Reflect and Assess	Thinking About Point of View, 305 Analyzing Characterization, 305	Evaluating Growth, 304 Producing a Proposal, 304	Relating to the Theme, 304 Building Your Portfolio, 305	

LEGEND DLS – Daily Language SkillBuilder Green type – Teacher's Edition

UNIT TWO
RESOURCE MANAGEMENT GUIDE
PART 1

To introduce the theme of this unit, use Fine Art Transparencies T22–24 in the Communications Transparencies and Copymasters.

	Unit Resource Book	Assessment	Integrated Technology and Media	**Additional Support** Literary Analysis Transparencies
I'm Nobody! Who Are You? It Seems I Test People Growing Pains *pp. 194–200*	• Active Reading p. 4 • Literary Analysis p. 5	• Selection Test, Formal Assessment pp. 29–30 • Test Generator	Audio Library	• Poetry: Figurative Language T19
Three Haiku *pp. 205–208*	• Active Reading p. 6 • Literary Analysis p. 7	• Selection Test, Formal Assessment pp. 31–32 • Test Generator	Audio Library LaserLinks, Teacher's SourceBook p. 18	• Form in Poetry: Rhyme and Meter T17
All Summer in a Day *pp. 209–218*	• Summary p. 8 • Active Reading p. 9 • Literary Analysis p. 10 • Words to Know p. 11 • Grammar p. 12 • Spelling p. 13 • Selection Quiz p. 14	• Selection Test, Formal Assessment pp. 33–34 • Test Generator	Audio Library Video: Literature in Performance, Video Resource Book, pp. 11–18 Research Starter www.mcdougallittell.com	
Chinatown, *from* **The Lost Garden** *pp. 219–229*	• Summary p. 15 • Active Reading p. 16 • Literary Analysis p. 17 • Words to Know p. 18 • Grammar p. 19 • Spelling p. 20 • Selection Quiz p. 21	• Selection Test, Formal Assessment pp. 35–36 • Test Generator	Audio Library LaserLinks, Teacher's SourceBook p. 19 Research Starter www.mcdougallittell.com	• Primary/Secondary Source T14

Writing Workshop: Original Poem

Unit Two Resource Book
• Prewriting p. 23
• Drafting and Elaboration p. 24
• Peer Response Guide pp. 25–26
• Revising, Editing, and Proofreading p. 27
• Student Models pp. 28–30
• Rubric for Evaluation p. 31

Writing Coach

Writing Transparencies T1–4, T16, T17, T35

Grammar Transparencies and Copymasters C84

Teacher's Guide to Assessment and Portfolio Use

Unit Assessment
• Unit Two, Part 1 Test, Formal Assessment pp. 37–40
• Test Generator
• Unit Two Integrated Test, Integrated Assessment pp. 7–12

Unit Technology
ClassZone www.mcdougallittell.com
Electronic Teacher Tools

Reading and Critical Thinking Transparencies	Grammar Transparencies and Copymasters	Vocabulary Transparencies and Copymasters	Writing Transparencies	Communications Transparencies and Copymasters
• Making Inferences T10	• Daily Language SkillBuilder T6 • Identifying Nouns and Pronouns C65		• Elaboration T13	• Dramatic Reading T12
• Noting Sensory Details T11	• Daily Language SkillBuilder T6		• Generating Writing Ideas T1	
• Evaluating T12	• Daily Language SkillBuilder T7 • Plural and Collective Nouns and Pronouns C66 • Using the Right Pronoun Case C72	• Using Context Clues C32	• Showing, Not Telling T22	• Appreciative Listening T2
• Distinguishing Fact from Opinion T26	• Daily Language SkillBuilder T7 • Collective Nouns C67 • Precise Nouns: Concrete and Abstract C70	• Using a Word Web C33 • Compound Words C34	• Focusing Your Report T12 • Dialogue T24 • Locating Information Using the Internet T47–48	

STUDENTS ACQUIRING ENGLISH

The **Spanish Study Guide,** pp. 34–48, includes language support for the following pages:
• Family and Community Involvement (per unit)

• Selection Summaries and Vocabulary
• Active Reading
• Literary Analysis

UNIT TWO
RESOURCE MANAGEMENT GUIDE
PART 2

To introduce the theme of this unit, use Fine Art Transparencies T22–24 in the Communications Transparencies and Copymasters.

	Unit Resource Book	Assessment	Integrated Technology and Media	Additional Support — Literary Analysis Transparencies
Aaron's Gift pp. 248–259	• Summary p. 32 • Active Reading p. 33 • Literary Analysis p. 34 • Words to Know p. 35 • Grammar p. 36 • Spelling p. 37 • Selection Quiz p. 38	• Selection Test, Formal Assessment pp. 39–40 Test Generator	Audio Library LaserLinks, Teacher's SourceBook p. 22	• Characterization T4
The Circuit pp. 264–274	• Summary p. 39 • Active Reading p. 40 • Literary Analysis p. 41 • Words to Know p. 42 • Grammar p. 43 • Spelling p. 44 • Selection Quiz p. 45	• Selection Test, Formal Assessment pp. 41–42 Test Generator	Audio Library LaserLinks, Teacher's SourceBook p. 24	• Characterization T4
Oh Broom, Get to Work pp. 275–283	• Summary p. 46 • Active Reading p. 47 • Literary Analysis p. 48 • Words to Know p. 49 • Grammar p. 50 • Spelling p. 51 • Selection Quiz p. 52	• Selection Test, Formal Assessment pp. 43–44 Test Generator	Audio Library	• Narrator and Point of View T22
Western Wagons / Night Journey pp. 284–288	• Active Reading p. 53 • Literary Analysis p. 54	• Selection Test, Formal Assessment pp. 45–46 Test Generator	Audio Library LaserLinks, Teacher's SourceBook pp. 25–26	• Poetry: Sound Devices T20

Writing Workshop: Character Sketch

		Unit Assessment	Unit Technology
Unit Two Resource Book • Prewriting p. 56 • Drafting and Elaboration p. 57 • Peer Response Guide pp. 58–59 • Revising, Editing, and Proofreading p. 60 • Student Models pp. 61–63 • Rubric for Evaluation p. 64	**Writing Coach** **Writing Transparencies** T1–4, T5, T8, T22, T24, T30 **Grammar Transparencies and Copymasters** C69 **Teacher's Guide to Assessment and Portfolio Use**	• Unit Two, Part 2 Test, Formal Assessment pp. 47–48 Test Generator • Unit Two Integrated Test, Integrated Assessment pp. 7–12	ClassZone www.mcdougallittell.com Electronic Teacher Tools

Reading and Critical Thinking Transparencies	Grammar Transparencies and Copymasters	Vocabulary Transparencies and Copymasters	Writing Transparencies	Communications Transparencies and Copymasters
• Predicting T7	• Daily Language SkillBuilder T8 • Possessive Nouns C68 • Verb Phrases: Main and Helping Verbs C78	• Using a Thesaurus C35	• How to Summarize T51	• Interview T9
• Making Inferences T10	• Daily Language SkillBuilder T8 • Avoiding Shifts in Tense C85 • Future Tense C82	• Using a Dictionary C36	• Point of View T23	• Nonverbal Strategies T15
• Connecting T2	• Daily Language SkillBuilder T9 • Two Kinds of Linking Verbs C80 • Vivid Verbs in Dialogue C86	• Example Clues C37	• Character Sketch T30	• Dramatic Reading T12
	• Daily Language SkillBuilder T9 • Contractions and Possessive Pronouns C75		• Showing, Not Telling T22	• Reading Aloud T11

STUDENTS ACQUIRING ENGLISH

The **Spanish Study Guide,** pp. 49–60, includes language support for the following pages:
• Family and Community Involvement (per unit)
• Selection Summaries and Vocabulary
• Active Reading
• Literary Analysis

Selection	SkillBuilder Sentences	Suggested Answers
I'm Nobody! Who Are You? It Seems I Test People Growing Pains	**1.** Her laughter fill the room. **2.** Things has gone wrong in the past.	**1.** Her laughter **fills** the room. **2.** Things **have** gone wrong in the past.
Three Haiku	**1.** The Milky Way are a galaxy, or a group of stars. **2.** Henry doesn't thinks that he can write haiku.	**1.** The Milky Way **is** a galaxy, or a group of stars. **2.** Henry doesn't **think** that he can write haiku.
All Summer in a Day	**1.** Tho Bradbury says, "A thousand forests had bin crushed under the rain," there are no forests on Venus. **2.** They still rememberd the sun as a gold coin in the ski.	**1.** **Though** Bradbury says, "A thousand forests had **been** crushed under the rain," there are no forests on Venus. **2.** They still **remembered** the sun as a gold coin in the **sky.**

Selection	SkillBuilder Sentences	Suggested Answers
Chinatown	**1.** The fair housing laws maked it illegal to deny someone housing because of race. **2.** When he is a kid, Laurence Yep was asked to sing a song in Chinese even though he didn't read the language.	**1.** The fair housing laws **made** it illegal to deny someone housing because of race. **2.** When he **was** a kid, Laurence Yep was asked to sing a song in Chinese even though he didn't read the language.
Aaron's Gift	**1.** Aarons grandmother lived in the Ukraine as a young girl. **2.** Gift's that come from the heart are the most treasured kind.	**1.** **Aaron's** grandmother lived in the Ukraine as a young girl. **2.** **Gifts** that come from the heart are the most treasured kind.
The Circuit	**1.** Panchito and Roberto run and hid in the vineyard yesterday. **2.** Mr. Lema is a kind teacher who caring about Panchito.	**1.** Panchito and Roberto **ran** and hid in the vineyard yesterday. **2.** Mr. Lema is a kind teacher who **cares** about Panchito.
Oh Broom, Get to Work	**1.** Can you teach me a magic trick with the broom **2.** Watch out	**1.** Can you teach me a magic trick with the broom? **2.** Watch out!

Selection	SkillBuilder Sentences	Suggested Answers
Western Wagons Night Journey	1. The Benéts say them will starve and freeze. 2. As I ride on the train, me view the beautiful scenery.	1. The Benéts say **they** will starve and freeze. 2. As I ride on the train, **I** view the beautiful scenery.

Grammar Focus by Unit	Unit One	Unit Two	Unit Three	Unit Four	Unit Five	Unit Six
	The Sentence and Its Parts	Nouns, Pronouns, and Verbs	Modifiers	Phrases	Compound and Complex Sentences	Review

The Language of Literature offers several options for integrating grammar instruction and literature.

- Each unit has a specific grammar focus. The grammar focus for this unit is highlighted on the planning chart. Categories of grammar skills for this unit are shown in red.

- The Pupil's Edition includes instructive features entitled *Grammar in Context*. The instruction in these features arises from the selections and relates to the grammar focus for each unit.

- The Writing Workshops in the Pupil's Edition include grammar tips that help the students produce error-free drafts.

- Mini Lessons in the Teacher's Edition complement the instruction in the *Grammar in Context* features. Additional Mini Lessons relate to the grammar focus for each unit as well as to the literature.

- Daily Language SkillBuilders in the Teacher's Edition provide students with ongoing proof-reading practice and reinforce punctuation, spelling, grammar and usage, and capitalization.

- Grammar Copymasters and Transparencies, which may be used independently or in conjunction with the Mini Lessons in the Teacher's Edition, present grammar in a traditional, systematic sequence.

PE instruction shown in black
TE Mini Lessons shown in green

Part 1

NOUNS
Identifying Nouns and Pronouns
"I'm Nobody/It Seems I Test People/Growing Pains," p. 200
Plural and Collective Nouns and Pronouns
"All Summer in a Day," p. 214
Collective Nouns
"Chinatown," p. 224

Proper Nouns
"Chinatown," p. 229
Precise Nouns: Concrete and Abstract
"Chinatown," p. 229

PRONOUNS
Replacing Nouns with Pronouns
"All Summer in a Day," p. 218
Using the Right Pronoun Case
"All Summer in a Day," p. 218

VERBS
Consistent Verb Tense
Writing Workshop, p. 240
Inconsistent Verb Tense
Assessment Practice, p. 241

Part 2

NOUNS
Possessive Nouns
"Aaron's Gift," p. 253
Possessive Nouns and Pronouns
Writing Workshop, p. 302
Possessive Nouns and Pronouns
Assessment Practice, p. 303

PRONOUNS
Contractions and Possessive Pronouns
"Western Wagons/Night Journey," p. 288

VERBS
Verb Phrases: Main and Helping Verbs
"Aaron's Gift," p. 259
Avoiding Shifts in Tense
"The Circuit," p. 268

Past and Present Verb Tenses
"The Circuit," p. 274
Future Tense
"The Circuit," p. 274
Vivid Verbs in Dialogue
"Oh Broom, Get to Work," p. 278

Action Verbs
"Oh Broom, Get to Work," p. 283
Two Kinds of Linking Verbs
"Oh Broom, Get to Work," p. 283

STYLE
Vivid Verbs
"Aaron's Gift," p. 259

OVERVIEW

Media Panel Discussion

Students conduct research and surveys to analyze the current image of children as portrayed by the media. They present their findings in a Media Panel Discussion.

Project at a glance The selections in Unit Two focus on the issues of identity and change. For this project, students will work in small groups to investigate how different forms of the media portray children and whether that portrayal is accurate. Each group will look at ads in a selected medium (magazines, television, newspaper, and radio). Then each group will conduct a survey to see if others think this image is accurate. They will also interview their peers (children) to find how they feel about their own image in the media. Group members will form panels to discuss their findings.

SCHEDULING
Panel discussions should take anywhere from 15 to 20 minutes. You may want to schedule the discussions over the course of this unit, or at the end of this unit depending on your purposes.

PROJECT OBJECTIVES
- To demonstrate the speaking and listening skills introduced in the activity
- To analyze the various images of children presented in the media
- To develop media awareness and critical-thinking skills
- To research various media and to interview people about the image presented by the media
- To draw conclusions about the image presented by the media
- To contribute to a panel discussion and present their findings

SUGGESTED GROUP SIZE
5–6 students per group

 ## Getting Started

Think about the resources available to you and about how you want to structure the project. If you have access to video and audio equipment, students can include television and radio in their investigations and presentations. Since students will be handing out surveys, you may want to make arrangements to use your school's photocopier.

Also decide whether you want to create evaluation forms. If so, have those ready at the end of the project.

Gather a wide selection of magazines and newspapers to get students started. Make sure the collection includes some aimed at children, some aimed at adults, some hard news, and some gossip papers. Find a few extreme examples that you can discuss later.

You can assign each group a bulletin board, or a section of one, on which to display their final projects. They also might be displayed in the main hall or lobby of the school.

If you are including videotaping as part of the project, you will need a television to view parts of the presentation. Make arrangements for one well ahead of time.

Writing Workshop Connection
As a springboard, students may use the Writing Workshop assignment **Problem-Solution Essay,** p. 430.

 ## Directing the Project

Preparing *(2 class periods)* Explain that students will be working in groups to find out how the media portray children and to draw conclusions about the accuracy of this image. Each group will analyze images of children in a different form of media (television, radio, print ads, and magazines). Groups will also interview teens and adults to find out whether they think that the children in the media represent all children. Groups will draw a conclusion based on the information and present their findings and supporting arguments in panel discussions. The panels will be composed of one representative from each media group. Panel members will share, explore, and compare their findings.

Assigning Roles Divide students into groups. Assign these roles for each group (students can have more than one role):

- presenter
- researcher
- surveyor
- interviewer
- materials collector
- writer
- moderator

▶ Have students browse through magazines and find children in ads. Discuss whether all children look like the one(s) in the ads, whether the ad gives a negative or positive impression of children, and whether this represents an accurate picture. Talk about what conclusions might be drawn by people who don't have much contact with children.

▶ Have students research advertising in their group's medium and write a description of the most common type of child they find. They will then create and conduct a survey by asking questions such as, "Children are often portrayed in the _____ media as _____. Do you think this is a fair and/or accurate image of children in general?"

▶ Encourage groups to survey as many types and ages of people as they can and to keep track of the results. You might hold a brief class discussion about the results and conclusions of the project. Before doing so, review with students the Speaking and Listening Skills listed on the next page.

Practicing *(1 class period)* Help students form panels. Since each student will be participating in a panel, everyone is expected to speak knowledgeably about his or her group's findings.

▶ During the rehearsal stage, check to make sure all the panels are running smoothly. Tell students that giving and receiving feedback during this stage is crucial. Refer them to the tips in the Feedback Center.

Presenting *(1 class period)* This project could culminate in a schoolwide presentation.

▶ **EVALUATION** Let students know that they will be rating their own performances as well as those of other members after the discussions. You can hand out evaluation sheets at the end of the discussions.

Teaching the Speaking and Listening Skills

The student is expected to:

Monitor and seek clarification as needed

Teaching Suggestions: Tell students that they can take an active role in their own learning. This means monitoring their own understanding and asking for clarification if necessary. Remind them that it is likely that if they don't understand something, others may not understand it either. Tell the panelists that, during the discussion, they will be expected to ask questions of one another, challenge claims made by the speaker(s), and ask for clarification if they don't understand.

Evaluate a spoken message in terms of its content, credibility, and delivery

Teaching Suggestions: Tell students that, whether they are listening to a radio program, watching television, reading a magazine, or listening to a live presentation, they must evaluate the speaker and the message. To do this, they should keep the following questions in mind: Is the delivery effective (clear and direct)? Is the presentation well organized? Is the research up-to-date and from credible sources? Are the main ideas supported by good evidence? Does the speaker present a fair description of the material, or is there a detectable bias that affects the message?

Identify facts, identify opinions, and distinguish the two

Teaching Suggestions: Tell students that to become educated consumers they need to be on the lookout for opinions presented as facts. Remind students that facts are statements that can be proved, while opinions express the judgements or feelings of the speaker and cannot be proved. During the panel discussion, have students try to distinguish facts from opinions. Can they identify judgmental statements or opinions presented as facts? If so, they should seek clarification from the speaker as to the validity of the statement or evidence to support the claim.

Feedback Center

Students can use the following guidelines when giving and receiving feedback during this project:

Giving Feedback

▶ Ask questions concerning content, delivery, purpose, and point of view (for instance, does the speaker have a detectable bias?).

▶ Provide feedback about the coherence and logic of the content, delivery, and overall impact on the listener.

▶ Comment on the verbal and nonverbal delivery (pitch, pace, volume, body language) and its impact on the listener.

▶ Respond to persuasive messages with questions, challenges, or affirmations.

▶ Question the evidence to support the speaker's claims and conclusions.

Receiving Feedback

▶ Listen to constructive criticism with an open mind.

▶ Use audience feedback and modify the presentation to clarify meaning or organization.

3 ▶ Assessing the Project

The following rubric can be used for group or individual assessment.

3 Full Accomplishment

The group followed directions to create a coherent description of children as portrayed by the media and used this successfully as the basis for a survey. Group members drew coherent conclusions and presented their information in an organized fashion in their panel discussion. Statements and claims were well supported by facts. All of the Speaking and Listening Skills were demonstrated.

2 Substantial Accomplishment

The group created a description, completed a survey, and drew adequate conclusions based on this information. Most of the information students presented in panel discussions was supported, and speakers were reasonably prepared. Two out of three of the Speaking and Listening Skills were demonstrated.

1 Little Accomplishment

The group's description and/or survey was incomplete or did not fulfill the requirements of the assignment. Panelists were unprepared, and their presentation seemed to lack several key elements. Only one of the Speaking and Listening Skills was demonstrated.

PART 1   The Need to Belong

Reflecting on the Theme   You can't have growth without change. Growing up isn't always easy, but a sense of belonging makes change less scary. Being part of something that matters to you can help. Some people feel they belong to a place. Others feel at home in groups. As you read the selections, think about your own sense of belonging. How does it feel when you don't fit in? Are there ever times when you don't want to belong?

ACTIVITY

Using a web similar to the one shown, brainstorm a list of ideas that could help a student who is new to your school. For example, what are some organizations or activities that someone your age could join? What else might help someone to meet people and to feel at home? Compare your web with those of other students.

188

LEARNING the Language of *Literature*

$\mathcal{P}$oetry

There are pictures in poems and poems in pictures.

—William Scarborough, translator

It has been said that **poetry** is an attempt to paint the color of the wind. A good poem leaves the reader with a powerful image or feeling. That's because poets carefully choose words that pack a great deal of energy and **sound** into a small space. When you read a poem, try to picture the **images**. Think about why the poet is expressing particular feelings.

In addition to the elements listed below, most poems have a **speaker** or voice through which the poem is told. If a poem has a strong voice, it will probably stay with you.

Key Elements of Poetry
- form
- sound
- imagery
- figurative language

189

Objectives
- understand the following literary terms:

form	free verse
line	repetition
stanza	alliteration
sound	speaker
onomatopoeia	imagery
rhyme	figurative language
rhythm	simile
meter	metaphor
personification	

- understand and appreciate poetry
- recognize the distinguishing features of poetry

Teaching the Lesson

This lesson analyzes the basic elements of poetry and shows how they work together in a poem to produce emotion and meaning.

Introducing the Concepts
Ask students to think about a poem or a song—a poem set to music—they have recently read or heard. Have them describe what makes that poem or song memorable.

📋 Use **Literary Analysis Transparencies,** p. 17–21, for additional support.

Presenting the Concepts
Form
Have students look through the book
to discover some of the different forms
that poems can take. Ask them to point
out the most unusual examples.

YOUR TURN
Possible Response: The first of the
two stanzas contains five lines which
make up a sentence. The second stanza
contains four lines and also makes a
sentence.

Form

Have you ever noticed the shape of a poem? The way a poem
looks—the arrangement of the words on a page—is its **form.** Poems
are made up of **lines,** which may or may not be sentences. In
some cases, the lines are arranged in groups, called **stanzas.**

When you read a poem, remember that the poet thought carefully
about how the words and lines should be organized. A poem's
form can often help you understand its meaning. Some poems
have a formal structure while others sound more like conversation
—these are called **free verse.** Another form of poetry in this book
is known as **concrete poetry,** in which the shape of a poem
reflects its subject.

YOUR TURN Read the excerpt at the top right, from "Change"
by Charlotte Zolotow. Can you describe its form?
Refer to the numbers of lines and stanzas.

FORM

The summer
still hangs
heavy and sweet
with sunlight
as it did last year.

The autumn
still comes
showering gold and crimson
as it did last year.

— Charlotte Zolotow,
"Change"

Examples of a poetic
form called limerick
appear on p. 564.

The poetic form
called haiku
appears on p. 206.

The sonnet is a poetic
form consisting of 14 lines.

Sound

Some people say that poetry is like music—it should be listened to and enjoyed. In fact, most poems have their own sound, beat, or rhythm. To hear the "music" of a poem, close your eyes while listening to someone read it aloud. You can also try reading it aloud to yourself.

Poets use many techniques to create special sounds. One is **onomatopoeia**—the use of words whose sounds suggest their meaning. When spoken, words like *slither, thunder,* and *clap* sound like the actions they describe. Here are other sound devices used in poetry:

- **Rhyme** occurs when two words have the same ending sound, like *moon* and *spoon.* Many poems contain rhyming words at the ends of lines.

YOUR TURN Read the passage from "Life Doesn't Frighten Me." Make a list of the rhyming words in the lines. Where are they placed in the lines? Which phrase is repeated?

- **Rhythm** is a "beat" created by a pattern of stressed and unstressed syllables. Stressed syllables are read with more emphasis, and unstressed syllables with less emphasis. Read the lines at the right from Lewis Carroll's "The Walrus and the Carpenter" aloud. Listen for the stressed (′) and unstressed (˘) syllables.

In some poems a rhythmic pattern is repeated over and over. Such a pattern is called a **meter.** Poems that do not have a particular rhythm are said to be written in **free verse.**

- **Repetition** is the use of sounds, words, phrases, or whole lines more than once. A poet can use repetition to emphasize an idea or feeling. Repetition can also add a musical quality to a poem. **Alliteration** is the repetition of consonant sounds at the beginning of two or more words. Look at the lines at the right from "Life Doesn't Frighten Me" by Maya Angelou. In the first line, two words begin with an *m* sound. In the second, two words begin with an *l* sound.

> **RHYME AND REPETITION**
>
> Shadows on the wall
> Noises down the hall
> Life doesn't frighten me at all
> Bad dogs barking loud
> Big ghosts in a cloud
> Life doesn't frighten me at all.
>
> — Maya Angelou,
> "Life Doesn't Frighten Me"

> **RHYTHM**
>
> The sea was wet as wet could be,
> The sands were dry as dry.
>
> — Lewis Carroll,
> "The Walrus and the Carpenter"

> **ALLITERATION**
>
> Mean old Mother Goose
> Lions on the loose
>
> — Maya Angelou,
> "Life Doesn't Frighten Me"

Sound
Explain to students that sound devices in poetry can help make the poem's meaning more vivid and the emotion of the work more apparent.

Rhyme/Rhythm
Ask two volunteers to select a poem that uses rhyme from this unit to read aloud. The first reader should use his or her voice to stress the rhyme; the second reader should emphasize the rhythm.

YOUR TURN
Possible Response: Rhyming words: *wall, hall/ all, all/ loud, cloud.* All the rhyming words are placed at the end of the lines. The phrase "Life doesn't frighten me at all" is repeated.

Repetition
Have students think about a familiar nursery rhyme or the lyrics to a song. Ask them to note which word or words are repeated.

Alliteration
Point out to students that the use of alliteration in poetry makes the language more musical and easier to remember.

Imagery and Figurative Language
Have students consider what images they would want to create if they were writing a scary poem. Ask them to give an example of imagery for each of the five senses. Ask students to speculate on why poets find figurative language useful.

Similes
Invite students to brainstorm a list of similes that complete the phrase: "Friendship is like a(n) _____."

Metaphors
Have students omit the word *like* from their phrases to change their similes into metaphors.

Personification
Point out to students that this term contains the word *person*.

YOUR TURN
Possible Response: "They" represents proud words. Sandburg is using personification by giving words pride and having them wear boots.

Speaker
Ask students if they can think of a poem that is written from a point of view different from that of the poet.

Imagery and Figurative Language

"Blistering sun," "piercing rain," "cotton-candy clouds"—each of these is an example of imagery. Do the images call up certain feelings for you? Do they remind you of places you've been or experiences you've had? **Imagery** includes any words and phrases that appeal to a reader's five senses—sight, hearing, smell, taste, and touch. Poets use imagery to draw the reader into a scene, to create a picture in the reader's mind, or to remind the reader of a familiar sensation.

Figurative language is language that presents ordinary things in new or unusual ways. There are three main types of figurative language.

> **FIGURATIVE LANGUAGE**
>
> Look out how you use proud words.
> When you let proud words go, it is not easy to call them back.
> They wear long boots, hard boots; they walk off proud; they can't hear you calling—
> Look out how you use proud words.
>
> —Carl Sandburg,
> "Primer Lesson"

- **Similes** are comparisons of things that have something in common. In the comparison, the writer uses the words *like* or *as.* "His hands were as cold as ice" is an example of a simile.
- **Metaphors,** like similes, are comparisons. A metaphor, however, does not contain the word *like* or *as.* "The branches of the old tree were long fingers scratching at the window" is an example of a metaphor.
- The metaphor about the old tree also illustrates a kind of figurative language called **personification**—giving human qualities to an animal, object, or idea. Describing branches as human fingers creates a powerful image.

YOUR TURN Read Carl Sandburg's poem "Primer Lesson" above. What does the "they" in the poem represent? What metaphor is Sandburg using? What human qualities do "they" have?

Speaker

Every poem has a **speaker,** or "voice," from whom the words come. Many readers think that every poem's speaker is the poet who wrote the poem, but this is not always true. Just as a story can be narrated, or told, by a made-up character, a poem can be spoken in any voice the poet chooses.

From "It Seems I Test People"

People often write poetry to express feelings. A poem's **form, sound, imagery, figurative language,** and **speaker** all work together to help the reader imagine the experience the poet is sharing. The following reading strategies can help you get the most from every poem.

Reading Poetry

How to Apply the Strategies

Preview the poem and read it aloud a few times. You'll be able to make sense of a poem if you hear how it sounds. Notice the poem's form: its shape on the page, the number of lines, and whether the lines are divided into stanzas. Look for end punctuation to help you find where each thought ends. As you read, listen for rhymes and rhythm and for the overall sound of the words.

Visualize the images. In your mind's eye, picture the images and comparisons you find in the poem. Do the images remind you of feelings or experiences you have had?

Clarify words and phrases. Allow yourself to wonder about any phrases or words that stand out. How does the choice of words add to the meaning or feeling of the poem?

Evaluate the poem's theme. Ask, what message is the poet trying to send or help me understand? Think about the speaker of the poem. What is his or her particular view of life? Look for clues that will help you **make inferences,** logical conclusions based on the evidence about the speaker's experiences, attitudes, and personality.

Let your understanding grow. Think about what the poem is saying to you. Does it relate to anything in your own life? Does it give you a new way of looking at something? Over time, your rereading of the poem, your discussions in class, and the other poetry you read will add to your understanding.

> **Here's how Carine uses the strategies:**
>
> *"Usually, I read a poem aloud so I can get a feel for the sound and rhythm. This helps me **visualize** the images. I sometimes memorize a poem and it becomes mine forever."*

Need More Help?

Remember that active readers use the essential reading strategies explained on page 4: • visualize • predict • clarify • question • connect • evaluate • monitor.

THE ACTIVE READER **193**

OVERVIEW

Objectives
• understand poetry by applying a variety of strategies
• appreciate poetry by listening to its rhyme, rhythm, and overall sound

Teaching the Lesson

The strategies on this page will help students learn and apply various skills for appreciating and understanding poetry.

Presenting the Strategies
Tell students that this page can help them to get the most out of a poem. They should keep these strategies in mind before they read the poetry in this unit and throughout the book.

PREVIEW
Tell students that reading the poem aloud a few times can help them get an overall feel for the language, rhyme, and rhythm of the poem.

VISUALIZE THE IMAGES
Remind students of the quotation on page 189: "There are pictures in poems and poems in pictures." Ask how this statement relates to visualizing as you read poetry.

CLARIFY WORDS AND PHRASES
Ask students to take another look at some poems they've read before and enjoyed. What words and phrases in these poems do they particularly like?

EVALUATE THE POEM'S THEME
As students read poems in the book, ask them to determine how each relates to the theme of the Unit/Part.

**LET YOUR
UNDERSTANDING GROW**
Explain that perhaps the most important thing about a poem is the effect it has on its readers. If the reader can find truth in what the poet says, the poet has done his or her job.

Use **Reading and Critical Thinking Transparencies,** p. 1, for additional support.

Objectives
1. understand and appreciate a **poem** (Literary Analysis)
2. understand **figurative language** in a poem (**Literary Analysis**)
3. use the reading strategy of **making inferences** to help understand the language of a poem (**Active Reading**)

Summary
In "I'm Nobody! Who Are You?" Emily Dickinson examines worldly fame and concludes that it is of no value. In "It Seems I Test People," James Berry describes the reactions he believes he evokes as he encounters others. In Jean Little's "Growing Pains," the poet recounts feeling stunned by an incident in which her mother expresses her anger, apologizes and explains why she is upset.

Thematic Link
This grouping of three poems explores various aspects of belonging. Dickinson has no use for any sense of belonging that requires one to achieve fame. Berry seems to boldly challenge others to find a sense of belonging to him. Little questions whether or not it is fair for her mother to share her pain with Little.

5-Minute Warm-Up

Daily Language SkillBuilder

Have students **proofread** the display sentences on page 187i and write them correctly. The sentences also appear on Transparency 6 of **Grammar Transparencies and Copymasters.**

PREPARING to *Read*

I'm Nobody! Who Are You?
Poetry by
EMILY DICKINSON

It Seems I Test People
Poetry by
JAMES BERRY

Growing Pains
Poetry by
JEAN LITTLE

> (**Connect to Your Life**)
>
> **Fitting In** How important do you think it is to belong? Do you think it is better to "go with the flow" or to make your presence known?

Build Background

Breaking Tradition Emily Dickinson was born in 1830. At that time, almost all poets wrote in strict forms, using traditional rhythms and rhyme schemes. Dickinson generally did so too, but she also experimented with poetic forms.

Dickinson's poetry paved the way for new, unstructured forms, like free verse—poetry without regular patterns of rhythm, rhyme, or line length. Free verse sounds more like the way people speak, and it became popular in the 20th century. "It Seems I Test People" and "Growing Pains" are examples of free verse.

Here you see a detail from Emily Dickinson's handwritten manuscript of "I'm Nobody! Who Are You?" Notice the dashes, which Dickinson used to break up the regular rhythms of her poetry.

Focus Your Reading

LITERARY ANALYSIS **FIGURATIVE LANGUAGE** Language that conveys ideas beyond the literal meanings of words is called **figurative language.** The two most common types of figurative language are similes and metaphors.

In a **simile** two things are compared by means of the word *like* or *as.* For example: *My skin sun-mixed like basic earth.*

In a **metaphor** the word *like* or *as* does not appear. Instead, one thing is spoken of as if it actually were another. For example: *My skin is sun-mixed earth.*

ACTIVE READING **MAKING INFERENCES** An **inference** is a logical judgment you make based on a writer's words and on your own knowledge and experience. By making inferences, you can fill in details about what you are reading. Consider, for example, the second line of "It Seems I Test People":

> *my voice having tones of thunder*

As you probably know from your own experience, thunder is loud. You can infer that the speaker's voice is loud and booming.

READER'S NOTEBOOK As you read these poems, look for words and phrases that help you make inferences. Focus on similes and metaphors. Record an example of each, along with the inferences that you make from them.

LESSON RESOURCES

UNIT TWO RESOURCE BOOK, pp. 4–5

ASSESSMENT
Formal Assessment, pp. 29–30
Teacher's Guide to Assessment and Portfolio Use
Test Generator

SKILLS TRANSPARENCIES AND COPYMASTERS
Literary Analysis
• Poetry: Figurative Language, TR 19 (for Paired Activity, p. 198)

Reading and Critical Thinking
• Making Inferences, TR 10 (for Thinking Through the Literature, p. 198)
Grammar
• Identifying Nouns and Pronouns, CM 65 (for Mini Lesson, p. 200)

INTEGRATED TECHNOLOGY
Audio Library

Visit our website:
www.mcdougallittell.com

I'm Nobody! Who Are You?

by Emily Dickinson

Clara in Front of Hydrangeas and Mirror (1978),
Norman Locks.

I'm Nobody! Who are you?
Are you—Nobody—Too?
Then there's a pair of us!
Don't tell! they'd advertise—
    you know!

5 How dreary—to be—Somebody!
How public—like a Frog—
To tell one's name—
    the livelong June—
To an admiring Bog!

Thinking Through the Literature

1. How does the speaker in this poem feel about being "Nobody" instead of "Somebody"?
2. According to the speaker, how is a "Somebody" like a frog?
3. What do you think are the pros and cons of being well-known and of being unknown?

POEMS BY DICKINSON, BERRY, AND LITTLE **195**

Ask students to make inferences in answer to the following questions and explain their reasoning:

Is the speaker of Berry's poem a gloomy or a cheerful person?

Possible Response: He is a cheerful person because he speaks of laughing and suggests that he is ready to greet people with a hello.

A Is the relationship between the speaker in Little's poem and her mother generally calm or stormy?

Possible Response: It seems to be stormy, because the speaker says that her mother is "forever nagging." Later she says she yells at her mother often.

Use **Unit Two Resource Book,** p. 4 for more practice. Use **Reading and Critical Thinking Transparencies,** p. 10, for additional support.

Literary Analysis
| FIGURATIVE LANGUAGE |

To help students appreciate the importance of literary devices such as figurative language, ask them to rewrite the second stanza of "It Seems I Test People"—without using figurative language.

Possible Response: I always expect people to move away when I approach. I always wait to see changes taking place as a result of my entering. Though I am friendly, people leave when I arrive. It seems I make people think about serious issues when I approach.

Use **Unit Two Resource Book,** p. 5 for more practice. Use **Literary Analysis Transparencies,** p. 19, for additional support.

It Seems I Test People

by James Berry

Freedom Now, Charles White. Collection of the California African American Museum of Art and Culture, Los Angeles; courtesy Heritage Gallery, Los Angeles.

My skin sun-mixed like basic earth
my voice having tones of thunder
my laughter working all of me as I laugh
my walk motioning strong swings
5   it seems I test people

Always awaiting a move
waiting always to recreate my view
my eyes packed with hellos behind them
my arrival bringing departures
10   it seems I test people

Teaching Options

 Viewing and Representing

Freedom Now
by Charles White

ART APPRECIATION Charles White (1918–1979) was a prolific printmaker and painter. He produced vivid images of African-American life and culture.

Instruction Discuss how visual media can add to the impact of writing when it echoes similar themes. Begin by pointing out that the boy in the painting is just a small part of the whole. The artist made a deliberate decision to paint the boy this way, forcing the viewer to examine the background.

Application Ask how the visual technique of framing the portrait of the boy with a large background reflects the message of the poem.

Possible Response: The boy is presented to us with a background that seems connected to him and leads us to make assumptions about his own background and the kind of person he is. Likewise the speaker of the poem finds that his background, as suggested by his skin color, is challenging to people and that they make assumptions about him based on it.

GROWING PAINS

by
Jean Little

Mother got mad at me tonight and bawled me out.
She said I was lazy and self-centered.
She said my room was a pigsty.
She said she was sick and tired of forever nagging
    but I gave her no choice.
5 She went on and on until I began to cry.
I hate crying in front of people. It was horrible.

I got away, though, and went to bed and it was over.
I knew things would be okay in the morning;
Stiff with being sorry, too polite, but okay.
10 I was glad to be by myself.

Then she came to my room and apologized.
She explained, too.
Things had gone wrong all day at the store.
She hadn't had a letter from my sister and she was
    worried.
15 Dad had also done something to hurt her.
She even told me about that.
Then *she* cried.
I kept saying, "It's all right. Don't worry."
And wishing she'd stop.

20 I'm just a kid.
I can forgive her getting mad at me. That's easy.
But her sadness . . .
I don't know what to do with her sadness.
I yell at her often, "You don't understand me!"
25 But I don't want to have to understand her.
That's expecting too much.

 Speaking and Listening

PRESENTING A POEM ORALLY
Prepare Have students present dramatic interpretations of the poems. Point out to students that they should vary their reading of a poem depending on the content. In order to communicate well, they should first ask themselves questions such as these: *Should the poem be read quickly or slowly? Should it be read very loudly, in a high pitch or low pitch, and in what tone?* For example, they might choose to read the Berry poem in a bold, rhythmic voice that reflects the personality of the speaker. The Little poem might be read in a softer tone, one that shows the speaker's feelings of discomfort with her situation. Have students work in pairs to practice their reading of one of the poems in this selection.

Present Reserve time for students to present their readings individually. As each reads, the other students can play the roles, of audience and critic, commenting specifically on how well each has adapted the presentation to the subject matter.

Use **Communication Transparencies and Copymasters**, p. 12, for additional support.

Connect to the Literature

What Do You Think?

1. Responses will vary. Some students may be reminded of relationships in their own lives. Others may respond by saying that the speaker should be more understanding of her mother.

Comprehension Check

- When he arrives, people depart.
- The mother said that the speaker was lazy and selfish, that the speaker's room was messy, and that the speaker gave the mother no choice but to nag.
- The mother expects too much by expecting the speaker, a child, to understand her.

Think Critically

2. **Possible Response:** Some students may say that the speaker feels overwhelmed by the mother's sadness and also feels responsible for making the mother happy.

3. **Possible Response:** Some students may say that the growing pains are those of becoming an adult and having to see your parents as people with problems. Others may interpret "growing pains" more literally, as the pain of being yelled at by your mother.

4. Responses should list specific inferences made and mention reasons why personal experiences helped to make those inferences.

 Use **Reading and Critical Thinking Transparencies,** p. 10, for additional support.

Literary Analysis

Figurative Language Responses should reflect an understanding of similes and metaphors and list instances accurately. Rewritten figures of speech should present the same subject of comparison as the original but form a new analogy.

Use **Literary Analysis Transparencies,** p. 19, for additional support.

Connect to the Literature

1. **What Do You Think?** What do you think about the relationship between the speaker and the mother in "Growing Pains"?

Comprehension Check
- What happens when the speaker in "It Seems I Test People" arrives somewhere?
- What did the mother say when she "bawled out" the child in "Growing Pains"?
- What does the speaker in "Growing Pains" think is "expecting too much"?

Think Critically

2. Why do you think the speaker in "Growing Pains" finds the mother's sadness harder to accept than her anger?

 THINK ABOUT
- what the speaker means by "I don't know what to do with her sadness"
- the speaker's reaction to the mother's anger
- the speaker's comment "I'm just a kid"

3. What do you think are the "growing pains" referred to in the poem's title? Support your answer.

4. **ACTIVE READING** **MAKING INFERENCES**
Compare the **inferences** you recorded in your **READER'S NOTEBOOK** with those of a classmate. Discuss how your own experience helped you make the inferences.

Extend Interpretations

5. **What If?** What do you think would happen if the speakers of these three poems met? What would they talk about?

6. **Connect to Life** Which of the poems best expresses your own feelings about growing up and fitting in? Explain your answer.

Literary Analysis

FIGURATIVE LANGUAGE Poets and other writers use figurative language to convey vivid images to their readers. Two kinds of **figurative language** are similes and metaphors. Both are comparisons of things that have something in common, even though they may not be much alike on the surface. In a **simile** the word *like* or *as* is used, as in the sentence "The sun was hot as an oven." A **metaphor** is a direct comparison, without *like* or *as*. You can compare the sun to an oven simply by saying "The sun baked us."

Paired Activity Choose one simile and one metaphor to rewrite. Compare the poet's subject to something other than what the poet compared it to. Read your simile and metaphor to a partner. Discuss what images they create.

FREE VERSE Poetry with no regular pattern of rhyme, rhythm, or line length is called **free verse.** Free verse often sounds like conversation. Read "Growing Pains" aloud as naturally as you can. Do you think free verse is a good way of presenting the ideas in the poem? Explain.

Extend Interpretations

5. **What If?** One possible response is that, assuming the poets were like the speakers in their poems, Dickinson and Little would have much in common to talk about, but Berry might be so brash that he would make the others keep silent. To get students started on this activity, have them divide into groups of three and role-play the various poets.

6. **Connect to Life** Responses may indicate any one of the three poems. Many students will probably pick "Growing Pains" because it deals with a young person's thoughts and feelings. Explanations should be thoughtful and well reasoned.

Writing Options

1. Advice Column Imagine that you are an advice columnist for a newspaper. One of the poems' speakers has written to you for advice. Write an advice column in which you respond to his or her request.

Dear "Just a Kid,"
I think you should give your mom a break. She shouldn't expect you to be an adult, but when she needs someone to talk to, you should try to listen. Sometimes it's tough to be a grown-up, too!

2. Letter to the Poet Write Emily Dickinson a letter telling her what you liked or disliked about her poem. Be sure to give reasons for your opinions.

3. Free Verse Think about one of your experiences in growing up. Write a poem in free verse, describing that experience. Think about the sounds and meanings of the words you choose. Place your poem in your **Working Portfolio.**

Activities & Explorations

1. Poetry in Music Many song lyrics are considered poetry. Find a song about growing up. Read the words of the song to your class. Explain to the class what the song means to you. What does it express about growing up? If possible, play the song for your class. ~ **SPEAKING AND LISTENING**

2. Portrait Draw, paint, or sculpt a portrait of one of the poems' speakers. Choose a line or phrase from the poem to use as a title for your portrait. ~ **ART**

3. Role-play Think about the personality and feelings expressed in one of the poems. Then, with a partner, improvise a scene in which one of you takes the role of the poem's speaker. The scene should have some conflict so that the speaker can express his or her point of view. ~ **PERFORMING**

Inquiry & Research

Rhyme Time There was a time when poets were seen as a small, select group of people. Today, poetry shows up in all walks of life, from song lyrics on radio and TV to posters on city subways and buses. With a partner, brainstorm a list of public places where you have seen poetry. Discuss how and why you think poetry plays a part in our daily lives. Then write a statement that explains your personal feelings about poetry. Is it important to you? Why or why not?

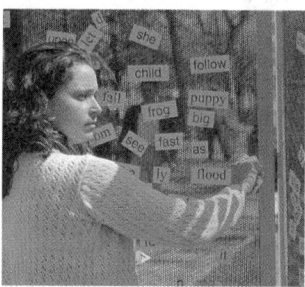

Communities across the nation have celebrated Poetry Month with magnetic bulletin boards where passersby can compose their own poems.

 Real World Link As part of your preparation, read "Calling All 'Nobodies'" on page 201.

Writing Options

1. Advice Column Responses should indicate a clear choice of poems, present the request for advice coherently, and offer a reasonable response to the request. To get students started on this activity, hand out samples of an advice column from a local newspaper, preferably one dealing with advice on personal matters.

2. Letter to the Poet Responses should cite specific points in the poem and support the opinions given with sound reasoning. **To make this activity more challenging,** ask students to add a response from Dickinson defending her poem against any objections raised to it.

3. Free Verse Poems should reflect an attempt to join word meanings and sounds in a portrayal of a childhood experience. **To make this activity easier,** suggest a specific target for the number of lines—perhaps five to ten.

Activities & Explorations

1. Poetry in Music Songs should touch on some aspect of growing up. Good resources for this activity are books with music and lyrics of popular songs, which may be available in the school or local library.

2. Portrait The portrait should evoke the speaker of the chosen poem in some demonstrable way. To get students started in this activity, have them study the painting on page 196.

3. Role-Play The improvised scene should include some recognizable expression of the speaker's point of view. To get students started on this activity, brainstorm possible sources of conflict for the speaker of each poem.

Inquiry & Research

Rhyme Time Students can formulate questions and develop ideas by doing research to see some of the ways people enjoy poetry in our society every day. Suggest that each student find at least five ways that people experience poetry outside of school and books.

✓ **Assessment** **Informal Assessment**

WRITING SIMILES AND METAPHORS
Explain to students that figurative language can enliven their writing. You can informally assess students' understanding of two types of figurative language by having them write similes and metaphors that summarize the poems. Ask them to create a simile or metaphor to describe a character or situation described in each poem. For example, they might write: "To be nobody is like being free," or "My mother is a tidal wave of sadness."

RUBRIC
3 Full Accomplishment Response reflects a full understanding of the situations and characters described and the use of metaphor or simile.

2 Substantial Accomplishment Response shows a general understanding of some or all of the situations and characters described or uses metaphor and simile ineffectively.

1 Little or Partial Accomplishment Response shows little understanding of the poems or the uses of metaphor and simile.

Emily Dickinson

In 1862, Dickinson sent some poems to a professional writer, Thomas Wentworth Higginson, asking him if he thought them worthwhile. He did not think them worth publishing, but he was intrigued enough to write to her and even visit her. He later reported: "I was never with any one who drained my nerve power so much. Without touching her, she drew from me. I am glad not to live near her."

Author Activity

Outsiders Students may work in small groups to choose and discuss poems. Allow ample time for research in the school or public library.

James Berry

A teacher as well as an author, James Berry conducts writing workshops for children. Besides *When I Dance,* another of his books has won an award: *A Thief in the Village and Other Stories,* a 1988 Coretta Scott King Award honor book. It is told from the point of view of a Jamaican child and grew out of his own childhood experiences.

Jean Little

Jean Little's eye problems prevent her from reading now, but she continues to write with the help of a talking computer. Little gives the following advice to young writers: "Read and write a lot. You have a storehouse in your head. If you don't put anything in it, there's nothing to draw on."

"a Book, is only the Heart's Portrait—every Page a Pulse."

Emily Dickinson
1830–1886

Shut-in Emily Dickinson was born in Amherst, Massachusetts, where she lived her whole life. She gradually withdrew from society until she became a total recluse, never leaving her home. Though she rarely spoke to strangers, she got along well with the neighborhood children. She would lower them treats of gingerbread in a basket from her second-floor window.

From Nobody to Somebody Dickinson's poetry was practically unknown in her lifetime. She published only seven poems. After her death, however, her sister found a collection of nearly 1,800 poems in her room. Now many people consider Dickinson one of the greatest American poets.

AUTHOR ACTIVITY
Outsiders Read some other works that express feelings of not belonging. You might read *Nilda* by Nicholasa Mohr or *The Whispering Wind: Poetry by Young American Indians,* edited by Terry Allen. Choose a favorite work and discuss with a group why you like it.

"It's the function of writers and poets to bring in the left-out side of the human family."

James Berry
born 1925

A Remembered Childhood James Berry moved to England in 1948 but never forgot his youth in Jamaica. The poems in *When I Dance,* which won a *Signal* Poetry Award, are written in Caribbean dialect. These rhythmic, humorous poems focus on the good and the bad parts of daily life and on the uniqueness of the individual. According to one poem, "Nobody can get into my clothes for me / or feel my fall for me, or do my running. / Nobody hears my music for me, either."

"The single most important thing that I have done to help myself become an able writer is to read."

Jean Little
born 1932

Writing from Experience Jean Little's poems and stories are based on her own experiences and portray young people's lives realistically. Little was legally blind at birth. By fourth grade, her vision had improved enough for her to attend regular classes. Many of her characters have physical disabilities, such as cerebral palsy or blindness. Although there are no magical cures in Little's books, her characters learn to cope and survive.

Teaching Options

Mini Lesson Grammar

IDENTIFYING NOUNS AND PRONOUNS Remind students that nouns refer to people, places, things, and ideas. Pronouns are words that can take the place of nouns or other pronouns. Write the following lines on the chalkboard:

My walk motioning strong swings

It seems I test people

Ask students to identify the nouns and pronouns. As they do so, underline the nouns and circle the pronouns.

My walk motioning strong swings.

It seems I test people.

Exercise Have students identify nouns and pronouns in the sentences below by underlining the nouns and circling the pronouns.

1. My arrival brings departures.
2. I knew things would be okay in the morning.
3. She even told me about that.
4. Some people tell their names to the bog.
5. We are a pair of unknown people.

 Use **Grammar Transparencies and Copymasters,** p. 65.

 Use McDougal Littell's *Language Network,* Chapters 2 and 3, for more instruction and practice in identifying nouns and pronouns.

Living · Arts

Calling All "Nobodies"

SPECIAL REPORT

by Francis X. Clines

Washington, March 16, 1998—If there is a more lyrical way to celebrate the approaching millennium than by letting an average American recite T. S. Eliot's "The Love Song of J. Alfred Prufrock," then Robert Pinsky, poet laureate of the United States, is dedicated to finding it.

In the meantime, Mr. Pinsky rates it an offbeat contender for a poetry archive he plans to begin building next month as a kind of soul-print of the nation for future cultural historians. All sorts of ordinary citizens from all the states will be invited to record audio- and videotape recitations of their favorite poems as a measure of the nation's "collective cultural consciousness" at the millennial turning.

"A gift to the nation's future," Mr. Pinsky said as he outlined his big plans to invite Americans to try out for the poesy pool. About 1,200 of them will make the final cut, but tens of thousands of others will be put into a database.

Beau Sia, 19, reads poetry in a New York cafe.

Reading for Information

A newspaper article that includes only facts can be boring. Sensory details, personal anecdotes, and direct quotes can add variety, fill out a story, and expand on ideas. A writer who elaborates on basic information creates a stronger, more informative piece.

ELABORATING   To **elaborate** is to work something out with great care and detail, to develop it completely. In writing, you elaborate when you support or develop a main idea with details—facts, descriptions, explanations, examples and stories, or quotations. By including such details you can create a vivid mental image for the reader.

YOUR TURN *Use this article with the questions and activities below to identify elaboration and to practice elaborating.*

 The writer describes Mr. Pinsky's archive as "a kind of soul-print of the nation for future cultural historians." A quotation from Mr. Pinsky and other details elaborate on that thought. Find another example in the article where a quotation provides more detail.

REAL WORLD LINK   **201**

Real WORLD Link

Newspaper Article

Objectives
• read and analyze a newspaper article
• explore the difference between fact and opinion
• examine the technique of elaboration in a piece of journalism

Connecting to the Literature
"Calling All 'Nobodies'" can help students understand that everyone has a poetic voice and a right to his or her opinions on the poetry of the past and present. In keeping with the great traditions of democracy in the United States, the organizer of the poetry archive, Robert Pinsky, is seeking the views of people from all walks of life. After reading about Pinsky's effort, students may be better able to appreciate the basic message of Dickinson's poem—that fame, is overrated.

Reading for Information
Tell students that the article appeared in a newspaper in March 1998, well before the celebration of the year 2000. As you examine the essay with students, have them use the material in the right-hand column as a guide to reading newspaper articles. The following are possible responses to the numbered exercises.

1 The quotation at the bottom of page 203 ("I'm not particularly interested in celebrities") adds detail to the discussion of the "motley chorus" of people who will be beginning the archive in a public performance at Town Hall in New York.

Use **Writing Transparencies,** p. 13, for additional support.

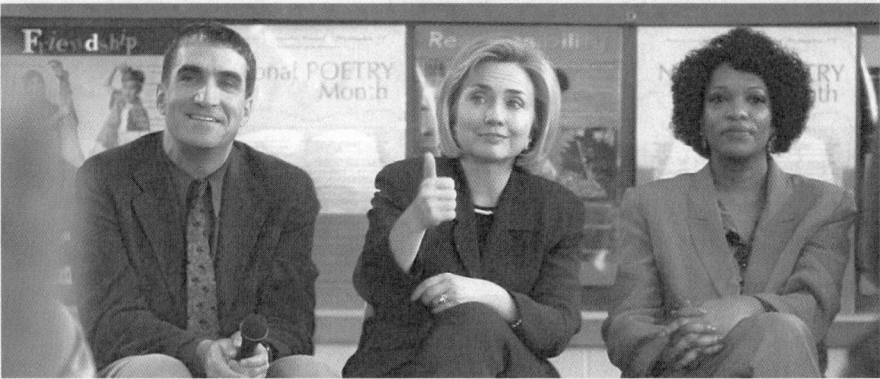

Poet laureates Robert Pinsky (left) and Rita Dove (far right) with Hillary Rodham Clinton at a Washington poetry contest.

"Poetry slows me down, makes me think, and it touches my heart," explained one of the most avid archive participants, Louise Hartzog, 97, a Sunday school teacher in Greenwood, S.C., with a prodigious[1] memory for a lifetime of favorite poets. She can speak riffs that dart from Wordsworth to Dorothy Parker. She laughingly applies some Emily Dickinson to explain her archive credentials:

> "I'm Nobody! Who are you?
> Are you—Nobody—too?
> Then there's the pair of us!"

Mr. Pinsky thought of the archive as a way to play off the mass cultural events that will be center stage during the millennial celebrations. "The pleasure and admiration for the mass arts, I believe, creates an appetite, in reaction, for a kind of art that is personal and individual," he said. "Poetry is individual; it's a voice."

The archive will invite people to say why they chose their particular poems. "And the explanations are wonderful," Mr. Pinsky said of some early samplings here at the Library of Congress where the archive is to be stored.

Professional poets need not apply. The only requirement is that volunteers not read their own poetry, a simple rule that Mr. Pinsky is confident will guarantee the broadest mix of great poets read by ordinary enthusiasts.

The Favorite Poem Archive will be one of the humbler, least graphic markings of the nation's millennium celebration. But Mr. Pinsky is

---

1. **prodigious** (prə-dĭj′əs): enormous, of impressive size.

convinced it will be one of the better heeded across time as an educational tool. From his travels, he already expects tens of thousands of volunteers to wind up in the database that will describe precisely what sorts of people like what sorts of poems these days, and why.

Even without a formal announcement, word of mouth has already prompted more than 800 poetry lovers to offer their voice and favorite poem. There is an Alaska woman who uses poetry to stave off depression in the long winters; she wants to read Stevie Smith's "Not Waving But Drowning." There is a retired Maryland parole officer who regularly recited Langston Hughes's "Hold Fast to Dreams" for his troubled clients.

"It isn't so much the people and it isn't so much the poems," said Mr. Pinsky. "It's the relationship between the person and the poem, the attachment, that makes it interesting."

Mr. Pinsky will make all final decisions with the help of the Library of Congress and the New England Foundation for the Arts. The archive formally begins its work on April 1, 1998, at Town Hall in New York, where the Academy of American Poets will line up a motley chorus—from an immigrant using poetry in his literacy training to some more public voices like Ed Bradley of "60 Minutes."

"I'm not particularly interested in celebrities," the laureate said. "The point of all this has to do not with celebrity but with our life together as Americans."

Reading for Information *continued*

❷ A writer can elaborate through the careful choice of descriptive words. For example, using vivid adjectives and sensory details of sound, smell, and taste to describe a meal can help build a complete mental picture of the event. What words and phrases does the writer use to describe Louise Hartzog as she quoted Emily Dickinson? How do the writer's descriptive words, combined with the facts of her age and occupation, create a more detailed image of Louise Hartzog?

❸ A **fact** is any piece of information that can be proved true. Which facts in this paragraph help support Mr. Pinsky's expectation that tens of thousands of readings will eventually be placed in the database?

❹ A writer may include a story or example to elaborate on a thought, making what you read easier to understand. Here, the writer uses the phrase "motley chorus," meaning a mixed group, to describe the people who will contribute to the poetry archive. What specific examples did the writer include in the article to show that the contributors are indeed a mixed group?

2 He says that she "laughingly" quotes Dickinson. The suggestion that she is laughing at herself and at her own credentials combines with the facts of her advanced age to suggest a spry, sharp-witted person.

3 Hundreds of poetry lovers found out about the project and responded even before a formal announcement was made. The writer cites two examples, a woman in Alaska and a man in Maryland.

4 The writer includes the specific examples of an immigrant using poetry in literacy training and a figure from the national news media.

Some Americans eminent in civic life, on the other hand, must be included, Mr. Pinsky said. "Whitman had this vision of poetry as holding together a country that might be fragmented," he explained. "So certain figures that have to do with our life together, our communal life, should be well-represented: a civil rights leader, someone who works with the home-less." But he guarantees that 85 percent of the archive participants will be the Dickinsonian nobodies who crave and read poetry in their lives.

"One of the beautiful things about the art of poetry is that the medium is the human body as its voice, but not necessarily the artist's body," Mr. Pinsky said of his search for the nobodies. "When you say a poem by Whitman or Dickinson, your voice is that artist's medium."

Peter McClenahan reads his favorite poem, "Kubla Khan," by Samuel Taylor Coleridge, at a poetry reading in Brookline, Massachusetts.

Inquiry & Research

Activity Link: "I'm Nobody! Who Are You?," "It Seems I Test People," "Growing Pains," p. 199. What poems do you know? Which one would you submit to an archive such as Mr. Pinsky's? Read several of your favorites aloud before making your final choice. Write a brief description of what the poem means to you. Elaborate, giving details or examples that help explain why the poem is important to you. With your classmates, create a poetry archive for your class. Record each student's favorite poem on audio tape, videotape, or in writing.

 Mini Lesson Inquiry & Research

Instruction Students can start the activity by reviewing poems in this textbook that appeal to them. They can also think about poems they have read in previous years of study. You may wish to provide some sources for students to look through—anthologies of commonly loved poems or of poems for young people. Stress the requirement that they read their poems aloud before making their final choice, as their opinions of which is their favorite may shift as they experience the poem in oral presentation. Point out the connection between the assignment and the Reading for Information questions in their text. Both deal with elaboration of a description.

Practice Students can take turns recording their favorite poems for the archive. Each student should add a brief description of what is appealing about the poem he or she has chosen. If you wish to have students record their choices in writing, you may want to have them compile the poems in a book, either handwritten or produced on a computer.

Three Haiku

Poetry by BASHŌ, ISSA, *and* RAYMOND R. PATTERSON

Connect to Your Life

Capture the Moment The unusual poems you are about to read capture moments that have been meaningful to three poets. With a partner, choose an object in the room. Then, on your own, try to observe that object as though you were seeing it for the first time. List five words that describe the object. Compare lists with your partner. Did the two of you describe the object in different ways?

Build Background

CONNECT TO HISTORY Japanese poets have been writing haiku for several hundred years. The haiku developed from the *tanka,* a five-line poem. In the late 1600s some Japanese poets began to write poems in a form that was like the first three lines of a tanka. These poems came to be known as haiku.

Western poets learned of the haiku form in 1868, when Japan was reopened to the West. There had been no trade or communication between the two cultures for 250 years.

After World War II, growing interest in Japanese culture made the haiku form popular in the United States. No other country has ever surpassed Japan in its appreciation of haiku, however. Today, Japan still has more haiku poets than any other country in the world.

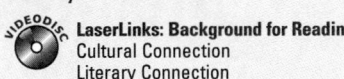 **LaserLinks: Background for Reading**
Cultural Connection
Literary Connection

Focus Your Reading

LITERARY ANALYSIS HAIKU A **haiku** is a three-line, unrhymed poem. In Japanese haiku, the first and third lines contain five syllables, and the second line contains seven syllables. (Haiku written in English or translated into English may have different numbers of syllables.)

1 2 3 4 5
When the wind passes

1 2 3 4 5 6 7
The sparrows in the branches

1 2 3 4 5
They cling so tightly.

As you read these three poems, think about how a haiku describes a single moment with a few chosen words.

ACTIVE READING NOTING SENSORY DETAILS One way that haiku convey meaning is through sensory details. A **sensory detail** is a word or phrase that helps the reader imagine the look, feel, sound, taste, or smell of something.

READER'S NOTEBOOK As you read the three haiku, pay attention to the images and sensory details in each one. Identify the main image in each poem and record it in your notebook. Then list the sensory details that you find.

THREE HAIKU **205**

Three Haiku

In my new clothing
I feel so different
I must
Look like someone else.

BY BASHŌ

Beautiful, seen through holes
Made in a paper screen:
The Milky Way.

BY ISSA

Glory, Glory . . .

Across Grandmother's knees
A kindly sun
Laid a yellow quilt.

BY RAYMOND R. PATTERSON

Incense wrapper (Edo period, Japan; 17th–18th centuries) attributed to Ogata Korin, 1658–1716. Wrapper mounted on hanging scroll, ink and color on gold-ground paper, 33 × 24.1 cm, The Art Institute of Chicago, Russell Tyson Purchase Fund (1966.470). Photograph © 1994, The Art Institute of Chicago, all rights reserved.

 Multicultural Link **Traditional Poetry**

Many nations have forms of poetry, like haiku, that are traditionally linked to their culture. For example, India has its Sanskrit poetry, which began some 4,000 years ago. Its most ancient form is the *Veda,* the hymns to the gods. Vedic poets used meter, rhyme, and onomatopoeia. Their poetic form was the basis of classical Sanskrit poetry, which followed after the Vedas. The great epics of classical Sanskrit include the *Mahabharata,* which has one hundred thousand couplets! Greece's oldest traditional poetry is the Homeric epics, composed orally by poets who probably lived around 700 B.C. It lives on: One recent poet, Nikos Kazantzakis, wrote a 33,333-line continuation of the Homeric poems. Norway and Iceland have the poems of Old Norse, written in two styles, the Eddic and Skaldic. These arose as early as A.D. 800–1000. One Skaldic poem, *Draumkvædet* (The Dream Vision), was composed around 1200 and then passed down from singer to singer until the 1800s, when it was finally written down.

Thinking through the LITERATURE

Connect to the Literature

1. **What Do You Think?** Read the poems slowly a second or third time. Do you notice or feel anything that you didn't notice or feel in your first reading? Discuss your reactions with a partner.

Think Critically

2. **ACTIVE READING** **NOTING SENSORY DETAILS**
   Look back at the word web you made in your **READER'S NOTEBOOK**. Exchange word webs with a partner and discuss other words or images that you could add.

3. Think about Bashō's haiku and the saying "Clothes make the man." Do you think the haiku and the saying have the same message? Explain your answer.

4. Which haiku best conveys the experience of being in a special place? Support your choice with details from the poem.

   THINK ABOUT
   - which **sensory details** in the poems present the clearest images
   - how many of the five senses each poem appeals to

Extend Interpretations

5. **What If?** Traditionally, haiku have no titles. Suppose you were asked to make up titles for the first two poems. What would your titles be?

6. **Connect to Life** Revisit the list you made in the Connect to Your Life activity on page 205. Write a haiku about the object you observed, using as many words from your list as possible.

7. **Art Connection** The artwork pictured on page 206 is a Japanese incense wrapper from the late 1600s. It was made by painting on thick gold paper. By decorating a wrapper—something intended to be thrown away—with a lovely work of art, the artist suggests that beauty passes away quickly. How might this idea apply to the images in haiku?

Literary Analysis

HAIKU The **haiku** is a traditional form of Japanese poetry. It presents a single moment, feeling, or object in three unrhymed lines. In traditional haiku, the first and third lines contain five syllables, and the second line contains seven syllables.

Originally, haiku were written to convey images of nature, but poets have used the form to write about everything from furniture to construction work.

Paired Activity With a partner, copy the three haiku in this lesson on a sheet of paper. Count the syllables in each line. (Keep in mind that haiku translated into English or written in English may not have the traditional pattern of five, seven, and five syllables.) Discuss with your partner the message that each haiku conveys to you.

THREE HAIKU **207**

Extend Interpretations

5. **What If?** Possible Responses: "The Imposter," "Night Sky." To get students started on this activity, read them these sample responses and have them come up with others.

6. **Connect to Life** Responses will vary. Students should include as many words from their Reader's Notebook list as possible. To get students started on this activity, have them write a single sentence about the object they observed, using the words from their list, and then try to write the sentence in haiku form.

7. **Art Connection** Possible Response: Both the life of the wrapper and the actual haiku are brief, as is the moment considered in a haiku.

GUIDING STUDENT RESPONSE

Connect to the Literature

1. **What Do You Think?**
   Responses will vary. Some students will say that they noticed a feeling of peacefulness the second time they read the haiku. Others may comment on the way the poets paint scenes using just a few descriptive details.

Think Critically

2. Have students note whether they used all their senses in choosing words to fill in their web.
3. Most students will respond that the saying and the haiku have the same message, because both say that putting on certain clothes can make you look and feel different. The wearer changes to fit the image of the clothes he or she puts on.
4. Responses will vary. Students should cite the senses that they used when reading their chosen haiku.

Use **Reading and Critical Thinking Transparencies,** p. 11, for additional support.

Literary Analysis

Haiku Students should be able to distinguish individual syllables and count them accurately. They should also discuss their personal experiences of the various haiku.

Use **Literary Analysis Transparencies,** p. 17, for additional support.

Writing Options

1. **Opinion Statement** Responses should express an opinion clearly and offer supporting explanations. **To make this activity more challenging,** have students write a free verse poem and a structured poem on the same topic to illustrate their points.

2. **Your Own Haiku** Responses should include the topics of growth and change and be presented in the haiku form. To get students started on this activity, discuss with them ways in which they have changed over the past few years.

 Use **Writing Transparencies,** p. 1, for additional support.

Activities & Explorations

1. **Recycled Haiku** Haiku generated in the activity should make sense. **To make this activity easier,** allow students to use some blank cards that can be filled in as needed to complete a haiku.

Author Activity

Pioneering Poets Have students work in special "poet research teams." Each team could be assigned a poet and each student on the team could have the task of finding out something about the poet from a different source.

Issa

During especially difficult periods of his youth, Issa would flee to the outdoors. Thus as a child he learned to associate the natural world with freedom, imagination, and possibility.

Bashō

Born Matsuo Menefusa, Bashō had no source of income except for his art. He frequently taught poetry writing and judged poetry contests.

Raymond R. Patterson

Patterson's most popular work, *Riot Rimes U.S.A.,* is an 85-poem sequence that depicts the Harlem riot of 1965.

Writing Options

1. **Opinion Statement** Unlike free verse, haiku are written in a very strict form. Write a paragraph explaining which kind of poetry you like better and why.

2. **Your Own Haiku** Try writing three haiku of your own. Write about things that suggest growth and change. Place the haiku in your **Working Portfolio.**

Activities & Explorations

Recycled Haiku Write each word in the three haiku on a separate card. Then, compose several new haiku using the words on the cards, plus a few of your own. Read your poems to the rest of the class. ~ SPEAKING AND LISTENING

Author Activity

Pioneering Poets Who were some other important haiku poets? What did they write? Use your library to find out. Read examples of their work to the class.

". . . a poem written is a poem discovered."

Raymond R. Patterson
born 1929

Teacher, Writer Raymond Patterson was born in New York City. After college, he worked in social services and taught English in public schools. In 1968 Patterson became a lecturer in English at City College in New York, where he is now professor emeritus. He received a Borestone Mountain Award in 1950 and a National Endowment for the Arts grant.

Issa
1763–1827

A Life of Tragedy Issa, born Kobayashi Nobuyuki, led a life full of poverty, illness, and tragedy. His mother died when he was three, and his stepmother mistreated him. At age 13, he left home for Edo (now Tokyo). There he studied haiku and took the pen name Issa (meaning "cup of tea"). The poet's first wife died young, and only one of his many children survived infancy. Issa's troubles helped him understand the struggles of ordinary people. His haiku use simple language to describe everyday subjects with great sensitivity.

Bashō
1644–1694

A Wandering Poet Matsuo Bashō is considered one of Japan's greatest poets. The son of a samurai, he worked as the companion of a noble family's son. When the son died, Bashō was greatly upset. He left the family's service and became a wandering poet. His innovations in haiku influenced many later poets. He created strict rules for the form and preferred to write about nature, especially the seasons. In addition to the haiku for which he is famous, Bashō wrote many beautiful travel diaries.

Teaching Options

 Assessment Informal Assessment

INFERRING A CONTEXT

Explain to students that haiku are powerful because they leave it up to the reader to infer a context based on the hints given in a poem. You can assess students' understanding of the selection by having them describe a larger context or situation in which each haiku might be set. For example, students might describe a visit by Patterson to his grandmother in a nursing home. Encourage students to use their imaginations, as long as they do not suggest anything that is contrary to the evidence in the poems.

RUBRIC

3 **Full Accomplishment** Response reflects understanding of the main message of each haiku, expressing inferences clearly.

2 **Substantial Accomplishment** Response shows understanding of the haiku and ability to draw inferences about their contexts, but either understanding or inferences are incomplete.

1 **Little or Partial Accomplishment** Response shows little understanding of the haiku or shows poor inferences about their contexts.

ACROSS the CURRICULUM
SCIENCE

All Summer in a Day

Short Story by RAY BRADBURY

Connect to Your Life

How do weather and temperature affect you?

Build Background "All Summer in a Day" is set on Venus, the second planet from the sun. Thanks to advances in space exploration technology, we now know far more about Venus than we did in 1954, when Ray Bradbury's story was first published.

Atmosphere on Venus :
96% CO_2 (carbon dioxide)
3% N_2 (nitrogen)
<1% H_2O (water)

SUN

MERCURY

Venus orbits the Sun between Earth and Mercury.

EARTH

67 million mi.

900°F

Cloud layer is composed of droplets of sulphuric acid.

Thick clouds reflect light and hold heat in.

Magellan spacecraft collected data from Venus, 1991–1994

Surface has been shaped by volcanic activity.

VENUS

Hurricane-force winds (up to 230 mph) in upper atmosphere

Focus Your Reading

LITERARY ANALYSIS SCIENCE FICTION Stories that are based on advances in science and technology are called **science fiction.** Many of these stories are set in the future and in imaginary places. As you read this story, look for:
- unusual settings
- effects of science or technology
- messages about the future

WORDS TO KNOW **Vocabulary Preview**
apparatus   resilient   tumultuously
concussion   savor

ACTIVE READING EVALUATING To **evaluate** a story is to make a judgment about it. Saying that a story is good or bad is not enough. You need to have reasons for your opinions. When you evaluate a story, ask yourself, Were all parts of the story believable? Did it hold my interest? What did I think about as I finished reading? As you read "All Summer in a Day," record your opinions about the plot, setting, characters, and theme in your READER'S NOTEBOOK. Be sure to support your opinions with reasons.

ALL SUMMER IN A DAY   **209**

LESSON RESOURCES

UNIT TWO RESOURCE BOOK, pp. 8–14

ASSESSMENT
Formal Assessment, pp. 33–34
Teacher's Guide to Assessment and Portfolio Use
Test Generator

SKILLS TRANSPARENCIES AND COPYMASTERS
Reading and Critical Thinking
• Evaluating, TR 12 (for Thinking Through the Literature, p. 216)

Grammar
• Using the Right Pronoun Case CM 72 (for Mini Lessson, p. 218)
• Plural and Collective Nouns and Pronouns, CM 66 (for Mini Lesson, p. 214)
Vocabulary
• Using Context Clues, CM 32 (for Mini Lesson, p. 211)

INTEGRATED TECHNOLOGY
Audio Library
Video: Literature in Performance
• "All Summer in a Day." See **Video Resource Book,** pp. 11–18
Internet: Research Starter

Visit our website:
www.mcdougallittell.com

OVERVIEW

 This selection is included in the **Grade 6 InterActive Reader.**

Objectives
1. understand and appreciate a **short story (Literary Analysis)**
2. appreciate **science fiction (Literary Analysis)**
3. use the reading strategy of **evaluating** to help understand a short story **(Active Reading)**

Summary
Margot's classmates resent her because she seems to be different. They were born on rainy Venus, but Margot comes from Earth and can remember what the sun was like. As the story opens, the sun is about to shine—as it does for one hour every seven years. Margot yearns to see it, but moments before it appears, her classmates lock her in a closet. After their hour of sunlit play, her classmates suddenly think of her and let her out. They have gained a new understanding of her need for the sun.

Thematic Link
To whom does Margot belong? To the underground dwellers on rain-swept Venus, or to the Earth dwellers who enjoy the blue sky and sun? Her playmates give her a definitive answer, but in so doing, discover that they, too, still belong to the Earth they have never known.

5-Minute Warm-Up

Daily Language SkillBuilder

Have students **proofread** the display sentences on page 187i and write them correctly. The sentences also appear on Transparency 7 of **Grammar Transparencies and Copymasters.**

Mini Lesson **Preteaching Vocabulary**
If you would like to preteach the WORDS TO KNOW for this selection, use the Mini Lesson, p. 211.

**Reading Skills and Strategies:
PREVIEW**

Briefly describe the situation of the people who live on Venus in this story, without mentioning how Margot is shut in the closet. Explain that according to the story, the people on Venus see the sun for only one hour every seven years. Ask students how the young people on Venus who could not remember ever seeing the sun would feel as they waited for it to reappear.
Possible Responses: eager, full of wonder and curiosity, perhaps fearful

Active Reading | EVALUATING |

Write the following questions on the board to help students evaluate the story during and after reading: Are believable reasons given for the actions of the characters? Is the end of the story satisfying? Why or why not?

Use **Unit Two Resource Book,** p. 9 for more practice.
Use **Reading and Critical Thinking Transparencies,** p. 12, for additional support.

Literary Analysis | SCIENCE FICTION |

Students should be able to identify the purposes of different types of texts. Point out that though we now know enough about Venus to see that Bradbury's story could not take place on that planet, his story is still of value. It says something about who we are as humans and what we need—including basic things like the sun and understanding of one another's differences. Ask students to look for other insights about people as they read this story.

Use **Unit Two Resource Book,** p. 10 for more practice.

ALL SUMMER IN A DAY
BY RAY BRADBURY

Detail of *The Sower* (1888), Vincent van Gogh. Oil on canvas, Rijksmuseum Kroeller-Mueller, Otterlo, The Netherlands, Erich Lessing/Art Resource, New York. Photo copyright © Erich Lessing.

Background photo copyright © 1994 Thomas Wiewandt.

210

Teaching Options

Mini Lesson — Viewing and Representing

Detail of *The Sower*
by Vincent van Gogh

ART APPRECIATION The paintings of Vincent van Gogh (1853–1890) have been among the most influential in modern art, though only one of his 1,500-plus paintings and drawings was sold in his lifetime.
Instruction Students should be able to describe how an illustrator's choice of style or the artwork chosen to accompany a text represents a text's meaning. Point out the use of broad brush strokes and bold colors, both van Gogh hallmarks. Tell

students that artists often use complementary colors—colors opposite to one another on the color wheel—to give vibrancy to their depictions of a scene. Have students list the colors used here to show the radiant light of the sun.
Answer: yellow, gold, green, red
Application Ask students to examine the rough, bare, plowed field in the foreground of the painting and list the colors van Gogh used to paint it.
Answer: blue, gold, green, white, red, black, and possibly others

"Ready?"

"Ready."

"Now?"

"Soon."

"Do the scientists really know? Will it happen today, will it?"

"Look, look; see for yourself!"

The children pressed to each other like so many roses, so many weeds, intermixed, peering out for a look at the hidden sun.

It rained.

It had been raining for seven years; thousands upon thousands of days compounded and filled from one end to the other with rain, with the drum and gush of water, with the sweet crystal fall of showers and the <u>concussion</u> of storms so heavy they were tidal waves come over the islands. A thousand forests had been crushed under the rain and grown up a thousand times to be crushed again. And this was the way life was forever on the planet Venus, and this was the schoolroom of the children of the rocket men and women who had come to a raining world to set up civilization and live out their lives.

"It's stopping, it's stopping!"

"Yes, yes!"

Margot stood apart from them, from these children who could never remember a time when there wasn't rain and rain and rain. They were all nine years old, and if there had been a day, seven years ago, when the sun came out for an hour and showed its face to the stunned world, they could not recall. Sometimes, at night, she heard them stir, in remembrance, and she knew they were dreaming and remembering gold or a yellow crayon or a coin large enough to buy the world with. She knew that they thought they remembered a warmness, like a blushing in the face, in the body, in the arms and legs and

trembling hands. But then they always awoke to the tatting drum, the endless shaking down of clear bead necklaces upon the roof, the walk, the gardens, the forest; and their dreams were gone.

> It had been raining for seven years; thousands upon thousands of days . . .

All day yesterday they had read in class about the sun, about how like a lemon it was and how hot. And they had written small stories or essays or poems about it:

> I think the sun is a flower,
> That blooms for just one hour.

That was Margot's poem, read in a quiet voice in the still classroom while the rain was falling outside.

"Aw, you didn't write that!" protested one of the boys.

"I did," said Margot. "I *did*."

"William!" said the teacher.

But that was yesterday. Now, the rain was slackening, and the children were crushed to the great thick windows.

"Where's teacher?"

"She'll be back."

"She'd better hurry; we'll miss it!"

They turned on themselves, like a feverish wheel, all tumbling spokes.

Margot stood alone. She was a very <u>frail</u> girl who looked as if she had been lost in the rain for years, and the rain had washed out the blue from her eyes and the red from her mouth and the yellow from her hair. She was an old <u>photograph dusted from an album, whitened away</u>;

WORDS TO KNOW	**concussion** (kən-kŭsh′ən) *n.* a strong shaking

211

Customizing Instruction

Less Proficient Readers

Set a Purpose Ask students to discuss how they feel when someone shows them dislike, and what do they do when they dislike someone. Then have them read to find out why Margot's classmates dislike her and how they treat her.

Students Acquiring English

Use **Spanish Study Guide**, pp. 43–45 for additional support.

Gifted and Talented

Have students note the vivid language Bradbury uses to describe Venus as they read. Tell them to think how they would use vivid language to describe their own environment.

Multiple Learning Styles

Logical/Mathematical Learners

1 Point out that Bradbury says "It had been raining for seven years; thousands upon thousands of days . . ." Ask students to figure out if there really are thousands and thousands of days in seven years. Suggest that they also do research to find out the length of a day and a year on Venus in case Bradbury is referring to Venusian days and years.

Answer: There are only 2,555 days in seven years on Earth, so Bradbury's statement is barely accurate. He would be even more incorrect if he were referring to days and years on Venus. The year on Venus (the time it takes the planet to orbit once around the Sun) is 225 Earth days long; the day on Venus (the time it takes the planet to rotate once on its axis) is 243 Earth days long—so the day on Venus is actually longer than its year! Seven years on Venus would take only 6.48 Venusian days. The length of a day on Venus was not known when Bradbury wrote his story.

 Preteaching Vocabulary

USING CONTEXT CLUES

Instruction Remind students that when they come across an unfamiliar word, they should examine the context carefully to see if they can infer its meaning. Write the following sentence on the chalkboard:

Though he knew little about machines, he managed to get the <u>apparatus</u> *to work.*

Point out that the context suggests that an apparatus is a kind of machine.

Exercises Have students use context clues to infer the meanings of the underlined WORDS TO KNOW in the following sentences:

1. The vegetation was springy and <u>resilient</u>, and bounced back when bent over by the rain.
2. With wild shrieking and shouting, the children spilled <u>tumultuously</u> out of the school.
3. Margot planned to sit quietly in the sunlight and happily <u>savor</u> its warmth.
4. The storms shook and rattled the buildings with repeated <u>concussions</u>.

Use **Unit Two Resource Book**, p. 11 for practice.

Use **Vocabulary Transparencies and Copymasters**, p. 32, for additional support.

Reading Skills and Strategies:
RECOGNIZE CAUSE AND EFFECT

Students should be able to use a text's structure to locate and recall information. Tell them that certain words indicate cause and effect relationships: *because, therefore, so,* and others. Remind them that sometimes cause and effect is shown indirectly, without the use of these marker words. Ask them to use marker words and inferences to find the causes behind the children's dislike of Margot.

Possible Responses: They dislike her because she will not play games with them or sing with them unless they sing about the sun and the summer. She has seen the sun and remembers what it was like.

Literary Analysis:
METAPHORS AND SIMILES

A Remind students that a comparison of two things is called a simile if *like* or *as* is used, and a metaphor if no such word is used. Have students identify metaphors or similes in this dialogue.

Possible Response: "Like a penny" and "like a fire in the stove" are both similes. There are no metaphors used.

Reading Skills and Strategies:
PREDICT

B Point out that one of the things that good readers do is ask questions about the outcome of the story. These questions are a first step toward predicting what will happen—a way of exploring several possible outcomes. Ask students to formulate questions about what will happen once Margot is locked in the closet.

Possible Responses: Will she get out? Will she miss the sun? How will the other students feel afterward if she fails to see the sun?

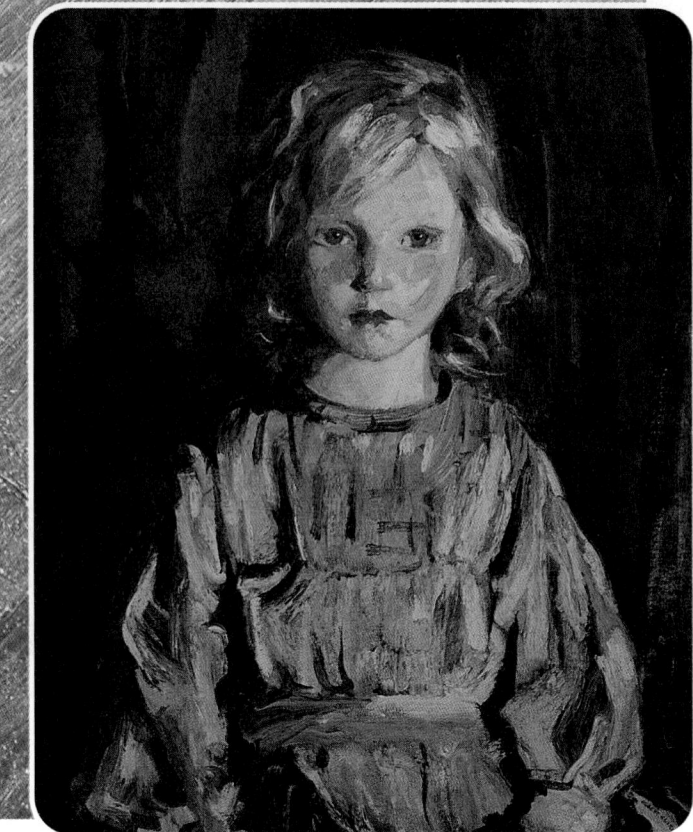

Wee Maureen (1926), Robert Henri. Oil on canvas, 24″ × 20″, The Pennsylvania Academy of the Fine Arts, Philadelphia, gift of Mrs. Herbert Cameron Morris.

and if she spoke at all, her voice would be a ghost. Now she stood, separate, staring at the rain and the loud, wet world beyond the huge glass.

"What're *you* looking at?" said William.

Margot said nothing.

"Speak when you're spoken to." He gave her a shove. But she did not move; rather, she let herself be moved only by him and nothing else.

They edged away from her; they would not look at her. She felt them go away. And this

was because she would play no games with them in the echoing tunnels of the underground city. If they tagged her and ran, she stood blinking after them and did not follow. When the class sang songs about happiness and life and games, her lips barely moved. Only when they sang about the sun and the summer did her lips move as she watched the drenched windows.

And then, of course, the biggest crime of all was that she had come here only five years ago from Earth, and she remembered the sun and the way the sun was and the sky was when she was four, in Ohio. And they, they had been on Venus all their lives, and they had been only two years old when last the sun came out and had long since forgotten the color and heat of it and the way that it really was. But Margot remembered.

"It's like a penny," she said once, eyes closed.

"No, it's not!" the children cried.

"It's like a fire," she said, "in the stove."

"You're lying; you don't remember!" cried the children.

But she remembered and stood quietly apart from all of them and watched the patterning windows. And once, a month ago, she had refused to shower in the school shower rooms, had clutched her hands to her ears and over her head, screaming the water mustn't touch her head. So after that, dimly, dimly, she sensed

1

A

Teaching Options

 Mini Lesson ## Viewing and Representing

Wee Maureen
by Robert Henri

ART APPRECIATION American artist Robert Henri (1865–1929) loved to paint pictures of children. However, his pictures never idealized children or childhood, but tried to express the emotions children actually experience.

Instruction Point out that portrait paintings use color, light, and the sitter's pose to describe the sitter. Ask students what kind of person Wee Maureen might be.

Possible Responses: She seems like an open person who is not shy, because of the way the artist painted her facing him and looking straight at him.

Application Compare the painting to Bradbury's description of Margot on pp. 211–212.

Possible Response: The girl in the picture has a washed out, "whitened" look, like Margot. Both the girl in the painting and Margot have blonde hair and blue eyes.

it; she was different, and they knew her difference and kept away.

There was talk that her father and mother were taking her back to Earth next year; it seemed vital to her that they do so, though it would mean the loss of thousands of dollars to her family. And so, the children hated her for all these reasons, of big and little consequence. They hated her pale, snow face, her waiting silence, her thinness, and her possible future.

"Get away!" The boy gave her another push. "What're you waiting for?"

Then, for the first time, she turned and looked at him. And what she was waiting for was in her eyes.

"Well, don't wait around here!" cried the boy, savagely. "You won't see nothing!"

Her lips moved.

"Nothing!" he cried. "It was all a joke, wasn't it?" He turned to the other children. "Nothing's happening today. *Is* it?"

They all blinked at him and then, understanding, laughed and shook their heads. "Nothing, nothing!"

"Oh, but," Margot whispered, her eyes helpless. "But, this is the day, the scientists predict, they say, they *know*, the sun . . ."

"All a joke!" said the boy and seized her roughly. "Hey, everyone, let's put her in a closet before teacher comes!"

"No," said Margot, falling back.

They surged about her, caught her up, and bore her, protesting and then pleading and then crying, back into a tunnel, a room, a closet, where they slammed and locked the door. They stood looking at the door and saw it tremble from her beating and throwing herself against it. They heard her muffled cries. Then, smiling, they turned and went out and back down the tunnel, just as the teacher arrived.

"Ready, children?" She glanced at her watch.
"Yes!" said everyone.
"Are we all here?"
"Yes!"

The rain slackened still more.

They crowded to the huge door.

The rain stopped.

It was as if, in the midst of a film concerning an avalanche, a tornado, a hurricane, a volcanic eruption, something had, first, gone wrong with the sound apparatus, thus muffling and finally cutting off all noise, all of the blasts and repercussions and thunders, and then, secondly, ripped the film from the projector and inserted in its place a peaceful tropical slide which did not move or tremor. The world ground to a standstill. The silence was so immense and unbelievable that you felt that your ears had been stuffed or you had lost your hearing altogether. The children put their hands to their ears. They stood apart. The door slid back, and the smell of the silent, waiting world came in to them.

The sun came out.

Then, for the first time, she turned and looked at him. And what she was waiting for was in her eyes.

WORDS TO KNOW

apparatus (ăp′ə-rā′təs) *n.* a device or set of equipment used for a specific purpose

213

Literary Analysis | SCIENCE FICTION |

Remind students that one of the features of science fiction is the description of unusual settings, especially on other planets or in future times. Ask students to identify descriptions on this page that show that the writing is science fiction.

Possible Responses: The Venusian jungle is like "a nest of octopuses, clustering up great arms of fleshlike weed, wavering . . . It was the color of rubber and ash." The floor of the jungle is described as a mattress that "sighs and squeaks under them, resilient and alive." When the rain comes back it is described as falling "in tons and avalanches everywhere and forever".

Active Reading | EVALUATING |

Ask students to evaluate the children's actions by asking these questions:

• Is the description of the children's response to the Venusian "spring" accurate? Explain.
  Possible Response: Yes; it would be very natural for children to run and shout in the sunlight when they had a chance.

• What is the author suggesting when he says that one of the children "gave a little cry" when he or she remembered Margot?
  Possible Response: He is suggesting that the child felt remorse for having shut Margot away and forgotten her.

• Is it believable that the children cannot look at each other as they think about having left Margot in the closet?
  Possible Response: Yes, because they are feeling extreme shame for what they have done. It was only when they experienced how wonderful the sun was that they could understand why Margot acted so strangely.

It was the color of flaming bronze, and it was very large. And the sky around it was a blazing blue tile color. And the jungle burned with sunlight as the children, released from their spell, rushed out, yelling, into the summertime.

"Now, don't go too far," called the teacher after them. "You've only one hour, you know. You wouldn't want to get caught out!"

But they were running and turning their faces up to the sky and feeling the sun on their cheeks like a warm iron; they were taking off their jackets and letting the sun burn their arms.

"Oh, it's better than the sun lamps, isn't it?"

"Much, much better!"

They stopped running and stood in the great jungle that covered Venus, that grew and never stopped growing, <u>tumultuously</u>, even as you watched it. It was a nest of octopuses, clustering up great arms of fleshlike weed, wavering, flowering in this brief spring. It was the color of rubber and ash, this jungle, from the many years without sun. It was the color of stones and white cheeses and ink.

The children lay out, laughing, on the jungle mattress and heard it sigh and squeak under them, <u>resilient</u> and alive. They ran among the trees, they slipped and fell, they pushed each other, they played hide-and-seek and tag; but most of all they squinted at the sun until tears ran down their faces, they put their hands up at that yellowness and that amazing blueness, and they breathed of the fresh, fresh air and listened and listened to the silence which suspended them in a blessed sea of no sound and no motion. They looked at everything and <u>savored</u> everything. Then, wildly, like animals escaped from their caves, they ran and ran in shouting circles. They ran for an hour and did not stop running.

And then—

In the midst of their running, one of the girls wailed.

Everyone stopped.

The girl, standing in the open, held out her hand.

"Oh, look, look," she said, trembling.

They came slowly to look at her opened palm.

In the center of it, cupped and huge, was a single raindrop.

She began to cry, looking at it.

They glanced quickly at the sky.

"Oh. Oh."

A few cold drops fell on their noses and their cheeks and their mouths. The sun faded behind a stir of mist. A wind blew cool around them. They turned and started to walk back toward the underground house, their hands at their sides, their smiles vanishing away.

A boom of thunder startled them, and like leaves before a new hurricane, they tumbled upon each other and ran. Lightning struck ten miles away, five miles away, a mile, a half mile. The sky darkened into midnight in a flash.

They stood in the doorway of the underground for a moment until it was raining hard. Then they closed the door and heard the gigantic sound of the rain falling in tons and avalanches everywhere and forever.

"Will it be seven more years?"

"Yes. Seven."

Then one of them gave a little cry.

"Margot!"

"What?"

"She's still in the closet where we locked her."

"Margot."

They stood as if someone had driven them, like so many stakes, into the floor. They looked

WORDS
TO
KNOW

tumultuously (tōō-mŭl′chōō-əs-lē) *adv.* in a wild and disorderly way
resilient (rĭ-zĭl′yənt) *adj.* flexible and springy
savor (sā′vər) *v.* to take great pleasure in

214

 Grammar

PLURAL AND COLLECTIVE NOUNS AND PRONOUNS
Instruction A collective noun is one that names a group of people, places, things, or ideas. A collective noun, unlike a plural noun, takes a singular verb. Write the following sentence on the board and ask students to rewrite it, substituting the collective noun *class* for the plural noun *children:* The children love the sun. (*The <u>class loves</u> the sun.*)
Tell students that pronouns that refer back to collective nouns should also be singular: The class is small. <u>It</u> is made up of children who have never seen blue sky before.

Exercises In the sentences below, have students supply the type of word described in parentheses.

1. The group (present verb) in circles. (Possible responses: runs, dances)

2. The company sent (possessive pronoun) people to Venus to work. (its)

 Use **Unit 2 Resource Book**, p. 12·
Use **Grammar Transparencies and Copymasters**, p. 66.

 Use McDougal Littell's *Language Network*, Chapters 2 and 3, for more instruction and practice in collectives.

at each other and then looked away. They glanced out at the world that was raining now and raining and raining steadily. They could not meet each other's glances. Their faces were solemn and pale. They looked at their hands and feet, their faces down.

"Margot."

One of the girls said, "Well . . . ?"

No one moved.

"Go on," whispered the girl.

They walked slowly down the hall in the sound of cold rain. They turned through the doorway to the room, in the sound of the storm and thunder, lightning on their faces, blue and terrible. They walked over to the closet door slowly and stood by it.

Behind the closet door was only silence.

They unlocked the door, even more slowly, and let Margot out. ❖

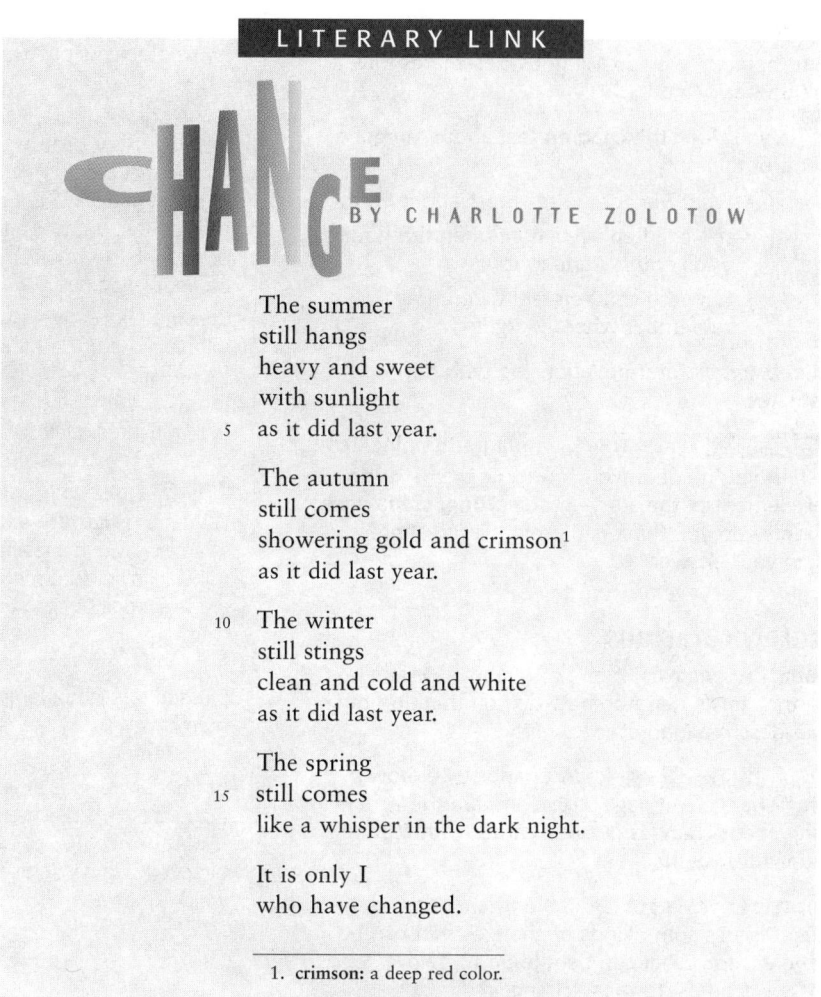

LITERARY LINK

CHANGE
BY CHARLOTTE ZOLOTOW

The summer
still hangs
heavy and sweet
with sunlight
5 as it did last year.

The autumn
still comes
showering gold and crimson[1]
as it did last year.

10 The winter
still stings
clean and cold and white
as it did last year.

The spring
15 still comes
like a whisper in the dark night.

It is only I
who have changed.

———
1. **crimson:** a deep red color.

ALL SUMMER IN A DAY   **215**

Customizing Instruction

Less Proficient Readers
Help students summarize what happens when the rain stops.
• How does the environment change when the rain stops?
  Possible Response: The sun comes out, and it becomes warm.
• What do the children find outside?
  Possible Response: A jungle the color of rubber, ash, stones, white cheeses, and ink.
• Why doesn't Margot get to see this change?
  Answer: She is locked in the closet.
Set a Purpose Have students read on to discover how the children feel at the end of the story.

LITERARY LINK

Charlotte Zolotow (1915–) began her career as a children's book editor. She has published over sixty books for young readers.
Explore the poem by asking the following questions:
• In Zolotow's poem, are the seasons seen as things that change or things that stay the same?
  Possible Response: Even though the seasons cycle, they are seen as things that stay the same.
• Does the speaker feel that life has changed? How do you know?
  Possible Response: The speaker says "I . . . have changed"; this suggests that life is very different for the speaker.
• How is Margot's situation different from that of the speaker of the poem?
  Possible Response: Margot believes she needs the changes of the seasons to be happy; in the poem, the changes of the seasons only remind the speaker that the important changes are those that take place inside oneself.

✓ Assessment   Standardized Test Practice

UNDERSTANDING CAUSE AND EFFECT On some standardized tests, students will be asked to choose an option that indicates a cause or effect described in a selection. Read aloud or write on the board the following question:

Which of the following statements best describes why the children go wild when the rain stops?

A. They are glad Margot can't see the sun.

B. They are ready for their daily recess.

C. They are only allowed out once a week.

D. They cannot remember having seen the sun.

Lead students through the process of choosing the correct option. In discussion, bring students to see that option A is not correct because the children have forgotten about Margot, as becomes clear later. Option B is incorrect because they do not have daily recess outdoors; nor is Option C correct, since they are not allowed out on a weekly basis. This leaves option D, the correct choice, which is supported by evidence in the story—the sun only shines once every seven years, and the last time it shone, the children were only two years old.

GUIDING STUDENT RESPONSE

Connect to the Literature

1. What Do You Think?
Students may respond that they felt sorry for Margot at the end of the story, that Margot must feel sad that she missed the sun, and that the other children seem to feel badly about what they did to Margot.

Comprehension Check
• The story takes place on Venus in the future.
• Margot was living on Earth until five years ago, whereas the other children were born on Venus.
• Margot is locked in a closet.

 Use Selection Quiz
Unit Two Resource Book, p. 14.

Think Critically

2. **Possible Response:** They envy her experiences in the sunlight.
3. **Possible Response:** After experiencing the sun, the children seem to understand Margot better and why she misses Earth so much. Now that they understand why Margot is different from them, they act guilty and serious about locking her in the closet.
4. **Possible Responses:** The relationship may improve because now everyone has seen the sun and the children feel guilty about locking Margot in the closet. The relationship may get worse because Margot may not be able to forgive or forget their cruel treatment of her.
5. Responses will vary.

 Use **Reading and Critical Thinking Transparencies,** p. 12, for additional support.

Literary Analysis

Science Fiction Discussion should lead to an awareness that despite the unusual nature of the setting, the children in the story deal with common human issues of dislike, isolation, depression, and spitefulness.

Connect to the Literature

1. What Do You Think?
Discuss the end of the story. How do you think Margot feels? How do you think the other children feel?

Comprehension Check
• Where and when does the story take place?
• Why is Margot the only child who remembers the sun?
• Where is Margot when the sun comes out?

Think Critically

2. In your opinion, why do Margot's classmates play a prank on her?

3. How do you think the children feel about Margot at the end of the story?

 THINK ABOUT
  • what Margot misses most about Earth
  • the children's reaction when the hour ends and it starts to rain
  • how the children feel when they remember where Margot is

4. Predict Margot's future relationship with her classmates.

5. **ACTIVE READING** **EVALUATING** With a partner, look over the chart you made in your **READER'S NOTEBOOK**. What element of the story—**plot, setting, characters,** or **theme**—do you think is the most interesting? Explain your answer.

Extend Interpretations

6. **Different Perspectives** If one of Margot's classmates were the story's narrator, how do you think he or she would describe Margot?

7. **COMPARING TEXTS** Read Charlotte Zolotow's poem "Change" on page 215. Compare the speaker's feeling about changes in the weather with Margot's reactions to weather.

8. **Connect to Life** Margot is unable to adapt to life on Venus. Discuss some kinds of changes that can be hard to accept. What can people do to help themselves adjust to those changes?

Literary Analysis

SCIENCE FICTION Fiction based on real or possible effects of progress in science and technology is called **science fiction.** Much science fiction is set in the future and in places where humans have never lived. The problems the characters face, however, are usually similar to the problems people face today.

Some science fiction writers call their work "speculative fiction" (fiction that predicts). In "All Summer in a Day," Bradbury predicts that humans will develop the technology to live on another planet.

Cooperative Learning Activity
With a group of classmates, look for realistic details in the story. Discuss whether the future that Bradbury predicts is similar to or different from the present.

REVIEW **FIGURATIVE LANGUAGE**
Writers use **figurative language** to create vivid images in readers' minds. Similes and metaphors are two types of figurative language.

In Bradbury's story, "The children pressed to each other like so many roses, . . ." is an example of a **simile.**

"It [the jungle] was a nest of octopuses, . . ." is a metaphor. A **metaphor** compares two things directly, but a simile uses the word *like* or *as.*

Extend Interpretations

6. **Different Perspectives** Student responses will vary, but should include some of the description from pages 211–212. To help students get started on this, ask them whether the classmate is describing Margot at the beginning or at the end of the story.
7. **Comparing Texts** Possible Response: The speaker in the poem finds the predictability of the seasons reassuring. Margot is frustrated by the predictability of the weather on Venus, and is anxious to see the sun.

8. **Connect to Life** Possible Response: Moving, changing schools, and a new member of the family are examples of changes that might be hard to accept. To get students started on this activity, discuss the need for communication, support from family and friends, and willingness to find new friends or just good features in new situations.

Writing Options

1. Character Contrasts In what ways are Margot and her classmates different? Use a chart like the one shown here to list the differences. Then write a paragraph about how these differences create conflict in the story.

Contrasts	
Main Character	**Her Classmates**
1.	
2.	

2. Final Scene Reread the ending of the story. Then write an additional scene, telling what happens after Margot is let out of the closet.

Writing Handbook
See p. R33: Narrative Writing.

Activities & Explorations

1. Plot Comparison As you view the film of "All Summer in a Day," take notes in a sequence-of-events chart. Afterward, compare and contrast the plot of the film with that of the short story. With a small group, discuss why you think the filmmakers changed Bradbury's story.
~ VIEWING AND REPRESENTING

 Side by Side: Literature in Performance

Inquiry & Research

Find out what scientists have discovered about Venus. Compare and contrast the environments of Venus and Earth. Record the similarities and differences in a Venn diagram, and share it with the class.

 More Online: Research Starter
www.mcdougallittell.com

Art Connection

Look again on page 210, at the photograph by Thomas Wiewandt, and the detail from *The Sower* by Vincent van Gogh. Find sensory details in "All Summer in a Day" that remind you of the color, texture, and mood of each artwork.

Writing Options

1. **Character Contrasts** Charts should list relevant contrasting characteristics. To get students started on this activity, have them skim the passage of the selection in which Margot is described.
2. **Final Scene** Responses should build on the existing story. **To make this activity more challenging,** ask students to incorporate science fiction elements into their final scenes.

Use **Writing Transparencies,** p. 22, for additional support.

Activities & Explorations

1. **Plot Comparison** You may suggest that students circle events which take place in the film but not in the short story to help them get started.

Use **Communications Transparencies and Copymasters,** p. 2, for additional support.

Inquiry & Research

Earth vs. Venus Diagrams should demonstrate research and present facts effectively.

Art Connection

Responses should link details from the story appropriately with the art.

Vocabulary in Action

EXERCISE: CONTEXT CLUES On your paper, write the Words to Know that best fill the blanks.

Instead of sleeping, Jamie shined a flashlight on the pages of his new science fiction book and began to __1__ the first chapter. The main character, Samma, was in trouble. Her spaceship's engine and other mechanical __2__ were malfunctioning. An explosion rocked the ship with a powerful __3__. Samma steered toward the nearest planet, and jumped ship. Her jet packs carried her into the planet's atmosphere, where she was tossed __4__ by strong winds. Jamie was glad to read that Samma landed safely, with the rainy planet's __5__ surface cushioning her fall.

Building Vocabulary
For an in-depth lesson on context clues, see p. 79.

WORDS TO KNOW	apparatus	concussion	resilient	savor	tumultuously

Vocabulary in Action

1. savor
2. apparatus
3. concussion
4. tumultuously
5. resilient

Grammar in Context

WRITING EXERCISE
Responses will vary. Possible responses are shown.
1. Margot remembered the sun. She said it was like fire in a stove.
2. The children watched the rain. They shouted when it stopped.
3. The class locked Margot in. They watched the door as she shook it.

Connect to the Literature

Accept all paragraphs where nouns are replaced with pronouns. Students should notice how substituting all pronouns makes the paragraph vague.

Author Activity

Responses should demonstrate a solid acquaintance with the two short stories and focus on a comparison of the effects of scientific change as reflected in each story.

Ray Bradbury

Ray Bradbury has won many awards for science fiction and fantasy writing. Unlike some other science fiction writers who are dazzled by high-tech gadgets, Bradbury is concerned with how technology and science affect ordinary people.

Grammar in Context: Replacing Nouns with Pronouns

By repeating **pronouns** rather than using specific names or other nouns, Ray Bradbury creates the scary sense of a mob overpowering an individual.

> **They** edged away from her; **they** would not look at her. **She** felt them go away.

Pronouns take different forms to show how they function in sentences. A **subject pronoun** functions as the subject of a sentence. Subject pronouns include the following words: *I, we, he, she, it, they, who.*

An **object pronoun** can function as a direct object or as the object of a preposition. The following words are object pronouns: *me, us, him, her, it, them, whom.*

WRITING EXERCISE Rewrite each pair of sentences. Choose effective places to replace nouns with pronouns.

Example: *Original* Margot was different from other children. The children didn't like Margot.

Rewritten Margot was different from them. They didn't like her.

1. Margot remembered the sun. Margot said the sun was like fire in a stove.
2. The children watched the rain. The children shouted when the rain stopped.
3. The class locked Margot in. The class watched the door as Margot shook the door.

Connect to the Literature In a paragraph from the story, replace nouns with pronouns. What effect is lost?

Grammar Handbook Using Nouns and Pronouns, p. R63

"I don't need an alarm clock. My ideas wake me."

Ray Bradbury
born 1920

Imaginary Worlds As a boy in Illinois, Ray Bradbury had a passion for adventure stories, secret-code rings, and comic strips. He started writing to create imaginary worlds of his own. In these worlds, Bradbury says, "I could be excellent all to myself."

First Love By the time he was in high school, Bradbury was writing about a thousand words a day. He wrote and illustrated his own magazines. About his early writing, Bradbury says, "I was in love with everything I did. I did

not warm to a subject, I boiled over." In the early 1940s, he began selling his stories.

A Grown-Up Child Though he writes about future technology and space travel, Bradbury is a bit old-fashioned. He has never learned to drive a car, preferring to get around by riding a bicycle. According to one critic, Bradbury is "the grown-up child who still remembers, still believes."

AUTHOR ACTIVITY

Changes Many of Bradbury's writings explore the impact of scientific developments on people. Find copies of his short stories "The Flying Machine" and "The Million-Year Picnic" and read the two stories. Compare the effects that scientific changes have on the lives of the stories' characters.

Teaching Options

USING THE RIGHT PRONOUN CASE
Explain to students that pronouns come in different forms, called *cases*. Write the following examples on the chalkboard:

Subject: They shut Margot in the closet.
Possessive: Margot did not join their games.
Object: No wonder she disliked them!

Point out to students how the form of the pronoun changes depending on its use in the sentence. Write the following list on the board to help students understand pronoun case use:

 Grammar (Mini Lesson)

Subject forms: I, you, he, she, it, we, you, they
Possessive forms: My (mine), your(s), his, her(s), its, ours, your(s), their(s)
Object: me, you, him, her, it, us, you, them
Exercise Have students change the pronoun in parentheses so that it is the correct case or form. In some sentences, the form is already correct.

1. (Them) thought she was strange. *(They)*
2. (Her) did not join in their games. *(She)*
3. We now know more about (it) climate. *(its)*

4. It does not have a jungle on (its). *(it)*
5. (Your) would not want to live as they did. *(You)*

Use **Unit Two Resource Book**, p. 12.
Use **Grammar Transparencies and Copymasters**, p. 72.

Use McDougal Littell's ***Language Network***, Chapter 3, for more instruction and practice in pronoun case.

Chinatown *from* The Lost Garden

Memoir by LAURENCE YEP

"How could I pretend to be somebody else when I didn't even know who I was?"

Connect to Your Life

Map Your Community What are the characteristics of your own neighborhood or community? Draw a simple map of your community, labeling the parts that are important to you. Share your map with a partner.

Build Background

CONNECT TO HISTORY In the 1800s the Chinese population in California rose dramatically. The gold rush of 1849 drew thousands of Chinese immigrants to San Francisco. In the 1860s, many Chinese laborers came to work on the Central Pacific Railroad. But as the Chinese-American population grew, many people began to view the newcomers as an economic burden. Laws were passed to restrict Chinese immigration. Other laws isolated Chinese Americans in communities called Chinatowns.

Not until the 1960s were immigration laws changed to end bias based on race. Fair housing laws were passed that allowed Chinese Americans to live where they wished.

 LaserLinks: Background for Reading
Historical Connection
Cultural Connection

WORDS TO KNOW **Vocabulary Preview**		
entice	remotely	tenement
gaudy	shunned	vulgar
immensely	stereotype	
palatial	taboo	

Focus Your Reading

LITERARY ANALYSIS **PRIMARY SOURCE** Information comes from various kinds of sources. A **primary source** conveys direct, firsthand knowledge. Autobiographies, journals, diaries, letters, and memoirs are all primary sources. "Chinatown" is a primary source because it is Laurence Yep's account of his own personal experience. As you read "Chinatown," notice how the details that Yep remembers help you understand what life was like for one Chinese American in San Francisco during the 1950s.

ACTIVE READING **DISTINGUISHING FACT FROM OPINION** A **fact** is a statement that can be proved, such as "U.S. teens watch an average of 20 hours of television a week." An **opinion** is a statement that expresses a person's beliefs or feelings. "U.S. teens watch too much television" is one person's opinion. You can tell a fact from an opinion by asking yourself, Can this statement be proved, or does it express what one person believes?

READER'S NOTEBOOK As you read "Chinatown," list in your notebook at least three facts and three opinions that you find.

Facts · Opinions
There is little plant life in Chinatown.

LESSON RESOURCES

UNIT TWO RESOURCE BOOK, pp. 15–21

ASSESSMENT
Formal Assessment, pp. 35–36
Teacher's Guide to Assessment and Portfolio Use
Test Generator

SKILLS TRANSPARENCIES AND COPYMASTERS
Literary Analysis
• Primary/Secondary Source, TR 14 (for Paired Activity, p. 227)

Reading and Critical Thinking
• Distinguishing Fact from Opinion, TR 26 (for Thinking Through the Literature, p. 227)
Grammar
• Collective Nouns, CM 67 (for Mini Lesson, p. 224)
• Precise Nouns: Concrete and Abstract, CM 70 (for Mini Lesson, p. 229)
Vocabulary
• Using a Word Web, CM 33 (for Mini Lesson, p. 220)
• Compound Words, CM 34 (for Mini Lesson, p. 223)

INTEGRATED TECHNOLOGY
Audio Library
LaserLinks
• Historical Connection; Cultural Connection; Author Background. See **Teacher's SourceBook,** p. 19
Internet: Research Starter

Visit our website:
www.mcdougallittell.com

 This selection is included in the **Grade 6 InterActive Reader.**

Objectives
1. understand and appreciate a **memoir** (Literary Analysis)
2. recognize **primary sources** (Literary Analysis)
3. **distinguish fact from opinion** (Active Reading)

Summary
In this memoir of his childhood in San Francisco, writer Laurence Yep describes how he felt like an outsider. Although he is Chinese American, Yep lived outside of Chinatown and did not learn how to speak Chinese. As a result, he missed the jokes that his friends told each other in Chinese. He didn't understand the different rules that governed the games Chinese boys played. Unlike the rest of his family, he wasn't a natural athlete. As he remembers feeling like an outsider, Yep also recalls wrestling with questions about his identity.

Thematic Link
Laurence Yep struggles to achieve a sense of belonging. As a Chinese American living in an African-American neighborhood, Yep explores Chinatown as an outsider. He tries to understand where he fits in.

5-Minute Warm-Up

Daily Language SkillBuilder

Have students **proofread** the display sentences on page 187j and write them correctly. The sentences also appear on Transparency 7 of **Grammar Transparencies and Copymasters.**

Mini Lesson **Preteaching Vocabulary**
If you would like to preteach the WORDS TO KNOW for this selection, use the Mini Lesson, p. 220.

Reading Skills and Strategies:
PREVIEW

Briefly summarize "Chinatown," without identifying the main theme—Yep's struggle to find his place in the world. Have students look through the story. Ask them to make predictions about what they think the selection will be about. Have them establish a purpose for reading.

Literary Analysis | PRIMARY SOURCE |

Have students begin a list of the details that indicate "Chinatown" is a primary source. Engage them in a discussion about other works they have read that are primary sources.

 Use **Unit Two Resource Book,** p. 17 for more practice.
Use **Literary Analysis Transparencies,** p. 14, for additional support.

Active Reading | DISTINGUISHING FACT FROM OPINION |

Distinguishing fact from opinion is an important reading skill. Once you identify a writer's opinions, you can better understand his or her personality, as well as his or her perspective on the world. As they read, tell students to think about what they know about Laurence Yep from tracking his opinions and distinguishing them from the facts.

Possible Response: It is a *fact* that Yep's parents and brother were athletic. It is a *fact* that Yep was not as athletic as his family, but it is Yep's *opinion* that his lack of athletic ability made him a major disappointment to his family.

 Use **Unit Two Resource Book,** p. 16 for more practice.
Use **Reading and Critical Thinking Transparencies,** p. 26, for additional support.

Chinatown

Celebration, Chinatown (1940), Dong Kingman.
Private collection.

from
The
Lost
Garden

by Laurence Yep

Teaching Options

 Preteaching Vocabulary

USING A WORD WEB Call students' attention to the list of WORDS TO KNOW. Tell them that making a word web can help them understand and remember the meanings of unfamiliar words.
Instruction
• Write the word web on the board.
• Ask a volunteer to explain how the words in each circle are related.
• Discuss the relationships of the words.

(The main headings are types of housing; the words under them are words that might describe them.)
Application Have students use the same kind of web with another WORD TO KNOW.

 Use **Unit Two Resource Book,** p. 18 for exercises. Use **Vocabulary Transparencies and Copymasters,** p. 33, for additional support.

This selection is a chapter from Laurence Yep's memoir The Lost Garden. *Yep grew up as a Chinese American in an African-American neighborhood of San Francisco. He attended school in Chinatown, although he did not speak or understand Chinese. His lack of knowledge of Chinese, among other things, made him an outsider in Chinatown—sometimes even among his friends.*

f Uncle Francis and other members of our family left Chinatown to explore America, my experience was the reverse because I was always going into Chinatown to explore the streets and perhaps find the key to the pieces of the puzzle. But the search only seemed to increase the number of pieces.

When I was a boy, Chinatown was much more like a small town than it is now. It was small not only in terms of population but in physical area as well. Its boundaries were pretty well set by Pacific Avenue on the north next to the Italian neighborhood of North Beach, Kearny Street on the east, Sacramento Street on the south, and Stockton Street on the west—an area only of a few city blocks.

There is a <u>stereotype</u> that the Chinese lived in Chinatown because they wanted to. The fact was that before the fair housing laws[1] they often had no choice.

For years there was a little cottage on an ivy-covered hill in the southwest corner of Chinatown just above the Stockton tunnel. There was—and still is—very little plant life in Chinatown, so the only color green I saw was the paint on my school. The kind of green that is alive—lawns, bushes, and trees—was something I had to leave Chinatown to see, except for that ivy-covered slope. On windy days, the ivy itself would stir and move like a living sea; and overlooking the ivy was a

cottage that was charm itself. However, as much as I admired the house—on occasion I was disloyal enough to the Pearl Apartments to want to live in it—I knew it wasn't for us. My Auntie Mary had once tried to rent it and had been refused because she was Chinese.

Out of some forty-five or so students in my class, I was one of the few who lived outside of Chinatown. Now, thanks to the fair housing laws that were passed in the 1960s, almost none of my former classmates live there; and

There is a stereotype that the Chinese lived in Chinatown because they wanted to.

Chinatown itself has spilled out of its traditional boundaries.

When I was a boy, though, we could see the results of white money and power on three sides of us. To the east we could stare up at the high-rise office buildings of the business district; and to the west, up the steep streets, were the fancy hotels of Nob Hill.[2] Southward lay downtown and the fancy department stores.

Grant Avenue led directly to downtown; but for years I always thought of the Stockton tunnel as the symbolic end to Chinatown. When it had been cut right through a hill, my father and his young friends had held foot races through it after midnight, hooting and hollering so that the echoes seemed to be the

---

1. **fair housing laws:** the civil rights acts of 1964 and 1968, which outlawed racial discrimination in the sale and rental of property, private as well as public.

2. **Nob Hill:** a wealthy neighborhood in northeastern San Francisco. It adjoins Chinatown and is noted for its large luxury hotels, such as the Fairmont and the Mark Hopkins.

WORDS
TO
KNOW

stereotype (stĕr′ē-ə-tīp′) *n.* a fixed idea, especially about the way a group of people looks or acts

221

Mini Lesson **Viewing and Representing**

Celebration, Chinatown
by Dong Kingman

ART APPRECIATION Dong Kingman (b. 1911) is a Chinese-American watercolor artist and educator. His paintings and murals are in many collections in the United States and Hong Kong.
Instruction Ask students to describe the setting of this watercolor. Have them explain how they can tell whether this scene shows the past, the present, or the future.
Possible Response: This scene depicts the past,

shown by the style of the car and the old-fashioned lamppost.
Application Ask students to think about the connection between this work of art and the title of the book from which this selection is taken, *The Lost Garden*. Encourage students to consider what the title of the book and the artwork reveal about the story.
Possible Response: The title suggests that the author is writing about a beautiful time that is now gone. The art sets the story in a specific time period.

Literary Analysis: MEMOIR

Ask students to give two examples that show that "Chinatown" is a memoir—a story about a person's life told by that person.

Possible Responses: Yep's story about following his friend Harold on his paper route shows that this is based on his childhood and therefore is a memoir. His story about his friend Paul is another example.

Literary Analysis: POINT OF VIEW

Ask students to identify the point of view of the selection, first-person or third-person, and explain how they know this.

Possible Response: The selection is written from the first-person point of view. The author uses the first-person pronouns *I* and *me*. He is writing a memoir about his own childhood experiences.

Active Reading | DISTINGUISHING FACT FROM OPINION

A Ask students to identify one thing that Yep says about the Chinatown projects that is a fact and one thing that is an opinion.

Possible Response: Yep presents a fact when he says that many of his schoolmates lived in the Chinatown projects. He gives an opinion when he says that he wasn't sure if living there was any better than living in the projects near his family's store.

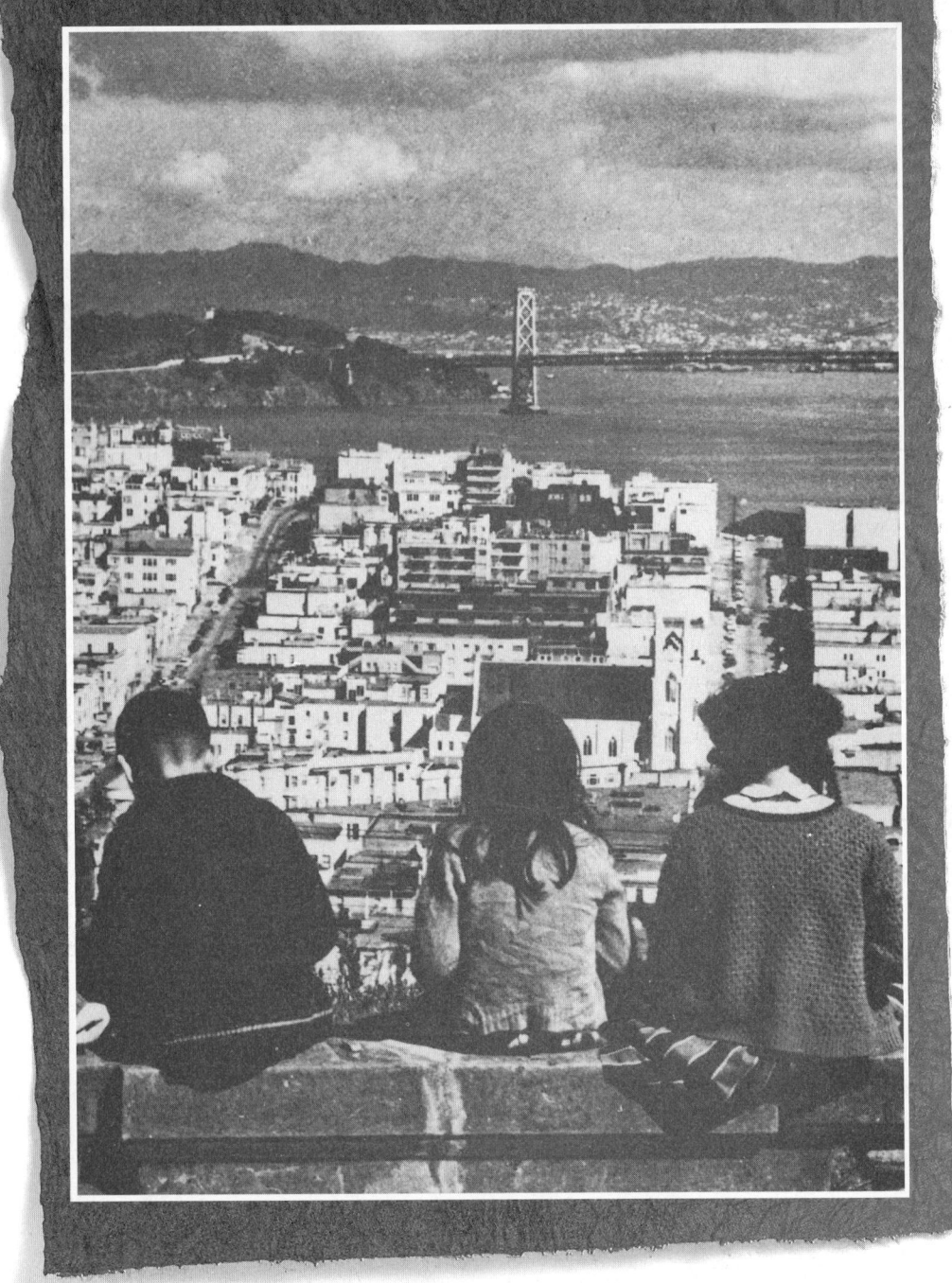

Detail. Young Chinese Americans enjoy a view of San Francisco Bay and the Bay Bridge. Courtesy California Historical Society, San Francisco.

222 UNIT TWO PART 1: THE NEED TO BELONG

Teaching Options

BLOCK SCHEDULING: MANAGING TIME

If your schedule requires that you cover the lesson objectives in a shorter time, use . . .
- Preparing to Read, p. 219
- Thinking Through the Literature, p. 227
- Vocabulary and Spelling, p. 228
- Grammar in Context, p. 229

If you would like to take advantage of longer class time, use . . .
- TE Teaching Options: Preteaching Vocabulary, p. 220; Viewing and Representing, p. 221; Vocabulary Strategy, p. 223; Grammar, p. 224, 229; Multicultural Link, p. 225; Standardized Test Practice, p. 226; Spelling, p. 228
- Choices & Challenges and Author Activity, pp. 228–229

cheers of a huge crowd. The rich white world began just on the other side of the tunnel.

There were also invisible barriers that separated the wealthy whites from the Chinese who cleaned their apartments or waited on

The world looked just the same whether it was a Chinese eye or an American one.

their tables. The Chinese could see and even touch the good life; but they could not join in.

One of my classmates, Harold, had a paper route on Nob Hill. I still find it hard to believe that, up hills that angled some forty degrees or so, he carried a kind of poncho loaded with papers in front and back. But he did that every afternoon. Once I went along with him; and I followed him into one of the fanciest hotels on Nob Hill, past the elaborately uniformed doorman, over the plush carpets, under the ornate chandeliers, and around in back, down concrete hallways as bleak as the ones in the Chinatown housing projects that were painted a cheap, gaudy yellow—a shade which my friend referred to as "landlord yellow." Harold would deliver the afternoon newspapers to the laundrymen and other workers. And with my friend that day, I wandered all around the roots of that palatial dream of wealth.

When the poncho was flat, my friend and I returned to his tenement apartment where there was only one toilet to a floor; and the toilet lacked both a door and toilet paper. When you went, you brought in your own toilet paper. Nothing could be done about the door except changing your attitude about privacy.

Many of my schoolmates lived in the Chinatown projects, and I wasn't sure if life was any better in them than life in the projects near our store. Another newspaper carrier named Paul lived there. As the oldest boy, Paul was expected to look after his younger brothers and sisters while his parents worked—a common practice among many Chinese families. However, as a result, Paul had failed to develop many social skills let alone improve his English. I remember the nun sending him out on an errand and then asking the rest of the class to act as his special friend—which was easy for her to say because she was an adult.

As far as I knew, he hung around with his own group in the projects rather than with anyone from school. His group, though, must have been pretty rough because one of them threw a knife that "accidentally" hit Paul in the eye. Fortunately, there was a charity that arranged an operation; and he was given a new eye from someone who had recently died.

We never knew the identity of the donor, but Paul amused himself by claiming it was a rich white. First, he would clap a hand over his new eye and roll his remaining Chinese eye around. Then he would put his hand over his old one and gaze around elaborately with his new American eye. And then he would announce to us that the world looked just the same whether it was a Chinese eye or an American one.

Paul had shot up early and was a giant compared to the rest of us. When he ran, he looked like an ostrich with arms. He would kick out his legs explosively while his arms flailed the air, so it was hard not to laugh; but we didn't because he was also immensely strong.

WORDS TO KNOW	**gaudy** (gô'dē) *adj.* bright and showy in a way that displays bad taste
	palatial (pə-lā'shəl) *adj.* large and richly decorated, like a palace
	tenement (tĕn'ə-mənt) *n.* a crowded, rundown apartment building
	immensely (ĭ-mĕns'lē) *adv.* to a great extent; enormously

223

**Reading Skills and Strategies:
MAKING INFERENCES**

A Ask students what inferences they can draw about the author's childhood feelings toward Paul.

Possible Response: Yep thought that Paul was awkward, but he admired Paul for his size and strength.

**Reading Skills and Strategies:
IDENTIFYING EFFECTS OF AUTHOR'S PERSPECTIVE**

B Explain that an author's perspective has a big effect on his or her writing. Tell students that an author's bias is revealed through the use of particular words and phrases. Ask students to look for clues to Yep's bias toward the playground director.

Possible Response: When Yep writes about the playground director, he says that he was always urging him on to "one disaster after another." The playground director did not mean to bring about disasters for Yep. Yep felt that way because he wasn't a natural athlete.

The playground at St. Mary's was only a concrete basketball court below. Up above, there was a kind of patio between the convent and the school where the younger children could play. However, the nuns were so worried about our knocking one another down that they forbade us to run during recess. About the only thing we could play under those conditions was a kind of slow-motion tag.

At noon, we could go across the street to the Chinese Playground—the playground where my father had once been the director. In those days, it consisted of levels. The first level near the alley that became known as Hang Ah Alley was a volleyball and a tennis court. Down the steps was the next level with a sandbox (which was usually full of fleas), a small director's building, a Ping-Pong table, an area covered by tan bark that housed a slide, a set of bars, and a set of swings and other simple equipment. The level next to the Chinese Baptist church was the basketball court.

We had Physical Education once a week there. The playground director taught the boys, and I suppose the nun handled the girls. Sometimes it was calisthenics; other times it was baseball played with a tennis ball on the tennis court. There was no pitcher. Rather, the "batter" threw up the ball and hit it with his fist. Because of his size and added arm strength from his own paper route, Paul could hit a home run almost every time, sending the tennis ball flying over the high wire mesh fence.

However, my experience was frequently the reverse. Because the present director knew that my father had once been the director of the playground, he was always urging me on to one disaster after another.

The worst happened when he wasn't present, though. In third grade, we had a very sweet nun, Sister Bridget, who used to play kickball with us. Kickball was like baseball except that the pitcher bowled a ball the size of a basketball over the ground and the "batter" kicked it. One time someone kicked a ball so that it rolled foul. Retrieving it, I threw it to Sister; but as fate would have it, she had turned her head right at that moment to look at something else. I wound up hitting her in the head; and though there was no physical harm, I broke her glasses. Even though my parents paid for replacements, the rest of my class treated me as if I were <u>taboo</u> for striking a nun. I learned what it meant to be <u>shunned</u> and to be invisible.

The only sport that I was remotely good at was football.

The experience also reinforced my belief that I was terrible at sports. Despite all the practice and coaching from my father, I was hopeless when it came to catching any ball in any shape or size. Nor could I dribble a basketball, even though my father sometimes kept me practicing in the little courtyard until it was almost too dark to see.

The only sport that I was <u>remotely</u> good at was football. Having worked and lifted crates in the store made me fairly strong. As a result, I was a good lineman at blocking and rushing—like my hero, Leo Nomellini. However, I was still hopeless at catching a pass. I still remember one game where I dropped three touchdown passes in a row. I was so bad that our opponents stopped covering me. Our quarterback, unable to resist a wide-open target, persisted in

WORDS	**taboo** (tə-bōō′) *adj.* not to be noticed or mentioned
TO	**shunned** (shŭnd) *adj.* avoided; shut out **shun** *v.*
KNOW	**remotely** (rĭ-mōt′lē) *adv.* to a small degree; slightly

224

Teaching Options

 Grammar

COLLECTIVE NOUNS

Instruction A collective noun is a singular noun that names a group of people or things: *class, crew, audience, band.* Even though it means more than one person or thing, it takes a singular verb. Ask students to find the collective noun in the highlighted sentence on p. 225. *(family)*. Remind students that a singular pronoun is used to replace a collective noun:
The chess <u>club</u> disbanded. <u>It</u> was unpopular.

Exercise Have students choose the correct verb or pronoun to agree with each collective noun.

1. The team (play, <u>plays</u>) on the playground.
2. Yep's family (come, <u>comes</u>) to the games.
3. Harold had a huge bunch of newspapers. (<u>It</u>, They) was too heavy to carry.
4. The group (shun, <u>shuns</u>) Laurence.

 Use **Unit Two Resource Book**, p. 19.
Use **Grammar Transparencies and Copymasters**, p. 67.

Use McDougal Littell's **Language Network**, Chapter 2, for more instruction and practice in collective nouns.

Detail. Chinese-American children reading with their teacher.
Courtesy California Historical Society, San Francisco.

very site of most of my failures. I often felt as if I were a major disappointment to my family.

Moreover, my lack of Chinese made me an outsider in Chinatown—sometimes even among my friends. Since it was a Catholic school taught by nuns, my friends would always tell dirty jokes in Chinese so the nuns wouldn't understand. However, neither did I, so I missed out on a good deal of humor when I was a boy. What Chinese I did pick up was the Chinese that got spoken in the playground—mostly insults and <u>vulgar</u> names.

There were times even with a good friend like Harold when I felt different. Though Harold and I would go see American war movies, he could also open up a closet and show me the exotic Chinese weapons his father, a gardener, would fashion in his spare time, and I could sense a gulf between my experience and that of Harold. It was as if we belonged to two different worlds.

Even my friends' games and entertainments in Chinatown could sometimes take their own different spin. They weren't quite like the games I saw American boys playing on television or read about in Homer Price. Handball was played with the all-purpose tennis ball against a brick wall in the courtyard.

Nor do I remember anyone ever drawing a circle with chalk and shooting marbles in the American way. Instead, someone would set up

throwing to me—and I dropped yet a fourth pass that could have been a touchdown.

The fact that my whole family was athletic only added to my disgrace. My father had played both basketball and football. My mother had also played basketball as well as being a track star, winning gold medals at the Chinese Olympics—a track event held for Chinese Americans. My brother was also excellent at basketball as well as bowling. Even worse, my father had coached championship teams when he had been a director at Chinese Playground—the

WORDS
TO   **vulgar** (vŭl′gər) *adj.* crudely disrespectful and displaying bad taste
KNOW

225

Customizing Instruction

Less Proficient Readers
1 Ask students to tell why Yep felt a "gulf" between himself and Harold.
Possible Response: Yep felt that he and Harold belonged to different worlds, because Harold was a part of the Chinese world that Yep felt shut out of.

Students Acquiring English
2 Point out the use of the word *spin* in the second to last paragraph on page 225. Explain to students that in this context, *spin* means "version or style." Tell them that the word *spin* is also used to refer to an interpretation of a politician's words. Tell students that this is a relatively new use of the word.

Games of Skill and Strategy

Like some of the games mentioned in "Chinatown," many games have been played by generations of children around the world. Depending on where the game is played, the rules may change. Some games have long histories. For example, it is believed that the game of dominoes originated in China in the 12th century, and was first played in Europe in the mid-18th century. Over the years, the small rectangular tiles have been made of wood, ivory, bone, and, more

recently, plastic. Mancala, or wari, originated in ancient Egypt and is now popular around the world. Players have a number of pebbles or stones that are distributed in a series of pockets around the wooden playing board. At each move, the player must make estimates, requiring numerical skill and good judgment, in order to win the game.

Literary Analysis | PRIMARY SOURCE |

Ask students to explain why "Chinatown" is a primary source.

Possible Response: Yep writes about his own experiences growing up in Chinatown. He conveys facts about life in San Francisco during the 1950's based on firsthand knowledge.

Active Reading | DISTINGUISHING FACT FROM OPINION |

A Ask students to identify one fact and one opinion in this paragraph.

Possible Response: It is a fact that the other kids sang in Chinese. It is Yep's opinion that the audience was charmed with the costumed Chinese children.

Literary Analysis: THEME

Engage students in a discussion of the last two paragraphs. Ask them to think about why there is a change in Yep's feelings about dressing up.

Possible Response: Yep is more concerned at this point with figuring out who he is than he is with trying on a different identity. He feels that his own identity is a puzzle, and he wants to find the missing pieces and put them all together.

marbles on one side of the basketball court at St. Mary's and invite the others to try to hit them. If they did, they got the marbles. If they didn't, the boy would quickly snatch up their shooters. The ideal spot, of course, was where irregularities in the paving created bumps or dips to protect the owner's marbles. At times, one edge of the courtyard would resemble a bazaar with different boys trying to <u>entice</u> shooters to try their particular setup with various shouted jingles.

Other times, they would set up baseball or football cards. Trading cards weren't meant to be collector's items but were used like marbles. In the case of cards, the shooter would send a card flying with a flick of the wrist. Mint cards[3] did not always fly the truest; and certain cards with the right bends and folds became deadly treasures.

But that sense of being different became sharpest the time I was asked to sing. Our school had a quartet that they sent around to build goodwill. The two girls and two boys dressed up in outfits that were meant to be Chinese: the girls in colored silk pajamas and headdresses with pom-poms, the boys in robes with black vests and caps topped by red knobs.

How could I pretend to be somebody else when I didn't even know who I was?

However, one day in December, one of the boys took sick, so the nuns chose me to take his place. Musical ability was not a consideration; the fit of the costume was the important thing. We were brought to sing before a group of

elderly people. I can remember following a cowboy with an accordion and a cowgirl with a short, spangled skirt who sang Christmas carols with a country twang.

Then we were ushered out on the small stage and I could look out at the sea of elderly faces. I think they were quite charmed with the costumed Chinese children. Opening their mouths, the others began to sing in Chinese. Now during all this, no one had bothered to find out if I could sing, let alone sing in Chinese. I recognized the tune as "Silent Night" but the words were all in Chinese. I tried to fake it, but I was always one note and one pretend-syllable behind the others. Then they swung into "It Came Upon a Midnight Clear." This time they sang in English, so I tried to sing along and ranged all over the musical scale except the notes I was supposed to be singing. Finally, one of the girls elbowed me in the ribs and from the side of her mouth, she whispered fiercely, "Just mouth the words."

Up until then I had enjoyed putting on costumes and even had a variety of hats, including cowboy and Robin Hood outfits as well as a French Foreign Legion hat and a Roman helmet; but the experience cured me of wanting to dress up and be something else. How could I pretend to be somebody else when I didn't even know who I was?

In trying to find solutions, I had created more pieces to the puzzle: the athlete's son who was not an athlete, the boy who got "A's" in Chinese school without learning Chinese, the boy who could sing neither in key nor in Chinese with everyone else. ❖

---

3. **mint cards:** freshly unwrapped trading cards, not yet damaged by handling.

WORDS TO KNOW | **entice** (ĕn-tīs′) v. to lure; to attract with promise of some reward

✓ **Assessment** **Standardized Test Practice**

CHOOSING THE BEST SUMMARY For some standardized tests, students will be asked to choose the best summary of a passage. To provide students with help in choosing the best summary, read aloud or write on the board the following question:

Which of the following statements best summarizes the theme of "Chinatown"?

A. Laurence Yep had a happy childhood growing up in San Francisco's Chinatown.

B. People in Chinatown conspired against Yep to make him feel like an outsider.

C. As a child, Laurence Yep felt like an outsider because he grew up outside of San Francisco's Chinatown, although he was Chinese American.

D. Because Laurence Yep's friends teased him and told jokes that he didn't understand, he felt like an outsider.

Lead students through the process of choosing the best summary. Help them to understand that C is the best choice. A and B contain false information, D is not completely accurate, but C contains all accurate information.

Connect to the Literature

1. **What Do You Think?**
   As you read this selection, what thoughts did you have about Yep's childhood?

   > **Comprehension Check**
   > - According to Yep, what stereotype exists about Chinese Americans living in Chinatown?
   > - How did Yep feel about his athletic abilities as a child?
   > - Why was it difficult for Yep to perform in the school quartet?

Think Critically

2. Yep writes, "In trying to find solutions, I had created more pieces to the puzzle." How would you describe the puzzle he was trying to solve?

    THINK ABOUT
   - the community in which he lived
   - his parents' expectations
   - the language barrier

3. What are some ways in which Yep might have handled his problem of feeling like an outsider?

4. **ACTIVE READING** | **DISTINGUISHING FACT FROM OPINION**
   Look over the **facts** and **opinions** you listed in your **READER'S NOTEBOOK**. Trade lists with a classmate and discuss how each of you knew what was fact and what was opinion.

Extend Interpretations

5. **COMPARING TEXTS** Ray Bradbury's story "All Summer in a Day" on page 209 is science fiction, while Laurence Yep's "Chinatown" is a retelling of his own memories. What account do you feel gives a more powerful sense of being torn between two worlds? What phrases in each selection create this feeling?

6. **Different Perspectives** How would "Chinatown" be different if Yep's story were told by someone other than Yep himself? Support your answer with details from the selection.

7. **Connect to Life** Laurence Yep longed to fit into the culture in which he lived. Later, however, he learned to appreciate his Chinese heritage. How important do you think it is for people to know and understand their heritage? Explain your opinion.

Literary Analysis

PRIMARY SOURCE A **primary source** conveys direct, firsthand knowledge to the reader. "Chinatown" is a primary source because in it Laurence Yep tells about things he has experienced personally. Primary sources are valuable for research because they provide eyewitness accounts by people who lived through particular times or events.

A **secondary source** is an account of events by someone who did not experience them directly. Authors of secondary sources get their information through research, not personal experience. Biographies and most newspaper articles are examples of secondary sources.

Paired Activity Become a "primary source" by writing on a sheet of paper some memories of your life. Then trade papers with a partner. After reading your partner's work, become a "secondary source" by rewriting it in your own words. (You may ask questions to gather more information.) Read the two versions to the class. Discuss the differences you notice in the two types of sources.

CHINATOWN **227**

Connect to the Literature

1. **What Do You Think?**
   Responses will vary but should address the fact that Yep felt out of place in his own world.

Comprehension Check
- They lived in Chinatown because they wanted to, not because they were forced to.
- He was ashamed because he didn't excel at sports.
- He couldn't carry a tune and didn't know the Chinese language.

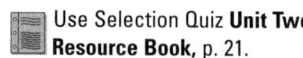 Use Selection Quiz **Unit Two Resource Book**, p. 21.

Think Critically

2. Most students will say that the puzzle Yep is trying to solve has to do with finding out who he is and where he fits in.
3. Some students may suggest that he could have learned more about his Chinese heritage. He could have learned the language.
4. Answers will vary, but should demonstrate the criteria students used to decide whether a piece of information was a fact or an opinion.

Use **Reading and Critical Thinking Transparencies**, p. 26, for additional support.

Literary Analysis

Primary Source Students' primary sources should be written in the first person, while their secondary sources should be written in the third person. Both versions should include details that reveal something about the time and place in which students live.

Use **Literary Analysis Transparencies**, p. 14, for additional support.

Extend Interpretations

5. Answers will vary. Phrases chosen should support students' choices.
6. **Different Perspectives** Students should understand that if the story had been told by someone else, the reader would not know as much about Yep's feelings.

7. **Connect to Life** Responses will vary. Students may stress that it is important to know about where you came from and to belong to a community of people who have a similar cultural background. Other students may say that it is important to fit into the culture in which you live, even if it is different from your original culture.

Writing Options

1. Imaginary Dialogue Responses will vary but should contain examples from the selection that show students' understanding of Yep's feelings. Students can place their work in their Working Portfolios.

 Use **Writing Transparencies,** p. 24, for additional support.

2. Role Web Students' paragraphs should include thoughts about Yep's role as an athlete's son, as a friend to Paul or Harold, and as a student at St. Mary's. Students should tell why they chose a particular role and explain why they think Yep found it to be the most challenging of all his roles.

Activities & Explorations

1. Heritage Collage Students' collages should contain pictures or artifacts that show or symbolize where their family or Yep's family comes from; the kinds of food they eat; and the traditions that they observe, such as holiday celebrations.

2. Games Chart Charts should be clear and readable. They should include specific information comparing two different versions of the same game.

Inquiry & Research

Immigrant Communities Students could work in small groups on this assignment. Each student picks one form of research, such as travel guides, encyclopedias, or the Internet. Students do their research individually, taking notes as they read. When they finish their research, all group members convene to share their information. Students decide as a group how to organize their poster. The finished product should capture the highlights and the flavor of the neighborhood.

 Use **Writing Transparencies,** pp. 47-48, for additional support.

Vocabulary and Spelling

Exercise A
1. vulgar, 2. tenement, 3. palatial, 4. gaudy, 5. entice, 6. shunned, 7. immensely, 8. remotely, 9. stereotype, 10. taboo

Exercise B
Possible Responses:
selection, population, bushes, traditional, plush, shade, social, special, shot, condition, mesh, shunned, shooter, sharpest, ushered, solutions

---

Writing Options

1. Imaginary Dialogue Write an imaginary dialogue between Yep as a young man and Yep as an older man. In the younger Yep's speeches, include questions about the confusion of living in two worlds. What words of advice might the older Yep offer?
Writing Handbook
See page R33: Narrative Writing.

2. Role Web Son or daughter, student or employee—people may play many roles in their lives. Use a diagram like the one shown here to record the roles that Yep played as a boy. Then write a paragraph explaining which role seems most challenging.

Activities & Explorations

1. Heritage Collage Create a "heritage collage" for yourself or Laurence Yep. Use pictures and objects to illustrate family origins and background. You might include photographs, drawings, and magazine pictures. ~ **ART**

2. Games Chart Yep mentions that the way children played marbles in Chinatown was different from other communities. Make a chart in which you compare the two ways of playing marbles (or two ways of playing another familiar game, such as checkers). ~ **VIEWING AND REPRESENTING**

Inquiry & Research

Immigrant Communities Like San Francisco's Chinatown, "Japantown" in San Francisco and "Little Italy" in New York City have become tourist attractions because of their unique shops, restaurants, and appearance. Use the Internet, travel guides, or an encyclopedia to research another well-known city neighborhood settled by immigrants. Make a poster that describes the history of the neighborhood.

 More Online:
Research Starter
www.mcdougallittell.com

Vocabulary and Spelling

EXERCISE A: ANTONYMS On a sheet of paper, write the Words to Know with meanings most nearly opposite to the meanings of the words below.

1. polite
2. mansion
3. tiny
4. plain
5. repel
6. welcomed
7. barely
8. certainly
9. fact
10. acceptable

Building Vocabulary
For an in-depth lesson on antonyms, see p. 230.

EXERCISE B: SPELLING |SH| The |sh| sound, as in *shun*, is usually spelled with the two letters *sh*. The |sh| sound can also be spelled *ti*, as in *palatial*, *ci*, as in *special*, and *ss*, as in *pressure*.

Find at least seven words from "Chinatown" that have the |sh| sound. Write the words on your paper, and underline the spelling of |sh| in each word.

Spelling Handbook p. R86

WORDS TO KNOW	entice	immensely	remotely	stereotype	tenement
	gaudy	palatial	shunned	taboo	vulgar

Teaching Options

 Mini Lesson **Spelling**

SPELLING /sh/
Instruction Explain that the /sh/ sound can be spelled in a number of different ways. List the following examples on the chalkboard:

- sh   *shark, shun*
- ti   *action, palatial*
- s   *sure, sugar*
- ss   *tissue, pressure*
- ci   *delicious, social*

Exercise Have students choose the correct /sh/ word from the list to complete each sentence.

mesh   traditional   issue   vicious   sugar

1. Yep's family was not a _____ Chinese American family. (*traditional*)
2. On his paper route, Paul ran away from some _____ dogs. (*vicious*)
3. Some people don't eat a lot of _____ because they're not fond of sweets. (*sugar*)
4. Being a good athlete was a major _____ in Yep's family. (*issue*)
5. The playground was surrounded by a wire _____ fence. (*mesh*)

 Use **Unit Two Resource Book,** p. 20.

Grammar in Context: Proper Nouns

Laurence Yep uses specific names of people, places, and even songs, to create a vivid picture of his childhood:

> One of my classmates, Harold, had a paper route on Nob Hill.

A **common noun** is the general name of a person, place, thing, or idea. A **proper noun** is the specific name of a person, place, thing, or idea. Notice the proper nouns in red.

uncle	Uncle Francis
hill	Nob Hill
song	Blue Moon
time	December

Usage Tip: Remember that proper nouns are capitalized; common nouns are not.

Apply to Your Writing: For vivid description, replace common nouns with proper nouns where possible.

WRITING EXERCISE Replace common nouns with proper nouns in the following sentences.

Example: *Original* The choir from our school will travel to another city.

Rewritten The Riverside School Chorus will travel to Atlanta.

1. We like to help our teacher.
2. Our school is on a street.
3. Our principal does a lot for our community.

Connect to the Literature Make a list of proper nouns in "Chinatown." Beside each one, write a common noun that could replace it.

Grammar Handbook Using Nouns and Pronouns, p. R63

"Chinatown is not so much a place as a state of mind—or to be more accurate, a state of heart. . . ."

Laurence Yep
born 1948

Making the Grade Laurence Yep began writing in school, when a teacher promised an A to any student who published an article in a national magazine. He earned the A with a science-fiction story that he sold for a penny per word.

An Outsider Yep's first book, *Sweetwater,* is about a young man who belongs to a minority group of transplanted aliens on another planet. According to Yep, "Probably the reason that much of my writing has found its way to a teenage audience is that I'm always pursuing

the theme of being an outsider—an alien—and many teenagers feel they're aliens." Yep also writes realistic and historical fiction. His novel *Dragonwings* has received 15 awards, including selection as a Newbery Honor Book.

AUTHOR ACTIVITY

Common Theme In much of his writing, Laurence Yep explores what it's like to be an outsider. Read one of his other stories or books and then describe it to a small group of classmates. With the group, discuss how Yep conveys the experience of being an outsider. Compare the feelings of his characters with Yep's own feelings about being an outsider in "Chinatown."

 LaserLinks: Background for Reading Author Background

CHINATOWN **229**

Grammar in Context

WRITING EXERCISE
Possible Responses:

1. Oscar and I like to help Mr. Gomez.
2. Lincoln School is on Park Drive.
3. Mrs. Lee does a lot for San Francisco.

CONNECT TO THE LITERATURE
Some proper nouns that students might find are *Pacific Avenue* (street), *Auntie Mary* (aunt or relative), *Nob Hill* (neighborhood), *St. Mary's* (a school), and *Hang Ah Alley* (a playground).

Author Activity

Common Theme Give students adequate time to find, read, and discuss other Yep stories.

Laurence Yep

A third-generation Chinese American, Laurence Yep sharpened his understanding of Chinese traditions and ideas through reading. Many of his books, including *Child of the Owl* and *Sea Glass,* focus on characters caught between two cultures. Yep has taught at various schools, including the University of California at Berkeley and the University of California at Santa Barbara, where he was a writer in residence.

 Mini Lesson

Grammar

PRECISE NOUNS: CONCRETE AND ABSTRACT
Instruction Explain that all nouns are either concrete or abstract. Concrete nouns name something that can be perceived with the senses: *banana, wind, computer.* Abstract nouns name something that cannot be perceived with the senses: *justice, idea, happiness.* Whether concrete or abstract, precise nouns make writing clearer.

Concrete: General: *furniture;* Precise: *sofa*
Abstract: General: *feeling;* Precise: *anger*

Exercise Have students complete each sentence with a more precise form of the general word in parentheses.

1. I'd like to learn more about (a religion). *(Buddhism)*
2. Our goal for the year is (a quality). *(peace)*
3. (A characteristic) is very important for people who work with the sick. *(compassion)*

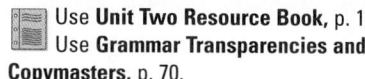 Use **Unit Two Resource Book,** p. 19.
Use **Grammar Transparencies and Copymasters,** p. 70.

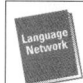 Use McDougal Littell's *Language Network,* Chapter 2, for more instruction and practice in using precise nouns.

Objectives

- understand the relation of word meanings in synonyms and antonyms
- learn to choose exact synonyms and antonyms for words

EXERCISE

Possible answers:

1. icy; boiling
2. giving; stingy
3. shabby; neat
4. frightening; calming
5. elderly; young
6. nasty; loving
7. uncomplicated; complicated
8. gorgeous; ugly
9. calm; disorderly
10. corrupt; honorable

Use **Unit Two Resource Book,** p. 22.
Use **Vocabulary Transparencies and Copymasters,** pp. 10–11, for additional support.

Shades of Meaning

Being able to use a variety of vivid and precise language is an important skill for a writer. Words that have similar meanings are **synonyms.** Words with opposite meanings are **antonyms.**

Which synonym do you think has the power of and the meaning closest to *vulgar?*

> What Chinese I did pick up was the Chinese that got spoken in the playground—mostly insults and vulgar names.
>
> —Laurence Yep, "Chinatown"

synonyms	rude	crude
	disrespectful	disgusting
	impolite	distasteful

Strategies for Building Vocabulary

Words not only express meaning, they help readers to feel a certain way. For example, suppose *vulgar* was replaced by the word *unpleasant* in the sentence above by Laurence Yep.

Notice how *unpleasant* does not have the suggestive power of *vulgar. Vulgar* expresses a strong feeling of disgust. *Unpleasant* suggests only mild discomfort. Writers learn to use these differences to express shades of meaning, or **connotations.**

❶ **Understand Synonyms** Notice the word *immensely* in the following passage.

> He would kick out his legs explosively while his arms flailed the air, so it was hard not to laugh; but we didn't because he was so immensely strong.
>
> —Laurence Yep, "Chinatown"

Now replace the word *immensely* with the word *very.* Although the words have similar meanings, notice that *very* does not create as strong a picture of the character. A better synonym for *immensely* might be *tremendously.* It has the same power.

❷ **Choose Exact Antonyms** Rereading the passage, think of a word that would be an exact antonym of the word *immensely.* The root word *immense* gives a picture of something extremely large.

An opposite word also needs to express an extreme idea. For example, *faintly* might work. The word *faint* refers to something extremely weak or barely visible, just as the word *immense* refers to something that is not just big, but gigantic.

EXERCISE For each word below, write one synonym and one antonym. Try to make your choices vivid and precise.

1. freezing
2. generous
3. sloppy
4. terrifying
5. old
6. hateful
7. simple
8. beautiful
9. peaceful
10. evil

Flowers and Freckle Cream

BY ELIZABETH ELLIS

Siri (1970), Andrew Wyeth. Tempera on panel, 30″ × 30½″. Collection of the Brandywine River Museum, Chadds Ford, Pennsylvania. Copyright © 1970 Andrew Wyeth.

When I was a kid about twelve years old, I was already as tall as I am now, and I had a lot of freckles. I had reached the age when I had begun to really look at myself in the mirror, and I was underwhelmed.[1] Apparently my mother was too, because sometimes she'd look at me and shake her head and say, "You can't make a silk purse out of a sow's ear."[2]

I had a cousin whose name was Janette Elizabeth, and Janette Elizabeth looked exactly like her name sounds. She had a waist so small that men could put their hands around it . . . and they did. She had waist-length naturally curly blond hair too, but to me her unforgivable sin was that she had a flawless peaches-and-cream complexion. I couldn't help comparing myself with her and thinking that my life would be a lot different if I had beautiful skin too—skin that was all one color.

And then, in the back pages of Janette Elizabeth's *True Confessions* magazine, I found the answer: an advertisement for freckle-remover cream. I knew that I could afford it if I saved my

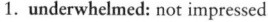

1. **underwhelmed:** not impressed.
2. **a silk purse out of a sow's ear:** something beautiful and of high quality from something inferior or ugly.

Possible Objectives
You can use this selection to achieve one or more of the following objectives:
- enjoy silent sustained reading
- read and analyze literature with a group (Option One)
- use the Reader's Notebook to write in response to literature (Option Two)

Summary
The narrator of this story looks back at herself as a freckled, awkward twelve-year-old. Envious of her cousin Janette Elizabeth's beautiful skin, the narrator sends away for freckle-removing cream. When the package finally arrives, she puts the cream on before going outside to hoe tobacco. The cream turns out to have disastrous effects when exposed to the sun: at the end of the day, the narrator has even more freckles than before! Horrified at her reflection in the mirror, she runs weeping from the house. Her grandfather, learning what has happened, tells her, "But child, there are all kinds of flowers, and they are all beautiful." She responds, "I've never seen a flower with freckles!" and retreats in misery to her room. The next morning she finds a freckled tiger lily on her pillow, placed there by her grandfather.

Art
The painter of *Siri,* Andrew Wyeth, born in 1917 in Pennsylvania, is known for his paintings of ordinary people in a realistic style. Many of his paintings focus on the loneliness of people and their environments. Siri Ericson, the subject of this painting, was from Cushing, Maine, near the Wyeth family's summer home. Andrew's father was the well-known book illustrator N.C. Wyeth, and Andrew's son Jamie is also an artist.

Shared Reading Groups

You may assign students to groups or allow them to choose their own. Students can read the selection together, alternately reading sections aloud, or they can read independently and meet to cooperate in a project that portrays some element of the story.

Possible Projects

- Pairs of students can write the dialogue for a possible conversation between the narrator and her grandfather after she sees the lily on her pillow. They can focus on the lesson she may have learned from her grandfather and how it will affect her future actions. They can perform the conversation for the rest of the class.

- Students can collaboratively create a setting for the performance of the dialogue, choosing one of the locations mentioned in the story.

Option Two
Reader's Notebook

- Students can use information from the text to create portraits of the narrator and her cousin.

- Ask students to describe the character of the narrator and to analyze in some detail why the freckle cream is so important to her.

- Ask students to read the selection, pausing at the end of the first column on page 231. At that point, ask students to predict what they think is going to happen in the rest of the story. Have them write their predictions in their Reader's Notebook.
  At the end of the story, students will return to their predictions. Ask them to note if their predictions were accurate.

- Ask students to write a note from the narrator's point of view thanking her grandfather for the lily and explaining what it meant to her.

Superb Lilies #2
(1966), Alex Katz. Oil
on canvas, 72″ × 144″.
Courtesy of Robert
Miller Gallery,
New York. Copyright
© 1996 Alex
Katz/Licensed by
VAGA, New York.

money, and I did. The ad assured me that the product would arrive in a "plain brown wrapper." Plain brown freckle color. For three weeks I went to the mailbox every day precisely at the time the mail was delivered. I knew that if someone else in my family got the mail, I would never hear the end of it. There was no way that they would let me open the box in private. Finally, after three weeks of scheduling my entire day around the mail truck's arrival, my package came.

I went to my room with it, sat on the edge of my bed, and opened it. I was sure that I was looking at a miracle. But I had gotten so worked up about the magical package that I couldn't bring myself to put the cream on. What if it didn't work? What would I do then?

I fell asleep that night without even trying the stuff. And when I got up the next morning and looked at my freckles in the mirror, I said, "Elizabeth, this is silly. You have to do it now!" I smeared the cream all over my body. There wasn't as much of it as I had thought there would be, and I could see that I was going to need a part-time job to keep me in freckle remover.

Later that day I took my hoe and went with my brother and cousins to the head of the holler[3] to hoe tobacco, as we did nearly every day in the summer. Of course, when you stay out hoeing tobacco all day, you're not working in the shade. And there was something important I hadn't realized about freckle remover: if you wear it in the sun, it seems to have a reverse effect. Instead of developing a peaches-and-cream complexion, you just get more and darker freckles.

By the end of the day I looked as though I had leopard blood in my veins, although I didn't realize it yet. When I came back to the house, my family, knowing nothing about the freckle-remover cream, began to say things like, "I've never seen you with that many freckles before." When I saw myself in the mirror, I dissolved into tears and hid in the bathroom.

My mother called me to the dinner table, but I ignored her. When she came to the

---

3. **head of the holler:** dialect for "head of the hollow," the end of a small valley.

bathroom door and demanded that I come out and eat, I burst out the door and ran by her, crying. I ran out to the well house[4] and threw myself down, and I was still sobbing when my grandfather came out to see what was wrong with me. I told him about how I'd sent for the freckle remover, and he didn't laugh—though he did suggest that one might get equally good results from burying a dead black cat when the moon was full.

It was clear that Grandpa didn't understand, so I tried to explain why I didn't want to have freckles and why I felt so inadequate when I compared my appearance with Janette Elizabeth's. He looked at me in stunned surprise, shook his head, and said, "But child, there are all kinds of flowers, and they are all beautiful." I said, "I've never seen a flower with freckles!" and ran back to my room, slamming the door.

When my mother came and knocked, I told her to go away. She started to say the kinds of things that parents say at times like that, but my grandfather said, "Nancy, leave the child alone." She was a grown-up, but he was her father. So she left me alone.

I don't know where Grandpa found it. It isn't at all common in the mountains where we lived then. But I know he put it in my room because my mother told me later. I had cried myself to sleep that night, and when I opened my swollen, sticky eyes the next morning, the first thing I saw, lying on the pillow next to my head, was a tiger lily. ❖

---

4. **well house:** a shed covering a deep hole from which water is drawn.

"Sometimes I feel guilty because I have so much fun."

Elizabeth Ellis
born 1943

Dallas Librarian Elizabeth Ellis was born in Kentucky and grew up in Tennessee, amid the Appalachian Mountains. After graduating from college she worked for 10 years as a children's librarian in Dallas, Texas. There, she says, "I realized it was the storytelling part of my job that I enjoyed the most—and the card-filing part that I liked the least."

Telling Tales In 1979, after attending the National Storytelling Festival in Tennessee, and realizing that people made their living telling stories, Ellis left the library and became a storyteller. For the past 16 years, she has charmed audiences of all ages with more than 500 stories about Texas, Appalachia, personal experiences, and—her favorite—unknown heroic women. Ellis performs throughout North America at festivals, schools, and libraries.

Too Much Fun? Many of Ellis's stories she heard from her grandfather, a circuit-riding minister who collected stories as he traveled. The story "Flowers and Freckle Cream" is based on her experiences while spending summers with her grandfather in Kentucky. She resides in Dallas, where she continues to share her stories. "It's a charming way to make a living. Sometimes I feel guilty because I have so much fun."

FLOWERS AND FRECKLE CREAM **233**

Possible Activities
Independent Activities
• Have gifted students skim over the story, noting details, facts and descriptions about the narrator's relationship with her family. Ask them to write in their Reader's Notebook their analysis of the relationship between the narrator and her grandfather and what this relationship reveals about both characters.
• Have students review the Learning the Language of Literature and Active Reader pages, pp. 189–193, in Unit Two. Ask them to note which skills and strategies they used while reading this selection.

Discussion Activities
• Use the questions formulated by the students in their Reader's Notebooks as the start of a discussion about this story.
• Ask students if they think that the narrator's perception of herself will change as a result of this experience. If so, how do they think her actions will change?

Assessment Opportunities
• You can assess students' comprehension of the story by evaluating the questions they formulate in their Reader's Notebook.
• You can use any of the discussion questions as essay questions.
• You can have students turn one of their Reader's Notebook entries into an essay.

Art
Superb Lilies #2 was painted by Alex Katz, born in 1927 in Brooklyn, New York.
He has often painted colossal pictures of flowers, working directly from nature. The 6-by-12-foot canvas shown on page 232 was one of his experiments in size and scale.

ELIZABETH ELLIS
Elizabeth Ellis conducts workshops to teach other people how to develop their skills in storytelling. Two of the little-known heroic women featured in Ellis's stories are Deborah Sampson, who disguised herself as a man to serve in the Revolutionary War, and Delia Akeley, a pioneer explorer in Africa around the turn of the last century.

Same Song
by Pat Mora

While my sixteen-year-old son sleeps,
my twelve-year-old daughter
stumbles into the bathroom at six a.m.
plugs in the curling iron
5   squeezes into faded jeans
curls her hair carefully
strokes Aztec Blue shadow on her eyelids
smooths Frosted Mauve blusher on her cheeks
outlines her mouth in Neon Pink
10 peers into the mirror, mirror on the wall
frowns at her face, her eyes, her skin,
not fair.

At night this daughter
stumbles off to bed at nine
15 eyes half-shut while my son
jogs a mile in the cold dark
then lifts weights in the garage
curls and bench presses
expanding biceps, triceps, pectorals,
20 one-handed push-ups, one hundred sit-ups
peers into that mirror, mirror and frowns too.

La misma canción

translated by Ina Cumpiano

A los dieciséis, mi hijo duerme
mientras que mi hija, que tiene doce,
a tropiezos llega al baño a las seis de la mañana
enchufa el rizador de pelo
5   se apretuja en sus mahones descoloridos
se riza el cabello con todo cuidado,
se pinta los párpados de Azul Azteca,
se acaricia en la mejilla un color de Malva Escarcha
se traza la boca de Rosa Neón
10   se escudriña en el espejo . . . espejo, espejo, dime espejo . . .
frunce la frente al verse la cara, los ojos, la piel;
no hay justicia.

Por la noche esta hija
a tropiezos cae a la cama a las nueve
15   los ojos los tiene a medio cerrar mientras mi hijo
corre una milla en la fría oscuridad
luego levanta pesas en el garaje . . .
cosa de arranque y de envión
y de expandir los biceps, los triceps, los pectorales,
20   de hacer tracciones de una mano, cien sentadas
se examina en el espejo, espejo, espejo, dime espejo,
y también frunce la frente.

Objectives
- write an original poem
- use a written text as a model for writing
- revise a draft to improve sound devices
- use verb tenses consistently

Introducing the Workshop

Original Poem Discuss with students some of their favorite poems. You might suggest poetry by Shel Silverstein, Jack Prelutsky, or Maya Angelou. Engage students in a discussion about why certain poems are especially appealing. Encourage students to talk about the rhythm of the language, the sound of particular words together, and the images that those words convey.

Basics in a Box
Using the Graphic Explain to students that a poem contains certain elements. It begins with an idea. That idea is expressed with vivid words that clearly represent the idea. Figurative language, including metaphor, simile, and personification, are also used to express the idea. Poems also contain "sound effects" made by words with the same beginning or ending sound, words with the same vowel sound, and words that sound like what they mean.

Presenting the Rubric To better understand the assignment, students may refer to the Standards for Writing a Successful Poem. You may also want to share with them the complete rubric, which describes several levels of proficiency.

 Use McDougal Littell's *Language Network,* Chapters 10–17, for more instruction on essential writing skills.

 Power Presentation

To engage students visually, use **Power Presentation** 1, Original Poem.

Poetry all around you . . .

From Reading to Writing Good poems capture a mood and feeling. They can take any form and can be written about anything imaginable— a feeling such as joy or sorrow, an image such as a beautiful sunset, or an everyday object such as an old tire lying by the side of the road. James Berry's poem "It Seems I Test People" shares the speaker's ideas about what others think of him. Jean Little's poem "Growing Pains" explores how upsetting it can be when people act differently from the way you expect. Writing an **original poem** gives you a chance to share your feelings and create pictures in the minds of your readers with carefully chosen words.

For Your Portfolio

WRITING PROMPT Write a poem that describes an experience, an idea, a place, a person, or a feeling.

Purpose: To express yourself
Audience: Anyone interested in hearing your poem

Basics in a Box

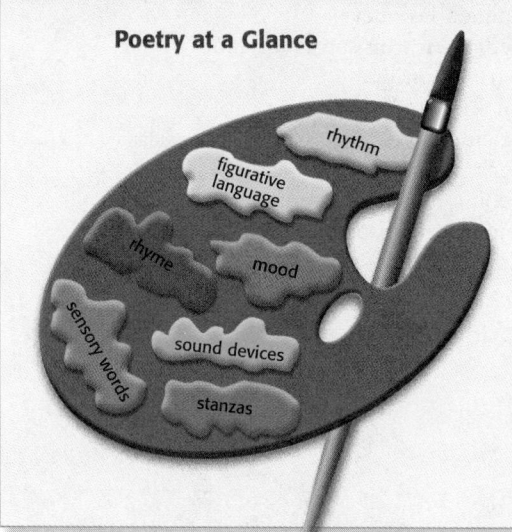

Poetry at a Glance

rhythm
figurative language
rhyme
mood
sensory words
sound devices
stanzas

RUBRIC **STANDARDS FOR WRITING**

A successful poem should
- focus on a single experience, idea, or feeling
- use precise, sensory words in a fresh, interesting way
- include figurative language such as similes and metaphors
- include sound devices such as alliteration and rhyme to support the meaning of the poem

236 UNIT TWO   PART 1: THE NEED TO BELONG

LESSON RESOURCES

USING PRINT RESOURCES
Unit Two Resource Book
- Prewriting, p. 23
- Drafting, p. 24
- Peer Response, pp. 25–26
- Revising, Editing, and Proofreading, p. 27
- Student Models, pp. 28–30
- Rubric, p. 31

Writing Transparencies
- Writing Process Transparencies, TR 1–TR 4
- Writing Style Transparencies: Sensory Word List, TR 16; Figurative Language and Sound Devices, TR 17
- Writing Template Transparencies: Poem, TR 35

Grammar Transparencies and Copymasters
- Inconsistent Verb Tense, CM 84 (for Mini Lesson, p. 241)

INTEGRATED TECHNOLOGY
LaserLinks
Writing Springboards
See **Teacher's SourceBook** p. 56 for bar codes.

Writing Coach CD-ROM
Visit our website:
www.mcdougallittell.com

Analyzing Published Student Models

See the Communication Handbook, p. R100 for speaking and presenting tips.

SPEAKING OPPORTUNITY

Carolyn Nash
published in *Stone Soup* magazine

Whistle

A sleepy <u>darkness</u> coats my bedroom,
    <u>seeping</u> into the corners and <u>wrapping</u> me in a
        <u>blanket</u> of night.
Like snowflakes aimlessly swirling through the air,
    memories flood through my mind
    of times vanished and years past.
I remember, like remembering a dream,
    <u>sitting on my father's lap, in the first days of spring</u>.
His whistle, calm and soft,
    would sail with the wind and sing with the birds,
    <u>wrapping around trees like a satin ribbon</u>.
My head tucked gently under his chin,
    I listened to the music,
    as it mingled among the clouds.
In time, the birds would flock around us,
    their angel <u>w</u>ings painted <u>w</u>ith brilliant colors,
    and they <u>w</u>ould <u>w</u>atch over us.

In the first days of this spring,
    I will walk past the trees
    and whistle my own songs to the birds
And every note that soars through the branches,
    will carry higher than the last,
    until the birds flock to me,
    and we sing together.

RUBRIC IN ACTION

❶ Uses precise sensory words

❷ Focuses on a single experience

❸ Uses an unexpected simile comparing her father's whistle to a satin ribbon

❹ Alliteration with the *w* sound draws attention to the line.

❺ The writer creates a separate stanza to indicate a shift in time (past to future).

Other Options
- Do not use separate stanzas.
- Use a rhyme scheme.

Teaching the Lesson

Analyzing the Model
"Whistle"

The student model is a poem about a memory associated with early spring. As spring approaches, the writer recalls her father's whistle. She remembers that his whistle was in harmony with the wind, the birds, and the trees. At the end of the poem, the writer links her memory to the present as she says that *she* will whistle to the birds this spring.

Have a volunteer read the poem aloud, and then discuss the Rubric in Action with students. Point out the key words and phrases in the student model that correspond to the elements mentioned in the Rubric in Action.

1 Ask students why it is important to begin a poem with a single experience.
   Possible Response: Readers are immediately drawn into the poem by the clear focus.

2 Ask students to identify the precise, sensory words that create a vivid image.
   Possible Response: snowflakes aimlessly swirling; memories flood. . .

3 Have students think about their response to the simile–the comparison of the father's whistle to a ribbon.
   Possible Response: I imagined his whistle wrapping around and around the tree, so I liked the image.

4 Ask students to discuss the alliteration of the *w* sound.
   Possible Response: When you repeat a sound, it draws your attention.

5 Discuss the change of time in the last stanza and how the poet shows this change.
   Possible Response: By creating a separate stanza, the author makes a clear break in time.

Mini Lesson
Viewing and Representing

PICTURING TEXT STRUCTURE

Instruction One way to structure a poem is to list the images that come to mind as one considers the topic. The poet arranges the images in a particular order to suit the feeling and meaning of the poem. In "Whistle" the images flow smoothly from one to the next.

Activity Have students analyze the organization of the student model by making a sequence chain like the one shown.

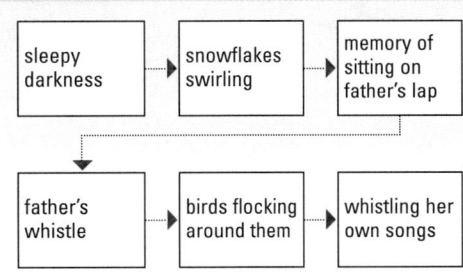

sleepy darkness → snowflakes swirling → memory of sitting on father's lap → father's whistle → birds flocking around them → whistling her own songs

Use **Reading and Critical Thinking Transparencies**, p. 39, for additional support.

Analyzing the Model
"Animal"

In this model, the poet writes about his experience learning how to hit a baseball. He uses the image of a caged animal to represent his own feelings of being trapped and wanting to get out and show that he can play.

1 Ask students to explain the comparison between the writer of this poem and a caged animal.
Possible Response: Just like an animal trapped in a cage, the writer of this poem wants a chance to get out and prove himself.

2 Have students analyze the effect of the internal rhyme "link clinks."
Possible Response: I can almost hear the rattling of the chain link fence behind the poet/batter.

3 Ask students to discuss how the dialogue brings readers closer to the poet's experience.
Possible Response: By hearing what other people are saying, I can imagine being there alongside the writer.

4 Ask students to point out the words that are repeated.
Possible Response: step, dig, twirl, wiggle

5 Ask students to explain how alternating between dialogue and regular wording creates a certain rhythm and tension.
Possible Response: The back-and-forth of dialogue and regular wording mimics the rhythm of the pitcher and the batter.

6 Ask students why it is effective to repeat the cage metaphor.
Possible Response: By repeating the cage metaphor, the writer reinforces its role as the strongest image in the poem.

Cody Banks
published in *Stone Soup* magazine

Animal

Coaches train me
to play a game I like.
They put me in a cage.
I'm the animal.
I want out.
I want to play.
Give me a bat;
I'll show you.

Chain link clinks
in the wind.
"Batter, batter, batter!"
someone yells.
I don't hear it.
Sounds like silence.
I know it's not.

Step, step, step.
Dig, dig, dig.
Twirl, twirl, twirl the bat.
Wiggle, wiggle, wiggle.
"Swing, batter!"
I don't.
"Ball one."
"Swing, batter!"
I don't.
"Ball two."
"Swing, batter!"
I do.
"Strike one!"

Eye to eye
across the field
with the pitcher.
He claws the ball.
He throws and it's mine.
Boom!
It's outta there.
Crowd screams.
Sounds like silence.
But I know it's not.

I performed.
Now, I'm in the cage.
Trained to play a game I like.

RUBRIC
IN ACTION

❶ Uses a metaphor to introduce his theme, comparing himself to an animal in a cage

❷ Rhymed words within the line create sound effects.

❸ Dialogue helps readers to experience the speaker's feeling.

❹ The writer uses repetition to speed up the rhythm.

❺ The writer alternates between dialogue and regular wording to build rhythm and tension.

❻ The cage metaphor appears again, bringing the poem full circle.

Writing Your Poem

❶ Prewriting

Poetry = the best words in the best order.
—Samuel Taylor Coleridge, British poet

Chances are that there is a poet inside you. Start noticing words and phrases that capture your imagination because of their sound, rhythm or meaning. **List** things you see, hear, taste, touch, and smell during the day. **Jot down** your feelings. See the **Idea Bank** in the margin for more suggestions. After you choose a subject, follow the steps below.

Planning Your Poem

▶ **1. Freewrite about your subject.** Write as much as you can about your subject. Let your ideas flow. Experiment with images, ideas, words, and meanings. Keep the ones you like and add new ones.

▶ **2. Decide on the mood.** Do you want your poem to be happy or sad? humorous or thoughtful? How will you accomplish this? Will you use rhyme or free verse? Will your poem be written in phrases or complete sentences?

▶ **3. Choose a focus.** Which word, line or image captures your attention? Which makes you think of interesting images and ideas? Look for one powerful line that can be the focus of your poem.

❷ Drafting

Now you can begin putting your images and words into a poem. Most poets rewrite their poems several times, so don't worry if your poem doesn't sound perfect at first.

- **Find the poem within the poem.** Experiment by rearranging words. Try using different line lengths. Cut out extra words until you are left with the strongest ones.

- **Play with images.** Create images with vivid words and sensory details. Try using similes and metaphors to make a comparison between two things.

- **Read your poem aloud.** Listen for vowel and consonant sounds that create a certain mood or effect. Decide what kind of sound devices fit your subject.

IDEABank

1. Your Working Portfolio
Look for ideas in the **Writing Options** that you completed earlier in this unit.
- **Free Verse,** p. 199
- **Your Own Haiku,** p. 208

2. Borrowed Quotes
Listen carefully to people's conversations. Choose a line of dialogue that you find interesting. Use it as the first line of your poem.

3. Who Am I?
Write a poem that captures how you think people see you and feel about you. Ask friends, family, and classmates for ideas.

Have a question?
See the **Writing Handbook**
Using Language Effectively, p. R30
Descriptive Writing, p. R31

Ask Your Peer Reader

- How did you feel when you read my poem? What was the overall mood?

- What ideas or meanings did you get from my poem?

- Which words helped you to picture what I was describing?

Prewriting

Choosing a Subject
If after reading the Idea Bank students have difficulty choosing a subject for their poem, suggest that they try the following:

- Make a list of personal experiences that you find yourself thinking about often. Choose one that you think would lend itself well to comparisons and vivid language.

- Think of an idea that you would like to express. It can be serious, sad, funny, or silly.

Planning the Poem

1. As students freewrite, check in with individuals to see who needs direction. Encourage hesitant writers to go forward with their ideas. Remind students not to be judgmental of their own ideas as they freewrite. Tell them they will make decisions once they are finished writing.

2. Once students have established the mood of their poem, encourage them to experiment with the form. Tell them to try writing one version in rhyme and another in free verse.

3. Remind students that it is effective to repeat their most powerful image.

Drafting

Remind students that the words that make up a poem should evoke its topic. Suggest that students brainstorm words and phrases that sound like the subject of their poem. For example, a poem about a warm spring day might include words such as *swaying leaves, soft breeze, sunshine soaked sky,* and so on.

Revising
USING SOUND DEVICES

Ask students to work with a partner. Students take turns reading aloud their poems to each other. Tell the student who is listening to offer praise for words that evoke the topic of the poem. Listeners may also give suggestions for additional or alternative words that would enhance the poem.

 Use **Writing Transparencies,** p. 17, for additional support.

Editing and Proofreading
CONSISTENT VERB TENSE

Tell students that they don't have to limit themselves to the same tense within a poem. Suggest that they reread "Whistle" and notice the different verb tenses. Point out that the writer uses the device of memory to make it clear that she is writing about the past. Tell students that they may change tenses within a poem, but they must make the transitions clear.

 Use **Grammar Copymasters,** p. 84, for practice.

Reflecting

Encourage students to write an entry in their Reader's Notebook about the experience of writing their poem. Tell them that they will not have to share this entry with anyone else, so they should feel free to write candidly about their experience.

Option
Teaching Tip

When students are finished writing their poems, invite volunteers to put together a poetry magazine featuring poems by class members or their favorite works by published poets. Distribute the booklet to other classes or organize a poetry reading.

Need revising help?

Review the **Rubric,** p. 236.

Consider **peer reader** comments.

Check **Revision Guidelines,** p. R23.

SPELLING
From Writing

 As you revise your work, look back at the words you misspelled and determine why you made the errors you did. For additional help, refer to the strategies and generalizations in the **Spelling Handbook** on page R86.

Stumped by verb tense?

See the **Grammar Handbook,** Using Verbs Correctly, p. R68.

Publishing
IDEAS

- Find pictures that illustrate the subject of your poem. Lay out a page with your poem and these visual images.

- Perform your poem. Use dramatic movement to draw attention to important ideas in the poem. Choose music to play in the background.

More Online:
Publishing Options
www.mcdougallittell.com

---

❸ Revising

TARGET SKILL ▶ USING SOUND DEVICES As you read your work aloud, listen to the sounds. **Alliteration,** the repetition of beginning sounds, may speed up the rhythm. For instance, in a poem about a snake, you might use words beginning with *s. The snake slithers slowly* . . . The *s* sound makes your listener think of the hissing of a snake.

> would sail ~~on~~ the ~~breeze~~ and sing with the birds,
> *with wind*
>
> wrapping around trees like a satin ribbon.

❹ Editing and Proofreading

TARGET SKILL ▶ CONSISTENT VERB TENSE It's easy to get confused about verb tense when you are writing a poem or telling a story. This is especially true if your subject thinks about the future or remembers the past. Go through your poem and look at all your verbs. Use the same tense when two or more actions occur at the same time or in sequence.

> He claws the ball.
> He ~~threw~~ *throws* and it's mine.
>
> Boom!
>
> It's outta there.
> Crowd ~~screamed.~~ *screams*

❺ Reflecting

FOR YOUR WORKING PORTFOLIO How did writing a poem help you understand how you felt? What did you learn about poetry that you didn't know before? Attach your answers to your finished poem. Save your original poem in your **Working Portfolio.**

Assessment Practice Revising & Editing

Read the passage below. The underlined sections may include the following kinds of errors:

- **lack of subject-verb agreement**
- **comma errors**
- **spelling errors**
- **inconsistent verb tense**

For each underlined section, choose the revision that most improves the writing.

<u>Before I started to write my poem I sat down in the kitchen and looked around.</u> <u>I pick</u> an apple up off of the table. When I looked at it
(1)   (2)
closely, I could see my reflection. Then I <u>bit</u> into it. The first bite made
                                            (3)
my taste buds water. The taste was <u>incredable</u>. The flesh of the fruit
                                     (4)
snapped and crunched under my teeth. I <u>breathed</u> deeply. The <u>apple's</u>
                                          (5)   (6)
<u>smell were delicate</u> and sweet.

---

1. **A.** Before I started, to write my poem I sat down in the kitchen and looked around.
   B. Before I started to write my poem, I sat down in the kitchen and looked around.
   C. Before I started to write my poem I sat down, in the kitchen and looked around.
   D. Correct as is

2. **A.** I picked
   B. I was picking
   C. I was going to pick
   D. Correct as is

3. **A.** bite
   B. biting
   C. bitten
   D. Correct as is

4. **A.** increduble
   B. incredouble
   C. incredible
   D. Correct as is

5. **A.** breethed
   B. brethed
   C. breathd
   D. Correct as is

6. **A.** apple's smell was delicate
   B. apple's smell is delicate
   C. apple's smell are delicate
   D. Correct as is

Need extra help?

See the **Grammar Handbook.**

Quick Reference: Punctuation, p. R56

Making Subjects and Verbs Agree, p. R60

Using Verbs Correctly, R68

Assessment Practice

Tell students to read the passage completely before they begin to correct the errors. Then explain that B is the correct answer to the first question because the introductory prepositional phrase is "Before I started to write my poem."

Answers: 1. B; **2.** A; **3.** D; **4.** C; **5.** D; **6.** A

 Grammar

CONSISTENT VERB TENSE

Instruction For use with Editing and Proofreading, p. 240. Point out that good poems, as well as good stories and essays, keep verb tenses consistent. Inconsistent verb tenses confuse readers.

Practice Have students explain the confusion in each of the following sentences and suggest changes to correct the errors.

1. Tomorrow we went on a school field trip to the symphony. *(will go)*

2. When my mother heard about that camp, she decides to get an application for me and my sister. *(decided)*

3. If you get tickets to that basketball game, you saw two of the best teams in the league. *(will see)*

4. If you had understood last night's assignment, you will have no problem completing this one. *(understood)*

5. When we went on our camping trip last year, we hike three miles before we took a rest. *(hiked)*

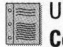 Use **Grammar Transparencies and Copymasters,** p. 84, for practice.

 Use McDougal Littell's *Language Network,* Chapter 4, for more instruction and practice in verb tenses.

Reflecting on the Theme It is said that you have to know where you come from to know where you are going. As you read this part of Unit Two, think about the home and heritage of the fictional characters and real people in the selections. How do home and heritage shape their growth? Think about how your own home and heritage make you the person you are.

ACTIVITY

With a partner, brainstorm a list of "What if?" questions that have to do with home and heritage. Use your imagination to think of ideas that would make good stories. For example, What if you learned of an ancestor you never knew you had? Pick one idea that you think would make an interesting short story. Outline the story, paying attention to how your characters might change.

242

Character and Setting

> *I've been asked if I always like my characters.*
> *It goes deeper than that. I have to understand them.*
>
> —Jean Fritz, writer

Have you ever dreamed up a talking spider, like the one in *Charlotte's Web*, or a girl like Dorothy in *The Wizard of Oz*? Perhaps you've pictured a futuristic family living near the North Pole or, better yet, on the planet Mars. Whenever you make up such people or creatures, you are creating characters.

Characters are people, or even animals, who take part in the action of a story. They live in a world created by the writer. This world is the story's **setting**—the place and time in which the story takes place. Setting can play an important part in the way a character grows and changes. It can provide clues about a character's past. It can also help you to understand a character's hopes and fears. Use the passages on the next few pages to help you learn about character and setting.

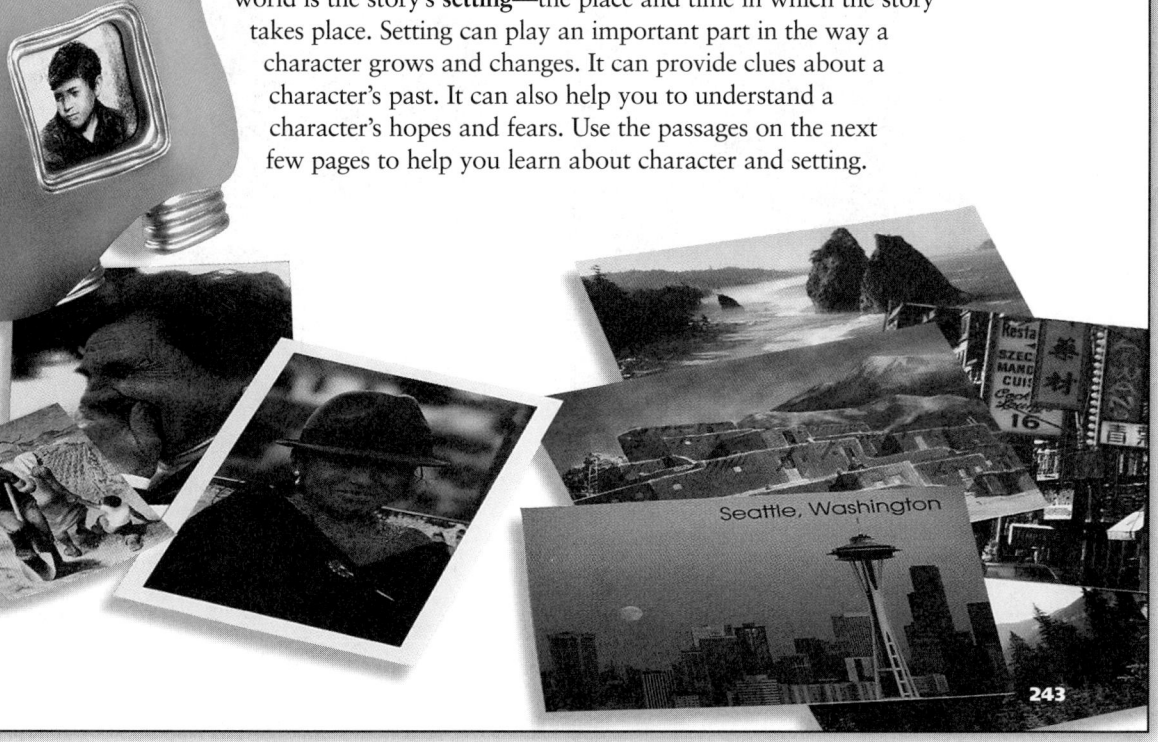

Seattle, Washington

243

LEARNING the Language of LITERATURE

OVERVIEW

Objectives
• understand the following literary terms:
    main character
    minor character
    characterization
    setting
    mood
• understand the relationship between characters and setting
• recognize how mood contributes to the effect of the text

Teaching the Lesson

This lesson analyzes the importance of characters in literary works and shows how setting and mood affect the actions and nature of these characters.

Introducing the Concepts
Ask students to put together a list of their favorite characters from books, film, or television. Have them explain why these characters appeal to them.

Use **Literary Analysis Transparencies**, pp. 2–4, 6, 26, for additional support.

Presenting the Concepts
Main and Minor Characters

Have students think of minor characters from fiction, film, or television. Ask them to analyze why these are minor characters and why these particular minor characters are memorable.

YOUR TURN

Possible Response: The main character is Mako. The minor characters are his mother and grandfather. Mako is the main character because he is the only one identified by name. The other two are identified only by their relationship to him.

Main and Minor Characters

Usually, a short story centers on events in the life of one person or creature. This person or creature is the story's **main character.** In addition, there may be one or more **minor characters** in the story. Minor characters sometimes serve as part of a story's background. More often, they interact with the main character and with one another. Their words and actions help to move the plot along.

YOUR TURN Read the passage at the right. Who do you think is the main character? Who are the minor characters? What clues helped you decide?

MAIN AND MINOR CHARACTERS

Mako's eyes glistened. "Thirty acres of land and a sailing canoe. How I should love to win that reward!"

Grandfather nodded, but Mako's mother scolded her son for such foolish talk. "Be quiet now, son, and go to sleep."

—Armstrong Sperry, "Ghost of the Lagoon"

From "Aaron's Gift"

From "Ghost of the Lagoon"

From "Tuesday of the Other June"

244   UNIT TWO   PART 2: HOME AND HERITAGE

Characterization

When you first get to know people, you learn about them in different ways. Perhaps you watch their actions and listen to what they say. You probably notice their physical appearance. You may also listen to what others say about them. These are the same methods writers use to help readers get to know their characters. The process by which a character's **traits,** or qualities, are revealed is known as **characterization.** When you read a story, novel, or play, look for clues to each character's traits in

- descriptions of the character's physical appearance
- the character's speech, thoughts, feelings, and actions
- the writer's direct statements about the character
- the thoughts, speech, and actions of other characters

YOUR TURN The above passage at the right contains details about Margot, the main character of "All Summer in a Day." What are some of her character traits? How do you know?

CHARACTERIZATION

Margot stood alone. She was a very frail girl who looked as if she had been lost in the rain for years, and the rain had washed out the blue from her eyes and the red from her mouth and the yellow from her hair. She was an old photograph dusted from an album, whitened away; and if she spoke at all, her voice would be a ghost. Now she stood, separate, staring at the rain and the loud, wet world beyond the huge glass.

"What're *you* looking at?" said William.

Margot said nothing.

"Speak when you're spoken to." He gave her a shove. But she did not move. . . .

—Ray Bradbury, "All Summer in a Day"

From "All Summer in a Day"

Characterization
Point out to students that a writer can make a character come alive for the reader through descriptions of the character's appearance, through the character's words and actions, through the words and actions of other characters, and through direct judgment statements about the character.

YOUR TURN
Possible Response: She seems to be frail, colorless, isolated, and not very lively. The author's descriptions of her appearance and her attitude convey these traits.

Setting and Mood

Setting is the place and time of a story. Setting can affect a character's personality. It can also shape his or her desires and experiences. You may find it helpful to think of **setting** as a movie set—full of details, lighting, and sounds. Can you describe the setting you are in right now? Can you hear birds singing or cars whizzing by?

The **mood** of a work is its feeling or atmosphere. Mood often originates in the setting. Perhaps a door creaks, a heart goes *thump thump,* or a gentle summer breeze blows a willow branch back and forth. Such descriptive details help to create a mood. As you read a story, or poem, think about how it makes you feel. Is the setting cold and dreary, or is it bright and full of activity? Are characters friendly toward one another, or angry and bitter? Your answers to these questions will help you identify the story's mood.

YOUR TURN Read the above passage at the right. How does the setting help to create a mood?

SETTING AND MOOD

The garage was worn out by the years. It had no windows. The walls, eaten by termites, strained to support the roof full of holes. The loose dirt floor, populated by earthworms, looked like a gray road map.

—Francisco Jiménez, "The Circuit"

From "Night Journey"

You're about to leave the house, and you hear thunder rumbling in the distance. You look up, and the sky is dark and overcast. You predict that it will rain, and you decide to wear a raincoat. Predicting means thinking about what might happen in the future on the basis of clues. An active reader can also predict, or make a logical inference, about a story's outcome.

$\mathcal{P}$redicting

How to Apply the Strategy

To **PREDICT,** an active reader will:
• Note clues and details
• Think about what will happen next
• **Connect** new information to prior knowledge
• **Evaluate** and revise the prediction
• Use a chart like this one to help you make predictions:

| clues + prior experience | prediction | new details | revised prediction |

Try It Now!

Read the example below. Predict what will happen next.

Then [the pigeon] strutted over to the crumbs, its head bobbing forth-back, forth-back, as if it were marching a little in front of the rest of the body—perfectly normal, except for that half-open wing which seemed to make the bird stagger sideways every so often.
  The pigeon began eating the crumbs as Aaron quickly unbuttoned his shirt and pulled it off. Very slowly, he edged toward the bird, . . .
—Myron Levoy, "Aaron's Gift"

Here's how Mike uses the strategy:

"To **predict** *what will happen in 'Aaron's Gift,' I look for clues in the title, illustrations, and the story. I think about the details— the injured pigeon and Aaron removing his shirt. These lead me to predict that Aaron will capture the bird."*

Need More Help?

Remember that active readers use the essential reading strategies explained on page 4: • **visualize** • **predict** • **clarify** • **question** • **connect** • **evaluate** • **monitor.**

THE ACTIVE READER **247**

OVERVIEW

Objectives
• make predictions and support them with textual evidence and prior knowledge
• use clues and details to make and revise predictions

Teaching the Lesson

The strategies on this page will help students apply the skill of predicting to the fiction selections they read.

Presenting the Strategies
PREDICT
Make sure students understand predicting and supporting their predictions with evidence and their own prior knowledge by discussing the incident described in the box on this page.

CONNECT
The combination of what they read and what they already know from their own experience of life is the key that allows good readers to make predictions.

EVALUATE
Remind students that predictions can change as new information is presented in the story. Adding details will help them to revise and refine their predictions as they continue to read.
Ask: What new details might be added to the thunder incident described in the box that could change your prediction?
Possible Response: As you go to get a raincoat, you notice that the rain has stopped and the sun has come out suddenly.

OVERVIEW

Objectives

1. understand and appreciate a **short story** (Literary Analysis)
2. understand the author's use of **characterization** (Literary Analysis)
3. use **predicting** to help understand the traits, motivations, and changes in the main character (**Active Reading**)

Summary

While roller-skating in the park, Aaron Kandel finds a pigeon with a broken wing. Aaron brings "Pidge" home, certain that his bird-loving grandmother will be pleased. As Pidge's wing heals, Aaron begins training him to be a carrier pigeon. When a neighborhood gang hears about the pigeon, they offer to let Aaron join if he will let them use Pidge as their mascot. When Aaron appears at the gang meeting, the boys build a fire and try to throw his bird into it. Aaron rescues Pidge, but the bird flies away during the struggle. Aaron is heartbroken because he had planned to give Pidge to his grandmother for her birthday, believing that the pigeon would replace the beloved pet goat she had as a girl in the Ukraine—a goat that was cruelly killed. Aaron runs home and tearfully tells his family about his own encounter with cruelty and about the loss of his grandmother's gift. Instead of being disappointed, Aaron's grandmother tells him that he has given her a greater gift than the pigeon. Aaron later understands that he has given the gift of freedom.

Thematic Link

Understanding one's home and heritage helps a person develop fully. In this story, Aaron learns more about himself through Pidge and his grandmother, helping him to grow and to develop his character.

5-Minute Warm-Up

Daily Language SkillBuilder

Have students **proofread** the display sentences on page 187j and write them correctly. The sentences also appear on Transparency 8 of **Grammar Transparencies and Copymasters**

"Aaron didn't really understand his grandmother, . . ."

Aaron's Gift

Short Story by MYRON LEVOY

Connect to Your Life

The Best Gifts in Life What is the best gift you ever gave or received, or heard about someone else giving? What made that gift so special?

Build Background

CONNECT TO HISTORY   In this story, the main character's grandmother grew up in a Jewish village in the Ukraine. During the late 19th century the Ukraine was part of the Russian Empire. The brutal leader of the empire was Czar Alexander the Third. At that time, Jews in the Ukraine lived in constant fear of Cossacks—soldiers loyal to the czar. These soldiers frequently attacked Jewish communities in raids known as pogroms. During Alexander the Third's rule, thousands of Jews left the Ukraine and came to the United States.

A 19th-century Ukrainian family gathering.

WORDS TO KNOW
Vocabulary Preview
assassinate   stoop
frenzied   thrashing
mascot

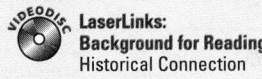

LaserLinks:
Background for Reading
Historical Connection

Focus Your Reading

LITERARY ANALYSIS CHARACTERIZATION
The way in which writers create and develop **characters** is called **characterization.** One way a writer can show a character's traits, or qualities, is by describing the character's actions. In the following passage, the author of "Aaron's Gift" characterizes Aaron as a gentle person by showing how Aaron treats a pigeon:

> *Aaron felt under the shirt, gently, and gently took hold of the wounded pigeon.*

As you read the story, look for other ways in which the author brings the characters to life.

ACTIVE READING PREDICTING   When you try to guess what might happen next, you are **predicting.** To make predictions, look for the following information:

- details that tell you what the characters are like
- details about the setting, from the story and the illustrations
- conflicts that hint at what might happen next

READER'S NOTEBOOK As you read, jot down at least three predictions about what will happen later in the story. Note the reasons for your predictions.

LESSON RESOURCES

UNIT TWO RESOURCE BOOK,
pp. 32–38

ASSESSMENT
Formal Assessment, pp. 39–40
Teacher's Guide to Assessment and Portfolio Use
Test Generator

SKILLS TRANSPARENCIES AND COPYMASTERS
Literary Analysis
- Characterization, TR 4 (for Paired Activity, p. 257)
Reading and Critical Thinking
- Predicting, TR 7 (for Thinking Through the Literature, p. 257)

Grammar
- Possessive Nouns, CM 68 (for Mini Lesson, p. 253)
- Verb Phrases: Main and Helping Verbs, CM 78 (for Mini Lesson, p. 259)
Vocabulary
- Using a Thesaurus, CM 35 (for Mini Lesson, p. 249)
Writing
- How to Summarize, TR 51

Communications
- Interviewing, TR 9

INTEGRATED TECHNOLOGY
Audio Library
LaserLinks
- Historical Connection. See Teacher's SourceBook, p. 22

Visit our website:
www.mcdougallittell.com

Aaron's Gift

by Myron Levoy

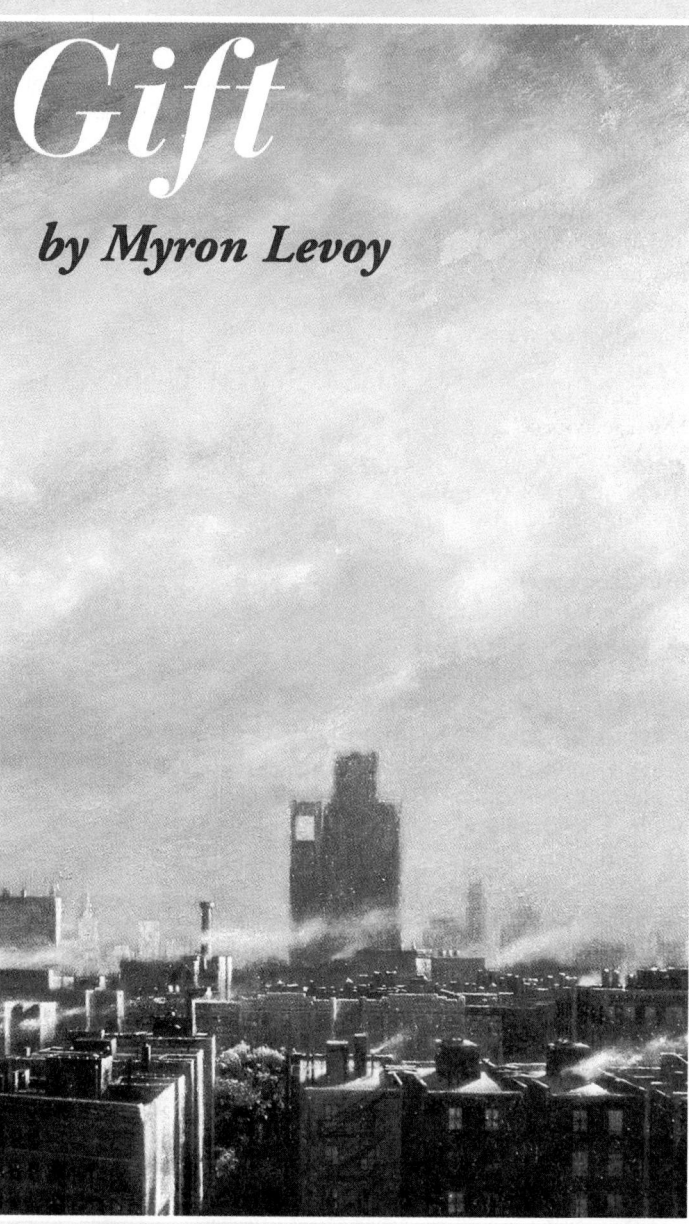

Detail of *Autumn* (1980–1981), Craig McPherson. Oil on canvas, 54" × 48", Museum of the City of New York (83.4), gift of the American Institute of Arts and Letters.

249

Literary Analysis

CHARACTERIZATION

Ask students to think about the kind of boy Aaron is and to provide examples from the text to support their answers.

Possible Response: Aaron is kind and gentle: he talks softly to the pigeon.

 Use **Unit Two Resource Book,** p. 34 for more practice.
Use **Literary Analysis Transparencies,** p. 4, for additional support.

Active Reading   **PREDICTING**

Ask students to use the name of the story and what has happened so far to predict what Aaron's gift might be.

Possible Responses: Maybe Aaron's "gift" is he got the pigeon; Maybe he will give the pigeon away.

 Use **Unit Two Resource Book,** p. 33 for more practice.
Use **Reading and Critical Thinking Transparencies,** p. 7, for additional support.

Reading Skills and Strategies:
SENSORY DETAILS

A Noting sensory words is a strategy that can help students visualize and draw inferences. In this description, ask students to find examples of how things look, sound, feel, smell, or taste.

Possible Responses: See the pigeon fluttering in a frenzied dance. Hear the beating and jerking of wings and the clacking of skates. Feel or taste the cookie crumbs.

ACTIVE READING

B **PREDICT** Possible Response: Aaron will take the pigeon home and fix its wing.

Aaron Kandel had come to Tompkins Square Park to roller-skate, for the streets near Second Avenue were always too crowded with children and peddlers and old ladies and baby buggies. Though few children had bicycles in those days, almost every child owned a pair of roller skates. And Aaron was, it must be said, a Class A, triple-fantastic roller skater.

1

Aaron skated back and forth on the wide walkway of the park, pretending he was an aviator in an air race zooming around pylons,[1] which were actually two lampposts. During his third lap around the racecourse, he noticed a pigeon on the grass, behaving very strangely. Aaron skated to the line of benches, then climbed over onto the lawn.

The pigeon was trying to fly, but all it could manage was to flutter and turn round and round in a large circle, as if it were performing a <u>frenzied</u> dance. The left wing was only half open and was beating in a clumsy, jerking fashion; it was clearly broken.

A

Luckily, Aaron hadn't eaten the cookies he'd stuffed into his pocket before he'd gone clacking down the three flights of stairs from his apartment, his skates already on. He broke a cookie into small crumbs and tossed some toward the pigeon. "Here pidge, here pidge," he called. The pigeon spotted the cookie crumbs and, after a moment, stopped <u>thrashing</u> about. It folded its wings as best it could, but the broken wing still stuck half out. Then it strutted over to the crumbs, its head bobbing forth-back, forth-back, as if it were marching a little in front of the rest of the body—perfectly normal, except for that half-open wing which seemed to make the bird stagger sideways every so often.

The pigeon began eating the crumbs as Aaron quickly unbuttoned his shirt and pulled it off. Very slowly, he edged toward the bird, making little kissing sounds like the ones he heard his grandmother make when she fed the sparrows on the back fire escape.

Then suddenly Aaron plunged. The shirt, in both hands, came down like a torn parachute.

The pigeon beat its wings, but Aaron held the shirt to the ground, and the bird couldn't escape. Aaron felt under the shirt, gently, and gently took hold of the wounded pigeon.

"Yes, yes, pidge," he said, very softly. "There's a good boy. Good pigeon, good."

The pigeon struggled in his hands, but little by little Aaron managed to soothe it. "Good boy, pidge. That's your new name. Pidge. I'm gonna take you home, Pidge. Yes, yes, *ssh.* Good boy. I'm gonna fix you up. Easy, Pidge, easy does it. Easy, boy."

Aaron squeezed through an opening between the row of benches and skated slowly out of the park, while holding the pigeon carefully with both hands as if it were one of his mother's rare, precious cups from the old country. How fast the pigeon's heart was beating! Was he afraid? Or did all pigeons' hearts beat fast?

"That's your new name. Pidge"

ACTIVE READING

PREDICT What will Aaron do with the pigeon?

B

---

1. **pylons** (pī'lŏnz'): towers marking turning points for airplanes in a race.

WORDS
TO
KNOW

frenzied (frĕn'zēd) *adj.* wildly excited; frantic
thrashing (thrăsh'ĭng) *n.* moving wildly **thrash** *v.*

250

BLOCK SCHEDULING: MANAGING TIME

If your schedule requires that you cover the lesson objectives in a shorter time, use . . .
- Preparing to Read, p. 248
- Thinking Through the Literature, p. 257
- Vocabulary and Spelling, p. 258
- Grammar in Context, p. 259

If you want to take advantage of longer class time, use . . .
- TE Teaching Options: Preteaching Vocabulary, p. 249, Viewing and Representing, pp. 251, 254, Cross Curricular Link p. 252, Grammar, pp. 253, 259, Spelling, p. 258, Multicultural Link p. 255, Standardized Test Practice, p. 256
- Choices & Challenges, pp. 258–259

Bobby (ca. 1943), Jack Humphrey. Oil on masonite. Used by permission of the Humphrey Estate. Photo courtesy of the collection of John Corey.

It was fortunate that Aaron was an excellent skater, for he had to skate six blocks to his apartment, over broken pavement and sudden gratings and curbs and cobblestones. But when he reached home, he asked Noreen Callahan, who was playing on the stoop, to take off his skates for him. He would not chance going up three flights on roller skates this time.

"Is he sick?" asked Noreen.

"Broken wing," said Aaron. "I'm gonna fix him up and make him into a carrier pigeon[2] or something."

"Can I watch?" asked Noreen.

"Watch what?"

"The operation. I'm gonna be a nurse when I grow up."

"OK," said Aaron. "You can even help. You can help hold him while I fix him up."

Aaron wasn't quite certain what his mother would say about his newfound pet, but he was pretty sure he knew what his grandmother would think. His grandmother had lived with them ever since his grandfather had died three years ago. And she fed the sparrows and jays and crows and robins on the back fire escape with every spare crumb she could find. In fact, Aaron noticed that she sometimes created crumbs where they didn't exist, by squeezing and tearing pieces of her breakfast roll when his mother wasn't looking.

Aaron didn't really understand his grandmother, for he often saw her by the window having long conversations with the birds, telling them about her days as a little girl in the Ukraine. And once he saw her take her mirror from her handbag and hold it out toward the birds. She told Aaron that she wanted them to see how beautiful they were. Very strange. But Aaron did know that she would love Pidge, because she loved everything.

---

2. **carrier pigeon:** a pigeon trained to carry messages from place to place.

WORDS
TO   **stoop** (sto͞op) *n.* a small porch outside the main door of a building
KNOW

251

Good readers are able to monitor their own comprehension as they read. One way to do that is by clarifying a confusing passage as you read it.

A Ask students to summarize this paragraph to help them clarify and comprehend.

Possible Response: Aaron's mother allowed him to keep the pigeon temporarily because it was sick and she could relate to it being all alone in the world.

Literary Analysis

CHARACTERIZATION

B Ask students to think about Aaron's strong desire to be a part of the gang. What does this tell them about Aaron's character?

Possible Response: It may mean that Aaron does not have many friends, that he is lonely, and that he wants desperately to be accepted by the older boys.

Active Reading PREDICTING

C Ask students to predict what Aaron will give his grandmother for her birthday. As they read, have them check their predictions.

Possible Responses: Aaron might make a gift, like a box or a drawing. He might give his grandmother Pidge.

Literary Analysis: POINT OF VIEW

D So far this story has been told as though the narrator knows Aaron's thoughts. Now the point of view expands. Whose thoughts and feelings are revealed by the narrator in the next three paragraphs?

Answer: They are told from the grandmother's point of view.

A To his surprise, his mother said he could keep the pigeon, temporarily, because it was sick, and we were all strangers in the land of Egypt,[3] and it might not be bad for Aaron to have a pet. *Temporarily.*

The wing was surprisingly easy to fix, for the break showed clearly and Pidge was remarkably patient and still, as if he knew he was being helped. Or perhaps he was just exhausted from all the thrashing about he had done. Two Popsicle sticks served as splints, and strips from an old undershirt were used to tie them in place. Another strip held the wing to the bird's body.

Aaron's father arrived home and stared at the pigeon. Aaron waited for the expected storm. But instead, Mr. Kandel asked, "Who *did* this?"

"Me," said Aaron. "And Noreen Callahan."

"Sophie!" he called to his wife. "Did you see this! Ten years old and it's better than Dr. Belasco could do. He's a genius!"

1 As the days passed, Aaron began training Pidge to be a carrier pigeon. He tied a little cardboard tube to Pidge's left leg and stuck tiny rolled-up sheets of paper with secret messages into it: THE ENEMY IS ATTACKING AT DAWN. Or: THE GUNS ARE HIDDEN IN THE TRUNK OF THE CAR. Or: VINCENT DEMARCO IS A BRITISH SPY. Then Aaron would set Pidge down at one end of the living room and put some popcorn at the other end. And Pidge would waddle slowly across the room, cooing softly, while the ends of his bandages trailed along the floor.

At the other end of the room, one of Aaron's friends would take out the message, stick a new one in, turn Pidge around, and aim him at the popcorn that Aaron put down on his side of the room.

And Pidge grew fat and contented on all the popcorn and crumbs and corn and crackers and Aaron's grandmother's breakfast rolls.

Aaron had told all the children about Pidge, but he only let his very best friends come up and play carrier pigeon with him. But telling everyone had been a mistake. A group of older boys from down the block had a club— Aaron's mother called it a gang—and Aaron had longed to join as he had never longed for anything else. To be with them and share their secrets, the secrets of older boys. To be able to enter their clubhouse shack on the empty lot on the next street. To know the password and swear the secret oath. To belong.

About a month after Aaron had brought the pigeon home, Carl, the gang leader, walked over to Aaron in the street and told him he could be a member if he'd bring the pigeon down to be the club <u>mascot</u>. Aaron couldn't believe it; he immediately raced home to get Pidge. But his mother told Aaron to stay away from those boys, or else. And Aaron, miserable, argued with his mother and pleaded and cried and coaxed. It was no use. Not with those boys. No.

---

3. **we were all . . . Egypt:** a reference to the biblical command to the Hebrews "Love ye therefore the stranger: for ye were strangers in the land of Egypt" (Deuteronomy 10:19).

WORDS TO KNOW

mascot (măs'kŏt') *n.* a person, an animal, or an object that is believed to bring good luck, especially one serving as the symbol of an organization (such as a sports team)

Teaching Options

Cross Curricular Link **Geography**

UKRAINE Ukraine is an independent country located in eastern Europe, south and west of Russia and north of the Black Sea. Its territory measures about 600,000 square kilometers. (235,000 square miles) The economy of Ukraine is split between the mining industry, iron and steel manufacturing, and agriculture. Ukraine has a mild climate, and good fertile soil is found in the central and southern portions. In 1986, the world's worst nuclear power plant disaster took place in Chernobyl, Ukraine.

The original name of Ukraine, Kievan Rus, got its name both from the Russ people and from Ukraine's capital city, Kiev. Over the centuries, the region has been ruled by a number of countries, including Russia, Poland, Lithuania, the Ottoman Empire, and Austria-Hungary. Ukraine was most recently a part of the Soviet Union. When the USSR fell in 1991, Ukraine once again achieved its independence.

Aaron's mother tried to change the subject. She told him that it would soon be his grandmother's sixtieth birthday, a very special birthday indeed, and all the family from Brooklyn and the East Side would be coming to their apartment for a dinner and celebration. Would Aaron try to build something or make something for Grandma? A present made with his own hands would be nice. A decorated box for her hairpins or a crayon picture for her room or anything he liked.

In a flash Aaron knew what to give her: Pidge! Pidge would be her present! Pidge with his wing healed, who might be able to carry messages for her to the doctor or his Aunt Rachel or other people his grandmother seemed to go to a lot. It would be a surprise for everyone. And Pidge would make up for what had happened to Grandma when she'd been a little girl in the Ukraine, wherever that was.

In a flash Aaron knew what to give her.

Often, in the evening, Aaron's grandmother would talk about the old days long ago in the Ukraine, in the same way that she talked to the birds on the back fire escape. She had lived in a village near a place called Kishinev[4] with hundreds of other poor peasant families like her own. Things hadn't been too bad under someone called Czar Alexander the Second,[5] whom Aaron always pictured as a tall, handsome man in a gold uniform. But Alexander the Second was <u>assassinated</u>, and Alexander the Third,[6] whom Aaron pictured as an ugly man in a black cape, became the czar. And the Jewish people of the Ukraine had no peace anymore.

One day, a thundering of horses was heard coming toward the village from the direction of Kishinev. "The Cossacks! The Cossacks!" someone had shouted. The czar's horsemen! Quickly, quickly, everyone in Aaron's grandmother's family had climbed down to the cellar through a little trap door hidden under a mat in the big central room of their shack. But his grandmother's pet goat, whom she'd loved as much as Aaron loved Pidge and more, had to be left above, because if it had made a sound in the cellar, they would never have lived to see the next morning. They all hid under the wood in the woodbin and waited, hardly breathing.

Suddenly, from above, they heard shouts and calls and screams at a distance. And then the noise was in their house. Boots pounding on the floor, and everything breaking and crashing overhead. The smell of smoke and the shouts of a dozen men.

The terror went on for an hour, and then the sound of horses' hooves faded into the distance. They waited another hour to make sure, and then the father went up out of the cellar and the rest of the family followed. The door to the house had been torn from its hinges, and every piece of furniture was broken. Every window, every dish, every stitch of clothing was totally destroyed, and one wall had been completely bashed in. And on the

---

4. **Kishinev** (kĭsh′ə-nĕf′): a city (known today as Chisinau) that is now the capital of the country of Moldova.

5. **Czar Alexander the Second:** emperor of Russia from 1855 to 1881.

6. **Alexander the Third:** emperor of Russia from 1881 to 1894.

WORDS TO KNOW   **assassinate** (ə-săs′ə-nāt′) *v.* to murder by surprise attack for political reasons

253

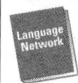 **Grammar**

POSSESSIVE NOUNS Remind students that a possessive noun shows who or what has or owns something.

Instruction Have students read the highlighted sentence on page 253. Ask them to notice that the grandmother owned the pet goat and that the *'s* is added to *grandmother* to form the possessive of a singular noun.

Point out that when a plural noun ends in *s,* simply adding an apostrophe to the end of the word makes it possessive.

Explain that when a plural noun does not end in *s,* an *'s* is added. (*children, children's*)

Application Have students write several sentences related to the content of the story, including both singular and plural possessive nouns.

📖 Use **Grammar Transparencies and Copymasters**, p. 68.

Use McDougal Littell's *Language Network*, Chapter 2, for more practice in using possessive nouns.

Reading and Analyzing

Reading Skills and Strategies: SENSORY DETAILS

Ask students to identify the sensory details used in the description of the *pogrom* and to describe the effect of these details.

Possible Responses: Details include: shouts and calls and screams at a distance, boots pounding, everything breaking and crashing, the smell of smoke, shouts of a dozen men, the sound of horses' hooves fading into the distance, the goat lying quietly, a young girl weeping. These details support the terror and horror of the scene being described.

ACTIVE READING

B PREDICT Possible Responses: Carl will try to hurt Pidge. Carl will use Pidge to force Aaron to do something he does not want to do.

Literary Analysis: PLOT

C The plot has been building toward a climactic event. Have students identify the turning point in this section and discuss how this event may influence the story's conclusion.

Possible Response: The gang is trying to kill Pidge. This leads to a turning point because Aaron really wants to be in the gang, and yet he loves Pidge and is looking forward to giving him to his grandmother. When Aaron "leap(s) right across the fire at Carl," he is choosing to defend Pidge rather than to belong to the gang.

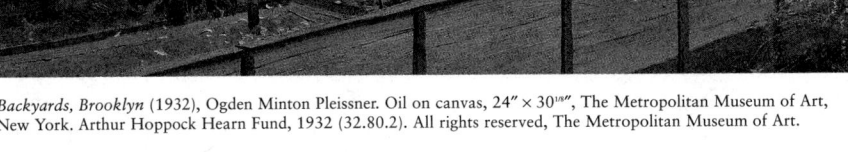

Backyards, Brooklyn (1932), Ogden Minton Pleissner. Oil on canvas, 24″ × 30⅛″, The Metropolitan Museum of Art, New York. Arthur Hoppock Hearn Fund, 1932 (32.80.2). All rights reserved, The Metropolitan Museum of Art.

floor was the goat, lying quietly. Aaron's grandmother, who was just a little girl of eight at the time, had wept over the goat all day and all night and could not be consoled.

ACTIVE READING

CLARIFY What happened to Aaron's grandmother?

But they had been lucky. For other houses had been burned to the ground. And everywhere, not goats alone, nor sheep, but men and women and children lay quietly on the ground. The word for this sort of massacre, Aaron had learned, was *pogrom*. It had been a pogrom. And the men on the horses were Cossacks. Hated word. Cossacks.

And so Pidge would replace that goat of long ago. A pigeon on Second Avenue where no one needed trap doors or secret escape passages or woodpiles to hide under. A pigeon for his grandmother's sixtieth birthday. *Oh wing, heal quickly so my grandmother can send you flying to everywhere she wants!*

But a few days later, Aaron met Carl in the street again. And Carl told Aaron that there was going to be a meeting that afternoon in which a map was going to be drawn up to show where a secret treasure lay buried on the

Teaching Options

Mini Lesson: Viewing and Representing

Backyards, Brooklyn **by Ogden Minton Pleissner**

ART APPRECIATION As a boy growing up in Brooklyn, Ogden Minton Pleissner (1905–1983) drew constantly. After finishing art school in 1929, he lived and worked in a studio where he painted this backyard scene.

Instruction The art chosen to illustrate a story can help the reader understand the setting. Ask students to describe the neighborhood in this painting. How does if help them visualize the setting for this story?

Possible Responses: The tenement houses are three-story buildings, similar to the one Aaron lived in. The houses are covered with vines and face the street. The backyards show clotheslines, trees, fenced yards with gates, and plenty of places for birds to land. You can imagine Aaron's grandmother on a fire escape feeding those birds. The neighborhood looks like it comes from the time period of the story.

empty lot. "Bring the pigeon and you can come into the shack. We got a badge for you. A new kinda membership badge with a secret code on the back."

Aaron ran home, his heart pounding almost as fast as the pigeon's. He took Pidge in his hands and carried him out the door while his mother was busy in the kitchen making stuffed cabbage, his father's favorite dish. And by the time he reached the street, Aaron had decided to take the bandages off. Pidge would look like a real pigeon again, and none of the older boys would laugh or call him a bundle of rags.

Gently, gently he removed the bandages and the splints and put them in his pocket in case he should need them again. But Pidge seemed to hold his wing properly in place.

When he reached the empty lot, Aaron walked up to the shack, then hesitated. Four bigger boys were there. After a moment, Carl came out and commanded Aaron to hand Pidge over.

ACTIVE READING

B **PREDICT** What will happen to Pidge?

"Be careful," said Aaron. "I just took the bandages off."

"Oh sure, don't worry," said Carl. By now Pidge was used to people holding him, and he remained calm in Carl's hands.

"OK," said Carl. "Give him the badge." And one of the older boys handed Aaron his badge with the code on the back. "Now light the fire," said Carl.

"What . . . what fire?" asked Aaron.

"The fire. You'll see," Carl answered.

"You didn't say nothing about a fire," said Aaron. "You didn't say nothing to—"

"Hey!" said Carl. "I'm the leader here. And you don't talk unless I tell you that you have p'mission. Light the fire, Al."

The boy named Al went out to the side of the shack, where some wood and cardboard and old newspapers had been piled into a huge mound. He struck a match and held it to the newspapers.

"OK," said Carl. "Let's get 'er good and hot. Blow on it. Everybody blow."

Aaron's eyes stung from the smoke, but he blew alongside the others, going from side to side as the smoke shifted toward them and away.

"Let's fan it," said Al.

In a few minutes, the fire was crackling and glowing with a bright yellow-orange flame.

"Get me the rope," said Carl.

One of the boys brought Carl some cord and Carl, without a word, wound it twice around the pigeon, so that its wings were tight against its body.

"What . . . what are you *doing!*" shouted Aaron. "You're hurting his wing!"

"Don't worry about his wing," said Carl. "We're gonna throw him into the fire. And when we do, we're gonna swear an oath of loyalty to—"

"No! *No!*" shouted Aaron, moving toward Carl.

"Grab him!" called Carl. "Don't let him get the pigeon!"

But Aaron had leaped right across the fire at Carl, taking him completely by surprise. He threw Carl back against the shack and hit out at his face with both fists. Carl slid down to the ground, and the pigeon rolled out of his hands. Aaron scooped up the pigeon and ran,

Gently, gently he removed the bandages.

C

Customizing Instruction

Students Acquiring English

1 Point out that Carl uses ungrammatical (*We got* instead of *We have*) and informal (*kinda* instead of *kind of*) language when talking to Aaron. Ask students how this affects their perception of Carl.

Less Proficient Readers
Ask students the following questions to help guide them through the reading:
1. Where did Aaron's grandmother live when she was a little girl?
   Answer: She lived in a village near Kishinev in the Ukraine.
2. Why do you think the passage about Aaron's grandmother and her goat is included in the story?
   Possible Responses: It helps explain why Aaron wants to give her the pigeon for her birthday. It helps us to understand Aaron's grandmother and her relationship with Aaron.

Gifted and Talented
As students read the remainder of the story, have them discuss the significance of the parallel between the story about Aaron and the story about his grandmother. How are the two stories similar? What purpose do these parallel stories serve?

Possible Responses: Both stories are concerned with the experiences of young children who must deal with violence and with the loss of a pet. The parallel stories strengthen the bond between Aaron and his grandmother and explain why Aaron decides to give Pidge to his grandmother as a birthday present.

Multicultural Link ## Immigration

Between 1880 and 1920, nearly 2.5 million Jewish people immigrated to the United States from a variety of eastern European countries. Many of these immigrants settled in industrial cites in the East—such as Boston, New York, and Philadelphia—and the Midwest. However, by 1920 most Americans were opposed to immigration and wanted to retrict it. In 1924 a new law put a sharp limit on the number of immigrants permitted to come to the United States. This law also established national quotas aimed at reducing immigration from southern and eastern European countries on the grounds that such immigrants were not as likely to make good Americans as those from northern and western Europe. Asians had already been restricted since the 1880s.

(A) Ask students if they agree or disagree with Aaron's calling the boys Cossacks. Have them explain their point of view.

Possible Responses: Students may agree with Aaron because the boys are behaving in a violent and destructive way like Cossacks; they are trying to kill the pigeon, just as the Cossacks killed the grandmother's goat. They may disagree because the boys are not killing thousands of people with government support, as the Cossacks did; they are just being mean to one boy and his pet.

Reading Skills and Strategies:
QUESTION

Ask students to imagine they are in Carl's gang and to respond to the dramatic scene between the gang and Aaron by generating questions the gang may have asked after they reassembled in their clubhouse.

Possible Responses: What are Cossacks? Why was Aaron yelling that at us? Why did the bird mean so much to him? Do you think Aaron is crazy?

Literary Analysis

| CHARACTERIZATION |

Encountering difficult situations often helps people to grow and mature. Ask students if they feel Aaron's character was strengthened by his run-in with the gang. Have them meet with a partner and discuss how the author shows this new strength.

Possible Responses: Yes; Aaron's character was strengthened because he realizes that belonging to a gang is not really important. Aaron also sees that setting the pigeon free was a better gift than the pigeon itself.

---

pretending he was on roller skates so that he would go faster and faster. And as he ran across the lot he pulled the cord off Pidge and tried to find a place, *any* place, to hide him. But the boys were on top of him, and the pigeon slipped from Aaron's hands.

"Get him!" shouted Carl.

(A) Aaron thought of the worst, the most horrible thing he could shout at the boys. "Cossacks!" he screamed. "You're all Cossacks!"

Two boys held Aaron back while the others tried to catch the pigeon. Pidge fluttered along the ground just out of reach, skittering one way and then the other. Then the boys came at him from two directions. But suddenly Pidge beat his wings in rhythm, and rose up, up, over the roof of the nearest tenement, up over Second Avenue toward the park.

With the pigeon gone, the boys turned toward Aaron and tackled him to the ground and punched him and tore his clothes and punched him some more. Aaron twisted and turned and kicked and punched back, shouting "Cossacks! Cossacks!" And somehow the word gave him the strength to tear away from them.

When Aaron reached home, he tried to go past the kitchen quickly so his mother wouldn't see his bloody face and torn clothing. But it was no use; his father was home from work early that night and was seated in the living room. In a moment Aaron was surrounded by his mother, father, and grandmother, and in another moment he had told them everything

> Pidge beat his wings in rhythm, and rose.

that had happened, the words tumbling out between his broken sobs. Told them of the present he had planned, of the pigeon for a goat, of the gang, of the badge with the secret code on the back, of the shack, and the fire, and the pigeon's flight over the tenement roof.

And Aaron's grandmother kissed him and thanked him for his present which was even better than the pigeon.

"What present?" asked Aaron, trying to stop the series of sobs.

And his grandmother opened her pocketbook and handed Aaron her mirror and asked him to look. But all Aaron saw was his dirty, bruised face and his torn shirt.

Aaron thought he understood, and then, again, he thought he didn't. How could she be so happy when there really was no present? And why pretend that there was?

Later that night, just before he fell asleep, Aaron tried to imagine what his grandmother might have done with the pigeon. She would have fed it, and she certainly would have talked to it, as she did to all the birds, and . . . and then she would have let it go free. Yes, of course. Pidge's flight to freedom must have been the gift that had made his grandmother so happy. Her goat has escaped from the Cossacks at last, Aaron thought, half dreaming. And he fell asleep with a smile. ❖

Teaching Options

✓ **Assessment Standardized Test Practice**

PREDICTING OUTCOMES In some standardized tests, students are asked to predict probable future actions and outcomes, based on a passage they have read. Write this question on the chalkboard or read it aloud:

What probably happens the next time that Carl approaches Aaron about joining his gang?

A. Aaron goes along with Carl and joins.

B. Aaron decides to ask Noreen, his mother, and his grandmother for advice.

C. Aaron walks away from Carl, and will not join the gang.

D. Aaron finds a different gang to join.

Guide students through the process of selecting the correct answer. A is against Aaron's character—he was appalled by Carl's earlier actions and is not likely to ever join his gang. B is possible, but Aaron is not likely to ask his grandmother or mother because he knows what their answer will be. D is unlikely for the same reasons as A. C is the best answer, based on what we know of Aaron's character.

Connect to the Literature

1. What Do You Think?
What scene, object, or character stands out most in your memory of this story?

.... **Comprehension Check** ....
- What does Aaron notice about the pigeon he finds in the park?
- Why does Aaron want to give his grandmother the pigeon?
- How does the pigeon escape danger?

Think Critically

2. **ACTIVE READING** **PREDICTING** How accurate were the **predictions** in your **READER'S NOTEBOOK?** Discuss with a classmate the **details** in the story that either helped or misled you.

3. What kind of person is Aaron? Describe his character and values.

THINK ABOUT
- his feelings about the gang
- his behavior toward Pidge
- his relationships with his family and with his friend Noreen

4. How does Aaron's heritage affect his encounter with the gang members at the end of the story?

5. In your opinion, what is Aaron's gift to his grandmother? Explain your answer.

Extend Interpretations

6. **COMPARING TEXTS** Look back at the other selections in this book in which animals play important roles: "Ghost of the Lagoon" on page 124 and the excerpt from *Woodsong* on page 165. Compare and contrast the role of Tupa or Scarhead with the role of Pidge in "Aaron's Gift."

7. Connect to Life Compare Aaron's gift with the gift you discussed in Connect to Your Life on page 248. How is Aaron's gift similar to or different from the gift you chose?

Literary Analysis

CHARACTERIZATION The way that a writer builds **characters** and makes them believable is called **characterization.** A writer can develop a character in four basic ways:

- by physically describing the character
- by presenting the character's thoughts, speech, and actions
- by presenting what others say or think about the character
- by directly commenting on the character's nature

In this passage from the story, the author uses Aaron's thoughts about his grandmother to characterize her:

But Aaron did know that she would love Pidge, because she loved everything.

Paired Activity Working with a partner, make a chart like the one shown below. Use the chart to analyze how Levoy develops Aaron's character. Go through the story to find examples of each of the four types of characterization listed above.

Characterization of Aaron	
Physical Descriptions	
Character's Thoughts, Speech, or Actions	He broke a cookie into small crumbs....
Thoughts and Speech of Others	
Author's Direct Comments	

Extend Interpretations

6. Comparing Texts Possible Responses: Pidge helps Aaron to realize his potential as a caring person and teaches him a valuable lesson about bravery, determination, and the gift of freedom. Tupa threatens the safety of Mako and Afa and teaches Mako a valuable lesson about bravery, determination, and heroism. Scarhead threatens the safety of Paulsen at first but teaches him a valuable lesson about the need for respect and distance in dealing with wild animals.

7. Connect to Life Students' responses will vary based on the gift they discussed. Students should support their answers with reasons why Aaron's gift is similar to or different from the gifts they chose.

Connect to the Literature

1. What Do You Think?
Responses will vary. Some students may cite Pidge flying away from danger as the most memorable scene.

Comprehension Check
- The pigeon has a broken wing.
- Aaron wants the pigeon to replace the pet goat that was killed in a *pogrom* when his grandmother was a girl. He also thinks that the pigeon can be helpful to her by carrying messages.
- The pigeon flies over the tenement buildings toward the park.

 Use Selection Quiz **Unit Two Resource Book,** p. 38.

Think Critically

2. Have students note whether they used all the information available to them when they made their predictions.

3. Possible Responses: Aaron is a caring, thoughtful boy. He fixes Pidge's broken wing, plans to give his grandmother the best gift he can think of, and shares an important task with Noreen.

4. Possible Responses: Aaron's knowledge of his grandmother's life in the Ukraine makes him react strongly to being bullied by the members of Carl's gang. He thinks that the bullies are like the Cossacks who hurt his grandmother. He wants to protect Pidge at all costs because his grandmother's favorite childhood pet was killed and he has decided to replace it.

5. Most students will say that giving Pidge his freedom was Aaron's gift to his grandmother. Some will also say that Aaron's bravery and determination to save Pidge's life is his gift.

Literary Analysis

Characterization Students should complete the chart with examples from the story. They may want to focus on examples about Aaron, or they may find examples about Aaron's grandmother, Carl, or another character.

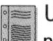 Use **Literary Analysis Transparencies,** p. 4, for additional support.

Writing Options

1. **Story Summary** Students should complete the sequence chart prior to writing their summary. They may want to work with a partner to complete the chart, and then work individually to write the summary.

   Use **Writing Transparencies**, p. 51, for additional support.

2. **Diary Entry** Students should write in the first person as if they are Aaron's grandmother. They should include feelings and thoughts consistent with her character.

Activities & Explorations

1. **Investigating Patterns** Students will need time and support for locating the information. This activity may work best with small groups of students each studying one immigrant group, and then presenting the information to the whole class.

Inquiry & Research

Let's Talk Students may wish to work in small groups to interview an older person. They can take turns asking questions, or they can designate a spokesperson to answer questions prepared by the group.

   Use **Communications Transparencies and Copymasters**, p. 9, for additional support.

Vocabulary and Spelling

EXERCISE A: 1 (a), 2 (b), 3 (c), 4 (a), 5 (d)
EXERCISE B: 1. says, birthdays; 2. flies, families; 3. stayed, qualified; staying, qualifying

---

Choices & CHALLENGES

Writing Options

1. Story Summary Filling in a sequence-of-events chart can help you understand "Aaron's Gift." Make a chart like the one shown here. Record one event in each box. Add boxes and events until you have described the entire story. Then use your chart as a reference to write a summary of "Aaron's Gift."

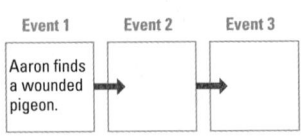

Event 1	Event 2	Event 3
Aaron finds a wounded pigeon.		

2. Diary Entry Pretend you are Aaron's grandmother. Write a **diary entry** for the day Pidge flies away. What does Pidge's freedom mean to you? Place the prediction in your **Working Portfolio.**

Activities & Explorations

1. Investigating Patterns Aaron's grandmother immigrated from the Ukraine. Use history books to find out why other immigrant groups left their homelands. How did they travel? Where did they settle? Present your findings to the class. ~ **SPEAKING AND LISTENING**

Inquiry & Research

Let's Talk With your teacher's guidance, arrange to interview an older person to find out what life was like when he or she was your age. Then write up the best parts of the interview. Use library resources and primary sources, such as documents and photographs, to add factual background. Include at least two sources other than your interview.

Real World Link Read "Your Family's History Will Come Alive" on p. 260 before you begin your research.

Vocabulary and Spelling

EXERCISE A: ASSESSMENT PRACTICE On your paper, write the letter of the word that does not belong with the other words in each set The Words to Know are shown in boldface.

1. (a) roof (b) **stoop** (c) steps (d) porch
2. (a) **frenzied** (b) fragile (c) frantic (d) wild
3. (a) pet (b) **mascot** (c) opponent (d) symbol
4. (a) assist (b) kill (c) murder (d) **assassinate**
5. (a) struggling (b) flailing (c) **thrashing** (d) sailing

Building Vocabulary
For an in-depth lesson on synonyms and antonyms, see p. 230.

EXERCISE B: FINAL *Y* WORDS AND SUFFIXES The spelling of some nouns and verbs ending in *y* changes when a suffix is added. When the letter before a final *y* is a vowel, the *y* does not change when a suffix is added, as in *plays*. When the letter before a final *y* is a consonant, change the *y* to *i* when adding *-es* or *-ed*, as in *frenzied*. When adding the suffix *-ing,* do not change the *y* to *i*, as in *carrying*.

1. Add the suffix *-s* to the following words.
   say   birthday
2. Add the suffix *-es* to the following words.
   fly   family
3. Add the suffixes *-ed* and *-ing* to the following words.
   stay   qualify

Spelling Handbook p. R86

Teaching Options

Mini Lesson Spelling

FINAL *Y* WORDS AND SUFFIXES
Instruction Remind students that when a suffix is added to many words ending in *y*, the *y* is changed to *i* before the suffix is added. Use these examples with students:
frenzy + ed = frenzied (*y* to *i*; add *ed*)
lady + s = ladies (*y* to *i*, add *es*)
Application Have students look through "Aaron's Gift" and/or their own writing for other examples of the *y* to *i* rule. Ask them to share the examples.

Exercises
Have students add the suffixes to the following words.
1. clumsy + ness (*clumsiness*)
2. lonely + ness (*loneliness*)
3. lucky + ly (*luckily*)
4. country + s (*countries*)
5. carry + er (*carrier*)
6. happy + er (*happier*)
7. spy + ed (*spied*)

 Use **Unit Two Resource Book,** p. 37 for more practice.

Grammar in Context: Vivid Verbs

Myron Levoy paints a colorful picture of the action in "Aaron's Gift." Notice his use of **vivid verbs,** shown in red type below:

> And Pidge would **waddle** slowly across the room, **cooing** softly, while the ends of his bandages **trailed** along the floor.

Suppose Levoy had used the verb "to move" in place of *waddle* above. The word *move* doesn't add any detail to the description. The sentences above would become dull and the vivid picture of the injured pigeon would be lost.

Apply to Your Writing: Replace dull, overused verbs with vivid verbs to add color and vitality to your writing.

WRITING EXERCISE Rewrite each sentence. Replace the underlined <u>dull verbs</u> with vivid verbs.

Example: *Original* Aaron's eyes <u>hurt</u> from the smoke.

Rewritten Aaron's eyes stung from the smoke.

1. Smoke <u>moved</u> toward them and away.
2. Aaron <u>ran</u> right across the fire to rescue Pidge.
3. Carl <u>fell</u> to the ground, and the pigeon <u>dropped</u> out of his hands.
4. Pidge <u>moved</u> along the ground and <u>walked</u> one way and then the other.

Grammar Handbook Quick Reference: Parts of Speech, p. R54

Connect to the Literature Reread the last page of "Aaron's Gift." Make a list of vivid verbs.

"My continuing concern has been for the 'outsider,' the loner."

Myron Levoy
born 1930

Engineer Turned Writer Myron Levoy was born in New York City in 1930 and worked as a chemical engineer before becoming a professional writer. In describing his poetry, plays, and short stories, he says, "My continuing concern has been for the 'outsider,' the loner."

Between Two Worlds In *Alan and Naomi*, Levoy writes about a Jewish boy facing anti-Semitism who befriends a troubled refugee girl. In another novel, *A Shadow Like a Leopard*, Levoy depicts a boy from the ghetto who is torn between two worlds. Each of these people, says Levoy, must grow and struggle to discover who he or she is.

Critical Success In 1982, *A Shadow Like a Leopard* was named one of the best books for young adults by the American Library Association. *The Witch of Fourth Street and Other Stories*, from which "Aaron's Gift" is taken, was named a *Book World* honor book.

AUTHOR ACTIVITY

New York Childhood "Aaron's Gift" takes place on New York City's Lower East Side. Find out what neighborhood of New York City Levoy grew up in. Research what the area was like when he was a child in the 1930s and 1940s. Discuss with a group the autobiographical details found in the setting of "Aaron's Gift" and other Levoy works you've read.

Grammar in Context
WRITING EXERCISE
Possible Responses:
1. Smoke **shifted** toward them and away.
2. Aaron **leaped** right across the fire to rescue Pidge.
3. Carl **slid** to the ground, and the pigeon **rolled** out of his hands.
4. Pidge **fluttered** along the ground and **skittered** one way and then the other.
CONNECT TO THE LITERATURE
Answers will vary. Vivid verbs include: pulled, slipped, screamed, held, catch, fluttered, skittering, beat, rose, tackled, punched, tore, twisted, turned, kicked, shouting, tear, surrounded, tumbling, kissed, thanked, understood, pretend, imagine, escaped, dreaming.

Author Activity
Students will need time and support to research Myron Levoy, his childhood, and the neighborhoods of New York City's Lower East Side.

Myron Levoy
New York Childhood The title of Myron Levoy's book *The Witch of Fourth Street and Other Stories* refers to East Fourth Street on New York City's Lower East Side. The book's eight stories portray events in the lives of immigrants who lived in that area during the 1920s.

 Grammar

VERB PHRASES: MAIN AND HELPING VERBS
Remind students that a verb may be a single word or a group of words. When there are two or more words in the verb, the last word is the main verb. Other words are helping verbs.
Instruction Read the following sentence aloud: Aaron was planning to give Pidge to his grandmother for her birthday.
Have students identify the main (*planning*) and helping (*was*) verbs. Remind students that the main and helping verbs are not always together in the sentence. (Example—Mother *has* never *liked* Carl's gang)

Application Have students locate sentences from *Aaron's Gift* that contain more than one verb. Have them write the sentences down, identifying the main and helping verbs in each.

Use **Unit Two Resource Book,** p. 36.
Use **Grammar Transparencies and Copymasters,** p. 78.

 Use McDougal Littell's *Language Network,* Chapter 4, for more instruction and practice in main and helping verbs.

Objectives
- read and analyze news sources
- recognize distinctive characteristics of primary and secondary sources
- become aware of material available on the Internet
- find out about the American Family Immigration History Center

Connecting to the Literature
Reading the Internet article "Your Family's History Will Come Alive" can help your students connect with characters like Aaron's grandmother in "Aaron's Gift." It is likely that Aaron's grandmother immigrated to the United States between 1892 and 1924, the years of the American Family Immigration History Center's research project, since many Jews left the Ukraine during those years. As students learn personal facts about immigrants, they may be able to make connections to Aaron's grandmother and other immigrant characters they read about.

Real WORLD Link   Internet Article

Source: *Statue of Liberty–Ellis Island Foundation, Inc.*

| Back | Forward | Reload | Home | Search | Images | Print | Security | Stop |

YOUR Family's History
WILL COME Alive

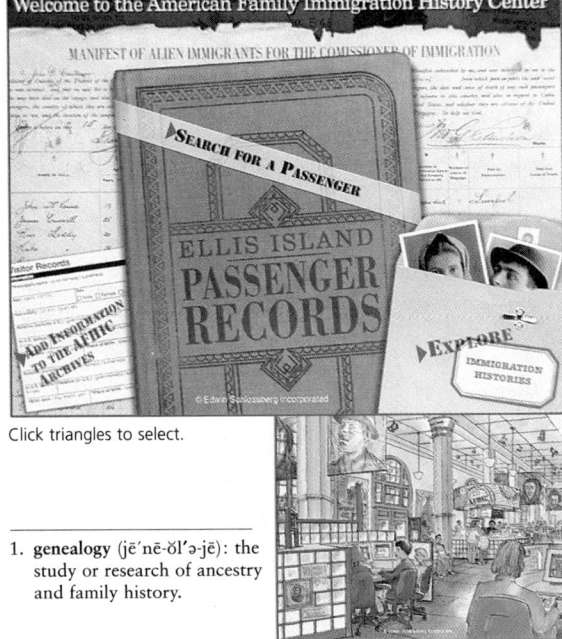

Welcome to the American Family Immigration History Center

MANIFEST OF ALIEN IMMIGRANTS FOR THE COMMISSIONER OF IMMIGRATION

SEARCH FOR A PASSENGER

ELLIS ISLAND PASSENGER RECORDS

ADD INFORMATION TO THE ATTIC ARCHIVES

EXPLORE IMMIGRATION HISTORIES

© Edwin Schlossberg Incorporated

Click triangles to select.

---

1. **genealogy** (jē′nē-ŏl′ə-jē): the study or research of ancestry and family history.

The Statue of Liberty–Ellis Island Foundation, Inc. has announced the development of an exciting new family genealogy[1] facility. To be housed in the Ellis Island Immigration Museum, **The American Family Immigration History Center**™ will use state-of-the-art interactive computer technology to bring the immigration records on ancestors who came to this country as long as a century ago to one's fingertips.

Over 113 million Americans are presently engaged in family history research. This innovative center will provide guidance to both adults and children in the fascinating task of tracing one's roots.

This Web site describes The American Family Immigration History Center™, a research center for the Ellis Island Immigration Museum. On the Center's electronic database, searchers can find the names of ships that brought immigrants to this country, when they arrived, and more. An electronic database is just one source of information.

This ambitious project is gathering the information on the more than 17 million people who immigrated through the port of New York from 1892–1924, the peak years of Ellis Island processing. The data is being taken directly from the ships' passenger manifests,[2] which are currently on microfilm at the National Archives and Records Administration.

❶

LIST OR MANIFEST OF ALIEN PASSENGERS FOR THE UNITED

A ship's manifest. Click to enlarge.

---

2. **manifests:** lists of cargo or passengers carried by a ship or airplane.

USING MULTIPLE SOURCES Sources can be unreliable or incomplete. That's why it is always wise to check more than one source when reading for information. Writers as well as readers gather information from sources such as experts, eyewitnesses, encyclopedias, nonfiction books, magazines, newspapers, and the Internet. A librarian can direct you to sources that will answer specific questions.

When reading for information, consider the type of source:

- **primary source:** a book, document, or living person that provides direct, first-hand knowledge. For example, an original photograph, letter, diary, or record book is a primary source.
- **secondary source:** one that gives indirect, secondhand knowledge. For example, each driver involved in a traffic accident is a primary source of information. A news article about the accident is a secondary source.

YOUR TURN *Read the article and complete the questions and activities below.*

❶ What is the primary source of the data the Center is gathering? Where are the original documents?

Reading for Information

Tell students that this site tells about a project underway to help millions of families research their own ancestors' immigration to the United States. As they read through the article, have them use the information in the right hand column as a guide.

Use **Literary Analysis Transparencies,** p. 14, for additional support.

Using Multiple Sources

Ask students if any of them have ancestors who came through Ellis Island, and if they know when they arrived. If students have access to the Internet, they may want to visit the Statue of Liberty–Ellis Island Foundation. Expain that if an ancestor were still alive, this person would be a primary source of information. If the student gets information from someone else who spoke with the ancestor who immigrated—one of their parents, perhaps—that person would be a secondary source. Help students to see how the information in this article can connect with their lives.

The following are possible responses to the four questions and activities.

1 The primary data source is the manifest from the ship. It is a handwritten list of all the passengers on the ship, along with some information about each passenger. The original documents are on microfilm at the National Archives and Records Administration.

Back Forward Reload Home Search Images Print Security Stop

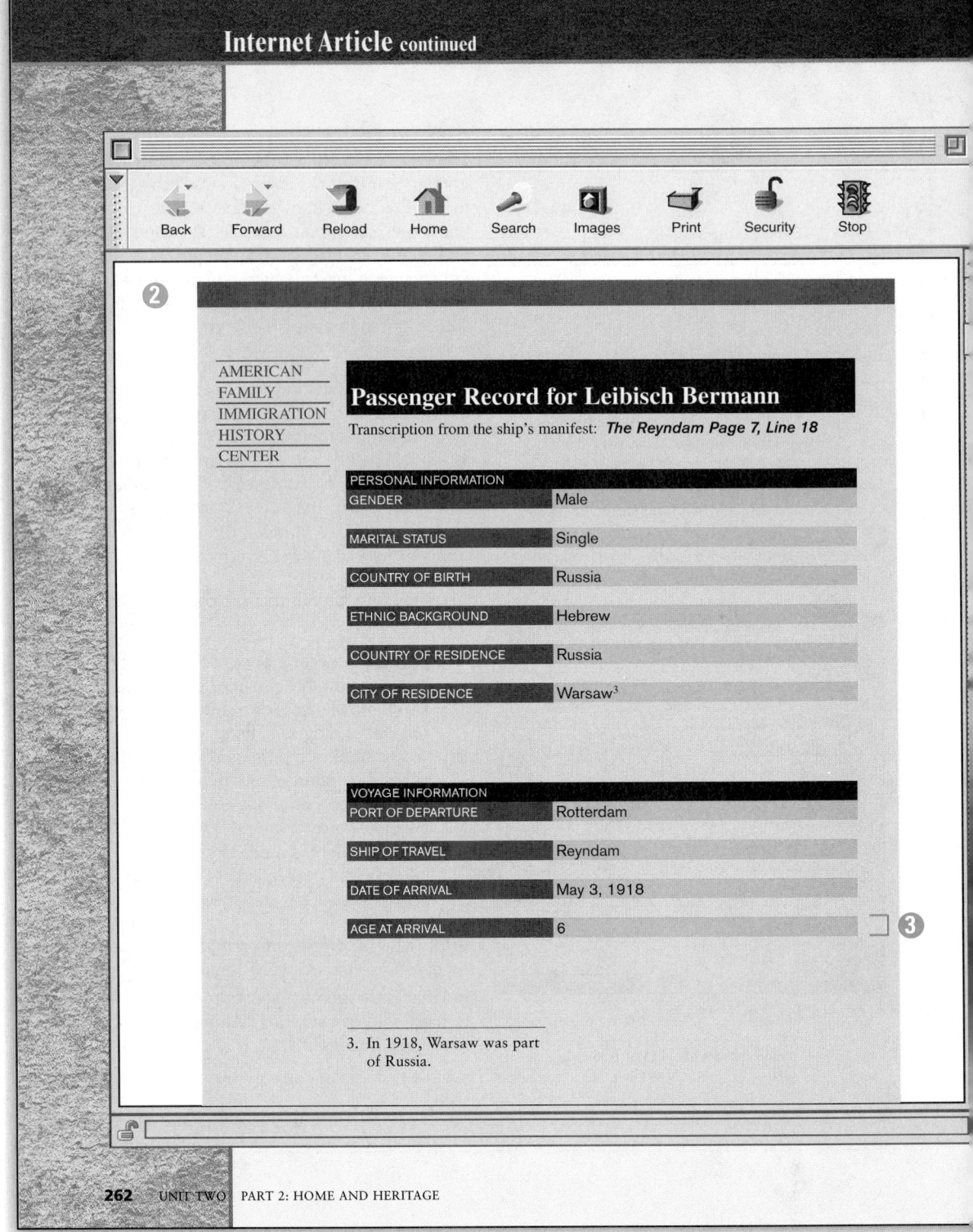

AMERICAN
FAMILY
IMMIGRATION
HISTORY
CENTER

Passenger Record for Leibisch Bermann

Transcription from the ship's manifest: *The Reyndam Page 7, Line 18*

PERSONAL INFORMATION	
GENDER	Male
MARITAL STATUS	Single
COUNTRY OF BIRTH	Russia
ETHNIC BACKGROUND	Hebrew
COUNTRY OF RESIDENCE	Russia
CITY OF RESIDENCE	Warsaw[3]

VOYAGE INFORMATION	
PORT OF DEPARTURE	Rotterdam
SHIP OF TRAVEL	Reyndam
DATE OF ARRIVAL	May 3, 1918
AGE AT ARRIVAL	6

3. In 1918, Warsaw was part
   of Russia.

Back **Forward** **Reload** **Home** **Search**

These valuable documents are, for the first time, being digitized, scanned and entered into an electronic database for easy access. The information will cover 11 fields of information, including:

④
- Immigrant's given name
- Immigrant's surname[4]
- Ship name
- Port of origin
- Arrival date
- Line number on manifest
- Gender
- Age
- Marital status
- Nationality
- Last residence (town and country)

For a nominal fee, visitors will be given the opportunity to receive a printout of their family's data as well as a scanned reproduction of the original ship's manifest on which their ancestor's entry appears, and a picture of the ship on which they arrived.

---

4. **surname:** a family name; a shared name that identifies the members of a family.

Reading for Information *continued*

② Compare this image with the image of the original manifest on page 261. What are some differences between the primary source and the typed record? Why might you want to read both an original document and its typed copy on a database?

③ This record states that Leibisch Bermann arrived in the United States on May 3, 1918. How old was he? What would you need to do to find out the date of his birth? List some primary and secondary sources you might use to find out more about Ellis Island immigrants.

④ Suppose you visit this site and tell a relative what you learned. You describe the center's purpose and the type of information it provides. Are you a primary source or a secondary source of information about the center? Explain. If you wanted more information about the center, what other sources might you check?

Inquiry & Research

Activity Link: "Aaron's Gift," p. 258.
Suppose you are reporting on immigration history. Use the information in the passenger record for Leibisch Bermann to write a paragraph about him. Include his age, where he was born, and the path he might have taken to reach the United States. Be sure to include the source of your information in your paragraph.

2 The original manifest is handwritten in cursive, while the Internet image is typed. The original has all the information about a passenger following his/her name, and the image has a chart format. You might want to read both the original and the typed copy so that you could verify the information. The original might have some additional information that didn't fit the chart. It is also interesting to see your ancestor's name on the original document.

3 Leibisch Bermann was 6 years old when he arrived in the United States. You cannot figure out Leibisch Bermann's birthday with the information from this chart. To find the date of his birth, you would need to talk to someone who knew him, get a copy of his birth certificate, or search the original of the manifest to see if it was listed there.

4 You would be a secondary source if you were telling someone about the site. The site itself is the primary source. If more information is wanted about the Immigration Center, you could write them a letter, visit Ellis Island, or call them. Usually this information can be found on the Internet site.

Connecting to Life Ask students if any of them have visited Ellis Island. Invite them to share stories, memories, and photographs from their trips to Ellis Island. Have them discuss how their trips added to their understanding of family history, immigration, and the diverse culture of the United States.

Inquiry & Research

This activity links to the Inquiry & Research section of the Choices & Challenges following "Aaron's Gift," in which students interview an older person.

Instruction Students will need time and support with a world map to trace the route Leibisch Bermann might have taken. You may want to use the Internet to explore various routes, or use print materials from the library. Students may also need

guidelines for report writing.

Application Students may want to present their report to their classmates, either through an oral presentation or by making a poster to represent what they found about Leibisch.

OVERVIEW

ℹ️ This selection is included in the **Grade 6 InterActive Reader.**
This selection appears in Spanish in the **Spanish Study Guide.**

Objectives

1. understand and appreciate a **short story** (Literary Analysis)
2. understand author's use of **description** (Literary Analysis)
3. use the reading strategy of **making inferences** to help understand the traits, motivations, relationships, and changes of the main character **(Active Reading)**

Summary

Panchito, a young Mexican-American boy, tells this story about life on "the circuit" in California—the regular route from harvest to harvest that migrant farm workers travel. As the story begins, Panchito's family have finished picking strawberries and are packing their jalopy with their few possessions. They find their next job picking grapes near Fresno, where an old garage serves as their temporary home. Each day Panchito and his older brother, Roberto, work alongside their father. When grape season ends in November, Panchito is free to enter sixth grade. On his first day at school, he feels shy and awkward at having to speak English for the first time in months. His teacher, Mr. Lema, is eager to help. Soon they form a friendship, and Panchito is thrilled when Mr. Lema offers to teach him the trumpet. He hurries home to tell his parents, only to find it is time to move again.

Thematic Link

When a family moves, many aspects of home and heritage change. In this story, Panchito struggles with frequent moves, but the love of his family is constant. The opportunities of education become more highly valued.

5-Minute Warm-Up

Daily Language SkillBuilder

Have students **proofread** the display sentences on page 187j and write them correctly. The sentences also appear on Transparency 8 of **Grammar Transparencies and Copymasters.**

The Circuit

Short Story by FRANCISCO JIMÉNEZ

"As we drove away, I felt a lump in my throat."

Connect to Your Life

Moving Day How would frequent moves affect your emotions, your experiences in school, and your friendships?

Build Background

CONNECT TO SOCIAL STUDIES This story is about the problems faced by Panchito, a young Mexican American boy in a family of migrant farm workers in California. Migrant farm workers are laborers who migrate, or move, from one agricultural area to another in search of work. The workers often move in a circuit—a regular route of travel—that follows the harvest seasons in different places.

California

Santa Rosa
San Francisco
Fresno
CALIFORNIA
Pacific Ocean
N W E S
Los Angeles
Miles
0   80   160

This map shows the great distances that migrant workers may travel looking for work in California. Much of "The Circuit" takes place in Fresno.

 LaserLinks: Background for Reading Cultural Connection

WORDS TO KNOW **Vocabulary Preview**
hesitantly   jalopy   vineyard
instinct   surplus

Focus Your Reading

LITERARY ANALYSIS DESCRIPTION One of the methods of **characterization** that writers use is **description.** Writers use description to help the reader understand a character's life and surroundings. Descriptions also help readers form mental pictures of a story's **setting** and events. Note the description in this passage from the story you are about to read:

I was completely soaked in sweat, and my mouth felt as if I had been chewing on a handkerchief.

Look for other vivid descriptions as you read.

ACTIVE READING MAKING INFERENCES When you **make inferences,** you are figuring out what the writer means but is not stating directly. From the description above, you can infer that Panchito is hot, tired, and thirsty. To make inferences, use the following strategies:

• look for **details** that the writer provides about the characters, setting, and events
• think about what you already know about the topic
• connect to experiences from your own life

📖 **READER'S NOTEBOOK** As you read, jot down at least two inferences about each character.

LESSON SUPPORT

UNIT TWO RESOURCE BOOK, pp. 39–45

ASSESSMENT
Formal Assessment, pp. 41–42
Teacher's Guide to Assessment and Portfolio Use
Test Generator

SKILLS TRANSPARENCIES AND COPYMASTERS
Literary Analysis
• Description, TR 4 (for Cooperative Activity, p. 272)
Reading and Critical Thinking
• Making Inferences, TR 10 (for Thinking Through the Literature, p. 272)

Grammar
• Avoiding Shifts in Tense, CM 85 (for Mini Lesson, p. 268)
• Future Tense, CM 82 (for Mini Lesson, p. 274)
Vocabulary
• Using a Dictionary CM 36 (for Mini Lesson, p. 265)
Writing
• Point of View, TR 23

Communications
• Nonverbal Strategies, TR 15

INTEGRATED TECHNOLOGY
Audio Library
LaserLinks
• Cultural Connection. See Teacher's SourceBook, p. 24

Visit our website:
www.mcdougallittell.com

The Circuit

by

Francisco Jiménez

Hot Day in the Field © 1999 Richard Haynes.

It was that time of year again. Ito, the strawberry sharecropper, did not smile. It was natural. The peak of the strawberry season was over and the last few days the workers, most of them *braceros*,[1] were not picking as many boxes as they had during the months of June and July.

As the last days of August disappeared, so did the number of *braceros*. Sunday, only one— the best picker—came to work. I liked him. Sometimes we talked during our half-hour lunch break. That is how I found out he was from Jalisco,[2] the same state in Mexico my family was from. That Sunday was the last time I saw him.

---

1. *braceros* (brä-sĕ′rôs) *Spanish:* Hispanic farm workers.
2. **Jalisco** (hä-lēs′kô).

Students Acquiring English
Point out that this story includes many Spanish words. Encourage Spanish speaking students to help their classmates with the pronunciation of Spanish words.

 Use **Spanish Study Guide,** pp. 52–54 for additional support.

Less Proficient Readers
Explain to students that "The Circuit" refers to the seasonal trips that migrant farm workers make around the countryside in order to find jobs.
Set a Purpose Ask students to read to find out what happens to Panchito and his family on the circuit.

Gifted and Talented
Have students think about how the story would be different if either Panchito's father or his mother told it. When students have finished reading, they can write a short version of the story from one of those viewpoints. Ask students, as they read, to jot down ideas that they can use in their rewritten stories.

Multiple Learning Styles
Visual Learners
Have students view the painting on page 265. Ask them to think about the life of a migrant farm worker. How does the picture help to shape their image? Ask them to describe what they think the life of a migrant worker would be like. As they read, they should remember these descriptions to help them understand the story.

 Mini Lesson **Preteaching Vocabulary**

USING A DICTIONARY
Instruction Remind students that there are several strategies to use when they encounter unknown words in reading. Using a dictionary can help students determine meanings for words they don't know. Combining context clues with meanings listed in the dictionary will help determine the correct meaning for each word.
Exercises Each of the following sentences contains one of the WORDS TO KNOW. Have students look up each underlined word and use the context of the sentence to decide which dictionary meaning is appropriate.

1. Panchito responded <u>hesitantly</u> when Mr. Lema called on him.
2. Papa was so proud of his old <u>jalopy</u>.
3. Papa worked long, hard hours in the <u>vineyard</u>.
4. Mama bought the cookpot at the army <u>surplus</u> store.
5. Upon seeing the school bus, our first <u>instinct</u> was to hide.

Use **Unit Two Resource Book,** p. 42 for more practice. Use **Vocabulary Transparencies and Copymasters,** p. 36, for additional support.

Literary Analysis | DESCRIPTION |

A Ask students to explain what they know about Papa from reading the description of how he chose his car.

Possible Response: Papa is a proud man, knowledgeable, cautious, and patient.

📖 Use **Unit Two Resource Book,** p. 41 for more practice. Use **Literary Analysis Transparencies,** p. 4, for additional support.

Active Reading | MAKING INFERENCES |

B Why does finding a blue necktie behind the rear seat of the car make Papa think that an important man must have owned the car?

Possible Response: In Papa's experience, the only men who wore neckties were important people.

📖 Use **Unit Two Resource Book,** p. 40 for more practice. Use **Reading and Critical Thinking Transparencies,** p. 10, for additional support.

Literary Analysis: SYMBOL

C The family has two cherished possessions: the car and the cookpot. Ask what these two objects may symbolize.

Possible Response: The car may be a symbol of the family's constant travel. The cookpot may symbolize stability. Wherever they live, they will always have the cookpot.

Literary Analysis | DESCRIPTION |

D Have students explain how the author's description of the garage helps them to draw a mental image.

Possible Response: The garage is old, dilapidated, and dark. There is no electricity or furniture. This makes it seem sad and lonely.

When the sun had tired and sunk behind the mountains, Ito signaled us that it was time to go home. "*Ya esora,*"[3] he yelled in his broken Spanish. Those were the words I waited for twelve hours a day, every day, seven days a week, week after week. And the thought of not hearing them again saddened me.

As we drove home, Papa did not say a word. With both hands on the wheel, he stared at the dirt road. My older brother, Roberto, was also silent. He leaned his head back and closed his eyes. Once in a while he cleared from his throat the dust that blew in from outside.

Yes, it was that time of year. When I opened the front door to the shack, I stopped. Everything we owned was neatly packed in cardboard boxes. Suddenly I felt even more the weight of hours, days, weeks, and months of work. I sat down on a box. The thought of having to move to Fresno and knowing what was in store for me there brought tears to my eyes.

That night I could not sleep. I lay in bed thinking about how much I hated this move.

A little before five o'clock in the morning, Papa woke everyone up. A few minutes later, the yelling and screaming of my little brothers and sisters, for whom the move was a great adventure, broke the silence of dawn. Shortly, the barking of the dogs accompanied them.

While we packed the breakfast dishes, Papa went outside to start the "Carcanchita." That was the name Papa gave his old '38 black Plymouth. He bought it in a used-car lot in Santa Rosa in the winter of 1949. Papa was very proud of his car. "*Mi Carcanchita,*"[4] my little jalopy, he called it. He had a right to be proud of it. He spent a lot of time looking at other cars before buying this one. When he finally chose the "Carcanchita," he checked it thoroughly before driving it out of the car lot.

He examined every inch of the car. He listened to the motor, tilting his head from side to side like a parrot, trying to detect any noises that spelled car trouble. After being satisfied with the looks and sounds of the car, Papa then insisted on knowing who the original owner was. He never did find out from the car salesman. But he bought the car anyway. Papa figured the original owner must have been an important man, because behind the rear seat of the car he found a blue necktie.

Papa parked the car out in front and left the motor running. "*Listo,*"[5] he yelled. Without saying a word, Roberto and I began to carry the boxes out to the car. Roberto carried the two big boxes and I carried the smaller ones. Papa then threw the mattress on top of the car roof and tied it with ropes to the front and rear bumpers.

Everything was packed except Mama's pot. It was an old large galvanized pot she had picked up at an army surplus store in Santa Maria the year I was born. The pot was full of dents and nicks, and the more dents and nicks it had, the more Mama liked it. "*Mi olla,*"[6] she used to say proudly.

I held the front door open as Mama carefully carried out her pot by both handles, making sure not to spill the cooked beans. When she

---

3. **Ya esora:** a made-up spelling for the sharecropper's pronunciation of the Spanish expression *Ya es hora* (yä'ĕs-ô'rä), which means "It is time."

4. **Mi Carcanchita** (mē kär-kän-chē'tä) *Spanish:* jalopy.

5. **listo** (lĕ'stô) *Spanish:* ready.

6. **mi olla** (mē ô'yä) *Spanish:* my pot.

WORDS
TO
KNOW
jalopy (jə-lŏp'ē) *n.* a shabby old car
surplus (sûr'pləs) *n.* extra material or supplies; leftovers

Teaching Options

BLOCK SCHEDULING: MANAGING TIME

If your schedule requires that you cover the lesson objectives in a shorter time, use . . .
- Preparing to Read, p. 264
- Thinking Through the Literature, p. 272
- Vocabulary in Action, p. 273
- Grammar in Context, p. 274

If you want to take advantage of longer class time, use . . .
- TE Teaching Options: Preteaching Vocabulary, p. 265, Cross Curricular Link, p. 267, Grammar, pp. 268, 274, Viewing and Representing, p. 269, Spelling, p. 270, Informal Assessment, p. 273
- Literary Link, p. 271
- Choices & Challenges, pp. 273-274

got to the car, Papa reached out to help her with it. Roberto opened the rear car door, and Papa gently placed it on the floor behind the front seat. All of us then climbed in. Papa sighed, wiped the sweat off his forehead with his sleeve, and said wearily: "*Es todo.*"[7]

Around

nine o'clock

the temperature

had risen to almost

one hundred

degrees.

As we drove away, I felt a lump in my throat. I turned around and looked at our little shack for the last time.

At sunset we drove into a labor camp near Fresno. Since Papa did not speak English, Mama asked the camp foreman if he needed any more workers. "We don't need no more," said the foreman, scratching his head. "Check with Sullivan down the road. Can't miss him. He lives in a big white house with a fence around it."

When we got there, Mama walked up to the house. She went through a white gate, past a row of rose bushes, up the stairs to the front door. She rang the doorbell. The porch light went on and a tall husky man came out. They exchanged a few words. After the man went in, Mama clasped her hands and hurried back to the car. "We have work! Mr. Sullivan said we can stay there the whole season," she said, gasping and pointing to an old garage near the stables.

The garage was worn out by the years. It had no windows. The walls, eaten by termites, strained to support the roof full of holes. The loose dirt floor, populated by earthworms, looked like a gray road map.

That night, by the light of a kerosene lamp, we unpacked and cleaned our new home. Roberto swept away the loose dirt, leaving the hard ground. Papa plugged the holes in the walls with old newspapers and tin can tops. Mama fed my little brothers and sisters. Papa and Roberto then brought in the mattress and placed it in the far corner of the garage. "Mama, you and the little ones sleep on the mattress. Roberto, Panchito, and I will sleep outside under the trees," Papa said.

Early next morning Mr. Sullivan showed us where his crop was, and after breakfast, Papa, Roberto, and I headed for the vineyard to pick.

Around nine o'clock the temperature had risen to almost one hundred degrees. I was completely soaked in sweat, and my mouth felt as if I had been chewing on a handkerchief.

---

7. **Es todo** (ĕs tŏ′dô) *Spanish:* That's everything.

WORDS
TO
KNOW
    vineyard (vĭn′yərd) *n.* an area where grapevines have been planted

Cross Curricular Link History

ON THE ROAD A sizable group of migrant farm workers first arose in the Midwest after the Homestead Act of 1862. Some people who tried farming in the Great Plains were unsuccessful and took to the road. On the East Coast, the end of World War II brought poor African Americans from the rural South to find work in Florida and other eastern states. California has had large groups of migrant workers of various nationalities since the 1870s. Among the newest groups are Mixtec Indians from the Mexican state of Oaxaca who began to move northward from southern Mexico during the late 1980s. Many speak neither English nor Spanish, but an ancient language of their own.

Literary Analysis: SENSORY DETAILS

 A Have students find the sensory details the author uses to describe the difficult working conditions of Panchito and his family.

Possible Responses: Panchito was soaked in sweat, his mouth felt as if he had been chewing on a handkerchief, and he fell on the hot, sandy ground.

Active Reading | MAKING INFERENCES |

B Ask students to explain why Papa is so alarmed when the school bus comes by.

Possible Response: Since by law all children must go to school, Papa may be frightened that the bus driver will report him for not sending his sons to school.

Reading Skills and Strategies: CONNECT

C Ask students whether they have ever "ached all over" from hard work or exercise. If so, have them describe how it felt and tell what they did to feel better.

Reading Skills and Strategies: EVALUATE

Tell students that as they've read this story, they've probably formed some opinions about migrant farm workers. Ask students to think about Francisco Jiménez's purpose for writing this story, and to choose several events from the story to evaluate.

Possible Responses: Students may select any event in the story, but may choose to talk about loading the car or Panchito's fall caused by the heat. They should express emotions and opinions about these events. Students should conclude that Jiménez wants his reader to know the harsh realities of the migrant farm worker's life.

A I walked over to the end of the row, picked up the jug of water we had brought, and began drinking. "Don't drink too much; you'll get sick," Roberto shouted. No sooner had he said that than I felt sick to my stomach. I dropped to my knees and let the jug roll off my hands. I remained motionless with my eyes glued on the hot, sandy ground. All I could hear was the drone of insects. Slowly I began to recover. I poured water over my face and neck and watched the black mud run down my arms and hit the ground.

I still felt a little dizzy when we took a break to eat lunch. It was past two o'clock and we sat underneath a large walnut tree that was on the side of the road. While we ate, Papa jotted down the number of boxes we had picked. Roberto drew designs on the ground with a stick. Suddenly I noticed Papa's face turn pale as he looked down the road. "Here **B** comes the school bus," he whispered loudly in alarm. Instinctively, Roberto and I ran and hid in the vineyards. We did not want to get in trouble for not going to school. The yellow bus stopped in front of Mr. Sullivan's house. Two neatly dressed boys about my age got off. They carried books under their arms. After they crossed the street, the bus drove away. Roberto and I came out from hiding and joined Papa. "*Tienen que tener cuidado,*"[8] he warned us.

After lunch we went back to work. The sun kept beating down. The buzzing insects, the wet sweat, and the hot dry dust made the afternoon seem to last forever. Finally the mountains around the valley reached out and swallowed the sun. Within an hour it was too dark to continue picking. The vines blanketed the grapes, making it difficult to see the bunches. "*Vámonos,*"[9] said Papa, signaling to us that it was time to quit work. Papa then took out a pencil and began to figure out how much we had earned our first day. He wrote

down numbers, crossed some out, wrote down some more. "*Quince,*"[10] he murmured.

When we arrived home, we took a cold shower underneath a waterhose. We then sat down to eat dinner around some wooden crates that served as a table. Mama had cooked a special meal for us. We had rice and tortillas with *carne con chile,*[11] my favorite dish.

The next morning I could hardly move. My **C** body ached all over. I felt little control over my arms and legs. This feeling went on every morning for days, until my muscles finally got used to the work.

It was Monday, the first week of November. The grape season was over and I could now go to school. I woke up early that morning and lay in bed, looking at the stars and savoring the thought of not going to work and of starting sixth grade for the first time that year. Since I could not sleep, I decided to get up and join Papa and Roberto at breakfast. I sat at the table across from Roberto, but I kept my head down. I did not want to look up and face him. I knew he was sad. He was not going to school today. He was not going tomorrow, or next week, or next month. He would not go until the cotton season was over, and that was sometime in February. I rubbed my hands together and watched the dry, acid-stained skin fall to the floor in little rolls.

When Papa and Roberto left for work, I felt relief. I walked to the top of a small grade next

---

8. *Tienen que tener cuidado* (tyĕ-nĕn′ kĕ tĕ-nĕr′ kwĕ-dä′dô) *Spanish:* you have to be careful.

9. *Vámonos* (vä′mô-nôs) *Spanish:* Let's go.

10. *Quince* (kēn′sĕ) *Spanish:* fifteen.

11. *carne con chile* (kär′nĕ kôn chē′lĕ) *Spanish:* a mixture of meat and spicy red peppers.

Teaching Options

Mini Lesson **Grammar**

AVOIDING SHIFTS IN TENSE

Instruction Remind students that different forms of a verb are used to show time.

Present tense tells about an action or a state of being that is happening now.

Past tense tells about an action or a state of being that was completed in the past.

Future tense tells about an action or a state of being that will happen in the future.

When telling a story or relating events, students should choose one tense and be consistent. Ask students to reread the highlighted passage in the text. Which tense is the author using? (past).

Have them notice the past-tense verbs used throughout the paragraph.

Application

Have students write summary sentences about the content of the story, avoiding shifts in tenses as they do.

Use **Grammar Transparencies and Copymasters,** p. 85.

Use McDougal Littell's *Language Network,* Chapter 4, for more instruction and practice in avoiding shifts in tense.

Harvest Hope
© 1999 Richard Haynes.

269

 Mini Lesson **Viewing and Representing**

Harvest Hope
by Richard Haynes

ART APPRECIATION

Instruction Ask students to study the art. Have them think about the bright, vivid colors the artist used. Ask them to discuss what the colors might represent.

Possible Response: The bright reds, yellows, and oranges may represent the sunshine and how hot it is for the farm workers. Also, the boldness of the colors shows strength.

Instruction Ask students to write about why they think this painting was selected for this story. Have them talk with a partner and share their reasons.

Possible Responses: The boy in this painting could be Roberto or Panchito. Some of the baskets are full of fruit, but not all. This could show us that the work is never done, and there is always more to pick. Also, the figure is sitting down, as if to rest, and this reminds us of Panchito when he fell down from the heat and lack of water.

A In this section, Panchito says he feels nervous and empty. Ask students to infer why he feels this way.

Possible Response: Everyone is ignoring him, and he's not sure he will like school or be able to do well.

Reading Skills and Strategies: EVALUATE

Have students discuss how people treat Panchito on his first day at school.

Possible Responses: The other students and the woman in the principal's office seem unfriendly and indifferent; the teacher seems more sympathetic.

Reading Skills and Strategies: CONNECT

Ask students to recall their first day at a new school and the feelings and expectations they had. Ask them to discuss how their experiences were similar to or different from Panchito's.

Possible Responses: Students may say that they felt alone and afraid just like Panchito and didn't like to read aloud either. They may say that they didn't feel like Panchito because all the kids were experiencing the same things.

Literary Analysis CHARACTERIZATION

B Have students describe the kind of person Mr. Lema is.

Possible Response: He is enthusiastic, polite, sensitive, and caring.

---

to the shack and watched the "Carcanchita" disappear in the distance in a cloud of dust.

Two hours later, around eight o'clock, I stood by the side of the road waiting for school bus number twenty. When it arrived I climbed in. No one noticed me. Everyone was busy either talking or yelling. I sat in an empty seat in the back.

I was startled. I had not heard English for months.

A When the bus stopped in front of the school, I felt very nervous. I looked out the bus window and saw boys and girls carrying books under their arms. I felt empty. I put my hands in my pants pockets and walked to the principal's office. When I entered I heard a woman's voice say: "May I help you?" I was startled. I had not heard English for months. For a few seconds I remained speechless. I looked at the lady who waited for an answer. My first <u>instinct</u> was to answer her in Spanish, but I held back. Finally, after struggling for English words I managed to tell her that I

wanted to enroll in the sixth grade. After answering many questions, I was led to the classroom.

Mr. Lema, the sixth-grade teacher, greeted me and assigned me a desk. He then introduced me to the class. I was so nervous and scared at that moment when everyone's eyes were on me that I wished I were with Papa and Roberto picking cotton. After taking roll, Mr. Lema gave the class the assignment for the first hour. "The first thing we have to do this morning is finish reading the story we began yesterday," he said enthusiastically. He walked up to me, handed me an English book, and asked me to read. "We are on page 125," he said politely. When I heard this, I felt my blood rush to my head; I felt dizzy. "Would you like to read?" he asked <u>hesitantly</u>. I opened the book to page 125. My mouth was dry. My eyes began to water. I could not begin. "You can read later," Mr. Lema said understandingly.

For the rest of the reading period, I kept getting angrier and angrier with myself. I should have read, I thought to myself.

During recess I went into the restroom and opened my English book to page 125. I began to read in a low voice, pretending I was in class. There were many words I did not know. I closed the book and headed back to the classroom.

Mr. Lema was sitting at his desk correcting papers. When I entered he looked up at me and smiled. I felt better. I walked up to him and asked if he could help me with the new words. "Gladly," he said.

The rest of the month I spent my lunch hours working on English with Mr. Lema, my best friend at school.

<table>
<tr><td rowspan="2">WORDS TO KNOW</td><td>instinct (ĭn'stĭngkt') n. a natural or automatic way of behaving</td></tr>
<tr><td>hesitantly (hĕz'ĭ-tənt-lē) adv. with pauses or uncertainty</td></tr>
</table>

270

Teaching Options

 Mini Lesson **Spelling**

LONG I: I, IE, IGH, IG, I-E, Y

Instruction Remind students that there are many ways to spell the long *i* sound. Have them think of words with the long *i* sound and list the spelling patterns across the chalkboard (*i, ie, igh, ig, i-e, y*)

Exercise Have students write these long *i* words from the selection under the appropriate pattern on the chalkboard: *July, liked, behind, time, eyes, while, night, silence, right, driving, side, trying, necktie, tied, climbed, sighed, wiped, white, light, termites, designs, hiding, finally, vines, rice.*

Ask them to add several more words of their own to each list.

Application Ask students to write a descriptive paragraph. The subject should be a trip where there is a temporary home—a hotel, a friend's house, or a campsite, for example. Have students underline all the words containing the long *i* sound.

Use **Unit Two Resource Book,** p. 44.

One Friday during lunch hour, Mr. Lema asked me to take a walk with him to the music room. "Do you like music?" he asked me as we entered the building.

"Yes, I like Mexican *corridos*,"[12] I answered. He then picked up a trumpet, blew on it and handed it to me. The sound gave me goose bumps. I knew that sound. I had heard it in many Mexican *corridos*. "How would you like to learn how to play it?" he asked. He must have read my face, because before I could answer, he added:

"I'll teach you how to play it during our lunch hours."

That day I could hardly wait to get home to tell Papa and Mama the great news. As I got off the bus, my little brothers and sisters ran up to meet me. They were yelling and screaming. I thought they were happy to see me, but when I opened the door to our shack, I saw that everything we owned was neatly packed in cardboard boxes. ❖

---

12. *corridos* (kô-rē′dôs) *Spanish:* slow, romantic songs.

the 1st

by Lucille Clifton

what I remember about that day
is boxes stacked across the walk
and couch springs curling through the air
and drawers and tables balanced on the curb
and us, hollering,
leaping up and around
happy to have a playground;

nothing about the emptied rooms
nothing about the emptied family

Connect to the Literature

1. What Do You Think?
Many students will respond that the ending surprised them. Others will respond that they found it sad that Panchito's family's move will prevent him from learning to play the trumpet, which he was very excited about.

Comprehension Check
• The peak of the strawberry season is over, and the family has to move to an area where there are crops to be picked.
• He must pick cotton to help support the family.
• Panchito's family has to move again.

 Use Selection Quiz **Unit Two Resource Book,** p. 45.

Think Critically

2. Have students note whether they used all the evidence available to them when they made inferences.
3. Possible Response: He is hardworking at school and in the fields. Also, he is sensitive, emotional, and shy.
4. Possible Responses: Yes; the memory of Mr. Lema's kindness and generosity can make Panchito trust other teachers. Also, Mr Lema taught Panchito an important lesson about how fun learning could be.
5. Possible Response: His experiences make the story more realistic, because he knows what it's like to move a lot and to work in the fields and to continue attending school.

Literary Analysis

Description Students should work cooperatively to complete the chart. When all groups have completed the work, they may want to share their charts with the whole class.

Connect to the Literature

1. What Do You Think?
How did you react to the end of the story? Explain.

Comprehension Check
• Why does Panchito's family have to move to Fresno?
• Why can't Roberto join Panchito at school?
• Why won't Mr. Lema be able to teach Panchito the trumpet?

Think Critically

2. **ACTIVE READING** **MAKING INFERENCES** How did the **inferences** you made in your **READER'S NOTEBOOK** help you know or understand the characters? Compare your inferences with a classmate's and discuss the details from the story that helped you.

3. How would you describe Panchito, the narrator of the story?

THINK ABOUT
• his attitude toward work and school
• his feelings about his brother
• his feelings about frequent moves

4. Do you think the narrator's friendship with Mr. Lema will have a lasting effect? Explain why or why not.

5. Francisco Jiménez's parents were migrant farm workers when he was young. Do you think he could have written this story without these firsthand experiences? Explain.

Extend Interpretations

6. **COMPARING TEXTS** Compare and contrast the feelings about moving that are expressed in "The Circuit" and the Literary Link poem "the 1st" on page 271.

7. The Writer's Style Jiménez uses many words in the story from the first language of Panchito and his family. Panchito frequently uses a Spanish word and then explains its meaning. What do you think the use of the original language adds to the story?

8. Connect to Life Revisit your response to the Connect to Your Life activity on page 264. After reading the story, what are your feelings about moving? Have they changed? Explain your response.

Literary Analysis

DESCRIPTION The process of using words to paint a picture of a **setting,** an event, or a **character** is called **description.** For descriptions, writers choose **details** carefully—details that appeal to readers' senses of sight, hearing, smell, touch, and taste. Descriptions often use figurative language, too. Notice the use of **simile** and vivid verbs in this description:

The walls, eaten by termites, strained to support the roof full of holes. The loose dirt floor, populated by earthworms, looked like a gray road map.

Cooperative Learning Activity
With a group, find descriptive passages from the story and read them aloud. Identify which senses the details appeal to. Also identify whether the description is about a person, a place, or an action. Record the group's answers in a chart like the one shown.

Details	Senses Used	Description of a . . .
drone of insects	hearing	place

REVIEW **CHARACTERIZATION**
The ways a writer develops characters are called characterization. Types of characterization include:
• descriptions of the character
• character's speech, thoughts, or actions
• comments or actions by others
• direct comments by the author

Extend Interpretations

6. Comparing Texts Possible Response: In both selections, moving is seen as damaging. In the poem, the narrator as a younger person didn't realize the unhappiness connected with moving; in the story, Panchito, though young, is sad about the frequent moves.

7. The Writer's Style Possible Response: The Spanish words help remind you that even though most of the story is written in English, the family's first language is Spanish. It says in the story that Papa doesn't speak any English, and when Panchito starts school he realizes he hasn't heard English spoken for months, so the family probably uses only Spanish when they talk among themselves.

8. Connect to Life Responses will vary, but students should discuss their feelings about moving and relate them to their earlier thoughts. They should explain if and why their feelings have changed after reading the story.

Writing Options

1. A Story Retold What if the story were told by either Panchito's father or his mother? How would the story be different? Write a short story from one of these viewpoints. Place the story in your **Working Portfolio.**

2. Letter to Mr. Lema Write the letter that Panchito might send to Mr. Lema from the next town along "the circuit."

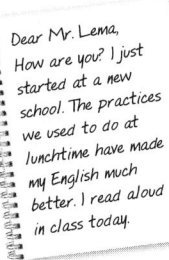

*Dear Mr. Lema,
How are you? I just started at a new school. The practices we used to do at lunchtime have made my English much better. I read aloud in class today.*

3. Predicting the Future What will life be like for the narrator of "The Circuit" ten years after the story? Write a prediction, and give reasons for it.

Activities & Explorations

1. Persuasive Speech Look back at Panchito's experiences in "The Circuit." Prepare a speech to convince members of a committee to begin a program that gives school supplies and books to families that do migrant farm work. Present your speech to the class. ~ **SPEAKING AND LISTENING**

2. Family Budget Imagine that Panchito's family has saved and put aside $50 for school supplies. Create a budget showing the best use of the money to prepare Panchito for his first day at school. ~ **MATH**

Inquiry & Research

The Fight for Farm Workers' Rights Who was Cesar Chavez? How did he affect the lives of migrant farm workers? Find books about Chavez or refer to an encyclopedia. Write a short essay about Chavez and his work.

LaserLinks: Background for Reading Cultural Connection

Vocabulary in Action

EXERCISE A: CONTEXT CLUES On a sheet of paper, write the vocabulary word that best completes each sentence.

1. Panchito crept into the classroom _____ because he wasn't sure he was in the right place.
2. Mama got her pots and pans at the army _____ store, where supplies that the military does not need are sold to the public.
3. Papa says that the sweetest grapes come from a _____ in Fresno.
4. Roberto didn't even think about what he should do when he saw the school bus; his _____ was to hide.
5. Panchito's family had to have a car in order to follow the harvests, but they could afford only a run-down _____.

EXERCISE B Make a chart like the one shown. Fill in the columns for each vocabulary word. Use a dictionary if you need help.

Word	Definition	Synonym	Example Sentence

Building Vocabulary
For an in-depth lesson on using context clues, see p. 79.

WORDS TO KNOW	hesitantly	instinct	jalopy	surplus	vineyard

Writing Options

1. **A Story Retold** Students should write in the first person, and retell this story from another viewpoint. It may be necessary to review first-person narrative writing.

   Use **Writing Transparencies,** p. 23, for additional support.

2. **Letter to Mr. Lema** Students should review the style of a friendly letter before beginning. They should also keep their writing consistent with the style of Panchito's language.

3. **Predicting the Future** Students may want to consider what experiences in the story form a lasting impression on Panchito. This will affect the way they write their prediction.

Activities & Explorations

1. **Persuasive Speech** Students may want to include statistics and visual aids in their presentations. Time and support may be needed to research this topic in the library.

   Use **Communications Transparencies and Copymasters,** p. 15, for additional support.

2. **Family Budget** Students may need school supply catalogs or flyers and calculators.

Inquiry & Research

The Fight for Farm Workers' Rights Students may want to work with a partner to research Cesar Chavez and to write their essay.

Vocabulary in Action

EXERCISE A
1. hesitantly, 2. surplus, 3. vineyard, 4. instinct, 5. jalopy
EXERCISE B
Charts will vary.

✓**Assessment** **Informal Assessment**

DESCRIPTION Good readers monitor their comprehension as they read. One way they do this is by creating mental images. Many authors use descriptive language to help readers paint these vivid mental pictures.

Ask students to pretend their family will be traveling a *circuit,* and space on the journey is limited—as in Panchito's family's old jalopy. Students can take only their most prized possession on the trip. Ask students to write a description of their most prized possession and include the reason for their choice.

RUBRIC

3 Full Accomplishment Response is a clear, vivid description of a prized possession and includes a strong supporting reason for the selection of this possession.

2 Substantial Accomplishment Response is a clear description of a prized possession, and contains vague reasons for choice of possession.

1 Little or Partial Accomplishment Response is not descriptive writing, but merely the naming of a possession and listing of one or more attributes. No reason is given, or the reason is weak and unclear.

Grammar in Context

WRITING EXERCISE

Answers

1. During recess I went to the library and opened my English book to page 125.
2. There were many words I did not know.
3. I closed the book and headed back.
4. I walked up to him and asked if he could help.

Author Activity

Students may want to talk to classmates and others in the community who are bilingual. They may also need library time to locate and read other books by Francisco Jiménez.

Francisco Jiménez

In 1973, Francisco Jiménez won an annual award from Arizona Quarterly for "The Circuit." He has also received a Ford Foundation grant and the Distinguished Leadership in Education Award from the California Teachers Association. His work appears widely in periodicals and in anthologies. In 1998, Jiménez's collected stories, *The Circuit: Stories from the Life of a Migrant Child,* won the coveted Boston Globe-Horn Book Award for fiction.

Grammar in Context: Past and Present Verb Tenses

A story told in the **present tense** conveys a sense of being there.

> Here comes the school bus.

A story told in the **past tense** relates events that have already occurred.

> The school bus stopped at my house.

Francisco Jiménez draws the reader into a past-tense world of memory in "The Circuit":

> When I opened the front door to the shack, I stopped. Everything we owned was neatly packed in cardboard boxes. Suddenly I felt even more the weight of hours, days, weeks, and months of work. I sat down on a box.

Usage Tip: When telling a story or relating events, choose one tense and stay with it.

> **Present Tense: The grape season is over and I can go to school.**
> **Past Tense: The grape season was over and I could go to school.**

WRITING EXERCISE Rewrite the following sentences using a consistent tense.

Example: *Original* Papa wipes the sweat off his forehead and said wearily: "Es todo."

Rewritten Papa wiped the sweat off his forehead and said wearily: "Es todo."

1. During recess I go to the library and opened my English book to page 125.
2. There were many words I do not know.
3. I close the book and headed back.
4. I walk up to him and asked if he could help.

Grammar Handbook Using Verbs Correctly, p. R68

"Learning and knowledge were the only stable things in my life."

Francisco Jiménez
born 1943

Migrant Childhood Francisco Jiménez was born in Mexico. He immigrated to the United States with his parents in 1947. Jiménez's parents were farm workers, and he helped them in the fields. Like Panchito, Jiménez enjoyed school because it meant he didn't have to pick crops. He also realized that school would help him escape "the circuit."

Professor and Writer A guidance counselor helped Jiménez get a scholarship to attend

college. Jiménez now teaches Spanish and literature at the University of Santa Clara in California. "The Circuit" comes from his book *The Circuit: Stories from the Life of a Migrant Child,* which contains other stories about Panchito and his family.

AUTHOR ACTIVITY

Between Two Languages How does Jiménez's knowledge of languages and his experience of learning affect his writing? Reread "The Circuit" and look at other stories by Jiménez. Write a paragraph explaining how the author's bilingual ability helps his storytelling.

 LaserLinks: Background for Reading Author Background

Teaching Options

 Mini Lesson Grammar

FUTURE TENSE

Instruction Verbs that tell about something that will happen in the future are in the future tense. One way to check to see if you are writing in future tense is to see if the word *tomorrow* makes sense in your sentence. Read the following sentence aloud: "Panchito will go to school when he gets to the next town."

Ask students if this sentence is in the future tense, and help them to see that they could say, "*Tomorrow* Panchito *will go* to school...."

Application Ask students to write a short paragraph in the future tense, describing the next

place on the circuit that Panchito's family will work. Students may want to include information about the farm work, their new home, or Panchito's experiences at a new school.

 Use **Unit Two Resource Book,** p. 43.
Use **Grammar Transparencies and Copymasters,** p. 82.

> Use McDougal Littell's ***Language Network,*** Chapter 4, for more practice in future tense verbs.

Oh Broom, Get to Work

Memoir by YOSHIKO UCHIDA (yō′shē-kō ōō-chē′dä)

"I stomped out of the living room without even a word of greeting to our guest, . . ."

Connect to Your Life

Houseguests This selection tells how a girl reacts to having too many visitors in her home. How would you deal with an unwanted guest?

Build Background

Immigrant Life Author Yoshiko Uchida and her sister, Keiko (kā′kō), grew up near San Francisco, California. Uchida's parents were issei (ēs′sā′)—Japanese immigrants to the United States—who welcomed many household guests. They were eager to help Japanese students who had come to study in this country. Most of their visitors were students at the University of California or other area schools.

Like this student at the Pacific School of Religion, many guests of the Uchidas were studying to become Christian ministers.

Focus Your Reading

LITERARY ANALYSIS **POINT OF VIEW** A writer chooses a **point of view** as a way of presenting events. The **narrator** is the voice or character that tells about the events. Most stories and nonfiction works are told from either a first-person or a third-person point of view. In a work told from a **first-person point of view,** the narrator participates in the events that he or she describes. The narrator uses the pronouns *I, me,* and *we,* as in this passage from the selection you are about to read:

> *I knew if I looked at Keiko we would both explode. But I did. And we did.*

As you read "Oh Broom, Get to Work," consider how the use of a first-person point of view affects the presentation of the events.

ACTIVE READING **CONNECTING** When you relate your reading to things you already know or to events in your own life, you are making **connections.** Connecting can help you understand the people that you read about.

📖 **READER'S NOTEBOOK** As you read this selection, ask yourself, What does this remind me of? Jot down at least three ways in which you connect the selection with your own knowledge or experience.

WORDS TO KNOW
Vocabulary Preview

audacious	indifferent
deprive	intrusion
devise	laden
dispense	pious
dread	pompous

OH BROOM, GET TO WORK **275**

Objectives
1. understand and appreciate a **memoir** (Literary Analysis)
2. understand **point of view** and its effect on a story (Literary Analysis)
3. use **connecting** to help understand a story (Active Reading)

Summary
Yoshiko Uchida reaches back to her childhood to recall the steady parade of Japanese visitors who came to her parents' home in California. In the author's view, all these visitors—with a few rare exceptions—were boring. Uchida's mother was unfailingly kind to the guests, a trait not shared by her resentful daughter. In fact, Uchida gleefully relates that she once followed an old Japanese tradition for getting rid of unwanted visitors: she put an upside-down broom with a cloth draped over it in view of a tiresome guest. When he saw it, he knew he was not wanted and soon departed.

Thematic Link
Uchida's home life helped her to appreciate her heritage, which included a tradition of courtesy and hospitality toward guests. The humor in her story arises from her refusal as a child to practice those family traditions even while she is slowly absorbing them.

5-Minute Warm-Up

Daily Language SkillBuilder

Have students **proofread** the display sentences on page 187j and write them correctly. The sentences also appear on Transparency 9 of **Grammar Transparencies and Copymasters.**

Mini Lesson **Preteaching Vocabulary**

If you would like to preteach the WORDS TO KNOW for this selection, use the Mini Lesson p. 276.

LESSON RESOURCES

Reading and Analyzing

Literary Analysis | POINT OF VIEW

Explain to students that the selection is written in the first person, which means that the narrator uses the pronouns *I, me, mine,* and sometimes *we, us,* and *our.* Have students think, as they read, about how the story would be different if it were written in the third person.

 Use **Unit Two Resource Book,** p. 48 for more practice.
Use **Literary Analysis Transparencies,** p. 22, for additional support.

Active Reading | CONNECTING

Students should be able to compare the text to their own experiences. Suggest ways in which they can do this: They can recall times they have had visitors in their own homes; they can recall when they had difficulty restraining their laughter; they can think of annoying things their parents do.

Use **Unit Two Resource Book,** p. 47 for more practice.
Use **Reading and Critical Thinking Transparencies,** p. 2, for additional support.

Reading Skills and Strategies:
EVALUATE

Remind students to evaluate the story as they read—to ask if its characters behave in believable ways, to consider whether or not they enjoy it, and to reflect on whether or not they agree with the central theme. Point out that "standing back" to think about a selection is an important part of any reading experience.

Oh Broom,

Teaching Options

 Mini Lesson   **Preteaching Vocabulary**

EXAMPLE CLUES
Instruction Explain to students that examples sometimes give valuable clues to the meaning of an unknown word. In the sentence, "Soldiers, astronauts, and mountain climbers all have to be audacious at times," they should be able to figure out from the examples that *audacious* means "bold".

Exercises The sentences below use examples to explain some of the WORDS TO KNOW. Have students write a definition of each underlined word based on the examples given.

1. Nightmares and thoughts of monsters cause <u>dread</u> in some children.

2. Robbers, thieves, and cheats all <u>deprive</u> people of their money.

3. Doctors, nurses, and pharmacists can legally <u>dispense</u> medicines to people.

4. After bursting in on a church service and crashing a party, he became known for his <u>intrusions</u>.

5. Edison and Einstein were famous because they <u>devised</u> new things or ideas.

 Use **Unit Two Resource Book,** p. 49 for more practice.
Use **Vocabulary Transparencies and Copymasters,** p. 37, for additional support.

Get to Work

by Yoshiko Uchida

I was on my way home from school when I found it. A little dead sparrow. It lay still and stiff, its legs thrust in the air like two sticks. It was the first dead creature I had seen close up, and it filled me with both <u>dread</u> and fascination.

I knew what I would do. I would give the bird a nice funeral. Mama would find a piece of soft red silk for me from her bag of sewing scraps. I would wrap the bird in a silken shroud,[1] put it in a candy box, and bury it beneath the peach tree. Maybe I would have Mama say a prayer for it, like the minister did at real funerals.

I picked up the bird carefully, cupping it in both hands, and ran home. I rushed through the kitchen and flung open the swinging door to the dining room.

"Look, Mama! I found a dead sparrow!"

But Mama was busy. She was sitting in the easy chair, knitting quietly. Sitting across from her on the sofa was a squat blob of a man— balding and gray—as silent as a mushroom.

The only sound was the soft ticking of the Chelsea clock on the mantel above the fireplace. I could see dust motes floating in the

> Poor Mama was stuck with company again.

shaft of late afternoon sun that filtered in from the small west window.

Poor Mama was stuck with company again. She and the guest had both run out of things to say, but the visitor didn't want to leave.

"Hello, Yo Chan," my mother called. She seemed happy for the <u>intrusion</u>. "How was school today?"

But all I thought was, company again! It wasn't the first time a visitor had <u>deprived</u> me of my mother's time and attention, and I was tired of having them intrude into our lives uninvited. I stomped out of the living room without even a word of greeting to our guest, and knew I would have to bury the sparrow by myself.

Mama might have sung a Japanese hymn for me in her high, slightly off-key voice, and she certainly would have offered a better prayer than I could <u>devise</u>. But I did the best I could.

"Dear Heavenly Father," I began. "Please bless this little bird. It never hurt anybody. Thank you. Amen."

---

1. **shroud** (shroud): a cloth used to wrap a body for burial.

WORDS TO KNOW	
	dread (drĕd) *n.* deep fear; terror
	intrusion (ĭn-trōō'zhən) *n.* an act of coming in rudely or inappropriately
	deprive (dĭ-prīv') *v.* to take something away from
	devise (dĭ-vīz') *v.* to form or plan in the mind; think up

277

Literary Analysis: ANECDOTE

A Explain to students that an anecdote is a short, amusing account often included within a larger work. Ask students why Uchida included this brief anecdote about the minister and the bathtub.

Possible Responses: It is humorous because many people might not expect such behavior from a minister, although Yoshiko's mother's explanation shows that the sisters may have jumped to the wrong conclusion about why he left the water. The anecdote also reinforces Yoshiko's claim that having guests created more work for her mother.

Literary Analysis: CHARACTERIZATION

Students should be able to analyze characters, including their traits, motivations, conflicts, points of view, and relationships. Ask students to describe the characters of Yoshiko and her mother, giving examples of characterization up to this point in the story.

Possible Responses: Yoshiko is a caring person who worries about a sparrow, but she is also feisty and independent. She runs out of the room without being polite to a guest. She likes to be entertained, as is clear from the example of Reverend Kimura. Her mother is also a caring, self-sacrificing person. She feels it's her duty to spend time with and feed her guests. She even cleans the bathtub without complaint, looking on the bright side of the situation.

I buried the box beneath a mound of soft, loose dirt, picked a few nasturtiums to lay on top, and made a cross out of two small twigs.

The gray-blob mushroom was just another of the countless visitors, usually from Japan, who came to see my parents. They were both graduates of Doshisha, one of Japan's leading Christian universities, and had close ties with many of its professors. This meant that many of our visitors were ministers or young men studying to become ministers at the Pacific School of Religion in Berkeley.

Once in a while, one of the visitors would be a pleasant surprise. Like the Reverend Kimura, who sang the books of the Bible to the tune of an old folk song.

1 *"Mah-tai, Mah-ko, Luka, Yoha-neh-deh-un . . ."* he sang out in a loud, clear voice. *"Shito, Roma, Corinto, Zen-ko-sho . . ."* He clapped in time as he sang.

I saw Mama's eyes light up as she listened, and soon she joined in, clapping and singing and laughing at the pure joy of it.

Mama surprised me sometimes. She could be a lot of fun depending on whom she was with. It was too bad, I thought, that so much of the time she had to be serious and proper, while visiting ministers smothered her with their <u>pious</u> attitudes.

To me they were all achingly and endlessly boring. It was only once in a great while that a Reverend Kimura turned up, like a red jelly bean in a jar full of black licorice.

A One <u>pompous</u> minister from Japan not only stayed overnight, which was bad enough, but left his dirty bathwater in the tub for Mama to wash out.

Yoshiko Uchida (right) and her older sister, Keiko, in the 1920s. Courtesy of the Bancroft Library, Berkeley, California.

"What nerve!" Keiko fumed.
"I'll say!" I echoed.

But Mama explained that in Japan everyone washed and rinsed outside the tub and got in just to soak. "That way the water in the tub stays clean, and you leave it for the next person."

Mama got down on her knees to wash out the tub, saying, "We're lucky he didn't try to wash himself outside the tub and flood the bathroom."

Some kind of luck, I thought. **2**

WORDS TO KNOW

pious (pī′əs) *adj.* showing religious feeling, especially in a way designed to draw attention

pompous (pŏm′pəs) *adj.* having excessive self-esteem or showing exaggerated dignity

278

Teaching Options

VIVID VERBS IN DIALOGUE Direct students' attention to the lines indicated by the highlighted area. Explain that Uchida could have used a plain verb here, such as "said." Instead she chose to make the dialogue more colorful. She made Keiko "fume" like a miniature volcano of righteousness, and showed herself "echoing" Keiko's wrath. Other vivid verbs for *say* used in the story are: *call, begin, murmur, add, answer, reply,* and *shout.*

Exercises Have students rewrite the following sentences with more vivid verbs for *said.*

Mini Lesson **Grammar**

1. "Look, Mama! A dead sparrow!" I said. *(exclaimed.)*
2. "I really like Reverend Kimura," I said. *(chimed.)*
3. Keiko said, "Please don't make me laugh." *(snickered)*
4. "That's the way we did it in Japan," said Mama. *(fumed)*
5. "You shouldn't have to do that for anyone," I said to Mama. *(sobbed)*

 Use **Grammar Transparencies and Copymasters,** p. 86.

 Use McDougal Littell's *Language Network,* Chapter 4, for more practice in using vivid verbs.

I didn't feel at all lucky about the seminary[2] students who often dropped in, plunked themselves down on our sofa, and stayed until they were invited to have supper with us.

"Poor boys, they're lonely and homesick," Mama would say.

"They just need some of Mama's kind heart and good cooking," Papa would add. And if they needed some fatherly advice, he was more than willing to <u>dispense</u> plenty of that as well.

Both my parents had grown up poor, and they also knew what it was to be lonely. They cared deeply about other people and were always ready to lend a helping hand to anyone. Mama couldn't bear to think of her children ever being less than kind and caring.

"Don't ever be <u>indifferent</u>," she would say to Keiko and me. "That's the worst fault of all."

It was a fault she certainly never had. She would even send vitamins or herbs to some ailing person she had just met at the dentist's waiting room.

On holidays all the Japanese students from the Pacific School of Religion—sometimes as many as five or six—were invited to dinner. Keiko and I always complained shamelessly when they came.

3 "Aw, Mama . . . do you *have* to invite them?"

But we knew what we were expected to do. We flicked the dust cloth over the furniture, added extra boards to the dining room table so it filled up the entire room, and set it with Mama's good linen tablecloth and the company china.

If it was to be a turkey dinner, we put out the large plates and good silverware. If it was a sukiyaki[3] dinner, we put out the rice bowls, smaller dishes, and black lacquer[4] chopsticks.

The men came in their best clothes, their squeaky shoes shined, their hair smelling of camellia hair oil. Papa didn't cook much else, but he was an expert when it came to making sukiyaki, and cooked it right at the table with gas piped in from the kitchen stove. As the men arrived, he would start the fat sizzling in the small iron pan.

Soon Mama would bring out huge platters <u>laden</u> with thin slivers of beef, slices of bean curd[5] cake, scallions, bamboo shoots, spinach, celery, and yam noodle threads. Then Papa would combine a little of everything in broth flavored with soy sauce, sugar, and wine, and the mouth-watering smells would drift through the entire house.

One evening in the middle of a sukiyaki dinner, one of the guests, Mr. Okada, suddenly rose from the table and hurried into the kitchen. We all stopped eating as the scholarly Mr. Okada vanished without explanation.

"Mama," I began, "he's going the wrong way if he has to . . ."

Mama stopped me with a firm hand on my knee. My sister and I looked at each other. What did he want in the kitchen anyway? More rice? Water? What?

It seemed a half hour before Mr. Okada finally reappeared. But he was smiling and seemed much happier.

---

2. **seminary** (sĕm′ə-nĕr′ē): a school for the training of priests, ministers, or rabbis.
3. **sukiyaki** (sōō′kē-yä′kē): a Japanese dish of sliced meat, bean curd, and vegetables seasoned and fried together.
4. **lacquer** (lăk′ər): a shiny substance used as a decorative coating on wooden objects.
5. **bean curd:** a food made from soybeans—also known as tofu.

WORDS TO KNOW	**dispense** (dĭ-spĕns′) *v.* to give out; distribute
	indifferent (ĭn-dĭf′ər-ənt) *adj.* not interested; unconcerned
	laden (lād′n) *adj.* weighed down; heavy

279

Customizing Instruction

Students Acquiring English
1 Explain to students that Reverend Kimura is singing the books of the part of the Christian Bible called the New Testament. He sings them in the form they take in Japanese: *Mah-tai* (Matthew), *Mah-ko* (Mark), *Luka* (Luke), *Yoha-neh-deh-un* (John), *Shito* (Acts), *Roma* (Romans), *Corinto* (Corinthians).

2 Point out that the phrase "some kind of luck" is sarcastic. It means something like "That's not really luck."

3 Indicate the italicized word *have* to students. Explain that it is printed in this way because Yoshiko emphasizes it when she says it. Read the sentence aloud, demonstrating this emphasis.

Multiple Learning Styles
Musical Learners
Ask students to study Japanese folk music by listening to a recorded collection. They should try to pick up a tune that they can then use to sing Reverend Kimura's words.

Less Proficient Readers
Ask the following questions to make sure students understand the visiting situation at the Uchida home:
1. Who are the visitors?
   Possible Response: Ministers and seminary students visit, usually from Japan.
2. Why is Yoshiko's mother willing to entertain so many guests?
   Possible Response: They are lonely and homesick, and she is a kind and generous person.

Speaking and Listening

READERS THEATER

Prepare Have students prepare to give a presentation of the story by reading it aloud. Assign the roles of narrator, Yoshiko, Keiko, Yoshiko's mother and father, Reverend Kimura, Mr. Okada, Mrs. Wasa, and the two characters in the joke—the visitor and the San Franciscan. To include more students, divide the narration and other roles among several students. Have students practice their roles in small groups, using tone, pitch, and volume to convey character and action vividly. For example, when Keiko and Yoshiko complain about the visitors, student readers should adopt loud, high pitched, whining tones. The mother can speak in a low, soothing, quiet voice.

Present Students should present their Readers Theater version of the story from beginning to end without pausing. Encourage them to think of it as a drama that must go on no matter what slight mistakes may be made.

BLOCK SCHEDULING This activity is particularly well suited for longer class periods.

Use **Communications Transparencies and Copymasters,** p. 12, for additional support.

"I'm sorry," he murmured, "but it was so warm I had to remove my winter undershirt." He wiped his face with a big handkerchief and added, "I feel much better now."

I knew if I looked at Keiko we would both explode. But I did. And we did. We laughed so hard we had to leave the table and rush into the kitchen holding our sides. Keiko and I often got the giggles at company dinners, and the harder we tried to stop, the harder we laughed. The only solution was for us not ever to glance at each other if we felt the giggles coming on.

In spite of all our grumbling, Keiko and I often enjoyed ourselves at these dinners. Sometimes it was Papa who provided the laughs. He loved to talk, and everyone always liked listening to his stories. Sometimes he would tell a joke he had heard at the office:

A visitor from Japan looked up at the sky. "Beautiful pigeons!" he says to a native San Franciscan.

"No, no," answers the native. "Those aren't pigeons, they're gulls."

The visitor replies, smiling, "Well, gulls or boys, they're beautiful pigeons!"

Much laughter all around.

After dinner Papa liked to gather everyone around the piano. He had a good baritone voice, often sang solos at church, and even organized the church choir. Keiko played the piano, and we sang everything from "Old Black Joe"[6] to "In the Good Old Summertime."

Sometimes Keiko and I added to the entertainment by playing duets for our guests —a fairly <u>audacious</u> act since most of the time I hadn't practiced all week. It never occurred to me then, but I suppose we were just as

boring to them as they so often seemed to us.

I once thought I'd found the perfect solution for getting rid of unwanted guests. Mrs. Wasa, who was like an adopted grandmother, told me one day of an old Japanese superstition.

"If you want someone to leave," she said, "just drape a cloth over the bristles of a broom and stand it upside down. It always works!"

I filed that wonderful bit of information inside my head, and the very next time Mama was trapped in the living room with another silent mushroom, I gave it a try. I did just as Mrs. Wasa instructed and stood the broom at the crack of the swinging door leading to the dining and living rooms.

"Oh, broom," I murmured. "Get to work!"

I kept a watchful eye on our visitor, and before too long, he actually got up and left.

"Mama, it worked! It worked!" I shouted, dancing into the living room with the broom. "He left! I got him to leave!"

But Mama was horrified.

"*Mah*, Yo Chan," she said. "You put the broom at the doorway where he could see?"

I nodded. "I didn't think he'd notice."

Only then did I realize that our visitor had not only seen the broom, but had probably left because he knew a few Japanese superstitions himself.

I'd always thought the seminary on the hill was bent on endlessly churning out dull ministers to try my soul. But that afternoon I felt as though I'd evened the score just a little. ❖

Before too long, he actually got up and left.

---

6. **"Old Black Joe":** a song by Stephen Foster (1826–1864), a composer of songs celebrating life in the Old South.

WORDS TO KNOW **audacious** (ô-dā′shəs) *adj.* fearlessly and recklessly daring; bold

280

Connect to the Literature

1. **What Do You Think?**
   What is your opinion of young Yoshiko Uchida's behavior?

   ┌───┐
   Comprehension Check
   - Who were the family's visitors?
   - In what ways did the visitors annoy Yoshiko?
   - At the end of the selection, why did the visitor leave?
   └───┘

Think Critically

2. **ACTIVE READING** **CONNECTING** With a group of classmates, discuss the connections that you recorded in your **READER'S NOTEBOOK**. Did you and your classmates relate to Yoshiko's situation?

3. In your opinion, how well did Yoshiko cope with her family's many visitors?

   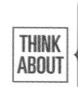
   THINK ABOUT
   - her descriptions of the visitors and the activities the family shared with them
   - her feelings toward her family
   - the expectations her parents had of her

4. Yoshiko's mother used to say, "Don't ever be indifferent. That's the worst fault of all." Why might being indifferent be such a terrible fault?

Extend Interpretations

5. **The Writer's Style** Uchida uses **sensory details** to make her writing interesting. Phrases such as "hair smelling of camellia hair oil" appeal to the reader's senses. Find other examples of sensory details in the selection and record them in a chart like the one shown. Note which sense or senses each detail uses.

Sensory Details	Sense(s) Used
hair smelling of camellia hair oil	smell

6. **Connect to Life** What is your idea of the perfect host and the perfect guest? Using ideas from the story and from your own experience, describe them.

Literary Analysis

POINT OF VIEW When events are told from a **first-person point of view,** the **narrator** (the person or character who tells about them) is involved in the events. The narrator refers to himself or herself as *I* or *me*.

When events are told from a **third-person point of view,** the narrator describes the events but does not take part in them. A third-person narrator refers to all the people or characters in the story as *he, she,* or *they*. The story "All Summer in a Day" is told from a third-person point of view. In this sentence from that story, the narrator describes the actions of Margot and her classmates:

> **If they tagged her and ran, she stood blinking after them.**

Cooperative Learning Activity
With a group of classmates, choose a short (one- or two-paragraph) scene from "Oh Broom, Get to Work." Write three retellings of the scene from different points of view. Try telling it from the mother's point of view (first person), a visitor's point of view (first person), or the point of view of a narrator not involved in the events (third person).

Extend Interpretations

5. **The Writer's Style** Possible Responses: "The soft ticking of the Chelsea clock" appeals to the sense of hearing. "Dust motes floating in the shaft of late afternoon sun" and "like a red jellybean in a jar full of black licorice" appeal to the sense of sight.
   You may wish to have students work in small groups to find examples of sensory details.

6. **Connect to Life** Students may say that the perfect guest is one who is entertaining but doesn't stay too long, and that the perfect host is one who is kind and generous and doesn't rush the guests to leave. To get students started on this assignment, review with them the things that Yoshiko does not like about guests.

Connect to the Literature

1. **What Do You Think?**
   Responses will vary, but may include that she was selfish or impatient.

Comprehension Check
- They were seminary students or ministers from Japan.
- They take her mother's attention; they come uninvited and they stay too long; they make extra work for the Uchidas.
- Yoshiko, following an old Japanese superstition that is supposed to cause unwelcome guests to leave, turned a broom upside down and covered it with a cloth. The guest saw the broom and left because he knew the same superstition.

Use Selection Quiz **Unit Two Resource Book,** p. 52.

Think Critically

2. Responses will vary. Possible Responses: Yes; I've had many dinners with my parents' friends when I was so bored I wanted to shout. Also I hate when my mother starts cleaning the house for "company." My friend and I once started laughing in the library. We tried to stop and we couldn't.

3. Possible Response: Yoshiko deals effectively with her family's many visitors. She lets her parents know that the visitors bore her, but she doesn't mean to be rude.

4. Possible Response: Being indifferent is an even worse fault than being mean—if you are indifferent towards someone, you don't even think the person is worth talking to.

Literary Analysis

Point of View Students should be able to shift from one point of view to another, and should also understand the difference between first-person and third-person tellings of an event.

Writing Options

1. **Guest Rules** Responses should list the suggested number of rules, and each rule should be applicable to the role of a good visitor. **To make this activity more challenging,** ask students to also list rules for a good host family.

2. **Personality Profile** Profiles should accurately sum up Yoshiko's personality, citing instances from the story in support of statements made, and including both good and bad qualities. To get students started on this activity, have them skim the selection and jot down good qualities and bad as they refresh their memories by reading.

 Use **Writing Transparencies,** p. 30, for additional support.

Activities & Explorations

1. **Monologue** Monologues should tell about a scene from the point of view of the speaker.

 Use **Communications Transparencies and Copymasters,** p. 12, for additional support.

2. **Display** Displays should include information about and examples of lacquerware.

Inquiry & Research

What's for Dinner? Menus should accurately describe dishes at a Japanese dinner. A good source of information for this activity, aside from cookbooks featuring Japanese cooking exclusively, would be Asian or international cookbooks that include Japanese recipes.

Writing Options

1. Guest Rules If you were to create a list of rules for guests, what would they be? Write five to eight guidelines for visitors in your home.

2. Personality Profile A profile is a description of a person's most important traits and actions. Write a profile of young Yoshiko. What was she like? What were her good and not-so-good points? Place the profile in your **Working Portfolio.**

Activities & Explorations

1. Monologue A monologue is a speech. In it, the character describes his or her thoughts and feelings. Choose a scene from this selection and rewrite it as a monologue. Perform your monologue for the class. ~ **PERFORMING**

2. Display The Uchidas use black lacquer chopsticks. What is lacquerware? How is it made? Make a display about this traditional Asian art form. Use drawings, pictures, and actual objects, if possible. ~ **ART**

Inquiry & Research

What's for Dinner? The Uchidas sometimes served their guests sukiyaki. What are some other Japanese dishes the family might have served? Using cookbooks or books about Japanese culture, create a menu for a Japanese dinner. Include a description of each dish on your menu.

Vocabulary in Action

EXERCISE A: MEANING CLUES Write the vocabulary word suggested by each clue.

1. Unconcerned about others' troubles
2. What you do with advice
3. Someone who is stuffy and proud
4. When you are unprepared for a test
5. Someone's barging into your room
6. To think up an excuse
7. Carrying a heavy backpack
8. People in a house of worship
9. To take something from someone
10. Description of a stunt person

EXERCISE B Work with a partner to solve each riddle with a Word to Know. Then try writing your own vocabulary riddles.

1. Cherries and apples have strong beliefs, but what are they?
2. Cheerleaders who brag a lot are _____.
3. We're outrageous, but not at night. What are we?
4. When is a ladle filled to the brim? When it's _____.

Building Vocabulary
For a lesson on definition and restatement clues, see p. 79.

WORDS TO KNOW				
audacious	devise	dread	intrusion	pious
deprive	dispense	indifferent	laden	pompous

Vocabulary in Action

Exercise A
1. indifferent
2. dispense
3. pompous
4. dread
5. intrusion
6. devise
7. laden
8. pious
9. deprive
10. audacious

Exercise B
1. pious
2. pompous
3. audacious
4. laden

Grammar in Context: Action Verbs

Author Yoshiko Uchida uses **action verbs** to show a child's energy and excitement in "Oh Broom, Get to Work."

> **I rushed through the kitchen and flung open the swinging door. . . .**

Compare these sentences:

> **I felt in a big hurry.**
> **I rushed through the kitchen.**

The second sentence, which uses an action verb, is more forceful and vivid than the first.

Usage Tip: An **action verb** can show **physical action**, or an **action of the mind**:

> **They cared deeply about other people.**

WRITING EXERCISE Rewrite each sentence using action verbs.

Example: *Original* Yo Chan seemed rude.
Rewritten Yo Chan fidgeted.

1. The sukiyaki was delicious.
2. The man seemed so dull.
3. Our conversation felt uncomfortable.
4. Mother's song sounded sweet.

Grammar Handbook Quick Reference: Parts of Speech, p. R54

Connect to the Literature Look back at the selection to find more examples of action verbs. Find two examples of verbs showing physical action, and two examples of verbs that show action of the mind.

> *"I write to celebrate our common humanity, for the basic elements of humanity are present in all our strivings."*

Yoshiko Uchida
1921–1992

Leading Family An author and educator, Yoshiko Uchida grew up in Berkeley, California. Her parents—leaders of Berkeley's Japanese-American community—filled their home with homesick seminary students, ministers, and graduates of Doshisha University.

War Experiences After the United States declared war on Japan in 1941, many Japanese Americans were arrested and placed in internment camps. The Uchidas were split up and sent to camps in Montana and Utah.

"Don't Think in Terms of Labels" Though Uchida's parents taught their daughters Japanese customs, the family's loyalty to the United States was strong. In 1984 Uchida said that she hoped that children could be "caring human beings who don't think in terms of labels—foreigners or Asians or whatever—but think of people as human beings."

AUTHOR ACTIVITY

Internment Camps Yoshiko Uchida's first successful writings were about her family's experiences during World War II. Find a copy of her autobiography *The Invisible Thread,* from which "Oh Broom, Get to Work" is taken. Read about her experiences in an internment camp during the war, and write a paragraph describing what happened.

Grammar in Context
WRITING EXERCISE
Possible Responses:

1. We gobbled up the delicious sukiyaki.
2. The dull man said nothing.
3. Our conversation included uncomfortable topics.
4. Mother sang a sweet song.

CONNECT TO THE LITERATURE
Verbs chosen will vary. Possible Response: wash, rinsed (physical action); thought, meant (action of the mind)

Author Activity
Responses should indicate acquaintance with Uchida's autobiography and focus on her experiences in the internment camp, summarizing them in an intelligible fashion. Students may find more information about Uchida's internment years in her book *Desert Exile: The Uprooting of a Japanese American Family.*

Yoshiko Uchida
Uchida's big break came when she followed the advice of an editor at *The New Yorker* magazine, who suggested that Uchida write about her experiences in the internment camps. In time, she also began to explore her other experiences as an American-born daughter of Japanese parents.

 Grammar

TWO KINDS OF LINKING VERBS Explain to students that there are two kinds of linking verbs. The first kind is used only as a linking verb: *be (am, is, are, was, were, being, been), become,* and *seem.* The second kind are those that can be used as linking verbs *or* as action verbs: *appear, remain, feel, grow, look, sound,* and *taste.* Discuss these examples with students:
LINKING The sky appears blue.
ACTION The sun appears at dawn.
LINKING The meat tasted delicious.
ACTION I tasted the delicious meat.
Point out that the difference in each case is that when used as a linking verb, the verb

indicates a state of being, not an action. A good trick for telling action and linking verbs apart is to substitute the appropriate form of the verb *seem* for the verb in the sentence. If the sentence still makes some kind of sense, the original verb is a linking verb.

Exercise Have students copy the following sentences and indicate whether the verbs in them are action verbs or linking verbs. Answers are given in parentheses.

1. Yo Chan remained happy. *(linking)*
2. She grew sick of the visits. *(linking)*
3. She smelled the sukiyaki her dad made. *(action)*

4. She looked for the broom. *(action)*
5. The poor student looked lonely. *(linking)*

Use **Unit Two Resource Book,** p. 50.
Use **Grammar Transparencies and Copymasters,** p. 80.

 Use McDougal Littell's ***Language Network,*** Chapter 4, for more practice in linking verbs.

This selection is included in the **Grade 6 InterActive Reader.**

Objectives

1. understand and appreciate a **poem** (Literary Analysis)
2. understand author's use of **sound devices** (Literary Analysis)
3. use **reading aloud** to help understand poetry better **(Active Reading)**

Summary

The two poems in this selection deal with travel across the western United States. In the first, Rosemary and Steven Vincent Benét describe westward expansion in an easy-going rhyme reminiscent of a traditional song. In the second, Theodore Roethke recounts in lilting verse an experience of traveling westward by train.

Thematic Link

The Benéts and Roethke are concerned with the nature of our homeland, the United States. While the Benéts revel in the legends of expansion that form the mythic history of our heritage, Roethke focuses on its physical beauty.

5-Minute Warm-Up

Daily Language SkillBuilder

Have students **proofread** the display sentences on page 187k and write them correctly. The sentences also appear on Transparency 9 of **Grammar Transparencies and Copymasters.**

PREPARING to *Read*

ACROSS the CURRICULUM
SOCIAL STUDIES

Western Wagons
Poetry by ROSEMARY *and* STEPHEN VINCENT BENÉT

Night Journey
Poetry by THEODORE ROETHKE

Connect to Your Life

In what ways do you think travel changes you or helps you grow?

Build Background The two poems you are about to read describe experiences of travelers in the West. The ease and popularity of westward travel has increased with its speed.

Before 1850 A pioneer family might live out of the interior of a Conestoga wagon. **Travel time, New York to San Francisco: over two months**

After 1850 Rail passengers could travel in comfortable trains, complete with dining cars. **New York to San Francisco: less than one week**

After 1920 The popularity of cars led to the construction of a national highway network. **New York to San Francisco: two and a half days, not including stops**

After 1970 Jet travel became the preferred method of cross-country travel. **New York to San Francisco: about five hours**

Transportation Milestones

1807	1831	1869	1908	1958
Robert Fulton invents the steamboat.	First U.S. steam railroad for passengers opens.	First U.S. transcontinental railroad completed.	Henry Ford begins mass producing automobiles.	First domestic jet passenger service.

Focus Your Reading

LITERARY ANALYSIS | **SOUND DEVICES** Rhyme, rhythm, and repetition are sound devices that can add feeling and music to poetry. Words that end with the same sound are said to **rhyme.**

Many poems also have **rhythm**—a pattern of stressed and unstressed syllables. (Stressed syllables are spoken with more emphasis.) The use of a word, phrase, or even a stanza more than once is called **repetition.**

ACTIVE READING | **READING ALOUD** Poets choose and arrange words to create the sounds they want listeners to hear. Try reading these two poems aloud. Pay attention to the patterns of sounds that you hear. In your **READER'S NOTEBOOK** list at least three pairs of lines that end with rhyming words.

LaserLinks: Background for Reading Historical Connection

LESSON RESOURCES

UNIT TWO RESOURCE BOOK, pp. 53–54

ASSESSMENT
Formal Assessment, pp. 45–46
Teacher's Guide to Assessment and Portfolio Use
Test Generator

SKILLS TRANSPARENCIES AND COPYMASTERS
Literary Analysis
• Poetry: Sound Devices, TR 20 (for Paired Activity, p. 287)

Grammar
• Contractions and Possessive Pronouns, CM 75 (for Mini Lesson, p. 288)

INTEGRATED TECHNOLOGY
Audio Library
LaserLinks
• Historical Connection. See Teacher's SourceBook, pp. 25– 26

Visit our website:
www.mcdougallittell.com

WESTERN WAGONS

by Rosemary and Stephen Vincent Benét

They went with axe and rifle, when the trail was still to blaze,
They went with wife and children, in the prairie-schooner days,
With banjo and with frying pan—Susanna, don't you cry!
For I'm off to California to get rich out there or die!

5 We've broken land and cleared it, but we're tired of where we are.
They say that wild Nebraska is a better place by far.
There's gold in far Wyoming, there's black earth in Ioway,
So pack up the kids and blankets, for we're moving out today!

The cowards never started and the weak died on the road,
10 And all across the continent the endless campfires glowed.
We'd taken land and settled—but a traveler passed by—
And we're going West tomorrow—Lordy, never ask us why!

We're going West tomorrow, where the promises can't fail.
O'er the hills in legions, boys, and crowd the dusty trail!
15 We shall starve and freeze and suffer. We shall die, and tame the lands.
But we're going West tomorrow, with our fortune in our hands.

Thinking Through the Literature

1. **Comprehension Check** What things are the pioneers taking
   with them?

2. On the basis of the poem, what kind of people do you
   think pioneers are?

3. Recall your responses to the question in Connect to Your
   Life on page 284. How do you think the people in this poem
   will be changed by their experiences on the trail?

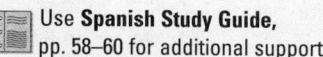 **History**

WESTWARD EXPANSION Settlers moving west depended on guidebooks that told them what trails to follow and what to expect. One of these, published by Lansford W. Hastings in 1845, paints what he considered an attractive picture of the future West: "The time is not distant, when those wild forests, trackless plains, untrodden valleys, and the unbounded ocean, will present one grand scene, of continuous improvements, universal enterprise, and unparalleled commerce: when those vast forests shall have disappeared, before the hardy pioneer; those extensive plains shall abound with innumerable herds of domestic animals; those fertile valleys shall groan under the immense weight of their abundant products; when those numerous rivers shall teem with countless steam-boats, steam-ships, ships, barques, and brigs; when the entire country will be everywhere intersected with turnpike roads, railroads, and canals; and when all the vastly numerous and rich resources of that now almost unknown region will be fully and advantageously developed."

TEACHING THE LITERATURE

Customizing Instruction

Less Proficient Readers
Set a Purpose Ask students to read to find out how the writers of the poems use sound to express their thoughts about traveling west.

Students Acquiring English
Help students read the rhyming words at the end of the lines in the poems. They may not perceive at first, for instance, that "road" and "glowed" are rhymes.

Use **Spanish Study Guide,** pp. 58–60 for additional support.

Gifted and Talented
Students may be interested in reading other poetry by Roethke. The poem "The Sloth," about that slow-moving animal, is amusing and appropriate for good readers. Other students might enjoy "A Nonsense Song," a love poem written by Stephen Vincent Benét for his wife.

Thinking Through the Literature

1. **Comprehension Check** They are taking tools, rifles, musical instruments, and household goods.
2. **Possible Responses:** strong, hardy, adaptable, independent, restless
3. Responses will vary, but should include reasonable predictions.

Active Reading [READING ALOUD]

The key to appreciating both poems in this selection will be reading them aloud. The Benéts' poem has long, musical sounding lines full of vivid imagery and dialect of the Old West. Students should find reading it out loud highly entertaining. The Roethke poem has a clickety-clack rhythm that mimics a rushing train. This will become clear to students as they inter-pret the poem aloud. Have students take turns reading stanzas of the Benéts' poem. Break up the Roethke poem according to sense in the follow-ing portions: lines 1–5; 6–11; 12–15; 16–19; 20–23; and line 24 to the end.

📖 Use **Unit Two Resource Book**, p. 53 for more practice. Use **Communications Transparencies and Copymasters**, p. 11, for additional support.

Literary Analysis [SOUND DEVICES]

After reading the poems aloud with stu-dents, point out that the rhythm in "Night Journey" is much like that of the rocking train described in the first two lines. The shortness of the lines and the strong rhymes that cap them reinforce this rhythm. Ask students to compare and contrast the sound devices used in "Night Journey" and "Western Wagons."

Possible Response: The lines in "Western Wagons" are long and musi-cal, while the lines in "Night Journey" are short and clipped. Both poems use strong rhyme. There is also repetition, such as in "Western Wagons" the repeat phrase "We're going West tomorrow."

📖 Use **Unit Two Resource Book**, p. 54 for more practice. Use **Literary Analysis Transparencies**, p. 20, for additional support

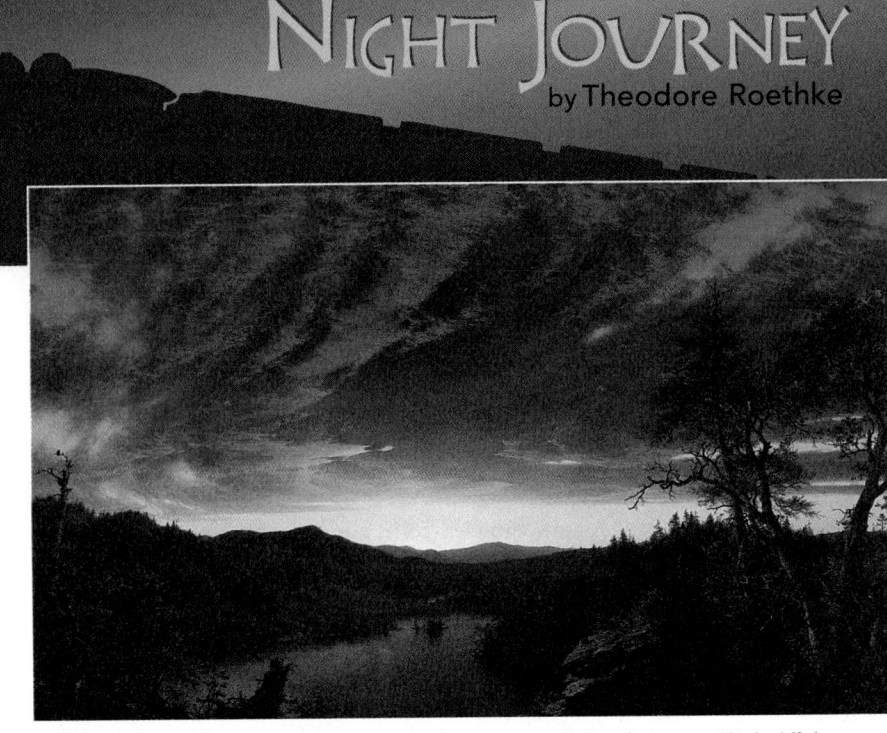

NIGHT JOURNEY
by Theodore Roethke

Twilight in the Wilderness, by Frederick Edwin Church, American (1826–1900), Oil on canvas, 101.6 x 162.6 cm, © 1999 The Cleveland Museum of Art, Mr. and Mrs. William H. Marlatt Fund, 1965.233.

Now as the train bears west,
Its rhythm rocks the earth,
And from my Pullman berth
I stare into the night
5   While others take their rest.
Bridges of iron lace,
A suddenness of trees,
A lap of mountain mist
All cross my line of sight,
10   Then a bleak wasted place,
And a lake below my knees.
Full on my neck I feel
The straining at a curve;
My muscles move with steel,

15   I wake in every nerve.
I watch a beacon swing
From dark to blazing bright,
We thunder through ravines
And gullies washed with light.
20   Beyond the mountain pass
Mist deepens on the pane,
We rush into a rain
That rattles double glass.
Wheels shake the roadbed stone,
25   The pistons jerk and shove,
I stay up half the night
To see the land I love.

Teaching Options

✓ Assessment **Informal Assessment**

SOUND DEVICES Students are expected to analyze the use of aesthetic language for its effects and to use literary devices effectively. Have them write 16 more lines for "Night Journey" describing other features of the landscape—perhaps a mountain range, a canyon, or a river. They should use the sound devices of rhyme, rhythm, and repetition as much as possible. Then they should write a para-graph explaining what sound devices they used and what effects the sounds create.

RUBRIC

3 Full Accomplishment Response reflects a full understanding of the use of sound devices in Roethke's poem and continues them in a similar style and rhyme pattern.

2 Substantial Accomplishment Response shows some understanding of Roethke's use of sound devices, but does not use them consistently in the poetic lines.

1 Little or Partial Accomplishment Response shows little understanding of sound devices.

Thinking through the LITERATURE

Connect to the Literature

1. What Do You Think?
What are your impressions of the speaker of "Night Journey"?

Comprehension Check
• Where is the speaker?
• What is the speaker doing?
• Name at least three things that the speaker sees, hears, or feels.

Think Critically

2. How do you think the speaker of "Night Journey" will feel about the end of his or her trip?

3. **ACTIVE READING** **READING ALOUD** Share with a partner the pairs of rhyming lines you listed in your READER'S NOTEBOOK. Discuss the effects created by the rhymes in the two poems.

4. How is seeing the world from a moving train different from experiencing it on foot or from a horse-drawn wagon?

> **THINK ABOUT**
> • the achievements and hardships of the pioneers
> • the observations that the speaker of "Night Journey" makes from the train
> • your own experiences traveling on foot versus traveling by car, bus, or subway

5. Which of the journeys presented in these poems would you most like to go on? Explain your response.

Extend Interpretations

6. **COMPARING TEXTS** Compare and contrast the journeys in "Western Wagons" and "Night Journey" with the journey of Amelia Earhart in the selection from *The Fun of It* (page 135). How are the travelers' experiences and reasons for traveling similar? How are they different?

7. **Connect to Life** Do you think you have to leave home to go on a journey or to explore? Why or why not?

Literary Analysis

SOUND DEVICES Poets often use rhyme, rhythm, and repetition to give their poems distinctive "sounds."

Words that end with the same sounds are said to **rhyme.** Many poems contain rhyming words at the ends of lines:

The cowards never started and the weak died on the road,

And all across the continent the endless campfires glowed.

Rhythm is a pattern of stressed(ˊ) and unstressed(˘) syllables. When the pattern repeats within a poem, the poem is said to have a regular rhythm.

> *Ĭts rhýthm rócks thĕ éarth,*
> *Ănd fróm mўy Púllmăn bérth*

The use of a sound, word, or phrase more than once is called **repetition.** In "Western Wagons," the repetition of "we're going West tomorrow" emphasizes the pioneers' determination.

Paired Activity With a partner, choose four or more lines in one of the poems. Copy the lines on your paper and mark the stressed and unstressed syllables. (Look at the example above for help.) Take turns reading the lines aloud. How does the sound of the poem change if you stress the unstressed syllables?

WESTERN WAGONS / NIGHT JOURNEY **287**

Writing Options

1. **Travel Narrative** Responses should show that the student has connected with the chosen poem and understood the basic outline of the action that underlies it. To get students started on this activity, hold a brainstorming session in which they offer suggestions on possible storylines behind the poems.

 Use **Writing Transparencies,** p. 22, for additional support.

2. **Travel Poem** Responses should focus on growth and change brought about by traveling. They should exhibit one or more of the sound devices listed.

Activities & Explorations

1. **Musical Accompaniment** Tunes chosen or composed should be musically appropriate for the poem in question. An example of a tune to accompany the poem "Western Wagons" is "Oh, Susanna," by Stephen Foster, which the poem very nearly fits.

Inquiry & Research

Roads and Rails Responses should include maps showing road and rail routes. A good source of information for this activity is *The First Transcontinental Railroad,* by John Debo Galloway (New York: Dorset Press, 1989).

Writing Options

1. **Travel Narrative** In prose, write your own version of the story that one of these poems tells. Write in the voice of the speaker or as a third-person narrator.

Writing Handbook
See p. R33: Narrative Writing.

2. **Travel Poem** Write a poem about the growth and change that travel can bring. Try using sound devices such as rhyme, rhythm, and repetition.

Activities & Explorations

1. **Musical Accompaniment** Many tales of the Old West were told in folk songs and ballads (songs that tell stories). Listen to some examples of these traditional songs—such as *Lonesome Whistle,* a folk song about the railroad. Then choose or create music to go with either of the poems in this lesson.
~ **MUSIC**

Inquiry & Research

SOCIAL STUDIES | ROADS AND RAILS

By the end of the 1800s, roads and railways crisscrossed the United States. With a partner, research the development of these transportation networks. Study historical atlases, and create a historical transportation map showing road and rail routes. Label key routes and intersections.

 LaserLinks: Background for Reading Historical Connection

Rosemary Benét
1898–1962

Stephen Vincent Benét
1898–1943

". . . I have tried to put [the details of my life] down in poems as barely and honestly as possible."

Theodore Roethke
1908–1963

A Literary Family Stephen Vincent Benét grew up in a family of writers. His father and grandfather had kept written records of their wartime experiences, and the family encouraged the literary interests of its younger members. Benét's brother and sister also became writers. Benét published his first book when he was just 17. In 1920 Benét received a fellowship that allowed him to study in France. It was there that he met Rosemary Carr, who was working in Paris as a journalist. During a later stay in France, Benét wrote his Pulitzer Prize–winning poem *John Brown's Body.* Stephen and Rosemary often combined their writing talents, especially when bringing stories from American history to life for children.

Childhood Theodore Roethke's father owned a floral business. Roethke grew up helping to tend the flowers in the family greenhouse. His father's death when Roethke was 14 affected the poet deeply. Much of his poetry explores his memories of his father.

Self Direction After graduating from the University of Michigan, Roethke supported himself by teaching in colleges. In 1947 he went west to take a job at the University of Washington in Seattle. He enjoyed teaching and was a favorite of his students, a number of whom became important poets themselves. In 1954, Roethke was awarded the Pulitzer Prize for his collection *The Waking.*

Teaching Options

 Mini Lesson **Grammar**

CONTRACTIONS AND POSSESSIVE PRONOUNS
Instruction It's useful to know how to use apostrophes in contractions and possessives. Write the following on the chalkboard:

> Your dream is to go west.
> You're [You are] going west.
> Their land is tamed.
> They're [They are] taming the lands.
> The West offered its land.
> It's [It is] a place to find land.

Exercise Have students form a contraction or possessive to fit the context.
1. The train rolls on (it) way. *(its)*
2. Look, (it) another mountain! *(it's)*
3. (You) looking ready to travel. *(You're)*
4. (They) train is faster than mine. *(Their)*
5. (They) trying to go west. *(They're)*

 Use **Grammar Transparencies and Copymasters,** p. 75.

 Use McDougal Littell's *Language Network,* Chapter 3, for more practice in possessive pronouns.

Words that Sound Alike

Words can have many meanings. Words like *pound* (a measure of weight) and *pound* (to beat) are called **homonyms**. They have the same spelling and sound but different meanings. But some words that sound the same have different spellings and different meanings. These are **homophones**.

Homonyms	
examples: *row, row*	
same	• spelling
	• pronunciation
different	• meaning

Homophones	
examples: *or, oar*	
same	• pronunciation
different	• spelling
	• meaning

> . . . when he reached home, he asked Noreen Callahan, who was playing on the stoop, to take off his skates for him.
>
> —Myron Levoy, *"Aaron's Gift"*

In this passage, **stoop** means: *a small porch or platform at the entrance of a home.*

But **stoop** can also mean: *to bend down.*

Strategies for Building Vocabulary

Homonyms and homophones can be confusing to readers, and can plague writers. In most cases the **context** makes clear the correct meaning of a homonym.

For example, in the Levoy passage above, it is clear that *stoop* is the noun that means "a small porch," not the verb meaning "to bend down."

❶ Understand Homonyms There may be times when you see a familiar word in a new context that just doesn't make sense.

How many meanings can you think of for the word *bark?* You know "the dog's bark," and "the tree's bark." What about "We set sail in a bark"? You can either consider **context** or use a **dictionary** to determine that *bark* also means "a sailing ship."

❷ Use Homophones in Your Writing The most difficult thing about using homophones in writing is that many common words (*our, hour; write, right*) have homophones. Use these words freely in your first drafts without worrying about spelling. Then, in revising, check carefully for homophones. See whether the words you chose match their contexts.

If you find different spellings hard to remember, you can keep a chart of hints such as the one on this page.

Homophones	Hints
here	in this place
hear	hear with the ear
herd	the shepherd's flock
heard	past tense of hear
their	belonging to them
they're	they are
there	there, not here

❸ Word Play You can also use homonyms and homophones creatively in your writing, for humor and for fun. Many poets, ad copywriters, and even comedians use pairs of words as puns: *Which witch? The nose knows!*

EXERCISE Look up each word's meaning in a dictionary. Then find the meaning of either a homonym or a homophone. Jot down both definitions, along with a sentence using each one. Tell whether you have used homonyms or homophones.

1. pair
2. weather
3. desert
4. shore
5. mind
6. piece
7. lie
8. mean
9. past
10. brake

ON YOUR OWN

Possible Objectives

You can use this selection to achieve one or more of the following objectives:

- enjoy silent sustained reading (Option One)
- read and analyze literature with a group (Option Two)
- use the Reader's Notebook to formulate questions about literature (Option Three)
- write in response to literature (Option Three)

Summary

In 1947, Mary is almost eleven and dreading her birthday. It means that she and her cousin Roger Deer Leg, like other eleven-year-old Kaws, have to undergo an endurance test called Ta-Na-E-Ka, or "the flowering of adulthood." For five days and nights, they will have to survive alone in the woods. Mary and Roger are prepared by their grandfather, who teaches them which berries and insects to eat and tells them tales of Ta-Na-E-Ka in the past. They complain and cannot see how this tradition fits into modern American life. As the first day of Ta-Na-E-Ka draws near, Mary decides that she cannot eat grasshoppers and berries. Formulating a plan, she borrows five dollars from her teacher.

Mary and Roger set off into the woods and separate according to the rules. Mary heads for the river where she knows she will find a marina. She uses some of the five dollars to buy herself breakfast at a restaurant. Later, when the owner has gone for the night, she sneaks into the restaurant to sleep. Discovered by the owner the next morning, she explains about Ta-Na-E-Ka and he offers to let her stay for the five days. When Mary returns home, she finds Roger exhausted; of course, she looks suspiciously healthy. Mary confesses what she did and, to her surprise, her grandfather praises her for her insight into survival in the modern world.

Ta-Na-E-Ka

Children at Play, Oscar Howe. © 1983 Adelheid Howe.

BY MARY WHITEBIRD

290

As my birthday drew closer, I had awful nightmares about it. I was reaching the age at which all Kaw Indians had to participate in Ta-Na-E-Ka.

Well, not all Kaws. Many of the younger families on the reservation were beginning to give up the old customs. But my grandfather, Amos Deer Leg, was devoted to tradition. He still wore handmade beaded moccasins instead of shoes and kept his iron-gray hair in tight braids. He could speak English, but he spoke it only with white men. With his family he used a Sioux dialect.[1]

Grandfather was one of the last living Indians (he died in 1953, when he was eighty-one) who actually fought against the U.S. Cavalry. Not only did he fight, he was wounded in a skirmish at Rose Creek—a famous encounter in which the celebrated Kaw chief Flat Nose lost his life. At the time, my grandfather was only eleven years old.

Eleven was a magic word among the Kaws. It was the time of Ta-Na-E-Ka, the "flowering of adulthood." It was the age, my grandfather informed us hundreds of times, "when a boy could prove himself to be a warrior and a girl took the first steps to womanhood."

"I don't want to be a warrior," my cousin, Roger Deer Leg, confided to me. "I'm going to become an accountant."

"None of the other tribes make girls go through the endurance ritual," I complained to my mother.

"It won't be as bad as you think, Mary," my mother said, ignoring my protests. "Once you've gone through it, you'll certainly never forget it. You'll be proud."

I even complained to my teacher, Mrs. Richardson, feeling that, as a white woman, she would side with me.

She didn't. "All of us have rituals of one kind or another," Mrs. Richardson said. "And look at it this way: How many girls have the opportunity to compete on equal terms with boys? Don't look down on your heritage."

Heritage, indeed! I had no intention of living on a reservation for the rest of my life. I was a good student. I loved school. My fantasies were about knights in armor and fair ladies in flowing gowns, being saved from dragons. It never once occurred to me that being an Indian was exciting.

But I've always thought that the Kaw were the originators of the women's liberation movement. No other Indian tribe—and I've spent half a lifetime researching the subject—treated women more "equally" than the Kaw. Unlike most of the sub-tribes of the Sioux Nation, the Kaw allowed men and women to eat together. And hundreds of years before we were "acculturated,"[2] a Kaw woman had the right to refuse a prospective husband even if her father arranged the match.

The wisest women (generally wisdom was equated with age) often sat in tribal councils. Furthermore, most Kaw legends revolve around "Good Woman," a kind of supersquaw, a Joan of Arc[3] of the high plains. Good Woman led Kaw warriors into battle after battle, from which they always seemed to emerge victorious.

And girls as well as boys were required to undergo Ta-Na-E-Ka.

---

1. **Sioux** (s\=oo) dialect: a language spoken by Native Americans of the Great Plains.

2. **acculturated** (ə-kŭl′chə-rā′tĭd): made to adopt another people's culture—in this case, the culture of European Americans.

3. **Joan of Arc**: French heroine of the early 1400s. At age 17, she led her country's army against the English and drove them out of the city of Orléans.

Reading the Selection

Option One
Silent Sustained Reading
You might set aside time each week for independent reading. During this time, you and all of your students would read for enjoyment. "Ta-Na-E-Ka" will appeal to many students and can be read independently in about thirty minutes. If you want to encourage students to read for pleasure, you might forego any assignments related to this selection. Should you want to make assignments, Options Two and Three offer suggestions.

Option Two
Shared Reading Groups
You may assign students to groups or allow them to choose their own. Students can read the selection together, alternately reading sections aloud, or they can read independently and meet to cooperate in a project that portrays some element of the story.
Possible Projects
- Using details from the story, students can create illustrations of Mary at various stages, starting from when she sets out on the first day of the trial.
- Using elements from the story, students can write the script for a speech Mary gives at school after completing Ta-Na-E-Ka. In it, she can explain what she did and what she learned about herself and her heritage through the experience. Students can present the speech to the class.
- Students can illustrate the various story characters, add captions giving their important traits, and add speech-bubbles with especially characteristic quotations from the story.

• Ask students to describe the setting of "Ta-Na-E-Ka" and to describe the character of Mary in detail.

• Tell students to read the selection, pausing at the end of the first column on page 292. At that point, ask them to summarize in their Reader's Notebook their initial impressions of the story and of the two children. Have them write down any questions they have about the story or any questions they would like to ask Mary. At the end of the story, students will return to their questions. Ask them to note if any of their questions have been answered and to write down additional questions they have.

• Instead of presenting a speech to the class, students can write such a speech in their Reader's Notebooks.

The actual ceremony varied from tribe to tribe, but since the Indians' life on the plains was dedicated to survival, Ta-Na-E-Ka was a test of survival.

"Endurance is the loftiest[4] virtue of the Indian," my grandfather explained. "To survive, we must endure. When I was a boy, Ta-Na-E-Ka was more than the mere symbol it is now. We were painted white with the juice of a sacred herb and sent naked into the wilderness without so much as a knife. We couldn't return until the white had worn off. It wouldn't wash off. It took almost 18 days, and during that time we had to stay alive, trapping food, eating insects and roots and berries, and watching out for enemies. And we did have enemies—both the white soldiers and the Omaha warriors, who were always trying to capture Kaw boys and girls undergoing their endurance test. It was an exciting time."

"What happened if you couldn't make it?" Roger asked. He was born only three days after I was, and we were being trained for Ta-Na-E-Ka together. I was happy to know he was frightened, too.

"Many didn't return," Grandfather said. "Only the strongest and shrewdest.[5] Mothers were not allowed to weep over those who didn't return. If a Kaw couldn't survive, he or she wasn't worth weeping over. It was our way."

"What a lot of hooey," Roger whispered. "I'd give anything to get out of it."

"I don't see how we have any choice," I replied.

Roger gave my arm a little squeeze. "Well, it's only five days."

Five days! Maybe it was better than being painted white and sent out naked for eighteen days. But not much better.

We were to be sent, barefoot and in bathing suits, into the woods. Even our very traditional parents put their foot down when Grandfather suggested we go naked. For five days we'd have to live off the land, keeping warm as best we could, getting food where we could. It was May, but on the northernmost reaches of the Missouri River the days were still chilly and the nights were fiercely cold.

Grandfather was in charge of the month's training for Ta-Na-E-Ka. One day he caught a grasshopper and demonstrated how to pull its legs and wings off in one flick of the fingers and how to swallow it.

I felt sick, and Roger turned green. "It's a darn good thing it's 1947," I told Roger teasingly. "You'd make a terrible warrior." Roger just grimaced.[6]

I knew one thing. This particular Kaw Indian girl wasn't going to swallow a grasshopper no matter how hungry she got. And then I had an idea. Why hadn't I thought of it before? It would have saved nights of bad dreams about squooshy grasshoppers.

I headed straight for my teacher's house. "Mrs. Richardson," I said, "would you lend me five dollars?"

"Five dollars!" she exclaimed. "What for?"

"You remember the ceremony I talked about?"

"Ta-Na-E-Ka. Of course. Your parents have written me and asked me to excuse you from school so you can participate in it."

---

4. **loftiest:** highest; most noble.

5. **shrewdest:** most clever.

6. **grimaced** (grĭm′ĭst): made a disgusted face.

"Well, I need some things for the ceremony," I replied, in a half-truth. "I don't want to ask my parents for the money."

"It's not a crime to borrow money, Mary. But how can you pay it back?"

"I'll baby-sit for you ten times."

"That's more than fair," she said, going to her purse and handing me a crisp, new five-dollar bill. I'd never had that much money at once.

"I'm happy to know the money's going to be put to a good use," Mrs. Richardson said.

A few days later the ritual began with a long speech from my grandfather about how we had reached the age of decision, how we now had to fend for ourselves and prove that we could survive the most horrendous of ordeals. All the friends and relatives who had gathered at our house for dinner made jokes about their own Ta-Na-E-Ka experiences. They all advised us to fill up now, since for the next five days we'd be gorging[7] ourselves on crickets. Neither Roger nor I was very hungry. "I'll probably laugh about this when I'm an accountant," Roger said, trembling.

"Are you trembling?" I asked.

"What do you think?"

"I'm happy to know boys tremble, too," I said.

At six the next morning, we kissed our parents and went off to the woods. "Which side do you want?" Roger asked. According to the rules, Roger and I would stake out "territories" in separate areas of the woods, and we weren't to communicate during the entire ordeal.

"I'll go toward the river, if it's okay with you," I said.

> This particular Kaw Indian girl wasn't going to swallow a grasshopper no matter how hungry she got.

"Sure," Roger answered. "What difference does it make?"

To me, it made a lot of difference. There was a marina a few miles up the river, and there were boats moored there. At least, I hoped so. I figured that a boat was a better place to sleep than under a pile of leaves.

"Why do you keep holding your head?" Roger asked.

"Oh, nothing. Just nervous," I told him. Actually, I was afraid I'd lose the five-dollar bill, which I had tucked into my hair with a bobby pin. As we came to a fork in the trail, Roger shook my hand. "Good luck, Mary."

"N'ko-n'ta," I said. It was the Kaw word for "courage."

The sun was shining and it was warm, but my bare feet began to hurt immediately. I spied one of the berry bushes Grandfather had told us about. "You're lucky," he had said. "The berries are ripe in the spring, and they are delicious and nourishing." They were orange and fat, and I popped one into my mouth.

Argh! I spat it out. It was awful and bitter, and even grasshoppers were probably better tasting, although I never intended to find out.

I sat down to rest my feet. A rabbit hopped out from under the berry bush. He nuzzled the berry I'd spat out and ate it. He picked another one and ate that, too. He liked them. He looked at me, twitching his nose. I watched a red-headed woodpecker bore into an elm tree, and I caught a glimpse of a civet cat[8]

---

7. **gorging** (gôr'jĭng): filling with food; stuffing.
8. **civet** (sĭv'ĭt) **cat:** a spotted skunk.

Possible Activities
Independent Activities
- Have gifted students scan the story, jotting down details, facts and descriptions about the narrator's attitude towards her heritage. Ask them to write in their Reader's Notebooks their analysis of her true feelings before and after the ritual and to note any significant changes that occur during the story. Remind them to consider carefully the passages in which the narrator informs the reader about the Kaw people. Ask students to consider what these passages reveal about the narrator's feelings.
- Have students review the Learning the Language of Literature and Active Reader pages, pp. 243–247. Ask them to note which skills and strategies they used while reading this selection.

Discussion Activities
- Use the questions formulated by the students in their Reader's Notebooks as the start of a discussion about this story.
- Ask students to consider what rituals in their lives might signal coming of age as the Ta-Na-E-Ka did for Mary and Roger.

Assessment Opportunities
- You can assess student comprehension of the story by evaluating the questions they formulate in their Reader's Notebook.
- You can use any of the discussion questions as essay questions.
- You can have students turn any one of their Reader's Notebook entries into an essay. Ask them to expand and clarify their ideas in the essay.

waddling through some twigs. All of a sudden I realized I was no longer frightened. Ta-Na-E-Ka might be more fun than I'd anticipated. I got up and headed toward the marina.

"Not one boat," I said to myself dejectedly. But the restaurant on the shore, "Ernie's Riverside," was open. I walked in, feeling silly in my bathing suit. The man at the counter was big and tough-looking. He wore a sweatshirt with the words "Fort Sheridan, 1944," and he had only three fingers on one of his hands. He asked me what I wanted.

"A hamburger and a milkshake," I said, holding the five-dollar bill in my hand so he'd know I had money.

"That's a pretty heavy breakfast, honey," he murmured.

"That's what I always have for breakfast," I lied.

"Forty-five cents," he said, bringing me the food. (Back in 1947, hamburgers were twenty-five cents and milkshakes were twenty cents.) "Delicious," I thought. "Better'n grasshoppers—and Grandfather never once mentioned that I couldn't eat hamburgers."

While I was eating, I had a grand idea. Why not sleep in the restaurant? I went to the ladies room and made sure the window was unlocked. Then I went back outside and played along the riverbank, watching the water birds and trying to identify each one. I planned to look for a beaver dam the next day.

The restaurant closed at sunset, and I watched the three-fingered man drive away. Then I climbed in the unlocked window. There was a night light on, so I didn't turn on any lights. But there was a radio on the counter. I turned it on to a music program. It was warm in the restaurant, and I was hungry. I helped myself to a glass of milk and a piece of pie,

I walked in, feeling silly in my bathing suit.

intending to keep a list of what I'd eaten so I could leave money. I also planned to get up early, sneak out through the window, and head for the woods before the three-fingered man returned. I turned off the radio, wrapped myself in the man's apron, and in spite of the hardness of the floor, fell asleep.

"What the heck are you doing here, kid?" It was the man's voice.

It was morning. I'd overslept. I was scared.

"Hold it, kid. I just wanna know what you're doing here. You lost? You must be from the reservation. Your folks must be worried sick about you. Do they have a phone?"

"Yes, yes," I answered. "But don't call them."

I was shivering. The man, who told me his name was Ernie, made me a cup of hot chocolate while I explained about Ta-Na-E-Ka.

"Darnedest thing I ever heard," he said, when I was through. "Lived next to the reservation all my life and this is the first I've heard of Ta-Na whatever-you-call-it." He looked at me, all goose bumps in my bathing suit. "Pretty silly thing to do to a kid," he muttered.

That was just what I'd been thinking for months, but when Ernie said it, I became angry. "No, it isn't silly. It's a custom of the Kaw. We've been doing this for hundreds of years. My mother and my grandfather and everybody in my family went through this ceremony. It's why the Kaw are great warriors."

"Okay, great warrior," Ernie chuckled, "suit yourself. And, if you want to stick around, it's okay with me." Ernie went to the broom closet and tossed me a bundle. "That's the lost-and-found closet," he said. "Stuff people left on boats. Maybe there's something to keep you warm."

Sisson's Diner, John Baeder, 7⁵⁄₈″ x 11″, watercolor on paper, © 1977.

The sweater fitted loosely, but it felt good. I felt good. And I'd found a new friend. Most important, I was surviving Ta-Na-E-Ka.

My grandfather had said the experience would be filled with adventure, and I was having my fill. And Grandfather had never said we couldn't accept hospitality.

I stayed at Ernie's Riverside for the entire period. In the mornings I went into the woods and watched the animals and picked flowers for each of the tables in Ernie's. I had never felt better. I was up early enough to watch the sun rise on the Missouri, and I went to bed after it set. I ate everything I wanted—insisting that Ernie take all my money for the food. "I'll keep this in trust for you, Mary," Ernie promised, "in case you are ever desperate for five dollars." (He did, too, but that's another story.)

I was sorry when the five days were over. I'd enjoyed every minute with Ernie. He taught me how to make Western omelets and to make Chili Ernie Style (still one of my favorite dishes). And I told Ernie all about the legends of the Kaw. I hadn't realized I knew so much about my people.

But Ta-Na-E-Ka was over, and as I approached my house, at about nine-thirty in the evening, I became nervous all over again. What if Grandfather asked me about the berries and the grasshoppers? And my feet were hardly cut. I hadn't lost a pound and my hair was combed.

"They'll be so happy to see me," I told myself hopefully, "that they won't ask too many questions."

I opened the door. My grandfather was in the front room. He was wearing the ceremonial beaded deerskin shirt which had belonged to *his* grandfather. "*N'g'da'ma,*" he said. "Welcome back."

I embraced my parents warmly, letting go only when I saw my cousin Roger sprawled on the couch. His eyes were red and swollen. He'd lost weight. His feet were an unsightly mass of blood and blisters, and he was moaning: "I made it, see. I made it. I'm a warrior. A warrior."

My grandfather looked at me strangely. I was clean, obviously well-fed, and radiantly healthy. My parents got the message. My uncle and aunt gazed at me with hostility.

Finally my grandfather asked, "What did you eat to keep you so well?"

I sucked in my breath and blurted out the truth: "Hamburgers and milkshakes."

"Hamburgers!" my grandfather growled.

"Milkshakes!" Roger moaned.

"You didn't say we *had* to eat grasshoppers," I said sheepishly.

"Tell us all about your Ta-Na-E-Ka," my grandfather commanded.

I told them everything, from borrowing the five dollars, to Ernie's kindness, to observing the beaver.

"That's not what I trained you for," my grandfather said sadly.

I stood up. "Grandfather, I learned that Ta-Na-E-Ka *is* important. I didn't think so during training. I was scared stiff of it. I handled it my way. And I learned I had nothing to be afraid of. There's no reason in 1947 to eat grasshoppers when you can eat a hamburger."

I was inwardly shocked at my own audacity. But I liked it. "Grandfather, I'll bet you never ate one of those rotten berries yourself."

Grandfather laughed! He laughed aloud! My mother and father and aunt and uncle were all dumbfounded. Grandfather never laughed. Never.

"Those berries—they are terrible," Grandfather admitted. "I could never swallow them. I found a dead deer on the first day of my Ta-Na-E-Ka—shot by a soldier, probably—and he kept my belly full for the entire period of the test!"

Grandfather stopped laughing. "We should send you out again," he said.

I looked at Roger. "You're pretty smart, Mary," Roger groaned. "I'd never have thought of what you did."

"Accountants just have to be good at arithmetic," I said comfortingly. "I'm terrible at arithmetic."

Roger tried to smile but couldn't. My grandfather called me to him. "You should have done what your cousin did. But I think you are more alert to what is happening to our people today than we are. I think you would have passed the test under any circumstances, in any time. Somehow, you know how to exist in a world that wasn't made for Indians. I don't think you're going to have any trouble surviving."

Grandfather wasn't entirely right. But I'll tell about that another time. ❖

Background: The Kaw Nation

Homeland Mary Whitebird is a member of the Kaw, or Kansa, Nation—a Native American group related to the Sioux. The names *Kaw* and *Kansa* both mean "people of the south wind." The original homeland of the Kansa was the plains of what is now Kansas. There they hunted buffalo and farmed. They lived in domed lodges made of wood, reeds, and earth.

Contact and Clash Because the Kansas and Missouri rivers were important means of transportation, the Kansa were among the first Native Americans of the plains to meet European explorers. In the early 1700s many Kansa began to die from smallpox carried by the Europeans. In the early 1800s the Kansa lost much of their land in treaties with the United States government. Later the government forced them onto a reservation in Oklahoma, where many of the nation's members live today.

 LaserLinks: Background for Reading
Historical Connection
Art Gallery

SAGUARO

BY FRANK ASCH

Stand
still.
Grow
slow.
Lift
high
your arms to the sun.
Stand
still.
Grow
slow.
Lift
high
your
flowers to the sky.
Stand
still.
Grow
slow.
Hold
tight
your
water
inside.
Stand
still.
Grow
slow
and let your roots spread wide and let your roots spread wide.

LITERARY LINK

SAGUARO **297**

Objectives
- write a character sketch
- use a written text as a model for writing
- revise a draft to add dialogue
- use possessive nouns and pronouns correctly

Introducing the Workshop

Character Sketch Discuss with students some character sketches that they have read. Elicit from students the kinds of details that make a character sketch memorable. Have students talk about funny, unusual, or fascinating traits and anecdotes that add to a good character sketch. Point out that while it is fun to read about famous people, sometimes it is even more inspiring to read about everyday people who have done extraordinary things.

Basics in a Box
Using the Graphic Tell students that the elements that make up a character sketch blend together to create a vivid and complete portrait. All of the components are equally important. Just as the viewer of a sculpture walks around the piece to see it in its entirety, the reader of a character sketch needs to see as many facets of a person as possible.

Presenting the Rubric To better understand the assignment, students can refer to the Standards for Writing a Successful Character Sketch. You may also want to share with them the complete rubric, which describes several levels of proficiency.

 Use McDougal Littell's *Language Network,* Chapters 10–17 for more instruction on essential writing skills.

 Power Presentation

To engage students visually, use **Power Presentation 2,** Character Sketch.

Writing Workshop
Character Sketch

Drawing a portrait with words ...

From Reading to Writing A character sketch is a portrait of a person drawn in words. It describes what he or she is like, inside and out. In "Oh Broom, Get to Work," Yoshiko Uchida shows her mother's generous nature. In "Aaron's Gift," Myron Levoy draws the portrait of a caring and brave boy who risks his own safety to rescue a pigeon. Writing a **character sketch** can help you to get to know someone and discover what sets that person apart from others.

For Your Portfolio

WRITING PROMPT Write a character sketch of someone you know or admire.

Purpose: To help readers understand an individual's personality
Audience: Classmates, family, or general readers

Basics in a Box

Character Sketch at a Glance

person's actions and speech

physical description

mannerisms of person

Main Impression of Subject

writer's feelings about the person

surroundings

other people's reactions to the person

RUBRIC STANDARDS FOR WRITING

A successful character sketch should
- present a vivid picture of the personality and physical appearance of the person
- give a main impression of the person
- include dialogue, mannerisms, descriptions and other devices that show, rather than tell what the person is like
- reveal the writer's response to the person
- place the person in surroundings that help readers understand him or her
- have a clear structure, a strong beginning and a strong conclusion

298 UNIT TWO   PART 2: HOME AND HERITAGE

LESSON RESOURCES

USING PRINT RESOURCES
Unit Two Resource Book
- Prewriting, p. 56
- Drafting and Elaboration, p. 57
- Peer Response Guide, pp. 58–59
- Revising, Editing, and Proofreading, p. 60
- Student Models, pp. 61–63
- Rubric for Evaluation, p. 64
Writing Transparencies
- Writing Process Transparencies, TR 1–TR 4

- Writing Structure Transparencies Identifying Paragraphs, TR 5; Achieving Unity, TR 8
- Writing Style Transparencies Dialogue, TR 24; Showing, Not Telling, TR 22
- Writing Template Transparencies Character Sketch, TR 30
Reading and Critical Transparencies
- Spider Map/Mind Map, TR 37

Grammar Transparencies and Copymasters
- Possessive Nouns and Pronouns, CM 69

INTEGRATED TECHNOLOGY
LaserLinks
Writing Springboards
See **Teacher's SourceBook** p. 56 for bar codes.

Writing Coach CD-ROM
Visit our website:
www.mcdougallittell.com

Analyzing a Student Model

SPEAKING OPPORTUNITY
See the Communication Handbook, p. R100 for speaking and presenting tips.

**Tiffany George
Princess Anne Middle School**

The Nurse: A Character Sketch

Grandma's friends call her "The Nurse" because she is always taking care of people. People come to her when they are not feeling well or when they need some support. She holds their hands and speaks softly to them, as though they were members of her own family. I know people are comforted by the warmth and strength in her green eyes, the way she leans in and listens, and the patience in her voice. There is a picture of her mother hanging in her house. She has the same high cheekbones and serious expression. Although she is in her seventies, Grandma has no wrinkles. She still looks young, even with all the responsibility on her shoulders. I know my grandfather appreciates everything she does, even if he cannot show it.

For seven years my grandmother has taken care of my grandfather—almost twenty-four hours a day, seven days a week. He is unable to take care of himself because he has Alzheimer's disease and recently suffered a stroke. Grandma felt that he needed more care than the nursing home could provide, so she decided to care for him herself. Because of this, she rarely gets to go to church anymore. If she needs to run an errand, she has to arrange for a relative to come and care for my grandfather or do the errand for her. She never leaves my grandfather alone.

Every morning, after she has had her cup of tea, Grandma makes my grandfather's bed and coaxes him to roll over so she can wash him up. "Rise and shine!" she announces as she opens the shutters to let the sun in. After that she helps him get ready for the day. She keeps him company when he eats his meals. Sometimes she just watches him. Often she will gently rub his back or smooth his hair.

RUBRIC IN ACTION

❶ Attention-getting beginning describes an important characteristic.

❷ States important mannerisms
Other Option:
• Use a quotation said by someone else to introduce main impression.

❸ Uses physical description to show character.

❹ Writer includes specific details. She places the person in natural surroundings to show personality.

WRITING WORKSHOP **299**

Teaching the Lesson

Analyzing the Model
"The Nurse: A Character Sketch"
The student model is a character sketch of the writer's grandmother. The writer lovingly calls her grandmother "the nurse" not because she is a real nurse, but because she provides care to so many people. The writer tells how her grandmother has devoted herself to caring for her husband, who has Alzheimer's disease. The writer describes a typical day in Grandma's life. The writer shows her affection and admiration by saying that even though they are the same height now, she still looks up to her grandmother.
Have a volunteer read the model aloud and discuss the Rubric in Action with students. Point out the key words and phrases in the student model that correspond to the elements mentioned in the Rubric in Action.

1/2 Ask why it is effective to begin with one of the character's important traits. What are three significant aspects of the character's personality mentioned in the first few sentences?
Possible Response: Readers can get a clear picture of the strength the person conveys. She speaks softly, is a good listener, and is patient.

3 Ask students to discuss the effect of the physical description.
Possible Response: The physical description helps me to visualize the writer's grandmother and her actions.

4 What details show her strength and warmth?
Possible Response: She speaks cheerfully despite her husband's illness; she thinks he needs more care than a nursing home can give.

 Mini Lesson

Viewing and Representing

PICTURING TEXT STRUCTURE
Instruction While vivid description and strong examples are critical to a successful character sketch, the structure—the way in which the ideas are organized—also plays a key role.
Activity Have students analyze the structure of the student model by making a diagram to show how the writer organized her character sketch. The following chart is an example.

Use **Reading and Critical Thinking Transparencies,** TR 37, for additional support.

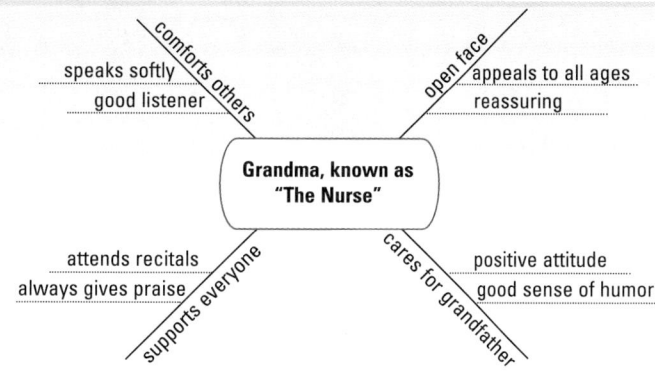

WRITING WORKSHOP **299**

5 Have students imagine this part of the character sketch without the dialogue. How would it be different?

Possible Response: If the writer just described what her grandmother said, instead of using dialogue, this part wouldn't have been as lively. The dialogue adds a bright, spontaneous element to the description. It helps me to imagine her grandmother talking.

6 Ask students to tell why the final details are important.

Possible Response: The final details tell more about the writer's relationship with her grandmother. Most of the character sketch tells about how her grandmother cares for others, especially for her grandfather, but the end shows how her grandmother expresses her love for the writer. It also shows how the writer feels toward her grandmother.

Sometimes, when he doesn't do what she tells him to do, she will good-naturedly say, <u>"Stop, or I'll fetch the fly-swatter!"</u> Then they share a laugh. She shakes all over and throws her head back when she laughs. Her laughter can fill a whole room.

Grandma makes people feel good just by being there for them. In the four years that I have been playing piano, she hasn't missed even one of my recitals. Whenever I've messed up, she says, "I didn't notice. It sounded good to me!" Grandma shows her whole family the same love and patience she shows my grandfather. She supports me so I show her respect. Even though I am as tall as she is now, about 5'3", I still look up to her!

❺ Uses dialogue to bring the character to life

❻ Adds final thoughts to reveal writer's respect and love for her grandmother

Writing Your Character Sketch

❶ Prewriting

A writer should create living people.
—Ernest Hemingway, American writer

Write down the names of people you respect or admire. Consider family members, friends, teachers, neighbors, or others in your community. What makes them interesting? Is it how they look or act? Do they have mysterious pasts or unusual hobbies? Do they have a quirky habit or have they made a great accomplishment in their lives? What about someone who always makes you laugh or whom you know you can trust? See the **Idea Bank** in the margin for more suggestions.

Planning Your Character Sketch

▶ 1. **Choose your character.** Look over your list of interesting people. Which one stands out the most?

▶ 2. **Get to know your character.** Collect details about how the person looks, dresses, talks, and moves. Then list characteristics such as talents, hobbies, likes, and dislikes. Also note how others react to your character. If you don't know your subject, you may want to talk to others who do, or interview the person yourself. Use a chart like the one below to organize your information.

How character looks	What character says	What character does	How others react

▶ 3. **Decide on a focus.** What qualities do you want to focus on? What is your main feeling about the person? What do you want your readers to know about him or her? Before you begin writing, focus on the two or three qualities, or traits, that best describe your subject.

▶ 4. **Choose a setting or situation for your character.** Showing how your subject reacts in a situation can help show his or her personality. Which setting will best show how your character acts around others? Which setting will reveal your character's inner self?

❷ Drafting

Close your eyes for a minute and just think about your character. What do you have to say about him or her? Start writing down your thoughts in any order. You don't have to make it sound perfect. Just get it all down on the page. You can reorganize your writing later.

• **Show rather than tell.** Good writing doesn't just tell readers what's going on. It lets them see for themselves by including vivid details, incidents, and dialogue. For example, the narrator in "The Nurse" shows her grandmother's patience and devotion when she describes how her grandmother spends each day taking care of her grandfather.

IDEABank

1. Your Working Portfolio 📁
Look for ideas in the Writing Options you completed earlier in this unit.
• **Diary Entry,** p. 258
• **A Story Retold,** p. 273
• **Personality Profile,** p. 282

2. Changing Places
Think about people with whom you would like to switch places for a day or two. Choose as your subject the person you would most like to be.

3. Real-Life Characters
Make a list of your favorite characters from the works that you've read. Then think of people in real life who interest you for the same reasons. Choose the person most similar to a favorite character.

Have a question?

See the **Writing Handbook.**
Using Language
Effectively, p. R30
Focus on Character, p. R34

Ask Your Peer Reader

• How do you think I feel about this person?
• How would you describe the person's personality?
• What details help you picture the person?
• Was there anything that confused you about my essay?

Prewriting
Choosing a Subject
If after reading the Idea Bank students have difficulty choosing a subject for their character sketch, suggest that they try the following:

• List three people who you think are especially strong and confident. Write down examples of things they have done that illustrate their strength.

• Think about someone you know who has a job that you would like to do. Think about why their job seems appealing and why they are good at doing it.

Planning the Character Sketch
1. Remind students that the person who stands out most may not necessarily be the one with the most exciting job but the one who, overall, has the most interesting or admirable personality.

2. After students have collected details about the person, suggest that they write a journal entry from that person's point of view.

3. Once students have chosen the two or three qualities that they will focus on, have them list two examples showing each of those traits.

4. Remind students to use dialogue to show how their subject acts in different situations.

Drafting
Suggest that students trade each other's rough drafts with a partner. Have students read each other's drafts and make suggestions for more dialogue, more vivid physical descriptions, clearer examples of character traits, and so on.

Revising
ADDING DIALOGUE

To help students locate places to insert dialogue, suggest that they look for a passage with a description that seems a little dull. Tell them that adding dialogue will help the description come to life and will make the subject of their character sketch appear more real to readers.

 Use **Writing Transparencies,** p. 24, for additional support.

Editing and Proofreading
POSSESSIVE NOUNS AND PRONOUNS

Remind students to be careful not to confuse possessive pronouns with contractions. For example:

The soccer team played *its* last game.

It's a beautiful day for a picnic.

Explain that in the first sentence, *its* is a possessive pronoun, and it does not have an apostrophe. In the second sentence, *It's* is a contraction, which stands for *It is*.

Reflecting

As they write their reflections, encourage students to think about what they learned about their subjects and whether they feel differently about a person as a result of writing a character sketch.

Option
Teaching Tip

Suggest that each student prepare a copy of their character sketch for the person who is the subject of the writing. Encourage students to make the copies especially neat, place each in a folder, and make a date to present it to the person about whom it was written.

Need revising help?

Review the **Rubric,** p. 298

Consider **peer reader** comments

Check **Revision Guidelines,** p. R23

SPELLING
From Writing

As you revise your work, look back at the words you misspelled and determine why you made the errors you did. For additional help, refer to the strategies and generalizations in the **Spelling Handbook** on page R86.

Puzzled by the possessive form?

See the **Grammar Handbook,** Using Nouns and Pronouns, p. R63

Publishing
IDEAS

- Create a photo essay by gathering pictures that show a person's character traits. Write captions for each photo.
- Collect slides and rewrite your sketch as narration for a slide show.

More Online:
Publishing Options
www.mcdougallittell.com

302 UNIT TWO PART 2: HOME AND HERITAGE

- **Remember your focus** A good character sketch gives a picture of a person that is so complete that the readers can predict how she or he would behave in other situations. As you write, ask yourself, Will this help the reader better understand my character?

❸ Revising

TARGET SKILL ▶ ADDING DIALOGUE Reading the exact words that a character says can tell you a lot about his or her personality. As you revise your character sketch, look for places where you can add dialogue. For example, if you are trying to show that the person has a great sense of humor, quote something funny that the person said.

> Sometimes when he doesn't do what she tells him to do, she will good-naturedly ~~tell him to stop.~~ say, "Stop, or I'll fetch the fly swatter!"

❹ Editing and Proofreading

TARGET SKILL ▶ POSSESSIVE NOUNS AND PRONOUNS
Possessive nouns show who or what owns something. For most singular possessive nouns, place the apostrophe before the *s*, as in *one boy's book*. For plural nouns that end in the letter *s*, place the apostrophe after the *s*, as in *all of the girls' pictures*. Possessive pronouns, such as *my, mine, his, her,* and *our,* do not have apostrophes.

> Every morning, after she has had her cup of tea, Grandma makes my grandfather's bed and coaxes him to roll over so she can wash him up.

❺ Reflecting

FOR YOUR WORKING PORTFOLIO If your character sketch is about someone you didn't know, what surprising thing did you learn about the person while doing this assignment? What other people would you like to sketch? Why? Attach your answers to your finished character sketch. Save your character sketch in your **Working Portfolio.**

Assessment Practice Revising & Editing

Read this passage from the first draft of a character sketch. The underlined sections may include the following kinds of errors:

- **incorrect possessive forms**
- **sentence fragments**
- **lack of subject-verb agreement**
- **capitalization errors**

For each underlined section, choose the revision that most improves the writing.

> Often a character I'm reading about reminds me of someone I know. <u>My aunt Bessie reminds me of mama</u> in "Oh Broom, Get to Work." ₍₁₎ <u>Because she is hospitable.</u> Her house is a true home. <u>She always welcome</u> ₍₂₎ ₍₃₎ visitors to her house. Even if my <u>Grandpa Joe and Cousin Sal arrives</u> at ₍₄₎ an inconvenient time <u>she always ask</u> them to sit down and have some ₍₅₎ refreshments. <u>When she invites guests over, she cooks. their favorite</u> ₍₆₎ foods. <u>Aunt Bessies</u> favorite saying is, "Happiness is doubled when you ₍₇₎ share what you have."

1. A. My Aunt Bessie reminds me of Mama
   B. My Aunt Bessie reminds me of mama
   C. My aunt Bessie reminds me of Mama
   D. Correct as is

2. A. She is hospitable.
   B. Bessie is hospitable.
   C. Because Bessie is hospitable.
   D. Correct as is

3. A. She always will welcome
   B. She always welcoming
   C. She always welcomes
   D. Correct as is

4. A. Grandpa Joe and Cousin Sal is arriving
   B. Grandpa Joe and Cousin Sal arrive

C. Grandpa Joe and Cousin Sal are arriving
   D. Correct as is

5. A. she always asked
   B. she always did ask
   C. she always asks
   D. Correct as is

6. A. When she invites guests over, She cooks their favorite foods.
   B. When she invites guests. Over she cooks their favorite foods.
   C. When she invites guests over, she cooks their favorite foods.
   D. Correct as is

7. A. Aunt Bessie's
   B. Aunt Bessies'
   C. Aunt Bessie's'
   D. Correct as is

Need extra help?

See the **Grammar Handbook.**

Quick Reference: Capitalization, p. R58

Writing Complete Sentences, p. R59

Making Subjects and Verbs Agree, p. R60

 Grammar

POSSESSIVE NOUNS AND PRONOUNS

Instruction For use with Editing and Proofreading, p. 302. Possessive nouns and pronouns such as *my, mine, his, her, hers, its, our, ours, their, theirs, your,* and *yours* show ownership or relationship: Please give me Bob's book. This is *our* favorite class.

Some possessive pronouns are easy to confuse with other words that sound the same, though:

Their house is next door. (possessive pronoun)
They're moving next week. (contraction)
The book is over *there.* (adverb)

Practice Have students choose the correct word in parentheses to complete each sentence.

1. Did you bring (<u>your</u>, you're) watch with you?

2. The cat cleaned (it's, <u>its</u>) tail with (it's, <u>its</u>) rough, pink tongue.

3. Your mother is waiting for you over (their, <u>there</u>)

4. I can't believe (your, <u>you're</u>) going to Paris!

5. (<u>They're</u>, Their) feeding my cat while I'm away.

 Use **Grammar Transparencies and Copymasters,** p. 69, for additional support.

 Use McDougal Littell's *Language Network,* Chapters 2–3, for more practice in possessive nouns and pronouns.

Objectives
- reflect on unit themes
- determine a text's main or major ideas
- connect, compare, and contrast ideas, themes, and issues across texts
- review literary analysis skills used in the unit
- assess and build portfolios

Reflecting on the Theme

Option 1

A successful response will
- identify qualities that show growth or maturity in the characters in this unit
- evaluate the growth of four characters
- include productive spoken interaction with a partner

Option 2

A successful response will
- analyze the selections in the unit according to their adaptability to a television format
- develop a proposal presenting the selections in terms of the growth and change of the characters
- paraphrase and summarize text to recall, inform, or organize ideas
- support choices with logical reasoning

Option 3

A successful response will
- relate the chosen selections with the theme of each part of the unit and with the overall unit theme
- give appropriate reasons for opinions given
- present ideas in clear and grammatically correct prose

Self Assessment
Students should demonstrate active assessment of their work on a chosen option. They should be able to connect their own experiences with the possible experiences of others. Extend the activity by having students present their responses orally.

Growth and Change

The selections in this unit are about growth and change in people, in society, and in the natural world. On the basis of your reading, what do you think causes growth and change? How do growth and change make people feel? Explore these questions by completing one or more of the options in each of the following sections.

Reflecting on the Theme

OPTION 1

Evaluating Growth What qualities do you think are signs of growth in a person? Make a list of the qualities shown by characters in this unit, as well as other qualities that you think are signs of growth or maturity. Use the list to evaluate four of the characters. In your opinion, which character grows the most as events unfold? Discuss your choice with a partner.

OPTION 2

Producing a Proposal Pretend that your class is a TV production company. Your job is to produce a series of hour-long shows called "Growth and Change," aimed at viewers your age. With two classmates, decide which selections in the unit would make the best television programs. Write a proposal in which you summarize the selections and give reasons for your choices.

OPTION 3

Relating to the Theme Choose one selection from each part of the unit. Write a paragraph about each selection, telling how it illustrates the theme of the part in which it appears—"The Need to Belong" or "Home and Heritage." Be sure to support your ideas with examples from the selection. Then write another paragraph about each selection, telling how it relates to the unit theme "Growth and Change."

Self ASSESSMENT

📖 READER'S NOTEBOOK

Imagine that another class is about to try the activities at the left. Write a brief note recommending the activity you chose. Explain what completing the activity revealed to you about the theme "Growth and Change." What might the other class want to do differently from the way you did it?

REVIEWING YOUR PERSONAL WORDList

Vocabulary Review the new words you learned in this unit. If necessary, use a dictionary to check the meaning of each word.

Spelling Review your list of spelling words. If you're not sure of the correct spelling, use a dictionary or refer to the **Spelling Handbook** on page R86.

Reviewing Literary Concepts

OPTION 1

Thinking About Point of View Most stories and poems use either a first-person point of view or a third-person point of view. Make a list of the titles of this unit's selections. Next to each title, record the point of view used, as well as the effect produced by that point of view. Then circle titles of selections in which the choice of point of view had a strong effect on you.

OPTION 2

Analyzing Characterization Choose one character from each selection in this unit (except for poems). Then use a chart like the one shown to analyze how each character is developed. Which character do you think you came to know best? Explain your choice.

| What does the character look like? | What are the character's thoughts? |
| What do others think about the character? | How does the author describe the character's personality? |

Building Your Portfolio

- **Writing Options** A few of the Writing Options in this unit were invitations to write poems. From your responses, choose the one in which you feel you expressed yourself the best. Write a note explaining the reasons for your choice. Then attach the note to the poem and place it in your **Presentation Portfolio.**

- **Writing Workshops** In this unit you wrote a poem. You also wrote a character sketch. Reread these two pieces and decide which you think shows a better use of vivid language and sensory details. Write a cover note explaining the reasons for your choice, attach it to the piece, and place it in your **Presentation Portfolio.**

- **Additional Activities** Think back to the assignments you completed for **Activities & Explorations** and **Inquiry & Research.** Keep a record in your portfolio of any assignments that you especially enjoyed, found helpful, or would like to do further work on.

Self ASSESSMENT

📖 READER'S NOTEBOOK

On a sheet of paper, copy the following literary terms introduced in this unit. Next to each term, jot down a brief definition. If you don't understand a term very well, refer to the **Glossary of Literary and Reading Terms** on page R6.

figurative language	characterization
simile	dialogue
metaphor	description
science fiction	point of view
haiku	rhyme
free verse	rhythm
	repetition

Self ASSESSMENT

At this point, you should have several pieces in your portfolio. Consider the different types of writing that are represented. What other types of writing do you want to add to your portfolio?

Setting GOALS

What one problem are you having with reading or writing that you would like to work on? What will you do to improve in this area? Write your answers on a sheet of colored paper. Use it as a reminder while you are working on the next unit.

Reviewing Literary Concepts

Option 1

A successful response will
- list the titles of the unit completely and correctly
- determine and record accurately the point of view of each selection
- make a determination about which points of view had the greatest personal impact

Option 2

Use the Unit Two Resource Book, page 65, to provide students a ready-made, full-depth chart for recording and analyzing characterization.

Building Your Portfolio

Students should evaluate the items in their Working Portfolios and choose pieces that represent their highest quality work for their Presentation Portfolios.

Before students write their notes, remind them that they will be reviewing their notes months from now. They should indicate their reasons clearly so that they will be able to understand them when reviewing them in the future.

Self Assessment and Setting Goals

Point out to students that part of the process of building any kind of portfolio is checking to ensure its breadth and depth of coverage. An assessment activity of this type helps to monitor the variety of materials in the portfolio.

Give the following examples of problems students may be having: visualizing as they read; pausing or rereading to clarify; making active predictions as they read; keeping structures in their writing parallel; using appropriate verb tenses.

For more information on using Portfolios, see *Teacher's Guide to Assessment and Portfolio Use* beginning on page 53.

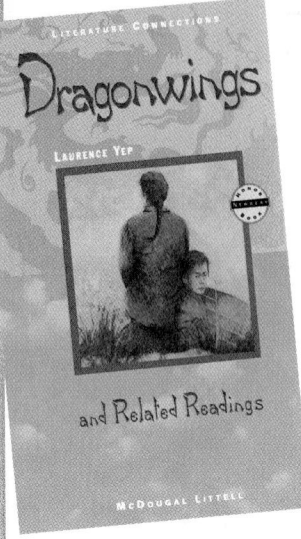

LITERATURE CONNECTIONS
Dragonwings

BY LAURENCE YEP

In this historical novel about the risks of growth and change, a young Chinese immigrant comes to San Francisco to join his father. Father and son encounter prejudice and danger and meet new friends. Along with relatives already settled in Chinatown, they learn how to preserve heritage while pursuing long-held dreams. Laurence Yep draws on historical documents from the early 1900s in this Newbery Honor Book.

These thematically related readings are provided along with *Dragonwings:*

The Flying Machine
BY RAY BRADBURY

Crazy Boys
BY BEVERLY MCLOUGHLAND

The Skydivers
BY JOSEPH COLIN MURPHY

"The Chinese Must Go"
BY BERNARD A. WEISBERGER

Ginger for the Heart
BY PAUL YEE

The Story of an Eyewitness
BY JACK LONDON

And Even *More* . . .

The Circuit: Stories from the Life of a Migrant Child

BY FRANCISCO JIMÉNEZ

The main character, Panchito, struggles to grow up in a world of constant change. The tales are based on Jiménez's own years as a child of migrant farm workers. He uses interviews, photographs, and even old music in his writing process, in order for "readers to hear the child's voice."

Books

Homesick: My Own Story
BY JEAN FRITZ
A memoir of an American child growing up in China

The Tree Is Older than You Are
EDITED BY NAOMI SHIHAB NYE
"A bilingual gathering of poems and stories from Mexico with paintings by Mexican artists"

Going Home
BY NICHOLASA MOHR
An 11-year-old girl visits relatives in Puerto Rico and feels like an outsider.

Roll of Thunder, Hear My Cry

BY MILDRED D. TAYLOR

Set in Mississippi during the Great Depression, Mildred Taylor's novel describes the members of the Logan family and their relationships with the land, their neighbors, and each other. When disturbing actions threaten their close-knit family, the Logans draw together in a fight to keep their 400-acre cotton farm.

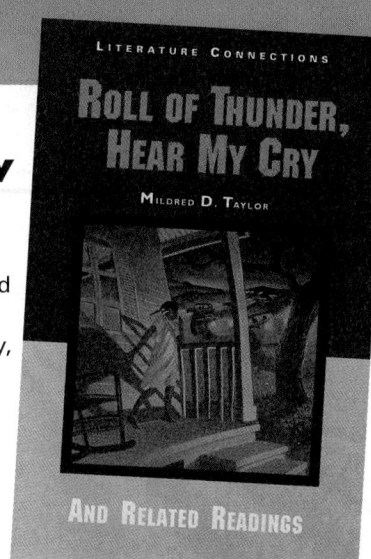

These thematically related readings are provided along with *Roll of Thunder, Hear My Cry:*

from Growing Up in the Great Depression
BY RICHARD WORMSER

Depression
BY ISABEL JOSHLIN GLASER

The Stolen Party
BY LILIANA HEKER
TRANSLATED BY ALBERTO MANGUEL

from Black Women in White America
BY GERDA LERNER

Incident
BY COUNTEE CULLEN

Equal Opportunity
BY JIM WONG-CHU

The Clearing
BY JESSE STUART

The Five-Dollar Dive
BY YVONNE NELSON-PERRY

Missing May
BY CYNTHIA RYLANT
An orphan learns about family.

Spirits of the High Mesa
BY FLOYD MARTINEZ
A boy torn between his grandfather's values and the lure of modern life

On the Way Home
BY LAURA INGALLS WILDER
Wilder's diary describes events along a frontier journey.

Other Media
On the Pulse of Morning: The Inaugural Poem
Maya Angelou reads her poem that delivered hope to a changing nation.
RANDOM HOUSE AUDIO
(AUDIOCASSETTE)

Sarah, Plain and Tall
Patricia MacLachlan's Sarah gives up her home for a new life.
HALLMARK HOME VIDEO
(VIDEOCASSETTE)

American Eyes
Many perspectives on a changing land
CANADIAN BROADCASTING CORPORATION
(VIDEOCASSETTE)

The Oregon Trail II
Fighting sickness and starvation on the historic trail west
THE LEARNING COMPANY
(CD-ROM)

The Reading and Writing for Assessment feature provides practice in taking standardized tests. As students work through this lesson, they will learn strategies for reading comprehension questions, multiple-choice questions, and essay and short-answer questions. Boxed strategies located alongside the text will help guide students through the activities. These strategies model processes students can use as they take standardized tests.

This feature is based on and will help to prepare students for state assessments, including end-of-course assessments.

OBJECTIVES
- understand and apply strategies for reading a test selection
- recognize literary techniques in a test selection
- understand and apply strategies for answering multiple-choice questions about a test selection
- respond to a writing prompt and present ideas in a logical order
- understand and apply strategies for revising and proofreading a test response

Reading&Writing for Assessment

Throughout middle school, you will be tested on your ability to read and understand many different kinds of reading selections. The following pages will give you test-taking strategies. Practice applying these strategies by working through the following models.

PART 1 How to Read the Test Selection

In many tests, you will read a passage and then answer multiple-choice questions. Applying the following basic test-taking strategies can help you focus on the right information.

STRATEGIES FOR READING A TEST SELECTION

▶ **Before you begin reading, skim the questions that follow the passage.** These can help focus your reading.

▶ **Use active reading strategies such as analyzing, predicting, and questioning.** Make notes in the margin only if the test directions allow you to mark on the test itself.

▶ **Think about the title, the message, and the theme.** What does the title suggest about the overall selection? What larger lesson can you draw from the passage?

▶ **Look for main ideas.** These are often stated at the beginning or end of paragraphs. Sometimes they are implied, not stated. After reading each paragraph, ask, What was this passage about?

▶ **Examine the sequence of ideas.** Are the ideas developed in chronological order, order of importance, or in some other way?

▶ **Evaluate literary elements and techniques used by the writer.** How well does the writer use tone (writer's attitude toward the subject), point of view, figurative language, or other elements to create a certain effect or to get the message across?

▶ **Unlock word meanings.** Use context clues and word parts to help you unlock the meaning of unfamiliar words.

---

308   UNIT TWO   GROWTH AND CHANGE

① Why Don't They Roam?

by Patricia Akhimie

1　Have you ever seen a buffalo? Maybe you've seen one in a zoo or on the back of an old nickel. Only a few hundred years ago it was not uncommon for the American plains to turn to ② black seas with the millions of moving heads of the buffalo herds. Now, it is unusual to see many buffalo. What led to the decrease in population?

2　With a thick woolly hide, humped back, and curved horns, the buffalo is hard to mistake for any other animal. However, the North American buffalo is not really a buffalo at all! The true name of the American buffalo is "bison." French explorers called the animals "boeufs" (buhf) because of their resemblance to cattle. English settlers adopted the name "buffalo" from a type of ox found in Asia.

3　The prehistoric ancestors of the modern buffalo came to North America from Asia during the last ice age. At that time there was a land bridge between Asia and what is now Alaska. ③ These buffalo evolved in the new climate and multiplied to number in the millions, roaming in herds over the plains.

4　The herds were hunted by nomadic Native Americans, who revered and honored the animal. Every part of the buffalo was valuable to them. They used buffalo skin, horns, and bones in everyday life. Almost all of the buffalo could be eaten as food, or made into clothes or tools.

5　Native American hunting did not hurt the buffalo population, which numbered in the tens of millions. However, with the arrival of the first Europeans in the 1500s things began to change. Spanish explorers introduced horses. By the 1800s horses were being used by the Native Americans to chase or quickly corner the buffalo. Soon guns replaced the bow and arrow, creating a much deadlier hunter.

6　④ The number of buffalo began to fall as the number of hunters began to rise. White settlers continued to arrive throughout the 1800s. Fur traders and trappers found a

STRATEGIES IN ACTION

① Think about the title.

ONE STUDENT'S THOUGHTS

"I wonder who 'they' are. Maybe they're animals, because people don't usually roam."

② Evaluate the effectiveness of figurative language.

"The writer compares herds of buffalo to black seas. It creates an impression in the reader's mind."

YOUR TURN
Determine the writer's purpose.

③ Look for main ideas.

"It's amazing that there were so many buffalo once. What happened to them?"

YOUR TURN
Find one or two other key ideas in this selection.

④ Read actively by asking questions.

"How were the Native Americans affected when so many buffalo were killed?"

Teaching the Lesson

Begin by previewing the text. Then read through the multiple-choice questions on page 311. As you read each question, ask students what they will need to look for as they read.

1 Students might recognize the title as coming from the old song "Home on the Range," in particular the lyrics, "O, give me a home, where the buffalo roam . . ."

2 Discuss ways in which the buffalo were like a black sea: they seemed to roll like waves and go on forever.

YOUR TURN By using this image, the writer is able to show how immense the buffalo herds were. This helps the reader understand the magnitude of the destruction of this natural resource.

3 To help students understand what the main idea is, read these examples and ask students if they are main ideas or not: A picture of the buffalo used to appear on the nickel (no); the arrival of the Europeans signaled a change in the fate of the buffalo herds (yes); in 1872, President Grant created Yellowstone Park (no).

YOUR TURN At one time, there were millions of buffalo; now there are only a few thousand. Native Americans hunted the buffalo and used every bit of the animal. Legislators and researchers have taken action to increase the number of buffalo.

4 Ask students to formulate other questions such as: Why were the carcasses left to rot? What did the Native Americans use to replace the buffalo as food? What else is being done today to protect buffalo?

5 Remind students that sometimes they will encounter words they do not understand in the text. First they should determine whether the word is important to understanding the selection. If not, they may not need to spend time determining its meaning. However, if it relates to a key event or idea in the selection, they should take a few minutes to apply their reading strategies to decipher it:

• Look at the surrounding words and sentences for context clues, such as examples, restatement, and definitions.

• Use word parts such as prefixes, suffixes, and roots to determine the meaning of the word.

• Try out different meanings for the word in the sentence. If the meaning is still not clear, make a general guess, then read on to see if there are more clues later in the selection.

6 Other words that convey the writer's tone are *revered, shocking, did a lot of damage,* and *"civilized"* (the quotation marks suggest irony).

YOUR TURN The writer talks about the enormous effort that was needed to preserve the buffalo at all.

7 Point out that skimming the questions before they read will help students find the information they need to answer the questions later on.

YOUR TURN The writer mentions Native Americans' hunting as a contrast to the wasteful ways in which white settlers used the buffalo, almost causing its extinction.

Check Your Understanding

Have students use the following questions to test their understanding of the selection before they answer the questions in their texts.

• What is the topic of the selection?
• What is the writer's attitude toward the subject?
• For what purpose did the author probably write the selection?
• Did the selection answer all your questions about the subject? If not, what questions remain unanswered?

good business in selling buffalo meat and hides.

7   Train companies also did a lot of damage. The demand for buffalo products, like fur coats and decorative horns, increased. The railroads promoted shooting buffalo for sport from the windows of the moving train. What is perhaps more shocking is that most of the ⑤ carcasses were simply left behind to rot.

8   By the 1860s buffalo hunting had become popular. The famous "Buffalo Bill" Cody killed over four thousand in two years. The destruction of the buffalo was considered a way to hurt Native Americans who still fought with the settlers. Killing the buffalo would take away their source of food and way of life. The settlers thought this would force the Native Americans to become "civilized."

9   Only a few thousand buffalo remained by 1880, but they were still hunted. In 1872, The United States Congress had created Yellowstone, the world's first national park, to preserve America's scenery and wildlife. However, the herds continued to decline, because poachers sneaked into the park and shot them. In 1894, there were only twenty buffalo in all of Yellowstone!

10   Shocked by the ⑥ tragic drop in numbers, Congress passed a law against hunting in national parks, but the buffalo herd remained small. Through the efforts of some important animal researchers, buffaloes from ranches and zoos were sent to Yellowstone to increase the herds, and to establish other wild herds on protected land.

11   Today there are over two thousand American bison in Yellowstone, with other smaller herds across the country. The buffalo very nearly became extinct in a short period of time. From the loss of so many great animals, we should learn a lesson not to abuse nature's resources.

⑤ **Use context clues to understand vocabulary.**

"It seems like *carcasses* means the dead bodies of the buffalo."

⑥ **Look for examples of tone.**

"Words like *tragic* show the attitude of the writer toward the subject."

YOUR TURN

How else does the writer get her point across?

⑦ **Skim the questions that follow the passage.**

"There was a question about what led to the killing off of the buffalo. The selection mentions hunting by Native Americans and white settlers, as well as damage from railroad expansion."

YOUR TURN

Why does the writer mention Native Americans' hunting if it didn't harm the population?

Use the strategies and notes in the side column to help you answer the questions below and on the following pages.

Based on the selection you have just read, choose the best answer for each of the following questions.

1. Why does the writer include statistics?
   A. because research reports are supposed to include statistics
   B. to support her statement that the buffalo almost became extinct
   C. to show that the land could not support the herds
   D. to convince the reader that she is telling the truth

2. In paragraph 7, why does the writer say that the fact that the carcasses were not eaten is more shocking than the way the buffalo were killed?
   A. She thinks the killing was pointless.
   B. She thinks it was a hazard to the environment.
   C. She does not believe in killing animals of any kind.
   D. She thinks people should have eaten the buffalo.

3. According to the writer, what did a lot of damage to the buffalo population?
   A. the land bridge
   B. famine
   C. disease
   D. train companies

4. What seems to be the writer's attitude toward the buffalo?
   A. She doesn't feel strongly about the buffalo.
   B. She respects the buffalo and wants to protect it.
   C. She thinks it is fair to kill animals for any reason.
   D. She feels the buffalo were a nuisance to begin with.

5. How does the title of the article relate to the article's theme?
   A. It does not relate to the theme.
   B. It refers to the population decrease of the Native Americans on the open plains.
   C. It refers to the settlers who built their houses on the open plains.
   D. It raises the question of what happened to the buffalo.

STRATEGIES FOR ANSWERING MULTIPLE-CHOICE QUESTIONS

▶ **Ask questions** that help you eliminate some of the choices.
▶ **Pay attention** to choices such as "all of the above" or "none of the above." To eliminate them, all you need to find is one answer that doesn't fit.
▶ **Skim your notes.** Details you noticed as you read may provide answers.

STRATEGIES IN ACTION

Skim your notes.
ONE STUDENT'S THOUGHTS
"She doesn't mention disease. I can eliminate choice *C*."

YOUR TURN
What other choices can you eliminate?

Ask questions. *What makes sense in the context of the essay?*
"She might have been talking about Native Americans but the essay's introduction and conclusion are about buffalo, not people. I can eliminate choice *B*."

YOUR TURN
Which other choice doesn't make sense?

Guiding Student Response

Multiple-Choice Questions
1. B
2. A
3. D

YOUR TURN Choice A can be eliminated because the selection says the land bridge was the way the buffalo got to America; Choice B can be eliminated because the author does not mention famine. That leaves Choice D, the correct option.

4. B
5. D

YOUR TURN She might mean the settlers, but the title asks why they *don't* roam. The settlers were people who came from other areas—roamed—to find new land. So option C can be eliminated.

Short-Answer Question

The writer wants to persuade people to respect nature's resources, not abuse them. She does so by using the near-extinction of the buffalo as an example.

YOUR TURN The writer's tone is one clue that she wants to persuade people to respect nature. She is appalled at the way the buffalo was nearly brought to extinction by the carelessness of white settlers.

Essay Question

When tens of millions of buffalo roamed the plains, the Native Americans who lived there were never at a loss for food. They hunted the massive animals, using hide, horns, bones, and meat for food, clothes, tools, and other necessities. Because they killed only as many as they needed, the buffalo herds did not decline. It was this way for thousands of years.

When Europeans reached America, things changed. They also hunted the buffalo for meat, hides, and other products, but in such huge numbers that the herds began to dwindle. This meant that the Native Americans could no longer pursue their own way of life. Buffalo became scarce, and Native Americans had to compete with white hunters. Without their traditional source of food and skins, the Native Americans' way of life changed forever.

YOUR TURN The main points are the decline of the buffalo herd and the reasons for this decline, as well as the fact that without the buffalo, the Native Americans could no longer live the way they had lived for centuries.

PART 3 ## How to Respond in Writing

You may be asked to write answers to questions about a reading passage. **Short-answer questions** often ask you to answer in a sentence or two. **Essay questions** require a fully developed piece of writing.

Short-Answer Question

STRATEGIES FOR RESPONDING TO SHORT-ANSWER QUESTIONS

▶ **Identify key words** in the writing prompt that tell you the ideas to discuss. Make sure you know what each word means.
▶ **Make your response direct** and to the point.
▶ **Support your ideas** using evidence from the selection.
▶ **Use correct grammar.**

> **Sample Question**
>
> Answer the following question in one or two sentences.
>
> Explain what you think the writer's purpose was in researching and reporting on the history of the buffalo.

Essay Question

STRATEGIES FOR ANSWERING ESSAY QUESTIONS

▶ **Look for direction words** in the writing prompt such as *essay, analyze, describe,* or *compare and contrast.*

▶ **List the points** you want to make before beginning to write.

▶ **Write an introduction** that presents your main point.

▶ **Develop your ideas** by using evidence from the selection.

▶ **Write a conclusion** that summarizes your points.

▶ **Check your work for correct grammar.**

> **Sample Prompt**
>
> Write an essay in which you explain how the killing of so many buffalo affected the Native Americans' way of life.

STRATEGIES IN ACTION

Identify Key Words

ONE STUDENT'S THOUGHTS
"The key words are *explain* and *purpose.* This means that I'll have to decide why the writer wrote the article and tell why I think so."

YOUR TURN
What clues to the writer's purpose can you find in the selection?

Look for Direction Words

ONE STUDENT'S THOUGHTS
"The important words are *essay* and *explain.* This means I'll have to create a fully developed piece of writing that explains the connections between things."

YOUR TURN
What are the main points you will need to cover?

Here is a student's first draft in response to the essay prompt at the bottom of page 312. Read and answer the multiple-choice questions that follow.

1	The Native Americans centered their lives around the
2	buffalo. The decline in the buffalo population hurt the
3	Native Americans.
4	Tribes might have had to travel and look elsewhere for
5	food. Because of this, they would not be able easily to
6	defend themselves and their land against them.

1. What is the BEST way to combine the sentences in lines 1–3 ("The Native Americans . . . the Native Americans.")?

   A. Because Native Americans centered their lives around the buffalo, the declining buffalo population hurt them.

   B. Since the Native Americans centered their lives around the buffalo, but the declining population hurt them.

   C. Even though the Native Americans centered their lives around the buffalo, the declining population hurt them.

   D. Make no change.

2. The BEST way to make the connection between paragraphs clear would be to add which of the following words to the beginning of line 4 ("Tribes might have . . .")?

   A. However,

   B. For example,

   C. In conclusion,

   D. Make no change.

3. What is the BEST change, if any, to the sentence in lines 5 and 6 ("Because of this . . . against them.")?

   A. Because of this, the white settlers would not be able easily to defend themselves and their land against the Native Americans.

   B. Because of this, the Native Americans would not be able easily to defend themselves and their land against the white settlers.

   C. Because of this, they would not be able easily to defend themselves and their land against the Native Americans.

   D. Make no change.

STRATEGIES FOR REVISING, EDITING, AND PROOFREADING

▶ **Read the passage carefully.**

▶ **Note the parts that are confusing** or don't make sense. What kinds of errors do they signal?

▶ **Look for errors** in grammar, usage, spelling, and capitalization. Common errors include:
   • run-on sentences
   • sentence fragments
   • lack of subject-verb agreement
   • lack of transition words

Answers
1. A
2. B
3. B

Check Your Understanding
Have students reread their own response to the short-answer and essay questions. Then have them use the following questions to guide them as they revise and edit their own work.

• Have I responded directly to the direction words in the writing prompt?

• Have I presented the points I wanted to make?

• Have I begun with an interesting introduction?

• Have I supported my ideas with evidence from the selection?

• Have I presented my ideas in a logical order?

• Have I written a conclusion that summarizes my points?

• Have I used correct grammar?

ACROSS the CURRICULUM

Space Exploration Game

OVERVIEW

While humans do not have the technology that would be necessary to colonize other planets as in "All Summer in a Day," we have made tremendous advances in space exploration in the second half of the 20th century. From the launching of the first artificial satellite, *Sputnik,* in 1957 by the Soviet Union to the first-ever moon landing in 1969, made by the United States, to the first space shuttle flight in 1981, humans' ability to travel, live, and work in space is ever-increasing.

Research Questions

• What have humans accomplished in space exploration?

• What obstacles must be overcome to explore more of the universe?

Investigation Working in small groups, students will create board or computer games based on a space exploration theme. Each group will plan and execute a rules pamphlet, game board and playing pieces (or the equivalent on the computer). Games should be directed at a particular group or age level.

Wrap-up The project should culminate in a Game Day where families, other students, and community members can examine or play the games. Elimination tournament play might be arranged in which players advance as they win.

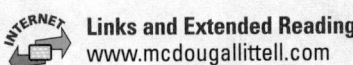

Links and Extended Reading
www.mcdougallittell.com

PREPARING to Read

All Summer in a Day
Short Story by RAY BRADBURY

Connect to Your Life
How do weather and temperature affect you?

Build Background "All Summer in a Day" is set on Venus, the second planet from the sun. Thanks to advances in space exploration technology, we now know far more about Venus than we did in 1954, when Ray Bradbury's story was first published.

Atmosphere on Venus :
96% CO_2 (carbon dioxide)
3% N_2 (nitrogen)
<1% H_2O (water)

SUN
MERCURY

900°F
67 million mi.

Venus orbits the Sun between Earth and Mercury.
EARTH

Cloud layer is composed of droplets of sulphuric acid.

Thick clouds reflect light and hold heat in.

Magellan spacecraft collected data from Venus, 1991–1994

VENUS

Surface has been shaped by volcanic activity.

Hurricane-force winds (up to 230 mph) in upper atmosphere

Focus Your Reading

LITERARY ANALYSIS SCIENCE FICTION Stories that are based on advances in science and technology are called **science fiction.** Many of these stories are set in the future and in imaginary places. As you read this story, look for:

• unusual settings
• effects of science or technology
• messages about the future

WORDS TO KNOW **Vocabulary Preview**
apparatus   resilient   tumultuously
concussion savor

ACTIVE READING EVALUATING To **evaluate** a story is to make a judgment about it. Saying that a story is good or bad is not enough. You need to have reasons for your opinions. When you evaluate a story, ask yourself, Were all parts of the story believable? Did it hold my interest? What did I think about as I finished reading? As you read "All Summer in a Day," record your opinions about the plot, setting, characters, and theme in your READER'S NOTEBOOK. Be sure to support your opinions with reasons.

ALL SUMMER IN A DAY   **209**

OBJECTIVES

❏ write rules for a game with a space exploration theme that fits a targeted audience

❏ research the history of space exploration and represent key events in a time line

❏ create a game board and playing pieces

❏ write and answer math problems about space travel

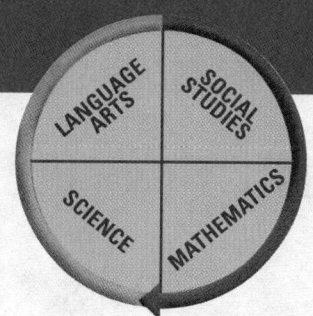

Team Teaching Assignments

CONNECT TO LANGUAGE ARTS Instruct students to develop and write the rules for a game based on the theme of space exploration. Have students examine commercial board (or computer) games and the rules of each for ideas. During brainstorming they should research and collect facts about space exploration (see activities below). They may wish to sketch ideas as they develop a game that is challenging and fun. When group members have agreed on the basic objectives and method of game play, they should write and publish a thorough guide to the rules of the game, keeping in mind the reading level of the group to which their game is targeted. You may also wish to have students complete the interdisciplinary assignments below.

YOU WILL NEED:
- board games or computer games for examination
- laser printer or art materials

CONNECT TO SOCIAL STUDIES The history of rocketry dates back over 1,500 years to the first use of explosives, in China. Later, the Chinese created gunpowder and used it to propel fireworks and weapons. Have students investigate the history of space travel and create a time line of key events. Encourage the groups to draw on this research as they create their games. They may wish to build their game around a time line.

YOU WILL NEED:
- Web access (optional)
- current reference materials on space exploration

CONNECT TO SCIENCE Probes sent to Venus have told us that the surface temperature of the planet is so high that no human could survive on its surface, even with protective equipment. After the groups have decided on the settings and goals of their games, ask them to consider what dangers explorers would face on missions to these settings. Also direct students to research the dangers of space travel in general. What challenges must people who travel and work in space overcome? (Direct students to use "Home on an Icy Planet," the Real World Link on page 588, as one resource.) Encourage students to base the conflicts that players encounter in their games on the real-life problems of space travel. Then have groups create the game boards and playing pieces (or computer graphics) for their games.

YOU WILL NEED:
- Web access (optional)
- current reference materials on space exploration
- art materials or graphics software

CONNECT TO MATHEMATICS Direct students to incorporate math into the scenario of their games. Tell students that the speed that a spacecraft needs to escape earth's gravity is 25,000 miles per hour (or about 7 miles per second). While in real life a spacecraft would not have a constant speed, by finding the distance from the earth to the destination and dividing by the spacecraft's average speed, students can estimate the amount of time the trip would take. Students may also wish to incorporate math problems into their games. They can write problems that players must answer correctly in order to advance in the game.

YOU WILL NEED:
- calculator

Oral Histories on Travel

OVERVIEW

The experience of travel has changed dramatically over the past 150 years. Innovations in production methods, such as Henry Ford's use of the assembly line in automobile factories, made cars affordable to a wider range of people starting in 1914. The invention of the jet engine in the 1930s has enabled us today to fly nonstop across the United States in just a few hours.

Research Questions

- How has travel changed over the last century?

- What transportation did Americans use in earlier times?

- What have been the most important advances in transportation technology in U.S. history so far?

Investigation Working in small groups and under supervision, students will interview some of the older members of their family, the neighborhood, or the community to gather oral histories. Students will formulate questions that will lead interview subjects to talk about their travel experiences and how they have seen transportation change over the years. These histories may be presented to the class on videotape or audiotape, in writing, or orally.

Wrap-up Schedule a day when the class's oral history presentations can be shared with families, other students, and community members. Written histories can also be displayed for a period of time on a bulletin board, and recorded histories can be made available for viewing or listening in the library.

More Online: Research Starter
www.mcdougallittell.com

LaserLinks: Background
Historical Connection

OBJECTIVES

- ❏ formulate interview questions and conduct oral interviews

- ❏ analyze interview data

- ❏ research the history of transportation in the United States

- ❏ graph the types of transportation used by interview subjects

Team Teaching Assignments

CONNECT TO **LANGUAGE ARTS** Instruct each group to work together to create a list of pertinent questions to ask their interviewee. These questions should be designed to encourage the interviewee to compare travel in an earlier time to travel today, not just tell a life story. After the group has a list of questions, members can interview several subjects and decide which candidate will provide the most interesting oral history. Then the group can conduct the final interview, taping it or writing it up for presentation. You may also wish to have students complete the interdisciplinary assignments below.

YOU WILL NEED:
- audio or video recorder and tapes (optional)
- paper and pencil

CONNECT TO **SOCIAL STUDIES** American suburbs experienced rapid growth in the 1950s. One important factor contributing to the rise of the suburbs was increased car ownership, resulting from a strong economy and lower prices. Cars allowed suburbanites to live outside cities in almost rural settings, yet still have access to jobs, shopping, and entertainment in more populous areas. Ask students to consider how changes in transportation technology affect society at large and the daily lives of individuals. Direct groups to analyze the results of their interviews and write a paragraph drawing conclusions about how interview subjects' personal histories fit into the larger picture of changes in American society.

YOU WILL NEED:
- oral histories (from language arts assignment)

CONNECT TO **SCIENCE** Guide students in creating a bulletin board on important advances in transportation technology of the nineteenth and twentieth centuries. Assign each group to research a different invention, such as the steam engine, the gasoline engine, or the jet engine. Students should combine text and pictures to discuss how the type of engine was invented and how it works. Have the bulletin board on display while the groups present their oral histories.

YOU WILL NEED:
- Web access (optional)
- encyclopedias and reference books
- art materials

CONNECT TO **MATHEMATICS** Have each group poll their interviewees (or another class or other group) about all the types of transportation they have used in their lives: car, bus, subway, train, boat, bicycle, plane, etc. Then have the class create a bar graph in which one axis represents the number of people and the other represents the type of transportation used.

YOU WILL NEED:
- chart-size paper
- colored pencils
- ruler

A Sense of Fairness

The selections in Unit Three present characters, both real and fictional, who have had to come to terms with unfair situations. The unit is divided into two parts: Part 1, "Between Friends," and Part 2, "Breaking Barriers." Selections in both parts contribute to the unit theme by presenting the many ways in which people fight to bring a sense of fairness to the world.

Part 1

Between Friends The selections in Part 1 focus on how friendship often helps people move past an argument or quarrel. A good strong friendship can also serve as a buffer to the hardships and unfair situations presented by life. In *Damon and Pythias,* a remarkable friendship sends out ripples felt throughout an entire kingdom.

Part 2

Breaking Barriers Part 2 further develops the theme of fairness in the larger world. How do we overcome the barriers each of us must face? An African prince struggles against the unfairness of slavery in America in "Abd al-Rahman Ibrahima." In "from *The Story of My Life,*" readers meet Helen Keller—blind, deaf, and unable to speak—who went on to become one of the most memorable achievers of her century.

UNIT THREE

A Sense of Fairness

We

must

move

past

indecision

to

action.

Dr. Martin Luther King, Jr.

American civil-rights leader

314

 Mini Lesson Viewing and Representing

Pushball
by Pavel Varfolomeevic Kusnezov

ART APPRECIATION
Instruction Pushball is a game in which two opposing teams attempt to push a heavy ball—6 feet in diameter—across a goal. Explain that the painter has used brush strokes that give the painting a sense of movement. The colors seem to form a halo around the ball, as if to indicate movement. There is also a sense of looseness and movement in the figures of the players themselves.

Ask: Why would a painting showing a competitive game be a good illustration for a unit named "A Sense of Fairness"?

Possible Responses: When you play games, it is important that everyone plays fairly and follows the rules. It might also mean that people need to work together and rely on teamwork to make the world a fairer place.

Pushball, Pavel Kusnetzov, Tretiakov Gallery, Moscow, Russia/Superstock. Copyright © Estate of Pavel Kusnetzov/Licensed by VAGA, New York, NY.

315

To help students explore the connections between the art, the quotation, and the unit theme, have them consider the following questions:

Ask: What do you think Dr. Martin Luther King, Jr. means in this quotation?

Possible Response: He may mean that it's not enough to just say that something is unfair. It's important to do something about it.

Ask: How would you define "A Sense of Fairness"?

Possible Response: Students may say that a sense of fairness is the idea that everybody should have a fair chance and an equal opportunity.

Ask: What do you think the people in the picture are doing, and how does it relate to a sense of fairness?

Possible Response: The people seem to be trying to lift a large, round, heavy object—possibly a symbol for the world. If each person does her or his fair share, the task can be done. Otherwise, it is hopeless. They also seem to be playing a game. In order to have fun, they must agree on the rules for fair play.

Features and Selections	Literary Analysis	Reading and Critical Thinking	Writing Opportunities	
A Sense of Fairness Between Friends				
Learning the Language of Literature Drama	Drama, 317			
The Active Reader Skills and Strategies		Reading Drama, 321		
DRAMA Damon and Pythias Difficulty Level: *Average*	Stage Directions, 322, 324, 328, 330 Review: Theme, 330	Story Mapping, 322, 324, 328, 330 Comparing Texts, 330 Standardized Test Practice, 327	Character Comparison Chart, 331 Scene Setting, 331 Director's Notes, 331	
SHORT STORY Cricket in the Road Difficulty Level: *Average* Literary Link Mean Song	Dialogue, 333, 334, 337 Review: Setting, 337	Predicting, 333, 334, 337 Standardized Test Practice, 338	Dramatic Dialogue, 338 Diary Entry, 338 Forgiveness Report, 338	
Real World Link Peers Talk It Out		Newspaper Article: Summarizing, 341		
POETRY The Quarrel Fable Difficulty Level: *Average* Building Vocabulary Literary Link: Analysis of Baseball	Narrative Poetry, 343, 334, 346	Connecting, 343, 344, 346 Comparing Texts, 346 Informal Assessment, 345	Imagined Conversation, 347 Advice Column, 347	
Communication Workshop: Staging a Scene Assessment Practice		Analyzing a Model Script, 356 Evaluating Your Staging Choices, 359	Staging Your Scene, 358	

Features and Selections	Literary Analysis	Reading and Critical Thinking	Writing Opportunities	
Breaking Barriers				
Learning the Language of Literature Autobiography and Biography	Autobiography and Biography, 362			
The Active Reader Skills and Strategies		Chronological Order, 364		
BIOGRAPHY Abd al-Rahman Ibrahima, *from* Now Is Your Time! Difficulty Level: *Challenging* Literary Link The Wolf and the House Dog	Sources of Information, 365, 366, 370, 374, 378	Chronological Order, 365, 366, 372, 378 Comparing Texts, 378 Standardized Test Practice, 375	Justice Speech, 379 Persuasion Pamphlet, 379 Interview Questions, 379	

LEGEND   DLS – Daily Language SkillBuilder   Green type – Teacher's Edition

Features and Selections	Literary Analysis	Reading and Critical Thinking	Writing Opportunities		
AUTOBIOGRAPHY *from* The Story of My Life **Difficulty Level:** *Challenging*	Sensory Details, 381, 382, 384, 385 Review: Autobiography, 385	Clarifying, 381, 382, 384, 385 Standardized Test Practice, 386	Word List, 386 Different Definitions, 386		
Real World Link High-tech Helping Hands		Magazine Article: Forming and Revising Research Questions, 389			
POETRY Street Corner Flight/Alas en la esquina Words Like Freedom **Difficulty Level:** *Average* **Building Vocabulary**	Speaker, 391, 392, 394, 395 Review: Repetition, 395	Connect to Your Life, 391 Making Inferences, 391, 392, 394, 395 Comparing Texts, 395 Informal Assessment, 394	Interior Monologue, 396 Concept Poem, 396		
AUTHOR STUDY Gary Soto					
SHORT STORY The School Play **Difficulty Level:** *Easy*	Tone, 402, 404, 409,	Monitoring Reading Strategies, 402, 404, 408, 409 Comparing Texts, 409 Standardized Test Practice, 408			
POETRY Ode to My Library **Difficulty Level:** *Easy*	Imagery, 411, 412, 415	Visualizing, 411, 412, 415 Standardized Test Practice, 413			
ESSAY Who Are Your Readers?	Audience, 416				
MEMOIR The Jacket **Difficulty Level:** *Average*	Humor, 418, 420, 424 Activity, 424 Review: Simile, 424	Identifying the Author's Purpose, 418, 420, 424 Standardized Test Practice, 422			
The Author's Style Author Study Project	Analysis of Style, 426	Active Reading, 426	Writing, 426 Personal Ode, 427 Embarrassing Moments Gallery, 427		
Writing Workshop: Problem-Solution Essay **Assessment Practice**		Analyzing a Student Model, 431 Supporting Ideas with Examples, 434	Writing Your Problem-Solution Essay, 433		
Reflect and Assess	Reviewing Literary Concepts, 437	Finding Inspiration, 436	Building Your Portfolio, 437		

LEGEND   DLS – Daily Language SkillBuilder   Green type – Teacher's Edition

To introduce the theme of this unit, use Fine Art Transparencies T25–27 in the Communications Transparencies and Copymasters.

	Unit Resource Book	Assessment	Integrated Technology and Media	Literary Analysis Transparencies
Damon and Pythias *pp. 322–332*	• Summary p. 4 • Active Reading p. 5 • Literary Analysis p. 6 • Words to Know p. 7 • Grammar p. 8 • Spelling p. 9 • Selection Quiz p. 10	• Selection Test, Formal Assessment pp. 49–50 Test Generator	Audio Library LaserLinks, Teacher's SourceBook, p. 30 Research Starter www.mcdougallittell.com	• Drama: Stage Directions T23
Cricket in the Road *pp. 333–339*	• Summary p. 11 • Active Reading p. 12 • Literary Analysis p. 13 • Words to Know p. 14 • Grammar p. 15 • Spelling p. 16 • Selection Quiz p. 17	• Selection Test, Formal Assessment pp. 51–52 Test Generator	Audio Library LaserLinks, Teacher's SourceBook, p. 31	• Dialogue T24
The Quarrel Fable *pp. 343–347*	• Active Reading p. 18 • Literary Analysis p. 19	• Selection Test, Formal Assessment pp. 53–54 Test Generator	Audio Library	• Setting T7

Communication Workshop: Staging a Scene

		Unit Assessment	Unit Technology	
Unit Three Resource Book • Planning and Drafting p. 21 • Practicing and Delivering p. 22 • Peer Response Guide pp. 23–24 • Refining Your Performance p. 25 • Rubric for Evaluation p. 26	**Writing Coach** **Communication Transparencies and Copymasters** T7, T8, T16 **Grammar Transparencies and Copymasters** C121 **Teacher's Guide to Assessment and Portfolio Use**	• Unit Three, Part 1 Test, Formal Assessment pp. 55–56 Test Generator • Unit Three Integrated Test, Integrated Assessment pp. 13–18	ClassZone www.mcdougallittell.com Electronic Teacher Tools	

Reading and Critical Thinking Transparencies	Grammar Transparencies and Copymasters	Vocabulary Transparencies and Copymasters	Writing Transparencies	Communications Transparencies and Copymasters
• Summarizing (Story Map) T13	• Daily Language SkillBuilder T10 • Forming Adjectives from Nouns and Pronouns C89 • Forming Adjectives from Verbs C90	• Using Word Webs C38	• Sensory Words List T16	
• Predicting T7	• Daily Language SkillBuilder T10 • Identifying Adverbs and the Words They Modify C92	• Comparison and Contrast Clues C39	• Dialogue T24	• Impromptu Speaking: Dialogue, Role-Play T13
• Connecting T2	• Daily Language SkillBuilder T11 • Articles and Demonstrative Adjectives C93		• Dialogue T24	• Dramatic Reading T12

STUDENTS ACQUIRING ENGLISH

The **Spanish Study Guide,** pp. 61–72, includes language support for the following pages:
• Family and Community Involvement (per unit)

• Selection Summaries and Vocabulary
• Active Reading
• Literary Analysis

UNIT THREE
RESOURCE MANAGEMENT GUIDE
PART 2

To introduce the theme of this unit, use Fine Art Transparencies T25–27 in the Communications Transparencies and Copymasters.

Additional Support

	Unit Resource Book	Assessment	Integrated Technology and Media	Literary Analysis Transparencies
Abd al-Rahman Ibrahima, *from* **Now Is Your Time!** *pp. 365–380*	• Summary p. 27 • Active Reading p. 28 • Literary Analysis p. 29 • Words to Know p. 30 • Grammar p. 31 • Spelling p. 32 • Selection Quiz p. 33	• Selection Test, Formal Assessment pp. 57–58 ⊙ Test Generator	⌢ Audio Library ◉ LaserLinks, Teacher's SourceBook, p. 32 ⇨ Research Starter www.mcdougallittell.com	• Primary/Secondary Source T14
from **The Story of My Life** *pp. 381–387*	• Summary p. 34 • Active Reading p. 35 • Literary Analysis p. 36 • Words to Know p. 37 • Grammar p. 38 • Spelling p. 39 • Selection Quiz p. 40	• Selection Test, Formal Assessment pp. 59–60 ⊙ Test Generator	⌢ Audio Library	
Street Corner Flight/ Alas en la esquina Words Like Freedom *pp. 391–396*	• Active Reading p. 41 • Literary Analysis p. 42	• Selection Test, Formal Assessment pp. 61–62 ⊙ Test Generator	⌢ Audio Library	• Poetry: Speaker T21
The School Play *pp. 402–410*	• Summary p. 44 • Active Reading p. 45 • Literary Analysis p. 46 • Words to Know p. 47 • Grammar p. 48 • Spelling p. 49 • Selection Quiz p. 50	• Selection Test, Formal Assessment pp. 63–64 ⊙ Test Generator	⌢ Audio Library ◉ LaserLinks, Teacher's SourceBook, p. 34 ◉ NetActivities	• Tone T25
Ode to My Library *pp. 411–415*	• Active Reading p. 51 • Literary Analysis p. 52	• Selection Test, Formal Assessment pp. 65–66 ⊙ Test Generator	⌢ Audio Library ◉ NetActivities	
The Jacket *pp. 418–425*	• Summary p. 53 • Active Reading p. 54 • Literary Analysis p. 55 • Words to Know p. 56 • Grammar p. 57 • Spelling p. 58 • Selection Quiz p. 59	• Selection Test, Formal Assessment pp. 66–67 ⊙ Test Generator	⌢ Audio Library ▭ Video: Literature in Performance, Video Resource Book pp. 19-24 ◉ NetActivities	

Writing Workshop: Problem-Solution Essay

		Unit Assessment	*Unit Technology*	
Unit Three Resource Book • Prewriting p. 60 • Drafting and Elaboration p. 61 • Peer Response Guide pp. 62–63 • Revising, Editing, and Proofreading p. 64 • Student Models pp. 65–67 • Rubric for Evaluation p. 68	◉ **Writing Coach** **Writing Transparencies** T1–4, T6, T33 **Grammar Transparencies and Copymasters** C83 **Teacher's Guide to Assessment and Portfolio Use**	• Unit Three, Part 2 Test, Formal Assessment pp. 69–70 ⊙ Test Generator • Unit Three Integrated Test, Integrated Assessment pp. 13–18	⇨ ClassZone www.mcdougallittell.com ◉ Electronic Teacher Tools	

Reading and Critical Thinking Transparencies	Grammar Transparencies and Copymasters	Vocabulary Transparencies and Copymasters	Writing Transparencies	Communications Transparencies and Copymasters
• Chronological Order T6	• Daily Language SkillBuilder T11 • Using *Less, Fewer, More, Many* C94 • Avoiding Double Comparative and Superlatives C97	• Analyzing Word Parts C40 • Prefixes and Suffixes C41	• Identifying Paragraphs T5	• Dramatic Reading T12 • Impromptu Speaking: Dialogue and Role-Play T13
• Noting Sensory Details T11	• Daily Language SkillBuilder T12 • Correcting Double Negatives C99	• Using a Dictionary C42	• Organizing your Writing T11 • Sensory Words List T16	
• Making Inferences T10	• Daily Language SkillBuilder T12 • Identifying Adjectives and the Words They Modify C91	• Analogies C43	• Figurative Language and Sound Devices T17 • Crediting Sources T55	• Appreciative Listening T2
• Strategies for Reading T1	• Daily Language SkillBuilder T13 • Punctuating a Series of Modifiers C124 • Choosing and Adjective or Adverb C95	• Definition and Restatement Clues C44		
• Visualizing T4 • Cluster Diagram T38	• Daily Language SkillBuilder T13 • Using Proper Adjectives C96		• Combining Sentences Using Conjunctions T19	
• Author's Purpose and Audience T8 • Visualizing T4	• Daily Language SkillBuilder T14 • Identifying Prepositions C100	• Definition and Restatement Clues T45	• Figurative Language and Sound Devices T17	• Giving and Using Feedback to Improve Performance T16

STUDENTS ACQUIRING ENGLISH

The **Spanish Study Guide,** pp. 73–90, includes language support for the following pages:
• Family and Community Involvement (per unit)

• Selection Summaries and Vocabulary
• Active Reading
• Literary Analysis

Selection	SkillBuilder Sentences	Suggested Answers
Damon and Pythias	1. Fan Kissen wrote playes for childrens.	1. Fan Kissen wrote **plays** for **children**.
	2. Mans jumped out of the bushs and tied his foots to a tree.	2. **Men** jumped out of the **bushes** and tied his **feet** to a tree.
Cricket in the Road	1. Selo, Vern, and Amy likes to play cricket.	1. Selo, Vern, and Amy **like** to play cricket.
	2. Selo throw the bat and ball in the bushes.	2. Selo **throws** the bat and ball in the bushes.
The Quarrel	1. I will have quarreled with my brother, but we soon were friends again.	1. I **had** quarreled with my brother, but we soon were friends again.
Fable	2. You be not as small as I be.	2. You **are** not as small as I **am**.

Selection	SkillBuilder Sentences	Suggested Answers
Abd al-Rahman Ibrahima	1. Them were brought as slaves to America. 2. Him and her went back to Africa.	1. **They** were brought as slaves to America. 2. **He** and **she** went back to Africa.
from The Story of My Life	1. Helen Keller couldn't read nothing when Miss Sullivan became her teacher. 2. Miss Sullivan never gave up on nobody.	1. Helen Keller couldn't read **anything** when Miss Sullivan became her teacher. 2. Miss Sullivan never gave up on **anybody**.
Street Corner Flight/Alas en la esquina Words Like Freedom	1. The young frightened child clung tightly to his sister's dirty scarred hand. 2. His mother sobbing and scared fought silently against the cold rushing water.	1. The young, frightened child clung tightly to his sister's dirty, scarred hand. 2. His mother, sobbing and scared, fought silently against the cold, rushing water.

Selection	SkillBuilder Sentences	Suggested Answers
The School Play	**1.** I like most of Gary Soto's stories, because I don't always understand them.	**1.** I like most of Gary Soto's stories, **but** I don't always understand them.
	2. I love to read poetry, or I really enjoy writing my own poems.	**2.** I love to read poetry, **and** I really enjoy writing my own poems.
Ode to My Library	**1.** you think that the author paints a vivid picture of the library?	**1.** **Don't** you think that the author paints a vivid picture of the library?
	2. the author mentions the Incas, he says that they lived two steps from heaven.	**2.** **When** the author mentions the Incas, he says that they lived two steps from heaven.
The Jacket	**1.** Gary Soto had always felt that his ugly jacket has been the cause of his unhappiness.	**1.** Gary Soto had always felt that his ugly jacket **was** the cause of his unhappiness.
	2. Even though he hated the jacket, Soto continues to wear it and even calls it his "brother."	**2.** Even though he hated the jacket, Soto **continued** to wear it and even **called** it his "brother."

Grammar Focus by Unit	Unit One	Unit Two	Unit Three	Unit Four	Unit Five	Unit Six
	The Sentence and Its Parts	Nouns, Pronouns, and Verbs	Modifiers	Phrases	Compound and Complex Sentences	Review

The Language of Literature offers several options for integrating grammar instruction and literature.

- Each unit has a specific grammar focus. The grammar focus for this unit is highlighted on the planning chart. Categories of grammar skills for this unit are shown in red.

- The Pupil's Edition includes instructive features entitled *Grammar in Context*. The instruction in these features arises from the selections and relates to the grammar focus for each unit.

- The Writing Workshops in the Pupil's Edition include grammar tips that help the students produce error-free drafts.

- Mini Lessons in the Teacher's Edition complement the instruction in the *Grammar in Context* features. Additional Mini Lessons relate to the grammar focus for each unit as well as to the literature.

- Daily Language SkillBuilders in the Teacher's Edition provide students with ongoing proofreading practice and reinforce punctuation, spelling, grammar and usage, and capitalization.

- Grammar Copymasters and Transparencies, which may be used independently or in conjunction with the Mini Lessons in the Teacher's Edition, present grammar in a traditional, systematic sequence.

PE instruction shown in black
TE Mini Lessons shown in green

Part 1

ADJECTIVES AND ADVERBS
Forming Adjectives from Nouns and Pronouns
"Damon and Pythias," p. 328

Using Adjectives for Precise Description
"Damon and Pythias," p. 332
Forming Adjectives from Verbs
"Damon and Pythias," p. 332

Using Adverbs for Excitement
"Cricket in the Road," p. 339
Identifying Adverbs and the Words They Modify
"Cricket in the Road," p. 339
Articles and Demonstrative Adjectives
"The Quarrel/Fable," p. 347

PUNCTUATION
Correctly Punctuating Dialogue
Assessment Practice, p. 360

Part 2

VERBS
Verb Tense Errors
Assessment Practice, p. 435

ADJECTIVES AND ADVERBS
Using *Less, Fewer, More, Many*
"Abd Al-Rahman Ibrahima," p. 372

Comparing with Adjectives
"Abd Al-Rahman Ibrahima," p. 380
Avoiding Double Comparatives and Superlatives
"Abd Al-Rahman Ibrahima," p. 380

Avoiding Confusion with Negatives
"The Story of My Life," p. 387
Correcting Double Negatives
"The Story of My Life," p. 387
Identifying Adjectives and the Words They Modify
"Street Corner Flight/Words Like Freedom," p. 396

Choosing Adjective or Adverb
"The School Play," p. 410
Choosing an Adjective or Adverb
"The School Play," p. 410
Using Proper Adjectives
"Ode to My Library," p. 412

Comparing with Adjectives and Adverbs
Writing Workshop, p. 434

PREPOSITIONS, CONJUNCTIONS, INTERJECTIONS
Describing with Prepositional Phrases
"The Jacket," p. 425
Identifying Prepositions
"The Jacket," p. 425

PUNCTUATION
Punctuating a Series of Modifiers
"The School Play," p. 406

OVERVIEW

Students work in small groups to present a persuasive speech on community involvement.

Points at a glance The selections in Unit Three focus on fairness. For this project, each group of students will identify an issue they feel is unfair in their school or community and deliver a speech proposing a way for the community to get involved. The issue could be anything from helping the handicapped (see "High-tech Helping Hands") to solving quarrels among students (see selections in Part 1). Students will research their idea, gather evidence, and write a persuasive speech. Members of each group will share responsibilities for researching the topic, writing the speech, and conducting interviews. Each topic should be well thought out, with a focus on a workable solution. Each student will present part of the speech so that everyone has a chance to speak.

SCHEDULING

Each group should take no more than ten minutes to present its persuasive speech. You may want to schedule the speeches over the course of 2–3 class periods. This project may take place over the course of the unit or at the end of the unit, depending on your scheduling purposes.

PROJECT OBJECTIVES

- To demonstrate the speaking and listening skills introduced in the activity
- To write a persuasive speech communicating the importance of solving a particular issue
- To present a convincing and workable plan
- To conduct in-depth research on their idea
- To effectively combine all parts of the speech into a coherent presentation

SUGGESTED GROUP SIZE

4–5 students per group

Persuasive Speech

1 Getting Started

Explain that students will be working in small groups to write and present a persuasive speech on community involvement. For some ideas on issues, see the Selections Overview for summaries of the stories in this unit.

Gather back copies of the op-ed section of local newspapers that deal with community issues. You might want to videotape a legislative session from a cable television channel so that students can get a flavor of the nature of persuasion. Also make sure students are familiar with the characteristics of a persuasive speech, found in the Communication Handbook, page R104.

You can have students give their speeches in your classroom. There should be chairs available for audience members and, if possible, a lectern from which students can address the audience. A row of chairs for group members should be positioned next to the lectern. You might invite other classes, parents, or teachers to act as judges or audience members. For their convenience, schedule any adults well ahead of time.

Writing Workshop Connection

As a springboard, students may use the Writing Workshop assignment **Problem-Solution Essay,** p. 430, which they will complete in Part 2 of this unit.

2 Directing the Project

Preparing (1 class period) As a class, have students discuss the issues covered in this unit, as well as any other issues in their school or community that they feel are unfair. Discuss the need for community involvement and the different forms it can take.

▶ Divide students into groups of four to five. Tell students that each person will write and present a segment of the speech so that everyone has a chance to speak. You can have students divide the speech into a five-paragraph essay format. For example, one student will write and present the introduction, another student will cover a body paragraph, and so on.

Assigning Roles Roles might include writer, interviewer, researcher, and so on. You might want to choose one student to write and present an introduction and conclusion for the entire class presentation (or you could fill this position yourself).

▶ Meet with groups after they have their ideas. Make sure there are no duplications. Later, help students write and refine the speech, identify visual aids, or just make suggestions about the project as a whole.

▶ Well before the presentation, have students check to make sure that all of their main points are supported with facts and examples. Also review with students the Speaking and Listening Skills listed on the next page.

Practicing (1 class period) You should leave enough time for groups to rehearse. The parts should have a similar feel and tone. Tell students that giving and receiving feedback during the rehearsal stage is crucial. Refer to the tips in the Feedback Center.

▶ Remind students that the point of a persuasive speech is to convince. Therefore, they should appear enthusiastic yet natural. Speakers should use gestures and facial expressions to fit the content. Their tone of voice should be loud enough to be heard but not so loud that they are shouting. If students are using visual aids such as posters, these should be neat and visible to the audience.

Presenting (1–2 class periods) This project could culminate in a presentation for the entire student body or just for your class.

▶ To begin, have students take a few deep breaths and focus on what they want to communicate. If they are using visual aids such as posters, these should be ready and on hand. Students should be seated in order of appearance next to the lectern so that they can quickly take the stage.

Teaching the Speaking and Listening Skills

The student is expected to:

Clarify and support spoken ideas with evidence, elaborations, and examples

Teaching Suggestions: Remind students that they are trying to persuade people who either have no opinion or who disagree with their own opinion. Evidence, including facts and statistics, expert testimony, and details such as sensory details make your ideas clearer and more convincing.

Set a purpose for listening

Teaching Suggestions: Discuss with students the purpose for listening to this speech. They might be listening to understand a different point of view, to learn something new, to solve a problem in their school or community, or to choose the best idea presented.

Eliminate barriers to effective listening

Teaching Suggestions: Tell students that barriers can prevent the listener from receiving the speaker's message. Review these strategies:

- Remove distracting noises.
- Rein in your mind if it starts to wander.
- List questions that occur to you as you listen.

- Keep your eyes on the speaker.
- Be aware of personal bias about the speaker or the message.

Analyze a speaker's persuasive techniques and credibility

Teaching Suggestions: Remind the student audience that an important part of critical listening is recognizing persuasive devices. These often involve faulty reasoning and might include inaccurate generalizations, either/or reasoning, bandwagon, or snob appeal. (These can be found in the Communication Handbook, page R102.) Have students assess the credibility of the speaker. Does the speaker appear knowledgeable about the subject matter? Has he or she done the necessary research? Are the claims and ideas backed up with facts and evidence?

Feedback Center

Students can use the following guidelines when giving and receiving feedback during this project:

Giving Feedback

▶ Ask questions concerning content, delivery, purpose, and point of view (for instance, is tone appropriate to purpose?).

▶ Provide feedback about the coherence and logic of the content, delivery, and overall impact on the listener.

▶ Comment on the verbal and nonverbal delivery (pitch, pace, volume, body language) and its impact on the listener.

▶ Respond to persuasive messages with questions, challenges, or affirmations.

▶ Question evidence to support the speaker's claims and conclusions.

Receiving Feedback

▶ Listen to constructive criticism with an open mind.

▶ Use audience feedback and modify the presentation to clarify meaning or organization.

3 ▶ Assessing the Project

The following rubric can be used for group or individual assessment.

3 Full Accomplishment

The group presented a persuasive speech that included a convincing plan for solving a particular issue. The ideas were well supported with evidence and clearly organized. Students worked effectively in a group and demonstrated all of the Speaking and Listening Skills listed, including effective communication skills, appropriate delivery of information, and logical presentation of the points.

2 Substantial Accomplishment

The group presented a persuasive speech, but it lacked focus or clarity of subject matter. There was some supporting evidence, but the speech lacked coherence. Two to three of the Speaking and Listening Skills were demonstrated.

1 Little Accomplishment

The group's segment was incomplete or did not fulfill the requirements of the assignment. The speech lacked a persuasive tone, the arguments were not supported, and only one of the Speaking and Listening Skills was demonstrated.

Reflecting on the Theme When life seems unfair, there's nothing like having a friend by your side. Friends can stand up for you, help you change what's wrong, or just lend an ear. Friendship can also test your own sense of fairness. Sometimes, if being fair means that things don't go your way, it's hard to be fair to others. In Part One of this unit, friendship offers a chance to learn what fairness really means.

ACTIVITY

Who has helped you learn to cope with unfairness? Make a list of people who have been positive role models in your life. Create a diagram like the one shown to explore your relationship with someone on your list. How has this person been important to you?

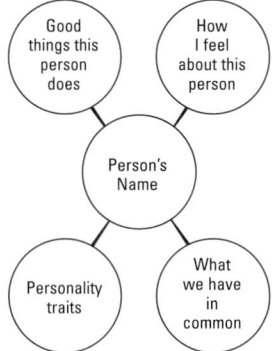

316

LEARNING *the Language of* Literature

Drama

> You need three things in the theatre—the play, the
> actors, and the audience, and each must give something.
> —Kenneth Haigh, writer

The stage is set. The lights begin to dim. As the heavy velvet curtain rises, a hush falls over the audience. One by one the actors take the stage. The drama is about to unfold.

When you go to a movie, watch a program on television, or see a play in a theater, you are experiencing a drama. A **drama** is a story that is meant to be acted out for an audience. It is written in a special form called a **script,** in which **lines** are written out for the characters to speak. All dramas share the elements of s**tage directions, plot, character,** and **dialogue.**

Key Elements of Drama

- stage directions
- plot
- character
- dialogue

317

OVERVIEW

Objectives
- understand and identify the following literary terms:
  - drama
  - stage directions
  - upstage
  - downstage
  - stage right
  - stage left
  - scenery
  - plot
  - conflict
  - climax
  - rising action
  - falling action
  - resolution
  - scenes
  - acts
  - main characters
  - minor characters
  - narrator
  - dialogue
- understand and appreciate drama
- appreciate a writer's craft
- compare communication in different forms such as contrasting a dramatic performance with a print version of the same story.

Teaching the Lesson

This lesson helps students understand and appreciate drama by defining and explaining its key elements.

Introducing the Concepts

Have students think about a play or musical they have seen performed on stage. Ask them to describe how they felt as the curtain rose and the play began. How does this experience compare with the feeling of being in a movie theater? If some of the students have participated in plays, ask them to describe their experiences from a behind-the-scenes perspective.

 Use **Literary Analysis Transparencies,** p. 24, for additional support.

Presenting the Concepts
Stage Directions
With students, discuss what kinds of scenery and props they would need in order to create the proper setting and mood for a dramatization of "Oh Broom, Get to Work," or one of the other selections in Unit 2.

YOUR TURN
Possible Response: The stage directions in this excerpt reveal the numbers mine as an eerie, dark but wondrous place. They also give the actors clues about how their voices should sound in such a place and the kind of movements they should make to reinforce a mood of awe.

Stage Directions

Stage directions are instructions for the actors, the director, and the stage crew. They are usually printed in italics in the script and might be enclosed in parentheses. Stage directions can tell the actors to move **upstage** or **downstage** or whether to enter and exit **stage right** or **stage left.** In addition, stage directions might describe an actor's tone of voice, the scenery, and the props. **Scenery** can include painted screens, backdrops, or other materials that help turn an ordinary stage into a different world. **Props** are objects that actors use during the play, such as books, telephones, or canes.

YOUR TURN How do stage directions in the excerpt to the right help create a mood for the scene?

STAGE DIRECTIONS

Dodecahedron. We're here. This is the numbers mine. *(Lights up a little, revealing Little Men digging and chopping, shoveling and scraping.)* Right this way and watch your step. *(His voice echoes and reverberates. Iridescent and glittery numbers seem to sparkle from everywhere.)*

—Norton Juster and Susan Nanus,
The Phantom Tollbooth

upstage

wings (off-stage)

upstage right — upstage center — upstage left

wings (off-stage)

stage right

center

stage left

downstage right — downstage center — downstage left

audience

Plot

Just as in fiction, **plot** in drama is made up of a series of main events in which a **conflict** develops, reaches a peak (**climax**), and then is resolved (**resolution**). (For more information about plot, see pages 443–445.) Just as a book is divided into chapters, the action in a drama is divided into **scenes**. When the setting or time changes, a new scene begins. Sometimes two or more scenes are grouped into an **act**.

YOUR TURN What conflict is suggested by the lines to the right from *Damon and Pythias?*

PLOT

King (*hard, cruel*). So, Pythias! They tell me you do not approve of the laws I make.

Pythias. I am not alone, Your Majesty, in thinking your laws are cruel. But you rule the people with such an iron hand that they dare not complain.

—Fan Kissen, *Damon and Pythias*

Characters

In a drama, the main characters and minor characters are listed in the cast of characters at the beginning of the script. Brief descriptions of the characters might also be included. **Main characters** are the most important characters in the play. The **minor characters** interact with the main character and help to further the plot. Sometimes there is a **narrator**. The narrator does not usually take part in the action. He or she sets the scene for the drama and might comment on what happens.

YOUR TURN Damon and Pythias are main characters in a play. What qualities do they show in the excerpt at the right?

CHARACTERS

Narrator. When Damon heard that his friend Pythias had been thrown into prison and the severe punishment that was to follow, he was heartbroken. He rushed to the prison and persuaded the guard to let him speak to his friend.

Damon. Oh, Pythias! How terrible to find you here! I wish I could do something to save you!

Pythias. Nothing can save me, Damon, my dear friend. I am prepared to die. But there is one thought that troubles me greatly.

Damon. What is it? I will do anything to help you.

Pythias. I'm worried about what will happen to my mother and my sister when I'm gone.

—Fan Kissen, *Damon and Pythias*

From *Damon and Pythias*

Plot

Remind students that the plot of a play contains the same elements as the plot of a short story or novel. The action in a play, however, is usually divided into acts, which are made up of several scenes each.

YOUR TURN

Possible Response: The conflict in this excerpt is between the king, who has made unjust and cruel laws, and Pythias, who has spoken out against these laws.

Characters

Explain to students that many plays provide a list of the cast of characters. Ask students to discuss why this would be helpful to the audience or the reader. Have them consider how it helps them identify characters and the relationships between them.

YOUR TURN

Possible Response: Damon exhibits compassion and determination. Pythias demonstrates bravery and loyalty.

Dialogue

Divide students into pairs. Have each pair create and write a dialogue between two players who are about to start off on an adventurous jouney. Ask for volunteers to perform their dialogue for the class.

YOUR TURN

Possible Response: This dialogue reveals that since Rhyme and Reason left, things have not been going smoothly. There is a difference of opinion about letting them return. It reveals that Humbug sides with whomever states an opinion and that Milo would like Rhyme and Reason to return while Azaz cannot see their return as a possibility.

Dialogue

Conversation, or **dialogue,** between the characters is what makes up most of a dramatic script. As a reader, you can get to know the characters' thoughts and feelings through the dialogue as the action of the drama takes place.

YOUR TURN What can you tell about the plot or the characters from reading the dialogue to the right?

From
The Phantom Tollbooth

DIALOGUE

Milo. Maybe you should let Rhyme and Reason return.

Azaz. How nice that would be. Even if they were a bother at times, things always went so well when they were here. But I'm afraid it can't be done.

Humbug. Certainly not. Can't be done.

Milo. Why not?

Humbug. *(Now siding with Milo.)* Why not, indeed?

Azaz. Much too difficult.

Humbug. Of course, much too difficult.

Milo. You could, if you really wanted to.

Humbug. By all means, if you really wanted to, you could.

—Norton Juster and Susan Nanus,
The Phantom Tollbooth

320   UNIT THREE   PART 1: BETWEEN FRIENDS

A drama can be as exciting on the page as it is on the stage. To read drama, you must be able to visualize the play as it unfolds. Exciting **characters** and **dialogue,** powerful **themes,** interesting **plots,** and detailed **stage directions** can all come alive as you read. The reading strategies explained here can help you get the most from every play.

*R*eading Drama

How to Apply the Strategies

Read the play silently. Before you read the play aloud with others, read it to yourself. You need to know the entire plot and understand the characters before you perform the play.

Read the stage directions carefully. Stage directions tell you where and when each scene is happening and help you understand the characters and the plot.

Get to know the characters. In a play, a character's words and actions tell you what he or she is like. Read the dialogue carefully.

Keep track of the plot. The plot of a play usually centers on a main conflict that the characters try to resolve. A story map is a chart that can help you keep track of the characters and events in the play.

Story Map for *Damon and Pythias*	
Characters:	Setting:
Conflict:	
Event 1: *Damon challenges the king.*	
Event 2:	
Event 3:	
Climax:	Resolution:

Read the play aloud with others. When you read a part, let yourself become the character. Be ready with your lines and read only the words your character says. Do not read the stage directions aloud.

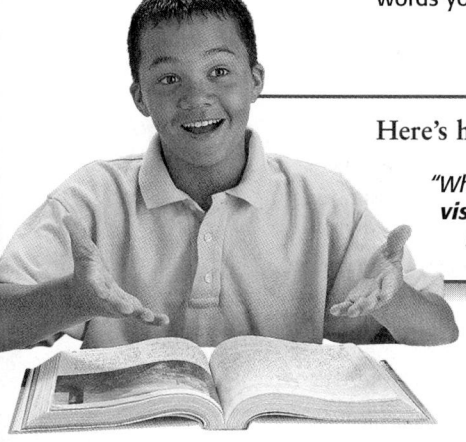

Here's how Ricky uses the strategies:

"When I read a play, I preview the stage directions and ***visualize*** *how a character looks and acts. Sometimes I make a* ***story map*** *to keep track of the plot."*

Need More Help?

Remember that active readers use the essential reading strategies explained on page 4: • **visualize** • **predict** • **clarify** • **question** • **connect** • **evaluate** • **monitor.**

THE ACTIVE READER **321**

OVERVIEW

Objectives
- understand and appreciate drama by analyzing elements of plot, character, setting, and theme
- identify stage directions to visualize the play as it unfolds
- use story mapping to keep track of the plot

Teaching the Lesson

Presenting the Strategies
The strategies on this page will help students interpret drama by focusing on the basic elements of its structure.

1 Read the Play, Including Stage Directions
Explain that in following any kind of directions, it is important to read them in their entirety before proceeding. This helps the reader to form the "big picture."

2 Get to Know the Characters
It is the interpretation of a character's words and actions that makes a play come alive. In order to do a thorough job, actors should get to know the characters they portray. Have small groups brainstorm a list of questions about each character: Who is the character? What does the he/she look like? What does she/he like? Is he/she a "good guy" or "bad guy" in the play—or neither? What makes you say that? Students may then work in small groups to come up with answers that describe each of the characters.

3 Keep Track of the Plot
What has happened? What is going to happen? In figuring out how a character reacts to a particular incident, for example, it's important that the reader keeps straight which events have already taken place and which haven't. A story map can help them to keep these events in order.

As students read *Damon and Pythias,* have them keep track of which events lead to the climax, what the climax is, and what events make up the resolution.

Use **Reading and Critical Thinking Transparencies,** p. 13, for additional support.

OVERVIEW

Objectives
- understand and appreciate a **drama** (Literary Analysis)
- understand author's use of **stage directions** (Literary Analysis)
- use **story mapping** to help understand drama better (**Active Reading**)

Summary
Damon and Pythias are best friends who openly criticize Sicily's evil king. When Pythias criticizes the king to his face, he is thrown in prison and sentenced to death. Pythias's only wish is to see his mother and sister before he dies. Damon offers to take his friend's place in prison so that he may travel to see them. Curious to test the limits of their friendship, the king agrees to this arrangement. Pythias makes the trip home safely but is attacked by robbers on his return journey. He arrives just before the execution and finds Damon—who has believed in Pythias throughout his absence—ready to die in his place. The king is so impressed by their loyalty and friendship that he sets both men free.

Thematic Link
Damon and Pythias demonstrate both a willingness to speak up for justice and a depth of trust. So powerful is this example of true friendship that it has survived in legend and literature to this day.

Editor's Note: With the permission of the author or copyright holder, the following alterations have been made to the text: The announcer has been deleted from the Cast of Characters and the announcer's only speech has been deleted from the beginning of the play.

5-Minute Warm-Up

Daily Language SkillBuilder

Have students **proofread** the display sentences on page 315i and write them correctly. The sentences also appear on Transparency 10 of **Grammar Transparencies and Copymasters.**

Damon and Pythias

Drama by FAN KISSEN

Connect to Your Life
What evidence of ancient Greek culture do you see in your world today?

Build Background Wherever the ancient Greeks traveled, they brought their culture. More than two thousand years ago, in settlements as far apart as Spain, North Africa, and Asia Minor, communities spoke Greek, performed Greek plays, and built temples in the Greek style. The city of Syracuse, where the famous friends Damon and Pythias lived, was one of the most powerful of these colonies.

Long, dry summers made it pleasant to spend time outside. Greeks built vast outdoor theaters and held drama festivals, where playwrights and actors competed for prizes.

Because steep, rocky mountains made land travel difficult, the ancient Greeks became expert sea travelers. They explored in boats such as this *trireme*, powered by about 170 rowers.

Focus Your Reading

LITERARY ANALYSIS **STAGE DIRECTIONS** The script of a play includes **stage directions.** These are instructions to the performers, the director, and the stage crew. Stage directions provide suggestions about music, sound effects, scenery, lighting, mood, and action.

VIDEODISC **LaserLinks: Background for Reading** Reading Connection

ACTIVE READING **STORY-MAPPING** A **story map** shows the most important elements in a story.

READER'S NOTEBOOK As you read, make a story map for the play. Start by writing down the title and author, then complete a chart like the one shown.

Characters: Damon Pythias King
Setting:
Conflict:
Key Events:
1.
2.

LESSON RESOURCES

UNIT THREE RESOURCE BOOK, pp. 4–10

ASSESSMENT
Formal Assessment, pp. 49–50
Teacher's Guide to Assessment and Portfolio Use
Test Generator

SKILLS TRANSPARENCIES AND COPYMASTERS
Literary Analysis
- Drama: Stage Directions TR 23 (for Cooperative Activity, p. 330)

Reading and Critical Thinking
- Summarizing (Story Map), TR 13 (for Thinking Through the Literature, p. 330)

Grammar
- Forming Adjectives from Nouns and Pronouns, CM 89 (for Mini Lesson, p. 328)
- Forming Adjectives from Verbs CM 90 (for Mini Lesson, p. 332)

Vocabulary
- Using Word Webs, CM 38 (for Mini Lesson, p. 324)

Writing
- Sensory Word List, TR 16

INTEGRATED TECHNOLOGY
Audio Library
LaserLinks
- Reading Connection. See **Teacher's SourceBook,** p. 30

Visit our website:
www.mcdougallittell.com

DAMON

AND

PYTHIAS

RETOLD BY FAN KISSEN

Top: Detail of statue of Diadoumenos (440 B.C.), unknown artist. Roman copy of Greek original, pentelic marble, The Metropolitan Museum of Art, Fletcher Fund, 1925 (25.78.56). Copyright © The Metropolitan Museum of Art. Bottom: Detail of Chiron the centaur teaching Achilles to play the lyre (first to third century A.D.), Roman fresco from Pompeii, Museo Archeologico Nazionale, Naples, Italy. Photo copyright © Erich Lessing/Art Resource, New York.

Less Proficient Readers
Set a Purpose Ask students to list characteristics that they think are important in a friend. Then have them read to find out whether Damon and Pythias have those qualities.

Students Acquiring English
Students may have some difficulty with the formal language of this Greek drama. Encourage students to restate dialogue in their own words to check their understanding of the drama.

 Use **Spanish Study Guide,** pp. 64–66 for additional support.

Gifted and Talented Students
Students should be able to recognize the distinguishing characteristics of literary forms such as legends. Have students think as they read about the universal appeal of the legend. Ask them to identify aspects of the legend that relate to an ancient time and place and aspects that relate to people in all times and places.

BLOCK SCHEDULING: MANAGING TIME

If your schedule requires that you cover the lesson objectives in a shorter time, use . . .
- Preparing to Read, p. 322
- Thinking Through the Literature, p. 330
- Grammar in Context, p. 332

If you would like to take advantage of longer class time, use . . .
- TE Teaching Options: Viewing and Representing, p. 326; Multicultural Link, p. 325; Standardized Test Practice, p. 327; Vocabulary Strategy, p. 324; Grammar, p. 328–329
- Choices & Challenges and Author Activity, pp. 331–332

Briefly summarize the events of the story, omitting the conclusion. Have students speculate on what the ending of the story might be, based on what you have told them.

Literary Analysis | STAGE DIRECTIONS |

Point out that the stage directions at the beginning of the story do not refer to sounds that actually occur in the narrative. Ask students why they are there. **Possible Response:** The sound called for in the stage directions is intended to get the listener's attention at the beginning of the play. Point out that the other stage directions in this radio play are used for two reasons—to describe a sound that gives the listener a clue to what is taking place or creates a mood, and to describe the tone of voice in which lines are spoken. Have students analyze each stage direction as they read to determine which of these purposes each one serves.

📖 Use **Unit Three Resource Book,** p. 6 for more practice. Use **Literary Analysis Transparencies,** p. 23, for additional support.

Active Reading | STORY MAPPING |

Point out that the stage directions give clues that will help with story mapping. They tell when each scene ends. Each scene will have at least one key event to be summarized on the story map.

📖 Use **Unit Three Resource Book,** p. 5 for more practice. Use **Reading and Critical Thinking Transparencies,** p. 13, for additional support.

| ACTIVE READING |

A CLARIFY Response: Pythias tells the king that his laws are cruel but that the people are afraid to speak out. The king sends Pythias to prison.

CAST OF CHARACTERS

Damon	Mother
Pythias	Narrator
King	First Voice
Soldier	Second Voice
First Robber	Third Voice
Second Robber	

(Sound: Iron door opens and shuts. Key in lock.)

(Music: Up full and out.)

Narrator. Long, long ago there lived on the island of Sicily[1] two young men named Damon and Pythias.[2] They were known far and wide for the strong friendship each had for the other. Their names have come down to our own times to mean true friendship. You may hear it said of two persons:

First Voice. Those two? Why, they're like Damon and Pythias!

Narrator. The king of that country was a cruel tyrant. He made cruel laws, and he showed no mercy toward anyone who broke his laws. Now, you might very well wonder:

Second Voice. Why didn't the people rebel?

Narrator. Well, the people didn't dare rebel because they feared the king's great and powerful army. No one dared say a word against the king or his laws—except Damon and Pythias. One day a soldier overheard Pythias speaking against a new law the king had proclaimed.

Soldier. Ho, there! Who are you that dares to speak so about our king?

Pythias *(unafraid).* I am called Pythias.

Soldier. Don't you know it is a crime to speak against the king or his laws? You are under arrest! Come and tell this opinion of yours to the king's face!

(Music: A few short bars in and out.)

Narrator. When Pythias was brought before the king, he showed no fear. He stood straight and quiet before the throne.

King *(hard, cruel).* So, Pythias! They tell me you do not approve of the laws I make.

Pythias. I am not alone, Your Majesty, in thinking your laws are cruel. But you rule the

---

1. **Sicily** (sĭs'ə-lē): large island off the southern tip of Italy.
2. **Damon** (dā'mən). . . **Pythias** (pĭth'ē-əs).

Teaching Options

Mini Lesson ## Vocabulary Strategy

USING WORD WEBS
Instruction Students should be able to use multiple reference aids in clarifying meanings and usages of words. Explain to students that one way to explore and understand the meaning of a word is to construct a word web. Show them how by writing the word *mock* in the center of a web formed by several rings linked by lines to the center. Then ask them for different meanings of the word. With the help of a dictionary they might suggest "make fun of" (as in "she mocks her little sister"), "imitation" (as in "mock apple pie"), "a person that is made fun of" (as in "a clown is the mock of everyone"),"insincere" (as in "mock-kindness"). As they suggest these meanings, write each one in one of the separate rings of the web.

Exercise Have students choose two or three other words from the selection and explore their meanings by creating word webs.

📖 Use **Unit Three Resource Book,** p. 7.
Use **Vocabulary Transparencies and Copymasters,** p. 38.

people with such an iron hand that they dare not complain.

King *(angry)*. But you have the daring to complain for them! Have they appointed you their champion?

Pythias. No, Your Majesty. I speak for myself alone. I have no wish to make trouble for anyone. But I am not afraid to tell you that the people are suffering under your rule. They want to have a voice in making the laws for themselves. You do not allow them to speak up for themselves.

King. In other words, you are calling me a tyrant! Well, you shall learn for yourself how a tyrant treats a rebel! Soldier! Throw this man into prison!

ACTIVE READING

CLARIFY Summarize the conversation between Pythias and the king.

Soldier. At once, Your Majesty! Don't try to resist, Pythias!

Pythias. I know better than to try to resist a soldier of the king! And for how long am I to remain in prison, Your Majesty, merely for speaking out for the people?

King *(cruel)*. Not for very long, Pythias. Two weeks from today, at noon, you shall be put to death in the public square as an example to anyone else who may dare to question my laws or acts. Off to prison with him, soldier!

(Music: In briefly and out.)

Narrator. When Damon heard that his friend Pythias had been thrown into prison and the severe punishment that was to follow, he was heartbroken. He rushed to the prison and persuaded the guard to let him speak to his friend.

Damon. Oh, Pythias! How terrible to find you here! I wish I could do something to save you!

Pythias. Nothing can save me, Damon, my dear friend. I am prepared to die. But there is one thought that troubles me greatly.

Damon. What is it? I will do anything to help you.

Pythias. I'm worried about what will happen to my mother and my sister when I'm gone.

Damon. I'll take care of them, Pythias, as if they were my own mother and sister.

Pythias. Thank you, Damon. I have money to leave them. But there are other things I must arrange. If only I could go to see them before I die! But they live two days' journey from here, you know.

Damon. I'll go to the king and beg him to give you your freedom for a few days. You'll give your word to return at the end of that time. Everyone in Sicily knows you for a man who has never broken his word.

Pythias. Do you believe for one moment that the king would let me leave this prison, no matter how good my word may have been all my life?

Damon. I'll tell him that I shall take your place in this prison cell. I'll tell him that if you do not return by the appointed day, he may kill me in your place!

Customizing Instruction

Less Proficient Readers
Ask students to describe Pythias.
Possible Responses: Students may say that Pythias is brave or foolish; idealistic or naive; stubborn or ready to die for a principle.

Students Acquiring English
Explain the following idioms to students:
1 *iron hand:* harsh authority or rule
2 *to have a voice in:* to participate in, to be able to express an opinion about
3 *when I'm gone:* after I'm dead
4 *to break one's word:* to go back on or break a promise

Gifted and Talented
Students are expected to interpret text ideas through means such as discussion. Point out to students that the penalty of death Pythias faces is undeniably harsh. But what about the principle that a ruler can punish those who speak out against his laws? If the king had given Pythias a lesser punishment, would that have been acceptable? Have students debate whether any kind of punishment is justifiable in this situation.

Multicultural Link — Other Legendary Friendships

One of the oldest friendships described in world literature is that of Gilgamesh and Enkidu. The epic that tells this story is Mesopotamian and dates from some time in the third millennium B.C. The Hebrew Bible, at a somewhat later date, describes David and Jonathan as the best of friends. In one notable incident, Jonathan protects David against Jonathan's father, Saul, when Saul wants to kill David.

Another legend from Greek times is the friendship of Orestes and Pylades. When they have been captured by an evil king, one is to be killed and the other spared if he will take letters back to his homeland. Each insists that the other be the one to carry the letters. Eventually they both win their freedom.

The medieval legend of Amis and Amiloun is told in a French epic poem. At one point in the epic, Amiloun learns from an angel that Amis can be cured of leprosy if Amiloun will sacrifice his own children. Relying on his faith in God, Amiloun slays his children and cures Amis. His children then miraculously come back to life.

Reading and Analyzing

ACTIVE READING

A **EVALUATE** Response: It sets up the situation where Pythias must return on time or his friend will be killed in his place.

Reading Skills and Strategies:
PREDICT

B Point out to students that the king has set a date for Pythias's return. Ask them how they think that might become important in the story.
Possible Response: Pythias's failure to return before the set time will test Damon's trust in his friend.

Literary Analysis: NARRATOR

C Ask students why the writer used a narrator to tell these events rather than have actors act them out.
Possible Response: It would take a lot of time to convey the long discussion between Damon and Pythias and the information about Pythias's long journey. The lines by the narrator allow the writer to keep the story moving at a rapid pace.

Literary Analysis: DIALOGUE

D Ask students to explain why the writer uses lines of dialogue among voices to evaluate Pythias's decision.
Possible Response: The dialogue of the different voices of the townspeople makes the ideas more lively and interesting.

Detail of procession of the court of Emperor Augustus (about 13–9 B.C.), unknown Roman artist. Museum of the Ara Pacis, Rome, Nimatallah/Art Resource, New York.

Pythias. No, no, Damon! You must not do such a foolish thing! I cannot—I will not—let you do this! Damon! Damon! Don't go! (*to himself*) Damon, my friend! You may find yourself in a cell beside me!

(*Music: In briefly and out.*)

Damon (*begging*). Your Majesty! I beg of you! Let Pythias go home for a few days to bid farewell to his mother and sister. He gives his word that he will return at your appointed time. Everyone knows that his word can be trusted.

King. In ordinary business affairs—perhaps. But he is now a man under sentence of death. To free him even for a few days would strain his honesty—any man's honesty—too far. Pythias would never return here! I consider him a traitor, but I'm certain he's no fool.

Damon. Your Majesty! I will take his place in the prison until he comes back. If he does not return, then you may take my life in his place.

King (*astonished*). What did you say, Damon?

Damon. I'm so certain of Pythias that I am offering to die in his place if he fails to return on time.

King. I can't believe you mean it!

ACTIVE READING

EVALUATE How does this scene help move the plot along?

Damon. I do mean it, Your Majesty.

King. You make me very curious, Damon, so curious that I'm willing to put you and Pythias to the test. This exchange of prisoners will be made. But Pythias must be back two weeks from today, at noon.

Teaching Options

Mini Lesson — Viewing and Representing

Procession of the Court of Emperor Augustus (detail)

ART APPRECIATION Tell students that the illustration shows part of the Ara Pacis, or Altar of Peace, built to honor the Roman emperor Augustus around 13–9 B.C. In fact, the Ara Pacis was part of Augustus's propaganda program. The emperor wanted people to honor him for the peace he'd brought to the empire.
Application Ask students what they think the role of this crowd is. How can they relate this picture to the crowd scenes in "Damon and Pythias"?

Possible Response: The people are probably all coming to praise and honor Emperor Augustus. The king in "Damon and Pythias" clearly wants his people to praise and honor him, too, which they do. But they may also say less flattering things behind his back. The people in the illustration from the Ara Pacis look as if they could be saying unflattering things about the emperor among themselves.

Students Acquiring English
Explain the meaning of the following idioms:

1 *to go by someone's hand:* to be delivered by someone in person

2 *to show no mercy:* to treat in a cruel manner

3 *death sentence:* the decision by a judge or other authority that a person must die; also, the actual carrying out of such a sentence

Less Proficient Readers
Students should be able to draw inferences about the text. Clarify the issues of the story by asking students why Pythias "did not like the king's bargain with Damon," and have them make an inference as to why he decides to go to see his family despite his reluctance.
Possible Response: Pythias loves Damon and does not want him to risk his life. However, he also loves his family and wants very much to visit them. He probably decided that although it was a risk to Damon, the king was basically forcing Damon to take that risk. Thus it would make little difference if Pythias took advantage of Damon's offer to travel to see his family.

Multiple Learning Styles
Interpersonal Learners
Have small groups of students write dialogue for additional characters to extend the discussion about Pythias' trustworthiness. Ask students to consider whether Pythias will return. Have the groups read this section aloud, adding the dialogue they've created.

Damon. Thank you, Your Majesty!

King. The order with my official seal[3] shall go by your own hand, Damon. But I warn you, if your friend does not return on time, you shall surely die in his place! I shall show no mercy!

(Music: In briefly and out.)

Narrator. Pythias did not like the king's bargain with Damon. He did not like to leave his friend in prison with the chance that he might lose his life if something went wrong. But at last Damon persuaded him to leave, and Pythias set out for his home. More than a week went by. The day set for the death sentence drew near. Pythias did not return. Everyone in the city knew of the condition on which the king had permitted Pythias to go home. Everywhere people met, the talk was sure to turn to the two friends.

First Voice. Do you suppose Pythias will come back?

Second Voice. Why should he stick his head under the king's axe once he's escaped?

Third Voice. Still, would an honorable man like Pythias let such a good friend die for him?

First Voice. There's no telling what a man will do when it's a question of his own life against another's.

Second Voice. But if Pythias doesn't come back before the time is up, he will be killing his friend.

Third Voice. Well, there's still a few days' time. I, for one, am certain that Pythias will return in time.

---

3. **official seal:** mark or stamp that shows that the order came from the king.

✓ **Assessment** **Standardized Test Practice**

IDENTIFYING THE BEST SUMMARY Some standardized tests require students to choose the best summary of a passage from several options. Offer students practice in this skill by writing the following question and possible answers on the board: Which of the following statements best summarizes the king's bargain with Damon?
A. Pythias and Damon will both go free if Pythias returns from his visit to his family.
B. Pythias's death will be postponed two weeks.
C. Pythias will try to get Damon to die in his place while Pythias visits his mother.

D. Pythias can visit his family temporarily if Damon guarantees his return with his own life.
Lead students through the process of identifying the best summary. A is incorrect because the king never promises to free Pythias. B is incorrect because the king says from the start that Pythias will die in two weeks' time. C is incorrect because Pythias does not want his friend Damon to die. D is the best summary of the king's bargain.

Remind students to be alert to the introduction of minor characters such as the mother and the robbers. These characters should all be included on the list of characters in the story map.

Literary Analysis: SUSPENSE

Tell students that a common way to create suspense is to use an event that slows down the action. This kind of dramatic device provides an obstacle and often brings on a crisis. The robbers serve such a function in the legend of Damon and Pythias. Ask students what the action of the legend would be like without the robbers.

Possible Response: Without the robbers, Pythias would have returned to the city a day early. There would have been no dramatic delay in which Damon's faith in his friend was tested to the utmost; and probably the king would not have been as impressed by Damon's loyalty as he was.

ACTIVE READING

A **QUESTION** Because Pythias is tied up, he can't get back to save Damon.

Literary Analysis STAGE DIRECTIONS

B Point out that it is a common technique in radio plays to make a character's voice fade out to indicate passing time or a break in the action. Ask what the stage direction "fade" is intended to show in this scene.

Possible Response: It shows that Pythias's protests continued for longer than the time we have heard them.

Second Voice. And I am just as certain that he will not. Friendship is friendship, but a man's own life is something stronger, I say!

Narrator. Two days before the time was up, the king himself visited Damon in his prison cell.

(Sound: Iron door unlocked and opened.)

King *(mocking).* You see now, Damon, that you were a fool to make this bargain. Your friend has tricked you! He will not come back here to be killed! He has deserted you!

Damon *(calm and firm).* I have faith in my friend. I know he will return.

King *(mocking).* We shall see!

(Sound: Iron door shut and locked.)

Narrator. Meanwhile, when Pythias reached the home of his family, he arranged his business affairs so that his mother and sister would be able to live comfortably for the rest of their years. Then he said a last farewell to them before starting back to the city.

Mother *(in tears).* Pythias, it will take you only two days to get back. Stay another day, I beg you!

Pythias. I dare not stay longer, Mother. Remember, Damon is locked up in my prison cell while I'm gone. Please don't make it harder for me! Farewell! Don't weep for me. My death may help to bring better days for all our people.

Narrator. So Pythias began his return journey in plenty of time. But bad luck struck him on the very first day. At twilight, as he walked along a lonely stretch of woodland, a rough voice called:

First Robber. Not so fast there, young man! Stop!

Pythias *(startled).* Oh! What is it? What do you want?

Second Robber. Your money bags.

Pythias. My money bags? I have only this small bag of coins. I shall need them for some last favors, perhaps, before I die.

First Robber. What do you mean, before you die? We don't mean to kill you, only to take your money.

Pythias. I'll give you my money, only don't delay me any longer. I am to die by the king's order three days from now. If I don't return to prison on time, my friend must die in my place.

First Robber. A likely story! What man would be fool enough to go back to prison ready to die?

Second Robber. And what man would be fool enough to die for you?

First Robber. We'll take your money, all right. And we'll tie you up while we get away.

ACTIVE READING

QUESTION Why is the robbery such a serious problem?

Pythias *(begging).* No! No! I must get back to free my friend! *(fade)* I must go back!

Narrator. But the two robbers took Pythias' money, tied him to a tree, and went off as fast as they could. Pythias struggled to free himself. He cried out for help as loud as he could for a long time. But no one traveled through that lonesome woodland after dark. The sun had been up for many hours before he finally managed to

---

Teaching Options

 Grammar

FORMING ADJECTIVES FROM NOUNS AND PRONOUNS

Instruction Explain to students that anything that modifies a noun is an adjective. A noun or a pronoun can be used in this way. For example, in the sentence "Pythias returned on *execution* day," the noun *execution* modifies the noun *day.*

The possessive form of a noun is also a kind of adjective, because it modifies another noun. In the sentence, "Pythias disliked the *king's* rule," the word *king's* is a possessive noun used as an adjective.

Pronouns are used as adjectives even more frequently than regular nouns. The possessive pronouns *my, your, his, hers, its, our,* and *their* all function as adjectives. Notice that sometimes a possesive pronoun is modified by the adjective *own* to make it more precise. Examples are:

Their names have come down to *our* own time.
I am not alone *Your* Majesty in thinking *your* laws are cruel.
That king is certainly cruel.
Any king could be kinder than he was.

free himself from the ropes that had tied him to the tree. He lay on the ground, hardly able to breathe.

(Music: In briefly and out.)

Narrator. After a while Pythias got to his feet. Weak and dizzy from hunger and thirst and his struggle to free himself, he set off again. Day and night he traveled without stopping, desperately trying to reach the city in time to save Damon's life.

(Music: Up and out.)

Narrator. On the last day, half an hour before noon, Damon's hands were tied behind his back, and he was taken into the public square. The people muttered angrily as Damon was led in by the jailer. Then the king entered and seated himself on a high platform.

(Sound: Crowd voices in and hold under single voices.)

Soldier *(loud)*. Long live the king!

First Voice *(low)*. The longer he lives, the more miserable our lives will be!

King *(loud, mocking)*. Well, Damon, your lifetime is nearly up. Where is your good friend Pythias now?

Damon *(firm)*. I have faith in my friend. If he has not returned, I'm certain it is through no fault of his own.

King *(mocking)*. The sun is almost overhead. The shadow is almost at the noon mark. And still your friend has not returned to give you back your life!

Damon *(quiet)*. I am ready, and happy, to die in his place.

King *(harsh)*. And you shall, Damon! Jailer, lead the prisoner to the—

(Sound: Crowd voices up to a roar, then under.)

First Voice *(over noise)*. Look! It's Pythias!

Second Voice *(over noise)*. Pythias has come back!

Pythias *(breathless)*. Let me through! Damon!

Damon. Pythias!

Pythias. Thank the gods I'm not too late!

Damon *(quiet, sincere)*. I would have died for you gladly, my friend.

Crowd Voices *(loud, demanding)*. Set them free! Set them both free!

King *(loud)*. People of the city! *(crowd voices out)* Never in all my life have I seen such faith and friendship, such loyalty between men. There are many among you who call me harsh and cruel. But I cannot kill any man who proves such strong and true friendship for another. Damon and Pythias, I set you both free. *(roar of approval from crowd)* I am king. I command a great army. I have stores of gold and precious jewels. But I would give all my money and my power for one friend like Damon or Pythias!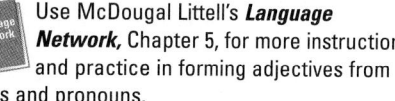

(Sound: Roar of approval from crowd up briefly and out.)

(Music: Up and out.) ❖

DAMON AND PYTHIAS **329**

DAMON AND PYTHIAS **329**

GUIDING STUDENT RESPONSE

Connect to the Literature

1. What Do You Think?
Possible Response: I felt relieved during the king's speech, though I had guessed that both Damon and Pythias would be safe in the end.

Comprehension Check
• He is arrested because he speaks out against one of the king's laws.
• Damon agrees to stay in prison while Pythias visits his family. If Pythias does not return, Damon will be killed in his place.
• Even the ordinarily merciless king cannot kill two people who have such a strong friendship that they are willing to die for one another.

 Use Selection Quiz
Unit Three Resource Book, p. 10.

Think Critically

2. Possible Response: They trust each other completely and keep their promises. Damon gives up his freedom for his friend. Pythias leaves his family early to make sure he gets to the city on time.

3. Possible Response: It is a generous thing to do but it is also foolish, because something could happen to Pythias (as it almost does). They both could have died. But if you loved a friend that much I would be willing to take that risk.

4. Possible Response: Damon is a greater hero, because he volunteers to trade places with Pythias; Pythias is a greater hero, because he speaks up against the king and keeps his promise; both are equally heroic.

5. Possible Response: This story shows the values of friendship, honor, and trust; the king discovers that friendship is more important than wealth or power.

6. Responses should include that the turning point, or climax, comes when Pythias returns.

 Use **Reading and Critical Thinking Transparencies,** p. 13, for additional support.

Connect to the Literature

1. What Do You Think?
What effect did the final scene have on you?

Comprehension Check
• Why is Pythias arrested?
• What bargain does the king strike with Damon?
• Why does the king free Damon and Pythias?

Think Critically

2. How would you describe the friendship between Damon and Pythias? Use examples from the play to support your answer.

3. Think about Damon's offer. Do you think taking Pythias's place is a wise and generous thing to do? What would you do if you were in Damon's position?

4. Who do you think is more of a hero—Damon or Pythias? Why?

5. What values do you think this story shows and supports?

 THINK ABOUT
• Damon's bargain with the king
• Pythias's words as he leaves his mother
• the king's speech at the end of the play

6. **ACTIVE READING** **STORY-MAPPING** Look at the story map you made in your **READER'S NOTEBOOK.** What would you say is the turning point of the story? Compare your story map with that of a classmate.

Extend Interpretations

7. **COMPARING TEXTS** Think back to how Nadia sought to keep her brother's memory alive in "Nadia the Willful" (page 67). How is her effort similar to Damon's effort to help Pythias? How would you compare the way these two characters face authority figures?

8. **Connect to Life** Imagine Damon and Pythias in our society today. What issues might they stand up for?

Literary Analysis

STAGE DIRECTIONS In the script of a play, instructions to the performers, the director, and the stage crew are called **stage directions.** Stage directions provide information about when and where the play takes place and give clues about characters and plot. Stage directions can help you **visualize** the play.

Cooperative Learning Activity
In a small group, go back through the play and read the stage directions. Discuss what you learned from these directions. What did they tell you about the characters? What did they tell you about the plot events? Did they help you visualize the setting? Then, make a three-column chart like the one shown.

Directions about characters	Directions about plot events	Directions about setting
Damon: "calm and firm"		

REVIEW **THEME** The **theme** of a literary work is a message about life or human nature that a writer wishes to share. Think about what theme this line might suggest: "I would give all my money and my power for one friend like Damon or Pythias!"

Literary Analysis

Stage Directions Responses will vary but should indicate awareness of how the stage directions contribute to the reader's knowledge of the characters and the changes in setting and time.

Use **Literary Analysis Transparencies,** p. 23, for additional support.

Extend Interpretations

7. Comparing Texts Nadia had a strong bond with her brother, and Damon and Pythias were as close as brothers. Both characters were willing to stand up to authority when they felt authority figures were acting unfairly.

8. Connect to Life Possible Response: Damon and Pythias would stand up for free speech and political participation. They might lead voter registration drives, uncover conspiracies, or seek to free political prisoners.

Writing Options

1. Character Comparison Chart
Make a two-column chart. In one column, list Damon's characteristics. In the other, list those of Pythias. What do the two characters have in common? How are they different?

2. Scene Setting Write a short essay describing the setting of the play. Refer to stage directions for details that will help you imagine the different scenes.

Writing Handbook
See p. R31: Descriptive Writing.

3. Director's Notes Jot down notes about what you imagine the characters are wearing, how they might speak, and how they behave. Put the notes in your **Working Portfolio.**

Activities & Explorations

1. Movie Poster Create a movie poster advertising a film version of *Damon and Pythias.* Include the names of the actors you would like to see in the movie, and make up quotes from reviewers. Hang your poster on a bulletin board. ~ **VIEWING AND REPRESENTING**

2. Dramatic Production If you were going to design a stage production of *Damon and Pythias,* how would you want the costumes to look? Use your impressions of the characters to sketch their costumes. ~ **ART**

Inquiry & Research

SOCIAL STUDIES **GREEK DRAMA**
Create a diorama of a scene in an ancient Greek theater. Refer to an encyclopedia or to books about ancient Greece for information on amphitheaters. Some theaters, like that of Epidavros, are still in use today. Use an empty box to create a stage against a painted background, or construct a more complex model of an amphitheater. Include masked figures to represent the actors.

Art Connection

During the fifth century B.C., Greek sculptors began creating figures with lifelike poses and expressions. Look at the statue below. What details seem realistic? How would you describe the expression on the face?

Writing Options

1. Character Comparison Chart
Responses may mention Damon's somewhat stubborn determination to help his friend and Pythias's intense concern for others, even at the risk of his own welfare. To get students started on this activity, set up a model chart on the blackboard and fill in some of the characteristics of Damon and Pythias, as volunteered by students.

2. Scene Setting Since the stage directions in this radio play give very little indication of setting, suggest that students read the narrator's speeches for indications as to how they might imagine the different scenes.

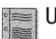 Use **Writing Transparencies,** p. 16, for additional support.

3. Director's Notes Point out that the stage directions do give some help as to how the characters speak. To get students started on this activity, have them close their eyes and use their imaginations to visualize the characters while you read a passage aloud.

Activities & Explorations

1. Movie Poster Student work should reflect appropriate casting based on the events and characters in the radio play. To get students started on this activity, have them suggest actors who might play the cruel king.

2. Dramatic Production Students can use the Director's Notes they wrote in the Writing Options activity as a starting point for their sketches.

Inquiry & Research

Greek Drama Take into account limitations of skill, time, and material in evaluating student response. Dioramas should, however, accurately reflect information from research sources. Be sure students understand that the selection is not a Greek drama but a modern radio play. **To make this activity more challenging,** have students create a puppet theater based on the design of ancient Greek theaters and act out the drama of Damon and Pythias with puppets.

Art Connection

Student responses will vary but may include the idea that the smooth soft curves of the face and the glance of the eyes look realistic and that the expression looks sad or thoughtful.

Grammar in Context

WRITING EXERCISE Answers will vary. Possible answers are shown.

1. The King of Sicily was an evil man who made unfair laws.
2. As Pythias walked the endless trail, he heard a booming voice.
3. Pythias set off on his most grueling day of travel.
4. Damon was ecstatic that his friend returned at the opportune hour.
5. There were never such devoted friends as these.

CONNECT TO THE LITERATURE Answers will vary. Possible response: angry, cruel.

Fan Kissen

Fan Kissen was an elementary school teacher in New York before she began writing radio scripts. However, after she started working on station WNYE, run by the board of education, her writing began to fill more of her time. During her long scripting career she won seven first place prizes for her educational radio plays. Some of her many volumes of collected scripts appeared as supplementary readers published by Houghton Mifflin between 1949 and 1961.

Grammar in Context: Using Adjectives for Precise Description

In the opening line of *Damon and Pythias,* the narrator tells us that

> …there lived on the island of Sicily two
> young men named Damon and Pythias.

The words shown in red above are **adjectives.** Adjectives are words used to describe a noun or pronoun. They tell **how many, what kind,** or **which one** about the word they modify. The adjective *two,* for example, tells how many young men there are. The adjective *young* tells what kind of men they are. In the following examples, the adjectives tell you which one the writer is talking about:

> So Pythias began his return journey. . . .
> On the last day, half an hour before noon, . . .

Apply to Your Writing Choose precise adjectives that give necessary information. They should help paint a clear picture of your description.

WRITING EXERCISE Find the adjectives in each sentence. Replace each one with a more specific word that tells what kind, how many, or which one.

Example: *Original* Pythias was a good man who fought the king's large army.

Rewritten Pythias was a brave man who fought the king's well-trained army.

1. The King of Sicily was a bad man who made bad laws.
2. As Pythias walked the long trail, he heard a loud voice.
3. Pythias set off on his worst day of travel.
4. Damon was happy that his friend returned at the perfect hour.
5. There were never such good friends as these.

Grammar Handbook Using Modifiers Effectively, p. R70

Connect to the Literature Reread one page of the play, paying attention to the stage directions. List the adjectives you find in stage directions only.

Fan Kissen
born 1904

Legendary Literature Fanny "Fan" Kissen was born in New York City and spent most of her career there. A former elementary school teacher, she became a successful radio scriptwriter. For 17 years she had her own award-winning radio series, *Tales from the Four Winds.* In this popular show she dramatized world folk tales and legends. Her plays, which are written as radio scripts, always include instructions for music and sound effects.

Travels and Tales Kissen visited the lands in which many of her stories take place. Her travels took her throughout Europe, South America, and the Near East. Most of her books are collections of plays written as radio scripts, including *The Straw Ox and Other Plays* and *The Bag of Fire and Other Plays.* In addition to writing radio plays, Kissen wrote several biographies of little-known historical figures for young people.

Teaching Options

FORMING ADJECTIVES FROM VERBS

Instruction Students should understand how they can form adjectives from verbs by creating participles. The simplest way to do this is to add *-ing* to the verb to form the present participle. For example, by adding *-ing* to *mutter,* we can create the adjective *muttering,* as in the phrase "the muttering crowd." The past participle can be formed by adding *-ed* to the verb, as in "The *muttered* complaints reached the king."

 Grammar

Exercises Have students form adjectives from the verbs underlined in these sentences:

1. The <u>terrify</u> man ran down the road. *(terrified)*
2. The <u>roar</u> crowd surprised the king. *(roaring)*
3. The <u>demand</u> voices were loud. *(demanding)*
4. The <u>amaze</u> king spared Pythias. *(amazed)*
5. The <u>rejoice</u> friends went home. *(rejoicing)*

 Use **Unit Three Resource Book,** p. 8.
Use **Grammar Transparencies and Copymasters,** p. 90.

Use McDougal Littell's ***Language Network,*** Chapter 5, for more instruction and practice in forming adjectives from verbs.

". . . I knew they were still very angry and would never forgive me."

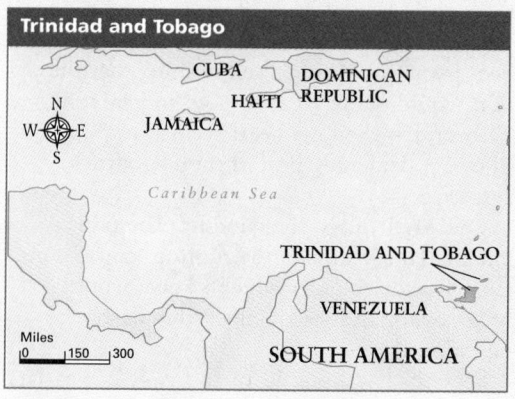

Cricket in the Road

Short Story by MICHAEL ANTHONY

Connect to Your Life

Fighting Words In the story you are about to read, a boy becomes upset with his friends over a game. Recall a disagreement you have had with a friend or a disagreement that you have read about. What caused it? How was it settled?

Build Background

CONNECT TO GEOGRAPHY The setting of this story is the village of Mayaro on the island of Trinidad. Trinidad is one of two islands that make up a country called Trinidad and Tobago, in the Caribbean Sea. Its climate is hot and humid, with a rainy season that lasts from about late May until December. Trinidad and Tobago was a colony of Great Britain until 1962 and still has many British customs. Cricket, a game somewhat like baseball, is popular in both countries.

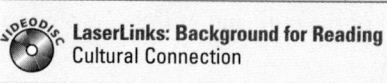

Trinidad and Tobago

CUBA
DOMINICAN REPUBLIC
HAITI
JAMAICA
Caribbean Sea
TRINIDAD AND TOBAGO
VENEZUELA
SOUTH AMERICA
Miles
0 150 300

LaserLinks: Background for Reading
Cultural Connection

WORDS TO KNOW Vocabulary Preview

dumbfounded	peal	tumult
fume	torrent	

Focus Your Reading

LITERARY ANALYSIS DIALOGUE The words that characters in a story speak aloud are called **dialogue.** In "Cricket in the Road," you will notice that some of the dialogue sounds different. This is because many people in Trinidad speak Trinidad English, a form of English that has been influenced by French and Spanish. Dialogue helps to move the plot along. It also helps to reveal the personalities of the characters.

ACTIVE READING PREDICTING When you make guesses about the outcome of a story, you are **predicting.** To make predictions, combine information from the story with your own knowledge. Try using the technique of story impressions to predict what might happen in "Cricket in the Road." The words and phrases shown refer to events in the story. What impression of the story do they give you? Write your predictions in your **READER'S NOTEBOOK.**

ball
bat
coin toss
tears
embarrassed
argument
rain clouds
Predictions:

Reading Skills and Strategies:
PREVIEW

Have students look over the illustrations and skim a few paragraphs. Ask them to tell what they think the story is about.

Set a Purpose Have students read to see if their predictions were correct.

Literary Analysis [DIALOGUE]

 Remind students that dialogue can give the reader a sense of the characters. Ask what the dialogue in this section tells the reader about the characters.

Possible Response: The characters' words show they are excited and how easily they can get angry at one another.

 Use **Unit Three Resource Book,** p. 13 for more practice.
Use **Literary Analysis Transparencies,** p. 13, for additional support.

Active Reading [PREDICTING]

Ask if students predicted that the children would argue. What information did they use to predict this?

Possible Response: The children all want to be first.

Use **Unit Three Resource Book,** p. 12 for more practice.
Use **Reading and Critical Thinking Transparencies,** p. 12, for additional support.

Literary Analysis: CONFLICT

Explain that internal conflict is a struggle within a character; external conflict is a struggle between a character and something outside himself or herself. Ask which type of conflict Selo's argument with Amy and Vern represents.

Answer: external

CRICKET in the ROAD

by Michael Anthony

In the rainy season we got few chances to play cricket in the road, for whenever we were at the game, the rains came down, chasing us into the yard again. That was the way it was in Mayaro in the rainy season. The skies were always overcast, and over the sea the rain clouds hung low and gray and scowling, and the winds blew in and whipped angrily through the palms. And when the winds were strongest and raging, the low-hanging clouds would become dense and black, and the sea would roar, and the <u>torrents</u> of rain would come sweeping with all their <u>tumult</u> upon us.

We had just run in from the rain. Amy and Vern from next door were in good spirits and laughing, for oddly enough they seemed to enjoy the downpour as much as playing cricket in the road. Amy was in our yard, giggling and pretending to drink the falling rain, with her face all wet and her clothes drenched, and Vern, who was sheltering under the eaves,[1] excitedly jumped out to join her. "Rain, rain, go to Spain," they shouted. And presently their mother, who must have heard the noise and knew, appeared from next door, and Vern and Amy vanished through the hedge.

I stood there, depressed about the rain, and then I put Vern's bat and ball underneath the house and went indoors. "Stupes!" I said to myself. I had been batting when the rains came down. It was only when *I* was batting that the rains came down! I wiped my feet so I wouldn't soil the sheets and went up on the bed. I was sitting, sad, and wishing that the rain would really go away—go to Spain, as Vern said—when my heart seemed to jump out of me. A deafening <u>peal</u> of thunder struck across the sky.

Quickly I closed the window. The rain hammered awfully on the rooftop, and I kept tense for the thunder which I knew would break again and for the unearthly flashes of lightning.

Secretly I was afraid of the violent weather. I was afraid of the rain, and of the thunder and

_____
1. **eaves** (ēvz): overhanging edges of a roof.

WORDS
TO
KNOW

torrent (tôr'ənt) *n.* a heavy downpour
tumult (tōō'mŭlt') *n.* a noisy uproar
peal (pēl) *n.* a loud burst of noise

334

Teaching Options

Instruction Students should be able to apply knowledge of context to recognize words. Tell students that often the context gives clues to a word's meaning. Comparison and contrast clues compare or contrast a word with something known. These clues may be introduced by the words *like, as, similar to, but, not, although, however,* or *on the other hand.* Write the following example on the board or read it aloud:

(Mini Lesson) Preteaching Vocabulary

The storm caused a <u>tumult,</u> but was not as loud as I had feared.

Show students how the contrast clue contained in the context should lead them to infer that *tumult* means a loud noise.

Exercises Have students infer the meanings of the underlined words from the context clues:

1. The <u>torrent</u> soon slowed to a trickle of water.

2. Although at first <u>dumbfounded,</u> Vern soon understood what Selo was up to.

3. I <u>fumed</u> for months, but then my anger cooled.

4. The <u>peals</u> of thunder in Trinidad were like the clanging of fierce bells.

Use **Unit Three Resource Book,** p. 14. Use **Vocabulary Transparencies and Copymasters,** p. 39, for additional support.

the lightning that came with them, and of the sea beating against the headlands,[2] and of the storm winds, and of everything being so deathlike when the rains were gone. I started[3] again at another flash of lightning, and before I had recovered from this, yet another terrifying peal of thunder hit the air. I screamed. I heard my mother running into the room. Thunder struck again, and I dashed under the bed.

"Selo! Selo! First bat!" Vern shouted from the road. The rains had ceased and the sun had come out, but I was not quite recovered yet. I brought myself reluctantly to look out from the front door, and there was Vern, grinning and impatient and beckoning to me.

"First bat," he said. And as if noting my indifference, he looked toward Amy, who was just coming out to play. "Who second bat?" he said.

"Me!" I said.

"Me!" shouted Amy almost at the same time.

"Amy second bat," Vern said.

"No, I said 'Me' first," I protested.

Vern grew impatient while Amy and I argued. Then an idea seemed to strike him. He took out a penny from his pocket. "Toss for it," he said. "What you want?"

"Heads," I called.

"Tail," cried Amy. "Tail bound to come!"[4]

The coin went up in the air, fell down and overturned, showing tail.

"I'm *not* playing!" I cried, stung. And as that did not seem to disturb enough, I ran toward

Schoolboys, Frané Lessac. From *Caribbean Canvas*, Macmillan Press, Ltd. By permission of the artist.

where I had put Vern's bat and ball and disappeared with them behind our house. Then I flung them with all my strength into the bushes.

When I came back to the front of the house, Vern was standing there <u>dumbfounded</u>. "Selo, where's the bat and ball?" he said.

I was <u>fuming</u>. "I don't know about *any* bat and ball!"

---

2. **headlands:** points of land that jut out into the water.

3. **started:** jumped suddenly in surprise.

4. **Toss for it. . . . Tail bound to come!:** Vern is flipping a coin to determine who will bat second. Selo calls that it will come up heads, so Amy roots for it to come up tails.

WORDS TO KNOW

dumbfounded (dŭm'foun'dĭd) *adj.* speechless with shock; astonished **dumbfound** *v.*
fume (fyōōm) *v.* to burn with anger

335

Mini Lesson — Viewing and Representing

Schoolboys
by Frané Lessac

ART APPRECIATION This colorful representation of schoolboys in the Caribbean is from a book titled *Caribbean Canvas*.
Instruction Explain that artists use color, line, and composition, or the arrangement of objects or people in a painting, to create mood in their artwork. As an example, point out the contrasts between the three boys on the left and the boy on the right. In what ways are the boys all alike? In what ways are they different?

Possible Response: The boys are all wearing the same shirts and shorts—maybe a school uniform. The poses of the three boys on the left, with the contrasting lines formed by their legs, suggest energy, enthusiasm, and good-natured activity, while the posture of the boy on the right is more formal and serious. He also has his shirt neatly tucked in and is wearing a belt.

Literary Analysis: DIALECT

 Students should identify how language use reflects regions and cultures. Explain to students that a dialect is a variety of a language that can be found in a specific region. It differs from the standard form of the language in important ways. Point out these pieces of dialect: "He throw them away" and "Who second bat?" They are Trinidad dialect for the Standard English "He threw them away" and "Who's batting second" or "Who's second at bat?" Much of the dialogue of the story is written in dialect; however, the narration is written in Standard English. Ask students how you would say, "You first bat" in Standard English.

Possible Response: "You be first [at] bat."

Reading Skills and Stategies: MAKE JUDGMENTS

Ask students to make a judgment about whether Selo does the right thing in walking away from the game when he is angry. On what do they base this judgment?

Possible Responses: Some may say Selo is foolish to make his friends angry over such a silly thing. Some may say he avoids a worse confrontation by walking away. Students may say that their judgments are based on their own experience.

LITERARY LINK

Use the following questions to help students analyze the poem.
- What kind of mood do the nonsense words suggest? *(anger)*
- Suggest a meaning for one of the lines of nonsense words in the poem. *(Responses will vary.)*

Teaching Options

"Tell on him," Amy cried. "He throw them away."

Vern's mouth twisted into a forced smile. "What's an old bat and ball," he said.

But as he walked out of the yard, I saw tears glinting from the corners of his eyes.

For the rest of that rainy season, we never played cricket in the road again. Sometimes the rains ceased and the sun came out brightly, and I heard the voices of Amy and Vern on the other side of the fence. At such times I would go out into the road and whistle to myself, hoping they would hear me and come out, but they never did, and I knew they were still very angry and would never forgive me.

And so the rainy season went on. And it was as fearful as ever with the thunder and lightning and waves roaring in the bay, and the strong winds. But the people who talked of all this said that was the way Mayaro was, and they laughed about it. And sometimes when through the rain and even thunder I heard Vern's voice on the other side of the fence, shouting "Rain, rain, go to Spain," it puzzled me how it could be so. For often I had made up my mind I would be brave, but when the thunder cracked I always dashed under the bed.

It was the beginning of the new year when I saw Vern and Amy again. The rainy season was, happily, long past, and the day was hot and bright, and as I walked toward home I saw that I was walking toward Vern and Amy just about to start cricket in the road. My heart thumped violently. They looked strange and new, as if they had gone away, far, and did not want to come back anymore. They did not notice me until I came up quite near, and then I saw Amy start, her face all lit up.

"Vern—" she cried, "Vern look—look Selo!"

Embarrassed, I looked at the ground and at the trees, and at the orange sky, and I was so happy I did not know what to say. Vern stared at me, a strange grin on his face. He was ripping the cellophane paper off a brand new bat.

"Selo, here—*you* first bat," he said gleefully.

And I cried as though it were raining and I was afraid. ❖

LITERARY LINK

Mean Song
by Eve Merriam

Snickles and podes,
Ribble and grodes:
That's what I wish you.

A nox in the groot,
A root in the stoot
And a gock in the forebeshaw, too.

Keep out of sight
For fear that I might
Glom you a gravely snave.

Don't show your face
Around any place
Or you'll get one flack snack in the bave.

BLOCK SCHEDULING: MANAGING TIME

If your schedule requires that you cover the lesson objectives in a shorter time, use . . .
- Preparing to Read, p. 333
- Thinking Through the Literature, p. 337
- Grammar in Context, p. 339

If you would like to take advantage of longer class time, use . . .
- TE Teaching Options: Viewing and Representing, p. 335; Standardized Test Practice, p. 338; Preteaching Vocabulary, p. 334; Grammar, p. 339
- Literary Link, p. 336
- Choices & Challenges and Author Activity, pp. 338–339

Connect to the Literature

1. What Do You Think?
What were your thoughts about the three friends as you finished reading?

Comprehension Check
• Why do Selo and Amy argue?
• How does Vern try to resolve their disagreement?
• How is the disagreement finally resolved?

Think Critically

2. It is obvious that Selo wants to play with Vern and Amy. Why, then, do you think he is reluctant to talk to them after the disagreement occurs?

3. In what ways are Selo and Vern alike? In what ways are they different?

> **THINK ABOUT**
> • their actions during the downpour
> • the way they determine the batting order
> • their reactions to seeing each other after the rainy season

4. **ACTIVE READING** **PREDICTING** Look at the notes you made in your **READER'S NOTEBOOK**. Did the impressions you developed before reading help you to make predictions? How do your predictions compare with the events of the story? Share your notes with a partner.

Extend Interpretations

5. What If? If Vern had not reached out to Selo, what do you think would have happened to their friendship?

6. Connect to Life In your opinion, what is the fairest and fastest way to settle a disagreement between friends? Support your opinion with ideas from "Cricket in the Road" as well as the experience you discussed before reading.

Literary Analysis

DIALOGUE In a story, spoken language is called **dialogue.** In "Cricket in the Road," the author writes the dialogue of the characters just as it would sound. This lets you "hear" how the characters speak. It also helps you to understand their feelings and why the characters act as they do.

Paired Activity With a partner, look over the story. Discuss how the dialogue helps the author tell the story. How would the story have been different if the author had used descriptions in place of dialogue?

REVIEW SETTING The **setting** of a story is the time and place of the action. How does the setting of "Cricket in the Road" affect the characters?

Extend Interpretations

5. What If? Possible Responses: If Vern had not reached out to Selo, the two boys would never have been reunited; or Selo would eventually have swallowed his pride and apologized to Amy and Vern.

6. Connect to Life Responses will vary. Make sure that the students include ideas from the selection and from their own experience.

Connect to the Literature

1. What Do You Think?
Responses will vary. Students may say that the three friends seem to have decided that friendship is more important than anything else. They may say that Amy's warmth, Vern's generosity, and Selo's tears prove how important the friendship was to all involved. Some students may say that Selo acted like a bad sport, and that Amy and Vern showed they were good friends when they forgave him for this.

Comprehension Check
• Both think they should be second bat.
• Vern tries to resolve the disagreement between Amy and Selo by tossing a coin.
• The quarrel is finally resolved when Vern makes the first move, letting Selo use his new bat first.

 Use Selection Quiz
Unit Three Resource Book, p. 17.

Think Critically

2. Possible Response: Selo is afraid of rejection. He is embarrassed about and ashamed of his behavior.

3. Possible Response: Selo and Vern enjoy many of the same activities, such as cricket, but are very different in temperament. Vern enjoys the rainy season, for example, while Selo is terrified of the thunder and lightning.

4. Answers will vary.

Use **Reading and Critical Thinking Transparencies,** p. 7, for additional support.

Literary Analysis

Dialogue Students should be aware that the dialogue makes the story more vivid and lively, as well as giving it a flavor of the region in which the action takes place.

Use **Literary Analysis Transparencies,** p. 24, for additional support.

Writing Options

1. **Dramatic Dialogue** Responses should indicate an accurate understanding of how the disagreement started and reflect the underlying causes of the problem in the suggested remedies. To get students started on this activity, have them hold improvised role-playing discussions in groups of three.

 Use **Writing Transparencies**, p. 24, for additional support.
Use **Communications Transparencies and Copymasters**, p. 13, for additional support.

2. **Diary Entry** Responses should indicate an awareness of Selo's shame at his own behavior and his longing for forgiveness.

3. **Forgiveness Poem** Offer students the option of writing a fictional poem if they find the assignment too personal. Assess responses on how well they reflect an understanding of the process of forgiveness.

Activities & Explorations

1. **Game Plan** Responses should show a clear understanding of the game and the ability to convey it to others in words and diagrams. A good source of information for this activity is an encyclopedia.

2. **Trinidad Brochure** Brochures should reflect research on Trinidad and the use of vivid writing. To get students started on this activity, provide some sample brochures.

Inquiry & Research

To adapt this activity for **visual learners,** have students create symbols to represent various conflict resolution techniques and display them.

Writing Options

1. **Dramatic Dialogue** Write a dialogue in which Selo, Amy, and Vern talk about their disagreement. Include ideas about how to avoid future problems. Place it in your **Working Portfolio.**

2. **Diary Entry** What lessons do you think Selo learned from his experience? Write a diary entry that Selo might write, describing what he learned.

3. **Forgiveness Poem** Write a poem about a time when you forgave someone or were forgiven by someone important to you.

Activities & Explorations

1. **Game Plan** Research the game of cricket and write a description of it. Add diagrams and present the information on a poster.
~ VIEWING AND REPRESENTING

2. **Trinidad Brochure** Design and write a travel brochure advertising Trinidad. Find out about tourist attractions and the island's history. Include pictures of Trinidad or your own drawings.
~ ART

Inquiry & Research

Friend or Foe? What makes a friendship strong? Can friends—like Vern, Amy, and Selo—disagree and still remain friends? How can friends who disagree still work or play together? With three or four classmates, brainstorm a list of ways to resolve conflicts, to calm down when angry, and to renew a friendship. Then check newspapers and nonfiction books to add more methods to your list.

Real World Link As part of your research, read "Peers Talk It Out" on p. 340.

Vocabulary and Spelling

EXERCISE A: ASSESSMENT PRACTICE Which sentence best expresses the meaning of each word as it is used in "Cricket in the Road"?

1. **tumult**
   a. The sudden rain annoyed Selo.
   b. Selo was overjoyed after the rain.
   c. The storms created a noisy uproar.

2. **peal**
   a. The banana skin fell from the tree.
   b. The organ could hardly be heard.
   c. The thunder made a deafening noise.

3. **torrent**
   a. The clouds brought a downpour.
   b. The stream was overflowing.
   c. Amy shouted a poem about the rain.

4. **dumbfounded**
   a. Vern's information was faulty.
   b. Selo's behavior left Vern speechless.
   c. Amy's stories amused her listeners.

5. **fume**
   a. The car's exhaust had a strong odor.
   b. Selo stormed off angrily.
   c. Waves crashed against the shore.

EXERCISE B: SILENT LETTERS Many words are difficult to spell because they contain silent consonants. Such words include *dumbfounded, whistle, crumb, answer,* and *sign.* You can invent your own catchy reminder to help you remember difficult spellings. These reminders are called *mnemonic devices.* Here is an example:

> *Dumb, thumb, and crumb*
> *All have a letter that's mum.*
> *To spell them correctly,*
> *End each with a "b."*

Create your own mnemonic device for a word that contains a silent letter.

Spelling Handbook p. R86

Teaching Options

✓ **Assessment Standardized Test Practice**

UNDERSTANDING THE FEELINGS AND EMOTIONS OF CHARACTERS Students are expected to analyze characters, including their traits, motivations, conflicts, points of view, relationships, and the changes they undergo. Some standardized tests will ask them to identify the emotions of characters. Help them practice this skill by posing the following question:

What choice below best describes the emotions Selo is feeling at the end of the story?
A. Sad and frightened
B. Gleeful and generous
C. Relieved and happy
D. Angry and upset

Discuss the options with students. Point out that A is incorrect because the narrator says he cried as *though* he were afraid—he is not really afraid. B is incorrect because he would not be crying if he felt gleeful. D is incorrect because at the end of the story he is happy, though embarrassed at his past actions. Thus, option C best describes the narrator's feelings at the end of the story.

Grammar in Context: Using Adverbs for Excitement

In "Cricket in the Road," Michael Anthony describes Selo's reaction to a thunderstorm. Notice how the words in red type add excitement and clarity to the writing:

> Quickly I closed the window. The rain hammered awfully on the rooftop, and I kept tense for the thunder which I knew would break again and for the unearthly flashes of lightning.
>
> Secretly I was afraid of the violent weather.

The words shown in red above are **adverbs.** An adverb modifies, or describes, a verb, an adjective, or another adverb. An adverb answers the question *how, when, where,* or *to what extent* about the word it modifies.

WRITING EXERCISE Rewrite each of the sentences, adding an adverb that answers the question in parentheses.

Example: *Original* The winds whipped (how?) through the palms.
Rewritten The winds whipped fiercely through the palms.

1. I screamed (how?) when the thunder pealed.
2. I wanted to bat (when?).
3. The thunder was (how?) loud.
4. My heart thumped (how?).
5. Selo felt (to what extent?) terrified.

Connect to the Literature Find four more exciting adverbs from "Cricket in the Road."

Grammar Handbook Using Modifiers Effectively, p. R70

"I feel very strongly about the brotherhood of mankind."

Michael Anthony
born 1932

Island Life Michael Anthony writes tales about life on the island of Trinidad. His stories offer readers a taste of Caribbean culture and a chance to consider the most important things in life—like friendship. His other works include *The Games Were Coming* and *Green Days by the River.*

Jobs and Journeys Born in Mayaro, in Trinidad and Tobago, Anthony began working in an iron foundry at the age of 15. Eight years later he went to England, where he held a variety of factory jobs and eventually became a journalist. From England he went to Brazil. After a two-year stay, he and his wife and four children returned to Trinidad to live.

Hoping for Peace The selection you have just read is from a short story collection that is also titled *Cricket in the Road.* Anthony has published novels and poems as well as stories. An optimist who would like to see all the nations of the world join together to become one strong nation, he says, "One of my main hopes is that human beings will find a way to live together without friction."

AUTHOR ACTIVITY
Caribbean View Read another one of Anthony's stories that is set in Trinidad. Look for details about the setting of the island and the customs of its people. What are your impressions of everyday life in Trinidad? Draw a scene based on Anthony's descriptions.

CRICKET IN THE ROAD **339**

 Grammar

IDENTIFYING ADVERBS AND THE WORDS THEY MODIFY Remind students that an adverb is a word used to modify a verb, an adjective, or another adverb. Adverbs tell how, when, where, or to what extent. Write the sentence below and point out that *extremely* modifies the adjective *rainy* by telling to what extent:

Trinidad can be extremely rainy.

Ask students to identify the adverbs and the words they modify in the following sentences:
1. Selo's life was fearfully full of thunder. *(fearfully modifies full)*
2. It rained hard in Mayaro. *(hard modifies rained)*

3. Selo wept very gratefully. (*gratefully* modifies *wept,* and *very* modifies *gratefully*)
4. Selo, Amy, and Vern played happily and peacefully. (*happily* and *peacefully* both modify *played*)

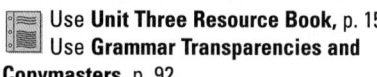 Use **Unit Three Resource Book,** p. 15.
Use **Grammar Transparencies and Copymasters,** p. 92.

 Use McDougal Littell's *Language Network,* Chapter 5, for more practice in identifying adverbs and the words they modify.

Objectives
- read and analyze a newspaper article
- practice summarizing information from text
- examine the concept of peer mediation

Connecting to the Literature

"Peers Talk It Out" presents the notion that in many situations it is young people who can best solve disputes between their peers. By connecting this real-world idea to what students have just read in "Cricket in the Road," students can explore the way the fictitious argument in the short story reflects disputes and misunderstandings that go on around them every day.

Metro·Region

❶ Peers Talk It Out

SPECIAL REPORT

by Janis Leibs Dworkis

Does a 10-year-old really know enough to help other students solve their problems? Can he understand more than one side of an issue? Can she be fair and impartial if she knows the students involved?

❷ About 10 percent of the 85,000 schools in the United States offer some form of peer mediation. The Dallas Independent School District offers peer mediation in about half of its almost 200 schools. And almost every school district in the Dallas–Fort Worth area offers a similar program in at least some of its schools.

The peer mediation concept is simple: two or more students who have a disagreement talk over their problem in front of one or two of their peers, with no adults present. The peer mediators, who remain neutral, help the students come to a mutually agreeable solution.

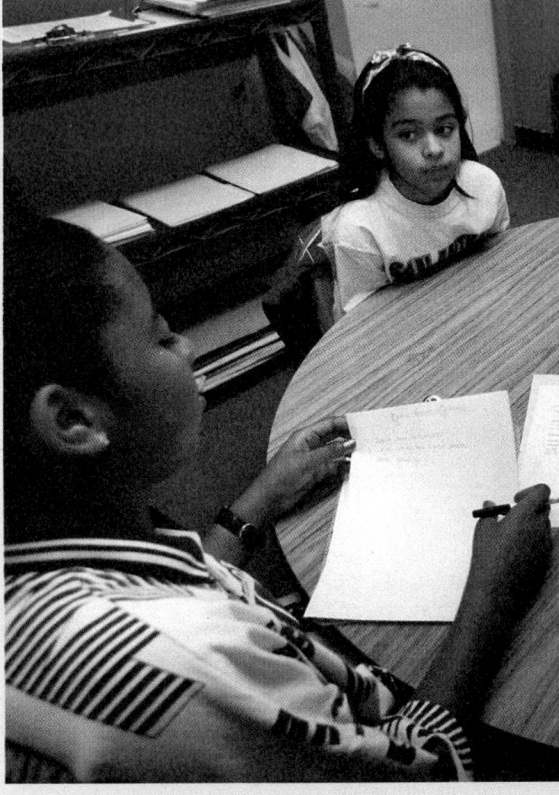

At the Nathaniel Hawthorne Elementary School, sixth graders Earnestine Glosson (front left) and Rocio De Leon (front right) mediate a misunderstanding between fourth graders Laura Rios and Quaniqua Davis (back, left and right).

340 UNIT THREE   PART 1: BETWEEN FRIENDS

Reading for Information

"What did you do in school today?"
"How was the movie?"
"What's that book about?"
If you don't summarize, your answer to any of these questions could take hours. When you **summarize** something you have read, you focus on the main idea or ideas and reword that information into a brief, understandable description. Summaries can be useful in everyday discussion as well as when you do research or study for tests.

SUMMARIZING To summarize a piece of writing is to tell the main ideas and important details briefly, in your own words. When summarizing, you condense a writer's ideas into precise statements, leaving out the less important details. A good summary is accurate, includes the important details, and reads smoothly.

YOUR TURN *Use the activities below to help you summarize the article.*

1 You must understand what you have read before you can summarize it. Read the article carefully. Look for any features—title, headings, photographs— that help explain what the article is about. What is the main idea of this article?

2 What important facts are given in this paragraph? Reread the article, making a list of other important facts, ideas, and events. Decide what will make your summary short but accurate. Edit your list so there are only three or four main points.

Reading for Information

Students may be familiar with the notion of peer mediation already if their school has such a program in place. If so, ask them to approach the concept as if it were new to them. As you examine the article with students, have them use the material in the right-hand column as a guide to reading newspaper articles. The following are possible responses to the numbered activities.

1 The main idea of the article is that peer mediators can solve many problems between young people more effectively than adults can.

2 Important facts in this paragraph include these: 10 percent of the 85,000 schools in the United States offer some form of peer mediation; the Dallas Independent School District has peer mediation in about half of its 200 schools; almost every school district in the Dallas-Fort Worth area offers a similar program in at least some of its schools.

3 The paragraphs give an example of how peer mediation works in one elementary school. They suggest that mediation works because peers listen well and understand the issues involved.

 Use **Writing Transparencies,** pp. 51, 52, for additional support.

P eer mediators don't dictate an outcome. If no solution can be found, which rarely happens, the mediation ends. Although peer mediators usually address problems related to rumors, gossip or other friendship issues, they have also handled problems related to racism and gangs.

Once the peer mediators are trained and put into action, they tend to be very successful. According to the National Institute for Dispute Resolution, peer mediation programs have reduced the need for adult

> "If they had been sent to an adult, . . . they would probably just have been told not to do a fight."

intervention in student conflicts by up to 80 percent in some schools. Some experts say that's because students can understand the problems other students face better than adults can.

Sixth-grader Rocio De Leon is serving her third year as a student mediator at Hawthorne. She remembers one particular mediation involving five or six fourth-grade girls who were fighting about some rumors circulating around school.

"We listened to what they had to say real well. That's so important in mediation. And we asked them what they wanted to have happen. They decided they just wanted to be friends. And they still are very good friends," Rocio says.

"If they had been sent to an adult, instead of coming to mediation, they would probably just have been told not to do a fight. But the adult wouldn't really understand them. It's a lot easier for a child to understand because you're talking to a person who is actually your age and having some of the same problems as you are."

Those who work with peer mediation hope that, in the long run, these problem-solving skills will lessen the occurrence of fighting—not only at school, but elsewhere, too.

Reading for Information continued

3 Review the article again. This time, look for supporting details that help make the main idea more understandable. How do these paragraphs help explain peer mediation?

Inquiry & Research

Activity Link: "Cricket in the Road," p. 338. After finalizing your list of important main ideas and supporting details, write a three- or four-sentence summary of "Peers Talk It Out." Then add a brief description of how peer mediation might have worked for Vern, Amy, and Selo. How could they have used peer mediation to settle their argument?

Mini Lesson **Inquiry & Research**

Instruction The Inquiry & Research activity on this page links the newspaper article to the story "Cricket in the Road." As they practice the summarizing skills called for here, students will gain an understanding of the process of peer mediation. They will then be able to apply that knowledge to the situation in the story.

First make sure that students understand what a peer is. They should realize that their peers are those who are approximately their own age and from their own basic background. For instance, a peer would be someone from their school.

After students have had a chance to summarize "Peers Talk It Out," review peer mediation with them. Observe that peer mediators do not dictate an outcome. Their success comes through listening and making all parties feel heard. Once those who are in dispute feel heard, they can move on to a solution that feels fair to everyone.

Practice Ask students to focus on what Vern, Amy, and Selo might have said if they had been telling their peers about their argument. Airing feelings would have been part of a solution.

The Quarrel

Poetry by ELEANOR FARJEON

Fable

Poetry by RALPH WALDO EMERSON

OVERVIEW

Objectives
1. understand and appreciate a **narrative poem (Literary Analysis)**
2. understand author's use of **theme** in a narrative poem **(Literary Analysis)**
3. Use **connecting** to help understand the theme better **(Active Reading)**

Summary
In "The Quarrel," two siblings have a dispute that ends when one generously admits to being in the wrong and proposes that they end the quarrel. In "Fable," the mountain and the squirrel also quarrel, and the mountain calls the squirrel a "little prig." The squirrel points out that being small has its advantages and insists upon respect.

Thematic Link
These two selections continue the theme of fairness between friends. In "The Quarrel," the poet explores the value of rising above petty disagreement. In "Fable," the poet uses a fictitious argument to point out that power and ability do not always belong to the large or mighty.

5-Minute Warm-Up

Daily Language SkillBuilder

Have students proofread the display sentences on page 315i and write them correctly. The sentences also appear on Transparency 11 of Grammar Transparencies and Copymasters.

(Connect to Your Life)

Despite Our Differences At one time or another, nearly everyone has had a fight or disagreement that seemed impossible to resolve. Can you think of a time when it felt like you and someone else would never see eye to eye, but still you managed to work things out? What happened? How did you come to a resolution?

Build Background

Poems with a Past Narrative poems are poems that tell stories. Narrative poetry has been important to cultures around the world for thousands of years, from ancient India to the ancient native cultures of the American Southwest.

   Long ago, people often told stories in the form of poems, because the rhythm of the poetry helped them to learn and remember the stories. As a result, people who did not read were able to pass on the beliefs, tales, and lessons they most valued by learning, and then sharing, narrative poems. All narrative poetry comes from this important tradition, from epic poems that tell about grand adventures of heroes to brief poems like the ones you are about to read.

The *Ellesmere Manuscript* contains Geoffrey Chaucer's 14th-century poem *The Canterbury Tales.*

Focus Your Reading

LITERARY ANALYSIS NARRATIVE POETRY Poetry that tells a story is called **narrative poetry.** Like any story, a narrative poem contains **characters,** a **setting,** and a **plot.** For example, the plot of each poem you are about to read involves characters who have a quarrel and then come to a resolution.

ACTIVE READING CONNECTING When your reading brings to mind things you know about or have experienced, you are **connecting.** As you read these poems, think about ways in which you can relate to the events described in the poems.

READER'S NOTEBOOK After you read each poem, think about what connections you can make between the experiences of the characters and your own knowledge or experiences. Record the details that triggered these connections, as well as your own related thoughts.

THE QUARREL / FABLE **343**

LESSON RESOURCES

Reading and Analyzing

Literary Analysis
NARRATIVE POETRY

Have students paraphrase the events of both poems, tell who the characters are, and describe any details of settings. Then ask them to give a statement of the theme for each poem.

Use **Unit Three Resource Book**, p. 19 for more practice. Use **Literary Analysis Transparencies**, p. 7, for additional support.

Active Reading CONNECTING

Students are expected to make connections in response to texts. Ask students to connect the selections to at least one thing in their own lives. Suggest that they use a chart to note their connections.

Use **Unit Three Resource Book**, p. 18 for more practice. Use **Reading and Critical Thinking Transparencies**, p. 2, for additional support.

Thinking Through the Literature

1. **Comprehension Check:** Possible Response: Two siblings have a quarrel, then make up.
2. Possible Response: They weren't even quarreling about anything important (they can't remember what started it), the quarrel seems like it will ruin the day, and the brother just wants it to be over.
3. Possible Response: The last line says that the brother's position was the right one to take in this situation.

Two Birds, One Worm (1989), © William Wegman.
Watercolor on paper, 11" × 14".

THE Quarrel
by Eleanor Farjeon

I quarreled with my brother,
I don't know what about,
One thing led to another
And somehow we fell out.
5   The start of it was slight,
The end of it was strong,
He said he was right,
I knew he was wrong!
We hated one another.
10   The afternoon turned black.
Then suddenly my brother
Thumped me on the back,
And said, "Oh, come along!
We can't go on all night—
15   I was in the wrong."
So he was in the right.

Thinking Through the Literature

1. **Comprehension Check** What happens in this poem?
2. Why do you think the brother tries to end the quarrel?

    THINK ABOUT
   - what the speaker says about the cause of the quarrel
   - the effects of the quarrel
   - the brother's words to the speaker

3. What does the last line of the poem mean?

Teaching Options

 Mini Lesson **Viewing and Representing**

Two Birds, One Worm **by William Wegman**

ART APPRECIATION William Wegman's simple watercolor is full of the drama of natural life. Wegman is perhaps best known for his photographs of Weimaraners dressed as people, but in this work, two birds compete over their dinner.
Instruction Point out how simple the watercolor image is and yet how full of meaning it is. Ask students to explain how it echoes the theme of the poem "The Quarrel."

Possible Response: The painting, like the poem, is about a dispute between two creatures.
Application Ask students how the quarrel in the watercolor could have the same outcome as the quarrel in the poem.
Possible Response: If one bird decided to give in to the other, and the second bird decided to share the worm, then the two birds would stop their quarrel.

Fable
by Ralph Waldo Emerson

Sunrise at Fujiyama, Japan (1928), Lillian Miller (1885–1943). Woodblock print, 37.3 × 51.6 cm, Lillian Miller Collection, Scripps College, Claremont. Photo: G+B Photo, Pasadena, Calif.

The mountain and the squirrel
Had a quarrel,
And the former[1] called the latter[2] "Little Prig";
Bun replied,
5 "You are doubtless very big;
But all sorts of things and weather
Must be taken in together,
To make up a year
And a sphere.
10 And I think it no disgrace
To occupy my place.
If I'm not so large as you,
You are not so small as I,
And not half so spry.[3]
15 I'll not deny you make
A very pretty squirrel track;
Talents differ; all is well and wisely put;
If I cannot carry forests on my back,
Neither can you crack a nut."

---

1. **former:** the first of two things.
2. **latter:** the second of two things.
3. **spry:** lively and active.

FABLE **345**

 Assessment Informal Assessment

WRITING A MORAL Explain to students that many traditional stories were written to teach a lesson or moral—that is, to tell people how they should behave. The teller of the story often summed up the lesson in a short statement at the end that was called a "moral." Tell them that much like such folklore, each of these poems relates a short incident that is intended to convey a lesson or moral. Have them sum up the messages of the poems by writing a moral for each.

RUBRIC
3 Full Accomplishment Response reflects a full understanding of the overall theme or lesson of each selection.
2 Substantial Accomplishment Response shows a general understanding of the theme or lesson of the selections, but fails to articulate the lesson in a moral.
1 Little or Partial Accomplishment Response shows little understanding of the theme or lesson of the selections or how to summarize it in a moral.

GUIDING STUDENT RESPONSE

Connect to the Literature

1. What Do You Think?
Possible Response: The squirrel has good sense to stand up for itself with such a calm and reasonable argument.

Comprehension Check
- The mountain is big and supports forests (home to the squirrel).
- The squirrel is small and spry and can crack nuts (impossible for the mountain).

Think Critically

2. Answers will vary, but the message is something to this effect: Everyone has necessary talents, so it is foolish to quarrel over who is most important. The squirrel responds to the mountain's insult ("Little Prig," line 3) by telling the mountain that they are each valuable. Each person (or element in nature) is uniquely valuable, so it is pointless to insult each other and quarrel over who is most important.

3. Possible Response: The squirrel is self-confident, outspoken, fair, reasonable, thoughtful, expressive, and so on. Though small, the squirrel stands up for itself to the mountain; it knows and values its own talents while acknowledging the mountain's talents.

4. Responses will vary. Students might identify with the sibling characters in "The Quarrel," who lost track of why they were fighting. Alternately, they may identify with the squirrel in "Fable," which stood up for itself in response to an insult.

Use **Reading and Critical Thinking Transparencies,** p. 2, for additional support.

Connect to the Literature

1. What Do You Think?
How did you react to the words of the squirrel?

Comprehension Check
- What are named as the mountain's most important traits?
- What does the squirrel name as its most important traits?

Think Critically

2. What do you think is the main message of the squirrel's speech?

THINK ABOUT
- the differences between the squirrel and the mountain
- the unique qualities of each
- the last two lines of the poem

3. How would you describe the squirrel in "Fable"? Support your answer by referring to the poem.

4. **ACTIVE READING** **MAKING CONNECTIONS** Which poem did you relate to more? Give reasons for your answer based on the details you recorded in your **READER'S NOTEBOOK**.

Extend Interpretations

5. **COMPARING TEXTS** Compare the quarrels in these poems with the quarrel in "Cricket in the Road" on page 333. How are they similar? What are the biggest differences? Support your opinions with details from the selections.

6. Connect to Life After reading these poems, what helpful tips for resolving a real argument can you offer? Use words and examples from the poem to elaborate on your tips.

Literary Analysis

NARRATIVE POETRY Poetry that tells a story is called **narrative poetry.** Like other stories, a narrative poem includes **characters,** a **setting,** and a **plot.** Narrative poetry may contain such elements of poetry as **rhyme, rhythm, imagery,** and **personification.** The description of the mountain "carrying a forest on its back" is an example of imagery. It is also an example of personification, or giving human qualities to something that is not human, because it uses the words *carry* and *back.*

Paired Activity Working with a partner, prepare one of these poems each for a dramatic reading to your class. First, practice reciting the poem for each other. Read in a way that brings to life the characters in the poem and the action of the plot. Speak slowly and make sure your words are clear and distinct.

Literary Analysis

Narrative Poetry Students should concentrate on presenting poems calmly and deliberately so that their messages, or themes, can be understood. **To make this activity more challenging,** have students work in larger groups and pantomime the action of the poems as they recite.

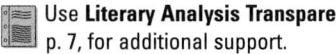 Use **Literary Analysis Transparencies,** p. 7, for additional support.

Extend Interpretations

5. Comparing Texts Possible Responses: Differences: "The Quarrel" does not give details about the disagreement, where "Cricket in the Road" does. The brother capitulates in "The Quarrel," and the characters in "Cricket" make up, while the squirrel defends itself. Similarities: Both poems and the story say the quarrels are foolish or pointless, the issues insignificant or invalid, and the division between characters hurtful and unnecessary.

6. Connect to Life Responses will vary. The poems could encourage combatants to consider the importance of what they argue about; the damage that may result; the value of others, despite differences; the possibility of giving in to end a stalemate; and the possibility of standing up for themselves calmly and rationally when points of view differ.

Writing Options

1. Imagined Conversation Go back to the poem you found most interesting. If the characters in this poem could have a conversation about friendship, what do you think they would say? Write down a possible dialogue.

2. Advice Column Imagine that the speaker in "The Quarrel" wrote to an advice columnist.

Write the speaker's letter and a letter of advice you think an expert would write in return.

Activities & Explorations

1. Dramatic Reading With a partner, practice the imagined conversation you prepared for Writing Option 1. Rehearse your parts, then present your conversation for the class. **~ SPEAKING AND LISTENING**

2. Public Opinion Poll Identify a heated issue affecting your school or community. Poll your classmates to see how they think the problem should be resolved. Present your findings in a bar graph. **~ MATH**

Inquiry & Research

Stories in Verse Research nursery rhymes. Which ones are narrative poems? Share your findings with the class.

"It would have been . . . as unnatural not to read as not to eat."

Eleanor Farjeon
1881–1965

A Passion for Words Eleanor Farjeon grew up in London, England. She gained much of her education at home, by reading books in her father's library and talking with the writers and stage performers who were family friends. She began writing poems and stories when she was seven. At 16, she co-wrote a libretto (the script for an opera) that was performed at London's famous Royal Academy of Music.

International Success Although Farjeon lived and wrote in England, her work was read and enjoyed in many countries. She wrote for more than 70 years, publishing poems, short stories, and novels. Her poems are often included in collections of favorite verse for children.

"Nothing great was ever achieved without enthusiasm."

Ralph Waldo Emerson
1803–1882

Claims to Fame Emerson was one of the most famous poets and thinkers of the 19th century. Trained as a minister, he later dedicated himself to writing and lecturing about his ideas on religion, nature, and society. Some of Emerson's beliefs are expressed in his well-known essay "Self-Reliance," which encourages people to make up their own minds about what they believe to be right.

A Lasting Influence Emerson's friends and followers included poet Walt Whitman and writer Henry David Thoreau. In his poetry, Emerson used clearer images, simpler words, and freer verse forms than most of the poets before him. His style helped shape modern poetry.

Writing Options

1. Imagined Conversation Answers should reflect the relationship between the characters in the given poem. To get students started on this activity, review the characters and their concerns in a class discussion.

 Use **Writing Transparencies,** p. 24, for additional support.

2. Advice Column Letters should accurately represent the conflict and resolution in the selection. A good source of information for this activity would be advice columns from a newspaper that could be used as models.

Activities & Explorations

1. Dramatic Reading Presentations should use appropriate dramatic movement and voice.

Use **Communications Transparencies and Copymasters,** p. 12, for additional support.

2. Public Opinion Poll Check the topics chosen for polling before students begin their work. Bar graphs should use appropriate parameters.

Inquiry & Research

Stories in Verse Responses should indicate thorough research and an understanding of what makes a narrative poem. A good source would be the children's section of a local library.

Eleanor Farjeon

When Farjeon began her writing at age seven, she did not bother with pen and paper. Instead she began tapping away at her father's typewriter as if she knew she had to hurry to finish seventy years' worth of writing!

Ralph Waldo Emerson

Though Emerson is now known mostly for his philosophy, his poetry was once highly regarded. American writer Nathaniel Hawthorne said of him that he admired Emerson "as a poet of deep beauty . . . but sought nothing from him as a philosopher."

 Mini Lesson ## Grammar

ARTICLES AND DEMONSTRATIVE ADJECTIVES

Instruction The words *a, an* and *the* are articles, a type of adjective that indicates whether a thing is indefinite (*a* or *an*) or definite (*the*).The demonstrative adjectives or pronouns are *this, that, these,* and *those.* They are used to "demonstrate," or point out, which particular thing is being talked about.

Exercises Ask students to identify the underlined words as indefinite or definite articles or demonstrative adjectives.

1. The mountain had a quarrel. (*definite article*)

2. A squirrel spoke up. (*indefinite article*)

3. Those two had better stop arguing. (*demonstrative adjective*)

4. That comment is not one I would make to a mountain. (*demonstrative adjective*)

5. The comment hurt feelings. (*definite article*)

 Use **Grammar Transparencies and Copymasters,** p. 93.

 Use McDougal Littell's *Language Network,* Chapter 3, for more practice in demonstrative pronouns.

Objectives

- identify the relation of word meanings in analogies
- recognize a variety of types of word relationships

EXERCISE

1. line
2. moist
3. hero
4. love
5. book

Use **Unit Three Resource Book,** p. 20.
Use **Vocabulary Transparencies and Copymasters,** p. 14, for additional support.

Word Relationships

An **analogy** contains two word pairs. The words in each pair have similar relationships. Words may be related as synonyms or as antonyms, for example, or one word might describe another. Analogies can help you understand these word relationships.

> Sitting across from her on the sofa was a squat blob of a man—balding and gray— as silent as a mushroom. . . .
> —Yoshiko Uchida, "Oh Broom, Get to Work"

The word *squat* means "short and thick; low and broad."

Squat is to mushroom as tall is to skyscraper.

Written in a formal way, an analogy looks like this:

SQUAT : MUSHROOM :: tall : skyscraper

Notice that in both pairs, the relationship is descriptive.

Strategies for Building Vocabulary

The following tips can help you understand and complete analogies.

❶ **Read Analogies** The words *happy* and *contented* are **synonyms,** as are the words *sad* and *depressed.* An analogy for these word pairs would be written this way:

HAPPY : CONTENTED :: sad : depressed

You would read the statement like this:

Happy relates to contented
as **sad** relates to depressed.

On a test, you might be asked to complete an analogy by filling in the appropriate word:

HAPPY : CONTENTED :: sad : ___?___

❷ **State the Relationship** In completing an analogy, it helps to read it aloud, restating it more precisely. For example, if the words are synonyms, you can use the phrase "means almost the same as." If the words are antonyms, say "means the opposite of."

SILENT : NOISY :: sad : ___?___

Say the analogy as though it were a sentence:

Silent means the opposite of noisy
as **sad** means the opposite of what?

❸ **Review Your Choice** First, determine the relationship expressed in the first word pair. Next, choose a word to complete the second word pair. Finally, test your choice by reading the complete statement. For example:

Silent means the opposite of noisy
as **sad** means the opposite of happy.

Here are some common word relationships.

Relationship	Example
Synonyms	BIG : LARGE :: shiny : bright
Antonyms	FRIEND : ENEMY :: bottom : top
Part to Whole	LEAF : TREE :: spoke : wheel
Item to Category	POODLE : DOG :: daisy : flower
Descriptive	ROUND : CIRCLE :: pointy : arrow

EXERCISE For each exercise write a word that completes the analogy.

1. ROUND : CIRCLE :: straight : ___?___
2. BIG : LARGE :: damp : ___?___
3. FRIEND : ENEMY :: coward : ___?___
4. PUSH : SHOVE :: like : ___?___
5. LEAF : TREE :: page : ___?___

The Southpaw
by Judith Viorst

Dear Richard,

Don't invite me to your birthday party because I'm not coming. And give back the Disneyland sweat shirt I said you could wear. If I'm not good enough to play on your team, I'm not good enough to be friends with.

Your former friend, Janet

P.S. I hope when you go to the dentist he finds twenty cavities.

Dear Janet,

Here is your stupid Disneyland sweat shirt, if that's how you're going to be. I want my comic books now—finished or not. No girl has ever played on the Mapes Street baseball team, and as long as I'm captain, no girl ever will.

Your former friend, Richard

P.S. I hope when you go for your checkup you need a tetanus shot.

Possible Objectives
- read and analyze literature with a group (Option One)
- use the Reader's Notebook to formulate questions about literature (Option Two)
- write in response to literature (Option Two)

Summary
This story is told through the exchange of letters between two friends who are arguing about the right of one of them to play on the neighborhood baseball team. Richard is the captain of the Mapes Street baseball team. Janet is his friend who wants to play on the team. She has been left out because she is a girl. Janet tries to blackmail Richard into putting her on the team by taking back things she'd given him, such as her sweatshirt, and by not inviting him for ice cream. Richard continues to refuse. As the summer wears on, however, his team loses game after game and his players drop out one by one. Finally, he is forced to ask Janet to play on the team, which she agrees to do only if she can pitch and the other neighborhood girls can play as well.

Reading the Selection

Option One
Shared Reading Groups
You may assign students to groups or allow them to choose their own. Students can read the selection together, alternately reading sections aloud, or they can read independently and meet to cooperate in a project that portrays some element of the story.

Possible Projects
- Students can collaborate on writing, in letter form, a different ending to the story in which Richard and Janet do not reach an agreement.
- Students can role-play an interview of Janet and Richard by a reporter for the school newspaper following Janet's first game.

Art

The painting on this page by Katherine Desjardins captures the feeling of conversations between friends. What are they saying? Who is saying what to whom?

While the people in the painting are realistic looking, the background isn't. Sometimes the shapes seem to link the friends, and sometimes they seem to separate them.

Ask: Why do you think this artwork has been chosen to illustrate "The Southpaw"?

Untitled (1998), Katherine Desjardins. Oil and resin on wood, 24" × 124". Photo: Dan Soper.

Why don't you forget about baseball and learn something nice like knitting?

I understand you're the laughingstock of New Jersey.

Dear Richard,

I'm changing my goldfish's name from Richard to Stanley. Don't count on my vote for class president next year. Just because I'm a member of the ballet club doesn't mean I'm not a terrific ballplayer.

Your former friend, Janet

P.S. I see you lost your first game, 28–0.

Dear Janet,

I'm not saving any more seats for you on the bus. For all I care you can stand the whole way to school. Why don't you forget about baseball and learn something nice like knitting?

Your former friend, Richard

P.S. Wait until Wednesday.

Dear Richard,

My father said I could call someone to go with us for a ride and hot-fudge sundaes. In case you didn't notice, I didn't call you.

Your former friend, Janet

P.S. I see you lost your second game, 34–0.

Dear Janet,

Remember when I took the laces out of my blue-and-white sneakers and gave them to you? I want them back.

Your former friend, Richard

P.S. Wait until Friday.

Dear Richard,

Congratulations on your unbroken record. Eight straight losses, wow! I understand you're the laughingstock of New Jersey.

Your former friend, Janet

P.S. Why don't you and your team forget about baseball and learn something nice like knitting, maybe?

Dear Janet,

Here's the silver horseback-riding trophy that you gave me. I don't think I want to keep it anymore.

Your former friend, Richard

P.S. I didn't think you'd be the kind who'd kick a man when he's down.

Dear Richard,

I wasn't kicking exactly. I was kicking back.

Your former friend, Janet

P.S. In case you were wondering my batting average is .345.

Dear Janet,

Alfie is having his tonsils out tomorrow. We might be able to let you catch next week.

Richard

Dear Richard,

I pitch.

Janet

Dear Janet,

Joel is moving to Kansas and Danny sprained his wrist. How about a permanent place in the outfield?

Richard

Dear Richard,

I pitch.

Janet

THE SOUTHPAW **351**

Art Note

The collage on this page, *Corrugated Catcher* by Saul Steinberg, takes a humorous look at baseball. The Romanian-born artist (1914–1999) was a keen observer of American culture, often using his sense of humor to comment on life in cartoons for the *New Yorker* magazine. This collage, which features the material often found in shipping boxes, has a light, whimsical attitude, which matches the tone of Viorst's storytelling style.

Corrugated Catcher (1954), Saul Steinberg, 29" × 20", courtesy of Jason Van Dalen. Copyright © 2001 Estate of Saul Steinberg/Artists Rights Society (ARS), New York.

I'll give you first base. That's my final offer.   I pitch.

Dear Janet,
  Ronnie caught the chicken pox and Leo broke his toe and Elwood has these stupid violin lessons. I'll give you first base. That's my final offer.
  Richard

Dear Richard,
  Susan Reilly plays first base, Marilyn Jackson catches, Ethel Kahn plays center field, I pitch. It's a package deal.
Janet
P.S. Sorry about your 12-game losing streak.

Dear Janet,
  Please! Not Marilyn Jackson.
  Richard

Dear Richard,
  Nobody ever said that I was unreasonable. How about Lizzie Martindale instead?
Janet

Dear Janet,
  At least could you call your goldfish Richard again?
  Your friend, Richard ❖

"I always, always, always wanted to be a writer."

Judith Viorst
born 1931

A Lifelong Writer Judith Viorst began writing poetry as a young child. "I took my writing very seriously," she says, "and thought everything I wrote was a masterpiece." After college she worked as an editor and journalist. While raising her children, she discovered that motherhood provided an endless source of material. The names and antics of her three sons made their way into her writing for children—most famously in her classic picture book *Alexander and the Terrible, Horrible, No Good, Very Bad Day.* This book was recently made into a musical, for which Viorst wrote many of the lyrics.

On the Go Viorst's writing is praised for its unique sense of humor and its sympathetic portrayals of life's everyday struggles. "It helps to understand that the losses of life . . . are part of the human condition," Viorst says. For nearly 40 years she has lived in Washington, D.C., with her husband, Milton Viorst, who is also a writer. Energetic and organized, she usually seems to be doing several things at the same time: once she cooked an entire chicken dinner while on the phone answering questions for a radio show. She has written dozens of books, ranging from collections of comic poetry to serious nonfiction books about psychology.

THE SOUTHPAW **353**

JUDITH VIORST
Judith Viorst's three children are perhaps the greatest source of inspiration for her writing. She wrote several of her books in response to problems that one or another of her own children was facing. Although she knew the books wouldn't solve their problems, she hoped that the books would help her boys "laugh at their problems, or look at them in less troubled, less hopeless ways."

Among the books that she wrote with her own children in mind are *I'll Fix Anthony,* which she wrote for her son Nick who bore the brunt of his older brother Anthony's teasing, and *Sunday Morning,* which features Anthony and Nick in a series of early morning adventures while their parents are still sleeping.

Analysis of Baseball
by May Swenson

It's about
the ball,
the bat,
and the mitt.
5 Ball hits
bat, or it
hits mitt.
Bat doesn't
hit ball, bat
10 meets it.
Ball bounces
off bat, flies
air, or thuds
ground (dud)
15 or it
fits mitt.

Bat waits
for ball
to mate.
20 Ball hates
to take bat's
bait. Ball
flirts, bat's
late, don't
25 keep the date.
Ball goes in
(thwack) to mitt,
and goes out
(thwack) back
30 to mitt.

Ball fits
mitt, but
not all
the time.
35 Sometimes
ball gets hit
(pow) when bat
meets it,
and sails
40 to a place
where mitt
has to quit
in disgrace.
That's about
45 the bases
loaded,
about 40,000
fans exploded.

It's about
50 the ball,
the bat,
the mitt,
the bases
and the fans.
55 It's done
on a diamond,
and for fun.
It's about
home, and it's
60 about run.

Communication Workshop — Staging a Scene

Preparing to present a play . . .

SPEAKING OPPORTUNITY — See the Communication Handbook, p. R100 for speaking and presenting tips.

From Reading to Staging Think of your favorite actors. They make acting look easy. However, there are many steps to creating a great movie or play. Someone has to choose or create a script, and decide on costumes and lighting. This is in addition to *blocking*—planning the actors' positions for each scene, and deciding how they will move around the stage. It's hard but interesting work. This is why **staging a scene** can help you appreciate how plays and movies bring a script to life.

For Your Portfolio

WRITING PROMPT Create a staged presentation of a scene from *Damon and Pythias.*

Purpose: To interpret and perform a scene

Audience: Your classmates and other interested students and adults

---

Basics in a Box

GUIDELINES AND STANDARDS   STAGING A SCENE

A successful script should

- include a description of the setting, props, lighting, and costumes
- include specific stage directions that describe gestures, movements, and the tone of voice the performers should use
- note details of pacing and stage location

A successful performance should

- show an awareness of the audience— actors' voices should be loud enough, and the audience should have an unblocked view of the action
- follow the script
- maintain the audience's interest through strong acting, good pacing, and effective staging

---

Communication Workshop
Staging a Scene

Objectives
- stage a scene
- punctuate dialogue correctly
- refine a performance by using standards to evaluate the effectiveness of the presentation

Introducing the Workshop

Staging a Scene Ask students to name any plays that they have seen. They may mention school plays, performances by local community theater groups, or professional productions. Engage them in a discussion about the aspects of the plays that they remember best—the music, costumes, scenery, particular actors and actresses, and so on. Have them think about why those features stand out in their minds.

Basics in a Box
Presenting the Guidelines and Standards Use the Guidelines and Standards for Staging a Scene to further clarify the assignment. The elements that make up a successful script provide everyone involved in a production all the information that they need to stage a play. The elements that make up a successful performance come together to effectively communicate the message of the play to the audience.

> Use McDougal Littell's *Language Network*, Chapters 29–30, for more instruction in essential skills.

> **Power Presentation**
>
> To engage students visually, use **Power Presentation 1**, Staging a Scene.

LESSON RESOURCES

Analyzing the Model

"Excerpts from Director's Script *Damon and Pythias*"

The model script supplies all the information that the cast and crew need to produce this scene. Tell students that the cast consists of the actors and actresses in the play, while the crew is made up of all the people who work "behind-the-scenes," doing music, lighting, costumes, props, scenery, and sound effects.

Have students read the model script. Then discuss the Guidelines in Action.

- Ask students why the beginning of the script contains a description of setting, lighting, and costumes, as well as props.
  Possible Response: This information is crucial for everyone involved in the play. It lays the groundwork, giving everyone the basic facts about the production and stating what is needed.

- Characters are listed in order of appearance, not importance. Why?
  Possible Response: Managing the "traffic" of a play is important, so it's essential to know who comes on stage and when.

- Ask students why a sketch of the stage is helpful.
  Possible Response: A sketch of the stage helps everyone to visualize how the scene will look. It tells where things and people go on stage.

- Ask students to explain the purpose of the handwritten notes in the margin of the script.
  Possible Response: These notes give the actors specific information about their actions and gestures. It also gives them some insight into their characters' personalities.

Analyzing a Model Script

Excerpts from Director's Script
Damon and Pythias

Setting and Lighting
Two settings are shown: the king's throne room, center stage, and the prison, back left. Lights focus on action, while rest of the stage is dark. Narrator stands front right. When narrator speaks, spotlight is used.

Characters
King, Pythias, Soldier, Narrator, Prison Guard, and Damon

Props
Throne for king; prison bars; crown for king; sandals, simple robes tied at the waist with a rope for other actors, shields and helmets for soldier and guard; cassette player with recorded music cued on cassette tape

GUIDELINES
IN ACTION

- A description of setting, lighting, and costumes appears at the beginning of the script.
- Performers are listed in the order in which they appear, along with a prop list.
- A sketch of the stage shows the positions of the actors and their movements.
- Handwritten notes show specific stage directions, tone of voice, gestures, and actions the actors should use.

throne — Guard — prison cell — Damon enters — King — Soldier — Pythias — stage right — stage left — Narrator

Soldier grabs Pythias roughly. → **King.** . . . Soldier! Throw this man into prison!

Soldier. At once, Your Majesty! Don't try to resist, Pythias!

Pythias is calm but folds his arms proudly. → **Pythias.** I know better than to try to resist a soldier of the king! And for how long am I to remain in prison, Your Majesty, merely for speaking out for the people?

King nods toward the prison. → **King.** (*cruel*). Not for very long, Pythias. Two weeks from today, at noon, you shall be put to death in the public square as an example to anyone else who may dare to question my laws or acts. Off to prison with him, soldier!

(*Music: In briefly and out.*)

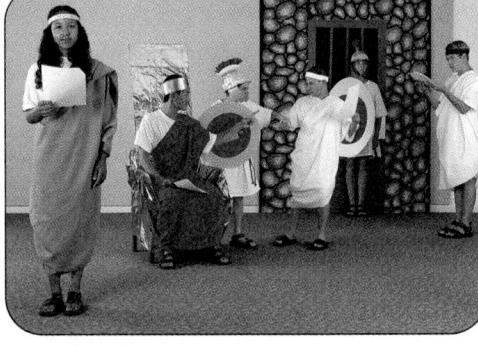

Damon is seen offering the guard money and clasping hands together in begging gesture.

Narrator. When Damon heard that his friend Pythias had been thrown into prison and the severe punishment that was to follow, he was heartbroken. He rushed to the prison and persuaded the guard to let him speak to his friend.

Damon grasps the bars and reaches toward his friend.

Damon. Oh, Pythias! How terrible to find you here! I wish I could do something to save you!

Pythias smiles and speaks calmly.

Pythias. Nothing can save me, Damon, my dear friend. I am prepared to die. But there is one thought that troubles me greatly.

Damon. What is it? I will do anything to help you.

Pythias. I'm worried about what will happen to my mother and my sister when I'm gone.

Damon. I'll take care of them, Pythias, as if they were my own mother and sister.

Pythias turns to stage left and looks into the distance.

Pythias. Thank you, Damon. I have money to leave them. But there are other things I must arrange. If only I could go to see them before I die! But they live two days' journey from here, you know.

Damon paces back and forth in front of the prison cell. His arm sweeps toward the audience when he says "Everyone in Sicily . . ."

Damon. I'll go to the king and beg him to give you your freedom for a few days. You'll give your word to return at the end of that time. Everyone in Sicily knows you for a man who has never broken his word.

Pythias shakes his head hopelessly.

Pythias. Do you believe for one moment that the king would let me leave this prison, no matter how good my word may have been all my life?

Damon. I'll tell him that I shall take your place in this prison cell. I'll tell him that if you do not return by the appointed day, he may kill me in your place!

Pythias tries to grab Damon. His voice is desperate. He holds his head in his hands as he speaks to himself.

Damon strides away with determination toward the king while Pythias is still calling to him.

Pythias. No, no, Damon! You must not do such a foolish thing! I cannot—I will not—let you do this! Damon! Damon! Don't go! (*to himself*) Damon, my friend! You may find yourself in a cell beside me!

All the lights dim.

(*Music: In briefly and out.*)

- Ask students why it is important to direct Damon to offer the guard money and clasp his hands together in a begging gesture.
  Possible Response: Because there are no lines in the script calling for Damon to verbally offer the guard money, the offer must be communicated through Damon's body language.
- Ask students why there is a note telling Pythias to turn toward the left and look into the distance.
  Possible Response: As Pythias delivers his lines about wanting to see his mother and sister, he needs to look in the direction of their home.
- Have students tell why Damon sweeps his arm toward the audience.
  Possible Response: Damon is imagining that the members of the audience are residents of Sicily. This device helps to engage the audience, making them feel as if they are part of the play.
- Ask students why it is important to note that Damon "strides away with determination toward the king"?
  Possible Response: It must be clear to the audience that Damon means business when he says that he'll go to the king. The purpose underlying his action must be clearly understood.

Staging Your Scene

Choosing a Scene

If students are having difficulty selecting a scene after they have read the suggestions in the Idea Bank, have them try the following:

- Choose a scene that seems difficult. Work together to break it down into parts and simplify what seems complicated.
- Select a scene that features your favorite character in a positive light.

Planning Your Scene

1. Ask if students are unfamiliar with any of the jobs mentioned. Invite volunteers to explain those jobs. If necessary, provide students with explanations.
2. Have students work in small teams to do the various jobs. Within each team, students decide who will be responsible for specific tasks. For example, if three students are on the prop crew, they will decide, as a team, on the props that are needed for the scene. Then individuals will volunteer to find or make specific props.
3. Tell students that the director works together with the lighting, sound, and scenery crew as well as the actors to make decisions.
4. Tell students to post a list of needed costumes, props, and set pieces. Students can sign up to bring in things that they already have at home.

Developing Your Stage Presentation

Tell students to write their notes clearly and simply so they will be easy to refer to. At the same time, the crew should be noting things they need to do.

IDEABank

1. Your Working Portfolio
Look for ideas in the **Writing Options** that you completed earlier in this unit.
- **Director's Notes,** p. 331
- **Dramatic Dialogue,** p. 338

2. Hidden Treasure
Choose a scene that might not seem important if someone were reading the play silently. Make it your goal to bring out the importance of what happens in this scene.

3. Playing Favorites
Choose your favorite scene from the play. If members of your group have more than one favorite, try staging parts from several scenes.

Staging Your Scene

❶ Planning Your Scene

With your classmates, choose a scene from *Damon and Pythias* to stage. **List** all of the important parts of the play. (The play is divided into sections by the stage directions that call for music.) Then pick your favorite scene. See the **Idea Bank** in the margin for other suggestions. After selecting a scene, follow the steps below.

Planning Your Scene

▶ **1. List responsibilities.** In addition to the acting roles, what other tasks need to be filled? Here are some possibilities:

- director
- prop manager
- sound manager
- lighting manager
- prompter
- prop crew
- set designer
- costume designer
- acting coach

▶ **2. Assign responsibilities.** Some members may have to take on more than one job. If one actor has two roles, make sure that both characters are not on stage at the same time. Choose jobs by volunteering or by drawing names.

▶ **3. Create a director's script.** The director should mark up a copy of the script with notes on where actors will stand, how they will move around the stage, and how they will speak their lines. Any lighting, sound, and scenery requirements should also be noted.

▶ **4. Gather costumes, props, and set decorations for staging.** What costumes and props will make the characters and actions seem real? Which will help to create the mood you want?

❷ Developing Your Stage Presentation

Actors make notes. Make sure that everyone in the group has read and discussed the scene thoroughly. Each actor should mark up his or her script with notes on tone of voice, actions, facial expressions, and stage position and movements for his or her part.

Crew jumps in. The crew should make notes on lighting, sound, and props that are needed. Everyone should have a responsibility. Those who do not have speaking parts can help during rehearsals by prompting the actors or coaching them.

❸ Practicing and Presenting

The entire cast should practice several times before presenting the scene.

- **Read through the scene.** Before using any movement, form a circle and have actors read their parts aloud. Practice tone of voice and emotion.
- **Walk through the scene.** Have actors take positions on the stage. Direct them through the movement, or *blocking*, while they are reading. Eliminate distracting or awkward movements. After a few run-throughs, practice using props. Then throw down the scripts!
- **Plug in the music and turn on the lights.** Test to be sure that the music and other sound effects aren't too loud. Try out various settings for the lights. Have the actors use props and costumes. Stop to make adjustments.
- **Stage a last rehearsal.** Run through the scene without pausing. Ask for comments from people watching.

Practicing TIP

Have someone videotape a rehearsal so that you can listen and watch for the parts of your presentation that are and are not working, and so that you can see whether the lighting, sound, and scenery need to be adjusted.

Ask Your Peer Reviewers

- What did you like most about the performance?
- What parts were hard to follow? Why?
- Was the staging effective? Was there enough movement? Was there any time when characters were difficult to see or hear?
- What actions and emotions seemed most believable?

❹ Refining Your Performance

TARGET SKILL ▶ EVALUATING YOUR STAGING CHOICES

You've had your rehearsals and gotten comments from peer reviewers. Now it's time to make adjustments. Think about the decisions you made. Use the following standards to evaluate your scene:

- **Awareness of audience.** Was the audience able to hear the actors? Were they able to see everything that happened?
- **Following the script.** Did all of the actors remember their lines? Did your performance stay true to the script that the playwright wrote?
- **Creating mood and character.** Did the actors' performances make the audience care about the characters? Was the scene presented too fast, too slow, or just right? Did your staging give added drama to the scene?

❺ Reflecting

FOR YOUR WORKING PORTFOLIO How did working to stage a scene help you appreciate the work that goes into movies and plays? What role in a stage production would you like to take next time? Why? Attach your answers to your marked-up script. Save your script in your **Working Portfolio.**

Publishing IDEAS

- Make a rehearsal videotape and compare it to a video of the actual performance. Comment on the changes you see.
- Take your show on the road and stage the scene for other classes.

More Online: Publishing Options
www.mcdougallittell.com

Practicing and Presenting

Invite a small group of students from another class to sit in on your dress rehearsal. Ask for their input at the end. Have each student who worked on the scene explain the job he or she had in the production of the scene. Emphasize the importance of every part, especially the behind-the-scenes jobs that are easily overlooked.

📖 Use **Communications Transparencies and Copymasters,** p. 16, for additional support.

Refining Your Performance

EVALUATING YOUR STAGING CHOICES

As students assess their decisions, tell them that a play is a dynamic creation. Although every play is based on a script, and performers need to recite the lines as they were written, there is much room for creativity. A director's interpretation of the script colors all the decisions that are made. You might mention that there have been many versions of the Shakespearean plays. Each one is distinctive, depending on the director's ideas about what Shakespeare had in mind.

📖 Use **Communications Transparencies and Copymasters,** p. 8, for additional support.

Reflecting

🗂 As they write about their experiences, tell students to think about the various steps that they took in preparing to stage their scene. Encourage them to think about the importance of each step.

Option

Teaching Tip

Obtain videotapes of two very different versions of the same play. Watch the videos with students. Discuss the differences between the two versions. Ask students to tell which one they preferred, and why.

📖 Use **Communications Transparencies and Copymasters,** p. 7, for additional support.

Assessment Practice Revising & Editing

Read this paragraph from a student essay. The underlined sections may include the following kinds of errors:

- **incorrect pronoun case**
- **verb tense errors**
- **incorrectly punctuated dialogue**
- **incorrectly used adverb and adjective modifiers**

For each underlined section, choose the revision that most improves the writing.

> <u>Sam Liu and me saw</u> a performance of *Damon and Pythias*
> (1)
> yesterday. <u>We watched enthusiastic.</u> The best moment was when
> (2)
> Damon proclaimed, <u>"I'll tell him that I shall take your place in this</u>
> (3)
> <u>prison cell."</u> It showed the strong friendship <u>between he and Pythias.</u>
> (4)
> <u>Damon then will stride off</u> to find the king and make his offer. <u>The king</u>
> (5)   (6)
> <u>didn't take Damon serious.</u> Damon meant what he said, however, and he
> and Pythias proved their friendship in the end.

1. A. Sam Liu and me seen
   B. Sam Liu and I saw
   C. Me and Sam Liu saw
   D. Correct as is

2. A. We watched enthusiastically.
   B. We watched very enthusiastic.
   C. We watched enthusiasm.
   D. Correct as is

3. A. Damon proclaimed I'll tell him that I shall take your place in this prison cell.
   B. Damon proclaimed, I'll tell him that I shall take your place in this prison cell.
   C. Damon proclaimed "I'll tell him that I shall take your place in this prison cell."
   D. Correct as is

4. A. between him and Pythias.
   B. between his and Pythias.
   C. between they.
   D. Correct as is

5. A. Damon then is striding off
   B. Damon then have strode off
   C. Damon then strode off
   D. Correct as is

6. A. The king didn't take Damon more serious.
   B. The king didn't take Damon seriously.
   C. The king didn't take Damon very serious.
   D. Correct as is

Need extra help?

See the **Grammar Handbook.**

Using Nouns and Pronouns, p. R65

Using Verbs Correctly, p. R68

Using Modifiers Effectively, p. R70

Correcting Punctuation, p. R78

 Mini Lesson Grammar

CORRECTLY PUNCTUATING DIALOGUE

Instruction Tell students that it is essential to use correct punctuation in dialogue. If the punctuation is wrong, then readers will not understand where narrative ends and speech begins. In addition to quotation marks, commas are used to separate narrative from dialogue.

Practice Have students read each of the following sentences, and then correct the punctuation.

1. Romeo said Oh, speak again, bright angel. (*said, "Oh/angel."*)
2. Juliet answered O Romeo, Romeo. Wherefore art thou Romeo? (*answered, "O/Romeo?"*)
3. The Montagues and the Capulets were rival families, said the narrator. (*"The/families,"*)
4. Come hither, Puck said Oberon to the merry wanderer. (*"Come hither, Puck,"*)

 Use **Grammar Transparencies and Copymasters**, p. 121.

 Use McDougal Littell's *Language Network*, Chapter 9, for more instruction and practice in punctuation.

Reflecting on the Theme Fairness is important with friends and family. It's also important in the larger world, where many people face barriers that make it difficult for them to pursue their goals. What do you think the world would be like if everyone had a fair chance to show what he or she could do?

ACTIVITY

Imagine that your proposal for a science project has been copied by a student who had "innocently" questioned you about it. What could you do to right this wrong? With classmates playing the roles of the other student and your teacher, role-play various ways of handling the situation. In your notebook, record your ideas about these possible resolutions.

- *help other student brainstorm*
- *give a warning*

361

Objectives
- understand and identify the following literary terms:
    - autobiography
    - biography
    - first-person point of view
    - third-person point of view
    - primary source
    - secondary source
    - author's perspective
    - bias
    - tone
- understand and appreciate autobiographies and biographies
- recognize the distinguishing features of autobiography and biography
- describe how the author's perspective or point of view affects the text

Teaching the Lesson

This lesson analyzes the basic elements of autobiographies and biographies and explains how the two types of nonfiction differ from each other.

Introducing the Concepts
Ask students to think about an event or incident from their own lives that they might want to write about. Ask for volunteers to share their topic, a possible opening sentence, and the reason they would want to write about this experience.

Presenting the Concepts
Point of View

Explain to students that an autobiography, which is written from the first-person point of view can reveal much about the author's personality. In a biography, written from the third person point-of-view, the writer tells about the experiences of the subject's life in the writer's own style and language.

YOUR TURN
Possible Response: The use of the pronouns "I" and "me" indicates that this excerpt is autobiographical.

Use **Literary Analysis Transparencies,** pp. 10, 11, 14, 22, 25, for additional support.

LEARNING the Language of Literature

Autobiography and Biography

> *[Before I write a biography, a] character in history will suddenly step right out of the past and demand a book. Once my character and I reach an understanding, then I begin the detective work.*
>
> —Jean Fritz, writer

Have you ever read the story of someone's life? If so, you have entered a world of emotions and experiences you could not have known otherwise. **Autobiographies** and **biographies** are two types of nonfiction that tell a life story. The main difference between them is in who does the telling. In an autobiography, the writer tells the story of his or her own life. A biography, however, is the story of someone's life written by another person. The stories the author chooses to include in a biography may help readers to understand the **author's perspective** on his or her subject, and the **author's purpose** for writing.

Point of View

Autobiographies are usually written from the **first-person point of view.** The writer tells about his or her own personal experiences and uses the pronouns *I, me,* and *we.* Biographies, on the other hand, are usually written from the **third-person point of view.** You know a piece is a biography because the writer is outside the story and uses pronouns such as *he, she,* and *they.*

YOUR TURN Is this excerpt from *The Story of My Life* by Helen Keller autobiographical or biographical?

POINT OF VIEW

I did not know what the future held of marvel or surprise for me. Anger and bitterness had preyed upon me continually for weeks and a deep languor had succeeded this passionate struggle.

The Story of My Life by Helen Keller

Primary and Secondary Sources

In order to gather information about a person's life, biographers and other writers of nonfiction use primary and secondary sources. **Primary sources** include materials like **autobiographies, journals, diaries, memoirs, letters, photographs,** and **legal documents.** They provide direct, firsthand knowledge. **Secondary sources** provide indirect, secondhand knowledge. Examples of secondary sources include **articles, reference books, reports,** and **biographies.**

Libraries are a good place to start looking for primary and secondary sources. The Internet also features good primary and secondary sources on a variety of subjects. For example, you can use the Internet to find interesting material on Helen Keller. If you decide to use an online source, always make sure it is trustworthy.

YOUR TURN What kinds of sources might the author have used to write this biography of Ibrahima, the son of an African chief?

Author's Perspective

The way an author sees the world is called the **author's perspective.** The author's ideas, attitudes, feelings, beliefs, and values can often be found in his or her tone. The **tone** of a work shows the author's attitude toward the subject. For example, the tone might be humorous, admiring, angry, or sad. Other clues to the author's perspective include direct statements, the ways in which the author describes important individuals, and the author's background. In nonfiction, it is important to look for the author's **biases,** or preferences and prejudices. Recognizing bias will help you determine the **author's purpose** for writing, and help you decide if the author's ideas are fair and truthful.

SOURCES

For Ibrahima there was confusion and pain. What was he to do? A few months before, he had been a learned man and a leader among his people. Now he was a captive in a strange land where he neither spoke the language nor understood the customs. Was he never to see his family again? Were his sons forever lost to him?

As a Fula, Ibrahima wore his hair long; Foster insisted that it be cut. Ibrahima's clothing had been taken from him, and his sandals. Now the last remaining symbol of his people, his long hair, had been taken as well.

—Walter Dean Myers,
"Abd al-Rahman Ibrahima," from *Now Is Your Time!*

From "Abd al-Rahman Ibrahima"

Primary and Secondary Sources
Ask students to create a plan for researching the life of Albert Einstein. Where would they look first? How would they progress from there? Ask them to explain their reasoning for each step.

YOUR TURN
Possible Response: The author may have used secondary sources, such as biographies of slaves and former slaves and reference books on life in Africa and on slavery. The author may also have used primary sources, such as memoirs and autobiographies of slaves and former slaves, legal documents that describe the rights of slave owners, and journals and diaries written by both slave owners and abolitionists.

Author's Perspective
Have students think of a biography they have previously read as a class. Ask them to identify the tone of the work and to discuss how they think the author views the person he or she was writing about. What do these two things reveal about the author of the work?

LEARNING THE LANGUAGE OF LITERATURE **363**

OVERVIEW

Objectives

- develop effective strategies, such as using a time line, for understanding chronological order
- learn to use a text's structure or progression of ideas such as chronology to locate and recall information

Teaching the Lesson

The strategies on this page will help students understand and recognize chronological order.

Presenting the Strategies

Help students understand the strategies by asking for volunteers to read them aloud. Emphasize to students that they will be using these skills as they read various selections in this book.

Skim for Words That Signal Time

Remind students that when they see words like *first, second, next, then, finally, after, before,* and *soon,* they should stop and clearly place the event being signaled in its chronology.

Question and Clarify

Tell students that by asking themselves when an event takes place in relation to another event, they can clarify what is happening. Using a time line will help them keep these events in chronological order.

Evaluate

Sometimes a story is not told in chronological order. For example, a writer might alternate current events with flashbacks. In that case, it is up to the reader to put the pieces of information together in a meaningful way.

Use **Reading and Critical Thinking Transparencies,** p. 6, for additional support.

Have you ever asked an older person about your family's history? If so, he or she may have said something like this: "My father was born in 1910 in Great Britain. Then when he was eight, he moved to the United States." When events are presented as they occurred in time, it is called chronological order. Knowing this skill can help you keep track of information.

Chronological Order

How to Apply the Skill

To understand **chronological order,** an active reader will:
- Skim the selection for dates and words that signal time
- Ask **questions** about what happens first, next, last
- **Clarify** the sequence of events with a time line
- **Evaluate** whether the order of events make sense

Try It Now!

The time line below shows some of the events described in "Abd al-Rahman Ibrahima." How can a time line like this one help you keep track of events?

1762
Ibrahima
is born.

1781
Dr. Cox comes
to the village.

1760   1770   1780   1790   1800   1810   1820

1788
Ibrahima is sold
into slavery.

Here's how Jillian uses the skill:

"When I read 'Abd al-Rahman Ibrahima,' I looked for dates. I took notes on major events and time periods.
"Sometimes while reading I make a time line that starts when someone was born. I mark the time line with even spaces, every 5, 10, or 20 years. Then I add the events. I can then clarify the order of events by seeing what happened in what sequence."

Need More Help?

Remember that active readers use the essential reading strategies explained on page 4: • **visualize** • **predict** • **clarify** • **question** • **connect** • **evaluate** • **monitor.**

364   UNIT THREE   PART 2: BREAKING BARRIERS

Abd al-Rahman Ibrahima
from Now Is Your Time!

Biography by WALTER DEAN MYERS

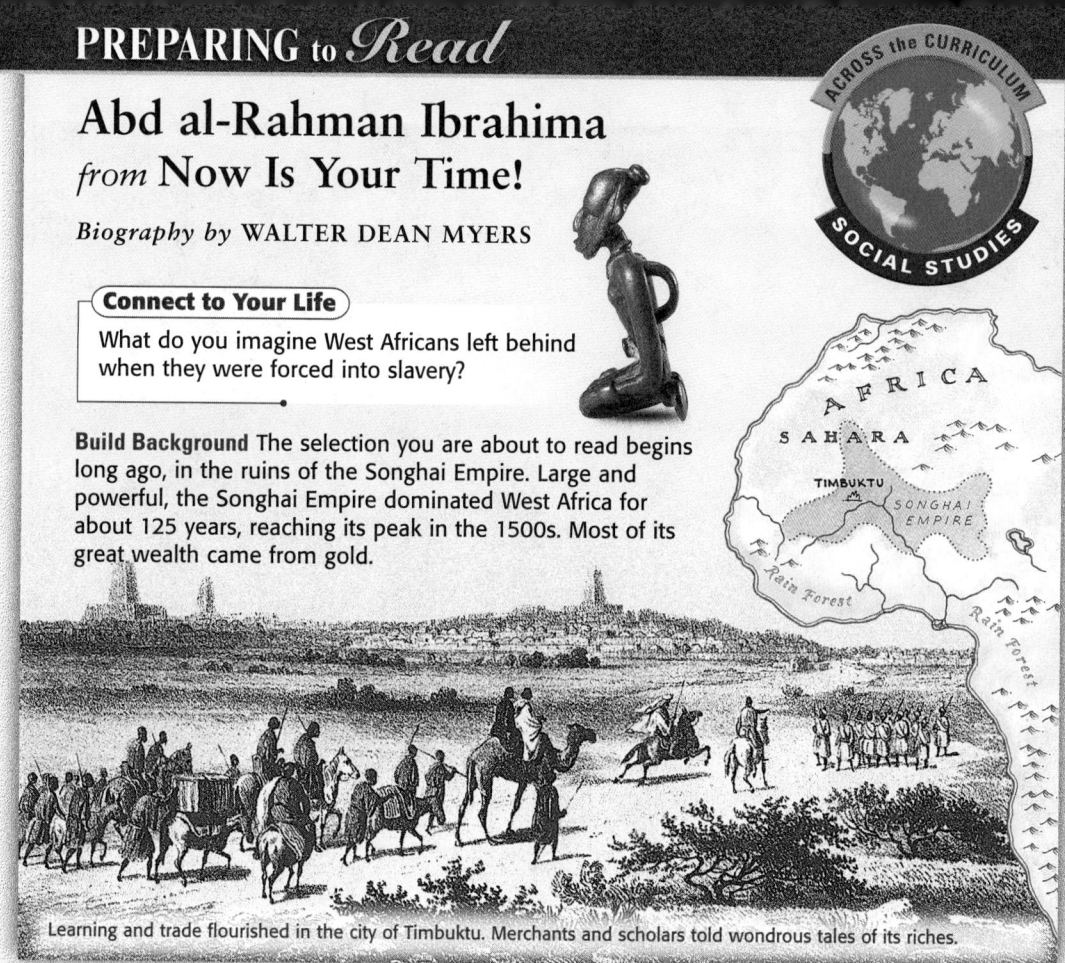

ACROSS the CURRICULUM
SOCIAL STUDIES

Connect to Your Life

What do you imagine West Africans left behind when they were forced into slavery?

Build Background The selection you are about to read begins long ago, in the ruins of the Songhai Empire. Large and powerful, the Songhai Empire dominated West Africa for about 125 years, reaching its peak in the 1500s. Most of its great wealth came from gold.

AFRICA
SAHARA
TIMBUKTU
SONGHAI EMPIRE
Rain Forest
Rain Forest

Learning and trade flourished in the city of Timbuktu. Merchants and scholars told wondrous tales of its riches.

Focus Your Reading

LITERARY ANALYSIS   SOURCES OF INFORMATION

The information that writers of nonfiction present comes from various sources. A **primary source** conveys firsthand knowledge based on someone's own experience. "Abd al-Rahman Ibrahima" is a **secondary source,** since the information it contains comes from Walter Dean Myers's research.

WORDS TO KNOW **Vocabulary Preview**

bondage	inhabitant	prosper	status
chaos	premise	reservation	trek
dynasty	procedure		

ACTIVE READING   CHRONOLOGICAL ORDER

Chronological order is the order in which events happen in time. In some narratives, events are related in chronological order. Other narratives move backward and forward in time.

 READER'S NOTEBOOK "Abd al-Rahman Ibrahima" covers one man's life from his birth in 1762 to his death in 1829. Make a time line to keep track of events. As you read, write in the years and events mentioned in the selection.

LaserLinks: Background for Reading
Cultural Connection
Historical Connection

OVERVIEW

This selection is included in the **Grade 6 InterActive Reader.** This selection appears in Spanish in the **Spanish Study Guide.**

Objectives
1. understand and appreciate a **biography** (Literary Analysis)
2. understand author's use of **sources of information** (Literary Analysis)
3. use **chronological order** to help understand the sequence of events in a biography (**Active Reading**)

Summary
Abd al-Rahman Ibrahima was born in Africa in 1762, the son of a Fula chieftain. Ibrahima was captured during an intertribal battle, sold to slave traders, and shipped to America. There, a Mississippi farmer named Thomas Foster bought him. To Foster, the African's claims to nobility meant nothing—he was simply a possession. After 20 years as a slave, he met John Cox, an Irish doctor who had lived with the Fula in Africa years before. Cox began a campaign to free Ibrahima. The African gained his freedom through the intervention of the Moroccan and American governments. In 1829, Ibrahima sailed with his wife to return to his homeland. He never reached his people, however. He died in the West African colony of Liberia that year.

Thematic Link
The story of Ibrahima and Dr. Cox shows how people can break through the barriers of culture to find a common human bond that transcends all.

5-Minute Warm-Up

Daily Language SkillBuilder

Have students **proofread** the display sentences on page 315j and write them correctly. The sentences also appear on Transparency 11 of **Grammar Transparencies and Copymasters.**

Mini Lesson Preteaching Vocabulary

If you would like to preteach the WORDS TO KNOW for this selection, use the Mini Lesson p. 367.

LESSON RESOURCES

UNIT THREE RESOURCE BOOK, pp. 27–33

ASSESSMENT
Formal Assessment, pp. 57–58
Teacher's Guide to Assessment and Portfolio Use
Test Generator

SKILLS TRANSPARENCIES AND COPYMASTERS
Literary Analysis
• Primary/Secondary Source, TR 14 (for Coop. Activity, p. 378)
Reading and Critical Thinking
• Chronological Order, TR 6 (for Thinking Through the Literature, p. 378)

Grammar
• Using *Less, Fewer, More, Many* CM 94 (for Mini Lesson, p. 372)
• Avoiding Double Comparatives and Superlatives, CM 97 (for Mini Lesson, p. 380)
Vocabulary
• Analyzing Word Parts, CM 40 (for Mini Lesson, p. 367)
• Prefixes and Suffixes, CM 41 (for Mini Lesson, p. 370)
Communications
• Dramatic Reading, TR 12 (for Mini Lesson, p. 374)

INTEGRATED TECHNOLOGY
Audio Library
LaserLinks
• Historical Connection; Religious Connection. See **Teacher's SourceBook,** p. 32
Internet: Research Starter

Visit our website:
www.mcdougallittell.com

Active Reading

CHRONOLOGICAL ORDER

Students are expected to use the text's structure or progression of ideas such as cause and effect or chronology to locate and recall information. Have students give examples of narratives (either in print or in films) that are told in chronological order. Then have them give contrasting examples of narratives told in non-chronological order. They may be able to think of narratives that use flashbacks, for example. Then explain that "Abd al-Rahman Ibrahima" is written in chronological order. Ask them to consider, as they read, how flashbacks might have been used to tell the story.

 Use **Unit Three Resource Book,** p. 28 for more practice.

Literary Analysis

SOURCES OF INFORMATION

Ask students to think as they read about the kind of primary sources Walter Dean Myers might have used to get the facts on which to base his story. When they have finished reading, discuss these possible sources with them to determine which would be trustworthy and which would not.

Possible Response: Myers might have consulted newspaper accounts of the time, government documents, records of abolitionist societies, and personal letters. Students should be aware that some sources might not be as trustworthy as others because they are based on incomplete information or personal opinion.

 Use **Unit Three Resource Book,** p. 29 for more practice.

Into Bondage (1936), Aaron Douglas. The Evans-Tibbs Collection, Washington, D.C.

Teaching Options

 Mini Lesson **Viewing and Representing**

Into Bondage
by Aaron Douglas

ART APPRECIATION This mural by Harlem Renaissance artist Aaron Douglas (1899–1979) depicts the enslavement of Africans and their removal from their homeland. The 60-by-60-inch mural was commissioned for the Texas Centennial Exposition in 1936.

Instruction Explain that the artist has included several symbolic elements in his painting. Symbolic elements can often be recognized because they depart from strict realism. Point out that ships in the painting are probably intended to be symbols, as they are not shown in correct scale, and would not be sailing at full speed directly for the coast. Ask students what the ships represent.

Possible Response: The ships represent the voyage away from the African homeland into bondage in the Americas.

Application Ask students what the star represents.

Possible Response: It may represent the distant hope of achieving freedom again.

Abd al-Rahman Ibrahima

from NOW IS YOUR TIME!

by Walter Dean Myers

. . . The Africans came from many countries, and from many cultures. Like the Native Americans, they established their territories based on centuries of tradition. Most, but not all, of the Africans who were brought to the colonies came from central and West Africa. Among them was a man named Abd al-Rahman Ibrahima.

 Mini Lesson ## Preteaching Vocabulary

ANALYZING WORD PARTS
Instruction Explain to students that they can often determine the meaning of unfamiliar words by breaking them down into parts. The main parts of words are prefixes (added to the beginning of a word), suffixes (added to the end), and roots (bases of words, often from Greek, Latin, or another language). Common prefixes are *in-, pro-, pre-,* and *re-.* Common suffixes are *-age, -ant, -ure,* and *-tion.* Show students how to analyze the word *inhabitant.* (*In-* is a prefix, *-ant* is a suffix, and *habit* is the root.) Tell students that the root *habit* means "to live [somewhere]." Have them look up the prefix and suffix in a dictionary to determine what the word *inhabitant* means and explain. (It means someone *[-ant]* who lives *[habit]* in *[in-]* a place.)
Exercises Have students analyze the parts of the following words:
1. premise (prefix: *pre-;* root: *mis*)
2. procedure (prefix: *pro-;* root: *ced;* suffix: *-ure*)
3. reservation (prefix: *re-;* root: *serv;* suffix: *-tion*)

 Use **Unit Three Resource Book,** p. 30 for more practice. Use **Vocabulary Transparencies and Copymasters,** p. 40, for more practice.

Literary Analysis: PLOT

A Students are expected to recognize and analyze story plot, setting, and problem resolution. Explain to students that a story's plot usually begins with an exposition, in which an author provides background for understanding the story and sets up the story's major theme. Ask students what important information is provided in the exposition to this selection.

Possible Response: The exposition gives important background information about how life in Africa changed drastically after the arrival of European invaders, which will be important in understanding what happens to Ibrahima.

ACTIVE READING

B **CLARIFY** Make sure that students' responses indicate an awareness of how privileged Ibrahima's life has been so far.

Literary Analysis: DESCRIPTION

C Have a volunteer read aloud the description of John Coates Cox. Ask students what mental image forms in their minds as they listen to the description.

Possible Response: He is a small white man with a patch over one eye who hobbles on one leg into the village, favoring a leg with a wound that is badly infected.

A he European invaders, along with those Africans who cooperated with them, had made the times dangerous. African nations that had lived peacefully together for centuries now eyed each other warily. Slight insults led to major battles. Bands of outlaws roamed the countryside attacking the small villages, kidnapping those unfortunate enough to have wandered from the protection of their people. The stories that came from the coast were frightening. Those kidnapped were taken to the sea and sold to whites, put on boats, and taken across the sea. No one knew what happened then.

Abd al-Rahman Ibrahima was born in 1762 in Fouta Djallon, a district of the present country of Guinea.[1] It is a beautiful land of green mountains rising majestically from grassy plains, a land rich with minerals, especially bauxite.

Ibrahima was a member of the powerful and influential Fula people and a son of one of their chieftains. The religion of Islam had swept across Africa centuries before, and the young Ibrahima was raised in the tradition of the Moslems.[2]

1 The Fula were taller and lighter in complexion than the other <u>inhabitants</u> of Africa's west coast; they had silky hair, which they often wore long. A pastoral[3] people, the Fula had a complex system of government, with the state divided into nine provinces and each province divided again into smaller districts. Each province had its chief and its subchiefs.

As the son of a chief, Ibrahima was expected to assume a role of political leadership when he came of age. He would also be expected to set a moral example and to be well versed in

his religion. When he reached twelve he was sent to Timbuktu[4] to study.

Under the Songhai[5] <u>dynasty</u> leader Askia the Great, Timbuktu had become a center of learning and one of the largest cities in the Songhai Empire. The young Ibrahima knew he was privileged to attend the best-known school in West Africa. Large and sophisticated, with wide, tree-lined streets, the city attracted scholars from Africa, Europe, and Asia. Islamic law, medicine, and mathematics were taught to the young men destined to become the leaders of their nations. It was a good place for a young man to be. The city was well guarded, too. It had to be, to prevent the <u>chaos</u> that, more and more, dominated African life nearer the coast.

Ibrahima learned first to recite from the Koran, the Moslem holy book, and then to read it in Arabic. From the Koran, it was felt, came all other knowledge. After Ibrahima had finished his studies in Timbuktu, he returned to Fouta Djallon to continue to prepare himself to be a chief.

ACTIVE READING

B **CLARIFY** What was Ibrahima's life like up to this point?

The Fula had little contact with whites, and what little contact they did have was filled with

---

1. **Fouta Djallon** (füt'ə-jə-lōn'). . . **Guinea** (gĭn'ē): Fouta Djallon is a small, mountainous region in Guinea, a small nation on the west coast of Africa.
2. **Islam** (ĭs-läm'). . . **Moslems** (mŏz'ləmz): refers to the Moslem merchants who traveled the gold-salt routes of wealthy West African empires and introduced Islam to the region. (A Moslem is a believer in the religion of Islam.)
3. **pastoral** (păs'tər-əl): having a way of life based on raising livestock.
4. **Timbuktu** (tĭm'bŭk-tōō'): now known as Tombouctou, a city in the part of Africa now known as Mali.
5. **Songhai** (sông'hī'): a West African empire that thrived in the 1400s and 1500s.

WORDS TO KNOW
inhabitant (ĭn-hăb'ĭ-tənt) *n.* someone living in a particular place
dynasty (dī'nə-stē) *n.* a series of rulers who are members of the same family
chaos (kā'ŏs) *n.* a state of great disorder

BLOCK SCHEDULING: MANAGING TIME

If your schedule requires that you cover the lesson objectives in a shorter time, use . . .
- Preparing to Read, p. 365
- Thinking Through the Literature, p. 378
- Vocabulary in Action, p. 379
- Grammar in Context, p. 380

If you want to take advantage of longer class time, use . . .
- TE Teaching Options: Viewing and Representing, pp. 366, 376; Preteaching Vocabulary, p. 367; Cross Curricular Links, pp. 369, 371, 373; Vocabulary Strategy, p. 370; Grammar, pp. 372, 380; Speaking and Listening, p. 374; Standardized Test Practice, p. 375
- Literary Link, pp. 376–377
- Choices & Challenges and Author Activity, pp. 379–380

danger. So when, in 1781, a white man claiming to be a ship's surgeon stumbled into one of their villages, they were greatly surprised.

John Coates Cox hardly appeared to be a threat. A slight man, blind in one eye, he had been lost for days in the forested regions bordering the mountains. He had injured his leg, and it had become badly infected as he tried to find help. By the time he was found and brought to the Fula chiefs, he was more dead than alive.

Dr. Cox, an Irishman, told of being separated from a hunting party that had left from a ship on which he had sailed as ship's surgeon. The Fula chief decided that he would help Cox. He was taken into a hut, and a healer was assigned the task of curing his infected leg.

During the months Dr. Cox stayed with the Fula, he met Ibrahima, now a tall, brown-skinned youth who had reached manhood. His bearing reflected his status as the son of a major chief. Dr. Cox had learned some Fulani, the Fula language, and the two men spoke. Ibrahima was doubtless curious about the white man's world, and Dr. Cox was as impressed by Ibrahima's education as he had been by the kindness of his people.

When Dr. Cox was well enough to leave, he was provided with a guard; but before he left, he warned the Fula about the danger of venturing too near the ships that docked off the coast of Guinea. The white doctor knew that the ships were there to take captives.

Cox and Ibrahima embraced fondly and said their good-byes, thinking they would never meet again.

Ibrahima married and became the father of several children. He was in his mid-twenties when he found himself leading the Fula cavalry in their war with the Mandingo.[6]

The first battles went well, with the enemy retreating before the advancing Fula. The foot warriors attacked first, breaking the enemy's ranks and making them easy prey for the well-trained Fula cavalry. With the enemy in full rout[7] the infantry returned to their towns while the horsemen, led by Ibrahima, chased the remaining stragglers. The Fula fought their enemies with spears, bows, slings, swords, and courage.

His bearing reflected his status as the son of a major chief.

The path of pursuit led along a path that narrowed sharply as the forests thickened. The fleeing warriors disappeared into the forest that covered a sharply rising mountain. Thinking the enemy had gone for good, Ibrahima felt it would be useless to chase them further.

"We could not see them," he would write later.

But against his better judgment, he decided to look for them. The horsemen dismounted at the foot of a hill and began the steep climb on

---

6. **Mandingo** (măn-dĭng'gō): any of various peoples of West Africa.

7. **in full rout:** in complete retreat.

WORDS
TO
KNOW
status (stā'təs) *n.* one's position in society; rank

369

Cross Curricular Link **History**

WEST AFRICAN TRIBES Inhabited West Africa is formed of two zones: the savanna, or grasslands, in the interior and the rain forest along the coast. In the savanna, there are three main groups of people: the Mande, including the Bambara, the Malinke, the Soninke, and others; the Voltaic group, including the Senufo, Lobi, Grunshi, Dogon, and Mossi; and the non-Muslim peoples of northern Nigeria, Niger, and Cameroon. Mingled with these non-Muslim tribes are the Muslim Fula or Fulani, the tribe to which Ibrahima belonged. (The enemies of the Fula, the Mandingo, belong to the Mande group.)

Along the Nigerian coast are found the Igbo, Ibibio, Edo, and Yoruba, and to the west can be found the Edo, Yorba, Fon, Ewe, Ga, Ashanti, Anyi, Fanti, Kru, Mende, Dyula, and the Wolof people. Generally the people of the savanna were herders and used horses for transport, as did Ibrahima's people. The rain forest was unsuitable for both cattle and horses, so people there survived by farming in forest clearings and by trade.

Literary Analysis: RISING ACTION

Explain to students that the term *rising action* refers to the part of a plot in which the main character encounters problems and complications. Ask students to identify the point at which they can see a clear example of rising action.
Possible Response: The moment at which Ibrahima is captured is clearly an example of rising action.

Reading Skills and Strategies: SUMMARIZE

A Have students summarize how Ibrahima came to be captured.
Possible Response: He was leading the Fula against another people, the Mandingo. Although the Mandingo seemed to be retreating, they were actually leading the Fula into a trap. Although Ibrahima tried to escape with his soldiers, and then to defend himself, he was knocked unconscious.

Literary Analysis
SOURCES OF INFORMATION

Have students speculate about what sources Myers might have used to reconstruct what happened to Ibrahima during the attack on the Mandingo.
Possible Response: He might have used an account by someone Ibrahima talked to in America.

Use **Literary Analysis Transparencies**, p. 14, for additional support.

Reading Skills and Strategies: PREDICT

Ask students to predict what will happen when Ibrahima is captured.
Possible Response: Students should be able to guess that Ibrahima will be sold into slavery in the Americas.

foot. Halfway up the hill the Fula realized they had been lured into a trap! Ibrahima heard the rifles firing, saw the smoke from the powder and the men about him falling to the ground, screaming in agony. Some died instantly. Many horses, hit by the gunfire, thrashed about in pain and panic. The firing was coming from both sides, and Ibrahima ordered his men to the top of the hill, where they could, if time and Allah permitted it, try a charge using the speed and momentum of their remaining horses.

Ibrahima was among the first to mount, and urged his animal onward. The enemy warriors came out of the forests, some with bows and arrows, others with muskets that he knew they had obtained from the Europeans. The courage of the Fula could not match the fury of the guns. Ibrahima called out to his men to save **A** themselves, to flee as they could. Many tried to escape, rushing madly past the guns. Few survived.

Those who did clustered about their young leader, determined to make one last, desperate stand. Ibrahima was hit in the back by an arrow, but the aim was not true and the arrow merely cut his broad shoulder. Then something smashed against his head from the rear.

The next thing Ibrahima knew was that he was choking. Then he felt himself being lifted from water. He tried to move his arms, but they had been fastened securely behind his back. He had been captured.

1 When he came to his full senses, he looked around him. Those of his noble cavalry who had not been captured were already dead. Ibrahima was unsteady on his legs as his clothes and sandals were stripped from him. The victorious Mandingo warriors now pushed him roughly into file with his men. They began the long <u>trek</u> that would lead them to the sea.

In Fouta Djallon being captured by the enemy meant being forced to do someone else's bidding,[8] sometimes for years. If you could get a message to your people, you could, perhaps, buy your freedom. Otherwise, it was only if you were well liked, or if you married one of your captor's women, that you would be allowed to go free or to live like a free person.

Ibrahima sensed that things would not go well for him.

The journey to the sea took weeks. Ibrahima was tied to other men, with ropes around their necks. Each day they walked from dawn to dusk. Those who were slow were knocked brutally to the ground. Some of those who could no longer walk were speared and left to die in agony. It was the lucky ones who were killed outright if they fell.

T he journey to the sea took weeks. Ibrahima was tied to other men, with ropes around their necks.

When they reached the sea, they remained bound hand and foot. There were men and women tied together. Small children clung to their mothers as they waited for the boats to come and the bargaining to begin.

---

8. **do someone else's bidding:** follow another's orders.

WORDS TO KNOW   **trek** (trĕk) *n.* a slow, difficult journey

370

Mini Lesson Vocabulary Strategy

PREFIXES AND SUFFIXES
Instruction Students are expected to be able to use structural analysis to identify root words with prefixes. Explain to students that a prefix is a letter or group of letters at the beginning of a word that has meaning when attached to a root. A suffix is similar, but added to the end of a word. Both prefixes and suffixes change the meaning of the root or base word. Suffixes often show changes in number (*-s, -es*), changes in tense (*-ed*), changes in degree of comparison (*-er, -est*), or changes in part of speech (*-y, -ly*).

Exercises Have students explain how the addition of a prefix or suffix changes the meaning in the following word pairs. Have students check the meanings of the added word part in question in a dictionary if necessary.

1. bond, bondage (*makes into something that describes a state or condition*)
2. proceed, procedure (*makes into a noun that is a process*)
3. reserve, reservation (*makes into a noun*)

Use **Vocabulary Transparencies and Copymasters**, p. 41.

Mecklenberg County: High Cotton Mother and Child (1978), Romare Bearden. Courtesy of the Estate of Romare Bearden.
Copyright © Romare Bearden Foundation/Licensed by VAGA, New York, NY.

Ibrahima, listening to the conversations of the men who held him captive, could understand those who spoke Arabic. These Africans were a low class of men, made powerful by the guns they had been given, made evil by the white man's goods. But it didn't matter who was evil and who was good. It only mattered who held the gun.

Ibrahima was inspected on the shore, then put into irons and herded into a small boat that took him out to a ship that was larger than any he had ever seen.

The ship onto which Ibrahima was taken was already crowded with black captives. Some shook in fear; others, still tied, fought by hurling their bodies at their captors. The beating and the killing continued until the ones who were left knew that their lot was hopeless.

On board the ship there were more whites with guns, who shoved them toward the open hatch. Some of the Africans hesitated at the hatch, and were clubbed down and pushed belowdecks.

It was dark beneath the deck, and difficult to breathe. Bodies were pressed close against other bodies. In the section of the ship he was in, men prayed to various gods in various languages. It seemed that the whites would never stop pushing men into the already crowded space. Two sailors pushed the Africans into position so that each would lie in the smallest space possible. The sailors panted and sweated as they untied the men and then chained them to a railing that ran the length of the ship.

The ship rolled against its mooring as the anchor was lifted, and the journey began. The

Cross Curricular Link Geography

THE SLAVE TRIANGLE The trade routes on which slaves were shipped formed a triangle between Europe, West Africa, and the Americas. For example, a British ship would typically sail to Africa on the first leg, loaded with rum and other goods. It would exchange these items for slaves and then sail on the so-called Middle Passage to the Americas. (This Middle Passage has become notorious for the tremendous loss of life that resulted from inhuman conditions on board the slave ships.) The third leg of the triangular route brought ships back to Britain with goods from the Americas, including molasses. This product of sugar cane farming could be distilled into rum, which could then be carried back to Africa to trade for more slaves.

372

Reading and Analyzing

ACTIVE READING

A **CHRONOLOGICAL ORDER**

Possible Response: The Africans were crammed into small spaces and chained. Once a day they were taken on deck to exercise and be fed beans or rice and yams and water. Many of them got sick and died.

Literary Analysis: PLOT

Ask students to explain why the sale of Ibrahima as a slave is an important moment in the plot.

Possible Response: It is at this point in the plot that the complete change in his life begins to become clear.

ACTIVE READING

B **CLARIFY** Ibrahima had no way to get back to Africa, and he lived in a society ruled by white people.

Active Reading

CHRONOLOGICAL ORDER

Students are expected to use the text's structure such as chronology to locate and recall information. Write the following list of events and have students determine the order in which they take place:

- Ibrahima is whipped. (4)
- Ibrahima is sold to Foster. (1)
- Ibrahima escapes. (5)
- Ibrahima tries to explain who he is to Foster. (2)
- Ibrahima decides to work for Foster. (6)
- Ibrahima's hair is cut. (3)

Use **Reading and Critical Thinking Transparencies,** p. 6, for additional support.

---

boards of the ship creaked and moaned as it lifted and fell in the sea. Some of the men got sick, vomiting upon themselves in the wretched darkness. They lay cramped, muscles aching, irons cutting into their legs and wrists, gasping for air.

Once a day they would be brought out on deck and made to jump about for exercise. They were each given a handful of either beans or rice cooked with yams, and water from a cask. The white sailors looked hardly better than the Africans, but it was they who held the guns.

Illness and the stifling conditions on the ships caused many deaths. How many depended largely on how fast the ships could be loaded with Africans and how long the voyage from Africa took. It was not unusual for 10 percent of the Africans to die if the trip took longer than the usual twenty-five to thirty-five days.

Ibrahima, now twenty-six years old, reached Mississippi in 1788. As the ship approached land, the Africans were brought onto the deck and fed. Some had oil put on their skins so they would look better; their sores were treated or covered with pitch. Then they were given garments to wear in an obvious effort to improve their appearance.

ACTIVE READING

CHRONOLOGICAL ORDER
In your own words, describe the sequence of events of Ibrahima's journey by ship.

A

Although Ibrahima could not speak English, he understood he was being bargained for. The white man who stood on the platform with him made him turn around, and several other white men neared him, touched his limbs, examined his teeth, looked into his eyes, and made him move about.

Thomas Foster, a tobacco grower and a hard-working man, had come from South Carolina with his family and had settled on

---

the rich lands that took their minerals from the Mississippi River. He already held one captive, a young boy. In August 1788 he bought two more. One of them was named Sambo, which means "second son." The other was Ibrahima.

For Ibrahima there was confusion and pain. What was he to do?

Foster agreed to pay $930 for the two Africans. He paid $150 down and signed an agreement to pay another $250 the following January and the remaining $530 in January of the following year.

When Ibrahima arrived at Foster's farm, he tried to find someone who could explain to the white man who he was—the son of a chief. He wanted to offer a ransom for his own release, but Foster wasn't interested. He understood, perhaps from the boy whom he had purchased previously, that this new African was claiming to be an important person. Foster had probably never heard of the Fula or their culture; he had paid good money for the African, and wasn't about to give him up. Foster gave Ibrahima a new name: He called him Prince.

For Ibrahima there was confusion and pain. What was he to do? A few months before, he had been a learned man and a leader among his people. Now he was a captive in a strange land where he neither spoke the language nor understood the customs. Was he never to see

---

Teaching Options

USING *LESS, FEWER, MORE, MANY*
Instruction Explain that *less* is used to speak of things that cannot be individually counted, while *fewer* is used for things that can be counted. Give the example, "Fewer slaves meant less cotton."

Explain that *more* is the comparative form of the adjective *many.* It is only used when two things are being compared. Give the example, "There were many slaves in Mississippi, but more in the South as a whole." Point out that *more* is used here because the number of

---

 **Grammar**

slaves in the South is being compared to the number in Mississippi.

Exercises Have students use these rules to choose the correct word in the following sentences.

1. The slave ships sailed for (more/many) days. *(many)*
2. Foster wanted to grow (more/many) cotton than he used to. *(more)*
3. Ibrahima was auctioned off with (more/many) other slaves. *(many)*

---

4. Foster actually paid (less/fewer) dollars than the agreed total. *(fewer)*
5. Foster had (less/fewer) understanding of human rights than most Americans today. *(less)*

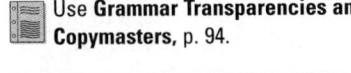 Use **Grammar Transparencies and Copymasters,** p. 94.

Use McDougal Littell's *Language Network,* Chapter 5, for more instruction and practice in using and comparing adjectives.

his family again? Were his sons forever lost to him?

As a Fula, Ibrahima wore his hair long; Foster insisted that it be cut. Ibrahima's clothing had been taken from him, and his sandals. Now the last remaining symbol of his people, his long hair, had been taken as well.

He was told to work in the fields. He refused, and he was tied and whipped. The sting of the whip across his naked flesh was terribly painful, but it was nothing like the pain he felt within. The whippings forced him to work.

For Ibrahima this was not life, but a mockery of life. There was the waking in the morning and the sleeping at night; he worked, he ate, but this was not life. What was more, he could not see an end to it. It was this feeling that made him attempt to escape.

Ibrahima escaped to the backwoods regions of Natchez.[9] He hid there, eating wild berries and fruit, not daring to show his face to any man, white or black. There was no telling who could be trusted. Sometimes he saw men with dogs and knew they were searching for runaways, perhaps him.

Where was he to run? What was he to do? He didn't know the country, he didn't know how far it was from Fouta Djallon or how to get back to his homeland. He could tell that this place was ruled by white men who held him in captivity. The other blacks he had seen were from all parts of Africa. Some he recognized by their tribal markings, some he did not. None were allowed to speak their native tongues around the white men. Some already knew nothing of the languages of their people.

As time passed, Ibrahima's despair deepened. His choices were simple. He could stay in the woods and probably die, or he could submit his body back into bondage. There is no place in Islamic law for a man to take his own life. Ibrahima returned to Thomas Foster.

Foster still owed money to the man from whom he had purchased Ibrahima. The debt would remain whether he still possessed the African or not. Foster was undoubtedly glad to see that the African had returned. Thin, nearly starving, Ibrahima was put to work.

Ibrahima submitted himself to the will of Thomas Foster. He was a captive, held in bondage not only by Foster but by the society in which he found himself. Ibrahima maintained his beliefs in the religion of Islam and kept its rituals as best he could. He was determined to be the same person he had always been: Abd al-Rahman Ibrahima of Fouta Djallon and of the proud Fula people.

By 1807 the area had become the Mississippi Territory. Ibrahima was forty-five and had been in bondage for twenty years. During those years he met and married a woman whom Foster had purchased, and they began to raise a family. Fouta Djallon was more and more distant, and he had become resigned to the idea that he would never see it or his family again.

Thomas Foster had grown wealthy and had become an important man in the territory. At forty-five Ibrahima was considered old. He was less useful to Foster, who now let the tall African grow a few vegetables on a side plot and sell them in town, since there was

ACTIVE READING

CLARIFY Summarize the reasons that Ibrahima remained with Thomas Foster.

---

9. **Natchez** (năch′ĭz): an early settlement in what is now the state of Mississippi.

WORDS
TO   **bondage** (bŏn′dĭj) *n.* slavery
KNOW

373

Cross Curricular Link **History**

SLAVERY IN UNITED STATES HISTORY The first captive Africans arrived in Virginia in 1619. As the settlers there did not have any legal provision for slave ownership, these first captives were viewed as indentured servants. However, the legal device of perpetual servitude was soon established. By 1681 there were 2,000 African slaves in Virginia. The colonies (later states) of the South developed economies dependent upon slave labor to produce their major cash crops: tobacco, rice, and cotton. Because tobacco rapidly exhausted the soil, it was failing as a cash crop by the time of the Revolution, and it seemed at that time that slavery would fade out. However, the boom in cotton production reversed this trend, and by 1860 there were some 4,441,000 slaves in the southern states. Thus, slavery can be linked to the plantation economy of the southern states. The division between the slave holding states of the South and the free states of the North was one of the tensions—though not the only one—that led to the Civil War.

Literary Analysis: FALLING ACTION

Explain to students that falling action in a narrative occurs after the climax or turning point. Have them discuss when the falling action begins in the story of Ibrahima.

Possible Responses: Some may say that the falling action begins after Ibrahima's unsuccessful attempt to escape from Foster. Others may say that it occurs after Ibrahima meets Dr. Cox.

Literary Analysis

SOURCES OF INFORMATION

A Point out that Myers describes the basic premise of slavery as "a premise that Foster *must have believed* without reservation" (emphasis added). Ask why Myers made his statement about Foster's belief in these words.

Possible Response: Myers did not have any primary sources that could definitely support his statement about Foster's belief, so he is letting us know that this statement is a conjecture on his part, based on the evidence of Foster's behavior.

Literary Analysis: BIOGRAPHY

Students should be able to identify the purposes of different types of texts. Ask students what Walter Dean Myers's purpose was in writing this biography of Ibrahima's life.

Possible Responses: Myers wanted to tell an interesting story about a remarkable man whose life was totally changed by slavery, but who managed to hold on to his identity as a cultured person, free in spirit, if not in fact; Myers wanted to make us appreciate our own liberty and to increase our respect for the rights of others.

nowhere in the territory that the black man could go where he would not be captured by some other white man and returned.

It was during one of these visits to town that Ibrahima saw a white man who looked familiar. The smallish man walked slowly and with a limp. Ibrahima cautiously approached the man and spoke to him. The man looked closely at Ibrahima, then spoke his name. It was Dr. Cox.

The two men shook hands, and Dr. Cox, who now lived in the territory, took Ibrahima to his home. John Cox had not <u>prospered</u> over the years, but he was still hopeful. He listened carefully as Ibrahima told his story—the battle near Fouta Djallon, the defeat, the long journey across the Atlantic Ocean, and, finally, his sale to Thomas Foster and the years of labor.

Dr. Cox and Ibrahima went to the Foster plantation. Meeting with Foster, he explained how he had met the tall black man. Surely, he reasoned, knowing that Ibrahima was of royal blood, Foster would free him? The answer was a firm, but polite, no. No amount of pleading would make Foster change his mind. It didn't matter that Dr. Cox had supported what Ibrahima had told Foster so many years before, that he was a prince. To Foster the man was merely his property.

Dr. Cox had to leave the man whose people had saved his life, but he told Ibrahima that he would never stop working for his freedom.

Andrew Marschalk, the son of a Dutch baker, was a printer, a pioneer in his field, and a man of great curiosity. By the time Marschalk heard about it, Cox had told a great many people in the Natchez district the story of African royalty being held in slavery in America. Marschalk was fascinated. He

suggested that Ibrahima write a letter to his people, telling them of his whereabouts and asking them to ransom him. But Ibrahima had not been to his homeland in twenty years. The people there were still being captured by slave traders. He would have to send a messenger who knew the countryside, and who knew the Fula. Where would he find such a man?

For a long time Ibrahima did nothing. Finally, some time after the death of Dr. Cox in 1816, Ibrahima wrote the letter that Marschalk suggested. He had little faith in the <u>procedure</u> but felt he had nothing to lose. Marschalk was surprised when Ibrahima appeared with the letter written neatly in Arabic. Since one place in Africa was the same as the next to Marschalk, he sent the letter not to Fouta Djallon but to Morocco.

he government of Morocco did not know Ibrahima but understood from his letter that he was a Moslem. Moroccan officials, in a letter to President James Monroe, pleaded for the release of Ibrahima. The letter reached Henry Clay, the American secretary of state.

The United States had recently ended a bitter war with Tripoli in North Africa and welcomed the idea of establishing good relations with Morocco, another North African country. Clay wrote to Foster about Ibrahima.

Foster resented the idea of releasing Ibrahima. The very idea that the government of Morocco had written to Clay and discussed a religion that Ibrahima shared with other Africans gave Ibrahima a past that Foster had long denied, a past as honorable as Foster's.

<table>
<tr><td>WORDS
TO
KNOW</td><td>prosper (prŏs′pər) v. to be successful; thrive
procedure (prə-sē′jər) n. a course of action</td></tr>
</table>

374

 Mini Lesson ## Speaking and Listening

VOICE-OVER

Prepare Students are expected to communicate by presenting dramatic interpretations of experiences, stories, poems, or plays. Explain that a voice-over is the voice of an unseen narrator in a movie or television program, or the voice of a character that tells his or her thoughts—even though his/her lips are not moving at the time to indicate that it is speech. Ask students to imagine a voice-over of Ibrahima's thoughts as they read the narrative. For instance, when Ibrahima is taken on board the slave ship he might be thinking:

"What is happening to us? Why are these men taking us away? I'll try to stay out of their way, but I'll keep looking for some way to escape from all this." These thoughts could become a voice-over.

Present After students have had time to think about the type of voice-over they will do, divide up the text into scenes and have students improvise their voice-overs aloud for the class.

Use **Communications Transparencies and Copymasters**, p. 12, for additional support.

This idea challenged a basic <u>premise</u> of slavery—a premise that Foster must have believed without <u>reservation</u>: that the Africans had been nothing but savages, with no humanity or human feelings, and therefore it was all right to enslave them. But after more letters and pressure from the State Department, Foster agreed to release Ibrahima if he could be assured that Ibrahima would leave the country and return to Fouta Djallon.

Many people who believed that slavery was wrong also believed that Africans could not live among white Americans. The American Colonization Society had been formed expressly to send freed Africans back to Africa. The society bought land, and a colony called Liberia was established on the west coast of Africa. Foster was assured that Ibrahima would be sent there.

By then Ibrahima's cause had been taken up by a number of abolitionist[10] groups in the North as well as by many free Africans. They raised money to buy his wife's freedom as well.

On February 7, 1829, Ibrahima and his wife sailed on the ship *Harriet* for Africa. The ship reached Liberia, and Ibrahima now had to find a way to reach his people again. He never found that way. Abd al-Rahman Ibrahima died in Liberia in July 1829.

Who was Ibrahima? He was one of millions of Africans taken by force from their native lands. He was the son of a chief, a warrior, and a scholar. But to Ibrahima the only thing that mattered was that he had lost his freedom. If he had been a herder in Fouta Djallon, or an artist in Benin, or a farmer along the Gambia, it would have been the same. Ibrahima was an African who loved freedom no less than other beings on earth. And he was denied that freedom. ❖

---

10. **abolitionist** (ăb′ə-lĭsh′ə-nĭst): favoring the end of slavery.

WORDS TO KNOW

premise (prĕm′ĭs) *n.* an idea that forms the basis of an argument
reservation (rĕz′ər-vā′shən) *n.* a doubt; an exception

375

Use the following questions to help students analyze and understand the fable.

1. Why does the idea of living as a House Dog appeal to the Wolf at first?

   Possible Response: He thinks of all the wonderful things he would have to eat.

2. Why does the Wolf decide that being a House Dog is not so wonderful?

   Possible Response: He asks about the place on the Dog's neck that was worn away by the collar and finds out that the House Dog is not always free.

Aesop

The name Aesop is given to a legendary figure associated with animal fables that arose in Greece at least as early as the fifth century B.C. Various writers invented "facts" about him, but there is no reason to accept any of these biographical details as true.

The first collection of fables said to be by Aesop was made by Demetrius Phalareus in the fourth century B.C. The fables were retold by many writers thereafter. One of the most well-known retellers was Jean de La Fontaine, a French poet of the seventeenth century.

The WOLF and the HOUSE DOG

by Aesop

*T*here once was a Wolf who got very little to eat because the Dogs of the village were so wide awake and watchful. He was really nothing but skin and bones, and it made him very downhearted to think of it.

One night this Wolf happened to fall in with a fine fat House Dog who had wandered a little too far from home. The Wolf would gladly have eaten him then and there, but the House Dog looked strong enough to leave his marks should he try it. So the Wolf spoke very humbly to the Dog, complimenting him on his fine appearance.

"You can be as well-fed as I am if you want to," replied the Dog. "Leave the woods; there you live miserably. Why, you have to fight hard for every bite you get. Follow my example and you will get along beautifully."

"What must I do?" asked the Wolf.

"Hardly anything," answered the House Dog. "Chase people who carry canes, bark at beggars, and fawn on the people of the house. In return you will get tidbits of every kind, chicken bones, choice bits of meat, sugar, cake and much more besides, not to speak of kind words and caresses."

Teaching Options

 Mini Lesson **Viewing and Representing**

Dog
by Alberto Giacometti

ART APPRECIATION The art of Alberto Giacometti (1901–1966) includes sculptures, paintings, and poetry. His later sculptures are characterized by the extreme thinness seen in his statue of the dog reproduced here.

Instruction Students are expected to describe how artists' choice of style, elements, and media help to represent or extend the text's meaning. Point out that the sculptor used lines and shapes

to express a mood or emotion in his sculpture of the dog. The designer chose this sculpture specifically because those lines and shapes, and the mood or emotion they present, represent the mood and emotion of the text.

Application Ask students what mood the sculpture expresses and how it represents or extends the meaning of the text.

Possible Response: The bowed head of the sculpture makes the dog look downtrodden and expresses the lack of freedom of the dog in the fable.

Dog, Alberto Giacometti. Hirshhorn Museum and Sculpture Garden, Smithsonian Institution, gift of Joseph H. Hirshhorn, 1966. Photo: Ricardo Blanc. Copyright © 2001 Artists Rights Society (ARS), New York/ADAGP, Paris.

Customizing Instruction

Students Acquiring English

1 Point out that *downhearted* means depressed, or low in spirit.

Gifted and Talented

2 Note the moral, or lesson, of the story which is printed in italics at the end of the fable. Have students think of other fables or stories they have heard, then write morals for them.

The Wolf had such a beautiful vision of his coming happiness that he almost wept. But just then he noticed that the hair on the Dog's neck was worn and the skin chafed.

"What's that on your neck?"

"Nothing at all," replied the Dog.

"What! Nothing!"

"Oh, just a trifle!"

"But please tell me."

"Perhaps you see the mark of the collar to which my chain is fastened."

"What! A chain!" cried the Wolf. "Don't you go wherever you please?"

"Not always! But what's the difference?" replied the Dog.

"All the difference in the world! I don't care a rap for your feasts and I wouldn't take all the tender young lambs in the world at that price." And away ran the Wolf to the woods.

There is nothing worth so much as liberty. ❖ **2**

GUIDING STUDENT RESPONSE

Connect to the Literature

1. What Do You Think?
Responses will vary. Students might say that Ibrahima's life shows the terrible cost of slavery—that a human being could be treated as property. They might say that Ibrahima should be proud of who he was and where he came from, regardless of the position he held in American society

Comprehension Check
- The Mandingos capture Ibrahima and sell him to the whites, who put him on a slave ship bound for the United States.
- He becomes enslaved to Thomas Foster.
- There is no way he could have gotten back there, even if he had escaped.

 Use Selection Quiz
Unit Three Resource Book, p. 33.

Think Critically

2. Possible Response: Dr. Cox might have told Foster about how the Fula people had taken care of him when he was injured, and about how educated Ibrahima was. He might have added that Foster's basic premise—that these people were savages without human feelings— was untrue.
3. Answers will vary, but should include the inhumanity of enslaving another person.
4. Students' retellings will vary, but should be in chronological order.

 Use **Reading and Critical Thinking Transparencies,** p. 6, for additional support.

5. Responses will vary. Students should support their answers with details from the selection, comparing what they now know to what they knew before they began reading.

Literary Analysis

Sources of Information Students' lists should indicate an understanding of what sources are secondary and what sources are primary. They should list appropriate sources, such as official records, school records, and letters to friends and family.

 Use **Literary Analysis Transparencies,** p. 14, for additional support.

378   UNIT THREE   PART 2

Connect to the Literature

1. What Do You Think?
If you could say one thing about Ibrahima's life, what would it be?

Comprehension Check
- How does Ibrahima come to be sold into slavery?
- What happens to Ibrahima in the United States?
- Why doesn't Ibrahima return to his home in Fouta Djallon?

Think Critically

2. Walter Dean Myers notes that Thomas Foster must have believed deeply in the "basic premise of slavery" to treat Ibrahima as he did. What do you think Dr. Cox would say to Foster about those beliefs?

 THINK ABOUT
- Dr. Cox's experiences in Fouta Djallon
- his relationship with Ibrahima
- his parting words to Ibrahima

3. If you were teaching this selection, what two or three main ideas would you want your students to remember?

4. **ACTIVE READING   CHRONOLOGICAL ORDER**   With a partner, take turns retelling the story of Ibrahima's life in your own words. Refer to the time line you made in your **READER'S NOTEBOOK** to keep track of chronological order.

5. What information about slavery did you find most surprising or disturbing?

Extend Interpretations

6. **COMPARING TEXTS**   Read "The Wolf and the House Dog" on page 376. What ideas about freedom does this fable present? Do you think Ibrahima would agree with these ideas? Why?

7. Connect to Life   Many people go to great lengths to find out about their backgrounds and ancestors. Why do you think finding out about their pasts matters so much to some people?

Extend Interpretations

6. Comparing Texts Possible Response: The fable's moral says that nothing is better than freedom. Ibrahima would agree, since he had to live most of his life without it.
7. Connect to Life Possible Response: People want to know about their heritage to understand who they are and where they came from. Ibrahima's knowledge of his heritage helped him preserve his dignity while he was a slave and empowered him to write to Marschalk, which secured his freedom.

Literary Analysis

SOURCES OF INFORMATION
The writer of a biography does research to find out about a person's life and the time in which he or she lived. A biographer may use both primary and secondary sources. **Primary sources,** such as personal papers and state records, convey firsthand knowledge. **Secondary sources,** such as other biographies and nonfiction books, convey secondhand knowledge.

Cooperative Learning Activity
What kinds of research might a biographer do in order to find out about your life? In a small group, make a list of primary and secondary sources that you think would be helpful.

Primary Sources:
- photographs

Secondary Sources:
- school newspaper

Choices & CHALLENGES

Writing Options

1. Justice Speech Write a speech about an issue of fairness in today's society. Tell why it is important to learn from the past. Place it in your **Working Portfolio.**

2. Persuasive Pamphlet Suppose that Andrew Marschalk is preparing a pamphlet that argues against slavery. **Summarize** Ibrahima's story for the pamphlet.

3. Interview Questions Imagine that you are a reporter interviewing Ibrahima and his wife just before they set sail to Liberia. Write the questions you would ask.

Activities & Explorations

1. Dramatic Scene With a partner, make up a conversation that Ibrahima and Dr. Cox might have had when they met in the United States. Act out the scene for the class. ~ **PERFORMING**

2. Portrait Pair Skim the selection for details that describe how Ibrahima looked and dressed. Draw or paint two pictures of him. In one picture, show him as a young man in his homeland. In the other, show him as an older man in the United States. ~ **ART**

Inquiry & Research

SOCIAL STUDIES **EMPIRE MAPS**

Research the Songhai Empire, along with the kingdoms of Benin, Kush, Kanem-Bornu, Ethiopia, and Mali. Make a map of Africa, showing the region that each kingdom occupied and the period in which each existed. Add images that represent each kingdom.

More Online: Research Starter
www.mcdougallittell.com

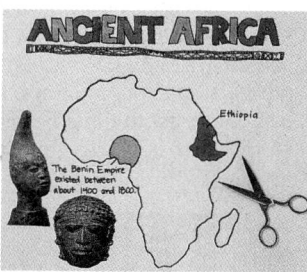

Vocabulary in Action

EXERCISE: ANALOGIES An analogy contains two pairs of words that are related in the same way. Consider this example:

   LARGE : HUGE :: quiet : silent.
This analogy is read as
   "Large is to *huge* as *quiet* is to *silent."*
The two pairs of words are related because they are pairs of synonyms.

  For each analogy, figure out the relationship between the words in the first pair. Then, decide which vocabulary word best completes the second pair of words.

1. NOISE : UPROAR :: _____ : resident
2. IDEA : OPINION :: _____ : doubt
3. FILTHY : CLEAN :: _____ : calmness
4. REGION : AREA :: _____ : rank
5. RESPONSE : ANSWER :: _____ : hike
6. TRUTH : FALSEHOOD :: _____ : freedom
7. SHUT : OPEN :: _____ : lose
8. FRIEND : COMPANION :: _____ : method
9. DECORATION : ORNAMENT :: _____ : belief
10. CAR : AUTOMOBILE :: _____ : empire

Building Vocabulary
For an in-depth lesson on analogies, see p. 348.

WORDS TO KNOW				
bondage	dynasty	premise	prosper	status
chaos	inhabitant	procedure	reservation	trek

Writing Options

1. Justice Speech Speeches should discuss a valid fairness issue and incorporate reasoning about the value of knowledge of the past. **To make this activity more challenging,** have students pair off and deliver differing points of view on the same issue.

2. Persuasive Pamphlet Summaries should outline the story in a coherent fashion. To get students started on this activity, have them skim the story, taking notes as they read.

Use **Writing Transparencies,** p. 51, for additional support.

3. Interview Questions Questions should focus on main issues and not dwell on trivial matters. To get students started on this activity, have the class as a whole discuss what things they might most want to ask Ibrahima.

Activities & Explorations

1. Dramatic Scene Scenes should follow the outlines of the meeting as given in the selection and include plausible dialogue.

Use **Communications Transparencies and Copymasters,** p. 13, for additional support.

2. Portrait Pair Portraits should provide imaginative images of Ibrahima based on the clues in the story. **To make this activity easier,** review the story with students to find the clues to Ibrahima's appearance.

Inquiry & Research

Empire Maps Student maps should be copied or traced from an actual printed map and should show the approximate boundaries of the kingdoms in question accurately. Labels should be clear and appropriate. **A good source of information for this activity** might be historical atlases or history texts that include information about the history of West Africa.

Vocabulary in Action

EXERCISE

1. inhabitant
2. reservation
3. chaos
4. status
5. trek

6. bondage
7. prosper
8. procedure
9. premise
10. dynasty

Grammar in Context

WRITING EXERCISE

1. older
2. more painful
3. saddest

Author Activity

Heroic Tales Students' time lines should show a clear understanding of chronological order and isolate the main events of the selected biography.

 Use **Reading and Critical Thinking Transparencies,** p. 6, for additional support.

Walter Dean Myers

Among the many challenges Myers overcame as a child was a speech impediment. As an adult he has struggled to find his way through the creative process, and has weathered personal difficulties such as divorce. His output includes stories and novels about his childhood home, the Harlem section of New York City. One of his poems recently won the Michael Printz Award. He has remarried and today lives in Jersey City, New Jersey.

Grammar in Context: Comparing with Adjectives

"Abd al-Rahman Ibrahima" contains many **adjectives** that compare people, things, or ideas. Notice how the words in red type add drama:

> . . . a ship that was **larger** than any he had ever seen.
> Fouta Djallon was **more and more distant.**

Writers use the **comparative form** of an adjective to compare one thing to another. For many adjectives, you can form the comparative by adding *-er* to the end of the word. For others, you need to place the word *less, more, better,* or *worse* in front of the adjective.

The **superlative form** of an adjective compares something to two or more things, or to an entire group or category of things. Form the superlative by adding *-est* to the adjective or by using the words *most, least, best,* or *worst.*

> Timbuktu became the **largest** city in the Songhai Empire.
> Ibrahima attended the **best-known** school.

WRITING EXERCISE Rewrite each sentence. Add the adjective form defined in parentheses.

Example: *Original* The Fula were the (superlative of *tall*) people.

Rewritten The Fula were the tallest people.

1. Now that he was (comparative of *old*), Ibrahima tended his own garden.
2. It was (comparative of *painful*) to starve in the woods than to live in slavery.
3. The (superlative of *sad*) part of the story was when Ibrahima died.

Grammar Handbook Using Modifiers Effectively, p. R71

". . . I want to . . . touch the lives of my characters and, through them, those of my readers."

Walter Dean Myers

born 1937

Early Obstacles The early years of Walter Dean Myers's life were marked by hardship. When this West Virginia native was two years old, his mother died. He was put into foster care at the age of three. As Myers grew into a bright and talented teenager in New York City's Harlem, he turned to writing as a way of expressing himself. In 1970, after a brief period in the army and a series of unsatisfying jobs, Myers became an editor for a publishing company. He wrote part-time for several years, and in 1977 he began to write full-time.

Many Talents Best known for his young people's novels about Harlem youth, Myers has also written ghost stories, adventure tales, modern fairy tales, and nonfiction. The selection "Abd al-Rahman Ibrahima" is a chapter from the nonfiction book *Now Is Your Time! The African-American Struggle for Freedom.* This book, like Myers's novels *Slam, Fallen Angels, The Young Landlords,* and *Motown and Didi: A Love Story,* won a Coretta Scott King Award. His novels *Somewhere in the Darkness* and *Scorpions* were Newbery Honor Books.

AUTHOR ACTIVITY

Heroic Tales Read another extraordinary life story in *Now Is Your Time!* Prepare a time line of the biography and a series of illustrations covering major events in the subject's life. Hang them on a bulletin board in your classroom.

Teaching Options

AVOIDING DOUBLE COMPARATIVES AND SUPERLATIVES

Instruction Remind students that a comparative form of a modifier is one that is used to compare two things; a superlative is the form used to compare more than two things. The comparative of most one-syllable words and some two-syllable words is formed by adding *-er,* while the superlative is formed by adding *-est.* Some modifiers of two syllables, and most modifiers of more than two syllables, form the comparative and superlative by using *more* and *most* before the word.

(Mini Lesson) Grammar

Point out that using the two ways of forming these at the same time results in a double comparative *(more faster)* or double superlative *(most fastest).* Both should be avoided.

Exercises Have students replace the underlined double comparatives and superlatives in these sentences with the correct single form.

1. The Fula had a more complexer form of government than many societies of that time. *(more complex)*
2. Timbuktu was one of the most importantest cities in Africa. *(most important)*

3. Dr. Cox was more harmlesser than the Fula expected. *(more harmless)*
4. Ibrahima rode more faster than his men. *(faster)*

 Use **Unit Three Resource Book,** p. 31.
Use **Grammar Transparencies and Copymasters,** p. 97.

Language Network Use McDougal Littell's *Language Network,* Chapter 5, for more practice in avoiding double comparatives and superlatives.

from The Story of My Life

Autobiography by HELEN KELLER

"'Light! Give me light!' was the wordless cry of my soul, . . . "

Connect to Your Life

Aha! In the selection you are about to read, Helen Keller describes a childhood experience when she had an exciting breakthrough. Think of a time when you were suddenly able to do or understand something important. What happened? What did it feel like?

Build Background

CONNECT TO HISTORY The first school for the hearing impaired opened in Hartford, Connecticut, in 1817. It was established by Thomas Gallaudet, a Hartford minister, and Laurent Clerc, a deaf teacher from the Royal Institute of Deaf Mutes in Paris, France. Gallaudet and Clerc created an American sign language, which, combined with several visual languages from the United States, became American Sign Language (ASL). Other schools for the hearing impaired followed, including Gallaudet University. Today, many schools offer programs and services to help students learn ASL.

ASL combines signs, gestures, facial expressions, and a hand alphabet. It is now the fourth most used language in the United States. As more people learn sign language, those with hearing loss face fewer barriers in today's society.

American Sign Language Manual Alphabet

A B C D E F
G H I J K

WORDS TO KNOW **Vocabulary Preview**

bitterness	persist	repentance	sentiment	tangible
impress	prey	reveal	succeed	vainly

Focus Your Reading

LITERARY ANALYSIS SENSORY DETAILS Words and phrases that help readers see, hear, taste, smell, and feel what a writer is describing are called **sensory details.** Note the details related to sight and touch in this line from the selection:

> *The afternoon sun penetrated the mass of honeysuckle that covered the porch.*

As you read, look for other sensory details.

ACTIVE READING CLARIFYING When you stop to quickly review events or unfamiliar words while you are reading, you are **clarifying.** Clarifying can help you find answers to any questions you might have. It can also help you make sense of what you read.

READER'S NOTEBOOK As you read, stop every two or three paragraphs to clarify what you have just read. Record the main events of the selection.

Helen has a temper tantrum. Teacher (Anne) arrives.

THE STORY OF MY LIFE **381**

LESSON RESOURCES

UNIT THREE RESOURCE BOOK, pp. 34–40

ASSESSMENT
Formal Assessment, pp. 59–60
Teacher's Guide to Assessment and Portfolio Use
Test Generator

SKILLS TRANSPARENCIES AND COPYMASTERS
Reading and Critical Thinking
• Noting Sensory Details, TR 11 (for Paired Activity, p. 385)

Grammar
• Correcting Double Negatives, CM 99 (for Mini Lesson, p. 387)
Vocabulary
• Using a Dictionary, CM 42 (for Mini Lesson, p. 382)

INTEGRATED TECHNOLOGY
Audio Library

Visit our website:
www.mcdougallittell.com

OVERVIEW

This selection is included in the **Grade 6 InterActive Reader.**

Objectives
1. understand and appreciate an **autobiography (Literary Analysis)**
2. understand author's use of **sensory details (Literary Analysis)**
3. use **clarifying** as a reading strategy to help understand autobiography better **(Active Reading)**

Summary
In this excerpt from Helen Keller's autobiography, *The Story of My Life,* Helen recounts the beginning of her relationship with her teacher, Miss Anne Sullivan. She tells of the day Miss Sullivan arrived, and how she taught Helen to sign the names of familiar objects. Helen remembers that normal feelings and emotions were not part of her life at the time, and how that changed as she realized the power that came with knowing objects had names.

Thematic Link
Helen Keller lived at a time when many deaf and blind people were institutionalized and never learned to function in the wider world. Because of Anne Sullivan's and Helen's determination, these women were able to break an important barrier for people with disabilities of all kinds. This short excerpt offers readers the hope that perhaps their own barriers can be overcome.

5-Minute Warm-Up

Daily Language SkillBuilder

Have students **proofread** the display sentences on page 315j and write them correctly. The sentences also appear on Transparency 12 of **Grammar Transparencies and Copymasters.**

Mini Lesson **Preteaching Vocabulary**

If you would like to preteach the WORDS TO KNOW for this selection, use the Mini Lesson, p. 382.

Literary Analysis SENSORY DETAILS

A Since Helen can neither see nor hear, she relies on her other senses. Ask what examples show her use of the sense of touch in this paragraph. Possible Responses: The sun touched her face; her fingers touched the leaves and blossoms.

Use **Reading and Critical Thinking Transparencies,** p. 11, for additional support. Use **Unit Three Resource Book,** p. 36 for more practice.

Active Reading CLARIFYING

B Ask students to think about the analogy Helen makes between herself before schooling and a ship in a dense fog. Ask them to explain how they think Helen felt before her education. Possible Response: Helen felt like searching for something more, yet didn't know what it was or how to find it.

Use **Unit Three Resource Book,** p. 35 for more practice.

Reading Skills and Strategies: EVALUATE

C Ask students to speculate why Miss Sullivan began to teach Helen by signing such words as *doll, pin, hat,* and *cup.* Possible Response: She began with words for objects that Helen was familiar with and that she used regularly.

Literary Analysis: CHARACTERIZATION

Have students describe Miss Sullivan. Possible Responses: She is patient, intelligent, persistent, and kind.

Teaching Options

from
The Story of My Life
by Helen Keller

 Mini Lesson **Preteaching Vocabulary**

USING A DICTIONARY Remind students that among the strategies for learning the meanings of words are using context and using a dictionary. **Instruction** Have students find the word *tangible* on page 383. Ask them to read the sentence the word appears in and try to find context clues that define it. Since there are none in the sentence, have students look the word up in a dictionary. Have them read the definition and decide whether it makes sense in the sentence. **Application** Divide students into pairs or small groups, giving each pair or group one of the

words from the WORDS TO KNOW list. Ask them to follow the above procedure to define each word. Have them share findings with the class and generate a class definition. Write the words and definitions on the chalkboard. Have students individually write a descriptive paragraph using as many of the WORDS TO KNOW as possible.

Use **Unit Three Resource Book,** p. 37 for more practice. Use **Vocabulary Transparencies and Copymasters,** p. 42, for more practice.

The most important day I remember in all my life is the one on which my teacher, Anne Mansfield Sullivan, came to me. I am filled with wonder when I consider the immeasurable contrasts between the two lives which it connects. It was the third of March, 1887, three months before I was seven years old.

On the afternoon of that eventful day, I stood on the porch, dumb, expectant. I guessed vaguely from my mother's signs and from the hurrying to and fro in the house that something unusual was about to happen, so I went to the door and waited on the steps. The afternoon sun penetrated the mass of honeysuckle that covered the porch, and fell on my upturned face. My fingers lingered almost unconsciously on the familiar leaves and blossoms which had just come forth to greet the sweet southern spring. I did not know what the future held of marvel or surprise for me. Anger and <u>bitterness</u> had <u>preyed</u> upon me continually for weeks and a deep languor had <u>succeeded</u> this passionate struggle.

Have you ever been at sea in a dense fog, when it seemed as if a <u>tangible</u> white darkness shut you in, and the great ship, tense and anxious, groped her way toward the shore with plummet and sounding-line,[1] and you waited with beating heart for something to happen? I was like that ship before my education began, only I was without compass or sounding-line, and had no way of knowing how near the harbor was. "Light! Give me light!" was the wordless cry of my soul, and the light of love shone on me in that very hour.

I felt approaching footsteps. I stretched out my hand as I supposed to my mother. Someone took it, and I was caught up and held close in the arms of her who had come to <u>reveal</u> all things to me, and, more than all things else, to love me.

The morning after my teacher came she led me into her room and gave me a doll. The little blind children at the Perkins Institution had sent it and Laura Bridgman had dressed it; but I did not know this until afterward. When I had played with it a little while, Miss Sullivan slowly spelled into my hand the word "d-o-l-l." I was at once interested in this finger play and tried to imitate it. When I finally succeeded in making the letters correctly I was flushed with childish pleasure and pride. Running downstairs to my mother I held up my hand and made the letters for *doll*. I did not know that I was spelling a word or even that words existed; I was simply making my fingers go in monkey-like imitation. In the days that followed I learned to spell in this uncomprehending way a great many words, among them *pin, hat, cup* and a few verbs like *sit, stand,* and *walk*. But my teacher had been with me several weeks before I understood that everything has a name.

One day, while I was playing with my new doll, Miss Sullivan put my big rag doll into my lap also, spelled "d-o-l-l" and tried to make me understand that "d-o-l-l" applied to both. Earlier in the day we had had a tussle[2] over the words "m-u-g" and "w-a-t-e-r." Miss Sullivan

---

1. **plummet** (plŭm′ĭt) **and sounding-line:** a metal weight tied to the end of a rope, used to determine water depth.

2. **tussle** (tŭs′əl): a rough struggle.

WORDS TO KNOW	**bitterness** (bĭt′ər-nĭs) *n.* a feeling of disgust or resentment
	prey (prā) *v.* to have a harmful effect
	succeed (sək-sēd′) *v.* to come after; follow
	tangible (tăn′jə-bəl) *adj.* able to be touched or grasped
	reveal (rĭ-vēl′) *v.* to bring to view; to show

383

Literary Analysis SENSORY DETAILS

Ask students to think about how Helen Keller made sense of her world using only her senses of touch and smell. What words does she use to help us understand her silent world?

Possible Responses: warm sunshine, hop and skip with pleasure, fragrance of honeysuckle, cool stream gushed

Active Reading CLARIFYING

Have students think about the events that led Helen to realize she had emotions. Ask them to summarize those events.

Possible Response: Miss Sullivan begins to teach Helen to sign, Helen and Miss Sullivan argue over *mug* and *water,* and Helen breaks the doll. They walk to the well-house where Helen finally understands *water.* Upon returning home, Helen touches many objects, eager to learn their names. She tries to put the doll back together and realizes she feels sorry for what she's done.

Reading Skills and Strategies: QUESTION

Ask students to brainstorm a list of questions that Helen might have asked Miss Sullivan once Helen understood language and was able to sign fluently.

Possible Responses: Answers will vary, but should reflect the kinds of things someone who had lived in silence for so long would ask once they had discovered language.

Reading Skills and Strategies: MAKE JUDGMENTS

Ask students to reflect on and to speculate as to why Helen Keller chose to recall these particular events in her life. Ask them to write down several reasons and then to discuss them with a partner.

---

had tried to <u>impress</u> upon me that "m-u-g" is *mug* and that "w-a-t-e-r" is *water,* but I <u>persisted</u> in confounding[3] the two. In despair she had dropped the subject for the time, only to renew it at the first opportunity. I became impatient at her repeated attempts and, seizing the new doll, I dashed it upon the floor. I was keenly delighted when I felt the fragments of the broken doll at my feet. Neither sorrow nor regret followed my passionate outburst. I had not loved the doll. In the still, dark world in which I lived there was no strong <u>sentiment</u> or tenderness. I felt my teacher sweep the fragments to one side of the hearth and I had a sense of satisfaction that the cause of my discomfort was removed. She brought me my hat, and I knew I was going out into the warm sunshine. This thought, if a wordless sensation may be called a thought, made me hop and skip with pleasure.

We walked down the path to the well-house, attracted by the fragrance of the honeysuckle with which it was covered. Someone was drawing water and my teacher placed my hand under the spout. As the cool stream gushed over one hand she spelled into the other the word *water,* first slowly, then rapidly. I stood still, my whole attention fixed upon the motions of her fingers. Suddenly I felt a misty consciousness as of something forgotten—a thrill of returning thought; and somehow the mystery of language was revealed to me. I knew then that "w-a-t-e-r"

meant the wonderful cool something that was flowing over my hand. That living word awakened my soul, gave it light, hope, joy, set it free! There were barriers still, it is true, but barriers that could in time be swept away.

I left the well-house eager to learn. Everything had a name, and each name gave birth to a new thought. As we returned to the house every object which I touched seemed to quiver with life. That was because I saw everything with the strange, new sight that had come to me. On entering the door I remembered the doll I had broken. I felt my way to the hearth and picked up the pieces. I tried <u>vainly</u> to put them together. Then my eyes filled with tears; for I realized what I had done, and for the first time I felt <u>repentance</u> and sorrow.

I learned a great many new words that day. I do not remember what they all were; but I do know that *mother, father, sister, teacher* were among them—words that were to make the world blossom for me, "like Aaron's rod, with flowers."[4] It would have been difficult to find a happier child than I was as I lay in my crib at the close of that eventful day and lived over the joys it had brought me, and for the first time longed for a new day to come. ❖

---

3. **confounding:** confusing.
4. **"like Aaron's rod, with flowers":** a reference to a passage of the Bible in which a wooden rod miraculously bears flowers and fruit (Numbers 17:8).

WORDS TO KNOW	
	impress (ĭm-prĕs') *v.* to implant firmly in the mind; convey vividly
	persist (pər-sĭst') *v.* to continue stubbornly
	sentiment (sĕn'tə-mənt) *n.* emotion
	vainly (vān'lē) *adv.* without success
	repentance (rĭ-pĕn'təns) *n.* a regret for past behavior

384

Teaching Options

Mini Lesson Spelling

VCCV AND CVC PATTERNS Remind students that being able to apply familiar syllable patterns to polysyllabic words will help them decode unknown words.

Instruction Model the VCCV pattern with words such as *pillow* or *dentist,* and the CVC pattern with *pilot* and *grateful.* Ask students to note that in the VCCV pattern, the second syllable begins with the second consonant. Knowing these patterns can help them in decoding unknown words. Write these words on the board: *frantic, trophy, papyrus, banquet, muscular, cymbal, widower.* Ask

students to read the words aloud, identify the pattern, and discuss how knowing this pattern helped them to pronounce the word.

Application Ask students to look through the selection to locate other words that fit these patterns. Have them use several of those words in an autobiographical paragraph.

Use **Unit Three Resource Book,** p. 39.

Connect to the Literature

1. What Do You Think?
In reading about Helen Keller's experience, what impressed you the most?

Comprehension Check
• What made Helen's world "still" and "dark"?
• How old was Helen when her teacher arrived?
• What happened at the well-house?

Think Critically

2. `ACTIVE READING` `CLARIFYING` How did her teacher's arrival affect Helen Keller's life? To support your answer, refer to the notes you made in your **READER'S NOTEBOOK.**

3. How would you describe Helen's life before she learned to use words? How would you describe it afterward?

4. Why did Helen's feelings about the doll change?

5. Based on this selection, what kind of person do you think Helen Keller was as a young girl?

THINK ABOUT
• the difficulties she faced
• what she learned
• her feelings about her teacher

6. How does reading Helen's own words make the events come alive? Support your answer with details from the selection.

Extend Interpretations

7. Different Perspectives Suppose that Helen's teacher, Anne Sullivan, had written about these events. What would be different about her account?

8. Connect to Life Imagine that Keller were a child today. How might her life be different?

Literary Analysis

`SENSORY DETAILS` The words and phrases that writers use to help readers imagine that they can see, hear, taste, smell, and feel what is being described are called **sensory details.** Keller uses sensory details to help her reader understand her experiences. For example, writing that the "sun . . . fell on my upturned face" appeals to the reader's sense of touch, or feeling. It helps the reader imagine the sun's warmth.

Paired Activity Working with a partner, look back through the selection to find sensory details. Record them on a chart as shown. Do you find details for every sense? What senses are triggered most often?

Sensory Details	
Smell	
Touch	sun . . . fell on my upturned face
Taste	
Sight	
Hearing	

`REVIEW` `AUTOBIOGRAPHY`
An **autobiography** is the story of a person's life, told by that person. The selection you have just read was taken from Helen Keller's autobiography.

Extend Interpretations

7. Different Perspectives Sullivan probably would have described Helen, both upon meeting her and as she watched her progress. She would also have described her own feelings and thoughts about working with Helen, but would have known less about Helen's thoughts and feelings.

8. Connect to Life Today, Helen would have many more public resources available to her, for example, Braille signs in many buildings, a communicating keyboard, and specially trained teachers in school settings. She probably would not have a teacher living with her family and constantly available. She still would have to learn to live with her disabilities because there are still no cures for many types of blindness and deafness.

Connect to the Literature

1. What Do You Think?
Possible Responses: Students might be impressed by the anger and bitterness Keller felt before her teacher's arrival, by Sullivan's patience and skill, or by the speed of Helen's learning.

Comprehension Check
• Helen Keller could not see, hear, or speak.
• Helen was six years old, almost seven, when her teacher arrived.
• She understood for the first time that things have names.

Use Selection Quiz **Unit Three Resource Book,** p. 40.

Think Critically

2. Possible Response: Before her teacher's arrival, Helen Keller could not express thoughts or feelings. Afterwards, Keller could communicate with sign language.

3. Possible Response: Helen's life before she learned to communicate was "dark" and "still." After she began to learn words, the world opened up to her.

4. Possible Response: Helen seemed to realize that the doll, being a gift, represented someone else's concern for her, something she could not understand before she had experienced her teacher's gift of love and language.

5. Possible Response: Helen was angry and bitter before she learned to communicate, but she was also intelligent, determined, successful, and grateful for love and for opportunities.

6. Possible Response: We feel what it was like for Helen to be deaf, blind, and mute. For example, she notices what honeysuckle leaves feel like; she also uses the "ship at sea in a dense fog" analogy to help the reader understand what her early life was like.

Literary Analysis

Sensory Details Students may find that smell, touch, and taste are triggered more often, since those senses are more acutely developed in Helen.

Use **Reading and Critical Thinking Transparencies,** p. 11, for additional support.

Writing Options

1. **Word List** Students should include words and phrases they may have heard from books or movies. They may also want to think about their own experiences of temporary loss of senses (for example, no feeling when the dentist numbs their mouth for a filling or a dark room before they acquire night vision).

2. **Different Definitions** Ask students to list as many words as they can before looking in a dictionary. They may also want to look in a thesaurus for additional ideas.

 Use **Writing Transparencies,** p. 16, for additional support.

Activities & Explorations

1. **Verbal Cues** Students may want to switch partners and try the activity a second time to see if they get better at their descriptions over time.

2. **Language Lesson** Students will need time to practice the use of the hand alphabet and ASL. There are many books that include this information; you may want to provide some for the students to use.

3. **Helping Invention** Remind students that the poster must contain all pertinent information, such as the disability, the name and description of the invention, and how it will help people with this disability. Adding color and pictures to the poster will make it more appealing.

Inquiry & Research

To make this activity easier, have students work in small groups to brainstorm helping occupations and to classify them according to kinds of help they provide, for example, medical, educational, and so on.

Writing Options

1. **Word List** Brainstorm a list of words or phrases that come to mind when you think about losing all or part of your sight or hearing. Share your list with a classmate.

2. **Different Definitions** Take the word *doll* or the word *water* and define it using only sensory details that do not relate to sight. Compare your definition with a dictionary definition of the word.

3. **Helping Invention** Identify a problem faced by a person with a disability. Imagine an invention that would help someone overcome that problem in everyday life. Make a poster that explains what the invention is and how it works. Add your explanation to your **Working Portfolio.** 📁

Activities & Explorations

1. **Verbal Cues** Draw a simple figure on graph paper. Describe the figure to a partner who cannot see it. Have your partner try to draw the shape you described. How do your pictures compare? **~ SPEAKING AND LISTENING**

2. **Language Lesson** Learn to spell your name using the hand alphabet. In addition, learn five signs in American Sign Language. Show your classmates how you fingerspell your name, and teach them the signs you learned. **~ SPEAKING AND LISTENING**

Inquiry & Research

Helping Hands Helen Keller felt lonely and frustrated before help arrived in the form of her teacher, Anne Sullivan. Many people find that the care and support of a helping professional can open doors for them. Think about careers that focus on helping people overcome challenges. For example, teachers instruct students, helping them develop lifelong learning skills. What careers focus on finding new and innovative ways of helping others? Whom do they help? What types of help do they provide?

 Real World Link
Read "High-tech Helping Hands" on p. 388 before searching for information about people who work to help others.

Vocabulary in Action

EXERCISE A: LEARNING AND REMEMBERING NEW WORDS On your paper, complete a chart like the one below. Use a dictionary to research the definition and origin, or etymology, of each vocabulary word below. Then use each word in a sentence related to the story. *Reveal* has been started for you as an example.

EXERCISE B: PREFIXES AND SUFFIXES Think about how knowing the origins of words can help you understand new words. Use the chart that you created to help you write definitions for *sentimental* and *impression.* Check your definitions in a dictionary.

Building Vocabulary

For an in-depth lesson on researching word origins see p. 663.

Word	Definition	Origin	Sentence
reveal	to make known	Middle English: *revelen;* Old French *reveler;* Latin *revēlāre;* (re- + *vēlāre,* to cover)	

WORDS TO KNOW				
bitterness	persist	repentance	sentiment	tangible
impress	prey	reveal	succeed	vainly

Teaching Options

✓ **Assessment** **Standardized Test Practice**

IDENTIFYING THE IMPLIED MAIN IDEA On some standardized tests, students are asked to determine a text's main idea. In some texts the main idea is implied, and students will need to draw a logical conclusion from the details provided. Write the following question on the board or read it aloud:

Based on "The Story of My Life," which statement is most likely the implied main idea?

A. Helen Keller enjoyed her life before Anne Sullivan.

B. Helen Keller did not want Anne Sullivan to intrude into her world.

C. Helen Keller's world changed drastically due to the teachings of Anne Sullivan.

D. Helen Keller and Anne Sullivan became true and lasting friends.

Guide students through the process of selecting the correct answer. A is not true, because Helen describes her prior life as being like a ship at sea in a dense fog. B may have been true at first, but is not the main idea of this excerpt. D may also be true, but is not addressed in this excerpt. C is the correct response.

Grammar in Context: Avoiding Confusion with Negatives

In *The Story of My Life* Helen Keller remarks:

> **I did not know what the future held of marvel or surprise for me.**

The word in red is a **negative.** A negative is a word that says "no." It "negates," or reverses, the meaning of the words around it. Negatives include *no, not, none, nothing, nobody, never,* and *nowhere.*

Writers and speakers of standard English never use two negatives together in the same sentence. That kind of construction, called a **double negative,** actually reverses the meaning of the negative. If Helen Keller had written, "I did not know nothing of what the future held," her words would lose their meaning. "I did not know nothing" is an awkward way of saying, "I knew something."

WRITING EXERCISE Rewrite each sentence using the negative in parentheses.

Example: *Original* Helen knew what to expect from her new teacher. (not)

Rewritten Helen did not know what to expect from her new teacher.

1. Helen guessed right away what the letters meant. (not)
2. Helen was horrified when she realized the doll was broken. (not)
3. She felt tenderness for the doll. (no)
4. At first Helen cared about the irritation she caused others. (nothing)

Grammar Handbook Using Modifiers Effectively, p. R70

Vocabulary in Action

Exercise A Students should complete the chart as modeled, using the WORDS TO KNOW.
Exercise B Students should write their own definitions prior to using a dictionary.

Grammar in Context

WRITING EXERCISE
Possible Responses:
1. Helen could not guess what the letters meant right away.
2. Helen was not horrified when she realized the doll was broken.
3. She felt no tenderness for the doll.
4. At first Helen cared nothing about the irritation she caused others.

Author Activity

Vivid Words Students will need access to the book *The Story of My Life.* It might be advantageous to have multiple copies available for students to work cooperatively on this activity. If only one copy is available, you may want to read other sections aloud.

"Life is either a daring adventure, or nothing."

Helen Keller
1880–1968

Silent Darkness Helen Keller was born in Tuscumbia, Alabama. Before she turned two, an illness left her blind and deaf. As a child, she invented 60 signs to identify objects and people.

A Life-Changing Visitor The director of the famous Perkins Institute for the Blind sent Anne Mansfield Sullivan to be a teacher for Helen. Sullivan herself had been nearly blind, but she had undergone operations that partially restored her sight. With patience and hard work, Sullivan won Keller's trust and became not only her teacher but her friend for life.

Education and Activism With Sullivan's help, Keller attended schools for the blind and deaf, and graduated from Radcliffe College, part of Harvard University. She wrote, lectured, and traveled the world, working for the rights of women, the poor, and the blind and deaf. In 1964, Keller received the Presidential Medal of Freedom from President Johnson.

AUTHOR ACTIVITY

Vivid Words Read further in *The Story of My Life.* How do you think Keller's early experiences might have affected her writing style?

Mini Lesson Grammar

CORRECTING DOUBLE NEGATIVES Explain that the word *not* is an adverb that often causes problems. It is a negative, a word that says "no." It changes the meaning of the verb, making it negative. When two negatives appear in one sentence, they result in a double negative. Remind students that many contractions contain the word *not,* represented as *n't.* It's easy to forget that contractions with an *n't* are negatives and should not be combined with words meaning "not."

Instruction Write the following sentence on the board: Helen Keller didn't have no fun before she learned words.

Ask students to identify the double negative *(didn't, no)* and correct the sentence.

Exercises Ask students to eliminate each double negative in the following sentences.

1. It wasn't never easy for Helen to learn to read. *(wasn't easy)*
2. Miss Sullivan wouldn't not give up; she was persistent. *(would not)*
3. Helen didn't think she could go to no college. *(to college)*

4. She wouldn't fail at nothing once she had tasted of the world of communication. *(at anything)*

 Use **Unit Three Resource Book,** p. 38.
Use **Grammar Transparencies and Copymasters,** p. 99.

Use McDougal Littell's *Language Network,* Chapter 5, for more practice correcting double negatives.

Source: *National Geographic World*

Objectives
- read for information
- read and analyze a magazine article
- form and revise research questions
- learn about inventions that help people with disabilities

Connecting to the Literature
An article such as "High-Tech Helping Hands" can help students make connections to nonfiction works such as "The Story of My Life." As students read this article, ask them to think about how some of these high-tech inventions could have helped Helen Keller. They may also want to think of other high-tech inventions that could have helped Keller as she learned to read, write, and communicate with others.

HIGH-TECH HELPING HANDS
By Jane R. McGoldrick

KIDS HELP RESEARCHERS INVENT HIGH-TECH TOOLS FOR PEOPLE WITH DISABILITIES.

C. J. Marconi's hand motions are "read" by his gloves and then displayed on a computer monitor.

POWER USERS

Power users, techno testers—kids like C. J. Marconi, 12, are both. Through a program in Wilmington, Delaware, C. J. and others ages 9 and up test high-tech devices designed to assist people with disabilities like their own. Here, C. J., who is deaf, tests a computer sign-language system. As C. J. makes the sign for "cat," his gloves "read" the sign. The figure on the monitor behind him is starting to mimic his movements.

SIGN ON! IT'S CHAT TIME

"It's cool—and a good learning tool, too," says C. J. of Fort Meyers, Florida. That's his description of the sign-language recognition and animation system he tested while staying in Delaware. The system displays an animated figure on a monitor. The figure mimics signs made by a tester. Researchers hope the system eventually will allow any person who doesn't sign to "speak" with someone who does sign. As the nonsigner types or speaks, a computer converts the words into signs. The signer "reads" the monitor. As the signer replies, the computer converts the signs into spoken or written words.

TESTING HANDS AND ARMS

When Krista Caudill tested a finger-spelling robot hand she immediately put her finger on the problem. The robot hand shifted into neutral between each letter it spelled, creating unnatural delays. Now, thanks to Krista's help, engineers are refining the motions.

Reading for Information

When you begin researching a topic, keep a specific question in mind. However, you may find that as you answer one question, your research raises new questions.

FORMING AND REVISING RESEARCH QUESTIONS

Your first step in any research project is to choose a topic. Form a clear, specific, and interesting question to answer through your research. But be prepared. You will find that you usually need to revise your original question as you collect information.

For example, you might begin to research "What was life like in the 19th century?" Then, as you do further research, you gradually revise the question to be more focused. Your final research question might be, "In the 19th century, what support and devices were available to people who were hearing-impaired?"

YOUR TURN *Use this article with the questions and activities below to help you learn how to form and revise research questions.*

1 Before you read this article, scan the title and the photos. What questions come to mind? List two or three questions you would like to have answered, or think will be answered by the article.

2 Suppose that after scanning this photo you wondered: "Who is this person and why is he wearing those gloves?" After reading the caption and the article, you learn more—C. J. Marconi is testing gloves that "read" sign language. Yet this doesn't explain everything about C. J. and his work. Write one or two questions about C. J. that go beyond the simple who-and-why question.

Tell students that this magazine article appeared in *National Geographic World,* as noted in the line that begins "Source." As they read through the article, have them use the material in the right-hand column as a guide to reading. The following are possible responses to the four numbered activities.

1 Students should preview the article prior to reading, taking note of the title and photograph. They may want to look at the photograph on the next page as well. The questions they generate should be prompted by their preview.
Possible Responses: What kinds of inventions are there for helping people with disabilities? How did these kids get involved with helping researchers? How do these inventions help disabled people?

2 Students should generate more questions based on the photograph on page 388 and on the information from the article.
Possible Responses: How do the gloves that C.J. is wearing help deaf people communicate? Are the gloves wired to the computer? How does that work?

 Use **Writing Transparencies,** p. 40, for additional support.

REAL WORLD LINK **389**

3 Students' questions should reflect details presented in the paragraph. **Possible Responses:** What is finger spelling, and how do people learn to do it? How did kids like Krista get involved with research? How are these inventions marketed and sold?

4 Students should think of questions that this article has prompted yet are not explicitly discussed in the article. **Possible Responses:** What kinds of video games could people with disabilities play? What is cerebral palsy, and what inventions help people who have it?

Revising Research Questions

With students, reread the research question provided in the text, "What are people doing to help others with physical disabilities?" Have students read through all the questions they have generated, then revise this question to have a more specific focus. They may want to work in small groups and generate several revised questions.

Reading for Information continued

 This paragraph includes information about a girl who helps engineers develop and test equipment. What detailed and specific research question might you ask about this topic?

4 Sometimes during research you find yourself attracted to a topic that differs from your original focus. For example, suppose your original question was "In what ways is technology used to help people with disabilities?" After reading about Julia Nelson, you might decide instead to ask how people with physical disabilities stay fit. That's fine, especially if you find the topic more interesting, and think others will, too. Think of one or two new focus questions that this article raises.

Inquiry & Research

Activity Link: from *The Story of My Life*, p. 386. Review the article and consider this focus question: "What devices, services, or training available today could have helped Helen Keller as a child?" Research how children with disabilities similar to Helen Keller's are given help, support, and training. Write a brief report of your findings.

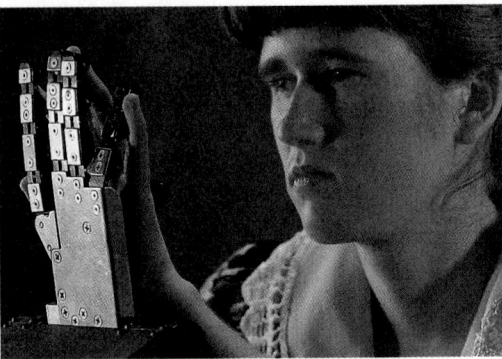

"THE PEOPLE I WORK WITH REALLY VALUE MY OPINION. IT MAKES ME FEEL GOOD THAT PEOPLE CAN LEARN FROM ME." **KRISTA CAUDILL**

 Krista is deaf and blind. To communicate, she often uses fingerspelling—forming shapes that stand for letters in the palm of the hand of her "listener." Krista helps engineers who work at the A.I. DuPont Institute in Wilmington, Delaware. They develop and test equipment to help people with disabilities. Krista is one of about a dozen young people with disabilities from the area who serve as consumer researchers before the devices are ready to be sold.

"We ask the researchers to attend team meetings and give us ongoing feedback," says director Richard Foulds. "They're a major part of our team."

Bern Gavlick, 16, has been testing a robot arm that attaches to his wheelchair. Because of his cerebral palsy, Bern cannot easily control the movements of his limbs. The arm can take a book off a shelf or open a door for him. Julia Nelson, 16, also has cerebral palsy. She tested a video game system designed for fun and fitness. "I love trying out the latest products," says Julia. "As a disabled teen, I'm looking to a future of trying to be independent," she adds. "It gives me hope that there are people working on products to help me achieve that goal."

 Inquiry & Research

The Inquiry & Research activity on this page links to the activity on page 386 from the Choices & Challenges following "The Story of My Life."

Instruction This article will serve as a starting point for researching the focus question; however, students will need time and support with print and electronic materials to gather additional information. Remind students of the requirements for writing a brief report. Students may benefit from working with a partner on this activity.

Application Students may want to do further research using one of the questions they generated during the reading of this magazine article and share it with the class.

Use **Writing Transparencies,** p. 41, for additional support.

PREPARING to *Read*

Street Corner Flight
Poetry by NORMA LANDA FLORES

Words Like Freedom
Poetry by LANGSTON HUGHES

Connect to Your Life

To Be Free What comes to mind when you think about freedom? What words and images express your thoughts and feelings about what it means to be free? Use a web like the one shown to explore your ideas.

Build Background

Words to Live By People have always struggled toward great ideals and imagined better ways of living. From national anthems to poems to simple proverbs, these ideals are often expressed in words and images. The Declaration of Independence proclaimed the importance of "life, liberty, and the pursuit of happiness." A famous African-American spiritual sang out hope for a time when slaves would "cross the mighty river" and know freedom. In the poems you are about to read, Langston Hughes and Norma Landa Flores use images and words to convey their thoughts about freedom.

Focus Your Reading

LITERARY ANALYSIS | **SPEAKER** In a poem, the speaker is the voice that talks to the reader—like the narrator in a work of fiction. Listen for the speaker's voice in this line from "Words Like Freedom":

> *There are words like* Liberty
> *That almost make me cry.*

A poem's speaker is not necessarily the poet.

ACTIVE READING | **MAKING INFERENCES** An **inference** is a logical guess based on evidence. A good reader makes inferences about the speaker of a poem.

READER'S NOTEBOOK As you read each poem, jot down any inferences you can make about the speaker. How old is the speaker? Might the poet be the speaker? Provide evidence to support your inferences. Evidence may come from the poem, your experience, or the author biographies.

STREET CORNER FLIGHT / WORDS LIKE FREEDOM **391**

Objectives
1. understand and appreciate a **poem** (Literary Analysis)
2. understand author's use of **speaker** (Literary Analysis)
3. **make inferences** to help understand poetry (**Active Reading**)

Summary
In "Street Corner Flight," Norma Landa Flores describes a city scene: two small boys release pigeons to fly away free. From her descriptive language, we get the image of the birds' view from the air, and we feel the sense of flying free, away from the problems and woes that must be facing the young boys. In "Words Like Freedom," the poet Langston Hughes provides powerful images. He evokes the deep significance the words *Freedom* and *Liberty* hold for the speaker. By looking at both poems, the reader gets a sense of how freedom may mean different things to different people—and for different reasons.

Thematic Link
The ways to break barriers are as many and as varied as the barriers themselves. Overcoming the barriers to liberty and freedom is a major theme in literature, as it is in life.

5-Minute Warm-Up

Daily Language SkillBuilder

Have students **proofread** the display sentences on page 315j and write them correctly. The sentences also appear on Transparency 12 of **Grammar Transparencies and Copymasters.**

LESSON RESOURCES

UNIT THREE RESOURCE BOOK, pp. 41–42

ASSESSMENT
Formal Assessment, pp. 61–62
Teacher's Guide to Assessment and Portfolio Use
Test Generator

SKILLS TRANSPARENCIES AND COPYMASTERS
Literary Analysis
• Poetry: Speaker, TR 21 (for Paired Activity, p. 395)

READING AND CRITICAL THINKING
• Making Inferences TR 10 (for Thinking Through the Literature, p. 395)

Grammar
• Identifying Adjectives and the Words They Modify, CM 91 (for Mini Lesson, p. 396)

Vocabulary
• Analogies, CM 43 (for Mini Lesson, p. 392)

INTEGRATED TECHNOLOGY
Audio Library

Visit our website:
www.mcdougallittell.com

Literary Analysis | SPEAKER |

Ask students to think about the poem, "Street Corner Flight," and to discuss the message of the speaker's voice.

Possible Response: The speaker describes how the pigeons are free to fly away from the hardships of life, while the boys must still face those hardships. The speaker may be trying to give us hope—that if the birds can find a better life, perhaps we can too.

 Use **Unit Three Resource Book,** p. 42 for more practice.

Active Reading | MAKING INFERENCES |

Ask students to draw inferences about who the speaker is and support this inference with evidence from the poem.

Possible Responses: The speaker may be the poet herself remembering how it was when she grew up in a similar place. She may have seen boys releasing pigeons and written this poem to portray the feeling she had of wanting to fly to freedom like the pigeons.

 Use **Unit Three Resource Book,** p. 41 for more practice.

Literary Analysis: VOICE

Set a Purpose Ask students to listen for the voice in the next poem, and to compare it to the voice in this first poem.

Thinking Through the Literature

1. **Comprehension Check**
   The boys set the pigeons free and they flew away.
2. **Think Critically** They are probably excited, sad, envious, and wishful.

Teaching Options

Street CORNER Flight

by Norma Landa Flores

From this side . . .
   of their concrete barrio
      two small boys hold
         fat white pigeons
5 trapped in their trembling hands.

Then,
   gently,
      not disturbing
         their powers of flight,
10   release them
into the air.

They were free
   to glide above
      rushing traffic
15   soar beyond
            labyrinths of
food stamps . . . loneliness . . . and want.

They were free
   to fly
20   toward the other side . . .
a world away.

Thinking Through the Literature

1. **Comprehension Check** What happens to the pigeons in "Street Corner Flight"?
2. **Think Critically** What do you think the boys in the poem are feeling?

 Vocabulary Strategy

ANALOGIES Remind students that one way to learn new words is through analogies. An analogy contains two word pairs with the words in each pair having similar relationships. The words in the second pair are related in the same way as those in the first pair. The words are separated by *is to* and *as* or by the symbols : and ::.

Instruction Tell students that some of the most common relationships used in analogies are synonyms and antonyms. Write these examples on the board and discuss them:

LIGHT is to DARK as UP is to DOWN (antonyms)

BRIGHT : SHINY :: COLD : FRIGID (synonyms)

Exercises Ask students to complete the analogies, using words from the two poems.

1. VILLAGE is to TOWN as NEIGHBORHOOD is to _____ (barrio)
2. FREEDOM is to SLAVERY as _____ is to CONSTRAINT (liberty)
3. PUZZLE : MYSTERY :: MAZE : _____ (labyrinth)
4. SLIDE : SLIP :: _____ : SOAR (glide)

 Use **Vocabulary Transparencies and Copymasters,** p. 43.

Alas EN la esquina

translated by F. E. Albi

De este lado . . .
   en su barrio de hormigo,
    dos muchachitos guardan
     palomas blancas, gordas,
5 presas en manos temblorosas.

En ese entonces,
  suavemente,
   sin contener
    sus ganas de volar,
10   las sueltan
en el aire.

Y fueron libres
  de planear por encima
   del loco trafico,
15   y subir mas alla de
     laberintos
de estampillas de comida . . . soledad . . .
  y miseria.

Libres
  de volar
20   hacia el otro lado . . .
un mundo aparte.

STREET CORNER FLIGHT   **393**

Customizing Instruction

Less Proficient Readers
Ask students to whom they think *they* refers in lines 12 and 18?
Possible Responses: It may refer to the pigeons flying above the city. The word also seems to refer to the boys, who, through the birds, can symbolically fly to a world beyond the barrio.
Set a Purpose: Have students read the second poem to learn what another poet has to say about freedom.

Students Acquiring English
For students whose native language is Spanish, have them read the poem in its Spanish translation. They may want to share with the class any differences in meaning that came through with the translation. Non-Spanish-speaking students might enjoy hearing this poem read aloud in Spanish.

Use **Spanish Study Guide** for additional support, pp. 79–81.

Multiple Learning Styles
Visual Learners
Have students read the poem by Langston Hughes on the next page and look closely at the artwork found there. Ask students to discuss what they see in the painting and to use that to help them understand the poem.

 Multicultural Link   **Barrios**

The word *barrio* comes from the Arabic *barr,* which means "an open area." Originally, the term referred to an urban district or quarter in a Spanish-speaking country. It has come to mean a chiefly Spanish-speaking community or neighborhood in a U.S. city.

Literary Analysis `SPEAKER`

Ask students who they think the speaker is or represents in this poem.

Possible Responses: The speaker is someone who has learned about the importance of freedom and liberty first-hand. The speaker may represent a group of people who have had a common experience.

 Use **Literary Analysis Transparencies,** p. 21, for additional support.

Active Reading `MAKING INFERENCES`

Ask students to draw inferences about what the speaker is trying to tell the reader. What evidence in the text supports those inferences?

Possible Responses: The speaker is telling the reader that simple words like *freedom* and *liberty* mean different things to different people. To the speaker, they are precious and powerful words that cause strong responses and emotions.

 Use **Reading and Critical Thinking Transparencies,** p. 10, for additional support.

Literary Analysis: REPETITION

The repetition of a word or phrase in a literary work is used to make a point. Ask students to identify the repetition in this poem and to interpret its meaning.

Possible Response: The repetition is of the phrase "There are words like." The poet may be using those words to remind the reader that there are many words we hear regularly and don't think about, but these words have very special meaning to some people.

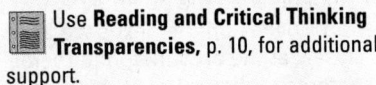

Words Like FREEDOM

by Langston Hughes

There are words like *Freedom*
Sweet and wonderful to say.
On my heartstrings freedom sings
All day everyday.

There are words like *Liberty*
That almost make me cry.
If you had known what I know
You would know why.

Freedom Now, Reginald Gammon.

Teaching Options

✓**Assessment Informal Assessment**

PARAPHRASE POEMS Students use a variety of strategies to help them understand what they read. One helpful strategy is to paraphrase and summarize text to recall, inform, or organize ideas. To help students comprehend poetry, ask them to paraphrase each of the two poems in this lesson. Remind them that to paraphrase means to retell the poem in their own words.

RUBRIC

3 Full Accomplishment Response shows a full understanding of the poems' meanings, and is thoughtfully written.

2 Substantial Accomplishment Response shows a substantial understanding of the poems and their meanings. Writing is appropriate for sixth grade.

1 Little or Partial Accomplishment Response shows little or partial understanding of the meaning of the poems. Writing is less than adequate.

Connect to the Literature

1. What Do You Think?
After reading "Words Like Freedom," what image stays in your mind?

> **Comprehension Check**
> • What effects do words like *freedom* and *liberty* have on the poem's speaker?

Think Critically

2. How would you describe the mood, or feeling, of "Words Like Freedom"?

3. What experiences might have made the poem's speaker appreciate freedom and liberty?

 THINK ABOUT
- times when you appreciate freedom and liberty
- events in history linked to these words
- emotions the speaker implies

4. [ACTIVE READING] [MAKING INFERENCES] Who do you imagine is the speaker in each poem? To support your answers, refer to the notes in your READER'S NOTEBOOK. What lines from the poems support your ideas?

Extend Interpretations

5. [COMPARING TEXTS] Choose either "Street Corner Flight" or "Words Like Freedom" and compare it to "I'm Nobody! Who Are You?," "It Seems I Test People," or "Growing Pains" (page 194). Compare the poetic form, use of figurative language, and theme, or message, of the two poems.

6. What If? Imagine that the speaker in "Words Like Freedom" could talk to the boys in "Street Corner Flight." What advice might he give them?

7. Connect to Life What new impressions or understandings of freedom did you gain from these poems? Share your thoughts with your classmates.

Literary Analysis

[LITERARY ANALYSIS] [SPEAKER]
In a poem, the **speaker** is the voice that talks to the reader. The speaker is not necessarily the poet, but the speaker may express the feelings of the poet. The speaker's words are carefully chosen to convey thoughts and feelings about a scene or subject.

Paired Activity Working with a partner, go back through the poems. Look for words and phrases that help you make inferences about each speaker. What do these words suggest about the speaker's experience? What do they suggest about the speaker's thoughts and feelings about freedom?

Speaker in "Words Like Freedom"
- "if you had known what I know"
- something has made him appreciate freedom

[REVIEW] [REPETITION] The use of a sound, word, or phrase more than once is called **repetition.** Writers use repetition to draw special attention to certain ideas, sounds, or feelings.

Connect to the Literature

1. What Do You Think?
Answers will vary.

Comprehension Check
• They make the speaker both happy and sad.

Think Critically

2. Possible Response: The mood is one of celebration mixed with the sadness of remembering.

3. Possible Response: If the speaker is African American, he may be remembering slavery and thinking about racism.

4. Possible Response: The speaker in "Words Like Freedom" is probably an adult African American, possibly Hughes himself. The speaker in "Street Corner Flight" is probably an adult, an observer who might or might not be the poet, possibly poor and/or Hispanic, since (s)he seems to understand the boys and situation.

Use **Reading and Critical Thinking Transparencies,** p. 10, for additional support.

Literary Analysis

Speaker As students work with their partners, encourage them to write down only those words and phrases that give them insight into each speaker. Have them think about the experiences, thoughts, and feelings they had when reading the poems to help them connect with the speaker. Have students keep two lists, one for the speaker of each poem.

Use **Literary Analysis Transparencies,** p. 21, for additional support.

Extend Interpretations

5. Comparing Texts Answers will vary depending on the poems students choose to compare, but they should be able to support their comparisons with evidence from the poems.

6. What If? Students might say the speaker in "Words Like Freedom" would tell the boys to value freedom; to learn from others' examples how to become free; to go to school, work hard, organize to live in better conditions as they grow up, and so on. He might also offer to help them.

7. Connect to Life Students may realize that poverty traps people: to be free, people need opportunities and options, and some people don't have those. Some people cannot take freedom for granted, and when they gain it, they rejoice in it.

Use **Communications Transparencies and Copymasters,** p. 2, for additional support.

Writing Options

1. **Interior Monologue** Students' monologues may include emotions and ideas they had as they read the poem, and should be written in the first person.
2. **Concept Poem** Encourage students to select a word that has an emotional meaning to them. Remind them that poetry can rhyme or it can be free verse.

 Use **Writing Transparencies,** p. 17, for additional support.

Activities & Explorations

Audio Imagery You might want to elicit the help of a music teacher to locate appropriate music.

Inquiry & Research

Famous Freedom Words If your school's computer has an encyclopedia program, you may want to provide students the opportunity to look for *freedom* quotes there.

 Use **Writing Transparencies,** p. 55, for additional support.

Author Activity

Read On Provide students with time to gather and read more works by Hughes. Students can work in small groups to discuss the major themes and topics in Hughes' work.

Writing Options

1. **Interior Monologue** What were the boys thinking when they released the pigeons? Speaking as one of the boys, write a monologue describing your impressions, thoughts, and feelings.

2. **Concept Poem** The words *liberty* and *freedom* are very meaningful to the speaker of "Words Like Freedom." Choose a word that holds great meaning for you. Write a poem about how that word makes you feel.

Activities & Explorations

Audio Imagery Select a piece of music that conveys the feelings of the speaker of one of the poems. Create a tape recording that combines the music and the poem.
~ **SPEAKING AND LISTENING**

Inquiry & Research

Famous Freedom Words In a book of quotations, look up *freedom.* Choose quotations that seem particularly meaningful and create a poster of famous sayings about freedom. Be sure to credit the person who said, wrote, or sang each line.

"My soul has grown deep like the rivers."

Langston Hughes
1902–1967

A Legend in His Time Born in Joplin, Missouri, Hughes had a lonely childhood during which his family moved often. After graduating from Lincoln University, he lived outside New York City and held odd jobs while writing poetry. Eventually, his works included poetry, songs, plays, short stories, novels, nonfiction, and a newspaper column. Hughes became a key figure in the Harlem Renaissance, the great literary movement that blossomed in New York City's Harlem during the 1920s.

AUTHOR ACTIVITY

Read On Read several more poems by Langston Hughes. With classmates, identify and discuss some of the themes, or important messages, that you see in his work.

"Out of midnight's cold winter air illusions become realities."

Norma Landa Flores

Winning Words At the time Norma Landa Flores wrote "Street Corner Flight," she was a student in California's lower San Joaquín Valley. She submitted entries to a writing contest sponsored by the Chicano Studies Department of Bakersfield College in Bakersfield, California. "Street Corner Flight" was one of several winning poems by Flores (another, "Through a Blue Room's Door," is quoted above). These poems were later published in *Sighs and Songs of Aztlán,* an anthology of new Chicano literature.

Teaching Options

Mini Lesson Grammar

IDENTIFYING ADJECTIVES AND THE WORDS THEY MODIFY Remind students that well-chosen descriptive words help readers understand the text, as well as make it more interesting to read.

Instruction Write the following sentence on the board: The sleek, white pigeons flew slowly toward the bright yellow sun.

Ask students to identify the adjectives in this sentence (*sleek, white* and *bright, yellow*) and the noun(s) they modify (*pigeons* and *sun*). Discuss how this description helps us get a mental image of the pigeons as they flew away towards the sun.

Exercises Ask students to underline the adjectives and circle the words they modify in each sentence.

1. The small, young boys watched intently as the birds became smaller and smaller.
2. As they flew, the pigeons climbed into the cloud-filled sky, until they were no longer visible.
3. Back in the hot, dusty barrio, the busy streets and noisy lives went on.

4. The cool, sparkling water was like liquid hope on that hot summer day in the city.

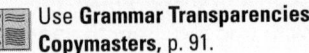 Use **Grammar Transparencies and Copymasters,** p. 91.

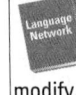 Use McDougal Littell's **Language Network,** Chapter 5, for more practice in identifying adjectives and the words they modify.

Breaking It Down

When you read a word you don't recognize, look for a **base word** you do know. Then look for a familiar **prefix**, a word part attached before the base word, or a familiar **suffix**, a word part attached to the end of the word.

> Bands of outlaws roamed the countryside . . . kidnapping those **unfortunate** enough to have wandered from the protection of their people.
>
> —Walter Dean Myers,
> "Abd al-Rahman Ibrahima"

You can divide the word into three parts to help determine its meaning.

unfortunate

prefix **un-** means "not"   suffix **-ate** means "having or filled with"

base word **fortune** means "luck"

Put the three parts together to determine the meaning of *unfortunate*: "not having luck."

Strategies for Building Vocabulary

Knowing the meanings of common prefixes and suffixes can help you understand new words. Here are some strategies for using prefixes and suffixes.

❶ Take the Word Apart To find the meaning of an unfamiliar word, divide it into parts. Think about the meaning of the prefix, the base word, and/or the suffix. Guess at a definition. Then check to see if it makes sense in context. Look at the following example:

> The Fula were taller and lighter in complexion than the other *inhabitants* of Africa's west coast; . . .
>
> —Walter Dean Myers,
> "Abd al-Rahman Ibrahima"

You can divide the word *inhabitants* into three parts as shown:

Prefix	Base Word	Suffix
in-	*habit*	*-ants*
"in, into"	"dwell"	"those who"

❷ Learn Common Prefixes and Suffixes You may already be familiar with many prefixes and suffixes. The following charts contain some of the most common ones.

Prefix	Meanings	Example
ex-	out, from	export
in-	in, into, not	incite
pre-	before	preface
pro-	forward, favoring	propose
re-	again, back	rebound
trans-	across, beyond	transmit
un-	not, opposite of	unhappy

Suffix	Meanings	Example
-al	of, like	trivial
-ant, -ent	one who	dominant
-ist	one performing or believing in	bicyclist
-ion, -tion	act or state of	suspension
-ous, -ious	marked by	pompous
-less	without	hopeless
-ment	act or state of	contentment

EXERCISE Divide each word to show its base word, prefix, and suffix. Then write a possible definition of the word. Use a dictionary to review the actual definition.

1. renewal
2. expression
3. proactive
4. insubstantial
5. abandonment

Building Vocabulary

Objectives
- understand the meanings of prefixes and suffixes
- apply meanings of prefixes and suffixes to understand unfamiliar words

EXERCISE
Possible Answers:
1. re/new/al—the act of making new again
2. ex/press/ion—the act of setting forth in words
3. pro/active—acting in advance (to deal with an expected difficulty)
4. in/substant/ial—of, or related to, having no substance or material
5. ab/andon/ment—the state of withdrawing support from

Use **Unit Three Resource Book,** p. 43. Use **Vocabulary Transparencies and Copymasters,** pp. 7–8, for additional support.

OVERVIEW

Objectives
- appreciate the works of a contemporary author and poet
- interpret the possible influences of personal events in Soto's life on his writing
- look at the descriptive writing techniques used by Soto

The Author Study offers a special opportunity for students to focus on the work of a popular contemporary author. Students will be exposed to information about Soto's life, which will give them insight into the person behind the stories. They will explore some aspects of the author's craft and apply these to their own writing.

Author Study GARY SOTO

CONTENTS

From Field to Fame

"Because I believe in literature and the depth of living it adds to our years, my task is to start Chicanos reading."

born 1952

CARDBOARD IN HIS SHOES

Gary Soto was born in Fresno, California, in a neighborhood surrounded by the factories where many of his relatives worked. His grandparents had left Mexico in 1914, but almost 40 years later the family was still struggling. Soto remembers walking around with cardboard in his shoes and wearing "socks with holes big enough to be ski masks." When Soto was five, his family moved to a new neighborhood. Soon afterward, his father was

Gary, his brother Rick (left), and sister Debra in 1957

His LIFE and TIMES

1952 Born April 12 in Fresno, California	**1957** Father dies.	**1970–1974** Attends college; begins to write poetry

Gary, age six

1950   **1960**   **1970**

1957 Soviets launch Sputnik satellite.	**1963** President Kennedy is assassinated.	**1965–1973** U.S. ground troops in Vietnam War

killed in an accident while helping to re-roof a friend's house. After the funeral, Soto recalls going into an empty room in the still-new house and making as much noise as possible so that "I could not hear the things in my heart."

HARD LABOR

As a child, Soto first wanted to be a priest, then a hobo, and even a paleontologist, a scientist who studies dinosaurs. But one of his first real jobs was picking grapes. When he was younger he had played in the vineyards while his mother worked, but he had no idea how difficult the work truly was. He soon found out when, as an adolescent, he began to pick grapes himself. Soto picked grapes off and on until he was 15. Later on, he and his brother hoed and chopped cotton, earning $1.25 an hour for work that was backbreaking. Soto also worked in car washes and at a tire factory.

AN ARTIST AWAKENS

While growing up, Soto had no great love of school, and his teachers considered him difficult. "I was no good at school," he recalls. "I could not sing, do art, or figure out math problems. I was deathly scared of the stage, yet jealous when my

Gary at age 20, around the time he started writing poetry

Family Struggles

A Most of Soto's family worked in the Sun-Maid Raisin factory on Braly Street where the author lived when he was a boy. Soto's grandfather, grandmother, father, three uncles, an aunt, and a dog—who accompanied his grandfather, a security guard, on rounds—worked at this factory.

Making a Living

B Soto began looking for work when he was still a boy. His search began one year when he tried to get the neighbors to pay him for raking leaves—in the summer when there were no leaves on the ground! He found some odd jobs, such as going to the store and weeding, to earn a little spending money. When he was older, he picked grapes with his mother each summer. It was hard, backbreaking work, and the pay was low, but it allowed Soto to buy new clothes for the next school year. One summer, he and his brother Rick got jobs chopping cotton—dusty, hot, and difficult work.

Poetry

C Soto's family was largely uneducated, and there were few books in his house when he was growing up. No one encouraged him to read. He began writing poetry in college after discovering a book of poems that made him think, "This is terrific: I'd like to do something like this." Soto was influenced and guided by the poet Philip Levine, his writing instructor at California State University, Fresno. His first poems were for adults, but in 1990, he began writing books of poetry for young people.

1975
Marries Carolyn Sadako Oda

1977
Publishes first book, *The Elements of San Joaquín*

1990
Publishes *Baseball in April*, his first book for young readers

1995
Is a finalist for the National Book Award

1980

1990

2000

1979
Egypt and Israel sign peace agreement.

1989–1990
Cold War between U.S. and USSR ends.

1993
South Africa adopts majority rule constitution.

1997
U.S. spacecraft transmits pictures from Mars.

GARY SOTO **399**

School Visits

D Soto says that one of his goals is to get Chicano kids reading. He wants to encourage them to read, partly because there was no one there to encourage him when he was a child. He enjoys spending time with young people and frequently visits with them at schools. Many of his stories reflect real issues that a lot of kids face, so this encourages students to connect with him.

friends got up on the stage and sang with gusto." His thoughts about school changed, however, when he received his draft notice for the Vietnam War in 1970. As a college student, Soto would be able to put off entering the army, so he enrolled at Fresno City College. During his second year, he discovered poetry. On his own, he read a poem called "Unwanted" that expressed many of his own feelings of being alone and isolated. This inspired him to write poetry of his own. Three years later, he won a national prize for his poetry.

A WRITER ON THE ROAD

D Today, Soto is an important American poet and writer. He is also dedicated to working with young people. He travels around California and the Southwest to promote Chicano literacy and literature. Although Soto has won much praise for his writing for adult audiences, he has become even better known by young readers. "I think I'm very childlike," he says, "and I often write youthful poems. It's sort of a silly act, writing itself . . . I like the youth in my poetry, sort of a craziness. For me that's really important. I don't want to take a dreary look at the world." Soto lives in Berkeley, California, with his wife and daughter.

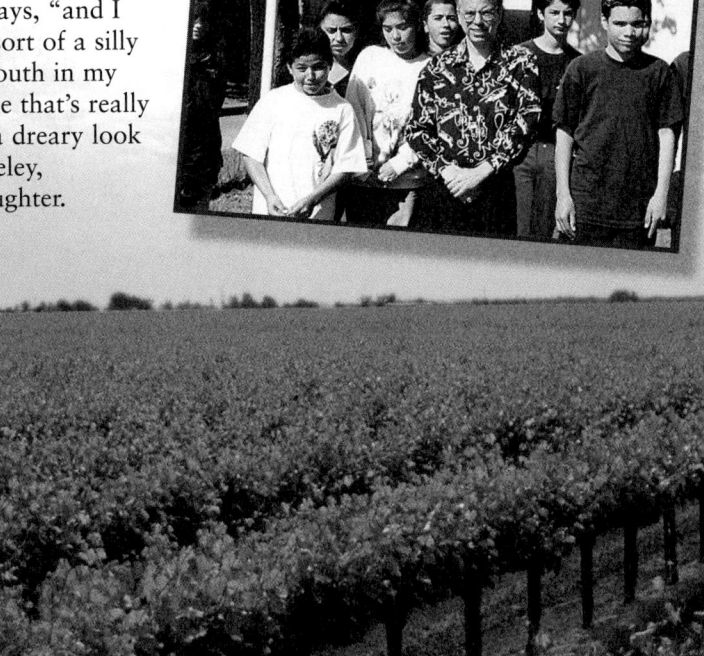

Gary Soto visits with students at the Washington School in Cloverdale, California.

400

Gary Soto loves traveling around to schools and meeting students.

TALKING WITH GARY SOTO

Q: Do you ever write in Spanish or just English?

A: Like most writers who have two languages, I choose to write in only one. English is my writing language. I leave the Spanish translations to Spanish experts.

Q: Which do you find easier to write—fiction or poetry?

A: I find it easier to write fiction, although poetry is what I truly love to write. My style of poetry is narrative (each poem has a story), so I guess I like to tell stories. With poetry, as opposed to fiction, I enjoy the challenge of telling that story with minimum words that still sound musical to my ear.

Q: One of the kids in my class didn't realize that you are Mexican, too, and he got really angry about one of your stories. He thought the story made it seem like all Mexicans were poor, or not educated. Have other people reacted to any of your stories like that? What do you say when they do?

A: Some of my characters are in fact poor, but there is nothing wrong about seeing poor people march across the page, especially if these people happen to be Chicano/Mexican American. People go to extremes to stay away from the poor, while in my own personal life I go to extremes to be with them. I'm thinking of my church, where most of our members are day laborers, domestic helpers, baby sitters, roofers, gardeners.

In short, I think the poor should be written about and those stories should come from people who come from their ranks.

Q: Have you ever experienced stage fright like the character Robert in "The School Play"?

A: Yes, I did, age 10 and in fifth grade. Cast as a Gold Rush 49er, I was supposed to say, "I have the glasses." But I was so busy admiring my costume beard that I forgot what to say. The beard, I remember, was red.

Q: The characters in your stories seem so true to life. Are they based on people in your family and people you know?

A: Yes, in books such as *Living Up the Street* and *A Summer Life* I have drawn on my childhood and, thus, the unavoidable presence of family, which, at times, was wild as pirates. While we may lament that our childhoods are boring, they in fact become the stuff of poems and storytelling. This is particularly true if you grew up poor, where there were not a lot of material gifts. Instead, the work of invention was at hand. What does my family think of this? Well, they don't really read my work, so they're not fully aware of how they've been brought to the page.

 LaserLinks: Background for Reading
Author Background

 More Online: Author Link
www.mcdougallittell.com

 NetActivities: Author Exploration

Variety

E Soto is currently writing novels, plays, essays, and poetry for adults and young readers. His passion at the moment is writing plays. He feels it is natural for contemporary writers to try their hand at many kinds of writing, and feels he is still "mulling over my intentions."

Chicano Influence

F Soto's themes are universal and speak to all adolescents, but his stories are clearly set in Mexican-American communities. He calls himself a Chicano and says he feels a certain obligation to that ethnic group. He includes many Spanish words in his writings because these are a part of the memories he draws from when he writes.

Grandmother

G A major influence in Soto's life was his grandmother, and even though she may not read his work, she is proud of him. She worked for over twenty years at the Sun-Maid Raisin factory to make a meager living for her family. She would stand at a conveyor belt, plucking out leaves and pebbles from raisins on their way to being boxed. She is the subject of some of Soto's poems, and his admiration for her shows through in his work.

OVERVIEW

Objectives

1. understand and appreciate a **short story** (Literary Analysis)
2. understand author's use of **tone** (Literary Analysis)
3. use **monitoring reading strategies** as an aid to understanding (**Active Reading**)

Summary

In this short story, author Gary Soto tells about a boy who is assigned a small speaking part in a school play. Although Robert knows his two lines well, he must deliver them to Belinda, the classroom bully, known for beating up boys and even taking on a pit bull terrier! Despite Belinda's menacing presence, Robert is determined to deliver his lines flawlessly and please his teacher, his family, and himself.

Thematic Link

Bullies like Belinda create barriers by making others feel inferior. Robert must overcome his fear of Belinda, as well as his own fear of failure, and prove to himself that he can perform without making mistakes.

5-Minute Warm-Up

Daily Language SkillBuilder

Have students **proofread** the display sentences on page 315k and write them correctly. The sentences also appear on Transparency 13 of **Grammar Transparencies and Copymasters.**

"He prayed that his line would come back to him."

The School Play

Short Story by GARY SOTO

Connect to Your Life

You're On! Think back to your own experiences of performing or speaking to a group. What do you remember most?

Build Background

CONNECT TO HISTORY In "The School Play," a class is preparing to perform *The Last Stand,* a play based on a tragic incident. In 1846 a group of about 90 pioneers from Illinois and nearby states set out for California. The group was led by George and Jacob Donner.

When trying to cross the Sierra Nevada mountain range in eastern California, the Donner party became snowbound, and the travelers ran out of food. Many began dying of starvation.

In their desperation, some of the remaining members of the party resorted to eating the bodies of the dead to survive. Only 47 made it through that grim winter. Donner Pass is now a national landmark.

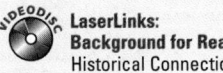
LaserLinks: Background for Reading Historical Connection

WORDS TO KNOW
Vocabulary Preview

depleted   quiver   smirk
prop   relentless

Focus Your Reading

LITERARY ANALYSIS   TONE The attitude that a writer has toward his or her subject is called **tone.** The tone can be humorous, sad, serious, frightening, or a combination of attitudes. Tone affects the **mood** of a story.

ACTIVE READING   MONITORING READING STRATEGIES You may be halfway through a story when you realize that you've forgotten who a certain character is, or that you don't understand what happened in a particular scene. To avoid these problems, it is helpful to **monitor** how you are reading. Pause every so often as you read. If you lose track of the characters, go back to an earlier scene to reread for details.

READER'S NOTEBOOK As you read, refer to the strategies in this chart. Make note of places where one or more of the strategies helped your understanding.

Reading Strategies	
Questioning	Question what happens as you read.
Connecting	Connect personally with the story.
Predicting	Predict what might happen next.
Clarifying	Stop occasionally for a quick review.
Visualizing	Form mental images of the story.
Evaluating	Form opinions about the story.

402   UNIT THREE   **AUTHOR STUDY**

LESSON RESOURCES

UNIT THREE RESOURCE BOOK, pp. 44–50

ASSESSMENT
Formal Assessment, pp. 63–64
Teacher's Guide to Assessment and Portfolio Use
Test Generator

SKILLS TRANSPARENCIES AND COPYMASTERS
Literary Analysis
• Tone, TR 25 (for Cooperative Activity, p. 409)
Reading and Critical Thinking
• Strategies for Reading, TR 1 (for Thinking Through the Literature, p. 409)

Grammar
• Choosing an Adjective or Adverb, CM 95 (for Mini Lesson, p. 410)
• Punctuating a Series of Modifiers, CM 124 (for Mini Lesson, p. 406)
Vocabulary
• Context Clues: Definition and Restatement, CM 44 (for Mini Lesson, p. 403)

INTEGRATED TECHNOLOGY
Audio Library
LaserLinks
• Historical Connection; Author Background; Art Gallery. See **Teacher's SourceBook,** p. 34

Visit our website:
www.mcdougallittell.com

THE SCHOOL PLAY

BY GARY SOTO

I n the school play at the end of his sixth-grade year, all Robert Suarez had to remember to say was, "Nothing's wrong. I can see," to a pioneer woman, who was really Belinda Lopez. Instead of a pioneer woman, Belinda was one of the toughest girls since the beginning of the world. She was known to slap boys and grind their faces into the grass so that they bit into chunks of wormy earth. More than once Robert had witnessed Belinda staring down the janitor's pit bull, who licked his frothing chops but didn't dare mess with her.

The class rehearsed for three weeks, at first without costumes. Early one morning Mrs. Bunnin wobbled into the classroom lugging a large cardboard box. She wiped her brow and said, "Thanks for the help, Robert."

Robert was at his desk scribbling a ballpoint tattoo that spelled DUDE on the tops of his knuckles. He looked up and stared, blinking at his teacher. "Oh, did you need some help?" he asked.

"NOTHING'S

WRONG.

I CAN SEE."

She rolled her eyes at him and told him to stop writing on his skin. "You'll look like a criminal," she scolded.

Robert stuffed his hands into his pockets as he rose from his seat. "What's in the box?" he asked.

She muttered under her breath. She popped open the taped top and brought out skirts, hats, snowshoes, scarves, and vests. She tossed Robert a red beard, which he held up to his face, thinking it made him look handsome.

"I like it," Robert said. He sneezed and ran his hand across his moist nose.

His classmates were coming into the classroom and looked at Robert in awe. "That's bad," Ruben said. "What do I get?"

Mrs. Bunnin threw him a wrinkled shirt. Ruben raised it to his chest and said, "My dad could wear this. Can I give it to him after the play is done?"

Mrs. Bunnin turned away in silence.

Most of the actors didn't have speaking

THE SCHOOL PLAY **403**

Literary Analysis [TONE]

Ask students to consider the author's tone and think about how it contributes to the effect of the text. Have students cite an example that reflects the tone of the story.

Possible Response: The tone is humorous and a little scary. When Belinda says, "Sucka, is there something wrong with your eye-balls?" it's funny. But because she's so tough, Belinda might have beaten up Robert if he made a mistake, so that was a little scary.

 Use **Unit Three Resource Book,** p. 46 for more practice. Use **Literary Analysis Transparencies,** p. 25, for additional support.

Active Reading

[MONITORING READING STRATEGIES]

Remind students that as they read, they may need to go back and reread certain parts in order to keep track of what's going on. Model monitoring by saying that now that Belinda's been fooling around with her line, you forget what she's really supposed to say. Have students go back and find her actual line.

Answer: "Is there something wrong with your eyes?"

 Use **Unit Three Resource Book,** p. 45 for more practice. Use **Reading and Critical Thinking Transparencies,** p. 1, for additional support.

Literary Analysis: CHARACTERS

Who are the main characters and what do you know about their traits?

Possible Response: The main characters are Robert, Belinda, and Mrs. Bunnin. Robert must be a good speller, because he got a speaking part in the play. He's nervous about his part and intimidated by Belinda, who is a bully. Mrs. Bunnin is a tough, wise teacher.

Teaching Options

The Old and the New Year (1953), Pablo Picasso. Musée d'Art et d'Histoire, St. Denis, France. Giraudon/Art Resource, New York. Copyright © 2001 Estate of Pablo Picasso/Artists Rights Society (ARS), New York.

 Viewing and Representing

The Old and the New Year
by Pablo Picasso

ART APPRECIATION Spanish artist Pablo Picasso (1881–1973) is one of the 20th century's most important artists. Picasso created a wealth of paintings, sculptures, etchings, and ceramics.
Instruction Discuss the subject matter of this work of art. Ask students to interpret what they see.
Possible Response: I think you could look at this work of art in two ways. First, you could say that a young boy is removing a mask of an old man. Maybe the boy is imagining what it might be like to be old. Or you could interpret it to mean that the old man is looking for the young boy inside of him. Maybe the painting is a statement about the child inside all of us.
Application Ask students to relate this work of art to "The School Play."
Possible Response: Like the boy in the painting, Robert wears a mask when he is in the play. Acting is like wearing a mask and pretending to be someone else.

parts. They just got cutout crepe-paper snowflakes to pin to their shirts or crepe-paper leaves to wear.

During the blizzard in which Robert delivered his line, Belinda asked, "Is there something wrong with your eyes?" Robert looked at the audience, which at the moment was a classroom of empty chairs, a dented world globe that had been dropped by almost everyone, one limp flag, one wastebasket, and a picture of George Washington, whose eyes followed you around the room when you got up to sharpen your pencil. Robert answered, "Nothing's wrong. I can see."

Mrs. Bunnin, biting on the end of her pencil, said, "Louder, both of you."

Belinda stepped up, nostrils flaring so that the shadows on her nose quivered, and said louder, "Sucka, is there something wrong with your eye-balls?"

"Nothing's wrong. I can see."

"Louder! Make sure the audience can hear you," Mrs. Bunnin directed. She tapped her pencil hard against the desk. She scolded, "Robert, I'm not going to tell you again to quit fooling with the beard."

"It's itchy."

"We can't do anything about that. Actors need props. You're an actor. Now try again."

Robert and Belinda stood center stage as they waited for Mrs. Bunnin to call "Action!" When she did, Belinda approached Robert slowly. "Sucka face, is there anything wrong with your mug?" Belinda asked. Her eyes were squinted in anger. For a moment Robert saw his head grinding into the playground grass.

"NOTHING'S WRONG. I CAN SEE."

"Nothing's wrong. I can see."

Robert giggled behind his red beard. Belinda popped her gum and smirked. She stood with her hands on her hips.

"What? What did you say?" Mrs. Bunnin asked, pulling off her glasses. "Are you chewing gum, Belinda?"

"No, Mrs. Bunnin," Belinda lied. "I just forgot my lines."

Belinda turned to face the snowflake boys clumped together in the back. She rolled out her tongue, on which rested a ball of gray gum, depleted of sweetness under her relentless chomp. She whispered "sucka" and giggled so that her nose quivered dark shadows.

The play, *The Last Stand*, was about the Donner party just before they got hungry and started eating each other. Everyone who scored at least twelve out of fifteen on their spelling tests got to say at least one line. Everyone else had to stand and be trees or snowflakes.

Mrs. Bunnin wanted the play to be a success. She couldn't risk having kids with bad memories on stage. The nonspeaking trees and snowflakes stood humming snow flurries, blistering wind, and hail, which they produced by clacking their teeth.

Robert's mother was proud of him because he was living up to the legend of Robert De Niro,[1] for whom he was named. Over dinner he said, "Nothing's wrong. I can see," when his brother asked him to pass the dishtowel,

---

1. **Robert De Niro** (də nîr′ō): a well-known American movie actor.

WORDS TO KNOW	
quiver (kwĭv′ər) v. to shake with a rapid trembling movement
prop (prŏp) n. an object an actor uses in a play
smirk (smûrk) v. to smile in an insulting, self-satisfied manner
depleted (dĭ-plē′tĭd) adj. emptied; drained **deplete** v.
relentless (rĭ-lĕnt′lĭs) adj. refusing to stop or give up

405

their communal napkin. His sister said, "It's your turn to do dishes," and he said, "Nothing's wrong. I can see." His dog, Queenie, begged him for more than water and a dog biscuit. He touched his dog's own hairy beard and said, "Nothing's wrong. I can see."

One warm spring night, Robert lay on his back in the backyard, counting shooting stars. He was up to three when David, a friend who was really his brother's friend, hopped the fence and asked, "What's the matter with you?"

"Nothing's wrong. I can see," Robert answered. He sat up, feeling good because the line came naturally, without much thought. He leaned back on his elbow and asked David what he wanted to be when he grew up.

"I don't know yet," David said, plucking at the grass. "Maybe a fighter pilot. What do you want to be?"

"I want to guard the president. I could wrestle the assassins and be on television. But I'd pin those dudes, and people would say, 'That's him, our hero.'" David plucked at a stalk of grass and thought deeply.

Robert thought of telling David that he really wanted to be someone with a supergreat memory, who could recall facts that most people thought were unimportant. He didn't know if there was such a job, but he thought it would be great to sit at home by the telephone waiting for scientists to call him and ask hard questions.

The three weeks passed quickly. The day before the play, Robert felt happy as he walked home from school with no homework. As he turned onto his street, he found a dollar floating over the currents of wind.

"A buck," he screamed to himself. He snapped it up and looked for others. But he didn't find any more. It was his lucky day,

"NOTHING'S

WRONG.

I CAN SEE."

though. At recess he had hit a home run on a fluke bunt—a fluke because the catcher had kicked the ball, another player had thrown it into center field, and the pitcher wasn't looking when Robert slowed down at third, then burst home with dust flying behind him.

That night, it was his sister's turn to do the dishes. They had eaten enchiladas with the works, so she slaved with suds up to her elbows. Robert bathed in bubble bath, the suds peaked high like the Donner Pass.

He thought about how full he was and how those poor people had had nothing to eat but snow. I can live on nothing, he thought and whistled like wind through a mountain pass, raking flat the suds with his palm.

The next day, after lunch, he was ready for the play, red beard in hand and his one line trembling on his lips. Classes herded into the auditorium. As the actors dressed and argued about stepping on each other's feet, Robert stood near a cardboard barrel full of toys, whispering over and over to himself, "Nothing's wrong. I can see." He was hot, itchy, and confused when he tied on the beard. He sneezed when a strand of the beard entered his nostril. He said louder, "Nothing's wrong. I can see," but the words seemed to get caught in the beard. "Nothing, no, no. I can see great," he said louder, then under his breath because the words seemed wrong. "Nothing's wrong, can't you see? Nothing's wrong. I can see you." Worried, he approached Belinda and asked if she remembered his line. Balling her hand into a fist, Belinda warned, "Sucka, I'm gonna bury your ugly face in the ground if you mess up."

"I won't," Robert said as he walked away. He bit a nail and looked into the barrel of toys. A clown's mask stared back at him. He

---

 Grammar

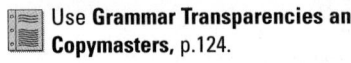
---

prayed that his line would come back to him. He would hate to disappoint his teacher and didn't like the thought of his face being rubbed into spiky grass.

The curtain parted slightly, and the principal came out smiling onto the stage. She said some words about pioneer history and then, stern faced, warned the audience not to scrape the chairs on the just-waxed floor. The principal then introduced Mrs. Bunnin, who told the audience about how they had rehearsed for weeks.

Meanwhile, the class stood quietly in place with lunchtime spaghetti on their breath. They were ready. Belinda had swallowed her gum because she knew this was for real. The snowflakes clumped together and began howling.

Customizing Instruction

Students Acquiring English

1 Explain a *fluke bunt* by telling students that a *fluke* is something that happens by chance. A *bunt* is a baseball term for a hit made by tapping the ball lightly so that the ball rolls slowly in front of the infielders.

2 Explain that Robert's sister isn't really a slave. When the word is used as a verb, it means to work very hard.

Less Proficient Readers

3 Ask students why Robert is so nervous about his two lines.

Possible Response: Robert is nervous because he's afraid that if he makes a mistake, he will disappoint his teacher and Belinda will beat him up.

Closing Scene (1963), David Hockney. Oil on canvas, 48" × 48", © David Hockney.

 Viewing and Representing

Closing Scene
by David Hockney

ART APPRECIATION David Hockney (b.1937) is a British painter, photographer, and stage designer. Hockney has designed sets for both opera and ballet. *Closing Scene* is an example of his interest in the theater.

Instruction Lead a discussion about the subject of *Closing Scene.* Ask students to describe what they see.

Possible Response: The curtain is probably closing at the end of a play. The backdrop, which shows the sky, mountains, and a tree, is visible. The woman on the right side probably had a role in the play. She is happy and maybe a little relieved that the play is over.

Application Ask students to consider why *Closing Scene* is a good choice to illustrate "The School Play."

Possible Response: The closing curtain signals the end of a play. Robert is looking forward to the end of his play. He is excited and nervous and probably looking forward to having it behind him.

Literary Analysis: SHORT STORY

Ask students to tell why they think Gary Soto chose to use the short story form to tell this particular story.

Possible Response: Gary Soto probably wrote "The School Play" as a short story because the events he writes about have a distinct beginning, middle, and end. It wouldn't have worked as a poem, and there isn't enough going on to turn it into a novel, so the short story form is perfect.

Active Reading

MONITORING READING STRATEGIES

After Robert delivers his line, the story says he "joined the snowflakes and trees." Ask students what this means and where they should look to find the information if they don't remember.

Possible Response: These were the students who did not have speaking parts. On page 405 it says, "Everyone else had to stand and be trees or snowflakes."

Use **Reading and Critical Thinking Transparencies,** p. 1, for additional support.

Literary Analysis: SIMILE

Ask students to find a simile on page 408. Then ask them to explain what it means.

Possible Response: "He howled wind like a baying hound . . ." is a simile. It means that Robert sounded like a hound dog howling at the moon.

Robert retied his beard. Belinda, smoothing her skirt, looked at him and said, "If you know what's good for you, you'd better do it right." Robert grew nervous when the curtain parted and his classmates who were assigned to do snow, wind, and hail broke into song.

Alfonso stepped forward with his narrative about a blot on American history that would live with us forever. He looked at the audience, lost for a minute. He continued by saying that if the Donner party could come back, hungry from not eating for over a hundred years, they would be sorry for what they had done.

The play began with some boys in snowshoes shuffling around the stage, muttering that the blizzard would cut them off from civilization. They looked up, held out their hands, and said in unison, "Snow." One stepped center stage and said, "I wish I had never left the prairie." Another one said, "California is just over there." He pointed, and some of the first graders looked in the direction of the piano.

"What are we going to do?" one kid asked, brushing pretend snow off his vest.

"I'm getting pretty hungry," another said, rubbing her stomach.

The audience seemed to be following the play. A ribbon of sweat ran down Robert's face. When his scene came up, he staggered to center stage and dropped to the floor, just as Mrs. Bunnin had said, just as he had seen Robert De Niro do in that movie about a boxer. Belinda, bending over with an "Oh, my," yanked him up so hard that something clicked in his elbow. She boomed, "Is there anything wrong with your eyes?"

Robert rubbed his elbow, then his eyes, and said, "I can see nothing wrong. Wrong is nothing, I can see."

"NOTHING'S WRONG. I CAN SEE."

"How are we going to get through?" she boomed, wringing her hands together at the audience, some of whom had their mouths taped shut because they were known talkers. "My husband needs a doctor." The drama advanced through snow, wind, and hail that sounded like chattering teeth.

Belinda turned to Robert and muttered, "You mess-up. You're gonna hate life."

But Robert thought he'd done okay. At least, he reasoned to himself, I got the words right. Just not in the right order.

With his part of the play done, he joined the snowflakes and trees, chattering his teeth the loudest. He howled wind like a baying hound and snapped his fingers furiously in a snow flurry. He trembled from the cold.

The play ended with Alfonso saying that if they came back to life, the Donner party would be sorry for eating each other. "It's just not right," he argued. "You gotta suck it up in bad times."

Robert figured that Alfonso was right. He remembered how one day his sister had locked him in the closet and he didn't eat or drink for five hours. When he got out, he hit his sister, but not so hard as to leave a bruise. He then ate three sandwiches and felt a whole lot better.

The cast then paraded up the aisle into the audience. Belinda pinched Robert hard, but only once because she was thinking that it could have been worse. As he passed a smiling and relieved Mrs. Bunnin, she patted Robert's shoulder and said, "Almost perfect."

Robert was happy. He'd made it through without passing out from fear. Now the first and second graders were looking at him and clapping. He was sure everyone wondered who the actor was behind that smooth voice and red, red beard. ❖

Teaching Options

✓ **Assessment** **Standardized Test Practice**

RECOGNIZING CAUSE AND EFFECT For some standardized tests, students will be asked to read a passage or story and identify cause and effect. To provide students with practice in recognizing cause and effect, read aloud or write on the board the following question:

Which of the following statements is an accurate cause-and-effect statement about what happens in "The School Play"?

A. Because Mrs. Bunnin is so mean, Robert is nervous about delivering his two lines.

B. Because he fears Belinda will beat him up and Mrs. Bunnin will be disappointed, Robert is nervous about delivering his two lines.

C. Since he has never acted in a play, Robert is nervous about going on stage.

D. Robert rehearsed his lines so many times, how could he have possibly made a mistake?

Lead students through the process of choosing the most accurate cause-and-effect statement. A and C are inaccurate. D isn't a cause-and-effect statement. Help them understand why B is the best choice.

Connect to the Literature

1. **What Do You Think?** What words would you use to describe Robert's feelings at the end of the story?

   Comprehension Check
   • Before the play, why did Robert repeat his line again and again?
   • What happened during the play?

Think Critically

2. Near the end of *The Last Stand*, Alfonso, the play's narrator, says, "You gotta suck it up in bad times." How well do you think Robert lives up to that statement?

   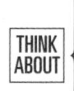 THINK ABOUT
   • how he behaves at home
   • what happens to him the day before the performance
   • how he behaves backstage just before the play begins

3. In later years, what do you think Robert would remember most about *The Last Stand?* Why?

4. **ACTIVE READING** **MONITORING READING STRATEGIES** Refer to the notes made in your **READER'S NOTEBOOK.** Which reading strategies helped you? Compare with a partner.

Extend Interpretations

5. **What If?** What if Belinda had been the one who forgot her lines? How do you think Robert would have responded? How might the story have ended?

6. **COMPARING TEXTS** The characters of Rachel in "Eleven," on page 26, and Robert in this selection both struggle to express themselves. Compare the way they face their situations. What do you think Robert might say to Rachel about the consequences of a day gone wrong?

7. **Connect to Life** How would you feel if you were in a play and forgot your lines after practicing for many weeks? How would you react during the performance?

Literary Analysis

 TONE The writer's attitude toward his or her subject is called **tone.** You can identify the tone by paying attention to **details** and your response to them. Consider this example from "The School Play":

Another one said, "California is just over there." He pointed, and some of the first graders looked in the direction of the piano.

This description shows that awkward and humorous things can happen when putting on a play. What attitude toward the subject might this show?

Cooperative Learning Activity In a small group, reread "The School Play." How would you describe the tone of the story? What details, dialogue, and descriptions help create the tone? You might use a web to organize your answer. In the center of the web, state the tone. In the ovals outside, give examples to support your statement.

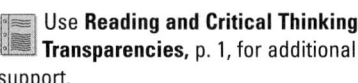

Detail: Belinda's gray chewing gum

Detail:

Tone:

Detail:

Detail:

Connect to the Literature

1. **What Do You Think?** Students may say that Robert is relieved, happy, proud. Their answers should reveal their understanding that even though Robert didn't do a perfect job, he is satisfied with himself.

   Comprehension Check
   • Robert kept reciting his lines because he was afraid that if he forgot them, Belinda would beat him up and Mrs. Bunnin would be disappointed.
   • During the play, Robert mixes up his lines.

    Use Selection Quiz **Unit Three Resource Book,** p. 50.

Think Critically

2. **Possible Responses:** He did not really live up to that statement because he let the pressure of the moment get to him; he did live up to that statement because he tried to take care of his nervousness by rehearsing, and when he messed up he was able to look on the bright side.

3. **Possible Response:** Robert will probably remember that he got through his lines and felt great once the play was over.

4. **Possible Response:** Students' choice of strategies will vary.

   Use **Reading and Critical Thinking Transparencies,** p. 1, for additional support.

Literary Analysis

Tone Students' webs should include examples that show that the tone of the story is humorous.

   Use **Literary Analysis Transparencies,** p. 25, for additional support.

Extend Interpretations

5. **What If?** Students may say that if Belinda had forgotten her lines, Robert might have felt so good that he would have had a sudden surge of confidence. At the end of the play, he would have felt great. Maybe Belinda would have even apologized for all the threats she made.

6. **Comparing Texts** Students may say that Robert would tell Rachel that just when you think your whole life is terrible, things change. He might tell her that one bad day doesn't mean anything. Everything could change tomorrow, once all the kids see Phyllis Lopez wearing the red sweater.

7. **Connect to Life** Responses will vary. Students may say that they would make up lines that made sense even though they weren't right.

Grammar in Context

WRITING EXERCISE

1. Robert wanted the play to go <u>well</u>.
2. Robert's mother thought he performed as <u>well</u> as Robert De Niro.
3. The pioneers in the play were <u>badly</u> prepared for winter.
4. David played with the grass and thought <u>deeply</u>.
5. Who was the actor whose voice sounded so <u>smooth</u>?

Vocabulary in Action

Exercise A
1. b
2. c
3. a
4. c
5. b

Exercise B
1. incorrect
2. correct
3. incorrect
4. incorrect
5. incorrect
Sentences will vary.

Grammar in Context: Choosing Adjective or Adverb

In "The School Play" Gary Soto describes a moment when Robert is confident:

> He sat up, feeling good because the line came naturally, without much thought.

Notice that Soto used the word *good,* not *well. Good* is an **adjective.** In this sentence it modifies the pronoun *he.* The word *well* is an **adverb** that means "capably" or "in a satisfactory way." The following example shows *well* modifying the verb *performing:*

> Robert dreamed of performing well in the play.

Another tricky pair of words is *bad* and *badly. Bad* is an adjective. It is used after linking verbs such as *to be, to feel, to taste,* or *to smell.*

> He felt bad for a minute when he forgot his line.

Badly is an adverb that means "not capably." Use *badly* after action verbs:

> He flubbed his line badly.

WRITING EXERCISE Rewrite the sentences, choosing the correct adjective or adverb.

Example: *Original* She tried to make Robert feel (bad, badly).

Rewritten She tried to make Robert feel bad.

1. Robert wanted the play to go (good, well).
2. Robert's mother thought he performed as (good, well) as Robert De Niro.
3. The pioneers in the play were (bad, badly) prepared for winter.
4. David played with the grass and thought (deep, deeply).
5. Who was the actor whose voice sounded so (smooth, smoothly)?

<u>Grammar Handbook</u> Using Modifiers Effectively, p. R70

Vocabulary in Action

EXERCISE A: ASSESSMENT PRACTICE Write the letter of the word or phrase that is closest in meaning to the vocabulary word.

1. **quiver** (a) still (b) shake (c) quiet
2. **prop** (a) script (b) scenery (c) object
3. **smirk** (a) insulting smile (b) self-satisfied frown (c) self-conscious sneeze
4. **depleted** (a) filled (b) replenished (c) emptied
5. **relentless** (a) brief (b) constant (c) often

EXERCISE B: WORD MEANING Decide whether the boldfaced vocabulary word is used correctly in each sentence below. On your paper, write "correct" or "incorrect." For each incorrectly used word, write a sentence that uses it correctly.

1. The lead actor said his lines clearly and with a confident **quiver** in his voice.
2. I wanted to **smirk** when my rival messed up.
3. I studied the script to memorize my **prop.**
4. I was glad to see our **depleted** supply of snow, because it meant we had a lot left.
5. The **relentless** applause ended quickly.

Building Vocabulary
For an in-depth lesson on synonyms, see p. 230.

Teaching Options

 Grammar

CHOOSING AN ADJECTIVE OR ADVERB

Instruction: Remind students that it isn't just *good, well, bad,* and *badly* that can be confusing. It's easy to get confused about whether to use an adjective or an adverb. Remember: Adjectives tell *which one, what kind,* or *how many* about nouns or pronouns only. Adverbs tell *how, where, when,* or *to what extent* about verbs, adjectives, or other adverbs.

Exercises: In the sentences below, have students choose the correct word—adjective or adverb—from the suggested pair.

1. Robert's mother felt (<u>proud</u>, proudly) because he had a speaking part in the play.
2. Robert saw Belinda's (<u>angry</u>, angrily) face looking at him.
3. Belinda's gum sat (sad, <u>sadly</u>) on her tongue.
4. *The Last Stand* is a (real, <u>really</u>) good play.

 Use **Unit Three Resource Book,** p. 48.
Use **Grammar Transparencies and Copymasters,** p. 95.

> Use McDougal Littell's *Language Network,* Chapter 5, for more practice in choosing adjective or adverb.

Ode to My Library

Poetry by GARY SOTO

(Connect to Your Life)

Poems that Praise Odes are a writer's way of honoring someone or something that has meaning or power in his or her life. Poets have written odes to their pets, relatives, and even favorite foods such as French fries and watermelons. What might you like to honor in an ode?

Build Background

CONNECT TO HISTORY The speaker of the poem is proud of the Aztec warrior he helped paint in a mural. The Aztecs lived in what is now Mexico and built a great empire that lasted until the Spanish invaded in the 16th century. Some Aztec males were trained to be warriors from the time they were born. At the age of ten, a boy's hair was cut so that a section of hair lay on the back of his neck. He was not allowed to cut this hair until he had brought back from battle at least one live prisoner.

An image of Montezuma II (1466?–1520), Mexico's most famous Aztec emperor.

Focus Your Reading

LITERARY ANALYSIS IMAGERY In his poetry, Gary Soto uses **imagery,** or words and phrases that appeal to his readers' senses. Consider how he describes the warrior in the mural:

> *I made the cuts*
> *Of muscle on*
> *His stomach*
> *And put a boulder*
> *Of strength in each arm.*

This vivid description helps readers to create an image of the warrior in their minds.

ACTIVE READING VISUALIZING When you use your imagination to form a picture of something in your mind, you are **visualizing.** Gary Soto's poetry is a workout for the senses. His language encourages readers to see, hear, touch, smell, and taste as they read.

READER'S NOTEBOOK As you read "Ode to My Library," think about what sense Soto is trying to get you to use with each new description. Write down words and phrases that trigger your senses.

 LaserLinks: Background for Reading
Art Gallery

Reading and Analyzing

Reading Skills and Strategies: PREVIEW

Have students look through "Ode to My Library." Ask students to think about what the poem might be about.

Active Reading | VISUALIZING |

To visualize is to create a mental image. Tell students that sometimes they can better appreciate a story or poem if they visualize what they are reading. Ask students to tell which of the images on page 413 they visualized as they read this part of the poem.

Possible Response: I visualized an old, small library. I focused on the pencil sharpener, with a small piece of crayon stuck inside. Then I saw the librarian with her glasses hanging down instead of on her eyes.

Use **Unit Three Resource Book,** p. 51 for more practice. Use **Reading and Critical Thinking Transparencies,** p. 4, for additional support.

Literary Analysis | IMAGERY |

Ask students to identify some of the images that they find especially effective or memorable.

Possible Response: I think the image of the fish making *jeta* is memorable because I can picture it perfectly.

Use **Unit Three Resource Book,** p. 52 for more practice.

Teaching Options

 Mini Lesson **Grammar**

USING PROPER ADJECTIVES Remind students that, like proper nouns, proper adjectives should be capitalized unless they have lost the association with the nouns from which they were derived.

Exercises Have students read the sentences below and make any necessary corrections to the proper adjectives.

1. What is the spanish word for *library*? *(Spanish)*
2. Georgia is a southern state. *(Southern)*
3. Many mexican people live in California. *(Mexican)*
4. The library is next to the catholic church. *(Catholic)*
5. Young Gary dreamed of the ancient aztec warriors. *(Aztec)*

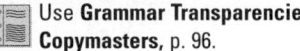 Use **Grammar Transparencies and Copymasters,** p. 96.

 Use McDougal Littell's *Language Network,* Chapter 5, for more instruction and practice in using proper adjectives.

Ode TO MY Library

BY GARY SOTO

It's small
With two rooms
Of books, a globe
That I once
5 Dropped, some maps
Of the United States and México,
And a fish tank with
A blue fish that
Is always making *jeta*.[1]
10 There are tables and chairs,
And a pencil sharpener
On the wall: a crayon is stuck
In it, but I didn't do it.

It's funny, but the
15 Water fountain
Is cooled by a motor,
And the librarian reads
Books with her
Glasses hanging

Rainbow,
© Synthia Saint James.

---

1. *jeta* (hĕ'tä) *Spanish:* fat, pouting lips.

Less Proficient Readers
Have students keep these questions in mind as they read:
- How does the author feel toward his library?
- Why does the author have strong feelings toward his library?
- Who would the author like to bring to his library? Why?

Students Acquiring English

 Use **Spanish Study Guide,** pp. 85–87 for additional support.

Gifted and Talented
"Ode to My Library" is filled with poetic imagery. Ask students to make a list of their favorite images and explain why they like those images.

 Use **Writing Transparencies,** p. 19, for additional support.

✓ Assessment Standardized Test Practice

DESCRIBING THE SETTING OF A STORY Tell students that some standardized tests will ask them to read a story or poem and then describe the setting. To provide students with help in describing setting, read aloud or write on the board the following question:

Which of the following statements best describes the setting of "Ode to My Library"?

A. The setting is a classroom with lots of books, globes, and maps.

B. The setting is a dusty ranch in Mexico.

C. The setting is a small library in California.

D. The setting is the speaker's room.

Lead students through the process of choosing the statement that best expresses the setting of the poem. Consider each choice. Explain that while A, B, and D all name things related to the poem, C is the answer that actually describes the setting.

Literary Analysis: FREE VERSE

Explain to students that free verse has no rhyme scheme. In fact, there are often no rhymes at all in free verse. Ask students whether "Ode to My Library" is an example of free verse, and have them tell why. Then ask them whether it has a certain rhythm even though it lacks rhyme.

Possible Response: "Ode to My Library" is an example of free verse because it doesn't have end rhymes. The poem does have rhythm, which makes it easy to read.

Literary Analysis: SENSORY DETAILS

Tell students that poets use sensory details to appeal to readers' sense of smell, taste, touch, sight, and hearing. Ask students to name two sensory details and tell to which sense each one appeals.

Possible Response: The detail of the birds talking loudly from the window appeals to the sense of hearing. The detail of his grandparents touching the speaker's hair appeals to the sense of touch.

Reading Skills and Strategies: CONNECT

Ask students to explain how they connected this poem with their own experiences.

Possible Response: I understand how the author feels, because I love my library, too. Although my library is different from the one described in the poem, it is a special place where I spend a lot of time reading and learning.

20 From her neck. If she
Put them on
She would see me
Studying the Incas
Who lived two steps
25 From heaven, way in the mountains.

The place says, "Quiet, please,"
But three birds
Talk to us
Loudly from the window.
30 What's best is this:
A phonograph
That doesn't work.
When I put on the headphones,
I'm the captain of a jet,
35 And my passengers
Are *mis abuelitos*[2]
Coming from a dusty ranch
In Monterrey. I want
To fly them to California,
40 But then walk
Them to my library.
I want to show them
The thirty books I devoured
In the summer read-a-thon.

45 I want to show them
The mural I helped paint.
In the mural,
An Aztec warrior
Is standing on a mountain
50 With a machete[3]
And a band of feathers
On his noble head.
I made the cuts
Of muscle on
55 His stomach
And put a boulder
Of strength in each arm.
He could gather
Enough firewood
60 With one fist.
He could slice
Open a mountain
With that machete,
And with the wave of his arm
65 Send our enemies tumbling.

If I could fly,
I would bring
Mis abuelitos to California.
They would touch my hair
70 When I showed
Them my library;
The fish making *jeta*,
The globe that I dropped,
The birds fluttering
75 Their wings at the window.
They would stand me
Between them,
When I showed them
My thirty books,
80 And the cuts
On the warrior,
Our family of people.

---

2. *mis abuelitos* (mēs ä-bwĕ-lē'tôs)
   Spanish: my grandparents.

3. **machete** (mə-shĕt'ē): a large knife with a broad blade.

Cross Curricular Link Social Studies

THE AZTECS The Aztec empire reached its height under Montezuma II, in the early 1500s. The capital city was Tenochtitlán (tay NOHCH tee TLAHN), located on an island in southern Mexico, where Mexico City stands today. At its peak, the city boasted a population of several hundred thousand. There was a large pyramid temple and an emperor's palace in the city. There were also "floating gardens"—artificial islands made of reed mats and earth on which beans, corn, and squash were raised. They provided the extra farmland needed by the growing population. The Aztecs prayed to many gods, including gods of corn, rain, sun, and war. The Aztec calendar told which month was sacred to each god and goddess. Priests performed ceremonies—including human sacrifice—intended to please these gods.

The Aztecs were a warlike people. They defeated many neighboring towns and cities and then forced the conquered people to give them tribute: food, feathers from tropical birds, gold, and cotton. Many prisoners of war became human sacrifices.

Connect to the Literature

1. What Do You Think?
How does the speaker make you feel about his library?

Comprehension Check
• Who does the speaker pretend to be when he puts on the earphones?
• What would he show to his grandparents?

Think Critically

2. After reading this poem, what image of the library is most vivid for you?

3. Each stanza of this poem is like a different photograph of the library. The last stanza puts them together to create the entire picture. What pictures did each stanza create in your mind as you read the poem?

4. What do you think this poem reveals about the speaker?

THINK ABOUT
• what the speaker thinks is "best" about the library, and why
• the aspects of the library that the speaker seems to be most proud of

5. **ACTIVE READING** **VISUALIZING** Look back at the words and phrases you listed in your ▯ **READER'S NOTEBOOK.** What sense did you use most while reading this poem? When did you use it?

6. Gary Soto is very active in encouraging children, especially Chicano children, to read. How do you think this poem relates to that goal?

Extend Interpretations

7. The Writer's Style Reread the poem, paying attention to how sentences are broken up and where capital letters are used. Then rewrite a stanza as a paragraph, using standard capitalization. How is the effect different?

8. Connect to Life Think about a special place that makes you feel safe, happy, or inspired. What words would you use to create a picture of this place?

Literary Analysis

IMAGERY Words and phrases that appeal to the senses are called **imagery.** Imagery helps readers use their imagination to see, feel, hear, taste, or smell what a writer describes. Readers are able to "see" the Aztec warrior when Soto describes him:

> *. . . standing on a mountain*
> *With a machete*
> *And a band of feathers*
> *On his noble head.*

Readers can also "hear" the fluttering of the birds' wings at the window.

Paired Activity With a partner, reread the poem. Pay attention to Soto's use of imagery. Which words and phrases cause you to see, feel, hear, taste, or smell something in your imagination? Describe the mental images the words and phrases created.

Extend Interpretations

7. The Writer's Style Responses will vary, but students should show an understanding of the effect of poetry. They should understand how the concise form of a poem enables poets to convey a message in a simple but powerful way. They should understand that the particular words form images that evoke the subject matter of the poem. In rewriting a stanza as a paragraph, students should see that adding words can have a diluting effect, weakening the effect of the poetic images and ideas.

8. Connect to Life Students should be able to name several aspects of the place that make it special or pleasant for them. Encourage them to make their images as sharp and clear as possible. Students may find it helpful to use a word web.

▤ Use **Reading and Critical Thinking Transparencies,** p. 38, for additional support.

Connect to the Literature

1. What Do You Think?
Students might say that the speaker makes them feel that his library is a wonderful place that comes to life when he is there.

Comprehension Check
• He pretends to be the captain of a jet.
• He would show them the thirty books, the fish, the globe, the birds, and the warrior.

Think Critically

2. Responses will vary. Students may mention the phonograph that doesn't work, the mural with the Aztec warrior, the fish making *jeta*.

3. Possible Responses: First stanza—the library as inviting, friendly, and full of familiar things; second stanza—what the librarian and the speaker are doing in the present; third stanza— imaginations at work and dreams of going beyond the real world; fourth stanza—a concrete and vivid image of the Aztec warrior.

4. Possible Responses: The speaker loves to imagine things; reading thirty books was a big achievement and the speaker is very proud of it; the speaker feels that family and ancestors are important; the speaker is probably of Mexican heritage.

5. Students may say that they used their ability to see the most while envisioning the rooms in the library, the speaker, and the mural.

▤ Use **Reading and Critical Thinking Transparencies,** p. 4, for additional support.

6. Possible Responses: Gary Soto wants his readers to think of libraries as friendly, safe places and as fun and inspirational.

Literary Analysis

Imagery Partners will likely discuss the librarian with her glasses dangling, the birds fluttering, the warrior in the mural, and his grandparents visiting.

Focus Your Reading
Literary Analysis: AUDIENCE

As they read, students may want to write down who Soto's readers are and how he meets them. After they complete the reading, ask them to discuss how knowing his audience helps Soto write.

Literary Analysis: DESCRIPTION

Soto's writing is vivid and full of humorous description. Ask students to identify some of the sensory words and descriptive phrases that Soto uses in this essay. Ask them to further discuss how the use of these words helps them to comprehend the text.

Possible Responses: *her brow creases deep enough to sow seeds, entirely decorated in red, spinning red lights of a fire engine pulsating on our faces, square head, big ears, spooked eyes*

These phrases help to paint pictures in the mind of the reader. We feel like we can see exactly the image that Soto is describing.

WHO ARE YOUR READERS?

by Gary Soto

Preparing to Read

Focus Your Reading

LITERARY ANALYSIS AUDIENCE

The group of people with whom a writer hopes to share his or her words is the **audience.** A writer thinks about his or her audience when deciding on a **subject,** a **purpose** for writing, and a **tone** in which to write.

In this essay by Gary Soto, he responds to the question "Who are your readers?" In doing so, he describes some of the unusual ways he meets the people who are his audience.

My first book of poems, *The Elements of San Joaquín,* was published in spring 1977 and dedicated in part to *mi abuelita.* My grandmother fled Mexico in 1914, somewhere in the middle of the Mexican Revolution, and like many other early immigrants could read neither Spanish nor English. As a young man of twenty-five, I did my duty by giving her a copy of my book. Grandma's reaction was to smile, and bunch her brow into creases deep enough to sow seeds; she realized an occasion was upon her and fixed me a glorious meal on her four-burner stove—eggs, frijoles, and tortillas. I don't remember what came first, the meal or her hunt for a picture frame into which she fit my book. She placed it on a coffee table in her living room that was entirely decorated in red— sofa, curtains, carpet, and cute ceramic sculptures. In that museum of bad taste, my book was the centerpiece.

Would Grandma be typical of my readership? Would others smile at my book, pat my shoulder for my effort to promote Chicano literacy and literature, and then put it in a picture frame? How do you get people to read your work, I wondered. The agony of writing is a terror in itself, but to build an audience once a book is published?

Unlike most other contemporary poets and writers, I've taken the show on the road and built a name among *la gente,* the people. I have ventured into schools where I have played baseball and basketball with young people, sung songs, acted in skits, delivered commencement speeches, learned three chords on a Mexican guitar to serenade teachers, formed a touring *teatro,* seen that my opera *Nerd-Landia* was mounted in high schools, established scholarships, and given away thousands of dollars to Chicano cultural centers.

My readership is strung from large cities, such as Los Angeles, to dinky Del Rey where peach trees outnumber the population by many thousands. Once,

Courtesy of Gary Soto.

I was a given a parade in Huron, California. The town, nearly all Mexican or Mexican American, numbered four thousand that winter when the mayor proclaimed Gary Soto Day. Because the town was small—three commercial blocks long—we had to start the parade of eight hundred celebrants in the grape vineyards, the spinning red lights of a fire engine pulsating on our faces. I sat in the back of a Chevy convertible while waving to the Spanish-speaking crowd.

© James Prigoff.

Sure, I felt silly, but it had to be done. The crowds watched as we made our way toward the school. There, I premiered my little 16mm film, *The Bike*, which featured the good people from Huron as the principal actors. Why go to the San Francisco Film Festival when a school cafeteria will do? I showed the film on a clean wall but not before a bike was auctioned off and my uncle Shorty, one of the actors, was assigned the duty of judging the Gary Soto portraits done by first graders. I was portrayed with a square head, big ears, spooked eyes—all the body parts of a happy-go-lucky Frankenstein.

Are these my readers? Is this my fame, my earthly reward played out in the grape fields I had wanted so much to escape? That night I had to stack the chairs and later pay for dinner—treating sixteen kids at a Mexican restaurant was an unwise move on my part! Of course, when I speak to college students I put on another face, one that is nearly serene, a college professor's face.

But, teaching is someone else's business. My business is to make readers from non-readers, and if you think it's easy, then join me anytime and see how, where, and why it's done. On the "where" front, I have slept on a lot of floors and couches, and on the "why" front I recall the kinder, gentler America that was proposed several years ago. And where is that America? Because I believe in literature, my task is to start Chicanos reading. If it's my poetry, great. If it's Sandra Cisneros's prose, that's great as well. If Chicanos start with other writers, say Hemingway or Kaye Gibbons, that's fine too. As for me, I start with kindergartners, and move up to college students, not to mention those *abuelitas* who are curious to see how I turned out after all the stupid antics I portrayed in *Living Up the Street*. I'm in their lives and in their hearts. I'm searching for a family whose grandmother, an illiterate, fits a book into a picture frame, the centerpiece for a household that will in time quiet down and throw open the cover. ❖

Thinking Through the Literature

1. **LITERARY ANALYSIS** **AUDIENCE** Now that you have read this essay, how would you answer the question "Who are Gary Soto's readers?"

2. What effect do you think meeting Soto has on his readers?

3. Based on this essay, what advice do you think Soto might give younger writers?

Thinking Through the Literature

1. **Possible Response:** Chicano readers, especially children and young people

2. **Possible Response:** Soto's readers are probably amazed to meet such a famous writer who is also a down-to-earth person.

3. **Possible Response:** Soto would probably tell young writers to write about what they know best.

OVERVIEW

Objectives

1. understand and appreciate a **memoir (Literary Analysis)**
2. understand the author's use of **humor (Literary Analysis)**
3. identify **author's purpose** to better understand a memoir **(Active Reading)**

Summary

In this memoir, author Gary Soto recounts how an ugly jacket had a deep, lasting effect on his formative years. Soto remembers the disappointment he felt when he came home to discover that his mother had bought him a jacket the color of "day-old guacamole." He had wanted a black leather jacket that would make him feel strong and tough. Instead he got a jacket that haunted him throughout his middle school years.

Thematic Link

"The Jacket" provides a vivid picture of how barriers are erected among kids. It shows how small things, such as clothing, can determine one's status, allowing kids to be either "in" or "out" of the dominant group. Preteens feel a strong need to be accepted by their peers. This story expresses the anxieties that one boy felt as he became aware of the social barriers in his world.

5-Minute Warm-Up

Daily Language SkillBuilder

Have students **proofread** the display sentences on page 315k and write them correctly. The sentences also appear on Transparency 14 of **Grammar Transparencies and Copymasters.**

The Jacket

Memoir by GARY SOTO

"I heard the buzz-buzz of gossip and even laughter that I knew was meant for me."

Connect to Your Life

Worn Out Have you ever had to wear a piece of clothing that someone else picked out, or that you thought was uncomfortable or ugly? How did you feel?

Build Background

CONNECT TO **GEOGRAPHY** The setting for "The Jacket" is Fresno, California, where Gary Soto grew up. He spent his childhood in a Mexican-American neighborhood where most people were "just getting by." Opposite his house was a factory, "while on the right . . . was a junkyard that dealt in metals—aluminum, iron, sheet metal, and copper stripped from refrigerators."

Fresno, which means "ash tree" in Spanish, is located in central California. Begining in the 1920s, farmers needed cheap labor, and Mexican laborers came to work in the fields of cotton, grapes, and beets that surrounded the town. Over time, Fresno's Hispanic and Chicano community grew. Fresno gradually became an industrial city as factories were built to process and market farm produce. Gary Soto's stories are often set in Fresno.

> WORDS TO KNOW
> **Vocabulary Preview**
> mope   terrorist
> profile   vinyl
> swoop

Focus Your Reading

LITERARY ANALYSIS **HUMOR** The quality that makes a literary work funny or amusing is called **humor.** One way Gary Soto creates humor in "The Jacket" is by exaggerating, or overstating, things. He also makes surprising comparisons. For example, he describes feeling "bitter as a penny."

ACTIVE READING **IDENTIFYING THE AUTHOR'S PURPOSE** Writers usually write for a particular reason or purpose. The **author's purpose** might be to **entertain,** to **inform,** to **express an opinion,** or to **persuade** readers to do or believe something. You can find clues to the author's purpose in the subject and tone of the work, the audience for which it was written, and the effect that it has on readers.

READER'S NOTEBOOK As you read "The Jacket," think about what the author's purpose seems to be. Jot down events, images, or description that suggest Gary Soto's purpose for writing the memoir.

LESSON RESOURCES

UNIT THREE RESOURCE BOOK, pp. 53–59

ASSESSMENT
Formal Assessment, pp. 67–68
Teacher's Guide to Assessment and Portfolio Use
Test Generator

SKILLS TRANSPARENCIES AND COPYMASTERS
Reading and Critical Thinking
• Author's Purpose and Audience, TR 8 (for Thinking Through the Literature, p. 424)

Grammar
• Identifying Prepositions, CM 100 (for Mini Lesson, p. 425)
Vocabulary
• Context Clues: Definition and Restatement, CM 45 (for Mini Lesson, p. 419)
Communications
• Giving and Using Feedback to Improve Performance, TR 16 (for Mini Lesson, p. 423)

INTEGRATED TECHNOLOGY
Audio Library
Video: Literature in Performance
• *The Pool Party.* See **Video Resource Book,** pp. 19–23

Net Activities

Visit our website:
www.mcdougallittell.com

The Jacket

by Gary Soto

My clothes have failed me.

I remember the green coat that I wore in fifth
and sixth grades when you either danced like a
champ or pressed yourself against a greasy wall,
bitter as a penny toward the happy couples.

When I needed a new jacket and my mother asked what kind I wanted, I described something like bikers wear: black leather and silver studs with enough belts to hold down a small town. We were in the kitchen, steam on the windows from her cooking. She listened so long while stirring dinner that I thought she understood for sure the kind I wanted. The next day when I got home from school, I discovered draped on my bedpost a jacket the color of day-old guacamole. I threw my books on the bed and approached the jacket slowly, as if it were a stranger whose hand I had to shake. I touched the <u>vinyl</u> sleeve, the collar, and peeked at the mustard-colored lining.

From the kitchen mother yelled that my jacket was in the closet. I closed the door to her voice and pulled at the rack of clothes in the closet, hoping the jacket on the bedpost wasn't for me but my mean brother. No luck. I gave up. From my bed, I stared at the jacket. I wanted to cry because it was so ugly and so big that I knew I'd have to wear it a long time. I was a small kid, thin as a young tree, and it would be years before I'd have a new one. I stared at the jacket, like an enemy, thinking bad things before I took off my old jacket whose sleeves climbed halfway to my elbow.

I put the big jacket on.

I zipped it up and down several times, and rolled the cuffs up so they didn't cover my hands. I put my hands in the pockets and flapped the jacket like a bird's wings. I stood in front of the mirror, full face, then <u>profile</u>, and then looked over my shoulder as if someone had called me. I sat on the bed, stood against the bed, and combed my hair to see what I would look like doing something natural. I looked ugly. I threw it on my brother's bed and looked at it for a long time before I slipped it on and went out to the backyard, smiling a "thank you" to my mom as I passed her in the kitchen. With my hands in my pockets I kicked a ball against the fence, and then climbed it to sit looking into the alley. I hurled orange peels at the mouth of an open garbage can and when the peels were gone I watched the white puffs of my breath thin to nothing.

I jumped down, hands in my pockets, and in the backyard on my knees I teased my dog, Brownie, by <u>swooping</u> my arms while making bird calls. He jumped at me and missed. He jumped again and again, until a tooth sunk deep, ripping an L-shaped tear on my left sleeve. I pushed Brownie away to study the tear as I would a cut on my arm. There was no blood, only a few loose pieces of fuzz. Dumb dog, I thought, and pushed him away hard when he tried to bite again. I got up from my knees and went to my bedroom to sit with my jacket on my lap, with the lights out.

WORDS TO KNOW	
vinyl (vī′nəl) *n.* a tough, shiny plastic	
profile (prō′fīl′) *n.* a side view	
swoop (swōōp) *v.* to move in a sudden sweep	

420

That was the first afternoon with my new jacket. The next day I wore it to sixth grade and got a D on a math quiz. During the morning recess Frankie T., the playground <u>terrorist</u>, pushed me to the ground and told me to stay there until recess was over. My best friend, Steve Negrete, ate an apple while looking at me, and the girls turned away to whisper on the monkey bars. The teachers were no help: they looked my way and talked about how foolish I looked in my new jacket. I saw their heads bob with laughter, their hands half-covering their mouths.

Even though it was cold, I took off the jacket during lunch and played kickball in a thin shirt, my arms feeling like braille from goose bumps. But when I returned to class I slipped the jacket on and shivered until I was warm. I sat on my hands, heating them up, while my teeth chattered like a cup of crooked dice. Finally warm, I slid out of the jacket but a few minutes later put it back on when the fire bell rang. We paraded out into the yard where we, the sixth graders, walked past all the other grades to stand against the back fence. Everybody saw me. Although they didn't say out loud, "Man, that's ugly," I heard the buzz-buzz of gossip and even laughter that I knew was meant for me.

And so I went, in my guacamole-colored jacket. So embarrassed, so hurt, I couldn't even do my homework. I received Cs on quizzes, and forgot the state capitals and the rivers of South America, our friendly neighbor. Even the girls who had been friendly blew away like loose flowers to follow the boys in neat jackets.

I wore that thing for three years until the sleeves grew short and my forearms stuck out like the necks of turtles. All during that time no love came to me—no little dark

girl in a Sunday dress she wore on Monday. At lunchtime I stayed with the ugly boys who leaned against the chainlink fence and looked around with propellers of grass spinning in our mouths. We saw girls walk by alone, saw couples, hand in hand, their heads like bookends pressing air together. We saw them and spun our propellers so fast our faces were blurs.

I blame that jacket for those bad years. I blame my mother for her bad taste and her cheap ways. It was a sad time for the heart. With a friend I spent my sixth-grade year in a tree in the alley, waiting for something good to happen to me in that jacket, which had become the ugly brother who tagged along wherever I went. And it was about that time that I began to grow. My chest puffed up with muscle and, strangely, a few more ribs. Even my hands, those fleshy hammers, showed bravely through the cuffs, the fingers already hardening for the coming fights. But that L-shaped rip on the left sleeve got bigger, bits

WORDS
TO
KNOW
terrorist (tĕr′ər-ĭst) *n.* one who uses or theatens to use unlawful force

421

Customizing Instruction

Less Proficient Readers

1 Ask students why the narrator doesn't do well in school after he gets the jacket.

Possible Response: He is so upset by having to wear the ugly jacket that he can't concentrate on his schoolwork. He may not do well for another reason, but he blames everything bad on the jacket.

Multiple Learning Styles
Visual Learners

2 Tell students that sometimes it helps to make a mental image of a scene. Tell students to visualize and then draw a picture of the playground at recess on the day that Frankie T. pushed the narrator.

 Use **Reading and Critical Thinking Transparencies**, p. 4, for additional support.

Mini Lesson **Spelling**

SPELLING LONG *O*

Instruction Remind students that words with the long *o* sound have the sound heard in the words *hold*, *so*, and *slow*. This sound is most often spelled *o*, but sometimes it is spelled *oa, oe, ou, ow, ough,* or *ew.*

coat	elbow	shoulder
although	sew	foe

Exercise Have students look on pages 420–421 for three examples of words with the long *o* sound. Then tell them to think of seven more words with this sound, so that they create a list of ten words containing the long *o* sound. Ask students to write a poem containing these and other words with the long *o* sound. When students have completed their poems, encourage them to read them aloud to the class.

 Use **Unit Three Resource Book**, p. 58.

Literary Analysis: MEMOIR

Ask students to tell how they know that "The Jacket" is a memoir—a story about a person's life told by that person.

Possible Responses: The author is remembering a specific time in his life, and that is what a memoir does. He also writes about feelings that only he would know about.

Literary Analysis: EXAGGERATION

Ⓐ Ask students to find an example of exaggeration—an abnormal or unnatural representation of the truth. Then have students explain why they think the author chose to exaggerate.

Possible Response: The "vicious spelling tests" are an exaggeration. The author probably called the spelling tests *vicious* because he was having such a bad year at school that even the tests he had to take seemed mean.

Reading Skills and Strategies: EVALUATE/MAKE JUDGMENTS

Ask students whether they think Soto really hated the jacket and whether he really felt that his mother was to blame for his unhappiness.

Possible Response: The fact that Soto called the jacket his "ugly brother" shows his mixed feelings. He became attached to it even though it wasn't at all what he had wanted. He needed someone or something to blame for his unhappiness, and his mother and the jacket were the easiest targets.

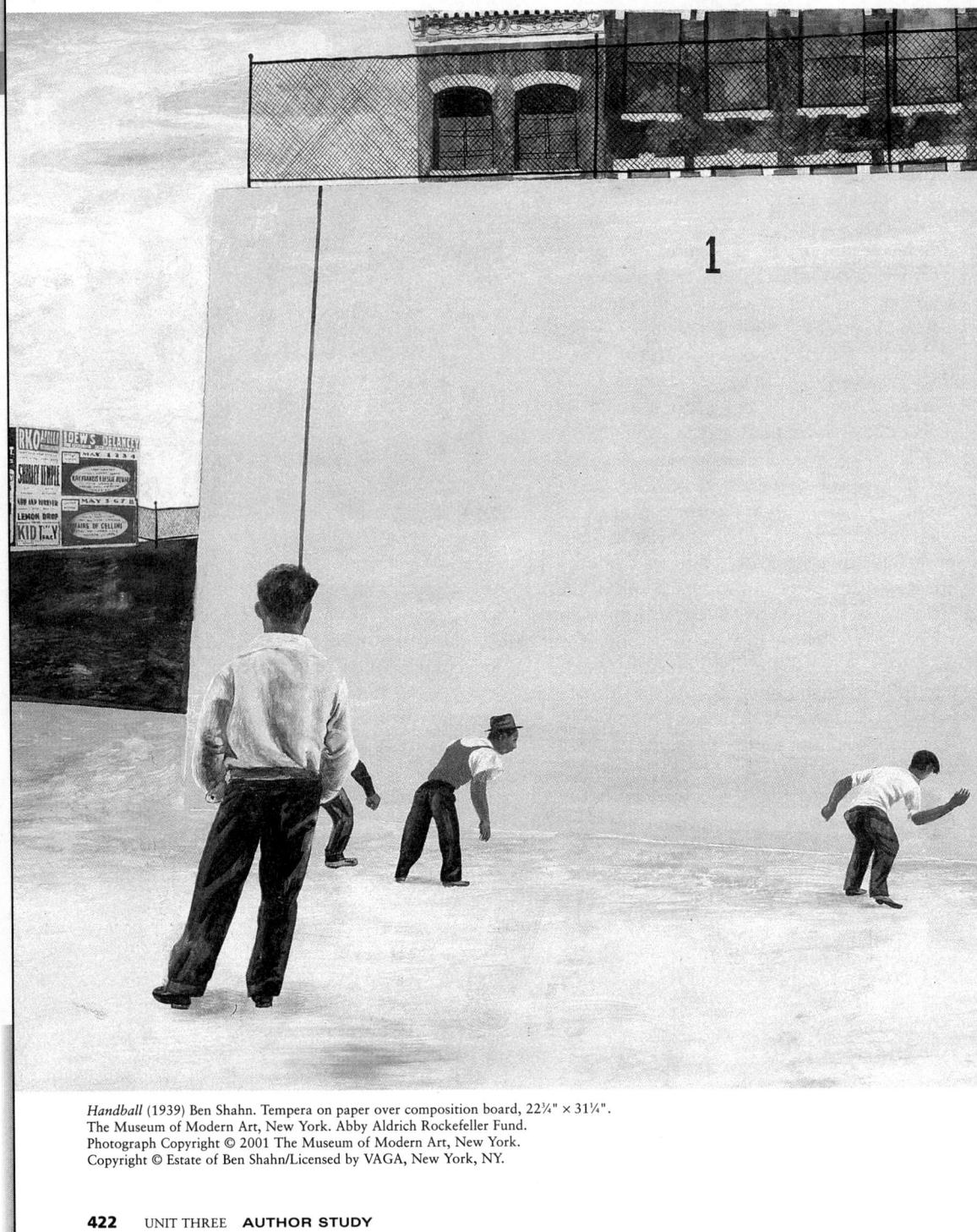

Handball (1939) Ben Shahn. Tempera on paper over composition board, 22¼" × 31¼".
The Museum of Modern Art, New York. Abby Aldrich Rockefeller Fund.
Photograph Copyright © 2001 The Museum of Modern Art, New York.
Copyright © Estate of Ben Shahn/Licensed by VAGA, New York, NY.

422 UNIT THREE **AUTHOR STUDY**

Teaching Options

✓ Assessment Standardized Test Practice

EVALUATING AND MAKING JUDGMENTS Tell students that for some standardized tests, they will be asked to read a passage and then make a judgment about what they have read. Tell students to reread the final paragraph of "The Jacket." Which of the following statements is the most accurate evaluation of the final paragraph?

A. Soto hated the jacket so much that he wanted to burn it.

B. Soto disliked the jacket but became attached to it because it had become so familiar.

C. Soto really liked the jacket but needed something to blame for his unhappiness.

D. Soto would never wear the jacket again.

Lead students through the process of choosing the best judgment. Consider each choice. Point out that D is not true, and even though answers A and C both contain some true information, B is the most accurate and complete evaluation.

of stuffing coughed out from its wound after a hard day of play. I finally Scotch-taped it closed, but in rain or cold weather the tape peeled off like a scab and more stuffing fell out until that sleeve shriveled into a palsied[1] arm. That winter the elbows began to crack and whole chunks of green began to fall off. I showed the cracks to my mother, who always seemed to be at the stove with steamed-up glasses, and she said that there were children in Mexico who would love that jacket. I told her that this was America and yelled that Debbie, my sister, didn't have a jacket like mine. I ran outside, ready to cry, and climbed the tree by the alley to think bad thoughts and watch my breath puff white and disappear.

But whole pieces still casually flew off my jacket when I played hard, read quietly, or took vicious spelling tests at school. When it became so spotted that my brother began to call me "camouflage," I flung it over the fence into the alley. Later, however, I swiped the jacket off the ground and went inside to drape it across my lap and <u>mope</u>.

I was called to dinner: steam silvered my mother's glasses as she said grace; my brother and sister with their heads bowed made ugly faces at their glasses of powdered milk. I gagged too, but eagerly ate big rips of buttered tortilla that held scooped-up beans. Finished, I went outside with my jacket across my arm. It was a cold sky. The faces of clouds were piled up, hurting. I climbed the fence, jumping down with a grunt. I started up the alley and soon slipped into my jacket, that green ugly brother who breathed over my shoulder that day and ever since. ❖

---
1. **palsied** (pôl′zēd): withered by disease.

WORDS TO KNOW **mope** (mōp) *v.* to be gloomy or in low spirits

423

Mini Lesson **Speaking and Listening**

PERSUASIVE SPEECH
Prepare Have students prepare a speech intended to persuade Soto's mother to exchange the jacket. Have them work in cooperative groups to write the speech. Tell students to come up with at least three good reasons why she should return the jacket. As they prepare their speech, remind students that a persuasive argument is strengthened by facts, not emotions.

Have students take turns presenting the speech. Encourage them to give each other positive feedback, as well as pointers on how to improve their presentation.

Present Groups can decide how to present their persuasive speech. Students who are listening should imagine that they are Soto's mother. They should evaluate whether the speech was successful in persuading her to return the jacket.

BLOCK SCHEDULING This activity is particularly well suited for longer class periods.

 Use **Communications Transparencies and Copymasters**, p. 16, for additional support.

GUIDING STUDENT RESPONSE

Connect to the Literature

1. What Do You Think?
Responses will vary but should reflect students' understanding of the author's mixed feelings toward the jacket.

Comprehension Check
- The narrator's mother gave him the jacket.
- His friends and teachers ignore him or talk about the jacket in a mean way.
- At the end of the story, the narrator puts the jacket on. He's going to keep it.

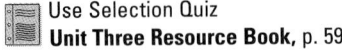 Use Selection Quiz
Unit Three Resource Book, p. 59.

Think Critically

2. Most students will say that the author exaggerated the jacket's role in his life. They may say that he would have been unhappy anyway, and the jacket was just a convenient excuse.

3. Possible Responses: He knew that his mother couldn't afford to buy him another one; if he got rid of it, he wouldn't be able to blame it for all his problems; he didn't want to hurt his mother's feelings; he knew his mother would be angry and not sympathetic.

4. Students may say that the author makes this comparison because, like an ugly brother, he has grown fond of the jacket even though it is imperfect.

5. Students' notes will vary. They may say that Gary Soto wanted to share how hard growing up is.

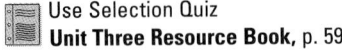 Use **Reading and Critical Thinking Transparencies,** p. 8, for additional support.

Literary Analysis

Humor Students' charts should include examples that contain exaggeration, unlikely comparisons, or funny details. Their explanations should be clear.

Connect to the Literature

1. What Do You Think?
What were your thoughts as you finished reading this selection?

Comprehension Check
- Who gives Soto the jacket?
- How do his friends and teachers react to him in the jacket?
- What does he do with the jacket at the end of the selection?

Think Critically

2. Do you think that the jacket really affected the author's life as much as he claims it did? Explain.

3. Why do you think the author did not get rid of the jacket?

 THINK ABOUT
- his family's circumstances
- the role the jacket plays in his life while he has it
- his mother's reaction when he shows her how worn out it is

4. Why do you think Soto compares the jacket to an "ugly brother"?

5. **ACTIVE READING** **IDENTIFYING THE AUTHOR'S PURPOSE**
Review the passages you wrote down in your **READER'S NOTEBOOK.** Based on your notes, why do you think Gary Soto wrote this memoir?

Extend Interpretations

6. What If? How would this memoir have been different if the author had gotten the jacket he wanted?

7. Different Perspectives How do you think the author's mother would have told this story? What might she say about the jacket and why she bought it?

8. Connect to Life What would you do if every day you had to wear a jacket that you hated?

424 UNIT THREE **AUTHOR STUDY**

Literary Analysis

HUMOR **Humor** is something that amuses readers or makes them laugh. Much of the humor in "The Jacket" comes from Gary Soto's exaggerated descriptions, his choice of funny details, and his comparisons between things that would normally appear to have nothing in common. For example, he compares the new coat to "a stranger whose hand I had to shake." This unlikely comparison between the coat and a stranger is humorous because it exaggerates the author's feeling of discomfort.

Activity Reread "The Jacket," paying close attention to phrases or passages that you find humorous. Make a chart listing at least five examples of humor. Next to each entry, explain briefly why you find it humorous. Compare your chart with that of a classmate.

REVIEW **SIMILE** A **simile** is a comparison of two things, using the words *as* or *like.* For instance, Soto uses a simile when he says that he was "thin as a young tree."

Extend Interpretations

6. What If? Possible Responses: He would have felt more confident and thus been more successful socially; he would still have felt unpopular and would have blamed it on the other jacket; he would have found other excuses for his problems.

7. Different Perspectives Responses will vary. Students might say that the author's mother would explain that she bought the jacket because it was inexpensive.

8. Connect to Life Responses will vary. Students may discuss finding ways to earn money to buy a new jacket. Or they might say that knowing they won't have to wear the jacket forever, they can cope with it.

Choices & CHALLENGES

Grammar in Context: Describing with Prepositional Phrases

Gary Soto often uses phrases to add detail rather than single-word adjectives and adverbs. Notice how the highlighted phrases make the following description clear:

> **With my hands clenched** I kicked a ball **against the fence.**

A **preposition** is a word that shows a relationship between other words. Common prepositions are *at, by, in, of, to, through, like,* and *with.* A **prepositional phrase** is a group of words made up of a preposition, a noun or pronoun, and any modifiers that go with the noun or pronoun. A prepositional phrase may be used as an adjective or adverb. For example, the phrase in red type above is used in place of an adjective to modify the word *I.* The phrase in orange is an adverb phrase, modifying the word *kicked.*

Apply to Your Writing Sometimes a one-word modifier (an adjective or adverb) does not paint a very clear picture of what it is describing. In your writing, look for places where prepositional phrases can pinpoint the exact look or position of something.

WRITING EXERCISE Make up a prepositional phrase to answer the question in parentheses. Rewrite the sentences, including your prepositional phrases.

Example: *Original* The other students stared. (Where?)

Rewritten The other students stared at me.

1. I threw my books. (Where?)
2. I combed my hair. (How?)
3. I wore the jacket. (When?)
4. My mother made me wear the jacket. (What kind?)

Connect to the Literature Find three more prepositional phrases in "The Jacket" that are used as adjectives or adverbs.

Grammar Handbook Quick Reference: Parts of Speech, p. R54

Vocabulary in Action

EXERCISE A: CONTEXT CLUES On your paper, write the vocabulary word that best completes the sentence.

1. My new jacket was ugly and made out of _____, just like an uncomfortable couch.
2. I tried on the jacket and looked at myself in the mirror from the side, hoping that at least my _____ was cool-looking.
3. When I am feeling unhappy, I _____ my arms at the dog like a big, wild bird.
4. Frankie T. was the playground _____ who bullied many sixth-grade students, including me.
5. The jacket was so ugly that it made me sad; I could only _____ around the house.

EXERCISE B Write a news story using all of the vocabulary words. Invent details to describe the event you are reporting. Include quotations from "interviews" with participants or witnesses.

Building Vocabulary
For an in-depth lesson on learning and remembering new words, see p. 491.

WORDS TO KNOW	mope	profile	swoop	terrorist	vinyl

Mini Lesson Grammar

IDENTIFYING PREPOSITIONS

Instruction Remind students that prepositions are words that show relationships. Some common prepositions are *at, by, in, of, to, through, like, with, on, under,* and *above.* They show how a noun or pronoun relates to another word. Explain that students should choose their prepositions carefully to make their meaning clear. Changing a preposition can make the meaning of a sentence entirely different. Write the following sentences on the board as examples:

Kim is waiting on the stairs.

Kim is waiting under the stairs.

Discuss the fact that meeting Kim would involve knowing which preposition describes where she is waiting.

Exercises: In the sentences below, have students underline the prepositions.

1. The narrator's dog jumped onto his jacket and ripped the sleeve with his teeth.
2. On the second day that the narrator wore his jacket, he was pushed by the playground terrorist.
3. During lunchtime, the narrator stood by the fence with the ugly boys.
4. In the cold weather, the pieces of tape that the narrator had put on the rip peeled off.
5. At the end of the story, the narrator puts the jacket on, knowing that it is his for keeps.

Use **Unit Three Resource Book**, p. 57.
Use **Grammar Transparencies and Copymasters**, p. 100.

 Use McDougal Littell's *Language Network,* Chapter 6, for more instruction and practice in identifying prepositions.

Soto's writing provides a vivid picture of growing up Chicano and poor. An analysis of his style can help reveal the techniques he uses to write. Students will be made aware of Soto's style through the Key Points and then they will find examples in the three excerpts on the right side of the page.

Key Points

First Activity

A **Exaggerated Details** Soto may use exaggerated details to make sure the reader understands his description. He wants us to really understand that Belinda is tough and that there were a lot of belts on the jacket. He is emphasizing something that he feels is important.

Second Activity

B **Unlikely Comparisons** By making unlikely comparisons, Soto forces the reader to pay close attention to the text. He helps the reader feel the way he did when he first saw and put on his new jacket.

Third Activity

C **Fresh Adjectives** Adjectives such as *wormy*, *frothing*, *gray*, and *relentless* help add zing to Soto's writing.

THE AUTHOR'S STYLE

Soto's Dramatic Descriptions

Gary Soto describes himself as "an imagist, that is, someone who paints a vivid picture. . . . I do employ dialogue, but most of my writing is descriptive. You come away with clear pictures of the scene, and hopefully they stay with you for a while." Many of Soto's dramatic descriptions include humor based on exaggeration and unlikely comparisons.

Key Style Points

A **Exaggerated Details** Soto uses exaggerated details to create memorable images and to emphasize certain points. Why do you think he uses these exaggerations in "The School Play" and "The Jacket"?

B **Unlikely Comparisons** By using unlikely comparisons, Soto creates humor and vivid images. He points out surprising similarities between things that usually seem unrelated. What effect do the comparisons in this passage from "The Jacket" have?

C **Fresh Adjectives** To add "zing" to his writing, Soto uses fresh adjectives. What adjectives in the descriptions listed here make them interesting?

Exaggerated Details

. . . Belinda was one of the toughest girls since the beginning of the world.
—"The School Play"

. . . I described something like bikers wear: black leather and silver studs with enough belts to hold down a small town.
—"The Jacket"

Unlikely Comparisons

I was a small kid, thin as a young tree, and it would be years before I'd have a new one. I stared at the jacket, like an enemy, thinking bad things . . .
—"The Jacket"

Fresh Adjectives

. . . they bit into chunks of wormy earth.
. . . the janitor's pit bull, who licked his frothing chops. . . .
. . . a ball of gray gum, depleted of sweetness under her relentless chomp.
—"The School Play"

Applications

1. **Active Reading** Look back over the selections in this author study. Find two examples for each of the three types of descriptive language listed above. Compare your examples with those of a classmate.

2. **Writing** Recall a humorous experience in your own life. Write a short essay about it, using Soto's descriptive techniques.

3. **Speaking and Listening** With a partner, choose a passage from a Soto selection to read aloud. Use your voice, facial expressions, and gestures to emphasize aspects of Soto's style. Take turns practicing your reading and commenting on each other's performance.

Applications

1. **Active Reading** Answers will vary, but examples should include exaggerated details, unlikely comparisons, and fresh adjectives.

2. **Writing** Answers will vary, but should include the descriptive techniques described on this page.

3. **Speaking and Listening** Suggest that students work together to make up a checklist on which to "grade" each other's performance.

Writing Options

1. Personal Ode Write an ode to a person, place, or thing that has had an impact on your life.

2. Embarrassing Moments Gallery Write an essay describing an embarrassing moment of your own, or one you've heard about. Add an illustration. Along with classmates, display your essay on a bulletin board.

Activities & Explorations

1. Soto Illustrated Read another short story by Gary Soto. Draw a comic strip about the events in the story. ~ ART

2. Film Review View Gary Soto's short film "The Pool Party." Write a review of it. Include references to Soto's literary works. ~ VIEWING AND REPRESENTING

 Literature in Performance

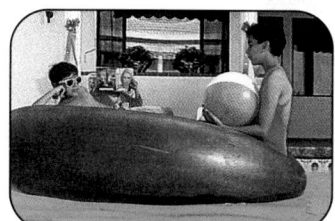

3. Tabloid Newspaper Make the cover for a tabloid newspaper, using exaggerated headlines about moments in the author study selections. Hang it on a bulletin board. ~ VIEWING AND REPRESENTING

Inquiry & Research

Justice in the Fields Soto cares about the struggles of farm workers. Do research to learn about the United Farm Workers union. What gains have been made in the last decade? Present your findings in a poster.

Author Study Project
On Stage

Now's the chance to bring Gary Soto's vivid descriptions to life! Present a dramatic version of one of the selections in this author study.

❶ Brainstorm Ideas With your team, brainstorm about presenting your scene. Decide whether you will use a narrator.

❷ Create a Script Rewrite the piece in the form of a script, with a cast of characters, stage directions, and lines of dialogue. Decide whether roles should be deleted or rearranged.

❸ Build the Scene Create a background for your scene by drawing scenery or arranging furniture. In addition, gather or make any props and costumes.

❹ Practice and Perform Practice your scene. Actors should speak with strong, clear voices and use dramatic gestures. Invite another class to see your production. If equipment is available, you can videotape the performance and watch it together afterward, or share it with family members.

Writing Options

1. Personal Ode Students' odes should give a clear impression of the subject and tell why the subject is worthy of an ode. Encourage students to include vivid images like those Soto employs.

2. Embarrassing Moments Gallery Keep in mind that some moments are too embarrassing for students to share. You might suggest moments that were embarrassing at the time, but now can be seen with humor.

 Use **Writing Transparencies**, p. 6, for additional support.

Activities & Explorations

1. Soto Illustrated Students' illustrations should reflect an understanding of the works on which they are based.

2. Film Review Provide published movie reviews as models for students. **To make this activity easier,** hold a class discussion of the Soto video before students begin writing their reviews.

3. Tabloid Newspaper Before making their tabloid newspapers, students may wish to discuss some of the exaggerated headlines they've seen on such newspapers. **To make this activity more challenging,** have students write the story to go with the headline.

Inquiry & Research

Justice in the Fields One book on Cesar Chavez that students might enjoy is the bilingual edition (English and Spanish) of *Cesar Chavez: Hope for the People,* by David Goodwin.

Author Study Project

On Stage Make sure that each group includes students who enjoy performing as well as students who can create backgrounds or sets, find music, or collect props.

MULTIMEDIA PROJECT
Students can make a multimedia project of their skits by filming them and arranging them with narration to give a fuller picture of Gary Soto's life. They can also add introductory and background music, as well as sound effects. They could also do this project as a radio play, paying special attention to the music and sound.

Other Works by GARY SOTO

The characters in Gary Soto's books grapple with rough kids and bad jobs, tough times and lousy luck. They also find humor in the most unexpected places. In his short stories, novels, and poems, Soto's wise observations touch subjects ranging from baseball and first kisses to racism and poverty.

Baseball in April and Other Stories 1990

ALA Best Book for Young Adults

Set in Soto's hometown of Fresno, California, this award-winning short-story collection focuses on the hopes, dreams, and hardships of young Mexican Americans growing up in the barrio.

Taking Sides 1991

Fourteen-year-old Lincoln Mendoza's world changes when he moves from a San Francisco barrio into a well-to-do suburb. Suddenly, he must struggle to find a place for himself. Among the stresses he deals with are racism at school, his mom's new boyfriend, and a basketball tournament that pits his new school against his old.

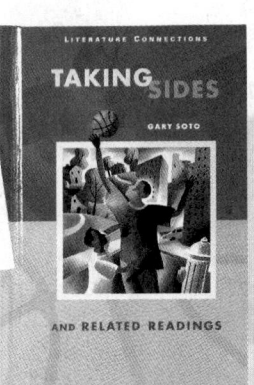

Pacific Crossing 1992

In this sequel to *Taking Sides*, Lincoln is chosen to be a summer exchange student at a small farm in Japan. Living in a different culture gives him a chance to learn about martial arts and meet new friends. It also helps him figure out what being Mexican American really means.

The Pool Party 1993

When Rudy Herrera is invited to a pool party by the rich and popular Tiffany Perez, he discovers that getting ready will be a family affair. It seems like everyone from his sister to his grandfather has already decided how Rudy should behave at the big event.

Local News 1993

One boy tries to save the planet by becoming a vegetarian. Another seeks to blackmail his older brother with pictures taken of him in the shower. These are just two of the funny, believable tales of teenage life in this companion to *Baseball in April*.

A Fire in My Hands 1990

Rich in detail, this poetry collection explores the emotions surrounding first love, family life, and the drama of friendship. Each poem has a brief introduction by the author that tells how he was inspired to write it.

Writing Workshop
Problem-Solution Essay

Objectives
- write a problem-solution essay
- use a written text as a model for writing
- revise a draft to provide examples
- use the correct comparative adjectives and adverbs

Introducing the Workshop

Problem-Solution Essay Begin by discussing with students the problem-solution essay form. Tell them that many people write problem-solution essays to help other people who have similar problems, to record how they solved a specific problem, or to persuade someone to solve a problem. Ask them if they have ever read a problem-solution essay, and what it was about.

Ask students to begin thinking about this essay by brainstorming problems that would be worthy of solving. Help focus their discussion on appropriate ideas.

Basics in a Box
Using the Graphic A problem-solution essay begins with a clear and concise explanation of the problem and its significance, proposes a workable solution and includes details that explain and support it, and concludes by restating the problem and the proposed solution. Point out that this graphic organizer helps students to visualize the problem-solution essay.

Presenting the Rubric To help students better understand the assignment, review the Standards for Writing a Successful Problem-Solution Essay. You may also want to share with them the complete rubric, which describes several levels of proficiency.

 Use McDougal Littell's **Language Network,** Chapters 10–17, for more instruction on essential writing skills.

 Power Presentation

To engage students visually, use **Power Presentation** 2, Problem-Solution Essay.

Writing Workshop
Problem-Solution Essay

Offering a solution to a problem . . .

From Reading to Writing Life can present difficult problems, from pollution and crime to simply forgetting your homework. Tackling a problem creatively and patiently makes all the difference. Think of Helen Keller. As a child she lost the use of sight, speech, and hearing. Her teacher, Anne Sullivan, helped solve this problem by teaching Helen sign language. Are there problems you would like to solve? Writing a **problem-solution essay** can help you explore a problem and work on solving it.

For Your Portfolio

WRITING PROMPT Identify an important problem and offer a solution.

Purpose: To inform readers about the problem and persuade them to consider your solution

Audience: People who might experience a similar problem, or who can help with the solution

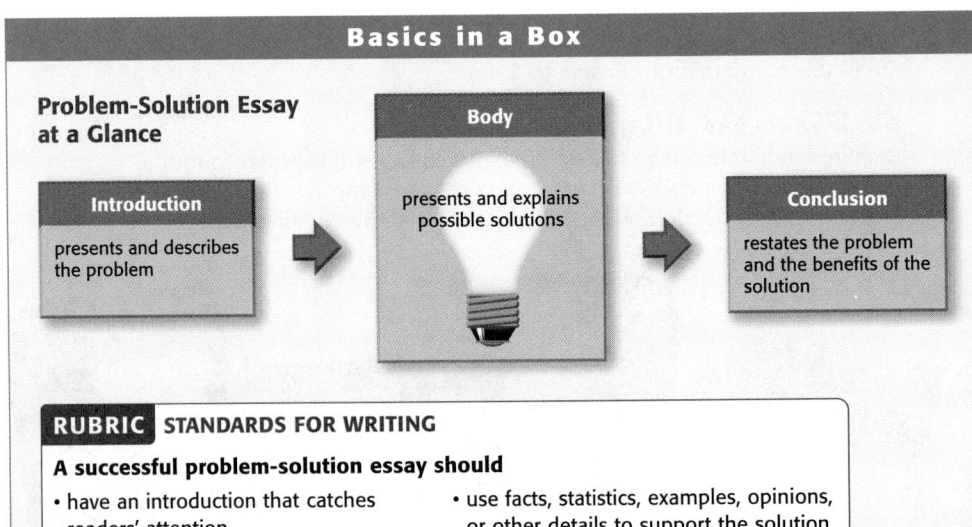

Basics in a Box

Problem-Solution Essay at a Glance

Introduction	Body	Conclusion
presents and describes the problem	presents and explains possible solutions	restates the problem and the benefits of the solution

RUBRIC STANDARDS FOR WRITING

A successful problem-solution essay should

- have an introduction that catches readers' attention
- give a clear picture of the problem
- explore all aspects of the problem, including its causes and effects
- offer a reasonable solution and explain how to put it into effect
- use facts, statistics, examples, opinions, or other details to support the solution
- use logical reasoning to convince the reader
- have a strong conclusion

LESSON RESOURCES

USING PRINT RESOURCES
Unit Three Resource Book
- Prewriting, p. 60
- Drafting, p. 61
- Peer Response, pp. 62–63
- Revising, Editing, and Proofreading, p. 64
- Student Models, pp. 65–67
- Rubric, p. 68

Writing Transparencies
- Writing Process Transparencies, TR 1–TR 4
- Writing Structure Transparencies: Structuring the Essay, TR 6
- Writing Template Transparencies: Problem-Solution Essay, TR 33

Grammar Transparencies and Copymasters
- Verb Tense Errors, CM 83

INTEGRATED TECHNOLOGY
LaserLinks
Writing Springboards
See **Teacher's SourceBook** p. 56 for bar codes.

Writing Coach CD-ROM

Visit our website:
www.mcdougallittell.com

Analyzing a Student Model

M. McGoff
St. Clement's Elementary School

See the Communication Handbook, p. R100 for speaking and presenting tips.

SPEAKING OPPORTUNITY

A Trip to the Grocery Store

Can you imagine the challenges that people with disabilities face each day? Even simple tasks like grocery shopping can be difficult. Perhaps they can't reach a can of soup on the shelf, or are unable to open a freezer door to get some ice cream. They may not be able to push a cart. They may have vision problems that stop them from reading labels or knowing what choices they have. In cases like these, shopping becomes a real challenge. However, I think grocery stores can do a lot to make shopping easier for people with disabilities.

Because of the different needs of disabled shoppers, I would like to see a shopping assistance program developed in grocery stores. People with disablities would register with the store in advance, letting managers know their needs and problems. The store would then hire an occupational therapist to interview shoppers to find out how the store could support them in becoming more independent. The main purpose of the program would be to find out how each person with a disability needs support and, with the help of an occupational therapist, come up with a plan to help each person shop as independently as possible. This program would also help shoppers feel more supported by the community.

For instance, a shopper might not be able to reach or lift groceries off the shelf but would like the experience of browsing through the aisles. With the help of mechanized devices, this person might tape-record a shopping list or choose things that he or she wants from a store checklist. Then a store assistant could get the items and meet the shopper at the checkout area. The shopper would be able to join the line at the checkout like everyone else. In other cases, a shopper could become perfectly independent with the use of a motorized shopping cart and a long mechanical arm device that could extend to get items from higher places. Still another shopper might require a store employee to walk with him or her to read labels or describe selections.

Despite the program's advantages, store owners might have

RUBRIC IN ACTION

❶ Introduction briefly presents the problem and the need for a solution

❷ A detailed explanation of the problem helps the reader understand what needs to be done.

❸ The writer presents a workable and definite solution.

❹ Supports the main idea of the paragraph with examples

Other options:
- Support with statistics
- Use description

Teaching the Lesson

Analyzing the Model
"A Trip to the Grocery Store"

The essay writer describes the challenges faced by disabled people as they attempt the simple task of grocery shopping. The essay explores several support systems and solutions to helping disabled persons have success when grocery shopping.

Have student volunteers read the essay aloud. Discuss the Rubric in Action with students. Point out key words and phrases in the student model that correspond to the elements mentioned in the Rubric in Action.

1 Posing a question is a good way to start a problem-solution essay because it lets the reader know immediately what problem the essay is addressing. Ask students to think of other questions that could be used to begin this essay.
   Possible Response: Have you ever tried to grocery shop on crutches or in a wheelchair?

2 Tell students that giving specific details about the problem helps convince readers of the validity of the problem. Ask them to list some of the details provided in this paragraph.
   Possible Responses: Shoppers can't reach items on shelves, may not be able to push a cart, or can't read labels.

3 Ask students to notice how the writer puts a clear, workable solution early in the essay. Ask students to suggest other workable solutions for this problem.
   Possible Response: The store could hire people to shop for the disabled person and bring the food to his or her home.

4 Point out that the essay continues to add supporting details for the proposed solution. Ask students to select the detail they like most and tell a partner why.

5 Tell students that the writer has pointed out both pros and cons to the proposed solution. Ask them to think of other possible objections to the proposed solution.
Possible Response: Disabled people might feel discriminated against if they were treated differently than other shoppers.

6 The writer has given a clear plan which deals with the possible objections to the proposed solution. Tell students that the more support and explanation the essay provides, the more likely it is to impact the readers. Ask students to discuss what they think of this solution.
Possible Responses: I think the solution is good and well thought out, and I can see some grocery stores trying this. I don't think this is a good plan because grocery stores don't care that much about the people who shop there.

7 The conclusion of the essay should restate the problem, clarify and repeat the solution, and provide the benefits of the proposed solution. Ask students to compare the first and last paragraphs of the essay to see what elements were repeated.
Possible Response: Simple grocery shopping tasks might be difficult or impossible to people with disabilities. Grocery stores could do simple things that would make shopping possible and pleasurable for disabled persons.

objections. They might feel it would cost too much money to hire extra employees to help people with disabilities. They might think that it isn't good business to spend money on a program that won't be profitable. The store owners might also feel there are not enough people who need this service.

> **❺** The writer raises possible objections to the plan.

Contrary to what store owners might believe, solving the problem is easier than it appears. Occupational therapists might be willing to volunteer a couple of hours a week, or the stores could pay therapists only for the number of hours they work. Since customers with disabilities would be shopping at different times, the stores could train employees working on different shifts to assist them. Middle- or high-school students also could volunteer to help disabled shoppers during a few hours after school. This would give the students valuable experience in helping their community.

> **❻** The body provides a step-by-step strategy for action.

Finally, the stores might also get government or town funding for equipment that would help people with disabilities shop more comfortably. As you can see, it is not just the disabled who would benefit from a program like this. I believe that everyone involved could benefit: store owners, volunteers, therapists, and store employees. The program could also create good publicity for the store. People would know that the store cares about its customers. They would want to shop there because of its reputation as a supportive, caring, community store. More people shopping at the store could help pay for the program.

Buying a pint of ice cream might not seem like a big deal, but to someone who has never had the freedom to do this it is a sign of independence. To get involved, you can contact your local grocery stores and ask them to create programs for the disabled. By doing what you can to solve some of the problems faced by these members of your community, you are helping to create a better world.

> **❼** The writer tells the reader how to get involved. She restates the benefits of the program to create a strong conclusion.

432   UNIT THREE   PART 2: BREAKING BARRIERS

 Viewing and Representing

PICTURING TEXT STRUCTURE

Instruction One good way to structure a good problem-solution essay is to think about the main points—stating the problem, offering a solution, and restating the problem and solution—and then to consider the details that support the problem and the solution. Tell students that using a graphic organizer can help them to organize their essay.

Activity Have students analyze the organization of the student model by constructing a diagram similar to the one shown here.

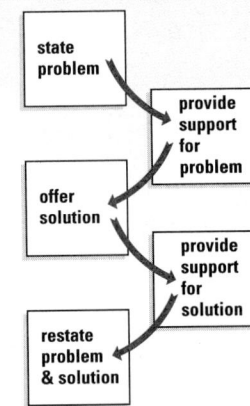

state problem → provide support for problem

offer solution → provide support for solution

restate problem & solution

Use **Writing Transparencies**, p. 6, for additional support.

Writing Your Problem-Solution Essay

❶ Prewriting

The best way to escape from a problem is to solve it.
—Alan Saporta, writer

Brainstorm problems that you see around you. **List** school problems, community problems, and world problems. See the **Idea Bank** in the margin for more suggestions. After you have selected a problem, follow these steps.

Planning Your Problem-Solution Essay

▶ **1. Define your problem.** What is the problem you want to solve? If it is too big to explain in one essay, write about one part of the problem. Ask the following questions: How did it start? Who is affected by it? What would happen if it isn't solved? Has anyone else tried to solve it?

▶ **2. Find information.** Research answers to your questions about the problem. Interview people who might be directly affected by it. If you're interested in a world problem, you can do research at the library and on the Internet. This will help you come up with solutions.

▶ **3. Brainstorm solutions.** How might the problem be solved? Write down as many possibilities as you can think of.

▶ **4. Choose the best solution.** Evaluate your solutions. Based on your research, which solutions have been successful in the past? Which might seem too difficult to put into practice? Discuss with classmates, teachers, family members, or people affected by the problem. Then choose the best solution.

❷ Drafting

Include as much information as you can in your first draft. Later you can go back and revise your draft.

- In your introduction, **identify** the problem.
- **Explain** the **causes and effects** of the problem and the reasons it must be solved.
- Describe your solution. **Prove** that it is a workable solution.
- In your conclusion, tell what you want to do about the problem and **explain** how you and others can do it.

IDEABank

1. Your Working Portfolio
Look for ideas in the **Writing Options** you completed earlier in the unit.
- **Justice Speech**, p. 379
- **Helping Invention**, p. 386

2. Take a Survey
Ask four or five people to name two problems that they think need solutions. List their answers and choose one of the problems for your essay.

3. Take It Personally
Think of the problems that directly affect you, such as overcrowded classrooms, old gym or lab equipment, or not enough money for class trips. Choose the one you feel most strongly about.

Have a question?

See the **Writing Handbook.**
Problem-Solution Writing, p. R37
Documenting Your Sources, p. R43

Ask Your Peer Reader

- Why is solving this problem important?
- Whom does the problem affect?
- Do you think this solution is the best one? Why or why not?
- Which information did you find most and least convincing?

Guiding Student Writing

Prewriting

Choosing a Subject
If after reading the Idea Bank, students have difficulty choosing a problem for their problem-solution essay, suggest they try the following:
- go back to their brainstormed lists of problems from the beginning of the lesson
- think about the things in their own lives that trouble them
- talk with a partner about their lives at home, school, and in the community

Planning the Problem-Solution Essay
1. Students may want to share their problem with a partner as they try to answer the questions posed. The most common error for students is to select a problem that is too big for one essay. Encourage students to help their partners think about how to narrow down the problem.
2. Encourage students to talk to family members and others involved with the problem. If it's a school-based problem, allow them time to talk with the personnel involved.
3. Have students do this task individually during a quiet time of free writing. During this time, students should write down any solution, whether they think it's a good one or not.
4. Once students have generated a list of possible solutions, have them talk with many people to help them get a good feeling for the most probable solution. Remind them that they will have to be able to support this solution in their essay, so they may want to take notes as they talk to other people.

Drafting

Suggest that students jot down the boldfaced key words in the margin where they occur in their first draft. This will help ensure that they get them all, and will make it easier for the peer reader to evaluate. Ask students to read the peer reader question box prior to beginning to write.

Revising
SUPPORTING IDEAS WITH EXAMPLES

Ask students to find a sentence in their essay that could use more details. Ask a volunteer to read one aloud, and help them to see how they can add more examples to support their problem or solution. Remind students to read their entire essay and to revise by adding more examples.

Editing and Proofreading
COMPARING WITH ADJECTIVES AND ADVERBS

Help students to identify comparative adjectives and adverbs in their essays. Check to see if they've used them correctly by asking students to read them aloud.

Reflecting

Encourage students to be specific in reflecting about their essay writing. Ask them to think about who they might want to read the essay and why.

Option
Teaching Tip

It is often helpful to pre-select student work to share with the class. As you are reading and conferencing with students on their writing pieces, and you see something you'd like to use in a future lesson, mention it to the students. Have them mark their rough draft, and make a note of it yourself. This way you can be sure to have a student volunteer when you ask. Another way is to ask students for permission to copy their piece and make an overhead transparency of it. You can then use the paper during the appropriate instruction.

Need Revising Help?

Review the **Rubric**, p. 430

Consider **peer reader** comments

Check **Revision Guidelines**, p. R23

SPELLING From Writing

As you revise your work, look back at the words you misspelled and determine why you made the errors you did. For additional help, refer to the strategies and generalizations in the **Spelling Handbook** on page R86.

Confused about Comparatives and Superlatives?

See the **Grammar Handbook**, p. R71

Publishing IDEAS

- Create a problem-solution bulletin board. Feature one problem and its solution each week.
- Choose essays that address common problems. Submit them to your school newspaper.

More Online: Publishing Options www.mcdougallittell.com

---

❸ Revising
TARGET SKILL ▶ SUPPORTING IDEAS WITH EXAMPLES
Supporting your points with examples helps to show that the problem needs to be solved and that your solution is a good one. In the following passage, the writer adds examples to show how her plan might work.

> For instance, if a shopper could not reach or lift groceries on the shelf but would like the experience of browsing through the aisles, he or she might ~~be helped in a couple of ways.~~ tape-record a shopping list or select items from a store checklist.

❹ Editing and Proofreading
TARGET SKILL ▶ COMPARING WITH ADJECTIVES AND ADVERBS When writing a problem-solution essay, you may want to make comparisons between your solution and the existing problem. Words like *better, happier,* and *more* signal a comparison. Most comparative adjectives and adverbs are formed by adding *-er* to short words or by using the word *more* with longer words. After you read the example below, check your essay to see if you have used comparative adjectives and adverbs correctly.

> Contrary to what store owners might believe, solving the problem is ~~more easy~~ easier than it appears.

❺ Reflecting
FOR YOUR WORKING PORTFOLIO What did you learn about the problem from writing your problem-solution essay? What did you learn about possible solutions? Attach these answers to your finished essay. Save your problem-solution essay in your **Working Portfolio.**

Assessment Practice Revising & Editing

Read this passage from the first draft of a problem-solution essay. The underlined sections may include the following kinds of errors.

- **incorrect comparative forms**
- **verb tense errors**
- **incorrect adverb and adjective choice**
- **incorrect capitalization**

For each underlined section, choose the revision that most improves the writing.

> Our river, <u>the Hialeah river,</u> <u>is the more polluted river</u> in the state.
> (1)   (2)
> The level of toxic chemicals in the water is high, so the river's fish
> population is <u>not doing good.</u> Many more <u>fish live</u> in the river ten years
> (3)   (4)
> ago. Not only are there chemicals in the water, <u>but a greater number of</u>
> (5)
> <u>people</u> use the river as a dumpster than ever before. It makes me sad to
> think that this beautiful <u>Old American river</u> is being destroyed.
> (6)

1. A. the hialeah river
   B. the hialeah River
   C. the Hialeah River
   D. Correct as is

2. A. is the most polluted river
   B. is the most pollutedest river
   C. is the much polluted river
   D. Correct as is

3. A. not doing more better
   B. not doing well
   C. not doing best
   D. Correct as is

4. A. fish have lived
   B. fish lived
   C. fish are living
   D. Correct as is

5. A. but a great number of people
   B. but a number of people
   C. but the greatest number of people
   D. Correct as is

6. A. old American River
   B. old American river
   C. Old American River
   D. Correct as is

Need extra help?

See the **Grammar Handbook.**

Using Verbs Correctly, p. R68

Using Modifiers Effectively, p. R70

Correcting Capitalization, p. R73

Grammar

VERB TENSE ERRORS

Instruction Remind students that verb tense shows the time of an action or condition. Writers sometimes cause confusion when they use different verb tenses in describing actions that occur at the same time. When two or more actions occur at the same time or in sequence, use the same verb tense to describe the actions.

Patsy lives in Detroit. She drives about fifteen minutes to work each day.

Ask students to note that *lives* and *drives* are both present tense.

Exercises Ask students to identify the correct verb in each sentence.

At our bus stop, many students are (<u>causing</u>, caused) problems. Don (liked, <u>likes</u>) to take the newspaper out of the box. Tisha (picked, <u>picks</u>) up pinecones and (<u>throws</u>, throwed) them at passing cars. Once, Katy (kicks, <u>kicked</u>) some pebbles into the grass. None of us (lived, <u>live</u>) in this house, and if this problem doesn't stop, our bus stop will get (move, <u>moved</u>) further away. The people who (<u>live</u>, lived) at the house are not very happy!

 Use **Grammar Transparencies and Copymasters,** p. 83, for additional support.

  Use McDougal Littell's *Language Network,* Chapter 4, for more instruction in verb tense errors.

Objectives
• reflect on and assess student understanding of the unit
• review literary analysis skills introduced in the unit
• assess and build portfolios

Reflecting on the Theme

OPTION 1

A successful response will
• identify ten personal qualities which at least three fictional characters or real people in this unit exhibited.
• list the identities of those characters next to their personal traits.
• demonstrate how these traits and qualities helped each character relate to success and/or failure.

OPTION 2

A successful response will
• include thoughtful discussion of the quote from Ibrahima's letter.
• result in interesting role-play with the three story characters identified.
• contain examples from characters' lives which demonstrate their response in struggling towards goals.

OPTION 3

A successful response will
• begin with discussion of the ways people encourage or are encouraged by others.
• evaluate the fictional characters and real people in this selection to discover the ways in which they overcome difficulties and pursue their goals.
• include appropriate quotations from the selections which provide support for tips on the chart.
• reflect the personal goal setting experiences of the student.

Use Unit 3 Resource Book page 69 to provide students a ready-made chart for listing their tips.

Self Assessment
Students should recall all the stories in this unit and think about how both fictional characters and real people behaved when faced with unfairness. The paragraphs should include these ideas, as well as ideas drawn from the student's personal experiences.

436   UNIT THREE

A Sense of Fairness

By reading the selections in this unit, you have learned about a wide range of unfair situations and an equally wide range of responses to them. What new thoughts about coping with difficulties have formed in your mind? To explore this question, complete one or more of the options in each of the following sections.

Reflecting on the Theme

OPTION 1

Making a Top-Ten List In dealing with life's injustices, which individuals in this unit responded with hope, with wisdom, or with determination? Working in a group, consider how these fictional characters and real people reacted to success or failure. Brainstorm a list of the top ten personal qualities it takes to deal with an unjust situation. Next to each quality, write the name of the characters or people in this unit who displayed it.

OPTION 2

Role-Playing a Response In "Abd al-Rahman Ibrahima," the author says that when Ibrahima wrote a letter asking for help, "he had little faith in the procedure but felt he had nothing to lose." In a group of three, taking the roles of Janet in "The Southpaw," Helen Keller, and Robert in "The School Play," respond to this quote about Ibrahima. What would each individual say about the importance of asking for help? What would each say about the value of struggling toward a goal?

OPTION 3

Finding Inspiration Look over the selections in this unit to find ways in which fictional characters and real people encourage themselves or are encouraged by others. Then create a chart titled "How to Reach Your Goals." List tips for overcoming difficulties and pursuing goals based on the experiences of the individuals. Include any quotes from the selections that you find helpful or inspiring.

436   UNIT THREE   A SENSE OF FAIRNESS

Self ASSESSMENT

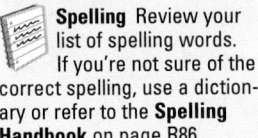 **READER'S NOTEBOOK**

After reading the selections in Unit Three, what have you learned about how to deal with unfair situations? Write a paragraph describing how you could use what you have learned in a real-life situation.

REVIEWING YOUR PERSONAL WORDList

Vocabulary Review the new words you learned in this unit. If necessary, use a dictionary to check the meaning of each word.

Spelling Review your list of spelling words. If you're not sure of the correct spelling, use a dictionary or refer to the **Spelling Handbook** on page R86.

Reviewing Literary Concepts

OPTION 1

Thinking About Dialogue Choose two selections from this unit that you think have especially effective dialogue. With a partner, read aloud dialogue from each selection in a way that emphasizes the feelings of the characters. How do the spoken lines bring the characters to life? What can you learn about their traits from the words they speak?

OPTION 2

Considering Tone The tone of a story or poem expresses the writer's attitude about the subject. A tone can be serious or humorous; it can be kind, critical, or neutral. Look through these selections to find examples of three or four different tones. Jot down details and dialogue that show the writer's attitude. Then, with a few classmates, discuss how the tone of each selection affected your emotions as you read.

Building Your Portfolio

- **Writing Options** Several of the Writing Options in this unit asked you to write letters. Choose the one that you feel most successfully allows your voice (or the voice of a character) to come through. Write a cover note explaining the reasons for your choice. Then attach the note to the letter and place it in your **Presentation Portfolio.**

- **Writing Workshops** In one Writing Workshop you wrote director's notes. In another, you wrote a problem-solution essay. Reread these two pieces and decide which one does a better job of showing your strengths as a writer. Explain your choice in a cover note, attach it to the piece you selected, and place it in your **Presentation Portfolio.**

- **Additional Activities** Think back to the assignments you completed for **Activities & Explorations** and **Inquiry & Research.** In your portfolio, keep a record of any assignments that you particularly enjoyed, found helpful, or would like to explore further.

Self ASSESSMENT

READER'S NOTEBOOK

Copy down the following literary terms introduced or reviewed in this unit. Put a question mark next to each one that you do not fully understand. Look at the **Glossary of Literary and Reading Terms** (page R6) to clarify the meanings of the terms you've marked.

stage directions	sensory details
dialogue	speaker
narrative poetry	repetition
primary sources	humor
	simile
secondary sources	tone
	imagery
autobiography	
biography	

Self ASSESSMENT

Compare your choices for your portfolio in Unit Three with the choices you made earlier. Write a note comparing a recent piece with an early one. Point out improvements that the recent piece shows.

Setting GOALS

How well are you working with others in group situations? Are you willing to share your ideas? Do you listen carefully to the ideas of other group members? Write down some practical tips to keep on hand during the next unit.

Reviewing Literary Concepts

OPTION 1

It may be helpful to pair students up according to the two selections they choose. Allow them time to practice reading the dialogue and to discuss their interpretation with their partner. The questions posed in this option might be used to form the basis of this discussion and interpretation.

OPTION 2

A successful response will
- begin with critical analysis of each selection, with individual students identifying several author tones.
- provide examples from the selections of each of the tones chosen.
- include thoughtful discussion of each tone and the effect each had on the reader.

Building Your Portfolio

Students should evaluate the letters in their Working Portfolios and choose the one that represents their best use of voice. Likewise, they should evaluate the other two pieces and select the one which represents their best work to include in their Presentation Portfolio.

As students attach notes to the items they transfer to their Presentation Portfolios, remind them to write the reasoning for their choices clearly so they will understand the notes several months from now.

Self Assessment
It may work well to have students use a different color paper to write the comparison notes. Remind them to be reflective and explicit in the comparison, as this will help them as they work on their writing.

For more information on using Portfolios, use *Teacher's Guide to Assessment and Portfolio* beginning on page 53.

Setting Goals
Help students to focus on the questions, to evaluate themselves honestly, and to set realistic, clear goals.

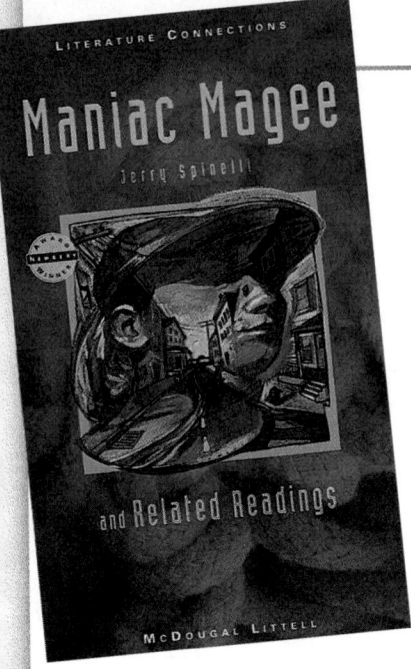

LITERATURE CONNECTIONS
Maniac Magee

BY JERRY SPINELLI

This Newbery Medal winner tells of homeless wanderer "Maniac" Magee, who can move like no one else the town has ever seen. He intercepts a football on a field of players twice his size, hits a home run without a baseball, and wins a race running backward. But there are two challenges he can't outrun: the strong racial divisions in his hometown, and his need for a loving family.

These thematically related readings are provided along with *Maniac Magee:*

from Freedom's Children
BY ELLEN LEVINE

Where the Rainbow Ends
BY RICHARD RIVE

Those Who Don't
BY SANDRA CISNEROS

A Lesson for Kings
BY MARGARET READ MACDONALD

Runner
BY DONNA LUONGO STEIN

Final Curve
BY LANGSTON HUGHES

The Boy with Yellow Eyes
BY GLORIA GONZALEZ

Stormalong
BY MARY POPE OSBORNE

And Even *More* . . .

Many Thousand Gone: African Americans from Slavery to Freedom

BY VIRGINIA HAMILTON

Award-winning author Virginia Hamilton has written a "joyous anthem of freedom" consisting of over 30 real-life stories of African-Americans, from the 1600s through the Civil War. The book honors the courage and dignity of those who experienced the horrors of slavery.

Books

Bullies Are a Pain in the Brain
BY TREVOR ROMAIN
A humorous but practical guide on how to deal with bullies

Escape to Freedom
BY OSSIE DAVIS
This play is about Frederick Douglass, orator, author, diplomat, and former slave.

Louis Braille: The Boy Who Invented Books for the Blind
BY MARGARET DAVIDSON
How Louis Braille, blinded at the age of 3, invented a system to allow the blind to read

The Clay Marble

BY MINFONG HO

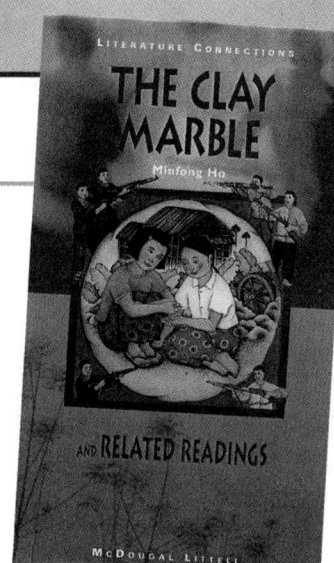

This historical novel is set in a Cambodian refugee camp in the early 1980s. Twelve-year-old Dara—with courage, quick thinking, and perseverance—copes with the horrors of war, helped by stories, a good friend, and a "magical" marble.

These thematically related readings are provided along with *The Clay Marble*:

All the People of Khmer Were Very Troubled
BY VEN YEM

My Life Story
BY LAN NGUYEN

Oppression
BY LANGSTON HUGHES

Birthday Box
BY JANE YOLEN

Holes
BY LILLIAN MORRISON

from **Childhood and Poetry**
BY PABLO NERUDA

All-Ball
BY MARY POPE OSBORNE

Dear World, January 17, 1994
BY ALMA LUZ VILLANUEVA

The Secret Garden
BY FRANCES HODGSON BURNETT
A friendless orphan discovers a secret garden.

Sees Behind Trees
BY MICHAEL DORRIS
A 16th-century Native American with impaired sight finds he has an extraordinary gift.

Very Best (Almost) Friends: A Collection of Friendship Poetry
SELECTED BY PAUL B. JANECZKO
A collection of poems about the good and the bad of friendship

Other Media

Frank and Ollie
True story of old friends who worked together for years making cartoons
WALT DISNEY HOME VIDEO
(VIDEOCASSETTE)

Martin Luther King, Jr.— "I Have a Dream"
The entire "I Have a Dream" speech as well as coverage of related events
MPI HOME VIDEO
(VIDEOCASSETTE)

Waiting for the Rain
Sheila Gordon's novel of two boys, one white, one black, struggle to remain friends in segregated South Africa.
RECORDED BOOKS
(AUDIOCASSETTE)

The Miracle Worker
The story of how Helen Keller learned to communicate with the help of her teacher, Anne Sullivan
MGM/UA HOME ENTERTAINMENT
(VIDEOCASSETTE)

Ancient Greece Fair

OVERVIEW

Greece has been called "the cradle of Western civilization." Foundations of Western culture such as drama, democracy, and art and architecture developed thousands of years ago in this small, mountainous area surrounded by sea. Influences from the culture of Greek antiquity are still felt today, particularly in Europe and North America. The following project could be part of a larger unit on ancient Greece.

Research Questions

• What was the culture of ancient Greece like?

• What gods and goddesses, foods, forms of entertainment, and styles of architecture were important in Greece some 2,000 years ago?

Investigation The class will work as a team to create an "ancient Greece fair" that creatively presents their research about Greek theatre, mythology, food, and architecture. Students will work together to generate posters, brochures, and other media. They will set up tables—perhaps clusters of desks—to display the materials they have created as well as books and media used in their research, with bookmarks at images that would be of particular interest to visitors. The visitors will move among the tables to explore the information. Students at each table could have a poster displaying "Ask me" questions to prompt discussion—for example: How long did plays last at ancient Greek theater festivals? Who are the most important Greek gods and goddesses? Students might also set up game or activity booths such as face-painting, posing for photos with a mythological character, an or "oracle" booth giving messages.

Wrap-up Students will invite other classes or family members to attend the ancient Greece fair, review their displays, ask questions, and take home various materials. They may wish to wear togas and sandals for the event or dress in the person of a mythological character, mortal or immortal.

Links and Extended Reading
www.mcdougallittell.com

LaserLinks: Background Reading Connection

OBJECTIVES

❑ describe and define theater terms having origins in ancient Greece

❑ recognize and represent the deities and tales from Greek mythology

❑ research the foodstuffs of ancient Greece

❑ create a floor plan representing a classical Greek temple

Team Teaching Assignments

CONNECT TO **LANGUAGE ARTS** From the earliest days when *tragoidia,* or goat songs, first became part of the ancient festivals of Dionysius in Athens, performance was central to Hellenic culture. More than 2,000 years ago, Greek playwrights created the first European works of drama, some of which are still performed. Particularly well known playwrights include Aeschylus, Sophocles, Euripides, and Aristophanes. Students should research terms relevant to the drama of ancient Greece—such as, *tragedy, comedy, chorus, prologue, epilogue, proscenium, amphitheater, antagonist, protagonist,* and *mask*—and compose a glossary of terms describing their meanings and historical origins. A group of students can work to create a model or diagram of an amphitheater such as the theater at Epidaurus, and attach their definitions of theater terms to the illustration. Alternately students might be guided to perform a reading of the play in Unit Three, *Damon and Pythias.* They should prepare a program for the play which includes their glossary of theater terms. *(3–5 class periods)*

YOU WILL NEED:
- Web access (optional)
- encyclopedia
- history books
- art materials as desired

CONNECT TO **SOCIAL STUDIES** It has been said that in Western literature, only the Bible has been more influential than Greek mythology. Students should make a poster that depicts the pantheon of the thirteen primary Olympian gods and goddesses, along with their various symbols (e.g., a trident for Poseidon, an owl for Athena). Family relationships should also be noted. The poster can be displayed during the fair. In addition, students might be assigned the roles of the various Olympians, to portray during the fair. A student should dress as his or her role, carrying appropriate props and preparing a brief one-paragraph self-introduction with which to greet visitors. Next, working in pairs, students should select a favorite Greek myth, summarize it, and create a black-and-white illustration. These will be collected, photocopied, and stapled together for visitors to take home. *(4–5 class periods)*

YOU WILL NEED:
- encyclopedias
- colored pencils or markers
- posterboard
- atlas
- books of mythology
- drawing paper
- photocopier (optional)

CONNECT TO **SCIENCE** Greece is a barren and rocky country, much of it desolate and dry, with relatively little arable land. Yet the feasts of ancient Greece are legendary, and myths tell of foods coveted by gods and mortals alike. Students should use reference books to find out what the ancient Greeks ate. How did they satisfy their nutritional needs with the resources available to them? (For example, olive trees yielded oil as well as fruit; goats provided meat, milk, and cheese.) Students should make a list of these foodstuffs. Next, they should organize them in a "food pyramid" large enough so that drawings of the foods may be included. In addition, on an 8½" by 11" sheet of paper, they should make up a decorative menu for a Greek festival and photocopy it for visitors to take along. *(2–3 class periods)*

YOU WILL NEED:
- books of Greek history
- posterboard
- colored pens and pencils
- food-pyramid example
- photocopier

CONNECT TO **MATHEMATICS** The ancient Greeks applied rigorous mathematical ideals to architecture. The peripteral temple—having a colonnade on four sides—was developed in the seventh century B.C. Provide students with pictures and measurements of the most famous such temple, the Parthenon. On graph paper they should make a floor plan that represents the temple, using circles for the columns. Ask them to consider the following points: What is meant by *symmetry*? How is this temple symmetrical? Next, share with them the formula for classical proportions of column placement: x represents each of the short sides of the temple, and $2x + 1$ represents each of the long sides. How does this apply to the Parthenon? Is x an even or an odd number? What effect does this fact have on the symmetry of the temple when viewed from the front? Students should display their plans and answers to the questions, along with pictures of the temples. *(2–4 class periods)*

YOU WILL NEED:
- reference photos of the Parthenon
- graph paper
- rulers and circle templates

Book of African Empires

OVERVIEW

For more than 1,000 years—from the rise of the Ghana Empire in the fourth century until the fall of the Songhai Empire in 1591—the area surrounding the present-day African nation of Mali was dominated by powerful empires. Bordered by the continent's famous Gold Coast and comprising trade routes that reached to Europe and Asia, these empires were centers of economy, scholarship, and culture.

Research Questions

• What kingdoms and empires once dominated West Africa?

• What were their greatest natural and cultural resources?

Investigation The class will act as a team to produce a book about the empires and kingdoms of West Africa. Students will work together to generate articles, locate images, and lay out the final product. The book will include descriptions of the cultural history of the area, detailed maps, information about gold (the base of this area's historical wealth), and estimates of distances traveled by merchants and scholars. If possible, students should use a scanner and a word-processing program with a desktop publishing program. Otherwise, students may simply assemble and then photocopy the various components. The project may be bound using a three-hole punch and ribbon, or simply secured with staples.

Wrap-up Enough copies should be made so that each student may have his or her own book. In addition, students may wish to distribute books in other classrooms, and to leave copies on display in the school library. If possible, the class might visit a book bindery or printing studio, or have a professional writer visit the classroom.

 Links and Extended Reading
www.mcdougallittell.com

 LaserLinks: Background
Cultural Connection
Historical Connection

OBJECTIVES

❑ research and write about the empires of historical West Africa

❑ create maps that show the range of each empire

❑ describe the properties and uses of gold

❑ represent distances traveled by visitors and tradespeople

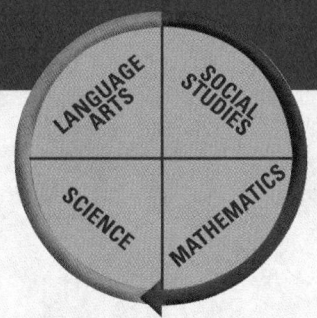

Team Teaching Assignments

CONNECT TO LANGUAGE ARTS Students should use reference books and the Internet to learn about the people and culture of these African empires. Students might be divided into four teams. One team will research groups key to the development of this region, such as the Arabs, the Almoravids, the Tuareg, and the Mandingos. Another will explore the importance of trade, including the extent of trade routes for salt and gold. Another will investigate the arrival of Islam and its impact on learning, art, and architecture. The fourth team will focus on the significance of Timbuktu as a center of trade and scholarship. Working in pairs, students should read what they can find about their subject. Next, they should write a feature article summarizing their findings. They might include images and intriguing facts about their area of research. *(4–5 class periods)*

YOU WILL NEED:
- Web access (optional)
- reference books
- notebook

CONNECT TO SOCIAL STUDIES The groups that ruled the area around present-day Mali changed over the centuries, as did their range and number. First, students should carefully draw a map of Africa, including geographical features such as lakes and rivers. They may wish to use graph paper for greater accuracy. Next, they should make one photocopy of the map for each kingdom they choose to explore. (A basic exploration might cover the empires of Ghana, Mali, and Songhai.) On each photocopy, students should label a particular kingdom and indicate its area. Approximate dates and a key would be helpful. Along with these maps, students might find it interesting to include in their book a map of Africa today. *(3–4 class periods)*

YOU WILL NEED:
- atlas
- reference books
- photocopier or scanner
- markers

CONNECT TO SCIENCE Gold has been a source of wealth in West Africa for centuries. Some scholars believe that gold, which has been valued since prehistoric times, was the first metal used by humans. Why have people found it so versatile? Students should do research to learn what makes this element unique. Why have people known it to be useful that gold is *chemically inactive*? What does it mean to say that gold is *ductile*? Why do the makers of jewelry and coins like the fact that gold is *malleable*? In what form is gold found? If possible, examine samples of gold wire and gold leaf, from art- or craft-supply stores. Students should compile their findings in a list of facts about gold and its properties. They may wish to accompany it with a list of uses to which gold was put in West Africa. *(1–2 class periods)*

YOU WILL NEED:
- reference books
- paper and pencils
- (optional) gold wire or gold leaf

CONNECT TO MATHEMATICS By the Middle Ages, the empires of this area were a center of trade across the African continent as well as into Europe, the Near East, and Asia. Today, it can take travelers a great deal of time by plane to reach Mali. However, many people visited that area centuries ago, when travel was far more difficult. Ask students to use a map and map scale to measure the distance between Timbuktu and a specific point on the African coast. Then consider: If a dromedary camel carrying a rider can travel an average of 100 miles a day, how long would it take someone to reach Timbuktu from that point? Have students calculate various round-trip distances and compile their findings in a chart called "Traveling to Timbuktu." *(1–2 class periods)*

YOU WILL NEED:
- atlas
- graph paper or plain paper
- rulers and calculators

Wondrous Worlds

There are worlds within and worlds without. In Unit Four, students will read about both kinds. Part 1, "Animal Wonders," introduces some animals, both exotic and ordinary, who open people's eyes to the wonders of nature. Part 2, "Imaginary Worlds," takes readers on a journey to the most exciting place of all—their own imaginations!

——— Part 1 ———

Animal Wonders Anyone who has ever loved an animal or wondered how the birds know when it is time to fly south will be enchanted by the selections in Part 1. "Lob's Girl" tells the story of an amazing pet who forever enriches the life of an entire family. These selections take the reader into worlds they may never have known existed.

——— Part 2 ———

Imaginary Worlds The worlds we create inside our heads may be the best of all, because in the imagination, anything is possible! Milo, the main character of the charming drama *The Phantom Tollbooth*, drives through a mysterious tollbooth that takes him to a land where words and numbers are more important than he ever dreamed possible.

WONDROUS WORLDS

In books,

I have traveled not

only to other worlds,

but into my own.

ANNA QUINDLEN
American journalist

Party Animals, Julia Lucich.
Pastel over acrylic, 17" × 22".

440

 Mini Lesson ## Viewing and Representing

Party Animals
by Julia Lucich

ART APPRECIATION

Instruction Explain that while the giraffes in this painting are very realistic looking in one way, they are fantastic looking in another way. Who has ever seen a blue or red giraffe? The artist explains, "If I had just used brown and tan, it might have been boring. Their astonishing shapes and contours seemed to cry out for a dif- ferent approach. . . . Sometimes we all wish that the world was more vibrant, filled with more fun and enthusiasm."

Ask: What do you notice about the background of the painting? Why do you think the painter chose to show it this way?

Possible Response: While the giraffes are shown very clearly, the background is hazy. The giraffes appear to be standing in weeds or grass. The background leaves a lot to the imagination.

To help students explore the connections between the art, the quotation, and the unit theme, have them consider the following questions:

Ask: What are some of the wonders of the world that amaze you? Why?

Possible Response: Students' responses will vary, but should provide reasons why they think these wonders are so fascinating.

Ask: How would you paraphrase the quotation by Anna Quindlen on page 440?

Possible Response: Books are a way to learn about the outside world and also a way to learn about yourself.

Ask: What do you think the giraffes in the painting are doing? What might they be looking at?

Possible Response: They may be looking for food or watching to make sure no enemies are nearby.

Ask: What kinds of stories and experiences might you expect to read about in a unit called "Wondrous Worlds"?

Possible Response: You might expect to read about some unusual things that have happened and some strange creatures. You might also read fantasies—stories set in places that exist only in the imagination.

441

Features and Selections	Literary Analysis	Reading and Critical Thinking	Writing Opportunities		
Wondrous Worlds **Animal Wonders**					
Learning the Language of Literature Plot	Plot, 443				
The Active Reader Skills and Strategies		Recognizing Cause and Effect, 446			
SHORT STORY Lob's Girl **Difficulty Level:** *Challenging*	Foreshadowing, 447, 448, 450, 456, 458, 459 Mood, 459	Cause and Effect, 447, 448, 450, 452, 456, 458, 459 Informal Assessment, 452 Standardized Test Practice, 460	Dog Care Instructions, 460 Pros-and-Cons Chart, 460 Newspaper Article, 460		
Real World Link Animals to the Rescue		Magazine Article: Making Judgements, 463			
ESSAY My First Dive with the Dolphins **Difficulty Level:** *Average*	Essay, 465, 466, 473 Specialized Language, 473	Making Generalizations, 465, 466, 473 Activity, 473 Standardized Test Practice, 471	New Point of View, 474 Time Line, 474		
POETRY Something Told the Wild Geese Questioning Faces **Difficulty Level:** *Average*	Sound Devices, 476, 478, 479	Word Choice, 476, 478, 479 Standardized Test Practice, 478	Field Diary, 480 Rhyming Couplets, 480		
SHORT STORY Zlateh the Goat **Difficulty Level:** *Average* **Building Vocabulary** **Literary Link** Chang McTang McQuarter Cat	Climax and Resolution, 481, 482, 486, 488	Story Mapping, 481, 482, 484, 486, 488 Activity, 488 Standardized Test Practice, 489	Persuasive Argument, 489 Dialogue with Zlateh, 489		
Writing Workshop: Process Description **Assessment Practice**		Analyzing a Student Model, 501	Writing Your Process Description, 503		

UNIT FOUR
PART 2 SKILLS TRACE

Imaginary Worlds					
Learning the Language of Literature Science Fiction and Fantasy	Science Fiction and Fantasy, 507				
The Active Reader Skills and Strategies		Visualizing, 511			

LEGEND   DLS – Daily Language SkillBuilder   Green type – Teacher's Edition

Features and Selections	Literary Analysis	Reading and Critical Thinking	Writing Opportunities	
DRAMA **The Phantom Tollbooth** Difficulty Level: *Challenging* Literary Link **All That Is Gold**	Fantasy, 512, 514, 518, 530, 546, 552	Visualizing, 512, 514, 526, 538, 552 Activity, 552 Standardized Test Practice, 530, 550 Informal Assessment, 539, 546 **TAAS READING OBJ. 1, 2, 4** **TAAS WRITING OBJ. 1, 2, 3, 4**	Plot Analysis, 553 Fantasy Word Play, 553	
POETRY **The Walrus and the Carpenter** **Fairy Lullaby,** *from* A **Midsummer Night's Dream** Difficulty Level: *Challenging*	Realistic and Fantastic Details, 555, 556, 561 Review: Narrative Poetry, 561	Visualizing, 555, 556, 561 Comparing Texts, 561 Standardized Test Practice, 557	Narrative Poem, 562 Eloquent Speech, 562	
POETRY **Three Limericks** Difficulty Level: *Easy* **Building Vocabulary**	Poetic Form: Limerick, 563, 564, 566 Review: Rhythm, 566	Reading Aloud, 563, 564, 566 Standardized Test Practice, 565	Limerick Retelling, 567 Your Own Limericks, 567	
COMPARING LITERATURE **Science Fiction**	Science Fiction, 572	Points of Comparison, 573	Comparison-and-Contrast Essay, 573	
SHORT STORY **The Fun They Had** Difficulty Level: *Easy*	Setting, 574, 576, 579	Purposes for Reading, 574, 576, 579 Informal Assessment, 578		
SHORT STORY **The Sand Castle** Difficulty Level: *Average*	Setting, 580, 582, 585	Compare and Contrast, 580, 582, 585 Informal Assessment, 584	Movie Outline, 586 Futuristic Setting Description, 586	
Comparing Literature: Assessment Practice		Reading the Prompt, 587	Planning a Comparison-and-Contrast Essay, 587	
Real World Link **Home on an Icy Planet**		Taking Notes and Outlining Ideas, 589		
Writing Workshop: Short Story Assessment Practice		Analyzing a Student Model, 593	Writing Your Short Story, 595	
Reflect and Assess	Analyzing Plot Structure, 599 Analyzing Fantasy and Science Fiction Elements, 599		Judging Impact, 598 Analyzing the Theme, 598 Thinking About Genre, 598 Building Your Portfolio, 599	

LEGEND   DLS – Daily Language SkillBuilder   Green type – Teacher's Edition

To introduce the theme of this unit, use Fine Art Transparencies T28–30 in the Communications Transparencies and Copymasters.

	Unit Resource Book	Assessment	Integrated Technology and Media	Additional Support — Literary Analysis Transparencies
Lob's Girl *pp. 447–461*	• Summary p. 4 • Active Reading p. 5 • Literary Analysis p. 6 • Words to Know p. 7 • Grammar p. 8 • Spelling p. 9 • Selection Quiz p. 10	• Selection Test, Formal Assessment pp. 79–80 Test Generator	Audio Library	• Foreshadowing T27
My First Dive with the Dolphins *pp. 465–475*	• Summary p. 11 • Active Reading p. 12 • Literary Analysis p. 13 • Words to Know p. 14 • Grammar p. 15 • Spelling p. 16 • Selection Quiz p. 17	• Selection Test, Formal Assessment pp. 81–82 Test Generator	Audio Library LaserLinks, Teacher's SourceBook p. 37 Research Starter www.mcdougallittell.com	
Something Told the Wild Geese **Questioning Faces** *pp. 476–480*	• Active Reading p. 18 • Literary Analysis p. 19	• Selection Test, Formal Assessment pp. 83–84 Test Generator	Audio Library LaserLinks, Teacher's SourceBook p. 38 Research Starter www.mcdougallittell.com	• Poetry: Sound Devices T20
Zlateh the Goat *pp. 481–490*	• Summary p. 20 • Active Reading p. 21 • Literary Analysis p. 22 • Words to Know p. 23 • Grammar p. 24 • Spelling p. 25 • Selection Quiz p. 26	• Selection Test, Formal Assessment pp. 85–86 Test Generator	Audio Library LaserLinks, Teacher's SourceBook p. 39	• Conflict T8

Writing Workshop: Process Description

		Unit Assessment	Unit Technology	
Unit Four Resource Book • Prewriting p. 28 • Drafting and Elaboration p. 29 • Peer Response Guide pp. 30–31 • Revising, Editing, and Proofreading p. 32 • Student Models pp. 33–35 • Rubric for Evaluation p. 36	**Writing Coach** **Writing Transparencies** T1–4, T6, T9, T31 **Grammar Transparencies and Copymasters** C112 **Teacher's Guide to Assessment and Portfolio Use**	• Unit Four, Part 1 Test, Formal Assessment pp. 87–89 Test Generator • Unit Four Integrated Test, Integrated Assessment pp. 19–24	ClassZone www.mcdougallittell.com Electronic Teacher Tools	

Reading and Critical Thinking Transparencies	Grammar Transparencies and Copymasters	Vocabulary Transparencies and Copymasters	Writing Transparencies	Communications Transparencies and Copymasters
• Cause and Effect T5	• Daily Language SkillBuilder T14 • Sentence Variety with Prepositional Phrases C105 • Identifying Prepositions and Their Objects C101	• Context Clues C46 • Learning and Remembering New Words C47	• Transitional Words and Phrases T9	
• Making Generalizations T14 • Main Idea and Supporting Details T25	• Daily Language SkillBuilder T15 • Combining Sentences Using Conjunctions C111 • Identifying Conjunctions C109	• Using a Dictionary: Guide Words C48 • Word Parts: Root Words and Base Words T6	• Point of View T23 • Locating Information Using the Internet T47 • Combining Sentences Using Conjunctions T19	• Appreciative Listening T2 • Impromptu Speaking: Dialogue, Role-Play T13
• Analyzing Word Choice T15	• Daily Language SkillBuilder T15		• Sensory Word List T16 • Locating Information Using the Internet T45	
• Summarizing Story Map T13	• Daily Language SkillBuilder T16 • Punctuating Appositives C125	• Using Compare and Contrast Clues C49	• Dialogue T24 • Figurative Language and Sound Devices T17	• Reading Aloud T11

STUDENTS ACQUIRING ENGLISH

The **Spanish Study Guide,** pp. 91–105, includes language support for the following pages:
• Family and Community Involvement (per unit)

• Selection Summaries and Vocabulary
• Active Reading
• Literary Analysis

UNIT FOUR
RESOURCE MANAGEMENT GUIDE
PART 2

To introduce the theme of this unit, use Fine Art Transparencies T28–30 in the Communications Transparencies and Copymasters.

Additional Support

	Unit Resource Book	Assessment	Integrated Technology and Media	Literary Analysis Transparencies
The Phantom Tollbooth *pp. 512–554*	• Summary p. 37 • Active Reading p. 38 • Literary Analysis p. 39 • Words to Know p. 40 • Grammar p. 41 • Spelling p. 42 • Selection Quiz p. 43	• Selection Test, Formal Assessment pp. 89–90 Test Generator	Audio Library	• Drama: Stage Directions T23
The Walrus and the Carpenter **Fairy Lullaby,** *from* **A Midsummer Night's Dream** *pp . 555–562*	• Active Reading p. 44 • Literary Analysis p. 45	• Selection Test, Formal Assessment pp. 91–92 Test Generator	Audio Library LaserLinks, Teacher's SourceBook p. 42	
Three Limericks *pp. 563–567*	• Active Reading p. 46 • Literary Analysis p. 47	• Selection Test, Formal Assessment pp. 93–94 Test Generator	Audio Library	• Form in Poetry: Rhyme and Meter T17
The Fun They Had *pp. 574–579*	• Summary p. 49 • Active Reading p. 50 • Literary Analysis p. 51 • Words to Know p. 52 • Grammar p. 53 • Spelling p. 54 • Selection Quiz p. 55	• Selection Test, Formal Assessment pp. 95–96 Test Generator	Audio Library LaserLinks, Teacher's SourceBook p. 43	• Setting T6
The Sand Castle *pp. 580–586*	• Summary p. 56 • Active Reading p. 57 • Literary Analysis p. 58 • Words to Know p. 59 • Grammar p. 60 • Spelling p. 61 • Selection Quiz p. 62	• Selection Test, Formal Assessment pp. 97–98 Test Generator	Audio Library	• Setting T6

Writing Workshop: Short Story

Unit Four Resource Book
• Prewriting p. 64
• Drafting and Elaboration p. 65
• Peer Response Guide pp. 66–67
• Revising, Editing, and Proofreading p. 68
• Student Models pp. 69–71
• Rubric for Evaluation p. 72

Writing Coach

Writing Transparencies T1–4, T23, T34

Grammar Transparencies and Copymasters C64, C127

Teacher's Guide to Assessment and Portfolio Use

Unit Assessment

• Unit Four, Part 2 Test, Formal Assessment pp. 99–100
Test Generator
• Unit Four Integrated Test, Integrated Assessment pp. 19–24

Unit Technology

ClassZone www.mcdougallittell.com
Electronic Teacher Tools

Reading and Critical Thinking Transparencies	Grammar Transparencies and Copymasters	Vocabulary Transparencies and Copymasters	Writing Transparencies	Communications Transparencies and Copymasters
• Visualizing T4 • Summarizing (Story Map) T13	• Daily Language SkillBuilder T16 • Identifying Adverb Phrases and the Words They Modify C104 • Identifying Adjective Phrases and the Words They Modify C103 • Using Commas to Prevent Misreading C123 • Punctuating Prepositional Phrases C126	• Word Parts: Prefixes and Suffixes C50 • Synonyms C51 • Denotation and Connotation C52 • Using Context Clues C53 • Homonyms and Homophones C54 • Prefixes and Suffixes C55 • Commonly Confused Homophones C56	• Locating Information Using Print Resources T45	• Impromptu Speaking: Dialogue, Role-Play T13 • Dramatic Reading T12
• Visualizing T4	• Daily Language SkillBuilder T17	• Using Antonyms C57	• Figurative Language and Sound Devices T17 • Effective Language T15	• Dramatic Reading T12 • Evaluation Matrix: Entertainment T5
	• Daily Language SkillBuilder T17 • Humor with Adjective Phrases C108			
• Setting Purpose T16	• Daily Language SkillBuilder T18 • Adverb Phrases That Show Time C106	• Context Clues: Definition and Restatement C58		
• Compare and Contrast T17	• Daily Language SkillBuilder T18 • Identifying Prepositions and Their Objects T102	• Word Parts C59	• Showing, Not Telling T22 • Using an Outline T54 • Comparison and Contrast Essay T29	• Interviewing T9

STUDENTS ACQUIRING ENGLISH

The **Spanish Study Guide,** pp. 106–120, includes language support for the following pages:
• Family and Community Involvement (per unit)
• Selection Summaries and Vocabulary
• Active Reading
• Literary Analysis

Selection	SkillBuilder Sentences	Suggested Answers
Lob's Girl	1. A dog would be a good pet for my brother and I. 2. Animals can provide protection and love for we.	1. A dog would be a good pet for my brother and **me.** 2. Animals can provide protection and love for **us.**
My First Dive with the Dolphins	1. Did you knew that dolphins has distinct personalities? 2. Researchers have discovers that some dolphins is aggressive, while others are quite playful.	1. Did you **know** that dolphins **have** distinct personalities? 2. Researchers have **discovered** that some dolphins **are** aggressive, while others are quite playful.
Something Told the Wild Geese Questioning Faces	1. I've always wondered how birds could fly so good. 2. I wanted to call the veterinarian, because the baby bird didn't sound so well.	1. I've always wondered how birds could fly so **well.** 2. I wanted to call the veterinarian, because the baby bird didn't sound so **good.**

Selection	SkillBuilder Sentences	Suggested Answers
Zlateh the Goat	1. The families goat was named Zlateh	1. The **family's** goat was named Zlateh.
	2. The goats production of milk had become very small.	2. The **goat's** production of milk had become very small.
The Phantom Tollbooth	1. Mom's car gets worser gas mileage than Milo's toy car.	1. Mom's car gets **worse** gas mileage than Milo's toy car.
	2. "The Phantom Tollbooth" is the excitingest and goodest play that I have ever read.	2. "The Phantom Tollbooth" is the **most exciting** and **best** play that I have ever read.
The Walrus and the Carpenter Fairy Lullaby	1. Isn't it funny that the Walrus and the Carpenter wants seven maids with seven mops to sweep away the sand?	1. Isn't it funny that the Walrus and the Carpenter **want** seven maids with seven mops to sweep away the sand?
	2. Do you and your friends like to read poetry that are silly and nonsensical?	2. Do you and your friends like to read poetry that **is** silly and nonsensical?

Selection	SkillBuilder Sentences	Suggested Answers
Three Limericks	1. Even though limericks are silly, them must conform to a definite rhyme scheme.	1. Even though limericks are silly, **they** must conform to a definite rhyme scheme.
	2. Shakespeare wrote poems, but he is best known for him plays.	2. Shakespeare wrote poems, but he is best known for **his** plays.
The Fun They Had	1. We will all be living in the future very soonly.	1. We will all be living in the future very **soon.**
	2. Computers can process information quite rapid.	2. Computers can process information quite **rapidly.**
The Sand Castle	1. "I think it would be great fun to have a computer for a teacher laughed Samuel.	1. "I think it would be great fun to have a computer for a teacher," laughed Samuel.
	2. Some day, said Marianne I'd like to build a time travel machine.	2. "Some day," said Marianne, "I'd like to build a time travel machine."

	Unit One	Unit Two	Unit Three	Unit Four	Unit Five	Unit Six
Grammar Focus by Unit	The Sentence and Its Parts	Nouns, Pronouns, and Verbs	Modifiers	Phrases	Compound and Complex Sentences	Review

The Language of Literature offers several options for integrating grammar instruction and literature.

- Each unit has a specific grammar focus. The grammar focus for this unit is highlighted on the planning chart. Categories of grammar skills for this unit are shown in red.
- The Pupil's Edition includes instructive features entitled *Grammar in Context*. The instruction in these features arises from the selections and relates to the grammar focus for each unit.
- The Writing Workshops in the Pupil's Edition include grammar tips that help the students produce error-free drafts.
- Mini Lessons in the Teacher's Edition complement the instruction in the *Grammar in Context* features. Additional Mini Lessons relate to the grammar focus for each unit as well as to the literature.
- Daily Language SkillBuilders in the Teacher's Edition provide students with ongoing proofreading practice and reinforce punctuation, spelling, grammar and usage, and capitalization.
- Grammar Copymasters and Transparencies, which may be used independently or in conjunction with the Mini Lessons in the Teacher's Edition, present grammar in a traditional, systematic sequence.

PE instruction shown in black
TE Mini Lessons shown in green

Part 1

THE SENTENCE AND ITS PARTS
Appositives and Appositive Phrases
"Zlateh the Goat," p. 490

PREPOSITIONS, CONJUNCTIONS, INTERJECTIONS
Sentence Variety with Prepositional Phrases
"Lob's Girl," p. 456

Using Prepositional Phrases as Transitions
"Lob's Girl," p. 461
Identifying Prepositions and Their Objects
"Lob's Girl," p. 461
Combining Sentences Using Conjunctions
"My First Dive with the Dolphins," p. 470

Combining Sentences by Joining Phrases
"My First Dive with the Dolphins," p. 475
Identifying Conjunctions
"My First Dive with the Dolphins," p. 475

Transitional Words and Phrases
Writing Workshop, p. 504
Transitional Words and Phrases
Assessment Practice, p. 505

PUNCTUATION
Punctuating Appositives
"Zlateh the Goat," p. 490

Part 2

THE SENTENCE AND ITS PARTS
Parts of Speech
"The Walrus and the Carpenter/Fairy Lullaby," p. 562

Appositive Phrases
Writing Workshop, p. 596
Appositive Phrases
Assessment Practice, p. 597

PREPOSITIONS, CONJUNCTIONS, INTERJECTIONS
Identifying Adverb Phrases and the Words They Modify
The Phantom Tollbooth, p. 535
Identifying Adjective Phrases and the Words They Modify
The Phantom Tollbooth, p. 540

Pinpointing with Prepositions
The Phantom Tollbooth, p. 554
Humor with Adjective Phrases
"Three Limericks," p. 567
Adverb Phrases That Show Time
"The Fun They Had," p. 577
Identifying Prepositions and Their Objects
"The Sand Castle," p. 586

PUNCTUATION
Using Commas to Prevent Misreading
The Phantom Tollbooth, p. 549
Punctuating Prepositional Phrases
The Phantom Tollbooth, p. 554
Punctuating, Choosing, and Incorporating Quotations
Writing Workshop, p. 596

OVERVIEW

Students explore imaginative worlds and characters by working in small groups to produce and perform original skits for an audience.

Project at a glance Many of the selections in Unit Four focus on fantastic worlds and characters (especially Part 2, Imaginary Worlds). For this project, students will write and act in skits that are set in a futuristic or fantastic world. Skits may be humorous or serious. All skits will be performed in front of a live audience and should be complete with costumes, scenery, and props (insofar as they are practical). This project might be coordinated with a schoolwide Talent Show, or the skits might be scheduled for a time when families can be invited to watch.

SCHEDULING

Skits should take no more than 15 minutes each. You may want to schedule the skits over the course of this unit, or at the end of this unit, depending on your purposes.

PROJECT OBJECTIVES

- To demonstrate the speaking and listening skills introduced in the activity
- To explore the theme of imagination through characters in a dramatic script
- To plan, prepare, and present an original skit
- To develop listening and viewing skills by watching and evaluating the performance of others

SUGGESTED GROUP SIZE

4–6 students per group

Dramatization

Getting Started

Explain that students will be working in groups to plan, write, and act out skits that are set in futuristic or fantastic worlds. You might ask students to make a list of TV shows that deal with science fiction or fantastic characters, worlds, or details.

Use the resources in your school. Invite your school's drama teacher or a volunteer from a local theater group to a few rehearsals. If students will be painting props, make arrangements for materials with your school's art teacher. Also consider borrowing musical instruments from your music department.

If your school has an auditorium, schedule time for each group to hold at least one dress rehearsal. If the skits are to take place in the classroom, arrange for side screens or curtains where students can go "off-stage" during performances.

This project lends itself to everything from a classroom to a schoolwide performance. You may even want to schedule an evening show and sell tickets to give students experience in advertising, sales, and management.

Writing Workshop Connection

As a springboard, students may use the Writing Workshop assignment **Short Story**, p. 506, which they will complete in Part 2.

Directing the Project

Preparing (1 class period) Discuss all that is needed in a theatrical production. Remind students that skits should follow the general format of exposition, conflict, and resolution.

▶ Divide students into groups. Each group should brainstorm ideas about the focus of their skit. You may want to have them create main characters who must solve a problem. When they have developed an idea, individual assignments can be made. Encourage everyone to contribute to the writing and acting, as well as to the behind-the-scenes duties. Entrances, exits, and other movements should be indicated in the scripts.

Assigning Roles In addition to individual character roles, you may want to choose a director, stage manager, acting coach, costume designer, and prop person (or people).

▶ After students have done the preliminary planning, they should submit a list and description of characters, and a plot summary. Meet with each group to discuss the scenario before students begin writing. Attend two or more rehearsals for the skit to offer advice and note progress.

▶ You should also work with students to create a set of guidelines for evaluation (i.e.

What Makes a Good Skit) to be filled out after the final performances.

Practicing (1 class period) Have each group read their parts aloud several times to make sure they understand the words and events of the plot. Then stage a walk-through, in which they perform their movements, gestures, and facial expressions as they say their lines. Students should do a final rehearsal using the actual props, lighting, and so on.

▶ Tell students that giving and receiving feedback during the rehearsal stage is crucial. Refer to the tips in the Feedback Center.

Presenting (2–3 class periods) This project could culminate in a Talent Show for the entire student body or just for your class.

▶ To begin, have students take a few deep breaths. Make sure props are in place and that there is adequate seating.

▶ **EVALUATION** Have student audience members complete a brief evaluation after each performance, as well as complete evaluations of their own performances. These should be turned in to you at the end of each performance and can be used for later discussion.

Teaching the Speaking and Listening Skills

The student is expected to:

Analyze the use of aesthetic language for its effects

Teaching Suggestions: Discuss with students how language can be used to create certain effects on an audience. Explain how certain words, phrasings, and rhyme patterns are pleasing to the ear, while others create a sense of disharmony. Also discuss how metaphors, similes, and other forms of figurative language can create pictures in an audience's mind. Have students incorporate these elements into their scripts. For more information, have students turn to the Communication Handbook, page R102.

Generate criteria to evaluate presentations of others and generate criteria to evaluate his/her own presentations

Teaching Suggestions: Tell students that before they perform their skits, they must develop a set of guidelines to evaluate their own as well as others' performances. Ask for suggestions about what makes an effective skit—in particular, notes about voice, delivery, pacing, and so on. From this discussion, you can create worksheets for students to use during the final performances. It will also be helpful to have students rate their own performances according to these guidelines.

Compare perceptions with perceptions of others

Teaching Suggestions: After each group has presented and has been evaluated by the class, have students compare their self-evaluations with the evaluations given by others. To do this, you might want to set a list of standards for discussion and explain what is meant by "constructive criticism." This might work best if you act as moderator.

Feedback Center

Students can use the following guidelines when giving and receiving feedback during this project:

Giving Feedback

▶ Provide feedback about the story idea (Does the story make sense?).

▶ Question the characters' tone and motivation (Are they appropriate to the subject?).

▶ Comment on the verbal and nonverbal delivery (pitch, pace, volume, body language) and its impact on the listener.

Receiving Feedback

▶ Listen to constructive criticism with an open mind.

▶ Use audience feedback and modify the presentation to clarify meaning or organization.

 Assessing the Project

The following rubric can be used for group or individual assessment.

3 *Full Accomplishment*

The group followed directions and produced a creative and engaging skit set in a futuristic or fantastic world. Group used aesthetic language effectively in their skit. Students evaluated their own performance as well as the performance of others and demonstrated thoughtful reflection on strengths and weaknesses. Students demonstrated all three of the Speaking and Listening Skills listed.

2 *Substantial Accomplishment*

Students produced a skit, but the script is incomplete. It shows some use of futuristic or fantastic elements and some use of aesthetic language. Two out of the three Speaking and Listening Skills were demonstrated.

1 *Little Accomplishment*

Students' script and skit are incomplete or do not fulfill the requirements of the assignment. Students did not work effectively in a group and demonstrated only one of the Speaking and Listening Skills.

Reflecting on the Theme What animals are you most curious about? Some people find it fascinating to watch birds at a bird feeder or squirrels in the park. Many pet owners will tell you that their pet is one of their best friends. The question of how animals contribute to our world and to our lives intrigues many writers.

LEARNING the Language of *Literature*

*P*lot

I have a notebook for plots. . . . If I get the germ of an idea, I scribble it in the notebook. . . . Perhaps after three years, perhaps after seven, there comes a time when I look at it and I see that it is ripe for writing.

—Roald Dahl, writer

Plots can be found in all types of stories—fiction, drama, biography, even narrative poetry. The **plot** of a story is a series of events. For writer Roald Dahl, good plots don't just "happen." Sometimes they can take years to develop! That is because the elements of a plot must fit together like pieces of a puzzle.

In the **exposition,** or the beginning of a plot, the stage is set. The characters and setting are introduced. Then the **rising action** begins— there is usually a conflict that the main character must face. Suspense builds and events move toward a **climax,** which is the turning point in the story. The climax occurs and leads to the **falling action** (sometimes called *resolution*), in which loose ends are tied up.

PLOT AT A GLANCE

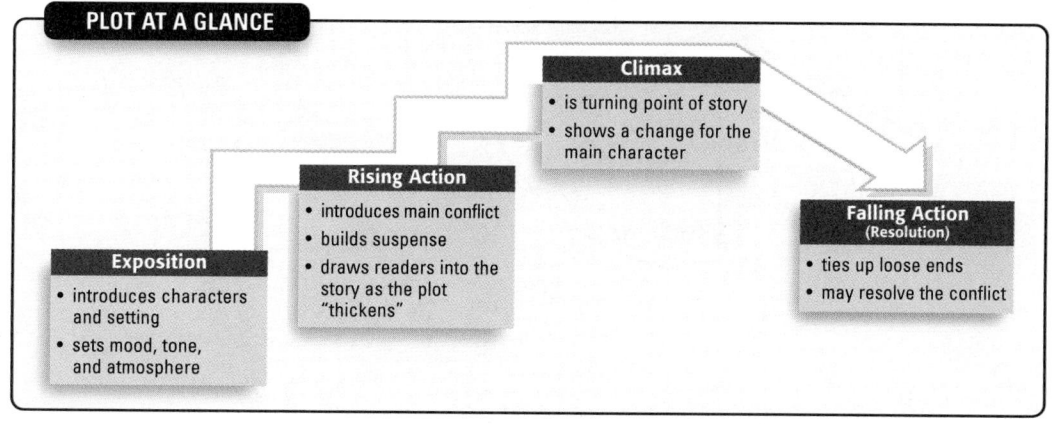

Climax
- is turning point of story
- shows a change for the main character

Rising Action
- introduces main conflict
- builds suspense
- draws readers into the story as the plot "thickens"

Exposition
- introduces characters and setting
- sets mood, tone, and atmosphere

Falling Action (Resolution)
- ties up loose ends
- may resolve the conflict

OVERVIEW

Objectives
- understand and identify the following literary terms:
  plot
  exposition
  rising action
  climax
  falling action
  resolution
  story structure
  conflict
  sequence of events
  external conflict
  internal conflict
  change
- recognize and analyze story plot, setting, and problem resolution
- analyze characters, including their traits, conflicts, and the changes they undergo

 Use **Literary Analysis Transparencies,** pp. 3, 5, 6, 8, 12, for additional support.

Teaching the Lesson

This lesson helps students understand the concept of plot by analyzing its basic elements through text and visual aids.

Introducing the Concepts
Have students think of a film they have recently seen or a book they have recently read. Ask them to identify the central conflict of the work, its climax, and the falling action, or resolution of the conflict. Using the chart on this page as a model, ask volunteers to chart their responses on the board.

Presenting the Concepts
Sequence of Events

Divide students into small groups. Have each group think of a cause-effect relationship that they could center a story or essay around. Ask them to discuss the possible sequence of events and details surrounding this relationship. Some ideas for a cause-effect relationship might be missing the bus to school, forgetting lunch money, or not doing homework. Have each group share their responses with the class.

YOUR TURN
Answer: Robert fools with his beard during rehearsal.

Sequence of Events

Every story has a **story structure.** The plot moves from the introduction of the **conflict** to the **resolution** through a **sequence of events.** These events are usually written in the order in which they happen. They often have a cause-and-effect relationship. The event that happens first is the cause, and the one that follows is the effect.

YOUR TURN Look at the story wheel below for one scene in "The School Play" by Gary Soto. What event causes Mrs. Bunnin to scold Robert?

From "The School Play"

1. Mrs. Bunnin brings a box of props into the classroom.
2. Robert tries on the red beard that Mrs. Bunnin gives him.
3. Robert sneezes.
4. Robert and Belinda rehearse their lines.
5. Robert fools with his beard during rehearsal.
6. Mrs. Bunnin scolds Robert.

444 UNIT FOUR   PART 1: ANIMAL WONDERS

Conflict

Conflict is a struggle or clash between opposing forces. Nearly every story revolves around a conflict. A conflict may involve something the main character wants and cannot get, or it might center on a problem the main character is trying to solve. Conflict may be **external**—a struggle between a character and an outside force, such as nature or another character. Conflict may also be **internal**—a struggle between opposing desires within a character.

YOUR TURN In the excerpt at right, what does Pythias want? What is standing in his way?

> ### CONFLICT
>
> **Pythias.** I'm worried about what will happen to my mother and my sister when I'm gone.
> **Damon.** I'll take care of them, Pythias, as if they were my own mother and sister.
> **Pythias.** Thank you, Damon. I have money to leave them. But there are other things I must arrange. If only I could go to see them before I die! But they live two days' journey from here, you know.
>
> —Fan Kissen, *Damon and Pythias*

Change

By the end of a story, often a character or a character's situation has changed as a result of an experience. You can learn about the author's perspective and purpose for writing by looking at the **change** that has taken place in a story and determining what events caused the change.

YOUR TURN In this excerpt, how did Helen Keller change? What do you think caused this change?

> ### CHANGE
>
> I left the well-house eager to learn. Everything had a name, and each name gave birth to a new thought. As we returned to the house every object which I touched seemed to quiver with life. That was because I saw everything with the strange, new sight that had come to me. On entering the door I remembered the doll I had broken. I felt my way to the hearth and picked up the pieces. I tried vainly to put them together. Then my eyes filled with tears; for I realized what I had done, and for the first time I felt repentance and sorrow.
>
> —Helen Keller,
> *The Story of My Life*

Conflict
Ask students to discuss examples of an external conflict that a character in a story might face and examples of an internal conflict that a character might face.

YOUR TURN
Possible Response: Pythias wants to see his mother and sister before he dies, but they live too far away.

Change
Have students think about stories they have read as a class and decide what kinds of changes any of the main characters underwent. Ask them to discuss what they think caused the changes in these characters. Can they determine the author's purpose from the changes the characters experienced? If so, what is it?

YOUR TURN
Possible Response: Helen Keller suddenly realized that things had names and she wanted to learn and understand. She experienced remorse and sorrow for the first time when she realized what she had done to the doll. This change was possibly caused by her new ability to communicate and understand language.

OVERVIEW

Objectives
• develop effective strategies for recognizing cause and effect.
• use the text's structure or progression of ideas such as cause and effect to locate and recall information.
• analyze ways authors organize and present ideas such as through cause and effect.

Teaching the Lesson

The strategies on this page will help students understand and recognize cause and effect in the literature they read.

Presenting the Strategies
Explain to students that the strategies on this page will help them use cause and effect as a way of understanding the events of a story or piece of nonfiction.

Signal Words
Helps students brainstorm a list of signal words that often indicate a cause and effect relationship: *because, since, therefore, in order that, if/then, so/that,* and *as a result.*

Clarify and Question
Remind students to reread any parts of a selection that are unclear and to ask questions about the sequence of events and about which events were the cause of others.

Connect
As a class, have the students discuss events in their own lives, telling what the cause and effect was in each one.

Use **Reading and Critical Thinking Transparencies,** p. 1, for additional support.

If you have ever walked into a dark room and turned on a lamp, then you understand cause and effect. Your turning on the lamp caused the room to become bright. The brightness in the room is the effect. The same can be true of events in a story. When something happens that leads to something else, the events are said to be related as cause and effect.

Recognizing Cause and Effect

How to Apply the Skill

To **recognize cause and effect,** an active reader will:
• Identify signal words that indicate cause and effect, such as *because, therefore, since,* and *so*
• **Clarify** the action by making a cause-effect chart
• **Question** what happened and why
• **Connect** the reading with personal experiences

Try It Now!
Read the excerpt below. Look for cause and effect.

> Jean Pengelly said, "Sandy, your Aunt Rebecca says she's lonesome because Uncle Will Hoskins has gone out trawling, and she wants one of you to go and spend the evening with her. You go, dear; you can take your homework with you."
>
> —Joan Aiken, "Lob's Girl"

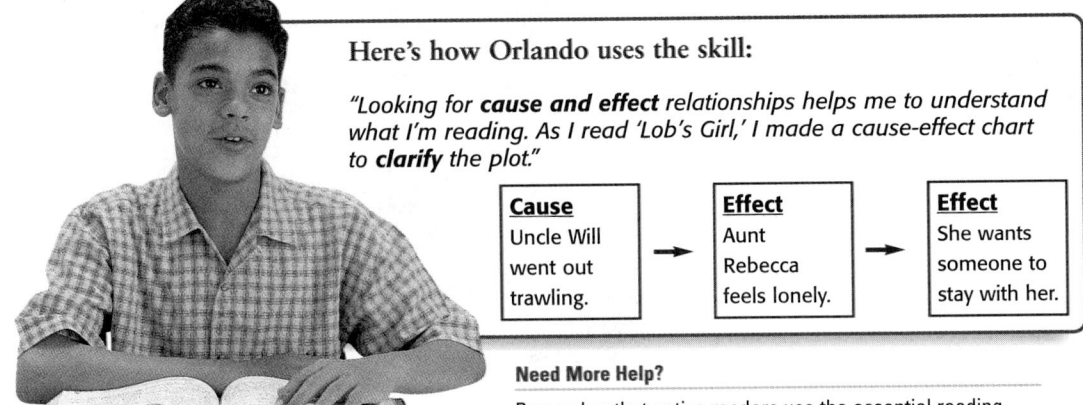

Here's how Orlando uses the skill:

*"Looking for **cause and effect** relationships helps me to understand what I'm reading. As I read 'Lob's Girl,' I made a cause-effect chart to **clarify** the plot."*

Cause	Effect	Effect
Uncle Will went out trawling.	Aunt Rebecca feels lonely.	She wants someone to stay with her.

Need More Help?

Remember that active readers use the essential reading strategies explained on page 4: • **visualize** • **predict** • **question** • **connect** • **evaluate** • **clarify** • **monitor.**

446   UNIT FOUR   PART 1: ANIMAL WONDERS

Lob's Girl

Short Story by JOAN AIKEN

"*Some people choose their dogs, and some dogs choose their people.*"

Connect to Your Life

Creature Features Have you ever witnessed a pet helping its owner in an extraordinary way? Describe what happened.

Build Background

CONNECT TO **GEOGRAPHY** The setting of this story is Cornwall, England. Cornwall is a peninsula, bordered by the Atlantic Ocean and the English Channel. The coast of Cornwall is made up of rocky cliffs.

Several of the characters in "Lob's Girl" come from Liverpool, a large city on England's western coast, about 400 miles north of Cornwall. While the harbors in Cornwall are used mainly by fishing boats, the ships that dock in Liverpool carry goods to and from England.

North Sea

UNITED KINGDOM

Liverpool

London

Atlantic Ocean

English Channel

Cornwall

Focus Your Reading

LITERARY ANALYSIS **FORESHADOWING** A technique that writers use to hint at future events in a story is called **foreshadowing**. Writers use descriptive words and events to foreshadow future outcomes and to build suspense.

For example, the narrator in "Lob's Girl" describes a "steep, twisting hillroad." This part of the setting will be important to events later in the story. As you read, note words and phrases used to foreshadow events.

ACTIVE READING **CAUSE AND EFFECT** When one event brings about another, they are said to have a **cause-and-effect** relationship. The event that happens first is the cause. The event that results from the cause is called the effect. One event may cause many things to happen. Some stories have a chain of causes and effects, in which one event causes another, which in turn causes another, and so on.

READER'S NOTEBOOK As you read "Lob's Girl," list cause-and-effect events in a chart like the one shown. Be on the lookout for events that cause more than one effect and for effects that cause other effects.

Cause	Effect(s)	Effect(s)
Lob jumps through the window.	He knocks a pudding off the windowsill.	The Pengellys hear a crash.

WORDS TO KNOW Vocabulary Preview

agitate	atone	conceal	inquire	rivet
assured	coma	draft	melancholy	transfusion

LOB'S GIRL **447**

OVERVIEW

 This selection is included in the **Grade 6 InterActive Reader.**

Objectives
1. understand and appreciate a **short story** (Literary Analysis)
2. understand the author's use of **foreshadowing** (Literary Analysis)
3. understand the use of **mood** (Literary Analysis)
4. recognize **cause and effect** to help understand foreshadowing (Active Reading)

Summary
Sandy is a five-year-old girl living in Cornwall, England, when she first meets the German shepherd, Lob. He soon adopts her and becomes the family pet. When Sandy is a teenager, she is struck by a speeding truck and seriously injured. The doctors are unable to help her and she lies in a coma with not much hope in sight. One day as Sandy's grandmother comes to visit, she sees Lob waiting outside the hospital, and she persuades the hospital staff to let her bring Lob in to see Sandy. Sandy responds to Lob and wakes long enough to rub his head and whisper his name. As Lob runs from the room, Sandy's shocked parents tell the grandmother that Lob had been killed in the accident that injured Sandy.

Thematic Link
Lob stands by Sandy—to the end and perhaps beyond. The author invents a wondrous world in which some events defy explanation.

5-Minute Warm-Up

Daily Language SkillBuilder

Have students **proofread** the display sentences on page 441i and write them correctly. The sentences also appear on Transparency 14 of **Grammar Transparencies and Copymasters.**

Mini Lesson **Preteaching Vocabulary**

If you would like to preteach the WORDS TO KNOW for this selection, use the Mini Lesson, p. 451.

LESSON RESOURCES

UNIT FOUR RESOURCE BOOK, pp. 4–10

ASSESSMENT
Formal Assessment, pp. 79–80
Teacher's Guide to Assessment and Portfolio Use
Test Generator

SKILLS TRANSPARENCIES AND COPYMASTERS
Literary Analysis
• Foreshadowing, TR 28 (for Paired Activity, p. 459)
Reading and Critical Thinking
• Cause and Effect, TR 5 (for Thinking Through the Literature, p. 459)

Grammar
• Identifying Prepositions and Their Objects, CM 101 (for Mini Lesson, p. 461)
• Sentence Variety with Prepositional Phrases, CM 105 (for Mini Lesson, p. 456)
Vocabulary
• Context Clues, CM 46 (for Mini Lesson, p. 451)
• Learning and Remembering New Words, CM 47 (for Mini Lesson, p. 458)

INTEGRATED TECHNOLOGY
Audio Library

Visit our website:
www.mcdougallittell.com

Literary Analysis FORESHADOWING

Remind students that a hint about an event that will occur later in a story is called foreshadowing.

Set a Purpose As students read, ask them to look for descriptive words or phrases that the author uses to foreshadow events.

 Use **Unit Four Resource Book,** p. 6 for more practice.

Active Reading CAUSE AND EFFECT

Remind students that when one event brings about another, the events are said to have a cause and effect relationship. Ask students to name the events that are related as cause and effect on this page. Help them to fill in the chart they began on page 447.

Possible Response: The picture of the queen in Granny's kitchen is the *cause* of Sandy being named Alexandra—the *effect.*

Set a Purpose As they read, ask students to continue filling in the cause and effect graphic organizer.

 Use **Unit Four Resource Book,** p. 5 for more practice.

Reading Skills and Strategies: PREDICT

Ask students to think ahead to what might happen in the story, and to predict probable and future actions and outcomes. Remind them to use the information the author has given them.

Possible Responses: The story will be about Lob and Sandy, because Lob chose Sandy. Lob might have to rescue Sandy from the water, because this story takes place near a beach.

Teaching Options

 Viewing and Representing

Maggie
by Judith S. Rubin

ART APPRECIATION This watercolor painting of a German shepherd was done by the artist in 1991.
Instruction Ask students to study the portrait of the dog, noticing the details, which are somewhat blurred by the loose, light strokes of the brush. What kind of animal do they think this dog is—that is, what are his or her traits? How would it make them feel to have a dog like this?

Possible Responses: This dog looks strong and protective, but he/she might also have a soft, loving side. The dog has a kind face. Having a dog like this might make students feel protected and loved.

Application Have students read the description of Lob on page 450. Ask them if this painting is similar to the way they visualized Lob.

Possible Response: Yes, this dog looks the way Lob is described in the story.

Girl

BY

JOAN AIKEN

**Some people choose their dogs,
and some dogs choose their people.**

The Pengelly family had no say in the choosing of Lob; he came to them in the second way, and very decisively.

It began on the beach, the summer when Sandy was five, Don, her older brother, twelve, and the twins were three. Sandy was really Alexandra, because her grandmother had a beautiful picture of a queen in a diamond tiara and high collar of pearls. It hung by Granny Pearce's kitchen sink and was as familiar as the doormat. When Sandy was born everyone agreed that she was the living spit[1] of the picture, and so she was called Alexandra and Sandy for short.

---

1. the living spit: an exact likeness.

Maggie (1991),
J. Rubin, watercolor
on paper.

449

Less Proficient Readers
To help students understand the characters in this story, ask them who they have met so far.

Answer: They've met the Pengelly family—Sandy, Don, and the twins; Sandy's Grandmother Pearce, and the dog Lob.

Set a Purpose Ask students to read on to find out how Lob affects the lives of the Pengelly family.

Students Acquiring English
As students read this story, they will encounter examples of British English, such as "the living spit," "Christmas puddings," and so on. Help them relate these terms and expressions to the American English they are learning.

 Use **Spanish Study Guide,** pp. 94–96 for additional support.

Gifted and Talented
Ask students to discuss how they were named and if their names hold any special meanings. Ask them to think about how that name or meaning has influenced them so far. Have them consider the reason for Sandy's name, and to speculate what effect it might have in this story.

Multiple Learning Styles
Visual Learners
Ask students to draw the scene on the beach the day Lob attaches himself to Sandy and her family. Since the author doesn't provide many clues on this page, remind students of the description of Cornwall given on page 447.

BLOCK SCHEDULING: MANAGING TIME

If your schedule requires that you cover the lesson objectives in a shorter time, use…
- Preparing to Read, p. 447
- Thinking Through the Literature, p. 459
- Vocabulary in Action, p. 460
- Grammar in Context, p. 461

If you want to take advantage of longer class time, use…
- TE Teaching Options: Viewing and Representing, pp. 448, 450; Preteaching Vocabulary, p. 451; Assessment, pp. 452, 460; Multicultural Link, p. 453; Spelling, p. 454; Cross Curricular Link, pp. 455, 457; Grammar, pp. 456, 461; Vocabulary Strategy, p. 458
- Choices & Challenges, pp. 460-461

Literary Analysis: SETTING

A The author uses vivid descriptions of people and places in this section. Ask students to describe the setting.

Possible Response: It is a quiet, warm, summer day. The twins are playing in the seaweed, Father and Don are working on the fishing boat, Mother is making Christmas puddings, and Sandy is lying in the sand.

ACTIVE READING

B QUESTION This is the gray-haired man's dog

Reading Skills and Strategies: VISUALIZE

C Ask students to describe the mental image they had as they read about Lob finding Sandy lying on the beach.

Possible Response: Just as Sandy is rolling over on the sand, a big dog jumps on her and starts licking her face wagging his tail.

Literary Analysis FORESHADOWING

D Ask students whether this comment might foreshadow events yet to come. Have them discuss what might happen.

Possible Response: Lob might come to live with them permanently, so they could play with him every day.

Use **Literary Analysis Transparencies,** p. 28, for additional support.

Active Reading CAUSE AND EFFECT

Remind students to be looking for cause-and-effect relationships. Ask them to share and record any relationships they found on these pages.

Possible Responses: Lob jumps on Sandy causing her to be covered with sand, which in turn causes Lob to lick her face.

Use **Reading and Critical Thinking Transparencies,** p. 5, for additional support.

---

*O*n this summer day she was lying peacefully reading a comic and not keeping an eye on the twins, who didn't need it because they were occupied in seeing which of them could wrap the most seaweed around the other one's legs. Father—Bert Pengelly—and Don were up on the Hard[2] painting the bottom boards of the boat in which Father went fishing for pilchards.[3] And Mother—Jean Pengelly—was getting ahead with making the Christmas puddings because she never felt easy in her mind if they weren't made and safely put away by the end of August. As usual, each member of the family was happily getting on with his or her own affairs. Little did they guess how soon this state of things would be changed by the large new member who was going to erupt into their midst.

Sandy rolled onto her back to make sure that the twins were not climbing on slippery rocks or getting cut off by the tide. At the same moment a large body struck her forcibly in the midriff, and she was covered by flying sand. Instinctively she shut her eyes and felt the sand being wiped off her face by something that seemed like a warm, rough, damp flannel. She opened her eyes and looked. It was a tongue. Its owner was a large and bouncy young Alsatian, or German

Breakers at Flood Tide (1909), Frederick Judd Waugh, 35" × 40", The Butler Institute of American Art, Youngstown, Ohio.

shepherd, with topaz eyes, black-tipped prick ears, a thick, soft coat, and a bushy, black-tipped tail.

"*Lob!*" shouted a man farther up the beach. "Lob, come here!"

But Lob, as if trying to <u>atone</u> for the surprise he had given her, went on licking the sand off Sandy's face, wagging his tail so hard while he kept on knocking up more clouds of sand. His owner, a gray-haired man with a limp, walked over as quickly as he could and seized him by the collar.

"I hope he didn't give you a fright?" the man said to Sandy. "He meant it in play—he's only young."

"Oh, no, I think he's *beautiful*," said Sandy truly. She picked up a bit of driftwood and

---

2. **Hard:** *British,* a landing place for boats.
3. **pilchards:** small fish, similar to sardines.

ACTIVE READING

QUESTION Whose dog is this?

WORDS
TO
KNOW **atone** (ə-tōn´) *v.* to make amends

450

Teaching Options

 Viewing and Representing

Breakers at Flood Tide
by Frederick Judd Waugh

ART APPRECIATION Frederick Judd Waugh (1861–1940) was born in New Jersey. He studied art in Philadelphia and later in Paris. From 1901 to 1907, he lived in England and worked as an illustrator for newspapers and magazines. He settled in Massachusetts in 1907 and painted over 2,500 seascapes.

Instruction Ask students what mood the painting creates. How is it similar to or different from the mood created in the beach scene on these pages?

Possible Response: The mood of the painting is peaceful and calm, though the sea looks a bit rough. The sun is shining, and it looks pleasant. This might be the scene the Pengelly family saw as they worked and played on the beach.

threw it. Lob, whisking easily out of his master's grip, was after it like a sand-colored bullet. He came back with the stick, beaming, and gave it to Sandy. At the same time he gave himself, though no one else was aware of this at the time. But with Sandy, too, it was love at first sight, and when, after a lot more stick-throwing, she and the twins joined Father and Don to go home for tea, they cast many a backward glance at Lob being led firmly away by his master.

"I wish we could play with him every day," Tess sighed.

"Why can't we?" said Tim.

Sandy explained. "Because Mr. Dodsworth, who owns him, is from Liverpool, and he is only staying at the Fisherman's Arms till Saturday."

"Is Liverpool a long way off?"

"Right at the other end of England from Cornwall, I'm afraid."

It was a Cornish fishing village where the Pengelly family lived, with rocks and cliffs and a strip of beach and a little round harbor, and palm trees growing in the gardens of the little whitewashed stone houses. The village was approached by a narrow, steep, twisting hillroad and guarded by a notice that said LOW GEAR FOR 1½ MILES, DANGEROUS TO CYCLISTS.

The Pengelly children went home to scones with Cornish cream and jam, thinking they had seen the last of Lob. But they were much mistaken. The whole family was playing cards by the fire in the front room after supper when there was a loud thump and a crash of china in the kitchen.

"My Christmas puddings!" exclaimed Jean, and ran out.

"Did you put TNT[4] in them, then?" her husband said.

But it was Lob, who, finding the front door shut, had gone around to the back and bounced in through the open kitchen window, where the puddings were cooling on the sill.

"I hope he didn't give you a fright?"

Luckily only the smallest was knocked down and broken.

Lob stood on his hind legs and plastered Sandy's face with licks. Then he did the same for the twins, who shrieked with joy.

"Where does this friend of yours come from?" inquired Mr. Pengelly.

"He's staying at the Fisherman's Arms—I mean his owner is."

"Then he must go back there. Find a bit of string, Sandy, to tie to his collar."

"I wonder how he found his way here," Mrs. Pengelly said, when the reluctant Lob had been led whining away and Sandy had explained about their afternoon's game on the beach. "Fisherman's Arms is right round the other side of the harbor."

Lob's owner scolded him and thanked Mr. Pengelly for bringing him back. Jean Pengelly warned the children that they had better not encourage Lob any more if they met him on the beach, or it would only lead to more trouble. So they dutifully took no notice of him the next day until he spoiled their good resolutions by dashing up to them with joyful barks, wagging his tail so hard that he winded Tess and knocked Tim's legs from under him.

---

4. TNT: trinitrotoluene, a powerful explosive.

WORDS TO KNOW
inquire (ĭn-kwīr') v. to question; ask

451

Customizing Instruction

Less Proficient Readers
To help less proficient readers understand the text, ask them the following questions:
• How does Sandy meet Lob?
  Answer: Lob finds Sandy lying on the beach, and he jumps on her.
• Who owns Lob?
  Answer: Mr. Dodsworth, who lives in Liverpool and is only visiting Cornwall, owns him.

Set a Purpose Ask students to read on to find out how Lob gets to live with the Pengellys.

Multiple Learning Styles
Kinesthetic Learners

Ask students to act out the scene on the beach with the Pengelly family and Lob. Help them to think about each character in the story and to choose a role with which they can most identify.

Mini Lesson Preteaching Vocabulary

CONTEXT CLUES Remind students that when they are reading and they come across words they don't know, they can often find clues in the rest of the sentence or paragraph to help explain the meaning of the unfamiliar word. This is called using context clues.
Instruction Ask students to locate the word *tiara* on page 449. Ask them if they can tell what *tiara* means from the context. They should be able to use the clues "queen" and "diamond" to help them figure out that a tiara is a kind of crown. Explain that not all clues are words. For example, the fact

that the word *inquired* is preceded by a question mark on page 451 is a clue to its meaning.
Application Ask students to preview the selection, looking for the WORDS TO KNOW. Instruct students to cover the definitions provided at the bottom of each page and try to determine the meaning of the words from their contexts. Have them list the context clues they used.

Use **Unit Four Resource Book,** p. 7 for more practice. Use **Vocabulary Transparencies and Copymasters,** p. 46, for more practice.

ACTIVE READING

A **CAUSE AND EFFECT** It makes Sandy feel sad.

Active Reading | **CAUSE AND EFFECT**

B Ask students what caused Lob's feet to be worn, dusty, tarry, and cut. Ask them if this effect caused any other events.

Possible Response: Lob walked all the way from Liverpool to Cornwall—about 400 miles! His being hurt causes Sandy and her mother to clean him up and to contact Lob's owner.

Literary Analysis: MOOD

A mood is a feeling that a literary work conveys to readers. Writers carefully choose words and phrases to create moods such as sadness, excitement, and anger. Sometimes authors create several moods in the same story to help readers experience many emotions. Ask students to talk about the various moods in this story and to give examples of what creates each mood.

Possible Response: The author creates a sad mood when Sandy watches Lob leave on the train. Words such as "drooping ears and tail," and "melancholy wail" help create that mood.

They had a happy day, playing on the sand.

The next day was Saturday. Sandy had found out that Mr. Dodsworth was to catch the half-past-nine train. She went out secretly, down to the station, nodded to Mr. Hoskins, the stationmaster, who wouldn't dream of charging any local for a platform ticket, and climbed up on the footbridge that led over the tracks. She didn't want to be seen, but she did want to see. She saw Mr. Dodsworth get on the train, accompanied by an unhappy-looking Lob with drooping ears and tail. Then she saw the train slide away out of sight around the next headland, with a <u>melancholy</u> wail that sounded like Lob's last good-bye.

ACTIVE READING

A **CAUSE AND EFFECT** How does seeing Lob make Sandy feel?

Sandy wished she hadn't had the idea of coming to the station. She walked home miserably, with her shoulders hunched and her hands in her pockets. For the rest of the day, she was so cross and unlike herself that Tess and Tim were quite surprised, and her mother gave her a dose of senna.[5]

1 A week passed. Then, one evening, Mrs. Pengelly and the younger children were in the front room playing snakes and ladders. Mr. Pengelly and Don had gone fishing on the evening tide. If your father is a fisherman, he will never be home at the same time from one week to the next.

Suddenly, history repeating itself, there was a crash from the kitchen. Jean Pengelly leaped up, crying, "My blackberry jelly!" She and the children had spent the morning picking and the afternoon boiling fruit.

But Sandy was ahead of her mother. With flushed cheeks and eyes like stars she had darted into the kitchen, where she and Lob were hugging one another in a frenzy of joy. About a yard of his tongue was out, and he was licking every part of her that he could reach.

"Good heavens!" exclaimed Jean. "How in the world did *he* get here?"

"He must have walked," said Sandy. "Look at his feet."

They were worn, dusty, and tarry. One had a cut on the pad. **B**

"They ought to be bathed," said Jean Pengelly. "Sandy, run a bowl of warm water while I get the disinfectant."

"What'll we do about him, Mother?" said Sandy anxiously.

Mrs. Pengelly looked at her daughter's pleading eyes and sighed.

"He must go back to his owner, of course," she said, making her voice firm. "Your dad can get the address from the Fisherman's tomorrow, and phone him or send a telegram.

"How in the world did he get here?"

In the meantime he'd better have a long drink and a good meal."

Lob was very grateful for the drink and the meal, and made no objection to having his feet washed. Then he flopped down on the hearth rug and slept in front of the fire they had lit because it was a cold, wet evening, with his head on Sandy's feet. He was a very tired dog. He had walked all the way from Liverpool to

---

5. **senna:** a medicine made from senna leaves.

WORDS TO KNOW **melancholy** (měl′ən-kŏl′ē) *adj.* sad; gloomy

452

Teaching Options

✓ **Assessment** **Informal Assessment**

UNDERSTAND THE FEELINGS AND EMOTIONS OF CHARACTERS To help students understand the feelings and emotions of characters, remind them that writers use descriptive words to "paint" a picture for the reader. Writers also use characters' words and actions to show their emotions. Ask students to think about Sandy and her relationship with Lob. Ask them to use clues the author has given to write a short description of what Sandy feels about Lob, and what these emotions tell about her character.

RUBRIC

3 Full Accomplishment Response shows full understanding of the feelings of Sandy's character.

2 Substantial Accomplishment Response shows substantial understanding of Sandy's feelings.

1 Little or Partial Accomplishment Response shows little or partial understanding of the feelings of Sandy's character.

Cornwall, which is more than four hundred miles.

The next day Mr. Pengelly phoned Lob's owner, and the following morning Mr. Dodsworth arrived off the night train, decidedly put out, to take his pet home. That parting was worse than the first. Lob whined, Don walked out of the house, the twins burst out crying, and Sandy crept up to her bedroom afterward and lay with her face pressed into the quilt, feeling as if she were bruised all over.

Jean Pengelly took them all into Plymouth to see the circus on the next day and the twins cheered up a little, but even the hour's ride in the train each way and the Liberty horses and performing seals could not cure Sandy's sore heart.

Child in Thought, Francisco Benitez. Courtesy of Chase Gallery, Boston.

She need not have bothered, though. In ten days' time Lob was back—limping this time, with a torn ear and a patch missing out of his furry coat, as if he had met and tangled with an enemy or two in the course of his four-hundred-mile walk.

Bert Pengelly rang up Liverpool again. Mr. Dodsworth, when he answered, sounded weary. He said, "That dog has already cost me two days that I can't spare away from my work—plus endless time in police stations and drafting newspaper advertisements. I'm too old for these ups and downs. I think we'd better face the fact, Mr. Pengelly, that it's your family

he wants to stay with—that is, if you want to have him."

Bert Pengelly gulped. He was not a rich man, and Lob was a pedigreed dog. He said cautiously, "How much would you be asking for him?"

"Good heavens, man, I'm not suggesting I'd *sell* him to you. You must have him as a gift. Think of the train fares I'll be saving. You'll be doing me a good turn."

"Is he a big eater?" Bert asked doubtfully.

By this time the children, breathless in the background listening to one side of

453

Customizing Instruction

Less Proficient Readers
Make sure students understand what is happening with Lob and the Pengelly family by asking the following questions:
- Why does Sandy go to the train station?
  Answer: She goes to watch Lob leave for Liverpool with Mr. Dodsworth.
- How does Lob get back to Cornwall?
  Answer: He walks.
- How do the Pengellys get Lob back to Mr. Dodsworth?
  Answer: They call Mr. Dodsworth to come and get him.
- What happens next?
  Answer: Lob runs away to Cornwall again. The family contacts Mr. Dodsworth, but he doesn't want to come and get Lob this time.

Gifted and Talented
Ask students to think about whom the painting on this page might represent. What mood does the painting set? Ask students to compare the mood in the story to the mood in the painting. Ask them to discuss why this particular painting may have been included in this story.

Possible Response: The painting may represent Sandy in the story and shows how sad and gloomy she feels when Lob has to return home to Liverpool. The story has several moods, but the painting seems to capture the sadness the author creates.

Students Acquiring English
1 Tell students that *snakes and ladders* is a board game, similar to an American game called Chutes and Ladders.

2 Explain that *rang up* is the British way of saying "called on the phone."

Life in a Fishing Village

Life in a fishing village revolves around the sea, and many of the inhabitants make their living from it. Depending on the location, the kind of fish varies, as does the method. People who fish do so with lines, nets, and even spears. Some boats stay out for days, and others set out each morning or evening, depending on the tide. Back on shore, the fish are sold in markets, shipped inland, or canned, frozen, or dried. The people who help maintain the boats, nets, traps, and other equipment have important jobs.

Many fishing villages boast restaurants that specialize in serving up the fresh catch of the day. Some villages attract tourists and artists because of their unspoiled beauty. Tourism has become an important industry in some villages where the fish have become less plentiful, providing a new source of work for the inhabitants. Some formerly "quaint" villages are now overcrowded tourist sites, however. Fishing is hard, dangerous work, but a love of the sea and the outdoors, coupled with an independent lifestyle, makes it worthwhile.

this conversation, had realized what was in the wind and were dancing up and down with their hands clasped beseechingly.

"Oh, not for his size," Lob's owner <u>assured</u> Bert. "Two or three pounds of meat a day and some vegetables and gravy and biscuits—he does very well on that."

Alexandra's father looked over the telephone at his daughter's swimming eyes and trembling lips. He reached a decision. "Well, then, Mr. Dodsworth," he said briskly, "we'll accept your offer and thank you very much. The children will be overjoyed and you can be sure Lob has come to a good home. They'll look after him and see he gets enough exercise. But I can tell you," he ended firmly, "if he wants to settle in with us, he'll have to learn to eat a lot of fish."

So that was how Lob came to live with the Pengelly family. Everybody loved him and he loved them all. But there was never any question who came first with him. He was Sandy's dog. He slept by her bed and followed her everywhere he was allowed.

Nine years went by, and each summer Mr. Dodsworth came back to stay at the Fisherman's Arms and call on his erstwhile dog. Lob always met him with recognition and dignified pleasure, accompanied him for a walk or two—but showed no signs of wishing to return to Liverpool. His place, he intimated, was definitely with the Pengellys.

In the course of nine years Lob changed less than Sandy. As she went into her teens he became a little slower, a little stiffer, there was

a touch of gray on his nose, but he was still a handsome dog. He and Sandy still loved one another devotedly.

In the course of nine years Lob changed less than Sandy.

One evening in October all the summer visitors had left, and the little fishing town looked empty and secretive. It was a wet, windy dusk. When the children came home from school—even the twins were at high school[6] now, and Don was a full-fledged fisherman—Jean Pengelly said, "Sandy, your Aunt Rebecca says she's lonesome because Uncle Will Hoskins has gone out trawling,[7] and she wants one of you to go and spend the evening with her. You go, dear; you can take your homework with you."

Sandy looked far from enthusiastic.

"Can I take Lob with me?"

"You know Aunt Becky doesn't really like dogs—Oh, very well." Mrs. Pengelly sighed. "I suppose she'll have to put up with him as well as you."

Reluctantly Sandy tidied herself, took her schoolbag, put on the damp raincoat she had just taken off, fastened Lob's lead to his collar, and set off to walk through the dusk to Aunt Becky's cottage, which was five minutes' climb up the steep hill.

---

6. **high school:** In Great Britain, students leave elementary school and begin attending high school when they are about 11 years old.

7. **trawling:** fishing with a net pulled behind a boat.

454

The wind was howling through the shrouds[8] of boats drawn up on the Hard.

"Put some cheerful music on, do," said Jean Pengelly to the nearest twin. "Anything to drown that wretched sound while I make your dad's supper." So Don, who had just come in, put on some rock music, loud. Which was why the Pengellys did not hear the truck hurtle down the hill and crash against the post office wall a few minutes later.

Dr. Travers was driving through Cornwall with his wife, taking a late holiday before patients began coming down with winter colds and flu. He saw the sign that said STEEP HILL. LOW GEAR FOR 1½ MILES. Dutifully he changed into second gear.

"We must be nearly there," said his wife, looking out of her window. "I noticed a sign on the coast road that said the Fisherman's Arms was two miles. What a narrow, dangerous hill! But the cottages are very pretty—Oh, Frank, stop, *stop!* There's a child, I'm sure it's a child—by the wall over there!"

B

Dr. Travers jammed on his brakes and brought the car to a stop. A little stream ran down by the road in a shallow stone culvert,[9] and half in the water lay something that looked, in the dusk, like a pile of clothes—or was it the body of a child? Mrs. Travers was out of the car in a flash, but her husband was quicker.

1

"Don't touch her, Emily!" he said sharply. "She's been hit. Can't be more than a few minutes. Remember that truck that overtook us half a mile back, speeding like the devil? Here, quick, go into that cottage and phone for an ambulance. The girl's in a bad way. I'll stay here and do what I can to stop the bleeding. Don't waste a minute."

Doctors are expert at stopping dangerous bleeding, for they know the right places to press. This Dr. Travers was able to do, but he didn't dare do more; the girl was lying in a queerly crumpled heap, and he guessed she had a number of bones broken and that it would be highly dangerous to move her. He watched her with great concentration, wondering where the truck had got to and what other damage it had done.

Mrs. Travers was very quick. She had seen plenty of accident cases and knew the importance of speed. The first cottage she tried had a phone; in four minutes she was back, and in six an ambulance was wailing down the hill.

Its attendants lifted the child onto a stretcher as carefully as if she were made of fine thistledown. The ambulance sped off to Plymouth—for the local cottage hospital did not take serious accident cases—and Dr. Travers went down to the police station to report what he had done.

2

ACTIVE READING

PREDICT Will Sandy survive? Why or why not?

He found that the police already knew about the speeding truck—which had suffered from loss of brakes and ended up with its radiator halfway through the post-office wall. The driver was concussed[10] and shocked, but the police thought he was the only person injured—until Dr. Travers told his tale.

At half-past nine that night Aunt Rebecca Hoskins was sitting by her fire thinking aggrieved thoughts about the inconsiderateness of nieces who were asked to supper and never turned up, when she was startled by a

---

8. **shrouds:** ropes or cables on a boat's mast.
9. **culvert:** a gutter or tunnel that runs along or under a road.
10. **concussed:** suffering from a concussion, an injury that results from being struck in the head.

Cross Curricular Link Math

MILES TO KILOMETERS In the United States it is common to see distances written in both miles (mi.) and kilometers (km). However, there are many countries that use only the metric system. It is helpful for students to have a general understanding of the relationship between customary/standard measures and those in the metric system. Provide students with these approximate measures:

• 1 inch is about 2.5 centimeters
• 1 meter is about 39 inches
• 1 mile is about 1.6 kilometers

• Ask students to figure out about how many kilometers it is from Liverpool to Cornwall, the distance Lob walked to be with Sandy. *(400 miles is about 600 km.)*
• Ask students to write these units in order from greatest to least: cm, mi., km, yd., m, in., ft. *(mi., km, m, yd., ft., in., cm)*
• Discuss with students why they think the U.S. has not completely switched over to the metric system, even though it was officially adopted in 1975.

Ask students to think about the chain of effects that occurs because Sandy is struck by the truck. Ask them to make a list of these effects and to add it to their graphic organizer.

Possible Response: Sandy is hurt, she is taken to the hospital, she has a blood transfusion, and she is in a coma. Lob is missing. The Pengellys are sad and upset, and their house is lonely and quiet.

Literary Analysis | FORESHADOWING

A In this paragraph, the author, Joan Aiken, foreshadows events yet to come. Ask students to think about the events so far and the details and clues the author has provided. Have them predict what events are still to come based on the content of this paragraph.

Possible Response: Aiken is foreshadowing the return of Lob and his visit to Sandy to help her to get better.

Reading Skills and Strategies: PREDICT

B Ask students to predict whether the dog will be allowed in the hospital with Granny Pearce.

Literary Analysis: CLIMAX

Tell students that in the plot of a story, the climax is the point of greatest interest. At the climax, the outcome of the story may become clear.

Set a Purpose Ask students to read to find out how the story ends. Ask them to look for details and events that uncover the climax.

---

neighbor, who burst in, exclaiming, "Have you heard about Sandy Pengelly, then, Mrs. Hoskins? Terrible thing, poor little soul, and they don't know if she's likely to live. Police have got the truck driver that hit her—ah, it didn't ought to be allowed, speeding through the place like that at umpty miles an hour, they ought to jail him for life—not that that'd be any comfort to poor Bert and Jean."

Horrified, Aunt Rebecca put on a coat and went down to her brother's house. She found the family with white shocked faces; Bert and Jean were about to drive off to the hospital where Sandy had been taken, and the twins were crying bitterly. Lob was nowhere to be seen. But Aunt Rebecca was not interested in dogs; she did not inquire about him.

"Thank the Lord you've come, Beck," said her brother. "Will you stay the night with Don and the twins? Don's out looking for Lob and heaven knows when we'll be back; we may get a bed with Jean's mother in Plymouth."

"Oh, if only I'd never invited the poor child," wailed Mrs. Hoskins. But Bert and Jean hardly heard her.

That night seemed to last forever. The twins cried themselves to sleep. Don came home very late and grim-faced. Bert and Jean sat in a waiting room of the Western Counties Hospital, but Sandy was unconscious, they were told, and she remained so. All that could be done for her was done. She was given <u>transfusions</u> to replace all the blood she had

Study of a Road Near Rottingdean, Sir Edward Coley Burne-Jones. Courtesy Brighton and Hove Council, The Royal Pavilion Libraries and Museums, Brighton, U.K.

lost. The broken bones were set and put in slings and cradles.

"Is she a healthy girl? Has she a good constitution?"[11] the emergency doctor asked.

"Aye, Doctor, she is that," Bert said hoarsely. The lump in Jean's throat prevented her from answering; she merely nodded.

"Then she ought to have a chance. But I won't <u>conceal</u> from you that her condition is very serious, unless she shows signs of coming out from this <u>coma</u>."

But as hour succeeded hour, Sandy showed no signs of recovering consciousness. Her parents sat in the waiting room with haggard faces; sometimes one of them would go to telephone the family at home, or to try to get a little sleep at the home of Granny Pearce, not far away.

---

11. **constitution:** physical makeup.

WORDS TO KNOW	**transfusion** (trăns-fyoo'zhən) *n.* an injection of blood, usually to replace a loss due to bleeding
	conceal (kən-sēl') *v.* to hide
	coma (kō'mə) *n.* a sleeplike state in which a person cannot sense or respond to light, sound, or touch

456

Teaching Options

 Mini Lesson **Grammar**

SENTENCE VARIETY WITH PREPOSITIONAL PHRASES

Instruction Tell students that a prepositional phrase is a group of words that begins with a preposition and ends with its object. Remind them that using prepositional phrases can add variety to their sentences, making their writing more interesting. Locate the highlighted sentence on page 456. Ask students to identify the prepositional phrases in that sentence, and to notice how the author uses these phrases to include important details.

Exercises Ask students to use the following

prepositional phrases in sentences, placing them at different points to show variety.

1. during the dark storm
2. toward her smiling face
3. above the glistening waves
4. upon the cold, hard stone

 Use **Grammar Transparencies and Copymasters,** p. 105.

Use McDougal Littell's *Language Network,* Chapter 6, for more instruction and practice in sentence variety.

At noon next day Dr. and Mrs. Travers went to the Pengelly cottage to inquire how Sandy was doing, but the report was gloomy: "Still in a very serious condition." The twins were miserably unhappy. They forgot that they had sometimes called their elder sister bossy and only remembered how often she had shared her pocket money with them, how she read to them and took them for picnics and helped with their homework. Now there was no Sandy, no Mother and Dad, Don went around with a gray, shuttered face, and worse still, there was no Lob.

The Western Counties Hospital is a large one, with dozens of different departments and five or six connected buildings, each with three or four entrances. By that afternoon it became noticeable that a dog seemed to have taken up position outside the hospital, with the fixed intention of getting in. Patiently he would try first one entrance and then another, all the way around, and then begin again. Sometimes he would get a little way inside, following a visitor, but animals were, of course, forbidden, and he was always kindly but firmly turned out again. Sometimes the guard at the main entrance gave him a pat or offered him a bit of sandwich—he looked so wet and beseeching and desperate. But he never ate the sandwich. No one seemed to own him or to know where he came from; Plymouth is a large city and he might have belonged to anybody.

At tea time Granny Pearce came through the pouring rain to bring a flask of hot tea to her daughter and son-in-law. Just as she reached the main entrance the guard was gently but forcibly shoving out a large, <u>agitated</u>, soaking-wet Alsatian dog.

"No, old fellow, you can *not* come in. Hospitals are for people, not for dogs."

"Why, bless me," exclaimed old Mrs. Pearce. "That's Lob! Here, Lob, Lobby boy!"

Lob ran to her, whining. Mrs. Pearce walked up to the desk.

"I'm sorry, madam, you can't bring that dog in here," the guard said.

Mrs. Pearce was a very determined old lady. She looked the porter in the eye.

"Now, see here, young man. That dog has walked twenty miles from St. Killan to get to my granddaughter. Heaven knows how he knew she was here, but it's plain he knows. And he ought to have his rights! He ought to get to see her! Do you know," she went on, bristling, "that dog has walked the length of England—*twice*—to be with that girl? And you think you can keep him out with your fiddling rules and regulations?"

"I'll have to ask the medical officer," the guard said weakly.

"You do that, young man." Granny Pearce sat down in a determined manner, shutting her umbrella, and Lob sat patiently dripping at her feet. Every now and then he shook his head, as if to dislodge something heavy that was tied around his neck.

That night seemed to last forever.

Presently a tired, thin, intelligent-looking man in a white coat came downstairs, with an impressive, silver-haired man in a dark suit, and there was a low-voiced discussion. Granny Pearce eyed them, biding her time.

"Frankly . . . not much to lose," said the older man. The man in the white coat approached Granny Pearce.

WORDS TO KNOW	**agitated** (ăj′ĭ-tā′tĭd) *adj.* disturbed; upset **agitate** *v.*

457

Customizing Instruction

Less Proficient Readers
Ask students to explain what they see in the picture on page 456 and how it fits in the story. Remind them that they can use illustrations to help them understand what they are reading.
Possible Response: The photograph shows a curvy, hilly road at night, with a small house nearby. It could be the way the road by Sandy's house looks or the road where she is walking when she is hit.

Students Acquiring English
1 Make sure students understand that the "lump in Jean's throat" does not mean a physical lump. It means that she is so overwhelmed with emotion that she can barely speak.

Multiple Learning Styles
Interpersonal Learners

2 Ask students to work as a group to discuss a plan for getting Lob into the hospital. Have them make a list of strategies Granny might use to persuade the hospital officials to let Lob visit Sandy.
Possible Response: Students should think of strategies that would help Granny persuade the hospital to let Lob in, such as Granny telling the story of how Lob came to be Sandy's pet.

Cross Curricular Link **Health and Science**

HEALTH BENEFITS OF PET OWNERSHIP Owning a pet can bring companionship, pleasure, and protection. But did you know that owning a pet may also be good for your health? Numerous medical studies have been done on the health benefits of pet ownership. Results show that pet owners have significantly lower blood pressure and lower triglycerides than non-pet owners do. In some cases, cholesterol was lowered in new pet owners, and fewer heart problems were reported. Pet owners were found to visit the doctor less often, and reported a significant reduction in minor health problems, such as headaches, backaches, colds and flu, insomnia, and general tiredness. Pet owners also get more exercise than non-owners and seem to experience positive health effects over the long term.

A CAUSE AND EFFECT This is such a serious case that they are making an exception.

Literary Analysis: SETTING

As students read the description of Sandy's hospital room, ask them to note the details that the author uses to help the reader visualize the setting. Ask them to identify some of these vivid words.

Possible Response: green-floored corridor; door half-shut; terribly quiet; white-coated man; high, narrow bed; gadgets; very flat; very still.

Active Reading | CAUSE AND EFFECT |

B Ask students what causes Sandy to wake from her coma. Remind them to enter this relationship on their chart.

Possible Response: Lob's presence in Sandy's room causes her to wake up, call his name, and touch his head.

Literary Analysis: CLIMAX

Ask students what the climax is and to discuss how they felt when they read the ending. Did the author give them any hints about the twist of events?

Possible Response: The climax is when a dog that looks like Lob visits Sandy in the hospital, helping her to get well.

Literary Analysis | FORESHADOWING |

C Now that students know Lob was buried at sea, sunk by a weight on his collar, ask them to think back on details that foreshadowed this ending in the scene where Lob waits at the hospital.

Possible Response: The guard says Lob looked wet; Lob sat dripping at Granny's feet; he shook his head as if trying to dislodge something heavy around his neck.

"It's strictly against every rule, but as it's such a serious case we are making an exception," he said to her quietly. "But only *outside* her bedroom door—and only for a moment or two."

ACTIVE READING

A CAUSE AND EFFECT
What caused the guard to allow Lob into the hospital?

Without a word, Granny Pearce rose and stumped upstairs. Lob followed close to her skirts, as if he knew his hope lay with her.

They waited in the green-floored corridor outside Sandy's room. The door was half-shut. Bert and Jean were inside. Everything was terribly quiet. A nurse came out. The white-coated man asked her something and she shook her head. She had left the door ajar and through it could now be seen a high, narrow bed with a lot of gadgets around it. Sandy lay there, very flat under the covers, very still. Her head was turned away. All Lob's attention was <u>riveted</u> on the bed. He strained toward it, but Granny Pearce clasped his collar firmly.

"I've done a lot for you, my boy, now you behave yourself," she whispered grimly. Lob let out a faint whine, anxious and pleading.

At the sound of that whine, Sandy stirred just a little. She sighed and moved her head the least fraction. Lob whined again. And then Sandy turned her head right over. Her eyes opened, looking at the door.

"Lob?" she murmured—no more than a breath of sound. "Lobby, boy?"

The doctor by Granny Pearce drew a quick, sharp breath. Sandy moved her left arm—the one that was not broken—from below the covers and let her hand dangle down, feeling, as she always did in the mornings, for Lob's furry head. The doctor nodded slowly.

"All right," he whispered. "Let him go to the bedside. But keep a hold of him."

Granny Pearce and Lob moved to the bedside. Now she could see Bert and Jean, white-faced and shocked, on the far side of the bed. But she didn't look at them. She looked at the smile on her granddaughter's face as the groping fingers found Lob's wet ears and gently pulled them. "Good boy," whispered Sandy, and fell asleep again.

Granny Pearce led Lob out into the passage again. There she let go of him, and he ran off swiftly down the stairs. She would have followed him, but Bert and Jean had come out into the passage, and she spoke to Bert fiercely.

"*I* don't know why you were so foolish as not to bring the dog before! Leaving him to find the way here himself—"

"But, Mother!" said Jean Pengelly. "That can't have been Lob. What a chance to take! Suppose Sandy hadn't—" She stopped, with her handkerchief pressed to her mouth.

"Not Lob? I've known that dog nine years! I suppose I ought to know my own granddaughter's dog?"

"Listen, Mother," said Bert. "Lob was killed by the same truck that hit Sandy. Don found him—when he went to look for Sandy's schoolbag. He was—he was dead. Ribs all smashed. No question of that. Don told me on the phone—he and Will Hoskins rowed a half mile out to sea and sank the dog with a lump of concrete tied to his collar. Poor old boy. Still—he was getting on. Couldn't have lasted forever."

"*Sank him at sea?* Then what—?"

Slowly old Mrs. Pearce, and then the other two, turned to look at the trail of dripping-wet footprints that led down the hospital stairs.

In the Pengellys' garden they have a stone, under the palm tree. It says: "Lob. Sandy's dog. Buried at sea." ❖

WORDS
TO
KNOW

rivet (rĭv′ĭt) *v.* to fasten firmly

458

Teaching Options

LEARNING AND REMEMBERING NEW WORDS

Remind students that there are various strategies they can use when they encounter an unfamiliar word. They can:

• Use context clues   • Think of related words
• Analyze word parts   • Consult a dictionary

Instruction Tell students that to help them remember new words, they can use a graphic organizer like the one to the right.

Mini Lesson Vocabulary Strategy

Application Have students select five words from the selection that are/were unfamiliar and create a graphic organizer to help them learn and remember the new words.

📖 Use **Vocabulary Transparencies and Copymasters**, p. 47.

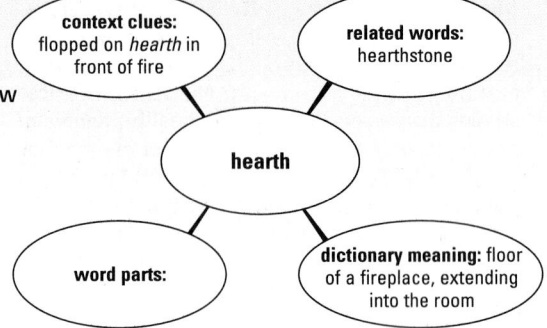

context clues: flopped on *hearth* in front of fire

related words: hearthstone

hearth

word parts:

dictionary meaning: floor of a fireplace, extending into the room

---

Connect to the Literature

1. **What Do You Think?** Did you expect the story to end the way it did? How did you feel about the ending?

Comprehension Check
- How does Lob become the Pengelly family pet?
- What caused the accident that injures Sandy?
- What helps Sandy recover?

Think Critically

2. Why do you think Sandy wishes she had not gone to the train station to see Lob leave?

3. Analyze the **plot structure** of "Lob's Girl" by identifying the **conflict** and the **climax** and then discussing the story's **resolution.**

4. How does Joan Aiken show the relationship between Lob and Sandy? Use examples from the story to explain your answer.

THINK ABOUT
- the way Lob and Sandy first meet
- why Mr. Dodsworth gives Lob away
- what happens when Granny Pearce visits the hospital

5. Lob is one of the main **characters** in this story, but he cannot speak. How do his actions show his character?

6. **ACTIVE READING** | **CAUSE AND EFFECT** Compare your **READER'S NOTEBOOK** chart on cause and effect with a classmate's. Discuss the causes of key events in the story. Did some events have more than one cause? Did some causes have multiple effects? Explain.

Extend Interpretations

7. **What If?** What if Mrs. Pengelly hadn't let Sandy take Lob with her to Aunt Rebecca's? With a partner, rewrite the end of the story so Lob does not go with Sandy. Tell what happens after Sandy is injured.

8. **Connect to Life** Have you ever experienced or shared with someone the loss of a pet? Discuss with a classmate how you think a pet's death affects its owner.

Literary Analysis

FORESHADOWING

Foreshadowing is a hint about an event or events that will occur later in a story. Writers create foreshadowing with descriptive words and events that often add an element of suspense to a story. Author Joan Aiken uses the technique of foreshadowing in "Lob's Girl." Early in the story, she describes the road where Sandy's accident later will occur. The road is described as "guarded by a notice that said LOW GEAR FOR 1½ MILES, DANGEROUS TO CYCLISTS."

The words *guarded* and *dangerous* suggest that something bad may happen in this place later in the story.

 MOOD The feeling or atmosphere in a story is called its **mood.** Often, writers create mood by describing details of setting, or by using actions and dialogue that reveal fear, excitement, happiness, or another emotion.

Paired Activity With a partner, go back through the story and list the words and events that foreshadow Lob coming to live with the Pengellys. Discuss how the author uses mood to make you feel that something is going to happen. Which scene in the story uses mood most effectively to foreshadow?

Extend Interpretations

7. **What If?** Accept rewritten endings that have Sandy going alone to her aunt's and that tell what happens after she is hit by the truck.

8. **Connect to Life** Students should draw on their own past experiences, family or friends' experiences, or on books or movies they've read or seen. Encourage them to share feelings as well as descriptions of events.

Literary Analysis

Foreshadowing Students' responses should identify a scene where the author sets a mood to foreshadow upcoming events.

 Use **Literary Analysis Transparencies,** p. 28, for additional support.

Connect to the Literature

1. **What Do You Think?** Possible Response: The ending was a surprise, but I was happy that Sandy got well.

Comprehension Check
- Lob keeps going to the Pengelly home so his owner tells the family to keep him.
- A truck that is driving too fast on the hill injures her.
- A dog that looks like Lob visits Sandy at the hospital.

Use Selection Quiz in **Unit Four Resource Book,** p. 10.

Think Critically

2. Possible Response: Watching the train take Lob away makes Sandy realize even more how much she is going to miss him.

3. Possible Response: The conflict is that Sandy is injured by a truck. The climax is that a dog who looks like Lob visits Sandy in the hospital, and his presence causes Sandy to get better. The resolution is the revelation that the dog in the hospital could not have been Lob because he died after the truck hit him. The resolution develops the author's theme by showing that Lob's love was so strong that not even death could keep him from Sandy.

4. Possible Response: Joan Aiken shows the relationship between Lob and Sandy by making it harder and harder for them to be together, but still having Lob find a way to get back to Sandy. Aiken shows Lob's complete devotion to Sandy by having him show up at the hospital to help her out of her coma.

5. Possible response: Lob's actions show his character because everything he does is enthusiastic and determined. When he first sees Sandy, he bumps into her and licks her face. Every time his owner takes him away, Lob gets back to Sandy.

6. Possible Response: Responses will vary.

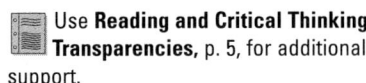 Use **Reading and Critical Thinking Transparencies,** p. 5, for additional support.

Writing Options

1. **Dog Care Instructions** Students may wish to access the Internet instead of using a book on pet care. Students may present the information as a booklet, a poster, or a written paper.
2. **Pros-and-Cons Chart** Students should draw and complete the chart. Encourage them to list as many in each column as they can, trying to keep their lists as even as possible.
3. **Newspaper Article** It would be helpful if students could read several newspaper articles to become familiar with the style of newspaper writing. Remind them to use quotation marks when quoting family members in their article.

Activities & Explorations

1. **Map of Lob's Route** Provide students with atlases or social studies textbooks that have detailed maps of England. **To make the activity more challenging,** students may also access the information on the Internet, perhaps using a map program to compare their route with one suggested by the computer.
2. **First Aid Presentation** Encourage students to talk to medical personnel, or arrange for a guest speaker to visit the classroom.

Inquiry & Research

No More Mystery Questions will vary.

Vocabulary in Action

EXERCISE A:
1. C, 2. A, 3. D, 4. I, 5. H, 6. B, 7. G, 8. E, 9. J, 10. F
EXERCISE B: Sentences will vary.

Choices & CHALLENGES

Writing Options

1. Dog Care Instructions Create a presentation to help new dog owners learn how to take care of their pets. Use the story, your own knowledge, and a book on pet care for dogs to make a list of instructions. Give your presentation for the class. Place your instructions in your **Working Portfolio.**

2. Pros-and-Cons Chart Reread the scene where Lob's owner offers to give Lob to the Pengellys. What are some reasons the family should or should not take the dog? Use a chart like the one shown to list the pros and cons.

Caring for Lob	
Pros	**Cons**
Will protect the family	Expensive to feed

3. Newspaper Article Imagine that you are a newspaper reporter. Write a news story about Lob's mysterious visit to the hospital. Include quotations from members of the Pengelly family, Mr. Dodsworth, the police, and the hospital staff.

Activities & Explorations

1. Map of Lob's Route Lob traveled 400 miles from his home in Liverpool to Sandy's home in Cornwall, England. Use an atlas to draw a map showing a route that Lob could have taken. Label towns and features such as rivers or harbors that he might have passed. ~ **ART**

2. First Aid Presentation Use a book on first aid or talk to the school nurse to find out how to help someone who is unconscious or has broken bones. Draw pictures that can remind you of the steps used to help an accident victim. Use the pictures in a class presentation on first aid.
~ **SPEAKING AND LISTENING**

Inquiry & Research

No More Mystery? Many people believe there is nothing new to learn about nature. Yet scientists continue to make discoveries about such animal behaviors as why birds sing, and how they can fly hundreds of miles in the dark without getting lost. What questions about animal behavior would you like answered? Use library resources to help you list two or three mysteries of animal behavior that interest you.

Real World Link Read the magazine article on page 462 before beginning your research.

Vocabulary in Action

EXERCISE A: ASSESSMENT PRACTICE On your paper, match each word on the left with its synonym on the right.

1. agitated   a. promise
2. assure   b. sketch
3. atone   c. disturbed
4. coma   d. repay
5. conceal   e. depressed
6. draft   f. transfer
7. inquire   g. question
8. melancholy   h. hide
9. rivet   i. blackout
10. transfusion   j. capture

EXERCISE B: LEARN AND REMEMBER NEW WORDS For each Word to Know, write a sentence that will help you remember the word's meaning. In each sentence, try to make the word's context vivid and precise.

Building Vocabulary

For an in-depth lesson on learning and remembering new words, see page 491.

Teaching Options

✓ Assessment **Standardized Test Practice**

PREDICTING In some standardized tests, students are asked to select a probable future action or outcome for a passage they have read. Write the following question on the board, or read it aloud:

What probably happens when Sandy gets home from the hospital?
A. She buys another dog that looks like Lob.
B. She searches along the seashore for Lob, and eventually finds him.
C. She gets on with her life and doesn't think about Lob at all.
D. She is sad for a while because she misses Lob, but slowly her life goes on.

Guide students through the process of selecting the correct answer. A is possible, but first look at the other choices. B is not possible: Lob died and Sandy would not be able to find him. C is not likely because Sandy loved Lob dearly and his memory would be a part of her life. D is the most probable: Lob's death was painful, but life does go on, as evidenced by the stone in the garden honoring Lob. Even though A is possible, D is the best answer.

Grammar in Context: Using Prepositional Phrases as Transitions

In "Lob's Girl" Joan Aiken uses prepositional phrases to make a smooth shift from one paragraph to another:

> On this summer day she was lying peacefully, . . .
>
> By this time the children, . . . had realized. . . .

The words shown in red are **prepositional phrases.** In the examples above, prepositional phrases set a new scene or show a transition, that is, a change in time.

In the examples, the words *on* and *by* are **prepositions,** words that show "position" in time, space, or in a relationship. A prepositional phrase includes a preposition followed by the **object of the preposition,** a noun or noun phrase.

WRITING EXERCISE Rewrite each sentence so that a prepositional phrase is used at the beginning to show transition.

Example: *Original* Sandy went to see her Aunt Becky on a lonely October evening.

Rewritten On a lonely October evening, Sandy went to see her Aunt Becky.

1. Dr. Travers discovered at the station that the police knew about the accident.

2. Sandy was unconscious for hour after hour.

3. Dr. and Mrs. Travers went to the cottage at noon the next day.

4. Granny saw the guard at the main entrance refuse to let Lob in.

5. Sandy stirred at the sound of Lob's whine.

Grammar Handbook Quick Reference: Parts of Speech, p. R54

"I knew from the age of five that I was going to be a writer. . . ."

Joan Aiken
born 1924

A Young Storyteller Joan Aiken, the daughter of the U.S. poet Conrad Aiken, grew up in England. Because there were no children of her age in the neighborhood, Aiken spent much of her time reading and making up stories to amuse herself and her younger stepbrother. She says, "I knew from the age of five that I was going to be a writer. . . ." Aiken says her writing process involves "a lot of revising and going back and crossing out words." She often gets her story ideas from interesting things she hears or reads, which she records in a notebook.

Tackling an Adult World As an adult, Aiken took jobs at a magazine and an advertising agency to support herself and her young children after she was widowed. To earn extra money, Aiken began writing and publishing short stories. She soon decided to become a full-time writer and has since authored dozens of books for children and adults. Aiken says her books for young people are "concerned with children tackling the problems of an adult world."

AUTHOR ACTIVITY

Thinking About Dialects Joan Aiken often writes in the dialects (different ways of speaking in different regions of a country) of England, her native land. Compare the language in "Lob's Girl" with other stories in this book that use dialects, such as "Cricket in the Road." How do the ways that characters speak help you appreciate a story?

 Mini Lesson Grammar

Real WORLD Link

Magazine Article

Objectives
- read for information
- read and analyze a magazine article
- use a written text to make judgments
- identify bias in a written text

Connecting to the Literature
This newspaper article is a useful companion piece to the short story "Lob's Girl" because it illustrates how, in real life, dogs have performed feats of great bravery under dangerous conditions in order to save the life of a human.

Real WORLD Link **Magazine Article**

Source: *National Geographic World*

Animals to the Rescue

① Why do animals act to save humans? No one really knows. Until recently scientists believed that animals were only creatures of instinct and training. Now they're not so sure. Some scientists say that animals may have emotions and thoughts like those of humans. Has your cat ever cuddled with you when you were sick in bed? If so, was it concerned and trying to make you feel better, did it want company . . . or was it just looking for a cozy spot? When an animal saves a human from injury, is it inspired by an emotion such as love, or simply acting on instinct? Read on to learn about animals who even risked their lives to help humans. Why did they do it? You be the judge.

Rattle of Terror

When 8-year-old Teresa Martinez of Loveland, Colorado, was picnicking one day, she accidentally wandered near a den of rattlesnakes. "I heard a rattle and froze. Then I started screaming for help," says Teresa. "Lady (Teresa's dog) raced over and started fighting the five snakes." That gave Teresa a chance to run for safety. Lady suffered three bites but survived thanks to quick medical attention. "Lady knew I was in trouble and wanted to protect me," adds Teresa. "She's a real hero."

Teresa Martinez with Lady, her rescuer.

Danger—Thin Ice

A shortcut across a frozen pond in 1995 could have killed Josh Mitchell, 15, of Indianapolis, Indiana. "There was a whoosh, and I fell through the ice," says Josh. Levi, a mixed golden and Labrador retriever, saw Josh fall. The dog bounded onto the ice and plunged into the cold water. Josh grabbed Levi around the neck and held on. Levi's owners, Denise and George Hamand, rushed to pull out Josh and Levi. Says Josh, "I guess that's why they call a dog 'man's best friend.'"

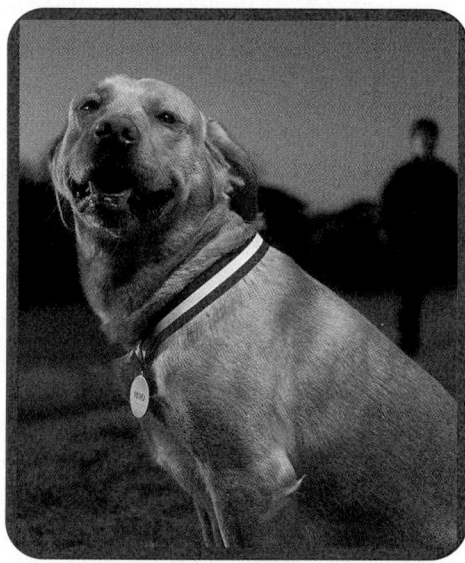

Levi saved Josh Mitchell from drowning.

Reading for Information

"There are two sides to every story." How many times have you heard that said? When reading for information, think carefully about what the writer is saying. Ask yourself:

- Would someone else have a different opinion?
- Is more than one viewpoint explained?
- Has the writer given me all the facts?
- Do I have enough information to judge whether or not the writer is truthful and accurate, or to decide whether I agree with the writer?

MAKING JUDGMENTS A **judgment** is a statement of opinion based on facts, observations, experience, and careful thought. Before you can make a wise judgment, you need to gather and review as much information as possible.

YOUR TURN *Use this article with the questions and activities below to find out more about making judgments.*

1 Before you can judge two opinions, you need to know what the two opinions are. Identify the two different reasons that might explain why animals rescue humans.

2 The author tells how Levi rescued Josh Mitchell. However, the article doesn't report that retrievers are types of dogs bred to fetch ducks from water; they have water-resistant fur and like to play in the water. Which opinion about animal rescues do these facts support?

3 Kelsey is a German shepherd, a breed of dogs often trained to protect and to attack aggressors. She could have deliberately kept the raccoon at bay in order to allow Ashley a chance to escape. The dog may have sensed Ashley's panic and reacted instinctively.

Identifying Bias

The people in the article may be biased because they are grateful to the dogs for saving their lives. They see the dogs as special and as more than mere animals.

Reading for Information *continued*

3 The author reports that Kelsey battled the raccoon, giving Ashley Gillen time to escape. Do you think Kelsey did that intentionally? What other reason might explain Kelsey's behavior? Hint: Discuss what type of dog Kelsey is. What do you know about German shepherds?

Identifying Bias A person's viewpoint, or **bias**, can influence his or her choice of words. The quotations from people rescued by dogs that acted "heroically" reflect a certain viewpoint. In what way might these people be biased?

Inquiry & Research

Activity Link: "Lob's Girl," p. 460. What else would you like to know before you judge which explanation of the dogs' behavior is correct? Use library resources to locate two or three more sources that discuss such rescues, as well as instinct, training, emotion, and thought in animals. Then form a judgment based on the facts you find along with your own observations and experience. Record your judgment in a brief essay, citing your sources.

Canine Courage

Kelsey, a German shepherd, fought off a rabid raccoon to save Ashley Gillen, of Weymouth, Massachusetts. In 1994, nine-year-old Ashley was playing outside her home when she heard a rustling sound. "A raccoon appeared. It chased me and bit me on the leg," she remembers. The dog ran out of the house and battled the raccoon until Ashley could escape. (Ashley and Kelsey both had follow-up shots to prevent rabies.) Says Ashley, as she gives her pooch a big hug, "Kelsey's a real hero. She saved my life."

Kelsey fought a rabid animal, saving her owner, Ashley.

 Inquiry & Research

The Inquiry & Research activity on this page links to the Inquiry & Research section of Choices and Challenges following "Lob's Girl."

Instruction Suggest that students be specific in their key word searches on the Internet and on-line systems at the library. Have them write a list of keywords to search, and suggest that they look under topics such as "animal rescues" as well.

Practice Suggest that students construct a chart or graph organizing the information they gather during their research. Once they have analyzed the material, have each student discuss his or her judgment with a partner before starting to write the essay.

Use **Writing Transparencies**, p. 47, for additional support.

PREPARING to *Read*

My First Dive with the Dolphins

Essay by DON C. REED

Connect to Your Life

What do you know about dolphins?
What would you like to learn about them?

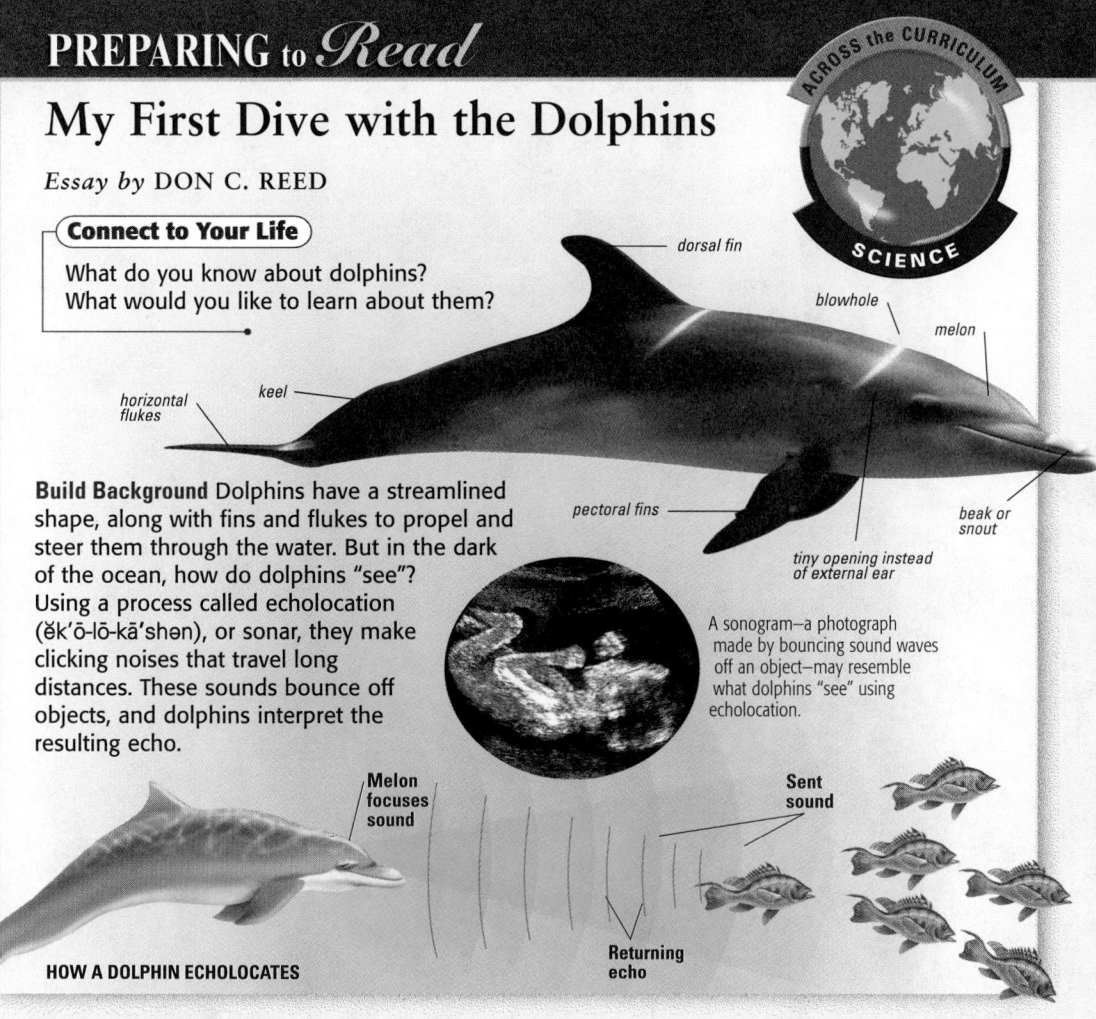

dorsal fin

blowhole

melon

horizontal flukes

keel

pectoral fins

beak or snout

tiny opening instead of external ear

A sonogram—a photograph made by bouncing sound waves off an object—may resemble what dolphins "see" using echolocation.

Build Background Dolphins have a streamlined shape, along with fins and flukes to propel and steer them through the water. But in the dark of the ocean, how do dolphins "see"? Using a process called echolocation (ĕk'ō-lō-kā'shən), or sonar, they make clicking noises that travel long distances. These sounds bounce off objects, and dolphins interpret the resulting echo.

Melon focuses sound

Sent sound

Returning echo

HOW A DOLPHIN ECHOLOCATES

Focus Your Reading

LITERARY ANALYSIS ESSAY An **essay** is a short work of nonfiction that deals with a single subject. The **purpose** of an essay may be to express feelings, entertain, explain, or persuade.

WORDS TO KNOW Vocabulary Preview

aggression	compressed	hurtle	sonar
camouflage	dominant	luminous	
coexistence	elegant	magnification	

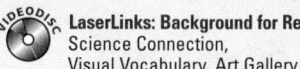 **LaserLinks: Background for Reading**
Science Connection,
Visual Vocabulary, Art Gallery

ACTIVE READING MAKING GENERALIZATIONS

A **generalization** is a conclusion you draw about a whole group of people or things. Making generalizations can help you understand the author's main ideas. Be careful not to make a generalization so broad that it is incorrect. For example, the generalization "All apples are red" is too broad. Some apples are green or yellow. As you read the essay, jot down at least three generalizations in your [] **READER'S NOTEBOOK**. Also note the evidence from the selection that supports your statements.

MY FIRST DIVE WITH THE DOLPHINS   **465**

Reading Skills and Strategies:
PREVIEW

Briefly summarize "My First Dive with the Dolphins." Have students look through the story. Tell them to make a prediction about what it would be like to dive with dolphins.

Literary Analysis ESSAY

Tell students that an essay is a short composition on a single subject. Usually the author of the essay conveys his or her personal view of the subject. Ask students to describe Don Reed's personal view of his work.

Possible Response: The author feels awkward as he embarks on his first day of work as a professional scuba diver.

 Use **Unit Four Resource Book,** p. 13 for more practice.

Active Reading
MAKING GENERALIZATIONS

Remind students that a generalization is a statement that applies to many examples. Encourage them to look for generalizations as they read "My First Dive with the Dolphins." Ask them to suggest some of the kinds of generalizations that they might encounter.

Possible Response: The author might make generalizations about how dolphins act toward people or about why dolphins are so fascinating to people.

Use **Unit Four Resource Book,** p. 12 for more practice. Use **Reading and Critical Thinking Transparencies,** p. 14, for additional support.

MY FIRST DIVE with the Dolphins

by Don C. Reed

466   UNIT FOUR   PART 1: ANIMAL WONDERS

Teaching Options

 Mini Lesson **Preteaching Vocabulary**

USING A DICTIONARY: GUIDE WORDS
Instruction Call students' attention to the list of WORDS TO KNOW. Remind them that they can learn the meaning of an unfamiliar word by using the dictionary. In order to find the word in the dictionary, students should use the guide words, the two words that appear at the top of each page. For example, if students want to look up the word *compress,* they might find it on a page with the guide words *compound* and *compromise* because *compress* comes between those two words.
Application Write the word *camouflage* on the board. Then write the following two pairs of

guide words. Ask students to identify the pair between which the word *camouflage* would fall.
camel   camera
camel   campaign
Now ask students to select another word from the WORDS TO KNOW list, look it up in the dictionary, and find the two guide words that appear on the page where that word is located.

Use **Unit Four Resource Book,** p. 14 for more practice. Use **Vocabulary Transparencies and Copymasters,** p. 48.

stood on a narrow, red-painted stage above half a million gallons of cold salt water.

A wave slashed foam onto the stage and across my bare feet. I had a black rubber wet suit on but neither a hood nor "booties," those heavy neoprene[1] shoes that divers take for granted nowadays. It didn't occur to me to ask the other divers why we had neither foot nor head protection. I wore what the other folks wore. I wasn't about to complain: if the other divers had jumped off the edge in their underwear, I would have just shrugged and done the same.

That cold, windy March day in 1972 was my first day of work as a professional scuba diver for Marine World, soon to become Marine World/Africa USA, an oceanarium-zoo in northern California. I didn't let on how strange everything felt. I was only six months out of deep-sea-diving school and had almost no idea of what to expect.

The hard rubber mouthpiece still felt foreign clenched between my teeth. It seemed clumsy to breathe through my mouth instead of my nose. Each breath had to be "asked for," pulled in by a conscious lifting of the chest, creating a vacuum to suck in the <u>compressed</u> air.

Not wanting to dangle my legs in the water, I stood awkwardly on one foot at a time as I fumbled into the big, floppy swim fins.

As I pulled the black plastic mask over my face, the strap tugged at my hair. When I opened my eyes, my field of vision was narrowed by the mask. It was like staring through a section of pipe.

I took one giant step forward and fell . . . into another world.

I heard the crash of the surface as it broke apart and thumped shut above me; I felt the massage of pressure and the cold water rushing down my neck and spine. Air bubbles slid ticklingly up my face, heading for the surface, while I headed the opposite way, falling, dragged down by the heavy lead work belt around my waist.

As the bubbles of my entry cleared, my vision returned. My fin tips folded softly underneath me as I landed on the green, algae-covered[2] floor.

Oddly, I didn't spot the dolphins right away. Perhaps their dark/light <u>camouflage</u> patterns broke up their outlines. Then, all at once, there they were—and so much bigger than I had expected. It's only the <u>magnification</u> down here, I told myself, a trick of underwater light. But I knew they

---

1. **neoprene** (nē′ə-prēn′): a weather-resistant synthetic rubber.

2. **algae-covered** (ăl′jē-kŭv′ərd): covered with algae, tiny plantlike organisms that grow in water.

WORDS TO KNOW	**compressed** (kəm-prĕst′) *adj.* under greater than normal pressure **compress** *v.*
	camouflage (kăm′ə-fläzh′) *n.* a disguise produced by blending in with the surroundings
	magnification (măg′nə-fĭ-kā′shən) *n.* the causing of objects to appear enlarged

467

Literary Analysis: SPECIALIZED LANGUAGE

Explain that specialized vocabulary tells about a specific topic. Tell students that this essay contains words that tell about scuba diving and words that tell about dolphins. Ask students to identify some of the specialized vocabulary on page 468. Then have them tell which topic the words relate to—scuba diving or dolphins.

Possible Response: Specialized vocabulary such as *air compressor* and *regulator* relate to scuba diving. *Sonar* relates to dolphins.

Reading Skills and Strategies: MAKE INFERENCES

A Tell students to reread the paragraph that begins, "I had always thought . . . " Ask them to make an inference about the author's feelings toward the dolphins at this point.

Possible Response: The author seems to be afraid of the dolphins. He's nervous about getting close to Arnie; he's not even sure which one Arnie is.

Reading Skills and Strategies: MAIN IDEA AND DETAILS

Ask students to identify the main idea of the text on page 469. Then tell them to name at least three of the details.

Possible Response: The main idea of the text on this page is that the scuba divers were responsible for scraping the algae off the tank. Some of the details include Ted's instructions to hold the brush upside-down, the reasons why the algae had to be removed, and the author's technique—making a stroke one-inch wide instead of six.

Use **Reading and Critical Thinking Transparencies**, p. 25, for additional support.

---

weighed between 300 and 400 pounds each, as much as a giant professional wrestler or the biggest lineman on a football team.

I tried to remember the one-minute human-dolphin <u>coexistence</u> lesson that head diver Ted Pintarelli had given me.

"Spock—that's the one with the hole in his fin—he won't bother you. Neither will Delbert: he's got a shark scar on his belly that makes him easy to spot. The smallest one's Ernestine; she's okay. Lucky is king bull, the toughest dolphin in the tank. You'll recognize him right away: there's a purple spot on his cheek, and he's big and all scarred up from fights, and . . . well, you'll know him!

"But Arnie, he's the one who'll give you trouble. He thinks he's bad, and he likes to try and scare new guys in the tank. Like he might swim fast at you or something. Just hold still if he does. Don't let him chase you out of the tank, or he'll make a game out of it, and you'll never get any work done. Don't look scared. He'll leave you alone . . . most of the time, anyway," the muscular, red-faced diver had added with a grin.

A had always thought of dolphins as sweet and gentle, like Flipper on the old TV show, who was sort of an oceangoing Lassie, man's best friend in the sea. Now I tried to figure out which one was Arnie. He was supposed to have a lower jaw shaped like a hook, whatever that meant. But it was no use: I couldn't tell the dolphins apart. They all looked like trouble to me.

As the streamlined but massive gray creatures cruised around me, I reminded myself they were not sharks. Their eighty-eight white, needlelike teeth, which I could see so clearly, were meant for snagging swift

herring on the run, not for ripping out a twenty-pound mouthful of flesh, as a white shark's teeth were. Dolphins were mammals, not fish, and the reason for the up-and-down motion of their tails was to bring them back up to the air.

1

> **"But Arnie, he's the one who'll give you trouble. . . . he likes to try and scare new guys in the tank."**

Some said dolphins were smart like people. Certainly dolphins could do things with <u>sonar</u> that we humans couldn't match. In one experiment I read about, dolphins were able to distinguish between two types of identical-looking plastic-coated wire—one with a lead core, the other with a copper core—just by sending their special clicking sounds inside them.

Well, I wasn't getting a whole lot of work done this way. In the distance I could see the three other divers, already lying down on the floor, their scrub brushes busy. As it was for them, cleaning algae off the underwater floors and walls and windows would be 95 percent of my job. The other 5 percent, the head diver had promised, would be magic.

None of the divers had air tanks. Each diver breathed through a thin yellow air hose leading up to the surface, where it was plugged into a brass outlet on an air compressor. I noticed the strange shape of the bubbles as they left my regulator and wobbled to the surface. They were not round but dome-shaped, flat

WORDS TO KNOW

coexistence (kō'ĭg-zĭs'təns) *n.* a state of living together in peace
sonar (sō'när') *n.* detection of objects by reflected sound waves

468

 Mini Lesson ## Speaking and Listening

DOLPHIN AND WHALE SOUNDS

Instruction Explain that dolphins use "echolocation," in which sounds are reflected off solid surfaces back to their ears. By using high-pitched whistles and squeaks, dolphins can detect the location of underwater objects, especially schools of fish and shrimp. Dolphins can also communicate with each other.

Marine biologists have made recordings of dolphin and whale sounds. Contact your local library or science center to acquire a recording, and play it for students.

Application After listening to a recording of dolphin and whale sounds, have students write a paragraph describing what they heard. Tell them to think about the meanings, or purposes, of the different sounds. Ask them to compare these sounds to the sounds of other wild animals they may be familiar with, such as birds and squirrels.

Use **Communications Transparencies and Copymasters**, p. 2, for additional support.

on the bottom, and they changed as they rose toward the mirrorlike surface twenty feet above.

In my hand was a short iron-handled scrub brush. I held it in the special way Ted had shown me.

"If you hold it the regular way, like a hairbrush, you can't get anything but wrist power behind it," Ted said. "But upside-down, the bristles are next to your palm, and you get your whole body into it. Switch hands every ten or twelve brush strokes, too, so you won't have to stop and rest."

Lying down in a sort of pushup position, I took an experimental scrub stroke at the floor. The brush was neither motorized nor self-operational. My tentative push did not accomplish much. Some scratches appeared in the green algae; that was all. The stuff clung like paint!

The algae has to be taken off, or it grows thicker and thicker and finally rots, breaking off at the roots, clouding the water, clogging the filtration system, and plugging up the windows. There are chemical ways to kill algae, of course, but these cannot be used because they are harmful to the dolphins' eyes.

So we divers scrubbed. Algae was our job security!

I turned the brush on edge, so that the stroke it made would be one inch wide instead of six, and leaned all my shoulder strength behind the stroke. Now the brush bit. There. I had a one-by-twelve-inch piece of clean white

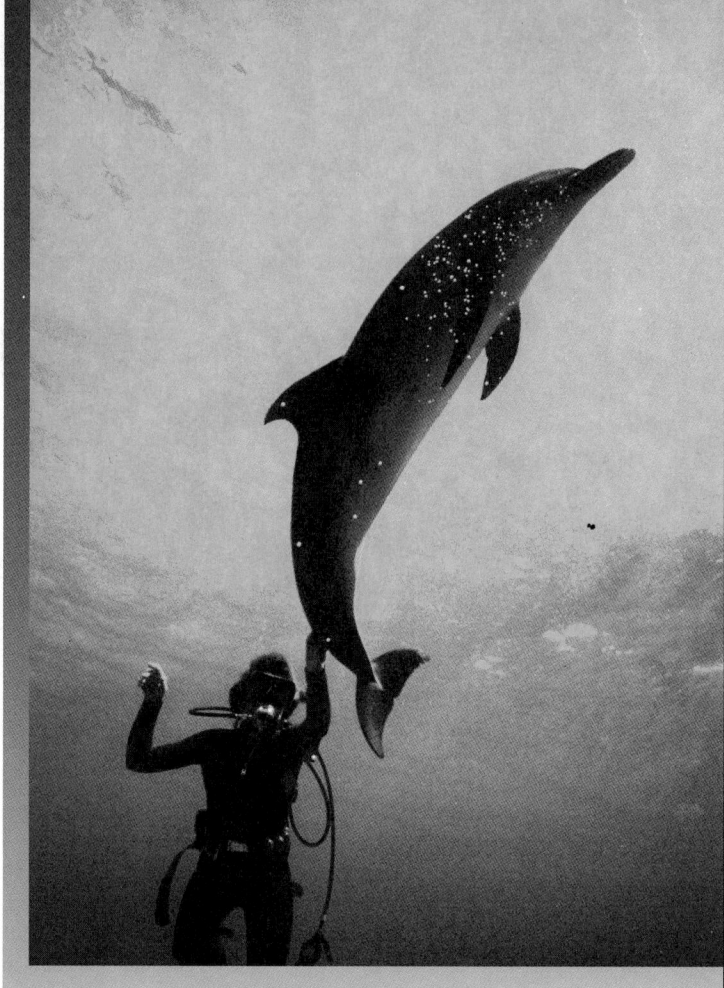

floor. Just eleven more strokes and I'd have one whole square foot finished. And since the tank was 60 by 80 feet, that meant there were only 4,799 more square feet to go.

Suddenly a blur of movement caught my eye. A dolphin was <u>hurtling</u> toward me. Although it was closing the distance between us unbelievably fast, I saw it as if it were in slow motion.

WORDS
TO   **hurtle** (hûr′tl) *v.* to move with great speed
KNOW

469

Mini Lesson Spelling

CHANGING *-T* TO *-CE*

Instruction Explain that some adjectives end in *-t*. Words such as *instant, dominant,* and *patient* end in *-t*. In order to form a noun from each of these words, you simply change the *-t* ending to *-ce*. Ask students to name the nouns that can be formed from the adjectives above. *(instance, dominance,* and *patience)*

Exercise Have students find a noun on pages 468–469 that ends in *-ce. (distance)* Tell them to

identify the related adjective. *(distant)* Ask them to change the *-t* on the following adjectives to make nouns, and then use each one in a sentence:
reluctant *(reluctance)*
significant *(significance)*
fragrant *(fragrance)*

Use **Unit Four Resource Book,** p. 16.

Literary Analysis: DESCRIPTIONS

 Have students tell why the description of Arnie is so effective.

Possible Response: The description of Arnie is effective because the author makes you feel as if you are there with him. By describing his first meeting with Arnie in great detail, he captures his own nervousness. I can completely understand what he was feeling.

Reading Skills and Strategies: CLARIFY

 Ask students to reread the paragraph on page 471 in which the author describes Ernestine making what looks like a halo. Ask students whether this passage was clear to them the first time they read it. Then ask them how they went about clarifying what they were reading.

Possible Response: I wasn't really sure what the author meant when he said the dolphin was "manufacturing a halo." I clarified what I was reading by reading on. After I read the paragraph that followed this description, I realized that the dolphin was playing in the water and making bubbles by exhaling air from her blowhole.

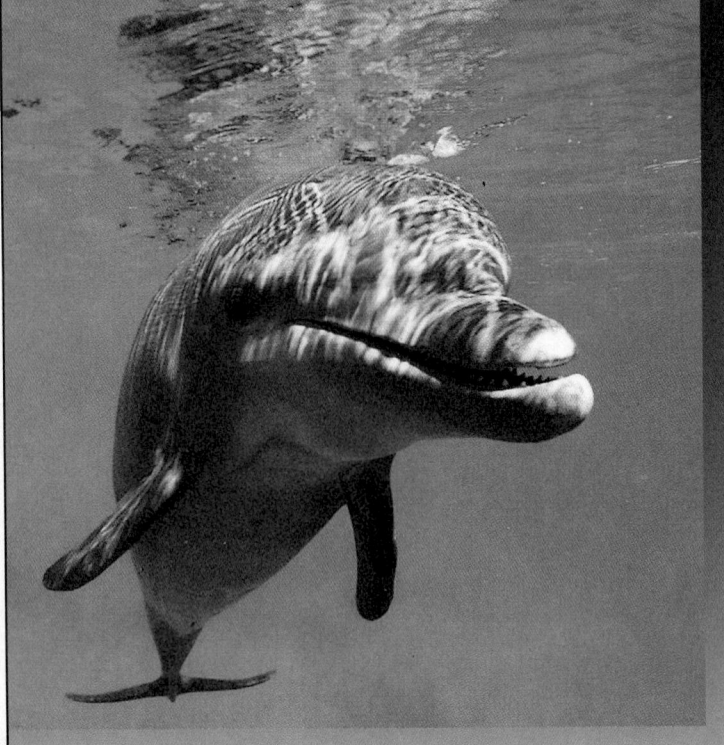

The dolphin's lower jaw hooked over its top one: it was Arnie. His head moved up and down violently, and his tail moved so fast that a trail of bubbles formed behind it. As the dolphin charged, I heard a roar of cavitation[3] as the very water tore, breaking into hydrogen and oxygen.

I didn't even have time to flinch properly. It was easy to do just what Ted recommended. I froze.

I knew that if the dolphin ran into me at that speed, whatever he hit would be broken. This was how dolphins were able to kill sharks: they smashed their insides with a high-speed ram.

Whooosh! I felt rather than heard a wash of water like a great wind. I saw the dolphin's stomach—he had a bellybutton!—then the animal turned like a veering jet.

But not to go away. No more than six feet from me, he stopped. I saw his narrow face, saw his jaws move, heard the *klonk* that I knew signaled aggression. His white teeth gleamed, sharp and clean as if they had been brushed. But dolphins do not fight seriously with their teeth.

In a motion so fast my mind had to reconstruct it afterward, the gristly ridge on the underside of the dolphin's tail flukes suddenly appeared right before my face. It was as if a baseball bat had been swung at my head—and stopped an inch before my face caved in.

Again I did nothing, but not through courage. My reflexes are slow. I had time to tell myself, Hold still; don't do anything to make him think you want to fight. I also had time to feel a wave of anger at this huge animal for picking on me for no reason at all.

Then another dolphin, heavy-bodied with a purple spot on the left side of his beak, eased into my vision, and Arnie casually swam off with him.

When my heart and breathing rates returned to relative normality, I went back to my work. I scrubbed and watched, and watched and scrubbed. My shoulders began to

---

3. **cavitation** (kăv′ĭ-tā′shən): sudden formation of bubbles in a liquid by an object moving rapidly through it.

WORDS
TO
KNOW

aggression (ə-grĕsh′ən) *n.* threatening behavior; hostility

470

Mini Lesson **Grammar**

COMBINING SENTENCES USING CONJUNCTIONS

Instruction Tell students that by using conjunctions, they can join two separate but related ideas, turning two sentences into one. Tell students that some conjunctions are *and, or, so, but, if, because, that, whether, although, since, when,* and *while.*

Exercises Write the following sentences on the board. Have students use a conjunction to join the two sentences.

1. The author didn't move when he saw Arnie. The author was afraid of the dolphin.

(The author didn't move when he saw Arnie, because he was afraid of the dolphin.)

2. The author feared Arnie. He was fascinated by Ernestine's beauty and grace. *(The author feared Arnie, but he was fascinated by Ernestine's beauty and grace.)*

 Use **Grammar Transparencies and Copymasters,** p. 111.

Use McDougal Littell's *Language Network,* Chapter 6, for more practice in streamlining with conjunctions.

feel pumped full of blood, as they do in weightlifting workouts.

Suddenly something shining caught my attention. I turned my head, and the whirring roar of the regulator seemed to disappear.

 n stillness like the hush in a cathedral, I saw the smallest dolphin move her head just slightly, and from the back of her neck something silvery emerged, as if she were manufacturing a halo.

Naah. Yes! There it was: a glistening, gleaming, silver bubble ring, rising. The dolphin flexed her neck again, and another ring emerged, rising faster, so that it joined its luminous relation and they merged, becoming first a figure eight and then a larger single circle, a Hula-Hoop of light.

After I'd spent nearly two hours in the water, the scrubbed-off algae was rising in darkening clouds, like night closing in.

I kept switching the brush back and forth, from hand to hand, trying not to think about Arnie. Long ago, in India, there was a saying that you should not worry about tigers, lest you bring one to you by the thought.

Still, I couldn't help wondering where he was. My head began to shift back and forth more rapidly as I tried to see but couldn't.

Just then, something touched me!

I rolled, ready to fight, and looked into the red-brown eye and the face of . . . whom?

It was definitely not the hook jaw of Arnie, and the purple spot of Lucky's cheek was not there. Spock was supposed to have a hole in his left pec fin, while Delbert had a shark scar. This must be Ernestine.

I told myself she wasn't really smiling: that happy look was just an accident of jaw formation, indicating nothing more than lines of bone and muscle. But looking at her made me feel happy just the same.

She was so beautiful. From a distance, the dolphins had looked simple, uncomplicated. But up close, everything about Ernestine was astonishing. The black pupil in the center of her red-brown eye seemed to radiate emotion. Six inches back from the eye was a fold of skin with an opening the size of a pinhole in it, the opening to her ear. Even the dolphin's skin was special: not perfectly smooth but textured with the tiniest of lines and colored with subtle gray patterns that were perfectly matched and fitted together, like the interlocking feathers on a hawk.

She was so beautiful. . . . up close, everything about Ernestine was astonishing.

She had pectoral (chest) fins to steer with, tail flukes for power, and a blowhole at the back of her head that could release breath at 200 miles per hour, punching a hole in the ocean spray so the dolphin could inhale relatively dry air and not drown in a storm. From the shape of her beak—the reason for the name "bottlenose"—to the elegant flare of her tail flukes, she was a creature of wonder. I felt I could study her for a thousand years and not see everything.

Ernestine nuzzled in beside me and laid her pectoral fin on my back.

This amazed me. A big animal I had never met before, and it swam up and touched me!

WORDS TO KNOW	luminous (lōō′mə-nəs) *adj.* full of light
	elegant (ĕl′ĭ-gənt) *adj.* beautiful in shape or style

471

Literary Analysis:
AUTHOR'S PURPOSE

Ask students to tell why they think the author wrote "My First Dive with the Dolphins." Did he write it to inform, entertain, persuade, or express an opinion? Tell students that sometimes an author has more than one purpose.

Possible Response: I think the author wrote this story to inform readers about dolphins and to express his own feelings about his first experience swimming in their tank.

Reading Skills and Strategies:
EVALUATE

Ask students to think about the opinions that they formed about the author as they read this selection.

Possible Response: I thought that the author was brave to do some of the things that he did. I admired him when he decided to swim along with Ernestine, and I thought he was smart to drift down and return to his scrubbing when he saw Lucky. He sensed that he should show respect to the dominant dolphin, and that turned out to be the right thing to do.

I couldn't resist her. Without conscious thought, my hand reached up and stroked her side. It felt smooth, soft, and firm, like the inside surface of a hard-boiled egg.

Suddenly the dolphin rolled, bringing the fin on her back into my hand. Then she took off.

The suddenness of the motion frightened me, and instantly I straightened my fingers, releasing the loose grip I had held so as not to make her feel restrained. Had I offended her?

But she turned and came back, rolling again to place her dorsal fin (the one on her back) in my right hand.

Why fight it? I thought, dropping my scrub brush.

This time, when Ernestine took off, I went along.

I left my human clumsiness behind. For glorious seconds I knew what it was to be the swiftest swimmer in the sea. She towed me, and I tried not to get in the way. I was conscious of my body's shape as an obstruction and tried to narrow myself.

We soared. The water rushed past my face and swirled around my body, and I felt the streaking lines of speed.

Klonk! At the sound, Ernestine flicked out and away from my hand and was gone in an instant. I hung in the water, becoming a sluggish human once again.

Before me "stood" a gray-white dolphin giant. There was no question as to his identity. I knew it was Lucky even before I saw the scars on his face and neck and shoulders and the dark spot on the left side of his jaw.

The <u>dominant</u> dolphin lowered his head slowly. Again I heard the noise of irritation,

threat, or challenge, and for an instant I thought he would give me trouble for getting too friendly with Ernestine. But the *klonk*ing sound was softer now, as if the point had already been made.

I was in the presence of a leader. Whether I labeled him "alpha male" or "dominant dolphin bull" or "king among his own kind" made no difference. This chunk of sea was Lucky's territory, and he was very definitely in charge.

There was depth to Lucky, and intelligence. It was an intelligence different from my own, perhaps, but certainly deserving of respect. He looked like he knew how to live and how to die, like an Apache[4] chieftain living in the wild, who would find hardship and danger at every turn and was content that it should be so.

I was in the presence of a leader.

I did not understand all this at once, of course. I had no words to express what I felt then. There were only raw emotions, ideas, possibilities. My brain felt staggered, like a computer with information overload.

Trying to show neither fear nor aggression (and certainly not disrespect!), I let myself drift down, settling slowly back to the floor of the tank, to my dropped scrub brush, to my work.

Lucky only watched me go and made no move to follow. ❖

---

4. **Apache** (ə-păch′ē): belonging to a Native American people of the southwestern United States and northern Mexico.

WORDS
TO
KNOW

dominant (dŏm′ə-nənt) *adj.* having the most influence; controlling all others

Teaching Options

Cross Curricular Link Science

DOLPHIN INTELLIGENCE Dolphins' social behavior and organization is thought to be among the most advanced in the animal kingdom. Because they survive well in captivity, dolphins have been the subject of many studies. Their relatively long life expectancy of 25 years gives scientists and marine biologists ample opportunity to study dolphin behavior.

Dolphins possess a complex communication and detection system. Through use of underwater sonar, dolphins can easily locate food that is 100 meters away. The time it takes for a reflected sound to return indicates how far away the object is from the dolphin.

Dolphins also use their ability to make sounds to communicate with each other. This skill is important in the open ocean, where there can be more than 1,000 dolphins in a living group, or pod.

Connect to the Literature

1. What Do You Think? How did you react to the author's experience with Lucky?

Comprehension Check
• What is Don C. Reed's job?
• What happens when Reed meets Arnie? Ernestine? Lucky?

Think Critically

2. How do you think Lucky might treat Reed the next time he enters the tank? Explain your response.

3. How do you think Reed feels during his first day on the job?

4. The head diver told Reed that 95 percent of his job would be cleaning and 5 percent would be fun and excitement. What was exciting about Reed's job?

5. What personality traits does Reed have that you think would be helpful in working with dolphins?

THINK ABOUT

- Reed's reaction to the diving gear he received
- how he dealt with the job of removing algae
- his reactions to Arnie, Ernestine, and Lucky

6. **ACTIVE READING** **MAKING GENERALIZATIONS** Exchange your **READER'S NOTEBOOK** entry with a classmate and discuss the generalizations you each made while reading the essay. What generalizations does the author make about dolphins?

Extend Interpretations

7. The Writer's Style Critics have praised the engaging details in Reed's writing. How does his use of **sensory details** contribute to your understanding of the selection?

8. Connect to Life On the basis of what you learned from the selection, would you want a job like the author's? Elaborate.

Literary Analysis

ESSAY An **essay** is a short piece of nonfiction that deals with one subject. Like other types of short nonfiction, an essay has an introduction, a body, and a conclusion. Both informal and formal essays often are found in magazines and newspapers. An informal essay writer's **purpose** usually is to **entertain** or **persuade** the reader, or to **describe** an incident that is significant to the writer. Writers of **informal essays** often present their own feelings and observations. For example, author Don C. Reed writes that he found Ernestine "beautiful" and "astonishing." **Formal essays** are rarely about personal subjects. They usually are written on scholarly topics.

Activity Look through a magazine or newspaper and find at least three examples of essays. Identify what you consider to be the author's purpose or purposes in each.

SPECIALIZED LANGUAGE
Words or phrases that relate to certain occupations, fields of study, or technology are called **specialized language.** "My First Dive with the Dolphins" contains many examples of specialized—or technical—language. You may wish to revisit unfamiliar terms, such as *alpha male* or *regulator,* and find their definitions in a dictionary.

Connect to the Literature

1. What Do You Think?
Encourage students to use specific details from the story to explain their thoughts.

Comprehension Check
• Reed's job is to scrub algae off the walls and floor of the dolphin tank.
• Arnie charges Reed and swings his tail at him. Ernestine puts her fluke in Reed's hand and tows him as she swims. Lucky makes an aggressive sound but leaves Reed alone.

 Use Selection Quiz **Unit Four Resource Book,** p. 17.

Think Critically

2. Possible Responses: Lucky would probably be less suspicious of Reed since Reed presented no threat to him; just because Lucky wasn't aggressive on Reed's first day in the tank doesn't mean that he won't be aggressive when Reed returns.

3. Possible Response: Reed has some moments of fear; however, his basic feelings range from excitement to a sense of wonder and respect.

4. Possible Responses: Simply being in the tank with the dolphins is exciting; being in actual contact with the dolphins is exciting.

5. Some students might suggest that Reed's enthusiasm is his most helpful trait. Because Reed wants to do a good job and make contact with the dolphins, he is willing to do the hard work and deal with a degree of risk.

6. Students may say that dolphins are intelligent or that dolphins are physically imposing.

Use **Reading and Critical Thinking Transparencies,** p. 14, for additional support.

Literary Analysis

Essay Encourage students to read some of the essays collected by their classmates. Then lead a discussion about the purposes of the various essays. Ask students if they agree with their classmates on the purposes of the collected essays.

Extend Interpretations

7. The Writer's Style Sample Response: By describing how swimming with the dolphins affects his senses, Reed makes readers feel as if they are there in the tank with him. For example, Reed describes the way the movement of the water feels when Arnie charges him and how Ernestine's skin feels when he touches it.

8. Connect to Life Some students may respond that Reed's job seems too difficult and dangerous. Other students may say that having a chance to spend time with the dolphins would make the job worthwhile.

Writing Options

1. New Point of View Tell students to include details in their scene that make it clear which dolphin they have chosen. Remind them that dolphins are intelligent creatures. Encourage students to try to get inside the mind of their dolphin and express what they think the dolphin is thinking and feeling.

2. Time Line Remind students to think about distinguishing the main idea from details as they decide which events to place on their time lines. Tell them that a time line should be clear and simple.

 Use **Writing Transparencies**, p. 23, for additional support.

Activities & Explorations

1. Underwater Illustration Students' artwork should capture some of the details that Reed provides in his essay. From looking at the drawing or painting, viewers who have read the story should be able to identify the scene that the artist has chosen.

2. Interview Role-Play Tell students to ask reasonable questions that Reed is likely to be able to answer. Suggest that students' questions pertain to information from the selection.

Use **Communications Transparencies and Copymasters,** p. 13, for additional support.

Inquiry & Research

Dolphin Facts Encourage students to make visual aids to accompany their oral presentations. Photos, charts, and illustrations will all make the information more appealing and more accessible to listeners. **To make this activity easier,** have students work in pairs or small groups, with each being responsible for a part of the task.

Use **Writing Transparencies,** p. 47, for additional support.

Writing Options

1. New Point of View Choose a scene from the essay. Rewrite the scene from the point of view of one of the dolphins.

2. Time Line Go through the essay and create a time line of the events that happened during Don C. Reed's first day on the job. Use a diagram like the one shown here.

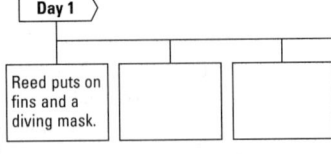

| Day 1 |

Reed puts on fins and a diving mask.

Place the completed time line in your **Working Portfolio.**

Activities & Explorations

1. Underwater Illustration Reed says, "I took one giant step forward and fell . . . into another world." Which of his descriptions helped you experience the feeling of being underwater? Draw or paint a scene that inspires you. **~ ART**

2. Interview Role-Play With a partner, write a list of questions you would ask Don C. Reed in an interview. Then role-play the interview, with one person taking the part of Reed and the other playing the interviewer. Halfway through, change roles. **~ SPEAKING AND LISTENING**

Inquiry & Research

SCIENCE **DOLPHIN FACTS**

Using the Internet, an encyclopedia, and books about dolphins, find out about the following:

- What areas of the world have dolphin populations?
- How do dolphins interact with other species?
- What do scientists know about dolphin intelligence?

Present your research to the class in the form of an oral presentation or a poster.

 More Online: Research Starter www.mcdougallittell.com

Vocabulary in Action

EXERCISE: CONTEXT CLUES On a sheet of paper, write the vocabulary word that best completes each sentence below.

1. While underwater, divers breathe _____ air from a tank or a hose.

2. The _____ of humans and dolphins at the oceanarium was mostly peaceful.

3. The dolphins' _____ makes them difficult to see underwater.

4. The _____ effect of water makes the dolphins look larger than they are.

5. Arnie swam so fast that he seemed to _____ through the water toward me.

6. An angry dolphin makes a special sound, one that is a sign of _____.

7. Dolphins use sounds called _____ to navigate underwater.

8. Ernestine created _____ rings that seemed to shine in the water.

9. From her red-brown eyes to her _____ flukes, Ernestine was beautiful.

10. Lucky was the _____ dolphin in the tank because of his toughness.

Building Vocabulary

For an in-depth lesson on specialized vocabulary, see p. 568.

WORDS TO KNOW				
aggression	coexistence	dominant	hurtle	magnification
camouflage	compressed	elegant	luminous	sonar

Vocabulary in Action

EXERCISE
1. compressed
2. coexistence
3. camouflage
4. magnification
5. hurtle
6. aggression
7. sonar
8. luminous
9. elegant
10. dominant

Choices & CHALLENGES

Grammar in Context: Combining Sentences by Joining Phrases

In "My First Dive with the Dolphins," Don C. Reed uses smooth, short sentences. For example:

> **Again I did nothing, but <u>not through courage</u>.**

The word shown in red is a **conjunction,** a word that joins other words or phrases. Common conjunctions include *and, but, for,* and *or.*

Compare the excerpt above to the choppy version below:

> **Again I did nothing. My doing nothing was <u>not through courage</u>.**

The second example uses too many words to say the same thing as the first. The underlined phrase can be combined with the previous sentence for more drama and a faster pace.

Apply to Your Writing Combining phrases can help you avoid repeating words unnecessarily.

WRITING EXERCISE Combine each pair of sentences using the conjunction in parentheses.

Example: *Original* A wave splashed on the stage. It splashed at my feet. (and)

Rewritten A wave splashed on the stage and at my feet.

1. Clouds of algae spread through the tank. They spread across the surface. (and)
2. I swam away from the shore. I swam into deeper water. (and)
3. Spock will play with you. Spock won't play with other dolphins. (but)

Connect to the Literature Find two examples of sentences in which phrases are joined by conjunctions. Write the sentences, and underline the conjunctions.

"I want my writing to be a positive force."

Don C. Reed
born 1945

Diving In Don C. Reed began his career as a scuba diver in 1972, at Marine World near San Francisco, California. The seaquarium later became Marine World/Africa USA, an oceanarium/zoo, and moved to Vallejo, California. Reed spent 15 years there, eventually becoming head diver.

A Positive Force Reed's adventures with a variety of sea creatures have provided the material for several articles and books. The

author views his writing as a way to "help the world." He states, "I want my writing to be a positive force. I will not write empty entertainment. I want my stuff to have . . . value." Although not a scientist, Reed believes humans and sea animals can coexist and may even be able to understand each other. "My First Dive with the Dolphins" is an excerpt from his book *The Dolphins and Me.*

AUTHOR ACTIVITY

Helping the World Read another article or chapter in a book by Don C. Reed. Based on "My First Dive with the Dolphins" and your other reading, evaluate the author's statement that he views his writing as a way to "help the world." Write a paragraph explaining what you think Reed hopes his writing will accomplish. How successful is he in achieving this?

 Grammar
Mini Lesson

IDENTIFYING CONJUNCTIONS

Instruction Students can make their writing flow more smoothly by using conjunctions. Write the following sentences on the board:

Don C. Reed was nervous about diving into the dolphin tank. He didn't let his fears stop him.

Don C. Reed was nervous about diving into the dolphin tank, but he didn't let his fears stop him.

Point out the way these two thoughts have been merged by using the conjunction *but.*

Exercise Tell students to read each pair of sentences and name a conjunction that they

could use to combine the two sentences.

1. Reed liked watching Ernestine. He particularly enjoyed touching her and swimming with her. *(and/ but)*
2. Reed purposely held still when Arnie approached him. That's what Ted had recommended. *(because)*
3. Reed sensed that Lucky commanded respect. He decided to drift down and return to his work. *(so)*
4. Ted had given Reed essential information about the dolphins. He knew it would help

Reed on his first dive. *(because)*
5. Reed says he used to think that all dolphins were gentle and sweet. He realizes that each one has a distinct personality. *(but)*

OVERVIEW

Objectives

1. understand and appreciate **poetry** (Literary Analysis)
2. understand author's use of **sound devices** (Literary Analysis)
3. think about **word choice** to help understand sound devices better (**Active Reading**)

Summary

Two poets ponder two birds. Rachel Field marvels at how wild geese know when it's time to fly south, while Robert Frost muses about the winter owl, admiring her grace as she veers away from a window.

Thematic Link

Through their poetry, Field and Frost express our desire to understand birds and our ability to appreciate their beauty. These two poems reflect our fascination with bird flight. How is it that these winged creatures know when and where to go?

5-Minute Warm-Up

Daily Language SkillBuilder

Have students **proofread** the display sentences on page 441i and write them correctly. The sentences also appear on Transparency 15 of **Grammar Transparencies and Copymasters.**

Something Told the Wild Geese

Poetry by RACHEL FIELD

Questioning Faces

Poetry by ROBERT FROST

(**Connect to Your Life**)

Birds of a Feather What have you noticed about the appearance and behavior of birds you see in your community?

Build Background

CONNECT TO **SCIENCE** In the two poems you are about to read, birds—wild geese and an owl—play important roles. Birds are different from most other animals because of their capacity for flight. Have you ever asked yourself why birds fly? One explanation is that they need to fly in order to survive. Like most animals, birds have adaptations, or special features, to help them live in certain habitats.

Birds need a steady, yearlong food supply, and many birds need to avoid very cold temperatures. These birds fly to warmer climates in the autumn and return in the spring.

Wild geese have webbed feet for swimming and broad, powerful wings to help them fly south for the winter.

Focus Your Reading

LITERARY ANALYSIS **SOUND DEVICES** Poets use **sound devices** to make their words more powerful. Common sound devices are rhyme, rhythm, and repetition. Words that end with the same sounds are said to **rhyme.** The pattern of stressed and unstressed syllables that guides your voice when reading is the poem's **rhythm.** The use of sounds, words, or phrases more than once is **repetition.** As you read, look for the patterns of rhyme, rhythm, and repetition. How do they add to the sense of wonder in each poem?

ACTIVE READING **WORD CHOICE** The words a poet chooses tell you a lot about his or her message. Specific words about a poem's subject add detail and flavor to a visual image. For example, it can be more interesting and accurate to describe a sky as *azure* instead of *blue.*

In poetry, both the sounds and the meanings of words are important. Well-chosen words help tie a poem's images to its theme and mood.

READER'S NOTEBOOK As you read each poem, list words and phrases you find especially powerful.

LESSON RESOURCES

UNIT FOUR RESOURCE BOOK, pp. 18–19

ASSESSMENT
Formal Assessment, pp. 83–84
Teacher's Guide to Assessment and Portfolio Use
Test Generator

SKILLS TRANSPARENCIES AND COPYMASTERS
Literary Analysis
• Poetry: Sound Devices, TR 20 (for Paired Activity, p. 479)
Reading and Critical Thinking
• Analyzing Word Choice, TR 15 (for Thinking Through the Literature, p. 479)

INTEGRATED TECHNOLOGY
Audio Library
LaserLinks
• Science Connection. See **Teacher's SourceBook,** p. 38
Internet: Research Starter

Visit our website:
www.mcdougallittell.com

Something Told the Wild Geese

by Rachel Field

Something told the wild geese
   It was time to go.
Though the fields lay golden
   Something whispered,—"Snow."
5 Leaves were green and stirring,
   Berries, luster-glossed,
But beneath warm feathers
   Something cautioned,—"Frost."
All the sagging orchards
10   Steamed with amber spice,
But each wild breast stiffened
   At remembered ice.
Something told the wild geese
   It was time to fly,—
15 Summer sun was on their wings,
   Winter in their cry.

Sunset, Kempenfelt Bay, Lawren Harris.
Collection of Power Corporation of Canada.

Thinking Through the Literature

1. **Comprehension Check** According to the speaker, what messages does nature send to the geese?
2. What time of year does "Something Told the Wild Geese" describe? What details tell you this?
3. Why might it be necessary for the geese to fly away?

TEACHING THE LITERATURE

Customizing Instruction

Less Proficient Readers
Have students keep these questions in mind as they read each poem.
• What is the subject of the poem?
• Why do you think the poet wrote this poem?

Students Acquiring English
Tell students that poets sometimes use personification, in which human traits are attributed to objects. Point out the line "Something whispered, —'Snow.'" Explain that this line doesn't mean that anyone actually said the word *snow*, but that there was a feeling of snow in the air.

Use **Spanish Study Guide,** pp. 100–102 for additional support.

Gifted and Talented
Encourage students to discuss other poems inspired by birds.

Thinking Through the Literature

1. **Comprehension Check** Nature tells them that it's "time to go," "snow," "frost."
2. It depicts late summer or early fall. "Fields lay golden" is a detail that shows this.
3. They are preparing to fly south for the winter because it will be too cold for them soon.

 Viewing and Representing

Sunset, Kempenfelt Bay
by Lawren Harris

ART APPRECIATION

Instruction *Sunset, Kempenfelt* Bay portrays sharp contrasts: between the vertical lines of the trees and the horizontal lines of the sky, the horizon, and the shoreline; and between the warm, light colors of the clouds and water and the cool, dark colors of the landforms and the trees. Point out to students that the poem also portrays a sharp contrast—that between the warmth and life of the late summer and the harsh cold of the coming winter. Ask them to discuss how the painting makes them feel about the changing of the seasons.

Application Ask students to describe how the poem makes them feel about the changing of the seasons. Then have them compare the impressions created by the poem and the painting.

Possible Response: Both the poem and the painting have a peaceful feeling, but the poem also talks about restless feelings. I sense both warm and cool in the painting, both sharpness and softness, dark and light. The poem also sets two opposites against each other: winter and summer.

Literary Analysis SOUND DEVICES

Ask students to identify the rhymes in the poem. Then have them look for *alliteration*—adjoining words that begin with the same sound.

Possible Response: The rhyming words are *pass* and *glass, aspread* and *red,* and *quill* and *sill.* Instances of alliteration include *straining suddenly* and *caught color.*

Use **Unit Four Resource Book,** p. 19, for more practice. Use **Literary Analysis Transparencies,** p. 20, for additional support.

Active Reading WORD CHOICE

A Ask students to consider the word *aspread.* Although they may not find this word in a dictionary, students should have little difficulty figuring out its meaning. Ask them why they think Frost chose this word.

Possible Responses: Frost might have chosen the word *aspread* because it sounds graceful. Because of the rhythm of the poem, a two-syllable word works here.

Use **Unit Four Resource Book,** p. 18, for more practice. Use **Reading and Critical Thinking Transparencies,** p. 15, for additional support.

Reading Skills and Strategies: MAKE INFERENCES

B Ask students to infer what Robert Frost means when he says that the owl's wings "caught color from the last of evening red."

Possible Response: Frost means that the owl's wings were reflecting the setting sun, which looked red.

Questioning Children (1949), Karel Appel. Courtesy of Grand Westin Hotel, Netherlands.

Questioning Faces

by Robert Frost

The winter owl banked just in time to pass

And save herself from breaking window glass.

And her wings straining suddenly aspread

Caught color from the last of evening red

In a display of underdown and quill

To glassed-in children at the window sill.

478 UNIT FOUR   PART 1: ANIMAL WONDERS

Teaching Options

✓ **Assessment Standardized Test Practice**

IMPLIED MAIN IDEA For some standardized tests, students will be asked to read a passage and identify the implied main idea. To give students practice in determining the implied main idea, read aloud or write on the board the following question.

Which of the following statements best expresses the implied main idea of "Questioning Faces"?

A. As an owl makes a sudden move to avoid crashing into a window, children watch and wonder about this mysterious creature.

B. The owl is an intriguing creature, but this one should be more careful so it doesn't crash into windows.

C. The winter owl is fun to watch.

D. The owl is a beautiful and fascinating creature. Lead students through the process of choosing the implied main idea. Consider each choice. A and B give too much detail to be the main idea—A is more like a summary of the poem. C is too general. Help students understand why D is the best choice.

Connect to the Literature

1. What Do You Think?
What images formed in your mind after reading Robert Frost's poem?

Comprehension Check
• In "Questioning Faces," why does the owl bank?
• Who is watching the owl?

Think Critically

2. How do you think the children feel about what they've witnessed?

3. How is "Questioning Faces" similar to "Something Told the Wild Geese"? How are these poems different?

THINK ABOUT
> • the picture each creates
> • the ways that humans view nature
> • the bird's-eye view of the world in each poem

4. **ACTIVE READING** **WORD CHOICE** Look at the list you made in your **READER'S NOTEBOOK**. With a classmate, discuss what these words and phrases add to the poems. Then select one word choice that you think is strong, and complete a web like the one shown.

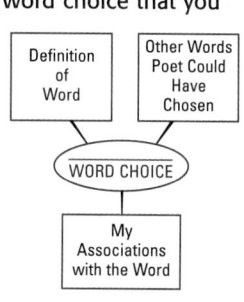

Extend Interpretations

5. **COMPARING TEXTS**
Compare the poems in this lesson with the three haiku on page 205. How are the ways in which Field and Frost describe nature similar to the way a haiku poet might do so?

6. Connect to Life What aspects of nature do you find fascinating or wonderful? Why?

Literary Analysis

SOUND DEVICES Poets use **sound devices** such as rhyme, rhythm, and repetition to create particular moods and emphasize certain ideas. Words that end with the same sound are said to **rhyme.** Robert Frost's poem is built with **rhyming couplets,** pairs of lines that end with rhyming words.

When a poem's **rhythm** has a regular beat, it gives the poem a musical quality. Your voice falls into a pattern when you read it aloud. In both of these poems, the rhyme pattern and rhythm stress the final word in each line.

Repeated words can emphasize the poet's ideas. Rachel Field's **repetition** of the word *something* invites you to wonder what that "something" is.

Paired Activity With a classmate, take turns reading the poems aloud. Then make a chart like the one below. Look at the poems again for examples of repetition and rhyme, and list them in your chart. Discuss how your knowledge of rhyme and repetition in the poems helps you hear their rhythms.

	Repeated Words	Rhyming Words
"Something Told the Wild Geese"	something	go/snow
"Questioning Faces"		

SOMETHING TOLD THE WILD GEESE / QUESTIONING FACES **479**

Extend Interpretations

5. Comparing Texts Possible Response: All five poets write about nature's wonders in very short, concise ways, but the haiku poets follow a different poetic form than Field and Frost. The haiku form is shorter, follows a five-seven-five pattern of syllables, and does not rhyme.

6. Connect to Life Answers will vary, but should include some reflection on students' feelings and thoughts about the natural world.

Writing Options

1. **Field Diary** Student responses will vary but should include their emotional responses as well as details that appeal to their senses. Tell students to feel free to make drawings of their observations in order to remember details. Students can place their field diaries in their Working Portfolios.

 Use **Writing Transparencies,** p. 16, for additional support.

2. **Rhyming Couplets** Suggest that students share their rhyming couplets with a partner. Invite volunteers to read aloud their couplets.

Activities & Explorations

1. **Multimedia Presentation** Give students a few days to prepare their presentations. **To make the activity easier,** allow them to spend some classroom time under your direction using reference books and the Internet to do research.

2. **Plan for Help** Students are likely to think of many different obstacles, including construction sites, fallen tree limbs, and downed power lines. Their warning ideas should be creative yet realistic.

Inquiry & Research

Bird Profile Students could work with partners on this assignment. Tell students it will make it easier for them to focus their writing if they keep the writing prompt in mind as they do their research: What makes this type of bird unique?

 Use **Writing Transparencies,** p. 45, for additional support.

Writing Options

1. **Field Diary** Rachel Field and Robert Frost probably got the ideas for their poems by observing nature. Gather details for a poem by watching something in the natural world. Record your observations in a field diary or journal entry. Note details that appeal to your senses in a sensory-details chart.

Sight	Hearing	Touch	Taste	Smell

2. **Rhyming Couplets** Try your hand at poetry by writing some rhyming couplets, pairs of lines that end with rhyming words. You might add some couplets to Frost's poem or start your own.

Activities & Explorations

1. **Multimedia Presentation** What do these poems convey about birds and about nature? Create a mini-multimedia presentation for the poems. Include music and artwork that express the poems' moods and images. If possible, include a tape-recorded reading of the poems. ~ **VIEWING AND REPRESENTING**

2. **Plan for Help** In Frost's poem, an owl is endangered by a window. What are some other obstacles that birds may encounter? With a partner, develop ways to warn birds away from windows and other hazards.

Present your ideas to the class. ~ **SPEAKING AND LISTENING**

Inquiry & Research

Bird Profile Learn more about wild geese or owls. Find out about physical features and adaptations, nesting and feeding habits, typical habitats and migration patterns, and how the birds are affected by humans. Write two to three paragraphs responding to the question, What makes this type of bird unique?

 More Online: Research Starter www.mcdougallittell.com

"I wasn't one of those children who are remembered . . . as clever and promising."

Rachel Field
1894–1942

Newbery Winner Rachel Field overcame severe learning difficulties to become a writer. In 1930, Field received the Newbery Medal for *Hitty: Her First Hundred Years* (1929). *Hitty* combined Field's interests in children's stories and history—particularly the history of pioneer life. Field's 1931 book about pioneers, *Calico Bush,* received a Newbery Honor Award.

"The poem begins in delight and ends in wisdom."

Robert Frost
1874–1963

A New England Poet Robert Frost farmed, taught school, and edited a newspaper before he achieved recognition as a poet. A four-time Pulitzer Prize winner, Frost received the first of these awards in 1924 for his collection *New Hampshire.* Frost more than achieved his life's goal, which he said was to write "a few poems it will be hard to get rid of."

PREPARING to *Read*

Zlateh the Goat

Short Story by ISAAC BASHEVIS SINGER

"He was a snow child, born of the snow, . . ."

Connect to Your Life

Working Relationship What roles do animals play in your life? How might you feel about an animal that helped your family to survive?

Build Background

CONNECT TO HISTORY Isaac Bashevis Singer grew up in and near Warsaw, Poland. His father was a rabbi, a scholar trained to interpret Jewish law. Most of Singer's stories for young people are rooted in the traditions of Jewish communities. As a boy, Singer lived in a simpler time and place. People clustered together in small villages, and survived on what they could produce on their farms or by trading goods with neighbors.

"Zlateh the Goat" takes place during Hanukkah. This Jewish religious festival celebrates a long-ago event in which one day's worth of lamp oil burned for eight days. Jews commemorate this miracle by lighting candles for eight nights, eating foods such as potato pancakes that are cooked in oil, and exchanging gifts.

WORDS TO KNOW	**Vocabulary Preview**		
astonish	dusk	penetrate	thatched
cleft	imp	regain	
content	indicate	splendor	

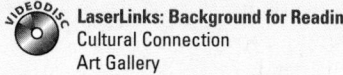

LaserLinks: Background for Reading
Cultural Connection
Art Gallery

Focus Your Reading

LITERARY ANALYSIS **CLIMAX AND RESOLUTION** Two important parts of a story's **plot** are climax and resolution. During the **rising action** characters attempt to solve their **conflicts,** or problems. This leads to the **climax**—the turning point of the story. The **resolution,** or **falling action,** is the part of the story in which the characters' conflicts are often solved. Sometimes the resolution occurs almost at the end of the story. For example, in "The Three Little Pigs," the wolf falls into the fireplace at the end of the story and the pig is safe. In "Zlateh the Goat," the resolution begins earlier. As you read, look for conflict. Then watch for the climax. It's your signal that the resolution is about to begin.

ACTIVE READING **STORY MAPPING** Understanding conflict, climax, and resolution can help you understand and enjoy your reading more. Sometimes it's hard to find these elements, however. They may blend into one another. Creating a **story map** can make the key elements and the key events easier to see.

READER'S NOTEBOOK As you read this story, make and fill in a story map similar to the one shown. Describe the main character, setting, and key events. Identify the conflict, climax, and resolution.

Characters:
Setting:
Conflict:
Key Events:
  1.
  2.
  3.
  (add more as needed)
Climax:
Resolution:

OVERVIEW

Objectives
1. understand and appreciate a **short story** (Literary Analysis)
2. understand author's use of **climax and resolution** (Literary Analysis)
3. use **story mapping** to help understand a short story better (**Active Reading**)

Summary
Reuven the furrier is having a bad year and decides he must sell the family's goat. He sends his son Aaron to town with the goat, Zlateh. The weather changes as they are on their way to the butcher's. Snow starts to fall. They lose their way and are forced to take shelter in a haystack. There, Zlateh is able to eat the hay, and Aaron drinks the goat's milk for nourishment. They survive the storm and return home, as Aaron has decided he will not sell the goat. Because cold weather has arrived, people need fur coats, so the family's situation is improved. Zlateh, instead of being sold, becomes more beloved to the family than before.

Thematic Link
Zlateh provides enough milk to keep Aaron alive during a blizzard. This interdependence of people and animals has provided endless fascination for writers and readers over the centuries.

5-Minute Warm-Up

Daily Language SkillBuilder

Have students **proofread** the display sentences on page 441j and write them correctly. The sentences also appear on Transparency 16 of **Grammar Transparencies and Copymasters.**

Mini Lesson **Preteaching Vocabulary**

If you would like to preteach the WORDS TO KNOW for this selection, use the Mini Lesson, p. 484.

LESSON RESOURCES

UNIT FOUR RESOURCE BOOK, pp. 20–26

ASSESSMENT
Formal Assessment, pp. 85–86
Teacher's Guide to Assessment and Portfolio Use
Test Generator

SKILLS TRANSPARENCIES AND COPYMASTERS
Literary Analysis
• Conflict, TR 8 (for Activity, p. 488)

Reading and Critical Thinking
• Summarizing (Story Map), TR 13 (for Thinking Through the Literature, p. 488)
Grammar
• Punctuating Appositives, CM 125 (for Mini Lesson, p. 490)
Vocabulary
• Context Clues: Compare/ Contrast, CM 49 (for Mini Lesson, p. 484)

INTEGRATED TECHNOLOGY
Audio Library
LaserLinks
• Cultural Connection; Art Gallery. See **Teacher's SourceBook,** p. 39

Visit our website:
www.mcdougallittell.com

Have students read the title of the story, examine the illustrations, and discuss what they think the story might be about.

Possible Response: Students might think the story will have animals in it, and that it takes place in winter.

Active Reading | STORY MAPPING |

Ask students to begin filling in their story maps.

Possible Responses: Main Characters: Zlateh the goat, Aaron; Setting: a village, during a mild winter; Conflict or Story Problem: The family needs money. Key Events: Event 1: Reuven decides to sell Zlateh.

Event 2: Aaron and Zlateh head toward the town.

 Use **Unit Four Resource Book,** p. 21 for more practice.

Literary Analysis
| CLIMAX AND RESOLUTION |

Remind students that the climax is the moment of greatest tension in a story. Ask students if it has happened yet.

Answer: No, it hasn't.

 Use **Unit Four Resource Book,** p. 22 for more practice.

Literary Analysis:
PLOT: RISING ACTION

Remind students that it will be helpful to them to recognize and analyze story plot. Ask what conflicts have been introduced.

Possible Response: The family needs money, so the father decides to sell their goat despite the family's love for her.

Teaching Options

Zlateh the Goat
by Isaac Bashevis Singer

The Goat, Pablo Picasso. Musée Picasso, Paris. Copyright © 2001 Estate of Pablo Picasso/Artists Rights Society (ARS), New York. Photo Copyright © RMN, Beatrice Hatala.

At Hanukkah time the road from the village to the town is usually covered with snow, but this year the winter had been a mild one. Hanukkah had almost come, yet little snow had fallen. The sun shone most of the time. The peasants complained that because of the dry weather there would be a poor harvest of winter grain. New grass sprouted, and the peasants sent their cattle out to pasture.

For Reuven the furrier[1] it was a bad year, and after long hesitation he decided to sell Zlateh the goat. She was old and gave little milk. Feyvel the town butcher had offered eight gulden[2] for her. Such a sum would buy Hanukkah candles, potatoes and oil for pancakes, gifts for the children, and other holiday necessaries for the house. Reuven told his oldest boy, Aaron, to take the goat to town.

Aaron understood what taking the goat to Feyvel meant, but he had to obey his father. Leah, his mother, wiped the tears from her eyes when she heard the news. Aaron's younger sisters, Anna and Miriam, cried loudly. Aaron put on his quilted jacket and a cap with earmuffs, bound a rope around Zlateh's neck, and took along two slices of bread

---

1. **furrier:** a person who makes or sells fur garments.
2. **gulden:** gold or silver coins.

 Viewing and Representing

La chèvre (Goat)
by Pablo Picasso

ART APPRECIATION Pablo Picasso (1881–1973) was one of the most important and prolific artists of the twentieth century. He is best known for his paintings, but also made significant contributions in other fields, including sculpture, though the public did not know the extent of his sculptures until he was 85 years old.

Instruction Explain that this goat, made in 1950, was cast in bronze. Picasso liked to use found objects in his sculptures. This goat's belly was actually formed from a wicker basket.

Application Ask students to describe how the choice of this sculpture helps to represent the story's meaning. How is this particular goat like Zlateh?

Possible Response: Students may say that this sculpture tells the reader more about what a goat is like than the story description does. The goat is scrawny, as we'd expect Zlateh to be, but also looks like she might have plenty of milk available. She looks cuddly like Zlateh, too.

with cheese to eat on the road. Aaron was supposed to deliver the goat by evening, spend the night at the butcher's, and return the next day with the money.

While the family said goodbye to the goat, and Aaron placed the rope around her neck, Zlateh stood as patiently and good-naturedly as ever. She licked Reuven's hand. She shook her small white beard. Zlateh trusted human beings. She knew that they always fed her and never did her any harm.

When Aaron brought her out on the road to town, she seemed somewhat <u>astonished</u>. She'd never been led in that direction before. She looked back at him questioningly, as if to say, "Where are you taking me?" But after a while she seemed to come to the conclusion that a goat shouldn't ask questions. Still, the road was different. They passed new fields, pastures, and huts with <u>thatched</u> roofs. Here and there a dog barked and came running after them, but Aaron chased it away with his stick.

The sun was shining when Aaron left the village. Suddenly the weather changed. A large black cloud with a bluish center appeared in the east and spread itself rapidly over the sky. A cold wind blew in with it. The crows flew low, croaking. At first it looked as if it would rain, but instead it began to hail as in summer. It was early in the day, but it became dark as <u>dusk</u>. After a while the hail turned to snow.

In his twelve years Aaron had seen all kinds of weather, but he had never experienced a snow like this one. It was so dense it shut out the light of the day. In a

I and the Village (1911), Marc Chagall. Oil on canvas, 75 ⅝" × 59 ⅝" (192.1 × 151.4 cm) The Museum of Modern Art, New York. Mrs. Simon Guggenheim Fund. Copyright © 2001 ARS, New York/ADAGP, Paris. Photograph © 2001 The Museum of Modern Art, New York.

WORDS TO KNOW	**astonished** (ə-stŏn′ĭsht) *adj.* surprised; amazed **astonish** *v.*
	thatched (thăcht) *adj.* made of or covered with reeds or straw **thatch** *v.*
	dusk (dŭsk) *n.* the time of day between sunset and complete darkness

483

 Mini Lesson ## Viewing and Representing

**I and the Village
by Marc Chagall**

ART APPRECIATION Marc Chagall (1887–1985) was a Russian-born painter who spent most of his adult life in France. *I and the Village* was painted in Paris in 1911.
Instruction Chagall painted in an expressionistic style, that is, he painted what he felt and imagined, rather than what he saw. Explain that Chagall could not have painted this from sight because he painted it in a big city—Paris—and it shows a village, perhaps like a village he knew in Russia.
Application Ask students to describe how the choice of art work helps to represent or extend the meaning of "Zlateh the Goat."
Possible Response The cow, the small houses, and the person with a tool all look like they could be in a village like Aaron's. An animal is prominent, as is a cow being milked, and milk is central to the story. The bright colors make it seem like a happy place.

Reading Skills and Strategies:
VISUALIZE

A Invite students to describe the mental images that descriptions of the storm in the text evoke.
Possible Response: Students might describe the swirling storm or the snow-coverd road, goat, and boy.

Reading Skills and Strategies:
PREDICT

B Ask students to speculate on what will happen next to Zlateh and Aaron.
Possible Responses: Students might predict that someone will appear to save them. Or students might predict that they will ride out the storm in the haystack, warm and safe.

Active Reading | STORY MAPPING |

Ask students to update their story maps.
Possible Responses: Event 3: They lose their way in a blizzard; Event 4: Aaron finds the haystack and they take shelter in it.

Use **Reading and Critical Thinking Transparencies,** p. 13, for additional support.

short time their path was completely covered. The wind became as cold as ice. The road to town was narrow and winding. Aaron no longer knew where he was. He could not see through the snow. The cold soon penetrated his quilted jacket.

At first Zlateh didn't seem to mind the change in weather. She too was twelve years old and knew what winter meant. But when her legs sank deeper and deeper into the snow, she began to turn her head and look at Aaron in wonderment. Her mild eyes seemed to ask, "Why are we out in such a storm?" Aaron hoped that a peasant would come along with his cart, but no one passed by.

The snow grew thicker, falling to the ground in large, whirling flakes. Beneath it Aaron's boots touched the softness of a plowed field. He realized that he was no longer on the road. He had gone astray. He could no longer figure out which was east or west, which way was the village, the town. The wind whistled, howled, whirled the snow about in eddies. It looked as if white imps were playing tag on the fields. A white dust rose above the ground. Zlateh stopped. She could walk no longer. Stubbornly she anchored her cleft hooves in the earth and bleated as if pleading to be taken home. Icicles hung from her white beard, and her horns were glazed with frost.

Aaron did not want to admit the danger, but he knew just the same that if they did not find shelter, they would freeze to death. This was no ordinary storm. It was a mighty blizzard. The snowfall had reached his knees. His hands were numb, and he could no longer feel his toes. He choked when he breathed. His nose felt

like wood, and he rubbed it with snow. Zlateh's bleating began to sound like crying. Those humans in whom she had so much confidence had dragged her into a trap. Aaron began to pray to God for himself and for the innocent animal.

Suddenly he made out the shape of a hill. He wondered what it could be. Who had piled snow into such a huge heap? He moved toward it, dragging Zlateh after him. When he came near it, he realized that it was a large haystack which the snow had blanketed.

Aaron realized immediately that they were saved. With great effort he dug his way through the snow. He was a village boy and knew what to do. When he reached the hay, he hollowed out a nest for himself and the goat. No matter how cold it may be outside, in the hay it is always warm. And hay was food for Zlateh. The moment she smelled it, she became contented and began to eat. Outside, the snow continued to fall. It quickly covered the passageway Aaron had dug. But a boy and an animal need to breathe, and there was hardly any air in their hide-out. Aaron bored a kind of a window through the hay and snow and carefully kept the passage clear.

Zlateh, having eaten her fill, sat down on her hind legs and seemed to have regained her confidence in man. Aaron ate his two slices of bread and cheese, but after the difficult journey he was still hungry. He looked at Zlateh and noticed her udders were full. He lay down next to her, placing himself so that when he milked her, he could squirt the milk into his mouth. It was rich and sweet. Zlateh was not accustomed to being milked that way, but she did not resist. On the contrary, she

WORDS
TO
KNOW

penetrate (pĕn′ĭ-trāt′) *v.* to pass through or enter into
imp (ĭmp) *n.* a small demon
cleft (klĕft) *adj.* divided; split
contented (kən-tĕn′tĭd) *adj.* happy with things as they are; satisfied
regain (rē-gān′) *v.* to get back; recover

484

Mini Lesson **Preteaching Vocabulary**

USING COMPARE AND CONTRAST CLUES
Remind students to draw on their own experiences to bring meaning to words in context.
Instruction Tell students that sentences often contain clues to help them find a word's meaning. A comparison clue compares a word to a similar word or idea and often uses *like* or *as*. Share the following sentence with students.
Zlateh was as astonished as a brand-new lottery winner when they left the yard behind.
Because a brand-new lottery winner would probably be surprised, *astonished* must mean

"surprised." Contrast clues use the opposite strategy: they compare a word to something very different from it. Look for signal words like *although, but, however,* or *on the other hand.* Share the following sentence.
It seemed like the cold of the storm should penetrate the haystack, but inside it was warm. The second half of the sentence shows that *penetrate* must mean "get through," because of the contrast of the cold on the outside and the warmth inside.

Exercises Ask students to read the following sentences and state whether each gives a compare or a contrast clue for the underlined word.
1. A thatched roof has as many reeds as a rainstorm has raindrops. (compare)
2. At dusk, the sun is setting, but at dawn, it is rising. (contrast)

Use **Unit Four Resource Book,** p. 23 for more practice. Use **Vocabulary Transparencies and Copymasters,** p. 49, for more practice.

January, (1940), Grant Wood. Oil on masonite panel, 18" × 24". Private Collection. Reproduced by permission.
Copyright © Estate of Grant Wood/Licensed by VAGA, New York, NY.

Customizing Instruction

Students Acquiring English

1 Point out that *astray*, which means "away from the correct path, " can be understood from reading the prior sentence.

Less Proficient Readers
Be sure students understand the importance of finding the haystack by asking:
• Why did Aaron know they were saved?
  Possible Response: He knew that the haystack would provide protection against the storm. He might also have known that Zlateh could eat the hay.

Gifted and Talented
Ask students to add the figurative language they find on these pages to their lists.
Possible Response:
Simile: wind became as cold as ice; his nose felt like wood
Personification: Zlateh . . . knew what winter meant. (and any other place where Zlateh's thoughts or meanings are inferred)

seemed eager to reward Aaron for bringing her to a shelter whose very walls, floor, and ceiling were made of food.

Through the window Aaron could catch a glimpse of the chaos outside. The wind carried before it whole drifts of snow. It was completely dark, and he did not know whether night had already come or whether it was the darkness of the storm. Thank God that in the hay it was not cold. The dried hay, grass, and field flowers exuded the warmth of the summer sun. Zlateh ate frequently; she nibbled from above, below, from the left and right. Her body gave forth an animal warmth, and Aaron cuddled up to her. He had always loved Zlateh, but now she was like a sister. He was alone, cut off from his family, and wanted to talk. He began to talk to Zlateh. "Zlateh, what do you think about what has happened to us?" he asked.

"Maaaa," Zlateh answered.

"If we hadn't found this stack of hay, we would both be frozen stiff by now," Aaron said.

"Maaaa," was the goat's reply.

"If the snow keeps on falling like this, we may have to stay here for days," Aaron explained.

"Maaaa," Zlateh bleated.

"What does 'Maaaa' mean?" Aaron asked. "You'd better speak up clearly."

"Maaaa. Maaaa," Zlateh tried.

"Well, let it be 'Maaaa' then," Aaron said patiently. "You can't speak, but I know you understand. I need you and you need me. Isn't that right?"

"Maaaa."

ZLATEH THE GOAT **485**

 Multicultural Link ## Hanukkah and Winter Festivals

Hanukkah, the celebration of the victory of a small band of Jews against the Syrians in 165 B.C., is just one of many holidays people celebrate in the winter months. In its use of light as a symbol, it has something in common with both Christmas and Kwanzaa. These holidays all fall near the winter solstice, the shortest day and longest night of the year in the Northern Hemisphere, so it makes sense that people use light in their celebrations.

Kwanzaa and Hanukkah celebrations both include ritual candle lightings, and the Christmas candle is a well-known symbol. Kwanzaa was created in 1966 as a way of bringing African Americans together. The holiday focuses on values such as unity, self-determination, collective work and responsibility, cooperative economics, purpose, creativity, and faith.

Literary Analysis

CLIMAX AND RESOLUTION

Ask students to pinpoint the climax.

Possible Response: A peasant gives Aaron and Zlateh directions to get back home. Aaron resolves that he will keep Zlateh.

 Use **Literary Analysis Transparencies,** p. 8, for additional support.

Remind students that they can recognize and analyze story plot, setting, and problem resolution. Ask them to describe the beginning of the story's resolution.

Possible Response: Aaron and Zlateh arrive home. The family is overjoyed to see them.

Active Reading **STORY MAPPING**

Ask students to complete their story maps.

Possible Response: Resolution: Zlateh, instead of being sold, becomes more beloved than ever.

Aaron became sleepy. He made a pillow out of some hay, leaned his head on it, and dozed off. Zlateh too fell asleep.

When Aaron opened his eyes, he didn't know whether it was morning or night. The snow had blocked up his window. He tried to clear it, but when he had bored through to the length of his arm, he still hadn't reached the outside. Luckily he had his stick with him and was able to break through to the open air. It was still dark outside. The snow continued to fall and the wind wailed, first with one voice and then with many. Sometimes it had the sound of devilish laughter. Zlateh too awoke, and when Aaron greeted her, she answered, "Maaaa." Yes, Zlateh's language consisted of only one word, but it meant many things. Now she was saying, "We must accept all that God gives us—heat, cold, hunger, satisfaction, light, and darkness."

Aaron had awakened hungry. He had eaten up his food, but Zlateh had plenty of milk.

For three days Aaron and Zlateh stayed in the haystack. Aaron had always loved Zlateh, but in these three days he loved her more and more. She fed him with her milk and helped him keep warm. She comforted him with her patience. He told her many stories, and she always cocked her ears and listened. When he patted her, she licked his hand and his face. Then she said, "Maaaa," and he knew it meant, I love you too.

The snow fell for three days, though after the first day it was not as thick and the wind quieted down. Sometimes Aaron felt that there could never have been a summer, that the snow had always fallen, ever since he could remember. He, Aaron, never had a father or mother or sisters. He was a snow child, born of the snow, and so was Zlateh. It was so quiet in the hay that his ears rang[3] in the stillness. Aaron and Zlateh slept all night and a good part of the day. As for Aaron's dreams, they were all about warm weather. He dreamed of green fields, trees covered with blossoms, clear brooks, and singing birds. By the third night the snow had stopped, but Aaron did not dare to find his way home in the darkness. The sky became clear and the moon shone, casting silvery nets on the snow. Aaron dug his way out and looked at the world. It was all white, quiet, dreaming dreams of heavenly splendor. The stars were large and close. The moon swam in the sky as in a sea.

On the morning of the fourth day, Aaron heard the ringing of sleigh bells. The haystack was not far from the road. The peasant who drove the sleigh pointed out the way to him—not to the town and Feyvel the butcher, but home to the village. Aaron had decided in the haystack that he would never part with Zlateh.

Aaron's family and their neighbors had searched for the boy and the goat but had found no trace of them during the storm. They feared they were lost. Aaron's mother and sisters cried for him: his father remained silent and gloomy. Suddenly one of the neighbors came running to their house with the news that Aaron and Zlateh were coming up the road.

There was great joy in the family. Aaron told them how he had found the stack of hay and how Zlateh had fed him with her milk. Aaron's sisters kissed and hugged Zlateh and gave her a special treat of chopped carrots and potato peels, which Zlateh gobbled up hungrily.

---

3. **his ears rang:** he heard a buzzing or humming sound.

WORDS
TO
KNOW   **splendor** (splĕn′dər) *n.* the condition of being brilliant or magnificent

486

Teaching Options

 Mini Lesson **Spelling**

WORDS WITH *EI* AND *IE*
Remind students that they need to use correct spelling for their work to have maximum impact.
Instruction If students are not already familiar with this rule, teach it to them: *i* before *e* except after *c*, and when sounding like *a* as in *neighbor* and *weigh*. Explain that this means that most words are spelled with *ie,* except when the vowels follow the letter *c,* or have the long *a* vowel sound. So the word *believe* follows the "*i* before *e*" part of the rule, and the word *ceiling* follows "except after *c.*"

Exercises Ask students to decide which vowel combination—*ei* or *ie*—is needed to spell each word correctly.
1. pat _ _ nce *(ie)*
2. dec _ _ ve *(ei)*
3. f _ _ lds *(ie)*
4. sl _ _ gh *(ei)*
5. rec _ _ ve *(ei)*
6. r _ _ gn *(ei)*
7. conc _ _ ve *(ei)*
8. y _ _ ld *(ie)*

 Use **Unit Four Resource Book,** p. 25 for more practice.

Orion in Winter, Charles Burchfield. Provenance: Museo Thyssen-Bornemisza, Madrid.

Nobody ever again thought of selling Zlateh, and now that the cold weather had finally set in, the villagers needed the services of Reuven the furrier once more. When Hanukkah came, Aaron's mother was able to fry pancakes every evening, and Zlateh got her portion too. Even though Zlateh had her own pen, she often came to the kitchen, knocking on the door with her horns to <u>indicate</u> that she was ready to visit, and she was always admitted. In the evening, Aaron, Miriam, and Anna played dreidel.[4] Zlateh sat near the stove, watching the children and the flickering of the Hanukkah candles.

Once in a while Aaron would ask her, "Zlateh, do you remember the three days we spent together?"

And Zlateh would scratch her neck with a horn, shake her white bearded head, and come out with the single sound which expressed all her thoughts, and all her love. ❖

---

4. **dreidel** (drād'l): a Hanukkah game played by spinning a four-sided top with a different Hebrew letter on each side.

WORDS
TO   **indicate** (ĭn'dĭ-kāt') *v.* to show or express
KNOW

487

GUIDING STUDENT RESPONSE

Connect to the Literature

1. What Do You Think?
Most students will be saddened by Zlateh's intended fate and relieved and uplifted by the ending. They may, however, appreciate the family's need to sell Zlateh.

Comprehension Check
- He is taking her to the butcher, because the family needs money.
- They are caught in a snowstorm and take shelter in a haystack.
- With joy and relief, the family decides to keep Zlateh after all.

 Use Selection Quiz
Unit Four Resource Book, p. 26.

Think Critically

2. Possible Response: Love is the most important because that is what motivates Aaron to keep Zlateh.
3. Most students will recognize that Zlateh is a valued member of the family, both because they need her and because they love her.
4. Possible Response: He is resourceful, strong, confident, and loyal.
5. Possible Response: He matures, learning to make his own decisions about how to survive the snowstorm and about keeping Zlateh.
6. Possible Response: Conflicts: Aaron's desire to save Zlateh and their mutual need to survive the snowstorm; Climax: when Aaron decides he must keep Zlateh; Resolution: Aaron and Zlateh are welcomed home

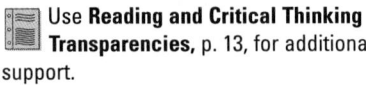 Use **Reading and Critical Thinking Transparencies,** p. 13, for additional support.

Literary Analysis

Climax and Resolution The conflicts in "Zlateh the Goat" are resolved—the family no longer needs to sell the goat, because their income is restored, and Zlateh and Aaron survive their ordeal. Students should be able to explain whether conflicts are resolved or not in two or more other stories.

 Use **Literary Analysis Transparencies,** p. 8, for additional support.

Connect to the Literature

1. What Do You Think?
How did you feel about the family's plan for Zlateh? What was your reaction to the story's ending?

Comprehension Check
- Where is Aaron taking Zlateh and why?
- How do Aaron and Zlateh save themselves from the storm?
- What does the family do with Zlateh at the end of the story?

Think Critically

2. What emotion do you think is most important in this story? Why?

3. How do you think Aaron and his family feel about Zlateh at the story's beginning? Support your answer.

4. What character traits do you think Aaron has that help him during his journey?

5. How does Aaron change as a result of his experiences with Zlateh?

 THINK ABOUT
- the way he makes decisions
- his relationship with his father
- what Zlateh teaches him during the journey

6. **ACTIVE READING STORY MAPPING** Look over the story map in your 📖 **READER'S NOTEBOOK.** Compare with a classmate what you recorded as the **conflict, climax,** and **resolution** of the story.

Extend Interpretations

7. **What If?** What if the snowstorm had not occurred? What actions might Aaron have taken because of his feelings for Zlateh?

8. **The Writer's Style** Why do you think Singer set his story during Hanukkah, a festival that celebrates a miracle and a new beginning for the Jewish people?

9. **Connect to Life** What do you think animals have to offer people? Does this story remind you of any animal-human relationships you've known about?

Literary Analysis

CLIMAX AND RESOLUTION In a story, **climax** is the main turning point. The **resolution,** which usually occurs at the story's conclusion, ties up loose ends and brings the story to a close. Conflicts in the story do not always disappear after the climax. Even if conflicts still are present, something in the story changes after the climax. You might notice a change in the characters or a change in the story's tone.

Activity Identify the conflicts in "Zlateh the Goat" and follow them from the time they are introduced until the story's resolution. Are the conflicts resolved or left unresolved at the end? Reexamine at least two other stories you have read in this book, and determine whether their conflicts are solved neatly or left open by each story's resolution.

Extend Interpretations

7. **What If?** Aaron would probably have tried to find some other way to save Zlateh. However, given his obedience to his father, he'd probably have ended up taking Zlateh to the butcher if no alternative could be found.

8. **The Writer's Style** It helps suggest the miracle of surviving the snowstorm and the new beginning for Zlateh and the family.

9. **Connect to Life** Students may say that animals offer companionship, work, and love. They may mention human-animal relationships from films, books, or personal experience.

Writing Options

1. Persuasive Argument Aaron doesn't want to sell Zlateh. Suppose he tried to change his father's mind? Write a persuasive argument that Aaron might use to show his father that the family should keep Zlateh. Place the argument in your **Working Portfolio.**

Writing Handbook
See p. R39: Persuasive Writing.

2. Dialogue with Zlateh Imagine that Zlateh really could talk. Reread what Aaron thinks she says to him. Then write your own version of one of their conversations.

Activities & Explorations

Live Storytelling Traditional stories are often shared orally. A good storyteller captures listeners with voice, gesture, and rhythm. Perform a live telling of "Zlateh the Goat." Work at conveying both suspense and character.
~ SPEAKING AND LISTENING

Inquiry & Research

Poland Today Compare and contrast modern Poland with the village world of "Zlateh the Goat." Write a few paragraphs about how the country has changed. Find information in social studies books or in the library.

Art Connection

I and the Village was painted in 1911 by Marc Chagall. His paintings are influenced by dreams and memories. The scenes in *I and the Village* flow together to create a feeling of village life. How do they help you understand the setting of "Zlateh the Goat"?

Writing Options

1. Persuasive Argument Students might argue that the family needs Zlateh's milk and that she is worth more to them alive than dead. They might have Aaron offer to find work himself; they might say that the weather is bound to turn colder if they can only hold out a bit longer, or they might say that it is not right to have a beloved animal killed for money.

2. Dialogue with Zlateh Students can **extend the activity** by pairing up with another student and reading each of their dialogues aloud.

Use **Writing Transparencies,** p. 24, for additional support.

Activities & Explorations

1. Live Storytelling Students may first wish to practice portraying each character, to make decisions about how high or low a voice the character speaks in, the speed of his or her speech, and so on, and to get used to keeping the character consistent, as well.

Use **Communications Transparencies and Copymasters,** p. 11, for additional support.

Inquiry & Research

Poland Today Students with an interest in history might also wish to find a map of Poland made just after World War I, and compare the borders with the current ones.

Art Connection

Answers will vary, but students should use story details as well as images from the painting to make their point.

Vocabulary and Spelling

EXERCISE A: RELATED WORDS On your paper, write the letter of the word that doesn't belong.

1. a) evening b) today c) twilight d) dusk
2. a) astonish b) alarm c) bore d) bewilder
3. a) uneasy b) content c) restless d) jumpy
4. a) rich b) darkness c) splendor d) grand
5. a) giant b) gnome c) imp d) elf
6. a) indicate b) gesture c) point d) observe
7. a) divided b) split c) cleft d) connected
8. a) drill b) penetrate c) leave d) enter
9. a) shed b) lose c) give d) regain
10. a) roofing b) cement c) thatched d) straw

EXERCISE B: FORMS OF THE PREFIX IN- The prefix *in-*, as in the vocabulary word *indicate*, may mean "in or into" or "not or without." The spelling of the prefix depends on the root to which the prefix is joined. For example:

in + direct = indirect
im + migrate = immigrate
im + mature = immature
il + legal = illegal
ir + resistable = irresistable

Make a new word by adding a form of the prefix *-in* to each root word below.

1. regular   3. literate   5. active
2. perfect   4. movable

Building Vocabulary
For a lesson on learning new words, see p. 491.

Vocabulary and Spelling

EXERCISE A
1. b   6. d
2. c   7. d
3. b   8. c
4. b   9. d
5. a   10. b

EXERCISE B
1. irregular
2. imperfect
3. illiterate
4. immovable
5. inactive

✓ Assessment **Standardized Test Practice**

DESCRIBING SETTING A standardized test will sometimes require students to tell where and when a story takes place. Read the following aloud and ask students to decide which setting correctly completes the sentence.

Aaron decides not to take Zlateh to the butcher when he is

A. still at home.
B. walking from the village to the town.
C. in the haystack.
D. walking back to the village after the storm.

Lead students through the process of choosing the correct answer. A is incorrect, because Aaron agrees to take the goat to the butcher. B is also incorrect, because Aaron is doing as he promised. C is correct: the story says directly that Aaron decided while in the haystack. D is incorrect, because Aaron has already made his decision and is walking Zlateh back home.

Grammar in Context

Possible Responses:

1. Aaron's father talked of selling Zlateh, the family pet.
2. Feuvel, a butcher from town, had offered eight gulden.
3. Aaron's shelter, a stack of sweet hay, was warm and dry.

Author Activity

Fantastic Stories Students can make a chart with two columns—one for realistic details, and one for fantastic details—for each story. When they have logged all three stories, they can decide how realistic or fantastic each story is and how they compare to one another on that scale.

Isaac Bashevis Singer

Singer was not the only literary member of his family. His older brother, Israel Joshua, who helped him get out of Poland, was a novelist he both admired and competed with. His sister, Hinde Esther, was also a published novelist.

Grammar in Context: Appositives and Appositive Phrases

Isaac Bashevis Singer introduces characters with words that clarify who they are:

> **Leah, his mother,** wiped the tears from her eyes. . . . Aaron's younger sisters, **Anna and Miriam,** cried loudly.

An **appositive** is a noun, pronoun, or noun phrase that renames another noun, pronoun, or noun phrase. Each phrase in red type above is an **appositive phrase.**

An appositive phrase might be short, as in the title "Zlateh the Goat."

An appositive might also be long and descriptive. It might even include a prepositional phrase, as shown here in red, modifying the noun:

> **Aaron, a boy from a small village,** learned something. . . .

Apply to Your Writing Use appositives to:
- give your reader clear information
- elaborate quickly and easily
- vary the rhythm of your sentences

WRITING EXERCISE Rewrite the sentences, using some or all of the information in parentheses to make an appositive phrase.

Punctuation Tip: Use a comma before and after an appositive phrase. For a phrase at the beginning or end of a sentence, use one comma.

Example: *Original* Hanukkah held no delight that year. (Hanukkah is a joyful holiday.)
Rewritten Hanukkah, a joyful holiday, held no delight that year.

1. Aaron's father talked of selling Zlateh. (Zlateh was the family pet.)
2. Feuvel had offered eight gulden. (Feuvel was a butcher from town.)
3. Aaron's shelter was warm and dry. (It was a stack of sweet hay.)

"Children are the best readers of genuine literature. . . ."

Isaac Bashevis Singer
1904–1991

Coming to America As the son of a rabbi, Isaac Bashevis Singer received a traditional Jewish education in Poland. In his twenties, Singer decided to become a writer, and in 1935 he followed his older brother to the United States to escape discrimination against Jews in Eastern Europe. After becoming a naturalized citizen, he wrote of his U.S. citizenship, "I would not trade it for all the money in the world."

Just a Storyteller Singer published his first children's book in 1966, noting that "children think about and ponder such matters as justice, the purpose of life, the why of suffering." Singer, a Newbery Honor winner three times, was awarded the Nobel Prize in literature in 1978. The award-winning author maintained, "I am nothing more than a storyteller."

AUTHOR ACTIVITY

Fantastic Stories Some of Singer's stories, like "Zlateh the Goat," are mostly realistic. Other stories are based more on folklore or imagination. Read at least two other stories in the collection *Zlateh the Goat.* Look for realistic and fantastic details.

Teaching Options

 Grammar

PUNCTUATING APPOSITIVES Remind students to punctuate appositive phrases correctly. **Instruction** Let students know that when an appositive phrase is not necessary for understanding the meaning of a sentence, it should be set off with a comma or commas. If the phrase is necessary, it should not be set off. Write the following on the board: Zlateh the goat seemed to understand Aaron. Aaron, a brave and obedient boy, loved Zlateh. Point out that in the first sentence, *the goat* is critical for understanding the meaning. In the

second sentence, the phrase in commas gives additional, nonessential information about Aaron. It could be omitted, and the sentence would still be clear.

Exercises Ask students to punctuate the following sentences.
1. Reuven the furrier decided to sell Zlateh. *(no commas)*
2. He asked Aaron his son to take the goat to the butcher. *(Aaron, his son,)*
3. The pair boy and goat lost their way. *(pair, boy and goat,)*

4. Luckily, they found a haystack a big thick mound. *(haystack, a big)*
5. Aaron decided never to sell Zlateh the goat. *(no commas)*

 Use **Unit Four Resource Book,** p. 24.
Use **Grammar Transparencies and Copymasters,** p. 125.

> Use McDougal Littell's ***Language Network,*** Chapter 9, for more instruction and practice in punctuating appositives.

Detecting Meaning

You have learned several methods of finding the meaning of an unfamiliar word. Using these methods, how would you determine the meaning of *magnification*?

❶ Look for clues in the surrounding text, such as the word bigger and the phrase "trick of underwater light."

❷ Then think of any similar words you know. You might be familiar with **magnify**, from using a magnifying glass.

❸ Divide the words into parts you recognize. The suffix **-tion** means "act or state of."

You could infer from any or all of these clues that *magnification* roughly means "making things appear larger."

> Then, all at once, there they were—and so much bigger than I had expected. It's only the **magnification** down here, I told myself, a trick of underwater light.
>
> —Don C. Reed, "My First Dive with the Dolphins"

Strategies for Building Vocabulary

Here are some ideas for learning and remembering new words.

❶ **Use Context Clues** Sometimes if you keep reading—or back up and reread a few lines—you'll find clues to the meaning in the text.

❷ **Think of Similar Words** Try to think of other words you know with the same base, or root. Then check whether the definition for that base word makes sense in the context of the sentence. The word *magnification*, for example, might remind you of the word *magnificent*, meaning "grand, stately." From this, you can infer that magnification has to do with making things large.

❸ **Take the Word Apart** If you know definitions of common prefixes, suffixes, and base words, you can often determine a word's meaning by analyzing its parts. For example:

co-   exist   -ence
"together"   "live"   "state of"

Coexistence, we can see, means "the state of living together."

❹ **Consult a Dictionary** After you use context and word parts to figure out a definition, check your definition in a dictionary. Consider all the definitions listed for the word and choose the one that fits the context. Noting a word's origin will help you connect it to other words.

❺ **Record and Use New Words** Once you learn the meaning of a new word, it's important to remember that word. Record new words and their definitions in your **Personal Word List.** Say each new word aloud and try to use it three or four times in your conversation or writing.

EXERCISE Define each underlined word. Identify the strategy you used to discover the meaning.

1. Pete tried to <u>conceal</u> his black eye by hiding it behind dark glasses.
2. Let's <u>inquire</u> at the lost-and-found office to see if anyone has turned in your watch.
3. The room was pitch dark except for the <u>luminous</u> white glow of the clock.
4. The members of a wolf pack always follow the lead of the <u>dominant</u> male.
5. After tripping over a crack in the ice, the skater struggled to <u>regain</u> her balance.

BUILDING VOCABULARY   **491**

Building Vocabulary

Objectives
• use context to determine the meaning of unfamiliar words
• apply meanings of roots and base words to comprehend unfamiliar words
• apply meanings of prefixes and suffixes to comprehend unfamiliar words
• use a personal word list to record and remember new words

EXERCISE
Students' individual decoding strategies will vary.
1. conceal: hide
2. inquire: ask
3. luminous: full of light
4. dominant: having the most influence; controlling all others
5. regain: recover possession of

Use **Unit Four Resource Book**, p. 27, for more practice.

ON YOUR OWN

Possible Objectives

You can use this selection to achieve one or more of the following objectives:

- enjoy silent sustained reading (Option One)
- read and analyze literature with a group (Option Two)
- use the Reader's Notebook to formulate questions about literature (Option Three)
- write in response to literature (Option Three)

Summary

The narrator tells how, while living in Africa for a short time, he and his family were given the responsibility of raising a baby lion rejected by its mother. No one expected it to live, but the family was determined that it would. First, they fed it diluted milk from a baby bottle. It seemed to do all right at first but as it got bigger, it seemed terribly weak. The family finds out that they need to add mutton broth to the lion cub's diet. They also find out that they need to brush its coat in order to make it healthy and clean. They call the cub Sullivan and, as he grows into a healthy young lion, they play with him and teach him how to eat on his own.

After studying the lion's behavior, the narrator notes that contrary to popular wisdom, lions are not just big cats: they have a dignity and grace all their own. Then the lion's caretakers have to leave Africa. Those who had doubted that the lion cub would live said that the foursome should take him back to England. The narrator knows, however, that Sullivan would never survive in England's climate and should be left in his homeland of Africa.

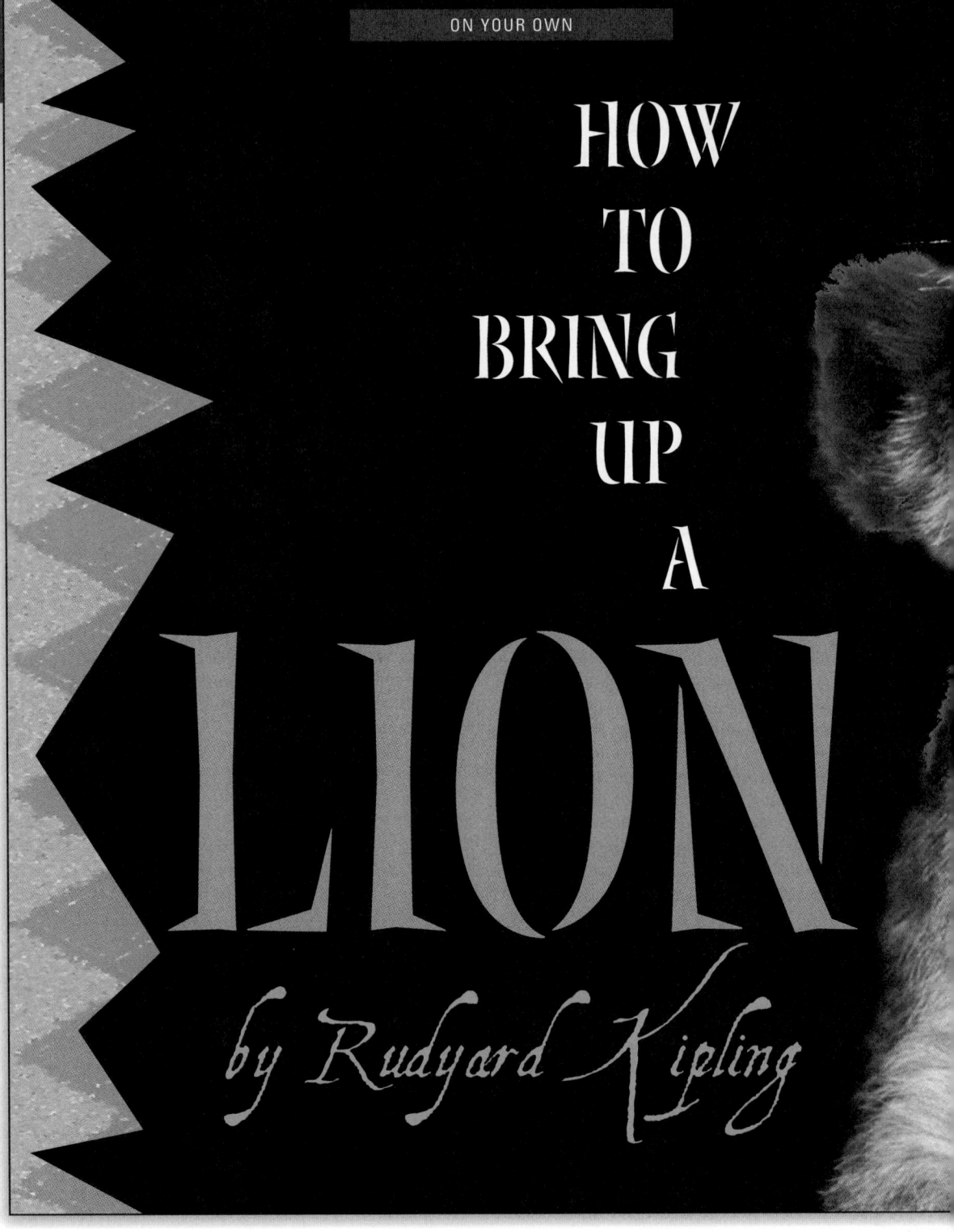

HOW TO BRING UP A LION

by Rudyard Kipling

Now this is a really-truly tale.
It all truthfully happened, and I
saw it and heard it.

Once there was a mother
lion that lived in a cage
halfway up a mountain
in Africa, behind the house
where I was living, and she
had two little baby lions. She
bit one of them so hard that
it died. But the keeper in
charge of the cages pulled
out the other little lion just in
time and carried him down
the hill. He put him
in an egg box, along with a
brindled bulldog puppy, called
Budge, to keep him warm.

HOW TO BRING UP A LION   **493**

Option One
Silent Sustained Reading

You might set aside time each week for independent reading. During this time, you and all of your students may read for enjoyment. "How to Bring Up a Lion" will appeal to many students and can be read independently in about twenty minutes. If you want to encourage students to read for pleasure, you might forego any assignment related to this selection. Should you want to make assignments, Options Two and Three offer suggestions.

Option Two
Shared Reading Groups

You may assign students to groups or allow them to choose their own. Students can read the selection together, alternately reading sections aloud, or they can read independently and meet to cooperate in a project that portrays some element of the story.

Possible Projects
- Using information from the story, students can prepare a presentation explaining how to raise an orphaned lion cub. They can list and describe the steps that the narrator and his family follow in order to keep the lion cub alive and healthy. They can give the presentation in front of the class.
- Students can use information from the story to create portraits of Sullivan, starting from the day he was brought to the narrator's house up to the day the narrator and his family leave Africa. Students' portraits should include all the changes that the narrator describes the lion going through. These portraits could be used as part of the presentation.
- Using information from the story, students could create a backdrop of the part of Africa in which this story is set to go along with the presentation.

• Ask students to read the selection, pausing at the end of the first column on page 493. At that point, ask students to consider the title of the selection and the passage they just read and to predict what they think is going to happen in this story and what its main point might be. Have them write their predictions in their Reader's Notebook. Have them also record any questions they have about the story as they continue to read. At the end of the story, students will return to their predictions and questions. Ask them to note if their predictions were accurate and if their questions were answered. They may want to write down any additional questions they have about the story.

• Ask students to give their impressions of how the narrator and his family felt about Sullivan the lion cub. Have them support their ideas with details from the story.

• Ask students to write a letter, written from the point of view of one of the children, to his or her classmates back home in England describing their adventures in bringing up a lion cub by hand.

When I went to look at the little thing, the keeper said, "This baby lion is going to die. Would you like to bring up this baby lion?" And I said, "Yes," and the keeper said, "Then I will send him to your house at once, because he is certainly going to die here, and you can bring him up by hand."

Then I went home and found Daniel and Una, who were little children, playing. I said, "We are going to bring up a baby lion by hand!" and both children said, "Hurrah! He can sleep in our nursery and not go away for ever and ever."

Then Daniel and Una's mother said to me, "What do you know about bringing up lions?" And I said, "Nothing whatever." And she said, "I thought so," and went into the house to give orders.

Soon the keeper came, carrying the egg box with the baby lion and Budge, the brindled bulldog pup, asleep inside. Behind the keeper walked a man with iron bars and a roll of wire netting and some picks and shovels. The men built a den for the baby lion in the backyard, and they put the box inside and said, "Now you can bring the lion up by hand. He is quite, quite certain to die."

The children's mother came out of the house with a bottle, the kind that you feed very small babies from, and she filled it with milk and warm water. She said, "I am going to bring up this baby lion, and he is *not* going to die."

She pulled out the baby lion (his eyes were all blue and watery and he couldn't see), and she turned him on his back and tilted the bottle into his little mouth. He moved all his four little paws like windmills, but he never let go of the bottle, not once, until it was quite empty and he was quite full.

The children's mother said, "Weigh him on the meat scales," and we did. He weighed four

"WE ARE GOING TO BRING UP A BABY LION BY HAND!"

pounds, three ounces. She said, "He will be weighed once every week, and he will be fed every three hours on warm milk and water—two parts milk and one part water. The bottle will be cleaned after each meal with boiling water."

I said, "What do you know about bringing up lions by hand?" and she said, "Nothing whatever, except that this lion is not going to die. *You* must find out how to bring up lions."

So I said, "The first thing to do is to stop Daniel and Una from hugging and dancing around him because if they hug him too hard or step on him he will surely die."

For ten days the baby lion ate and slept. He didn't say anything; he hardly opened his eyes. We made him a bed of wood shavings (they are better than straw), and we built him a real little house with a thick roof to keep the sun off. And whenever he looked at all hungry, it was time for him to be fed out of the bottle.

Budge tried to make him play, but the little lion wouldn't. When Budge chewed his ears too hard, he would stretch himself all over the puppy and Budge would crawl from under him, half choked.

We said, "It is an easy thing to bring up a lion," and then visitors began to call and give advice.

One man said, "Young lions all die of paralysis[1] of the hindquarters." And another man said, "They perish of rickets,[2] a condition that comes on just as they are cutting their first teeth."

We looked at the baby lion, and his hind legs were very weak indeed. He rolled over when he tried to walk, and his front paws doubled up under him. His eyes were dull and blind.

I went off to find someone who knew about animals' insides. "You must give him broth," I was told. "Milk isn't enough for him. Give him mutton broth at eight in the morning and four in the afternoon. You must also buy a dandy brush, same as they brush horses with, and brush him every day to make up for his own mother not being able to lick him with her tongue."

So we bought a dandy brush (a good hard one) and mutton for broth, and we gave him the broth from the bottle. In two days he was a different lion. His hind legs grew stronger, and his eyes grew lighter, and his furry, woolly skin grew cleaner.

We all said, "Now we must give him a real name of his own." We inquired into his family history and found that his parents were both Matabele[3] lions from the far north and that the Matabele word for lion was "umlibaan." But we called him Sullivan for short, and that very day he knocked a bit of skin off his nose trying to climb the wire fence.

He began to play with Daniel and Una—especially with Una, who walked all around the garden, hugging him till he squeaked.

One day, Una went out as usual and put her hand in Sullivan's house to drag him out, just as usual, and Sullivan flattened his little black-tipped ears back to his thick woolly head and opened his mouth and said "Ough! Ough! Ough!" like a monkey.

Una pulled her hand back and said, "I think

Sullivan has teeth. Come and look." And we saw that he had six or eight very pretty little teeth about a quarter of an inch long, so we said, "Why should we give up our time to feeding this monarch of the jungle every few hours with a bottle? Let him feed himself."

He weighed eight pounds, eight ounces, and he could run and jump and growl and scratch, but he did not like to feed himself.

For two days and two nights, he wouldn't feed himself at all. He sang for his supper, like little Tommy Tucker, and he sang for his breakfast and his dinner, making noises deep in his chest, high noises and low noises and coughing noises. Una ran about saying, "Please let my lion have his bottle!"

Daniel, who didn't speak very plainly, would go off to the lion's den, where poor Sullivan sat looking at a plate of cold broth. He would say, "Tullibun, Tullibun, eat up all your dinner or you'll be hungry."

At last Sullivan made up his mind that bottles would never come again and he put down his little nose and ate for dear life. I was told that the children's mother had been out in the early morning and dipped her finger in mutton broth and coaxed Sullivan to lick it off. She discovered that his tongue was as raspy as a file. Then we were sure he ought to feed himself.

So we weaned Sullivan, and he weighed ten pounds, two ounces, and the truly happy times of his life began. Every morning, Una and Daniel would let him out of the den. He was perfectly polite so long as no one put a hand into his house. He would come out at a steady,

---

1. **paralysis** (pə-răl'ĭ-sĭs): a loss of the ability to move a body part.

2. **rickets:** a disease in which bones fail to grow normally, caused by a lack of calcium, vitamin D, or sunlight.

3. **Matabele** (mä'tä-bĕl'ā): having to do with a people of southwestern Zimbabwe (a country in the southern part of Africa).

Possible Activities
Independent Activities
• Have gifted students skim over the story, noting details, facts, and descriptions about the narrator and the character of the children's mother. Ask them to write in their Reader's Notebook their impressions of these characters and their respective roles in the process of bringing up the lion.
• Have students review the Learning the Language of Literature and Active Reader features, pp. 443–446. Ask them to note which skills and strategies they used while reading this selection.

Discussion Activities
• Use the questions formulated by the students in their Reader's Notebooks as the start of a discussion about this story.
• Ask students if they think the family was right to leave the lion in Africa when they returned to England. What do students think would have happened if the family had taken Sullivan with them?

Assessment Opportunities
• You can assess student comprehension of the story by evaluating the questions they formulate in their Reader's Notebook.
• You can use any of the discussion questions as essay questions.
• You can have students turn any one of their Reader's Notebook entries into an essay.

RUDYARD KIPLING

Kipling's *Jungle Book,* considered to be one of his best works, was written in 1894 while he was living in Vermont with his wife and two baby daughters. The most popular story in the book tells the story of Mowgli, a young boy raised by wolves in the jungle.

In 1899, Kipling's daughter Josephine died from pneumonia, and Kipling coped by losing himself in his work. Two years later he published *Kim,*

thought by many to be his finest novel. It tells the story of an orphaned Irish boy who becomes involved in espionage and counterespionage in the hostilities between Great Britain and Russia in late nineteenth-century India.

In 1902 Kipling published the *Just So Stories* which he wrote for his two surviving children, Elsie and John. Written to be read aloud, their language is musical and playful.

rocking-horse canter that looked slow but was quicker even than Una's run.

He would be brushed, first on his yellow tummy and then on his yellow back, and then under his yellow chin where he dribbled mutton broth, and then on his dark yellow mane. The mane hair of a baby lion is a little thicker than the rest of his hair, and Sullivan's was tinged with black.

After his brushing, he would go out into the garden to watch Daniel and Una swing. Or he would hoist himself up on the porch to watch their mother sew or he would go into my room and lie under the couch. If I wished to get rid of him I had to call Una, for at her voice he would solemnly trundle out with his head lifted and help her chase butterflies among the hydrangeas. He never took any notice of me.

One of the many queer things about him was the way he matched his backgrounds. He would lie down on the bare tiled porch in the full glare of the sun, and you could step on him before you saw him. He would sit in the shadow of a wall or slide into a garden border, and, till he moved, you could not tell that he was there. That made him difficult to photograph.

Sudden noises, like banging doors, always annoyed him. He would go straight backward almost as fast as he ran forward, till he got his back up against a wall or a shrub. There he would lift one little broad paw and look wicked until he heard Una or Daniel call him.

If he smelled anything in the wind, he would stop quite still and lift his head high into the air, very slowly, until he had quite made up his mind. Then he would slowly steal upwind with his tail twitching a trifle at the very end.

The first time he played with a ball he struck it just as his grandfather must have struck at the big Matabele oxen in the far

ONE DAY I SHALL NEVER FORGET, HE BEGAN TO SEE OUT OF HIS EYES—REALLY SEE.

north—one paw above and one paw below, with a wrench and a twist—and the ball bounced over his shoulder.

He could use his paws as easily as a man can use his arms, and much more quickly. He always turned his back on you when he was examining anything. That was a signal that you were not to interfere with him.

We used to believe that little lions were only big cats, as the books say. But Sullivan taught us that lions are always lions. He would play in his own way at his own games, but he never chased his tail or patted a cork or a string or did any foolish, kitten tricks. He never forgot that he was a lion, not a dog or a cat, but a lion.

When he lay down, he would cross his paws and look like the big carved lions in Trafalgar Square.[4] When he rose and sniffed, he looked like a bronze lion, and when he lifted one paw and opened his mouth and wrinkled up his nose to be angry (as he did when we washed him all over with carbolic and water because of fleas), he looked like the lions the old Assyrians[5] drew on stone.

---

4. **Trafalgar** (trə-făl′gər) **Square:** a plaza in London, England, that is the site of a famous monument (Nelson's Column) surrounded by four large statues of lions.

5. **Assyrians** (ə-sîr′ē-ənz): a people of southwestern Asia whose powerful empire reached its peak from the ninth to the seventh century B.C.

He never did anything funny. He was never silly or amusing (not even when he had been dipped in carbolic and water), and he never behaved as though he were trying to show off. Kittens do.

He kept to himself more and more as he grew older. One day I shall never forget, he began to see out of his eyes—really see. Up till then his eyes had been dull and stupid, just like a young baby's eyes. But that day— I saw them first under the couch—they were grown-up lion's eyes, soft and blazing at the same time, without a wink in them, eyes that seemed to look right through you and out over all Africa.

Though he had been born in captivity, as were his parents, and though the only home he had ever known was on the slopes of the big Table Mountain where Africa ended, we never saw him once look up the hill when he lay down to do his solemn, serious thinking. He always faced squarely to the north, to the great open plains and the ragged, jagged mountains beyond them—looking up and into the big, sunny, dry Africa that had once belonged to his people.

That was curious. He would think and he would sigh, exactly like a man. He was full of curious, half-human noises, grunts and groans and mutters and rumbles.

He grew to weigh more than fifteen pounds when we had to leave him. We were very proud of this, and triumphed over the keeper and the other people who had said we could never bring him up by hand.

"You've certainly won the game," they said. "You can have this lion if you like and take him home and give him to the Zoological Gardens in London."

But we said, "No, Sullivan is one of the family, and if he were taken to a cold, wet, foggy zoo, he'd die. Let him stay here." ❖

"I write of all matters that lie within my understanding, and of many that do not."

Rudyard Kipling
1865–1936

Early Childhood Rudyard Kipling was born to a British family in India, which was a British colony at the time. He spent a great deal of time with his ayah (Indian nanny), who taught him about Indian culture and traditions. When he was five, his parents left him with a foster family in England, so that he could attend school there.

Inspired by India Kipling never forgot the land of his birth. He refused his family's offer to send him to a university, and in 1882 he returned to India. While working as a newspaper reporter, he published many short stories in newspapers and books. Kipling's attachment to India can also be seen in his novel *Kim,* about an Irish orphan who, like the author, finds a home in India.

Fame and Fortune In 1896 Kipling went back to England, where he found himself acclaimed as a great writer. There he wrote one of his best-loved books, *Just So Stories,* a collection of humorous tales that explain how different animals got their physical characteristics. "How to Bring Up a Lion" was inspired by a visit to South Africa in 1900. While in South Africa, Kipling wrote for a newspaper and raised funds for British military veterans. His powers of observation, imagination, and storytelling were recognized in 1907 with the Nobel Prize for literature.

The Nantucket Cat, Paul Stagg. From *The Mardi Gras Cat Book* by Paul Stagg and Naomi Lewis, published by Heineman Press. Copyright © The Stephanie Hoppen Picture Archive Ltd., London.

CHANG MCTANG MCQUARTER
CAT

by John Ciardi

Chang McTang McQuarter Cat
Is one part this and one part that.
One part is yowl, one part is purr.
One part is scratch, one part is fur.
5 One part, maybe even two,
Is how he sits and stares right through
You and you and you and you.
And when you feel my Chang-Cat stare
You wonder if you're really there.

10 Chang McTang McQuarter Cat
Is one part this and ten parts that.
He's one part saint, and two parts sin.
One part yawn, and three parts grin,
One part sleepy, four parts lightning,
15 One part cuddly, five parts fright'ning,
One part snarl, and six parts play.
One part is how he goes away
Inside himself, somewhere miles back
Behind his eyes, somewhere as black
20 And green and yellow as the night
A jungle makes in full moonlight.

Chang McTang McQuarter Cat
Is one part this and twenty that.
One part is statue, one part tricks—
25 (One part, or six, or thirty-six.)

One part (or twelve, or sixty-three)
Is—Chang McTang belongs to ME!

Don't ask, "How many parts is that?"
Addition's nothing to a cat.

30 If you knew Chang, then you'd know this:
He's one part everything there is.

 LaserLinks: Background for Reading
Science Connection

Objectives
- write a process description
- use a written text as a model for writing
- revise a draft to include the definitions of unfamiliar words
- use transitional words and phrases

Introducing the Workshop

Process Description Discuss with students the different kinds of process descriptions that they encounter every day at school, at home, and while pursuing their hobbies. Ask them to think about what makes a process description easy to follow.

Basics in a Box
Using the Graphic The graphic on this page illustrates how a process description can be broken down into three main parts. Point out that the graphic suggests elements that students should include when they draft their descriptions.

Presenting the Rubric To better understand the assignment, students can refer to the Standards for Writing a Successful Process Description. You may also want to share with them the complete rubric, which describes several levels of proficiency.

 Use McDougal Littell's **Language Network,** Chapters 10–17, for more instruction on essential writing skills.

 Power Presentation

To engage students visually, use **Power Presentation 1,** Process Description.

Writing Workshop — Process Description

Explaining one step at a time . . .

From Reading to Writing When you learned to log on to a computer for the first time, you had to follow step-by-step instructions. If you were given a wrong step, you might have accidentally logged off or retrieved the wrong file. Writing a **process description** is one way you can clarify steps. A process description is a step-by-step explanation of how to do something. You can learn how to do almost anything when the directions are broken down into steps.

For Your Portfolio

WRITING PROMPT Write an essay that tells how to do something or how something works. Focus on a task or a process that you know well.

Purpose: To inform and explain
Audience: Classmates, family, or readers with an interest in your subject

---

Basics in a Box

Process Description at a Glance

Part 1
- presents purpose and topic
- provides background information
- lists necessary equipment or materials

Part 2
- describes steps in logical order, using transitional words and phrases
- devotes a separate paragraph to each step

Part 3
- summarizes the process
- describes the outcome or final product

RUBRIC STANDARDS FOR WRITING

A successful process description should
- focus on a single activity
- begin with a clear statement of the topic and your purpose
- explain to readers how to do something or how something works
- present the steps of the process in a logical order
- give the meaning of terms that may be unfamiliar to readers and provide necessary background information
- use paragraphs and transitional words to signal the start of each new step

500   UNIT FOUR   PART 1: ANIMAL WONDERS

LESSON RESOURCES

USING PRINT RESOURCES
Unit Four Resource Book
- Prewriting, p. 28
- Drafting and Elaboration, p. 29
- Peer Response, pp. 30–31
- Revising, Editing, and Proofreading, p. 32
- Student Models, pp. 33–35
- Rubric for Evaluation, p. 36

Writing Transparencies and Copymasters
- Writing Process Transparencies, TR 1–TR 4

- Writing Structure Transparencies: Structuring the Essay, TR 6; Transitional Words and Phrases, TR 9
- Writing Template Transparencies: Process Description, TR 31

Grammar Transparencies and Copymasters
- Transitional Words and Phrases, CM 112

INTEGRATED TECHNOLOGY
LaserLinks
Writing Springboards
See **Teacher's SourceBook** p. 56 for bar codes.

Writing Coach CD-ROM

Visit our website:
www.mcdougallittell.com

Analyzing a Student Model

Weston Sager
The Paul School

SPEAKING OPPORTUNITY See the Communication Handbook, p. R100 for speaking and presenting tips.

Scrambling for Eggs

There is more to gathering farm-fresh eggs than you might think. Collecting eggs is fun and interesting, believe it or not. Keeping egg-laying hens is rewarding because you get farm-fresh eggs almost every day.

My family owns several six-year-old chickens. They are in good health and lay eggs almost every day. It's unusual to have chickens that are six years old and still lay eggs. My family thinks they are such good layers because in addition to providing them with shelter, and lots of water, we feed them good-quality table scraps and give them special care. As a result, our chickens give us some of the best eggs anywhere. Read on to learn about how to gather farm-fresh eggs.

First, you need to have a container to carry table scraps. This container should be able to hold about ten large eggs. A plastic bowl is ideal. You should always use a large container or you might drop some table scraps or eggs. That would be a disaster.

Next, you need to have some good table scraps. Hens like stale bread and cake, lettuce stalks, carrot shavings, and other vegetable or grain products. Stay away from pepper, meat, and crustacean shells or they will flavor and color the eggs. Don't use anything too strong-flavored either. You don't want to harm the chickens or make their eggs taste funny.

Third, throw your leftovers in the container instead of the trash. You should keep your container right in the kitchen. My mother puts leftover food in our table-scrap container every day. This way she never misses an opportunity to feed some scraps to the chickens.

After getting the container and the feed ready, make sure you are dressed in the right clothing. The chicken coop is very messy, so always wear sturdy shoes that are easy to clean. Wearing a jacket is a good idea if it is cold outside.

Now it is time to pick up the plastic container with the table scraps and walk outside to the chicken coop. The chicken coop is the shedlike house where the chickens are kept. Our coop is tucked away in a wooded area close to our house. A coop must be well sealed so that predators—animals that kill chickens—cannot get inside and eat the eggs and chickens.

RUBRIC
IN ACTION

❶ Begins with a strong introduction, which includes a clear statement of topic and purpose

❷ Mentions equipment and other supplies necessary for the task

❸ Explains each step in a separate paragraph in the order in which it must be done
Another Option:
• Use headings to identify each step.

❹ Defines specific words that may be unfamiliar to the reader

Teaching the Lesson

Analyzing the Model
"Scrambling for Eggs"

The student model is a process description of how to gather farm-fresh eggs. The writer starts the essay by describing the chickens and their environment, and then lays out the steps for gathering the eggs.

Have students think of a situation in which they had to follow written directions. Help students to see how the organization and the use of transitional words make the explanation of the process easy to follow.

Then point out the key words and phrases in the student model that correspond to the elements mentioned in the Rubric in Action.

1 Ask students to identify the author's purpose or purposes in this essay.
   Possible Responses: to describe how to gather eggs; to illustrate how the process of gathering eggs can be fun and interesting

2 Have students read the next two paragraphs omitting the transitional words. Ask them how this omission affects the essay.
   Possible Responses: The essay seems less organized and the steps more difficult to follow; the progress from one step to the next is not clearly defined.

3 Ask students to explain how the essay would change if all the steps were combined into one paragraph.
   Possible Responses: The process would be harder to follow and to read. Some of the steps described in the middle of a paragraph might be missed.

4 Ask students to explain why it is important to define unfamiliar or difficult words.
   Possible Response: Understanding the meaning of a sentence or a paragraph might depend upon knowing the definition of the word.

Mini Lesson Viewing and Representing

PICTURING TEXT STRUCTURE

Instruction While ideas and word choice play key roles in good writing, the structure of a text— the way in which ideas are organized and events unfold—also contributes to the effectiveness of the work.

Activity Have students analyze the organization of the student model by constructing a diagram or other graphic organizer. The following flow chart is an example.

Use **Writing Transparencies**, p. 6, for additional support.

• **Introduction:** introduces topic of egg gathering and explains that it is fun and interesting

• **Background:** gives information about chickens and describes equipment that is needed and why

• **Directions:** explains the steps involved in gathering eggs and managing chickens

• **Conclusion:** refers back to introduction in order to tie essay together

502 UNIT FOUR PART 1

5 Point out to students that the student author of this essay varies the introductory sentences of his paragraphs so that the essay is interesting to read and does not resemble a list of chores.

6 Point out the definition of *mulch* given in the essay.

7 Ask students how the student author connects the last paragraph of this essay to his introduction.

Possible Response: He gives examples of why gathering eggs can be interesting and fun and illustrates why he thinks it is a rewarding task.

Once you are at the coop, gently open the door. It may be dusty—our coop is! Make sure you do not scare the chickens. They are very timid and will jump and fly around if you startle them. The chickens know that you are there to feed them, and they will want their food immediately. When you hand out the scraps, be sure to tear up the large pieces so the chickens can eat them easily.

While the chickens are busy eating, look in the egg boxes for the fresh eggs. It is always a surprise. You might find twelve eggs, or, if the chickens have been lazy, you might find only one or two. The eggs are often warm to the touch. You should gather them every day, especially in the winter. If you don't gather them often in the winter, they can freeze and break.

❺ Uses a topic sentence in each paragraph, providing a transition from the previous paragraph

Next, collect the eggs and place them carefully in your now-empty container. You don't want the fragile eggs breaking, especially ones of such good quality. Before you leave, check each hen's feet and beak. If the feet and beak are turning bright yellow it means the hens have stopped laying. This is because all of the pigment that colors the egg yolk is being used by the chicken herself.

As you leave the chicken coop, shut and lock the door securely behind you. Scrape off the bottom of your shoes with a twig or rock. A special brush is also a good idea. Once you are back at your house, wash the eggs. The eggs are often sticky, so they pick up the mulch—ground leaves, straw, or mosses—that is used as cushioning in the egg boxes. You should wash them in cool water with a sponge. The eggs must be clean before you store them.

❻ Defines another unfamiliar word

Finally, you can store the eggs. The eggs will last for the longest time if they are put in the refrigerator. They can be stored at room temperature if no more room is available in the refrigerator. We store our eggs in recycled egg cartons. This helps the environment and it is free. You might want to give eggs away to friends and relatives because fresh eggs are so delicious. Ask people for extra egg cartons so that you never run out.

Eggs come in different sizes and colors but they are all the same. Brown eggs and white eggs have both the same nutrition and taste. Often, we get a huge gooselike egg that contains a double yolk. Occasionally, we have gotten an egg the size of a robin's. This egg was extremely small. No matter what size or color they are, our eggs are fun to gather, great tasting, and practically free. Once you have tried a farm-fresh egg, you will become an egghead just like me.

❼ Summarizes the benefits of collecting farm-fresh eggs

Writing Your Process Description

❶ Prewriting

Knowledge advances by steps.
—Thomas Macaulay, 19th-century British writer

In the course of the day, you do many things that involve a number of steps. Other people might not know how to do some of the tasks that you do easily. **List** the tasks that you do from the time you wake up until the time you go to sleep. Include activities like riding your bike, making lunch, or practicing a musical instrument. Then note activities of the people around you. See the **Idea Bank** in the margin for other suggestions. After you choose a process to describe, follow the steps below.

Planning Your Process Description

▶ **1. Know your audience.** Think about how much your audience knows about the topic. What background information will they need? Will your description be serious or humorous?

▶ **2. Gather the details.** List all the steps that you think are necessary to the process. Then make a note of all the equipment or supplies that you need to accomplish the task.

▶ **3. Organize your information.** Are your steps in order? Is there background information or details that need to be included? Have you included any unnecessary details?

❷ Drafting

Begin to write your process description. **First** tell what you are going to describe and why the process is important or interesting. **Then** describe the steps. **Finish** with a **summary** of the process and its end result.

- Use **vocabulary** that can be easily understood by your readers. Explain any words your readers might not know.
- Include a complete list of supplies and equipment.
- **Describe** each step fully in a separate paragraph.
- Show the **order** of steps by using transitional words such as *first, next, before, during,* or *after* to help your readers know when each step occurs.

IDEABank

1. For Your Working Portfolio
Look for ideas in the **Writing Options** that you completed earlier in this unit.
- **Dog Care Instructions**, p. 460
- **Time Line**, p. 474

2. Equipment Expertise
List pieces of equipment that you know how to operate, like a computer, VCR, or tape recorder. Explain to a partner how to complete a simple function with one of these items.

3. New Horizons
Think about tasks that you've always wanted to be able to do, such as baking bread or building a birdhouse. Interview someone who knows how to do your chosen task. Ask him or her what steps are involved.

Have a question?
See the **Writing Handbook.**
Transitions, p. R28
Elaboration, p. R29

Ask Your Peer Reader: EVALUATING

- How well did I explain my subject?
- Were the steps presented clearly?
- Did I use effective transitions?
- Did I include the necessary background information?

Guiding Student Writing

Prewriting
Choosing a Subject
If after reading the Idea Bank students have difficulty choosing a subject for their process description, suggest that they try the following:
- Look around and ask yourself how things work—in your house, in nature, in the car. List several processes that you would like to learn more about, such as how a caterpillar turns into a butterfly or how an engine works.
- Think about a hobby or activity you participate in, such as building models or collecting coins. Think about how you can explain this activity to someone who knows nothing about it.

Planning the Process Description
1. Encourage students to use precise language and vivid descriptions in order to make the process clear and interesting to read.
2. Suggest that students take notes while walking through the process they wish to describe to make sure they include all the steps.
3. Suggest that students use a time line, flow chart, or other diagram to organize their ideas and steps.

Drafting
If students have difficulty getting started, suggest they begin writing about the parts of the process they find most interesting or easiest to describe. Then have them go back and fill in details and missing steps.

Ask Your Peer Reader
Remind students to use the peer reviewer's feedback when revising their drafts.

Revising

DEFINING UNFAMILIAR TERMS

Review the change in the sample with students. To help students practice recognizing and defining unfamiliar words, ask volunteers to share paragraphs from their drafts. Have the rest of the class listen for words that they would like defined or explained.

Editing and Proofreading

TRANSITIONAL WORDS AND PHRASES

Remind students that transitional words and phrases alert the reader that new information is about to be discussed. Have students explain the change in the sample. For more practice, see the Grammar Mini Lesson at the bottom of page 505.

Reflecting

As they write their reflections, have students consider what they will be more aware of the next time they learn a new process.

Option

Managing the Paper Load

To cut down on the paper load as you make sure that all students are on track, read only the opening paragraph of each paper. Offer specific written comments rather than meeting with students individually.

Need revising help?

Review the **Rubric,** p. 500

Consider **peer reader** comments

Check **Revision Guidelines,** p. R23

SPELLING
From Writing

As you revise your work, look back at the words you misspelled and determine why you made the errors you did. For additional help, refer to the strategies and generalizations in the **Spelling Handbook** on page R86.

Perplexed by prepositions?

See the **Grammar Handbook,** p. R54

Publishing
IDEAS

- Choose a younger audience for your process description. Simplify the language so that your instructions will be understood.

- Create a do-it-yourself video by narrating your process description and either doing the process at the same time or showing illustrations of each step.

**More Online:
Publishing Options**
www.mcdougallittell.com

---

❸ Revising

TARGET SKILL ▶ DEFINING UNFAMILIAR TERMS

As you explain the steps in your process description, look for words or phrases that might be unfamiliar to your readers. If you have used an unfamiliar word, simply include a definition directly after it. For example, in a process description about making fudge, one student writes: *The fudge is done when it congeals, or becomes solid, in cold water.* Explaining the word *congealed* makes the instruction clear.

> —*ground leaves, straw, or mosses*—
>
> The eggs are often sticky, so they pick up the mulch ‸
>
> that is used as cushioning in the egg boxes.

❹ Editing and Proofreading

TARGET SKILL ▶ TRANSITIONAL WORDS AND PHRASES

The order of the steps in your process essay should be clear. You can signal the order of the steps by using transitional words and phrases. These include prepositions and prepositional phrases like *before, after, during, in addition to, prior to,* and *next to.*

> My mother puts leftover food in our table scrap
>
> container every day. This way she never misses an
>
> opportunity to feed some scraps to the chickens.
> *After getting the container and feed ready,*
> ‸You should make sure you are dressed in the
>
> right clothing.

❺ Reflecting

FOR YOUR WORKING PORTFOLIO What did you learn about your process or subject by writing a process description? Which part of writing the description was most difficult? What other processes or tasks would you like to describe? Attach your answers to your finished essay. Save your process description in your **Working Portfolio.**

Assessment Practice Revising & Editing

Read this paragraph from the first draft of a process description. The underlined sections may include the following kinds of errors:

- **spelling errors**
- **incorrectly used modifiers**
- **incorrect conjunctions**
- **comma errors**

For each underlined section, choose the revision that most improves the writing.

> Making fudge can be done <u>real easy</u> if you follow the necessary
> (1)
> steps. First, you should gather all of the ingredients and supplies. The
> recipe calls for the following items: <u>butter, sugar, chocolate, condensed
> milk, marshmallows</u>. In addition, you need a pan that will <u>distribute or
> (2)   (3)
> spread</u> the heat <u>even</u>. A measuring cup, a tablespoon, <u>a large wooden
> (4)   (5)
> spoon, a candy thermometer</u> are also needed. After you collect the
> supplies, you can begin to cook. If you follow all the directions, your
> fudge will be a <u>success</u>!
> (6)

1. A. really easily
   B. real easily
   C. really easier
   D. Correct as is

2. A. butter, sugar, chocolate condensed milk, marshmallows.
   B. butter, sugar, chocolate, condensed milk marshmallows.
   C. butter, sugar, chocolate, condensed, milk marshmallows.
   D. Correct as is

3. A. distribute, or spread,
   B. distribute or, spread
   C. distribute but spread
   D. Correct as is

4. A. evener
   B. evenly
   C. evenest
   D. Correct as is

5. A. a large wooden spoon, or a candy thermometer
   B. a large wooden spoon, and a candy thermometer
   C. a large wooden spoon, but a candy thermometer
   D. Correct as is

6. A. sucess
   B. succes
   C. sucses
   D. Correct as is

Need extra help?

See the **Grammar Handbook.**

Quick Reference: Parts of Speech, p. R54

Using Modifiers Effectively, p. R70

Correcting Punctuation, p. R76

Assessment Practice

Demonstrate how students can eliminate incorrect choices for the first question.

A. This choice correctly uses an adverb to modify an adverb.

B. This choice is incorrect because it uses an adjective to modify an adverb.

C. This choice is incorrect because "easier" is an adjective.

D. The original choice is incorrect because the underlined words are adjectives.

Answers:

1. A; 2. D; 3. A; 4. B; 5. B; 6. D.

 Mini Lesson Grammar

TRANSITIONAL WORDS AND PHRASES For use with Editing and Proofreading, p. 504. Tell students that when organizing the elements of a process into chronological order, transitional words and phrases can help make the order of events clear to the reader by showing relationships in time. Transitional words and phrases are usually placed at or near the beginning of a sentence.

Practice Have students make the following five sentences into a paragraph, using transitional words and phrases to clarify the order of events. *(Answers will vary.)*

1. We read about coral reefs.
2. We watched a video about the Great Barrier Reef.
3. Ellen's mother gave a presentation about snorkeling.
4. Our teacher helped us set up a salt water aquarium.
5. To end the unit on coral reefs, we visited the National Aquarium.

Possible Responses: To start the unit on coral reefs, we began by reading about coral reefs. Next, we watched a video about the Great Barrier Reef. A few days later, Ellen's mother gave a presentation about snorkeling, and then our teacher helped us set up a salt water aquarium. Finally, to end the unit, we visited the National Aquarium.

 Use McDougal Littell's *Language Network,* Chapter 6, for more practice in using prepositions.

Reflecting on the Theme   Have you ever been told you have an active imagination? Do you think that it's good to have lots of imagination? In this part of Unit Four, writers use their imaginations to invent new worlds or to imagine how our own world could be different.

ACTIVITY

Make a list of movies, television shows, comic books, and literary works that are set in imaginary worlds. Choose three and use a Venn diagram to compare and contrast them. Write what is similar about them in the middle of the diagram. List the aspects that are unique to each in the other sections of the diagram. Compare your diagram with a classmate's. Discuss the elements that works of imagination tend to have in common.

506

Science Fiction and Fantasy

> *Whether writing realism or fantasy, my concerns are the same—how we learn to be . . . human beings.*
> —Lloyd Alexander, writer

Can you imagine building a rocket and traveling to the moon? Writer Jules Verne imagined it. He wrote about it in his book *From Earth to the Moon* which was published in 1865—almost 100 years before man first set foot on the moon. Today, Jules Verne is considered to be one of the greatest science fiction writers of all time.

Science fiction is a literary genre in which the action of a story usually takes place in the future or in outer space. Imaginary objects and events are based on real or possible science and technology. Science fiction writers have predicted the invention of submarines, cell phones, and computers.

Fantasy is another literary genre that can introduce you to new worlds, unusual characters, and strange events. However, fantasy stories don't have to be based on science and technology. In fact, they are often based on myths and legends. In fantasy stories, there must be at least one completely unreal or fantastic element, such as elves, fairies, or talking plants.

OVERVIEW

Objectives
- understand and identify the following literary genres:
  science fiction
  fantasy
- understand common and disparate elements of science fiction and fantasy
- recognize common themes within each of the two genres

Teaching the Lesson

This lesson defines and analyzes science fiction and fantasy and helps students understand the similarities and differences between the two genres.

Introducing the Concepts
Have students think about a movie they have seen recently that might be considered science fiction. Ask them to explain why they consider this film science fiction. What elements do they think are required for a work to be considered science fiction?

Presenting the Concepts
Science Fiction

Working as a class, have students come up with the opening paragraph for a science fiction story. The paragraph should describe at least one character in detail and should also describe the setting of the story in vivid and specific detail. Remind students that their scientific details should be real or at least possible at some point in the future. Write their paragraph on the chalkboard.

YOUR TURN

Possible Response: "It had been raining for seven years," "A thousand forests had been crushed . . . and grown up a thousand times," "this was the way life was . . . on the planet Venus," "children of the rocket men and women"

Science Fiction

In **science fiction,** the descriptions of setting include details about technology and scientific developments. The technology seems fantastic but also appears to be possible. Science fiction writers use detailed descriptions to help readers visualize **futuristic settings.** In most science fiction stories, vivid details tell you how a place looks, what types of plants are there, what color the sky is, and how the place feels. Characters, too, are described in detail. The details about setting and characters help you compare and contrast the story with what you know about life on earth.

YOUR TURN What details in the excerpt from "All Summer in a Day" create a futuristic setting?

SCIENCE FICTION

It had been raining for seven years; thousands upon thousands of days compounded and filled from one end to the other with rain, with the drum and gush of water, with the sweet crystal fall of showers and the concussion of storms so heavy they were tidal waves come over the islands. A thousand forests had been crushed under the rain and grown up a thousand times to be crushed again. And this was the way life was forever on the planet Venus, and this was the schoolroom of the children of the rocket men and women who had come to a raining world to set up civilization and live out their lives.

—Ray Bradbury,
"All Summer in a Day"

From "All Summer in a Day"

Comparing
Science Fiction and Fantasy

Science Fiction
- real or possible science data
- often set in the future or in space
- often describes future technology

Both
- imaginative
- new worlds
- unusual characters
- strange events

Fantasy
- unrealistic or fantastic settings
- imaginary creatures
- impossible events
- elements of myths and legends

Fantasy

A work of fiction is **fantasy** if it includes at least one fantastic or unreal element. For example, you may read a fantasy story about a place in which everything seems realistic, except for the fact that the animals can talk. The author of a fantasy makes it possible for you to imagine the impossible. To make this happen, the author will include **imaginative settings, fantastic details, imaginary creatures,** or **impossible events.** For example, an author will try very hard to describe a setting exactly, so that when animal characters start talking, it seems surprising but believable.

YOUR TURN Look at the excerpt from "The Walrus and the Carpenter." Which details and events are possible, and which are not possible?

FANTASY

The sun was shining on the sea,
 Shining with all his might:
He did his very best to make
 The billows smooth and bright—
And this was odd, because it was
 The middle of the night.

The moon was shining sulkily,
 Because she thought the sun
Had got no business to be there
 After the day was done—
"It's very rude of him," she said,
 "To come and spoil the fun!"

—Lewis Carroll,
"The Walrus and the Carpenter"

From "The Walrus and the Carpenter"

LEARNING THE LANGUAGE OF LITERATURE **509**

Fantasy

Have students working as a group come up with an opening paragraph for a fantasy. Ask students to describe at least one character in detail and to describe the setting of the story in vivid and specific detail. Remind students that either the character or the setting should contain at least one imaginative, unrealistic element. Have them then compare this paragraph to their science fiction paragraph and to discuss the similarities and differences between them.

YOUR TURN
Possible Response: The sun shining in the night at the same time as the moon is ordinarily not possible; the moon speaking is not possible.

Theme

Have students look back at the paragraphs for the science fiction story and the fantasy they created. As a class, discuss possible themes for these stories based on the settings and characters that are described.

Use **Literary Analysis Transparencies,** p. 7, for additional support.

Theme

Theme is an important idea expressed in a work of literature. Think of it as a message or feeling about life or human nature that the writer wishes to share with readers. Sometimes a theme is stated directly. Usually, however, readers have to make inferences about the theme based on details in a story. A story's title, characters, setting, and plot can provide clues to theme.

Many science fiction pieces share two common themes: the dangers of taking the natural environment for granted, and the effect of technology on our society. In fantasy writing, themes often deal with good versus evil, the weak versus the powerful, or characters overcoming odds or completing difficult journeys.

THEME

Milo. But there's so much to learn.

Rhyme. That's true, but it's not just learning that's important. It's learning what to do with what you learn and learning why you learn things that matters.

—Norton Juster and Susan Nanus,
The Phantom Tollbooth

From *The Phantom Tollbooth*

Have you ever listened to someone talk about a great new movie? If so, you probably pictured the people and events as they were described. Whenever you create mental pictures, you are visualizing. You can visualize with literature, too. Active readers get the most from what they read by visualizing the settings, characters, and events in a story.

isualizing

How to Apply the Strategy

To **VISUALIZE,** an active reader will:
- Form mental pictures and images
- Look for details and descriptions that appeal to the senses
- Pay attention to the stage directions in a drama
- **Connect** with settings, characters, and events

Try It Now!

Read the excerpt below and visualize the scene.

> *(LIGHTS UP to reveal MILO'S bedroom. The CLOCK appears to be on a shelf in the room of a young boy—a room filled with books, toys, games, maps, papers, pencils, a bed, and a desk. . . . as well as records, a television, a toy car, and a large box that is wrapped and has an envelope taped to the top. The sound of FOOTSTEPS is heard, and then enter MILO dejectedly. He throws down his books and coat, flops into a chair, and sighs loudly.)*
>
> —Norton Juster and Susan Nanus,
> *The Phantom Tollbooth*

Here's how Brittany uses the strategy:

"After I read the stage directions in The Phantom Tollbooth, *I close my eyes and try to picture the scene. I imagine that I see the setting where the action takes place. As I read, I pay attention to how the characters move and speak. I look for details that appeal to my senses. This helps me to* **visualize** *each description. I feel a* **connection** *to this piece as I picture Milo coming in. This could almost be my bedroom."*

Need More Help?

Remember that active readers use the essential reading strategies explained on page 4: • **visualize** • **predict** • **clarify** • **question** • **connect** • **evaluate** • **monitor.**

THE ACTIVE READER **511**

OVERVIEW

Objectives
- develop effective strategies for visualizing
- describe mental images that text descriptions evoke
- respond to text by making connections to prior experiences

Teaching the Lesson

The strategies on this page will help students visualize the settings, characters, and events in the selections they read.

Presenting the Strategies
Help students understand the strategies by asking for volunteers to read them aloud. Emphasize to students that they will be using these strategies as they read the selections in this book.

1 Mental Images and Details
Tell students that as they read the excerpt from *The Phantom Tollbooth* they should note details that appeal to the senses as they try to form mental images.

2 Stage Directions
Remind students that since stage directions sometimes tell the actors what to do and where to move, they are a good source of visual information.

3 Connect
As a class, discuss how the material students read is easier to visualize if they relate the descriptions to their own life experiences.

Try It Now!
Answers will vary, but should include sensory details.

Use **Reading and Critical Thinking Transparencies,** p. 4, for additional support.

OVERVIEW

 Act I of this selection is included in the **Grade 6 InterActive Reader.**

Objectives

1. to understand and appreciate **fantasy (Literary Analysis)**
2. to understand and appreciate a **drama (Literary Analysis)**
3. to use **visualizing** to help understand character, setting, and action **(Active Reading)**

Summary

Milo is bored until he finds in his room one day a tollbooth. He gets into his toy car and sets off for Dictionopolis. He travels through Expectations and the Doldrums, and joins up with Tock, the Watchdog. In Dictionopolis, they meet the Spelling Bee, Humbug, and King Azaz, the ruler. Azaz and his brother, the Mathemagician, ruler of Digitopolis, banished their sisters, Rhyme and Reason, to the Castle-in-the-Air. Now Azaz wants them back, and Milo finds himself taking on the quest of rescuing the princesses with his friends Tock and Humbug. On their way, they encounter more strange characters. They return to the Land of Wisdom with the princesses, and Milo ends his journey back in his room, having learned many important lessons.

Thematic Link

Milo finds out that there are no limits to what someone can do with a little imagination.

5-Minute Warm-Up

Daily Language SkillBuilder

Have students **proofread** the display sentences on page 441j and write them correctly. The sentences also appear on Transparency 16 of **Grammar Transparencies and Copymasters.**

 Mini Lesson **Preteaching Vocabulary**

If you would like to preteach the WORDS TO KNOW for this selection, use the Mini Lesson, p. 514.

The Phantom Tollbooth

Novel by NORTON JUSTER *dramatized by* SUSAN NANUS

Connect to Your Life

What is the greatest number you can name?

In 1655, the English mathematician John Wallis introduced this symbol to represent infinity.

Build Background

As the main character in *The Phantom Tollbooth* finds out, the series of numbers has no end. No matter how great a number you imagine, you can always add 1 to it. When something has no end, we say that it is *infinite.*

Negative numbers   Positive numbers

-6 -5 -4 -3 -2 -1 0 1 2 3 4 5 6

Numbers are infinite in both "directions." This is why number lines have an arrow on each end. The arrows stand for the infinite progression of numbers on either side of zero.

Focus Your Reading

LITERARY ANALYSIS **FANTASY** The drama you are about to read is a **fantasy,** a work that contains one or more fantastic or unreal elements. *The Phantom Tollbooth* features fantastic characters and settings. For example, the main character, who is a boy, meets Tock, a talking "watchdog" with an alarm clock in his belly. Together these characters travel to imaginary lands.

WORDS TO KNOW **Vocabulary Preview**

acknowledge	deliberately	leisurely	petty
admonishing	destination	mourn	quest
ascend	fanfare	pantomime	vigorously
dejectedly	ignorance	perish	

ACTIVE READING **VISUALIZING** Writers of fantasy often provide vivid descriptions of unusual characters and settings. **Visualizing,** or forming pictures in your mind, can help you appreciate and understand a fantasy play, story, or poem. As you read, visualize the places and characters in *The Phantom Tollbooth.*

READER'S NOTEBOOK Jot down key phrases that help create images in your mind.

THE PHANTOM TOLLBOOTH

NOVEL BY
NORTON JUSTER

DRAMATIZED BY
SUSAN NANUS

TEACHING THE LITERATURE

Customizing Instruction

Less Proficient Readers
Remind students that drama is meant to be acted out. Review the importance of paying attention to stage directions, which describe the appearance, gestures, and movements of the actors and indicate the setting. Tell students that act and scene divisions organize the plot of a play.

Students Acquiring English
Help students to understand the title by defining *phantom* as "having appearance without substance" or "apparition." Explain that the purpose of a tollbooth is to collect the fees charged for using a public road. The "phantom tollbooth" will allow Milo to go into the realm of fantasy.

 Use **Spanish Study Guide,** pp. 106–108 for additional support.

Gifted and Talented
Ask students to consider, as they read, which of the following quotations from the novel *The Phantom Tollbooth* best describes what Milo learns during his journey. Discuss students' choices and their reasons at the end of their reading of the play.

". . . the way you see things depends a great deal on where you look at them from."
". . . [time] is our most valuable possession, more precious than diamonds."
". . . the most important reason for going from one place to another is to see what's in between."

 Mini Lesson **Viewing and Representing**

Milo and Rhyme and Reason

Instruction Tell students that this photograph is from a production of *The Phantom Tollbooth.* Pictured are Milo, Rhyme, and Reason. Ask students what they might infer about the characters from the picture.

Possible Responses: The costumes of Rhyme and Reason suggest that they are members of royalty. Rhyme and Reason appear as people. This prepares the reader to see other fantastic charac-

ters. Milo is young and seems to be looking for something off in the distance.

Application Ask students to react to seeing this image at the beginning of their reading. What does its placement here help them to do?

Possible Responses: Some may find it helpful because they gain an immediate sense of characters; others may say it helps them to form their own mental pictures of a stage production as they read.

Reading Skills and Strategies:
PREVIEW

Tell students that this is a play about Milo's journey to several destinations. Have students skim the play to get an idea of the characters that Milo meets and the adventures he has. Students should set a purpose before reading each scene.

Literary Analysis | FANTASY |

Remind students that this play contains elements of fantasy. Ask students which settings listed are realistic and which are fantasy settings.

Possible Responses: Milo's bedroom is realistic; the other settings are not.

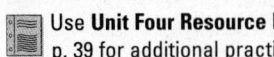 Use **Unit Four Resource Book,** p. 39 for additional practice.

Active Reading | VISUALIZING |

Ⓐ Ask students which details help them to create a mental image of Digitopolis.

Possible Responses: "glittering place without trees or greenery"; "full of shining rocks"; "hundreds of numbers shining"

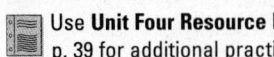 Use **Unit Four Resource Book,** p. 38 for additional practice. Use **Reading and Critical Thinking Transparencies,** p. 4, for additional support.

Literary Analysis:
CAST OF CHARACTERS

Tell students that many scripts like this one include a list of all the characters in the order in which they appear. Ask students to name the last new character that will be seen.

Answer: Senses Taker

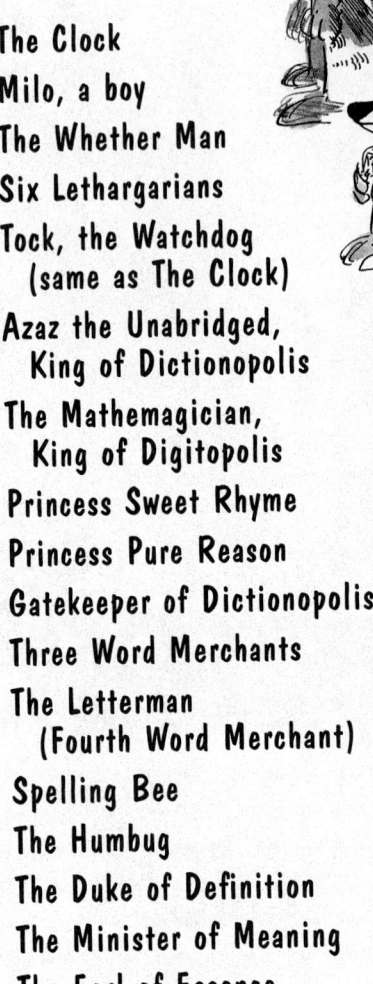

CAST
(in order of appearance)

The Clock
Milo, a boy
The Whether Man
Six Lethargarians
Tock, the Watchdog
  (same as The Clock)
Azaz the Unabridged,
  King of Dictionopolis
The Mathemagician,
  King of Digitopolis
Princess Sweet Rhyme
Princess Pure Reason
Gatekeeper of Dictionopolis
Three Word Merchants
The Letterman
  (Fourth Word Merchant)
Spelling Bee
The Humbug
The Duke of Definition
The Minister of Meaning
The Earl of Essence

The Count of Connotation
The Undersecretary of
  Understanding
A Page
Kakafonous A. Dischord,
  Doctor of Dissonance
The Awful Dynne
The Dodecahedron
Miners of the Numbers Mine
The Everpresent Wordsnatcher
The Terrible Trivium
The Demon of Insincerity
Senses Taker

Teaching Options

Mini Lesson **Preteaching Vocabulary**

WORD PARTS: PREFIXES AND SUFFIXES

Instruction Tell students that examining the prefix or suffix of an unfamiliar word may help them to define it. Display the following prefixes and meanings: *as, ad* – to, toward; *de* – away, from, off, down. Then tell students that suffixes often determine the word's function in the sentence: *ly* – adverbs (in a way that is); *ation, ion, tion, ance* – nouns (state or condition).

Exercise Have students analyze the prefixes and suffixes of the WORDS TO KNOW in the right column and match them with the definitions in the left.

1. to move toward the top
2. state of being uneducated
3. in a sad way
4. done with energy
5. warning away from

a. dejectedly
b. ascend
c. admonishing
d. ignorance
e. vigorously

ANSWERS: 1. b; 2. d; 3. a; 4. e; 5. c

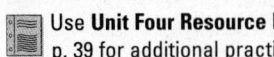 Use **Unit Four Resource Book,** p. 40 for more practice.
Use **Vocabulary Transparencies and Copymasters,** p. 50, for additional support.

The SETS

1. Milo's bedroom

With shelves, pennants, pictures on the wall, as well as suggestions of the characters of the Land of Wisdom.

2. The road to the Land of Wisdom

A forest, from which the Whether Man and the Lethargarians emerge.

3. Dictionopolis

A marketplace full of open-air stalls as well as little shops. Letters and signs should abound. There may be street signs and lampposts in the shapes of large letters (large O's and Q's) and all windows and doors can be in the shape of H's and A's.

4. Digitopolis

A dark, glittering place without trees or greenery, but full of shining rocks and cliffs, with hundreds of numbers shining everywhere. When the scene change is made to the Mathemagician's room, set pieces are simply carried in from the wings.

5. The Land of Ignorance

A gray, gloomy place full of cliffs and caves, with frightening faces. Different levels and heights should be suggested through one or two platforms or risers, with a set of stairs that lead to the castle in the air.

Reading Skills and Strategies: EVALUATE

 Have students sit in silence for 30 seconds. Then have students do an activity like copying something for 30 seconds. Ask them if they agree or disagree with the Clock's assessment of time.

Possible Response: Most will agree that when there is much to do, time goes quickly. When there is not much, time passes slowly.

Literary Analysis: THEME

B Ask students what important idea is conveyed by the Clock's words.

Possible Response: People should make every minute count and appreciate the time they have.

Literary Analysis: HUMOR

C Tell students that writers can add humor through exaggeration—overemphasis on minor events, or through witty dialogue, sarcasm, or irony. Ask students what device the writer uses here.

Answer: exaggeration

Literary Analysis: STAGE DIRECTIONS

D Tell students that stage directions contain instructions to the performers, director, and stage crew. They are usually italicized and in parentheses. If a play is read instead of viewed, the reader must examine the stage directions for important clues to action and character. Ask students what they learn from the stage directions describing Milo's room.

Possible Response: He has many possessions; he seems to be a typical young boy; images relating to future characters appear on various things in his room.

Use **Literary Analysis Transparencies,** p. 23, for additional support.

516 UNIT FOUR PART 2: IMAGINARY WORLDS

Teaching Options

Mini Lesson — Viewing and Representing

Illustration of Milo in his room
by Bruce Roberts

Instruction Remind students that an illustrator's choice of style, elements, and media help to represent or extend the text's meanings. Point out illustrator Bruce Roberts's take on Milo's room. He uses lots of color and loose brush strokes to create a casual, energetic feeling. Ask students how this illustration of Milo compares with the one from page 513, aside from the fact that one is a photograph and one is drawn.

Possible Response: Milo looks a little older in this illustration. You also get to see him in his own environment—his messy room.

Application Tell students to note the various objects in this illustration and to refer back to this page as they meet some of the characters in the course of the play. How are the characters related to what they see in Milo's room as the play begins?

ACT ONE
SCENE 1

The stage is completely dark and silent. Suddenly the sound of someone winding an alarm clock is heard, and after that, the sound of loud ticking is heard.

Lights up on the Clock, a huge alarm clock. The Clock reads 4:00. The lighting should make it appear that the Clock is suspended in mid-air (if possible). The Clock ticks for 30 seconds.

Clock. See that! Half a minute gone by. Seems like a long time when you're waiting for something to happen, doesn't it? Funny thing is, time can pass very slowly or very fast, and sometimes even both at once. The time now? Oh, a little after four, but what that means should depend on you. Too often, we do something simply because time tells us to. Time for school, time for bed, whoops, 12:00, time to be hungry. It can get a little silly, don't you think? Time is important, but it's what you do with it that makes it so. So my advice to you is to use it. Keep your eyes open and your ears perked. Otherwise it will pass before you know it, and you'll certainly have missed something!

Things have a habit of doing that, you know.

Being here one minute and gone the next.

In the twinkling of an eye.

In a jiffy.

In a flash!

I know a girl who yawned and missed a whole summer vacation. And what about that caveman who took a nap one afternoon, and woke up to find himself completely alone. You see, while he was sleeping, someone had invented the wheel and everyone had moved to the suburbs. And then of course, there is Milo. *(Lights up to reveal Milo's bedroom. The Clock appears to be on a shelf in the room of a young boy—a room filled with books, toys, games, maps, papers, pencils, a bed, a desk. There is a dartboard with numbers and the face of the Mathemagician, a bedspread made from King Azaz's cloak, a kite looking like the Spelling Bee, a punching bag with the Humbug's face, as well as records, a television, a toy car, and a large box that is wrapped and has*

 Speaking and Listening

INTRODUCE CAST OF CHARACTERS

Prepare Tell students that tone, volume, and expression can convey information. For example, if something is a secret, the speaker may use a stage whisper and hesitate frequently to show a reluctance to reveal the information. Have students review the cast of characters and jot down their impressions of each character from his or her name. They may wish to work in pairs or individually. Then have them practice conveying those impressions through their tone, expression, and volume.

Since the name Earl of Essence suggests dignity, his introduction might be given in a deep voice and formal tone.

Present Have students take turns introducing the characters. Ask audience members to describe the impression of each character that they receive from the way his or her name is spoken. After reading the play, ask students how their impressions of the characters changed or remained the same.

BLOCK SCHEDULING This activity is particularly well suited for longer class periods.

Reading and Analyzing

an envelope taped to the top. The sound of footsteps is heard, and then enter Milo <u>dejectedly</u>. He throws down his books and coat, flops into a chair, and sighs loudly.) Who never knows what to do with himself—not just sometimes, but always. When he's in school, he wants to be out, and when he's out, he wants to be in. *(During the following speech, Milo examines the various toys, tools, and other possessions in the room, trying them out and rejecting them.)* Wherever he is, he wants to be somewhere else—and when he gets there, so what. Everything is too much trouble or a waste of time. Books—he's already read them. Games—boring. T.V.—dumb. So what's left? Another long, boring afternoon. Unless he bothers to notice a very large package that happened to arrive today.

ACTIVE READING

A **CONNECT** Can you picture yourself in Milo's place? When do you feel bored?

Milo. *(Suddenly notices the package. He drags himself over to it, and disinterestedly reads the label.)* "For Milo, who has plenty of time." Well, that's true. *(Sighs and looks at it.)* No. *(Walks away.)* Well . . . *(Comes back. Rips open envelope and reads.)*

Voice. "One genuine turnpike tollbooth, easily assembled at home for use by those who have never traveled in lands beyond."

Milo. Beyond what? *(Continues reading.)*

Voice. "This package contains the following items:" *(Milo pulls the items out of the box and sets them up as they are mentioned.)* "One (1) genuine turnpike tollbooth to be erected according to directions. Three (3) precautionary signs to be used in a precautionary fashion. Assorted coins for paying tolls. One (1) map, strictly up to date, showing how to get from here to there. One (1) book of rules and traffic regulations which may not be bent or broken. Warning! Results are not guaranteed. If not perfectly satisfied, your wasted time will be refunded."

Milo. *(Skeptically.)* Come off it, who do you think you're kidding? *(Walks around and examines tollbooth.)* What am I supposed to do with this? *(The ticking of the Clock grows loud and impatient.)* Well . . . what else do I have to do. *(Milo gets into his toy car and drives up to the first sign. NOTE: The car may be an actual toy propelled by pedals or a small motor, or simply a cardboard imitation that Milo can fit into, and move by walking.)*

Voice. "Have your <u>destination</u> in mind."

Milo. *(Pulls out the map.)* Now, let's see. That's funny. I never heard of any of these places. Well, it doesn't matter anyway. Dictionopolis.[1] That's a weird name. I might as well go there. *(Begins to move, following map. Drives off.)*

Clock. See what I mean? You never know how things are going to get started. But when you're bored, what you need more than anything is a rude awakening.

(The alarm goes off very loudly as the stage darkens. The sound of the alarm is transformed into the honking of a car horn, and then is joined by the blasts, bleeps, roars and growls of heavy highway traffic. When the lights come up, Milo's bedroom is gone and we see a lonely road in the middle of nowhere.)

---

1. **Dictionopolis** (dĭk´shə-nŏp´ə-lĭs): an imaginary place name, formed from *dictionary* (an alphabetical listing of the words of a language) and the root *–polis*, meaning "city or state."

WORDS TO KNOW
dejectedly (dĭ-jĕk´tĭd-lē) *adv.* in a depressed manner
destination (dĕs´tə-nā´shən) *n.* the place to which one intends to go

518

SCENE 2

THE ROAD TO
DICTIONOPOLIS

*Enter Milo in
his car.*

Milo. This is weird! I don't recognize any of this scenery at all. *(A sign is held up before Milo, startling him.)* Huh? *(Reads.)* Welcome to Expectations. Information, predictions and advice cheerfully offered. Park here and blow horn. *(Milo blows horn.)*

Whether Man. *(A little man wearing a long coat and carrying an umbrella pops up from behind the sign that he was holding. He speaks very fast and excitedly.)* My, my, my, my, my, welcome, welcome, welcome, welcome to the Land of Expectations, Expectations, Expectations! We don't get many travelers these days; we certainly don't get many travelers. Now what can I do for you? I'm the Whether Man.

Milo. *(Referring to map.)* Uh . . . is this the right road to Dictionopolis?

Whether Man. Well now, well now, well now, I don't know of any wrong road to Dictionopolis, so if this road goes to Dictionopolis at all, it must be the right road, and if it doesn't, it must be the right road to somewhere else, because there are no wrong roads to anywhere. Do you think it will rain?

Milo. I thought you were the Weather Man.

Whether Man. Oh, no, I'm the Whether Man, not the weather man. *(Pulls out a sign or opens a flap of his coat, which reads: "Whether.")* After all, it's more important to know whether there will be weather than what the weather will be.

Milo. What kind of place is Expectations?

Whether Man. Good question, good question! Expectations is the place you must always go to before you get where you are going. Of course, some people never go beyond Expectations, but my job is to hurry them along whether they like it or not. Now what else can I do for you? *(Opens his umbrella.)*

Milo. I think I can find my own way.

Whether Man. Splendid, splendid, splendid! Whether or not you find your own way, you're bound to find some way. If you happen to find my way, please return it. I lost it years ago. I imagine by now it must be quite rusty. You did say it was going to rain, didn't you? *(Escorts Milo to the car under the open umbrella.)* I'm glad you made your own decision. I do so hate to make up my mind about anything, whether it's good or bad, up or down, rain or shine. Expect everything, I always say, and the unexpected never happens. Goodbye, goodbye, goodbye, good . . . *(A loud clap of thunder is heard.)* Oh dear! *(He looks up at the sky, puts out his hand to feel for rain and runs away. Milo watches puzzledly, and drives on.)*

Milo. I'd better get out of Expectations, but fast. Talking to a guy like that all day would get me nowhere for sure. *(He tries to speed up, but finds instead that he is moving slower and slower.)* Oh, oh, now what? *(He can

---

 Viewing and Representing

Illustration of Milo in his car
by Jules Feiffer

ART APPRECIATION Jules Feiffer (b. 1929) has been interested in art all his life. He began drawing cartoons after high school, and since then, his cartoons have been syndicated internationally. He illustrated the novel *The Phantom Tollbooth* in the early part of his career.
Instruction Tell students to notice Feiffer's style of drawing, which uses loose, sparse pen strokes. Although there is not a great deal of detail, a definite impression of the character is created. Ask

students what the portrait of Milo suggests about his character.
Possible Response: uncertainty; anxiety; wondering alertness as he moves into the unknown
Application Ask students whether this cartoon image of Milo matches their mental image. Have them explain why or why not.
Possible Responses: Some students may think the cartoon shows a more mature and older Milo than the text depicts. Others may see the artist's portrayal as just the sort of wide-eyed, curious boy they imagine.

A VISUALIZE Possible Responses:
"carry small pillows that look like rocks"; "colored in the same colors of the trees or the road"; "move very slowly"; "stop to rest"

Reading Skills and Strategies: CAUSE AND EFFECT

B Ask students to use the text's progression of ideas to locate the reason Milo is stuck in the Doldrums. What will he have to do to get out?

Possible Response: He stopped thinking. He'll have to start thinking again.

Literary Analysis: THEME

C Ask students what Milo is meant to learn from the Lethargarians.

Possible Response: People who waste time and do not use their minds go nowhere in life.

Active Reading: WORD PLAY

D Ask what the two meanings of "watchdog" are in the play.

Possible Responses: The first is literally a dog that contains a watch. The second is someone who tracks what others are doing or a guard dog.

Literary Analysis: IDIOM

E Ask students what effect the use of the idiom *killing time* has on their perception of time.

Possible Response: Time seems to be alive, so *killing* it becomes a terrible thing.

Literary Analysis: CHARACTERIZATION

F Ask students what the Watchdog's words and actions show about the kind of influence he will be on Milo.

Possible Response: He will be a positive influence.

barely move. Behind Milo, the Lethargarians[2] begin to enter from all parts of the stage. They are dressed to blend in with the scenery and carry small pillows that look like rocks. Whenever they fall asleep, they rest on the pillows.) Now I really am getting nowhere. I hope I didn't take a wrong turn. *(The car stops. He tries to start it. It won't move. He gets out and begins to tinker with it.)* I wonder where I am.

Lethargarian 1. You're . . . in . . . the . . . Dol . . . drums[3] . . . (Milo looks around.)

Lethargarian 2. Yes . . . in . . . the . . . Dol . . . drums . . . (A yawn is heard.)

Milo. *(Yelling.)* What are the Doldrums?

Lethargarian 3. The Doldrums, my friend, are where nothing ever happens and nothing ever changes. *(Parts of the scenery stand up or six people come out of the scenery colored in the same colors of the trees or the road. They move very slowly and as soon as they move, they stop to rest again.)* Allow me to introduce all of us. We are the Lethargarians at your service.

VISUALIZE Picture the Lethargarians. What words or phrases help you?

Milo. *(Uncertainly.)* Very pleased to meet you. I think I'm lost. Can you help me?

Lethargarian 4. Don't say think. *(He yawns.)* It's against the law.

Lethargarian 1. No one's allowed to think in the Doldrums. *(He falls asleep.)*

Lethargarian 2. Don't you have a rule book? It's local ordinance 175389-J. *(He falls asleep.)*

Milo. *(Pulls out rule book and reads.)* Ordinance 175389-J: "It shall be unlawful, illegal and unethical to think, think of thinking, surmise, presume, reason, meditate

or speculate while in the Doldrums. Anyone breaking this law shall be severely punished." That's a ridiculous law! Everybody thinks.

All the Lethargarians. We don't!

Lethargarian 2. And the most of the time, you don't, that's why you're here. You weren't thinking and you weren't paying attention either. People who don't pay attention often get stuck in the Doldrums. Face it, most of the time, you're just like us. *(Falls, snoring, to the ground. Milo laughs.)*

Lethargarian 5. Stop that at once. Laughing is against the law. Don't you have a rule book? It's local ordinance 574381-W.

Milo. *(Opens the rule book and reads.)* "In the Doldrums, laughter is frowned upon and smiling is permitted only on alternate Thursdays." Well, if you can't laugh or think, what can you do?

Lethargarian 6. Anything as long as it's nothing, and everything as long as it isn't anything. There's lots to do. We have a very busy schedule . . .

Lethargarian 1. At 8:00 we get up and then we spend from 8 to 9 daydreaming.

Lethargarian 2. From 9:00 to 9:30 we take our early midmorning nap . . .

Lethargarian 3. From 9:30 to 10:30 we dawdle and delay . . .

Lethargarian 4. From 10:30 to 11:30 we take our late early morning nap . . .

Lethargarian 5. From 11:30 to 12:00 we bide our time and then we eat our lunch.

---

2. **Lethargarians** (lĕth′ər-jär′ē-anz): a made-up name based on the word *lethargy*. A *Lethargarian* would thus be dull, inactive, or uncaring.

3. **in the doldrums** (dōl′drəmz′): the condition of being depressed or listless; here, *the Doldrums* refers to an imaginary land.

Mini Lesson Vocabulary Strategy

SYNONYMS

Instruction Remind students that synonyms are words that share similar meanings. Although using synonyms helps writers to avoid repetition, not all synonyms can be used interchangeably. Direct students' attention to Milo's speech at the bottom of the left column on page 520. Unlike *illegal*, something *unethical* is wrong because it goes against moral principles, not necessarily against the law.

Exercise Have students use a thesaurus or other reference work to help them choose the best synonym for the verb *think* to complete each sentence.

1. Milo (surmises, meditates) that the Lethargarians will never change.
2. The Lethargarians seem to (reason, presume) that Milo is willing to join them on their holiday.
3. It is unlawful to (speculate, presume) about the future in the Doldrums.
4. When Milo has time, he may (meditate, surmise) on his experiences to learn from them.

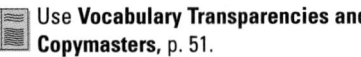

Use **Vocabulary Transparencies and Copymasters**, p. 51.

Lethargarian 6. From 1:00 to 2:00 we linger and loiter . . .

Lethargarian 1. From 2:00 to 2:30 we take our early afternoon nap . . .

Lethargarian 2. From 2:30 to 3:30 we put off for tomorrow what we could have done today . . .

Lethargarian 3. From 3:30 to 4:00 we take our early late afternoon nap . . .

Lethargarian 4. From 4:00 to 5:00 we loaf and lounge until dinner . . .

Lethargarian 5. From 6:00 to 7:00 we dilly-dally . . .

Lethargarian 6. From 7:00 to 8:00 we take our early evening nap and then for an hour before we go to bed, we waste time.

Lethargarian 1. *(Yawning.)* You see, it's really quite strenuous doing nothing all day long, and so once a week, we take a holiday and go nowhere.

Lethargarian 5. Which is just where we were going when you came along. Would you care to join us?

Milo. *(Yawning.)* That's where I seem to be going, anyway. *(Stretching.)* Tell me, does everyone here do nothing?

Lethargarian 3. Everyone but the terrible Watchdog. He's always sniffing around to see that nobody wastes time. A most unpleasant character.

Milo. The Watchdog?

Lethargarian 6. The Watchdog!

All the Lethargarians. *(Yelling at once.)* Run! Wake up! Run! Here he comes! The Watchdog! *(They all run off. Enter a large dog with the head, feet, and tail of a dog, and the body of a clock, having the same face as the character The Clock.)*

Watchdog. What are you doing here?

Milo. Nothing much. Just killing time. You see . . .

Watchdog. Killing time! *(His alarm rings in fury.)* It's bad enough wasting time without killing it. What are you doing in the Doldrums, anyway? Don't you have anywhere to go?

Milo. I think I was on my way to Dictionopolis when I got stuck here. Can you help me?

Watchdog. Help you! You've got to help yourself. I suppose you know why you got stuck.

Milo. I guess I just wasn't thinking.

Watchdog. Precisely. Now you're on your way.

Milo. I am?

Watchdog. Of course. Since you got here by not thinking, it seems reasonable that in order to get out, you must start thinking. Do you mind if I get in? I love automobile rides. *(He gets in. They wait.)* Well?

Milo. All right. I'll try. *(Screws up his face and thinks.)* Are we moving?

Watchdog. Not yet. Think harder.

Milo. I'm thinking as hard as I can.

Watchdog. Well, think just a little harder than that. Come on, you can do it.

Milo. All right, all right. . . . I'm thinking of all the planets in the solar system, and why water expands when it turns to ice, and all the words that begin with "q," and . . . *(The wheels begin to move.)* We're moving! We're moving!

Watchdog. Keep thinking.

Milo. *(Thinking.)* How a steam engine works and how to bake a pie and the difference between Fahrenheit and centigrade[4] . . .

---

4. **Fahrenheit** (făr′ən-hīt′) **and centigrade** (sĕn′tĭ-grād′): *Fahrenheit* is a temperature scale on which water freezes at 32 and boils at 212 degrees. On the centigrade (Celsius) scale, water freezes at 0 and boils at 100 degrees.

ACTIVE READING

(A) PREDICT Possible Responses: There will be words and letters scattered about, piled up, and arranged on shelves. Buildings might look like pages of a dictionary.

Literary Analysis: CHARACTER

(B) Ask students to explain what is suggested by the names of the two kings. Possible Responses: *Azaz* suggests the alphabet, the letters from A to Z; *Mathemagician* suggests that he can work magic with numbers.

Literary Analysis: FLASHBACK

(C) Explain to students that a flashback is a literary device in which a scene that took place at an earlier time is presented. Writers use flashback to provide background information. Ask students what they learn from this flashback. Possible Responses: Azaz and the Mathemagician don't agree on anything; the two princesses were banished because their brothers did not like the way they settled their argument.

Reading Skills and Strategies: WORD PLAY

(D) Have students explain the two meanings of *count* in this sentence. Possible Response: *Count* means numbers "are important" and "show numerical value."

Literary Analysis: PROPS

(E) Tell students that props are objects used on stage. They may be functional or symbolic. Ask students what the significance of the tollbooth is. Possible Response: It links back to the tollbooth found in Milo's room and indicates that another stage of Milo's journey is about to begin.

Watchdog. Dictionopolis, here we come.

Milo. Hey, Watchdog, are you coming along?

1 **Watchdog.** You can call me Tock, and keep your eyes on the road.

Milo. What kind of place is Dictionopolis, anyway?

ACTIVE READING

(A) **PREDICT** What do you think Dictionopolis will look like?

Tock. It's where all the words in the world come from. It used to be a marvelous place, but ever since Rhyme and Reason⁵ left, it hasn't been the same.

Milo. Rhyme and Reason?

(B) **Tock.** The two princesses. They used to settle all the arguments between their two brothers who rule over the Land of Wisdom. You see, Azaz is the king of Dictionopolis and the Mathemagician is the king of Digitopolis⁶ and they almost never see eye to eye on anything. It was the job of the Princesses Sweet Rhyme and Pure Reason to solve the differences between the two kings, and they always did so well that both sides usually went home feeling very satisfied. But then, **2** one day, the kings had an argument to end all arguments. . . .

(C) *(The lights dim on Tock and Milo, and come up on King Azaz of Dictionopolis on another part of the stage. Azaz has a great stomach, a gray beard reaching to his waist, a small crown and a long robe with the letters of the alphabet written all over it.)*

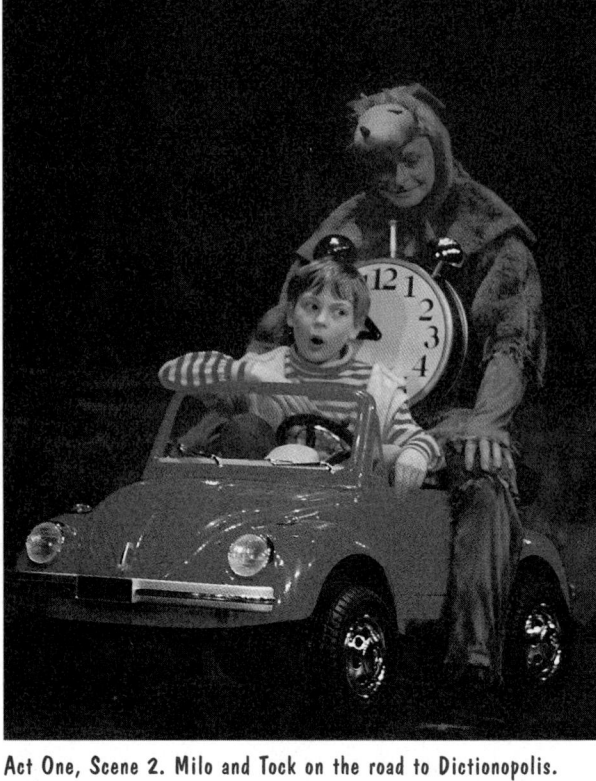

Act One, Scene 2. Milo and Tock on the road to Dictionopolis.

Azaz. Of course, I'll abide by the decision of Rhyme and Reason, though I have no doubt as to what it will be. They will choose words, of course. Everyone knows that words are more important than numbers any day of the week.

---

5. **Rhyme and Reason:** sense or explanation. The princesses try to establish order. When they disappear, there is "neither Rhyme nor Reason in this kingdom."

6. **Digitopolis** (dĭj´ə-tŏp´ə-lĭs): another made-up place name, this uses *digit* (any of the numbers 0–9) and the root –*polis* ("city or state") to describe a land of numbers.

 Mini Lesson **Viewing and Representing**

Milo and Tock on the road to Dictionopolis

Instruction Tell students that this photograph from a production of *The Phantom Tollbooth* illustrates how directors have their own visions of characters. In this image, Tock appears quite a bit larger than Milo. Ask students how this affects their impression of the relationship between the two characters.
Possible Response: Tock is seen as a protector for Milo and as a character whose wisdom and experience can help guide Milo.

Ask students to describe the look on Milo's face in this photograph.
Possible Response: He appears interested and happy.
Application Ask students if they agree with this director's portrayal of Tock and why or why not.
Possible Response: Many will agree that Tock's actions show him to be more mature and knowledgeable than Milo. This is shown when he leads Milo out of the Doldrums and fills him in on the background of Rhyme and Reason.

(The Mathemagician appears opposite Azaz. The Mathemagician wears a long flowing robe covered entirely with complex mathematical equations, and a tall pointed hat. He carries a long staff with a pencil point at one end and a large rubber eraser at the other.)

Mathemagician. That's what you think, Azaz. People wouldn't even know what day of the week it is without numbers. Haven't you ever looked at a calendar? Face it, Azaz. It's numbers that count.

Azaz. Don't be ridiculous. *(To audience, as if leading a cheer.)* Let's hear it for words!

Mathemagician. *(To audience, in the same manner.)* Cast your vote for numbers!

Azaz. A, B, C's!

Mathemagician. 1, 2, 3's! *(A fanfare is heard.)*

Azaz and Mathemagician. *(To each other.)* Quiet! Rhyme and Reason are about to announce their decision.

(Rhyme and Reason appear.)

Rhyme. Ladies and gentlemen, letters and numerals, fractions and punctuation marks—may we have your attention, please. After careful consideration of the problem set before us by King Azaz of Dictionopolis *(Azaz bows.)* and the Mathemagician of Digitopolis *(Mathemagician raises his hands in a victory salute.)* we have come to the following conclusion:

Reason. Words and numbers are of equal value, for in the cloak of knowledge, one is the warp and the other is the woof.[7]

Rhyme. It is no more important to count the sands than it is to name the stars.

Rhyme and Reason. Therefore, let both kingdoms, Dictionopolis and Digitopolis, live in peace.

(The sound of cheering is heard.)

Azaz. Boo! is what I say. Boo and Bah and Hiss! **3**

Mathemagician. What good are these girls if they can't even settle an argument in anyone's favor? I think I have come to a decision of my own.

Azaz. So have I.

Azaz and Mathemagician. *(To the Princesses.)* You are hereby banished from this land to the Castle-in-the-Air. *(To each other.)* And as for you, keep out of my way! *(They stalk off in opposite directions.)*

(During this time, the set has been changed to the Market Square of Dictionopolis. Lights come up on a deserted square.)

Tock. And ever since then, there has been neither Rhyme nor Reason in this kingdom. Words are misused and numbers mismanaged. The argument between the two kings has divided everyone and the real value of both words and numbers has been forgotten. What a waste!

Milo. Why doesn't somebody rescue the princesses and set everything straight again?

Tock. That is easier said than done. The Castle-in-the-Air is very far from here, and the one path which leads to it is guarded by ferocious demons. But hold on, here we are. *(A man appears, carrying a gate and a small tollbooth.)* **E**

---

7. **warp and . . . woof:** in weaving, the *warp* is made of parallel threads stretched on a loom. The *woof* is made of threads that wind between the warp to make cloth.

WORDS
TO   **fanfare** (făn'fâr') *n.* a loud blast of trumpets
KNOW

523

Customizing Instruction

Less Proficient Readers
Ask students the following questions:
1. Who are Rhyme and Reason?
   Possible Response: They are princesses, sisters of Azaz and the Mathemagician. The princesses gave order to the kingdoms of Dictionopolis and Digitopolis.
2. Why did they leave Dictionopolis?
   Possible Response: They were banished by their brothers, who didn't like the way they settled an argument.
3. Where did Rhyme and Reason go?
   Answer: The went to the Castle-in-the-Air.

Set a Purpose Have students read to find out what Dictionopolis looks like and whom Milo meets there.

Students Acquiring English
1 Have students figure out why the Watchdog is called Tock. (It is one of the sounds that a clock makes—*tick, tock.*)
2 Explain that "an argument to end all arguments" means "an especially bad quarrel."
3 Tell students that the sounds that Azaz makes show his unhappiness with the decision of Rhyme and Reason.

Multiple Learning Styles
Visual Learners
Have students draw King Azaz and the Mathemagician. Remind students to skim the text for details.

Logical Learners
Have students think of ways in which numbers and letters are important. Ask them whether they agree with Azaz or the Mathemagician.

Cross Curricular Link **History**

CASTLES Over the centuries, changes were made in both the design and material of castles. The first castles, built in northwest Europe in the ninth century, were made mostly of earth and wood. By the end of the twelfth century, however, stone was replacing timber, as more sophisticated designs spread to western Europe from the Holy Land. Castle construction reached its golden age by the thirteenth century, particularly in Great Britain. Several lines of defense had to be penetrated in the castles of the late thirteenth century before the invaders could reach the inner living quarters. Although the invention of gunpowder is considered a primary reason for the decline of the importance of the castle by the fifteenth century, economic and domestic factors also contributed. Central governments could afford to pay a large mercenary army with the money raised by merchant taxes, and people no longer wanted to live in damp, uncomfortable castles. Many times, castles were left to decay while new residences or palaces were built next to them.

Reading and Analyzing

Literary Analysis: REALISTIC AND FANTASTIC DETAILS

A Ask students what is realistic about the setting described here. What is fantastic?

Possible Response: The marketplace, with its merchants and vendors, is realistic. The sudden appearance of the market and the selling of words and letters are fantastic.

Ask students if a lack of realistic details would have changed the play's effect.

Possible Response: The play would have been more difficult to relate to and comprehend.

ACTIVE READING

B **VISUALIZE** **Possible Response:** The marketplace is a square filled with movement, crowds, and voices. Tock and Milo can be seen looking around.

Reading Skills and Strategies: CLARIFY

C Ask why it makes sense that *A* and *I* are more popular than *X* and *Z*.

Possible Response: They are tastier.

Literary Analysis: STAGE DIRECTIONS

D Ask students what impression of Humbug the stage directions create.

Possible Response: He seems dapper and perhaps vain; his actions of swinging his cane and clicking his heels attract attention.

Literary Analysis: CHARACTERIZATION

E Ask what the Spelling Bee's reaction to Humbug reveals about Humbug's stories.

Possible Response: Humbug is not always truthful.

Gatekeeper. AHHHHREMMMM! This is Dictionopolis, a happy kingdom, advantageously located in the foothills of Confusion and caressed by gentle breezes from the Sea of Knowledge. Today, by royal proclamation, is Market Day. Have you come to buy or sell?

Milo. I beg your pardon?

Gatekeeper. Buy or sell, buy or sell. Which is it? You must have come here for a reason.

Milo. Well, I . . .

Gatekeeper. Come now, if you don't have a reason, you must at least have an explanation or certainly an excuse.

Milo. *(Meekly.)* Uh . . . no.

Gatekeeper. *(Shaking his head.)* Very serious. You can't get in without a reason. *(Thoughtfully.)* Wait a minute. Maybe I have an old one you can use. *(Pulls out an old suitcase from the tollbooth and rummages through it.)* No . . . no . . . no . . . this won't do . . . hmmm . . .

Milo. *(To Tock.)* What's he looking for? *(Tock shrugs.)*

Gatekeeper. Ah! This is fine. *(Pulls out a medallion on a chain. Engraved in the medallion is: "Why not?")* Why not. That's a good reason for almost anything . . . a bit used, perhaps, but still quite serviceable. There you are, sir. Now I can truly say: Welcome to Dictionopolis.

A *(He opens the gate and walks off. Citizens and merchants appear on all levels of the stage, and Milo and Tock find themselves in the middle of a noisy marketplace. As some people buy and sell their wares, others hang a large banner which reads: Welcome to the Word Market.)*

Milo. Tock! Look!

Merchant 1. Hey-ya, hey-ya, hey-ya, step right up and take your pick. Juicy tempting words for sale. Get your fresh-picked "if's," "and's" and "but's"! Just take a look at these nice ripe "where's" and "when's."

Merchant 2. Step right up, step right up, fancy, best-quality words here for sale. Enrich your vocabulary and expand your speech with such elegant items as "quagmire," "flabbergast," or "upholstery."

Merchant 3. Words by the bag, buy them over here. Words by the bag for the more talkative customer. A pound of "happy's" at a very reasonable price . . . very useful for "Happy Birthday," "Happy New Year," "happy days," or "happy-go-lucky." Or how about a package of "good's," always handy for "good morning," "good afternoon," "good evening," and "goodbye."

Milo. I can't believe it. Did you ever see so many words?

Tock. They're fine if you have something to say. *(They come to a Do-It-Yourself Bin.)*

Milo. *(To Merchant 4 at the bin.)* Excuse me, but what are these?

Merchant 4. These are for people who like to make up their own words. You can pick any assortment you like or buy a special box complete with all the letters and a book of instructions. Here, taste an "A." They're very good. *(He pops one into Milo's mouth.)*

ACTIVE READING

VISUALIZE Close your eyes and picture the Word Market. Note details.

B

Milo. *(Tastes it hesitantly.)* It's sweet! *(He eats it.)*

Merchant 4. I knew you'd like it. "A" is one of our best-sellers. All of them aren't that good, you know. The "Z," for instance—very dry **C**

Teaching Options

and sawdusty. And the "X?" Tastes like a trunkful of stale air. But most of the others aren't bad at all. Here, try the "I."

Milo. *(Tasting.)* Cool! It tastes icy.

Merchant 4. *(To Tock.)* How about the "C" for you? It's as crunchy as a bone. Most people are just too lazy to make their own words, but take it from me, not only is it more fun, but it's also *de*-lightful, *(Holds up a "D.")* *e*-lating, *(Holds up an "E.")* and extremely useful! *(Holds up a "U.")*

Milo. But isn't it difficult? I'm not very good at making words.

(The Spelling Bee, a large colorful bee, comes up from behind.)

Spelling Bee. Perhaps I can be of some assistance . . . a-s-s-i-s-t-a-n-c-e. *(The Three turn around and see him.)* Don't be alarmed . . . a-l-a-r-m-e-d. I am the Spelling Bee. I can spell anything. Anything. A-n-y-t-h-i-n-g. Try me. Try me.

Milo. *(Backing off, Tock on his guard.)* Can you spell goodbye?

Spelling Bee. Perhaps you are under the misapprehension[8] . . . m-i-s-a-p-p-r-e-h-e-n-s-i-o-n that I am dangerous. Let me assure you that I am quite peaceful. Now, think of the most difficult word you can, and I'll spell it.

Milo. Uh . . . o.k. *(At this point, Milo may turn to the audience and ask them to help him chose a word or he may think of one on his own.)* How about . . . "Curiosity?"

Spelling Bee. *(Winking.)* Let's see now . . . uh . . . how much time do I have?

Milo. Just ten seconds. Count them off, Tock.

Spelling Bee. *(As Tock counts.)* Oh dear, oh dear. *(Just at the last moment, quickly.)* C-u-r-i-o-s-i-t-y.

Merchant 4. Correct! *(All cheer.)*

Milo. Can you spell anything?

Spelling Bee. *(Proudly.)* Just about. You see, years ago, I was an ordinary bee minding my own business, smelling flowers all day, occasionally picking up part-time work in people's bonnets. Then one day, I realized that I'd never amount to anything without an education, so I decided that . . .

Humbug. *(Coming up in a booming voice.)* Balderdash! *(He wears a lavish coat, striped pants, checked vest, spats and a derby hat.)* Let me repeat . . . Balderdash! *(Swings his cane and clicks his heels in the air.)* Well, well, what have we here? Isn't someone going to introduce me to the little boy?

Spelling Bee. *(Disdainfully.)* This is the Humbug. You can't trust a word he says.

Humbug. Nonsense! Everyone can trust a Humbug. As I was saying to the king just the other day . . .

Spelling Bee. You've never met the king. *(To Milo.)* Don't believe a thing he tells you.

Humbug. Bosh, my boy, pure bosh. The Humbugs are an old and noble family, honorable to the core. Why, we fought in the Crusades with Richard the Lion-hearted,[9] crossed the Atlantic with Columbus, blazed trails with the pioneers. History is full of Humbugs.

Spelling Bee. A very pretty speech . . . s-p-e-e-c-h. Now, why don't you go away? I

---

8. **misapprehension** (mĭs-ăp′rĭ-hĕn′shən): the misunderstanding of something.

9. **fought in the Crusades with Richard the Lion-hearted:** the Crusades were journeys undertaken by European Christians in the eleventh through thirteenth centuries to fight the Muslims for control of the Holy Land. Richard the Lion-hearted was an English king who led the Third Crusade (1190–1192).

Customizing Instruction

Less Proficient Readers
Ask students the following questions:

1. **What do the merchants sell on Market Day in Dictionopolis?**
   Possible Response: They sell words and letters.

2. **What options does the letter merchant offer?**
   Possible Response: Customers may buy an assortment or a box complete with all the letters and instructions.

3. **Whom does Milo meet in Dictionopolis?**
   Possible Response: He meets the Spelling Bee and Humbug.

Set a Purpose Have students read to find out who the five gentlemen are who appear in the marketplace.

Students Acquiring English

1 Read Merchant 1's speech aloud to students. Use your tone of voice to show how *hey-ya* is used to attract people's attention.

2 Tell students that *having a bee in your bonnet* is an idiom. It means "being upset or worked up about something."

3 Explain that *Balderdash* means nonsense.

4 *Bosh* is also a slang word for nonsense.

Multiple Learning Styles
Interpersonal Learners
Have students devise and perform a sales pitch for their favorite words.

Speaking and Listening

VERBAL SWORD FIGHT

Prepare Explain to students that the quick exchange of comments, often sarcastic, or the attempt to avoid answering awkward questions by making distracting remarks is known as fencing. Ask two volunteers to read the dialogue between Humbug and Spelling Bee aloud. Students should notice how the characters interrupt each other to create a fast-paced dialogue and how their comments develop from a word or phrase in the other's previous remark. Have students work in pairs to extend this dialogue. Encourage students

to improvise their comments. They should practice their timing, the tone, expression, and volume of their voice. Remind students to keep their comments in character.

Present As students perform their dialogues, audience members should generate criteria to evaluate the presentations.

BLOCK SCHEDULING This activity is particularly well suited for longer class periods.

Use **Communications Transparencies and Copymasters,** p. 13, for additional support.

Reading and Analyzing

Active Reading | VISUALIZING |

A Ask students to describe the mental image evoked by this passage of the text.

Possible Response: The Ministers, who are almost identical, stand in a line, reading or speaking one after the other. They all have very stuffy expressions.

Literary Analysis: HUMOR

B Ask students how the author's style makes this bit of dialogue humorous.

Possible Response: The author uses exaggeration. Five ministers saying essentially the same thing in different words several times is humorous.

Reading Skills and Strategies: EVALUATE

C Ask students whether they think the minister's comment that "one word is as good as another" is valid.

Possible Response: No; one word is not as good as another. Words have different dictionary definitions and different connotations.

---

was just advising the lad of the importance of proper spelling.

Humbug. Bah! As soon as you learn to spell one word, they ask you to spell another. You can never catch up, so why bother? (*Puts his arm around Milo.*) Take my advice, boy, and forget about it. As my great-great-great-grandfather George Washington Humbug used to say . . .

Spelling Bee. You, sir, are an impostor i-m-p-o-s-t-o-r who can't even spell his own name!

Humbug. What? You dare to doubt my word? The word of a Humbug? The word of a Humbug who has direct access to the ear of a king? And the king shall hear of this, I promise you . . .

Voice 1. Did someone call for the king?

Voice 2. Did you mention the monarch?

Voice 3. Speak of the sovereign?

Voice 4. Entreat the emperor?

Voice 5. Hail his highness?

A (*Five tall, thin gentlemen regally dressed in silks and satins, plumed hats and buckled shoes appear as they speak.*)

Milo. Who are they?

Spelling Bee. The king's advisors. Or in more formal terms, his cabinet.

Minister 1. Greetings!

Minister 2. Salutations!

Minister 3. Welcome!

Minister 4. Good afternoon!

B **Minister 5.** Hello!

Milo. Uh . . . Hi.

(*All the Ministers, from here on called by their numbers, unfold their scrolls and read in order.*)

Minister 1. By the order of Azaz the Unabridged . . .

Minister 2. King of Dictionopolis . . .

Minister 3. Monarch of letters . . .

Minister 4. Emperor of phrases, sentences, and miscellaneous figures of speech . . .

Minister 5. We offer you the hospitality of our kingdom . . .

Minister 1. Country

Minister 2. Nation

Minister 3. State

Minister 4. Commonwealth

Minister 5. Realm

Minister 1. Empire

Minister 2. Palatinate

Minister 3. Principality.

Milo. Do all those words mean the same thing?

Minister 1. Of course.

Minister 2. Certainly.

Minister 3. Precisely.

Minister 4. Exactly.

Minister 5. Yes.

Milo. Then why don't you just use one? Wouldn't that make a lot more sense?

Minister 1. Nonsense!

Minister 2. Ridiculous!

Minister 3. Fantastic!

Minister 4. Absurd!

Minister 5. Bosh!

Minister 1. We're not interested in making sense. It's not our job.

Minister 2. Besides, one word is as good as another, so why not use them all?

Minister 3. Then you don't have to choose which one is right.

Minister 4. Besides, if one is right, then ten are ten times as right.

Teaching Options

 Mini Lesson ## Vocabulary Strategy

DENOTATION AND CONNOTATION

Instruction Tell students that the dictionary definition of a word is its *denotation*. The attitudes or emotions associated with a word are its *connotations*. A good writer chooses a word for its connotation as well as the dictionary definition. Display this sentence to illustrate the importance of a word's connotation:

The details of the story are <u>fantastic</u>.

Have students substitute *absurd* for *fantastic*. Although both words share similar meanings, students should see that absurd has a connotation of silly, while fantastic has a more positive connotation.

Exercise Have students discuss how replacing the underlined word with the word in parentheses affects the meaning of the sentence.

1. Milo walked up to the door <u>timidly</u>. (cautiously)
2. Humbug <u>compliments</u> the King. (flatters)
3. The Lethargarians know how to <u>relax</u>. (loaf)

Use **Vocabulary Transparencies and Copymasters**, p. 52.

VIEW AND COMPARE

These images show Milo, Tock, and the Spelling Bee meeting the Humbug in the Word Market.

The animated musical film *The Phantom Tollbooth* was co-directed by Chuck Jones, well-known animator of popular characters from Bugs Bunny to the Grinch.

THE PHANTOM TOLLBOOTH ©1969 Turner Entertainment Co.
A Time Warner Company. All rights reserved.

OperaDelaware ventured into new territory with *The Phantom Tollbooth* adapted and performed as an opera, a drama set to music.

What are the advantages and disadvantages of using animation, compared with live actors, to tell the story **?**

Customizing Instruction

Less Proficient Readers
Ask students the following questions:
1. Who are the five gentlemen that speak to Milo?
   Possible Response: They are the King's advisors, or cabinet.
2. Describe the appearance of the advisors, as well as their speech.
   Possible Response: They are tall and thin and are dressed in silks and satins. They all say the same thing in different words.

Set a Purpose Have students read to find out what Milo chooses to eat at the Royal Banquet.

Students Acquiring English
Help students understand that the ministers use synonyms to express similar ideas in different words.

VIEW AND COMPARE
Remind students that they are expected to analyze ideas as represented in various media. Have students cite evidence from the text to support their response to the question.
Possible Response: With animation, the artist is able to make each character and scene look just the way she or he wants it to look. It's also easier to portray fantastic scenes when you draw them than it is to film them with live actors.

Reading and Analyzing

ACTIVE READING

A PREDICT Possible Responses: alphabet soup; foods served in alphabetical order, ranging from asparagus to zucchini; juggling letters; singing the A B C's

Reading Skills and Strategies: WORD PLAY

B Call on volunteers to explain the word play with *light*.

Possible Response: Milo means something not too filling, or heavy; Azaz literally serves light.

C Ask students to explain the play on the word *square*.

Possible Response: Milo means a well-balanced, nutritionally sound meal; Azaz serves squares.

Literary Analysis: FIGURATIVE LANGUAGE

D Remind students that figurative language communicates ideas beyond the dictionary definitions of the words. Ask students to find the figures of speech that are interpreted literally in Dictionopolis.

Possible Responses: "Eat my words," "just desserts," "half-baked ideas"

Reading Skills and Strategies: AUTHOR'S PURPOSE

Ask students to identify the author's purpose for including the banquet scene.

Possible Response: The author includes it to entertain the reader but is also showing how words can be played with, manipulated, and interpreted in different ways.

Minister 5. Obviously, you don't know who we are. *(Each presents himself and Milo acknowledges the introduction.)*

Minister 1. The Duke of Definition.

Minister 2. The Minister of Meaning.

Minister 3. The Earl of Essence.

Minister 4. The Count of Connotation.

Minister 5. The Undersecretary of Understanding.

A ACTIVE READING

PREDICT What sorts of food and entertainment might be offered at the banquet?

All Five. And we have come to invite you to the Royal Banquet.

Spelling Bee. The banquet! That's quite an honor, my boy. A real h-o-n-o-r.

Humbug. Don't be ridiculous! Everybody goes to the Royal Banquet these days.

Spelling Bee. *(To the Humbug.)* True, everybody does go. But some people are invited and others simply push their way in where they aren't wanted.

Humbug. How dare you? You buzzing little upstart, I'll show you who's not wanted . . . *(Raises his cane threateningly.)*

Spelling Bee. You just watch it! I'm warning w-a-r-n-i-n-g you! *(At that moment, an ear-shattering blast of trumpets, entirely off-key, is heard, and a Page appears.)*

Page. King Azaz the Unabridged is about to begin the Royal Banquet. All guests who do not appear promptly at the table will automatically lose their place. *(A huge table is carried out with King Azaz sitting in a large chair, carried out at the head of the table.)*

Azaz. Places. Everyone take your places. *(All the characters, including the Humbug and*

the *Spelling Bee, who forget their quarrel, rush to take their places at the table. Milo and Tock sit near the King. Azaz looks at Milo.)* And just who is this?

Milo. Your Highness, my name is Milo and this is Tock. Thank you very much for inviting us to your banquet, and I think your palace is beautiful!

Minister 1. Exquisite.

Minister 2. Lovely.

Minister 3. Handsome.

Minister 4. Pretty.

Minister 5. Charming.

Azaz. Silence! Now tell me, young man, what can you do to entertain us? Sing songs? Tell stories? Juggle plates? Do tumbling tricks? Which is it?

Milo. I can't do any of those things.

Azaz. What an ordinary little boy. Can't you do anything at all?

Milo. Well . . . I can count to a thousand.

Azaz. AARGH, numbers! Never mention numbers here. Only use them when we absolutely have to. Now, why don't we change the subject and have some dinner? Since you are the guest of honor, you may pick the menu.

Milo. Me? Well, uh . . . I'm not very hungry. Can we just have a light snack?

Azaz. A light snack it shall be!

(Azaz claps his hands. Waiters rush in with covered trays. When they are uncovered, shafts of light pour out. The light may be created through the use of battery-operated flashlights which are secured in the trays and covered with a false bottom. The guests help themselves.)

B

WORDS
TO
KNOW

acknowledge (ăk-nŏl′ĭj) *v.* to admit or to value the existence of

528

Teaching Options

 Mini Lesson **Vocabulary Strategy**

USING CONTEXT CLUES

Instruction Remind students that using context clues can help them to understand the meaning of an unfamiliar word. Contrast shows the difference between the unknown word and something that is known and uses words such as *but, not, although, however,* or *on the other hand* as clues. Write this sentence to show how *unabridged* can be defined as "complete" using the contrast presented.

King Azaz is <u>unabridged</u>, not shortened or abbreviated.

Exercise Have students use the strategy to define the underlined words in the sentences below.

1. People used to <u>swallow</u> that theory; however, it is now rejected.

2. His <u>rigmarole</u> was in contrast to the brief, well-organized comments of the other speaker.

3. Phonies change their loyalties, but real friends are <u>steadfast</u>.

4. The drive was <u>leisurely</u>, not frantic.

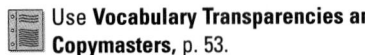 Use **Vocabulary Transparencies and Copymasters**, p. 53.

Humbug. Not a very substantial meal. Maybe you can suggest something a little more filling.

Milo. Well, in that case, I think we ought to have a square meal . . .

Azaz. (*Claps his hands.*) A square meal it is! (*Waiters serve trays of colored squares of all sizes. People serve themselves.*)

C

Spelling Bee. These are awful. (*Humbug coughs and all the guests do not care for the food.*)

Azaz. (*Claps his hands and the trays are (removed.*) Time for speeches. (*To Milo.*) You first.

Milo. (*Hesitantly.*) Your Majesty, ladies and gentlemen, I would like to take this opportunity to say that . . .

Azaz. That's quite enough. Musn't talk all day.

Milo. But I just started to . . .

Azaz. Next!

Humbug. (*Quickly.*) Roast turkey, mashed potatoes, vanilla ice cream.

Spelling Bee. Hamburgers, corn on the cob, chocolate pudding p-u-d-d-i-n-g. (*Each guest names two dishes and a dessert.*)

Azaz. (*The last.*) Pâté de fois gras, soupe a l'oignon, salade endives, fromage et fruits et demitasse.[11] (*He claps his hands. Waiters serve each guest his words.*) Dig on. (*To

Milo.*) Though I can't say I think much of your choice.

Milo. I didn't know I was going to have to eat my words.

1 D

Azaz. Of course, of course, everybody here does. Your speech should have been in better taste.

Minister 1. Here, try some somersault. It improves the flavor.

Minister 2. Have a rigamarole. (*Offers breadbasket.*)

2

Minister 3. Or a ragamuffin.

Minister 4. Perhaps you'd care for a synonym bun.

Minister 5. Why not wait for your just desserts?

Azaz. Ah yes, the dessert. We're having a special treat today . . . freshly made at the half-bakery.

Milo. The half-bakery?

Azaz. Of course, the half-bakery! Where do you think half-baked ideas come from? Now, please don't interrupt. By royal command, the pastry chefs have . . .

3

Milo. What's a half-baked idea?

(*Azaz gives up the idea of speaking as a cart is wheeled in and the guests help themselves.*)

Humbug. They're very tasty, but they don't always agree with you. Here's a good one. (*Humbug hands one to Milo.*)

Milo. (*Reads.*) "The earth is flat."

Spelling Bee. People swallowed that one for years. (*Picks up one and reads.*) "The moon is made of green cheese." Now, there's a half-baked idea.

---

11. **pâté de foie gras . . . demi-tasse** *French: pâté de foie gras* (pâ-tä′ də fwä grä): a paste made from goose liver; *soupe a l'oignon* (sōōp ä lô′nyôn): onion soup; *salade endives* (sä′läd än′dēv): lettuce salad; *fromage et fruits* (frô′mäzh ā frwē): cheese and fruit; *demitasse* (dĕmē′täs): a small cup of strong, black coffee.

THE PHANTOM TOLLBOOTH **529**

Customizing Instruction

Less Proficient Readers
• Ask students to describe the first meal that Milo orders.
  Possible Response: He orders a light snack. It turns out to be trays with rays of light coming from them.
• What is Milo's second request? How is it served?
  Possible Response: His second request is for a square meal, which consists of trays filled with colored squares.
• What happens after the guests make speeches?
  Possible Response: They eat their words.

Set a Purpose Have students read to find out what journey Milo and his friends are going to make and what obstacles they can anticipate.

Students Acquiring English
To help students appreciate the humor in the banquet scene, be sure they understand the figurative interpretations of the idioms.

1 Explain to students that "eating your words" is having to take back what you've said.

2 Help students to appreciate the humor created by using words unrelated to food but having the name of a food item in them or suggesting a food by their sound. *somersault* – salt; *rigmarole* – roll; *ragamuffin* – muffin; *synonym bun* – cinnamon bun

3 Explain that a "half-baked idea" is an idea that is not very sensible or well thought out.

Multicultural Link — Idioms Borrowed From Other Languages

Although many idioms seem as "American as apple pie," their origins may reach back as far as the ancient civilizations. Some of the best known expressions have been translated from other languages to take the form in which we know them. "Without rhyme or reason" was borrowed from the French of the late Middle Ages, who said *"na Ryme ne Raison."* The modern French phrase is *"ni rime ni raison."* English speakers have been using the phrase "without rhyme or reason" since the sixteenth century.

The English language has included the phrase "a castle in the air" since the late 1500s. The French, however, have used "a castle in Spain," to mean roughly the same thing since the 1300s, *"un château en Espagne."*

Over four hundred years ago, the Dutch gave English speakers the idiom "in a pretty pickle." Their saying was *"in de pekel zitten,"* which meant to literally sit in the salty liquid used to pickle. Anyone sitting in that liquid for too long would be in trouble!

Reading and Analyzing

Reading Skills and Strategies: CLARIFY

A Ask students why there is confusion in King Azaz's kingdom.

Possible Response: There is no Rhyme or Reason.

Literary Analysis: CHARACTERIZATION

B Students should be able to analyze characters, including their traits, by using the characters' words and actions. Ask students what is revealed about Humbug's character through his comments.

Possible Response: Humbug is easily influenced and wants to be on whichever side appears to be in favor.

Literary Analysis   FANTASY

C Ask students to identify fantastic details in this account.

Possible Responses: entering the Mountains of Ignorance; climbing a two-thousand-foot staircase without railings; fighting off frightening fiends

Literary Analysis: QUEST

Tell students that a quest is a journey of discovery, often motivated by a noble purpose. Ask students what is noble about Milo's quest.

Possible Response: His goal is to rescue the princesses.

What might Milo discover along the way?

Possible Responses: He might discover his own inner qualities. He might learn more about ignorance and obstacles on the path to success

---

(Everyone chooses one and eats. They include: "It Never Rains but Pours," "Night Air Is Bad Air," "Everything Happens for the Best," "Coffee Stunts Your Growth.")

Azaz. And now for a few closing words. Attention! Let me have your attention! *(Everyone leaps up and exits, except for Milo, Tock and the Humbug.)* Loyal subjects and friends, once again on this gala occasion, we have . . .

Milo. Excuse me, but everybody left.

Azaz. *(Sadly.)* I was hoping no one would notice. It happens every time.

Humbug. They've gone to dinner, and as soon as I finish this last bite, I shall join them.

Milo. That's ridiculous. How can they eat dinner right after a banquet?

Azaz. Scandalous! We'll put a stop to it at once. From now on, by royal command, everyone must eat dinner before the banquet.

Milo. But that's just as bad.

Humbug. Or just as good. Thing which are equally bad are also equally good. Try to look at the bright side of things.

A **Milo.** I don't know which side of anything to look at. Everything is so confusing, and all your words only make things worse.

Azaz. How true. There must be something we can do about it.

Humbug. Pass a law.

Azaz. We have almost as many laws as words.

Humbug. Offer a reward. *(Azaz shakes his head and looks madder at each suggestion.)* Send for help? Drive a bargain? Pull the switch? Lower the boom? Toe the line? *(As Azaz continues to scowl, the Humbug loses confidence and finally gives up.)*

Milo. Maybe you should let Rhyme and Reason return.

Azaz. How nice that would be. Even if they were a bother at times, things always went so well when they were here. But I'm afraid it can't be done.

Humbug. Certainly not. Can't be done.

Milo. Why not?

Humbug. *(Now siding with Milo.)* Why not, indeed?

Azaz. Much too difficult.

Humbug. Of course, much too difficult.

Milo. You could, if you really wanted to.

Humbug. By all means, if you really wanted to, you could.

Azaz. *(To Humbug.)* How?

Milo. *(Also to Humbug.)* Yeah, how?

Humbug. Why . . . uh, it's a simple task for a brave boy with a stout heart, a steadfast dog and a serviceable small automobile.

Azaz. Go on.

Humbug. Well, all that he would have to do is cross the dangerous, unknown countryside between here and Digitopolis, where he would have to persuade the Mathemagician to release the princesses, which we know to be impossible because the Mathemagician will never agree with Azaz about anything. Once achieving that, it's a simple matter of entering the Mountains of <u>Ignorance</u> from where no one has ever returned alive, an effortless climb up a two-thousand-foot stairway without railings in a high wind at night to the Castle-in-the-Air. After a pleasant chat with the princesses, all that remains is a <u>leisurely</u> ride back through those chaotic crags where the frightening fiends

B

C

WORDS TO KNOW
ignorance (ĭg′nər-əns) *n.* the state of being uneducated or unaware
leisurely (lē′zhər-lē) *adj.* unhurried

530

Teaching Options

✓ **Assessment Standardized Test Practice**

ARRANGING DETAILS IN SEQUENTIAL ORDER For some standardized tests, students will be asked questions about the order of events or other details. To provide students with some help in choosing the best answer, read aloud or write on the chalkboard the following question:
Which event happens immediately before Milo meets Tock?
A. Milo decides to drive to Dictionopolis.
B. The Lethargarians tell Milo about the Watchdog and then suddenly run off.

C. Milo meets the Whether Man.
D. Milo thinks his way out of the Doldrums.
Lead students through the process of choosing the correct answer. A is incorrect. This event precedes Milo meeting Tock but does not occur immediately before. C is incorrect because this encounter occurs at the beginning of the scene, before Milo arrives in the Doldrums. D is also incorrect. This occurs after he meets Tock. B is the correct answer: the Lethargarians run off, *then* Milo meets Tock.

have sworn to tear any intruder from limb to limb and devour him down to his belt buckle. And finally after doing all that, a triumphal parade! If, of course, there is anything left to parade . . . followed by hot chocolate and cookies for everyone.

Azaz. I never realized it would be so simple.

Milo. It sounds dangerous to me.

Tock. And just who is supposed to make that journey?

Azaz. A very good question. But there is one far more serious problem.

Milo. What's that?

Azaz. I'm afraid I can't tell you that until you return.

Milo. But wait a minute, I didn't . . .

Azaz. Dictionopolis will always be grateful to you, my boy and your dog. *(Azaz pats Tock and Milo.)*

Tock. Now, just one moment, sire . . .

Azaz. You will face many dangers on your journey, but fear not, for I can give you something for your protection. *(Azaz gives Milo a box.)* In this box are the letters of the alphabet. With them you can form all the words you will ever need to help you overcome the obstacles that may stand in your path. All you must do is use them well and in the right places.

Milo. *(Miserably.)* Thanks a lot.

Azaz. You will need a guide, of course, and since he knows the obstacles so well, the Humbug has cheerfully volunteered to accompany you.

Humbug. Now, see here . . . !

Azaz. You will find him dependable, brave, resourceful and loyal.

Humbug. *(Flattered.)* Oh, Your Majesty.

Milo. I'm sure he'll be a great help. *(They approach the car.)*

Tock. I hope so. It looks like we're going to need it.

(The lights darken and the King fades from view.)

Azaz. Good luck! Drive carefully! *(The three get into the car and begin to move. Suddenly a thunderously loud noise is heard. They slow down the car.)*

Milo. What was that?

Tock. It came from up ahead.

Humbug. It's something terrible. I just know it. Oh, no. Something dreadful is going to happen to us. I can feel it in my bones. *(The noise is repeated. They all look at each other fearfully as the lights fade.)*

END of ACT ONE

Thinking Through the Literature

1. **Comprehension Check**
   - How does Milo escape the Doldrums?
   - What caused Azaz and the Mathemagician to quarrel?

2. How does Milo change during Act One?

   THINK ABOUT
   - his reason for going on this journey
   - his experiences in the Doldrums
   - how he "volunteers" for the rescue

3. On page 526, the Ministers list synonyms for *country, certainly,* and *nonsense.* Using a thesaurus, how many other synonyms can you find for these words?

4. *The Phantom Tollbooth* is also a novel and an animated film. How do you think watching theater—a live performance of a literary work—is different from reading a book or watching a movie?

Reading Skills and Strategies: MONITOR

Have students pause to monitor their own comprehension by reviewing the major events of Act 1, rereading portions of the text if necessary. Discuss ways in which they might adjust their reading strategy in Act 2.

Literary Analysis: ACT

A Tell students that longer plays are divided into acts. An act is a major unit of action. Ask students what they anticipate happening during the second act.
Possible Responses: They might mention Milo visiting Digitopolis and meeting the Mathemagician or Milo's attempt to rescue the princesses.

Literary Analysis: HUMOR

B Ask students why Humbug's remark is humorous.
Possible Response: He literally will be standing behind Milo for protection.

Literary Analysis: CHARACTERIZATION

C Ask students to analyze the difference in the character traits of Milo as compared to Humbug.
Possible Response: Milo shows more courage and leadership than Humbug.

ACTIVE READING

D **VISUALIZE** **Possible Responses:** The dishes would crash noisily; the ant would be silent; and the octopus would snap and crinkle.

Teaching Options

Mini Lesson   Viewing and Representing

Illustration of Dr. Dischord
by Bruce Roberts
Instruction Point out the exuberance illustrator Bruce Roberts captures in this drawing of Dr. Dischord. Everything seems to be noisy and chaotic—just the way the scene is described. Objects fly everywhere, there seem to be explosions. Even the colors are loud and clashing!
Ask students what noises Dr. Dischord might be mixing with his mortar and pestle.

Possible Responses: car horns, explosions, popcorn, fireworks, screeching brakes, crashing cymbals.

Application Have students refer back to the illustration as they read the description of Dr. Dischord and his activities. Ask which of Dr. Dischord's noises they find particularly appealing—or particularly unappealing. What other noises would they add to his collection?

A ACT TWO
SCENE
1

The set of Digitopolis glitters in the background, while upstage right near the road, a small colorful wagon sits, looking quite deserted. On its side in large letters, a sign reads:

"KAKAFONOUS A. DISCHORD

Doctor of Dissonance"[12]

Enter Milo, Tock, and Humbug, fearfully. They look at the wagon.

Tock. There's no doubt about it. That's where the noise was coming from.

Humbug. *(To Milo.)* Well, go on.

Milo. Go on what?

Humbug. Go on and see who's making all that noise in there. We can't just ignore a creature like that.

Milo. Creature? What kind of creature? Do you think he's dangerous?

B **Humbug.** Go on, Milo. Knock on the door. We'll be right behind you.

Milo. O.K. Maybe he can tell us how much further it is to Digitopolis.

C *(Milo tiptoes up to the wagon door and knocks timidly. The moment he knocks, a terrible crash is heard inside the wagon, and Milo and the others jump back in fright. At the same time,* the door flies open and from the dark interior, a hoarse Voice inquires.)*

Voice. Have you ever heard a whole set of dishes dropped from the ceiling onto a hard stone floor? *(The others are speechless with fright. Milo shakes his head. Voice happily.)* Have you ever heard an ant wearing fur slippers walk across a thick wool carpet? *(Milo shakes his head again.)* Have you ever heard a blind-folded octopus unwrap a cellophane-covered bath-tub? *(Milo shakes his head a third time.)* Ha! I knew it. *(He hops out, a little man, wearing a white coat, with a stethoscope around his neck, and a small mirror attached to his forehead, and with very huge ears,*

D **ACTIVE READING**

VISUALIZE What would these events sound, feel, and look like?

---

12. **Kakafonous A. Dischord, Doctor of Dissonance:** the doctor's first name is a playful spelling of *cacophonous* (kə-kŏf′ə-nəs), which means having a loud, harsh, sound. *Dischord* (dĭs′ kôrd′) is an intentional misspelling of *discord,* which, along with *dissonance* (dĭs′ə-nəns), means clashing sounds.

THE PHANTOM TOLLBOOTH **533**

Speaking and Listening

READERS THEATER

Prepare Explain to students that a good dramatic reading brings events and characters to life for an audience. Tell students that dramatic readings allow them to vocally express their interpretations of characters by providing them with an opportunity to give each character a distinctive voice and style of speaking. To provide all students with a chance to participate, alternate the role assignments at scene breaks in Act 2. Have students prepare for their parts by listing the qualities they think best describe their character and by imagin-ing what type of voice would best express those qualities. Students playing the same part may wish to confer about their interpretations. Have students without speaking roles in each scene do the sound effects.

Present Have students perform Act 2. As part of a class discussion following the performance, ask students to comment on one aspect of the performance.

BLOCK SCHEDULING This activity is particularly well suited for longer class periods.

Use **Communications Transparencies and Copymasters,** p. 12, for additional support.

Reading Skills and Strategies:
WORD PLAY

A Point out to students how the mis-spelling and correct spelling of *discord* give rise to many meanings. Tell students that one definition of a *chord* is "a group of musical notes sounded together." Ask students what *dischord* suggests.

Possible Response: It suggests wrong notes, notes not played in harmony. Explain that another meaning of *discord* is disagreement. Ask students what conclusion might be drawn about loud, harsh noise from the doctor's name.

Possible Response: Loud noise leads to a lack of harmony and causes upset among people.

Active Reading: CONNECT

Ask students for examples of unpleasant sounds they hear regularly.

Possible Responses: sirens; screams; coughing; traffic noises

Reading Skills and Strategies:
CLARIFY

B Ask students to explain this sentence.

Possible Response: Sound is invisible, no matter how loud it is.

Literary Analysis: HUMOR

Ask students how Dynne brings humor into the play.

Possible Response: through his delight in unpleasant noises

Reading Skills and Strategies:
QUESTION

Discuss what questions students might have at this point in response to the text of the play.

Possible Response: What is Dr. Dischord's role in the play?

and a mortar and pestle[13] in his hands. He stares at Milo, Tock and Humbug.) None of you looks well at all! Tsk, tsk, not at all. *(He opens the top or side of his wagon, revealing a dusty interior resembling an old apothecary shop, with shelves lined with jars and boxes, a table, books, test tubes and bottles and measuring spoons.)*

Milo. *(Timidly.)* Are you a doctor?

A **Dischord.** *(Voice.)* I am Kakafonous A. Dischord, Doctor of Dissonance! *(Several small explosions and a grinding crash are heard.)*

Humbug. *(Stuttering with fear.)* What does the "A" stand for?

Dischord. AS LOUD AS POSSIBLE! *(Two screeches and a bump are heard.)* Now, step a little closer and stick out your tongues. *(Dischord examines them.)* Just as I expected. *(He opens a large dusty book and thumbs through the pages.)* You're all suffering from a severe lack of noise. *(Dischord begins **1** running around, collecting bottles, reading the labels to himself as he goes along.)* "Loud Cries." "Soft Cries." "Bangs, Bongs, Swishes, Swooshes." "Snaps and Crackles." "Whistles and Gongs." "Squeeks, Squacks, and Miscellaneous Uproar." *(As he reads them off, he pours a little of each into a large glass beaker and stirs the mixture with a wooden spoon. The concoction smokes and bubbles.)* Be ready in just a moment.

Milo. *(Suspiciously.)* Just what kind of doctor are you?

Dischord. Well, you might say, I'm a specialist. I specialize in noises, from the loudest to the softest, and from the slightly annoying to the terribly unpleasant. For instance, have you ever heard a square-wheeled steamroller ride over a street full of hard-boiled eggs? *(Very loud crunching sounds are heard.)*

Milo. *(Holding his ears.)* But who would want all those terrible noises?

Dischord. *(Surprised at the question.)* Everybody does. Why, I'm so busy I can hardly fill all the orders for noise pills, racket lotion, clamor salve and hubbub tonic.[14] That's all people seem to want these days. Years ago, everyone wanted pleasant sounds and business was terrible. But then the cities were built and there was a great need for honking horns, screeching trains, clanging bells and all the rest of those wonderfully unpleasant sounds we use so much today. I've been working overtime ever since and my medicine here is in great demand. All you have to do is take one spoonful every day, and you'll never have to hear another beautiful sound again. Here, try some.

Humbug. *(Backing away.)* If it's all the same to you, I'd rather not.

Milo. I don't want to be cured of beautiful sounds.

Tock. Besides, there's no such sickness as a lack of noise.

Dischord. How true. That's what makes it so difficult to cure. *(Takes a large glass bottle from the shelf.)* Very well, if you want to go all through life suffering from a noise deficiency, I'll just give this to Dynne for his lunch. *(Uncorks the bottle and pours the liquid into it. There is a rumbling and then a loud explosion accompanied by smoke, out of*

---

13. **mortar** (môr′tər) **and pestle** (pĕs′əl): a mortar is a container in which substances are ground with a hand-held tool (a pestle).

14. **clamor** (klăm′ər) **salve** (săv) **and hubbub** (hŭb′ŭb) **tonic:** a clamor is a loud outcry, and hubbub is noisy confusion. Salve is a healing cream, and tonic can also be a kind of medicine.

Mini Lesson Vocabulary Strategy

HOMONYMS AND HOMOPHONES

Instruction Remind students that homonyms are two or more words with the same spelling but different meanings and origins. Homophones are two or more words with the same pronunciation but different spellings, meanings, and origins. Tell students that context clues will help them to determine which meaning or word is intended. Display the sentences below:

Milo tried to figure the <u>mean</u> of the numbers.

The Bird describes Milo as <u>mean</u>.

Use context to define *mean* in the first sentence as "the average" and in the second sentence as "ill-tempered."

Application Have students work in pairs. Each partner should write a sentence for the different meanings of two of the word groups, using a dictionary if necessary. Then partners should exchange papers and use context clues to help them define the words.

1. threw/through 2. row/row 3. brake/break
4. right/right

 Use **Vocabulary Transparencies and Copymasters,** p. 54.

which Dynne,[15] *a smog-like creature with yellow eyes and a frowning mouth, appears.)*

Dynne. *(Smacking his lips.)* Ahhh, that was good, Master. I thought you'd never let me out. It was really cramped in there.

Dischord. This is my assistant, the awful Dynne. You must forgive his appearance, for he really doesn't have any.

Milo. What is a Dynne?

Dischord. You mean you've never heard of the awful Dynne? When you're playing in your room and making a great amount of noise, what do they tell you to stop?

Milo. That awful din.

Dischord. When the neighbors are playing their radio too loud late at night, what do you wish they'd turn down?

Tock. That awful din.

Dischord. And when the street on your block is being repaired and the drills are working all day, what does everyone complain of?

Humbug. *(Brightly.)* The dreadful row.[16]

Dynne. The Dreadful Rauw was my grandfather. He <u>perished</u> in the great silence epidemic of 1712. I certainly can't understand why you don't like noise. Why, I heard an explosion last week that was so lovely, I groaned with appreciation for two days. *(He gives a loud groan at the memory.)*

Dischord. He's right, you know. Noise is the most valuable thing in the world.

Milo. King Azaz says words are.

Dischord. Nonsense! Why, when a baby wants food, how does he ask?

Dynne. *(Happily.)* He screams!

Dischord. And when a racing car wants gas?

Dynne. *(Jumping for joy.)* It chokes!

Dischord. And what happens to the dawn when a new day begins?

Dynne. *(Delighted.)* It breaks!

Dischord. You see how simple it is? *(To Dynne.)* Isn't it time for us to go?

Milo. Where to? Maybe we're going the same way.

Dynne. I doubt it. *(Picking up empty sacks from the table.)* We're going on our collection rounds. Once a day, I travel throughout the kingdom and collect all the wonderfully horrible and beautifully unpleasant sounds I can find and bring them back to the doctor to use in his medicine.

Dischord. Where are you going?

Milo. To Digitopolis.

Dischord. Oh, there are a number of ways to get to Digitopolis, if you know how to follow directions. Just take a look at the sign at the fork in the road. Though why you'd ever want to go there, I'll never know.

Milo. We want to talk to the Mathemagician.

Humbug. About the release of the Princesses Rhyme and Reason.

Dischord. Rhyme and Reason? I remember them. Very nice girls, but a little too quiet for my taste. In fact, I've been meaning to send them something that Dynne brought home by mistake and which I have absolutely no use for. *(He rummages through the wagon.)* Ah, here it is . . . or maybe you'd like it for yourself. *(Hands Milo a package.)*

Milo. What is it?

---

15. **Dynne** (dĭn): this name is a play on the word *din*, a jumble of loud, confusing noises.

16. **row** (rou): a noisy disturbance.

> WORDS
> TO   **perish** (pĕr'ĭsh) *v.* to die, perhaps in an untimely or painful way
> KNOW

535

B

C

Customizing Instruction

Less Proficient Readers
Ask students the following questions:
1. What is Dr. Dischord's occupation?
   Possible Response: He is a specialist in unpleasant and annoying noises.
2. What does Dynne look like?
   Possible Response: He is a smog-like creature with yellow eyes and a frowning mouth.
3. What are Dynne and Dr. Dischord setting off to do?
   Possible Response: They are going to collect horrible sounds.

Set a Purpose Have students read to find out what Dr. Dischord gives Milo and who the Dodecahedron is.

Students Acquiring English
1 Be sure students know that the labels describe the kinds of noises found in the bottles.

Multiple Learning Styles
Auditory Learners
2 Have students duplicate the sounds described in this passage and desribe them.

Visual Learners
Have students draw their own image of the Awful Dynne.

  Grammar

IDENTIFYING ADVERB PHRASES AND THE WORDS THEY MODIFY

Instruction Remind students that an adverb phrase is a prepositional phrase that can modify adjectives, adverbs, or verbs. First identify the prepositional phrase and then look at the word it modifies. Point out the highlighted passage. The adverb phrase "on our collection rounds" answers the question "where?" about the verb *are going.*

Exercise Have students identify the adverb phrase(s), the modified word, and the part of speech of the modified word.

1. Milo felt quite *hungry* <u>after a few hours</u>. (adj.)
2. Dr. Discord *travels* <u>throughout the countryside</u>. (v.)
3. <u>Because of all the noise</u>, they *could* hardly *think*. (v.)
4. They arrived *late* <u>in the day</u>. (adv.)

▭ Use **Grammar Transparencies and Copymasters**, p. 104.

▭ Use McDougal Littell's ***Language Network***, Chapter 5, for more instruction and practice in adverb phrases.

Dischord. The sounds of laughter. They're so unpleasant to hear, it's almost unbearable. All those giggles and snickers and happy shouts of joy, I don't know what Dynne was thinking of when he collected them. Here, take them to the princesses or keep them for yourselves, I don't care. Well, time to move on. Goodbye now and good luck! *(He has shut the wagon by now and gets in. Loud noises begin to erupt as Dynne pulls the wagon offstage.)*

Milo. *(Calling after them.)* But wait! The fork in the road . . . you didn't tell us where it is . . .

Tock. It's too late. He can't hear a thing.

Humbug. I could use a fork of my own, at the moment. And a knife and a spoon to go with it. All of a sudden, I feel very hungry.

Milo. So do I, but it's no use thinking about it. There won't be anything to eat until we reach Digitopolis. *(They get into the car.)*

Humbug. *(Rubbing his stomach.)* Well, the sooner the better is what I say.

(A sign suddenly appears.)

Voice. *(A strange voice from nowhere.)* But which way will get you there sooner? That is the question.

Tock. Did you hear something?

Milo. Look! The fork in the road and a signpost to Digitopolis! *(They read the sign.)*

DIGITOPOLIS

5	Miles
1,600	Rods
8,800	Yards
26,400	Feet
316,800	Inches
633,600	Half Inches

AND THEN SOME

Humbug. Let's travel by miles, it's shorter.

Milo. Let's travel by half inches. It's quicker.

Tock. But which road should we take? It must make a difference.

Milo. Do you think so?

Tock. Well, I'm not sure, but . . .

Humbug. He could be right. On the other hand, he could also be wrong. Does it make a difference or not?

Voice. Yes, indeed, indeed it does, certainly, my yes, it does make a difference.

(The Dodecahedron appears, a 12-sided figure with a different face on each side, and with all the edges labeled with a small letter and all the angles labeled with a large letter. He wears a beret and peers at the others with a serious face. He doffs his cap and recites:)

Dodecahedron. My angles are many.
My sides are not few.
I'm the Dodecahedron.
Who are you?

Milo. What's a Dodecahedron?

Dodecahedron. *(Turning around slowly.)*

ACTIVE READING

VISUALIZE What would it be like to talk to a creature with 12 faces?

See for yourself. A Dodecahedron is a mathematical shape with 12 faces. *(All his faces appear as he turns, each face with a different expression. He points to them.)* I usually use one at a time. It saves wear and tear. What are you called?

Milo. Milo.

Dodecahedron. That's an odd name. *(Changing his smiling face to a frowning one.)* And you have only one face.

Milo. *(Making sure it is still there.)* Is that bad?

Dodecahedron. You'll soon wear it out using it for everything. Is everyone with one face called Milo?

 Mini Lesson **Spelling**

NUMBER PREFIXES
Instruction Tell students that knowing number prefixes can help them to spell mathematical terms and other words. Write some of the common prefixes on the chalkboard:

uni – one	penta – five	octa – eight
di – two	hexa – six	nona – nine
tri – three	hepta – seven	deca – ten
quadri – four		

Tell students that the spelling of the prefixes varies depending on the root word to which they are attached.

Exercise Have students add the appropriate prefix to the roots below.
1. six-sided figure (___gon)
2. solid figure with ten faces (___hedron)
3. three-angled figure (___angle)
4. one sided (___lateral)
5. solid figure with eight faces (___hedron)
Answers: *1. hexagon 2. decahedron 3. triangle 4. unilateral 5. octahedron*

Use **Unit Four Resource Book**, p. 42 for more practice.

VIEW AND COMPARE

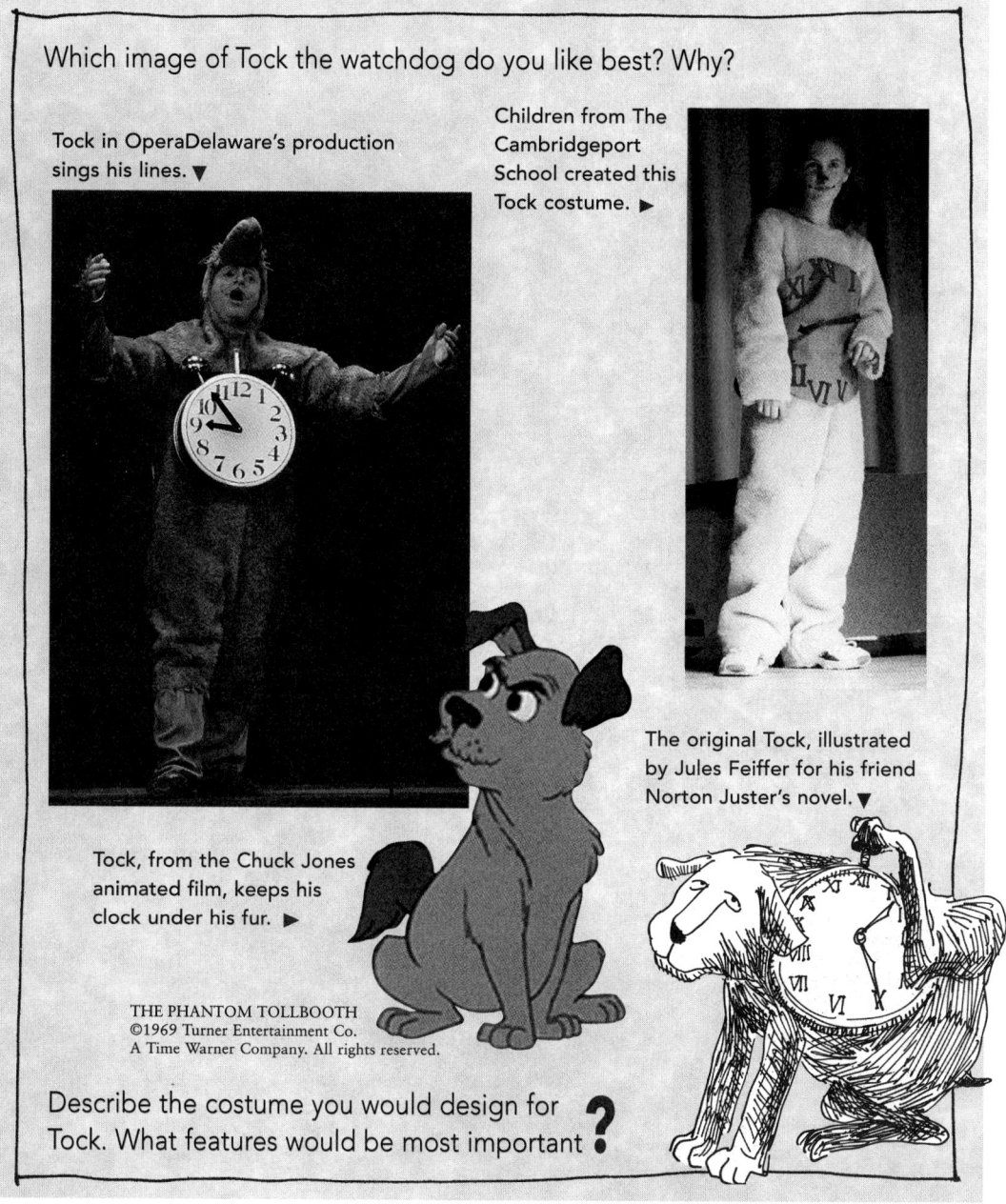

Which image of Tock the watchdog do you like best? Why?

Tock in OperaDelaware's production sings his lines. ▼

Children from The Cambridgeport School created this Tock costume. ▶

Tock, from the Chuck Jones animated film, keeps his clock under his fur. ▶

THE PHANTOM TOLLBOOTH
©1969 Turner Entertainment Co.
A Time Warner Company. All rights reserved.

The original Tock, illustrated by Jules Feiffer for his friend Norton Juster's novel. ▼

Describe the costume you would design for Tock. What features would be most important **?**

Customizing Instruction

Less Proficient Students
Ask students the following question:
1. What does Dr. Dischord give Milo to take to the princesses?
   Possible Response: He gives him the sounds of laughter.
2. How does he describe the sounds?
   Possible Response: He finds them unpleasant to hear.
3. Who is Dodecahedron?
   Possible Response: He is a twelve-sided figure who appears as the three travelers are deciding which road to take to Digitopolis.

Set a Purpose Have students read to find out how numbers are obtained.

Multiple Learning Styles
Logical/Mathematical Learners

1 Have students figure out which way is shortest. Tell students that 1 mile = 320 rods, 1760 yards, 5280 feet, 63,360 inches, and 126,720 half inches.

Answer: All roads are the same distance in different units of measurement.

VIEW AND COMPARE
Remind students that they are expected to compare, contrast, and critique various media treatments of the same subject.

Possible Response: Students' preferences will vary, but they should explain what they like about their first choice.

Possible Response: Students' descriptions of the costumes they would design should be consistent with the description of this character presented in the text.

Reading Skills and Strategies:
CLARIFY

A Ask students to eliminate all the details that do not relate to the problem.
Possible Responses: size of car; time of day; time of year; occupants of car
Ask students what becomes clear when the extra details have been omitted.
Possible Response: All cars will arrive at the same time.

Literary Analysis: IDIOM

B Ask students to think of other expressions that incorporate numbers.
Possible Responses: "six of one, half a dozen of the other," "high noon," "four corners," "two to tango," "three bears," "half and half," "fifty-fifty."

Active Reading | **VISUALIZING**

C Ask students to pick out details that enable them to hear what is happening in the mine.
Possible Responses: "digging and chopping"; "shoveling and scraping"; "His voice echoes and reverberates."

Literary Analysis: STAGE DIRECTIONS

D Ask students how the actor playing Humbug might show the feeling of being intimidated.
Possible Response: He would back away, speak softly, and smile uncertainly.

▮ **ACTIVE READING**

E EVALUATE: Possible Response
The author is saying that numbers are very precious.

Milo. Oh, no. Some are called Billy or Jeffery or Sally or Lisa or lots of other things.

Dodecahedron. How confusing. Here everything is called exactly what it is. The triangles are called triangles, the circles are called circles, and even the same numbers have the same name. Can you imagine what would happen if we named all the twos Billy or Jeffery or Sally or Lisa or lots of other things? You'd have to say Robert plus John equals four, and if the fours were named Albert, things would be hopeless.

Milo. I never thought of it that way.

Dodecahedron. *(With an admonishing face.)* Then I suggest you begin at once, for in Digitopolis, everything is quite precise.

Milo. Then perhaps you can help us decide which road we should take.

Dodecahedron. *(Happily.)* By all means. There's nothing to it. *(As he talks, the three others try to solve the problem on a large blackboard that is wheeled onstage for the occasion.)* Now, if a small car carrying three people at 30 miles an hour for 10 minutes along a road 5 miles long at 11:35 in the morning starts at the same time as 3 people who have been traveling in a little automobile at 20 miles an hour for 15 minutes on another road exactly twice as long as half the distance of the other, while a dog, a bug, and a boy travel an equal distance in the same time or the same distance in an equal time along a third road in mid-October, then which one arrives first and which is the best way to go?

Humbug. Seventeen!

Milo. *(Still figuring frantically.)* I'm not sure, but . . .

Dodecahedron. You'll have to do better than that.

Milo. I'm not very good at problems.

Dodecahedron. What a shame. They're so very useful. Why, did you know that if a beaver 2 feet long with a tail a foot and a half long can build a dam 12 feet high and 6 feet wide in 2 days, all you would need to build Boulder Dam is a beaver 68 feet long with a 51-foot tail?

Humbug. *(Grumbling as his pencil snaps.)* Where would you find a beaver that big?

Dodecahedron. I don't know, but if you did, you'd certainly know what to do with him.

Milo. That's crazy.

Dodecahedron. That may be true, but it's completely accurate, and as long as the answer is right, who cares if the question is wrong?

Tock. *(Who has been patiently doing the first problem.)* All three roads arrive at the same place at the same time.

Dodecahedron. Correct! And I'll take you there myself. *(The blackboard rolls off, and all four get into the car and drive off.)* Now you see how important problems are. If you hadn't done this one properly, you might have gone the wrong way.

Milo. But if all the roads arrive at the same place at the same time, then aren't they all the right road?

Dodecahedron. *(Glaring from his upset face.)* Certainly not! They're all the wrong way! Just because you have a choice, it doesn't mean that any of them has to be right. *(Pointing in another direction.)* That's the way to Digitopolis and we'll be there any moment. *(Suddenly the lighting grows*

WORDS
TO
KNOW

admonishing (ăd-mŏn′ĭsh-ĭng) *adj.* issuing a gentle warning **admonish** *v.*

Teaching Options

Multicultural Link **The Abacus**

The abacus is most commonly thought of as the Chinese device consisting of a small wooden frame with beads on wires. However, a similar device was developed in the West. The ancient Greeks and Romans most commonly did their calculations by moving counters, known to the Romans as "calculi," on a sanded table, wooden board, or a stone or marble tablet. The calculi were usually under an inch in diameter and were made of bone, ivory, or glass.

The abacus, or counting table, had symbols repre-senting the significant numerical values in the counting system. Counters would be placed next to the symbols. Subtraction, addition, multiplication, or other calculations could be done quite easily by adding to or subtracting from the original counters. For example, 1,252 would have one counter next to the 1,000 mark, two on the 100 line, one on the 50 line, and two on the 1 line. To subtract 1100 would mean removing the counter next to the 1000 and 1 of the counters from the 100 line. The remaining total could be easily figured out from the counters left on the table.

dimmer.) In fact, we're here. Welcome to the Land of Numbers.

Humbug. (*Looking around at the barren landscape.*) It doesn't look very inviting.

Milo. Is this the place where numbers are made?

Dodecahedron. They're not made. You have to dig for them. Don't you know anything at all about numbers?

Milo. Well, I never really thought they were very important.

Dodecahedron. Not important! Could you have tea for two without the 2? Or three blind mice without the 3? And how would you sail the seven seas without the 7?

Milo. All I meant was . . .

Dodecahedron. (*Continues shouting angrily.*) If you had high hopes, how would you know how high they were? And did you know that narrow escapes come in different widths? Would you travel the whole wide world without ever knowing how wide it was? And how could you do anything at long last without knowing how long the last was? Why, numbers are the most beautiful and valuable things in the world. Just follow me and I'll show you. (*He motions to them and pantomimes walking through rocky terrain with the others in tow. A doorway similar to the tollbooth appears and the Dodecahedron opens it and motions the others to follow him through.*) Come along, come along. I can't wait for you all day. (*They enter the doorway and the lights are dimmed very low, as to simulate the interior of a cave. The sounds of scrapings and tapping, scuffling and digging are heard all around them. He hands them helmets with flashlights attached.*) Put these on.

Milo. (*Whispering.*) Where are we going?

Dodecahedron. We're here. This is the numbers mine. (*Lights up a little, revealing little men digging and chopping, shoveling and scraping.*) Right this way and watch your step. (*His voice echoes and reverberates. Iridescent and glittery numbers seem to sparkle from everywhere.*)

Milo. (*Awed.*) Whose mine is it?

Voice of Mathemagician. By the four million eight hundred and twenty-seven thousand six hundred and fifty-nine hairs on my head, it's mine, of course! (*Enter the Mathemagician, carrying his long staff which looks like a giant pencil.*)

Humbug. (*Already intimidated.*) It's a lovely mine, really it is.

Mathemagician. (*Proudly.*) The biggest number mine in the kingdom.

Milo. (*Excitedly.*) Are there any precious stones in it?

Mathemagician. Precious stones! (*Then softly.*) By the eight million two hundred and forty-seven thousand three hundred and twelve threads in my robe, I'll say there are. Look here. (*Reaches in a cart, pulls out a small object, polishes it vigorously and holds it to the light, where it sparkles.*)

Milo. But that's a five.

Mathemagician. Exactly. As valuable a jewel as you'll find anywhere. Look at some of the others. (*Scoops up others and pours them into Milo's arms. They include all numbers from 1 to 9 and an assortment of zeroes.*)

ACTIVE READING

EVALUATE What is the author saying about numbers by comparing them to jewels?

WORDS TO KNOW

pantomime (păn′tə-mīm′) *v.* to express oneself using only gestures and facial expressions

vigorously (vĭg′ər-əs-lē) *adv.* done with force and energy

539

A Tell students that although not all plays use scenery to produce mood and create setting, in many plays, scenery is important. Point out how specific the instructions about scenery are in these stage directions. Ask students what ideas the scenery reinforces.

Possible Response: Mathematics enters into many aspects of life and is very important.

Reading Skills and Strategies: AUTHOR'S PURPOSE

B Ask students what the author accomplishes by emphasizing the power of math through the character of the Mathemagician.

Possible Response: The Mathemagician helps to persuade the reader that math is fun and nothing to be afraid of.

Reading Skills and Strategies: MAKE INFERENCES

C Ask students to draw an inference about Milo's math ability and support it with evidence from the text.

Possible Response: He has gained confidence in his mathematical ability; he has improved his math skills.

Dodecahedron. We dig them and polish them right here, and then send them all over the world. Marvelous, aren't they?

Tock. They are beautiful. (*He holds them up to compare them to the numbers on his clock body.*)

Milo. So that's where they come from. (*Looks at them and carefully hands them back, but drops a few which smash and break in half.*) Oh, I'm sorry!

Mathemagician. (*Scooping them up.*) Oh, don't worry about that. We use the broken ones for fractions. How about some lunch?

(*Takes out a little whistle and blows it. Two miners rush in carrying an immense cauldron which is bubbling and steaming. The workers put down their tools and gather around to eat.*)

Humbug. That looks delicious! (*Tock and Milo also look hungrily at the pot.*)

Mathemagician. Perhaps you'd care for something to eat?

Milo. Oh, yes, sir!

Tock. Thank you.

Humbug (*Already eating.*) Ummm . . . delicious! (*All finish their bowls immediately.*)

Mathemagician. Please have another portion. (*They eat and finish. Mathemagician serves them again.*) Don't stop now. (*They finish.*) Come on, no need to be bashful. (*Serves them again.*)

Milo. (*To Tock and Humbug as he finishes again.*) Do you want to hear something strange? Each one I eat makes me a little hungrier than before.

Mathemagician. Do have some more. (*He serves them again. They eat frantically, until the Mathemagician blows his whistle again and the pot is removed.*)

Humbug. (*Holding his stomach.*) Uggghhh! I think I'm starving.

Milo. Me, too, and I ate so much.

Dodecahedron. (*Wiping the gravy from several of his mouths.*) Yes, it was delicious, wasn't it? It's the specialty of the kingdom . . . subtraction stew.

Tock. (*Weak from hunger.*) I have more of an appetite than when I began.

Mathemagician. Certainly, what did you expect? The more you eat, the hungrier you get, everyone knows that.

Milo. They do? Then how do you get enough?

Mathemagician. Enough? Here in Digitopolis, we have our meals when we're full and eat until we're hungry. That way, when you don't have anything at all, you have more than enough. It's a very economical system. You must have been stuffed to have eaten so much.

Dodecahedron. It's completely logical. The more you want, the less you get, and the less you get, the more you have. Simple arithmetic, that's all. (*Tock, Milo and Humbug look at him blankly.*) Now, look, suppose you had something and added nothing to it. What would you have?

Milo. The same.

Dodecahedron. Splendid! And suppose you had something and added less than nothing to it? What would you have then?

Humbug. Starvation! Oh, I'm so hungry.

Dodecahedron. Now, now, it's not as bad as all that. In a few hours, you'll be nice and full again . . . just in time for dinner.

Milo. But I only eat when I'm hungry.

Mathemagician. (*Waving the eraser of his staff.*) What a curious idea. The next thing you'll have us believe is that you only sleep when you're tired.

 Mini Lesson **Grammar**

IDENTIFYING ADJECTIVE PHRASES AND THE WORDS THEY MODIFY

Instruction Remind students that a prepositional phrase may function as an adjective. The first step is to pick out the prepositional phrase and then to determine whether it tells more about a noun or pronoun in the sentence. Point out that in the highlighted passage *specialty* is modified by the phrase "of the kingdom."

Exercise Have students identify the adjective phrase(s) in each sentence and the noun or pronoun modified by the phrase.

1. The doctor gives Milo a *package* of laughter.
2. A giant *bee* with a sharp stinger could be scary.
3. The merchant pointed out the *letters* under the shelf and the *ones* in the bin.
4. The *meal* at the palace was not very filling.

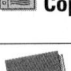 Use **Grammar Transparencies and Copymasters**, p. 103.

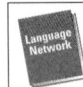 Use McDougal Littell's *Language Network*, Chapter 5, for more practice in adjective phrases.

(The mine has disappeared as well as the miners. This may be done by dropping a curtain in front of the mine, through a blackout[17] on the stage, while a single spotlight remains on the Mathemagician and the others, or through the use of multi-level platforms. The miners may fall behind the platforms, as two-dimensional props which depict the Mathemagician's room are dropped down or raised up.)

Humbug. Where did everyone go?

Mathemagician. Oh, they're still in the mine. I often find that the best way to get from one place to another is to erase everything and start again. Please make yourself at home.

(They find themselves in a very unique room, in which all the walls, tables, chairs, desks, cabinets and blackboards are labeled to show their heights, widths, depths and distances to and from each other. To one side is a gigantic notepad on an artist's easel, and from hooks and strings hang a collection of rulers, measures, weights and tapes, and all other measuring devices.)

Milo. Do you always travel that way? *(He looks around in wonder.)*

Mathemagician. No, indeed! *(He pulls a plumb line[18] from a hook and walks.)* Most of the time I take the shortest distance between any two points. And of course, when I have to be in several places at once . . . *(He writes $3 \times 1 = 3$ on the notepad with his staff.)* I simply multiply. *(Three figures looking like the Mathemagician appear on a platform above.)*

Milo. How did you do that?

Mathemagician and the Three. There's nothing

Act Two, Scene 1. The Mathemagician asks Milo to name the greatest number he can think of.

to it, if you have a magic staff. *(The Three cancel themselves out and disappear.)*

Humbug. That's nothing but a big pencil.

Mathemagician. True enough, but once you learn to use it, there's no end to what you can do.

Milo. Can you make things disappear?

Mathemagician. Just step a little closer and watch this. *(Shows them that there is nothing up his sleeve or in his hat. He writes:)* $4 + 9 - 2 \times 16 + 1 = 3 \times 6 - 67 + 8 \times 2 - 3 + 26 - 1 - 34 + 3 - 7 + 2 - 5 =$ *(He looks up expectantly.)*

Humbug. Seventeen?

Milo. It all comes to zero.

Mathemagician. Precisely. *(Makes a theatrical bow and rips off paper from notepad.)* Now, is there anything else you'd like to see? *(At*

---

17. **blackout:** the switching off of stage lights to mark the end of an act or scene.
18. **plumb line** (plŭm lĭn): a line from which a weight is hung to determine distance.

Customizing Instruction

Less Proficient Readers
Ask students the following questions:

1. What do Milo and his friends have for lunch?
   Answer: subtraction stew
2. What is the effect of subtraction stew?
   Possible Response: It makes people who eat it hungrier.
3. What does the Mathemagician show Milo when he asks about the biggest and longest numbers?
   Possible Response: The Mathemagician displays a huge "3" and a wide "8."
4. What does Milo learn about the number of greatest magnitude?
   Possible Response: No matter how great the number he thinks of, he can always add one.

Set a Purpose Have students read to find out how Milo convinces the Mathemagician to agree with Azaz about releasing the princesses.

Students Acquiring English

1 Tell students that Humbug's exclamation shows his surprise and dismay at being hungrier than he was before he ate.

2 Explain to students that *stuffed* is a colloquial expression that means "filled up with food" or "fully satisfied."

Multiple Learning Styles
Kinesthetic Learners

3 Have students act out this scene. Their performance should help to illustrate why the ruler of Digitopolis is known as the Mathemagician.

Interpersonal Learners
Remind students that Milo's task is to convince the Mathemagician to agree to release the princesses. Have students think of how they might persuade the Mathemagician to agree with Azaz.

Mini Lesson   Viewing and Representing

The Mathemagician asks a question

Instruction Tell students that costumes vary from production to production. Every director has a different interpretation of the characters and their roles, which costuming can enhance. Ask students how the appearance of the number miners differs from students' own images of how miners should look.
Possible Responses: Instead of being grimy from digging, the number miners look fresh and clean.

Ask students what they can infer about number mining from the way these miners are costumed.
Possible Response: Mining for numbers may not be as hard as mining for other substances.

Application Ask students which details of the Mathemagician's appearance are similar to their mental image of the ruler.
Possible Response: He is carrying a large pencil and is wearing a long robe. His hat is adorned with mathematical symbols.

Reading and Analyzing

Literary Analysis: HUMOR

A Students should be able to recognize how tone and mood contribute to the effect of the text. Ask why the Mathemagician's reaction is humorous.

Possible Response: No one could possibly understand his letter; yet he thinks he is being friendly and generous by writing it to his brother.

Reading Skills and Strategies: EVALUATE

B Ask students if "a seven is a seven everywhere."

Possible Response: Many will agree, but it is what the number is attached to that gives it meaning.

Literary Analysis: CHARACTERIZATION

C Ask students how Milo's interaction with the Mathemagician differs from what he would have done at the beginning of the play.

Possible Response: Milo doesn't give up or lose interest in the situation. He uses his reason to solve the problem.

Active Reading: PREDICT

D Ask students what the obstacle might be.

Possible Responses: The obstacle might be something that will trap them upon their return; the impossibility of getting back to the Land of Wisdom once they have left it; or becoming trapped in the castle.

---

this point, an appeal to the audience to see if anyone would like a problem solved.)

Milo. Well . . . can you show me the biggest number there is?

Mathemagician. Why, I'd be delighted. *(Opening a closet door.)* We keep it right here. It took four miners to dig it out. *(He shows them a huge "3" twice as high as the Mathemagician.)*

Milo. No, that's not what I mean. Can you show me the longest number there is?

Mathemagician. Sure. *(Opens another door.)* Here it is. It took three carts to carry it here. *(Door reveals an "8" that is wide as the "3" was high.)*

Milo. No, no, that's not what I meant either. *(Looks helplessly at Tock.)*

Tock. I think what you would like to see is the number of the greatest possible magnitude.

Mathemagician. Well, why didn't you say so? *(He busily measures them and all other things as he speaks, and marks it down.)* What's the greatest number you can think of? *(Here, an appeal can also be made to the audience or Milo may think of his own answers.)*

Milo. Uh . . . nine trillion, nine hundred and ninety-nine billion, nine hundred ninety-nine million, nine-hundred ninety-nine thousand, nine hundred and ninety-nine. *(He puffs.)*

Mathemagician. *(Writes that on the pad.)* Very good. Now add one to it. *(Milo or audience does.)* Now add one again. *(Milo or audience does so.)* Now add one again. Now add one again. Now add . . .

Milo. But when can I stop?

Mathemagician. Never. Because the number you want is always at least one more than the number you have, and it's so large that if you

started saying it yesterday, you wouldn't finish tomorrow.

Humbug. Where could you ever find a number so big?

Mathemagician. In the same place they have the smallest number there is, and you know what that is?

Milo. The smallest number . . . let's see . . . one one-millionth?

Mathemagician. Almost. Now all you have to do is divide that in half and then divide that in half and then divide that in half and then divide that . . .

Milo. Doesn't that ever stop either?

Mathemagician. How can it when you can always take half of what you have and divide it in half again? Look. *(Pointing offstage.)* You see that line?

Milo. You mean that long one out there?

Mathemagician. That's it. Now, if you just follow that line forever, and when you reach the end, turn left, you will find the Land of Infinity. That's where the tallest, the shortest, the biggest, the smallest and the most and the least of everything are kept.

Milo. But how can you follow anything forever? You know, I get the feeling that everything in Digitopolis is very difficult.

Mathemagician. But on the other hand, I think you'll find that the only thing you can do easily is be wrong, and that's hardly worth the effort.

Milo. But . . . what bothers me is . . . well, why is it that even when things are correct, they don't really seem to be right?

Mathemagician. *(Grows sad and quiet.)* How true. It's been that way ever since Rhyme and Reason were banished. *(Sadness turns to fury.)* And all because of that stubborn wretch Azaz! It's all his fault.

Teaching Options

 Mini Lesson ## Vocabulary Strategy

PREFIXES AND SUFFIXES

Instruction Tell students that the more prefixes and suffixes they know, the more words they will be able to figure out. Give students these prefixes and suffixes and their meanings:

Prefixes: *dis* – opposing, away; *non* – not; *over* – too much, above; *pre* – before; *trans* – across, beyond, into another state

Suffixes: *ary* – connected with; *ful* – full of; *less* – without; *ous* – characterized by

Exercise Ask students to use the prefixes and suffixes listed to help them think of the word

described by each phrase below.

1. full of resources *(resourceful)*
2. not sense *(nonsense)*
3. without worth *(worthless)*
4. characteristic of a villain *(villainous)*
5. fixed into another state *(transfixed)*

Application Have students find other words in the play with the prefixes or suffixes listed above.

Use **Vocabulary Transparencies and Copymasters,** p. 55.

Milo. Maybe if you discussed it with him . . .

Mathemagician. He's just too unreasonable! Why just last month, I sent him a very friendly letter, which he never had the courtesy to answer. See for yourself. (*Puts the letter on the easel. The letter reads:*)

4738 1919,
667 394107 5841 62589
85371 14 39588 7190434 203
27689 57131 481206.
5864 98053,
62179875073

Milo. But maybe he doesn't understand numbers.

Mathemagician. Nonsense! Everybody understands numbers. No matter what language you speak, they always mean the same thing. A seven is a seven everywhere in the world.

Milo. (*To Tock and Humbug.*) Everyone is so sensitive about what he knows best.

Tock. With your permission, sir, we'd like to rescue Rhyme and Reason.

Mathemagician. Has Azaz agreed to it?

Tock. Yes, sir.

Mathemagician. Then I don't! Ever since they've been banished, we've never agreed on anything, and we never will.

Milo. Never?

Mathemagician. Never! And if you can prove otherwise, you have my permission to go.

Milo. Well then, with whatever Azaz agrees, you disagree.

Mathemagician. Correct.

Milo. And whatever Azaz disagrees, you agree.

Mathemagician. (*Yawning, cleaning his nails.*) Also correct.

Milo. Then, each of you agree that he will disagree with whatever each of you agrees with, and if you both disagree with the same thing, aren't you really in agreement?

Mathemagician. I've been tricked! (*Figures it over, but comes up with the same answer.*)

Tock. And now may we go?

Mathemagician. (*Nods weakly.*) It's a long and dangerous journey. Long before you find them, the demons will know you're there. Watch out for them, because if you ever come face to face, it will be too late. But there is one other obstacle even more serious than that.

Milo. (*Terrified.*) What is it?

Mathemagician. I'm afraid I can't tell you until you return. But maybe I can give you something to help you out. (*Claps hands. Enter the Dodecahedron, carrying something on a pillow. The Mathemagician takes it.*) Here is your own magic staff. Use it well and there is nothing it can't do for you. (*Puts a small, gleaming pencil in Milo's breast pocket.*)

Humbug. Are you sure you can't tell about that serious obstacle?

Mathemagician. Only when you return. And now the Dodecahedron will escort you to the road that leads to the Castle-in-the-Air. Farewell, my friends, and good luck to you. (*They shake hands, say goodbye, and the Dodecahedron leads them off.*) Good luck to you! (*To himself.*) Because you're sure going to need it. (*He watches them through a telescope and marks down the calculations.*)

Dodecahedron. (*He re-enters.*) Well, they're on their way.

Mathemagician. So I see. (*Dodecahedron stands waiting.*) Well, what is it?

Dodecahedron. I was just wondering myself, your Numbership. What actually *is* the serious obstacle you were talking about?

Mathemagician. (*Looks at him in surprise.*) You mean you really don't know?

BLACKOUT

Cross Curricular Link **Mathematics**

INFINITY The Mathemagician makes the concept of infinity seem easy. That is part of his magic. In reality, though, the theory of infinity took centuries to explore and formulate.

Galileo, in the 17th century, was one of the first to advance mathematical ideas about infinity. Multiplying a number by itself equals a number called a square. For example, the square of 2 is 4, the square of 4 is 16, the square of 16 is 256. Galileo said that for every number, there is a square. Since numbers go on to infinity, then there must also be an infinite number of squares.

Furthermore, every number has a square so there are as many squares as there are numbers. Galileo did not want to use the word *equal* to describe the relationship between the numbers and their squares. He didn't think that infinite quantities could be proven to be equal, greater, or lesser. However, Georg Cantor, in the late 19th century, proved that those terms could be used in connection with infinity. He said that if two sets of numbers, like whole numbers and their squares, could be paired into infinity, then the sets had equal numbers of members.

Literary Analysis: COUPLET

A Define a couplet as two successive lines of poetry with the same end rhyme. Ask students to identify the rhyme in these four lines.

Answers: smart/heart; dreams/schemes

ACTIVE READING

B **CLARIFY** Possible Response: Rhyme speaks in rhyme. Reason is cool and logical.

Literary Analysis: SETTING

C Ask students what they learn about the Land of Ignorance from Milo's words.

Possible Response: It is very dark. Ask students to explain the significance of the dark setting.

Possible Response: People who are ignorant are figuratively "in the dark" because there is so much of which they are unaware or unknowing.

Reading Skills and Strategies: WORD PLAY

D Ask students to point out the homophones and homonyms that the Bird uses to play on Milo's words.

Possible Responses: morning/mourning; spend; sense/cents; mean/mean; weight/wait

ACTIVE READING

E **RECALL** Possible Response: Milo has received the tollbooth, some signs and coins, a map, a rule book, a box with letters of the alphabet, and the sound of laughter.

SCENE 2

THE LAND OF IGNORANCE

Lights up on Rhyme and Reason, in their castle, looking out two windows.

Rhyme. I'm worried sick, I
　　must confess
　I wonder if they'll have
　　success
All the others tried in vain,
And were never seen or heard again.

Reason. Now, Rhyme, there's no need to be so pessimistic. Milo, Tock, and Humbug have just as much chance of succeeding as they do of failing.

A

Rhyme. But the demons are so deadly smart
　They'll stuff your brain and fill your heart
　With <u>petty</u> thoughts and selfish dreams
　And trap you with their nasty schemes.

B

ACTIVE READING

CLARIFY How is the manner in which each princess speaks appropriate to her name?

Reason. Now, Rhyme, be reasonable, won't you? And calm down, you always talk in couplets when you get nervous. Milo has learned a lot from his journey. I think he's a match for the demons and that he might soon be knocking at our door. Now come on, cheer up, won't you?

Rhyme. I'll try.

(Lights fade on the Princesses and come up on the little car, traveling slowly.)

C

Milo. So this is the Land of Ignorance. It's so dark. I can hardly see a thing. Maybe we should wait until morning.

Voice. They'll be <u>mourning</u> for you soon enough. *(They look up and see a large, soiled, ugly bird with a dangerous beak and a malicious expression.)*

Milo. I don't think you understand. We're looking for a place to spend the night.

Bird. *(Shrieking.)* It's not yours to spend!

Milo. That doesn't make any sense, you see . . .

Bird. Dollars or cents, it's still not yours to spend.

Milo. But I don't mean . . .

Bird. Of course you're mean. Anybody who'd spend a night that doesn't belong to him is very mean.

Tock. Must you interrupt like that?

Bird. Naturally, it's my job. I take the words right out of your mouth. Haven't we met before? I'm the Everpresent Wordsnatcher.

Milo. Are you a demon?

Bird. I'm afraid not. I've tried, but the best I can manage to be is a nuisance. *(Suddenly gets nervous as he looks beyond the three.)* And I don't have time to waste with you. *(Starts to leave.)*

Tock. What is it? What's the matter?

Milo. Hey, don't leave. I wanted to ask you some questions. . . . Wait!

Bird. Weight? Twenty-seven pounds. Bye-bye. *(Disappears.)*

Milo. Well, he was no help.

Man. Perhaps I can be of some assistance to you? *(There appears a beautifully dressed man, very polished and clean.)* Hello, little boy. *(Shakes Milo's hand.)* And how's the faithful dog? *(Pats Tock.)* And who is this handsome creature? *(Tips his hat to Humbug.)*

| WORDS TO KNOW | **petty** (pĕt′ē) *adj.* narrow-minded; shallow |
| | **mourn** (môrn) *v.* to feel or express grief or sorrow |

544

Teaching Options

 Mini Lesson ## Vocabulary Strategy

COMMONLY CONFUSED HOMOPHONES

Instruction Tell students that using context clues will help them to choose the correct homophone. Although homophones sound the same, they have different meanings. Point out that the deliberate use of incorrect homophones by the Everpresent Wordsnatcher creates humor. However, most often, using the wrong homophone leads to confusion on the part of the reader.

Exercise Have students choose the homophone that best completes each sentence.

1. The Whether Man carried his umbrella in case of (reign, <u>rain</u>, rein).

2. The (sense, cents, <u>scents</u>) of the daydream awakened Tock's keen nose.

3. The (<u>ascent</u>, assent) up the mountain was filled with difficulty.

4. Milo wondered if his adventure was (reel, <u>real</u>) or a dream.

5. It was impossible for the demon of insincerity to tell the (<u>bare</u>, bear) truth.

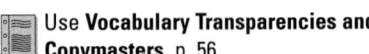 Use **Vocabulary Transparencies and Copymasters**, p. 56.

Humbug. *(To others.)* What a pleasant surprise to meet someone so nice in a place like this.

Man. But before I help you out, I wonder if first you could spare me a little of your time, and help me with a few small jobs?

Humbug. Why, certainly.

Tock. Gladly.

Milo. Sure, we'd be happy to.

Man. Splendid, for there are just three tasks. First, I would like to move this pile of sand from here to there. *(Indicates through pantomine a large pile of sand.)* But I'm afraid that all I have is this tiny tweezers. *(Hands it to Milo, who begins moving the sand one grain at a time.)* Second, I would like to empty this well and fill that other, but I have no bucket, so you'll have to use this eyedropper. *(Hands it to Tock, who begins to work.)* And finally, I must have a hole in this cliff, and here is a needle to dig it. *(Humbug eagerly begins. The man leans against a tree and stares vacantly off into space. The lights indicate the passage of time.)*

Milo. You know something? I've been working steadily for a long time, now, and I don't feel the least bit tired or hungry. I could go right on the same way forever.

Man. Maybe you will. *(He yawns.)*

Milo. *(Whispers to Tock.)* Well, I wish I knew how long it was going to take.

Tock. Why don't you use your magic staff and find out?

ACTIVE READING

RECALL Can you remember what other gifts Milo has received on his journey?

Milo. *(Takes out pencil and calculates to Man.)* Pardon me, sir, but it's going to take 837 years to finish these jobs.

Man. Is that so? What a shame. Well, then, you'd better get on with them.

Milo. But . . . it hardly seems worthwhile.

Man. Worthwhile! Of course they're not worthwhile. I wouldn't ask you to do anything that was worthwhile.

Tock. Then why bother?

Man. Because, my friends, what could be more important than doing unimportant things? If you stop to do enough of them, you'll never get where you are going. *(Laughs villainously.)*

Milo. *(Gasps.)* Oh, no. You must be . . .

Man. Quite correct! I am the Terrible Trivium,[19] demon of petty tasks and worthless jobs, ogre of wasted effort and monster of habit. *(They start to back away from him.)* Don't try to leave, there's so much to do, and you still have 837 years to go on the first job.

Milo. But why do unimportant things?

Man. Think of all the trouble it saves. If you spend all your time doing only the easy and useless jobs, you'll never have time to worry about the important ones which are so difficult. *(Walks toward them, whispering.)* Now do come and stay with me. We'll have such fun together. There are things to fill and things to empty, things to take away and things to bring back, things to pick up and things to put down . . . *(They are transfixed by his soothing voice. He is about to embrace them when a Voice screams.)*

Voice. Run! Run! *(They all wake up and run with the Trivium behind. As the Voice continues to call out directions, they follow until they lose the Trivium.)* Run! Run! This way! Over here! Over here! Up here! Down there! Quick, hurry up!

Tock. *(Panting.)* I think we lost him.

---

19. **Trivium** (trĭv′ē-əm): a made-up name, this uses the same root as *trivial*, which means utterly unimportant.

THE PHANTOM TOLLBOOTH **545**

Customizing Instruction

Less Proficient Readers
Ask students the following questions to check comprehension:

1. What does the Everpresent Word-snatcher do?
   Possible Response: He takes the words right out of people's mouths.

2. Describe the man asking for help with some jobs.
   Possible Response: He is beautifully dressed, very polished and clean.

3. Explain the jobs that Milo and the others have to do.
   Possible Responses: They have to move sand from a pile with tweezers; empty a well and fill another with an eyedropper; and dig a hole in a cliff with a needle

Set a Purpose Have students read to find out who the man is and what other obstacles threaten Milo's quest.

Students Acquiring English
1 Point out to students how the Bird uses homophones of Milo's words to add humor and play on the words.

Mini Lesson ## Viewing and Representing

Illustration of *Rhyme and Reason*
by Jules Feiffer

Instruction Students should recognize these figures as Rhyme and Reason. Ask students to look carefully at the facial expressions of the two princesses and decide which is Rhyme and which is Reason. Have students explain their choices.

Possible Response: The figure on the left is sweeter looking than the figure on the right. Because Reason would look at the logic of a situation and would not be swayed by emotion, she might be the one on the right, who appears more serious and who is holding a book in her hand. Rhyme's full title is Sweet Rhyme so that supports the idea that she is on the left. The order of their names would also suggest that Rhyme is on the left.

Application Ask students how this illustration suggests that these characters will react to Milo's rescue.

Possible Response: They will be helpful and quite calm. They will not lose their composure.

Literary Analysis: SYMBOL

Ⓐ Ask students to interpret the symbolism of the attractive appearances of the Terrible Trivium and the demon of Insincerity.

Possible Response: Sometimes evil is disguised as good and appears attractive and tempting, not frightening or repulsive. This deceptive appearance makes it more dangerous.

Reading Skills and Strategies: CAUSE AND EFFECT

Ask students what results when people are discovered to be insincere.

Possible Response: They can no longer be trusted because others can never be sure when they are telling the truth.

Literary Analysis: REALISTIC AND FANTASTIC DETAILS

Ask students to identify what is realistic and what is fantastic about the sequence where the three run from the demons.

Possible Responses: Their reactions are realistic; the demons and the location of the castle are fantastic.

Literary Analysis FANTASY

Ask students to analyze the effect of the fantasy setting of the Land of Ignorance.

Possible Response: It allows the writer to incorporate symbolic demons and create a frightening atmosphere without instilling real fear in the reader.

Voice. Keep going straight! Keep going straight! Now step up! Now step up!

Milo. Look out! *(They all fall into a trap.)* But he said "up!"

Voice. Well, I hope you didn't expect to get anywhere by listening to me.

Humbug. We're in a deep pit! We'll never get out of here.

Voice. That is quite an accurate evaluation of the situation.

Milo. *(Shouting angrily.)* Then why did you help us at all?

Ⓐ **Voice.** Oh, I'd do as much for anybody. Bad advice is my specialty. *(A little furry creature appears.)* I'm the demon of insincerity. I don't mean what I say; I don't mean what I do; and I don't mean what I am.

Milo. Then why don't you go away and leave us alone!

Insincerity. *(Voice.)* Now, there's no need to get angry. You're a very clever boy and I have complete confidence in you. You can certainly climb out of that pit . . . come on, try . . .

Milo. I'm not listening to one word you say! You're just telling me what you think I'd like to hear, and not what is important.

Insincerity. Well, if that's the way you feel about it . . .

Milo. That's the way I feel about it. We will manage by ourselves without any unnecessary advice from you.

Insincerity. *(Stamping his foot.)* Well, all right for you! Most people listen to what I say, but if that's the way you feel, then I'll just go home. *(Exits in a huff.)*

Humbug. *(Who has been quivering with fright.)* And don't you ever come back! Well, I guess we showed him, didn't we?

Milo. You know something? This place is a lot more dangerous than I ever imagined.

Tock. *(Who's been surveying the situation.)* I think I figured a way to get out. Here, hop on my back. *(Milo does so.)* Now you, Humbug, on top of Milo. *(He does so.)* Now hook your umbrella onto that tree and hold on. *(They climb over Humbug, then pull him up.)*

Humbug. *(As they climb.)* Watch it! Watch it, now. Ow, be careful of my back! My back! Easy, easy . . . oh, this is so difficult. Aren't you finished yet?

Tock. *(As he pulls up Humbug.)* There. Now, I'll lead for a while. Follow me, and we'll stay out of trouble. *(They walk and climb higher and higher.)*

Humbug. Can't we slow down a little?

Tock. Something tells me we better reach the Castle-in-the-Air as soon as possible, and not stop to rest for a single moment. *(They speed up.)*

Milo. What is it, Tock? Did you see something?

Tock. Just keep walking and don't look back.

Milo. You did see something!

Humbug. What is it? Another demon?

Tock. Not just one, I'm afraid. If you want to see what I'm talking about, then turn around.

Teaching Options

 Informal Assessment

LOG ENTRIES

You can informally assess students' understanding of the selection by having them write two travelogue entries. Students should place themselves in Milo's position and imagine that he kept a record of the places he visited, the people he met, and the events that he experienced in the course of his journey. Entries should include specific details, and each should be organized into one or two paragraphs.

RUBRIC

3 Full Accomplishment Students accurately narrate events, describe setting, and include complete details to support the main ideas.

2 Substantial Accomplishment Responses are organized into paragraphs and present several accurate details of events, character, and setting in a logical sequence.

1 Little or Partial Accomplishment Responses are not organized and include few details from the text.

(They turn around. The stage darkens and hundreds of Yellow Gleaming Eyes can be seen.)

Humbug. Good grief! Do you see how many there are? Hundreds! The Overbearing Know-it-all,[20] the Gross Exaggeration,[21] the Horrible Hopping Hindsight,[22] . . . and look over there! The Triple Demons of Compromise! Let's get out of here! (Starts to scurry.) Hurry up, you two! Must you be so slow about everything?

Milo. Look! There it is, up ahead! The Castle-in-the-Air! (They all run.)

Humbug. They're gaining!

Milo. But there it is!

Humbug. I see it! I see it!

(They reach the first step and are stopped by a little man in a frock coat, sleeping on a worn ledger. He has a long quill pen and a bottle of ink at his side. He is covered with ink stains over his clothes and wears spectacles.)

Tock. Shh! Be very careful. (They try to step over him but he wakes up.)

Senses Taker.[23] (From sleeping position.) Names? (He sits up.)

Humbug. Well, I . . .

Senses Taker. Names? (He opens book and begins to write, splattering himself with ink.)

Humbug. Uh . . . Humbug, Tock and this is Milo.

Senses Taker. Splendid, splendid. I haven't had an "M" in ages.

Milo. What do you want our names for? We're sort of in a hurry.

Senses Taker. Oh, this won't take along. I'm the official Senses Taker and I must have some information before I can take your sense. Now if you'll just tell me: (Handing them a form to fill. Speaking slowly and *deliberately*.) When you were born, where you were born, why you were born, how old you are now, how old you were then, how old you'll be in a little while . . .

Milo. I wish he'd hurry up. At this rate, the demons will be here before we know it!

Senses Taker. . . . Your mother's name, your father's name, where you live, how long you've lived there, the schools you've attended, the schools you haven't attended . . .

Humbug. I'm getting writer's cramp. `2`

Tock. I smell something very evil and it's getting stronger every second. (To Senses Taker.) May we go now?

Senses Taker. Just as soon as you tell me your height, your weight, the number of books you've read this year . . .

Milo. We have to go!

Senses Taker. All right, all right, I'll give you the short form. (Pulls out a small piece of paper.) Destination?

Milo. But we have to . . .

Senses Taker. Destination?

Milo, Tock and Humbug. The Castle-in-the-Air! (They throw down their papers and run past him up the first few stairs.)

Senses Taker. Stop! I'm sure you'd rather see

---

20. **Overbearing Know-it-all:** *overbearing* means pushy and arrogant.

21. **Gross Exaggeration:** a *gross* exaggeration is one that is obvious and overstated.

22. **Hindsight** (hīnd′sīt′): to view an event in hindsight means to consider its meaning after it has already occurred.

23. **Senses Taker:** A play on words: a *census taker* makes an official count of a population.

WORDS
TO   **deliberately** (dĭ-lĭb′ər-ĭt-lē) *adv.* done in a slow, purposeful manner
KNOW

547

Viewing and Representing

(Mini Lesson)

Illustration of Tock, Milo, and Humbug
by Jules Feiffer

Instruction Students will notice that this illustration has more background detail than those previously seen. Ask students how the artist uses this background to convey the difficulty of the escape from the pit.
Possible Response: It is shown as very deep, and the walls are smooth, meaning that there is nothing to give the characters a foothold. The ground looks rocky, which would make a fall very uncomfortable.

Application Ask students why Humbug, who is portrayed as the biggest of the three, is on top.
Possible Response: As the biggest, he will have the most strength to hold on as the other two characters climb over him to reach the top.
Ask students what the illustration emphasizes about the relationship of the three characters.
Possible Response: They have learned to work as a team to solve problems. Each one is willing to help the others.

Reading and Analyzing

Reading Skills and Strategies: CLARIFY

A Ask students why a particular image is shown to each character.

Possible Response: Each image appeals to the character's weakness or strongest sense.

Ask students to identify the sense to which each appeals.

Possible Response: Milo's—sight, sound, smell; Tock's—smell; Humbug's—sense of importance

Reading Skills and Strategies: CONNECT

B Have students use their knowledge and experience to comprehend what the Senses Taker is saying.

Reading Skills and Strategies: STORY MAPPING

Tell students that mapping this scene will help them review the events leading up to the climax. Have them design a flow chart and fill in events.

Possible Responses: Major conflict: rescuers vs. demons

Event 1: Rescuers enter Ignorance and encounter the Wordsnatcher; Event 2: Rescuers escape from the Terrible Trivium's trap; Event 3: Rescuers follow the demon of Insincerity and fall into a pit; Event 4: They escape from the pit and make it past the Senses Taker

ACTIVE READING

C **VISUALIZE** **Possible Responses:** The castle is rising out of the clouds; it has a moat, drawbridge, and several towers

ACTIVE READING

D **PREDICT** **Possible Responses:** Time goes quickly or in this situation, time literally flies. The rescuers and princesses will hang on to Tock and reach the ground.

---

what I have to show you. *(Snaps his fingers; they freeze.)* A circus of your very own. *(Circus music is heard. Milo seems to go into a trance.)* And wouldn't you enjoy this most wonderful smell? *(Tock sniffs and goes into a trance.)* And here's something I know you'll enjoy hearing . . . *(To Humbug. The sound of cheers and applause for Humbug is heard, and he goes into a trance.)* There we are. And now, I'll just sit back and let the demons catch up with you.

Act Two, Scene 2. The demons of insincerity pursue Milo, Tock, and the Humbug.

(Milo accidentally drops his package of gifts. The Package of Laughter from Dr. Dischord opens, and the Sounds of Laughter are heard. After a moment, Milo, Tock and Humbug join in laughing and the spells are broken.)

Milo. There was no circus.

Tock. There were no smells.

Humbug. The applause is gone.

Senses Taker. I warned you I was the Senses Taker. I'll steal your sense of purpose, your sense of duty, destroy your sense of proportion—and but for one thing, you'd be helpless yet.

Milo. What's that?

Senses Taker. As long as you have the sound of laughter, I cannot take your sense of humor. Agh! That horrible sense of humor.

Humbug. Here they come! Let's get out of here!

(The demons appear in nasty slithering hordes, running through the audience and up onto the stage, trying to attack Tock, Milo and Humbug. The three heroes run past the Senses Taker up the stairs toward the Castle-in-the-Air with the demons snarling behind them.)

ACTIVE READING

VISUALIZE Picture the Castle-in-the-Air. Think about size, color, and shape.

Milo. Don't look back! Just keep going! *(They reach the castle. The two Princesses appear in the windows.)*

Princesses. Hurry! Hurry! We've been expecting you.

Milo. You must be the princesses. We've come to rescue you.

 Speaking and Listening

Mini Lesson

BACKGROUND MUSIC

Prepare Explain to students that background music can help set the mood in a drama. Have the class divide into small groups and choose the chase scene or another brief scene. Give them time to listen to CDs from the school, public, or their own music libraries. Then have them work together to choose music that enhances the mood of the scene. Students should decide how much should be played as an introduction to the scene. Then students should practice reading the

characters' parts, working with the music to achieve maximum effectiveness.

Present Have groups present their scenes by playing the music and reading the dialogue. Audience members should evaluate how the choice of music and its incorporation into the scene affected their understanding and enjoyment of the play.

BLOCK SCHEDULING This activity is particularly well suited for longer class periods.

Humbug. And the demons are close behind!

Tock. We should leave right away.

Princesses. We're ready anytime you are.

Milo. Good, now if you'll just come out. But wait a minute—there's no door! How can we rescue you from the Castle-in-the-Air if there's no way to get in or out?

Humbug. Hurry, Milo! They're gaining on us.

Reason. Take your time, Milo, and think about it.

Milo. Ummm, all right . . . just give me a second or two. (*He thinks hard.*)

Humbug. I think I feel sick.

Milo. I've got it! Where's that package of presents? (*Opens the package of letters.*) Ah, here it is. (*Takes out the letters and sticks them on the door, spelling:*) E-N-T-R-A-N-C-E. Entrance. Now let's see. (*Rummages through and spells in smaller letters:*) P-u-s-h. Push. (*He pushes and a door opens. The Princesses come out of the castle. Slowly, the demons <u>ascend</u> the stairway.*)

Humbug. Oh, it's too late. They're coming up and there's no other way down!

Milo. Unless . . . (*Looks at Tock.*) Well . . . Time flies, doesn't it?

ACTIVE READING

PREDICT What are the two meanings of "time flies"? Predict what will happen next.

Tock. Quite often. Hold on, everyone, and I'll take you down.

Humbug. Can you carry us all?

Tock. We'll soon find out. Ready or not, here we go!

(*His alarm begins to ring. They jump off the platform and disappear. The demons, howling with rage, reach the top and find no one there. They see the Princesses and the heroes running across the stage and bound down the stairs after them and into the audience. There is a mad chase scene until they reach the stage again.*)

Humbug. I'm exhausted! I can't run another step.

Milo. We can't stop now . . .

Tock. Milo! Look out there! (*The armies of Azaz and Mathemagician appear at the back of the theatre, with the kings at their heads.*)

Azaz. (*As they march toward the stage.*) Don't worry, Milo, we'll take over now.

Mathemagician. Those demons may not know it, but their days are numbered!

Spelling Bee. Charge! C-H-A-R-G-E! Charge! (*They rush at the demons and battle until the demons run off howling. Everyone cheers. The Five Ministers of Azaz appear and shake Milo's hand.*)

Minister 1. Well done.

Minister 2. Fine job.

Minister 3. Good work!

Minister 4. Congratulations!

Minister 5. Cheers! (*Everyone cheers again. A fanfare interrupts. A page steps forward and reads from a large scroll:*)

Page. Henceforth, and forthwith,
Let it be known by one and all,
That Rhyme and Reason
Reign once more in Wisdom.
(*The Princesses bow gratefully and kiss their brothers, the kings.*)
And furthermore,
The boy named Milo,
The dog known as Tock,
And the insect hereinafter referred to as
   the Humbug

WORDS TO KNOW **ascend** (ə-sĕnd´) v. to move upward

549

 **Grammar**

USING COMMAS TO PREVENT MISREADING
Instruction Remind students that using the correct punctuation helps to eliminate confusion in writing. Placing commas after introductory phrases, between items in a series, and to set off names used in direct address will make the meaning clearer. Indicate the highlighted sentence. Have students read the sentence without the first comma. The meaning is changed. Instead of hanging onto Tock, the characters would be hanging onto each other and going nowhere.
Exercise Have students rewrite each sentence with the commas correctly placed.

1. He asked for pizza ice cream and banana pudding. (*pizza, ice cream,*)
2. I called Milo Tock to prepare him. (*Milo, Tock,*)
3. After the close call they had second thoughts. (*call,*)
4. Put your cane down Humbug. (*down,*)

Use **Grammar Transparencies and Copymasters,** p. 123.

Use McDougal Littell's *Language Network,* Chapter 9, for more instruction and practice in using commas.

Reading and Analyzing

Literary Analysis: HERO

(A) Ask students what characteristics of a hero they would associate with Milo.

Possible Responses: He showed courage; he didn't give up; he overcame obstacles; he accomplished his quest; he became a better person.

Literary Analysis: QUEST

(B) Ask students what broader purpose besides rescuing the princesses they see Milo's quest fulfilling.

Possible Response: It showed him that there was no limit to what he could accomplish if he tried.

ACTIVE READING

(C) EVALUATE Possible Response: Rhyme speaks in rhyme. Reason states everything clearly.

Literary Analysis: THEME

(D) Ask students what major idea of the play Reason's words support and reinforce.

Possible Response: Learning opens many roads into the future and prepares a person to overcome obstacles in his or her life. Learning is valuable if it is used to help others.

(A) Are hereby declared to be Heroes of the Realm. *(All bow and salute the heroes.)*

Milo. But we never could have done it without a lot of help.

Reason. That may be true, but you had the courage to try, and what you can do is often a matter of what you will do.

Azaz. That's why there was one very important thing about your <u>quest</u> we couldn't discuss until you returned.

Milo. I remember. What was it?

Azaz. Very simple. It was impossible!

Mathemagician. Completely impossible!

Humbug. Do you mean . . . ? *(Feeling faint.)* Oh, . . . I think I need to sit down.

Azaz. Yes, indeed, but if we'd told you then, you might not have gone.

(B) Mathemagician. And, as you discovered, many things are possible just as long as you don't know they're impossible.

Milo. I think I understand.

Rhyme. I'm afraid it's time to go now.

Reason. And you must say goodbye.

Milo. To everyone? *(Looks around at the crowd. To Tock and Humbug.)* Can't you two come with me?

Humbug. I'm afraid not, old man. I'd like to, but I've arranged for a lecture tour which will keep me occupied for years.

Tock. And they do need a watchdog here.

Milo. Well, O.K., then. *(Milo hugs the Humbug.)*

1 Humbug. *(Sadly.)* Oh, bah.

Milo. *(He hugs Tock, and then faces everyone.)* Well, goodbye. We all spent so much time together, I know I'm going to miss you. *(To Princesses.)* I guess we would have reached you a lot sooner if I hadn't made so many mistakes.

Reason. You must never feel badly about making mistakes, Milo, as long as you take the trouble to learn from them. Very often you learn more by being wrong for the right reasons than you do by being right for the wrong ones.

ACTIVE READING

EVALUATE What types of aesthetic, or pleasing, language do the princesses use?

Milo. But there's so much to learn.

Rhyme. That's true, but it's not just learning that's important. It's learning what to do with what you learn and learning why you learn things that matters.

Milo. I think I know what you mean, Princess. At least, I hope I do. *(The car is rolled forward and Milo climbs in.)* Goodbye! Goodbye! I'll be back someday! I will! Anyway, I'll try. *(As Milo drives, the set of the Land of Ignorance begins to move offstage.)*

Azaz. Goodbye! Always remember. Words! Words! Words!

Mathemagician. And numbers!

Azaz. Now, don't tell me you think numbers are as important as words?

Mathemagician. Is that so? Why I'll have you know . . . *(The set disappears, and Milo's room is seen onstage.)*

Milo. *(As he drives on.)* Oh, oh, I hope they don't start all over again. Because I don't think I'll have much time in the near future to help them out. *(The sound of loud ticking is heard. Milo finds himself in his room. He gets out of the car and looks around.)*

(D)

> WORDS
> TO
> KNOW
>
> **quest** (kwĕst) *n.* a journey in search of adventure or to perform a task

550

Teaching Options

✓ Assessment Standardized Test Practice

PREFIXES AND SUFFIXES

For some standardized tests, students will be asked to answer questions about words that show their knowledge of prefixes and suffixes. To provide students with some help in choosing the best answers, read aloud or write on the chalkboard the following:

The word <u>precautionary</u> means

A. a condition of roads

B. being filled with dangerous events

C. connected with taking care beforehand

D. without medicine

Lead students through the process of choosing the correct definition.

A is incorrect, because *caution* does not mean roads and *ary* does not mean condition. B is incorrect because *pre* does not mean dangerous, *caution* does not mean events, and *ary* does not mean full of. D is incorrect, too. *Caution* does not mean medicine, and *ary* does not mean without. C is the correct answer: *Pre* means beforehand, *caution* means to take care, and *ary* indicates being connected with.

Clock. Did someone mention time?

2 **Milo.** Boy, I must have been gone for an awful long time. I wonder what time it is. *(Looks at Clock.)* Five o'clock. I wonder what day it is. *(Looks at calendar.)* It's still today! I've only been gone for an hour! *(He continues to look at his calendar, and then begins to look at his books and toys and maps and chemistry set with great interest.)*

Clock. An hour. Sixty minutes. How long it really lasts depends on what you do with it. For some people, an hour seems to last forever. For others, just a moment, and so full of things to do.

Milo. *(Looks at clock.)* Six o'clock already?

Clock. In an instant. In a trice. Before you have time to blink. *(The stage goes black in less than no time at all.)* ❖

END

LITERARY LINK

All That Is Gold
by J. R. R. Tolkien

All that is gold does not glitter,

Not all those who wander are lost;

The old that is strong does not wither,

Deep roots are not reached by the frost.

From the ashes a fire shall be woken,

A light from the shadows shall spring;

Renewed shall be blade that was broken:

The crownless again shall be king.

THE PHANTOM TOLLBOOTH **551**

Customizing Instruction

Less Proficient Readers
Ask students:
• What couldn't Milo be told about his quest?
  Possible Response: It was impossible.

Students Acquiring English
1 Explain to students that there is a well-known expression, "Bah, humbug!" taken from a story by Charles Dickens.
2 Tell students that *Boy* expresses Milo's surprise, like the word "Wow" might.

Gifted and Talented
Have students consider whether Milo's adventure could have been a dream. They should support their views with evidence from the text. Ask students whether the theme would be altered if it were a dream.
Possible Response: Yes, it might be a dream. The length of time, the objects in Milo's room, which resemble the characters he meets, and the fact that he returns to his room support this view. The lessons he learned remain the same, even if the experience is a dream.

LITERARY LINK
J.R.R. Tolkien, who died in 1973, was the author of *The Hobbit* and *The Lord of the Rings* trilogy. This poem is taken from the trilogy's first book, *The Fellowship of the Ring*. It is spoken by Bilbo, who, like Milo, has returned from a successful quest from which he learned a great deal. Ask students to read the poem and compare the lessons that Bilbo and Milo have both learned.
Possible Responses: They have both learned that things are not always what they seem; that a defeat is not the end, it is only temporary; that imagination makes even the dullest things valuable.

**GUIDING STUDENT
RESPONSE**

Connect to the Literature

1. What Do You Think?
Answers will vary. Students should support their responses with selection details.

Comprehension Check
- Both take the same amount of time.
- He meets the Everpresent Wordsnatcher, the Terrible Trivium, the demon of Insincerity, and the Senses Taker.
- Using the letters that King Azaz gave him, Milo creates a doorway in the Castle-in-the-Air.

 Use Selection Quiz
Unit Four Resource Book, p. 43.

Think Critically

2. Possible Response: If Milo had known the quest was impossible, his expectations for success would have been very low. He might have been too discouraged to even try.

3. Possible Response: At first, Milo doesn't like school, and he gets bored easily, as do many children. He finds the situations that he encounters in the land beyond "weird" and is reluctant to try to rescue the princesses. His questions and reactions are much like the reader's would be in similar situations. The author made the main character realistic so that the reader could identify with him.

4. Possible Response: Milo becomes much more interested in learning and participating. In the beginning, he doesn't know what to do with himself and feels he has "plenty of time." He doesn't think he is very good at making words or solving problems. However, when Milo has reasons to work with words and numbers, he successfully does so. By the end of the play, Milo feels that time is too short to do everything that he wants to do.

5. Possible Responses: word market, the banquet, the armies fighting the demons

 Use **Reading and Critical Thinking Transparencies,** p. 4.

Connect to the Literature

1. What Do You Think?
Which scene or incident in the play did you find the most exciting? Why?

Comprehension Check
- Which route to Digitopolis is faster, 5 miles or 633,600 half inches?
- What creatures does Milo meet in the Land of Ignorance?
- How does Milo rescue the princesses?

Think Critically

2. How might Milo's quest have been affected if Azaz and the Mathemagician had told him ahead of time that it was impossible? Elaborate.

3. In what ways does Milo behave as an ordinary boy might? Why do you think the author chose to make the main character in this fantasy realistic?

4. How does Milo change over the course of the play?

 THINK ABOUT
- the questions he asks in Act Two
- his approach to problem-solving in Act Two
- what he says about learning at the end

5. **ACTIVE READING** **VISUALIZING** Share with a classmate the notes you made in your **READER'S NOTEBOOK.** Discuss the images you each pictured as you read the play. Which images do you think would make good scenes in a film of *The Phantom Tollbooth?*

Extend Interpretations

6. The Writer's Style Much of Norton Juster's word play is based on idioms. An idiom is a phrase whose meaning cannot be understood from the literal meanings of the words. "To eat your words" is an example of an idiom. It means to admit that you were wrong. How does Juster use idioms to add to the humor of the play?

7. Connect to Life On page 538, the Dodecahedron says it is a shame that Milo is "not good at problems," because "they're so very useful." Is mathematics useful in your life? When and how?

Literary Analysis

FANTASY A work of fiction that contains one or more fantastic, or unreal, elements is called a **fantasy.** The **setting** of a fantasy might be a totally imaginary world—like the "lands beyond" in *The Phantom Tollbooth*—or a realistic place where unrealistic things happen. The **plot** of a fantasy often involves magic or characters with extraordinary abilities, such as the Mathemagician in *The Phantom Tollbooth.* Although the play is a fantasy, the fanciful creatures that Milo meets often behave much the same way humans might.

An author's **purpose** in writing fantasy may be to entertain or to make a serious comment on reality. While Norton Juster's main purpose is to entertain, he also uses fantasy and humor to make a point about the importance of learning.

Activity In the center of a sheet of paper, draw one of the characters or settings from the play. Leave space around your drawing for labels. On the left side of the paper, label fantastic details of this creature or place, and on the right side, label the realistic details.

Extend Interpretations

6. The Writer's Style Milo encounters many idioms in the land beyond. They add humor because they often turn out to be literally true. For example, Milo really does have to eat his words at the banquet, and time really does fly when Tock helps Milo and the others escape from the demons.

7. Connect to Life Answers will vary.

Literary Analysis

Fantasy Have students choose a significant character, such as Humbug, or a major setting, such as Digitopolis. Students should review the text for realistic and fantastic details for their labels.

Writing Options

1. Plot Analysis To help you understand *The Phantom Tollbooth,* fill in a story map similar to the one below. Identify the play's main conflict, climax, and resolution. Then use your chart to write a summary of the plot. Place the summary in your **Working Portfolio.**

The Phantom Tollbooth	
Characters:	**Setting:**
Conflict:	
Event 1: *Milo receives a tollbooth.* **Event 2:** **Event 3:** (more key events)	
Climax:	**Resolution:**

2. Fantasy Word Play Write down three common idioms, such as "it's a piece of cake." (List ones that do not appear in *The Phantom Tollbooth.*) Then write a scene for a fantasy story using word play. Use the three idioms, along with homophone puns, riddles, and rhymes.

Activities & Explorations

1. Map of the Lands Beyond With a partner, create a map of Milo's journey. Label all the locations mentioned in the play, beginning with Milo's room. Beside each location, write a description of what happened there.

Display your map in the classroom. ~ **VIEWING AND REPRESENTING**

2. Dramatic Recording Make a dramatic recording of part or all of the play. Assign roles and find ways to produce sound effects. ~ **SPEAKING AND LISTENING**

Inquiry & Research

MATHEMATICS **SYSTEMS**

Research a counting system, such as Roman numerals or the numbers you use today. Find out about the origins of these symbols and how they have changed over time. Present your findings to the class using such visual aids as a poster or time line.

Vocabulary and Spelling

EXERCISE A: LEARNING AND REMEMBERING NEW WORDS Use a dictionary to look up the entire definition of each of the Words to Know. In your own words, paraphrase the definition in just one sentence. Then write another sentence that helps you remember the word in context.

The more imaginative your sentences are, the more they will help you remember new words. For example: *The talking tree gave me an* **admonishing** *look when I picked one of its apples.*

EXERCISE B: THE SUFFIX -*ANCE* The suffix -*ance* is often added to words to form nouns or adjectives. For example, the vocabulary word *ignorance* is formed by adding -*ance* to the word *ignore. Ignore* ends with a silent *e;* always drop a silent *e* before adding -*ance.*

1. Add -*ance* to the following words:
   guide   perform   insure
2. Find two other words in *The Phantom Tollbooth* that end with -*ance.* Write each word along with its root word.

Building Vocabulary

For an in-depth lesson on learning and remembering new words, see p. 491.

WORDS TO KNOW	acknowledge admonishing ascend	dejectedly deliberately destination	fanfare ignorance leisurely	mourn pantomime perish	petty quest vigorously

Mini Lesson Spelling

THE SUFFIX -*ANCE*

Instruction Tell students that the suffix -*ance* is commonly added to complete words or roots to form nouns. Words that end in silent *e* usually drop the *e* if a suffix beginning with a vowel is added. Therefore, most words will drop the final *e* when the suffix -*ance* is added. Display the example below:

ignore + ance = ignorance

Exercise Have students combine the word and the suffix and write the new word.

1. annoy + ance =

2. endure + ance =
3. accept + ance =
4. repent + ance =
5. observe + ance =

ANSWERS: *1. annoyance 2. endurance 3. acceptance 4. repentance 5. observance*

Application Have students use each word in an original sentence.

 Use **Unit Four Resource Book,** p. 42 for additional practice.

Writing Options

1. Plot Analysis Remind students that a summary includes the main ideas. **To make this assignment easier,** have students divide into groups, with each group working on a story map for one scene.

2. Fantasy Word Play To get students started on this assignment, have them brainstorm figures of speech as a class. Students should map out their scene and devise their puns ahead of time. **To adapt this activity for visual learners,** have them create a comic strip.

Use **Reading and Critical Thinking Transparencies,** p. 13, for additional support.

Activities & Explorations

1. Map of the Lands Beyond To get students started on this assignment, you may wish to show them an edition of the novel that includes a map. **To extend this assignment,** have students tape record a travelogue to accompany their map.

2. Dramatic Recording To get students started on this assignment, have them choose part of a scene with lively dialogue and distinguishing sound effects. They should experiment with sound effects. **To adapt this assignment for kinesthetic learners,** have students act out a scene and videotape it.

Use **Communications Transparencies and Copymasters,** p. 12, for additional support.

Inquiry & Research

Systems Students may find that the appendices of a dictionary are a good starting point. Some students may wish to generate slides on the computer for their presentation.

Use **Writing Transparencies,** p. 45, for additional support.

Vocabulary and Spelling

EXERCISE A
Accept reasonable responses.
EXERCISE B
1. guidance; performance; insurance
2. Possible responses include:

appearance	root: appear
assistance	root: assist
importance	root: import
dissonance	root: dissonant

Grammar in Context: Pinpointing with Prepositions

Notice how the settings in *The Phantom Tollbooth* are described. What words or phrases provide the details?

> Milo's bedroom—with <u>shelves, pennants, pictures</u> on <u>the wall</u>. . . .
> Digitopolis—a dark, glittering place without <u>trees or greenery</u>. . . .

The words shown in red are **prepositions,** words that help show the relationship between two words. In each example above, the underlined words are the **object of a preposition.** Together, the preposition and its object form a **prepositional phrase,** which works as an **adjective** to describe a noun or a pronoun.

A prepositional phrase can also work as an **adverb** to clarify an adjective or an adverb, or to pinpoint the action of a verb. Look at the adverb phrase in the following stage direction:

(His alarm rings **in fury**.)

The phrase "in fury" modifies the verb *rings.*

WRITING EXERCISE Expand each setting or stage direction by completing the prepositional phrase.

Example: *Original* The Doldrums—A gloomy land of . . .

Rewritten The Doldrums—A gloomy land of mist and shadow

1. Castle in the Air—A tower surrounded by . . .
2. **Dischord** (*Listens through . . .*).
3. The Marketplace—A mixture of . . .

Connect to the Literature Read some of the stage directions in *The Phantom Tollbooth.* Find and list three prepositional phrases, telling whether each phrase is used as an adjective or an adverb.

"In many ways I came to writing by accident."

Norton Juster
born 1929

From the City to the Country Norton Juster grew up in Brooklyn, New York. He studied architecture at the University of Pennsylvania and city planning at the University of Liverpool in England. After teaching at the Pratt Institute and practicing architecture in New York City, Juster and his family moved to a farm in western Massachusetts. There he is a partner in an architecture firm and teaches architectural design at Hampshire College.

Author and Architect Juster considers himself primarily an architect rather than a writer, but finds that the two vocations complement each other. He began writing *The Phantom Tollbooth,* his first book, in 1959 as a way to relax from the pressures of an architecture project. He has written several other books for children, including *Alberic the Wise* and *Silly as Knees, Busy as Bees: An Astounding Assortment of Similes,* as well as books for adults.

AUTHOR ACTIVITY
Play vs. Novel Find a copy of the novel *The Phantom Tollbooth,* on which the play is based. Locate a scene in the novel that was not included in the play. Write a brief summary of the scene and share it with the class.

Grammar in Context

WRITING EXERCISE
Possible Responses:
1. Castle in the Air – A tower surrounded by jagged rocks
2. Dischord (Listens through a stethoscope)
3. The Marketplace – A mixture of colors and sounds

CONNECT TO THE LITERATURE
Possible Response: at Tock (adverb), in surprise (adverb), on a pillow (adjective)

Author Activity

Play vs. Novel To extend this activity, assign each student a scene from the novel that was not in the play. Have students present their summaries in the order in which the scenes occur. **To make this assignment more challenging,** have students compare and contrast elements of the novel and the play and present their findings to the class.

Teaching Options Mini Lesson Grammar

PUNCTUATING PREPOSITIONAL PHRASES
Instruction Tell students that most prepositional phrases are not set off by commas. However, introductory phrases and phrases that break the flow of thought in a sentence must be set off by commas. Display the following sentence: At the end of his quest, Milo was surprised at his accomplishments.

Exercise Ask students to rewrite each of the sentences with the correct punctuation.
1. Throughout the journey Milo kept up his hopes. *(journey,)*
2. Reason inside the castle never doubted the success of the rescuers. *(, inside the castle,)*

3. With the magic pencil Milo and his friends escaped the Terrible Trivium's trap. *(pencil,)*
4. After the subtraction stew they were hungrier than ever. *(stew,)*

 Use **Unit Four Resource Book,** p. 41.
Use **Grammar Transparencies and Copymasters,** p. 126.

> Language Network
> Use McDougal Littell's *Language Network,* Chapter 9, for more practice in punctuating prepositional phrases.

The Walrus and the Carpenter

Poetry by LEWIS CARROLL

Fairy Lullaby

from A Midsummer Night's Dream

Song by WILLIAM SHAKESPEARE

OVERVIEW

This selection appears in Spanish in the **Spanish Study Guide**.

Objectives

1. understand and appreciate a **narrative poem and a song** (Literary Analysis)
2. understand author's use of **realistic and fantastic details** (Literary Analysis)
3. use **visualizing** to help understand realistic and fantastic details. **(Active Reading)**

Summary

Lewis Carroll's poem tells the tale of a walrus and a carpenter who invite a group of oysters to join them for a walk on a sunny beach in the middle of the night. The walk turns out to be a cruel trick, as every one of the oysters gets eaten. In "Fairy Lullaby," a group of fairies attends the fairy queen. Their soothing song is used to protect the queen from a variety of creepy creatures.

Thematic Link

Both selections take the reader into worlds that live only in the imagination. A land where walruses talk to oysters? One with tiny fairy creatures? Why not? Use your imagination! These writers did.

5-Minute Warm-Up

Daily Language SkillBuilder

Have students **proofread** the display sentences on page 441j and write them correctly. The sentences also appear on Transparency 17 of **Grammar Transparencies and Copymasters.**

Connect to Your Life

Tricky Tales Have you ever had a trick played on you, or have you ever read a story about someone who was tricked? What happened?

This illustration of Alice was created in 1865 by Sir John Tenniel, the first and most famous illustrator of *Alice's Adventures in Wonderland.*

Build Background

Fantasy in Poem and Song "The Walrus and the Carpenter" and "Fairy Lullaby" are examples of fantasy written in verse. Lewis Carroll's poem appears in *Through the Looking Glass,* the sequel to his famous fantasy novel *Alice's Adventures in Wonderland.* In England in the 1800s, when Carroll lived, schoolchildren were often asked to memorize long, dull poems meant to teach proper behavior. "The Walrus and the Carpenter" makes fun of this approach to education.

"Fairy Lullaby" appears in William Shakespeare's play *A Midsummer Night's Dream,* which was written around 1595. In this part of the play, Oberon, the king of the fairies, decides to play a trick on Titania, his queen. While Titania sleeps, Oberon plans to put drops in her eyes that will make her fall in love with the first thing she sees when she awakes. As Titania prepares for bed, her fairy attendants sing "Fairy Lullaby" to protect her from harm as she sleeps.

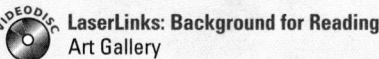

LaserLinks: Background for Reading Art Gallery

Focus Your Reading

LITERARY ANALYSIS **REALISTIC AND FANTASTIC DETAILS** These two poems are works of **fantasy.** A fantasy contains at least one fantastic, or unreal, element. In "The Walrus and the Carpenter," some of the **characters** are fantastic. The Walrus and the Oysters have the ability to speak, and the Oysters walk, as if they had legs. At the same time, some elements of the poem are realistic, such as the **setting** and the character of the Carpenter. As you read the poems, look for other examples of **realistic and fantastic details.**

ACTIVE READING **VISUALIZING** When you **visualize** something, you use your imagination to form a picture of it in your mind. To appreciate the realistic and fantastic details in the two poems, try to visualize the **setting** and the **characters.**

READER'S NOTEBOOK As you read the poems, pay attention to the realistic and fantastic details that help you visualize. Use a chart like the one shown here to record the details that you notice.

	Realistic Details	Fantastic Details
"The Walrus and the Carpenter"	sandy shore	sun at midnight
"Fairy Lullaby"		

LESSON RESOURCES

UNIT FOUR RESOURCE BOOK, pp. 44–45

ASSESSMENT
Formal Assessment, p. 91–92
Teacher's Guide to Assessment and Portfolio Use
Test Generator

SKILLS TRANSPARENCIES AND COPYMASTERS
Reading and Critical Thinking
• Visualizing, TR 4 (for Thinking Through the Literature, p. 561)
Vocabulary
• Using Antonyms, CM 57 (for Mini Lesson, p. 559)
Communications
• Dramatic Reading, TR 12 (for Mini Lesson, p. 558)

INTEGRATED TECHNOLOGY
Audio Library
LaserLinks
• Art Gallery; Biographical Connection. See **Teacher's SourceBook,** p. 42

Visit our website:
www.mcdougallittell.com

Literary Analysis

REALISTIC AND FANTASTIC DETAILS

Ask students to identify two realistic details and two fantastic details.

Possible Response: Two realistic details: "The sea was wet," and "The sands were dry as dry." Two fantastic details are the sun shining in the middle of the night and the moon thinking.

Use **Unit Four Resource Book,** p. 45 for more practice.

Active Reading VISUALIZING

Have students describe the mental images they picture as they read.

Possible Response: I imagine a beautiful beach, but the lighting is strange because the moon and the sun are both out. The Walrus and the Carpenter are walking side by side. The walrus is walking on his back flipper.

Use **Unit Four Resource Book,** p. 44 for more practice. Use **Reading and Critical Thinking Transparencies,** p. 4, for additional support.

ACTIVE READING

A VISUALIZE Students might say that the beach is realistic but the talking walrus and the talking moon are fantasy.

B CLARIFY The Walrus wants no more than four, so that he and the Carpenter can each hold two.

C QUESTION Perhaps he's afraid. He knows he shouldn't walk with strangers.

D VISUALIZE Students might say that the Oysters seem like eager toddlers; "eager," "hopping," "scrambling"

The
Walrus and the
Carpenter
by Lewis Carroll

The sun was shining on the sea,
 Shining with all his might:
He did his very best to make
 The billows smooth and bright—
5 And this was odd, because it was
 The middle of the night.

The moon was shining sulkily,
 Because she thought the sun
Had got no business to be there
10 After the day was done—
"It's very rude of him," she said,
 "To come and spoil the fun!"

The sea was wet as wet could be,
 The sands were dry as dry.
15 You could not see a cloud because
 No cloud was in the sky:
No birds were flying overhead—
 There were no birds to fly.

The Walrus and the Carpenter
20 Were walking close at hand:
They wept like anything to see
 Such quantities of sand:
"If this were only cleared away,"
 They said, "it *would* be grand!"

GUIDE FOR READING

4 billows: large waves.

7 sulkily (sŭl′kə-lē): in a gloomy, pouting way.

13–24 Picture the scene that Carroll describes. What parts are realistic? What parts are fantastic?

Teaching Options

BLOCK SCHEDULING: MANAGING TIME

If your schedule requires that you cover the lesson objectives in a shorter time, use . . .
- Preparing to Read, p. 555
- Thinking Through the Literature, p. 561

If you would like to take advantage of longer class time, use . . .
- TE Teaching Options: Standardized Test Practice, p.557; Speaking and Listening, p. 558; Vocabulary Strategy, p. 559; Grammar, p. 562
- Choices & Challenges, p. 562

25 "If seven maids with seven mops
    Swept it for half a year,
Do you suppose," the Walrus said,
    "That they could get it clear?"
"I doubt it," said the Carpenter,
30   And shed a bitter tear.

"O Oysters, come and walk with us!"
    The Walrus did beseech.
"A pleasant walk, a pleasant talk,
    Along the briny beach:
35 We cannot do with more than four,
    To give a hand to each."

The eldest Oyster looked at him,
    But never a word he said:
The eldest Oyster winked his eye,
40   And shook his heavy head—
Meaning to say he did not choose
    To leave the oyster-bed.

But four young Oysters hurried up,
    All eager for the treat:
45 Their coats were brushed, their faces washed,
    Their shoes were clean and neat—
And this was odd, because, you know,
    They hadn't any feet.

Four other Oysters followed them,
50   And yet another four;
And thick and fast they came at last,
    And more, and more, and more—
All hopping through the frothy waves,
    And scrambling to the shore.

35–36 Why does the Walrus say he wants only four Oysters to walk with him and the Carpenter?

37–42 Why do you think the eldest Oyster doesn't want to join the Walrus and the Carpenter? **C**

51–54 What images does Carroll's description of the Oysters bring to your mind? What words in this description make it especially vivid? **D**

THE WALRUS AND THE CARPENTER   **557**

Literary Analysis: IMAGERY

Ask students to read page 558 and name an image that they find especially easy to visualize, or create a mental image of, and explain why.

Possible Response: I think the image of the Oysters turning blue is easy to visualize, because they're frightened that they're about to be eaten. In literature, and in real life, creatures and people feeling fearful become cold, turn bluish, and shiver. Also colors are easy to visualize.

ACTIVE READING

A **VISUALIZE** Students might say they see slimy creatures scurrying or slithering over the forest floor, possibly a green snake, an orange newt, a pink worm.

55   The Walrus and the Carpenter
     Walked on a mile or so,
  And then they rested on a rock
     Conveniently low:
  And all the little Oysters stood
60   And waited in a row.

  "The time has come," the Walrus said,
     "To talk of many things:
  Of shoes—and ships—and sealing-wax—
     Of cabbages—and kings—
65   And why the sea is boiling hot—
     And whether pigs have wings."

  "But wait a bit," the Oysters cried,
     "Before we have our chat;
  For some of us are out of breath,
70   And all of us are fat!"
  "No hurry!" said the Carpenter.
     They thanked him much for that.

  "A loaf of bread," the Walrus said,
     "Is what we chiefly need:
75   Pepper and vinegar besides
     Are very good indeed—
  Now, if you're ready, Oysters dear,
     We can begin to feed."

  "But not on us!" the Oysters cried,
80   Turning a little blue.
  "After such kindness, that would be
     A dismal thing to do!"
  "The night is fine," the Walrus said.
     "Do you admire the view?

85   "It was so kind of you to come!
     And you are very nice!"
  The Carpenter said nothing but
     "Cut us another slice.
  I wish you were not quite so deaf—
90   I've had to ask you twice!"

  "It seems a shame," the Walrus said,
     "To play them such a trick.
  After we've brought them out so far,
     And made them trot so quick!"
95   The Carpenter said nothing but
     "The butter's spread too thick!"

  "I weep for you," the Walrus said:
     "I deeply sympathize."
  With sobs and tears he sorted out
100   Those of the largest size,
  Holding his pocket-handkerchief
     Before his streaming eyes.

  "O Oysters," said the Carpenter,
     "You've had a pleasant run!
105   Shall we be trotting home again?"
     But answer came there none—
  And this was scarcely odd, because
     They'd eaten every one.

Teaching Options

Speaking and Listening

RECITE A NARRATIVE POEM ALOUD

Prepare Ask students to prepare an oral reading of "The Walrus and the Carpenter."
Encourage them to work in groups of four. One student reads the narrative, one reads the part of the Walrus, one the part of the Carpenter, and one the part of the Oysters.

Suggest that students switch roles to see how it feels to read a different part. Encourage any interested students to read the whole poem by themselves.

Tell students to try out various rates, volumes, pitches, and tones of voice as they practice to ensure using the most effective ones.

Present Have students present their readings to the class. After each reading, have students discuss what they liked about each reading.

BLOCK SCHEDULING This activity is particularly well suited for longer class periods.

Use **Communications Transparencies and Copymasters,** p. 12, for additional support.

Fairy Lullaby

from A Midsummer Night's Dream
by William Shakespeare

First Fairy. You spotted snakes with double tongue,
           Thorny hedgehogs, be not seen,
           Newts and blind-worms, do not wrong,
           Come not near our fairy queen.

5 **Chorus.** Philomele, with melody,
           Sing in our sweet lullaby,
           Lulla, lulla, lullaby, lulla, lulla, lullaby.
           Never harm,
           Nor spell, nor charm,
10   Come our lovely lady nigh.
           So good night, with lullaby.

GUIDE FOR READING

1–3 Close your eyes and picture the animals described in the song. What do you see? **A**

5 Philomele (fĭl'ə-mē'lə): in Greek mythology, a princess from Athens who was turned into a nightingale.

Customizing Instruction

Less Proficient Readers
Some of the words in "Fairy Lullaby" may look strange to students. Tell students that *nigh* means "nearby," *hence* means "away from here," and *aloof* means "distant physically or emotionally."

Students Acquiring English
Explain that because this poem was written more than 350 years ago, the language and the syntax, or word order, are different from the way we speak today. Tell students to focus on the meaning of the poem and not to worry about the unusual word order. You might also explain archaic or unfamiliar words, such as those listed above.

FAIRY LULLABY **559**

 Vocabulary Strategy

USING ANTONYMS

Instruction Tell students that antonyms are words with opposite meanings. Explain that knowing antonyms can help students figure out the meaning of a confusing sentence, since antonyms can provide contrasting context clues.

Dictionaries of synonyms and antonyms, as well as most thesauruses, can help students find antonyms for a word.

Exercises Provide students with the following series of words, and ask them to choose an antonym for the word in bold type.

1. **sulk:** happy rejoice sad silk *(rejoice)*
2. **bitter:** sour sweet cruel bad *(sweet)*
3. **dismal:** joyous dim sad deep *(joyous)*
4. **admire:** like admit dislike love *(dislike)*

 Use **Vocabulary Transparencies and Copymasters,** p. 57.

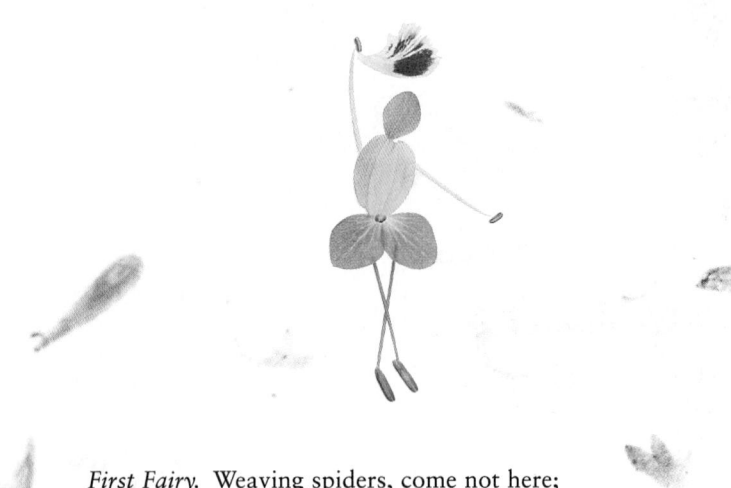

Reading and Analyzing

Literary Analysis: POETIC LANGUAGE

Tell students to look for poetic language as they read "Fairy Lullaby." Ask them to cite two examples. Then ask them to think about how this language sounds and how it makes them feel.

Possible Response: One example of poetic language is "Come our lovely lady nigh." Another example is the last two lines of the poem, "Hence, away! now all is well. One aloof stand sentinel." I think this language sounds old-fashioned, but beautiful. It makes me feel as if I'm living long ago.

Reading Skills and Strategies: CLARIFY

Ask students whether they understood the meaning of the last line—"Once aloof stand sentinel." Ask them how they figured it out.

Possible Response: I wasn't sure what the word *sentinel* meant, so I looked it up in the dictionary. Once I knew that it meant "to guard," I understood the line.

ACTIVE READING

A **EVALUATE** The rhythm and rhyme create a soothing, musical, lulling effect.

First Fairy. Weaving spiders, come not here;
  Hence, you long-legg'd spinners, hence!
  Beetles black, approach not near;
15 Worm nor snail, do no offense.

Chorus. Philomele, with melody,
  Sing in our sweet lullaby,
  Lulla, lulla, lullaby, lulla, lulla, lullaby.
  Never harm,
20 Nor spell, nor charm,
  Come our lovely lady nigh.
  So good night, with lullaby.

Second Fairy (spoken). Hence, away! now all is well.
  One aloof stand sentinel.

16–22 What effect does Shakespeare create through repetition and rhyme?

Thinking through the LITERATURE

Connect to the Literature

1. What Do You Think?
What was your reaction to the song? Explain.

Comprehension Check
- Who are the fairies trying to protect?
- What dangers do they fear?

Think Critically

2. Why do the fairies list particular animals? What do you think these creatures have in common?

3. Do you think that Carroll intends for you to feel sorry for the Oysters in "The Walrus and the Carpenter"? Support your answer.

4. "The Walrus and the Carpenter" and "Fairy Lullaby" are both fantasies, but they create very different effects. How would you describe the mood of the poem and the song?

THINK ABOUT
- sound devices
- word choice
- word play

5. **ACTIVE READING** **VISUALIZING** Look over the chart you made in your READER'S NOTEBOOK. With a partner, discuss which images in "The Walrus and the Carpenter" and "Fairy Lullaby" you enjoyed the most. Which did you respond to more strongly, realistic details or fantastic details? Why?

Extend Interpretations

6. **COMPARING TEXTS** Compare and contrast the humor in "The Walrus and the Carpenter" with the humor in *The Phantom Tollbooth* (page 512). What similarities do you see between the two works?

7. **Connect to Life** What kind of tricks do you think are mean? Are there tricks that you think are acceptable to play on people? Elaborate.

Literary Analysis

REALISTIC AND FANTASTIC DETAILS

"The Walrus and the Carpenter" and "Fairy Lullaby" are both examples of **fantasy.** Each contains fantastic, or unreal, elements. A fantasy may have a totally imaginary setting, or the setting may be a realistic place where impossible things happen, as in these two works.

As in most fantasies, this poem and song blend realistic **details,** with imaginary ones. For example, the animals mentioned in Shakespeare's song actually exist. The characters singing the song, however, are fairies—imaginary beings.

Paired Activity For each fantastic detail in "The Walrus and the Carpenter," suggest a realistic alternative. For example, what if the main characters were not a walrus and a carpenter, but a pair of chefs?

With a partner, discuss how the poem would be different if these details were realistic. How would these changes affect the poem's humor?

REVIEW **NARRATIVE POETRY**

A poem that tells a story is called a **narrative poem.** Like stories, narrative poems have characters, settings, plots, and sometimes dialogue. "The Walrus and the Carpenter" is an example of a narrative poem.

Extend Interpretations

6. Comparing Texts Possible Response: The humor in the two selections is similar. Both works contain fantastic characters, such as talking animals. Both works feature characters who play tricks on other characters. For example, in the "The Walrus and the Carpenter," the Walrus invites the Oysters to go for a walk, and then he and the Carpenter eat them. In "The Phantom Tollbooth," Milo orders a light snack at the banquet, and he is served actual light on a plate. In the Land of Ignorance, Milo meets the Everpresent Wordsnatcher, who deliberately misunderstands everything that Milo says.

7. Connect to Life Responses will vary.

Writing Options

1. Narrative Poem Student responses should be in the form of a narrative poem. Their poems should contain a story, and they should have several elements that are found in poetry, such as rhythm, rhyme, repetition, figurative language, and vivid imagery.

 Use **Writing Transparencies,** p. 17, for additional support.

2. Eloquent Speech Students' speeches should be clear and well-written. They should have strong arguments that would dissuade the Walrus and the Carpenter from eating the Oyster.

 Use **Writing Transparencies,** p. 15, for additional support.

Activities & Explorations

1. Poem Illustrations Students' drawings should depict key parts of the poem and should include humorous details mentioned in the poem.

2. Dramatic Reading Encourage students to work in small groups as they prepare the dramatic reading.

 Use **Communications Transparencies and Copymasters,** p. 12, for additional support.

Inquiry & Research

Comparing Performances Tell students to pay close attention to details such as sets, costumes, and the individual performances of the actors. Have them carefully consider why they prefer one performance over another.

 Use **Communications Transparencies and Copymasters,** p. 5, for additional support.

More About the Authors

In Lewis Carroll's *Through the Looking Glass,* everything seems backward. For example, Alice must walk away from a place in order to reach it and must run fast in order to remain where she is!

William Shakespeare is probably the English language's most quoted writer. In his plays and poetry, Shakespeare expressed deep thoughts and feelings in beautiful and powerful words. His mastery of the technical aspects of poetry—rhythm, image, metaphor—is considered unrivaled.

Choices & CHALLENGES

Writing Options

1. Narrative Poem Think of a story you would like to tell, and write a narrative poem of your own. Place the poem in your **Working Portfolio.**

2. Eloquent Speech Suppose that one of the Oysters wants to avoid being eaten. Help the Oyster by writing an eloquent speech to persuade the Walrus and the Carpenter to spare him or her.

Writing Handbook
See p. R39: Persuasive Writing.

Activities & Explorations

1. Poem Illustrations Create a series of drawings that illustrate the events of "The Walrus and the Carpenter." Try to reveal the poem's humor. ~ **ART**

2. Dramatic Reading Read a modern retelling of *A Midsummer Night's Dream,* such as Bruce Coville's illustrated version or Charles and Mary Lamb's *Tales from Shakespeare.* Present a dramatic reading of one scene.
~ **SPEAKING AND LISTENING**

Inquiry & Research

Comparing Performances Your school library or a public library may have performances of *Through the Looking Glass* and *A Midsummer Night's Dream* on videotape. Choose either work and view at least two different performances of it. Compare interpretations of "The Walrus and the Carpenter" or "Fairy Lullaby" in the different productions. Which performance do you prefer? Why?

"All the world's a stage, And all the men and women merely players: . . ."

William Shakespeare
1564–1616

Actor, Playwright, Poet William Shakespeare is probably the best-known English writer of all time. The son of a businessman, Shakespeare grew up in Stratford-upon-Avon, a town to which he returned periodically throughout his life. As a young man, he acted on the London stage and helped found the famous theater, the Globe. By his late twenties, Shakespeare had begun to write plays. He is equally famous for his comedies, such as *A Midsummer Night's Dream,* and his tragedies, like *Hamlet* and *Macbeth.* Shakespeare is also well-known for his poetry, especially his sonnets.

"Curiouser and curiouser!"

Lewis Carroll
1832–1898

Fun and Games Lewis Carroll was the pen name of the writer and mathematician Charles Lutwidge Dodgson. Although very intelligent, he was shy as a child and stammered when he spoke to adults. Throughout his life, Dodgson felt more comfortable around children and enjoyed making up puzzles and stories to entertain them. He invented "Alice's Adventures Underground" to amuse a ten-year-old friend, Alice Liddell. The story was published in 1865 as *Alice's Adventures in Wonderland.*

 LaserLinks: Background for Reading
Biographical Connection

Teaching Options

Mini Lesson ## Grammar

PARTS OF SPEECH

Instruction Review the various parts of speech—noun, pronoun, verb, adjective, adverb, preposition, and conjunction. Explain how each one functions within a sentence.

Exercises Write the following sentences on the chalkboard. Ask students to identify the parts of speech in each sentence.

1. Lewis Carroll loved to write silly, nonsensical poems. *(n, v, prep, v, adj, adj, n)*
2. What kind of poetry do you like to write? *(pron, adj, prep, n, v, pron, v, prep, v)*
3. The eldest Oyster was wise not to leave the oyster bed. *(art, adj, n, v, adj, adv, prep, v, art, adj, n)*
4. What did you think the Walrus was going to do with bread, pepper, and vinegar? *(pron, v, pron, v, art, n, v, v, prep, v, prep, n, n, conj, n)*

 Use **Grammar Transparencies and Copymasters,** p. 51.

Use McDougal Littell's **Language Network,** Chapter 6, for more practice in identifying parts of speech.

PREPARING to *Read*

Three Limericks

Poetry by EDWARD LEAR, OGDEN NASH,
and JACK PRELUTSKY

Connect to Your Life

Ever Get the Giggles? You probably can think of many times when something made you smile or chuckle or even laugh out loud. Maybe you were riding a roller coaster, watching a cartoon, or simply making a silly face. What makes you laugh? Try describing it in one sentence. Now try describing it in two lines that rhyme.

Build Background

CONNECT TO HISTORY The limerick is a form of poetry that first appeared in England in the early 1800s. Limericks were made popular by Edward Lear, who said he first saw the limerick form used in a nursery rhyme. Lear paired his poetry with his own humorous illustrations, as shown below, and published them in *A Book of Nonsense* in 1846.

Limericks didn't come to be called by that name until well after Lear's time. The name may have come from a party game in which people recited the poems aloud, pausing after each verse to insert this chorus: "We'll all come up, come up to Limerick." (The chorus came from a song Irish soldiers used to sing about a town in Ireland.) In the United States, the game evolved into a contest in which people made up their own limericks.

There was an Old Man who said, "Hush! I perceive a young bird in this bush!"
When they said, "Is it small?" he replied, "Not at all!
It is four times as big as the bush!"

Focus Your Reading

LITERARY ANALYSIS **POETIC FORM: LIMERICK**
Limericks are a form of nonsense verse. A typical limerick has five lines and follows the **rhyme scheme** *aabba*. Like other types of poetry, limericks often are meant to be read aloud.

ACTIVE READING **READING ALOUD** Reading aloud makes it easier to hear the careful arrangement of sounds and syllables in a limerick. To enjoy these poems fully, read them aloud, first to yourself and then to a partner. As you read, don't let yourself be hurried by the sing-song rhythm. Reading at a normal pace often better conveys the poem's humor.

READER'S NOTEBOOK As you read these poems, jot down words or lines that you find funny. Then note examples of the poems' sound devices, such as rhythm, rhyme, and repetition.

Literary Analysis

POETIC FORM: LIMERICK

In addition to the AABBA rhyme scheme, a limerick has other distinguishing features and structural requirements. Each line has a definite number of stressed syllables. Ask students to count the stressed syllables in each line to figure out the pattern.

Possible Response: The lines that rhyme have the same number of stressed syllables. For example, in Ogden Nash's limerick, lines 1, 2, and 5 all have three stressed syllables. Lines 3 and 4 contain two stressed syllables apiece.

Use **Unit Four Resource Book,** p. 47 for more practice.

Use **Literary Analysis Transparencies,** p. 17 for additional support.

Active Reading   READING ALOUD

After partners read the limericks aloud, have them discuss how it felt. Ask them whether they knew which words to stress the first time they read, and whether their reading improved with each successive try.

Possible Response: The first time I read the limericks aloud, I wasn't sure which words to emphasize. With practice, though, I got to know the poems and I understood where to place the stress.

Use **Unit Four Resource Book,** p. 46 for more practice.

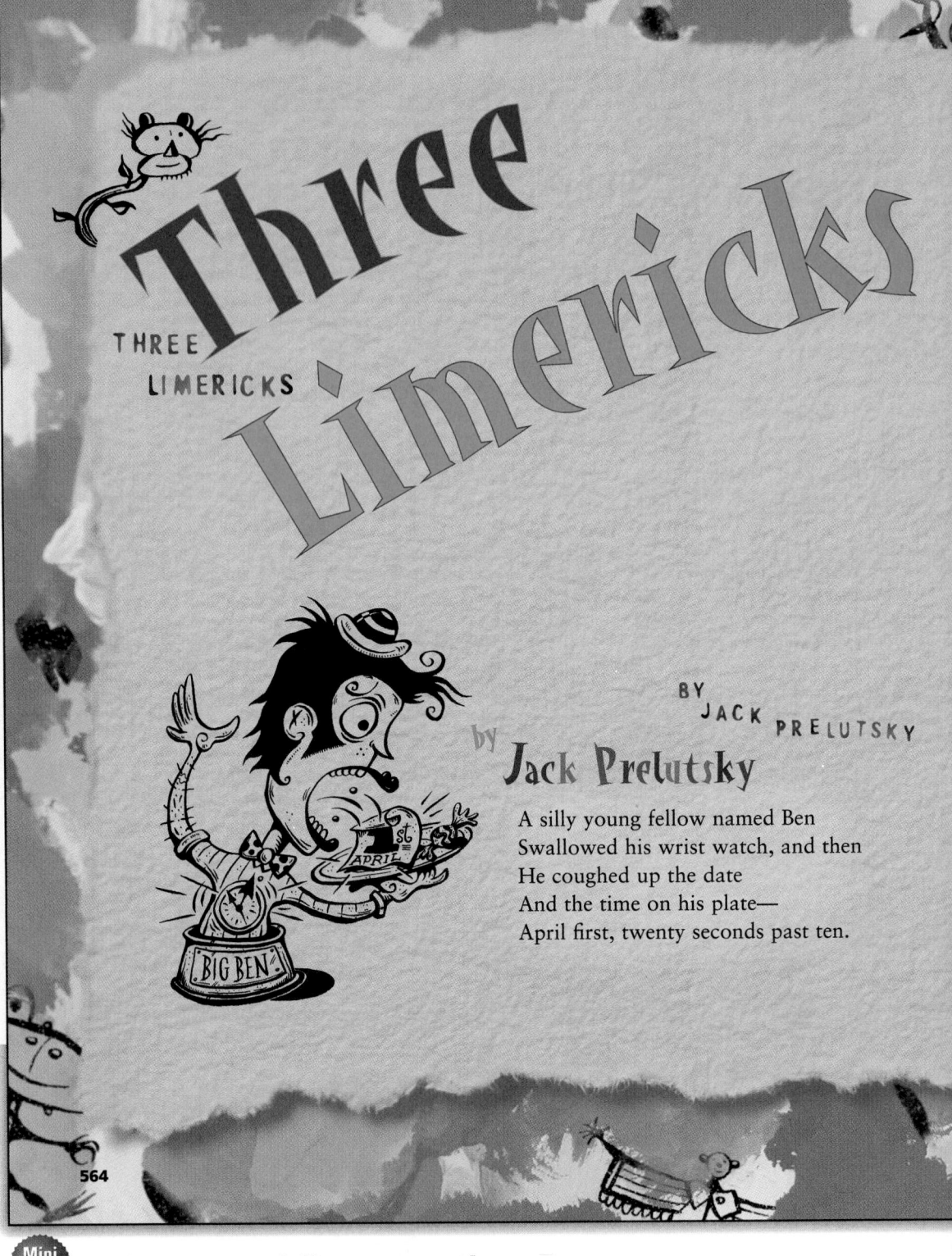

Three Limericks

THREE LIMERICKS

BY JACK PRELUTSKY

by Jack Prelutsky

A silly young fellow named Ben
Swallowed his wrist watch, and then
He coughed up the date
And the time on his plate—
April first, twenty seconds past ten.

564

Teaching Options

Mini Lesson **Viewing and Representing**

VIEW AND CREATE YOUR OWN ILLUSTRATIONS

Instruction Point out that the illustrations provided are all humorous character sketches. The artist has started with a human face and then altered it to fit the limerick.

Application Tell students to make their own pen and ink illustrations for the three limericks on pages 564–565. They should start with a pencil sketch, working into it with the eraser and the pencil until it becomes very exaggerated and expressive. Then have them use black felt-tipped pens to finish the final cartoon drawing. When the illustrations are complete, hang them up around the classroom. Invite volunteers to discuss their artwork.

BY OGDEN NASH

by
Ogden Nash

A bugler named Dougal MacDougal
Found ingenious ways to be frugal.
He learned how to sneeze
In various keys,
Thus saving the price of a bugle.

BY
EDWARD
LEAR

by
Edward Lear

There was an old man with a beard,
Who said, "It is just as I feared!—
Two owls and a hen, four larks and a wren,
Have all built their nests in my beard!"

✓ **Assessment Standardized Test Practice**

GUIDING STUDENT RESPONSE

Connect to the Literature

1. **What Do You Think?**
Answers will vary but should be clearly explained. Most students will say that the limericks are funny in a silly sort of way.

Think Critically

2. A number of birds make nests in the old man's beard.
3. Possible Response: Dougal McDougal is a cheapskate and is willing to do anything to save money. But he is also tricky and clever, and especially talented. he is probably a happy-go-lucky guy.
4. Possible Response: A boy with a wristwatch is realistic, but swallowing it is less so. Coughing up the time and date is complete fantasy. A musician being frugal could be realistic, but playing music by sneezing is fantastic. An old man with a long beard is common, but birds nesting in a beard is impossible.
5. Students' answers will vary.

Literary Analysis

Limericks Students' evaluations of the three limericks should be detailed and include an examination of rhythm, rhyme, and humor.

Use **Literary Analysis Transparencies,** p. 17.

Connect to the Literature

1. **What Do You Think?** Did you find these poems funny? Why or why not?

Think Critically

2. Explain what happens to the old man in Edward Lear's poem.

3. What kind of a person is Dougal MacDougal?

   THINK ABOUT { • what the word *frugal* means
   • what Dougal teaches himself, and why

4. In each poem, decide which details are realistic and which are fantastic. Which details came as a complete surprise to you?

5. **ACTIVE READING** **READING ALOUD** Look back at the words and lines you recorded in your **READER'S NOTEBOOK.** Then talk with a classmate about the parts of the poems each of you found to be funniest. Compare different ways of reading the poems to convey their humor.

Extend Interpretations

6. **COMPARING TEXTS** Compare and contrast the three limericks with "The Walrus and the Carpenter" (page 555). Consider structure, rhyme scheme, and rhythm. Also think about the humor in the poems.

7. **Connect to Life** Think back to the Connect to Your Life discussion on page 563. After reading these poems, can you add limericks to the list of things that make you laugh? Use details to explain why or why not.

Literary Analysis

LIMERICKS Limericks are humorous nonsense poems—the ideas in them may not make any sense. Limericks usually contain five lines, have a sing-song **rhythm,** and **rhyme.** The **rhyme scheme** or pattern consists of two **rhyming couplets** (pairs of lines that end with rhyming words) and a fifth line that rhymes with the first couplet. As you read, consider the way in which rhythm and rhyme add to the humor of these poems.

REVIEW **RHYTHM** **Rhythm** is the pattern of stressed and unstressed syllables in a poem. It guides your voice to emphasize certain words and sounds. In these poems, the rhythm has a musical, sing-song quality.

Paired Activity Working with a partner, study each limerick. Identify parts of the poem that are nonsense. Examine the rhyme scheme to identify the rhyming words. When you are finished, rate each poem for **humor, rhythm,** and **rhyme.** Which limerick works best? Why?

Extend Interpretations

6. **Comparing Texts** Possible Response: Both the limericks and "The Walrus and the Carpenter" use humor and fantasy. The limericks are very short and fit the standard limerick form and rhyme scheme. "Walrus" is a longer poem with several stanzas of rhyming lines.

7. **Connect to Life** Answers will vary, but students should be able to explain their opinions.

Writing Options

1. Limerick Retelling Retell in your own words the story of one of the limericks. Then add even more fantastic details to make an outrageous story.

2. Your Own Limericks Write three limericks of your own. Start by thinking of rhyming words. You might try a limerick about something clumsy you did, or about sports, or an animal friend.

Activities & Explorations

Incredible Feats Look in a book, such as the *Guinness Book of World Records,* that describes incredible things people have done. As a class, write limericks about these "achievements" and give a reading for another class. ~ **SPEAKING AND LISTENING.**

"I've been in love with words all my life."

Ogden Nash
1902–1971

Not for Grownups During Ogden Nash's childhood, his family divided its time between Savannah, Georgia, and a New York City suburb. He tried different jobs after college, including becoming a bond trader on Wall Street. When Nash tried to sell the poetry he had written for adults, he got absolutely nowhere. But when he began to write light verse intended for children, he found success. Nash has also edited a magazine, written film screenplays, and helped create a successful Broadway musical.

Writing Options

1. Limerick Retelling Tell students that this is one time when they can let their imagination run wild and be as silly as they want to be.

2. Your Own Limericks Students' limericks will vary, but should have the AABBA rhyme scheme, a discernible rhythm, and humor. **To make this activity easier,** provide students with pairs of rhyming words from which they can choose.

Activities & Explorations

Incredible Feats Encourage interested students to make illustrations to accompany the class limericks. Display the poems along with the drawings for other classes to enjoy.

"There was an Old Derry down Derry, / who loved to see little folks merry . . ."

Edward Lear
1812–1888

An Artist and Traveler Edward Lear was born in England, the second youngest of 21 children. He was raised by two older sisters who read him poetry and encouraged him to draw. Although he is best known for his nonsense verse, Lear first worked as an artist illustrating books about animals. He also gave art lessons. Queen Victoria of England was one of his students. Later he began writing light verse to entertain his employer's children. His *Book of Nonsense* made him famous in England. Lear traveled often, for pleasure and for his health. He wrote and sketched wherever he went.

"Poetry is . . . one way a human being can tell another human being what's going on inside."

Jack Prelutsky
born 1940

Try, Try Again Jack Prelutsky's first love was music; at one point, he trained to be an opera singer. Then he became a folk singer, combining his love of music with an interest in storytelling. However, once he began writing poetry for children, he never stopped. Prelutsky writes poems often—once he wrote six poems in one day. He also visits many schools, where, he says, "I try to tell kids that poetry is not boring or a chore. . . . It is one way a human being can tell another human being what's going on inside."

THREE LIMERICKS **567**

Mini Lesson Grammar

HUMOR WITH ADJECTIVE PHRASES

Instruction Tell students that an adjective phrase is a prepositional phrase that modifies a noun or pronoun, just as an adjective does. Because they describe, adjective phrases are often used to add humorous details. Point out the adjectival phrase in the following sentence.

The limericks in this collection are all very funny.

Exercises In the humorous sentences below, have students underline the adjective phrases.

1. There once was a woman in Denmark who fancied her meals in the pitch dark.

2. She ate by the light of the moon.

3. She had dreams of a silver spoon.

4. Her checks for the rent from her uncle were sent.

5. Her friends in the city could only take pity— they thought she was mad as a loon.

 Use **Grammar Transparencies and Copymasters,** p. 108.

 Use McDougal Littell's *Language Network,* Chapter 5, for more instruction and practice in adjective phrases.

Objectives

- expand vocabulary through wide reading
- use context to determine the meaning of specialized vocabulary
- use reference tools to determine word meanings

EXERCISE

1. **sector:** part; (Computer Science): A bit or set of bits on a magnetic storage system that makes up the smallest addressable unit of information.
2. **ozone layer:** A region of the upper atmosphere, between ten and twenty miles in altitude, containing a relatively high concentration of ozone that absorbs solar ultraviolet radiation in a wavelength range not screened by other atmospheric components.
3. **stimulus:** something that causes a response.
4. **altimeter:** An instrument for determining the elevation of an aircraft.
5. **dorsal:** Of or toward the back or upper surface.

Use **Unit Four Resource Book,** p. 48. Use **Vocabulary Transparencies and Copymasters,** p. 16 for additional support.

Technical Terms

When you watch a weather report, you may not know all the technical terms the meteorologist, or weather forecaster, uses. Still, you can understand the forecast. That's because you understand the context, the words around the technical or **specialized vocabulary.** You can do the same thing when you read.

> Mrs. Pavloff reached for her protective sun goggles that covered most of her face. It screened all ultraviolet light from the once life-giving sun; now, it, the sun, scorched the Earth, killing whatever it touched.
>
> —Alma Luz Villanueva, "The Sand Castle"

You can tell from the **clues** in the surrounding text that the sun produces **ultraviolet light** and that ultraviolet light can cause harm.

Strategies for Building Vocabulary

Professionals in many fields use and understand their own specialized vocabulary. The following strategies can help you understand the technical meanings of specialized vocabulary:

❶ **Use Context Clues** Often the **context,** or surrounding text, gives clues that help you infer the meaning of an unfamiliar term. Let's consider the following example.

> "Our television screen must have had a million books on it and it's good for plenty more. . . ."
> "Same with mine," said Margie. She was eleven and hadn't seen as many telebooks as Tommy had.
>
> —Isaac Asimov, "The Fun They Had"

In this example, the author invented the term *telebook.* The context helps us understand that a telebook is a book that appears on a television screen.

❷ **Use a Reference Tool** Sometimes context clues aren't enough to clarify the meaning. Textbooks often define a special term when it is first introduced. Look for definitions or restatement clues in parentheses. Also you can try to find definitions in footnotes, a glossary, or even a dictionary. If you still need more information, you can refer to a specialized reference, such as:

- an encyclopedia
- a field guide
- an atlas
- a user's manual
- a technical dictionary (such as a medical dictionary)

EXERCISE Use context clues to make a guess at the meaning of each underlined term. Then check a dictionary and revise your definition.

1. I can't run this software because my hard drive has a damaged <u>sector</u>. At least all my files aren't lost.
2. Holes in the <u>ozone layer</u>, that atmospheric layer of protection, may contribute to global warming.
3. The victim did not respond to any <u>stimulus</u>; she appeared to be in a coma.
4. The plane's <u>altimeter</u> indicated that it had climbed to 30,000 feet.
5. The dolphin slipped its <u>dorsal</u> fin into a ring that was floating on the water.

Where the Sidewalk **Ends**

by Shel Silverstein

There is a place where the sidewalk ends
And before the street begins,
And there the grass grows soft and white,
And there the sun burns crimson bright,
5   And there the moon-bird rests from his flight
To cool in the peppermint wind.

Let us leave this place where the smoke blows black
And the dark street winds and bends.
Past the pits where the asphalt flowers grow
10 We shall walk with a walk that is measured and slow,
And watch where the chalk-white arrows go
To the place where the sidewalk ends.

Yes we'll walk with a walk that is measured and slow,
And we'll go where the chalk-white arrows go,
15 For the children, they mark, and the children, they know
The place where the sidewalk ends.

WHERE THE SIDEWALK ENDS   **569**

Possible Objectives
- read and analyze poetry with a group (Option One)
- use the Reader's Notebook to formulate questions about poetry (Option Two)
- write in response to poetry (Option Two)

Summary
Shel Silverstein's poem "Where the Sidewalk Ends" describes a place that young children might imagine exists at the end of the entire length of the world's sidewalks. He describes the grass as being soft and white, the sun as especially bright, and the wind as cool as peppermint. In the poem, this special place offers refuge from the scariness of the real world. Similarly, Virginia Hamilton's poem "Under the Back Porch" describes a place of refuge for a child. In this case, it is a secret hiding place underneath the back porch of her white house. This is her special place where she can be alone, away from her brothers and sisters. She describes this space as being shaded and damp with the sunlight filtering through the slats of wood and the smell of damp, green moss.

Reading the Selections

Option One
Shared Reading Groups
You may assign students to groups or allow them to choose their own. Students can read the selections together, alternately reading sections aloud, or they can read independently and meet to cooperate in a project that portrays some element of the poems.

SHEL SILVERSTEIN

Shel Silverstein's varied and numerous creative abilities earned him the title of "Renaissance Man," or man of many talents, during his lifetime. As well as writing poetry and stories for children, which he illustrated himself, Silverstein also wrote and performed music. In 1969 he wrote a number one hit for country music star Johnny Cash, called "A Boy Named Sue." Eleven years later, he recorded an album of country music himself, called *The Great Conch Train Robbery.* Following on the heels of his recording successes, Silverstein branched out into theater work. In the eighties he wrote several hit plays and screenplays for movies.

UNDER THE BACK

by Virginia Hamilton

Possible Projects

- Using the descriptions from the poems, students could create illustrations for each poem by drawing or painting their own illustrations, or by finding art or photographs that represent their vision of the places in the poems.
- Students can memorize the poems and present them to the class, taking turns within each group so that all students get a chance to recite.

Option Two
Reader's Notebook

- Ask students to read the selections and to analyze their initial reactions to the special places that are described in these poems. Have them write their reactions in their Reader's Notebooks. Have them also write any questions they have about the poems or their meanings.
  After reading the selections a second time, students will return to their initial reactions and questions. Ask them to note if their impressions remained the same after rereading the poems and if their questions were answered. They may want to write down any additional questions.
- Ask students to note which descriptions in the poems seem most vivid to them and to explain why.
- Ask students to write a passage or a poem describing a special place where they go to be alone.

Our house is two stories high
shaped like a white box.
There is a yard stretched around it
and in back
5 a wooden porch.

Under the back porch is my place.
I rest there.
I go there when I have to be alone.
It is always shaded and damp.
10 Sunlight only slants through the slats
in long strips of light,
and the smell of the damp
is moist green,
like the moss that grows here.

PORCH

15 My sisters and brothers
can stand on the back porch
and never know
I am here
underneath.
20 It is my place.
All mine.

"I have ideas, and ideas are too good not to share."

Shel Silverstein
1932–1999

An Adult Who Thinks Like a Child Shel Silverstein started writing and drawing when he was around 12, although, he has said, "I would much rather have been a good baseball player." In addition to writing and illustrating poetry and stories, Silverstein was a songwriter. One of his songs, "A Boy Named Sue," became a hit when it was recorded by Johnny Cash in 1969. A critic once called Silverstein "that rare adult who can still think like a child." Perhaps because of this quality, Silverstein's work appeals to people of all ages. His books include *The Giving Tree* and *A Light in the Attic.*

"I write books because I love chasing after a good story. . . ."

Virginia Hamilton
born 1936

Writing from Roots As a child Virginia Hamilton loved to listen to her parents tell her family history, such as the story of her grandfather's escape from slavery. She knew then that she wanted to be a writer. Hamilton attended college in Ohio and then studied writing in New York. There she published her first book, *Zeely,* in 1967. Later, she moved back to her family's Ohio farm, where she has lived ever since. Hamilton's work has received, among many awards, the Newbery Medal, the National Book Award, and the Coretta Scott King Award.

UNDER THE BACK PORCH **571**

VIRGINIA HAMILITON

Storytelling was such a part of Virginia Hamilton's childhood that as she grew up, she "learned to think and to manage feelings in terms of stories." Many of the stories she heard as a child centered on her mother's ancestor, Levi Perry, a fugitive slave who eventually settled in the Ohio town of Yellow Springs. Virginia's fascination with her own history and culture is evident in the fiction she writes for children, but she has also written factual, historical accounts of African Americans. Her book *Many Thousand Gone: African-Americans from Slavery to Freedom* tells fascinating tales of famous and not so famous African American slaves from the beginning of slavery until the end of the Civil War.

OVERVIEW

This feature gives students an opportunity to compare, evaluate, and form opinions about two short science fiction selections. The focus of this comparison is on the settings of the stories.

Teaching Option

Because each work of science fiction is accompanied by its own introductory and response pages, teachers have the option of pairing the stories or teaching them individually. Used in conjunction with the Comparing Literature Assessment Practice on page 587, the selections may also be used to help students prepare for literature-based writing assessments.

COMPARING LITERATURE

Science Fiction

You are about to read two works of short fiction that take place in the future. Each of them tells a type of story known as **science fiction**—an imaginary look at how science and technology could change people's lives in surprising ways. "The Fun They Had" predicts the way students might learn in the year 2157, while "The Sand Castle" envisions the kind of environment that people might face in the future.

Short Story by ISAAC ASIMOV

THE Fun They Had

SELECTION 1

Short Story by ALMA LUZ VILLANUEVA

The Sand Castle

SELECTION 2

What Does the Future Hold?

Think of the ways that scientific advances have made your life different from the lives of your great-grandparents.

◆ How has technology affected communication?

◆ What effects have technology had on the environment?

◆ Which of these changes do you think are good ones, and which do you think are bad?

Discuss your responses with a small group of classmates.

POINTS OF COMPARISON

The most important difference between **science fiction** and other types of fiction is the **setting**. Science fiction is usually set in the future and often includes technology that doesn't exist today. In the pages that follow, you will compare and contrast the settings of two short works of science fiction. To help you note similarities and differences, keep these questions in mind as you read:

◆ What is the **time** and **place** of each story?

◆ In what ways are the **settings** of the stories similar to and different from each other?

◆ How do the settings compare to our world today?

Take notes on the settings in a diagram like the one shown above. After you read each selection, fill in the Details of Setting. After you have read *both* stories, complete the Venn diagram. Write details of the two stories' settings that are alike in the center of the diagram, where the two ovals overlap. Write unique details in the spaces on either side.

Assessment Option: Comparison-and-Contrast Essay

Writing After you have read "The Fun They Had" and "The Sand Castle," you will have the option of writing a comparison-and-contrast essay. Your chart will help you plan and write the essay.

"The Fun They Had"   **"The Sand Castle"**

Details of Setting	Details of Setting
• *takes place on May 17, 2157* • *set in the future* • *teacher is a machine*	

Connect to Your Life

Students may benefit from a whole class brainstorming session, listing scientific and technological advances that have occurred in the last fifty years. Students could then use this list to respond to the questions. Allow students time to rehearse prior to meeting with their small group.

Possible Responses: Students may suggest these forms of communication: cordless telephones, cellular phones, fax machines, pagers, high speed computer modems, interactive on-line websites and chat rooms, email. Their responses should include effects of these technological advances as well as which ones they think are good or bad and why.

Points of Comparison

Students will compare the setting across both stories. Have them copy the comparison chart in their notebooks, and remind them to add details as often as they want, making sure they come back to the chart at the end of each selection.

Assessment Option: Compare-Contrast Essay

Students should complete the points of comparison chart carefully, as this will serve as the basis for their essay.

The Fun They Had

Short Story by ISAAC ASIMOV

Objectives

1. understand and appreciate a **short story** (Literary Analysis)
2. understand author's use of **setting** in science fiction (**Literary Analysis**)
3. understand a short story better by identifying the **purposes for reading** (**Active Reading**)

Summary

In this futuristic story, set in 2157, two friends learn about schools of the past. When Tommy finds an old-fashioned book, one with real pages, he and Margie eagerly read it to find out about schools of long ago. When Margie compares those schools to her room at home with a mechanical teacher and her punch code assignments, she wishes she could have attended one of those old-fashioned schools. Students may delight in the irony that the *old-fashioned* schools sound like our current day schools.

Thematic Link

One imaginary world is the world of the future. Science fiction writers, like Isaac Asimov, are experts at imagining what technologies may develop and change, and how those changes might affect society as we know it.

Build Background

CONNECT TO **TECHNOLOGY** Isaac Asimov wrote "The Fun They Had" in 1951. Back then, computers were huge machines that had to be kept in refrigerated buildings. They were not user-friendly, and only a computer expert could operate them. Specialists stored information in computers by punching patterns of holes into cards or tape. (Notice that a character in the story uses this "punch code" method instead of a keyboard.) It was only after the invention of the silicon chip in the 1960s that computers became smaller, easier to use, and less expensive. In 1977, the first personal computers became available for home use.

Focus Your Reading

LITERARY ANALYSIS **SETTING** The time and place in which the action of a story happens is called the **setting.** In science fiction, setting is a key element. Almost all science fiction is set in the future. Many science fiction writers create settings that combine realistic details with elements of fantasy. In futuristic settings, imagined technological advances are often an important part of the landscape.

ACTIVE READING **PURPOSES FOR READING** People read for many different purposes. Two of the most common purposes are entertainment and understanding. Your purpose in reading "The Fun They Had" is to understand the story's setting so that you can compare it to the setting of the next selection, "The Sand Castle." Paying attention to the details of setting will help you understand how setting affects a story.

READER'S NOTEBOOK As you read, keep your purpose in mind. Jot down notes to help you answer the Points of Comparison questions on page 573.

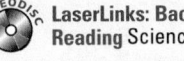

WORDS TO KNOW
Vocabulary Preview
dispute   scornful
loftily   sector
nonchalantly

LaserLinks: Background for Reading Science Connection

574   UNIT FOUR   PART 2: IMAGINARY WORLDS

5-Minute Warm-Up

Daily Language SkillBuilder

Have students **proofread** the display sentences on page 441k and write them correctly. The sentences also appear on Transparency 18 of **Grammar Transparencies and Copymasters.**

LESSON RESOURCES

THE F un
They Had

BY ISAAC ASIMOV

Margie even wrote about it that night in her diary. On the page headed May 17, 2157, she wrote, "Today Tommy found a real book!"

It was a very old book. Margie's grandfather once said that when he was a little boy, his grandfather told him that there was a time when all stories were printed on paper.

They turned the pages, which were yellow and crinkly, and it was awfully funny to read words that stood still instead of moving the way they were supposed to—on a screen, you know. And then, when they turned back to the page before, it had the same words on it that it had when they read it the first time.

TEACHING THE LITERATURE
Customizing Instruction

Less Proficient Readers
Engage students' interest in the selection by asking them if they have ever imagined what the future would be like. Ask them to brainstorm what their houses might be like, their towns, and their schools one hundred years in the future. Tell them that this story takes place in 2157 and things are very different from the way they are now.

Set a Purpose Ask students to read to find out how schools are different in the year 2157.

Students Acquiring English
If students have attended schools in other places that were different than their current school, ask them to share some of those differences. Tell them that this story will tell about a school in the future, and that it, too, will be different. Ask them to think about those differences as they read.

Use **Spanish Study Guide,** pp. 115–117 for additional support.

Gifted and Talented
Ask students to think about going 150 years *back* in time. Have them imagine what a young boy and girl might have thought about the schools of today (the future to them). Allow students to take time to share their thoughts with each other.

Multiple Learning Styles
Visual Learners
Ask students to study the drawing on the opening page and to discuss what they see and what it might represent. Remind them of the background information provided on page 574 and the opening paragraphs here. As they read the remainder of the story, they may wish to revisit this discussion.

 Preteaching Vocabulary

CONTEXT CLUES: DEFINITION AND RESTATEMENT
Remind students that when they read an unfamiliar word, they can find context clues around that word to help them figure out what it means. One kind of context clue is *restatement* or *definition clues.*

Instruction Tell students that sometimes unfamiliar words are accompanied by a definition clue or a restatement of the word's meaning. These context clues are often set off with dashes or signaled by a comma or by words such as *or, that is, in other words,* or *also called.* Write the following sentence on the board, or read it aloud:

Tommy and Margie had a *dispute,* or argument, about the old book.

Ask students what *dispute* means. How do they know?

Application Ask students to find each word in the WORDS TO KNOW list in the selection. Have them write a sentence for each word, using restatement or definition clues.

 Use **Unit Four Resource Book,** p. 52 for more practice.
Use **Vocabulary Transparencies and Copymasters,** p. 58, for additional support.

Literary Analysis SETTING

A Remind students to look for details that give information about the setting in this story and to record that information in the Points of Comparison charts they began earlier. Although many aspects of the setting are different from the present, some things may be the same. Ask students which elements of the setting are similar to those of today.
Possible Responses: The children live in houses with their parents. Tommy's house has an attic.

Use **Unit Four Resource Book,** p. 51 for more practice. Use **Literary Analysis Transparencies,** p. 6, for additional support.

Active Reading

PURPOSES FOR READING

Remind students that they are reading this selection for information. In particular they are looking for details that describe the setting of the story. Encourage them to look for descriptions of setting as they read, and to take notes.

Use **Unit Four Resource Book,** p. 50 for more practice. Use **Reading and Critical Thinking Transparencies,** p. 16, for additional support.

Reading Skills and Strategies:
CONNECT

B Ask students to reflect on the discussion Tommy and Margie have about their teachers and to discuss how this compares with experiences they have had with their own teachers.
Possible Responses: Students should talk about the obvious difference—human versus machine—but also the class size idea, the individualized curriculum, and the process for submitting homework.

"Gee," said Tommy, "what a waste. When you're through with the book, you just throw it away, I guess. Our television screen must have had a million books on it and it's good for plenty more. I wouldn't throw it away."

 "**A** man Can't Know as much as a teacher."

"Same with mine," said Margie. She was eleven and hadn't seen as many telebooks[1] as Tommy had. He was thirteen.

She said, "Where did you find it?"

"In my house." He pointed without looking, because he was busy reading. "In the attic."

"What's it about?"

"School."

Margie was scornful. "School? What's there to write about school? I hate school." Margie always hated school, but now she hated it more than ever. The mechanical teacher[2] had

been giving her test after test in geography, and she had been doing worse and worse until her mother had shaken her head sorrowfully and sent for the county inspector.

He was a round little man with a red face and a whole box of tools with dials and wires. He smiled at her and gave her an apple, then took the teacher apart. Margie had hoped he wouldn't know how to put it together again, but he knew how all right, and after an hour or so, there it was again, large and ugly, with a big screen on which all the lessons were shown and the questions were asked. That wasn't so bad. The part she hated most was the slot where she had to put homework and test papers. She always had to write them out in a punch code they made her learn when she was six years old, and the mechanical teacher calculated the mark in no time.

The inspector had smiled after he was finished and patted her head. He said to her mother, "It's not the little girl's fault, Mrs. Jones. I think the geography sector was geared a little too quick. Those things happen sometimes. I've slowed it up to an average ten-year level. Actually, the overall pattern of her progress is quite satisfactory." And he patted Margie's head again.

Margie was disappointed. She had been hoping they would take the teacher away altogether. They had once taken Tommy's teacher away for nearly a month because the history sector had blanked out completely.

So she said to Tommy, "Why would anyone write about school?"

---

1. **telebooks** (tĕl´ə-bŏŏks): books presented on a television screen.

2. **mechanical teacher:** a machine or computer that serves as a teacher.

WORDS TO KNOW
scornful (skôrn´fəl) *adj.* having an attitude of contempt; disdainful
sector (sĕk´tər) *n.* a part or division

Teaching Options

Mini Lesson **Speaking and Listening**

COMPUTER DIALOGUE IN A VARIETY OF VOICES
Prepare Tell students that during this dramatization, they will act out dialogue that they have created. The dialogue will be a lesson that Margie's mechanical teacher might teach her. Further, students will present the lesson with a mechanical voice, speaking as if they were the computer.
Present Ask students to work in small groups to create a simple lesson to teach Margie.

Ask them to prepare text for the computer screen, and to write it on either a poster board or on a real computer screen. If possible, allow them to listen to synthesized computer voices, and to practice speaking with similar sounding voices. Have students present their lessons to a group of classmates, using a voice they have chosen and practiced to represent a futuristic mechanical teacher.

BLOCK SCHEDULING This activity is particularly well suited for longer class periods.

Tommy looked at her with very superior eyes, "Because it's not our kind of school, stupid. This is the old kind of school that they had hundreds and hundreds of years ago." He added <u>loftily</u>, pronouncing the word carefully, "*Centuries* ago."

Margie was hurt. "Well, I don't know what kind of school they had all that time ago." She read the book over his shoulder for a while, then said, "Anyway, they had a teacher."

"Sure they had a teacher, but it wasn't a regular teacher. It was a man."

"A man? How could a man be a teacher?"

"Well, he just told the boys and girls things and gave them homework and asked them questions."

"A man isn't smart enough."

"Sure he is. My father knows as much as my teacher."

"He can't. A man can't know as much as a teacher."

"He knows almost as much I betcha."

Margie wasn't prepared to <u>dispute</u> that. She said, "I wouldn't want a strange man in my house to teach me."

Tommy screamed with laughter. "You don't know much, Margie. The teachers didn't live in the house. They had a special building and all the kids went there."

"And all the kids learned the same thing?"

"Sure, if they were all the same age."

"But my mother says a teacher has to be adjusted to fit the mind of each boy and girl it teaches and that each kid has to be taught differently."

"Just the same, they didn't do it that way then. If you don't like it, you don't have to read the book."

"I didn't say I didn't like it," Margie said quickly. She wanted to read about those funny schools.

They weren't even half finished when Margie's mother called, "Margie! School!"

Margie looked up. "Not yet, Mamma."

"Now," said Mrs. Jones. "And it's probably time for Tommy, too."

Margie said to Tommy, "Can I read the book some more with you after school?"

"Maybe," he said, <u>nonchalantly</u>. He walked

WORDS TO KNOW	**loftily** (lôf′tĭ-lē) *adv.* in a grand or pompous way
	dispute (dĭ-spyo͞ot′) *v.* to argue about; debate
	nonchalantly (nŏn′shə-länt′lē) *adv.* in a casual, unconcerned way

577

Literary Analysis: REALISTIC AND FANTASTIC DETAILS

In some science fiction stories, authors combine realistic and fantastic details to create their imaginary world. Ask students to create a two-column chart, with one side listing realistic elements in this story and the other side listing fantastic details. Ask them to discuss how these details merge to create a cohesive story.

Possible Responses: Realistic elements might include the children, their homes, parents, going to school, and doing homework. Fantastic details might include the mechanical teacher, the punch code homework, and the individualized nature of the lessons. The elements come together easily to create a scene that might actually happen in the future but isn't happening now.

Isaac Asimov

Isaac Asimov was a scientist and a writer. He combined his two loves into one career: writing for science fiction magazines, science textbooks, and science reference materials. He once said, "My novels are going to be interesting and are going to sell and be famous," and he was right about that. Asimov is one of the most well-known writers in the field of science fiction. When asked how to pronounce his last name, Asimov responded with, "Has Him Off and leave off the H's."

---

away whistling, the dusty old book tucked beneath his arm.

Margie went into the schoolroom. It was right next to her bedroom, and the mechanical teacher was on and waiting for her. It was always on at the same time every day except Saturday and Sunday, because her mother said little girls learned better if they learned at regular hours.

The screen was lit up, and it said: "Today's arithmetic lesson is on the addition of proper fractions. Please insert yesterday's homework in the proper slot."

> "**P**lease insert yesterday's homework in the proper slot."

Margie did so with a sigh. She was thinking about the old schools they had when her grandfather's grandfather was a little boy. All the kids from the whole neighborhood came, laughing and shouting in the schoolyard, sitting together in the schoolroom, going home together at the end of the day. They learned the same things so they could help one another on the homework and talk about it.

And the teachers were people. . . .

The mechanical teacher was flashing on the screen: "When we add the fractions $\frac{1}{2}$ and $\frac{1}{4}$—"

Margie was thinking about how the kids must have loved it in the old days. She was thinking about the fun they had. ❖

"I do not fear computers. I fear the lack of them."

Isaac Asimov
1920–1992

The Hardest-Working Writer The *New York Times* once called Isaac Asimov a "writing machine." Over his lifetime this acclaimed science fiction author wrote or edited more than 470 books—more than any other American writer. Asimov was born in Russia. When he was three years old he came to the United States with his parents. When he grew older he received an advanced science degree and served as a professor of biochemistry for several years before becoming a full-time writer at the age of 38.

A Little Story About School In the first volume of his autobiography, Asimov explains how he came to write "The Fun They Had." A friend had asked him to write a story for young readers. "I thought about it and decided to write a little story about school," Asimov says. "What could interest children more? It would be about a school of the future, by way of teaching machines, with children longing for the good old days when there were old-fashioned schools that children loved. I thought the kids would get a bang out of the irony."

Teaching Options

✓ Assessment Informal Assessment

LETTERS BETWEEN CHARACTERS One way to help students identify with and understand the stories they read is to ask them to recognize the feelings and emotions of characters. Ask students to think about the characters of Margie and Tommy. Tell them to select any character from a previous story in the book and to write a letter to that character, as if they were Tommy or Margie. The letter should express how they feel about the old-fashioned schools they have been learning about. Remind them to use specific details from the story.

RUBRICS

3 Full Accomplishment Letter shows a full understanding of the character's feelings, and all features of friendly letter writing are used.

2 Substantial Accomplishment Letter shows a substantial understanding of the character's feelings, and most features of letter writing are evident.

1 Little or Partial Accomplishment Letter shows little or partial understanding of the character's emotions, and few of the features of letter writing are used.

Connect to the Literature

1. **What Do You Think?**
   What was your reaction to the end of the story?

   Comprehension Check
   - What made Tommy think the book was "a waste"?
   - Why did Margie do badly in geography?
   - Where was Margie's "schoolroom"?

Think Critically

2. **ACTIVE READING** **PURPOSES FOR READING** Share the notes that you made in your **READER'S NOTEBOOK** with a classmate. Discuss how the author shows the reader that the setting is important.

3. **What If?** If Margie were to visit a school like yours, what might be her reaction? Do you think she would like it as much as she thinks she would in the story? Explain your answer.

4. **Connect to Life** Think of the tasks for which you use a computer. Make a list of these activities. With the class, share your opinions about the advantages and disadvantages of using computers for these purposes.

Literary Analysis

 SETTING The world that Isaac Asimov presents in "The Fun They Had" is very different from our own. Imagine what it would be like to be taught by a mechanical teacher, the way Margie is, instead of by a human teacher. Although there are many differences between Asimov's earth in 2157 and our world today, there are also many similarities. For example, children still have homework (although they must write it in punch code) and they still complain about it.

POINTS OF COMPARISON

Fill in the Details of Setting column for "The Fun They Had" in your Points of Comparison diagram. Several details are already listed for you.

Paired Activity Share the notes you made in your **READER'S NOTEBOOK** with a classmate. Together, discuss which details of the setting indicate that you are reading a science fiction story. In what ways might the setting be different if the story were not science fiction?

"The Fun They Had"   "The Sand Castle"

Details of Setting	Details of Setting
• takes place on May 17, 2157	
• set in the future	
• teacher is a machine	

THE FUN THEY HAD **579**

Connect to the Literature

1. **What Do You Think?**
   Accept all reasonable answers.

Comprehension Check
- Tommy thought the book was a waste because it could only tell one story as opposed to a computer, which can contain many books.
- Margie did poorly in geography because the geography sector of her mechanical teacher was set to a level too advanced for Margie.
- Margie's schoolroom was in her house, in the room next to her bedroom.

Use Selection Quiz
Unit Four Resource Book, p. 55.

Think Critically

2. Possible Responses: Students should discuss the futuristic setting, using specific examples drawn from the story.

Use **Reading and Critical Thinking Transparencies**, p. 16.

3. Answers will vary, but should be supported by evidence from the story.

4. Lists will vary. Students may wish to make a graphic organizer to keep track of the pros and cons they come up with.

Literary Analysis

Setting Ask students to discuss with a partner some of the similarities and differences found between the setting of Asimov's story and the current time. Students will use this discussion to complete the Points of Comparison activity.

Use **Literary Analysis Transparencies**, p. 6.

Points of Comparison

Ask students to refer to the diagram they drew at the beginning of the selection. Ask them to fill in all the details they can remember about the setting in this story. Remind them to draw on the information discussed with a partner earlier.

OVERVIEW

Objectives
1. understand and appreciate a **short story** (Literary Analysis)
2. understand author's use of **setting in science fiction** (Literary Analysis)
3. use **comparing and contrasting** to help understand a short story better (**Active Reading**)

Summary
Masha Pavloff is taking her grand-children to the beach to build a sand castle. However, in this story set in the future, the sun has ravaged the world. All people must wear protective cloth-ing and glasses when they go out dur-ing daylight hours. They may not go in the sea or touch the sand. As Masha reflects on her childhood memories of going to the beach, she tries to create the same kind of memories for her grandchildren. This story may cause readers to think about the effects of global warming and the depletion of the earth's ozone layer.

Thematic Link
The future world created by Villanueva in this piece is frightening. When science fiction depicts a future that is likely or possible, the stories have great impact on readers' imaginations.

5-Minute Warm-Up

Daily Language SkillBuilder

Have students **proofread** the display sentences on page 441k and write them correctly. The sentences also appear on Transparency 18 of **Grammar Transparencies and Copymasters.**

The Sand Castle

Short Story by ALMA LUZ VILLANUEVA

Build Background

CONNECT TO **SCIENCE** In recent decades, many scientists have been concerned that the earth could be in danger from the sun's rays, due to a thinning of the ozone layer. Ozone is a form of oxygen high up in the atmosphere that normally absorbs harmful ultraviolet rays from the sun before they reach the earth. But chemicals called CFCs— used in air conditioners, aerosol sprays, and other products—may have eaten away at the ozone layer allowing an increase in harmful ultraviolet radiation at the earth's surface. The long-term effects of ozone depletion could be deadly for marine life, birds, and even people.

Focus Your Reading

LITERARY ANALYSIS **SETTING** Almost all science fiction is set in the future, but writers often focus on different aspects of life in the future. In "The Fun They Had," Isaac Asimov focuses on how changes in technology affect people's lives. Ray Bradbury's "All Summer in a Day" (page 209) is an example of science fiction that emphasizes the impact of environment—in this case, the weather on Venus—on people. As you read "The Sand Castle," consider how both technology and environment affect the characters.

ACTIVE READING **COMPARE AND CONTRAST** When you **compare and contrast**, you look for similarities and differences. After reading "The Sand Castle," you will write a comparison-and-contrast essay focusing on setting. As you read this selection, find ways in which its setting is similar to and different from the setting of "The Fun They Had."

READER'S NOTEBOOK As you read, refer to the Points of Comparison questions on page 573. Take notes about similarities and differences in the settings of the two stories.

> WORDS TO KNOW
> **Vocabulary Preview**
> cumbersome   listlessly
> forlorn   ultraviolet
> hostile

LESSON RESOURCES

UNIT FOUR RESOURCE BOOK, pp. 56–62

ASSESSMENT
Formal Assessment, pp. 97–98
Teacher's Guide to Assessment and Portfolio Use
Test Generator

SKILLS TRANSPARENCIES AND COPYMASTERS
Literary Analysis
• Setting, TR 6 (for Paired Activity, p. 585)

Reading and Critical Thinking
• Compare and Contrast, TR 17 (for Thinking Through the Literature, p. 585)
Grammar
• Identifying Prepositions and Their Objects, CM 102 (for Mini Lesson, p. 586)
Vocabulary
• Word Parts, CM 59 (for Mini Lesson, p. 581)

INTEGRATED TECHNOLOGY
Audio Library

Visit our website:
www.mcdougallittell.com

The Sand Castle

by Alma Luz Villanueva

"**H**AVE YOU DRESSED YET?" their grandmother called. "Once a month in the sun and they must almost be forced," she muttered. "Well, poor things, they've forgotten the warmth of the sun on their little bodies, what it is to play in the sea, yes. . . ." Mrs. Pavloff reached for her protective sun goggles that covered most of her face. It screened all <u>ultraviolet</u> light from the once life-giving sun; now, it, the sun, scorched the Earth, killing whatever it touched. The sea, the continents, had changed. The weather, as they'd called it in the last century, was entirely predictable now: warming.

Mrs. Pavloff slipped on the thick, metallic gloves, listening to her grandchildren squabble and she heard her mother's voice calling her, "Masha, put your bathing suit under your clothes. It's so much easier that way without having to go to the bathhouse first. Hurry! Father's waiting!" She remembered the ride to the sea, the silence when the first shimmers of water became visible. Her father had always been first into the chilly water. "Good for the health!" he'd yell as he dove into it, swimming as far as he could, then back. Then he'd lie exhausted

WORDS
TO   **ultraviolet** (ŭl′trə-vī′ə-lĭt) *adj.* consisting of invisible radiation wavelengths
KNOW

THE SAND CASTLE   **581**

Tell students that there are actually two settings described here, one in the present time, and one in Mrs. Pavloff's memories. Ask them to compare and contrast the two settings, perhaps by making a two-column chart.

Possible Responses: The current setting is hot, barren, and unsafe to go outside without protection. Most people go out only at night, so it is usually dark when they see the outside. In Masha's memories the sun is warm, the sea is refreshing, and people walk outside during the day without protective clothing.

 Use **Unit Four Resource Book**, p. 58 for more practice.
Use **Literary Analysis Transparencies**, p. 6, for additional support.

Active Reading

| COMPARE AND CONTRAST |

Remind students to pay attention to the details of the setting so they can compare and contrast them with the setting of "The Fun They Had."

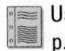 Use **Unit Four Resource Book**, p. 57 for more practice.
Use **Reading and Critical Thinking Transparencies**, p. 17, for additional support.

---

on the sand, stretched to the sun. Such happiness to be warmed by the sun.

Then the picnic. She could hear her mother's voice, "Stay to your knees, Masha! Only to your knees!" To herself: "She'd be a mermaid if I didn't watch," and she'd laugh. Masha would lie belly down, facing the sea, and let the last of the waves roll over her. She hadn't even been aware of the sun, only that she'd been warm or, if a cloud covered it, cold. It was always there, the sun: its light, its warmth. But the sea—they travelled to it. So, she'd given all of her attention to the beautiful sea.

She saw her father kneeling next to her, building the sand castle they always built when they went to the sea. Her job was to find seashells, bird feathers, and strips of seaweed to decorate it. How proud she'd felt as she placed her seashells where she chose, where they seemed most beautiful. Only then was the sand castle complete. She heard her father's voice, "The Princess's castle is ready, now, for her Prince! Come and look, Anna! What do you think?" She saw herself beaming with pride, and she heard her mother's laugh. "Fit for a queen, I'd say! Can I live in your castle, too, Masha? Please, Princess Masha?" "Of course, Mother! You can live with me always. . . ." She remembered her mother's laughing face, her auburn hair lit up by the sun, making her look bright and beautiful.

The sun, the sun, the sun. The scientists were saying that with the remedies they were employing now and the remedies begun twenty years ago—they'd stopped all nuclear testing[1] and all manufacturing of ozone-depleting[2] chemicals was banned worldwide—the scientists were saying that the sun, the global problem, would begin to get better. Perhaps for her grandchildren's children. Perhaps they would feel the sun on their unprotected bodies.

Perhaps they would feel the delicious warmth of the sun.

All vehicles were solar powered. The populations took buses when they needed transportation and people emerged mainly at night. So, most human activity was conducted after the sun was gone from the sky. Those who emerged during the day wore protective clothing. Everything was built to screen the sun's light. Sometimes she missed the natural light of her childhood streaming through the windows so intensely the urge to just run outside would overtake her. She missed the birds, the wild birds.

But today, they were going out, outside in the daytime, when the sun was still in the sky. Masha knew they were squabbling because they hated to dress up to go outside. The clothing, the gloves, the goggles, were uncomfortable and <u>cumbersome</u>. She sighed,

---

1. **nuclear testing:** experimental explosions of nuclear bombs.
2. **ozone-depleting** (ō′zōn′ dǐ-plē′tǐng) **chemicals:** substances that can damage the atmosphere's ozone layer, which helps to protect living things from the harmful ultraviolet radiation in sunlight.

WORDS
TO   **cumbersome** (kǔm′bər-səm) *adj.* uncomfortably heavy or bulky
KNOW

582

Teaching Options

BLOCK SCHEDULING: MANAGING TIME

If your schedule requires that you cover the lesson objectives in a shorter time, use…
- Preparing to Read, p. 580
- Thinking Through the Literature, p. 585
- Comparing Literature: Assessment Practice, p. 587

If you want to take advantage of longer class time, use…
- TE Teaching Options, Preteaching Vocabulary, p. 581, Cross Curricular Link, p. 583, Informal Assessment, p. 584, Grammar, p. 586
- Choices & Challenges, p. 586

tears coming to her eyes. Well, they're coming, Masha decided. They can remove their goggles and gloves on the bus.

The sea was closer now and the bus ride was comfortable within the temperature controlled interior. Those with memories of the sea signed up, bringing grandchildren, children, friends, or just went alone. Masha had taken her grandchildren before, but they'd sat on the sand, listlessly, sifting it through their gloved hands with bored little faces. She'd tried to interest them in the sea with stories of her father's swimming in it as far as he could. But they couldn't touch it, so it, the sea, didn't seem real to them. What was it: a mass of undrinkable, hostile water. Hostile like the sun. They'd taken no delight, no pleasure, in their journey to the sea.

But today, yes, today we will build a sand castle. Masha smiled at her secret. She'd packed everything late last night to surprise them at the sea.

Why haven't I thought of it before? Masha asked herself, and then she remembered the dream, months ago, of building a sand castle with her father at the sea. It made her want to weep because she'd forgotten. She'd actually forgotten one of the most joyful times of her girlhood. When the sea was still alive with life.

Today we build a sand castle.

They trudged on the thick, dense sand toward the hiss of pale blue. Only the older people picked up their step, excited by the smell of salt in the air. Masha's grandchildren knew they'd be here for two hours and then trudge all the way back to the bus. The darkened goggles made the sunlight bearable. They hated this forlorn place where the sun had obviously drained the life out of everything. They were too young to express it, but they felt it as they walked, with bored effort, beside their grandmother.

"We're going to build a sand castle today— what do you think of that?" Masha beamed, squinting to see their faces.

"What's a sand castle?" the boy mumbled.

"You'll see, I'll show you. . . ."

"Is it fun Grandmama?" the girl smiled, taking her grandmother's hand.

"Yes, it's so much fun. I've brought different sized containers to mold the sand, and, oh, you'll see!"

The boy gave an awkward skip and nearly shouted, "Show us, Grandmama, show us what you mean!"

Masha laughed, sounding almost like a girl. "We're almost there, yes, we're almost there!"

The first circle of sandy shapes was complete, and the children were so excited by what they were building they forgot about their protective gloves.

"Now, we'll put a pile of wet sand in the middle and build it up with our hands and then we'll do another circle, yes, children?"

The children rushed back and forth from the tide line carrying the dark, wet sand. They only had an hour left. Their eyes, beneath the goggles, darted with excitement.

"Just don't get your gloves in the water, a little wet sand won't hurt, don't worry, children. When I was a girl there were so many birds at the sea we'd scare them off because they'd try to steal our food. Seagulls, they were, big white birds that liked to scream at the sea, they sounded like eagles to me. . . ."

WORDS TO KNOW	**listlessly** (lĭst′lĭs-lē) *adv.* without energy or interest; sluggishly
	hostile (hŏs′təl) *adj.* unfavorable to health or well-being; dangerous
	forlorn (fər-lôrn′) *adj.* miserable and lonely; desolate

583

Customizing Instruction

Multiple Learning Styles
Kinesthetic Learners

1 Help students to recall the items that people have to wear when they go outside (goggles, thick, metallic gloves, full body suits). Ask them to discuss how it would feel to bundle up this way every time they went outside.

Possible Responses: It would be awful to not be able to touch anything outside. Such protective gear might be very awkward.

Visual Learners

2 Ask students to look at the image on these two pages and discuss what they see. Help them to connect the image with the content of the story.

Gifted and Talented

Ask students to think about the good things in this imaginary world. What advantages do the characters have that we don't? Ask them to brainstorm some of the positives that the story implies but may not state directly.

Less Proficient Readers

To help students understand the story, ask them the following questions:
1. How do Masha's grandchildren get to the beach?
   Answer: They ride in a solar powered, climate-controlled bus.
2. What do they do at the beach?
   Answer: They build a sand castle.
3. How does this trip compare with their last trip to the beach?
   Answer: Last time they sat on the sand, sifting sand through their gloved hands. This time they are having fun building the sand castle.

Set a Purpose Tell students to read on to find out if they build a sand castle, and what happens next.

Cross Curricular Link **Science**

EFFECTS OF THE SUN'S RAYS It seems we all like to work or play in the warm sunshine, but are we actually harming ourselves by doing so? Scientists are becoming increasingly concerned that we are. How did this happen? The sun's rays have always been dangerous for humans, but most of the sun's rays never reached us. The ozone in the earth's atmosphere filters most of the sun's ultraviolet rays, but in recent years, the ozone layer has eroded, and more dangerous rays are getting to earth. There are several reasons why the ozone is being depleted, but one major cause is the common use of certain chemicals, such as those in air conditioners, refrigerators, and aerosol sprays. Since 1987, leaders from over 160 countries have signed a treaty banning ozone depleting substances. The Environmental Protection Agency (EPA) works to enforce the bans in the United States. The EPA also educates people on the link between ultraviolet radiation and skin cancer, and promotes the following action steps: avoid midday sun; seek shade; wear SPF 15 or higher sunblock, a hat, full-length clothing, and 99–100% UV blocking glasses.

Reading Skills and Strategies
EVALUATE

Ask students to think about Mrs. Pavloff and her reasons for taking her grandchildren to the beach to build a sand castle. Ask students to evaluate her actions by discussing these questions. Do they agree or disagree with her? Why? Would they do the same in her place?

Possible Responses: Students may agree or disagree with Masha's decision. In either case they should be able to support their choices and to put themselves in a similar situation.

Literary Analysis:
AUTHOR'S PURPOSE

Many authors write stories to teach their readers something, or to cause them to think about issues and ideas. Ask students to discuss what purpose the author, Alma Luz Villanueva, may have had in writing this story.

Possible Response: She may have written this story so we would all think about what might happen to the earth if we don't stop depleting the ozone layer.

Author Activity

Allow students time to practice reciting the poems. They may want to do some of the poems with a partner, in a choral reading.

"You used to eat at the sea, Grandmama?" the girl asked incredulously.

"We used to call them picnics. . . ."

"What are eagles, Grandmama?" the boy wanted to know, shaping the dark sand with his gloved hands.

"They used to be one of the largest, most beautiful wild birds in the world. My grandfather pointed them out to me once. . . ." Until that moment, she'd forgotten that memory of nearly sixty years ago. They'd gone on a train, then a bus, to the village where he'd been born. She remembered her grandfather looking up toward a shrill, piercing cry that seemed to come from the sky. She'd seen the tears in her grandfather's eyes and on his cheeks. He'd pointed up to a large, dark flying-thing in the summer blue sky: "That's an eagle, my girl, the spirit of the people."

Sadness overtook Masha, but she refused to acknowledge its presence. The sand castle, Masha told herself sternly—the sand castle is what is important now. "I've brought a wonderful surprise, something to decorate the castle with when we're through building it."

"Show us Grandmama, please?"

"Yes, please, please show us now!"

Masha sighed with a terrible, sudden happiness as she brought out the plastic bag. Quickly, she removed each precious seashell from its protective cotton: eight perfect shells from all over the world.

"But grandmama, these are your special shells! You said the sea doesn't make them anymore. . . ."

"It will, Anna, it will." Masha hugged her granddaughter and made her voice brighten with laughter. "Today we will decorate our sand castle with the most beautiful shells in the world, yes!" ❖

"Writing takes all your courage. . . ."

Alma Luz Villanueva
born 1944

Villanueva's Themes Alma Luz Villanueva is a Mexican-American writer known for both her poetry and her prose. Two aspects of Villanueva's life have had a strong influence on her writing. One was her Mexican grandmother, with whom she lived until she was 11 years old and who taught her many stories and poems. The other was a stay in the Sierra Nevada mountains. Both of these influences—the role women play in passing along tradition, and the importance of our environment—are key themes in the story you have just read.

Poetry and Prose Villanueva grew up in the Mission district of San Francisco. After her grandmother died, she lived as an adolescent with her young mother and an aunt. In the late 1960s, Villanueva began writing poetry based largely on her childhood experiences. She has published a number of poetry books, novels, and a collection of short stories, from which this selection was taken.

AUTHOR ACTIVITY
Go to the library and choose a book of poetry by the author. Select your favorite poem and share it with a group.

Teaching Options

☑ **Assessment** **Informal Assessment**

VENN DIAGRAM COMPARISON To help students compare two pieces of literature, it is often helpful to use graphic representations. A Venn Diagram is especially useful when comparing two pieces of the same genre.
Ask students to construct two large, overlapping circles. Ask them to label one "The Fun They Had," and one "The Sand Castle." Ask students to fill in literary elements and details from each story in the corresponding circles. Elements that were common to both stories should be placed in the intersection of the circles.

RUBRICS
3 Full Accomplishment Response shows a full understanding of the stories and their corresponding literary elements.
2 Substantial Accomplishment Response shows a substantial understanding of the stories and their literary elements.
1 Little or Partial Accomplishment Response shows little or partial understanding of the stories and their literary elements.

Connect to the Literature

1. **What Do You Think?**
Did you enjoy "The Sand Castle" more or less than "The Fun They Had"? Explain.

Comprehension Check
- Why do the characters need to wear protective clothing to go outside during the day?
- Where does Mrs. Pavloff take her grandchildren?
- What are Mrs. Pavloff and her grandchildren going to use to decorate their sand castle?

Think Critically

2. **ACTIVE READING** **COMPARE AND CONTRAST** Did you find any clues that suggest how far into the future this story might be set? What about place? How do time and place compare between these two sections?

3. **Connect to Life** In what ways might your own grandparents' memories of sunning at the beach or just spending time outside be different from your experiences?

Literary Analysis

SETTING A science fiction writer's descriptions of the future often contain a message, or even a warning, about what the future might hold. Science fiction writers like to speculate, or guess, about how changes in technology or the environment would affect people. Sometimes the effects they envision are produced by people's actions today. In "The Sand Castle," Alma Luz Villanueva describes how damage to the earth's ozone layer affects the environment, and how the resulting environmental changes might affect people in the future.

POINTS OF COMPARISON

Fill in the Details of Setting column for "The Sand Castle" in your Points of Comparison diagram. Remember to consider the time and place of the story, and how it is similar to and different from our world today. Then fill in the Venn diagram for the two stories. In the center, write what the settings of the stories have in common. Then write details of the settings that are unique to one selection or the other in the spaces on either side.

Paired Activity With a partner, discuss the ways in which the setting of "The Sand Castle" is different from the world you know. Does the setting of "The Sand Castle" seem more or less unusual than the setting of "The Fun They Had"? Why?

"The Fun They Had" "The Sand Castle"

May 17, 2157
machine for
a teacher

future
earth

two generations
into the future

sun is dangerous

Details of Setting
- takes place on May 17, 2157
- set in the future
- teacher is a machine
- set on earth

Details of Setting
- takes place two generations in the future
- sun is dangerous to people

THE SAND CASTLE **585**

Points of Comparison

Ask students to complete the chart with the details about the setting in "The Sand Castle." Remind them to fill in the center of the Venn diagram with those elements of the setting that are common to both stories.

GUIDING STUDENT RESPONSE

Connect to the Literature

1. **What Do You Think?**
Accept all reasonable responses.

Comprehension Check
- There is too much ultraviolet light in the sunlight that reaches the earth, and people have to wear protective gear so that they aren't harmed by it.
- Mrs. Pavloff takes her grandchildren to the beach.
- Mrs. Pavloff and her grandchildren will decorate their sand castle with seashells.

 Use Selection Quiz
Unit Four Resource Book, p. 62.

Think Critically

2. **Possible Response:** Mrs. Pavloff's memories of her childhood (going to the shore, taking trains and busses, seeing birds) seem a lot like my childhood today, so this story could be set about two generations into the future.

Use **Reading and Critical Thinking Transparencies,** p. 17.

3. **Possible Response:** My grandparents didn't use sunscreen or worry too much about getting sunburned because they didn't know that the sun could be bad for you. Also sun exposure was less dangerous then, when the ozone layer was thicker.

Literary Analysis

Setting Provide students with time to meet with partners and discuss the posed questions in the paired activity. It might be helpful for them to consult their Reader's Notebook.

 Use **Literary Analysis Transparencies,** p. 6.

Writing Options

1. **Movie Outline** Students may benefit from looking at an actual screen play. If this isn't feasible, a whole class generated model might be appropriate.

2. **Futuristic Setting Description** Encourage students to revisit their comparison charts of the settings in these two stories. They may be able to draw on some of the ideas presented there.

 Use **Writing Transparencies**, p. 22, for additional support.

Activities & Explorations

1. **Keepsake Scrapbook** Students will need some time to complete this project. **To make this activity easier,** a classroom scrapbook could be developed first. Doing so would model the process for students, and provide memories of important events of the school year.

2. **Technology Interview** Encourage students to write their questions prior to conducting the interviews. It would be appropriate to develop the questions as a whole class activity, and each pair could then individualize the list of questions for their own interview.

 Use **Communications Transparencies and Copymasters,** p. 9, for additional support.

Inquiry & Research

Future Perfect The school librarian or media specialist may be able to recommend some older science fiction titles that would be appropriate.

Writing Options

1. **Movie Outline** Imagine that you are in charge of making one of the previous two stories into a science fiction film. Which story would you rather make into a movie? Why? Write a new title for your movie. Then write notes for each scene about the scenery, costumes, special effects, and other film techniques necessary to bring the story to the screen.

2. **Futuristic Setting Description** If you were to write a science fiction story with a strong message, what would the setting be like? Imagine and write a description of a futuristic setting. Consider the time and place and how this futuristic world is different from our world today. How do changes in technology or the environment affect your setting? Place the description in your **Working Portfolio.**

Activities & Explorations

1. **Keepsake Scrapbook** In the previous two stories, objects from the past—a book, seashells—remind characters of times gone by. Think of some of the objects or activities in your life that are special to you. Create a scrapbook that could help your grandchildren understand what your life is like now. Paste objects, pictures, or drawings onto paper to make a scrapbook. Include a brief description of each item you include. Display your scrapbook in the classroom. **~ VIEWING AND REPRESENTING**

2. **Technology Interview** With a partner, plan and conduct an interview with an older relative or friend. Ask about the changes in technology that have occurred in his or her lifetime. Focus on changes in the ways people communicate and changes in the environment. Share the results of your interview with the class. **~ SPEAKING AND LISTENING**

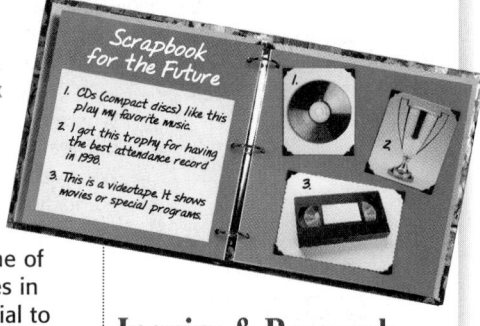

Scrapbook for the Future
1. CDs (compact discs) like this play my favorite music.
2. I got this trophy for having the best attendance record in 1998.
3. This is a videotape. It shows movies or special programs.

Inquiry & Research

Future Perfect Research old science fiction stories for descriptions of the future. Set up a chart like the one shown here to keep track of the descriptions you find and whether or not they are accurate today.

Story Name and Description	Today's Reality

 Real World Link Read "Home on an Icy Planet" on pages 588–591 before filling in your chart of descriptions.

Teaching Options

Mini Lesson · Grammar

IDENTIFYING PREPOSITIONS AND THEIR OBJECTS Tell students that a *preposition* shows how a noun or a pronoun relates to another word in a sentence. The noun or pronoun that follows a preposition is the *object of the preposition.*

Instruction Write the following sentence on the chalkboard:

I think it would be scary to live in the future.

Ask students to identify the preposition *(in)* and its object *(future).*

Exercises Have students create sentences using prepositions and objects from the lists below. For each sentence, they should choose one preposition and one object (not necessarily the one across from it). They may put more than one prepositional phrase in a sentence.

Prepositions	Objects
about	sunshine
toward	him
near	bicycle
beyond	them
under	teacher
during	candle light
upon	child
among	us
past	boxes
at	sea shells

 Use **Unit Four Resource Book,** p. 60. Use **Grammar Transparencies and Copymasters,** p. 102.

Language Network Use McDougal Littell's **Language Network,** Chapter 6, for more practice in identifying prepositions and their objects.

Assessment Practice

Comparing Literature
ASSESSMENT PRACTICE

PART 1 Reading the Prompt

On tests you are often asked to respond to a writing prompt like the one below. A writing prompt gives you a topic for an essay and often explains how to focus your writing. When you come across a writing prompt, first read the entire prompt carefully. Then read it again, looking for key words that can help you identify the purpose of the essay.

> **Write a Comparison-and-Contrast Essay**
>
> "The Fun They Had" and "The Sand Castle" both present visions of what the future might be like. In an essay, compare and contrast the settings of the ❶ two stories. Use examples from the stories to ❷ support your points. Conclude your essay by explaining which setting you think is more ❸ frightening and why.

STRATEGIES IN ACTION

❶ I have to **compare and contrast** the settings of two stories about the future.

❷ I need to use **examples** from the stories.

❸ I have to tell **which future** I think is scarier, and why.

PART 2 Planning a Comparison-and-Contrast Essay

- Review the Points of Comparison on pages 573 and 585.

- Use your Venn diagram to find examples of similarities and differences in the two stories' settings.

- Create an outline with headings for "Introduction," "Body," and "Conclusion."

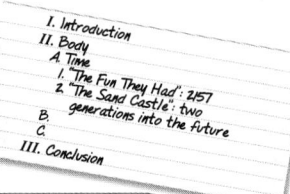

I. Introduction
II. Body
  A. Time
    1. "The Fun They Had": 2157
    2. "The Sand Castle": two generations into the future
  B.
  C.
III. Conclusion

PART 3 Drafting Your Essay

Introduction Clearly state your essay's purpose—to compare and contrast two science fiction settings. Briefly describe your understanding of a science fiction setting.

Body Decide how to organize your essay. One way is to use a separate paragraph to discuss each aspect of setting (time, place, what is similar to today's world, what is different from today's world). Start each paragraph with a topic sentence. Include examples from the stories. As you write, refer to your Points of Comparison diagram.

Conclusion Your conclusion should be your most lasting idea, such as which future you find more frightening.

Revising Reread your essay to make certain that it is free of mistakes. Check to make sure your writing is clear and that the reader always knows which story you are discussing.

Writing Handbook
See p. R35: Compare and Contrast.

Comparing Literature
ASSESSMENT PRACTICE

PART 1 Reading the Prompt
Model the process of reading a prompt.
- Read through the prompt in its entirety.
- Point out key words of the assignment (*compare, contrast, settings, examples, frightening*)
- Clarify the key words using the Strategies in Action to show how students can restate the prompts in their own words.

PART 2 Planning a Comparison-and-Contrast Essay
- Students can use the charts referenced on pages 573, 579, and 585.
- Have students use the outline on this page as a model for their own outline.
- Students may wish to fill in the outline with details about the setting of one story and then the other story, using the information from their Venn diagrams.

 Use **Unit Four Resource Book**, p. 63, for more practice. Use **Writing Transparencies**, p. 54, for additional support.

PART 3 Drafting Your Essay
Introduction Students should include that they will be talking about the two elements of setting—time and place. They may want to include that they will be comparing the two stories to each other, as well as to today's world.
Body Another way to organize would be to do all the elements of one story in one paragraph, all the elements of the other story in the next paragraph, and then write two more paragraphs comparing each story to today's world.
Conclusion Encourage students to not only tell which setting was more frightening, but to tell why. This will create a more powerful essay.
Revising Have students check each paragraph in the body for strong topic sentences. A strong topic sentence will help them to maintain their organization and will make the order of their comparison clear.

Use **Writing Transparencies**, p. 29, for additional support.

Real WORLD Link

Magazine Article

Objectives
- read and analyze a magazine article
- understand how main idea and supporting details are presented
- use the skills of note taking, paraphrasing, summarizing, and outlining
- learn about how some students have connected their own ideas and their school studies to create a realistic project

Connecting to the Literature
An article such as "Home on an Icy Planet" can help students make connections to stories such as "The Sand Castle" and "The Fun They Had." As students read, ask them to think about how the students in this article took ideas from science and from their imaginations and turned them into a realistic model.

HOME on an Icy Planet

From left to right, engineer Craig Smith, Adam Patinkin, Brian Freedman, alternate Dan Dresner, Matt Keenan, and teacher Barbara Janes with the winning model.

588   UNIT FOUR   PART 2: IMAGINARY WORLDS

Kids design a winning city for the future

It all began with a frozen planet named Hoth in the movie *The Empire Strikes Back*. What a cool place for a human colony! Four seventh-grade boys from Central School in Illinois decided to design a city on such a planet. Their city, Seolforis (See-*ol*-for-ees), won the $5,000 prize in the Future City Competition in Washington, D.C. The contest is held each February during National Engineers Week.

"The biggest challenge was balancing the atmosphere so that the ice wouldn't melt," says Adam Patinkin, 13. The boys decided to build the city near geothermal vents—deep cracks that let heat escape from a planet's hot core. The surface there would be warmest and most livable.

The boys built a model with plastic cups, boxes and Petri dishes. They could not spend more than $100.

Matt Keenan, 12, explains that humans would have come to Seolforis (early English for "silver ice") to mine rich pockets of silver. He planned the mines and a hydroponics system—a way to grow plants with water and nutrients but no soil.

Reading for Information

If you have difficulty understanding new ideas in a piece of writing, take notes using paraphrasing, summarizing, and outlining. When you use your own words to paraphrase and summarize the main points, it helps you understand what you read. Outlining is a way to organize your ideas, summaries, opinions, and additional questions. Outlining is also a useful way to draft a report.

TAKING NOTES AND OUTLINING IDEAS

Try organizing your notes on index cards. Using your own words, paraphrase and summarize the information. Write the main idea at the top of the card, followed by the paraphrased information or summary. Below that, write any new questions that arise. When you finish taking notes, sort your cards into groups of similar ideas. Then you can use the groups to create an **outline**, a visual display of the main ideas and supporting details. It is easier to create an outline if you first take notes.

YOUR TURN *Use the questions and activities below to help you take notes on this article.*

❶ **Paraphrasing** Often a subtitle gives the main idea of an article. Paraphrase the main idea of this article as it is given here. Record it on an index card.

❷ On a note card, record supporting details about the Future City Competition. Then write the main idea at the top of your card.

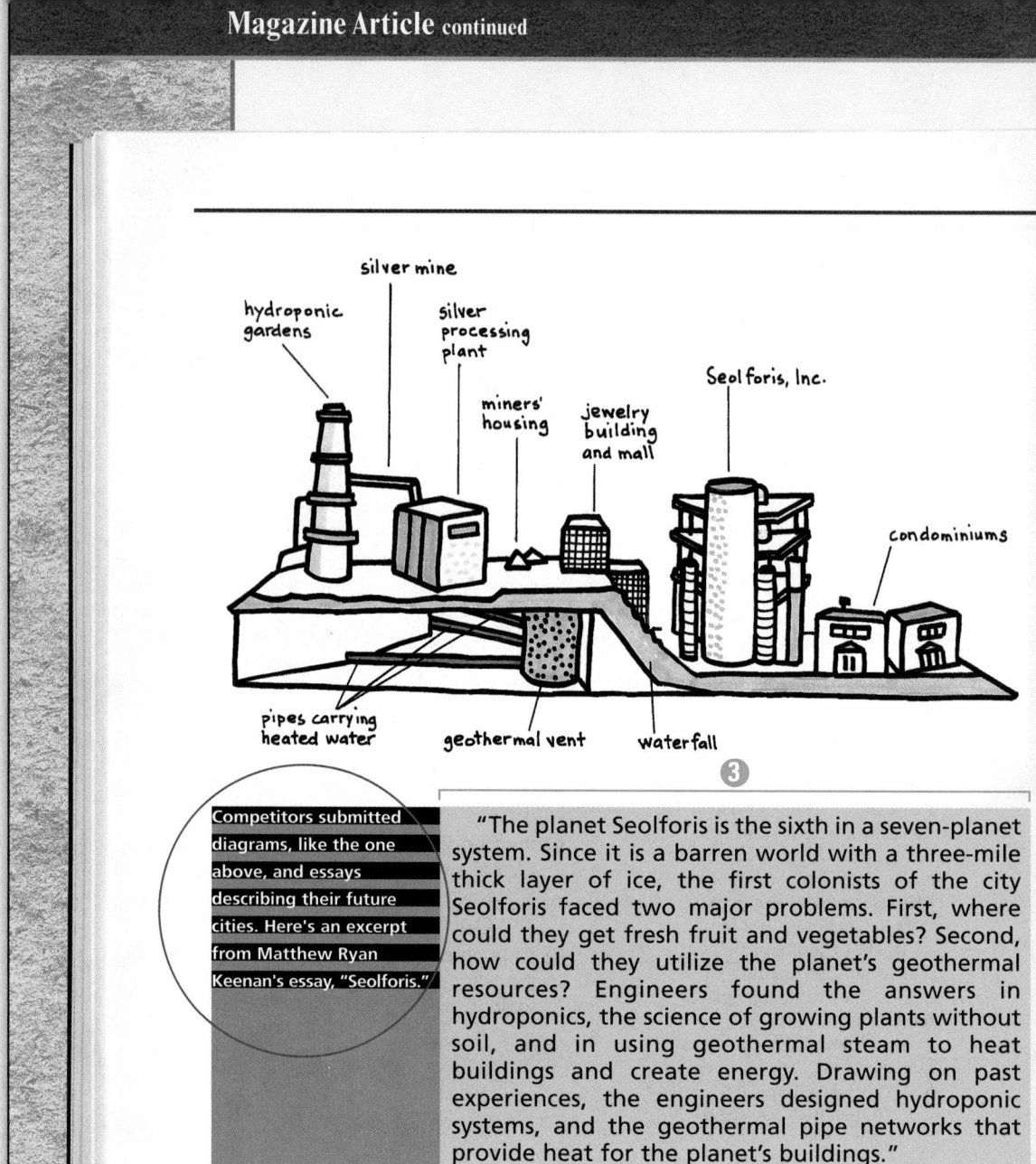

silver mine

hydroponic gardens

silver processing plant

miners' housing

jewelry building and mall

Seolforis, Inc.

condominiums

pipes carrying heated water

geothermal vent

waterfall

3

Competitors submitted diagrams, like the one above, and essays describing their future cities. Here's an excerpt from Matthew Ryan Keenan's essay, "Seolforis."

"The planet Seolforis is the sixth in a seven-planet system. Since it is a barren world with a three-mile thick layer of ice, the first colonists of the city Seolforis faced two major problems. First, where could they get fresh fruit and vegetables? Second, how could they utilize the planet's geothermal resources? Engineers found the answers in hydroponics, the science of growing plants without soil, and in using geothermal steam to heat buildings and create energy. Drawing on past experiences, the engineers designed hydroponic systems, and the geothermal pipe networks that provide heat for the planet's buildings."

Teaching Options

Brian Freedman, 13, was the city planner who made sure Seolforis would have everything its people might need, including education, jobs, recycling, food and lots of fun.

"Where we come from, a really small town, there isn't anything to do within 20 miles," says Brian, who built the city model with Dan Dresner. Lucky citizens could watch the Seolforis Miners play baseball on climate-controlled Koufax Field. They could also check out 3-D holographic movies.

Science teacher Barbara Janes and engineer Craig Smith helped the team. But the boys had to nail down tricky scientific details. "If we had it to do over, we would not put the city on an ice planet," says Adam. "It took us so long to figure everything out."

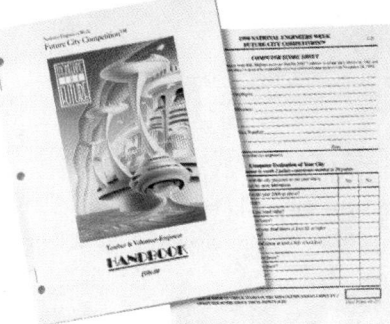

The Future City Competition Handbook contains the rules, regulations, and entry form for the contest.

Reading for Information *continued*

3 Paraphrase the main idea in this paragraph, then record any important thoughts or details that support it. Continue taking notes on the rest of the article. Remember to record each main idea at the top of an index card.

Outlining Important Ideas Now that you have finished taking notes on the article, create an outline like the one shown below. List main ideas as headings, next to Roman numerals. Below each main idea, list the details that support it. Use capital letters for the general details, and numbers and lowercase letters for more specific details. Remember to write down only the key points. Don't try to copy every word; summarize and paraphrase the information.

> I. Students Win Future City Competition
>   A. The Future City Competition
>   1. Goal is to design a future city
>   2. Held during National Engineers Week
>   a. Each February in Washington, D. C.
>   b. Who can enter?
>   3.

Inquiry & Research

Activity Link: "The Fun They Had" and "The Sand Castle," p. 586. Suppose you decide to enter the Future City Competition and want to create a city based on either "The Fun They Had" or "The Sand Castle." Use information from the story, as well as your own imagination, to create an outline that will help you plan, build, and prepare your model. Your outline may include your city's name, its location, the names of your advisors and team members and their roles or tasks, and the materials you will need to build your model.

---

3 Possible Response:
Main Idea:
Conditions on Seolforis posed two major problems for colonists, both of which were solved by engineering.
Supporting Ideas:
A. Problems
1. planet is barren, covered with ice
2. planet is cold
B. Engineering Solutions
1. hydroponics—agriculture without soil—used to grow fruits and vegetables
2. geothermal steam used for heat and to create energy
Students should follow the same format for each of the remaining paragraphs: List the main idea at the top of the card and some supporting details under the main idea.

Outlining Important Ideas Ask students to note how the sample outline uses brief statements, not complete thoughts or long sentences. Students should use their own note cards to create their outline. The one shown here is just a sample.

 Use **Writing Transparencies,** pp. 49, 54, for additional support. Use **Reading and Critical Thinking Transparencies,** p. 46, for additional support.

Mini Lesson **Inquiry & Research**

The Inquiry & Research activity on this page links to the Inquiry & Research activity on page 586 from the Choices & Challenges page following "The Fun They Had" and "The Sand Castle."

Instruction Lead a discussion reviewing the main ideas of the two selections, with a focus on the settings. Ask students to compare these settings with those given for the city created in the Future City contest. Remind students of the guidelines for outlining. Help them create an outline for their own Future City entry by modeling one of your

own, or from data gathered from the class. Focus the discussion on the setting of this Future City entry. Encourage students to be creative and to use past personal experiences as well as the material in the selections and the magazine article.

Application As students work on their outlines, provide opportunities for them to share with peers and to revise and adjust their outlines as appropriate. It may be fun to follow through with actually building a Future City.

Objectives
- write a short story
- use a written text as a model for writing
- revise a draft to include a consistent point of view
- use appositive phrases

Introducing the Workshop

Short Story Discuss with students short stories they have previously read as a class. Have them consider which stories are most memorable and ask them to explain why.

Basics in a Box
Using the Graphic The graphic on this page shows the three main parts of a short story. Point out that the graphic suggests elements for each part that students should include when they draft their stories.

Presenting the Rubric To better understand the assignment, students can refer to the standards for writing a successful short story. You may also want to share with them the complete rubric, which describes several levels of proficiency.

 Use McDougal Littell's **Language Network,** Chapters 10–17, for more instruction on essential writing skills.

 Power Presentation

To engage students visually, use **Power Presentation 2,** Short Story.

Writing Workshop — Short Story

Creating your own world . . .

From Reading to Writing What will the world be like in a hundred years? Isaac Asimov answers this question in the futuristic story "The Fun They Had." Even though the world of the story is imaginary, it seems real because of the vivid details and realistic dialogue between characters. As the writer of a **short story,** you, too, can build your own world and create the characters within it.

For Your Portfolio

WRITING PROMPT Write a short story about an imaginary world or place that interests you.

Purpose: To entertain
Audience: Your classmates, family, or general readers

Basics in a Box

Short Story at a Glance

Introduction	Body	Conclusion
Sets the stage by	**Develops the plot by**	**Finishes the story by**
• introducing the **characters**	• introducing the conflict	• resolving the **conflict**
• describing the **setting**	• telling a sequence of **events**	• telling the **last event**
	• developing **characters** through words and actions	
	• building toward a **climax**	

RUBRIC STANDARDS FOR WRITING

A successful short story should
- have a strong beginning and ending
- use the elements of character, setting, and plot to create a convincing world
- use techniques such as vivid sensory language, concrete details, and dialogue to create believable characters and setting
- have a main conflict
- present a clear sequence of events
- maintain a consistent point of view

LESSON RESOURCES

USING PRINT RESOURCES
Unit Four Resource Book
- Prewriting, p. 64
- Drafting and Elaboration, p. 65
- Peer Response Guide, pp. 66–67
- Revising, Editing, and Proofreading, p. 68
- Student Models, pp. 69–71
- Rubric for Evaluation, p. 72
Writing Transparencies
- Writing Process Transparencies, TR 1–TR 4

- Writing Template Transparencies: Short Story, TR 34
- Writing Style Transparencies: Point of View, TR 23
Reading and Critical Thinking Transparencies
- Sequence Chain, TR 39 (for Mini Lesson, p. 593)
Grammar Transparencies and Copymasters
- Punctuating, Choosing, and Incorporating Quotations, CM 127 (for Mini Lesson, p. 596)

- Appositive Phrases, CM 64 (for Mini Lesson, p. 597)

INTEGRATED TECHNOLOGY
LaserLinks
Writing Springboards
See **Teacher's SourceBook** p. 56 for bar codes.

Writing Coach CD-ROM
Visit our website:
www.mcdougallittell.com

Analyzing a Student Model

SPEAKING OPPORTUNITY
See the Communication Handbook, p. R100 for speaking and presenting tips.

Ben Wright
Somerville Charter School

A World of Color

"Clones! Awaken!" The Leader's booming voice echoed through the city. Bleary-eyed, Zolak sat up in bed and looked at the digital display on his wall. 6:00 A.M. He shook the dreams from his mind and quickly reviewed his day. Again, he would have to work hard with the other clones to maintain the city. He scanned the shelves of his cubicle for all of his necessities: a food-pellet processor, a single blue uniform, and a one-way communication unit that broadcasted his daily directives. He had everything he needed, but life on his planet was not easy. Each day his normal routine drew him out of the room and down to the work lines where all the clones stood together, building, repairing, and ripping down power lines and bridges, walls and gutters.

Zolak looked like all the others, but he had never quite fit in. Years ago, he had had fantastic dreams about a world of colors—a world of trees and flowers and birds—things you only saw in books. And of course there was the letter he still carried with him from his mother. "You are not a clone. You must never believe the Leader's lies." She had been terminated because of her strange ideas.

Zolak had kept quiet about the letter. He was lucky to be alive. Most plant and animal life had been destroyed during the Great War, so the Leaders had to clone people and animals to maintain life on the planet. The human clones were "born" at the age of fifteen, possessing all the knowledge they would need to work for the Leaders. Their lives would be terminated at age thirty by an electrical pulse sent through the bracelets they all wore. The world the Leaders had designed was extremely efficient and full of constant work.

As he swallowed his morning food pellet, he noticed for the first time that it was bland. Was something happening to him? Then the loud voice of the Leader interrupted him. "Zolak, today you are assigned to drill air holes in Sector Twenty-one." Zolak quickly walked out of his cubicle to join the other clones.

The clones moved in silent lines like ants. Every now and then, they would pass through the oxygen booths that provided a quick dose of pure oxygen. Without this oxygen, they would tire rapidly and couldn't work in the polluted subterranean atmosphere. The air holes that they were going to drill in Sector Twenty-one were the first step in constructing new oxygen booths. Zolak imagined that the world above

RUBRIC IN ACTION

❶ Captures reader's attention with a quote
Other Options:
- Begin with action
- Begin with a description

❷ Precise sensory details establish setting.

❸ Develops central conflict that was hinted at in the introduction

❹ Background information is ordered chronologically.

Teaching the Lesson

Analyzing the Model
"A World of Color"

The student model is a short story about a clone who lives in a colorless and restricted world but longs to live in a world of color and freedom. The student author uses vivid details and descriptions to help the reader visualize the setting and the characters.

Have students think of a short story they have read in which the setting is particularly memorable and easy to visualize. Help students to see how vivid details and sensory descriptions bring a story to life. Then point out the key words and phrases in the student model that correspond to the elements mentioned in the rubric in action.

1. Have students think of an alternative opening sentence.
   Possible Responses: Zolak opened his eyes and looked around his gray, colorless surroundings; Zolak leaped out of bed as the Leader's voice boomed over the city.

2. Ask students what impression they get of Zolak's life from this description.
   Possible Responses: Zolak's life is tedious and his days are filled with hard labor; the tasks that make up his daily life are never-ending and always the same.

3. Ask students to summarize the central conflict in their own words.
   Possible Response: Since most plant and animal life had been wiped out in the Great War, clones—like Zolak—that "live" for 15 years do all the work of the society.

4. Ask students why this background information is important to the story.
   Possible Responses: Because it reveals more about Zolak's life and his character; because it moves the story ahead to the ending events.

 Mini Lesson ## Viewing and Representing

PICTURING TEXT STRUCTURE

Instruction While word choice and ideas play key roles in good writing, the structure of a text—the way in which ideas are organized and events unfold—also contributes to the effectiveness of the work.

Activity Have students analyze the organization of the student model by constructing a diagram or other graphic organizer. The following flow chart is an example.

Use **Reading and Critical Thinking Transparencies**, p. 39, for additional support.

Setting is established and main character is introduced.

Central conflict is introduced and Zolak's situation is established.

Background information helps prepare the reader for the events that follow.

Zolak discovers the other world and is forced to make a decision.

Zolak acts and runs for freedom.

5. Ask students to describe the effect that is created by the third-person point of view.

Possible Responses: Suspense and tension is heightened because neither the reader nor the narrator knows what is going to happen; the reader has a sense of being outside Zolak's world, looking in.

6. Discuss the color images in this paragraph and how they contrast with Zolak's world.

Possible Responses: Zolak never saw green or blue, let alone *shades* of these colors, except in dreams. The color was the most important thing missing from his world.

7. Ask students to discuss how the student author creates tension and suspense in this paragraph.

Possible Responses: By including dialogue that increases the action; by using strong, active verbs; by emphasizing the strangeness of Zolak's situation.

8. Ask students to explain how the student author ties the conclusion of the story into the opening paragraphs.

Possible Response: The author places Zolak in the world of bright colors that he longed for in the beginning of the story.

---

had oxygen. He wondered what else it it might have? He stopped himself from wondering why none of the other clones had questions.

Zolak's bracelet beeped. While he had been lost in thought, the other clones had finished and were back in their cubicles. Zolak spoke into his bracelet. "I have one more hole to drill."

The piercing voice answered him. "You have thirty minutes to finish."

Zolak was alone. He tried to concentrate on his drilling. He finally finished the hole. Suddenly the area around it began to crack and crumble around him. He looked up. He was face to face with a pair of sparkling aqua eyes. He had never seen such a creature.

A high, singing voice said, "Zolak, we have been waiting a long time for you." Zolak was astonished. The creature had yellow hair and red lips. It motioned for him to come forward through the opening. Zolak looked through. All the shades of green, blue, yellow, pink, and other colors that he had only seen in his dreams washed over him. Hundreds of creatures, all shapes and sizes with high singing voices, surrounded him. They repeated his name. The creature, the one with the aqua eyes, took his hand and laughed. "You are one of us. This is your home." Zolak experienced joy for the first time in his life, but he had no word for it.

Just then, fear seized him. He looked at his bracelet. The piercing voice cut in, "Where are you, Zolak? Why is your heart beating so quickly?" Zolak tried to answer in his usual voice but couldn't. He was dizzy from all of the pure air he had breathed. It was difficult to think, and soon he was running back from the hole. The piercing voice demanded, "You are trying to escape."

"No, I'm coming. It took longer than I expected," Zolak gasped.

"That is a lie, Zolak. You must be terminated."

It was now or never. Zolak could die in the middle of this cold tunnel or he could try to escape to the world of colors. The voice began counting down: "10 . . . 9 . . . 8." Zolak turned back and sprinted with every ounce of strength he could muster. He could see the light now. "6 . . . 5 . . . ." The tunnel was beginning to get warmer. "4! . . . 3! . . . 2!" The voice was crazy, angry. But he was almost there. "1!" He leaped for the hole as the voice screamed "ZERO!" The glowing bracelet flashed and went dark. As he entered his new world, Zolak felt his bracelet rip from his wrist. Surrounded by singing and laughter under a deep blue sky, Zolak was finally free.

❺ Uses third-person point of view throughout the story

❻ Sensory details contrast the world above with Zolak's world below.

❼ Character's reactions make him seem believable.

❽ Conclusion resolves the conflict and ends the story at the climax.

Writing Your Short Story

❶ Prewriting

Stories are like fairy gold. The more you give away, the more you have.
—Polly McGuire

Write down familiar places and people and **imagine** how they would be different in a future or past world. **Listen** for stories or unusual happenings. **Read** information on the kind of space travel that is possible now. See the **Idea Bank** in the margin for more suggestions. After you select an idea, follow the steps below.

Planning Your Short Story

▶ **1. Plan the major parts of your story.**
   - **Characters.** You'll probably have one or more main characters plus some minor ones. Decide what background information is necessary to include.
   - **Setting.** Where will the story take place and when? Does the setting affect the characters and plot in any way?
   - **Plot.** Work out the major events of your story. What is the conflict? Decide what will happen at the beginning, middle, and end of the story.

▶ **2. Choose a narrator.** Who will tell your story? Do you want one of the characters to tell the story in the first person, or would you like your narrator to be outside of the action?

▶ **3. Create a mood.** Do you want your story to be sad, frightening, mysterious, humorous, or serious? How will you create that feeling through your characters and setting?

❷ Drafting

Begin writing your short story by introducing the setting, characters, or first event in your plot. Include dialogue that will help your reader get to know the characters and see the action unfolding. Also use sensory details to make your story come alive. For example, "The Fun They Had" gives readers the sensation of how antique pages look and feel: "They turned the pages, which were yellow and crinkly. . . ."

Ask Your Peer Reader: Evaluating

- Did I clearly describe the characters and setting?
- Was the plot engaging and logical?
- Was the tone appropriate to the content?
- Was my choice of a narrator appropriate and consistent?

IDEA Bank

1. Your Working Portfolio
Look for ideas in the **Writing Options** that you completed earlier in this unit.
- **Plot Analysis**, p. 553
- **Narrative Poem**, p. 562

2. Sequels
Think of stories that you've enjoyed. Imagine how you might go about writing a sequel, or follow-up story, to one of them, using the same characters but a different plot and setting.

3. Puzzle Pieces
Fold a piece of paper into nine squares. Write down three names of people, three feeling words, and three events—anything from a birthday party to a natural disaster. Then cut out the squares and turn them, face down. Choose two squares from the names section, one from the feeling section, and one from events. Put the words together and use them as a starting point for your story.

Have a question?

See the **Writing Handbook**
Description, p. R31
Narrative Writing, p. R33

Prewriting

Choosing a Subject

If after reading the Idea Bank students have difficulty choosing a subject for their short stories, suggest that they try the following:

- Think of a setting that would be ideal for a scary story, or for a fairy tale. Describe the setting in detail and then decide what kinds of characters would fit in with the setting. Build your story around the setting and the characters.
- Pick a wild animal whose habits you know something about, such as a rabbit or a squirrel, and write an imaginative story about how that animal might spend its day.

Planning the Short Story

1. Encourage students to brainstorm possible characters, plots, and settings.
2. Suggest that students write two versions of an introductory paragraph from two different points of view, then decide which one is more interesting and suitable for the story topic.
3. Suggest that students write a list of words that they think evoke the mood they wish to create. They can use these words as a starting point.

Drafting

Suggest that student volunteers read the dialogue and descriptions they've written to the class. Ask students to discuss ways to make the dialogue natural and exciting, and to add vivid and precise language in order to enhance the descriptions.

Ask Your Peer Reader

Remind students to use the peer reviewer's feedback when revising their drafts.

Revising
MAINTAINING A CONSISTENT POINT OF VIEW

Review the change in the sample with students. To help students practice maintaining a consistent point of view, have them share their drafts with a partner who will check the essay for inconsistencies.

 Use **Writing Transparencies**, p. 23, for additional support.

Editing and Proofreading
APPOSITIVE PHRASES

Remind students that appositive phrases usually follow a noun or pronoun and identify or explain it. Have students explain the change in the sample. For more practice, see the Grammar Mini Lesson at the bottom of page 597.

Reflecting

 As they write their reflections, have students consider what aspects of short stories they will be more aware of in the future.

Option
Managing the Paper Load

To reduce grading time, try reading students' stories quickly for enjoyment and then respond by using a check, a plus, or a minus sign rather than formal letter or number grades.

SPELLING From Writing

 As you revise your work, look back at the words you misspelled and determine why you made the errors you did. For additional help, refer to the strategies and generalizations in the **Spelling Handbook** on page R86.

Need revising help?

Review the **Rubric**, p. 593
Consider **peer reader** comments
Check **Revision Guidelines**, p. R23

Frantic about phrases?

See the **Grammar Handbook**, p. R75

Publishing IDEAS

- Organize your stories and those of your classmates into a short-story collection. Use a computer to print out copies for friends and family.
- Host a Read-Aloud Month. Invite students from other classes to come in and listen to various short stories being read out loud.

More Online: Publishing Options www.mcdougallittell.com

---

❸ Revising
TARGET SKILL ▶ MAINTAINING CONSISTENT POINT OF VIEW Because you do not want your readers to be confused, you must maintain a consistent point of view throughout your story. You may choose to use a first-person narrator who is one of the characters. When the narrator is a participant in the story and refers to him or herself as *I*, this indicates first-person point of view. When events are told by a narrator outside the story, using the pronouns *he, she, it,* and *they,* this indicates third-person point of view. Whichever point of view you choose, stay with it throughout your story.

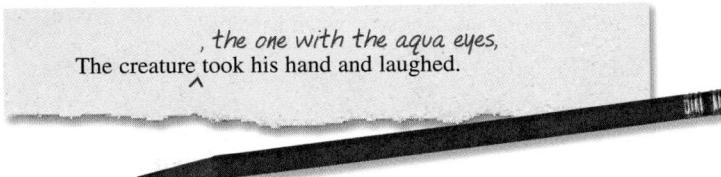

> Zolak spoke into his bracelet. "I have one more hole to drill." The piercing voice answered ~~me~~. of him

❹ Editing and Proofreading
TARGET SKILL ▶ APPOSITIVE PHRASES An appositive phrase renames something. It is used to give more details or information about a person, idea, or thing. For example, the appositive phrase in the following sentence gives added detail about the subject: *Ellen, a hard-working student, finished the book report before going out to play.* Make sure that you set off appositive phrases with commas.

> The creature took his hand and laughed.
> , the one with the aqua eyes,

❺ Reflecting
FOR YOUR WORKING PORTFOLIO Which parts of the writing process did you find most difficult? What did you learn about short stories from writing your own? Attach your answers to your finished work. Save your short story in your **Working Portfolio**.

(Mini Lesson) Grammar

PUNCTUATING, CHOOSING, AND INCORPORATING QUOTATIONS Tell students that using quotations will help make their writing interesting, active, and vivid. Remind them that the quotations should help reveal information about the character or setting, or should help move the action forward. Quotations should generally be set off by commas.
Practice Have students find the punctuation and placement errors in the following sentences and suggest corrections. Some are correct.

1. "Throw the ball here!" he yelled to his teammate. *(correct)*
2. She said regretfully. "No, I cannot come to your birthday party," *(regretfully, party.)*
3. "I" Caroline told her mother "would like to get a puppy." *(I, mother,)*
4. Sam whispered, "But I don't want to go swimming." *(correct)*
5. "The cat has." she confided to me. "run away." *(has, me,)*

 Use **Grammar Transparencies and Copymasters**, p. 127, for more practice.

 Use McDougal Littell's **Language Network**, Chapter 9, for more instruction on punctuation.

Assessment Practice | Revising & Editing

Read this paragraph from the first draft of a short story. The underlined sections may include the following kinds of errors:

- **errors in appositive phrases**
- **capitalization errors**
- **spelling errors**
- **sentence fragments**

For each underlined section, choose the version that most improves the writing.

> Sand stretched across the horizon. <u>The egyptian princess</u> began to
> (1)
> panic. She wondered aloud, "<u>Were are we?</u>" Her camels and most of her
> (2)
> water supply had been stolen <u>by soldiers of her enemy; Prince Neto.</u>
> (3)
> The princess walked alongside her loyal servants and guards. <u>Trudged</u>
> <u>in the heat for several hours.</u> Suddenly, clouds on the horizon signaled
> (4)
> the approach of other <u>travlers</u>. <u>The princess watched, frozen with fear,</u>
> (5) (6)
> <u>nervously.</u> Then she recognized the king coming to assist her.

1. A. The Egyptian princess
   B. The Egyptian Princess
   C. The egyptian Princess
   D. Correct as is

2. A. "Ware are we?"
   B. "Wear are we?"
   C. "Where are we?"
   D. Correct as is

3. A. by soldiers of her enemy.
         Prince Neto.
   B. by soldiers of her enemy:
         Prince Neto.
   C. by soldiers of her enemy,
         Prince Neto.
   D. Correct as is

4. A. Trudging in the heat for
         several hours.
   B. They trudged in the heat for
         several hours.
   C. They, trudging in the heat for
         several hours.
   D. Correct as is

5. A. travlerrs
   B. travvelers
   C. travelers
   D. Correct as is

6. A. The princess watched
         nervously frozen, with fear.
   B. The princess frozen with fear
         watched nervously.
   C. The princess, frozen with fear,
         watched nervously.
   D. Correct as is

Need extra help?

See the **Grammar Handbook**

Quick Reference: Punctuation p. R56

Quick Reference: Capitalization, p. R58

 Grammar

APPOSITIVE PHRASES For use with Editing and Proofreading, p. 596. Remind students that an appositive is a noun or a phrase that explains one or more words in a sentence. Appositives are set off by commas if they add extra information to the main idea. If they add an essential detail, such as a proper name, they are not set off by commas.

Practice Have students correct the punctuation errors in the following sentences. Some sentences are correct.

1. Harvey's, a famous restaurant, first opened for business in 1859. *(correct)*
2. South African president Nelson Mandela visited the White House last year. *(correct)*
3. The dog an old Labrador looked longingly at the hamburger. *(dog, Labrador,)*
4. The British monarch, Queen Elizabeth II, has reigned for many years. *(monarch (no comma); Elizabeth II (no comma))*
5. The old man, a golfer, made a hole in one. *(correct)*

Use **Unit Four Resource Book**, p. 68.
Use **Grammar Transparencies and Copymasters**, p. 64, for more practice.

 Use McDougal Littell's *Language Network*, Chapter 1, for more practice with the sentence and its parts.

Objectives
- reflect on and assess student understanding of the unit and its theme
- review literary concepts and skills introduced in the unit
- assess and build portfolios

Reflecting on the Theme

OPTION 1

A successful response will
- include a chosen selection from the unit and an explanation for its choice
- provide support for selection choice with examples of the "wondrous" elements each contains
- evaluate the author's craft in creating a "wondrous world"

OPTION 2

A successful response will
- begin with a detailed list of animals and the traits that make each animal wondrous
- include thoughtful writing with examples of the wondrous animals from each list
- conclude with a paragraph of summary, using ideas from each animal and its traits, to make a generalization about animals and their wondrous nature

OPTION 3

A successful response will
- include reflective discussion of the fantasy and science fiction genres, and the elements that make them unique
- provide specific examples from the selections in the unit to support that discussion
- compare these genres to realistic fiction and offer a concluding statement that reflects the theme of the unit

Self Assessment

It may be helpful for students to discuss the quotation with a partner or small group prior to the writing portion of the assessment. Encourage students to reflect on their peer discussion, the stories in this unit, and their own personal experiences, thoughts, and feelings.

598   UNIT FOUR

Wondrous Worlds

In the selections in this unit, you've seen that wondrous worlds are found not just in imaginary lands and made-up adventures, but in the everyday behavior of animals around us. How have these stories changed the way you view the world around you? Explore this question by completing one or more of the options in each of the following sections.

Party Animals, Julia Lucich.

Reflecting on the Theme

OPTION 1

Judging Impact Which works of literature in this unit inspire awe, surprise, or admiration? Choose the selection that made the biggest impression on you, and write two or three paragraphs about its "wondrous" elements. How do you think the author of the work achieves this impact?

OPTION 2

Analyzing the Theme Make a list of all the animals in Part One of this unit. Think about the part theme, "Animal Wonders." Next to each animal's name, make notes about how the animal relates to the theme. What about each animal or its behavior is wondrous? Read over your list, and then write a paragraph answering this question: What makes an animal a "wonder"? Support your explanation with examples from the selections.

OPTION 3

Thinking About Genre Why do you think some writers choose to write in the genres of fantasy and science fiction? What do these types of literature allow a writer to do that he or she cannot do in realistic fiction? Write a few paragraphs in response to these questions. As you write your response, keep in mind the elements of science fiction and fantasy and the theme of this unit.

Self ASSESSMENT

Reconsider the quotation at the beginning of the unit: "In books, I have traveled not only to other worlds, but into my own." Write a paragraph explaining how reading the selections in this unit has given you a better understanding of the quotation's meaning.

REVIEWING YOUR PERSONAL WORDList

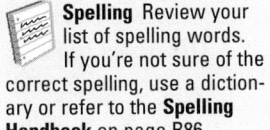

Vocabulary Review the new words you learned in this unit. If necessary, use a dictionary to check the meaning of each word.

Spelling Review your list of spelling words. If you're not sure of the correct spelling, use a dictionary or refer to the **Spelling Handbook** on page R86.

Reviewing Literary Concepts

OPTION 1

Analyzing Plot Structure Make a chart like the one shown to analyze the climax and resolution of each fiction selection you have read in this unit. Also note how a character or situation is changed by the events of each story's climax.

Story	Climax	Resolution	What Changes
Lob's Girl	Sandy comes out of a coma.	Granny finds out that Lob is dead.	The family understands Lob's love for Sandy.

OPTION 2

Analyzing Fantasy and Science Fiction Elements Create a fantasy and science fiction spectrum. Draw a horizontal line. Label one end of the line "Fantasy" and the other "Science Fiction." For each selection in Part Two of this unit, decide whether the selection is fantasy, science fiction, or a combination, and write its title on the line where you think it belongs. Discuss with the class where you placed each selection on the spectrum and why.

Building Your Portfolio

- **Writing Options** Several of the Writing Options in this unit asked you to write forms of poetry—rhyming couplets, a heroic ballad, a narrative poem, and a limerick. Choose the one that you feel best expresses a sense of wonder. Write a note explaining the reasons for your choice. Then attach the note to the poem and place it in your **Presentation Portfolio.**

- **Writing Workshops** In this unit you wrote a process description and a short story. Reread these two pieces and decide which you think is a stronger piece of writing. Write a cover note explaining the reasons for your choice, attach it to the piece, and place it in your **Presentation Portfolio.**

- **Additional Activities** Think back to any of the assignments you completed under **Activities & Explorations** and **Inquiry & Research.** Keep a record of the assignments that you especially enjoyed, found helpful, or would like to do further work on.

Self ASSESSMENT

📖 READER'S NOTEBOOK

On a sheet of paper, copy the following literary terms introduced in this unit, listing them in order of difficulty. Write down the concepts you find easiest first, and put at the bottom of the list the concepts you're not sure of. Use the **Glossary of Literary Terms** on page R6 to look up the terms in the lower half of your list.

story structure
foreshadowing
climax
essay
sound
  devices
resolution

realistic and
  fantastic
  details
fantasy
futuristic
  settings
mood

Self ASSESSMENT

Look over and compare the earliest work in your **Presentation Portfolio** 📁 with your more recent work. Write a note to yourself, describing what you now see as the strengths and weaknesses in your writing skills.

Setting GOALS

What reading or writing strategies do you want to work on as you complete the next unit? Write at least three goals on a sheet of paper. Exchange papers with a classmate and discuss ways that each of you might achieve your goals.

Reviewing Literary Concepts

OPTION 1

Use the Unit 4 Resource Book, page 73, to provide students a ready-made chart for analyzing plot structure. Have students complete the chart, including information about the climax and resolution of each selection. Make sure they analyze these elements of the plot carefully and thoughtfully and include discussion of how these events impacted the characters and situations in each story.

OPTION 2

Students should work independently on the spectrum, reflecting carefully before making each placement on the line. Encourage them to think of the evidence they will provide their classmates to support each placement. Students may want to share their spectrums with a small group prior to the whole class to allow them time to practice and reconsider each placement.

Building Your Portfolio

Students should evaluate the items in their Working Portfolios and choose pieces that represent their highest quality work for their Presentation Portfolio. As they attach notes to the items they transfer to their Presentation Portfolios, remind them to write the reasoning for their choices clearly so they will understand the notes several months from now.

📚 For more information on using Portfolios, use *Teacher's Guide to Assessment and Portfolio Use,* beginning on page 53.

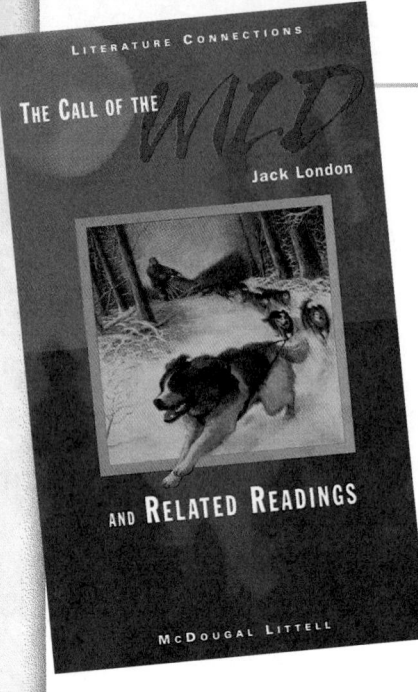

LITERATURE CONNECTIONS
The Call of the Wild

BY JACK LONDON

Buck, a beloved family pet, is stolen and shipped to Alaska during the 1890s Gold Rush. Mistreated, he learns to survive as a member of a dog sled team. Becoming more like a wolf and less like a domestic dog, Buck encounters many dangers. Jack London used his own experiences in the Klondike to write this classic tale of survival and adventure.

These thematically related readings are provided along with *The Call of the Wild*:

The Wolf and the Dog
BY MARIE DE FRANCE

from **The Hidden Life of Dogs**
BY ELIZABETH MARSHALL THOMAS

The Wolf Said to Francis
BY A. G. ROCHELLE

The Man Who Was a Horse
BY JULIUS LESTER

Unsentimental Mother
BY SALLY CARRIGHAR

Long Duel
BY ROBERT MURPHY

And Even *More* . . .

The Bat-Poet

By Randall Jarrell

A young bat keeps his eyes open during the day and discovers a wondrous world. He finds friends as he turns his amazement into poetry. Through poems, the little bat "captures" the chipmunk, mockingbird, and even the ferocious owl. About this book, Louis Untermeyer has written, "The combination of poetry and prose has never been bettered."

Books

A Newbery Zoo
BY M. GREENBERG, C. WAUGH
Animal fiction by authors Beverly Cleary, Robert Lawson, and others

My Friend Flicka
BY MARY O'HARA
After Kennie convinces his father to give him a colt, he proves his devotion.

The Lost Zoo
BY CHRISTOPHER CAT AND COUNTEE CULLEN
A menagerie of poems to each imaginary beast

A Wrinkle in Time

BY MADELEINE L'ENGLE

A science fiction novel about the struggle between good and evil, this absorbing story relates how Meg, her brother Charles Wallace, and her friend Calvin become involved with supernatural beings, inhabitants of distant planets, and a daring rescue.

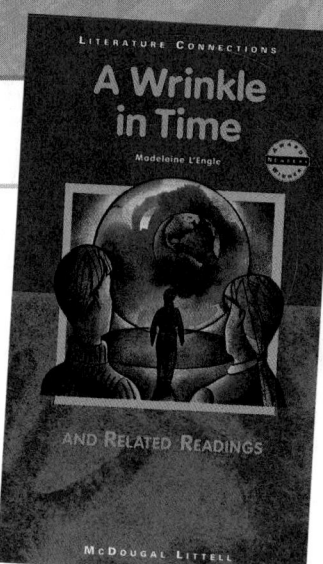

These thematically related readings are provided along with *A Wrinkle in Time*:

Odd Jobs
BY JUDITH GOROG

Reversible
BY OCTAVIO PAZ

Behind Bars
BY FADWA TUQAN

from **World of the Brain**
BY ALVIN AND VIRGINIA SILVERSTEIN

from **It's Our World, Too!**
BY PHILLIP HOOSE

The Dark Princess
BY RICHARD KENNEDY

The Sparrow
BY IVAN TURGENEV

Colony
BY RICK WERNLI

The Hobbit
BY J. R. R. TOLKIEN
Comfort-loving hobbit Bilbo ventures out to hunt a dragon.

The Remarkable Journey of Prince Jen
BY LLOYD ALEXANDER
A Chinese prince and two wise-cracking companions

The Ear, the Eye, and the Arm
BY NANCY FARMER
In Zimbabwe, 200 years in the future, a dangerous adventure

Other Media
The Original Adventures of Hank the Cowdog
Author John R. Erickson reads tales of Hank, West Texas mutt.
TEXAS MONTHLY PRESS
(AUDIOCASSETTE)

The Phantom Tollbooth
Milo drives through a tollbooth and enters an animated world.
MGM/UA HOME VIDEO
(VIDEOCASSETTE)

James and the Giant Peach
The movie version of Roald Dahl's classic describes the odd journey of James and his amazing animal friends.
WALT DISNEY PICTURES
(VIDEOCASSETTE)

Creatures 2
The Norn, a playful, peaceful race of aliens, need your help to survive.
MINDSCAPE ENTERTAINMENT
(CD-ROM)

This Reading and Writing for Assessment feature provides more practice in taking standardized tests. As students work through this lesson, they will have an opportunity to practice strategies for reading comprehension questions, multiple-choice questions, and essay and short-answer questions. Boxed strategies located alongside the text will help guide students through the activities. These strategies model processes for students to follow when taking standardized tests.

OBJECTIVES

- understand and apply strategies for reading a test selection
- recognize and answer questions about tone in a test selection
- analyze a literary excerpt included in a test selection
- understand and apply strategies for answering multiple-choice questions about a test selection
- respond to a prompt by extracting information from the text and presenting it in a written answer
- understand and apply strategies for revising and proofreading a test response

Reading&Writing — for Assessment

When you studied the test-taking strategies on pages 308-313, you learned helpful new techniques. The following pages will give you practice using these strategies and more.

PART 1 How to Read the Test Selection

Listed below are some basic reading strategies. By applying these strategies and by taking notes, you can identify the information you need in answering test questions.

> **STRATEGIES FOR READING A TEST SELECTION**
>
> ▶ **Before you begin reading, skim the questions that follow the passage.** These can help focus your reading.
>
> ▶ **Think about the title and message.** What does the title suggest about the overall message or theme of the selection?
>
> ▶ **Use active reading strategies such as analyzing, predicting, and questioning.** If the test directions allow you to mark on the test itself, make notes in the margin as you read.
>
> ▶ **Look for main ideas.** These are often stated at the beginning or end of paragraphs. Sometimes they are implied, not stated. After reading each paragraph, ask, What was this passage about?
>
> ▶ **Note the literary elements and techniques used by the writer.** Consider the effects of word choice, figurative language, and mood.
>
> ▶ **Evaluate the organization.** For a comparison-and-contrast essay, how well does the use of feature-by-feature or subject-by-subject organization work in the piece?
>
> ▶ **Look for expert testimony.** What supporting evidence or sources of information does the writer use? Why are these sources appropriate to the subject?
>
> ▶ **Make judgments about the writer's purpose.** Does the writer have a bias or use a particular tone? How does this affect the message and presentation of information?

① Moving On

by Asher Owens

1   For as long as I can remember, I've been falling asleep to the chirping of crickets. That is because I grew up on a farm that has been in our family for generations. Last year, when my dad's brother was old enough, he decided to take over the farm so that we could move into the city. ② I didn't know then that leaving the country behind me would take some adjusting.

2   The first thing I noticed about the city was the lack of open space. Growing up on a farm with the nearest house three miles away, I got used to the open landscape. I remember climbing the chestnut tree at the edge of our cornfield and looking out over ③ a huge quilt of green and gold. Every day after school, I'd climb to my post and look out. After the crops were harvested and the fields were completely empty, it was easy to imagine I was the only one left on the planet. In a city, you have to look harder to find that freedom. When I take the elevator up to the rooftop of my apartment building, I stare out across the blazing sky, swollen with buildings. The skyline looks as though it is on fire when the sun goes down.

3   The busy landscape isn't the only thing I've had to get used to since leaving the ④ rustic life. On a farm, things pretty much wind down when the sun sets. In the city, it is harder to find peace and quiet. For the first few months, sleeping was difficult because the traffic outside my window never stops. I had to learn how to tune out the blaring horns. Now I can just close my eyes and imagine I hear the wind rustling in the oaks outside. Sometimes I can even hear the crickets chirping, and this almost always puts me to sleep.

4   Some people think that life on a farm is boring, that there is nothing to do, but this is not the case. ⑤ Actually, I have more free time now that I live in the city. On the farm, I rarely stayed up too long after dinner because I had to get up early to do chores. As soon as I grew strong enough to carry the buckets of corn to the hogs, chores took up much of my daily life. Chores meant feeding the pigs, cleaning out their pens, and fixing whatever needed

① Think about the title.

ONE STUDENT'S THOUGHTS

"I wonder who is moving and what they are moving on from."

② Make judgments about the writer's purpose.

"The writer seems less complimentary about city life, at least at the beginning."

YOUR TURN

Determine the writer's purpose.

③ Note literary elements like the use of figurative language.

"The writer uses a metaphor, a 'quilt of green and gold,' to refer to the crops."

YOUR TURN

Why do you think the writer uses metaphor here?

④ Use context clues to understand vocabulary.

"It seems like *rustic* is the opposite of city life."

⑤ Read actively— analyze.

"If country life is so peaceful, why does the writer have more free time in the city?"

Begin by previewing the text. Note the title and ask students to identify the subject. Read through the questions and prompts at the end of the text. Discuss with students what they should look for as they read the selection.

1 Point out the dual meanings of *moving on*— "physical movement" and "moving on to a new stage of life." Suggest to students that the title of a test selection is likely to give important clues that will help them answer the test questions. The tone set by the title is often a clue to the tone of the selection.

2 Point out that the author is setting up a compare-and-contrast situation between city and country. So far, the writer seems to have a more positive attitude about the country.

YOUR TURN By setting up this compare-and-contrast situation, the writer is letting readers know that he is going to tell things he likes about both city and country, as well as the things he dislikes.

3 Ask students what other metaphor or simile the writer uses in this paragraph. (*He says the skyline looks as if it is on fire when the sun goes down.*)

YOUR TURN The metaphor "a quilt of green and gold" makes the country sound appealing and beautiful.

4 Remind students to use various kinds of context clues as they try to figure out unfamiliar words. They can search the words and sentences around the unfamiliar word for definition or restatement clues. They can look for comparisons and contrasts. They can also look for word parts, such as prefixes, suffixes, and roots, to give them clues to a word's meaning.

5 In order to analyze, remind students to ask questions as they read. For example, they might ask, "Is the writer starting to find good things about city living? What evidence in this paragraph points to that?" (*The writer has far fewer chores to do and can sleep later in the morning; he can also stay up later because he's not as tired from getting up early to do chores.*)

6 Ask students, What are the writer's feelings about mealtimes together? Where the family always ate dinner together on the farm, they are less likely to do so in the city where there are more activities competing for their time. Discuss the purpose of this comparison.

YOUR TURN Comparing this one feature allows the writer to tell in more depth how this change in mealtime togetherness affects the family.

7 Point out that skimming the questions will help students find the information they need as they look back at the text.

Check Your Understanding

Have students use the following questions to test their understanding of the selection before they answer the questions in their texts.

- What were the main ideas of the selection?
- How does the author use comparison and contrast to support his main ideas?
- What structure does the writer use in his comparison-and-contrast essay—feature by feature or subject by subject?
- What conclusion does the writer come to after comparing country and city life?

fixing. I rarely slept in on weekends. Now that I live in the city, I go to sleep later and get up later. My chores consist of taking out the trash on Wednesday and sweeping off the front step. This leaves me much more time to hang out with my friends and relax.

5   Because we are not as busy doing chores, you'd think my family and I would see more of each other, but this is not the case. **6** On the farm, no matter what you were doing during the day, dinnertime was sacred. Everyone had to be at the dinner table each night, no excuses. Now my siblings are involved in different activities and we rarely have dinner together. My two younger brothers are involved in sports, my sister is in the drama club, and my mother has enrolled in night classes. **7** She has also taken a part-time job teaching nursery school. This is something she had always wanted to do but couldn't because running the farm took so much of her time. We still spend some time together as a family, though. Every Sunday we take turns making a breakfast. When it is my turn, I make waffles with lots of whipped cream and, when they are in season, fresh blueberries or strawberries. We sit around the big kitchen table, the same one we had at our farm, and we laugh and take turns sharing stories about what has happened during our week.

6   Moving was a big change for all of us, but I have come to appreciate city life. I have also come to appreciate those things that have stayed the same. My mother still makes apple pies from scratch. We still have fresh squash and tomatoes in the summer; now they come from my father's rooftop garden. I still ride my bike a lot, and it is easier now because I don't have to ride on rocky dirt roads. The most important thing I have learned is that it really doesn't matter where you live as long as you have your family. In this respect, the farm and the city are exactly the same.

6 **Evaluate the writer's use of comparison and contrast.**

"One feature—dinnertime—is compared within a paragraph."

YOUR TURN
How well does the use of feature-by-feature organization work in the essay?

7 **Skim the questions that follow the passage.**

"There's a question about his mother's part-time job. The selection says that she could never have had this opportunity when they lived on the farm."

PART 2

How to Answer Multiple-Choice Questions

Use the strategies in the box and notes in the side column to help you answer the questions below and on the following pages.

Based on the selection you have just read, choose the best answer for each of the following questions.

1. Why do you think the essay is titled "Moving On"?
   A. People move faster in the city.
   B. The writer has moved on to a new life in the city.
   C. Everything on a farm is constantly moving.
   D. The writer's family needed help moving to the city.

2. Why does the writer begin with crickets chirping?
   A. He wants the reader to appreciate crickets and their contribution to the world.
   B. He wants to hook the reader with a statement that appeals to the senses.
   C. The thesis of the paper has to do with noise levels.
   D. He never has trouble sleeping.

3. What main idea does the writer support by mentioning that he saw a "quilt of green and gold" from the treetops?
   A. You rarely see those colors in the city.
   B. Tree climbing is excellent exercise and helps develop the muscles.
   C. There is much more open land in the country.
   D. Everything looks better when viewed from up high.

4. Why does the writer mention his mother's part-time job?
   A. To show that his mother has no time for the family.
   B. To show that everyone in his family is doing more meaningful work.
   C. To show that his family members see less of each other now.
   D. All of the above.

5. What is the writer's tone at the end of the essay?
   A. His attitude toward country life changes from positive to negative.
   B. His attitude toward the move has not changed at all.
   C. He appreciates both country and city life.
   D. He regrets the life he has lost.

STRATEGIES FOR ANSWERING MULTIPLE-CHOICE QUESTIONS

▶ **Ask questions** that help you eliminate some of the choices.

▶ **Pay attention to choices such as "all of the above" or "none of the above."** To eliminate them, all you need to find is one answer that does not fit.

▶ **Choose the one best answer.** More than one choice may be true, but only one will be true and answer the question completely.

STRATEGIES IN ACTION

Choose the one best answer.

ONE STUDENT'S THOUGHTS
"All these answers might be true, but this essay doesn't deal with exercise, so I can eliminate choice B."

YOUR TURN
What other choices can you eliminate?

Pay attention to choices such as "all of the above."

ONE STUDENT'S THOUGHTS
"I don't think the writer feels that his mother has no time for the family. He even says that she still makes apple pies from scratch. So I can eliminate choice A. That means that choice D—all of the above—can't be right either."

YOUR TURN
Which of the remaining choices makes the most sense?

Multiple-Choice Questions

1. B
2. B
3. C

YOUR TURN This essay is about the comparison between city and country life, not about how things look better from up high, so Choice D can be eliminated, as well.

4. C

YOUR TURN Choice C makes the most sense, because the writer says that the family sees less of each other now, and his mother's job is one of the examples he uses to explain what he means.

5. C

Short-Answer Question

The writer's purpose in comparing city and country life is to explain how he made the adjustment from one to the other. He concludes that both have advantages, but that being with the family counts the most.

YOUR TURN One clue is that the writer says the move took some adjusting on his part. He begins by thinking he won't like city life, but as he goes on, he sees some advantages that put the change in perspective.

Essay Question

City life differs from country life in several ways. First of all, there is the look of the city. In the country, there are vast, open spaces to see and explore. The city is more crowded, with buildings as far as the eye can see. The city is also noisy, with the sounds of traffic replacing the quiet country sound of crickets chirping. Life on a farm provides less leisure time, since there are always chores to be done and animals to tend. In the city, chores are fewer, so there is more time to relax and hang out. Finally, the busier pace and greater variety of activities mean that the family spends less time together. What time they do spend, though, might tend to be appreciated more, since they are spending it together by choice, not by necessity.

YOUR TURN Important points to include are the differences in the following: landscape, noise level, leisure time, and family time.

Check Your Understanding

Have students reread their own responses to the short-answer and essay questions. Then have them ask themselves the following questions as they revise and edit their own work.

• Have I responded directly to the direction words in the writing prompt?
• Have I covered the points I wanted to make?
• Do I have an introductory sentence?
• Have I supported my ideas with evidence?
• Have I written a conclusion?
• Have I used correct grammar?

PART 3 How to Respond in Writing

You may also be asked to write answers to questions about a reading passage. **Short-answer questions** often ask you to answer in a sentence or two. **Essay questions** require a fully developed piece of writing.

Short-Answer Question

> **STRATEGIES** FOR RESPONDING TO SHORT-ANSWER QUESTIONS
>
> ▶ **Identify the key words** in the writing prompt that tell you the ideas to discuss. Make sure you know what each key word means.
> ▶ **Make your response direct** and to the point.
> ▶ **Support your ideas** by using evidence from the selection.
> ▶ **Use correct grammar.**
>
> > **Sample Question**
> >
> > Answer the following question in one or two sentences.
> >
> > Explain what you think the writer's purpose was in comparing and contrasting country and city life.

Essay Question

> **STRATEGIES** FOR ANSWERING ESSAY QUESTIONS
>
> ▶ **Look for direction words** in the writing prompt that tell you what to write and what to do such as *essay, analyze, describe*, or *compare and contrast*.
> ▶ **List the points** you want to make before beginning to write.
> ▶ **Write an interesting introduction** that presents your main point.
> ▶ **Develop your ideas** by supporting your statements with evidence from the selection. Present ideas in a logical order.
> ▶ **Write a conclusion** that summarizes your points.
> ▶ **Check your work for correct grammar.**
>
> > **Sample Prompt**
> >
> > The writer of this selection sees many differences between life in the city and life in the country. Write an essay in which you **summarize** these differences.

STRATEGIES IN ACTION

Identify key words.

ONE STUDENT'S THOUGHTS
"The key words are *explain* and *purpose*. This means that I'll have to decide why the writer wrote the article and tell why I think that way."

YOUR TURN
What clues to the writer's purpose can you find in the selection?

Identify direction words.

ONE STUDENT'S THOUGHTS
"The key direction words are *essay* and *summarize*. This means that I'll have to discuss the differences in a fully developed piece of writing."

YOUR TURN
What important points will you have to include in your essay?

Here is a student's first draft in response to the writing prompt at the bottom of page 606. Read the paragraph and answer the multiple-choice questions that follow.

1	The writer says that city life differs from country life. He
2	mentions four major ways. First, the city landscape is
3	littered with buildings instead of being open and vast.
4	Second, there is more noise living in the city. Which the
5	writer has had to get used to. The amount of time he has is
6	also a difference. He spends less time with his family.
7	However, at least once a week the family shares a meal
8	together. Sunday breakfasts are special. He never misses it.

STRATEGIES FOR REVISING, EDITING, AND PROOFREADING

▸ **Read the passage carefully.**
▸ **Note the parts that are confusing.** What types of errors might cause that confusion?
▸ **Look for errors** in grammar, usage, spelling, and capitalization. Common errors include:
  • sentence fragments
  • lack of subject-verb agreement
  • pronoun antecedent problems
  • lack of transition words

1. What is the BEST way to combine the sentences in lines 1–2 (The writer says . . . four major ways.)?

   A. The writer says that city life differs from country life; four major ways.

   B. The writer says that city life differs from country life, but he mentions four major ways.

   C. The writer says that city life differs from country life, though he mentions four major ways.

   D. The writer says that city life differs from country life in four major ways.

2. What is the BEST way to revise the sentences in lines 4–5 (Second, there is . . . used to.)?

   A. Second, there is more noise living in the city of which the writer has had to get used to.

   B. Second, there is more noise living in the city: which the writer has had to get used to.

   C. Second, there is more noise and the writer has had to get used to it living in the city.

   D. Second, living in the city, the writer has had to get used to more noise.

3. What is the BEST way to revise the sentence in line 8 (He never misses it.)?

   A. They never miss it.

   B. They never miss him.

   C. He never misses them.

   D. They never misses it.

Dolphin Field Guide

OVERVIEW

The bottlenose dolphin—the type featured in "My First Dive with the Dolphins"—inhabits temperate and tropical waters worldwide, and is not an endangered species. The bottlenose is the most abundant species of dolphin along the eastern United States from Cape Cod through the Gulf of Mexico.

Research Questions

- How do dolphins, porpoises, and whales differ?

- What are the identifying features of the bottlenose and other species of dolphins?

- How does the top swimming speed of bottlenose dolphins compare to that of other marine animals?

Investigation Working in small groups or individually, students will publish field guides to dolphins. While researching and writing their guides, students should consider, among other things, dolphin biology and habitat, how to distinguish between dolphins, porpoises, and whales, as well as how to identify the bottlenose and other species of dolphins. Each guide will be enhanced with student-selected or student-authored poetry about dolphins. Guides will also include brief articles about conservation issues.

Wrap-up When the dolphin field guides are complete, invite other students, parents, and community members to view them. Place the guides in a "lending library" in the classroom or in the school library.

Links and Extended Reading
www.mcdougallittell.com

LaserLinks: Background
Science Connection
Visual Vocabulary
Art Gallery

OBJECTIVES

❑ read, discuss, and write poetry about marine animals

❑ research and report on the issue of dolphin injuries from tuna fishing

❑ research and write a "field guide" to dolphins

❑ create a bar graph comparing the swimming speeds of marine animals

Team Teaching Assignments

CONNECT TO | **LANGUAGE ARTS**   Have students read aloud and discuss poetry about dolphins and other marine creatures such as whales, killer whales, sharks, and fish. Students may wish to include some of this poetry in their field guides, or to write their own poetry about dolphins and publish it in their guides. Two good sources for animal poetry are *The Oxford Book of Animal Poems,* edited by Michael Harrison and Christopher Stuart-Clark, and *The Beauty of the Beast: Poems from the Animal Kingdom,* edited by Jack Prelutsky. *(2 class periods)*

> **YOU WILL NEED:**
> - animal poetry anthologies

CONNECT TO | **SOCIAL STUDIES**   Ask students if they have noticed "dolphin-safe" labels on tuna fish cans. In the early 1990s, the American public became very concerned about the number of dolphins dying in fishing nets. The estimated number of dolphin deaths worldwide due to tuna fishing has dropped from 133,000 in 1986 to 2,000 in 1998. Direct students to research what the "dolphin-safe" label means, what fishing practices endanger dolphins, and how fishing fleets have changed their practices. Each group of students should work together to write a short report on the issue of dolphins and tuna fishing or on another current conservation issue related to dolphins for inclusion in their field guides. *(2–3 class periods)*

> **YOU WILL NEED:**
> - Web access (optional)
> - current reference materials on dolphins and tuna fishing

CONNECT TO | **SCIENCE**   Have students form small groups and encourage them to examine sample field guides to see what type of information is included and how it is organized. Each group should create an outline of their dolphin field guide and then perform research to gather the necessary information. They will then write text and combine it with photographs and/or illustrations. Have students include any reports, fact sheets, graphs, or poetry from other team assignments and bind their field guides inside an illustrated cover. *(4 class periods)*

> **YOU WILL NEED:**
> - samples of field guides
> - Web access (optional)
> - reference books on dolphins
> - word processor (optional)
> - art materials for bookbinding

CONNECT TO | **MATHEMATICS**   Tell students that bottlenose dolphins can swim as fast as 20 miles per hour over short distances. Provide students with the following maximum swimming speeds of other marine animals, or have them research other animals' speeds: *gray whale: 12 mph; killer whale: 30 mph; porpoise: 24 mph; mako shark: 60 mph; sailfish: 68 mph.* Instruct each group of students to make a bar graph comparing the top speed of the bottlenose dolphin to that of other marine animals. Groups may include the bar graph in their field guide. *(1–2 class periods)*

> **YOU WILL NEED:**
> - colored pencils
> - graph paper

"About Time" Bulletin Board

OVERVIEW

Time is one concept that can seem infinite. The character Milo in *The Phantom Tollbooth* feels he has too much time. He even tries "killing time." Archaeological remains tell us that in almost every ancient culture people devised ways to measure and record the passage of time.

Research Questions

- When does time seem to pass slowly and quickly for you?

- What are time zones and why do we have them?

- How did people in various cultures tell time before there were clocks?

Investigation Working in small groups, students will create a classroom bulletin board about time. The bulletin board will be made up of creative writing about time, information on time zones, descriptions of timekeeping devices through history, and calculations of the amount of time left until students' next birthdays.

Wrap-up When the bulletin board is complete, encourage students to organize a presentation on the subject for a class of younger students. They may wish to create or select a musical recording or a short picture book to use in their presentation as an attention grabber.

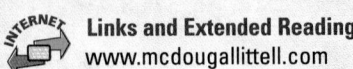

Links and Extended Reading
www.mcdougallittell.com

OBJECTIVES

- ❏ write a poem or a story about time

- ❏ map time zones, world cities, and their local times

- ❏ research and illustrate timekeeping devices through history

- ❏ use scientific notation to express the amount of time left until students' next birthdays

Team Teaching Assignments

CONNECT TO **LANGUAGE ARTS** Ask students if their perception of how quickly time passes is affected by what they are doing. Have them brainstorm a list of occasions when it seems that time passes slowly and those when it seems that time passes quickly. Record their responses on the board. Each student should then generate a piece of creative writing (a poem or a story) about one of the listed scenarios. Encourage students to provide vivid descriptions of what it feels like when time passes "quickly" or "slowly." *(2 class periods)*

YOU WILL NEED:
(no special materials needed)

CONNECT TO **SOCIAL STUDIES** Display a United States map with clearly marked time zones and their time differences. Quiz students about what time it is in United States time zones other than their own. Explain that there are different time zones all across the world. For example, when it is 8:00 A.M. standard time in New York City, it is 10:00 P.M. in Tokyo, Japan. Have students trace a map of the world from an atlas or an almanac. Have them label on the map the town in which their school is located. Then have them label other cities across the globe with the city's name and the local time in that city when it is 8:00 A.M. (or another time) at the students' school. *(2 class periods)*

YOU WILL NEED:
- Web access (optional)
- atlas
- chart-size paper
- colored pencils

CONNECT TO **SCIENCE** Sundials, which use the movement of the sun to indicate the time, were the first devices for telling time. The ancient Egyptians began using simple sundials as early as 3500 B.C. Sundials were followed by the development of increasingly accurate methods of telling time: water clocks, mechanical clocks, quartz clocks, and atomic clocks. Assign each group to research one of these devices and create illustrations and captions for the bulletin board explaining how it works and when and in what part(s) of the world it primarily is (or was) used. *(2–3 class periods)*

YOU WILL NEED:
- Web access (optional)
- reference books on the history of time
- art materials

CONNECT TO **MATHEMATICS** Scientific notation is a way of writing very large numbers so that they are easier to work with than when they are written out. Ask students to calculate the number of seconds until their next birthday. (Have them start by determining the number of days, and then multiplying by 86,400, the number of seconds in a day.) Then guide each student in expressing the number using scientific notation. Assign one group to create a chart titled "The Number of Seconds Until Class Members' Next Birthdays, as of [insert date and time]" for display on the bulletin board. *(2 class periods)*

YOU WILL NEED:
- calculator
- chart-size paper
- colored pencils

Making Your Mark

In Unit Five, students will read about how people have left their stamp on the world, both in the modern world and in ancient times. The selections in this unit may prompt students to consider how they can make their own marks in life.

——————— Part 1 ———————

Finding Your Voice In order to make your mark, you first have to find your voice—the way in which you can best express who you are. In *Words on a Page,* a young girl discovers that through her writing she is able to bring together the two parts of her life that she holds most dear.

——————— Part 2 ———————

Voices from the Past The voice of history is never stilled. Things that happened thousands of years ago still have an impact on today's world. In "The Dog of Pompeii," we get a glimpse of ordinary life almost 2,000 years ago and find how little some things have changed.

Making Your Mark

Not for power,

not for money,

but simply to say

"I was here for a

little while;

I left this mark."

WILLIAM FAULKNER
AMERICAN WRITER

608

Philip and Karen Smith, © Tony Stone Images.

 Viewing and Representing

Photograph of Cave Painting,
Cuevos Los Manos, Argentina

ART APPRECIATION

Instruction Ask if students remember when they were little and made tracings of their hands, impressions of their hands in clay, or other artworks using the shape of their hands. This ancient cave painting is a little bit like that, but the hands are many and of different shapes and colors. It seems like people have always wanted to make their mark, no matter how far back in history you go!

Ask: What do the hands in the painting appear to be doing?
Possible Response: Some of the hands look as if they may be reaching for something. Some look as if they want to touch each other.

Ask: Do you think everyone wants to leave a mark on the world? Why?
Possible Response: Yes, because everybody wants to be remembered for something.

609

Making Connections

To help students explore the connections between the art, the quotation, and the unit theme, have them consider the following questions:

Ask: What would you want the mark you make to say about you?
Possible Response: Students' responses will vary, but should involve things they would like to be remembered for, either by people they know or by future generations.

Ask: What question do you think William Faulkner might have been responding to in his quotation on page 608?
Possible Response: Faulkner might have been responding to a question about why he is a writer.

Ask: If you were to choose a title for this ancient cave painting, what would it be?
Possible Responses: "Making Your Mark"; "Hands On"; "Striving"

Ask: What kinds of stories and experiences might you expect to read about in a unit called "Making Your Mark"?
Possible Response: You might expect to read about some people who left their mark on the world, for better or for worse. You might also read about some historical events and archaeological finds.

Features and Selections	Literary Analysis	Reading and Critical Thinking	Writing Opportunities	
Making Your Mark **Finding Your Voice**				
Learning the Language of Literature Theme	Theme, 611			
The Active Reader Skills and Strategies		Drawing Conclusions, 613		
DRAMA Words on a Page **Difficulty Level: *Average*** Literary Link Bringing the Prairie Home	Theme, 614, 616, 618, 624, 630, 631, 633	Drawing Conclusions, 614, 616, 620, 622, 626, 630, 633 Comparing Texts, 633 Standardized Test Practice, 627 Informal Assessment, 630	Acceptance Speech, 634 Permission Letter, 634 Comparison Chart, 634 Self-Assessment, 634	
ESSAY *from* All I Really Need to Know I Learned in Kindergarten **Difficulty Level: *Average***	Personal Essay, 636, 638, 640	Identifying Main Idea and Details, 636, 638, 640 Standardized Test Practice, 641	Personal Credo, 641	
POETRY You Sing (Sonnet 52)/Soneto 52 How to Paint the Portrait of a Bird **Difficulty Level: *Challenging***	Onomatopoeia, 643, 644, 648 Review: Personification, 648	Noting Sensory Details, 643, 644, 646, 648 Comparing Texts, 648 Informal Assessment, 647	How-to Poem, 649 Sensory Description, 649	
Real World Link Flip Out!		Following Complex Directions, 651		
SHORT STORY The Scribe **Difficulty Level: *Easy*** Building Vocabulary	Characterization, 653, 654, 656, 658, 660, 661	Connect to Your Life, 653 Making Inferences About Characters, 653, 654, 656, 658, 660, 661 Test Practice, 660	Comparison Essay, 662 Day Narrative, 662 Letter to the Editor, 662	
AUTHOR STUDY **Lois Lowry**				
SHORT STORY Crow Call **Difficulty Level: *Average***	Symbol, 668, 670, 674	Recognizing Cause and Effect, 668, 670, 672, 674 Standardized Test Practice, 673		
SPEECH Newbury Acceptance Speech		Identifying the Author's Purpose, 676		
MEMOIR *from* Looking Back **Difficulty Level: *Easy***	Voice, 678, 680, 682, 684	Identifying Effects of Author's Perspective, 678, 680, 684 Comparing Texts, 684	Informal Assessment, 683	
The Author's Style Author Study Project	Analysis of Style, 686	Active Reading, 686	Writing, 686 Photo Essay, 687 Dramatic Dialogue, 687 Comparison Essay, 687	

LEGEND   **DLS – Daily Language SkillBuilder**   **Green type – Teacher's Edition**

Features and Selections	Literary Analysis	Reading and Critical Thinking	Writing Opportunities		
Writing Workshop: Opinion Statement Assessment Practice		Analyzing a Student Model, 691	Writing Your Opinion Statement, 693 Making Weak Endings Stronger, 694		

Voice From the Past					
Learning the Language of Literature Historical Fiction	Historical Fiction, 697				
The Active Reader Skills and Strategies		Distinguishing Fact from Opinion, 699			
SHORT STORY The Dog of Pompeii Difficulty Level: *Average*	Historical Fiction, 700, 702, 704, 706, 708, 710, 711 Review: Conflict, 711	Connect to Your Life, 700 Distinguishing Fact from Nonfact, 700, 702, 708, 710 Comparing Texts, 711 Standardized Test Practice, 709	Sensory Interview, 712		
Real World Link A 9,500-Year-Old Summer Home		SQ3R, 715			
INFORMATIVE NONFICTION Tutankhamen, *from* Lost Worlds Difficulty Level: *Challenging* **Literary Link** Ancestors	Informative Nonfiction, 718, 720, 725 Review: Sources of Information, 725	Analyzing Text Structure, 718, 720, 725	Archaeological Catalog, 726 Classification Essay, 726 Informal Assessment, 724		
INFORMATIVE NONFICTION The First Emperor, *from* The Tomb Robbers Difficulty Level: *Challenging*	Tone, 728, 730, 732, 734	SQ3R, 728, 730, 732, 734 Comparing Texts, 734 Test Practice, 735	Climactic Order Paragraph, 735 Log Entry, 735		
POETRY Barbara Frietchie Difficulty Level: *Average* **Building Vocabulary**	Poetic Form: Couplet, 737, 738, 740 Review: Sound Devices, 740	Clarifying, 737, 738, 740 Standardized Test Practice, 739	Frietchie Interview, 741 Rhymed Couplets, 741		
Communication Workshop: Multimedia Presentation Assessment Practice		Analyzing a Multimedia Presentation, 755			
Reflect and Assess	Looking at Symbols, 761 Thinking About Voice, 761	Comparing Qualities, 760	Predicting Outcomes, 760 Building Your Portfolio, 761		

LEGEND   DLS – Daily Language SkillBuilder   **Green type – Teacher's Edition**

UNIT FIVE
RESOURCE MANAGEMENT GUIDE
PART 1

To introduce the theme of this unit, use Fine Art Transparencies T31–33 in the Communications Transparencies and Copymasters.

	Unit Resource Book	Assessment	Integrated Technology and Media	Additional Support Literary Analysis Transparencies
Words on a Page pp. 614–635	• Summary p. 4 • Active Reading p. 5 • Literary Analysis p. 6 • Words to Know p. 7 • Grammar p. 8 • Spelling p. 9 • Selection Quiz p. 10	• Selection Test, Formal Assessment pp. 101–102 Test Generator	Audio Library Video: Literature in Performance, Video Resource Book pp. 26–30 Research Starter www.mcdougallittell.com	• Theme T7
from All I Really Need to Know I Learned in Kindergarten pp. 636–642	• Summary p. 11 • Active Reading p. 12 • Literary Analysis p. 13 • Words to Know p. 14 • Grammar p. 15 • Spelling p. 16 • Selection Quiz p. 17	• Selection Test, Formal Assessment pp. 103–104 Test Generator	Audio Library	
You Sing (Sonnet 52)/ Soneto 52 **How to Paint the Portrait of a Bird** pp. 643–649	• Active Reading p. 18 • Literary Analysis p. 19	• Selection Test, Formal Assessment pp. 105–106 Test Generator	Audio Library	• Poetry: Sound Devices T20
The Scribe pp. 653–662	• Summary p. 20 • Active Reading p. 21 • Literary Analysis p. 22 • Words to Know p. 23 • Grammar p. 24 • Spelling p. 25 • Selection Quiz p. 26	• Selection Test, Formal Assessment pp. 107–108 Test Generator	Audio Library	• Characterization T4
Crow Call pp. 668–675	• Summary p. 28 • Active Reading p. 29 • Literary Analysis p. 30 • Words to Know p. 31 • Grammar p. 32 • Spelling p. 33 • Selection Quiz p. 34	• Selection Test, Formal Assessment pp. 109–110 Test Generator	Audio Library More Online: Author Link www.mcdougallittell.com NetActivities	
from Looking Back pp. 678–685	• Summary p. 35 • Active Reading p. 36 • Literary Analysis p. 37 • Words to Know p. 38 • Grammar p. 39 • Spelling p. 40 • Selection Quiz p. 41	• Selection Test, Formal Assessment pp. 111–112 Test Generator	Audio Library Research Starter www.mcdougallittell.com NetActivities	• Author's Style T9

Writing Workshop: Opinion Statement

		Unit Assessment	Unit Technology	
Unit Five Resource Book • Prewriting p. 42 • Drafting and Elaboration p. 43 • Peer Response Guide pp. 44–45 • Revising, Editing, and Proofreading p. 46 • Student Models pp. 47–49 • Rubric for Evaluation p. 50	**Writing Coach** **Writing Transparencies** T1–4, T12, T27 **Reading and Critical Thinking Transparencies** T25 **Grammar Transparencies and Copymasters** C59, C128 **Teacher's Guide to Assessment and Portfolio Use**	• Unit Five, Part 1 Test, Formal Assessment pp. 113–114 Test Generator • Unit Five Integrated Test, Integrated Assessment pp. 25–30	ClassZone www.mcdougallittell.com Electronic Teacher Tools	

Reading and Critical Thinking Transparencies	Grammar Transparencies and Copymasters	Vocabulary Transparencies and Copymasters	Writing Transparencies	Communications Transparencies and Copymasters
• Drawing Conclusions T18	• Daily Language SkillBuilder T19 • Using Italics in Plays C132 • Ellipses C130 • Examples as Fragments C60	• Context Clues C60 • Word Origins C61 • Denotation and Connotation C62		• Impromptu Speaking: Dialogue, Role-Play T13 • Evaluation Matrix: Film/Video T7
• Main Idea/Details T25	• Daily Language SkillBuilder T19 • Using Colons for Sentence Variety C133	• Using a Thesaurus C63	• Achieving Conciseness T21 • Elaboration T13	
• Noting Sensory Details T11	• Daily Language SkillBuilder T20 • Using Conjunctions to Connect Ideas C110			
• Making Inferences T10 • Venn Diagram T35	• Daily Language SkillBuilder T20 • Capitalizing Proper Nouns, Pronouns, and Adjectives C118	• Idioms C64		• Dramatic Reading T12
• Cause and Effect T5 • Author's Purpose and Audience T8	• Daily Language SkillBuilder T21 • Subject Position in Interrogative and Exclamatory Sentences C56	• Analogies C65	• Varying Sentence Openers and Closers T18	
• Author's Purpose and Audience T8	• Daily Language SkillBuilder T21 • Combining Sentences Using Conjunctions C111	• Meaning Clues C66	• Dialogue T24	• Reading Aloud T11

STUDENTS ACQUIRING ENGLISH

The **Spanish Study Guide,** pp. 121–141, includes language support for the following pages:
• Family and Community Involvement (per unit)
• Selection Summaries and Vocabulary
• Active Reading
• Literary Analysis

UNIT FIVE
RESOURCE MANAGEMENT GUIDE
PART 2

To introduce the theme of this unit, use Fine Art Transparencies T31–33 in the Communications Transparencies and Copymasters.

	Unit Resource Book	Assessment	Integrated Technology and Media	Additional Support Literary Analysis Transparencies
The Dog of Pompeii *pp. 700–713*	• Summary p. 51 • Active Reading p. 52 • Literary Analysis p. 53 • Words to Know p. 54 • Grammar p. 55 • Spelling p. 56 • Selection Quiz p. 57	• Selection Test, Formal Assessment pp. 115–116 • Test Generator	Audio Library LaserLinks, Teacher's SourceBook p. 45	• Conflict T8
Tutankhamen, *from* **Lost Worlds** *pp. 718–727*	• Summary p. 58 • Active Reading p. 59 • Literary Analysis p. 60 • Words to Know p. 61 • Grammar p. 62 • Spelling p. 63 • Selection Quiz p. 64	• Selection Test, Formal Assessment pp. 117–118 • Test Generator	Audio Library LaserLinks, Teacher's SourceBook p. 46 Research Starter www.mcdougallittell.com	• Text Structure (Organization) C12
The First Emperor, *from* **The Tomb Robbers** *pp. 728–736*	• Summary p. 65 • Active Reading p. 66 • Literary Analysis p. 67 • Words to Know p. 68 • Grammar p. 69 • Spelling p. 70 • Selection Quiz p. 71	• Selection Test, Formal Assessment pp. 119–120 • Test Generator	Audio Library LaserLinks, Teacher's SourceBook p. 48 Research Starter www.mcdougallittell.com	• Tone T25
Barbara Frietchie *pp. 737–741*	• Active Reading p. 72 • Literary Analysis p. 73	• Selection Test, Formal Assessment pp. 121–122 • Test Generator	Audio Library LaserLinks, Teacher's SourceBook p. 50 Research Starter www.mcdougallittell.com	• Form in Poetry: Rhyme and Meter T17 • Mood T26

Communication Workshop: Speaking and Listening

Unit Five Resource Book
• Planning and Drafting p. 75
• Practicing and Delivering p. 76
• Peer Response Guide pp. 77–78
• Refining Your Performance p. 79
• Rubric for Evaluation p. 80

Writing Coach

Writing Transparencies T1–4, T11, T18, T39

Communication Transparencies and Copymasters T16

Grammar Transparencies and Copymasters C128, C137

Teacher's Guide to Assessment and Portfolio Use

Unit Assessment
• Unit Five, Part 2 Test, Formal Assessment pp. 123–124
• Test Generator
• Unit Five Integrated Test, Integrated Assessment pp. 25–30

Unit Technology
ClassZone www.mcdougallittell.com
Electronic Teacher Tools

Reading and Critical Thinking Transparencies	Grammar Transparencies and Copymasters	Vocabulary Transparencies and Copymasters	Writing Transparencies	Communications Transparencies and Copymasters
• Distonguishing Fact from Opinion T26	• Daily Language SkillBuilder T22 • Independent and Dependent Clauses C62	• Synonyms and Antonyms C67 • Analogies C68	• Sensory Words List T16 • Using Periodical Indexes T44	• Dramatic Reading T12
• Text Structure (Organization) T24	• Daily Language SkillBuilder T22 • Compound and Complex Sentences C63 • Using Dashes to Set Off Ideas C129	• Context Clues C69		
• SQ3R T48	• Daily Language SkillBuilder T23 • Adverb Phrases for Transitions C107	• Using Prefixes, Suffixes, and Roots C70		
• Strategies for Reading T2	• Daily Language SkillBuilder T23		• Dialogue T24	• Giving and Using Feedback to Improve Performance T16

STUDENTS ACQUIRING ENGLISH

The **Spanish Study Guide,** pp. 142–153, includes language support for the following pages:
• Family and Community Involvement (per unit)

• Selection Summaries and Vocabulary
• Active Reading
• Literary Analysis

Selection	SkillBuilder Sentences	Suggested Answers
Words on a Page	1. Some stories is wonderful to read out loud. 2. Can you give me an idea of how long this play last?	1. Some stories **are** wonderful to read out loud. 2. Can you give me an idea of how long this play **lasts**?
from All I Really Need to Know . . .	1. When he was young, his personal statements was lengthy. 2. He and I shares some of the same beliefs.	1. When he was young, his personal statements **were** lengthy. 2. He and I **share** some of the same beliefs.
You Sing (Sonnet 52)/Soneto 52 How to Paint the Portrait of a Bird	1. It might be a women's voice that is being described in the first poem. 2. One of the poet's is well known as a playwright also.	1. It might be a **woman's** voice that is being described in the first poem. 2. One of the **poets** is well known as a playwright also.
The Scribe	1. Like the boy in the story, my parents and me live in a city. 2. The people in the story were like people in mine neighborhood.	1. Like the boy in the story, my parents and **I** live in a city. 2. The people in the story were like people in **my** neighborhood.

Selection	SkillBuilder Sentences	Suggested Answers
Crow Call	1. Lois Lowry loves to garden cook play Bridge watch movies and read. 2. Lowry's dog Bandit is a Tibetan terrier and brings her great joy.	1. Lois Lowry loves to garden, cook, play Bridge, watch movies, and read. 2. Lowry's dog, Bandit, is a Tibetan terrier and brings her great joy.
from Looking Back	1. "My brother Jon was younger than I said Lois, and yet we had a lot in common." 2. I wanted to write something for his daughter to remember him by, Lois replied when asked about the book she wrote about her son.	1. "My brother Jon was younger than I," said Lois, "and yet we had a lot in common." 2. "I wanted to write something for his daughter to remember him by," Lois replied when asked about the book she wrote about her son.
The Dog of Pompeii	1. The eruption of Mount Vesuvius completely buried the city of Pompeii in ashs. 2. Because of this, we now know how mens and woman of that time dressed and lived.	1. The eruption of Mount Vesuvius completely buried the city of Pompeii in **ashes**. 2. Because of this, we now know how **men** and **women** of that time dressed and lived.
Tutankhamen	1. Lord Carnarvon the man who paid for Howard Carter's archaeological work. 2. Carter insisted that his team.	1. Lord Carnarvon **was** the man who paid for Howard Carter's archaeological work. 2. Carter insisted that his team **cover the entire area.**

Selection	SkillBuilder Sentences	Suggested Answers
The First Emperor	1. Ch'in Shih Huang Ti's tomb is one of the greatest archaeological finds ever it contains thousands of clay figures and covers a vast area. 2. The first emperor used his power to build the Great Wall. As well as a tomb for himself.	1. Ch'in Shih Huang Ti's tomb is one of the greatest archaeological finds ever. **It** contains thousands of clay figures and covers a vast area. 2. The first emperor used his power to build the Great Wall, **as** well as a tomb for himself.
Barbara Frietchie	1. Its a tragedy that so many soldiers died in the Civil War. 2. I think that this womans courage is truly admirable.	1. **It's** a tragedy that so many soldiers died in the Civil War. 2. I think that this **woman's** courage is truly admirable.

Grammar Focus by Unit	Unit One	Unit Two	Unit Three	Unit Four	Unit Five	Unit Six
	The Sentence and Its Parts	Nouns, Pronouns, and Verbs	Modifiers	Phrases	Compound and Complex Sentences	Review

The Language of Literature offers several options for integrating grammar instruction and literature.

- Each unit has a specific grammar focus. The grammar focus for this unit is highlighted on the planning chart. Categories of grammar skills for this unit are shown in red.

- The Pupil's Edition includes instructive features entitled *Grammar in Context*. The instruction in these features arises from the selections and relates to the grammar focus for each unit.

- The Writing Workshops in the Pupil's Edition include grammar tips that help the students produce error-free drafts.

- Mini Lessons in the Teacher's Edition complement the instruction in the *Grammar in Context* features. Additional Mini Lessons relate to the grammar focus for each unit as well as to the literature.

- Daily Language SkillBuilders in the Teacher's Edition provide students with ongoing proofreading practice and reinforce punctuation, spelling, grammar and usage, and capitalization.

- Grammar Copymasters and Transparencies, which may be used independently or in conjunction with the Mini Lessons in the Teacher's Edition, present grammar in a traditional, systematic sequence.

PE instruction shown in black
TE Mini Lessons shown in green

Part 1

THE SENTENCE AND ITS PARTS
Sentence Fragments and Run-on Sentences
"Words on a Page," p. 635
Examples as Fragments
"Words on a Page," p. 635
Subjects in Different Positions
"Crow Call," p. 675
Subject Position in Interrogative and Exclamatory Sentences
"Crow Call," p. 675

Correcting Sentence Fragments
Writing Workshop, p. 694
Correcting Sentence Fragments
Assessment Practice, p. 695

PREPOSITIONS, CONJUNCTIONS, INTERJECTIONS
Using Conjunctions to Connect Ideas
"You Sing/How to Paint the Portrait of a Bird," p. 649

Combining Sentences
"Looking Back," p. 685
Combining Sentences Using Conjunctions
"Looking Back," p. 685

CAPITALIZATION
Capitalizing Proper Nouns, Pronouns, and Adjectives
"The Scribe," p. 658

PUNCTUATION
Using Italics in Plays
"Words on a Page," p. 618
Ellipses
"Words on a Page," p. 621

Sentence Variety Using Colons
"All I Really Need to Know I Learned in Kindergarten," p. 642
Using Colons for Sentence Variety
"All I Really Need to Know I Learned in Kindergarten," p. 642
Punctuating, Choosing, and Incorporating Quotations
Writing Workshop, p. 692

Part 2

THE SENTENCE AND ITS PARTS
Independent and Dependent Clauses
"The Dog of Pompeii," p. 713
Compound and Complex Sentences
"Tutankhamen," p. 722

PREPOSITIONS, CONJUNCTIONS, INTERJECTIONS
Using Adverb Phrases for Sentence Variety
"The First Emperor," p. 736
Adverb Phrases for Transitions
"The First Emperor," p. 736

PUNCTUATION
Using Semicolons to Combine Sentences
"The Dog of Pompeii," p. 713
Appositives Set Off with Dashes
"Tutankhamen," p. 727
Using Dashes to Set Off Ideas
"Tutankhamen," p. 727

STYLE
Consistent Form
Writing Workshop, p. 758
Consistent Form
Assessment Practice, p. 759

OVERVIEW

Students work with partners to present staged interviews with historical figures.

Project at a glance Many of the selections in Unit Five, Part 2, focus on historical topics or people. For this project, each partnered team will choose a historical figure from the unit (or another figure that interests them) and deliver a staged interview session. Students will research the life of the historical figure, gather information and prepare an interview. Both partners will share responsibilities for researching and writing. Students might present the interviews in a "History Day."

SCHEDULING

Partners should take no more than ten minutes to present their interview. You may want to schedule the interviews over the course of 2–3 class periods and/or align them with one of your social studies units, if it is practical.

PROJECT OBJECTIVES

- To demonstrate the speaking and listening skills introduced in the activity
- To research the life and accomplishments of a historical figure
- To play the role of a historical figure and give an interview
- To demonstrate interviewing skills
- To answer questions from the audience

SUGGESTED GROUP SIZE

Partners

Historical Interview

 # Getting Started

Explain that students will be working with partners to present an interview with a historical figure. See the Selections Overview for summaries of the stories in this unit.

Before students begin, do a little research yourself to see if your school library has sufficient information (biographies, autobiographies) on historical figures. If it does not, arrange with a local library for these materials to be available to students.

You might also locate a collection of films or videos on historical figures of your choice. Students should be encouraged to "get into character," which might involve dressing up as the historical figure, with the appropriate costumes, props, makeup, and so on. You should make arrangements for these items to

be available, either from your school's drama department or from some other source.

This project should only require rearranging a bit of furniture in your classroom on the appropriate day. There should be two chairs in the front of the room, as well as seating for audience members. If you think students are ready for a real audience, you might create a History Day and invite other classes, parents, or teachers to act as judges or audience members.

Communication Workshop Connection

As a springboard, students may use the Communication Workshop assignment **Multimedia Presentation,** p. 754.

 # Directing the Project

Preparing As a class, briefly discuss the historical topics featured in this unit, as well as any other topics you might be covering in a social studies unit or another related unit.

▶ Divide students into pairs. Tell students that each team will write and present an interview with a historical figure. Have students choose a figure from the unit or another figure. They should decide who will act as the figure and the interviewer.

Assigning Roles Have students divide the work up evenly within each team. Roles might include writer, interviewer, researcher, and so on. You might want to choose one student to write and present an introduction and conclusion for the entire class presentation (or you could fill this position yourself).

▶ After teams have chosen their historical figure, they should begin researching. Meet with them to make sure there are no duplications. Students should collect information using multiple sources (films, videos, books, and so on) and choose an important event in their subject's life. They should then write an interview script based on that event. Or they may simply choose to focus on their subject's life in general.

▶ Later, meet with each team to refine the interview, offer help, or make suggestions. Before the presentation, students should check

to make sure all the main points are supported with facts and examples. Review with students the Speaking and Listening Strategies found in the Communication Handbook, page R102.

Practicing You should allow time for teams to rehearse their interviews. The interviewer should go over his or her notes, and the historical figure should be well prepared to answer questions.

▶ For this stage, both students may use notes to help prepare; however, this should be discouraged during the final presentation. Remind students to stay in character during the interview, as this is what will make it most convincing.

▶ Tell students that giving and receiving feedback during the rehearsal stage is crucial. Refer to the tips in the Feedback Center.

Presenting This project could culminate in a History Day for the entire student body or just for your class.

▶ To begin, have students take a few deep breaths and focus on what they want to communicate. Students should take their places in front of the audience. After the initial interview, you might open the forum to questions from the audience. The historical figure could then answer in character and provide further insights into his or her life and times.

Teaching the Speaking and Listening Skills

The student is expected to:

Adapt spoken language such as word choice, diction, and usage to the purpose, audience and occasion

Teaching Suggestions: Tell students that "getting into character" means learning about the culture and context of their historical figure. This will require research. Perhaps students can watch films set in their speaker's era. Students should adjust their message to fit their audience's knowledge and expectations, and adjust their speech and delivery to fit the occasion (formal vs. informal). Students should also try to match their language to the purpose of their message. Have students identify their purposes and discuss with them ways in which they might adjust their language to best suit those purposes.

Interpret a speaker's verbal and nonverbal message, purpose, and perspective

Teaching Suggestions: Discuss with students how body language can reflect a speaker's message. Ask students for suggestions as to the types of signals that indicate nonverbal messages (for instance, arms folded across one's chest might mean that the person is not open to new information). During the interview, have student audience members pay particular attention to the historical figure's verbal and nonverbal message. Decide how it reflects their purpose and perspective.

Listen to learn by taking notes, organizing ideas, and summarizing ideas

Teaching Suggestions: Have student audience members take notes during the interviews so that they are prepared to ask questions afterward. Briefly outline note-taking techniques and the use of outline form. Tell students that they don't need to write down everything that is said during an interview or speech; only the major ideas and perhaps a word or phrase that will jog their memory when it is time to ask questions. They should also jot down questions to be asked later. When asking a question, students should briefly summarize the character's point of view (for example, "Beethoven, I know your father was a singer. What did you learn about music from him?").

Feedback Center

Students can use the following guidelines when giving and receiving feedback during this project:

Giving Feedback

► Ask questions concerning content, delivery, purpose and point of view (for example, Is tone appropriate to purpose?).

► Provide feedback about the coherence and logic of the content, delivery and overall impact on the listener.

► Comment on the verbal and nonverbal delivery (pitch, pace, volume, body language) and its impact on the listener.

► Respond to persuasive messages with questions, challenges, or affirmations.

► Question the evidence to support the speaker's claims and conclusions.

Receiving Feedback

► Listen to constructive criticism with an open mind.

► Use audience feedback and modify the presentation to clarify meaning or organization.

 ## Assessing the Project

The following rubric can be used for group or individual assessment.

3 *Full Accomplishment*

Students followed directions and presented a coherent interview based on solid research and investigation. The ideas discussed were well supported with evidence and examples. Students worked effectively with partners and demonstrated all of the Speaking and Listening Skills listed.

2 *Substantial Accomplishment*

Students presented a coherent interview based on adequate research. There was some supporting evidence. Students worked adequately with partners, and the presentation, however lacking in originality or insight, met most of the Speaking and Listening points.

1 *Little Accomplishment*

Partners' interviews were incomplete or did not fulfill the requirements of the assignment. There was inadequate research, points were not supported with evidence, and the interview lacked a convincing tone.

Reflecting on the Theme Each person has unique talents, abilities, and ways of looking at life. Finding your voice is part of expressing who you are and what you believe. In Part One of this unit, real people and fictional characters have experiences that help them to find their voices.

Was there a time when you had a new experience, such as singing on stage or helping a neighbor, that led you to discover a talent or interest you didn't know you had? Make a collage that expresses how you felt.

610

LEARNING the Language of Literature

Theme

> To produce a mighty book, you must choose a mighty theme.
> —Herman Melville, author of Moby Dick

Theme is a story's main message. It is an observation about life that the writer shares with the reader. To find the theme, ask what important truths are revealed. What do the characters learn along their journey? You might also question the **author's purpose** or **perspective**. In other words, what do you think the author wanted you to learn or remember? In folk tales, themes are simple and may be stated directly. For example, in "The Wolf and the House Dog" there is a lesson about freedom stated at the end of the story. Most themes, however, become apparent as the story unfolds.

The Difference Between Subject and Theme

The **subject** of a story is what it is about. For example, the subject of *The Phantom Tollbooth* is a young boy's adventure in a land of words and numbers. The **theme**, or central truth of the play, might be stated as "With courage and caring, nothing is impossible." In other words, where there's a will there's a way. The theme can be determined from the passage at the right.

YOUR TURN: What words and phrases in this excerpt convey the theme?

THEME

(All bow and salute the heroes.)

Milo. But we never could have done it without a lot of help.

Reason. That may be true, but you had the courage to try, and what you can do is often a matter of what you will do.

—Norton Juster and Susan Nanus,
The Phantom Tollbooth

From *The Phantom Tollbooth*

611

Objectives
- understand and identify the following literary terms:
  theme
  author's purpose
  author's perspective
  subject
  title
  character
  setting
  plot
- appreciate a writer's craft
- recognize and analyze story plot, setting, and problem resolution
- connect, compare, and contrast ideas, themes, and issues across texts

Teaching the Lesson

This lesson teaches students how to identify the theme of a text by analyzing the other elements within the text. This lesson also shows how setting and plot help develop the theme.

Introducing the Concepts
Have students think of a favorite film or book. Ask them to describe the central idea of the work and to explain how they identified the central idea.

Presenting the Concepts
The Difference Between Subject and Theme
Have students think about the short stories they have read as a class. Ask them to identify the subjects of several of these stories, and have a volunteer note the subjects on the chalkboard. Then ask the students to identify the central idea, or theme, of each story. Discuss how the subject and the theme differ for each story.

Use **Literary Analysis Transparencies**, p. 7, for additional support.

YOUR TURN
Possible Response: ". . . What you can do is often a matter of what you will do."

Identifying Theme

Have students reread a short story they've previously read as a class. Ask them to discuss their interpretation of the title after reading the story. Then ask them to analyze changes in the main character and to explain how these changes could help them identify the theme.

Scanning the Story for Key Phrases

Divide students into small groups and assign each group a short story to analyze. Ask each group to identify the main theme of their story and to present a list of evidence, such as quotations, descriptions, and details from the story, to support their identification.

YOUR TURN
Possible Response: "Help people out."

Identifying Theme

You can often find clues to theme in the story title or in the story elements of character, setting, and plot. For instance, a theme of "The Scribe" is that people can use their talents to make positive changes in the world. Look at the chart to see how theme is conveyed in "The Scribe."

- **Title** The title of a story may give a clue about theme.
- **Character** Reviewing the actions, thoughts, and concerns of the main character can also give clues to theme. Ask yourself what the character has learned or how the character has changed.
- **Setting and Plot** Notice how setting affects the characters, plot, and mood. Think about how conflicts are resolved.

IDENTIFYING THEME IN "THE SCRIBE"	
Key Elements	**Clues**
Title	• *Scribe* means a public clerk or writer; title refers to a writer in the story who serves his community.
Character	• 13-year-old James notices illiteracy in his community; takes action by helping people through his writing abilities.
	• He changes from an observer to someone who acts for change.
Setting	• The setting shows inequality; his apartment seems warm compared to the "Silver Dollar Check Cashing Service."
Plot	• James is in conflict about unfair treatment and illiteracy in his neighborhood.
	• He has to overcome the community's fear and then his own fear in order to resolve the unfairness.

Scanning the Story for Key Phrases

After your first reading of a story, ask yourself what ideas about life the story conveyed to you. Then skim the story again to find evidence that supports these themes. Pay attention to

- the first line of each paragraph
- what characters say or think about themselves and each other
- what the narrator says about the characters
- how the setting is described
- descriptions of major conflicts or solutions

A story may have more than one theme, but often there is one theme that is central. After scanning the story for evidence, ask yourself which theme is most important.

YOUR TURN Read the passage at the right and pick out a key phrase that supports a larger theme.

KEY PHRASES

In our neighborhood, when they see a cop, people scatter. That was why the back of my neck was burning.

"What are you trying to do here, sonny?" the cop asks.

"Help people out," I tell him calmly though my knees are knocking together under the table.

—Kristin Hunter, "The Scribe"

From "The Scribe"

Have you ever walked inside a house and smelled something cooking? If you were able to guess what it was, you were drawing a conclusion based on past experiences and common sense. In life, drawing conclusions helps you understand the world. In literature, drawing conclusions gives you a fuller understanding of what you are reading.

Drawing Conclusions

How to Apply the Skill

To **draw conclusions,** an active reader will:
- Look for facts and details
- Consider experience and knowledge
- Make logical inferences
- **Evaluate** information
- **Connect** personally

Try It Now!

Read and draw conclusions from the excerpt below.

> **Miss Walker** (*quietly*). Lenore, that was beautiful!
> (*Lenore gives a shy, tentative smile.*) . . .
>
> **Girl #2.** It was just like a book.
> (*There is a silent moment after this pronouncement. Lenore looks at the other students, trying to suppress her excitement.*) . . .
>
> **Miss Walker.** I'm really very impressed, Lenore. Leave your story on my desk. There are some people I'd like to show it to.
> —Keith Leckie, *Words on a Page*

Here's how Talisa uses the skill:

*"I can **connect** to the happiness and pride that Lenore feels from getting so many compliments. After **evaluating** the class's reaction and Miss Walker's decision to show Lenore's story to other people, I conclude that Lenore will continue writing. She probably feels that writing is one of the most important things in her life."*

Need More Help?

Remember that active readers use the essential reading strategies explained on page 4: • **visualize** • **predict** • **question** • **connect** • **evaluate** • **clarify** • **monitor.**

THE ACTIVE READER **613**

Objectives
- draw conclusions
- support responses by referring to text evidence and one's own experiences

Teaching the Lesson

The strategies on this page will help students learn how to draw conclusions about plot, character, setting, and theme in a story.

Presenting the Strategies
Help students understand the strategies by asking for volunteers to read them aloud. Emphasize to students that they will be using these strategies as they read the selections in this book. Ask them to follow the strategies outlined on this page as they do the following:

Draw Conclusions
Choose a selection from this unit to read, and divide the class into small groups. Ask each group to use the strategies outlined on this page and list the significant facts and details in the story. Then have them discuss the inferences that they are able to draw from these facts and details.

Evaluate
Ask a volunteer from each group to share the conclusions they drew and explain how they arrived at these conclusions.

Connect
As a class, discuss connections that students could make between the elements in the story and their own life experiences that could help them draw conclusions.

Use **Reading and Critical Thinking Transparencies,** p. 1, for additional support.

Objectives

1. understand and appreciate **drama** (Literary Analysis)
2. understand and appreciate **theme** (Literary Analysis)
3. use the reading skill of **drawing conclusions** (Active Reading)

Summary

Lenore Green, an Ojibway teenager, is a promising writer. Her teacher enters Lenore's writing in the District Writing Competitions, giving Lenore the chance to appear before a panel of judges and win a scholarship. Lenore's father, a loving but somewhat bitter man, refuses to allow his daughter to participate, fearing that her encounters with the outside world will take her away from her home and Ojibway heritage and subject her to the same kind of humiliations he has suffered at the hands of white people. The deep understanding between father and daughter, even with all its conflicts, eventually solves the problem.

Thematic Link

Lenore Green has found her voice, but will it fall on deaf ears? Or will her message be so powerful that it cannot fail to make its mark?

5-Minute Warm-Up

Daily Language SkillBuilder

Have students **proofread** the display sentences on page 609i and write them correctly. The sentences also appear on Transparency 19 of **Grammar Transparencies and Copymasters.**

PREPARING to *Read*

ACROSS the CURRICULUM · SOCIAL STUDIES

Words on a Page

Drama by KEITH LECKIE

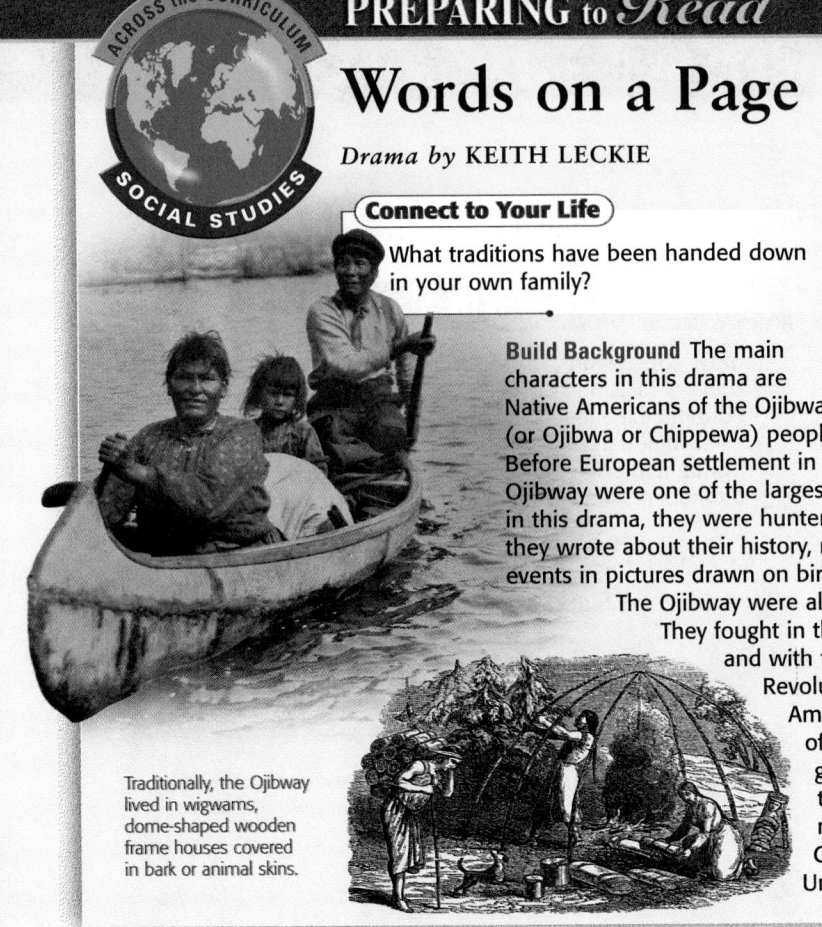

(Connect to Your Life)

What traditions have been handed down in your own family?

Build Background The main characters in this drama are Native Americans of the Ojibway (or Ojibwa or Chippewa) people. Before European settlement in North America, the Ojibway were one of the largest native groups. Like Pete in this drama, they were hunters and fishers. Like Lenore, they wrote about their history, recording important events in pictures drawn on birch bark.

The Ojibway were also known as warriors. They fought in the French and Indian War and with the British in the American Revolution. Like other Native Americans, they lost most of their land to the U.S. government. Today, they live primarily on reservations in the Upper Great Lakes region of the United States and Canada.

Traditionally, the Ojibway lived in wigwams, dome-shaped wooden frame houses covered in bark or animal skins.

Focus Your Reading

LITERARY ANALYSIS THEME In a work of literature, the **theme** is a message about life or human nature the writer wishes to share. A work may have more than one theme. As you read this drama, think about its message and the lessons you might learn from it.

ACTIVE READING DRAWING CONCLUSIONS When you pay attention to details as you are reading and make guesses about what they mean, you are **drawing conclusions.** In drawing conclusions, you use information from your reading as well as from your own experiences.

READER'S NOTEBOOK As you read, note words or phrases that point to a larger message, that state beliefs, or that comment on life. What details or prior knowledge helped you draw a conclusion?

WORDS TO KNOW **Vocabulary Preview**

abundance	expertise	gesture	tentative
anticipation	foliage	hover	
collective	foreground	momentum	

LESSON RESOURCES

Words on a Page
by Keith Leckie

Characters

Lenore Green, an Ojibway teenager

Pete Green, Lenore's father, a fisherman and trapper

Connie Green, Lenore's mother

Sadie Green, Lenore's younger sister

Miss Walker, Lenore's grade ten teacher

The Principal of Lenore's high school

Various Students

Driver

Man

Reading and Analyzing

Reading Skills and Strategies: PREVIEW

Have students look through the selection and note how it differs from the stories they've read. You might point out that this is not just a drama, but a teleplay, or a drama meant to be presented on television or film. Tell students to notice how the selection is divided and how the stage directions are shown.

Literary Analysis THEME

Remind students that the theme is an important statement the author makes about life. What statement is Lenore making about life in the piece she reads on this page?

Possible Response: She is saying that her home is important to her.

Use **Unit Five Resource Book**, p. 6 for more practice. Use **Literary Analysis Transparencies**, p. 7, for additional support.

Active Reading
DRAWING CONCLUSIONS

Ask students what inference or conclusion they can draw about what Girl #2 means when she says, "It was just like a book."

Possible Response: She means it was as well-written as a published book.

Use **Unit Five Resource Book,** p. 5 for more practice. Use **Reading and Critical Thinking Transparencies,** p. 18, for additional support.

Literary Analysis: TELEPLAY

Explain to students that a teleplay is a drama written for television. Ask them to note several words on this page that indicate this is a teleplay.

Possible Responses: camera, panning, holding, cuts, pulls focus

---

Scene 1   Interior. Classroom. Day.

1 *It is a sunny fall afternoon in Lenore's grade ten English class. Sunrays through dust particles in the air. There are a dozen classmates, a mixture of white and native, listening as Lenore reads a story she has written.*

Lenore. . . . So on that morning before she left, they went by canoe one last time to those favorite places. It was at first light, when the water is a mirror and the trees are still, as if nature is holding her breath.

2 *(A variety of young faces listen, all enthralled with her story. Camera moves slowly, panning across the classroom, holding on different faces.)*

And there was the beaver and the loon and the hawk circling above the treetops. And below the trout and the sturgeon slipped silently through the black water.

(Camera stops on one Girl, listening intently, then moves again. Camera holds on two Boys slouching close together, almost touching, but their eyes and attention are on Lenore at the front of the class.)

Creatures as powerful as the great moose, as small as a minnow. She and her father took their place among them.

3 *(Camera cuts to Miss Walker, the native teacher. She sits to one side of Lenore listening as intently as the rest. She is very impressed.*

4 *Camera pans and pulls focus to hold finally on Lenore as she finishes the story. She has memorized most of it and hardly has to look at the page. She speaks very well with skilled emphasis and a personal passion for her words.)*

And in this world there was a peace and harmony that she knew no matter how far she traveled, she would never find again. She understood now why her father had brought her here. She felt the morning sun on her face and the gentle rocking of the canoe and smiled because she knew that here would always be her home.

(Lenore stops speaking, holds the few pages against her chest with both arms and looks at Miss Walker a little anxiously. There is a hushed silence for a moment.)

Miss Walker *(quietly).* Lenore, that was beautiful!

(Lenore gives a shy, <u>tentative</u> smile.)

What did you think, class?

(The class gives a <u>collective</u> chatter of positive response, then . . .)

Girl #1. It was real sad.

Boy #1. It reminded me of . . . like around Shadow River.

Girl #2. It was just like a book.

(There is a silent moment after this pronouncement. Lenore looks at the other students, trying to suppress her excitement.)

(The bell rings signaling the end of class and the students quickly exit the classroom. When the wave of students has passed, Lenore is left still standing there. Miss Walker puts a hand on her shoulder.)

Miss Walker. I'm really very impressed, Lenore. Leave your story on my desk. There are some people I'd like to show it to.

(Miss Walker then exits, leaving Lenore alone. She takes a deep breath then allows herself a beaming smile as she hugs her story against herself.)

WORDS TO KNOW   **tentative** (tĕn′tə-tĭv) *adj.* uncertain; hesitant
collective (kə-lĕk′tĭv) *adj.* done by a number of people acting as a group

616

Teaching Options

BLOCK SCHEDULING: MANAGING TIME

If your schedule requires that you cover the lesson objectives in a shorter time, use . . .
- Preparing to Read, p. 614
- Thinking Through the Literature, p. 633
- Vocabulary in Action, p. 634
- Grammar in Context, p. 635

If you want to take advantage of longer class time, use . . .
- TE Teaching Options: Preteaching Vocabulary, p. 615; Viewing and Representing, pp. 617, 620, 629, 632; Grammar, pp. 618, 621, 635; Vocabulary Strategy, pp. 619, 624; Spelling, pp. 622, 625; Speaking and Listening, p. 623; Cross Curricular Links pp. 626, 631; Assessment, pp. 627, 630, 634; Multicultural Link, p. 628
- Choices & Challenges, p. 634

Good Afternoon #1, Alex Katz. Oil on canvas, 71½" × 96", Private Collection, Paris. Courtesy of Colby College Museum of Art. Copyright © Alex Katz/Licensed by VAGA, New York, NY/Marlborough Gallery, NY.

(Mini Lesson) Viewing and Representing

Good Afternoon #1
by Alex Katz

ART APPRECIATION Alex Katz, born in Brooklyn, New York in 1927, studied art in Skowhegan, Maine. He has donated hundreds of his works to Colby College's museum in Waterville, Maine.
Instruction This painting is one of a series of four paintings the artist did in 1974, depicting Coleman Lake, near his summer home in Maine, at different times of the day. The woman is paddling right toward you. A feeling of calm pervades the paint-ing. Point out that the canoe is made from birch bark, a material that the Ojibway used to record their history in drawings. Ask students how they think this painting may be related to the setting of this teleplay.

Possible Response: Lenore and her family might live in a place that looks like this. Since they fish, they may do so from canoes like this one, made out of birch bark.

Literary Analysis: TELEPLAY

A Point out that the term *stock shot* means a camera shot that is taken from stock, or from what is already on hand. Ask why filmmakers might use a stock shot of a beaver swimming rather than going out and shooting a new one.

Possible Response: Any shot of a beaver swimming would work here; it's often easier and cheaper to use stock shots in situations like this that do not include characters or important action.

Literary Analysis [THEME]

B Many times people tell stories like the one Lenore's father tells in order to make a point. What theme does her father seem to be getting at with his story about the beaver?

Possible Response: He might be saying that if you do things for the wrong reason, they will backfire on you.

ACTIVE READING

C **CONCLUSIONS** They seem to be close and are able to talk about a lot of things.

Literary Analysis: CONFLICT

D Ask what conflict this sentence that Lenore's father speaks might introduce.

Possible Response: He doesn't seem to like the idea of Lenore spending so much time on her schoolwork, while Lenore loves school and writing.

Literary Analysis: CHARACTERIZATION

E What does Lenore's comment about Pauline Johnson having a hard time getting gas for her outboard reveal about her character?

Possible Response: It shows that Lenore has a good sense of humor. Obviously, there were no outboard motors for boats a hundred years ago.

Scene 2A Exterior. Stream. Afternoon.

The prow of a cedar canoe cuts through the calm water. Lenore and her father Pete, in the stern, are canoeing their way up a quiet stream. It is late in the afternoon. The shadows are lengthening, and the sunlight retains the shimmering intensity of this time of day as it filters through the autumn <u>foliage</u>.

1 **Pete.** Good here for beaver. Heavy willow growth. Lots of food. *(Lenore notices a beaver swimming. She points.)*

2 **Lenore.** Look, Baba.

A *(Shot of beaver swimming. He suddenly slaps his tail loudly and dives—stock shot.)*

He's warning his friends about us.

Pete *(seriously).* You know that a long time ago the beaver only had a little skinny tail.

Lenore. Oh yeah?

(Lenore looks back smiling expectantly. She knows this is the opening to one of her father's crazy stories.)

B
3 **Pete** *(storytelling tone).* You see, one day Nanabozho was out paddling his big canoe. He's pretty lazy so he decided if he gave the beaver a big paddle tail, he could tie them on the back and they would push his canoe. But once he had given the beaver a paddle tail, the beaver was too quick to catch. So he didn't get a chance to try it.

Lenore *(only half serious).* D'you think it would work?

Pete. Cheemo and I tried it once.

Lenore. Really?

Pete. Sure! Roped a couple 70 pound beavers on the back of this canoe.

Lenore. What happened?

Pete. Well, they chewed a hole in the canoe and we all sank and they got away!

(Lenore laughs at this image and turns to look back at her father.)

Lenore. Serves you right.

(Pete laughs too. They continue paddling slowly, quietly.)

Scene 2B Exterior. Beaver pond. Day.

They canoe near a bubbling beaver dam with more beaver houses visible.

Pete. You said you had a dream to tell.

Lenore. Yes. *(She turns around in the canoe, facing him.)* It's pretty simple, I guess. I'm standing in the woods. There's a raven flying just above my head. It <u>hovers</u> there. It has something to tell me. *(pause, thinking)* It wants to land . . . but it can't. It only hovers there. It never lands.

(Pete thinks about the dream very seriously for a moment.)

C

ACTIVE READING

CONCLUSIONS
What can you conclude about Lenore's relationship with Pete?

Pete. Sounds like a good dream. Can't tell you what it means. Maybe it isn't finished with you yet. *(Lenore smiles. Pause)* You know Cheemo had the same dream for five nights in a row. He dreamed he was swimming underwater.

Lenore. Yeah?

Pete. Every night, same thing. Swimming underwater!

Lenore. Yeah?

Pete. On the sixth day, he couldn't stand it anymore. He jumped into the lake! And no more dream.

WORDS TO KNOW   **foliage** (fō′lē-ĭj) *n.* plant leaves, especially tree leaves, considered as a group
hover (hŭv′ər) *v.* to remain floating or suspended nearby

Teaching Options

Mini Lesson **Grammar**

USING ITALICS IN PLAYS

Instruction Stage directions and settings are usually printed in italics in order to differentiate them from dialogue. Stage directions are also usually in brackets or parentheses, while settings are in italics without brackets. Point out the examples of each in the highlighted text. Ask which words in italics give the setting and which are stage directions. *(The first italicized sentence is the setting. The rest of the italicized words and sentences are stage directions.)*

Exercise Have students add italics where needed in the scene that follows:

Scene 36: <u>Lenore and her father are in a car on the highway.</u>

Lenore: Well, Dad, were you surprised by what I wrote?

Pete: <u>(thinking and rubbing his jaw)</u> I was, Lenore. <u>(turning to look at her)</u> I guess I don't have so much to worry about after all.

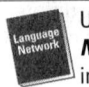 Use **Grammar Transparencies and Copymasters**, p. 132.

Use McDougal Littell's *Language Network*, Chapter 9, for more practice in using punctuation.

(They both laugh again.)

We'll go upstream to the next pond and . . .

Lenore *(hesitant).* Baba, I . . .

Pete. What?

Lenore *(feeling bad).* I've got all kinds of homework to do. We've got a lot of tests coming up . . .

Pete. Isn't it enough they have you all day at that school?

Lenore. I'm sorry, Baba.

Pete *(gruffly).* Never mind.

(Pete quickly backpaddles to turn the canoe around and they head back the way they came. Lenore looks unhappy.)

Scene 3   Exterior. Schoolyard. Day.

It is lunch break at school. A number of students are sitting around on the grass and walls eating lunch. Some play volleyball nearby. Lenore is sitting on a bench reading some poetry to a Classmate. Sadie, Lenore's sister, is listening in. Lenore reads with feeling from the book.

Lenore. "Up on the hill against the sky,
A fir tree rocking its lullaby,
Swings, swings,
Its emerald wings,
Swelling the song that my paddle sings."

Classmate #1. That's neat!

Lenore. Yeah. Pauline Johnson. She's a native poet who traveled all around these lakes almost 100 years ago. Musta been hard to get gas for her outboard then, eh? *(They laugh. Miss Walker comes up behind them with a letter in her hand. She crouches behind them.)*

Miss Walker *(excited, smiling).* Lenore? I've got some news for you. I sent your story in to the District Writing Competitions. You have been accepted as a finalist!

(She shows Lenore the letter. Lenore and Sadie read it together. Lenore is both excited and disbelieving.)

Next week you go down to Thunder Bay to read your story to the judges!

(Lenore and Sadie look at each other in amazement.)

This is wonderful! If you do well there, they could send you to a special high school in the south. Then maybe to study English at university!

Lenore *(mixed emotions).* University!

Miss Walker. Well, let's see how Thunder Bay goes. We just need a letter of permission from your parents and we're all set!

(Lenore looks at the letter again, confused and excited. Miss Walker smiles at her, then leans forward and gives her a little hug.)

I'm proud of you.

(Miss Walker gets up and leaves them. Again Sadie and Lenore look at each other.)

Sadie. Nice going!

Lenore *(grinning).* Yeah! I can't believe it! *(frowning)* I just wonder what Baba is going to say.

Scene 4   Interior. Kitchen (Lenore's home). Evening.

Lenore, Sadie, their mother Connie, and Pete are having fish dinner. Pete eats his food hungrily. Lenore looks up at him once, then again. Then she notices Sadie staring at her impatiently. Lenore glares at Sadie and they both resume eating.

Pete *(to all).* Good trout, eh? We caught them way north of Mulligan Bay. Cold and deep.

(He takes another huge mouthful.)

Connie. We should have enough in the freezer to last until Christmas.

Vocabulary Strategy

WORD ORIGINS
Instruction Knowing word origins, or where words come from, is an aid to understanding historical influences on English words. For example, the word *canoe* comes from the French word *canoe,* which in turn is borrowed from the Spanish *canoa,* but the word is of Carib origin. The Carib were a native people of northern South America, Central America, and the Caribbean islands of the Lesser Antilles. In order to find infor-

mation like this, students can use any good dictionary. Information about word origins is usually given at the end of the entry for a word.
Exercise Ask students to find the origins of these words: *moose, moccasin, pecan, toboggan. (All are of Native American origin.)*

Use **Vocabulary Transparencies and Copymasters,** p. 61.

Reading and Analyzing

Literary Analysis: STAGE DIRECTIONS

A What is Pete doing as Sadie is telling him Lenore has something to tell him? How do you know that?

Possible Response: He is eating fish for dinner and acting rather uninterested. The stage directions tell the reader that this is what is going on.

Active Reading

DRAWING CONCLUSIONS

B Students should be able to draw inferences such as conclusions and support them. What does Pete mean when he says "'Want' and 'Can' are not always the same thing"?

Possible Response: He means that you can't always have everything just because you want it.

C In her story, Lenore's character is talking to her father about why he won't let her go to the city to visit her aunt. What do you think she is really thinking about when she reads this?

Possible Response: She is probably thinking of the fact that her father won't let her go to Thunder Bay to read her story.

ACTIVE READING

D **MAKE INFERENCES** Possible Response: There are different ways of solving the same problem.

Untitled (1960), Henri Michaux. Copyright © 2001 Artists Rights Society (ARS), New York/ADGAP, Paris.

Pete. The King of France never ate better than this.

(There is a moment of silence. Sadie can wait no longer.)

Sadie. Baba, Lenore has something to ask you.

(Pete and Connie look up. Lenore glares at Sadie.)

Pete. Uh huh?

Lenore. Well . . . I've been doing some work at school . . .

Pete. Yeah. So?

Lenore. You know . . . like writing.

A *(Pete takes another large bite of fish, only vaguely interested.)*

Anyway . . . the new teacher, Miss Walker, said I've been doing real well . . . and there was a story I wrote . . .

Pete. A what?

Lenore *(hesitating).* Well, a story . . . and they, ah . . .

Sadie *(interrupting).* The story won a contest and now she has to go to Thunder Bay to read it and then they'll send her away to university!

(Lenore "looks daggers" at Sadie. Both Pete and Connie look at Lenore in surprise.)

Lenore. Can't you shut up!

Pete. University!

(Lenore passes Pete the letter.)

Lenore. Well, no! It's only if I win, but . . .

(Pete glances at the letter then pushes it away.)

Pete. That's crazy! You're only a young girl! You can forget about going to Thunder Bay.

Lenore. But I have to! I'm representing the school!

620 UNIT FIVE PART 1: FINDING YOUR VOICE

Teaching Options

 Mini Lesson ## Viewing and Representing

Untitled
by Henri Michaux

ART APPRECIATION Henri Michaux was a man of many talents. Born in Belgium in 1899, he traveled the world as a sailor, then settled in Paris in 1922. He was also a well-known poet and magazine editor. Many of his paintings explored the inner world of dreams and fantasies. He died in 1984.

Instruction Point out that sometimes artists intentionally leave their paintings untitled. In that way, they leave it up to the viewer's imagination to find meaning in the painting.

Application Ask students what this painting reminds them of. How do they think it might relate to the play?

Possible Responses: Students may say that the painting reminds them of the birds shown on the first page of the selection. They may also say that they appear to be random ink strokes which could become words on a page.

Pete. They can find someone else.

Lenore. But they want my story!

Pete. Then send the story to Thunder Bay.

Lenore *(approaching tears)*. But I want to go!!

B **Pete.** "Want" and "Can" are not always the same thing.

(Pete goes back to his dinner.)

Lenore. You never . . . !

(Lenore is about to continue her argument but her mother is signaling her not to continue along these lines. Lenore stands up and quickly exits the kitchen.)

Scene 5 Interior. Classroom. Day.

The classroom is empty except for Lenore standing at the front and Miss Walker sitting at a desk several rows back. Lenore is practicing reading her story with a compelling intensity.

Lenore. She found her father out behind the shed laying the steaming cedar strips across the frame of a new canoe, his strong hands molding the soft wood. "Baba," she said, "Why can't I visit Aunt Doreen for the summer? I'm not a child anymore. I want to ride a subway, Baba! I want to climb to the top of a skyscraper, and see a museum and go to a play. I want to see the world!" But her father turned away and would not look at her.

(Lenore stops and thinks about her father for a moment.)

Miss Walker *(quietly)*. Yes. Go on.

(Suddenly all of Lenore's <u>momentum</u> is gone. She appears weary.)

Lenore. Can we stop now?

Miss Walker. Sure. Sure, that's fine. It's coming along really well, Lenore. Parents' Night will be a good rehearsal for the finals.

(Pause, looking at Lenore who appears distracted)

Is everything all right?

Lenore. Yes, I'm just tired.

Miss Walker. Good. You get a good sleep. I'll see you tomorrow.

(Lenore gives her a half-hearted smile and leaves the classroom. Miss Walker looks after her, wondering if there is anything wrong.) **2**

Scene 6 Interior. Kitchen (Lenore's house). Day.

Lenore comes into the kitchen, tosses down her books and flops down at the table. Her mother is making bannock bread. They are alone. Her mother notices her unhappiness.

Connie. How was school?

Lenore. Okay. *(pause)* Actually it was lousy. *(sudden anger)* I just don't understand! Why won't he let me go?!

(Connie stops work and sits down across from her.)

Connie *(after a moment)*. He's afraid of what will happen to you.

Lenore. He wants to trap me!

Connie. It might seem like that, but he believes he's protecting you.

Lenore *(deflated)*. What am I going to do, Mom?

Connie. He's stubborn. The harder you push, the more he digs in his heels. *(pause)* D'you remember the story of the Sun and the Wind, how they had a contest to see who could get the coat off a passing man? The Wind blew as hard as he could, but the man held the coat on tightly. When the Sun had his

ACTIVE READING

MAKE INFERENCES
What is the theme or message of Connie's story?

621

Customizing Instruction

Less Proficient Readers
Help students summarize what has gone on in Scene 4 by asking:
- Why is Lenore uneasy about telling her father about the writing contest?
  Possible Response: She thinks that he won't let her go to Thunder Bay.
- Why is Lenore angry at her sister?
  Possible Response: She wants to tell her father in her own way, not just blurt it out like Sadie does.
- Why does Lenore stop arguing with her father?
  Possible Response: Her mother signals her to stop because she won't get anywhere with her father by arguing like this.

Students Acquiring English
1 Explain that "looks daggers" means to give a look to someone that is sharp and angry.
2 Demonstrate a "half-hearted smile," one that involves only your mouth, not your eyes. Explain that a half-hearted smile means that the person smiling isn't really feeling the happiness that usually goes behind a smile.

Multiple Learning Styles
Auditory Learners
Have students practice and perform Scene 4 to clarify the meanings of all the pauses and interruptions.

Grammar

ELLIPSES

Instruction Point out the ellipses (. . .) in the three highlighted sections. In the first, they indicate a pause or hesitation in what Lenore is saying. In the second, the ellipses indicate that Sadie interrupted Lenore before she could finish what she was saying. In the third section, they indicate that Lenore's voice started to say something, then trailed off as she saw her mother's signal to stop arguing. Explain that ellipses are sometimes used to show that a speaker starts in the middle of something, too.

Exercise Have students working in pairs or small groups look back at the selection so far and find other places where ellipses are used. Ask them to explain why they're used in each instance.

Use **Grammar Transparencies and Copymasters**, p. 130.

Literary Analysis: CONFLICT

 Students should be able to analyze characters, including their conflicts and relationships. What conflict does Lenore's excitement, followed by her subdued answer, indicate? Is this an internal conflict or an external one?

Possible Response: Lenore wants to please her father and enjoys being with him, but she doesn't want to miss school. The conflict is internal because it's inside Lenore's own mind.

Literary Analysis: TELEPLAY

B Point out the description of the scene under the heading "Scene 8." Ask students which direction tells how the scene is to be photographed, and why they think the filmmaker would want it to be seen that way.

Possible Response: The description says "Camera at stream level." By placing the camera at stream level, the film maker would be able to show both Lenore's and Pete's expressions.

C Point out the description of the scene under the heading "Scene 9." How does it indicate the dream sequence is to be shot? Why do you think the filmmaker would do this?

Possible Response: It says, "Shot in slightly slow motion." This could make it look dreamy and would also differentiate it from the rest of the film.

> ### ACTIVE READING
> **D** VISUALIZE **Possible Response:** The birds may look like the hawk in Lenore's story.

Active Reading

> **DRAWING CONCLUSIONS**

E What conclusion might you draw from the driver having to turn the bill right side up for Pete?

Possible Response: Pete can't read.

---

turn, he shone warm and bright and the man just took off his coat.

Lenore. I should be the sun?

(Connie nods.)

Connie. Maybe you could read your story to him.

Lenore. I have to read it on Parents' Night. But he'll never come.

Connie. Maybe this time, if you ask, he will.

(Lenore looks suddenly hopeful.)

Lenore. You think so?

Connie *(smiling).* Maybe.

(Lenore smiles happily.)

Scene 7   Exterior. Woods. Day.

A small cedar tree crashes to the ground near the banks of a stream. Pete stands beside the stump, axe in hand. He wipes a sleeve across his sweating forehead, then quickly begins to trim the branches.

With a smaller axe Lenore competently trims the branches of another downed cedar in the foreground. In the background we see a sturdy lean-to, three-quarters completed, large enough to sleep two or three people with provisions— side walls, open front, firepit. Lenore lifts her ten-foot cedar pole, takes it to the structure and fits it in place, resting on the center beam nailed between two trees.

Pete is suddenly beside her and places his pole beside hers which almost completes the superstructure of the roof. He smiles at her.

Pete. Now the tarp, a good layer of cedar boughs and one snowfall will make it warm and dry. Ron and I'll live here a week for trapping. *(looking at her)* What do you think? You want to come?

Lenore. Where?

Pete. Out on the new trapline in November with Ron and me?

Lenore *(excited).* Yeah! *(then subdued)* But I've got school.

(Pete turns away to adjust the crosspiece.)

(hopefully) But maybe I can get off for a couple of days.

Pete *(not looking at her).* You think about it.

Scene 8   Exterior. Rocky stream bed. Day.

Lenore kneels down on a flat rock. Holding her hair back she drinks from the surface of the black, bubbling stream. Camera at stream level. She looks up, satisfied, her face wet. She watches her father who puts his face right down in the water and shakes his head, splashing and blowing bubbles. He looks up at her and they both laugh, water dripping off their faces.

Pete cups some water in his hand and brings it to his lips to drink. Lenore watches him a moment.

Lenore. Sometimes I wish I could be a son for you, Baba.

(Pete looks up at her curiously at this statement out of the blue.)

Pete. A son?

Lenore. Yes. I know every father wants a son.

(Pete considers this as he fills a canteen with water.)

Pete. I would like a son. Maybe someday . . . *(pause)* but the first time I saw you and you smiled at me, I wouldn't have traded you for ten sons!

(Lenore smiles at this, watching him fill the canteen.)

Lenore. Baba?

> WORDS TO KNOW
>
> **foreground** (fôr′ground) *n.* the part of a scene or picture that is nearest to the viewer

---

Teaching Options

Mini Lesson   Spelling

APOSTROPHES IN CONTRACTIONS AND POSSESSIVES

Instruction Remind students that apostrophes are used to form contractions and possessives. In contractions, apostrophes stand for the letter(s) omitted: wouldn't = would not; I've = I have; he'll = he will.

Apostrophes are also used to show possession. To make a singular noun possessive, add 's: Lenore's story. To make a plural noun that ends in s possessive, simply add an apostrophe: Parents' night. If it does not end in s, add an 's: children's.

Exercises Have students choose the correct form of each possessive or contraction.

1. (Wel'l, <u>We'll</u>) be busy fishing that day.
2. The (bird's, <u>birds'</u>) heads slowly came into focus.
3. The water dripped down (<u>Pete's</u>, Petes) chin.
4. Lenore (did'nt, <u>didn't</u>) know how to tell her father about the writing contest.
5. (<u>Sadie's</u>, Sadies') interruption came at a bad time.

 Use **Unit Five Resource Book,** p. 9

Pete. Hummm?

Lenore. Parents' Night is on Wednesday.

Pete *(distastefully)*. Parents' Night?

Lenore. Yeah. I'm going to read something. Be real nice if you were there.

Pete. I don't have anything to say to those teachers.

Lenore. You don't have to say anything.

Pete *(resisting)*. And we're fishing next day. We'll be outfitting the boat.

Lenore. Just for a little while? Maybe? *(pause)* Please?

Pete. Okay. I'm not promising but I'll try.

(Lenore smiles, her eyes sparkling.)

Scene 9   Exterior. Open sky (dream). Day.

In slow motion against a blue sky background a single bird comes into frame. Shot in slightly slow motion. It hovers above the camera. After a moment it is joined by other birds . . . two, three, four, all hover in frame above the camera. It is not a threatening image. The motion is beautiful to watch. The sound of wings becomes steadily louder.

ACTIVE READING

VISUALIZE Imagine Lenore's dream. What do you think the birds look like?

Scene 10A   Interior. Lenore's bedroom. Night.

Lenore, with a little gasp, suddenly sits up in bed, staring out in front of her. Her tense body relaxes. She thinks for a moment about the images of the dream. She lies down again and rolls over, her face toward camera. She smiles with excitement and <u>anticipation</u>.

Scene 10B   Exterior. Spirit Bay docks. Late day.

A pick-up truck stops beside the docks. Pete is waiting. The Driver gets out and opens the tailgate.

Driver. Got your new nets, Pete.

(Pete inspects the three bundles of nets as the Driver drops them to the ground.)

Pete. Hey, they don't have floats!

(The Driver hands him the bill.)

Driver. See? Nothing about floats.

(Pete looks at the bill. The Driver looks at him, then turns the bill right side up for him to read. Pete glances at it and stuffs it into his pocket.) **Ⓔ**

Pete. Gonna take me all night to sew floats on these nets.

Driver. You want 'em or not?

(Pete nods. The Driver drops the last net on the ground, gets back in the truck and drives off. As the truck drives away, Pete checks his watch, looks unhappy, then carries the first bundle toward the boat.)

Scene 11   Interior. School auditorium. Evening.

It's Parents' Night in the small auditorium. There are about two dozen parents present, native and white. Tables display artwork of various kinds and highly graded tests and essays. There is a coffee and pastry table where parents stand in small groups talking with four or five teachers.

There is a podium[1] at the front of the auditorium. Lenore stands near it anxiously watching the doorway, holding the pages of her story.

---

1. **podium** (pō′dē-əm): an elevated platform or stand, as for a public speaker.

> **WORDS TO KNOW**   **anticipation** (ăn-tĭs′ə-pā′shən) *n.* the feeling of expecting something

623

Reading and Analyzing

Literary Analysis | THEME |

Ask students to summarize the theme of the play thus far.

Possible Response: The conflict between the different generations is one theme.

Ⓐ What is the theme of the Principal's speech?

Possible Response: There is so much to know in the modern world that a good education is even more important than ever.

Reading Skills and Strategies: VISUALIZE

Ⓑ Ask students to picture and then describe what the scene looks like after Lenore runs from the room.

Possible Response: The people probably sit quietly for a while, then they might start to talk among themselves and look outside the room to see what is going on. Some of them probably stare at Mrs. Green.

Reading Skills and Strategies: PREDICT

Ask students to predict whether they think Lenore will give up the chance to go to Thunder Bay and win the contest.

> **ACTIVE READING**
>
> **Ⓒ CONCLUSIONS** Possible Response: Lenore feels that if her father did not even come to hear her read at Parents' Night, he'll never allow her to go to Thunder Bay to compete, so there's no point to reading her story.

---

1 **Sadie.** Betcha he doesn't come.

Lenore. He'll come.

(Miss Walker approaches them.)

Miss Walker. Hi Lenore. Are you ready?

Lenore *(anxious).* I think so.

Miss Walker. You'll do great! Are your parents here yet? I was looking forward to meeting them.

2 **Lenore** *(eyeing the doorway).* They'll be here any minute.

(The Principal moves behind the podium to address those present. Conversation dwindles.)

Principal. Good evening, and welcome to the first Parents' Night of the year at Nipigon District Junior High School. Glad you could come out. In a moment I'll ask one of our students to come up and read a prize-winning story she's written . . .

(Principal's talk continues over dialogue between Lenore and Miss Walker, below.)

But first I would like to say a few words about the challenges facing us in the coming year. Never before has there been such an <u>abundance</u> of information and communication in our world . . .

(Lenore whispers anxiously to Miss Walker.)

Lenore. Wait! I can't do it yet!

Miss Walker. Don't worry. I'll stall him if necessary. *(smiling)* Mr. Crankhurst goes on forever, anyway.

(Lenore tries to smile. She looks at the Principal.)

Ⓐ **Principal.** It is almost overwhelming when you consider it. In the face of this, a sound education has never been more important. And so, our goal will remain a high standard of academic achievement and individual

excellence in all our endeavors. We are deeply aware of our responsibility here at Beardmore to mold the bright minds of young men and women who will in a few short years forge the destiny of our world!

(Connie comes through the door into the auditorium. She is alone. Lenore watches her. Connie stops, looks around the room and sees Lenore. She looks at her and shakes her head sadly. Pete is not coming. Lenore appears as if she's about to cry. Sadie takes this all in.)

So now let me introduce one of those bright young minds, to read her story that has been selected for the finals of the District Writing Competition . . . Lenore Green.

(There is polite applause. Lenore turns to Miss Walker in anger and frustration.)

Lenore. I'm not going to do it.

Miss Walker *(sudden alarm).* What!?

Lenore. Why bother!

(The applause dies out. The Principal and all others are looking expectantly at Lenore. With story in hand, Lenore turns and exits the auditorium. There are whispered comments in the audience of parents. Miss Walker quickly follows Lenore.)

Scene 12 Interior. Hallway (school). Evening.

The hallway is deserted. Lenore walks determinedly away from the auditorium. Miss Walker comes out the door and calls after her.

Miss Walker. Lenore! Lenore!

(Lenore stops and turns back. Miss Walker comes up to her.)

Miss Walker. What's wrong!? I don't understand.

Lenore. I don't want to read my story. And I don't want to go to Thunder Bay!

WORDS TO KNOW   **abundance** (ə-bŭn′dəns) *n.* a great amount

624

Teaching Options

 Mini Lesson **Vocabulary Strategy**

DENOTATION AND CONNOTATION

Instruction Remind students that *denotation* is the literal meaning of a word—what is given in a dictionary. A word's connotation includes the attitudes and feelings associated with a word. Words with similar meanings can have quite different connotations. Display the following example:

The dress was <u>cheap</u>.

The dress was <u>inexpensive</u>.

Discuss the fact that *cheap* is associated with being poorly made and shoddy, where *inexpensive*, while similar in denotation, has the connotation of being a good buy.

Exercise Have students work in pairs to decide how the underlined words, which are synonyms, differ in their connotation. Ask volunteers to explain the words' different connotations.

Lenore was <u>anxious</u> as Parents' Night was about to begin. She knew Miss Walker was <u>eager</u> to meet her parents.

(*Anxious* implies nervousness; *eager* implies a pleasant anticipation.)

Use **Vocabulary Transparencies and Copymasters,** p. 62.

Afternoon Light #6, © Lee Wallat Illustration. 8¼" × 11" pastel.

Miss Walker. But Lenore! This is a great opportunity! This is the first big step in your career.

Lenore. What career?!

Miss Walker. You could do anything—go to university, become a journalist or an English professor or a playwright. You've been given a talent. You can't turn your back on it!

Lenore. It's only a stupid story. I'm sorry I even wrote it.

ACTIVE READING

CONCLUSIONS Why do you think Lenore won't read her story?

(Lenore throws the story down on the floor, turns and walks away. After a beat Miss Walker reaches down and picks up the spilled pages. She looks at them, then watches Lenore walking away from her.)

Scene 13A Interior. Classroom. Morning.

Miss Walker is sitting at her desk marking tests in the empty classroom. She works quickly for a moment, but then her momentum slows, her eyes leave her work, and brows knitted she begins to think again about Lenore. She can't figure it out.

Sadie and Connie enter the room behind her. Connie is intimidated by a woman of her own generation with a university education. She looks uncomfortably around the room.

Sadie. Miss Walker?

Miss Walker *(turns around and stands).* Hi Sadie . . . and Mrs. Green. How are you?

(Connie nods shyly. It takes a moment to find the words, but she speaks them with determination.)

Students Acquiring English

1 Point out that *betcha* is slang for "I bet you." Sadie is so sure of her father not coming that she'd be willing to bet on it.

2 Help students figure out the meaning of *eyeing* by asking, "What do you do with your eyes?"

3 Demonstrate a face with *brows knitted.* Ask students what such an expression might indicate?

Possible Response: It might indicate concern, confusion, or deep thought.

Less Proficient Readers

Help students to see that Scene 12 is going on outside the room where Scene 11 took place. The people are still in the auditorium wondering what might have happened to Lenore to make her run out of the room as she did.

Ask students how much time has passed since the end of Scene 12 and the beginning of Scene 13A.

Answer: one night

 Mini Lesson **Spelling**

REGULAR AND IRREGULAR PLURALS

Instruction Remind students that most nouns make their plurals by adding *s* or *es* to the base word: *parent, parents.* Sometimes you have to change a *y* to *i* before adding *es: story, stories.* But irregular plurals follow no set pattern and you just have to learn them. Some change one or two letters: *man, men; woman, women; mouse, mice.* Some add an ending: *child, children; ox, oxen.* Some are the same in the singular and the plural: *moose; deer, fish.* Some are totally different in spelling: *person, people.*

Exercises Have students choose the correct plural form of the noun to complete each sentence. Tell them to use a dictionary if they need help.

1. Many of the (children, childs) at Lenore's school were Ojibway.
2. Mr. Green went fishing and caught a dozen (fish, fishs).
3. How many (deers, deer) did he see in the meadow?
4. Many (writeres, writers) begin young.

Literary Analysis: TELEPLAY

How many scenes are on these two pages?

Answer: five (or four and a half—13B only, 14, 15, 16, 17)

Literary Analysis: STAGE DIRECTIONS

A How is Connie feeling as she begins to talk to Miss Walker? How do you know?

Possible Response: She feels a little ashamed. The stage directions tell the reader that is how she's feeling.

Literary Analysis: CONFLICT

B The stage directions say that Pete feels bad. What internal conflict is making him feel that way?

Possible Response: He loves Lenore and wants to make her happy, but he is afraid to let her out into the world and away from the community.

Active Reading

DRAWING CONCLUSIONS

C Have students draw a conclusion, about why Connie wants so badly for Lenore to go to university.

Possible Response: Connie was a good student herself, but never took the opportunity to go to university, so now she really wants this for her daughter.

Connie. There is something you should know. Lenore loves to write more than anything. And she wants to go to Thunder Bay. But my husband . . . *(a little ashamed)* he won't let her.

Sadie. Baba doesn't believe in schools and books and stuff.

Miss Walker *(reflectively)*. I see. Please sit.

(Miss Walker gestures to a chair for Connie and another for Sadie.)

Scene 13B Exterior. Spirit Bay docks. Afternoon.

Pete is unloading his catch after a good day's fishing. He is on the dock. A Crewman hands him a tub full of ice and fish from the deck on the boat. There are several tubs on the dock.

Pete *(feigning pain)*. Uhhh! The only trouble with a good catch is it's bad for my back!

(The Crewman laughs. Pete lifts the tub of fish and walks a few steps to the other tubs when he notices Lenore. Lenore stands—with school books—at the far end of the dock watching Pete from a distance. Other students pass by behind her on their way home. Lenore and Pete look at each other a moment. Pete puts the tub down with the others and wiping his hands with a rag takes a step toward her. Lenore turns and quickly walks away. Pete stops and watches her, feeling bad.)

Scene 14 Interior. Classroom. Afternoon.

Connie and Sadie are talking to Miss Walker. Connie is more relaxed now. She is reflective.

Connie. When I was Lenore's age, I was real good at school too. Top of my class. I might have gone on to university, even! But I couldn't decide . . . and then I met Pete . . . *(pause, then with conviction)* I want this for Lenore!

Miss Walker. So do I.

Connie. We're having a roast Sunday. Why don't you come by?

(Connie and Miss Walker and Sadie share a conspiratorial smile.)

Miss Walker. Good! I will.

Scene 15 Exterior. Lenore's house. Day.

Establishing shot/time passage. A car and a pickup truck are parked outside.

Scene 16 Interior. Kitchen (Lenore's house). Day.

The table is nicely laid out with flowers and a bright, plastic tablecloth and a variety of food— fish, slices of moose, potatoes and other vegetables, and bannock bread. Miss Walker sits at one end of the table, Pete at the other. Sadie and Connie sit on one side, Lenore on the other.

Lenore is very quiet. She is angry at her father and embarrassed by Miss Walker being there. She is uncomfortable to be at the table with both of them.

Miss Walker takes a platter of meat from Lenore.

Miss Walker. Thanks, Lenore.

(Pete is eating his food hungrily, eyes on his plate. Miss Walker is talking mostly to Connie, although she watches Pete for any response.)

. . . and we're getting in a new portable classroom and adding to the library . . .

(Pete, without looking up, grunts his disfavor over this.)

And what I'm hoping for by the end of the year is a computer terminal for the students to use . . .

Pete *(grunts again)*. Pass the moose.

(Miss Walker finds the platter of moose beside her and passes it. Pete piles moose meat on his

WORDS TO KNOW

gesture (jĕs′chər) *v.* make a motion to express thought or emphasize words

Teaching Options

Cross Curricular Link **Social Studies**

OJIBWAY ART

If you go to Thunder Bay, Ontario, you can visit the Thunder Bay Museum, which features exhibits of Ojibway art. Among them are the stunning traditional beadwork for which the Ojibway are known.

Modern Ojibway have brought their art into the contemporary world, as well. Among the best-known artists is Norval Morrisseau. He is the founder of the school of art called "Legend" or "Woodland." Morrisseau was born on Sand Point

Reserve, near Beardmore, Ontario, in 1932. He was fascinated by the ancient rock art of his people, and when he began to paint, his style echoed some of what he had seen there. When he attempted to paint his dreams, thoughts, and visions, he was criticized by some Ojibway for revealing their legends and beliefs. He maintained that he wanted to restore cultural pride to his people, and has donated paintings to raise money for Ojibway causes.

Other Ojibway artists include Patrick DesJarlait, Francis Kaegig, and Daphne Odjig.

plate. Miss Walker looks at him, is about to say something to him, then thinks better of it.)

Miss Walker. One thing I'm excited about *(She looks at Pete.)* . . . and Mr. Crankhurst seems open to it . . . is an Ojibway Studies course.

(Pete looks up at this.)

Pete *(with disdain)*. Ojibway Studies?

Miss Walker. Yes. The language and customs and history . . .

Pete. Like one of them dead civilizations in a museum.

Miss Walker. No! Not at all. In fact, you trap and fish. Maybe you'd come in and give demonstrations of your <u>expertise</u>?

Pete. Expertise! If you get paid by the word, that's a ten dollar one for sure!

(Sadie giggles at this. Miss Walker is angry. The gloves are off.)

Miss Walker. I can see you don't think much of education, but it can give all kinds of things to a girl like Lenore.

Pete. You mean like a one-way ticket out of here.

(Miss Walker takes out the folded pages of Lenore's story and unfolds them.)

Miss Walker. Have you read this?

Pete. No.

(Connie looks worried.)

Miss Walker. Well I think you should read it!

Pete *(suddenly awkward)*. I will . . . later.

Miss Walker. Read it now! Just the first page.

(She stands up, reaches over and puts the manuscript[2] down in front of him. Pete moves it away. Miss Walker stays standing.)

Pete. No.

Miss Walker. Well if you don't care enough to even read . . .

(Pete stands up angrily.)

Pete. You saying I don't care about my daughter?!

Miss Walker. She has talent and imagination and desire! You can't imprison her here!

Pete. Prison!

Miss Walker. There's a whole world waiting for her out there!

(Lenore sits there becoming angry and frustrated listening to this.)

Pete. In that world she'll be an outsider! She'll be alone and unhappy and forget who she is!

(Lenore stands up and looks at Pete.)

Lenore. You don't know who I am! *(then at Miss Walker)* Neither of you! No one even cares what I want!

(Lenore turns away and exits the house. Pete and Miss Walker look at each other, now sorry that they have been so insensitive.)

Scene 17 Exterior. End of dock (Sunset Lodge). Day.

Lenore crouches on the end of the dock. She looks down at her reflection in the black water. She holds out a pebble and lets it drop into the reflection. When it clears a moment later, her father's reflection can be seen behind. He stands there a moment.

Lenore *(residual[3] anger)*. Why won't you read my story?

---

2. **manuscript** (măn′yə-skrĭpt′): an unpublished version of a book or other work.

3. **residual** (rĭ-zĭj′oō-əl): remaining after the feeling has mostly passed.

627

Customizing Instruction

Less Proficient Readers
Since there are many scene changes on these two pages, help students note or chart the changes and tell what happens in each location in their own words.

Students Acquiring English
 Explain that a *roast* is an event at which some kind of food—fish or meat, usually—is roasted and people gather to eat.

Multiple Learning Styles
Interpersonal Learners
Have students work in pairs to write new dialogue for Scene 16 in which both Miss Walker and Pete say what they really mean to each other. Have students discuss whether this straight-forward approach might have prevented an argument.

✓ **Assessment Standardized Test Practice**

RECOGNIZING PERSUASIVE DEVICES
Sometimes students will be asked on standardized tests to determine when a writer is trying to persuade them to do something or think in a particular way. Write the following sentences on the board:

A. Many artists try to present their culture to the world.

B. Artists should keep their culture to themselves.

C. Some of the finest Ojibway artists today are living and working in Canada.

D. I don't know why other people would be interested in the art of the Ojibway.

Lead students through the process of recognizing which sentence tries to persuade them. A and C both present factual information. D states an opinion on the part of the writer, but does not aim to persuade others to feel the same way. Sentence B is the correct answer. The word *should* is a clue that the writer is trying to tell the reader how to think or what to do.

Literary Analysis: CONFLICT

Ⓐ Ask students what conflict Pete faces here.

Possible Response: He has to either tell Lenore he can't read or let her think he doesn't care enough to read her story.

Literary Analysis: STAGE DIRECTIONS

Ⓑ What adverb tells how Pete feels as he says these words?

Answer: bitterly

ACTIVE READING

Ⓒ **CONCLUSIONS Possible Response:** They probably feel peaceful and as if they can talk about anything.

Literary Analysis: SYMBOL

Ⓓ Students should be able to recognize and interpret literary devices such as symbolism. What do the birds in Lenore's dream symbolize?

Possible Response: They symbolize her dreams of becoming a writer.

(Pete crouches down beside her and looks out at the water a moment. He doesn't look at her as he speaks.)

Ⓐ **Pete.** Because. . . I can't.

(Lenore looks at him in surprise.)

I never learned to read so good. You never knew, eh?

Ⓑ *(Lenore shakes her head; pause, then bitterly)*

When I went to school there was a teacher. . . If I didn't learn my lessons or talked Indian, he'd beat me with a switch and call me names. One day I took the switch away from him and never went back. Never been in school since.

(Lenore watches her father, her expression softening.)

Lenore. Come for a walk?

(Pete looks up at her for the first time, smiles and nods.)

Scene 18A Exterior. Spirit Bay Field. Day.

A telephoto lens shows Pete and Lenore walking side by side toward camera. The background shows the picturesque village of Spirit Bay on the edge of the lake. They walk in silence for a moment.

Pete. I'm afraid. *(pause)* Afraid that you'll go away and become a stranger to us.

Lenore. How could I do that?!

Pete. If you go south to school. It's very different there.

Scene 18B Exterior. Spirit Bay Road. Day.

Pete and Lenore walk toward camera, telephoto lens.

Lenore. I'll always be Nishnabe, Baba. And Spirit Bay is my home.

Pete. Others have said that and not come back.

Lenore. I'll come back! I want to learn to write

better so I can live here and tell about our people! That's why I want to write!

(Pete thinks about this hard as they walk along. They fall silent again.)

Scene 19 Exterior. Dreamer's Rock. Afternoon.

Pete and Lenore sit atop Dreamer's Rock facing the lake that stretches out before them to the horizon. The village can be seen below, and distant islands in the lake.

ACTIVE READING

CONCLUSIONS How do you think this setting makes Pete and Lenore feel?

Lenore. I've been waiting to tell you the last of the dreams. The dreams of the bird that wants to land.

Pete *(very interested).* Yes! Is it finished?

Lenore. It's finished.

Pete. How did it end?

Lenore. Remember I told you the bird was hovering and trying to land? *(Pete nods.)* Well then each night there were more birds— a few and then dozens . . . then hundreds of birds! *(pause, remembering)* And there was a wide open field of snow! And there they began to land, black against the white snow.

(Pete is listening intently.)

Pete. They all landed?

Lenore. Yes! And as each bird landed it became a letter. And the snow was like a page. And the bird-letters formed words. And the words sentences. *(looking at him)* They were my words, Baba! They were the words I wrote!

(Lenore stops, thinking about the images. Pete smiles at her, excited by the dream, but saddened by its meaning.)

Pete. Sounds like you were meant to be a writer. I won't stop you.

(Lenore is not satisfied.)

Multicultural Link ## Why Native Americans Are Called "Indians"

When Christopher Columbus landed in 1492 at the Caribbean island he called San Salvador, he thought that he had arrived in the Indies—a group of islands in Southeast Asia. Columbus had reasoned that, since the earth was a sphere, he could reach the Indies by sailing west. He was right about the direction. However, he had underestimated the circumference of the earth, and he did not know that there were two continents—North and South America—blocking his path.

Convinced that the islands where he landed were, indeed, the Indies, Columbus called the people who lived there "Indians." The name stuck and is still used, erroneously, today. Native Americans of North, South, and Central America comprise over 2,000 separate cultures. So the term "Indian" is inaccurate in more ways than one.

Courtesy of Christopher Pullman, WGBH, Boston.

Students Acquiring English

1 Ask students to find the smaller word in *picturesque*. (*picture*) Tell them that if a village is described as being *picturesque,* it is like something they might see in a picture of a village. Ask whether they think this means the village is pretty or not and to explain why.

Possible Response: It's probably pretty, since most things tend to be represented in their best light in pictures.

Multiple Learning Styles
Visual Learners
Have students draw a picture showing Lenore's dream.

Viewing and Representing

LOON POSTER

Instruction The image shown on this page was used as a poster to advertise a morning radio music program.

The central figure of this poster is the loon. This bird has a strange cry that mimics human laughter. Many people find it a haunting, lonely sound.

Application Ask students what things about the image make them think of morning.

Possible Response: The pink sky and shadowy hills look like morning. The feeling is very peaceful and quiet, like this time of day.

Application Why do you think this poster was chosen to accompany *Words on a Page?*

Possible Responses: It looks like the place where Pete and Lenore might sit and talk. The birds in the sky remind me of the birds in Lenore's dream.

Reading and Analyzing

Literary Analysis [THEME]

Ask students to elaborate on their earlier thoughts about the theme of this play.

Possible Response: The theme still has to do with a conflict between the generations. It also says that people must find their own way in the world, and having a strong sense of "home" gives them a better chance of finding who they really are.

ACTIVE READING

A CONCLUSIONS Possible Response: Lenore feels home and harmony with nature are the most important parts of her life.

Active Reading
[DRAWING CONCLUSIONS]

B Ask students if they think the behavior of the audience at the University in any way changed Pete's feelings about how his people are treated by outsiders.

Possible Responses: No, the people didn't seem to act very warmly toward Lenore and her story; Yes, after a while, everybody started to applaud for Lenore.

Lenore. But I need more, Baba. I don't know if I can do it alone. I need your help.

Pete. My help? I can't even read!

Lenore. Not that kind. I need your . . . *(pause, finding right word)* courage. Will you come to Thunder Bay and hear me read my story?

Pete *(unhappily)*. At the university?

(Lenore nods. Pete hesitates, then answers.)

I'll come.

(Lenore takes his hand and smiles at him happily.)

Scene 20A Exterior. Lakehead University. Day.

Establishing shot of university with an identifying sign.

Scene 20B Interior. University. Day.

Pete, Lenore, Sadie, Connie and Miss Walker approach a Man in a suit outside the lecture room doors. Pete looks around uncomfortably.

Miss Walker *(to Man)*. Is this the District Writing Finals?

Man *(officious)*. Yes. They're about to begin.

(Lenore is excited and scared. She hesitates at the door.)

Lenore. I . . . I don't think . . .

(Pete puts a hand on her shoulder. She looks up at him.)

Pete *(smiling)*. Read it to me. Just to me.

(Lenore takes heart in these instructions. She smiles and goes quickly inside followed by the others.)

Scene 21 Interior. Lecture hall. Day.

The lecture hall is quite full of people. A panel of six judges sits at a table at the front listening as Lenore reads her story.

Lenore. So on that morning before she left, they went by canoe one last time to those favorite places. It was at first light, when the water is

---

a mirror and the trees are still, as if nature is holding her breath.

(Near the front rows sit Miss Walker, Pete, Connie and Sadie listening. Lenore reads directly to her father, inspired by his presence. Pete listens intently.)

And there was the beaver and the loon and the hawk circling above the treetops. And below, the trout and the sturgeon slipped silently through the black water.

Creatures as powerful as the great moose, as small as the minnow. She and her father took their place among them.

(Pete, in his solemn features, reveals amazement at his daughter's ability and the touching sentiments of the story.)

And in this world there was a peace and harmony that she knew no matter how far she traveled, she would never find again.

She understood now why her father had brought her here. She felt the morning sun on her face and the gentle rocking of the canoe and smiled because she knew that here would always be her home.

ACTIVE READING
CONCLUSIONS
What conclusions can you draw about what is most important to Lenore?

(When Lenore finishes, the hall is silent. Pete, very moved by his daughter's story, rises immediately to his feet. He begins to applaud loudly—the only one in the hall. The Judges look at him with disfavor. But then Sadie applauds and stands and Connie and Miss Walker stand applauding and then others and finally the whole hall is on its feet applauding. Even two of the Judges give polite applause. Connie, Miss Walker and Sadie smile at Pete. Pete looks only at Lenore.)

(Pete and Lenore, with tears in her eyes, look at each other and smile meaningfully at one another.) ❖

Teaching Options

✓ **Assessment Informal Assessment**

ALTERNATIVE ENDING

You can informally assess students' understanding of the selection by having them imagine an alternative ending. For example, what might have happened if Lenore's father had not allowed her to go to Thunder Bay?

RUBRIC

3 Full Accomplishment Student writing reflects a full understanding of the importance of Pete's support to Lenore.

2 Substantial Accomplishment Student writing shows some understanding of the importance of Pete's support to Lenore, but does not fully reflect how this might influence the ending.

1 Little or Partial Accomplishment Student writing displays little or no understanding of the importance of Pete's support or of how it might influence the ending.

BRINGING THE PRAIRIE HOME

by Patricia MacLachlan

Place.

This is one of my favorite words, and I am a writer because of it.

Place.

I remember vividly the place where I was born: the smell of the earth, the look of the skies when storms came through; the softness of my mother's hollyhock blooms that grew by the back fence.

When I was ten years old, I fell in love with place. My parents and I drove through the prairie, great stretches of land between small towns named wonderful names like Spotted Horse, Rattlesnake, Sunrise. We stopped once for drinks that we fished out of cold-water lift-top tanks, and my mother and I walked out onto the prairie. Then my mother said something that changed my life forever. She took a step, looked down at her footprint, and said, "Someone long ago may have walked here, or maybe no one ever has. Either way it's history."

BRINGING THE PRAIRIE HOME **631**

Cross Curricular Link **Geography**

THE PRAIRIE

The great central plains of Canada and the United States are covered by prairie—flat, rolling grasslands. Rainfall averages 12 to 40 inches (30 to 51 cm) per year in this temperate land. Weather on the prairie can be harsh. Winter storms often blow across this open land, and hot summers can bring drought. However, some of the richest farmland in the world is in the North American prairie, giving it the nickname, "the nation's breadbasket."

Native Americans lived on the prairie for thousands of years, but in the 1800s, their land was taken by the U.S. government and given away to settlers who agreed to farm it. They toiled to plow through the prairie sod, the top layer of soil, which was held together by the thick, matted roots of the prairie grasses. The sod was so firm that it could be cut into brick-like pieces and used to build homes. But the rich soil was fertile for farming.

In the 1930s, many Great Plains farms were devastated by a severe drought. Without the prairie grass roots to hold the soil together, winds created great dust storms. The area most affected became known as the Dust Bowl, and thousands of farm families were forced from their land.

WORDS ON A PAGE **631**

I thought of those who might have come before me and those who might come after, but mostly I was face-to-face with the important, hopeful permanence of place, place that I knew was there long before I walked there, and would be there long after I was gone. I realized, in that moment, that the Earth is history. The Earth is like a character who has secrets; the Earth holds important clues to who we are, who we've been; who we will be. We are connected to the land and to those secrets.

It was after this event that I bought a diary and began writing all sorts of truths about myself, as if I, too, might leave clues about myself behind. I was becoming a writer. All because of place. Now I cannot write a story unless I know the place, the landscape that shapes the story and the people in the story. And to remind myself of the place that changed me, I have carried a small bag of prairie dirt with me for years.

I took that bag of prairie dirt with me once to a class of fourth graders, and I found that those children are connected to place, too. Some had moved from place to place many times: One boy's house had burned in a fire recently; another was about to move to a place he had never been.

"Maybe," I said, "I should toss this out onto my New England yard. I'll probably never live on the prairie again."

"*No!*" cried a boy, horrified. "It might blow away!"

And then a girl had a suggestion. "Maybe you should put that prairie dirt in a glass on your windowsill, so you can see it when you write. It would be like bringing the prairie home."

And that is where that little piece of my prairie is today; my place, my past, my landscape; in a glass on my windowsill. I have brought the prairie home so that I can look at it every day; write about it, write about me, and remind myself that the land is the connection that links us all.

Teaching Options

Mini Lesson · Viewing and Representing

VIDEO Once students have finished reading "Words on a Page," you may wish to show them the accompanying video.

Instruction Tell students that as they watch the video, they should keep in mind the stage directions and settings described in the teleplay they just read. They should also compare their own visualizations of the play with the actual video. Use the video sourcebook for additional instructional ideas.

Application After students have seen the video, conduct a discussion on how a particular scene (or scenes) in the written selection was presented on the screen. For example, if the stage directions indicated that a character said a line in a particular manner, was this followed in the video? Did the setting look the way it was described in the play?

BLOCK SCHEDULING This activity is particularly well suited for longer class periods.

 Use **Communications Transparencies and Copymasters,** p. 7, for additional support.

Connect to the Literature

1. **What Do You Think?**
   How did you feel about Lenore's writing?

   Comprehension Check
   - Why is Lenore invited to Thunder Bay?
   - What is her father's reaction to the invitation?
   - What secret does Pete share with Lenore at the end of the drama?

Think Critically

2. How does Lenore feel about her father and her community? What **conflict** do these feelings create for her?

3. Why do you think Lenore is angry at both Miss Walker and her father?

   THINK ABOUT
   - how they have treated Lenore
   - what each wants from Lenore
   - Lenore's wishes for her future

4. What does Pete want for Lenore's future? Why is he worried about her?

5. **ACTIVE READING** **DRAWING CONCLUSIONS** What are some of the conclusions you noted in your **READER'S NOTEBOOK?** Compare your notes with those of a classmate. How were your conclusions different? Would you change any of them now that you have finished reading the drama?

Extend Interpretations

6. **COMPARING TEXTS** Look back at "Aaron's Gift" on page 248. Both Aaron and Lenore seem to have a special bond with their family elders. How would you compare their feelings about family history? How do they show their feelings?

7. **Connect to Life** Pete hides the fact that he cannot read behind an attitude that school is not important. Why do you think it can be hard for a person to admit he or she cannot do something?

Literary Analysis

THEME The **theme** of a work of literature is an idea about life or human nature the writer hopes the reader will learn. Consider what *Words on a Page* seems to say about life and human nature. What might the author wish to express about the importance of home, family, and finding your voice?

Cooperative Learning Activity
In a small group, discuss the theme for this part of Unit Five, "Finding Your Voice." Together, make a list of statements based on this story that elaborate on the theme. Compare your list with that of another group.

- Support from others can help you find your voice.

Extend Interpretations

6. **Comparing Texts** Aaron is especially sad for what his grandmother had to go through in her youth because of prejudice against the Jews. Now that she knows what is behind it, Lenore is better able to understand her father's sometimes harsh attitude toward the outside world, as well.

7. **Connect to Life** Possible Response: They are embarrassed. They believe that others will think less of them for not knowing how to do something.

GUIDING STUDENT RESPONSE

Connect to the Literature

1. **What Do You Think?**
   Answers will vary, but students should support their opinions with information from the selection.

Comprehension Check
- She is invited to read her story at a contest.
- Her father forbids her to go.
- He finally tells her that he never learned to read.

 Use Selection Quiz
Unit Five Resource Book, p. 10.

Think Critically

2. Possible Response: Lenore loves her father and her community very much. She also loves to read, write, and learn. She wants to explore the world. This creates a conflict between her two sets of wishes and between her wishes and those of her father.

3. Answers will vary, but should note that both adults are planning Lenore's future based on their needs and wants. They are arguing with each other and ignoring Lenore as if she were a child too young to discuss her own future.

4. Possible Response: Pete wants her to stay in the Native American community. He thinks she'll be treated badly in the white community and also won't return home.

5. Students' conclusions will vary, but should be reasonable, based on the information presented.

 Use **Reading and Critical Thinking Transparencies,** p. 18, for additional support.

Literary Analysis

Theme Students' list of statements should connect the theme of this individual selection with the theme of other selections in Unit Five, Part One.

Use **Literary Analysis Transparencies,** p. 7, for additional support.

Writing Options

1. **Acceptance Speech** Most students will say that Lenore would thank her teacher and her mother and sister for helping her get to this point, but she would especially thank her father. She would probably say that her writing is a way to express her feelings about her heritage and to teach others.

2. **Permission Letter** Letters, whether giving permission or not, should be based on the parents' words and actions in the play.

3. **Comparison Chart** Their main area of overlap is in the area of the importance of home, family, and heritage. However, Pete doesn't want much to do with the outside world, and Lenore wants to learn more.

Activities & Explorations

Video Imagery Refer to page 632 for a Mini Lesson built around the video.

Inquiry & Research

The Ojibway Tell students that they may also find information about the Ojibway under these spellings: Ojibwe, Ojibwa, and Chippewa. **To make this activity easier,** suggest that students work in pairs or small groups.

Vocabulary in Action

EXERCISE:
1. foliage
2. hover
3. momentum
4. foreground
5. anticipation
6. abundance
7. expertise
8. gesture
9. tentative
10. collective

Writing Options

1. Acceptance Speech
Imagine that Lenore wins the Thunder Bay competition. Write her acceptance speech. Whom would she thank? What might she say that writing means to her?

2. Permission Letter If you were Lenore's parent, would you let her go to Thunder Bay? Write a letter from Connie and Pete explaining their reasons for letting her go, or not. Place it in your **Working Portfolio.**

3. Comparison Chart What values, traditions, experiences, and talents do Pete and Lenore share? What makes them different? Use a Venn diagram to explore your thoughts. Then write a paragraph comparing the two characters.

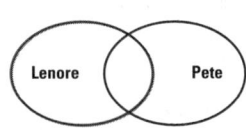

Activities & Explorations

Video Imagery View the video version of *Words on a Page.* How does the setting compare

with the way you visualized it as you read? Do Lenore and Pete perform their roles as you imagined?

~ VIEWING AND REPRESENTING

VIDEO **Literature in Performance**

Inquiry & Research

SOCIAL STUDIES   THE OJIBWAY

What are today's Ojibway communities like? What kinds of work do Ojibway adults do? How many people leave the community for school or work? Gather information from encyclopedias and the Internet. Then make a poster that presents your findings to the class.

INTERNET **More Online: Research Starter**
www.mcdougallittell.com

Vocabulary in Action

EXERCISE: CONTEXT CLUES On your paper, write the Word to Know that best completes each sentence.

1. The fall _____ dazzled Lenore with its shades of gold and crimson.

2. A gull can _____ as though it is suspended in midair.

3. Lenore slumped over her desk, her _____ gone.

4. The photograph showed a raven perched in the _____, while water gleamed in the background.

5. Backstage, Lenore clutched her essay, filled with eager _____.

6. Lenore's mother was amazed by the university's _____ of information.

7. The class listened as Pete shared his fishing _____.

8. The teacher began to _____ for Lenore to speak more loudly.

9. Lenore accepted Miss Walker's compliment with a shy, _____ smile.

10. At Parents' Night, Lenore's reading inspired _____ shouts of joy.

Building Vocabulary
For an in-depth lesson on using context clues, see p. 79.

WORDS TO KNOW				
abundance anticipation	collective expertise	foliage foreground	gesture hover	momentum tentative

Teaching Options

✓ **Assessment   Self-Assessment**

REWRITE In order to help students assess their own comprehension of "Words on a Page," ask them to rewrite the story, this time from the point of view of Pete. Point out that they need not write the story in play form, but they should be able to tell all the major events of the play as if Pete were telling the story. Ask them to keep the following in mind:

• How would Pete describe his family?
• What would Pete say about the school Lenore attends and the teachers there?
• How might the outcome of the story change?

RUBRIC

3 Full Accomplishment Rewrite successfully changes point of view and tells details from Pete's perspective.

2 Substantial Accomplishment Rewrite changes the point of view but does not tell details from Pete's perspective.

1 Little or Partial Accomplishment Rewrite shows little or no understanding of how the changed perspective affects the story.

Grammar in Context: Sentence Fragments and Run-on Sentences

A sentence contains a subject and a predicate, and it expresses a complete thought. Keith Leckie's characters often use phrases that do not express complete thoughts. Sometimes a writer will use this technique to mimic actual speech.

> Good here for beaver. Lots of food.

A **sentence fragment** is part of a sentence punctuated as if it were a complete sentence. You can fix a sentence fragment by adding the words that will complete the thought.

A **run-on sentence** has the opposite problem. It has two or more sentences written as one.

> The story won a contest now she has to go to Thunder Bay to read it then they'll send her away to university!

You can fix a run-on sentence by making it two or more sentences, or by adding a **comma** and a **coordinating conjunction.**

> The story won a contest, and now she has to go to Thunder Bay to read it. Then they'll send her away to university!

Apply to Your Writing Use sentence fragments and run-on sentences only when you are trying to show casual or broken speech.

WRITING EXERCISE Rewrite the sentences to fix fragments and run-ons.

Example: *Original* Sunrays through dust particles.
Rewritten Sunrays fell through dust particles.

1. Be really nice if you were there.
2. Your parents aren't here I was looking forward to meeting them.
3. Can't tell you what it means.
4. I'm excited about the course Mr. Crankhurst is open to it.

Grammar Handbook Writing Complete Sentences, p. R59

"Most of all, I want to write a good love story."

Keith Leckie
born 1952

Behind the Scenes Keith Leckie is a lifelong resident of Toronto, Ontario. He has worked in Canadian filmmaking since the mid-1970s. He started as part of a production crew, working with the many people who film scenes. Later he became a scriptwriter and director for both television and film.

Working for Change Leckie served as a volunteer for groups sending aid to Central America. Later, he researched that region's political history for a book. He has also written about the struggle for freedom by people in Afghanistan. Leckie enjoys creating fiction about lighter subjects as well. His other works include *The Seventh Gate* and *The Coco River.*

AUTHOR ACTIVITY

Reading Films Many popular film and TV dramas have been published. With a partner, read a key scene in a script for a film you enjoyed. How could the scene have been performed or filmed differently? Discuss.

WORDS ON A PAGE **635**

 Grammar
Mini Lesson

WORDS ON A PAGE **635**

OVERVIEW

Objectives

1. understand and appreciate **nonfiction (Literary Analysis)**
2. understand and appreciate a **personal essay (Literary Analysis)**
3. use the reading skill of **identifying main idea and details**

Summary

In this personal essay, Robert Fulghum tells how each spring, he writes a statement of personal belief. When he was young, his credo filled many pages as he tried to cover every eventuality. As he grew older, his statements became more abbreviated. Recently, he decided to condense his personal beliefs into one page. Upon reflection, he realized that the precepts he learned at a young age have been the foundation of his personal beliefs all along. Kindergarten taught him the importance of sharing, caring for others and the world's resources, appreciating the wonder around him, living a balanced life, and remembering that death comes to all. He concludes by observing that the world would be a better place if everyone lived by these principles.

Thematic Link

For Robert Fulghum, finding his voice means looking at the lessons he has learned in the past that have helped him to become who he is today.

5-Minute Warm-Up

Daily Language SkillBuilder

Have students **proofread** the display sentences on page 609i and write them correctly. The sentences also appear on Transparency 19 of **Grammar Transparencies and Copymasters.**

from All I Really Need to Know I Learned in Kindergarten

Essay by ROBERT FULGHUM (fool´jŭm)

"Everything you need to know is in there somewhere."

(Connect to Your Life)

Doing Your Best In the selection you are about to read, Robert Fulghum lists what he thinks a person needs to know in order to live a meaningful life. List three things you think everyone "needs to know" about life. Share your list with a partner.

Build Background

CONNECT TO **HISTORY** Many people set aside time once a year to think about how to improve their lives and make the world a better place. Some make a list of resolutions, statements of goals or ideas to keep in mind in the coming year.

For a number of people, January 1 is a traditional time to do this. January was named for Janus, the Roman god of gates and doorways, who is usually depicted with two faces: one looking back into the past and one looking forward into the future. For centuries, the beginning of January has been a popular time to think about the past and plan for the future.

Some people think through their goals for the next year at the start of a new school term. Some do so on a birthday. Others explore these ideas on a particular religious holiday.

WORDS TO KNOW
Vocabulary Preview
bland   idealism   sanitation
cynical   naive

Focus Your Reading

LITERARY ANALYSIS **PERSONAL ESSAY** A **personal essay,** or informal essay, is a short work of nonfiction in which a writer expresses his or her thoughts, feelings, and opinions about a subject. Usually, personal essays include anecdotes or personal experiences. The writer of a personal essay may seek to express his or her ideas. The writer may also wish to entertain, to inform, or to persuade readers to think or feel a particular way. As you read, think about why Robert Fulghum wrote this essay.

ACTIVE READING **IDENTIFYING MAIN IDEA AND DETAILS**
Most nonfiction writing is organized around a **main idea.** The main idea may appear as a statement, or it may be developed throughout the work. The main idea is supported by strong, well-chosen details. Identifying the main idea and supporting **details** can help you understand what you read.

📖 READER'S NOTEBOOK As you read, think about what the author's main idea seems to be. Jot down details you think support this main idea.

636   UNIT FIVE   PART 1: FINDING YOUR VOICE

LESSON RESOURCES

UNIT FIVE RESOURCE BOOK, pp. 11–17

ASSESSMENT
Formal Assessment, pp. 103–104
Teacher's Guide to Assessment and Portfolio Use
Test Generator

SKILLS TRANSPARENCIES AND COPYMASTERS
Reading and Critical Thinking
• Main Idea/Details, TR 25 (for Thinking Through the Literature, p. 640)
Grammar
• Using Colons for Sentence Variety, CM 133 (for Mini Lesson, p. 642)

Vocabulary
• Using a Thesaurus, CM 63 (for Mini Lesson, p. 637)
Writing
• Achieving Conciseness, TR 21 (for Mini Lesson, p. 638)

INTEGRATED TECHNOLOGY
Audio Library

Visit our website:
www.mcdougallittell.com

All I Really Need to Know I Learned in Kindergarten

by Robert Fulghum

Illustrations, by students of the Harlem School of the Arts, copyright © 1994 by Oxford University Press, Inc.

Each spring for many years, I have set myself the task of writing a personal statement of belief: a Credo. When I was younger, the statement ran for many pages, trying to cover every base, with no loose ends. It sounded like a Supreme Court brief, as if words could resolve all conflicts about the meaning of existence.

The Credo has grown shorter in recent years—sometimes <u>cynical</u>, sometimes comical, sometimes <u>bland</u>—but I keep working at it. Recently I set out to get the statement of personal belief down to one page in simple terms, fully understanding the <u>naive</u> <u>idealism</u> that implied.

WORDS TO KNOW

cynical (sĭn′ĭkəl) *adj.* expressing scorn and mockery
bland (blănd) *adj.* dull
naive (nä-ēv′) *adj.* as simple and believing as a young child
idealism (ī-dē′ə-lĭz′əm) *n.* the practice of imagining that things could be absolutely perfect

637

TEACHING THE LITERATURE

Customizing Instruction

Less Proficient Readers
Before beginning the selection, discuss with the class how a person's beliefs influence a person's actions. For example, if someone believed that the elderly should be treated with respect, he or she might give up a seat on a bus to an elderly person. Ask volunteers to share their beliefs and how they act on those beliefs.

Set a Purpose Have students read to find out what Robert Fulghum learned in kindergarten.

Students Acquiring English
Explain that a *credo* is a statement of beliefs. It comes from the Latin word meaning, "I believe."

 Use **Spanish Study Guide,** pp. 127–129 for additional support.

Gifted and Talented
Ask students to decide which rules are most important. Then have them group themselves with others in the class who think similarly and discuss why they have all chosen those particular rules. Set up a class debate in which each team argues for its choices.

Mini Lesson Preteaching Vocabulary

USING A THESAURUS

Instruction Remind students that a thesaurus helps them to find synonyms or words that share similar meanings. Using synonyms helps writers to avoid repetition and to express their meaning more precisely. For example, someone might be described as *tired.* However, the synonym *exhausted* may express more exactly how tired the person is. Tell students that in deciding which of the thesaurus's choices to use, they may wish to consult a dictionary to be sure that the word means what they think it does.

Exercises Have students use a thesaurus to find the best synonym for each of the underlined

WORDS TO KNOW in the following sentences.

1. His <u>idealism</u> helped him to see the good in people.
2. The sick child had to follow a <u>bland</u> diet.
3. People often become more <u>cynical</u> as they grow older.
4. She showed a <u>naive</u> pleasure in the simple activity.

 Use **Unit Five Resource Book,** p. 14 for more practice. Use **Vocabulary Transparencies and Copymasters,** p. 63, for more practice.

Ask students how Robert Fulghum achieves an informal style and how it contributes to the effect of the text.

Possible Responses: He uses sentence fragments, colloquial language, anecdotes, and direct address of the reader for a friendly, conversational tone.

 Use **Unit Five Resource Book,** p. 13 for more practice.

Active Reading | IDENTIFYING MAIN IDEA AND DETAILS

Remind students that a main idea is developed through several types of details. Ask students what kinds of supporting detail they find in this essay.

Possible Response: examples and incidents

 Use **Unit Five Resource Book,** p. 12 for more practice.

Use **Reading and Critical Thinking Transparencies,** p. 25, for additional support.

Literary Analysis: METAPHOR

A Ask students what the author compares himself to when he has trouble making an important decision.

Possible Response: He compares himself to his old car stalling.

Ask students what larger metaphor is implied through the car comparison.

Possible Response: Life is a journey.

Reading Skills and Strategies: ANALYZE COMMON PERSUASIVE TECHNIQUES

B Ask students how this conclusion reinforces the author's purpose.

Possible Response: The author's purpose is to persuade readers to live by the rules they learned in kindergarten. He offers specific examples and finishes by reiterating, in a memorable way, the most important point.

1
A
The inspiration for brevity[1] came to me at a gasoline station. I managed to fill an old car's tank with super-deluxe high-octane go-juice. My old hoopy couldn't handle it and got the willies—kept sputtering out at intersections and belching going downhill. I understood. My mind and my spirit get like that from time to time. Too much high-content information, and I get the existential[2] willies—keep sputtering out at intersections where life choices must be made and I either know too much or not enough. The examined life is no picnic.

All I really need to know about how to live and what to do and how to be I learned in kindergarten. Wisdom was not at the top of the graduate-school mountain, but there in a sand pile at Sunday school. These are the things I learned:

2

Share everything.

Play fair.

Don't hit people.

Put things back where you found them.

Clean up your own mess.

Don't take things that aren't yours.

Say you're sorry when you hurt somebody.

Wash your hands before you eat.

Flush.

Warm cookies and cold milk are good for you.

Live a balanced life—learn some and think some and draw and paint and sing and dance and play and work every day some.

Take a nap every afternoon.

When you go out into the world, watch out for traffic, hold hands and stick together.

Be aware of wonder. Remember the little seed in the Styrofoam cup: The roots go down and the plant goes up and nobody really knows how or why, but we are all like that.

Goldfish and hamsters and white mice and even little seeds in the Styrofoam cup—they all die. So do we.

And then remember the Dick-and-Jane books and the first word you learned—the biggest word of all—LOOK.

Everything you need to know is in there somewhere. The Golden Rule and love and basic <u>sanitation</u>. Ecology and politics and equality and sane living.

Take any one of those items and extrapolate[3] it into sophisticated adult terms and apply it to your family life or your work or your government or your world and it holds true and clear and firm. Think what a better world it would be if we all—the whole world—had cookies and milk about three o'clock every afternoon and then lay down with our blankies for a nap. Or if all governments had a basic policy to always put things back where they found them and to clean up their own mess.

And it is still true, no matter how old you are—when you go out into the world, it is best to hold hands and stick together. ❖

B

---

1. **brevity** (brĕv′ĭ-tē): being brief and to the point.
2. **existential** (ĕg′zĭ-stĕn′shəl): of or relating to existence.
3. **extrapolate** (ĭk-străp′ə-lāt′): to make predictions based on limited information.

WORDS TO KNOW   **sanitation** (săn′ĭ-tā′shən) *n.* the creation of rules designed to protect public health

638

Teaching Options

Mini Lesson **Speaking and Listening**

PERSONAL BELIEF STATEMENTS

Prepare Have students reflect on their personal beliefs and compose ten rules to live by. The rules should be organized in order of importance or by topic and should be written in a concise and straightforward style. Students should be prepared to defend their choices by giving examples or reasons or facts.

Present Have students share their rules with a partner and explain their choices. After both partners have presented their lists, have students discuss which rules of the partner they like or agree

with and why. Then have the pairs create a new list of rules to live by, which incorporates the ideas that they mutually agree on from each other's presentations. Student pairs can then share their mutual list with the class and offer their explanations for the new choices.

BLOCK SCHEDULING This activity is particularly well suited for longer class periods.

Use **Writing Transparencies,** p. 21, for additional support.

The Gifted Boy, Paul Klee. Super Stock. Copyright © 2001 Artists Rights Society (ARS), New York/VG Bild-Kunst, Bonn.

Customizing Instruction

Less Proficient Readers

Ask students what Robert Fulghum learned in kindergarten about how to treat other people.

Possible Response: He learned to treat others nicely and to be considerate of them.

• What did he learn to include in his life every day?

Possible Response: Some work, some play, some relaxation, some learning, and some happiness should be included in each day.

• What does he think would happen if all adults lived by these rules?

Possible Response: The world would be a better place.

Students Acquiring English

1 Explain that *old hoopy* refers to his old car and the *willies* are the shakes.

2 Have students take turns reading the rules aloud. Pause to discuss those that might be less familiar to students.

Multiple Learning Styles
Visual Learners

Have students create posters that could be used to remind kindergarten children of these rules in their classroom. Remind students that kindergarten children can't always read yet, so posters should include clear graphic illustrations.

Mini Lesson Viewing and Representing

The Gifted Boy
by Paul Klee

ART APPRECIATION Paul Klee's artistic direction was influenced by both people and events. A trip to Africa changed the way he felt about using colors. He described himself as becoming possessed by color after experiencing the intense light of Tunisia.

Instruction Tell students that color and line predominate in Klee's works. Point out to students how even the figure of the boy is composed of lines. Ask students to interpret the significance of the lines in this painting.

Possible Response: The boy is linked to the shapes in the background by the lines appearing in his own body. The shapes are structures, perhaps symbolic of his potential accomplishments. The structures resemble building blocks.

Application Ask students to relate this painting to the main idea of the essay.

Possible Response: If someone is given the right building blocks when he or she is young, there is no limit to what can be achieved.

GUIDING STUDENT RESPONSE

Connect to the Literature

1. What Do You Think?
Responses will vary. Students may think that the list makes sense. Others may find the list overly simple or too light-hearted to be practical.

Comprehension Check
• He was at the gas station.
• Don't hit people or take things that aren't yours.
• Governments should put things back where they find them and clean up their own mess.

 Use Selection Quiz
Unit Five Resource Book, p. 17.

Think Critically

2. Possible Responses: Sharing, playing fair, cleaning up after yourself, saying you're sorry, and sticking together are the most important. Following these rules will prevent conflicts and injustices that cause unhappiness.

3. Possible Responses: Fulghum means that life choices can be difficult, particularly when it seems that there are so many factors to consider in making them. It is easy to lose sight of the basics, such as those he lists in this essay, and become overwhelmed by too much complex information.

4. Possible Response: Writing a credo each year helps Fulghum keep the important things in mind. This helps him face conflicts and work to make his own life meaningful.

5. Possible Response: The main idea is that we already know all that we need to know in order to have a meaningful life and make good decisions. Fulghum supports this idea with his list of the most basic rules for social conduct, and by asking the reader to imagine what the world would be like if everyone followed these rules.

 Use **Reading and Critical Thinking Transparencies,** p. 25, for additional support.

Literary Analysis

Personal Essay Encourage students to list direct and indirect lessons that Fulghum shares, such as the importance of taking stock of one's life. Students will probably conclude that he wrote the essay to inform and persuade.

Connect to the Literature

1. What Do You Think? How did you react to Robert Fulghum's list of important things to know?

Comprehension Check
• Where was Fulghum when he was inspired to write his list?
• What are the two things he says not to do?
• What basic policy does he think governments should follow?

Think Critically

2. Look again at Fulghum's list of what he learned in kindergarten. Which five things do you think are most important? Explain.

3. Fulghum says the "examined life is no picnic." What do you think he means by this statement?

THINK ABOUT
{
• why he writes a credo
• how he feels when facing life choices
• how the credo relates to his life
}

4. Fulghum believes that words cannot resolve the conflicts about the meaning of life. If this is true, why do you think he continues to write a credo every year?

5. **ACTIVE READING** **IDENTIFYING MAIN IDEA AND DETAILS**
Look back through the notes you made in your **READER'S NOTEBOOK.** What do you think is the main idea of the essay? What details support it? Compare your thoughts with those of a partner.

Extend Interpretations

6. Critic's Corner One critic has said that Fulghum "specializes in the celebration of the everyday event." Do you think this is true of this selection? Why?

7. Connect to Life Do you agree with Fulghum's belief that all we need to know we learned in kindergarten? Explain your opinion.

Literary Analysis

PERSONAL ESSAY A **personal essay** is a short work of nonfiction about one subject. Personal essays are usually **autobiographical.** They focus on the author's own experiences and the lessons he or she has learned.

REVIEW **AUTHOR'S PURPOSE**
A writer usually writes for one or more purposes. To express oneself, to inform or explain, to persuade, to entertain, may all be purposes for writing.

Activity Review Fulghum's essay. Then jot down ideas about what he learned from his experiences and why he wrote the essay. Compare your notes with those of a partner.

What Fulghum learned:

His purpose for writing:

Extend Interpretations

6. Critic's Corner Possible Response: This is true because Fulghum says that little things, such as taking a nap and learning to share, should be appreciated because they are so important that they could even help to create world peace.

7. Connect to Life Possible Responses: I do agree, because if all the countries of the world followed these rules, there would not be war; I do not agree, because real-world decisions can be very complex and require advanced education and mature thought. For example, "playing fair" can be a complicated thing to define.

Choices & CHALLENGES

Writing Options

Personal Credo Look back through Fulghum's statements of personal belief. Then make a list of your own strongest beliefs about life. Write a paragraph or two elaborating on one of these beliefs. Place it in your **Working Portfolio.**

Strongest Beliefs
1. Everyone should be treated equally

Activities and Explorations

1. Belief Illustration Create a drawing that illustrates one of the beliefs from Fulghum's list, or one from your own list. For example, you might draw a picture of people watching out together for traffic, or a seed sprouting in a Styrofoam cup. Add a caption to your illustration. ~ **ART**

2. Public Poll Conduct a poll of your classmates to find out whether they agree with the idea that you learn all you really need to know in kindergarten. For those who disagree, ask at what age they think you learn everything you need to know. Present your findings in a bar graph. ~ **MATH**

3. Credo Speech Fulghum first shared much of his writing as a public speaker. Think of a statement you would include in a credo, and write a short speech elaborating on it. Entertain your audience by relating an incident or story that supports your statement. Present your speech for the class. ~ **SPEAKING AND LISTENING**

Vocabulary in Action

EXERCISE A: ASSESSMENT PRACTICE On your paper, write the letter of the phrase that best completes each sentence.

1. A **cynical** person believes that
   (a) people are not to be trusted.
   (b) people are basically good.
   (c) it is important to help others.

2. A soup with a **bland** taste
   (a) has too many strong spices.
   (b) has little flavor.
   (c) is surprisingly rich.

3. **Idealism** is often considered to be
   (a) a cruel way of thinking.
   (b) proof that a person is greedy.
   (c) a sign that a person is hopeful.

4. We knew my brother was **naive** because
   (a) he cheated his best friend.
   (b) he would not listen to our wild story.
   (c) he believed that pigs could fly.

5. After the **sanitation** workers quit,
   (a) people lost their electricity.
   (b) garbage piled up in the streets.
   (c) snow was left unplowed.

EXERCISE B For each of the Words to Know, write a new sentence that correctly uses the word. Then rewrite your sentences on a new sheet of paper and leave a blank where the Word to Know should be. Exchange papers with a classmate and fill in the correct vocabulary words for each other's sentences.

Building Vocabulary

For an in-depth lesson on learning new vocabulary words, see page 491.

Assessment Standardized Test Practice

IDENTIFYING THE MAIN IDEA For some standardized tests, students will be asked to identify the stated or implied main idea of a passage. To provide students with some help in making the best choice, read aloud or write on the board the following:

Based on the main idea of this essay, with which statement would Robert Fulghum probably agree?

A. Eating in between meals is not a healthy habit.

B. People will make good decisions if they remember the basic lessons that they learned at a young age.

C. Adults should live by a totally different set of rules than children do.

D. Life is too short to waste time in relaxing.

Lead students through the process of choosing the correct answer. A is incorrect. Obviously the author believes in snacks of milk and cookies. B is correct. This is the main idea of the essay. C is incorrect. One of his points is that adults can adapt the rules to their world. D is incorrect. A balanced life includes rest and relaxation.

Writing Options

Personal Credo To get students started on this assignment, have them refer back to the list of rules they created for the Speaking and Listening Mini Lesson on page 638 and choose the one that they feel is most important to live by or that encompasses the others. Have students develop their explanation of why this belief is important by offering several examples of how it affects their lives and could affect the lives of others.

 Use **Writing Transparencies,** p. 13, for additional support.

Activities & Explorations

1. **Belief Illustration** This activity is **well suited for visual learners. To adapt this assignment,** have students create a collage that incorporates all of their beliefs or the author's.

2. **Public Poll** Tell students to poll a sizable number of classmates in order to get a broad sampling of opinions. To get students started on this assignment, show them a bar graph and discuss how the data might be presented as numbers of people or percentages. Some students may wish to complete this assignment on the computer. **This assignment is well suited for logical learners. To make this assignment more challenging,** have students compile the data from everyone's graph into one.

3. **Credo Speech** To get students started on this assignment, have them review the personal credo they wrote. Encourage them to brainstorm incidents that led them to this belief or that taught them the validity of the rule. Have students rehearse their speeches with a partner.

Vocabulary in Action

EXERCISE A:

1. a
2. b
3. c
4. c
5. b

EXERCISE B:

Sentences will vary.

Grammar in Context

1. Live a balanced life: learn, think, draw, paint, sing, dance, play, and work.
2. This advice is good: watch for traffic, hold hands, and stick together.
3. There is one thing politicians do not know: clean up your mess.
4. All things die: goldfish, hamsters, white mice, and everything else.

Author Activity

Small Wonders To extend this assignment, have students discuss lessons that they might draw from the world around them.

Grammar in Context: Sentence Variety Using Colons

Robert Fulghum uses a **colon** to let us know that he's going to list the lessons he learned in kindergarten:

> These are the things I learned: Share everything. Play fair. . . .

The colon formally introduces the things that follow it. For example, it can introduce the following: a series, a summary, a restatement, or an explanation. You can also use a colon to join two related sentences:

> Remember the little seed in the Styrofoam cup: the roots go down and the plant goes up. . . .

Punctuation Tip: Use a colon after the salutation of a business letter and between hours and minutes in an expression of time. In a play or a script, a colon may appear between a speaker's name and what the speaker says.

WRITING EXERCISE Punctuate each sentence with a colon.

Example: ***Original*** Here's my credo all you really need to know you learn in kindergarten.

Rewritten Here's my credo: all you really need to know you learn in kindergarten.

1. Live a balanced life learn, think, draw, paint, sing, dance, play, and work.
2. This advice is good watch for traffic, hold hands, and stick together.
3. There is one thing politicians do not know clean up your mess.
4. All things die goldfish, hamsters, white mice, and everything else.

Grammar Handbook Quick Reference: Punctuation, p. R56

"I've always made a clear distinction between making a life and making a living."

Robert Fulghum
born 1937

Artist and Orator Before becoming a world-famous author, Robert Fulghum created motel art, taught folk music, and worked as a singing cowboy and amateur rodeo performer. Fulghum grew up in Waco, Texas, and left home after high school to explore the world. Eventually, he went to college and became a minister.

Popular Wisdom Most of Fulghum's best-selling 1988 book *All I Really Need to Know I Learned in Kindergarten: Uncommon Thoughts on Common Things* was originally written for his sermons and church newsletters. It has been published in 93 countries and in 27 languages.

The Importance of Fun Fulghum's books have sold more than 15 million copies. However, he does not take fame and fortune too seriously. "Any fool can make enough money to survive," Fulghum says. "It's another thing to keep yourself consistently entertained." His books include *It Was on Fire When I Lay Down on It* and *Uh-Oh: Some Observations from Both Sides of the Refrigerator Door.*

AUTHOR ACTIVITY

Small Wonders In his writing, Fulghum often examines what seems like a simple subject and finds great meaning in it. Look for some of these everyday subjects in Fulghum's other essays. Share your findings with the class.

642 UNIT FIVE PART 1: FINDING YOUR VOICE

Teaching Options

 Mini Lesson Grammar

USING COLONS FOR SENTENCE VARIETY
Instruction Remind students of the uses of the colon to introduce series, summaries, restatements, and explanations. Tell students that they must recognize when *not* to use a colon as well as when a colon is necessary. For example, in the following sentence, the colon is used incorrectly. On his grocery list, he wrote: milk.
The colon is incorrect because no series follows.
Exercises Have students rewrite each sentence correctly and explain the reason for their change.

1. Robert Fulghum has written many books: including this one. *(books, including)*
2. I have one personal belief think before you act. *(belief: think)*
3. After reading the essay: I felt better. *(essay, I)*

Use **Unit Five Resource Book**, p. 15.
Use **Grammar Transparencies and Copymasters**, p. 133.

 Use McDougal Littell's *Language Network*, Chapter 9, for more instruction and practice in using colons.

You Sing (Sonnet 52)
Poetry by PABLO NERUDA

How to Paint the Portrait of a Bird
Poetry by JACQUES PRÉVERT (zhäk prä'věr)

*"But I hear only
your voice,
your voice . . ."*

(Connect to Your Life)

What Inspires You? Something makes you sit up and take notice. Maybe it's a song on the radio or a beautiful sunrise. What stirs your feelings and your imagination? Discuss with a partner.

Build Background

Artistic Inspiration Each of us is moved to strong feelings by different things—the sound of a particular instrument, a favorite poem, a clear sky on a brilliant day. This feeling of being moved can bring artistic inspiration. Pablo Neruda once said that in the area where he grew up, "Nature . . . went to my head . . . I was barely ten at the time, but already a poet." As a writer and an artist, Jacques Prévert was inspired to create poems, plays, songs, and children's books, as well as pictures. In the poems that follow, Neruda and Prévert use poetry to capture sounds and images that move them.

Focus Your Reading

LITERARY ANALYSIS **ONOMATOPOEIA** The use of words whose sounds suggest their meaning is called **onomatopoeia** (ŏn'ə-măt'ə-pē'ə). For example, when you say the words *hiss, pow,* and *thud* aloud, they sound like what they mean. As you read the poems, listen for onomatopoeia.

ACTIVE READING **NOTING SENSORY DETAILS** Words and phrases that help the reader see, hear, taste, smell, and feel what the writer is describing are called **sensory details.** Noting sensory details helps you share the writer's experience. For example, the word *creak* lets you "hear" the sound of Neruda's caravan wheels.

READER'S NOTEBOOK As you read, jot down sensory details in a chart like the one shown.

Sound	Sight	Touch	Taste	Smell
creaking wheels				

Literary Analysis `ONOMATOPOEIA`

Ask students what effect the word *zing* in line 10 creates.

Possible Response: *Zing* suggests speed and the sound of the arrow's release from the bow.

Use **Unit Five Resource Book,** p. 19 for more practice.
Use **Literary Analysis Transparencies,** p. 20, for additional support.

Active Reading

`NOTING SENSORY DETAILS`

Ask students to describe the sounds in the second stanza.

Possible Response: The sounds created by the sensory details are clanging, harsh, painful, and metallic.

Ask students how these sounds are related to the sound of the voice.

Possible Response: The voice is in contrast to these noises and soars above them.

Use **Unit Five Resource Book,** p. 18 for more practice.
Use **Reading and Critical Thinking Transparencies,** p. 11, for additional support.

Literary Analysis: PERSONIFICATION

Ask students what object is given human characteristics in the first stanza.

Possible Response: The pine trees are personified.

Reading Skills and Strategies: MAKING INFERENCES

Ask students to infer from the last line the speaker's feelings toward the person whose voice is the subject of the poem.

Possible Response: It is the voice of someone he loves.

Teaching Options

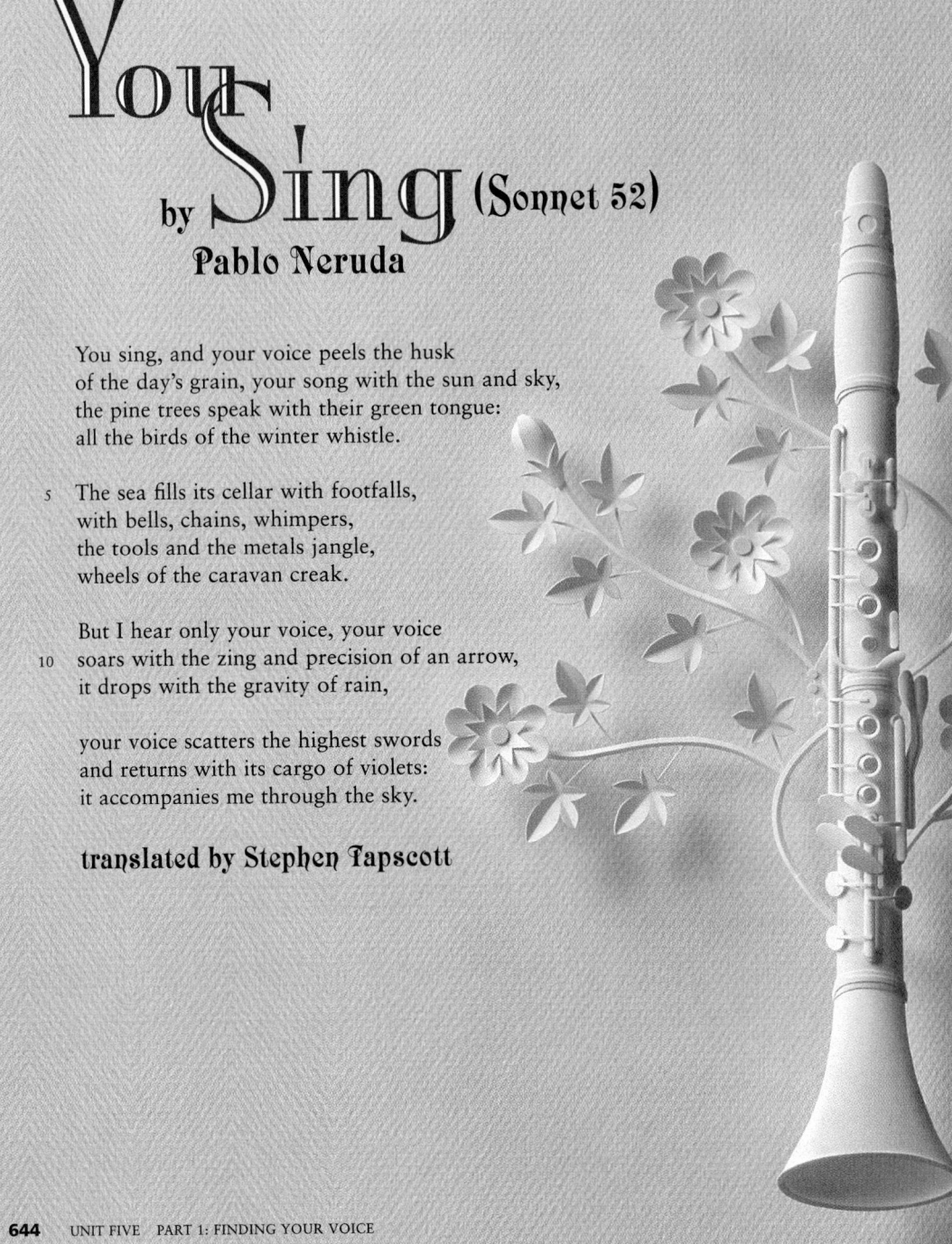

Your Sing (Sonnet 52)

by **Pablo Neruda**

You sing, and your voice peels the husk
of the day's grain, your song with the sun and sky,
the pine trees speak with their green tongue:
all the birds of the winter whistle.

5 The sea fills its cellar with footfalls,
with bells, chains, whimpers,
the tools and the metals jangle,
wheels of the caravan creak.

But I hear only your voice, your voice
10 soars with the zing and precision of an arrow,
it drops with the gravity of rain,

your voice scatters the highest swords
and returns with its cargo of violets:
it accompanies me through the sky.

translated by Stephen Tapscott

Multicultural Link

Nobel Prize for Literature

Pablo Neruda was the recipient of the Nobel Prize for Literature in 1971. This prize is given annually by the Swedish Academy for achievements in literature, language, or areas of general culture. Candidates for the prize cannot apply but must be nominated by members of the Swedish Academy or similar academies, former Nobel laureates, or others eminent in the fields of language and literature. The money for the prize comes from a fund created by the fortune left by Alfred Nobel, who died in 1896. The fund is managed by the Nobel Foundation.

Pablo Neruda was awarded the prize "for a poetry that, with the action of an elemental force, brings alive a continent's destiny and dreams." In his Nobel lecture, Neruda speaks about his decision to be politically active. He says that he saw his task "to join the extensive forces of the organized masses of the people," even if his actions led to criticism. He believes a poet's responsibilities "involve friendship not only with the rose . . . with exalted love . . . but also with unrelenting human occupations . . . "

Soneto 52

Cantas, y a sol y a cielo con tu canto
tu voz desgrana el cereal del día,
hablan los pinos con su lengua verde:
trinan todas las aves del invierno.

5 El mar llena sus sótanos de pasos,
de campanas, cadenas y gemidos,
tintinean metales y utensilios,
suenan las ruedas de la caravana.

Pero sólo tu voz escucho y sube
10 tu voz con vuelo y precisión de flecha,
baja tu voz con gravedad de lluvia,

tu voz esparce altísimas espadas,
vuelve tu voz cargada de violetas
y luego me acompaña por el cielo.

Thinking Through the Literature

1. **Comprehension Check** What does the speaker say is the only thing he hears?

2. How would you describe the speaker's feelings about the voice in this poem?

3. How does the speaker use comparison and contrast to explain his feelings? Refer to lines in the poem that support your answer.

YOU SING (SONNET 52) **645**

Customizing Instruction

Less Proficient Readers
Interest students in the poem by pairing them up and asking them to describe their partner's voice. Then read the poem aloud to the students before they read it silently.
- What does the poet associate with the voice in the first stanza?
  Possible Response: forces of nature
- What does the last line of the poem mean?
  Possible Response: The voice lives in the speaker's memory and heart.

Set a Purpose Have students read the next poem to find out the steps involved in painting the portrait of a bird.

Students Acquiring English
Have a Spanish-speaking volunteer read the poem in the original Spanish. Follow up by reading it to students in English and comparing the sound of the poem in each language. Focus on a few images, such as those in the first and fourth stanzas, that promote specific ideas about the voice.

 Use **Spanish Study Guide,** pp. 130–132 for additional support.

Gifted and Talented
Have students discuss pieces of music that use some of the sounds described in the poems. Ask how the music adds to students' understanding of the poet's description of the voice.

Thinking Through the Literature

1. **Comprehension Check** He only hears "your voice."
2. Possible Response: The speaker loves the voice and feels that it keeps him going through the day.
3. Possible Response: The speaker compares the voice to the *zing* of an arrow in line 10.

Mini Lesson Spelling

APOSTROPHES IN POSSESSIVES AND CONTRACTIONS

Instruction Explain that when two words are contracted to form one, the apostrophe takes the place of the missing letters. For example, the apostrophe in *doesn't* replaces the *o* of *not*. To form the possessive of a singular noun or a plural noun that does not end in *s*, add *'s*. To a plural noun ending in *s*, simply add an apostrophe. Remind students not to put an apostrophe in possessive pronouns such as *its* or *theirs*.

Exercises Have students correct the spelling errors in the following sentences.
1. The voices power could'nt be described. (*voice's; couldn't*)
2. You'r poem is very moving. (*Your*)
3. The birds song wouldv'e given it's location away if we hadn't already spotted it. (*bird's; would've; its*)
4. Peoples reactions to poetry are varied. (*People's*)

How to Paint the Portrait of a Bird

by Jacques Prévert ✑ translated by Paul Dehn

First paint a cage
with an open door
then paint
something pretty
5   something simple
something fine
something useful
for the bird
next place the canvas against a tree
10   in a garden
in a wood
or in a forest
hide behind the tree
A   without speaking
15   without moving . . .

Sometimes the bird comes quickly
but it can also take many years
before making up its mind
Don't be discouraged
20   wait
wait if necessary for years
the quickness or the slowness of the coming
of the bird having no relation
to the success of the picture
25   When the bird comes
if it comes
observe the deepest silence
wait for the bird to enter the cage
and when it has entered
30   gently close the door with the paint-brush
then
one by one paint out all the bars
taking care not to touch one feather of the bird
Next make a portrait of the tree
35   choosing the finest of its branches
for the bird
paint also the green leaves and the freshness of the wind
dust in the sun
and the sound of the insects in the summer grass
40   and wait for the bird to decide to sing
If the bird does not sing
it is a bad sign
a sign that the picture is bad
but if it sings it is a good sign
45   a sign that you are ready to sign
so then you pluck very gently
one of the quills[1] of the bird
and you write your name in a corner of the picture.

---

1. **quill** (kwĭl): any of the larger feathers of a bird; also, a
   writing pen made from such a feather.

Customizing Instruction

Less Proficient Readers
Ask students to list the steps that someone must follow to paint the portrait of a bird.

Possible Response: First, paint a cage with an open door; then place the picture of the cage in a natural setting and wait. When the bird enters the cage, push the door shut and paint out the bars. Next paint a tree and a beautiful scene for the bird. If the bird sings, sign the painting.

Students Acquiring English
1 Be sure students understand the two meanings of the word *sign* as it is used in this line. The first *sign* is an indication or signal; the last one means to write one's name.

Gifted and Talented
- To further discussion of "You Sing," point out the contradictions in the images used by the poet to describe the voice and ask students to consider how these paradoxes deepen the sense of the speaker's appreciation of the voice.
- As students read "How to Paint the Portrait of a Bird," ask them how this poem might express Prévert's credo, or statement of belief, about being a poet.

Possible Response: If this poem is read as Prévert's credo, he seems to be saying that inspiration is essential to write poetry. Also important is the treatment of that inspiration by the poet. If a poet is fortunate enough to receive inspiration, he must nurture it and show it off to its best advantage. If the finished poem is not authentic, or does not "sing," he has failed.

✓ Assessment Informal Assessment

RECOGNIZING POETIC DEVICES You can informally assess students' understanding of the poems by having them chart the poetic devices in each poem. Students should record the examples of sound devices, such as rhythm, rhyme, repetition, alliteration, and onomatopoeia, and instances of figurative language, such as simile, metaphor, and personification, that they find in each poem.

RUBRIC

3 Full Accomplishment Student responses include all possible examples and identify the type of device in each correctly.

2 Substantial Accomplishment Students accurately identify the devices within each poem and include a good number of examples.

1 Little or Partial Accomplishment Student responses inaccurately identify the poetic devices or fail to locate examples of sound devices or figurative language.

GUIDING STUDENT RESPONSE

Connect to the Literature

1. What Do You Think?
Possible Response: The image of an open birdcage waiting for a bird to enter is a very strong image that stays in my mind.

Comprehension Check
- First, paint a cage with an open door.
- You should pause in quiet when the bird comes, and then close the cage door and paint out its bars.
- The painting is good.

Think Critically

2. Possible Response: Sight is most important, as is appropriate to a poem about the visual medium of painting.

 Use **Reading and Critical Thinking Transparencies**, p. 11, for additional support.

3. Possible Response: The bird represents creativity. Sometimes creative inspiration takes a long time to come.

4. Possible Responses: Be open to life and its beauties; wait patiently for inspiration; seize creative opportunity when it comes; erase traces of your effort to make it look easy; strive to create art that seems alive.

Literary Analysis

Onomatopoeia Examples of onomatopoeia from "You Sing" include: *whimpers, jangle, creak, zing.*
An example from "How to Paint the Portrait of a Bird" is *pluck.*
Students' own choices for "You Sing" might include:
the pine trees *murmur*
the bells *clang*
the chains *rattle*
your voice *pings, whizzes*

 Use **Literary Analysis Transparencies,** p. 20, for additional support.

Personification Examples of personification from "You Sing" include "the pine trees speak" and "The sea fills its cellar."

Connect to the Literature

1. What Do You Think?
What image does this poem leave in your mind?

Comprehension Check
- How does the speaker say to begin painting?
- What does the speaker say you should do if the bird comes?
- What does it mean if the bird sings?

Think Critically

2. **ACTIVE READING** **NOTING SENSORY DETAILS** Which sense does this poem appeal to most? With a partner, use your ⬛ **READER'S NOTEBOOK** chart to discuss how sensory details bring the poem to life.

3. What do you think the bird represents? Why must the painter wait so patiently for the bird to come?

4. What advice do you think the speaker of this poem offers to readers?

Extend Interpretations

5. **COMPARING TEXTS** Compare the two poems. How are they similar and different? How would you describe the mood created by each poem?

6. **Critic's Corner** One critic has said that Neruda "does not describe, he glorifies." Do you think this is true of "You Sing"? Explain.

7. **Connect to Life** Recall your prereading discussion about finding inspiration. What experiences do you think inspire strong feelings in these two poets?

Extend Interpretations

5. Comparing Texts Possible Response: In "You Sing," the speaker is telling the person he addresses how that person brightens his life. In "How to Paint the Portrait of a Bird," the speaker is giving advice about how to be creative, and about how to live your life.

6. Critic's Corner Possible Response: Yes, because Neruda praises the good qualities of the person to whom the poem is addressed.

7. Connect to Life Possible Responses: The sound of a beloved person's voice inspires Neruda. Prévert is inspired by the beauty of nature. The fact that it is hard to capture seems to make it even more beautiful to him.

Literary Analysis

ONOMATOPOEIA Words such as *hiss* and *bang* that sound like what they mean are examples of **onomatopoeia.** These words are a kind of sensory language that helps writers create vivid images. Onomatopoeic words often describe movement, such as the *zing* of the arrow in "You Sing."

Cooperative Learning Activity
With a small group, search the poems for examples of onomatopoeia. Include both specific words and overall impressions created by sound. Then think of other onomatopoeic words that could help to describe the scenes in each poem. Write them down on index cards. Try reading them aloud with an emphasis on the dramatic sounds they make.

PERSONIFICATION The use of human qualities to describe an object, animal, or idea is called **personification.** For example, Neruda describes trees that "speak with their green tongue." What other examples of personification can you find in these two poems?

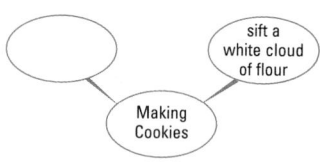

Writing Options

1. How-to Poem Think of an activity with which you are familiar. Write a how-to poem that describes how to do this activity. Plan the poem with a web.

- sift a white cloud of flour
- Making Cookies

2. Sensory Description Recall a vivid sound or image you have experienced. How did you feel? Write a description, using sensory language.

Activities & Explorations

1. Choose a Voice Listen to recordings to find a voice you think captures the effect Neruda describes. Share your recording with classmates. **~ MUSIC**

2. Paint a Portrait Imagine what it would be like to paint a portrait of a bird. What problems might you face? Then use observation, books, or your imagination to paint a portrait of a bird or other animal. **~ ART**

Inquiry & Research

Let Me Count the Ways List activities that make you feel happy or creative. Then think of three other activities you'd like to try. Write a paragraph about each, explaining how it might allow you to find your voice.

 Real World Link Before beginning your work, read "Flip Out!" on pages 650–652.

Writing Options

1. **How-to Poem** To get students started on this assignment, have them brainstorm the steps involved in the process and order them. Then fill in the web with phrases that use sound devices or figurative language to describe the process. Encourage students to use onomatopoeia and personification.

2. **Sensory Description** To get students started on this assignment, have them jot down, for two or three days, the sights, sounds, and other sensations that they experience before they choose a subject.

 Use **Writing Transparencies**, p. 16, for additional support.

Activities & Explorations

1. **Choose a Voice** Have students support their choices with references to specific lines from the poem. **To make this assignment more challenging,** have students record the voice of someone who is special to them and explain, using imagery, what they hear in that voice.

2. **Paint a Portrait** This assignment is **well suited to visual learners. To make this assignment more challenging,** have students observe a bird or other animal in nature and paint its portrait from memory.

Inquiry & Research

Let Me Count the Ways To make this assignment easier, have students brainstorm activities in small groups. Students may wish to research some of the activities mentioned by other students in their group.

"What could I ever say without my roots?"

Pablo Neruda
1904–1973

Born a Poet When Pablo Neruda was growing up in a small Chilean village, poetry seemed an unlikely career. But as a child, Neruda would say, "I'm going out hunting poems." First published when he was 15, by his college years Neruda was a well-known poet.

Freedom and Fame Declaring himself a poet of the people, Neruda wrote poems and prose supporting social change. In 1971 he received the Nobel Prize in literature. Neruda's work has been translated into dozens of languages. Collections of his poems include *Elementary Odes* and *Residence on Earth*.

"Don't joke about humor— humor is serious!"

Jacques Prévert
1900–1977

On Page and Screen Born in a small town in France, Jacques Prévert was educated in Paris, where he spent much of his adult life. A very popular poet, he is also regarded as one of his country's greatest screenwriters. He also wrote plays, song lyrics, and children's books.

Loved and Hated Critics are divided about Prévert's poetry. Some find his work moving; others claim he is often driven by anger. In "How To Paint the Portrait of a Bird," he seems to reveal at least part of his true nature. Prévert tells artists to seize life with gusto—yet still be patient.

YOU SING (SONNET 52) / HOW TO PAINT THE PORTRAIT OF A BIRD **649**

 Mini Lesson **Grammar**

USING CONJUNCTIONS TO CONNECT IDEAS
Instruction Tell students that using conjunctions will help show the relationship between ideas more clearly and eliminate wordiness in their writing. Give students the following example.

You paint a cage. You leave the door open.

Using a conjunction creates one sentence with a compound verb.

You paint a cage and leave the door open.

Remind students that a comma and a conjunction will connect two complete sentences that have closely related ideas.

Exercises Have students combine the ideas in each pair of sentences and rewrite the sentence.

1. The voice soars. The voice drops. *(soars and drops)*

2. His father objected. Pablo Neruda was determined to write poetry. *(objected, but Pablo)*

3. Noise will startle the bird. Movement will also. *(Noise and movement will)*

4. You may wait hours. You may wait weeks for the bird to come. *(wait hours or weeks for)*

 Use **Grammar Transparencies and Copymasters,** p. 110.

 Use McDougal Littell's *Language Network,* Chapter 6, for more practice in using conjunctions.

Objectives
- read to be informed
- use study strategies to understand complex directions
- monitor and adjust strategies to improve comprehension
- find out how to make a flipbook

Connecting to the Literature
"Flip Out!" is a nonfiction article that complements the poem "How to Paint the Portrait of a Bird" because it outlines the process for arriving at an end result. Both the article and the poem rely on the reader's ability to follow directions exactly and in order. Because it is obvious that omitting steps or doing them in the wrong sequence would sabotage the success of the flipbook, students can more easily understand the importance of following the steps in the poem to arrive at the full literal and metaphorical meaning.

Flip Out!

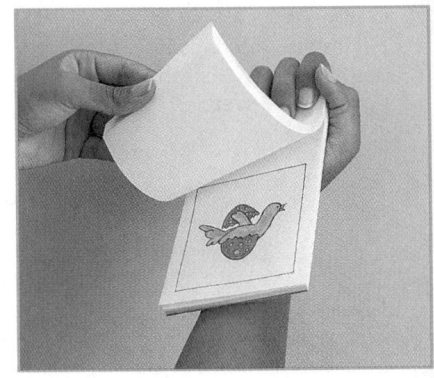

Without film or camera you can make simple cartoons jump to life. Even animators of big-budget, computer-rendered cartoons still test their pencil drawings in flipbooks before developing them for the big screen.

The pages of a flipbook show a series of drawings. Each page has one drawing that is changed in some small way from the previous drawing. By flipping the pages, you make the character or designs in the drawings appear to bounce, bend, change, or fly away. Below are instructions on how to make your own flipbook. Read the directions carefully before you begin.

Step 1. You'll need a small, blank, white stationery pad. A pad about 6" x 4" is a good size. The pad should contain about 100 sheets of paper.

Step 2. First, secure the top of the pad with small binder clips or masking tape. This will ensure that the pad does not fall apart as you use it and will keep your drawings in order.

2

Step 3. Next, open the pad to the last page. With a pencil, lightly mark a 3" x 3½" rectangle at the bottom of the page, leaving about a ¼" space from the edges. This is your work area, where you will create your drawings. Drawings too close to the bound edge of your pad will not be visible when you flip them.

Step 4. Decide what sort of movement you want to illustrate. It takes about 24 drawings to animate one second of movement, so keep it simple! Don't start by drawing a running horse or a baseball slugger. Instead, try something like a floating balloon, a hatching egg, or a sprouting seed. It is also fun to begin with a simple shape and "morph," or transform, it into a completely different shape.

Step 5. Using a pencil, place your first simple line drawing within the frame, or work area, on the last page. Make the drawing dark enough so that you will be able to see it through the second page of the pad. (You may not be able to see all the details, but its location should be clearly visible.)

Reading for Information

Some people have careers that not only help pay their bills but also give great pleasure, allowing them to make full use of their talents. Yet no matter how exciting a particular job may seem, there is usually some part of it that is difficult or time consuming. In order to make a difficult task easier, it pays to follow directions.

FOLLOWING COMPLEX DIRECTIONS The first and most important step in trying a new or complicated activity is to read through the directions.

Good directions are clear, complete, and in the correct order. Numbers or letters make the steps easy to follow. Look for words such as *first, second, next,* and *finally.* Read the steps in the given order.

Complex directions often include illustrations that make it easier for the reader to complete the activity. Make sure you examine any diagrams or illustrations, including their labels and captions.

Remember, if you don't understand the directions the first time, try rereading or asking for help. When you are sure you understand the directions, collect the materials and carry out the steps in order.

YOUR TURN *Use the questions and activities below to follow the directions.*

1 What is the first step in following any set of directions? Why do you think it is important?

2 What features of a good set of directions are used here?

3 The illustration shows that the drawings on each page are very similar and that you work from the back to the front. If this step were completed before Step 2, you would not be able to keep the pages in the correct order or keep them together to trace the drawings accurately.

4 Responses will vary. Step 10 might be paraphrased to read: Draw until every page is filled or you have finished the sketch. Adding a little more detail to each drawing will make the end result more eye-catching.

Activity
Students may suggest the following: that all the necessary supplies be listed under a separate heading at the beginning of the directions, instead of integrated with the steps; that the additional explanations of why something must be done a certain way be simplified; that more diagrams be included. For example, an illustration for Step 10 would be helpful to show how to make each drawing more complex.

Reading for Information *continued*

3 How does this illustration help make the directions easier to follow? What do you think might happen if you carried out this step before you did Step 2?

4 Remember to apply your study skills when you read new or complex material. If you still don't understand something after reading through all the directions, try paraphrasing. Choose one of the flipbook steps and paraphrase it.

When you have finished reading the directions, collect your materials and make your own flipbook. Note any steps that you had difficulty understanding or completing. How would you change the directions to make them easier to follow?

Inquiry & Research
Activity Link: "You Sing (Sonnet 52)," "How to Paint the Portrait of a Bird," p. 649. Write directions for an activity that was once new to you. You may choose to describe how to write a poem or how to carry out some other activity that you had difficulty learning or particularly enjoyed—a new sport, or your first part in a play, for example. Make sure your guidelines are clear, complete, and in the correct order.

 3

Step 6. Turn to the second page, the next-to-last page of your flipbook. Re-draw or trace your first drawing with some small change. For example, a hatching egg might begin to show a small crack.

Step 7. Repeat Step 6 until you have about 12 drawings.

Step 8. Check your drawings to see how they "move." Hold the top of the pad in one hand with the bottom of the pad against your palm and your fingers curled over the top. Hold the free edge of the pad with your other hand. Put your fingers on top and your thumb under the bottom page.

Step 9. Let pages flip down past your thumb so that you view them in the order in which you drew them, from bottom to top. Try it several times at different speeds. If your animation does not flow smoothly, adjust your drawings. If necessary, remove a page, but try not to do this often or the action will skip or "jump."

Step 10. Continue drawing on each remaining page until you have either drawn on every sheet in the pad or completed your cartoon. You may want to let your drawings get more complex, leading up to a big finish. **4**

 Inquiry & Research

The Inquiry & Research activity on this page links to the Inquiry & Research section of Choices & Challenges on page 649, following "You Sing" and "How to Paint the Portrait of a Bird."

Instruction Suggest that students choose an activity with which they are quite familiar or one that they have researched thoroughly. Have students brainstorm the steps necessary to complete the activity. Performing the activity may help to refresh their memories.

Practice Have students write each step on a separate index card. The order of the steps can then be easily changed or the step rewritten in more concise language. Each card should refer to the diagram or illustration that will accompany the step; students may prefer to attach the diagram to the card. Encourage students to check the accuracy of their directions and the clarity of their language by reading the instructions aloud to a partner.

PREPARING to *Read*

The Scribe

Short Story by KRISTIN HUNTER

"What are you trying to do here, sonny?"

Build Background

CONNECT TO **SOCIAL STUDIES**

One problem that exists in many communities is illiteracy. An illiterate person is someone who has not learned to read and write. In the United States, it is estimated that between 40 million and 44 million adults are functionally illiterate. This means they cannot read or write well enough to fill out a job application or address a letter so that it will reach its destination. Although many of these people have enrolled in school at some time in their lives, for various reasons they did not learn to read and write well.

Many communities have literacy volunteer groups. Volunteers help illiterate or low-literate adults learn to read and write. Some workplaces also offer classes to help employees improve their literacy skills.

Focus Your Reading

LITERARY ANALYSIS **CHARACTERIZATION** The way a writer creates and develops characters' personalities is known as **characterization.** A writer can make a character come alive through a description of the character's appearance, through the character's words and actions, and through the words and actions of other characters. Here, the author shows that a character is impatient by describing his actions:

> *He sighs, rolls his eyes to the ceiling, and bangs his fist on the form angrily.*

As you read, look for examples of characterization.

ACTIVE READING **MAKING INFERENCES ABOUT CHARACTERS**

An inference is a logical conclusion based on evidence. A good reader **makes inferences about characters** in a story. You can make an inference about a character's emotions or motivations, for example, or about the changes he or she might undergo.

READER'S NOTEBOOK As you read, notice how James responds to events. Why does he act as he does? Use your observations to write down inferences about James's character. Next to each inference, note evidence from the story that supports it.

OVERVIEW

Objectives
1. understand and appreciate a **short story (Literary Analysis)**
2. understand the role of **characterization** in fiction **(Literary Analysis)**
3. use the reading skill of **making inferences** to understand the characters in the story **(Active Reading)**

Summary
Thirteen-year-old James and his family live in an apartment above the Silver Dollar Check Cashing Service. James becomes angry when he learns how this shop makes money—by charging customers for services such as cashing checks and filling out forms. Many of the Silver Dollar's customers need these services because they cannot read or write. James decides to help these customers by reading and writing for them, just like the scribes in the Bible. When James sets up his free service in front of the Silver Dollar, people flock to his table, until a police officer arrives threatening to shut him down for not having a business license. Still determined to help, James reappears in front of the Silver Dollar the next day. This time, he tries to guide customers to a nearby bank that cashes checks for free. Only one person accepts, an elderly woman who proudly opens her first bank account. She inspires James to think about applying for a business license, so that he can continue to be a scribe.

Thematic Link
James discovers that he can have a voice in his community, first as a scribe and then as a friendly guide. He helps others and in turn is helped by them.
Note: Point out that slang, such as "Man!" and other dated expressions, can help readers identify the setting (mid-twentieth century). Encourage them to suggest modern equivalents.

Reading and Analyzing

Literary Analysis

CHARACTERIZATION

A Remind students that a story's narrator may be a character in the story. When the narrator is a character, readers learn his or her thoughts. This information can help them analyze characters and their traits, motivations, and conflicts. Ask students to describe what James thinks about the people who come into the Silver Dollar.

Possible Responses: They are in bad shape; they are treated badly.

Use **Unit Five Resource Book,** p. 22 for more practice. Use **Literary Analysis Transparencies,** p. 4, for additional support.

Active Reading   **MAKING INFERENCES ABOUT CHARACTERS**

B To help students make inferences and support them with text evidence and experience, ask students what evidence in the story suggests that the narrator does not like the way Mr. Silver treats customers.

Possible Responses: He takes their picture "like they're some kind of criminal"; he yells at them; he calls them by their first names.

C Why might the old man not want someone knowing that he can't fill in forms himself?

Possible Responses: He is embarrassed; he does not want to be yelled at.

Use **Unit Five Resource Book,** p. 21 for more practice. Use **Reading and Critical Thinking Transparencies,** p. 10, for additional support.

The Scribe
by Kristin Hunter

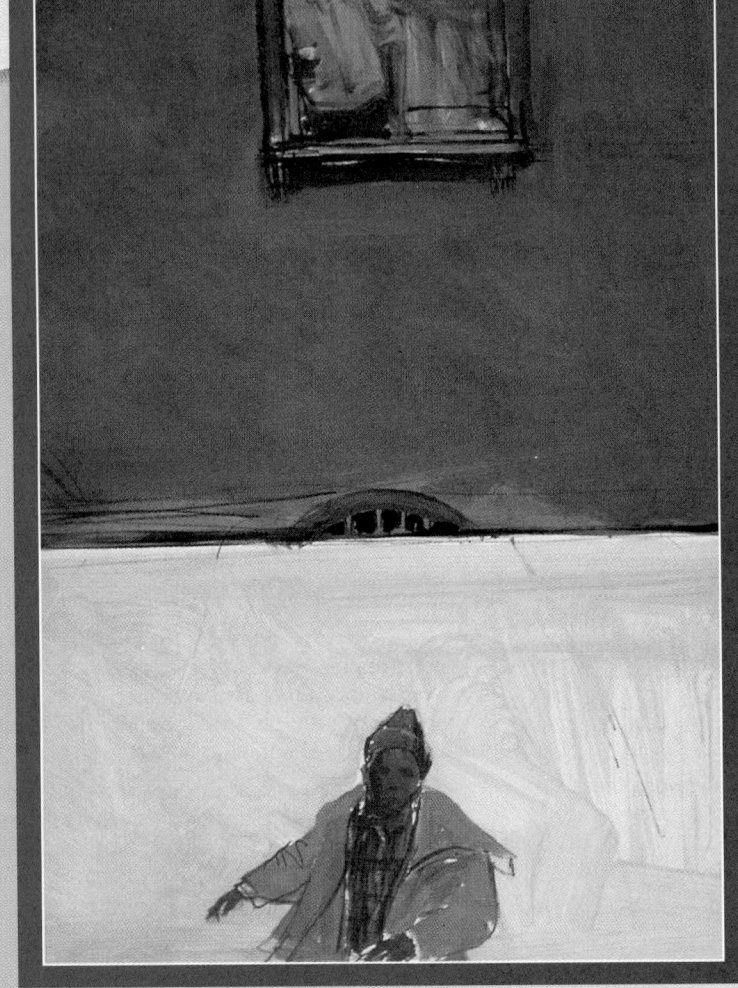

Copyright © Michael Paraskevas.

Teaching Options

Mini Lesson Vocabulary Strategy

IDIOMS

Instruction Tell students that idioms are expressions that cannot be understood from the meanings of the individual words. Point out the phrase *in bad shape,* and explain that the narrator is not talking about people's actual shape; he means that they have significant problems. Explain that many times students can draw on their own experiences to bring meaning to words in context, such as idioms.

Exercises Ask students to determine the meaning of the underlined words that follow:

1. After school, James liked to <u>hang around</u> the library until supper time. *(stay near)*
2. James sold a box of books and really <u>cleaned up</u> at that book sale. *(did a lot of business)*
3. If you don't leave here right away, I'm going to <u>run you off</u>. *(chase you away)*
4. At first James was angry, but then he <u>cooled off</u>. *(became calm)*
5. At first, people talked and laughed, but they <u>shut up</u> when the police came. *(became quiet)*

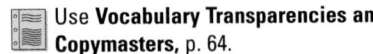 Use **Vocabulary Transparencies and Copymasters,** p. 64.

*W*e been living in the apartment over the Silver Dollar Check Cashing Service five years. But I never had any reason to go in there till two days ago, when Mom had to go to the Wash-a-Mat and asked me to get some change.

And man! Are those people who come in there in some bad shape.

Old man Silver and old man Dollar, who own the place, have signs tacked up everywhere:

NO LOUNGING, NO LOITERING[1]

THIS IS NOT A WAITING ROOM

and

MINIMUM CHECK CASHING FEE, 50¢

and

LETTERS ADDRESSED, 50¢

and

LETTERS READ, 75¢

and

LETTERS WRITTEN, ONE DOLLAR

And everybody who comes in there to cash a check gets their picture taken like they're some kind of criminal.

After I got my change, I stood around for a while digging the action. First comes an old lady with some kind of long form to fill out. The mean old man behind the counter points to the "One Dollar" sign. She nods. So he starts to fill it out for her.

"Name?"

"Muskogee Marie Lawson."

"SPELL it!" he hollers.

"M, m, u, s—well, I don't exactly know, sir."

"I'll put down 'Marie,' then. Age?"

"Sixty-three my last birthday."

"Date of birth?"

"March twenty-third"—a pause—"I think, 1900."

"Look, Marie," he says, which makes me mad, hearing him first-name a dignified old gray-haired lady like that, "if you'd been born in 1900, you'd be seventy-two. Either I put that down, or I put 1910."

"Whatever you think best, sir," she says timidly.

He sighs, rolls his eyes to the ceiling, and bangs his fist on the form angrily. Then he fills out the rest.

"One dollar," he says when he's finished. She pays like she's grateful to him for taking the trouble.

Next is a man with a cane, a veteran who has to let the government know he moved. He wants old man Silver to do this for him, but he doesn't want him to know he can't do it himself.

"My eyes are kind of bad, sir. Will you fill this thing out for me? Tell them I moved from 121 South 15th Street to 203 North Decatur Street."

Old man Silver doesn't blink an eye. Just fills out the form, and charges the crippled man a dollar.

And it goes on like that. People who can't read or write or count their change. People who don't know how to pay their gas bills, don't know how to fill out forms, don't know how to address envelopes. And old man Silver

---

1. **loitering** (loi′tər-ĭng): staying around without purpose.

THE SCRIBE **655**

Customizing Instruction

Less Proficient Readers
Explain the title to students by saying that a scribe is someone who writes or copies words. They will learn more about scribes as they read this story.
Set a Purpose Invite students to find out who the scribe is in this story and why that person is a scribe.

Students Acquiring English
Students may have difficulty with some of the idioms, regionalisms, and other examples of informal English:
1 Explain that *digging the action* means "enjoying what's going on."
2 When the narrator says "Old man Silver doesn't blink an eye," it means that he shows no emotion.

Use **Spanish Study Guide**, pp. 133–135 for additional support.

Gifted and Talented
Point out to students that the problem of illiteracy has still not been solved. Many state and local agencies offer courses for adults who cannot read at all, or who cannot read and write in English. Have students discuss how these agencies might get information about such courses to potential students, who are unable to read about them.

BLOCK SCHEDULING: MANAGING TIME

If your schedule requires that you cover the lesson objectives in a shorter time, use . . .
• Preparing to Read, p. 653
• Thinking Through the Literature, p. 661

If you want to take advantage of longer class time, use . . .
• TE Teaching Options: Vocabulary Strategy, p. 654; Viewing and Representing, p. 656; Multicultural Link, p. 657; Grammar, p. 658; Speaking and Listening, p. 659; Standardized Test Practice, p. 660
• Choices & Challenges and Author Activity, p. 662

> "There was a time in history when nobody could read or write except a special class of people."

and old man Dollar cleaning up on all of them. It's pitiful. It's disgusting. Makes me so mad I want to yell.

And I do, but mostly at Mom. "Mom, did you know there are hundreds of people in this city who can't read and write?"

Mom isn't upset. She's a wise woman. "Of course, James," she says. "A lot of the older people around here haven't had your advantages. They came from down South, and they had to quit school very young to go to work.

A "In the old days, nobody cared whether our people got an education. They were only interested in getting the crops in." She sighed. "Sometimes I think they *still* don't care. If we hadn't gotten you into that good school, you might not be able to read so well either. A lot of boys and girls your age can't, you know."

"But that's awful!" I say. "How do they expect us to make it in a big city? You can't even cross the streets if you can't read the 'Walk' and 'Don't Walk' signs."

"It's hard," Mom says, "but the important thing to remember is it's no disgrace. There was a time in history when nobody could read or write except a special class of people."

B And Mom takes down her Bible. She has three Bible study certificates and is always giving me lessons from Bible history. I don't

exactly go for all the stuff she believes in, but sometimes it *is* interesting.

"In ancient times," she says, "no one could read or write except a special class of people known as scribes. It was their job to write down the laws given by the rabbis and the judges.[2] No one else could do it.

"Jesus criticized the scribes," she goes on, "because they were so proud of themselves. But he needed them to write down his teachings."

"Man," I said when she finished, "that's something."

*M*y mind was working double time. I'm the best reader and writer in our class. Also it was summertime. I had nothing much to do except go to the park or hang around the library and read till my eyeballs were ready to fall out, and I was tired of doing both.

So the next morning, after my parents went to work, I took Mom's card table and a folding chair down to the sidewalk. I lettered a sign with a Magic Marker, and I was in business. My sign said:

C PUBLIC SCRIBE—ALL SERVICES FREE

1 I set my table up in front of the Silver Dollar and waited for business. Only one thing bothered me. If the people couldn't read, how would they know what I was there for?

D But five minutes had hardly passed when an old lady stopped and asked me to read her grandson's letter. She explained that she had just broken her glasses. I knew she was fibbing, but I kept quiet.

_____

2. **the rabbis and the judges:** the teachers and rulers of the ancient Hebrews.

Afternoon Glare—Main Street (1991), Carl J. Dalio. Collection of the artist. Copyright © 1991 Carl J. Dalio.

I read the grandson's letter. It said he was having a fine time in California but was a little short. He would send her some money as soon as he made another payday. I handed the letter back to her.

"Thank you, son," she said, and gave me a quarter.

I handed that back to her too.

The word got around. By noontime I had a whole crowd of customers around my table. I was kept busy writing letters, addressing envelopes, filling out forms, and explaining official-looking letters that scared people half to death.

I didn't blame them. The language in some of those letters—"Establish whether your disability is one-fourth, one-third, one-half, or total, and substantiate[3] in paragraph 3 (b) below"—would upset anybody. I mean, why can't the government write English like everybody else?

Most of my customers were old, but there were a few young ones too. Like the girl who had gotten a letter about her baby from the Health Service and didn't know what "immunization"[4] meant.

At noontime one old lady brought me some iced tea and a peach, and another gave me

---

3. **substantiate** (səb-stăn′shē-āt): to give evidence to prove a claim.

4. **immunization** (ĭm′yə-nĭ-zā′shən): medicine given to protect against disease.

Active Reading | MAKING INFERENCES ABOUT CHARACTERS |

A Ask students to infer how the narrator feels. Have them support their answer with text evidence and experience.

Possible Response: He's scared. His knees are knocking; people shiver when they are scared.

Reading Skills and Strategies:
CAUSE AND EFFECT

B Ask students why the narrator closes his business. Have them use the text's structure or progression of ideas such as cause and effect to recall information.

Possible Response: The policeman told him that he should charge money, but then he would be breaking the law unless he had a license.

Literary Analysis
| CHARACTERIZATION |

C Ask students what James's actions suggest about his character.

Possible Response: He is angry, but he realizes that he should not be taking his frustration out on the birds.

Active Reading | MAKING INFERENCES ABOUT CHARACTERS |

D Ask students to infer who the mother means by "our people."

Possible Response: She means African-American people; she says that some think that banks are only for white people.

---

some fried chicken wings. I was really having a good time when the shade of all the people standing around me suddenly vanished. The sun hit me like a ton of hot bricks.

Only one long shadow fell across my table. The shadow of a tall, heavy, blue-eyed cop. In our neighborhood, when they see a cop, people scatter. That was why the back of my neck was burning.

"What are you trying to do here, sonny?" the cop asks.

"Help people out," I tell him calmly, though my knees are knocking together under the table.

"Well, you know," he says, "Mr. Silver and Mr. Dollar have been in business a long time on this corner. They are very respected men in this neighborhood. Are you trying to run them out of business?"

"I'm not charging anybody," I pointed out.

"That," the cop says, "is exactly what they don't like. Mr. Silver says he is glad to have some help with the letter writing. Mr. Dollar says it's only a nuisance to them anyway and takes up too much time. But if you don't charge for your services, it's unfair competition."

Well, why not? I thought. After all, I could use a little profit.

"All right," I tell him. "I'll charge a quarter."

"Then it is my duty to warn you," the cop says, "that it's against the law to conduct a business without a license. The first time you accept a fee, I'll close you up and run you off this corner."

> He really had me there. What did I know about licenses? I'm only thirteen, after all.

He really had me there. What did I know about licenses? I'm only thirteen, after all. Suddenly I didn't feel like the big black businessman anymore. I felt like a little kid who wanted to holler for his mother. But she was at work, and so was Daddy.

"I'll leave," I said, and did, with all the cool I could muster. But inside I was burning up, and not from the sun.

One little old lady hollered "You big bully!" and shook her umbrella at the cop. But the rest of those people were so beaten down they didn't say anything. Just shuffled back on inside to give Mr. Silver and Mr. Dollar their hard-earned money like they always did.

I was so mad I didn't know what to do with myself that afternoon. I couldn't watch TV. It was all soap operas anyway, and they seemed dumber than ever. The library didn't appeal to me either. It's not air-conditioned, and the day was hot and muggy.

Finally I went to the park and threw stones at the swans in the lake. I was careful not to hit them, but they made good targets because they were so fat and white. Then after a while the sun got lower. I kind of cooled off and came to my senses. They were just big, dumb, beautiful birds and not my enemies. I threw them some crumbs from my sandwich and went home.

Mini Lesson   Grammar

CAPITALIZING PROPER NOUNS, PRONOUNS, AND ADJECTIVES

Instruction Explain that proper nouns are always capitalized. They name a particular person, place, thing, or idea. Proper nouns include names and titles of people (Mrs. Adams), the pronoun *I*, the names of religious writings (Bible), geographical areas (New York, the East), and historical periods (Depression).

Proper adjectives are formed from proper nouns, such as *Chinese* from *China*. Proper adjectives are also capitalized.

Application Have students find and list at least ten proper nouns or adjectives in the story. Have them compare their lists and be prepared to explain what category ("name of person," for example) each word or phrase fits into.

Use **Unit Five Resource Book**, p. 24.
Use **Grammar Transparencies and Copymasters**, p. 118.

| Language Network | Use McDougal Littell's *Language Network*, Chapter 8, for more practice in capitalization. |

"Daddy," I asked that night, "how come you and Mom never cash checks downstairs in the Silver Dollar?"

"Because," he said, "we have an account at the bank, where they cash our checks free."

"Well, why doesn't everybody do that?" I wanted to know.

"Because some people want all their money right away," he said. "The bank insists that you leave them a minimum balance."

"How much?" I asked him.

"Only five dollars."

"But that five dollars still belongs to you after you leave it there?"

"Sure," he says. "And if it's in a savings account, it earns interest."

"So why can't people see they lose money when they *pay* to have their checks cashed?"

"A lot of *our* people," Mom said, "are scared of banks, period. Some of them remember the Depression,[5] when all the banks closed and the people couldn't get their money out. And others think banks are only for white people. They think they'll be insulted, or maybe even arrested, if they go in there."

Wow. The more I learned, the more pitiful it was. "Are there any black people working at our bank?"

"There didn't use to be," Mom said, "but now they have Mr. Lovejoy and Mrs. Adams. You know Mrs. Adams, she's nice. She has a daughter your age."

"Hmmm," I said, and shut up before my folks started to wonder why I was asking all those questions.

The next morning, when the Silver Dollar opened, I was right there. I hung around near the door, pretending to read a copy of *Jet* magazine.

"Psst," I said to each person who came in. "I know where you can cash checks *free*."

It wasn't easy convincing them. A man blinked his red eyes at me like he didn't believe he had heard right. A carpenter with tools hanging all around his belt said he was on his lunch hour and didn't have time. And a big fat lady with two shopping bags pushed past me and almost knocked me down, she was in such a hurry to give Mr. Silver and Mr. Dollar her money.

But finally I had a little group who were interested. It wasn't much. Just three people. Two men—one young, one old—and the little old lady who'd asked me to read her the letter from California. Seemed the grandson had made his payday and sent her a money order.

"How far is this place?" asked the young man.

"Not far. Just six blocks," I told him.

"Aw shoot. I ain't walking all that way just to save fifty cents."

So then I only had two. I was careful not to tell them where we were going. When we finally got to the Establishment Trust National Bank, I said, "This is the place."

"I ain't goin' in there," said the old man. "No sir. Not me. You ain't gettin' me in *there*." And he walked away quickly, going back in the direction where we had come.

To tell the truth, the bank did look kind of scary. It was a big building with tall white marble pillars. A lot of Brink's armored trucks and Cadillacs were parked out front. Uniformed guards walked back and forth inside with guns. It might as well have a "Colored Keep Out" sign.

Whereas the Silver Dollar is small and dark and funky and dirty. It has trash on the floors and tape across the broken windows.

---

5. **Depression:** the Great Depression, a period of slow business activity and high unemployment from 1929 through the 1930s, before bank deposits were insured.

THE SCRIBE **659**

 Mini Lesson ## Speaking and Listening

DRAMATIC PRESENTATION
Prepare Tell students that they can present dramatic interpretations of stories to communicate what they have learned.

First, have students working in pairs or small groups select scenes to dramatize. Then have each student choose a character to portray in the scene. They should base their interpretations on details of characterization that they learned during reading or discussion. They can then use these details to develop gestures, expressions, and ways of speaking.

Present Have students take turns presenting their scenes to their classmates. Afterwards, you might encourage a group discussion, where students compare and contrast the presentations with their own interpretations of characters.

You may wish to combine this activity with the **Dramatic Scene** activity on page 662.

BLOCK SCHEDULING This activity is particularly well suited for longer class periods.

Use **Communications Transparencies and Copymasters**, p. 12, for additional support.

Active Reading | MAKING INFERENCES ABOUT CHARACTERS

Ⓐ Ask students to infer why Mrs. Adams and the narrator wink at each other.

Possible Responses: They know that glasses are not the problem; they know that the woman cannot read.

Literary Analysis

CHARACTERIZATION

Ⓑ Ask students what they learn about Mrs. Franklin when she winks at the narrator and then talks to him.

Possible Responses: She is bright and lively; she has the courage to try new things.

Literary Analysis

CHARACTERIZATION

Ⓒ To help students analyze characters and the changes they undergo, ask how the narrator changes by the end of the story. What is different about him?

Possible Responses: He is more determined to help; he knows what to do.

I looked at the little old lady. She smiled back bravely. "Well, we've come this far, son," she said. "Let's not turn back now."

So I took her inside. Fortunately Mrs. Adams's window was near the front.

"Hi, James," she said.

"I've brought you a customer," I told her.

Mrs. Adams took the old lady to a desk to fill out some forms. They were gone a long time, but finally they came back.

"Now, when you have more business with the bank, Mrs. Franklin, just bring it to me," Mrs. Adams said.

"I'll do that," the old lady said. She held out her shiny new bankbook. "Son, do me a favor and read that to me."

"Mrs. Minnie Franklin," I read aloud. "July 9, 1972. Thirty-seven dollars."

"That sounds real nice," Mrs. Franklin said. "I guess now I have a bankbook, I'll have to get me some glasses."

Ⓐ Mrs. Adams winked at me over the old lady's head, and I winked back.

> "Well, we've come this far, son," she said. "Let's not turn back now."

"Do you want me to walk you home?" I asked Mrs. Franklin.

"No thank you, son," she said. "I can cross streets by myself all right. I know red from green."

And then she winked at both of us, letting us know she knew what was happening.

"Son," she went on, "don't ever be afraid to try a thing just because you've never done it before. I took a bus up here from Alabama by myself forty-four years ago. I ain't thought once about going back. But I've stayed too long in one neighborhood since I've been in this city. Now I think I'll go out and take a look at *this* part of town."

Then she was gone. But she had really started me thinking. If an old lady like that wasn't afraid to go in a bank and open an account for the first time in her life, why should I be afraid to go up to City Hall and apply for a license?

Wonder how much they charge you to be a scribe? ❖

Teaching Options

✓ **Assessment** **Standardized Test Practice**

PREDICTING PROBABLE OUTCOMES In some standardized tests, students are asked to predict probable future actions and outcomes based on detailed story evidence and inferences. To provide students with some help in predicting probable outcomes, read aloud or write on the board the following:

Which of these is most likely to happen in the future?

A. The Silver Dollar Check Cashing Service will go out of business.

B. The police will return and arrest James.

C. James will apply for a business license.

D. Mrs. Franklin will learn how to read.

Lead students through the process of choosing the best answer. Help them recognize that no story evidence supports answers A, B, and D. However, the last two sentences of the story support answer C. Therefore, the best answer is C.

Connect to the Literature

1. **What Do You Think?**
Does anything about James remind you of yourself? Explain.

Comprehension Check
- What services do the owners of the Silver Dollar offer?
- Why don't James's parents cash checks at the Silver Dollar?
- Why does the police officer shut down James's business?

Think Critically

2. Why do you think James wants to help people?

3. What does James learn from Mrs. Franklin?

4. In your opinion, what effects do James's efforts to help others have on his community?

 THINK ABOUT
- the people he helps with reading and writing
- the people he tries to take to the bank
- the owners of the Silver Dollar

5. **ACTIVE READING** | **MAKING INFERENCES ABOUT CHARACTERS**
What does James's behavior toward his parents and toward the customers of the Silver Dollar tell you about him? Refer to the notes you made in your **READER'S NOTEBOOK**.

6. What do you think James will do after the story ends? Make a prediction based on James's character traits and the clues at the end of the story.

Extend Interpretations

7. **Different Perspectives** Imagine how this story would be different if it had been told by Mr. Silver. How might he view James's efforts?

8. **Connect to Life** Think about an unfair situation you have seen or experienced. How did you respond? What might you do differently now?

Literary Analysis

CHARACTERIZATION
The way a writer makes a character come alive is known as **characterization.** Writers develop characters in four basic ways:
- describing the character's physical appearance
- presenting the character's thoughts, speech, and actions
- presenting the thoughts, speech, and actions of other characters
- making direct comments on the character's nature

When James refers to "the mean old man behind the counter," the word *mean* conveys his thoughts about the other character. This helps to characterize the man.

Paired Activity Working with a partner, go through the story again and look for details that help create the character of James. Make a chart to organize these examples.

James's Thoughts, Speech, and Actions
—It's disgusting: Makes me so mad I want to yell.

Others' Thoughts, Speech, and Actions

James

What Adjectives Describe James?

THE SCRIBE **661**

Extend Interpretations

7. **Different Perspectives** Students' responses should show an appreciation of the fact that James is probably not viewed happily by Mr. Silver. He is likely to be seen as a nuisance or a threat.

8. **Connect to Life** Responses will vary. Some students will say that today they would behave just as they did then; others will say they would behave differently. Encourage students to give reasons for their responses.

Writing Options

1. **Comparison Essay** Suggest that **visual learners** create a two-column chart to organize their ideas. One column could be titled "James's Business" and the other column, "Silver Dollar."

2. **Day Narrative** Encourage **students acquiring English** to describe what problems they had before they learned any English. How did they know where to shop, for example, or how to take public transportation? This may help students imagine a typical day in the life of a non-reader.

3. **Letter to the Editor** Remind students that a letter to the editor should contain a statement of opinion and reasons to support it. **To make this activity easier,** have students work in pairs or small groups to brainstorm details of what they want to write about James.

Activities & Explorations

1. **Dramatic Scene** Encourage **kinesthetic learners** to participate in this activity. Remind students that gestures and expressions can be as important as words in a dramatization.

   Use **Communications Transparencies and Copymasters**, p. 12, for additional support.

2. **Bar Graph** Students will find literacy statistics in many almanacs. These may be included with other statistics about each country.

Inquiry & Research

Spreading the Word The first printed book appeared in China about 1000 A.D. Some centuries later—in 1438—Johann Gutenberg pioneered a movable-type printing press. Students may enjoy working cooperatively and presenting their research by means of a class time line.

Kristin Hunter

In one interview, Hunter said, "I have tried to show some of the positive values existing in the so-called ghetto—the closeness and warmth of family life, the willingness to extend help to strangers in trouble. . . . and the strong tradition of religious faith."

Choices & CHALLENGES

Writing Options

1. **Comparison Essay** In an essay, compare and contrast James's business and the Silver Dollar. How are the relationships between the business and the customer different?

   Writing Handbook
   See p. R35: Compare and Contrast.

2. **Day Narrative** What would a typical day be like for someone who cannot read or write? Write a narrative that describes the difficulties and challenges that person might face in one day.

   Writing Handbook
   See p. R33: Narrative Writing

3. **Letter to the Editor** Imagine you live in James's city. Write a letter to the local paper about James and his efforts to help people. Place your letter in your **Working Portfolio.**

Activities & Explorations

1. **Dramatic Scene** In a small group, dramatize an incident from the story. For example, you might recreate the scene between Mr. Silver and Muskogee Marie Lawson, or the scene between James and the policeman.
   ~ PERFORMING

2. **Bar Graph** Research literacy rates for several other countries and compare them to the United States. Make a two-tone bar graph to compare the literate population of each country to its total population. **~ MATH**

Inquiry & Research

Spreading the Word After the invention of the printing press by Johannes Gutenberg in 1450, literacy greatly increased in Europe. Use of the press gradually spread to other areas as well. Research the impact and development of the printing press, and present your findings to the class.

"I really cannot say when I didn't want to be a writer."

Kristin Hunter
born 1931

A Lifelong Writer At age 14, Hunter was a writer for the Philadelphia edition of the *Pittsburgh Courier.* On the job, she spent time in Philadelphia's South Street area, an African-American cultural center that inspired her fiction. Her writing includes novels, short stories, poems, and magazine articles for adults, young adults, and children. She has received numerous awards, including the Children's Prize of the Council on Interracial Books for Children, the Lewis Carroll Shelf Award for *Soul Brothers*

and *Sister Lou,* and the *Chicago Tribune* Book World Prize for *Guests in the Promised Land.*

A Message of Hope Hunter says "the bulk of my work has dealt—imaginatively, I hope—with relations between the white and black races in America." Her stories about urban life suggest that individuals can change their lives and improve their circumstances, however difficult, by believing in themselves and their ability to make a difference.

AUTHOR ACTIVITY
New Views Hunter had a middle-class upbringing, but came to know people who grew up with fewer advantages. Read more about Hunter and her childhood. Then create a Venn diagram comparing her upbringing with details about the character of James.

Teaching Options

Author Activity

New Views Encourage students to think about the writer's home, her upbringing, and her occupation when they compare details with those in the story. Even if students can find no additional details about the author, the ones on the pupil page will allow them to recognize that the character is in some ways like the writer.

Use **Reading and Critical Thinking Transparencies**, p. 35, for additional support.

The Story Behind the Words

The English language is like a collage made of words from different languages and periods in history.

Most English words can be traced to Greek, Latin, Old English, or another historical language.

> And in this world there was a peace and harmony that she knew no matter how far she traveled, she would never find again. She understood now why her father had brought her here.
>
> —Keith Leckie, *Words on a Page*

Latin *pax,* peace

Old English *faeder,* from the **Latin** *pater,* father.

Greek *harmos,* joint, something shared, a place where things come together.

Strategies for Building Vocabulary

When you study a word's history and origin, it's like going behind the scenes at a play. You find out when, where, and sometimes how it came to be. This information can help you see how the spelling and meaning of words are related. Use the following strategies to discover more about word origins.

❶ **Read Dictionary Entries** A complete dictionary includes each word's history and origin. Notice the highlighted part of this entry for *drama.*

> **dra•ma** (drä′mə) *n.* **1.** A work that is meant to be performed by actors. **2.** Theatrical works of a certain type or period in history. [Late Latin *drama, dramat-,* from Greek *dran,* to do or perform.]

This entry shows that the earliest form of the word *drama* was the Greek word *dran.* In many dictionaries, an appendix at the back of the book lists common word parts and their origins.

❷ **Discover How Words Begin** Many words have interesting histories. Some come from the names of people and places. A German engineer named Rudolf Diesel invented the type of engine now called a *diesel* engine.

Other words, like *mailbox, bookkeeping,* and *eggshell,* were created by joining two existing words.

❸ **Look for Word Families** Words with the same history often have meanings that are connected. For example, the words *remember, memory,* and *memorial* all grew from the Latin word *memor,* which means "mindful." Read the chart below to see other words related to each other by origin.

Latin Root:	*senus,* to sense or feel	**Greek Root:**	*aster,* star
English:	**sensory** perceived through one of the senses	**English:**	**asteroid** a small object in outer space
	sensitive responds to senses or feelings		**asterisk** a star-shaped punctuation mark
	sensation a perception or feeling		**astronomy** the study of outer space

EXERCISE Use a dictionary to find information about the history or origin of each of the following words. Paraphrase any information about roots and their meanings.

Example:

  cry: from Latin *quiritare,* to cry out

1. happy
2. sandwich
3. boardwalk
4. dairy
5. potato
6. captain
7. grammar
8. battle
9. klutz
10. tofu

BUILDING VOCABULARY **663**

Objectives

- research and use word origins as an aid to understanding meanings
- research word origins as an aid to spelling
- apply meanings of word roots and affixes to determine the meanings of unfamiliar words
- use a personal word list to record and remember new words

EXERCISE

1. from Middle English *hap,* "luck"
2. food named after John Montagu, the Fourth Earl of Sandwich
3. a walk made of planks or boards: combines the words *board* and *walk*
4. from Middle English *daie,* "dairymaid," from Old English *dæge,* "bread kneader"
5. from Spanish *patata* and Taino *batata,* "sweet potato"
6. from Latin *caput,* "head"
7. from Greek *gramma,* "letter"
8. from Latin *battuere,* "to beat"
9. from Yiddish *klotz,* from Middle High German *kloz,* "block, lump"
10. from Japanese *tofu,* from Chinese *doufu,* "curdled bean"

Use **Unit Five Resource Book,** p. 27, for more practice. Use **Vocabulary Transparencies and Copymasters,** p. 9, for additional support.

OVERVIEW

Objectives
- appreciate the works of a contemporary author
- interpret the possible influences of personal events in Lowry's life on her writing
- gain information on the genres of short story, speech, and memoir
- look at the lively language techniques used by Lowry

The Author Study offers a special opportunity for students to focus on the work of a popular contemporary author. Students will be exposed to information about Lowry's life, which will give them insight into the person behind the stories. They will explore some of the lively language techniques used by Lowry and apply these to their own writing.

Author Study Lois Lowry

CONTENTS

Through a Child's Eyes

"That is how I write—I go back to the child I was and see things through those eyes."

born 1937

A YOUNG TRAVELER, A YOUNG READER

Lois Lowry was born Cena Hammersberg on March 20, 1937, in Honolulu, Hawaii. She was named for her grandmother, who was not pleased by the gesture and insisted that her granddaughter be given a more common name. The baby was soon renamed Lois. Because Lowry's father was an army dentist, the family moved often, rarely settling in one place for more than a few years. Reading and imagination were always an important part of Lowry's life. "I was a solitary child who lived in the world of books and my own imagination," she says. By the time Lowry was three, she was able to read—an ability that set her apart from the rest of her nursery school class.

Her LIFE and TIMES

1937	1948	1956	1962
Born on March 20 in Honolulu, Hawaii	Moves to Japan	Leaves Brown University to marry Donald Lowry	Sister Helen's death from cancer

| **1940** | | **1950** | | **1960** |

1941	1945–1946	1950	
United States enters World War II.	Nazi leaders are tried and sentenced at Nuremberg trials.	Korean War begins.	Sculpture from Korean War Memorial in Washington, D.C.

WAR AND SEPARATION In December 1941, the Japanese bombed Pearl Harbor in Hawaii. When the attack ended, over 2,300 Americans had been killed and the United States was at war. More than 50 years later, Lowry still remembered "the fear in Mother's voice when she hear[d] the news on the radio." Lowry's father left home to fight in the war, and the rest of the family moved to Pennsylvania. In 1948 they rejoined Lowry's father, who was stationed in Japan. Lowry was overjoyed to be with her father again and viewed life in Japan as a grand adventure. Already filled with a writer's curiosity, she often sneaked out of the American compound to explore the neighborhoods of Tokyo. There she saw the tragedy and destruction of war. Entire families lived in packing crates because their houses had been destroyed by bombs. Two years later, when war broke out in nearby Korea, Lowry returned to the states with her mother, sister Helen, and brother Jon while her father remained in Japan.

Did You Know?

- For years Lowry made a living as a portrait photographer.
- She appeared on *Jeopardy!*
- She took the cover photographs on the first editions of *Number the Stars* and *The Giver*.
- She has traveled to Fiji, Antarctica, and the Serengeti.
- She didn't care if her children cleaned their rooms or ate their vegetables.
- She grows yellow helenium flowers in memory of her sister, Helen.

1972 Receives college degree after four years of part-time study

1977 Publishes *A Summer to Die*

1990 Wins Newbery Medal for *Number the Stars*

1994 Wins Newbery Medal for *The Giver*

| 1970 | 1980 | 1990 | 2000 |

1975 Vietnam War ends.

1976 Jimmy Carter is elected president.

1997 Madeleine Albright is sworn in as U.S. secretary of state.

1999 Computer experts prepare for the year 2000 ("Y2K").

LOIS LOWRY **665**

Books
Lowry describes herself as an introvert, a kid who hung out with books because she wasn't really comfortable with people. She wasn't an athlete, so when most kids were out on a ball field, she was curled up with a good book. It is in these books that she learned about language and the way to put together a story. Lowry says that reading brilliant paragraphs makes her want to write brilliant paragraphs. She is still an avid reader today and has an extensive personal library, which she has organized in her own eclectic way.

A Transient Life
After Lowry's birth in Hawaii, Lois' family moved to New York. When her father was called to World War II, her mother and siblings moved to her mother's hometown in Pennsylvania. After the war, the family moved to Japan to be with her father. Several years later, Lois, her brother, sister, and mother moved back to the United States, while her father stayed in Japan. Lowry attended high school in New York City. She attended college for two years at Brown University in Rhode Island, where she met and married her husband, Donald Lowry. He was also a military man, and they lived in California, Connecticut, Florida, South Carolina, Massachusetts, and Maine, where she raised her four children. Today she lives in Cambridge, Massachusetts.

Family
Lois's father was a dentist in the military, and her mother was a homemaker. Lois's older sister Helen was much like their mother, gentle and eager to please. Her younger brother, Jon, was always playing with electric trains and construction sets, and when he was older, tinkering with cars with their father.

Author Study Lois Lowry

A Writer's Beginnings

D Lowry didn't begin writing professionally until she was in her mid-thirties, even though as a child she had scribbled endless stories and poems in notebooks. She says her books have one general theme: the importance of human connections. Most of her stories come about because of people she knows and stories she's heard. She believes that all of her experiences have an influence on her writing and that eventually they end up in one of her books.

Emotional Healing

E When confronted with tough situations, Lowry finds comfort and healing in writing. Writing has become so much a part of her that it is what she turns to constantly. Some of her books have resulted from tragedy, as did *A Summer to Die,* a fictionalized account of her sister's death from cancer. One of her daughters has become disabled as a result of a disease of the central nervous system, and Lowry says since that time her books have reflected a new and passionate awareness of the importance of human connections that transcend physical differences. Her father, who, prior to his death had poor health and a failing memory, prompted images for *The Giver,* as she thought about how without memory there is no pain. And when her son, an Air Force pilot, was killed during a take-off, she wrote a sort of newsletter so that everyone would know the treasure she had lost.

Anastasia Krupnik

F Lowry created the character of Anastasia Krupnik in 1978, when Jimmy Carter was president of the United States. Lowry gives credit for the character of Anastasia Krupnik to Amy Carter, the president's daughter. Amy Carter's physical appearance and her behavior in public while her father was in office prompted Lowry to model the character of Anastasia after her.

FAMILY YEARS The family reunited in New York City just as Lowry was beginning the tenth grade. They lived on an army base on an island in the city's harbor, and Lowry traveled to school by ferry. Reading and writing were her favorite pursuits. Lowry's teachers encouraged her literary talent, and her classmates decorated her yearbook picture with the caption "Future Novelist." Brown University in Rhode Island granted her a scholarship to its creative writing program. After her second year there, however, she left college to marry Donald Lowry, a naval officer. For the next 15 years, Lowry put aside her dreams of writing while she raised their four children. The family moved often before settling in Maine. Lowry later said, "My children grew up in Maine. So did I."

FINALLY A WRITER "Now, when I write," says Lowry, "I draw a great deal from my own past." In the early 1970s, she finished her college degree and began writing stories based on her childhood. In 1977 she published her first novel, *A Summer to Die*, which was inspired by her sister Helen's death from cancer 15 years earlier. Lowry says the novel brought together "details and fragments that accompanied a time of saying good-bye in the lives of two sisters." In that same year, her marriage ended and she started a new life on her own. Since then she has written about two dozen novels, including two Newbery Medal winners, *Number the Stars* and *The Giver*, and the popular Anastasia Krupnik series. Lowry has earned the devotion of a generation of young readers. She lives and writes in Cambridge, Massachusetts, where she shares her home with a shaggy Tibetan terrier named Bandit.

666

When Lois Lowry meets with her readers, she often is asked about her reading and writing habits. Here, she responds to some of these questions.

TALKING WITH LOIS LOWRY

Q: What's your favorite place to sit and read?

A: Depends whether it is summer or winter. In summer I read in a hammock on the screened porch of my house in the country. I watch the birds come and go as I read. In winter I mostly read in the city house. My favorite spot is a pale yellow couch by the fireplace. That's my dog's favorite spot, too, so sometimes I have to fight him for it. I'm bigger than he is, so I always win.

Q: You have written about the impact that *The Yearling* had on you when you were young. What other stories or writers have influenced you?

A: I loved the book *A Tree Grows in Brooklyn*. I encountered it first when I was 11 years old, living in Pennsylvania. I had lived in Brooklyn as a small child, so the title attracted me to the book—then when I read it, I discovered a whole world unlike mine: a crowded, noisy, exuberant world of immigrant life. I moved right into it and lived there for the length of the book. A good book lets you do that.

Q: You used to work as a photographer. Do you still like to make photographs? What kinds of things are interesting to photograph?

A: I love photographing people, especially children. Mostly I photograph my grandchildren now—not the one who's almost 16, though. He's tired of having Grandma torment him with a camera. The little ones still don't mind.

Q: Are you glad you became a writer? Why?

A: I feel very fortunate because I make my living doing what I love most. A lot of people work at jobs that they dislike, or that bore them. Not me. Even before I was a Writer, I was a writer. It has always been a part of my life: my favorite part.

Q: What do you like most about yourself? Why?

A: I suppose what I like best is that I have always had an eager curiosity. That means that I am never bored. I don't understand boredom, really. There is so much to learn, to observe, to think about. What a waste of time to shrug and turn away from it all. I don't like people who do that. I want to poke them.

 More Online: Author Link
www.mcdougallittell.com

 NetActivities: Author Exploration

Other Favorites

Besides reading, there are other activities that occupy Lois Lowry's time. She enjoys gardening in the spring and summer and knitting in the winter. She has remained faithful to photography over the years, taking the pictures on the covers of *Number the Stars* and *The Giver*. She loves watching movies, eating Mexican food, and cooking. In fact, she has an extensive library of cookbooks. She also likes to play bridge, travel, and spend time with her children, grandchildren, and her dog Bandit.

Writing Today

Most mornings you can find Lowry at her computer and working by eight o'clock. She works all morning, sometimes stopping for a short lunch break. She works into the afternoon as well, usually stopping for the day in mid-afternoon. She has written novels, short stories, and essays. Mostly she writes for young people, but she also writes for herself and for members of her family. She varies the point-of-view of her stories, but says it's not a conscious decision. It just seems that some books need to be told from an omniscient, third-person viewpoint and others need the first person voice in all its uniqueness. She also says she doesn't set out to place a moral in each story, but that a message usually works its way into each story. Her goal when she sits down to write a story, though, is just to tell her readers a good story.

LOIS LOWRY **667**

OVERVIEW

Objectives

1. understand and appreciate a **short story** (Literary Analysis)
2. understand and appreciate a **symbol** (Literary Analysis)
3. use the reading skill of **recognizing cause and effect** (Active Reading)

Summary

In this short story, the narrator tells of a hunting trip she took with her father. She was nine years old, and her father had recently returned from the war. Before the trip, her father had bought her a large, plaid, man's hunting shirt, which she now wears proudly. When her father stops for breakfast, cherry pie is ordered for both, as it is her favorite food. When they get to the hunting ground, they traipse through the woods, talking about what in life scares them, until her father finds the spot. The narrator's job is to blow the crow call to get the crows awake and flying so her father can shoot. But the joy and fun that blowing the crow call brings the young girl also brings joy to her father, and they conclude their hunting trip without a single shot being fired.

Thematic Link

Learning about yourself can often be sparked by unusual situations. The narrator and her father share such a situation in this story. In living through it, the narrator learns about herself and maybe a little about who she will become.

5-Minute Warm-Up

Daily Language SkillBuilder

Have students **proofread** the display sentences on page 609j and write them correctly. The sentences also appear on Transparency 21 of **Grammar Transparencies and Copymasters.**

"I sat shyly in the front seat of the car next to the stranger who was my father, . . ."

Crow Call

Short Story by LOIS LOWRY

Connect to Your Life

Life Lessons Think about a time in your life when you shared an experience with someone special and, in the process, learned something about the person. Share your memory with a partner.

Build Background

CONNECT TO BIOLOGY In this story, the narrator and her father set off to hunt crows. Crows are omnivorous, meaning that they will eat just about anything. They eat berries, grains, insects, the eggs of other birds, and even the meat of dead animals. Farmers consider them pests because they like to eat corn, wheat, and other crops in the fields. For this reason, farmers often try to get rid of them by using scarecrows, or, if this doesn't work, by shooting them.

Common crows range from southern Canada to the southern United States. They are abundant, adaptable, and considered to be very intelligent. Some crows in captivity have been trained to "speak" and count. Crows can live up to 20 years in captivity.

WORDS TO KNOW
Vocabulary Preview

arrogantly	mannequin	ruddy
condescending	marred	subside
decoy	poised	
disgruntled	practical	

Focus Your Reading

LITERARY ANALYSIS **SYMBOL** A **symbol** is a person, a place, or an object that stands for something else. In literature, objects and images may be used to symbolize things that cannot be seen, such as ideas or feelings. In "Crow Call," a reader might see the narrator's hunting shirt as representing her desire for closeness with her father. As you read, look for other symbols.

ACTIVE READING **RECOGNIZING CAUSE AND EFFECT** A story usually is based on a chain of events, with one event causing another. Events in this chain are said to be related as **cause and effect.** Recognizing causes and their effects can help you understand the meaning of a story as it unfolds. It can also help you make predictions.

READER'S NOTEBOOK Use a chart like the one below to help recognize causes and their effects within the story. As you read, make a chart for each cause and effect that you find.

Cause
Narrator pauses by shop window.

↓

Effect
Father buys hunting shirt.

LESSON RESOURCES

UNIT FIVE RESOURCE BOOK, pp. 28–34

ASSESSMENT
Formal Assessment, pp. 109–110
Teacher's Guide to Assessment and Portfolio Use
Test Generator

SKILLS TRANSPARENCIES AND COPYMASTERS
Reading and Critical Thinking
• Cause and Effect, TR 5 (for Thinking Through the Literature, p. 674)

Grammar
• Subject Position in Interrogative and Exclamatory Sentences, CM 56 (for Mini Lesson, p. 675)
Vocabulary
• Analogies, CM 65 (for Mini Lesson, p. 669)

INTEGRATED TECHNOLOGY
Audio Library
More Online: Author Link

Visit our website:
www.mcdougallittell.com

CROW CALL

by Lois Lowry

Crow, Lucy White. Dye, resin, dishcloth on wood, 23″ × 23″ × 2″. Courtesy of the Bernard Toale Gallery.

 It was morning, early, barely light, cold for November. I was nine and the war was over. At home, in the bed next to mine, my older sister still slept, adolescent, her blond hair streaming over the edge of the sheet. I sat shyly in the front seat of the car next to the stranger who was my father, my blue-jeaned legs pulled up under the too-large wool shirt I was wearing, making a bosom of my knees.

"Daddy," I said, the title coming uncertainly, "I've never gone hunting before. What if I don't know what to do?"

"Well," he said, "I've been thinking about that, and I've decided to put you in charge of the crow call. Have you ever operated a crow call?"

I shook my head. "No."

"It's an art," he said. "No doubt about that. But I'm pretty sure you can handle it. Some people will blow and blow on a crow call and not a single crow will even wake up or bother to listen, much less answer. But I really think you can do it. Of course," he added, chuckling, "having that shirt will help."

CROW CALL   **669**

CROW CALL   **669**

 Mini Lesson ## Preteaching Vocabulary

A Ask students what two events occurred in this section. Which one was the cause, and which was the effect?

Possible Response: The narrator's pigtails being tucked in her shirt caused the waitress to think she was a boy.

Set a Purpose Remind students to look for cause-and-effect relationships as they read. They should fill in the chart in their Reader's Notebook each time they find a cause-and-effect relationship.

Use **Unit Five Resource Book,** p. 29 for more practice. Use **Reading and Critical Thinking Transparencies,** p. 5, for additional support.

Literary Analysis   SYMBOL

B Remind students that sometimes objects or events in stories can stand for something else. Ordering cherry pie for breakfast is certainly unusual. Ask students to think about what the cherry pie for breakfast may symbolize.

Possible Response: Cherry pie for breakfast might symbolize the special occasion of the narrator and her father getting to know each other again.

Use **Unit Five Resource Book,** p. 30 for more practice.

Reading Skills and Strategies: PREDICT

C Ask students to think about what might happen as the narrator and her father finally reach the hills for the hunt.

Possible Responses: They will be successful and shoot a crow; there will be an accident with her father's gun, and someone will get hurt; they will not hunt at all, but talk and rebuild their relationship.

I glanced over quickly to see if he was laughing at me, but his smile was inclusive; I chuckled too, hugging my shirt around me.

My father had bought the shirt for me. In town to buy groceries, he had noticed my hesitating in front of Kronenberg's window. The plaid hunting shirts had been in the store window for a month—the popular red-and-black and green-and-black ones toward the front, clothing <u>ruddy</u> <u>mannequins</u> holding guns and duck <u>decoys</u>; but my shirt, the rainbow plaid, hung separately on a wooden hanger toward the back of the display. I had lingered in front of Kronenberg's window every chance I had since the hunting shirts had appeared.

My sister had rolled her eyes in disdain. "Daddy," she pointed out to him as we entered Kronenberg's, "that's a *man's* shirt."

The salesman had smiled and said dubiously, "I don't quite think . . ."

"You know," my father had said to me as the salesman wrapped the shirt, "buying this shirt is probably a very <u>practical</u> thing to do. You will never *ever* outgrow this shirt."

Now, as I got out of the car in front of the diner where we were going to have breakfast, the shirt unfolded itself downward until the bottom of it reached my knees; from the bulky thickness of rolled-back cuffs my hands were exposed. I felt totally surrounded by shirt.

My father ordered coffee for himself. The waitress, middle-aged and dawn-sleepy, asked, "What about your boy? What does he want?"

My father winked at me, and I hoped that my pigtails would stay hidden inside the plaid wool collar. Holding my head very still, I looked at the menu. At home my usual breakfast was cereal with honey and milk.

> "What's your favorite thing to eat in the whole world?" asked my father...

My mother kept honey in a covered silver pitcher. The diner's menu, grease-spotted and <u>marred</u> with penciled notations and paper-clipped addenda,[1] seemed not to include honey.

"What's your favorite thing to eat in the whole world?" asked my father.

I smiled at him. If he hadn't been away for so long, he would have known. It was a family joke in a family that hadn't included him. "Cherry pie," I admitted.

My father handed back both menus to the waitress. "Three pieces of cherry pie," he told her.

"Three?" She looked at him sleepily, not writing the order down. "You mean two?"

"No," he said, "I mean three. One for me, with black coffee, and two for my hunting companion, with a large glass of milk."

She shrugged.

We ate quickly, watching the sun rise now across the Pennsylvania farm lands. Back in the car, I flipped my pigtails out from under my shirt collar and giggled.

"Hey, boy," my father said to me in an imitation of the groggy waitress's voice, "you sure you can eat all that cherry pie, boy?"

---

1. **addenda** (ə-dĕn′də): things that have been added, especially a supplement to a book.

WORDS TO KNOW	**ruddy** (rŭd′ē) *adj.* reddish; rosy **mannequin** (măn′ĭ-kĭn) *n.* a model of the human body, used for displaying clothes **decoy** (dē′-koi′) *n.* an artificial bird used to attract live birds within shooting range **practical** (prăk′tĭ-kəl) *adj.* useful **marred** (mär′d) *adj.* damaged; marked **mar** *v.*

670

Teaching Options

BLOCK SCHEDULING: MANAGING TIME

If your schedule requires that you cover the lesson objectives in a shorter time, use . . .
- Preparing to Read, p. 668
- Thinking Through the Literature, p. 674
- Grammar in Context, p. 675
- Vocabulary in Action, p. 675

If you want to take advantage of longer class time, use . . .
- TE Teaching Options: Preteaching Vocabulary, p. 669; Viewing and Representing, p. 671; Spelling, p. 672; Standardized Test Practice, p. 673; Grammar, p. 675

Cherry Pie (1962), Roy Lichtenstein, Oil on canvas.
20" × 24". Collection of Sydney and Frances Lewis/
Virginia Museum of Fine Art.

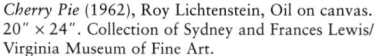

…"Cherry pie," I admitted.

Customizing Instruction

Less Proficient Readers

1 Help students to see that this section of the story is a flashback to another time in the narrator's life. She is telling the story to help us understand the importance of the hunting shirt. Students may be confused as to what is happening now, and what has already happened in the past.

Set a Purpose Ask students to read on to find out what happens on the hunting trip.

Multiple Learning Styles
Linguistic Learners

2 Have students listen to the beautiful, descriptive language in this section as you read it aloud. Ask them to identify which words in the description are most effective in helping them create their mental images.

Possible Responses: frozen, crunched, sharp, supremely clear, etched, brittle stillness, smooth, stamped, scamper, uneasy feeling

"Just you watch me, lady," I answered in a deep, I thought boyish, voice, pulling my face into stern, serious lines. We laughed again, driving out into the graygreen hills of the early morning.

Grass, frozen after its summer softness, crunched under our feet; the air was sharp and supremely clear, free from the floating pollens of summer, and our words seemed etched and breakable on the brittle stillness. I felt the smooth wood of the crow call in my pocket, moving my fingers against it for warmth, memorizing its ridges and shape. I stamped my feet hard against the ground now and then as my father did. I wanted to scamper ahead of him like a puppy, kicking the dead leaves and

reaching the unknown places first, but there was an uneasy feeling along the edge of my back at the thought of walking in front of someone carrying a gun. Carefully I stayed by his side.

It was quieter than summer. There were no animal sounds, no bird-waking noises; even the occasional leaf that fell within our vision did so in silence, spiraling slowly down to blend in brownly with the others. But most leaves were already gone from the trees; those that remained seemed caught there by accident, waiting for the wind that would free them. Our breath was steam.

"Daddy," I asked shyly, "were you scared in the war?"

CROW CALL   **671**

Viewing and Representing

Cherry Pie
by Roy Lichtenstein

ART APPRECIATION Roy Lichtenstein (1923–1997) was a teacher and artist who did much of his work in commercial art and design. He is considered a part of the Pop Art movement; his best known works from the 1960s are based on comic strip and advertising images.

Instruction Ask students to think about the senses to which this painting appeals, and to jot them down. Ask them to use descriptive words that help them to experience each sense.

Possible Responses: Smell: warm, cherry, sweet, baking crust, yummy; taste: sweet, juicy, tart, hot, delicious; sight: fresh, steaming, red, ripe berries, flaky crust.

Application Ask students to recall these descriptions as they reread the restaurant scene on page 670. Have students write a short paragraph describing the same scene, using their descriptions and sense memories. Have them share their paragraphs with a partner.

A Authors often use dialogue to move the plot forward and to reveal the personalities of the characters. Ask students to think about what this section of dialogue reveals about the narrator and her father.

Possible Responses: The narrator is afraid of her father's gun, she doesn't like death and killing, and she doesn't want to hunt the crows; her father knows what fear is and he didn't like the thought of killing anyone in the war; they both have a sense of humor and are learning to enjoy each other's company again.

Active Reading

> RECOGNIZING
> CAUSE AND EFFECT

B Remind students to fill in their cause-and-effect charts. In this section, the crows begin to stir, flutter, and call. Ask students to identify the cause of this action.

Possible Response: The narrator blew on the crow call and it caused the crows to wake up.

Reading Skills and Strategies: CONNECT

C Ask students to recall a meaningful experience they shared with a parent or other adult. Have them share their experiences with each other and talk about how the narrator's hunting trip might impact the relationship she has with her father.

Possible Response: Because the narrator had such a good time with her father, she will probably be able to share other happy times with him, and their relationship will get stronger.

"Listen, Daddy!
Do you hear them?

He looked ahead, up the hill, and rubbed the stock of his gun thoughtfully with one hand and said after a moment, "Yes. I was scared."

"Of what?"

"Lots of things. Of being alone. Of being hurt. Of hurting someone else."

"Are you still?"

He glanced down. "I don't think so. Those kind of scares go away."

"I'm scared sometimes," I confided.

He nodded, unsurprised. "I know," he said. "Are you scared now?"

I started to say no, and then answered, "Maybe of your gun, a little."

I looked quickly at his gun, his polished, waxed prize, and then at him. He nodded, not saying anything. We walked on.

"Daddy?"

"Mmmmmm?" He was watching the sky, the trees.

"I wish the crows didn't eat the crops."

"They don't know any better," he said. "Even people do bad things without meaning to."

"Yes, but . . ." I paused and then told him what I'd been thinking. "They might have babies to take care of. Baby crows."

"Not now, not this time of year," he said. "By now their babies are grown. It's a strange thing, but by now they don't even know who their babies are." He put his free arm over my shoulders for a moment.

"And their babies grow up and eat the crops too," I said, and sighed, knowing it to be true and unchangeable.

"It's too bad," he acknowledged. We began to climb the hill.

"Can you call anything else, Daddy? Or just crows?"

"Sure," he said. "Listen. *Moooooooo.* That's a cow call."

"Guess the cows didn't hear it," I teased him when we encountered silence.

"Well, of course, sometimes they choose not to answer. I can do tigers too. *Rrrrrrrrrrr.*"

"Ha. So can I. And bears. Better watch out, now. Bears might come out of the woods on this one. *Grrrrrrrrr.*"

He looked at me <u>arrogantly</u>. "You think you're so smart, doing bears. Listen to this. Giraffe call." He stood with his neck stretched out, soundless.

I tried not to laugh, wanting to do rabbits next, but couldn't keep from it. He looked so funny, with his neck pulled away from his shirt collar and a <u>condescending</u>, <u>poised</u>, giraffe look on his face. I giggled at him and we kept walking to the top of the hill.

From where we stood we could see almost back to town. We could look down on our car and follow the ribbon of road through the farm lands until it was lost in trees. Dark roofs of houses lay scattered, separated by pastures.

"Okay," said my father, "you can do the crow call now. This is a good place."

WORDS
TO
KNOW

arrogantly (ăr′ə-gənt-lē) *adv.* with excessive and often undeserved pride in oneself
condescending (kŏn′dĭ-sĕn′dĭng) *adj.* displaying an attitude of patronizing superiority **condescend** *v.*
poised (poĭzd) *adj.* seeming calm and well balanced **poise** *v.*

672

 Mini Lesson ## Spelling

DOUBLING CONSONANTS BEFORE FINAL -ED AND -Y Explain to students that when adding the suffixes -*ed* and -*y*, sometimes the final consonant is doubled. The final consonant is doubled when it is preceded by a single vowel, or in a multisyllabic word in which the final syllable is accented. **Instruction** Write the following examples on the board:

mar, marred; omit, omitted; fur, furry

Exercises Have students add the suffixes -*ed* and -*y* to each word as appropriate, doubling consonants when needed.

1. cough *(coughed)*
2. excel *(excelled)*
3. fun *(funny)*
4. dismiss *(dismissed)*
5. bush *(bushy)*
6. dad *(daddy)*
7. regret *(regretted)*
8. drag *(dragged)*

 Use **Unit Five Resource Book**, p. 33.

They think I'm their friend!"

I saw no crows. For a moment the fear of disappointing him struggled with my desire to blow into the smooth, polished tip of the crow call. But he was waiting, and I took it from my pocket, held it against my lips and blew softly.

The harsh, muted sound of a sleepy crow came as a surprise to me, and I smiled at it, at the delight of having made that sound myself. I did it again, softly.

From a grove of trees on another hill came an answer from a waking bird. Just one, and then silence.

Tentatively I called again, more loudly. The branches of a nearby tree rustled, and crows answered, fluttering and calling crossly. They flew briefly into the air and then settled on a branch—three of them.

"Look, Daddy," I whispered. "Do you see them? They think I'm a crow!"

He nodded, watching them.

I moved away from him with confidence and stood on a rock at the top of the hill and blew loudly several times. From all the trees rose crows. They screamed with harsh voices and I responded, blowing again and again as they flew from the hillside in circles, dipping and soaring; landing speculatively, lurching from the limbs in afterthought and then settling again with resolute and <u>disgruntled</u> shrieks.

"Listen, Daddy! Do you hear them? They think I'm their friend! Maybe their baby, all grown up!"

I ran about the top of the hill and then down, through the frozen grass, blowing the crow call over and over. The crows called back at me, and from all the trees they rose, from all the hills. They circled and circled, and the morning was filled with the patterns of calling crows as I looked back, still running. I could see my father sitting on a rock, his gun leaning against him, and I could see he was smiling.

My crow calling came in shorter and shorter spurts as I became breathless; finally I stopped and stood laughing at the foot of the hill, and the noise from the crows <u>subsided</u> as they circled irritably and settled back in the trees. They were waiting for me.

My father came down the hill to meet me coming up. He carried his gun carefully; and though I was grateful to him for not using it, I felt that there was no need to say thank you, for I felt that he knew. The crows would always be there and they would always eat the crops; and some other morning, on some other hill, he would shoot them.

I blew the crow call once more, to say good morning and good-by and everything that goes in between. Then I put it into the pocket of my shirt and reached over out of my enormous cuffs and took my father's hand. We stood there, he and I, halfway up the November hillside, and the newly up sun was a pink wash across the Pennsylvania sky. The brown grass and curled leaves were thick around our feet, and above our heads the air was filled with the answering sound of the circling crows. ❖

| WORDS TO KNOW | **disgruntled** (dĭs-grŭn'tld) *adj.* not happy |
| | **subside** (səb-sīd') *v.* to sink or settle down to a lower or normal level |

673

GUIDING STUDENT RESPONSE

Connect to the Literature

1. What Do You Think?
Possible Response: She is happy because she and her father enjoyed themselves and got to know each other again, and because she was successful at doing the crow call.

Comprehension Check
- The narrator has two pieces of cherry pie, and her father has one.
- The crows answer back and start to fly out of the trees.
- The crows think she's their friend or one of their babies that has grown up.

 Use Selection Quiz
Unit Five Resource Book, p. 34.

Think Critically

2. Possible Responses: The narrator's father wants to get reacquainted with her. He has just returned from war and knows that he has to readjust to family life and that the family has to readjust to him. He realizes that there is a lot he no longer knows about his children, so he sets time aside to be with them individually. The narrator's sister would obviously not be interested in this type of activity, and her presence would have spoiled it.

3. Possible Response: She thinks about breaking up the crows' families.

4. Possible Response: He knows that his daughter doesn't want to see the crows killed. This shows sensitivity, understanding, and the ability to be flexible.

5. Possible Response: The most important result was the renewed closeness with her father. The special treatment her father showed her caused this closeness to return.

 Use **Reading and Critical Thinking Transparencies,** p. 5, for additional support.

Literary Analysis

Symbol Students' charts will vary, but they should support their choice of symbols with evidence from the selection.

Connect to the Literature

1. What Do You Think?
What do you think the narrator is feeling as she walks down the hill with her father?

Comprehension Check
- What do the narrator and her father have for breakfast?
- What happens when the narrator blows the crow call?
- What does the narrator say the crows think she is?

Think Critically

2. Why do you think the narrator's father takes her on this hunting trip?

 THINK ABOUT
- the narrator's feelings about her father at the beginning of the story
- the fact that her sister isn't with them
- her father's recent experience

3. What thoughts does the narrator have about the crows as she climbs the hill?

4. Why do you think the narrator's father doesn't shoot the crows? What might this reveal about him?

5. **ACTIVE READING** **RECOGNIZING CAUSE AND EFFECT** Look back at the chart in your **READER'S NOTEBOOK.** What do you think was the most important result of this trip for the narrator? What caused this effect?

Extend Interpretations

6. Different Perspectives Imagine that this story was told by the father. What might he have been thinking as he looked at his daughter sitting next to him in the car?

7. Connect to Life Think about the narrator's experience of blowing the crow call. Was there ever a time when a simple act, such as riding a bicycle, gave you a feeling of power? Explain.

Literary Analysis

SYMBOL Writers use **symbols**—people, places, or objects that stand for something other than themselves—to represent ideas or feelings. Some symbols represent the same ideas in many literary works. For example, a rising sun often symbolizes a beginning or a fresh start. As the narrator and her father stand on the hill in "Crow Call," the sun has just risen. This might symbolize that the narrator's relationship with her father is entering a new stage. Other symbols—such as the hunting shirt—have meaning only within a particular story.

Paired Activity With a partner, reread "Crow Call," looking for symbols. Discuss what each symbol represents and how it adds to the meaning of the story. Organize your ideas in a chart like the one shown.

Symbol	What It Represents	Its Importance in the Story
hunting shirt	the narrator's father	When her father buys it, it shows he understands his daughter.

Extend Interpretations

6. Different Perspectives The father might have felt concerned and anxious about the success of the day. He may have felt that he didn't know his daughter very well. He might have been eager to spend some time alone with his daughter, without other distractions.

7. Connect to Life Encourage students to list activities that are meaningful to them, that foster partnership or cooperation, or that provide opportunities for quiet conversation. Students should provide specific reasons for their choices.

*Choices & * CHALLENGES

Grammar in Context: Subjects in Different Positions

Lois Lowry varies her sentences by not always placing the **subject** at the beginning.

> At home, in the bed next to mine, my older sister still slept. . . .

> Holding my head very still, I looked at the menu.

> Carefully I stayed by his side.

Subjects usually appear at the beginning of a sentence. Sometimes, however, a sentence can begin with a phrase or word that adds important information.

Apply to Your Writing Varying your sentences by using a phrase or descriptive word before the subject will make your writing more interesting.

WRITING EXERCISE Rewrite each sentence, moving the subject from the beginning.

Example: *Original* The leaf fell silently, spiraling slowly to the ground.

Rewritten Spiraling slowly to the ground, the leaf fell silently.

1. The grass crunched softly under our feet.
2. He stood with his neck stretched out, soundless.
3. The crows arose from the trees and the hills.
4. My father smiled as he watched me.

Connect to the Literature Skim "Crow Call." Find another example of a sentence that does not begin with its subject.

Grammar Handbook Correcting Punctuation, p. R76

Vocabulary in Action

EXERCISE A: ASSESSMENT PRACTICE
Determine the relationship between the first pair of words. Then decide which Word to Know best completes the analogy. The first sentence may be restated as *"Whitish* is to *pale* as *reddish* is to _____."*

1. WHITISH : PALE :: reddish : _____
2. MOVIE : FILM :: model : _____
3. HUMAN : DOLL :: bird : _____
4. USELESS : FUNCTIONAL :: silly : _____
5. INJURED : HURT :: damaged : _____
6. PLEASED : UNHAPPY :: satisfied : _____
7. INCREASE : RISE :: decrease : _____
8. BOLDLY : BRAVELY :: proudly : _____
9. TRUTHFUL : HONEST :: graceful : _____
10. CRANKY : GRUMPY :: patronizing : _____

EXERCISE B Write a sample page for a catalog of sportswear or camping equipment, using all the Words to Know. Add illustrations if you like.

Building Vocabulary

For an in-depth lesson on analogies, see p. 348.

WORDS TO KNOW				
arrogantly	decoy	mannequin	poised	ruddy
condescending	disgruntled	marred	practical	subside

CROW CALL **675**

TEACHING THE LITERATURE

Active Reading: IDENTIFYING AUTHOR'S PURPOSE

In this acceptance speech for *The Giver*'s Newbery Award, Lois Lowry explains some of her purposes for writing that book. Her speech also had a purpose. Ask students to think about the message the speech conveys and why they think she wrote the speech this way. Ask them to cite specific examples from the speech to validate their stance. They may be able to get these examples from the notes they made in their Reader's Notebook as they read.

📖 Use **Reading and Critical Thinking Transparencies,** p. 8, for additional support.

Literary Analysis: FLASHBACK

In her speech, Lowry looks back on several times in her life and uses examples to describe where she got her inspiration. Ask students to think about the use of flashback in her speech. Was it effective? Ask them to discuss what impact these examples had on the speech as a whole.

Possible Response: The use of flashback was effective because it showed how events in Lowry's life impacted the writing of *The Giver*. Specific examples, such as the time when she rode her bike out of the safe community again and again, show the audience how this idea of going beyond the comfortable ended up in *The Giver*.

Preparing to Read

Focus Your Reading

ACTIVE READING | **IDENTIFYING THE AUTHOR'S PURPOSE**

Authors write for many reasons: to entertain, to explain or inform, to express opinions, to persuade readers. Often a writer has more than one purpose for creating a piece. As you read, think about what Lois Lowry wants to share with her audience and why.

📖 **READER'S NOTEBOOK**

Lowry gave this speech to accept an award. But it is clear from reading it that she also had other purposes in mind. Jot down phrases or sentences that hint at these other purposes.

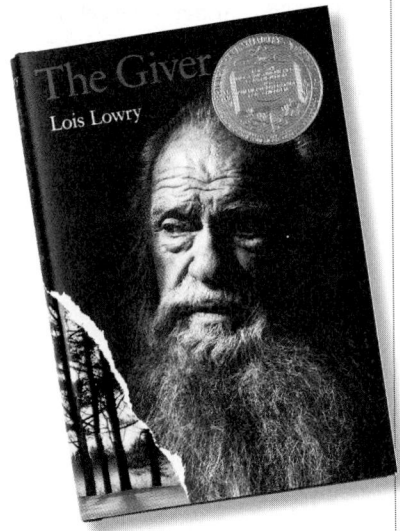

This evening it feels right to start by quoting a passage from *The Giver*, a scene set during the days in which the boy, Jonas, is beginning to look more deeply into the life that has been very superficial, beginning to see that his own past goes back further than he had ever known and has greater implications than he had ever suspected.

Now he saw the familiar wide river beside the path differently. He saw all of the light and color and history it contained and carried in its slow-moving water; and he knew that there was an Elsewhere from which it came, and an Elsewhere to which it was going.

Every author is asked again and again the question we probably each have come to dread the most: HOW DID YOU GET THIS IDEA?

I'd like, tonight, to try to tell you the origins of this book. It is a little like Jonas looking into the river and realizing that it carries with it everything that has come from an Elsewhere. A spring, perhaps, at the beginning, bubbling up from the earth; then a trickle from a glacier; a mountain stream entering farther along; and each tributary bringing with it the collected bits and pieces from the past, from the distant, from the countless Elsewheres: all of it moving, mingled, in the current.

For me, the tributaries are memories, and I've selected only a few. I'll tell them to you chronologically. I have to go way back. I'm starting forty-six years ago.

In 1948, I am eleven years old. I have gone with my mother, sister, and brother, to join my father, who has been in Tokyo for two years and will be there for several more.

We live there, in the center of that huge Japanese city, in a small American enclave with a very American name: Washington Heights. We live in an American-style house, with American neighbors, and our little community has its own movie theater, which shows American movies; and a small church, a tiny library, and an elementary school; and in many ways it is an odd replica of a United States village.

(In later, adult years I was to ask my mother why we had lived there instead of taking advantage of the opportunity to live within the Japanese community and to learn and experience a different way of life. But she seemed surprised by my question. She said that we lived where we did because it was comfortable. It was familiar. It was safe.)

I have a bicycle. Again and again—countless times—without my parents' knowledge, I ride my bicycle out the back gate of the fence that surrounds our comfortable, familiar, safe, American community. I ride down a hill because I am curious and I enter, riding down that hill, an unfamiliar, slightly uncomfortable, perhaps even unsafe—though I never feel it to be—area of Tokyo that throbs with life.

It is a district called Shibuya.

I remember, still, after all these years, the smells: fish and fertilizer and charcoal; the sounds: music and shouting and the clatter of wooden shoes and wooden sticks and wooden wheels; and the colors: I remember the babies and toddlers dressed in bright pink and orange and red, most of all; but I remember, too, the dark blue uniforms of the schoolchildren: the strangers who are my own age.

I wander through Shibuya day after day during those years when I am eleven, twelve, and thirteen. I love the feel of it, the vigor, and the garish brightness and the noise: all of such a contrast to my own life.

But I never talk to anyone. I am not frightened of the people, who are so different from me, but I am shy. I watch the children shouting and playing around a school, and they are children my age, and they watch me

in return; but we never speak to one another.

1991. I am in an auditorium somewhere. I have spoken at length about my book, *Number the Stars*, which has been honored with the 1990 Newbery Medal. A woman raises her hand. When the turn for her question comes, she sighs very loudly and says, "Why do we have to tell this Holocaust thing over and over? Is it really *necessary?*"

I answer her as well as I can—quoting, in fact, my German daughter-in-law, who has said to me, "No one knows better than we Germans that we must tell this again and again."

But I think about her question—and my answer—a great deal. Wouldn't it, I think, playing Devil's Advocate to myself, make for a more comfortable world to forget the Holocaust? And I remember once again how comfortable, familiar, and safe my parents had sought to make my childhood by shielding me from Elsewhere. But I remember, too, that my response had been to open the gate again and again. ❖

Thinking Through the Literature

1. According to Lowry's mother, why did the family live in the American community in Japan?

2. **ACTIVE READING** **AUTHOR'S PURPOSE** With a partner, share the information you noted in your **READER'S NOTEBOOK**. Decide what purposes Lowry accomplishes with her speech.

Thinking Through the Literature

1. They lived in the American community because it was safe, familiar, and comfortable.
2. **Possible Response:** Lowry's main purpose was to describe how her memories flow together to create ideas for her writing. She used *The Giver* as a specific example because she is being honored for that book.

NEWBERY ACCEPTANCE SPEECH **677**

OVERVIEW

Objectives
1. understand and appreciate **autobiography (Literary Analysis)**
2. understand and appreciate the writer's **voice (Literary Analysis)**
3. use the reading skill of **identifying effects of author's perspective (Active Reading)**

Summary
In this autobiographical essay, Lois Lowry uses family photographs to prompt memories of her childhood. She shares with her readers the thoughts and feelings she recalls as she looks at each picture. Through this unique format, we gain insight into Lois Lowry the child, and in the final vignette, we get a glimpse of the woman she is today.

Thematic Link
As one thinks about developing voice, this essay can help. It creates the opportunity for each reader to look at their own life through photographs and to explore, as Lois Lowry did, how these pictures help us recall events, emotions and attitudes—all defining elements of our own individual voice.

5-Minute Warm-Up

Daily Language SkillBuilder

Have students **proofread** the display sentences on page 609j and write them correctly. The sentences also appear on Transparency 21 of **Grammar Transparencies and Copymasters.**

---

from Looking Back
Memoir by LOIS LOWRY

Connect to Your Life

I Remember When In her book *Looking Back: A Book of Memories,* Lois Lowry shares photographs and memories of her family. She recalls funny moments, embarrassing incidents, and important experiences. What events in your life have been captured in photographs? Describe some of these moments.

Build Background

CONNECT TO HISTORY When she started to write *Looking Back,* Lois Lowry prompted her memories by looking at old photographs. The art of photography started in the 1830s in France with the daguerreotype (də-gâr'ə-tīp), an image that was created on a silver-covered copper plate. The subject of a daguerreotype portrait had to sit in full sunlight and remain absolutely still for several minutes. In the 1800s, millions of people who could not afford to have portraits painted relied on the daguerreotype to preserve images of important people in their lives. Now, in the age of instant photography, most families have albums full of pictures. These pictures are likely to be informal "snapshots" taken by family members.

> WORDS TO KNOW
> **Vocabulary Preview**
> modest   obnoxious   vigil
> mortification   peer

Focus Your Reading

LITERARY ANALYSIS VOICE A writer's **voice** is his or her style or way of writing. Voice is shaped by the writer's choice of words, the way he or she puts them together, and the incidents or ideas he or she chooses to write about. As you read, listen for Lois Lowry's voice. In *Looking Back* she writes as if she is talking to the reader. She even asks the reader questions.

ACTIVE READING IDENTIFYING EFFECTS OF AUTHOR'S PERSPECTIVE
Every writer looks at the world differently. A writer's **perspective** is influenced by his or her experiences, feelings, and beliefs. This perspective is communicated to the reader through the **tone** that the writer takes toward the subject and through concrete details. For example, Lowry's sister would provide different details than Lowry herself does.

Notice that one effect of the author's perspective is that the anecdotes are not presented chronologically. Instead, they emerge and fade like memories. The effect is that of a scrapbook or family album.

READER'S NOTEBOOK As you read, think about how Lowry's experience as a photographer may have led her to write a memoir based on looking at photographs. Note each place in which Lowry refers to details in photographic images.

678 UNIT FIVE **AUTHOR STUDY**

LESSON RESOURCES

UNIT FIVE RESOURCE BOOK, pp. 35—41

ASSESSMENT
Formal Assessment, pp. 111—112
Teacher's Guide to Assessment and Portfolio Use
Test Generator

SKILLS TRANSPARENCIES AND COPYMASTERS
Literary Analysis
• Author's Style, TR 9 (for Paired Activity, p. 684)

Reading and Critical Thinking
• Author's Purpose and Audience, TR 8 (for Thinking Through the Literature, p. 684)
Grammar
• Combining Sentences Using Conjunctions, CM 111 (for Mini Lesson, p. 685)
Vocabulary
• Meaning Clues, CM 66 (for Mini Lesson, p. 679)

Communications
• Reading Aloud, TR 11 (for Mini Lesson, p. 681)

INTEGRATED TECHNOLOGY
Audio Library
NetActivities
Internet: Research Starter

Visit our website:
www.mcdougallittell.com

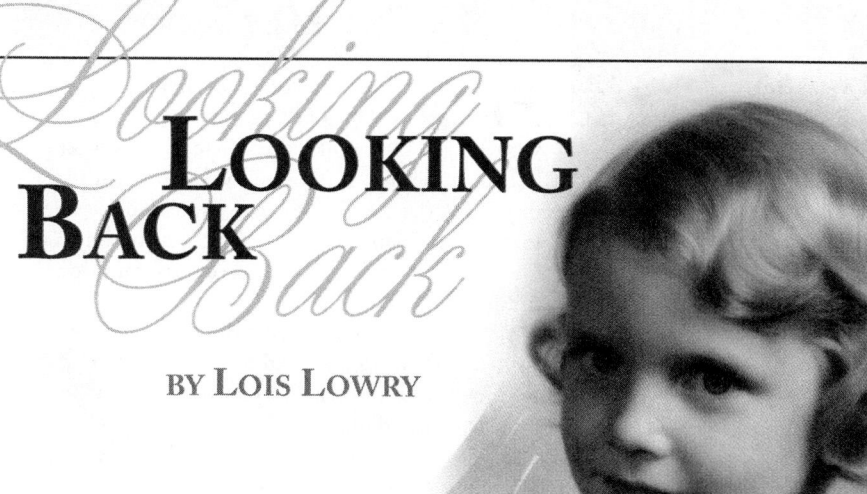

LOOKING BACK

BY LOIS LOWRY

❧1941❧

When I was very young, about four, I had a friend named <u>Modest</u> Storewrecker. That didn't seem unusual to me at the time, because when you are four, nothing seems unusual.

But later, when I was grown up, more literate, and living in a different place, I thought occasionally about Modest Storewrecker. I wondered if she was still at it. I pictured her blushing shyly (an immodest storewrecker would have been boastful and <u>obnoxious</u>) and explaining, "Ah, shucks, it was nothing. I just took my baseball bat and went into Woolworth's and bashed everything."

Then, visiting my elderly parents, I was looking at old photograph albums and came across a picture of three children: me, another little girl, named Betty June, and Modest Storewrecker, taken fifty years before. It had come loose from the page. I picked it up and smiled at the little girls staring self-consciously at the camera.

"Remember her?" I asked my mother. She <u>peered</u> through her bifocals at the picture.

"That's you," she said.

"No, I mean the *other* one."

"Betty June Rose."

"No, Mom, the other one."

She peered more closely. "Of course," she told me. "She lived just down the street. A nice little girl. Her name was Mardis Storacker."

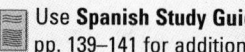

WORDS	**modest** (mŏd′ĭst) *adj.* not likely to call attention to oneself
TO	**obnoxious** (ŏb-nŏk′shəs) *adj.* worthy of disapproval or dislike
KNOW	**peer** (pîr) *v.* to look intently

679

IDENTIFYING EFFECTS OF AUTHOR'S PERSPECTIVE

A Ask students to think about how Lowry felt about the bathing suits. Ask them how these feelings are shown.

Possible Response: Lowry thought the bathing suits were ugly. She uses the words *hideous* and *wretched*.

Use **Unit Five Resource Book,** p. 36 for more practice. Use **Reading and Critical Thinking Transparencies,** p. 8, for additional support.

Literary Analysis   VOICE

B Remind students that the author's voice is what the reader hears while reading. What about this section helps us as readers to hear Lowry's voice?

Possible Response: She asks the reader questions. That helps us to feel like she is talking directly to us.

Use **Unit Five Resource Book,** p. 37 for more practice.

Reading Skills and Strategies: CONNECT

C Ask students to recall how *The Yearling* prompted this entire memory. Ask them to think about a book they've read that has meaning in their lives and to share the book and its meaning.

Literary Analysis: TONE

D The tone in this vignette is different from the preceding ones. Ask students to identify the tone and to speculate on why Lowry's tone is different here.

Possible Response: The tone of this piece is serious at times, where the other pieces were mostly funny. It may be serious because the sad events of the book were so important to Lowry at the time.

❦1942❦

A

Helen and I were probably five and eight in this snapshot. Her bathing suit was blue; mine was white, with blue polka dots. The photograph is black and white, as most photos were in those days. But I remember the colors, as well as the textures and smells. My bathing suit had a shiny quality to it, and when it was damp, an odor of mildew and pond scum.

I can't imagine that my mother, a kind woman, went into a store and said to a salesperson, "Please find me the two most hideous bathing suits in the world for my daughters."

So how did she end up buying these two wretched bathing suits? I have no idea.

❦1945❦

1

Having a little brother was, on the whole, an enjoyable thing. Sometimes, when he was little, Jon was a pest. Most of the time we got along pretty well, although I have never entirely forgiven him for the time he broke the china head of an antique doll that I loved.

But sometimes, when he was little, I was a bully and a torturer. When we lived in Japan, Jonny accumulated a collection of fireworks, which were plentiful, available, and legal there. He was seven when we returned to Pennsylvania, and he says that I told him he would be arrested if they caught him trying to bring Japanese fireworks into the United States. So as we crossed the Pacific, he says, he went out to the stern of the ship, all alone, and very solemnly and sadly threw his beloved fireworks into the sea.

I don't remember that at all. And Jon says he doesn't remember smashing the head of my doll.

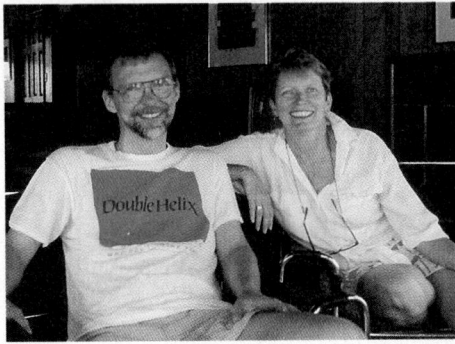

B

Isn't it amazing how we forget the things we are ashamed of?

(But isn't it amazing, too, how we forgive each other?)

Jon and I looked somewhat alike; I didn't know that then, but I can see it now, looking back. When I was eight and he was two, I wore glasses and he didn't. When I was nine and he was three, he wore glasses and I didn't. Now we both wear glasses. But now he has a beard, and I don't. So we are never *exactly* in sync; but still, we look somewhat alike.

Teaching Options

BLOCK SCHEDULING: MANAGING TIME

If your schedule requires that you cover the lesson objectives in a shorter time, use . . .
- Preparing to Read, p. 678
- Thinking Through the Literature, p. 684
- Vocabulary and Spelling, p. 685
- Grammar in Context, p. 685

If you want to take advantage of longer class time, use . . .
- TE Teaching Options: Preteaching Vocabulary, p. 679, Speaking and Listening, p. 681, Cross Curricular Link, p. 682, Informal Assessment, p. 683, Grammar, p. 685
- Choices & Challenges, p. 685

❧1946❧

My mother read *The Yearling* to Helen and me. I was nine; Helen was twelve. Mother sat in the hall outside our bedrooms and read aloud.

I thought *The Yearling* was the most wonderful book I'd ever encountered. It made me want to be a boy; I wanted to be poor and live in a swamp, where I would have animals as friends.

There was a picture in our copy of *The Yearling* which showed Jody sitting on the floor beside his father's bed. His father—Pa—had been bitten by a rattlesnake. "Snakebit," they said in the book.

In the picture, you can see Pa's face, looking almost dead because that was how you looked if you got snakebit. Jody looked very sad and beautiful, leaning against the patchwork quilt.

Sometimes I would sit on the floor beside my own bed, pretending to be Jody. I leaned my head the way he

did, and tried to look sad and beautiful.

The caption under the picture was "The Vigil." I didn't know what a vigil was. But a few pages earlier in the book, it said, of Jody: "The vigil was in his hands."

In the picture, Jody's right hand was clearly empty. So the vigil had to be in his left, which was sort of in shadows. A vigil had to be something fairly small, to fit into one left hand.

I put a crayon in my left hand and sat on the floor beside my bed. I leaned my head and closed my eyes and looked mournful. "The vigil was in her hands," I said to myself, even though secretly I knew it was only a crayon. I sighed, clasping the vigil tightly, and prayed for my snakebit Pa to get well.

My sister walked past my room, looked in, and groaned. "Mom," she called loudly down to the kitchen, "Lois is doing that weird thing by her bed again."

Reprinted with permission of Atheneum Books for Young Readers, an imprint of Simon & Schuster Children's Publishing Division, from THE YEARLING by Marjorie Kinnan Rawlings, illustrated by N.C. Wyeth. Illustrations copyright 1939 Charles Scribner's Sons; copyright renewed © 1967 Charles Scribner's Sons.

WORDS TO KNOW   **vigil** (vĭj′əl) *n.* a watch kept during normal sleeping hours

681

Customizing Instruction

Students Acquiring English
1 Ask students to share any stories they have of crossing a large body of water, perhaps from one country to another. Do they remember any rules or guidelines that were made known to them during the crossing? Help them to understand that different countries have different laws regarding what they can import.

Multiple Learning Styles
Visual Learners

Ask students to discuss each photograph or illustration and to add to the textual meaning from the details found in the pictures. Many times visual learners will pick up details that others don't see, and this discussion could bring new insight about Lowry into this author study.

Gifted and Talented
2 Ask students to think about the word *vigil*, and to discuss how Lowry constructed the meaning she did for it. Have them suggest ways she could have discovered the word's real meaning as a child. Ask them to speculate whether knowing the correct meaning was important to Lowry, and if it would have changed her attachment to *The Yearling*.

Mini Lesson   Speaking and Listening

READING A MEMOIR ALOUD

Prepare Remind students that a memoir is autobiographical and often presents the author's voice in a vivid and clear way. Have them think about Lois Lowry's voice as they reread the memoir.

Present Ask students to select one section of the memoir to read aloud to the class. Ask them to think about Lowry's voice and the tone in which she presents that particular vignette. Encourage them to use various tones of voice, expressions, and gestures to represent the mood Lowry sets in each vignette. Ask students to practice reading the memoir aloud with a partner. Each partner should listen carefully to the other's tone, and partners should discuss the reading. Then they should revise and rehearse as necessary.

BLOCK SCHEDULING This activity is particularly well suited for longer class periods.

Use **Communications Transparencies and Copymasters**, p. 11, for additional support.

Literary Analysis VOICE

A Ask students to identify what Lowry's voice sounds like in this section, and how she presents it to us.

Possible Response: At the beginning of the section, Lowry's voice is reflective as she thinks about her mother. Near the end, her voice becomes sarcastic; we read her sarcasm when she uses italics to emphasize important words, like *clothes* and *Not*.

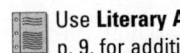 Use **Literary Analysis Transparencies,** p. 9, for additional support.

Literary Analysis: POINT OF VIEW

B This section is told from Lowry's point of view. Ask students to discuss how this photograph might be explained from Lowry's mother's point of view.

Possible Response: Lowry's mother probably thought Lois looked cute in it.

Reading Skills and Strategies: EVALUATE

C Ask students to think about Lowry's game and to evaluate the kind of person they think Lowry is to have devised such a game. Do they think this game would be fun to play? Why or why not?

Possible Response: Lowry is obviously a well-read person, who enjoys books and thinking. She is also clever. I think this game would be fun because I love to read books too.

❧1928❧

Long before she was married, back when she had just finished college, my mother had traveled in Europe. I have her passport, dated 1928; it shows a pretty young woman and tells me that she had a scar on her right eyelid (something I never knew, never noticed), and that she visited

Germany, Italy, France, Belgium, Switzerland, and England that summer, when she was twenty-two years old.

Now that I am grown, and now that she has been dead for several years, I feel glad on Mother's behalf that she had that opportunity when she was young. But when I was young, when I was seven and eight and nine years old, I wished that my mother had never ever visited any foreign country in her life.

She had, you see, brought back *clothes.* Children's clothes. I suppose even then, when she was twenty-two, she had looked forward to one day having children. Probably she had expected that her children would one day enjoy wearing the little foreign outfits she had brought back from several European countries.

Not, as my grandson would say today. [1]

[2]

❧1945❧

Here I am in my little boy's (okay, so she didn't know, when she was twenty-two, that she would have *girls*) lederhosen from Switzerland. Observe the socks, which were wool and itched. Observe the pants, which were leather and wouldn't bend. Observe the hat, which had a feather of the most embarrassing sort.

Observe the look on the little girl's face. Many words would describe that look. I choose *mortification*.

WORDS TO KNOW | **mortification** (môr′tə-fĭ-kā′shən) *n.* a feeling of shame or humiliation

682

Cross Curricular Link **Social Studies**

JAPAN AFTER WORLD WAR II Lowry moved to Japan with her family in 1948, approximately three years after World War II had ended. During World War II, the Japanese had suffered heavy losses of buildings and people. The atomic bombs dropped on Hiroshima and Nagasaki took many lives. After the war, Americans occupied much of the country and were involved in some of the rebuilding efforts. As Japan began to rebuild its war-damaged cities and industries, it became a strong and stable country once again. Only eight years after the war ended, Japan was producing more goods than it had been producing before the war began.

After the war, Japan established a new constitution and a new style of government. They began to have a prime minister as the head of their government and a legislative body called the Diet. The members of the Diet are elected by the people. This is very different from the imperial system Japan had in place before World War II. Japan kept its emperor, but he does not lead the government.

❀1945❀

Bobby Hobaugh, who lived next door, lent me his football uniform the Halloween that I was eight. I wanted to wear it forever. It made me feel powerful and brave, two things that I had never been.

I walked around the house wearing my football uniform and Bobby Hobaugh's sneakers, which were much too big, saying footbally sounding things like "Hike!" and "Hup!" in as masculine a voice as I could fake.

My brother, Jon, who was three, was scared of me when I turned into a football player. He whimpered when he saw me coming in those big sneakers.

My eleven-year-old sister, who was being a very serious ballerina, ignored me completely.

❀1984❀

Here's a game I like to play with my children, who are all grown up, and with my grandchildren, who are growing up very quickly, and with my friends, who are all ages. Age doesn't matter with this game. The only thing that matters is loving books.

The game is simply this. When you see a certain scene, you say, "What book does this remind you of?" and everybody who loves books will answer. Some will answer very quickly, and some will think a while and answer after a moment has passed.

There are no wrong answers.

For example, suppose you are walking through a meadow on a breezy day, with three friends. Suppose you stop walking, look around, and say, "What book does this remind you of?"

One friend (maybe he will be an elderly man wearing a tweed vest) will say, *"Wind in the Willows."* He will be right.

Another friend (maybe a tall, thin lady with sunglasses and a straw hat) will say, *"Gone with the Wind."* She will be right, too.

Maybe the third friend will be a very small boy with a freckled nose. Maybe he will say, after a moment of serious thinking, *"Where the Wild Things Are."* And of course—you guessed it—he, too, will be right. ❖

GUIDING STUDENT RESPONSE

Connect to the Literature

1. What Do You Think?
Answers will vary, but students should refer to one incident and offer reasons for their choice.

Comprehension Check
- The children are Helen, Lois, and Jon.
- Lowry remembers the football uniform, the Swiss outfit (lederhosen and hat), and the white bathing suit with blue polka dots.

 Use Selection Quiz
Unit Five Resource Book, p. 41.

Think Critically

2. Possible Response: Young Lois is imaginative, dramatic, self-conscious, mischievous, and forgiving.

3. Possible Response: It reveals her love of books and her fondness for sharing this love with her family.

4. Possible Response: Lowry's tone is mostly humorous. The details that she chooses highlight the humor in many situations and create a vivid sense of the people in her life. Lowry looks at her past with affection for the child she was and a sense of gratitude for the people who influenced her development and created a happy childhood for her.

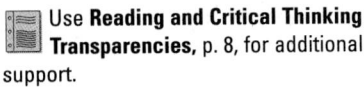 Use **Reading and Critical Thinking Transparencies**, p. 8, for additional support.

5. Possible Responses: Lowry may have chosen to write this book to relive some happy times in her life; to make sure that she remembered people no longer with her; or to preserve her family's history for other family members.

Literary Analysis

Voice Encourage students to work together to generate the list of words or phrases that depict Lowry's childlike voice.

 Use **Literary Analysis Transparencies**, p. 9, for additional support.

Connect to the Literature

1. What Do You Think?
Which of Lois Lowry's memories is your favorite? Why?

Comprehension Check
- List the children in Lois Lowry's family from oldest to youngest.
- What outfits does Lowry vividly remember from her childhood?

Think Critically

2. What words would you use to describe the young Lois Lowry?

 THINK ABOUT
- her reaction to *The Yearling*
- her feelings about the clothes her mother made her wear
- her relationships with her brother and sister

3. What does the game that Lowry enjoys playing with her children and grandchildren reveal about her?

4. **ACTIVE READING** | **IDENTIFYING EFFECTS OF AUTHOR'S PERSPECTIVE** Look back at the notes you made in your **READER'S NOTEBOOK**. What effect do you think Lowry's experiences might have on her ability to "see through a child's eyes"?

5. Lowry wrote *Looking Back* after her son was killed in an accident. What are some reasons she may have decided to write this kind of book?

Extend Interpretations

6. **COMPARING TEXTS** Compare the narrator's attitude toward clothing in "Crow Call" on page 668 with Lowry's attitude as revealed in *Looking Back*.

7. Connect to Life Think about your own memories. Which ones are most important to you? What people do you most want to remember? Why?

Extend Interpretations

6. Comparing Texts Both the narrator in "Crow Call" and Lowry see certain clothes as symbols of identities that they want to assume. For the narrator, the oversized hunting shirt gives her a sense of security and is a symbol of the adult world. For Lowry, the football uniform empowers her and gives her confidence that she does not otherwise possess.

7. Connect to Life Memories will vary, but students should be able to explain why each is important to them.

Literary Analysis

VOICE A writer's unique manner of expression is his or her **voice**. In *Looking Back*, Lowry has a friendly and conversational voice. One way she creates this voice is through a detailed description of her movements during each incident.

I put a crayon in my left hand and sat on the floor beside my bed. I leaned my head and closed my eyes and looked mournful.

Lowry carefully chooses words, such as *mournful*, that might have been in her head at the time. Her choice of incidents and details also helps to create her voice.

Paired Activity With a partner, look through the selection to see how Lowry captures a childlike voice by choosing particular words. Make a list of words that were spoken when she was young and words that she might have liked to use at the time.

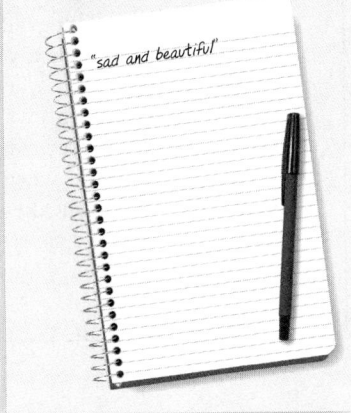
"sad and beautiful"

Choices & CHALLENGES

Grammar in Context: Combining Sentences

Notice that Lois Lowry often combines two sentences that have closely related ideas into one longer sentence by using a **comma** and a **coordinating conjunction.**

> He was seven when we returned to Pennsylvania, and he says that I told him he would be arrested if they caught him trying to bring Japanese fireworks into the United States.

You may combine two closely related sentences by connecting them with a comma followed by a coordinating conjunction such as *and, or,* or *but.*

Another way of combining closely related sentences is to use a **semicolon** and no coordinating conjunction.

> My Mother read *The Yearling* to Helen and me. I was nine; Helen was twelve.

WRITING EXERCISE Combine the sentences with a comma and a coordinating conjunction or with a semicolon.

Example: ***Original*** Many words could describe her look. I choose *mortification.*

Rewritten Many words could describe her look, but I choose *mortification.*

1. I don't remember about his fireworks. Jon doesn't remember smashing my doll.
2. Helen's bathing suit was blue. Mine was white, with blue polka dots.
3. I was eight. Jon was two.
4. Jon and I looked alike. I didn't know it then.

Grammar Handbook Clauses, p. R75

Vocabulary and Spelling

EXERCISE A: MEANING CLUES Read the following newspaper headlines. Then, on your paper, write the Word to Know that would be most likely to appear in the article that goes with each headline.

1. Brother Repeats Everything Sister Says
2. Prize Winner Describes Self as "Ordinary"
3. Boy Stays Awake All Night with Sick Puppy
4. Girl Spills Grape Juice on Friend
5. Judges Look Closely to Examine Photos

Building Vocabulary
For an in-depth lesson on meaning clues, see p. 79.

EXERCISE B: HARD AND SOFT G The letter *g* can have a soft sound or a hard sound. Notice the difference between the two sounds:

Soft *g*   *vigil*
Hard *g*   *legal*

Read aloud the following words from this selection: *photograph, page, living, college, Germany, glad.* Which words use a soft *g* sound? Which words use a hard *g*? Find ten other words that have hard and soft *g* sounds, either in your own writing or in this book. Make a list of these words. Indicate after each one whether it uses a hard or soft *g* sound.

Spelling Handbook p. R86

WORDS TO KNOW	modest	mortification	obnoxious	peer	vigil

 Mini Lesson Grammar

COMBINING SENTENCES USING CONJUNCTIONS
Remind students that when two sentences are closely related, they can be joined by adding a comma followed by a conjunction, such as *and, or,* or *but.*
Instruction Ask volunteers to suggest two related sentences. Write them on the board. Demonstrate how to combine them.
Application Have students work with a partner. Each student should write five pairs of related sentences, using information about Lois Lowry or topics from her stories and memoirs. After stu-

dents have written their individual sentences, have them trade papers and combine the pairs into five complete sentences. Ask partners to share their new sentences with the class.

Use **Unit Five Resource Book,** p. 39.
Use **Grammar Transparencies and Copymasters,** p. 136.

 Use McDougal Littell's *Language Network,* Chapter 11, for more practice in combining sentences.

Lowry's writings provide insight into her life and the events and people who have influenced her. An analysis of her style can help reveal the techniques she uses to write. Students will be made aware of Lowry's style through the Key Style Points and examples.

Key Style Points

First Activity
Varied Sentence Length and Type
The short sentence adds emphasis and draws attention to the idea that is expressed.

Second Activity
Realistic Dialogue He is encouraging and sensitive.

Third Activity
Word Choice: Sound and Image
Words that create sound include *screamed, harsh,* and *resolute* and *disgruntled shrieks.* Words that evoke visual images include *circles, dipping and soaring, landing speculatively,* and *lurching.*

The Author's Style

Lowry's Lively Language

When she was very young, Lois Lowry was thrilled to discover the power of language. "I remember the feeling of excitement that I had, the first time that I realized each letter had a sound and the sounds went together to make words, and the words became sentences and the sentences became stories. . . ." As a writer, Lowry reveals the power of words by choosing them skillfully.

Key Style Points

Varied Sentence Length and Type Lois Lowry uses a combination of sentence lengths and types to hold the reader's interest. What is the effect of the short sentence among the longer ones in this passage from *Looking Back?*

Realistic Dialogue Dialogue can move the action forward and reveal character traits. What do you learn about the narrator's father from his words to his daughter in this passage from "Crow Call"?

Word Choice: Sound and Image Lively writing doesn't tell the reader what he or she should hear or see. Instead, authors like Lois Lowry choose nouns, verbs, adjectives, and adverbs that re-create sounds and paint strong visual images. Which words in the third passage at the right evoke images or sounds?

Varied Sentences

When I was eight and he was two, I wore glasses and he didn't. When I was nine and he was three, he wore glasses and I didn't. Now we both wear glasses. But now he has a beard, and I don't.

—Looking Back

Realistic Dialogue

"Well," he said, "I've been thinking about that, and I've decided to put you in charge of the crow call. Have you ever operated a crow call?"

I shook my head. "No."

"It's an art," he said. "No doubt about that. But I'm pretty sure you can handle it. Some people will blow and blow on a crow call and not a single crow will even wake up or bother to listen, much less answer. But I really think you can do it. . . ."

—"Crow Call"

Word Choice

From all the trees rose crows. They screamed with harsh voices and I responded, blowing again and again as they flew from the hillside in circles, dipping and soaring; landing speculatively, lurching from the limbs in afterthought and then settling again with resolute and disgruntled shrieks.

—"Crow Call"

Applications

1. **Active Reading** Look back through the stories and personal memories in this author study to find examples of these three elements of Lowry's style.

2. **Writing** Recall a time in your childhood when you learned a new skill. Describe the experience in a few paragraphs. Choose words that evoke images and sounds.

3. **Speaking and Listening** With a partner, find a paragraph from one of the selections that uses a variety of sentence types and lengths. Rewrite it in short statements. Read each aloud. How is the effect different?

Applications

1. **Active Reading** Encourage students to draw from all of the selections to answer this question. Students should be able to defend their choices by explaining the effect of the varying sentence lengths, discussing what certain lines of dialogue reveal, and pointing out specific words that they feel are descriptive.

2. **Writing** To help students get started on this assignment, ask them to brainstorm incidents and choose the one they think is the most humorous. Allow the students to break into pairs and tell their stories to each other before writing them.

3. **Speaking and Listening** Students should hear the differences between the two versions. With a variety of sentence lengths and types, the writer keeps the reader interested and adds emphasis to important ideas. If all the sentences are uniformly simple and short, the writing sounds choppy, ideas are equally emphasized, and there is less unity in the paragraph.

Choices & CHALLENGES

Writing Options

1. Photo Essay Find an old photograph of yourself. In an essay, recall what you were like at that age. Place the essay in your **Working Portfolio.**

2. Dramatic Dialogue Write a dialogue that the narrator in "Crow Call" might have with her father on the way home. Reveal their personalities through their words.

3. Comparison Essay Read one of Lowry's Anastasia books. What similarities do you see between Anastasia and Lowry as a child? Make a Venn diagram. Then write an essay

explaining how the two are alike and different.

Activities & Explorations

1. Crow Symphony Reread the description of the crows in "Crow Call." Find musical recordings that suggest the motion of the birds. Bring in a recording to play for the class. ~ **MUSIC**

2. Memory Game Play your own version of the "What book?" game described in *Looking Back.* In a group, look at photographs or magazine images. What books do they bring to mind? ~ **VIEWING AND REPRESENTING**

Inquiry & Research

Photo Features Using nonfiction books, the Internet, and other media, find out what careers today use photography. Pick one career and write a brief report explaining why photography is important to it.

 More Online: Research Starter www.mcdougallittell.com

Author Study Project
Class Yearbook

When you look back on this year in school, what will you most want to remember? Create a yearbook that preserves your class's memories.

❶ **Create a List** In a small group, brainstorm a list of people and events you would like to remember. Choose the memories you will include and decide how you will organize them.

❷ **Find the Illustrations** Which memories will you illustrate? Gather photographs and make your own art.

❸ **Write the Descriptions** Write paragraphs that include lively descriptions of each memory. Match them with your illustrations.

❹ **Assemble the Book** Glue your illustrations and descriptions into a scrapbook. If you like, make a label for the cover. Invite other students to read your yearbook.

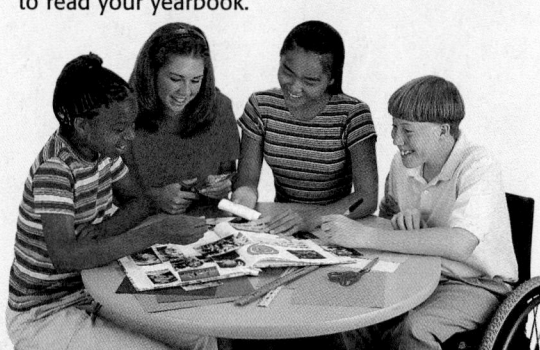

Writing Options

1. **Photo Essay** Students should locate several photographs and freewrite about them to see what they remember about each occasion and themselves at that age. Students should then choose the photograph that evokes the most complete memories and use their freewriting to help them shape their essays.

2. **Dramatic Dialogue** To get students started on this assignment, have them reread the dialogue in "Crow Call" and write down ideas for topics of conversation. Students might find it helpful to work with a partner who can take the part of one of the characters so that they can read their dialogues aloud.

📝 Use **Writing Transparencies,** p. 24, for additional support.

3. **Comparison Essay** Suggest that students take notes on the character of Anastasia as they read. They can use these notes to make their Venn diagrams. Then students should choose two or three of the most significant features to discuss.

Activities & Explorations

1. **Crow Symphony** Students who can play a musical instrument may choose to interpret this passage themselves. The sounds they play should suggest activity and liveliness, as well as the shrieking and cawing sounds of the crows.

2. **Memory Game** **To make this activity easier,** have groups brainstorm a list of books they have read. Encourage them to also think about books that have been read to them.

Author Study Project

CLASS YEARBOOK
Encourage students to assign each member of the group a specific role, such as collecting photographs and organizing them. All students in the group should be involved in writing descriptions of the events. Have them read their paragraphs aloud before making a final copy so that they can make adjustments in content and style.

As an alternative, students might want to do a Video Yearbook, in which video recordings of various events, as well as interviews with students and teachers, are included.

Inquiry & Research

Photo Features Encourage students to ask a librarian to lead them to Web sites that might be helpful.

Lois Lowry

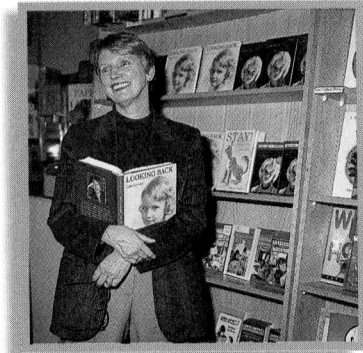

Lois Lowry's readers are drawn to the voice they find in her books, a voice that seems to know their own hearts and minds. It's no wonder Lowry's books are so believable. Many of the emotions she describes come from her own vivid memories. Whether exploring the world of family or the world at war, Lowry brings to life the challenges and discoveries that shape the years of becoming an adult.

The Giver   1994
Newbery Medal

This disturbing novel is set in a futuristic community that appears to have solved all of the world's problems. Because 12-year-old Jonas has special talents, he is chosen for a unique honor—to be an apprentice to the Giver, the society's keeper of all of its memories, both good and bad. Not until his apprenticeship begins does Jonas understand the true meaning of the Giver's work. With this new knowledge, he begins to doubt the deepest values of his community.

Number the Stars   1990
Newbery Medal

To young Annemarie Johansen, it feels as if war is all anyone can talk about since the Nazis occupied her home city in Denmark. But food shortages and soldiers in the streets seem like petty matters after Annemarie becomes part of a secret and dangerous plot. As tensions build, Annemarie and her family risk their lives to help their Jewish friends to safety in Sweden. This gripping novel was inspired by real-life events of World War II.

A Summer to Die   1977

International Reading Association's Children's Literature Award
Everything seems new the summer that Meg's family moves to the country. The change brings 13-year-old Meg new neighbors, new friends, and, unfortunately, a new room she has to share with her beautiful and popular 15-year-old sister, Molly. But when Molly falls ill, Meg finds she will need new strength more than anything.

Anastasia Krupnik   1979

Anastasia Krupnik is always in crisis. Her grandmother can't recall her name, her teacher doesn't understand her poetry, and a certain sixth-grade boy doesn't seem to know she exists. Worse, her parents have provided her with yet one more item for her "things I hate" list: they're adding a new baby to the family, and without consulting Anastasia first. This is the first novel in Lowry's popular and hilarious Anastasia Krupnik series.

Rabble Starkey   1987

Boston Globe–Horn Book Award, Golden Kite Award
Twelve-year-old Parable Ann "Rabble" Starkey and her mother have never had it easy. Her mother had Rabble when she was only 14, and struggles to support them by cleaning houses in their small mountain town. When they move in with Rabble's best friend, Veronica Bigelow, while Mrs. Bigelow is in the hospital, Rabble feels like she's found her dream home. How will Rabble cope when it's time to return to her old life?

Writing Workshop
Opinion Statement

Objectives
- write an Opinion Statement
- use a written text as a model for writing
- revise a draft to make weak endings stronger
- correct sentence fragments

Introducing the Workshop

Opinion Statement Locate and share with the class several short opinion statements, such as editorials and letters to the editor in newspapers and magazines. A student newspaper might be a good source for examples. Have them think about how successful the authors were at convincing their readers of their opinions. Ask them to consider what factors made some of the authors more successful than others.

Basics in a Box
Using the Graphic The graphic on this page illustrates how an opinion statement should be organized. Point out that the graphic suggests elements that students should include when they draft their own statements.

Presenting the Rubric To better understand the assignment, students can refer to the Standards for Writing a Successful Opinion Statement. You may also want to share with them the complete rubric, which describes several levels of proficiency.

 Use McDougal Littell's *Language Network,* Chapters 10–17, for more instruction on essential writing skills.

 Power Presentation

To engage students visually, use **Power Presentation 1**, Opinion Statement.

Writing Workshop
Opinion Statement

Telling what you think . . .

From Reading to Writing Can you remember what you learned in kindergarten? Do you believe the lessons you learned can guide you through the rest of your life? Robert Fulghum does. In his book *All I Really Need to Know I Learned in Kindergarten,* he gives reasons and examples to support his opinion. Writing an **opinion statement** is one way to make your voice heard. Backing up your statement with facts and evidence can help you convince others to see things your way.

For Your Portfolio

WRITING PROMPT Write an opinion statement about an issue that you care about.

Purpose: To share your opinion and help others understand it
Audience: Anyone interested in the same issue

Basics in a Box

Opinion Statement at a Glance

Introduction — Presents the issue and states opinion

Why I believe it

Body — Supporting Evidence | Supporting Evidence | Supporting Evidence

Conclusion — Summary of opinion

RUBRIC STANDARDS FOR WRITING

A successful opinion statement should
- clearly state the issue and your opinion in the introduction
- support your opinion with reasons, examples, and facts
- use language and details appropriate for your audience
- show clear reasoning
- sum up your opinion in the conclusion

LESSON RESOURCES

USING PRINT RESOURCES
Unit Five Resource Book
- Prewriting, p. 42
- Drafting, p. 43
- Peer Response, pp. 44–45
- Revising, Editing, and Proofreading, p. 46
- Student Models, pp. 47–49
- Rubric for Evaluation, p. 50

Reading and Critical Thinking Transparencies
- Main Idea and Supporting Details, TR 25

Grammar Transparencies and Copymasters
- Correcting Sentence Fragments, CM 59 (for Mini Lesson, p.695)
- Punctuating, Choosing, and Incorporating Quotations, CM 128

Writing Transparencies and Copymasters
- Writing Process Transparencies, TR 1–TR 4
- Writing Structure

Transparencies: Focusing the Report, TR 12
- Writing Template Transparencies: Opinion Statement, TR 27

INTEGRATED TECHNOLOGY
LaserLinks
Writing Springboards
See **Teacher's SourceBook** p. 56 for bar codes.

Writing Coach CD-ROM
Visit our website:
www.mcdougallittell.com

Analyzing a Student Model

SPEAKING OPPORTUNITY
See the Communication Handbook, p. R100 for speaking and presenting tips.

**Jared Taitel
Wilson Middle School**

For Art's Sake

There are a lot of reasons to live in my town. It has two libraries, three large parks, good restaurants, and a town fair in the summer. It also has acres and acres of apple trees as far as the eye can see. But my town doesn't have everything. It doesn't have an arts center.

My town needs an arts center for a few reasons. First, teenagers in our community need a safe place to express themselves. Right now there is a problem with teenagers hanging around the local stores after school and on the weekends. They get into trouble because there just isn't a lot to do in town. A community arts center could offer music and art classes. Teens could get involved in projects like painting murals or forming bands. I have been involved in community theater and drawing classes in other towns. These experiences have helped me to develop confidence, character, and creativity. An arts center would be a great place for kids to spend quality time without their parents having to worry about them.

Second, I believe that an arts center could solve the problems faced by our community's theater group. For example, right now the group puts on two plays and one musical each year. They have to rehearse in the basement of a church. This is very inconvenient and uncomfortable. The basement is drafty, and actors, especially the singers, find it difficult to rehearse. Also, the stage is small and the lighting is bad. The director just has to hope that the staging and special effects will look right on the night of the performance. Space for the performances is also hard to find. Often the high school auditorium is used. This creates scheduling problems for groups at the high school. If the theater group performed in an arts center, it could have a more comfortable place to rehearse and stage more productions.

RUBRIC IN ACTION

❶ States the issue and his position

❷ Gives first reason to support his opinion

Other Option:
• Present reasons first. Then examine objections.

❸ The writer presents a second reason.

❹ Includes facts and examples

WRITING WORKSHOP **691**

Teaching the Lesson

Analyzing the Model
"For Art's Sake"

The student model is an opinion statement about the need for an arts center in the writer's town. The student writer states his opinion that his town needs to provide an alternative meeting place for teenagers and those interested in the arts. He supports his assertions with examples and facts.

Have students think of a problem or issue about which they have a strong opinion. Help students see how supporting an argument with examples and details helps to clarify the argument and convince the readers. Then point out the key words and phrases in the student model that correspond to the elements mentioned in the Rubric in Action.

1. Ask students why they think the writer starts off with this description of his town.

   Possible Response: It starts the essay off on a positive note; it shows that the writer is able to see the good in the town as well as the problems.

2. Ask students to consider why the writer addresses the problems of the teens in the town first.

   Possible Responses: It is the most immediate and visible problem; it is a concern of all the town residents.

3. Point out that the student author uses a transitional word at the beginning of this paragraph to signal that he is moving on to another idea.

4. Ask students what impression is created by the facts and examples included in this paragraph.

   Possible Responses: The writer knows his facts and has thought his plan through; the situation of the theater group needs to be remedied.

Viewing and Representing
Mini Lesson

Instruction The effectiveness of a written text depends on word choice, ideas, and the structure of the text—the way in which ideas are organized and events unfold.

Activity Have students analyze the organization of the student model by listing the main idea and supporting details of the essay in a chart similar to the one shown here.

 Use **Reading and Critical Thinking Transparencies,** p. 25, for additional support.

Title:	For Art's Sake
Main Idea:	writer's town needs an arts center
Detail:	Teens need activities and a safe place in which to do them.
Detail:	The community theater group needs new facilities.
Detail:	The community already has a building that could be used as an arts center—the old Town Hall.

5. Ask students why they think the writer's third reason is significant to the essay.

Possible Responses: It provides a practical solution to the problem of where the center would go; it takes care of the problem of having a vacant building in the middle of the town; it anticipates the objections that it would be too expensive or complicated to create an arts center.

6. Ask students what effect this conclusion has on the reader.

Possible Responses: It reinforces the arguments that the author made; offers an easy way for the reader to get involved; makes the arts center seem logical and fairly easy to achieve.

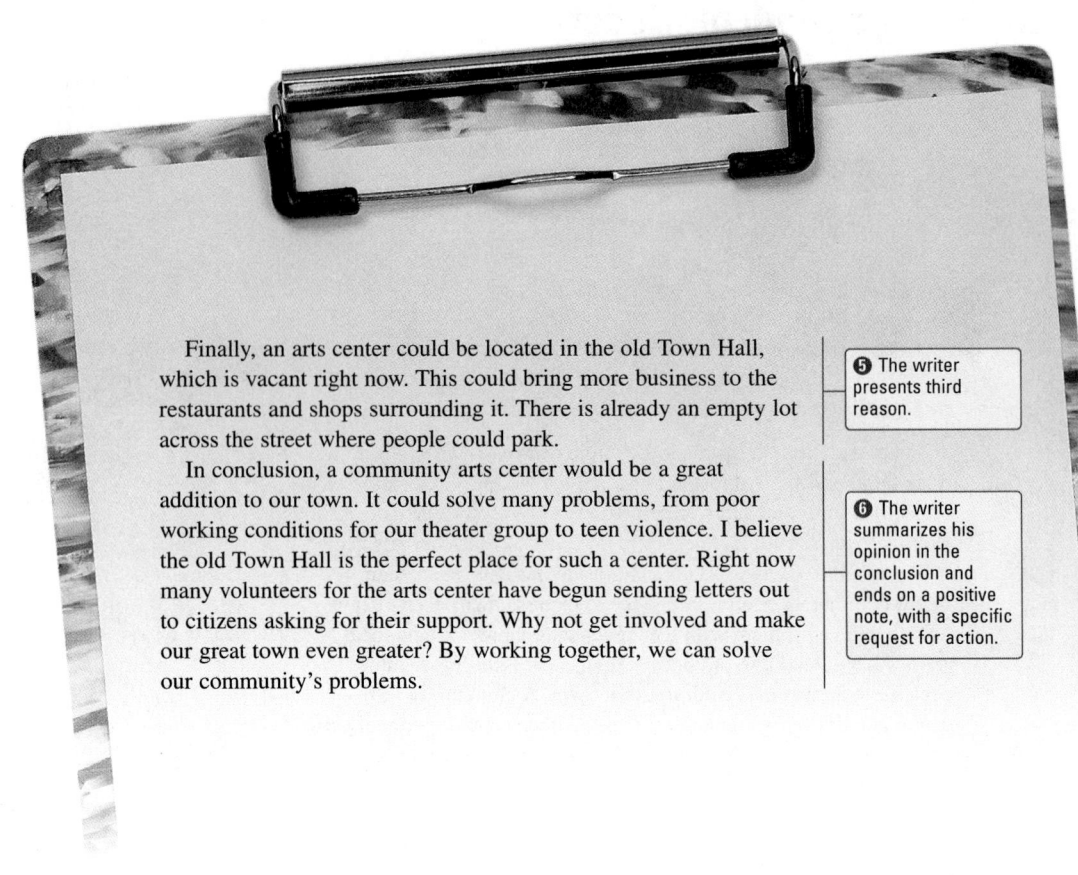

Finally, an arts center could be located in the old Town Hall, which is vacant right now. This could bring more business to the restaurants and shops surrounding it. There is already an empty lot across the street where people could park.

In conclusion, a community arts center would be a great addition to our town. It could solve many problems, from poor working conditions for our theater group to teen violence. I believe the old Town Hall is the perfect place for such a center. Right now many volunteers for the arts center have begun sending letters out to citizens asking for their support. Why not get involved and make our great town even greater? By working together, we can solve our community's problems.

❺ The writer presents third reason.

❻ The writer summarizes his opinion in the conclusion and ends on a positive note, with a specific request for action.

 Grammar

PUNCTUATING, CHOOSING, AND INCORPORATING QUOTATIONS Remind students that one way to strengthen the arguments in their opinion statements is to incorporate quotations from experts or from others involved in the issue. Quotations should be set off by commas and quotation marks.

Practice Have students add quotation marks and commas where they are needed in the following sentences.

1. When interviewed about the proposed arts center, the council chairman said, *"I wish we'd had an arts center when I was a kid."*

2. Johanna Lindsay, a sculptor who just moved to town, told me *"One of the reasons I like it here is that there is such strong support for the arts."*

3. *"It would be a shame to let the old Town Hall, which is a beautiful building, go to waste,"* said Historical Society President Allison Abate.

 Use **Grammar Transparencies and Copymasters**, p. 128.

Writing Your Opinion Statement

❶ Prewriting

Writing comes more easily if you have something to say.
—Sholem Asch, novelist

To find a subject for your opinion statement, **list** topics in your school or community about which you feel strongly. **Write down** changes you think need to be made or things that strike you as unfair. See the **Idea Bank** in the margin for more suggestions. After you have decided on an issue, follow the steps below.

> ### Planning Your Opinion Statement
>
> ▶ 1. **Decide on your focus.** Make sure you understand the issue. Is there one specific part you want to focus on? Can you state your opinion in one sentence?
>
> ▶ 2. **Think about the reasons for your opinion.** Why do you have this opinion? Which of your reasons are the most convincing?
>
> ▶ 3. **Find the facts.** What facts or examples support your reasons? Go to the library or talk to an expert to find out as much information as you can about your issue.
>
> ▶ 4. **Identify your audience.** Who will read your opinion statement? Which of your arguments will work best with the people reading your statement? How much background information do you need to give your readers?

❷ Drafting

Begin writing your opinion statement. Keep in mind that you can revise and rewrite it later, but remember that every reason for your opinion must be supported. When you write a reason, follow it up with the **facts** or **examples** that support it. You will probably want to put your reasons in order from weakest to strongest. Cover a different reason in each paragraph. Be sure to state your opinion in the **introduction** and summarize it in the **conclusion.**

IDEABank

1. Your Working Portfolio
Look for ideas in the **Writing Options** you completed earlier in this unit.
• **Personal Credo,** p. 641
• **Letter to the Editor,** p. 662

2. If I ruled the world . . .
Use the sentence starter above to come up with ideas to improve life for people in your school, home, city, state, or country.

3. Debate!
With a partner, decide on a topic that both of you are familiar with, such as a sport, a current event, or a local community issue. Choose opposite sides to create a debate. Take notes and use the information for your paper.

Have a question?

See the **Writing Handbook** Prewriting, R22

>
> ### Ask Your Peer Reader
>
> • What is my opinion about this issue?
> • Which reasons were most convincing? Where do I need more supporting evidence?
> • What information was not convincing?
> • How did you feel about the issue after reading my essay?

Revising
MAKING WEAK ENDINGS STRONGER

Review the changes in the sample with students. To help students practice writing strong endings, ask volunteers to share the conclusions from their drafts. Have the rest of the class suggest ways to make the conclusion stronger and more effective.

Editing and Proofreading
CORRECTING SENTENCE FRAGMENTS

Remind students always to express themselves in complete thoughts so that their readers are able to understand the argument. Have students explain the change in the sample. For more practice, see the Grammar Mini Lesson at the bottom of the next page.

Reflecting

 As they write their reflections, have students think about what they will look for in the editorials and letters to the editor that they read in the future.

Option
Managing the Paper Load

In order to decrease your grading time, tape-record your comments and reactions to students' papers rather than writing them down. Then have students listen to your remarks and make any changes in their essays.

Need revising help?

Review the **Rubric,** p. 690

Consider **peer reader** comments

Check **Revision Guidelines,** p. R23

SPELLING
From Writing

As you revise your work, look back at the words you misspelled and determine why you made the errors you did. For additional help, refer to the strategies and generalizations in the **Spelling Handbook** on page R86.

Wondering what part is missing?

See the **Grammar Handbook,** p. R55

Publishing
IDEAS

- Submit your opinion statement to your school or community newspaper.
- Turn your essay into a speech to convince others to think and feel the way that you do.

More Online:
Publishing Options
www.mcdougallittell.com

❸ Revising

TARGET SKILL ▶ **MAKING WEAK ENDINGS STRONGER**
The ending of your paper is often the part that readers will remember most. That is why it is important to restate your opinion and your strongest supporting arguments in your conclusion.

a community arts center would be a great addition,
In conclusion, ~~I think a community arts center is a good~~
to our town. It would solve many problems, from poor
~~idea. That is the end of my essay. I hope you agree!~~
working conditions for our theater group to teen violence.

❹ Editing and Proofreading

TARGET SKILL ▶ **CORRECTING SENTENCE FRAGMENTS**
A sentence fragment is a group of words that does not express a complete thought. It may be confusing to the reader because it is not a complete sentence. It may be lacking a subject, a predicate, or some final phrase that completes the thought. Avoid sentence fragments in order to make your writing more easily understood.

more business to the restaurants and shops surrounding it.
An arts center in this location could bring ˄

❺ Reflecting

FOR YOUR WORKING PORTFOLIO How did your opinion change or develop as you wrote your opinion statement? What did you learn about writing an opinion statement? What other issues would you like to write about? Attach your answers to your finished essay. Save your opinion statement in your **Working Portfolio.**

Read this passage from the first draft of an opinion statement. The underlined sections may include the following kinds of errors:

- **run-on sentences**
- **capitalization errors**
- **sentence fragments**
- **punctuation errors with quotes**

For each underlined section, choose the revision that most improves the writing.

> Our principal, Mr. Dolinger, says we don't need to have dances at
> (1)
> our school. He said "There are already too many activities here" It is
> (2)
> true that some students are involved in sports, while others participate
> in the newspaper and yearbook. However, only 40 percent of our
> (3)
> students. That statistic shows that a lot of us aren't doing anything
> with people in our school. Having dances on Valentine's day, the first
> (4)
> day of Spring, or on other special occasions would help to build school
> (5)
> spirit, to create a sense of friendship among students. One school
> (6)
> activity that everyone could enjoy.

1. A. Our Principal, Mr. Dolinger
   B. Our Principal, mr. dolinger,
   C. Our principal, mr. Dolinger,
   D. Correct as is

2. A. He said "There are already too many activities here.
   B. He said, "There are already too many activities here."
   C. He said, There are already too many activities here.
   D. Correct as is

3. A. only 40 percent of our students participate at all.
   B. only 40 percent of our students:
   C. only 40 percent.
   D. Correct as is

4. A. Valentine's Day, the first day of spring,
   B. valentine's day, the first day of spring,
   C. Valentine's Day, the first day of Spring,
   D. Correct as is

5. A. to build school spirit and to create a sense of friendship
   B. to build school spirit: to create a sense of friendship
   C. to build school spirit to create a sense of friendship
   D. Correct as is

6. A. Dances are one school activity
   B. Are one activity
   C. School activity
   D. Correct as is

Assessment Practice

Demonstrate how students can eliminate incorrect choices for the first question.

A. This choice incorrectly capitalizes *principal.*

B. This choice incorrectly capitalizes *principal* and does not capitalize the first letters of the proper name.

C. This choice is incorrect because the title *Mr.* is not capitalized.

D. The original sentence is correct.

Answers:

1. D; **2.** B; **3.** A; **4.** A; **5.** A; **6.** A.

Need extra help?

See the **Grammar Handbook.**

Writing Complete Sentences, p. R59

Correcting Capitalization, p. R73

Correcting Punctuation, p. R76

 Grammar

CORRECTING SENTENCE FRAGMENTS For use with Editing and Proofreading, p. 694. Tell students that sentences that do not express a complete thought—sentence fragments—lessen the effectiveness of their writing because their readers cannot know what is missing and cannot interpret the author's meaning. Sentence fragments can be corrected by supplying the missing information or by combining them with a complete sentence. **Exercises** Have students identify the sentence fragments in the following examples and suggest corrections. Some sentences are already correct.

1. Dogs are considered man's best friend.
2. Obedient and fun to play with. *(F)*
3. Cats tend to be more aloof.
4. And seem to be more independent. *(F)*
5. Trapped and unable to escape. *(F)*

Use **Grammar Transparencies and Copymasters,** p. 59.

 Use McDougal Littell's *Language Network,* Chapter 1, for more practice in correcting sentence fragments.

Reflecting on the Theme The selections in this part of Unit Five use literature to make the past come alive. You'll read about a courageous woman in the American Civil War, a natural disaster that shocked ancient Rome, and a boy who ruled Egypt when he was younger than you are now. Learning about the past can shape your understanding of the world today.

ACTIVITY

Imagine that you are making a time capsule that will help people of the future to understand what your life is like. Make a list of ten important things you would like to include. Share your list with a classmate.

Time Capsule:
• newspaper
• menu

LEARNING the Language of *Literature*

*H*istorical Fiction

> *Young readers write to me, "How did you learn about Indians?" or about life in colonial times? The answer of course, is research. . . . To me, it is an ever-fascinating game which I have likened to a scavenger hunt.*
> —*Elizabeth George Speare, novelist*

Can you imagine sitting down to eat a piece of apple pie with Abraham Lincoln? What about sailing alongside Christopher Columbus or attending the burial of the Egyptian pharaoh Tutankhamen? All of these notions are made possible through a type of literature called historical fiction.

Historical fiction is writing in which a particular period of history is brought to life through an author's imagination. It allows the reader to travel through time and meet the characters and events from another era. When writing historical fiction, a writer may use people from history and imaginary characters, as well as important dates, details, settings, and real events. Most writers of historical fiction spend long hours doing research to help them better understand the time period and create a convincing story.

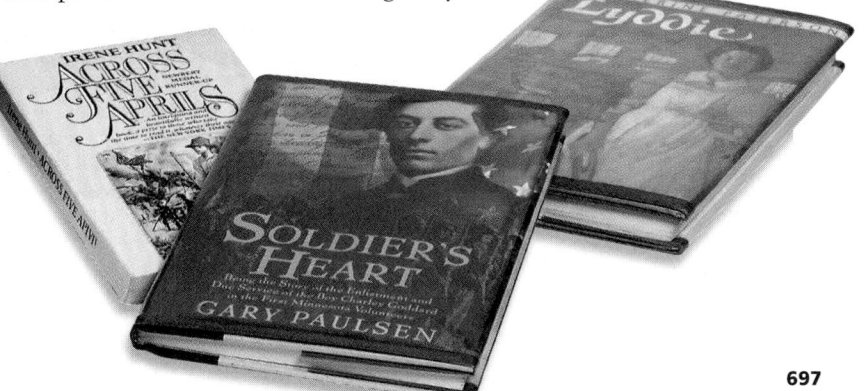

697

Objectives
- understand and identify the following literary terms:
  - historical fiction
  - real characters
  - setting
  - plot
- to appreciate the writer's craft
- recognize the distinguishing features of historical fiction.

Teaching the Lesson

This lesson analyzes the elements of historical fiction and shows how the writer uses these elements to create interest and reader involvement.

Introducing the Concepts
Ask students to think of a book they've recently read or a film they've recently seen that is based on a realistic story set in an earlier time. As a class, discuss what makes these works interesting and what students learned from reading or seeing them.

Presenting the Concepts
Characters: Real and Imaginary
Discuss with students ways in which they can distinguish between real characters and imaginary characters in historical fiction.

YOUR TURN
Possible Response: The author's use of vivid details makes Tito seem realistic. The writer describes Tito's senses and his emotions.

Setting
Ask students to imagine that they are to write a work of historical fiction. Ask them to describe the setting they would choose, including the time period and appropriate details.

YOUR TURN
Possible Response: The scene takes place in a crowded square in Pompeii, near the forum. The author describes the kinds of people in the square and their activities, and provides specific details, such as "displaying the latest fashions from Greece and Egypt," which place the scene in a specific era.

 Use **Literary Analysis Transparencies,** p. 6, for additional support.

Plot
Ask students to think about what historical event they would weave into a work of historical fiction. What role would the event have in the story? Ask for volunteers to share their ideas with the rest of the class.

YOUR TURN
Possible Response: The writer has placed Tito in the middle of the violent earthquake that shook Pompeii in A.D. 79.

Characters: Real and Imaginary

Historical fiction often includes real characters from history as well as invented ones. Writers of historical fiction often have their characters face problems that real people faced at that time in history. By creating dialogue, thoughts, and feelings for the characters, a writer shows the similarities and differences between people then and now.

YOUR TURN Read the excerpt at the right. How does the author make Tito, a fictional character, seem realistic?

Setting

Most writers of historical fiction use their imaginations to describe settings, but they try to be accurate in the way they show daily life, styles of architecture, modes of transportation, and people's beliefs during a particular time. The historical setting can make a story come alive for the reader.

YOUR TURN Read the excerpt at the right and think about how the author created this scene. Where does the scene take place? What details does the author use to recreate the historical period?

Plot

In historical fiction, plot is strongly influenced by the setting. This is because characters are involved in the events of their time. The writer weaves historical facts and actual events into the plot. Although the reader may know from studying history that an earthquake, a war, or a famine is going to happen, the author makes readers care about how the main character will cope with these events.

YOUR TURN What actual catastrophe does the writer describe in the excerpt at the right?

698 UNIT FIVE PART 2: VOICES FROM THE PAST

CHARACTERS

Tito was not the merriest boy in Pompeii. He could not romp with the other youngsters and play hare and hounds and I spy and follow-your-master and ball-against-the-building and jackstones and kings and robbers with them. But that did not make him sorry for himself. If he could not see the sights that delighted the lads of Pompeii, he could hear and smell things they never noticed.

—Louis Untermeyer, "The Dog of Pompeii"

SETTING

The forum was the favorite promenade for rich and poor. What with the priests arguing with the politicians, servants doing the day's shopping, tradesmen crying their wares, women displaying the latest fashions from Greece and Egypt, children playing hide-and-seek among the marble columns, knots of soldiers, sailors, peasants from the provinces—to say nothing of those who merely came to lounge and look on—the square was crowded to its last inch.

—Louis Untermeyer, "The Dog of Pompeii"

PLOT

He was getting drowsy, too drowsy to walk. But walk he must. He knew it. And Bimbo knew it; the sharp tugs told him so. Nor was it a moment too soon. The sacred ground of the forum was safe no longer. It was beginning to rock, then to pitch, then to split. As they stumbled out of the square, the earth wriggled like a caught snake, and all the columns of the temple of Jupiter came down. It was the end of the world—or so it seemed.

—Louis Untermeyer, "The Dog of Pompeii"

Suppose someone tells you, "*Star Wars* is the best movie ever made! It has an exciting plot, great actors, and terrific special effects." Someone else says, "*Star Wars* was released in 1977. It starred Mark Hamill, Carrie Fisher, and Harrison Ford." Can you tell which is fact and which is opinion? Being able to tell the difference will help you win arguments, defend your own opinions, and evaluate what you read.

Distinguishing Fact from Opinion

How to Apply the Skill

To **distinguish fact from opinion,** an active reader will:
• **Clarify** statements of fact as true or false
• Look for words or phrases that signal opinions
• **Evaluate** and analyze ideas and reasoning
• Look for supporting evidence

Try It Now!

Read and distinguish fact from opinion in the excerpt below.

> In November 1922, Carter and his crew began uncovering the area near the tomb of Rameses VI—the only section that had not been dug up in the Valley of the Kings. . . . To the eyes of most people their undertaking seemed absurd. Nearly everybody was convinced that Tutankhamen's tomb had already been found.
>
> —Anne Terry White, "Tutankhamen"

Here's how Chris uses the skill:

"The first statement about Carter is a fact because I can check the month and year the excavation began in a history book. Judgment words such as terrible, great, always, never, probably, all, most, *and* none, *and phrases—*I think, I feel, I believe, it seems—*help me to recognize an opinion. I* **evaluate** *the last sentences, to see that this part is an opinion. The words* most *and* seemed *and the phrase 'nearly everybody was convinced' can't be proved."*

Need More Help?

Remember that active readers use the essential reading strategies explained on page 4: • **visualize** • **predict** • **clarify** • **question** • **connect** • **evaluate** • **monitor.**

THE ACTIVE READER **699**

OVERVIEW

Objectives
• distinguish fact from opinion in various texts
• support responses by referring to relevant aspects of text

Teaching the Lesson

The strategies on this page will help students understand how to tell the difference between facts and opinions in written texts.

Presenting the Strategies
Help students understand the strategies by asking for volunteers to read them aloud. Emphasize to students that they will be using these strategies as they read the selections in this book.

Divide students into small groups. Choose a selection from this unit to read and divide it into sections. Assign one section to each group of students. Ask each group to use the strategies outlined on this page to identify the facts and opinions in their section.

1 Clarify
Have the students construct a chart listing the statements that are fact and those that are opinion. Suggest they also note words that signal opinions in the text.

2 Evaluate
Ask for a volunteer from each group to draw the chart on the board and explain their conclusions.

As a class, discuss with students additional ways of determining what is fact and what is opinion in written texts.

OVERVIEW

This selection is included in the **Grade 6 InterActive Reader.**

This selection appears in Spanish in the **Spanish Study Guide.**

Objectives

1. understand and appreciate a **short story (Literary Analysis)**
2. understand and appreciate **historical fiction (Literary Analysis)**
3. use details in the text to **distinguish fact from nonfact (Active Reading)**

Summary

In the ancient Roman city of Pompeii, the blind boy Tito and his dog Bimbo live a simple life together. Three times a day, Bimbo slips away to steal raisin cakes and scraps of food for them to live on. Together they roam Pompeii, exploring its smells and sounds. One night the city's people are especially merry as they celebrate the birthday of the Roman emperor. Afterward, Tito sleeps soundly, exhausted from the excitement. Early the next morning his dog pulls him awake and drags him toward the Forum. The ground trembles and volcanic ash fills the air—the nearby volcano, Mount Vesuvius, is erupting! Pompeiians crowd the street as buildings burn and pumice falls. Confused and frightened, Tito tries to head toward the center of town, but Bimbo forces him toward the sea. There someone lifts Tito safely into a boat, leaving Bimbo behind in the commotion. Centuries later, scientists find the skeleton of a dog in a Pompeiian bakery, a raisin cake still in its mouth.

Thematic Link

Although the physical voices of those from the past may be stilled, the artifacts that people leave behind speak for them.

5-Minute Warm-Up

Daily Language SkillBuilder

Have students **proofread** the display sentences on page 609j and write them correctly. The sentences also appear on Transparency 22 of **Grammar Transparencies and Copymasters.**

The Dog of Pompeii

Short Story by LOUIS UNTERMEYER

"The mountain was turning itself inside out."

Connect to Your Life

What do you know about the ancient city of Pompeii? In a chart like the one shown, record what you already know about this city, and what you would like to learn.

What I Know	What I Want to Learn	What I Learned
It was buried by a volcanic eruption.		

Build Background

CONNECT TO HISTORY In A.D. 79, the volcanic mountain Vesuvius in southern Italy erupted. It poured tons of burning lava and ashes over the countryside and buried Pompeii, a nearby city, under about 20 feet of ash and cinders. The blast was as strong as a nuclear explosion. Out of the estimated population of 20,000, nearly 2,000 were killed, many of them trapped in their homes. Other victims died trying to escape by boat.

Later eruptions continued to cover the ruins, and Pompeii lay undisturbed under lava deposits for almost 1,700 years. The ruins were first discovered in the late 1500s, but excavation did not begin until 1748. The excavations that followed uncovered Pompeii. The remains of the city, well preserved by the ashes, present a clear picture of what life was like in the ancient Roman Empire. We now know how people dressed, how children were taught, and even how foods were prepared.

> WORDS TO KNOW **Vocabulary Preview**
> dislodging   eruption   restore   shrine   vapor

  LaserLinks: Background for Reading
Historical Connection
Visual Vocabulary

Focus Your Reading

LITERARY ANALYSIS **HISTORICAL FICTION** When a writer bases all or part of a story on real people or events from the past, the result is called **historical fiction.** The writer may blend factual information about a time, a place, and historical persons with imaginary characters, dialogue, and events.

ACTIVE READING **DISTINGUISHING FACT FROM NONFACT** A fact is a statement that can be proven to be true. Fiction tells about imaginary people, places, and events. As you read, try to decide which elements are true and which are made up. Record facts and fiction in a two-column chart in your **READER'S NOTEBOOK.**

Fact	Nonfact
"Once a year the Caesar visited the pleasure city."	"The sacrifices in the forum were better than a show."

LESSON RESOURCES

UNIT FIVE RESOURCE BOOK
pp. 51–57

ASSESSMENT
Formal Assessment,
pp. 115–116
Teacher's Guide to Assessment and Portfolio Use
Test Generator

SKILLS TRANSPARENCIES AND COPYMASTERS
Literary Analysis
• Conflict, TR 8 (for Cooperative Activity, p. 711)

Reading and Critical Thinking
• Distinguishing Fact from Opinion, TR 26 (for Thinking Through the Literature, p. 711)
Grammar
• Independent and Dependent Clauses, CM 62 (for Mini Lesson, p. 713)
Vocabulary
• Synonyms and Antonyms, CM 67 (for Mini Lesson, p. 701)
• Analogies, CM 68 (for Mini Lesson, p. 710)

Communications
• Dramatic Reading, TR 12 (for Mini Lesson, p. 712)

INTEGRATED TECHNOLOGY
Audio Library
LaserLinks
• Historical Connection; Visual Vocabulary. See **Teacher's SourceBook,** p. 45

Visit our website:
www.mcdougallittell.com

THE DOG OF POMPEII

by Louis Untermeyer

Tito and his dog Bimbo lived (if you could call it living) under the wall where it joined the inner gate. They really didn't live there; they just slept there. They lived anywhere. Pompeii was one of the gayest of the old Latin towns, but although Tito was never an unhappy boy, he was not exactly a merry one. The streets were always lively with shining chariots and bright red trappings; the open-air

Cave Canem [Beware of dog], Roman mosaic. Museo Archeologico Nazionale, Naples, Italy. Scala/Art Resource, New York.

701

HISTORICAL FICTION

Ⓐ To help students recognize the distinguishing features of historical fiction, point out that this genre contains details about real places, events, and sometimes people. Ask students what real events and people are mentioned in the first paragraph.
Possible Responses: theatrical performances, sports, Caesar's visit; Caesar.

 Use **Unit Five Resource Book**, p. 53 for more practice.

Active Reading

DISTINGUISHING FACT FROM NONFACT

Ⓑ To help students distinguish fact from nonfact, ask which details in this paragraph are likely to come from the writer's imagination. In other words, which cannot be proved true or false?
Possible Responses: Tito dreaming; how Bimbo sat and yawned; Bimbo putting his paw on Tito's knee

 Use **Unit Five Resource Book**, p. 52 for more practice.
Use **Reading and Critical Thinking Transparencies**, p. 26, for additional support.

ACTIVE READING

Ⓒ **SUMMARIZE** Possible Response: Bimbo provides food three times a day.

Literary Analysis: NARRATOR

Remind students that a narrator is the person who tells a story. Ask students if the narrator of this story is a story character. Have them explain how they know.
Possible Response: No, he refers to all the characters in the third-person.

Ⓐ theaters rocked with laughing crowds; sham battles and athletic sports were free for the asking in the great stadium. Once a year the Caesar[1] visited the pleasure city, and the fireworks lasted for days; the sacrifices[2] in the forum were better than a show. But Tito saw none of these things. He was blind—had been blind from birth. He was known to everyone in the poorer quarters. But no one could say how old he was; no one remembered his parents; no one could tell where he came from. Bimbo was another mystery. As long as people could remember seeing Tito—about twelve or thirteen years—they had seen Bimbo. Bimbo had never left his side. He was not only dog but nurse, pillow, playmate, mother, and father to Tito.

Did I say Bimbo never left his master? (Perhaps I had better say comrade, for if anyone was the master, it was Bimbo.) I was wrong. Bimbo did trust Tito alone exactly three times a day. It was a fixed routine, a custom understood between boy and dog since the beginning of their friendship, and the way it worked was this: Early in the morning, shortly after dawn, while Tito was Ⓑ still dreaming, Bimbo would disappear. When Tito woke, Bimbo would be sitting quietly at his side, his ears cocked, his stump of a tail Ⓒ tapping the ground, and a fresh-baked bread—more like a large round roll—at his feet. Tito would stretch himself; Bimbo would yawn; then they would breakfast. At noon, no matter where they happened to be, Bimbo would put his paw on Tito's knee, and the two of them would return to the inner gate. Tito would curl **1** up in the corner (almost like a dog) and go to sleep, while Bimbo, looking quite important (almost like a boy), would disappear again. In

> **THERE WAS PLENTY OF EVERYTHING IN POMPEII IF YOU KNEW WHERE TO FIND IT—AND IF YOU HAD A DOG LIKE BIMBO.**

half an hour he'd be back with their lunch. Sometimes it would be a piece of fruit or a scrap of meat; often it was nothing but a dry crust. But sometimes there would be one of those flat, rich cakes, sprinkled with raisins and sugar, that Tito liked so much. At suppertime the same thing happened, although Ⓑ there was a little less of everything, for things were hard to snatch in the evening with the streets full of people. Besides, Bimbo didn't approve of too much food before going to sleep. A heavy supper made boys too restless and dogs too stodgy—and it was the business of a dog to sleep lightly with one ear open and muscles ready for action.

But whether there was much or little, hot or cold, fresh or dry, food was always there. Tito never asked where it came from, and Bimbo never told him. There was plenty of rainwater in the hollows of soft stones; the old egg-woman at the corner sometimes gave him a cupful of strong goat's milk; in the grape season the fat winemaker let him have drippings of the mild juice. So there was no danger of going hungry or thirsty. There was plenty of everything in Pompeii if you knew where to find it—and if you had a dog like Bimbo.

ACTIVE READING

SUMMARIZE How does Bimbo care for Tito?

As I said before, Tito was not the merriest boy in Pompeii. He could not romp with the other youngsters and play hare and hounds and I spy and follow-your-master and ball-against-the-building and

---

1. **the Caesar** (sē′zər): the Roman emperor.
2. **sacrifices:** offerings of animals or objects to the gods.

Teaching Options

BLOCK SCHEDULING: MANAGING TIME

If your schedule requires that you cover the lesson objectives in a shorter time, use . . .
- Preparing to Read, p. 700
- Thinking Through the Literature, p. 711
- Vocabulary in Action, p. 712
- Grammar in Context, p. 713

If you want to take advantage of longer class time, use . . .
- TE Teaching Options: Preteaching Vocabulary, p. 701; Viewing and Representing, pp. 703, 707; Cross-Curricular Links, pp. 704, 705; Multicultural Link, p. 706; Spelling, p. 708; Standardized Test Practice, p. 709; Vocabulary Strategy, p. 710; Speaking and Listening, p. 712; Grammar, p. 713;
- Choices & Challenges and Author Activity, pp. 712–713

jackstones and kings and robbers with them. But that did not make him sorry for himself. If he could not see the sights that delighted the lads of Pompeii, he could hear and smell things they never noticed. He could really see more with his ears and nose than they could with their eyes. When he and Bimbo went out walking, he knew just where they were going and exactly what was happening.

"Ah," he'd sniff and say as they passed a handsome villa, "Glaucus Pansa is giving a grand dinner tonight. They're going to have three kinds of bread, and roast pigling, and stuffed goose, and a great stew—I think bear stew—and a fig pie." And Bimbo would note that this would be a good place to visit tomorrow.

Or, "H'm," Tito would murmur, half through his lips, half through his nostrils. "The wife of Marcus Lucretius is expecting her

2

The Sorceress and the Traveler. Mosaic from Pompeii, House of the Dioscuri. Museo Archeologico Nazionale, Naples, Italy. Scala/Art Resource, New York.

ACTIVE READING

A FACT AND OPINION Possible Responses: Students might mention the following as true: There were no private houses, and buildings were replaced after the earthquake. Opinions might include the following: everything glittered, and citizens were ambitious.

ACTIVE READING

B FACT AND NONFACT Possible Responses: Imaginary parts of the conversation might include bath master Rufus's opinion that there will be no more earthquakes. Those based on fact include the two towns destroyed three times in 15 years by earthquakes.

Literary Analysis

HISTORICAL FICTION

Remind students that historical fiction is like any other fiction in many ways. To help students find similarities across texts, such as in treatment, scope, or organization, discuss what they already know about the elements of fiction. Have them identify the setting and characters and predict what the central conflict might be, based on story clues.

Possible Responses: The setting is ancient Pompeii; the characters include Tito and Bimbo; the central conflict will probably center around the eruption of Mount Vesuvius.

---

mother. She's shaking out every piece of goods in the house; she's going to use the best clothes—the ones she's been keeping in pine needles and camphor[3]—and there's an extra girl in the kitchen. Come, Bimbo, let's get out of the dust!"

Or, as they passed a small but elegant dwelling opposite the public baths, "Too bad! The tragic poet is ill again. It must be a bad fever this time, for they're trying smoke fumes instead of medicine. Whew! I'm glad I'm not a tragic poet!"

Or, as they neared the forum, "Mm-m! What good things they have in the macellum today!" (It really was a sort of butcher-grocer-marketplace, but Tito didn't know any better. He called it the macellum.) "Dates from Africa, and salt oysters from sea caves, and cuttlefish, and new honey, and sweet onions, and—ugh!—water-buffalo steaks. Come, let's see what's what in the forum." And Bimbo, just as curious as his comrade, hurried on. Being a dog, he trusted his ears and nose (like Tito) more than his eyes. And so the two of them entered the center of Pompeii.

The forum was the part of the town to which everybody came at least once during each day. It was the central square, and everything happened here. There were no private houses; all was public—the chief temples, the gold and red bazaars, the silk shops, the town hall, the booths belonging to the weavers and jewel merchants, the wealthy woolen market, the shrine of the household gods. Everything glittered here. The buildings looked as if they were new—which, in a sense, they were. The earthquake of twelve years ago had brought down all the old structures, and since the citizens of Pompeii were ambitious to

ACTIVE READING

FACT AND OPINION
Which parts of this description of the buildings could be proved to be true? Which are opinion?

rival Naples and even Rome, they had seized the opportunity to rebuild the whole town. And they had done it all within a dozen years. There was scarcely a building that was older than Tito.

Tito had heard a great deal about the earthquake, though being about a year old at the time, he could scarcely remember it. This particular quake had been a light one—as earthquakes go. The weaker houses had been shaken down; parts of the outworn wall had been wrecked; but there was little loss of life, and the brilliant new Pompeii had taken the place of the old. No one knew what caused these earthquakes. Records showed they had happened in the neighborhood since the beginning of time. Sailors said that it was to teach the lazy city folk a lesson and make them appreciate those who risked the dangers of the sea to bring them luxuries and protect their town from invaders. The priests said that the gods took this way of showing their anger to those who refused to worship properly and who failed to bring enough sacrifices to the altars and (though they didn't say it in so many words) presents to the priests. The tradesmen said that the foreign merchants had corrupted the ground and it was no longer safe to traffic in imported goods that came from strange places and carried a curse with them. Everyone had a different explanation—and everyone's explanation was louder and sillier than his neighbor's.

They were talking about it this afternoon as Tito and Bimbo came out of the side street

---

3. **camphor** (kăm′fər): a strong-smelling substance used as a moth repellent.

WORDS TO KNOW   **shrine** (shrīn) *n.* a place of worship

704

704   UNIT FIVE   PART 2

Teaching Options

Cross Curricular Link   Science

VOLCANOES Although Italy has seen some terrible eruptions, including the one that buried Pompeii, most active volcanoes form in a region called The Ring of Fire, an area that rims the Pacific Ocean. Here plates, or huge sections of the earth's crust, lying beneath the Pacific Ocean meet plates that lie beneath surrounding land forms. Many volcanoes form where plates meet.

Two famous Indonesian eruptions were said to be even more powerful than that of Vesuvius:

• In 1815, Mt. Tambora blew its top and created devastating tidal waves and storms. The ash from the eruption affected weather around the globe. Approximately 90,000 people died, either during the eruption itself or afterward.

• In 1883, Mt. Krakatoa exploded with a noise that could be heard thousands of miles away. The ash and tidal waves wiped out 36,000 people.

into the public square. The forum was the favorite promenade[4] for rich and poor. What with the priests arguing with the politicians, servants doing the day's shopping, tradesmen crying their wares, women displaying the latest fashions from Greece and Egypt, children playing hide-and-seek among the marble columns, knots of soldiers, sailors, peasants from the provinces[5]—to say nothing of those who merely came to lounge and look on—the square was crowded to its last inch. His ears even more than his nose guided Tito to the place where the talk was loudest. It was in front of the shrine of the household gods that, naturally enough, the householders were arguing.

"I tell you," rumbled a voice which Tito recognized as bath master Rufus's, "there won't be another earthquake in my lifetime or yours. There may be a tremble or two, but earthquakes, like lightnings, never strike twice in the same place."

"Do they not?" asked a thin voice Tito had never heard. It had a high, sharp ring to it, and Tito knew it as the accent of a stranger. "How about the two towns of Sicily that have been ruined three times within fifteen years by the eruptions of Mount Etna? And were they not warned? And does that column of smoke above Vesuvius mean nothing?"

ACTIVE READING

FACT AND NONFACT In your opinion, which elements of this conversation are imaginary? Which are based on fact?

"That?" Tito could hear the grunt with which one question answered another. "That's always there. We use it for our weather guide. When the smoke stands up straight, we know we'll have fair weather; when it flattens out, it's sure to be foggy; when it drifts to the east—"

"Yes, yes," cut in the edged voice. "I've heard about your mountain barometer. But the column of smoke seems hundreds of feet higher than usual, and it's thickening and spreading like a shadowy tree. They say in Naples—"

"Oh, Naples!" Tito knew this voice by the little squeak that went with it. It was Attilio, the cameo[6] cutter. "*They talk while we suffer.* Little help we got from them last time. Naples commits the crimes, and Pompeii pays the price. It's become a proverb with us. Let them mind their own business."

"Yes," grumbled Rufus, "and others, too."

"Very well, my confident friends," responded the thin voice, which now sounded curiously flat. "We also have a proverb—and it is this: Those who will not listen to men must be taught by the gods. I say no more. But I leave a last warning. Remember the holy ones. Look to your temples. And when the smoke tree above Vesuvius grows to the shape of an umbrella pine, look to your lives."

Tito could hear the air whistle as the speaker drew his toga about him, and the

> IT WAS THE CENTRAL SQUARE, AND EVERYTHING HAPPENED HERE. . . . EVERYTHING GLITTERED HERE.

---

4. **promenade** (prŏm'ə-nād'): a public place for leisurely walking.

5. **provinces:** areas of a country that are far from the capital.

6. **cameo** (kăm'ē-ō'): a gem or shell with a picture carved on it.

WORDS TO KNOW

eruption (ĭ-rŭp'shən) *n.* an outburst or throwing forth of lava, water, steam, and other materials

---

Customizing Instruction

Students Acquiring English

1 Be sure students understand that *Mm-m* represents a sound Tito makes to indicate his appreciation of the smell of food. Model the appropriate intonation of *mm-m!* and the exclamation "What good things they have in the macellum today!" In a similar way, explain the sound *ugh* two sentences later.

Less Proficient Readers

Ask the following questions to make sure students understand the story so far.

1. How does Tito know what is going on inside the houses?
   Possible Response: He smells things and knows how to interpret the smells.
2. Why was Pompeii rebuilt?
   Possible Response: An earthquake had destroyed many buildings, and the citizens had rebuilt the whole town.
3. What are the bath master and the stranger talking about?
   Possible Response: They are talking about whether there will be another earthquake—whether to worry about the smoke above Vesuvius or not.

Set a Purpose Have students read to find out if the stranger or the local people are correct.

Gifted and Talented

2 Students may wish to discover and explain why the smoke rises straight up in good weather and flattens out in foggy weather.

Cross Curricular Link **History**

POMPEII In A.D. 62, seventeen years before Vesuvius erupted, a strong earthquake had damaged Pompeii and the neighboring city of Herculaneum. Scientists now believe that Vesuvius was trying to erupt then, but that people did not understand the warning.
The blast that occurred in A.D. 79 was 10 times more powerful than the 1980 eruption of Mount St. Helens in the state of Washington.

Literary Analysis

HISTORICAL FICTION

A Ask students what they learn here about the activities in ancient Pompeii.
Possible Response: Caesar's birthday is celebrated with food and theater.

ACTIVE READING

B **VISUALIZE** Possible Responses: "The air was hot. And heavy", "[it] turned to . . . warm powder that stung his nostrils and burned his . . . eyes"; "Peculiar sounds"; "Hissings and groanings and muffled cries. . . ."

Active Reading

DISTINGUISHING FACT FROM NONFACT

Ask students which elements of this day are probably imaginary and which are based on fact. Discuss with students how writers might discover facts about something that happened long ago.
Possible Responses: The heat and heaviness of the air, the burning powder, the sounds, and the hot water are probably based on fact. The people's cries and movements are probably from the writer's imagination. Writers could learn the factual information through research.

quick shuffle of feet told him the stranger had gone.

"Now what," said the cameo cutter, "did he mean by that?"

"I wonder," grunted Rufus. "I wonder."

Tito wondered, too. And Bimbo, his head at a thoughtful angle, looked as if he had been doing a heavy piece of pondering. By nightfall the argument had been forgotten. If the smoke had increased, no one saw it in the dark. Besides, it was Caesar's birthday, and the town was in holiday mood. Tito and Bimbo were among the merrymakers, dodging the charioteers who shouted at them. A dozen times they almost upset baskets of sweets and jars of Vesuvian wine, said to be as fiery as the streams inside the volcano, and a dozen times they were cursed and cuffed. But Tito never missed his footing. He was thankful for his keen ears and quick instinct—most thankful of all for Bimbo.

A

> THE NOISES CAME FROM UNDERNEATH. HE NOT ONLY HEARD THEM—HE COULD FEEL THEM.

They visited the uncovered theater, and though Tito could not see the faces of the actors, he could follow the play better than most of the audience, for their attention wandered—they were distracted by the scenery, the costumes, the by-play, even by themselves— while Tito's whole attention was centered in what he heard. Then to the city walls, where the people of Pompeii watched a mock naval battle in which the city was attacked by the sea and saved after thousands of flaming arrows had been exchanged and countless colored torches had been burned. Though the thrill of flaring ships and lighted skies was lost to Tito, the shouts and cheers excited him as much as any, and he cried out with the loudest of them.

1

The next morning there were *two* of the beloved raisin and sugar cakes for his breakfast. Bimbo was unusually active and thumped his bit of a tail until Tito was afraid he would wear it out. The boy could not imagine whether Bimbo was urging him to some sort of game or was trying to tell him something. After a while, he ceased to notice Bimbo. He felt drowsy. Last night's late hours had tired him. Besides, there was a heavy mist in the air—no, a thick fog rather than a mist— a fog that got into his throat and scraped it and made him cough. He walked as far as the marine gate[7] to get a breath of the sea. But the blanket of haze had spread all over the bay, and even the salt air seemed smoky.

He went to bed before dusk and slept. But he did not sleep well. He had too many dreams— dreams of ships lurching in the forum, of losing his way in a screaming crowd, of armies marching across his chest, of being pulled over every rough pavement of Pompeii.

He woke early. Or, rather, he was pulled awake. Bimbo was doing the pulling. The dog had dragged Tito to his feet and was urging the boy along. Somewhere. Where, Tito did not know. His feet stumbled uncertainly; he was still half asleep. For a while he noticed nothing except the fact that it was hard to breathe. The air was hot. And heavy. So heavy that he could taste it. The air, it seemed, had turned

ACTIVE READING

B **VISUALIZE** What sensory details help you to visualize this description?

---

7. **marine gate:** a gate in the city wall, leading to the sea.

2

Teaching Options

Multicultural Link   Fireworks

This page mentions that fireworks are set off during the Caesar's visit to Pompeii. To help students articulate and discuss themes and connections that cross cultures, point out that a number of holidays worldwide are celebrated with fireworks.

- Many Chinese celebrate the New Year with fireworks, which are supposed to scare away evil spirits.
- Fireworks are part of the Indian festival called Diwali, or the Feast of Lights.

- In Vietnam, celebrants set off firecrackers on the last day of the Tet celebration.
- In some places in Mexico, the Day of the Dead is marked with fireworks that are set off to guide the spirits of loved ones home.
- In the United States, Independence Day, the Fourth of July, is usually marked by fireworks displays.

Mount Vesuvius in Eruption (1817), Joseph Mallord William Turner, R.A., 1775–1851. Yale Center for British Art, New Haven, Connecticut, Paul Mellon Collection.

to powder, a warm powder that stung his nostrils and burned his sightless eyes.

Then he began to hear sounds. Peculiar sounds. Like animals under the earth. Hissings and groanings and muffled cries that a dying creature might make dislodging the stones of his underground cave. There was no doubt of it now. The noises came from underneath. He not only heard them—he could feel them. The earth twitched; the twitching changed to an uneven shrugging of the soil. Then, as Bimbo half pulled, half coaxed him across, the ground jerked away from his feet and he was thrown against a stone fountain.

The water—hot water—splashing in his face revived him. He got to his feet, Bimbo steadying him, helping him on again. The noises grew louder; they came closer. The cries were even more animal-like than before, but now they came from human throats. A few people, quicker of foot and more hurried by fear, began to rush by. A family or two—then a section—then, it seemed, an army broken out of bounds. Tito, bewildered though he

WORDS
TO
KNOW

dislodging (dĭs-lŏj′ĭng) *adj.* moving from a settled position **dislodge** *v.*

707

Less Proficient Students

1 You may wish to help students by having them summarize in their own words what Tito does on this night: He celebrates Caesar's birthday with other townspeople, going to theater, where he listens to the performance.

To help students follow the story, ask the following questions:

1. What was Pompeii celebrating?
   Answer: Caesar's birthday
2. Why weren't people paying attention to the increasing smoke?
   Possible Response: They were too busy having fun.
3. What does Bimbo do in the morning, and what does Tito notice?
   Possible Responses: Bimbo gives Tito two cakes and pulls the boy along; Tito notices that the air has warm powder in it; he hears underground noises and yelling people.
4. What is scaring the people and causing the hot air, the rumbling noises, and the hot water in the fountain?
   Answer: Vesuvius is erupting.

Set a Purpose Instruct students to pay attention to what happens to Tito during the volcanic eruption.

Gifted and Talented

2 Many people believe that animals can predict seismic activity, such as earthquakes and eruptions. Ask students what animals might notice that humans do not.

Mini Lesson Viewing and Representing

Mount Vesuvius in Eruption
by Joseph Mallord William Turner, R. A. (1775–1851)

ART APPRECIATION The British artist J. M. W. Turner ranks among the greatest of all landscape painters. He liked to paint epic scenes of natural catastrophes, of which this painting is a prime example.

Instruction To help students interpret and evaluate the various ways visual image makers such as illustrators represent meaning, remind them that artists decide on a picture's color, composition, and style. When they look at paintings, they should look at the size and placement of objects, the color, and the overall message that these convey.

Application Ask students how the artist conveyed the size of the eruption, as well as its heat, its danger, and its effect on people.

Possible Responses: The volcano is in the center of the picture and the eruption fills most of the picture. The artist uses red and yellow to show the heat—even the water is red. The people look tiny by comparison, and they seem to be huddled at one edge of the picture.

Reading and Analyzing

A **CONNECT** Possible Responses:
Students might mention confusion,
fear, or some other strong emotion.

Literary Analysis: SIMILE

B Remind students that a simile is a
comparison of two things that have
some quality in common. Ask students
what two things the writer is comparing
here, and what the comparison suggests about what Tito is experiencing.
Possible Responses: He is comparing
the earth and a caught snake; it suggests how wildly the earth was moving.

Literary Analysis
HISTORICAL FICTION

C Point out that a piece of historical
fiction, like any other story, has a plot
that contains rising action that leads to
a climax. Ask students to identify details
that are part of the rising action and
those that are part of the climax.
Possible Responses: Rising action:
running with no sense of direction; the
worry about being trampled; Tito's collapse. Climax: reaching the gate and
fainting in the sand.

Active Reading
DISTINGUISHING FACT
FROM NONFACT

Ask students which parts of the description of the eruption are likely to be
based on factual information, and which
come from the writer's imagination.
Possible Responses: Students might
suggest that the following are based on
fact: the blackness; the wriggling earth;
people racing toward the sea gate; the
bubbling pools; the dust and pebbles
falling; the red hot ash. The rest of the
details are probably from the author's
imagination.

The volcanic ash that covered victims of the Pompeii disaster hardened over time. Archaeologists used the resulting "shells" as molds for body casts. © Krafft/Explorer, Photo Researchers.

ACTIVE READING

A **CONNECT** Do you recall a
personal experience in
which time seemed to
"stand still"? What
caused this feeling?

was, could recognize
Rufus as he bellowed
past him, like a water
buffalo gone mad. Time
was lost in a nightmare.

It was then the
crashing began. First a
sharp crackling, like a monstrous snapping
of twigs; then a roar like the fall of a whole
forest of trees; then an explosion that tore
earth and sky. The heavens, though Tito
could not see them, were shot through with
continual flickerings of fire. Lightnings above
were answered by thunders beneath. A house
fell. Then another. By a miracle the two
companions had escaped the dangerous side

streets and were in a more open space. It was
the forum. They rested here awhile—how long
he did not know.

Tito had no idea of the time of day. He
could *feel* it was black—an unnatural
blackness. Something inside—perhaps the lack
of breakfast and lunch—told him it was past
noon. But it didn't matter. Nothing seemed to
matter. He was getting drowsy, too drowsy to
walk. But walk he must. He knew it. And
Bimbo knew it; the sharp tugs told him so.
Nor was it a moment too soon. The sacred
ground of the forum was safe no longer. It was
beginning to rock, then to pitch, then to split.
As they stumbled out of the square, the earth
wriggled like a caught snake, and all the

Teaching Options

(Mini Lesson) Spelling

WORDS WITH SUFFIXES

Instruction To help students write with accurate
spelling of suffixes, remind them that when a suffix is added to a word that ends in silent *e*, the *e*
is dropped if the suffix begins with a vowel but is
kept if the suffix begins with a consonant.
Examples:
scarcely   wriggled   choked
Exercise Have students write the word produced
by adding each suffix.

1. hate + ing
2. irritate + ing
3. chime + ing
4. inflate + able
5. taste + ful
6. advise + able
7. peace + ful
8. blame + less
9. strange + ly
10. amuse + ment
11. hope + less
12. shame + ful

Ask students to look through the selection to find
more words that fit this pattern and to write them
in their personal word lists.

 Use **Unit Five Resource Book**, p. 56.

columns of the temple of Jupiter[8] came down. It was the end of the world—or so it seemed.

To walk was not enough now. They must run. Tito was too frightened to know what to do or where to go. He had lost all sense of direction. He started to go back to the inner gate; but Bimbo, straining his back to the last inch, almost pulled his clothes from him. What did the creature want? Had the dog gone mad?

Then, suddenly, he understood. Bimbo was telling him the way out—urging him there. The sea gate, of course. The sea gate—and then the sea. Far from falling buildings, heaving ground. He turned, Bimbo guiding him across open pits and dangerous pools of bubbling mud, away from buildings that had caught fire and were dropping their burning beams. Tito could no longer tell whether the noises were made by the shrieking sky or the agonized people. He and Bimbo ran on—the only silent beings in a howling world.

New dangers threatened. All Pompeii seemed to be thronging toward the marine gate; and, squeezing among the crowds, there was the chance of being trampled to death. But the chance had to be taken. It was growing harder and harder to breathe. What air there was choked him. It was all dust now—dust and pebbles, pebbles as large as beans. They fell on his head, his hands—pumice[9] stones from the black heart of Vesuvius. The mountain was turning itself inside out. Tito remembered a phrase that the

stranger had said in the forum two days ago: "Those who will not listen to men must be taught by the gods." The people of Pompeii had refused to heed the warnings; they were being taught now—if it was not too late.

Suddenly it seemed too late for Tito. The red hot ashes blistered his skin; the stinging vapors tore his throat. He could not go on. He staggered toward a small tree at the side of the road and fell. In a moment Bimbo was beside him. He coaxed. But there was no answer. He licked Tito's hands, his feet, his face. The boy did not stir. Then Bimbo did the last thing he could—the last thing he wanted to do. He bit his comrade, bit him deep in the arm. With a cry of pain, Tito jumped to his feet, Bimbo after him. Tito was in despair, but Bimbo was determined. He drove the boy on, snapping at his heels, worrying his way through the crowd; barking, baring his teeth, heedless of kicks or falling stones. Sick with hunger, half dead with fear and sulphur[10] fumes, Tito pounded on, pursued by Bimbo. How long he never knew. At last he staggered through the marine gate and felt soft sand under him. Then Tito fainted. . . .

Someone was dashing seawater over him. Someone was carrying him toward a boat. "Bimbo," he called. And then louder, "Bimbo!" But Bimbo had disappeared.

ALL POMPEII SEEMED TO BE THRONGING TOWARD THE MARINE GATE . . . . THERE WAS THE CHANCE OF BEING TRAMPLED TO DEATH.

---

8. **Jupiter:** the supreme god in Roman mythology.

9. **pumice** (pŭm'ĭs): a light rock formed from lava.

10. **sulphur** (sŭl'fər): a pale yellow chemical element that produces a choking fume when burned.

WORDS TO KNOW

vapor (vā'pər) *n.* fumes, mist, or smoke

709

Customizing Instruction

Students Acquiring English
Help students understand the following, which use inverted order or sentence fragments:
1 "But walk he must"
2 "The sea gate, of course. The sea gate—and then the sea. Far from falling buildings, heaving ground."

Multiple Learning Styles
Visual Learners
Ask students how they picture the flight from Pompeii. If they were illustrating this scene, what visual images would they select, and render to complement the story's meaning?
Possible Responses: They might show the flickering lightning, the heaving ground, the burning buildings, and the dog biting the boy.

Less Proficient Readers
Ask students whether they think that Tito could find his way to the sea gate without Bimbo's help.
Possible Response: No, because he has lost his sense of direction and wants to stop, and because he needs Bimbo to guide him around the obstacles.

Set a Purpose Have students read to find out what happens to Tito and Bimbo as the story concludes.

✓ **Assessment** **Standardized Test Practice**

DRAWING LOGICAL CONCLUSIONS In some standardized tests, students are asked to draw conclusions and to support them with text evidence and experience. To provide students with some help in evaluating, read aloud or write he following item:
The reader can tell that the eruption
A. was beautiful.
B. came without any warning.
C. terrified people.
D. killed every man, woman, and child.

Lead students through the process of choosing the best answer. Help them recognize that no evidence supports answer D. The smoking mountain and previous eruptions were warnings, so B is incorrect. Everyone's reaction is more of terror than of admiration, so C is a stronger choice than A. Several details, including rushing, crying people, "red hot ashes," "stinging vapors," and "pain," support answer C. Therefore, the best answer is C.

Petrified bread from Pompeii.
Museo Archeologico Nazionale,
Naples, Italy. Alinari/Art
Resource, New York.

Voices jarred against each other. "Hurry—hurry!" "To the boats!" "Can't you see the child's frightened and starving!" "He keeps calling for someone!" "Poor boy, he's out of his mind." "Here, child—take this!"

They tucked him in among them. The oarlocks creaked; the oars splashed; the boat rode over toppling waves. Tito was safe. But he wept continually.

"Bimbo!" he wailed. "Bimbo! Bimbo!" He could not be comforted.

Eighteen hundred years passed. Scientists were <u>restoring</u> the ancient city; excavators were working their way through the stones and trash that had buried the entire town. Much had already been brought to light—statues, bronze instruments, bright mosaics,[11] household articles; even delicate paintings had been preserved by the fall of ashes that had taken over two thousand lives. Columns were dug up, and the forum was beginning to emerge.

It was at a place where the ruins lay deepest that the director paused.

"Come here," he called to his assistant. "I think we've discovered the remains of a building in good shape. Here are four huge millstones that were most likely turned by slaves or mules—and here is a whole wall standing with shelves inside it. Why! It must have been a bakery. And here's a curious thing. What do you think I found under this heap where the ashes were thickest? The skeleton of a dog!"

"Amazing!" gasped his assistant. "You'd think a dog would have had sense enough to run away at the time. And what is that flat thing he's holding between his teeth? It can't be a stone."

"No. It must have come from this bakery. You know it looks to me like some sort of cake hardened with the years. And, bless me, if those little black pebbles aren't raisins. A raisin cake almost two thousand years old! I wonder what made him want it at such a moment."

"I wonder," murmured the assistant.

---

11. **mosaics** (mō-zā′ĭks): pictures or designs made by setting small colored stones or tiles into surfaces.

| WORDS TO KNOW | **restore** (rĭ-stôr′) v. to bring back to an original condition |

710

Connect to the Literature

1. What Do You Think? How did you feel after reading the story?

Comprehension Check
- How does Tito get the food he eats?
- Why does Bimbo pull Tito awake the morning after the emperor's birthday?
- How does Tito manage to escape?

Think Critically

2. Louis Untermeyer ends the story of the disaster 1,800 years later. Why do you think he does this?

3. Do you think Bimbo is a realistic character? Defend your answer with evidence from the story.

 THINK ABOUT
- Bimbo's role in Tito's everyday life
- how Bimbo responds to the volcanic eruption

4. **ACTIVE READING** **DISTINGUISHING FACT FROM NONFACT**
With a partner, go over the chart you made in your READER'S NOTEBOOK. Does the story seem more like history or more like fiction? Explain.

Extend Interpretations

5. **COMPARING TEXTS** Think back to Lob's relationship with Sandy in "Lob's Girl" (page 447). How is it similar to Bimbo's relationship with Tito? How do both dogs show courage and loyalty to their people?

6. Critic's Corner One critic believes that the role of historical fiction is to help readers see the "similarities and differences in people from other times and places." What similarities do you see between life in ancient Pompeii and the United States today?

7. Connect to Life What did you learn about the city of Pompeii that you didn't know before? Record any new information in the last column of the chart you made for the Connect to Your Life activity.

Literary Analysis

HISTORICAL FICTION Literature that brings a period of history to life through a writer's imagination is called **historical fiction.** From such literature you learn not only the facts about historical events but also the feelings people may have had. In reading "The Dog of Pompeii," what did you learn about how people may have felt when Mt. Vesuvius erupted?

REVIEW **CONFLICT** Most stories revolve around a **conflict**—a struggle between opposing forces. An **external conflict** is a struggle between a character and an outside force such as a natural disaster or a rival character. An **internal conflict** occurs within a character's mind. It may be the opposing ideas or feelings that arise in facing a tough decision.

Cooperative Learning Activity
In a small group, discuss how Louis Untermeyer uses the elements of fiction in "The Dog of Pompeii." Who are the main characters? What events lead to a climax, or turning point? How is the setting important? What do you think is the theme?

Connect to the Literature

1. What Do You Think?
Responses will vary. Students may feel wonder, surprise, or confusion about whether to believe the last scene.

Comprehension Check
- Bimbo steals raisin cakes and food scraps three times a day.
- Bimbo wakes Tito because the volcano has begun to erupt.
- Tito boards a boat and goes out to sea.

Use Selection Quiz
Unit Five Resource Book, p. 57.

Think Critically

2. Possible Response: The ending reveals what happened to Bimbo after Tito left the city. In addition, it shows Bimbo's loyalty and heroism because the raisin cake found in his mouth shows that he died trying to take care of Tito.

3. Possible Responses: He is realistic, because he acts like a loyal dog, caring for and protecting Tito. He is not realistic, because he shows too many human qualities.

4. Possible Responses: It has so many facts that it seems more like history. It has such a good plot that it seems more like a story.

Use **Reading and Critical Thinking Transparencies**, p. 26, for additional support.

Literary Analysis

Historical Fiction Students should mention as the main characters Bimbo and Tito. The events leading up to the climax might include overhearing the conversation on the street and awakening to the hot and heavy air. The setting is crucial because it creates the story's main conflict and affects the characters' actions. The theme might be a dog's loyalty, or that people need to show respect for nature's powers.

Use **Literary Analysis Transparencies**, p. 8, for additional support.

Extend Interpretations

5. Comparing Texts Both relationships are based on a deep bond that is revealed through daily interaction. Both dogs demonstrate their devotion in ways that seem amazing, touching, and even puzzling.

6. Critic's Corner Possible Responses: Pompeii and cities in the United States both have lively urban streets, crowding, and traffic. Both have theaters, athletic events, bakeries, public places, new buildings and various foods for sale. Both have wealthy citizens and people who live in the streets.

7. Connect to Life Responses will vary. Some students may be surprised that the eruption occurred so quickly that people could not escape. They may be interested that such a complex city existed so long ago. They may be surprised at some of the details about volcanic eruptions. **To extend this activity**, suggest that students do more research on one aspect that they recorded.

Writing Options

1. **Sensory Interview** Students' interviews should not contain any visual details. To get students started on this assignment, suggest that they begin by listing sensory details from the story and then use those details as the basis for their interviews.

📄 Use **Writing Transparencies**, p. 16, for additional support.

Activities & Explorations

1. **Live News Report** Students may enjoy working in teams, as many news professionals do. One announcer provides certain details and then switches to another announcer.

2. **Proverb Poster** Encourage **students acquiring English** to offer proverbs from their cultures. These might be displayed in the original languages as well as in English translations.

3. **Media Comparison** Students' comparisons should show a clear understanding of the relationships of the various characters to the animals in the stories.

Art Connection

Informative Images Encourage students to focus on the animal's posture and expression and its being leashed.

Inquiry & Research

Dig It Many times, archaeological discoveries are made during public works projects that include new highways and subway excavation. One way to learn about such discoveries would be to interview older residents.

📄 Use **Writing Transparencies**, p. 44, for additional support.

Vocabulary in Action

EXERCISE A
1. S—mist, gas
2. A—fix, rebuild
3. S—outburst, outbreak
4. S—sanctuary, chapel
5. A—loosening, removing

EXERCISE B
Students might enjoy making some of their drawings mosaic style, using graph paper to help them.

Writing Options

Sensory Interview Write an interview with Tito about his final day in Pompeii. Include only his sensory impressions of hearing, tasting, smelling, and feeling.

Activities & Explorations

1. **Live News Report** Naples and Pompeii lie on opposite sides of a large bay. Imagine you are safely in Naples on the day Vesuvius erupts. Write a live news report of what you see happening in Pompeii, and present it to your class.
~ **SPEAKING AND LISTENING**

2. **Proverb Poster** A stranger in the forum says, "Those who will not listen to men must be taught by the gods." Think of other proverbs or sayings that relate to the events in the story and display them on a poster with illustrations.
~ **VIEWING AND REPRESENTING**

3. **Media Comparison** Think about the similarities and differences between this story and other accounts of loyal pets, such as "Older Run" or "Zlateh the Goat." Use writing and illustration to present a brief summary of each story. Present your summaries and graphics in a poster, slide show, or videotape. ~ **VIEWING AND REPRESENTING**

Art Connection

Informative Images Look at the mosaic of the dog. In Pompeii, homeowners warned off robbers by placing mosaics like this at the entrance of their homes. On some of these mosaics, the words *Cave canem* (kä'wā kä'nĕm), meaning "Beware of Dog," appear. Even without this message, how can you tell that the mosaic serves as a warning?

Inquiry & Research

Dig It Archaeological discoveries have been made just about everywhere people have lived. In the United States, some scientists search landfills and dumps for information about recent decades. Using the library or the Internet, find a newspaper or magazine article describing an archaeological discovery in your state.

 Real World Link Before beginning your research, read "A 9,500-Year-Old Summer Home" on page 714.

Vocabulary in Action

EXERCISE A: SYNONYMS AND ANTONYMS Identify each pair of words as synonyms or antonyms by writing *synonym* or *antonym* next to each on your paper. Then write a new synonym for each Word to Know.

1. **vapor**—fume
2. **restore**—destroy
3. **eruption**—explosion
4. **shrine**—temple
5. **dislodging**—replacing

EXERCISE B Draw pictures that show the meaning of each Word to Know. Hang them on a bulletin board and invite your classmates to guess which word each picture illustrates.

Building Vocabulary
For an in-depth lesson on using synonyms and antonyms, see p. 230.

Teaching Options Mini Lesson **Speaking and Listening**

READING ALOUD
Prepare Tell students that reading aloud is a way of sharing stories and poems with others. To provide practice in reading aloud in ways that both reflect understanding of the text and engage the listeners, have students silently reread the conversation in the public square on page 705. Ask what they can do when they read this aloud to help listeners understand the scene and enjoy hearing it. *(Examples: They could read with expression. They could use gestures.)*
Have students work in groups to practice reading this part of the story aloud. First, they should

assign roles and practice reading them individually. Then they should all rehearse the entire scene.
Present Have students take turns presenting their scenes to their classmates and sharing feedback with each other on how they could improve their presentations.

BLOCK SCHEDULING This activity is particularly well suited for longer class periods.

📄 Use **Communications Transparencies and Copymasters**, p. 12, for additional support.

Grammar in Context: Using Semicolons to Combine Sentences

Louis Untermeyer uses **semicolons** to combine sentences in order to create the sense of a bustling, crowded place.

> The streets were always lively with shining chariots and bright red trappings; the open-air theaters rocked with laughing crowds; sham battles and athletic sports were free for the asking in the great stadium.

Untermeyer could have written this passage as three separate sentences. Because each element describes something entertaining you might have seen in Pompeii, however, he chose to include them in a single sentence.

Apply to Your Writing You can sometimes avoid short, choppy sentences by joining closely related ones with a semicolon. You can also use adverbs like *instead, however,* or *therefore* or transitional phrases like *as a result, for that reason,* or *all the same* after the semicolon.

WRITING EXERCISE Combine the sentences with a semicolon. Add an adverb or transitional phrase if necessary.

Example: *Original* They really didn't live in the inner gate. They just slept there.

Rewritten They really didn't live in the inner gate; instead, they just slept there.

1. When the Caesar visited, the fireworks lasted for days. The sacrifices in the forum were better than a show.
2. Glaucus Pansa was giving a grand dinner. Tito would not be invited.
3. He said that they would be taught by the gods. Events proved him correct.
4. The earth twitched. The twitching changed to a shrugging. Then the ground jerked and he was thrown down.

Grammar Handbook Quick Reference: Punctuation, p. R56

> *"Fantasy was the most important part of my boyhood—at least it is the only part I remember. "*

Louis Untermeyer
1885–1977

Dreaming Days As a boy, Louis Untermeyer disliked school but read constantly. A storyteller at an early age, at bedtime he would tell his brother fantastic tales of his own creation.

From Goldsmith to Wordsmith While working successfully in the jewelry business for more than 20 years, Untermeyer spent much of his free time writing poems. After publishing a book of poems, he decided to devote all his time to writing.

Making Poets Popular Untermeyer made a name for himself as a poet, critic, and novelist. He is best known, however, as an editor of major poetry collections, many of which have been used to teach the art of poetry. He edited 56 collections and is credited with introducing the works of Robert Frost to a large audience.

AUTHOR ACTIVITY
Poetic Works Browse through one of Louis Untermeyer's poetry anthologies, such as *The Paths of Poetry: Twenty-Five Poets and Their Poems.* Choose one poem and explain in a paragraph why you like it.

THE DOG OF POMPEII **713**

Grammar in Context
WRITING EXERCISE
Possible Responses:
1. When the Caesar visited, the fireworks lasted for days; the sacrifices in the forum were better than a show.
2. Glaucus Pansa was giving a grand dinner; however, Tito would not be invited.
3. He said that they would be taught by the gods; events proved him correct.
4. The earth twitched; the twitching changed to a shrugging. Then the ground jerked and he was thrown down.

Author Activity

Poetic Works Students' choices will vary, but they should be able to explain what appeals to them about the poem.

Louis Untermeyer

Untermeyer lived and wrote into his nineties. On his ninetieth birthday, he announced that he was writing his third biography. "The other two were premature," he explained.

 Grammar

INDEPENDENT AND DEPENDENT CLAUSES
Instruction To help students write in complete sentences, explain that a clause is a group of words that contains a subject and a verb. A clause that can stand by itself as a sentence is an independent clause, for example: *The man discovered something interesting.*
A clause that cannot stand by itself as a sentence is called a dependent clause. A dependent clause is a sentence fragment, like this example: *Where the ashes were thickest* Explain that this clause leaves readers wondering what happened where the ashes were

thickest. Dependent clauses begin with subordinating conjunctions, such as *where, while,* and *because.* Clauses that follow subordinating conjunctions must be joined to a main clause to make them complete. Demonstrate this by combining the two examples.

Exercises Have students identify which clauses are dependent and which are independent. Have them add to the dependent clauses to make complete sentences.
1. Vesuvius erupted in A.D. 79 *(I)*
2. Although the eruption was sudden *(D)*
3. Many were trapped and died *(I)*

4. Because the ruins were undisturbed *(D)*
5. Since the ash preserved so much *(D)*
6. Pompeii lay hidden from view for centuries *(I)*

Use **Unit Five Resource Book,** p.55.
Use **Grammar Transparencies and Copymasters,** p. 62 for more practice.

 Use McDougal Littell's *Language Network,* Chapter 1, for more instruction and practice in independent and dependent clauses.

THE DOG OF POMPEII **713**

Magazine Article

Objectives
You can use this selection to achieve one or more of the following objectives:
- read to be informed
- determine a text's main ideas and how those ideas are supported with details
- paraphrase and summarize informational text
- Use the strategy "survey, question, read, recite, review" to understand an informational article.
- use text organizers to locate and organize information, including headings

Connecting to the Literature
This newspaper article, "A 9,500-Year-Old Summer Home" is a companion piece to "The Dog of Pompeii" because it deals with a similar situation: the discovery of a site that had been buried by a volcanic eruption. However, unlike the historical fiction story, which takes place half a world away, this site is in the United States, and it was found recently. The article explains how the buried site was discovered in October of 1998, what the "house" contained, and what researchers learned from the buried artifacts.

Science

Excavators work on the floor of a 9,500-year-old house in Oregon that was preserved by a layer of volcanic ash.

A 9,500-Year-Old Summer Home

by Thomas H. Maugh II

Researchers in Oregon have found the remains of what appears to be the oldest house ever discovered in the United States, a 9,500-year-old lakeside dwelling that is providing new insights into the lives of some of the continent's earliest inhabitants.

The structural remains were unearthed in central Oregon by construction workers enlarging a road into the Newberry National Volcanic Monument, archaeologist[1] Tom Connolly of the University of Oregon will report today at the Great Basin Archaeology Conference in Eugene.

---

1. **archaeologist** (är′kē-ŏl′ə-jĭst): a scientist who studies the material evidence—such as buildings, tools, and pottery—remaining from past cultures.

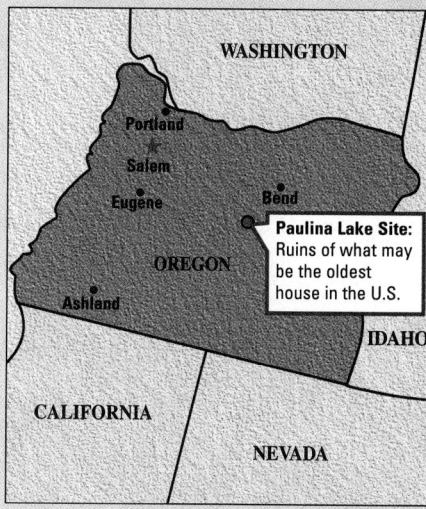

His team has discovered not only the remains of the house, but a variety of tools, food remnants and other artifacts that paint the most comprehensive picture available of everyday life not long after humans first arrived on this continent.

"This find adds a great deal of detail to our understanding of how these people lived their lives," Connolly said. "Our ideas were previously based on small bits of information gathered here and there—a kind of conjectural[2] view. Now we have lots of solid evidence."

Connolly has tentatively identified what appear to be the remains from several other dwellings nearby, suggesting that the site was a summer encampment on the shores of Paulina Lake in Newberry Crater.

"The site is unique . . . and the oldest in the United States as far as I know," said archaeologist Kenneth Ames of Portland State University. "The next oldest one dates from only 7,500 years before the present."

---

2. **conjectural** (kən-jĕk′chər-əl): based on partial evidence and logical guesswork.

Reading for Information

Archaeologists don't just pick a spot and start digging in the ground—they first make preparations and usually follow a carefully organized plan. By being prepared and following a plan, you can learn more from an informative article.

SQ3R One plan that can help you understand nonfiction is the process called **SQ3R**: Survey, Question, Read, Recite, and Review.

- **Survey** the selection quickly. Make a note of the general ideas as you preview, or skim, the article.
- **Question** what you would like to find out when you read.
- **Read** the selection carefully. Look for information that will answer the questions you formed in the second step.
- **Recite** or record in your own words the main idea of each paragraph as you read.
- **Review** the whole article. As you reread, ask yourself if all your questions have been answered. What else do you need to know?

YOUR TURN *Use SQ3R to get the most out of the article.*

❶ *Survey* the article by skimming to get the general topic. What ideas are conveyed by the title and graphics? Skim the entire article. List the general ideas you discover.

❷ Having surveyed the article for general ideas, record the *questions* you would like answered. Then continue by writing at least two questions that relate to the information in the first two paragraphs.

3. The main idea is that the site was protected because it was buried in a huge eruption of Mt. Mazama 7,500 years ago.

4. The article does not give a complete answer about how the road construction plans changed. Some students will say that their questions were answered, while others may need to do more research for full answers.

Use **Reading and Critical Thinking Transparencies,** p. 48, for additional support.

3

The site is fairly well preserved because it was buried in the massive eruption of Mt. Mazama about 7,500 years ago. That eruption, several times larger than the 1980 explosion at Mt. St. Helens, formed what is now Crater Lake. Although Newberry Crater is about 50 miles away from Mt. Mazama, it was nonetheless buried in at least two feet of volcanic ash, protecting the remains of the dwelling.

The burial also aided dating because anything below the ash has to be at least 7,500 years old, Connolly said.

Newberry Crater is a volcanic caldera,[3] formed from a massive eruption about 200,000 years ago. Researchers have found traces of 25 small eruptions in the caldera over the last 10,000 years, the most recent occurring about 1,300 years ago.

Alerted by construction workers, Connolly discovered a large fire hearth and the remains of structural posts enclosing an oval area about 14 feet across and 18 feet wide. Radiocarbon dating[4] of the posts indicates an age of about 9,490 years.

Charred fragments from the hearth are a few hundred years older, Connolly said, but the residents may have been burning fuel that had been dead for many years.

The dating indicates that the residents belonged to the Windust group of Native Americans, named after earlier discoveries in the Windust caves along the Columbia River. The Windust people, mobile tribes of hunter-gatherers, were in the region as early as 11,000 years ago. They did not settle down into permanent villages until about 4,000 to 5,000 years ago, according to Ames, which supports the idea that the newly discovered house was part of a temporary summer settlement.

Other scientists had previously unearthed about 70 pairs of sandals made of sagebrush bark, dating from the same period as the new Paulina Lake discovery, at Fort Rock Cave, about 25 miles away from the Paulina site.

Connolly's group also found chipped-stone and obsidian cutting, grinding and abrading tools, as well as a stone pestle that could have been used for pulping roots, breaking up bones and other purposes. The obsidian was traced to a site more than 60 miles away, indicating that the people "had a pretty substantial range" of movement, he said.

> **The Windust people, . . . were in the region as early as 11,000 years ago.**

Dr. Dennis Jenkins examines stone tools that may have been used for cutting meat and grinding food.

3. **caldera** (kăl-dâr′ə): a crater formed by a volcanic explosion.

4. **radiocarbon dating:** a method to tell the approximate age of an ancient object by the amount of carbon 14 that it contains.

716 UNIT FIVE PART 2: VOICES FROM THE PAST

Mini Lesson ## Inquiry & Research

The Inquiry & Research activity on this page links to the Inquiry & Research activity of Choices & Challenges on page 712, following "The Dog of Pompeii."

Instruction Explain that before students read the article they have chosen using the SQ3R method, they should think about the types of questions that will provide the most useful information. Remind them that reporters need to find answers to the following questions: *Who? What? Where? When? Why?* and *How?* Explain that such questions usually cover most of the important details.

Practice After students have found articles about archaeologists (or discoveries or methods), have them survey them. Then have them begin their questioning by asking questions that begin with *Who, What, Where, When, Why,* and *How.* Point out that they may wish to ask several questions that begin with some words, such as *How* and *Why.* After they have asked and answered these questions, they can make up additional questions if any important information was omitted.

The remains of the house were buried under at least two feet of ash from a volcanic explosion several times larger than the Mt. St. Helens eruption of 1980.

Blood traces on the tools suggest that the dwelling's residents hunted bison, rabbit, bear, sheep and deer or elk—all of which would have been abundant.

Remnants in the hearth indicate that they ate chokeberries, hazelnuts, blackberries and other fruits and nuts. They also processed hardwood bark, bulrushes and other plants to make baskets, clothing, and floor and roof coverings.

They kept warm and cooked with fires from lodgepole pine, ponderosa pine and sagebrush. The region was probably a ponderosa pine forest at the time, Connolly said, but destruction of the forest by Mazama's eruption allowed lodgepole pine to displace it.

Connolly has found another central hearth nearby and traces of other houses, but no other structural remains. "We have one house that we are sure of, and suggestions of others," he said.

4 And the modern road? That underwent "significant design changes" to protect the site, he said.

Reading for Information *continued*

3 Does this paragraph contain a main idea? Explain. In your own words, recite and record the main ideas you've read so far.

4 Suppose you wanted to know how the road construction plans changed after the site was uncovered. Does the article provide enough information to give a complete answer? Review the article. Which of your SQ3R questions have been answered? Which need more research to be answered fully?

Inquiry & Research

Activity Link: "The Dog of Pompeii," p. 712. In your library or on the Internet, locate an article about an archaeologist, an archaeological discovery, or an archaeological method. Use SQ3R to help you understand the article, then present your findings as a series of questions and answers.

OVERVIEW

This selection is included in the **Grade 6 InterActive Reader.**

Objectives

1. understand and appreciate **informative nonfiction (Literary Analysis)**
2. analyze text structure **(Active Reading)**

Summary

The archaeologist who led the team that discovered King Tut's tomb reaped the rewards after many years of hard work. The story of Howard Carter's fantastic find is fascinating, not only for the riches he unearthed, but also for the tale it tells about the value of persistence and thoroughness.

Thematic Link

The work of Howard Carter and other archaeologists reveals much about how ancient peoples lived—their beliefs, their food, their clothing, and even their furniture.

5-Minute Warm-Up

Daily Language SkillBuilder

Have students **proofread** the display sentences on page 609j and write them correctly. The sentences also appear on Transparency 22 of **Grammar Transparencies and Copymasters.**

Mini Lesson **Preteaching Vocabulary**

If you would like to preteach the WORDS TO KNOW for this selection, use the Mini Lesson, p. 720.

Tutankhamen
from Lost Worlds

Informative Nonfiction by ANNE TERRY WHITE

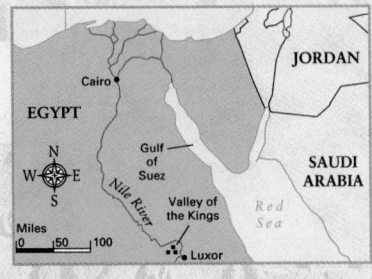

Connect to Your Life

What do you know about burial practices in ancient Egypt?

Build Background For more than 1,000 years, ancient Egyptians built great pyramids as tombs for their kings, or pharaohs (fâr′ōs). The treasures of these tombs were often stolen by grave robbers. By the 15th century B.C., pharaohs were no longer buried in pyramids. Instead, their tombs were hidden underground. More than 60 tombs have been discovered in what became known as the Valley of the Kings.

The Great Pyramid
king's burial chamber
passageway

The most famous pyramids, now thousands of years old, are near Cairo.

The jackal-headed god Anubis was believed to accompany the pharaohs after death.

Focus Your Reading

LITERARY ANALYSIS | **INFORMATIVE NONFICTION**

Writing that provides factual information is called **informative nonfiction.** Forms of informative nonfiction include science and history textbooks, encyclopedias, and most of the articles in magazines and newspapers.

WORDS TO KNOW **Vocabulary Preview**
dissuade   intact   sentinel   systematically   tedious

LaserLinks: Background for Reading
Historical Connection
Art Gallery

ACTIVE READING | **ANALYZING TEXT STRUCTURE**

If you know how facts are organized it is easier to recall them later. Informative nonfiction may be organized in many ways. For example, the **structure** of a piece may be **cause and effect, comparison and contrast, chronological order,** or **spatial order.** Or ideas may be presented using **inductive** or **deductive reasoning.** As you read, ask yourself how the piece is organized. How would you describe the structure? Make note in your **READER'S NOTEBOOK** of the most important idea or fact in each paragraph. Think about what holds the facts together.

718 UNIT FIVE PART 2: VOICES FROM THE PAST

LESSON RESOURCES

UNIT FIVE RESOURCE BOOK, pp. 58–64

ASSESSMENT
Formal Assessment, pp. 117–118
Teacher's Guide to Assessment and Portfolio Use
Test Generator

SKILLS TRANSPARENCIES AND COPYMASTERS
Literary Analysis
• Text Structure (Organization) TR 12 (for Activity, p. 725)

Reading and Critical Thinking
• Text Structure (Organization) TR 24 (for Thinking Through the Literature, p. 725)
Grammar
• Compound and Complex Sentences, CM 63 (for Mini Lesson, p. 722)
• Using Dashes to Set Off Ideas, CM 129 (for Mini Lesson, p. 727)
Vocabulary
• Context Clues, CM 69 (for Mini Lesson, p. 720)

INTEGRATED TECHNOLOGY
Audio Library
LaserLinks
• Historical Connection; Art Gallery. See **Teacher's SourceBook,** p. 46
Internet: Research Starter

Visit our website:
www.mcdougallittell.com

TUTANKHAMEN

FROM

LOST WORLDS

BY

ANNE TERRY WHITE

One of the four miniature coffins that contained Tutankhamen's internal organs. Copyright © Lee Boltin.

Less Proficient Readers
Have students keep these questions in mind as they read.
- Who is Howard Carter?
- What is Carter looking for?
- Why is Carter so determined?

Students Acquiring English
Tell students that this selection contains specialized vocabulary relating to archaeology. Many of the words are explained in footnotes, while others can be understood through context clues. Remind students to use their dictionaries to look up any words that don't have footnotes and are not easily understood through context.

Use **Spanish Study Guide,** pp. 145–147 for additional support.

Gifted and Talented
Encourage students to read a related book, either about life in ancient Egypt or about another archaeological dig in Egypt. Suggest that students present an oral report on the book that they read.

Mini Lesson — Viewing and Representing

Miniature Coffin for Tutankhamen

ART APPRECIATION This coffin, made of gold inlay and decorated with colored glass and quartz, is considered one of the great discoveries from Howard Carter's excavation.

Instruction Tell students that this coffin contains the internal organs of King Tutankhamen. In preparation for the afterlife, it was customary for the intestines, liver, lungs, and stomach to be removed and stored in containers called *canopic jars.* While the brain was not kept, the heart was left in place. Ancient Egyptians believed that a person's heart would be weighed on the Scales of Truth in the afterlife.

Application Ask students to tell what the coffin is made of and how it is decorated.

Possible Response: It is made of gold. Some parts are painted. The narrow column in the middle contains hieroglyphs, which are pictures and symbols that represent various ideas and objects from the Egyptians' lives.

Five seasons had passed and the British archaeologist Howard Carter and his financial supporter, Lord Carnarvon, had failed in their search for the tomb of Pharaoh Tutankh-amen. Howard Carter remained convinced that he was close to the 3,200-year-old tomb. Carter persuaded Lord Carnarvon that the tomb most likely lay in the center of the Valley of the Kings. In November 1922, Carter and his crew began uncovering the area near the tomb of Rameses VI—the only section that had not been dug up in the Valley of the Kings.

N ow Carnarvon and Carter were not planning to dig at random in the Valley of the Tombs of the Kings. They were on the lookout for a particular tomb, the tomb of the Pharaoh Tutankhamen, and they believed they had worked out the location where it lay. To the eyes of most people their undertaking seemed absurd. Nearly everybody was convinced that Tutankhamen's tomb had already been found. But Lord Carnarvon and Mr. Carter were not to be <u>dissuaded</u>, for they believed that the pit-tomb containing the fragments bearing the figures and names of Tutankhamen and his queen was far too small and insignificant for a king's burial. In their opinion the things had been placed there at some later time and did not indicate that the Pharaoh himself had been buried on the spot. They were convinced that the tomb of Tutankhamen was still to be found, and that the place they had chosen—the center of the Valley—was the best place to look for it. In that vicinity had been unearthed something which they considered very good evidence—two jars containing broken bits of

things that had been used at the funeral ceremonies of King Tutankhamen.

Nevertheless, when in the autumn of 1917 the excavators came out to look over the spot they had chosen and to begin their Valley campaign in earnest, even they thought it was a desperate undertaking. The site was piled high with refuse thrown out by former excavators. They would have to remove all that before they could begin excavating in virgin soil.[1] But they had made up their minds and meant to go through with it; even though it took many seasons, they would go <u>systematically</u> over every inch of ground.

In the years that followed, they did. They went over every inch, with the exception of a small area covered with the ruins of stone huts that had once sheltered workmen probably employed in building the tomb of Rameses VI.[2] These huts lay very near the tomb of the Pharaoh on a spot which Carter and Carnarvon had not touched for reasons of courtesy. The tomb of Rameses VI was a popular show place in the valley, and digging in the area of the huts would have cut off visitors to the tomb. They let it be, and turned instead to another site which they felt had possibilities.

The new ground proved, however, no better than the old, and now Lord Carnarvon began to wonder whether with so little to show for six seasons' work they were justified in going on. But Carter was firm. So long as a single area of unturned ground remained, he said, they ought to risk it. There was still the area

---

1. **virgin soil:** ground that has not been dug up or explored.
2. **Rameses** (răm′ĭ-sēz′) **VI:** a Pharaoh whose tomb was built higher on the hill, above Tutankhamen's.

720

Howard Carter (left) and Lord Carnarvon at the entrance to Pharoah Tutankhamen's tomb, February 1923.

The Griffith Institute, Ashmolean Museum, Oxford, England.

of the huts. He insisted on going back to it. On November first, 1922, he had his diggers back in the old spot.

And now things happened with such suddenness that Carter afterward declared they left him in a dazed condition. Coming to work on the fourth day after the digging on the little area had started, he saw at once that something extraordinary had happened. Things were too quiet; nobody was digging and hardly anybody was talking. He hurried forward, and there before him was a shallow step cut in the rock beneath the very first hut attacked! He could hardly believe his eyes. After all the disappointments of the past six seasons, was it possible that he was actually on the threshold[3] of a great discovery? He gave the command to dig, and the diggers fell to work with a will. By the next afternoon Carter was able to see the upper edges of a stairway on all its four sides, and before very long there stood revealed twelve steps, and at the level of the twelfth the upper part of a sealed and plastered doorway.

Carter's excitement was fast reaching fever pitch. Anything, literally anything, might lie beyond. It needed all his self-control to keep from breaking the doorway down and satisfying his curiosity then and there. But was it fair to see what lay beyond that door alone? Although Lord Carnarvon was in England, was it not his discovery as much as Carter's? To the astonishment of the workmen, the excavator gave orders to fill the stairway in again, and then he sent the following cable off to Carnarvon: "At last have made wonderful discovery in Valley. A magnificent tomb with seals <u>intact</u>. Recovered same for your arrival. Congratulations."

---

3. **threshold:** an entrance or beginning.

Customizing Instruction

Students Acquiring English

1 Point out the word *justified.* Ask students to try to figure out the meaning through using context clues. If necessary, explain that *justify* means "to prove to be just or right."

Less Proficient Readers

Use the following questions to help students understand Carter's actions.

1. Why does Carter give the command to dig?

   Possible Response: Carter gives the command to dig because the workers discovered a shallow step underneath the first stone hut.

2. What does Carter see that makes him so excited?

   Possible Response: Carter sees the upper edges of a stairway. This indicates that there is more below.

3. Why does Carter decide to delay breaking down the doorway?

   Possible Response: Carter knows that since Lord Carnarvon is funding this excavation, he would want to be there when they discover what's behind the door.

BLOCK SCHEDULING: MANAGING TIME

If your schedule requires that you cover the lesson objectives in a shorter time, use . . .
- Preparing to Read, p. 718
- Thinking Through the Literature, p. 725
- Vocabulary and Spelling, p. 726
- Grammar in Context, p. 727

If you want to take advantage of longer class time, use . . .
- TE Teaching Options: Viewing and Representing, p. 719; Preteaching Vocabulary, p. 720; Grammar, pp. 722, 727; Cross-Curricular Link, p. 723; Informal Assessment, p. 724
- Choices & Challenges and Author Activity, pp. 726-727

Some of the artifacts discovered in Tutankhamen's tomb. Note the numbered labels used to catalogue the objects.

Valley of the Kings antechamber, west side with numbers (Egyptian Dynasty XVIII, Thebes). Photo by Egyptian Expedition, The Metropolitan Museum of Art. Copyright © The Metropolitan Museum of Art, all rights reserved.

As he waited for Lord Carnarvon to come, Carter found it hard to persuade himself at times that the whole episode had not been a dream. The entrance to the tomb was only thirteen feet below the entrance to the tomb of Rameses VI. No one would have suspected the presence of a tomb so near the other. Had he actually found a flight of steps? Was it really there under the sand, waiting to conduct him to the great mystery?

I n two weeks' time Lord Carnarvon and his daughter were on the spot. Carter now ordered his men to clear the stairway once more, and there on the lower part of the sealed doorway the explorers beheld what almost took their breath away—the seal of the Pharaoh Tutankhamen. Now they knew. Beyond this doorway lay either the Pharaoh's secret treasure store or else the very tomb for which they were searching. Yet one thing made them uneasy. They noticed that part of the door was patched up and that in the patched-up part there stood out clearly the seal of the cemetery. It was evident that the door had been partly broken down—by robbers, of course—and then patched up again by cemetery officials. Had the robbers been caught in time? Did at least some of Tutankhamen's glory yet remain behind that twice-sealed doorway? Or would perhaps only barren walls reward their years of tedious toil?

WORDS
TO   **tedious** (tē′dē-əs) *adj.* long, tiring, and boring
KNOW

722

With pounding hearts they broke down the door. Beyond lay only another obstacle to their progress—a passage filled with stone. Had the robbers got beyond that? They began slowly to clear away the stone, and on the following day—"the day of days," Carter called it, "and one whose like I can never hope to see again"—they came upon a second sealed doorway, almost exactly like the first and also bearing distinct signs of opening and reclosing.

His hands trembling so that he could scarcely hold a tool, Carter managed to make a tiny hole in the door and to pass a candle through it. At first he could see nothing, but as his eyes grew accustomed to the light, "details of the room slowly emerged from the mist, strange animals, statues, and gold—everywhere the glint of gold."

"Can you see anything?" Carnarvon asked anxiously as Carter stood there dumb with amazement.

"Yes, wonderful things!" was all the explorer could get out.

And no wonder. What he saw was one of the most amazing sights anybody has ever been privileged to see. It seemed as if a whole museumful of objects was in that room. Three gilt[4] couches, their sides carved in the form of monstrous animals, and two statues of a king, facing each other like two <u>sentinels</u>, were the most prominent things in the room, but all around and between were hosts of other things—inlaid caskets, alabaster vases, shrines, beds, chairs, a golden inlaid throne, a heap of white boxes (which they later found were filled with trussed ducks and other food offerings), and a glistening pile of overturned chariots. When Carter and Carnarvon got their senses together again, they realized all at once that there was no coffin in the room. Was this then merely a hiding place for treasure? They

examined the room very intently once again, and now they saw that the two statues stood one on either side of a sealed doorway. Gradually the truth dawned on them. They were but on the threshold of their discovery. What they saw was just an antechamber.[5] Behind the guarded door there would be other rooms, perhaps a whole series of them, and in one of them, beyond any shadow of doubt they would find the Pharaoh lying.

But as they thought the thing over, the explorers were by no means certain that their first wild expectations would actually come to pass. Perhaps that sealed doorway, like the two before it, had also been re-opened. In that case there was no telling what lay behind it.

On the following day they took down the door through which they had been peeping, and just as soon as the electric connections had been made and they could see things clearly, they rushed over to the doubtful door between the royal sentinels. From a distance it had looked untouched, but when they examined it more closely, they saw that here again the robbers had been before them; near the bottom was distinct evidence that a small hole had been made and filled up and resealed. The robbers had indeed been stopped, but not before they had got into the inner chamber.

It took almost as much self-command not to break down that door and see how much damage the robbers had done as to have filled in the staircase after it had once been cleared. But Carter and Carnarvon were not treasure-seekers; they were archaeologists, and they

---

4. **gilt:** covered with a layer of gold.

5. **antechamber** (ăn′tē-chām′bər): a small room leading to a larger one.

WORDS TO KNOW
sentinel (sĕn′tə-nəl) *n.* one who keeps watch; guard

723

A

Cross Curricular Link Social Studies

KING TUTANKHAMEN AND LATER DISCOVERIES
King Tutankhamen, known as the Boy Pharaoh, ruled Egypt for about ten years in the mid-14th century B.C. Historians are uncertain how he died or who his parents were. Tutankhamen, encouraged by his minister of state, Ay, restored the ancient religion of Egypt, which recognized many gods and goddesses. After the Pharaoh's death, Ay directed his burial in the Valley of the Kings, and then he ruled briefly as king. Tutankhamen's tomb may be the most spectacular of the Egyptian tombs unearthed, but it was not the last. In 1996, archae-

ologists discovered a 2,000 year old cemetery at the Bahariya Oasis. The discovery was made after a donkey slipped into an opening to one of the tombs. More than 100 mummies of men, women, and children have been found. Perhaps the most amazing fact of all is that looters had never found this site, and therefore, it contains a wealth of well-preserved artifacts. It may take archaeologists a decade to examine everything.

Literary Analysis: CHRONOLOGICAL ORDER

Ask students to describe the order of events chronologically, beginning with the discovery of the first step.

Possible Response: On November 1, 1922, workers found the step. The next day, they unearthed the stairway and the upper part of a sealed doorway. Then Carter told the workers to fill in the stairway, and he sent a cable to Carnarvon. Two weeks later, Carnarvon and his daughter arrived. Workers cleared the stairway, revealing the doorway with Tutankhamen's seal. Workers broke down the doorway, revealing a passage filled with stone. They cleared the stones, then found a second sealed doorway. Carter made a small hole in the door and passed a candle through it, seeing many precious objects, but no coffin. The next day, workers removed the doorway to the antechamber. After entering the antechamber, the crew found another doorway that had been resealed. Then they discovered a small hole, looked through it, and saw another chamber filled with even more objects.

LITERARY LINK

Reading Skills and Strategies: CLARIFY

Have students read "Ancestors," paraphrase the questions that Dudley Randall poses, and explain their meaning.

Possible Response: Randall asks why history pays so much attention to royalty and so little to everyday people. He wonders whether everyone was a king. The questions posed by this poem say that history books make it seem as if only kings and princes were important.

---

would not take the chance of injuring the objects within the antechamber just to satisfy their curiosity. For the moment they let that go and turned their attention to the things already before them.

There was enough there to leave them altogether bewildered. But while they were yet going crazily from one object to another and calling excitedly to each other, they stumbled on yet another discovery. In the wall, hidden behind one of the monstrous couches, was a small, irregular hole, unquestionably made by the plunderers[6] and never re-sealed. They dragged their powerful electric light to the hole and looked in. Another chamber, smaller than the one they were in, but even more crowded with objects! And everything was in the most amazing mess they had ever seen. The cemetery officials had made some attempt to clean up the antechamber after the robbers and to pile up the funeral furniture in some sort of order, but in the annex they had left things just as they were, and the robbers had done their work "about as thoroughly as an earthquake." Not a single inch of floor space remained unlittered.

Carter and Carnarvon drew a long breath and sobered down. They realized now that the job before them was going to take months and months. It would be a monumental task to photograph, label, mend, pack, and ship all this furniture, clothing, food, these chariots, weapons, walking sticks, jewels—this museumful of treasures. ❖

---

6. **plunderers:** people who invade a place to rob and destroy it.

LITERARY LINK

ANCESTORS

BY DUDLEY RANDALL

Why are our ancestors
always kings or princes
and never the common people?

Was the Old Country a democracy
where every man was a king?
Or did the slavecatchers
take only the aristocracy[1]
and leave the fieldhands
laborers
streetcleaners
garbage collectors
dishwashers
cooks
and maids
behind?

My own ancestor
(research reveals)
was a swineherd
who tended the pigs
in the Royal Pigstye
and slept in the mud
among the hogs.

Yet I'm as proud of him
as of any king or prince
dreamed up in fantasies
of bygone glory.

---

1. **aristocracy** (ăr′ĭ-stŏk′rə-sē): nobility; rulers.

Teaching Options

 Assessment   **Informal Assessment**

WRITE A SUMMARY You can informally assess students' understanding of the selection by asking them to write a summary. Students should be able to produce a cohesive and coherent summary by organizing their ideas chronologically, using effective transitions, and choosing precise wording.

RUBRIC

3 Full Accomplishment Response reflects a complete understanding of the selection, placing events in correct chronological order.

2 Substantial Accomplishment Response shows solid understanding but may place some events in incorrect chronological order.

1 Little or Partial Accomplishment Response shows little understanding of the selection and places events in incorrect chronological order.

Connect to the Literature

1. What Do You Think?
How did you react to this account of the discovery of Tutankhamen's tomb?

Comprehension Check
- Why did people think Carter's search for the tomb was "absurd"?
- What did Carter hope to find in the tomb?
- What was behind each of the three sealed doors?

Think Critically

2. What traits do you think Carnarvon and Carter show in their efforts to locate the tomb?

3. Why did Carter feel it was important to find the king's coffin, even though they had already found so much?

4. Tutankhamen was not a particularly important ruler. Why is his tomb so interesting to historians?

 THINK ABOUT
- the condition of other tombs
- what might be learned from the objects found in the tomb

5. Based on the artifacts found in the tomb, what can you say about the beliefs of the ancient Egyptians? Give reasons for your answer.

6. **ACTIVE READING** **ANALYZING TEXT STRUCTURE** Look at your notes in your **READER'S NOTEBOOK**. How would you describe the structure of this piece? How did the text's **structure** help you to find or to remember the facts in the Comprehension Check questions above?

Extend Interpretations

7. The Writer's Style Recall that suspense is the feeling of tension and excitement that makes a reader curious about what happens next in a story. Reread the last page of the selection. What words and phrases help create suspense?

8. Connect to Life Dry air and sand preserved the buried treasures of Egyptian tombs for thousands of years. Do you think these artifacts should be left untouched, or made available for public viewing in museums? Explain your opinion.

Literary Analysis

INFORMATIVE NONFICTION

Writing that provides facts about a certain subject is called **informative nonfiction.** Because its main purpose is to inform, writing of this kind requires a great deal of research by the author to make sure the information is correct. Writers of informative nonfiction study materials such as log entries, letters, and other documents to gather information.

REVIEW **SOURCES OF INFORMATION**

A **primary source** conveys direct, firsthand knowledge. A **secondary source** conveys indirect, secondhand knowledge. If you were going to write a report on Carter's discoveries, what sources might you use?

Activity Look back through the selection. What are some sources Anne Terry White might have consulted before she wrote this account?

Extend Interpretations

7. The Writer's Style Possible Response: Words and phrases that help create suspense include *going crazily, calling excitedly.*

8. Connect to Life Possible Responses: Artifacts should be made available for public viewing in museums because museums work hard to preserve and protect the artifacts. *Or:* Artifacts should be left untouched because the people who enclosed them in the tombs wished for them to remain.

Literary Analysis

Informative Nonfiction Possible Responses: She would probably use primary sources, such as diaries or logs kept by Carter, Carnarvon, and others involved in the dig. She might also use secondary sources, such as museum catalogs and books about Carter.

 Use **Literary Analysis Transparencies**, p. 12, for additional support.

Connect to the Literature

1. What Do You Think?
Students may have been curious throughout about what would happen next.

Comprehension Check
- People called the search "absurd," because they thought that the tomb had already been found.
- Carter hoped to find the coffin and mummy of the king and many important artifacts.
- Behind the first door lay a passage filled with stone; behind the second door lay a room with statues and gold objects, but no coffin; behind the third door lay another chamber, which contained objects in "the most amazing mess."

 Use Selection Quiz
Unit Five Resource Book, p. 64.

Think Critically

2. Possible Response: Carnarvon and Carter were persistent, enthusiastic, considerate, and energetic.

3. Possible Response: It was important to find the king's coffin because it would prove that the king had been buried there.

4. Possible Response: Tutankhamen's tomb was important because it was one of the very few to be discovered intact, and all the objects in it revealed valuable information about the lives of the ancient Egyptians.

5. Possible Response: The ancient Egyptians believed in a life after death in which the spirit needed all the usual earthly comforts.

6. Responses will vary. Students may say that the piece is organized in both chronological and spatial order. Knowing the latter would help them answer the third Comprehension Check question in particular.

Use **Reading and Critical Thinking Transparencies,** p. 24, for additional support.

Writing Options

1. **Archaeological Catalog** Students' descriptions will vary, but should reflect some thought on the value of the objects chosen. As students compare their descriptions, remind them that some objects may have served several purposes.

2. **Classification Essay** Students' paragraphs should show an understanding of categorizing like things together.

Activities & Explorations

1. **Radio Drama** Students' scenes should show their knowledge of King Tutankhamen, as well as their insight into the methods and approach taken by Carter and Carnarvon.

2. **Tutankhamen Mural** Murals should reflect the chronological order of events as described in the selection. Students should refer to the text in order to place artifacts in the correct place on the mural.

Inquiry & Research

Hieroglyphics Students could work in pairs or small groups **to make this assignment easier.** Tell students that hieroglyphs can be read from left to right, right to left, or even top to bottom in vertical columns. Hieroglyphs are used to tell a person's name and what he or she did. Sometimes they express prayers for the owner.

Choices & CHALLENGES

Writing Options

1. Archaeological Catalog Choose several items found in the tomb and write a description of each. Tell why each item was important and what it revealed. Compare your catalog with that of a classmate. Then place it in your **Working Portfolio.**

2. Classification Essay An archaeologist studies objects from ancient cultures. Brainstorm a list of treasures found on Carter's expedition. Then write two or three paragraphs describing these objects by category.

Activities & Explorations

1. Radio Drama Adapt the events in the selection into a radio drama. With a partner, improvise a scene in which Carter and Carnarvon unearth the pharaoh's long-buried tomb. Tape-record your drama, and play it for the class. ~ **PERFORMING**

2. Tutankhamen Mural Create a mural that illustrates the events described in this selection. ~ **ART**

Inquiry & Research

An archaeological discovery in 1799 made it possible to read some hieroglyphics. Use encyclopedias and other reference materials to learn about this ancient form of Egyptian writing. Make a poster showing some common hieroglyphics and what they mean.

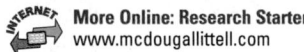

More Online: Research Starter
www.mcdougallittell.com

Vocabulary and Spelling

EXERCISE A: CONTEXT CLUES Write the Words to Know that best fill the blanks.

Those months in Egypt were the most exhausting of my life. Every day I spent long, __1__ hours digging under the hot sun. On the nights when I was the __2__, I stayed awake until dawn to guard our precious tools. My family wanted to __3__ me from this seemingly fruitless work, but I was too excited by the possibility of finding the tomb. Then one day, after we had __4__ examined miles of the valley, my shovel struck a buried door! My hands trembled as I scraped away the sand to reveal the beautiful gold seals, still __5__, that held it shut. Could the legendary tomb lie within?

Building Vocabulary

For an in-depth lesson on context clues, see p. 79.

EXERCISE B: WORDS ENDING IN -ALLY When forming an adverb with a word ending in the letter *c*, you should use the ending *-ally*, not *-ly*. For example, the correct form is *magically*, not *magicly*.

Use the correct form of the boldfaced word in each of the following sentences.

1. A selection such as "Tutankhamen" should be **historic** accurate.

2. Lord Carnarvon felt the tomb would **logic** be found in the center of the valley.

3. They **systematic** investigated the desert, inch by inch.

4. You might think that different parts of the valley looked **basic** the same.

Spelling Handbook p. R86

WORDS TO KNOW	dissuade	intact	sentinel	systematically	tedious

---

Teaching Options

Vocabulary and Spelling

Exercise A
1. tedious
2. sentinel
3. dissuade
4. systematically
5. intact

Exercise B
1. historically
2. logically
3. systematically
4. basically

Grammar in Context: Appositives Set Off with Dashes

Notice how Anne Terry White sometimes interrupts a sentence with an **appositive**.

> They were convinced that the tomb of Tutankhamen was still to be found, and that the place they had chosen—the center of the Valley—was the best place to look for it.

An appositive is a word or group of words that renames or tells more about a nearby noun or pronoun. This one tells about the place archaeologists chose to explore: the center of the Valley of the Kings. An appositive may be set off with a dash or a comma.

> In that vicinity had been unearthed something which they considered very good evidence—two jars containing broken bits of things that had been used at the funeral ceremonies of King Tutankhamen.

WRITING EXERCISE Rewrite the sentences, adding the information in parentheses as appositives set off by dashes or commas.

Example: *Original* It was a sight that took their breath away. (the seal of the Pharaoh Tutankhamen)

Rewritten The seal of the Pharaoh Tutankhamen—it was a sight that took their breath away.

1. Although they lost six years, they gained a treasure. (the treasure of Tutankhamen)
2. The objects in the room were amazing, and the men handled them carefully. (inlaid caskets, alabaster vases, shrines)
3. If you visit Cairo's Egyptian Museum you can see the treasures. (a massive building)

Connect to the Literature Look back through the selection to find another example of words set off by dashes.

Grammar Handbook Quick Reference: Punctuation, p. R57

> *"[Archaeology] has the fascination of the detective story, the charm of the jigsaw puzzle."*

Anne Terry White
1896–1980

Sharing the Classics The first book by Anne Terry White was about Hebrew Bible figures; her second book was about William Shakespeare. She wrote the books to introduce her daughters to great works of literature in a way that would be both entertaining and easy to understand.

Amazing True Stories "Tutankhamen" is an excerpt from White's book *Lost Worlds: The Romance of Archaeology.* Considered one of the foremost writers of nonfiction for young people, she retold myths, legends, and folktales. Her other works include *Prehistoric America* and *Odysseus Comes Home from the Sea.*

AUTHOR ACTIVITY
Long-Lost Worlds Find out what other ancient subjects White has explored in her books. In an oral report, tell which one of these topics you would most like to learn about and why.

TUTANKHAMEN **727**

Grammar in Context

WRITING EXERCISE
Possible Responses:

1. Although they lost six years, they gained a treasure—the treasure of Tutankhamen.
2. The objects in the room—inlaid caskets, alabaster vases, shrines—were amazing, and the men handled them carefully.
3. If you visit Cairo's Egyptian Museum—a massive building—you can see the treasures.

CONNECT TO THE LITERATURE
"In November 1922, Carter and his crew began uncovering the area near the tomb of Rameses VI—the only section that had not been dug up in the Valley of the Kings."

Author Activity

Long-Lost Worlds Anne Terry White also wrote books about the underground railroad, the Atlantic slave trade, and the forced removal of the Cherokees from Georgia. Her wide-ranging interests were expressed in her many books.
Anne Terry White came to the United States from the Ukraine when she was eight years old. Her interest in her background is reflected in her book of Russian folktales.

 Grammar
Mini Lesson

USING DASHES TO SET OFF IDEAS

Instruction Tell students that another use of dashes is to show an abrupt change in thought. They also add extra information to an already complete thought.
The expedition—assuming all goes well—will take two years.
The searchers—I'm sure they would agree—were getting impatient.

Exercises Have students use dashes to add the phrase in parentheses to each of these sentences.

1. Tutankhamen reigned for only nine years. (I'm pretty sure of this) *(after Tutankhamen)*

2. The antechamber contained precious objects. (the room that was so hard to find) *(after antechamber)*

 Use **Unit Five Resource Book,** p. 62.
Use **Grammar Transparencies and Copymasters,** p. 129 for more practice.

> Use McDougal Littell's *Language Network,* Chapter 9, for more practice in using hyphens, dashes, and parentheses.

OVERVIEW

Objectives

1. understand and appreciate informative nonfiction (**Literary Analysis**)
2. understand and identify **tone** (**Literary Analysis**)
3. use the reading skill of **SQ3R (Active Reading)**

Summary

Ch'in Shih Huang Ti, the first emperor of China, had an obsessive fear of his own death. Although he searched for the secret of immortality, he also had the foresight to begin construction on his own tomb, which took 30 years to complete. According to legend, the tomb's incredible contents included miniature reproductions of Shih Huang Ti's 270 palaces, a solid copper burial chamber, and loaded crossbows poised to shoot intruders. The tomb lay covered with earth for many centuries until 1974, when a peasant plowing a nearby field uncovered a life-sized clay statue of a warrior. Further excavations revealed thousands of similar statues, all part of the emperor's "spirit army," who were meant to serve the dead ruler in the next world. Whether the tomb has been robbed or still holds the legendary treasures remains to be seen, as Chinese archaeologists are still slowly and carefully working their way toward the tomb site.

Thematic Link

In this selection, the voices from the past appear in the guise of the thousands of sculptures that embody the wishes of the emperor, the skill of his sculptors, and offer a picture of people from long ago.

5-Minute Warm-Up

Daily Language SkillBuilder

Have students **proofread** the display sentences on page 609k and write them correctly. The sentences also appear on Transparency 23 of **Grammar Transparencies and Copymasters.**

"The farmers who lived in the area had heard stories that Mount Li contained the tomb ..."

The First Emperor
from The Tomb Robbers

Informative Nonfiction by DANIEL COHEN

(**Connect to Your Life**)

Life Without End In the selection you are about to read, an early Chinese ruler searches for a secret that would let him live forever. What would be the advantages of living forever? What would be the disadvantages?

Build Background

CONNECT TO **HISTORY** Three dynasties, or ruling families, known as the Xia (shyä), the Shang (shäng), and the Zhou (jō), controlled ancient China from about 2000 to 256 B.C. In 256 B.C., the feudal state of Ch'in defeated the last Zhou ruler. Ten years later a man named Cheng, the subject of this selection, became king of Ch'in. By 221 B.C., he had united all of China under the Ch'in dynasty.

Believing that he would live forever, and that his family's reign would last 10,000 generations, the new ruler created a new title. He added *shih* (shē), meaning "first," to *huang ti* (hwäng dē), meaning "emperor," and called himself Ch'in Shih Huang Ti. The Ch'in dynasty survived only 15 years, but it began 2,100 years of rule by emperors. Throughout the following seven major dynasties, Chinese emperors were called *huang ti.* Imperial rule lasted until 1912, when China became a republic.

> **WORDS TO KNOW**
> **Vocabulary Preview**
>
> | | | |
> |---|---|---|
> | consolidate | preservation | tyrant |
> | immortality | proclaim | unparalleled |
> | insignificant | reproduction | |
> | intricate | surpass | |

Focus Your Reading

LITERARY ANALYSIS **TONE** A writer's attitude toward a particular subject is called the **tone.** The tone of a piece of writing can be serious, playful, caring, sad, angry, or some combination of these. As you read "The First Emperor," pay attention to phrases and details that suggest the tone.

ACTIVE READING **SQ3R** To study a nonfiction selection, you may find it helpful to use the technique of **SQ3R.** It has five steps:

Survey. Get a general preview of what you will be reading by **skimming** the selection and **scanning** the images.

Question. Write down any study questions or your own questions that come to mind.

Read. Look for the answers to your questions as you read. Also, try to identify main ideas.

Recite. After you have finished reading, say the main answers to your questions to yourself, or write them in your ▭READER'S NOTEBOOK.

Review. Quickly reread your notes and the main ideas in the material so that you will remember them.

Try using the SQ3R study method as you read "The First Emperor."

 LaserLinks: Background for Reading
Historical Connection
Art Gallery

LESSON RESOURCES

UNIT FIVE RESOURCE BOOK,
pp. 65–71

ASSESSMENT
Formal Assessment,
pp. 119–120
Teacher's Guide to Assessment and Portfolio Use
Test Generator

SKILLS TRANSPARENCIES AND COPYMASTERS
Literary Analysis
• Tone, TR 25 (for Cooperative Activity, p. 734)

Reading and Critical Thinking
• SQ3R, TR 48 (for Thinking Through the Literature, p. 734)
Grammar
• Adverb Phrases for Transitions, CM 107 (for Mini Lesson, p. 736)
Vocabulary
• Using Prefixes, Suffixes, and Roots, CM 70 (for Mini Lesson, p. 729)

INTEGRATED TECHNOLOGY
Audio Library
LaserLinks
• Historical Connection; Art Gallery. See **Teacher's SourceBook,** p. 48
Internet: Research Starter

Visit our website:
www.mcdougallittell.com

AMBITION 志

DESTINY 命

永 ETERNITY

忠 LOYALTY

The First EMPEROR

from *The Tomb Robbers* by Daniel Cohen

729

Less Proficient Readers
Tell students that this selection is about a powerful ruler who lived in China more than two thousand years ago.
Set a Purpose Ask students to read to learn about the many accomplishments of the first emperor of China.

Students Acquiring English
Because much of this selection is speculative, words and phrases such as *may, it is said, according to legend,* and *authorities believe,* are sprinkled throughout. List them on the chalkboard, and explain to students that these words signal that whatever follows is a likely conclusion, but is not a hard fact.

 Use **Spanish Study Guide,** pp. 148–150 for additional support.

Gifted and Talented
Ask students to discuss why it might be difficult to protect the valuable artifacts uncovered in archaeological excavations.
Possible Response: Major threats to the artifacts are deterioration due to exposure, tomb robbers, and accidental damage caused by visitors.

Mini Lesson **Preteaching Vocabulary**

USING PREFIXES, SUFFIXES, AND ROOTS Remind students to determine meanings of words by applying knowledge of root words, prefixes, and suffixes.
Instruction Write *consolidate* on the chalkboard. Draw lines before and after the root *solid.* Explain that a prefix and suffix have been added to a root word to form this derivative word. Knowing that *solid* means "firm or compact" gives a clue to the meaning of *consolidate,* "to bring together, to make strong or secure." If students also know that *con-* means "together or with," and *-ate* means

"become, cause, or make," they have a good idea of the word's meaning.
Exercise Have students look up each of the other WORDS TO KNOW in a dictionary and list the roots, prefixes, and suffixes that make up each one. Then have them write a sentence using each word.

Use **Unit Five Resource Book,** p. 68.
Use **Vocabulary Transparencies and Copymasters,** p. 70, for additional support.

Terra cotta statues from the tomb of Ch'in Shih Huang Ti.
Copyright © An Keren/PPS/Photo Researchers.

There is what may turn out to be the greatest archaeological find of modern times, one that may ultimately outshine even the discovery of the tomb of Tutankhamen. It is the tomb of the emperor Ch'in Shih Huang Ti. Now admittedly the name Ch'in Shih Huang Ti is not exactly a household word in the West. But then neither was Tutankhamen until 1922. The major difference is that while Tutan-khamen himself was historically insignificant, Ch'in Shih Huang Ti was enormously important in Chinese history. In many respects he was really the founder of China.

The future emperor started out as the king of the small state Ch'in. At the time, the land was divided up among a number of small states, all constantly warring with one another. Ch'in was one of the smallest and weakest. Yet the king of Ch'in managed to overcome all his

WORDS
TO
KNOW

insignificant (ĭn′sĭg-nĭf′ĭ-kənt) *adj.* having little or no importance

730

rivals, and in the year 221 B.C. he proclaimed himself emperor of the land that we now know as China. From that date until the revolution of 1912, China was always ruled by an emperor. The name China itself comes from the name Ch'in.

Shih Huang Ti ruled his empire with ferocious efficiency. He had the Great Wall of China built to keep out the northern barbarians. The Great Wall, which stretches some fifteen hundred miles, is a building project that rivals and perhaps surpasses the Great Pyramid.[1] The Great Wall took thirty years to build and cost the lives of countless thousands of laborers. Today the Great Wall remains China's number one tourist attraction.

As he grew older, Shih Huang Ti became obsessed with the prospect of his own death. He had survived several assassination attempts and was terrified of another. He traveled constantly between his 270 different palaces, so that no one could ever be sure where he was going to be. He never slept in the same room for two nights in a row. Anyone who revealed the emperor's whereabouts was put to death along with his entire family.

Shih Huang Ti searched constantly for the secret of immortality. He became prey to a host of phony magicians and other fakers who promised much but could deliver nothing.

The emperor heard that there were immortals living on some far-off islands, so he sent a huge fleet to find them. The commander of the fleet knew that if he failed in his mission, the emperor would put him to death. So the fleet simply never returned. It is said that the fleet found the island of Japan and stayed there to become the ancestors of the modern Japanese.

In his desire to stay alive, Shih Huang Ti did not neglect the probability that he would die someday. He began construction of an immense tomb in the Black Horse hills near one of his favorite summer palaces. The tomb's construction took as long as the construction of the Great Wall—thirty years.

The emperor, of course, did die. Death came while he was visiting the eastern provinces. But his life had become so secretive that only a few high officials were aware of his death. They contrived to keep it a secret until they could consolidate their own power. The imperial procession headed back for the capital. Unfortunately, it was midsummer and the emperor's body began to rot and stink. So one of the plotters arranged to have a cart of fish follow the immense imperial chariot to hide the odor of the decomposing corpse. Finally, news of the emperor's death was made public. The body, or what was left of it, was buried in the tomb that he had been building for so long.

---

1. **Great Pyramid:** one of the largest pyramids built by the ancient Egyptians. It is made of more than 2 million stone blocks, each weighing about two tons. Each side of its base is longer than two football fields.

| WORDS TO KNOW | **proclaim** (prō-klām') v. to announce officially; declare
surpass (sər-păs') v. to be better or greater than
immortality (ĭm'ôr-tăl'ĭ-tē) n. endless life or existence
consolidate (kən-sŏl'ĭ-dāt') v. to make strong or secure |

731

Students Acquiring English

1 Explain to students that *in many respects* is a more formal way of saying "in many ways." Model using the phrase and suggest that students use it in their academic writing.

2 Have students calculate how long ago Shih Huang Ti became emperor.
Answer: Students should add 221 to the current year.
Then ask students how long ago Tutankhamen became pharaoh.
Answer: Add 1,347 to the current year.

Multiple Learning Styles
Logical/Mathematical

3 Invite students to guess the meaning of *whereabouts*. ("present location") If necessary, point out that the question word *where* is a clue to the meaning.

Less Proficient Readers

Ask students what the emperor's most famous achievement was.
Answer: He built the Great Wall of China.

Set a Purpose Have students look, in the next part of the selection, for details about what things the archaeologists expect to find in the emperor's tomb.

 ## Mini Lesson Spelling

FORMS OF THE PREFIX *IN-* Remind students that their work will have more impact if they write with accurate spelling.
Instruction Explain that the spelling of the prefix *in-* depends on the first letter of the word it is added to. Write the following chart.

in- becomes	before words beginning with
im-	m or p
ir-	r
il-	l

In all other cases, it remains *in-*. One meaning of *in-* is "not or without."

Exercises Have students add a form of the prefix *in-* to each underlined word. They will have to rewrite the sentence.

1. Stories about the tomb don't sound credible. *(Stories about the tomb sound incredible.)*
2. It wasn't possible for the emperor to live forever. *(It was impossible for the emperor to live forever.)*
3. Building 270 palaces doesn't sound logical. *(Building 270 palaces sounds illogical.)*

4. The smell from the emperor's body was not perfectly disguised by the fish. *(The smell from the emperor's body was imperfectly disguised by the fish.)*
5. Some people think it was not responsible of the emperor to spend so much money on his tomb. *(Some people think it was irresponsible of the emperor to spend so much money on his tomb.)*

 Use **Unit Five Resource Book,** p. 70 for more practice.

Remind students to look for answers to their questions as they read. They should also identify the main ideas in each section. If anything is unclear, they can add questions to their lists. When students have finished reading, ask them to answer their own questions, rereading if necessary. Finally, they should review their notes so the material stays clear in their minds.

Reading Skills and Strategies:
DISTINGUISH FACT FROM OPINION

Ⓐ Remind students to distinguish fact and opinion in various texts. Facts can be proven; opinions cannot. Ask whether the statement indicated is a fact or an opinion.
Answer: It is a fact.

Literary Analysis `TONE`

Ⓑ Ask students to report on the author's tone regarding China's slow approach to the excavation.
Possible Response: The author seems to have an approving tone, saying that the Chinese are not rushing, and that a few more years won't make much difference after all this time.

A soldier and his horse, two of many remarkable statues found in the tomb of the Emperor Shih Huang Ti.
Copyright © Laurie Platt Winfrey, Inc.

1 Stories about that tomb sound absolutely incredible. It was said to contain miniature <u>reproductions</u> of all the emperor's 270 palaces. A map of the entire empire with all the major rivers reproduced in mercury, which by some mechanical means was made to flow into a miniature ocean, was also part of the interior of the tomb. So was a reproduction of the stars and planets. According to legend, the burial chamber itself was filled with molten copper so that the emperor's remains were sealed inside a gigantic ingot.[2]

It was also said that loaded crossbows were set up all around the inside of the tomb and that anyone who did manage to penetrate the inner chambers would be shot full of arrows. But just to make sure that no one got that far, the pallbearers who had placed Shih Huang Ti's remains in the tomb were sealed inside with it. They were supposed to be the only ones who knew exactly how to get in and out of the <u>intricate</u> tomb. All of this was done to preserve the emperor's remains from the hands of tomb robbers. Did it work? We don't really know yet.

---

2. **ingot** (ĭng′gət): a mass of metal shaped as a bar or block.

WORDS TO KNOW
reproduction (rē′prə-dŭk′shən) n. a copy; an imitation
intricate (ĭn′-trĭ-kĭt) adj. full of complicated details

732

 Mini Lesson ## Viewing and Representing

A soldier and his horse, clay figures from the tomb of the Emperor Shih Huang Ti

ART APPRECIATION Explain that this figure was among those discovered at the burial site of Shih Huang Ti.
Instruction Sculptures of many different types of soldiers appear in the tomb. The military dress of this figure suggests that it was meant to help protect the emperor's tomb from invaders. What details show that this is a soldier?

Possible Response: He appears to have armor on his chest and is wearing some kind of helmet as well.
Application Ask how the photograph of the soldier and his horse helps students visualize the vast area taken up by the tomb.
Possible Response: The figures appear to be life-sized, so 6,000 of them would take up a lot of space.

There are two contradictory stories about the tomb of Ch'in Shih Huang Ti. The first says that it was covered up with earth to make it resemble an ordinary hill and that its location has remained unknown for centuries.

But a more accurate legend holds that there never was any attempt to disguise the existence of the tomb. Ch'in Shih Huang Ti had been building it for years, and everybody knew where it was. After his death the tomb was surrounded by walls enclosing an area of about five hundred acres. This was to be the emperor's "spirit city." Inside the spirit city were temples and all sorts of other sacred buildings and objects dedicated to the dead emperor.

Over the centuries the walls, the temples, indeed everything above ground was carried away by vandals. The top of the tomb was covered with earth and eventually came to resemble a large hill. Locally the hill is called Mount Li. But still the farmers who lived in the area had heard stories that Mount Li contained the tomb of Ch'in Shih Huang Ti or of some other important person.

In the spring of 1974 a peasant plowing a field near Mount Li uncovered a life-sized clay statue of a warrior. Further digging indicated that there was an entire army of statues beneath the ground. Though excavations are not yet complete, Chinese authorities believe that there are some six thousand life-sized clay statues of warriors, plus scores of life-sized statues of horses. Most of the statues are broken, but some are in an absolutely remarkable state of preservation. Each statue is finely made, and each shows a distinct individual, different from all the others.

This incredible collection is Shih Huang Ti's "spirit army." At one time Chinese kings practiced human sacrifice so that the victims could serve the dead king in the next world. Shih Huang Ti was willing to make do with the models. Men and horses were arranged in a military fashion in a three-acre underground chamber. The chamber may have been entered at some point. The roof certainly collapsed. But still the delicate figures have survived surprisingly well. Most of the damage was done when the roof caved in. That is why the Chinese archaeologists are so hopeful that when the tomb itself is excavated, it too will be found to have survived surprisingly well.

The Chinese are not rushing the excavations. They have only a limited number of trained people to do the job. After all, the tomb has been there for over two thousand years. A few more years won't make much difference.

Though once denounced as a tyrant, Ch'in Shih Huang Ti is now regarded as a national hero. His name is a household word in China. The Chinese government knows that it may have an unparalleled ancient treasure on its hands, and it wants to do the job well. Over the next few years we should be hearing much more about this truly remarkable find. ❖

WORDS TO KNOW	**preservation** (prĕz'ər-vā'shən) *n.* the condition of being kept perfect or unchanged
	tyrant (tī'rənt) *n.* a cruel, unjust ruler
	unparalleled (ŭn-păr'ə-lĕld') *adj.* having no equal; unmatched

733

Cross Curricular Link **Social Studies**

THE FIRST EMPEROR Ch'in Shih Huang Ti came to power in 246 B.C., at the age of 13. He gained control of much territory and divided the empire into 36 provinces, each with two officials—one governor and one defender. This brought unity to the empire and allowed the emperor to establish standard systems of money, measurement, and writing. Taking the land away from thousands of noble families, he put an end to the feudal system and allowed anyone who could pay taxes to own land. To protect his empire from possible invasion from the north, Shih Huang Ti used a forced-labor crew of hundreds of thousands to build the Great Wall of China. Lengthened and repaired over the centuries, this massive wall stretched for 4,000 miles by the time of the Ming Dynasty (1368–1644). Much of the emperor's burial site still remains to be uncovered. In addition to the clay army, archaeologists have found chariots, iron farm tools, objects of silk, linen, jade, and bone, and weapons such as spears and swords that remain sharp and shiny to this day.

GUIDING STUDENT RESPONSE

Connect to the Literature

1. What Do You Think?
Students may say that they are amazed by the contents of the emperor's tomb, by the power he exercised, or by his dramatic efforts to live forever.

Comprehension Check
• Shih Huang Ti was the first to rule over all the land, which was divided into small states.
• The Great Wall and his tomb were both constructed during his rule.
• The tomb was discovered in 1974 by a farmer who was plowing a field.

 Use Selection Quiz
Unit Five Resource Book, p. 71.

Think Critically

2. Possible Response: Shih Huang Ti accomplished important things such as unifying the country and protecting the people from northern invaders. However, he was also cruel. Working conditions on his projects were so bad that thousands of people died, and he killed anyone who told of his whereabouts.

3. Possible Response: Main ideas include the emperor's fear of death; his nearly unlimited power; the fact that he built his tomb while still alive; the incredible contents of that tomb; the fact that it was recently discovered by accident; and the fact that much remains to be excavated.

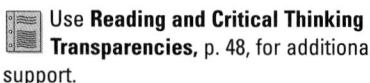 Use **Reading and Critical Thinking Transparencies,** p. 48, for additional support.

4. Possible Response: Archaeologists have learned about the clothing and weapons used by the emperor's soldiers and the artistic achievements of the people who made the statues.

5. Possible Response: Archaeologists might want to learn more about history, to find interesting and valuable objects, and to become famous. Opinions will vary.

Connect to the Literature

1. What Do You Think?
What were your thoughts as you finished reading this selection?

Comprehension Check
• Why is Shih Huang Ti called the first emperor of China?
• What two large-scale construction projects were carried out during his rule?
• When and how was the emperor's tomb discovered?

Think Critically

2. How would you describe Shih Huang Ti?

 THINK ABOUT
• his attempts to achieve immortality
• his accomplishments
• his effects on those he ruled

3. ACTIVE READING **SQ3R** Look over the notes you made in your READER'S NOTEBOOK. With a partner, restate the most important main ideas in the selection. Do you agree about which these are?

4. What kinds of information about Chinese history have archaeologists learned from the tomb so far?

5. Some archaeologists spend their lives searching for the remains of past civilizations. What do you think motivates them? In your opinion, do the time and effort equal the rewards?

Extend Interpretations

6. COMPARING TEXTS Now that you have read "The First Emperor," think back to "The Dog of Pompeii" (page 700) and "Tutankhamen" (page 718). Compare the ancient cultures of Pompeii, Egypt, and China as revealed by the artifacts described in each selection.

7. Connect to Life Many people would like to achieve a certain kind of immortality—that of having their names and achievements live on after their deaths. If you could choose one thing to be remembered by, centuries from now, what would it be?

Literary Analysis

TONE The attitude expressed by a piece of writing is called the **tone.** The tone of a literary work can vary greatly, from serious to humorous, from playful to sad. Sometimes, reading aloud can help you identify the tone. The emotions you express in reading can give clues to the tone of the work.

Cooperative Learning Activity
In a small group, read aloud a few paragraphs from "The First Emperor." Discuss how you would describe the tone of these paragraphs. Then look closely at the paragraphs to find words and phrases that help create this tone. Compare your findings with those of another group.

Extend Interpretations

6. Comparing Texts Responses will vary. Students should skim the other two selections and note similarities and differences among such areas as forms of government, interest in the arts, and belief in life after death.

7. Connect to Life Responses will vary. Students may wish to be remembered for their hobbies or concerns, from painting to baseball to caring for animals.

Literary Analysis

Tone Most students will agree that the tone is a serious one. They should be able to back up their statements with examples from the text.

 Use **Literary Analysis Transparencies,** p. 25, for additional support.

Writing Options

1. Climactic Order Paragraph
What amazed you most about the first Chinese emperor? Try writing a paragraph about Ch'in Shih Huang Ti. List a few of your ideas in climactic order—in order from least to most impressive. Then present them in paragraph form.

Writing Handbook
See p. R32: Climactic Order.

2. Log Entry Imagine you are a Chinese archaeologist in 1974. Write a log entry that describes your reactions to this discovery.

Activities & Explorations

Talk-Show Interview With a partner, do a talk-show interview with one of you as an archaeologist excavating the tomb and the other as the host. Invite class members to be the audience. ~ **SPEAKING AND LISTENING**

Inquiry & Research

Ancient Wonders Draw a map of the Great Wall, a floor plan of the tomb of Shih Huang Ti, or another ancient site mentioned in the selection. Present your drawing on a poster, along with important facts about the site.

More Online:
Research Starter
www.mcdougallittell.com

Art Connection

Amazing Individuals The terra cotta soldier and horse shown on page 732 were among the more than 6,000 statues discovered in the tomb. No two are alike. Look carefully at the figures. What details can you observe?

Writing Options

1. Climactic Order Paragraph Choices of most amazing details will vary; the most impressive detail should be presented last in the paragraph.

2. Log Entry Remind students to use first-person point of view. Tell them that the choice of tone is theirs.

Activities & Explorations

Talk-Show Interview **To make this activity more challenging,** have students research excavation techniques before beginning the interview.

Inquiry & Research

Ancient Wonders Because the Great Wall was built over a period of many years, if students choose to draw a map of it, they may wish to identify the age of each section in some way. Students may work in pairs or small groups **to make this activity easier.**

Art Connection

Amazing Individuals Students may point out the armor on the soldier's chest, the covering on the back of the horse, the stiffness of the horse's mane, and other details.

Vocabulary in Action

1. c
2. c
3. c
4. a
5. b
6. a
7. b
8. a
9. a
10. a

Vocabulary in Action

EXERCISE: ASSESSMENT PRACTICE On your paper, write the letter of the phrase that best explains the meaning of the boldfaced Word to Know.

1. A historically **insignificant** ruler was (a) important, (b) cruel, (c) not important.

2. The **intricate** security system of the tomb is thought to be (a) easy to get inside, (b) filled with cement, (c) complicated.

3. When Shih Huang Ti chose to **proclaim** himself emperor, he (a) was voted into the position, (b) won the title in a contest, (c) made himself emperor.

4. Obsessed with the thought of his death, the emperor sought **immortality,** (a) wanting to live forever, (b) needing more money, (c) hoping to die painlessly.

5. When officials **consolidate** power, each (a) gets a new job, (b) gets more power, (c) gets elected.

6. A small **reproduction** of the palace would look like (a) a miniature palace, (b) a blueprint, (c) a door key.

7. If the Great Wall did **surpass** all other monuments in its amount of stone, then it (a) used less stone, (b) used more stone, (c) used stone efficiently.

8. The **preservation** of the artifacts is amazing; they are (a) in terrific condition, (b) crumbling, (c) in a heap.

9. He was considered a **tyrant** because he could be (a) cruel, (b) lazy, (c) fair.

10. If the tomb is an **unparalleled** Chinese treasure, it is (a) unique in the world, (b) the oldest known, (c) a great treasure.

Building Vocabulary

For an in-depth lesson on learning and remembering new words, see p. 491.

✓ Assessment **Standardized Test Practice**

IDENTIFYING THE MAIN IDEA Standardized tests will sometimes require students to identify the stated or implied main idea of a passage. Read the first paragraph on page 730 aloud, then work with students to determine which answer gives the main idea of the passage.

A. Tutankhamen's name is more well-known than Ch'in Shih Huang Ti's.

B. Ch'in Shih Huang Ti was a more notable ruler than Tutankhamen.

C. Ch'in Shih Huang Ti's tomb may be the greatest archaeological find of modern times.

D. Ch'in Shih Huang Ti was the founder of China.

Statement A is true (in the United States at least) but it is not what the paragraph is about. Statement B and D are also true, but again, they are not the main idea of the passage. Statement C is the main idea—the rest of the information about Tutankhamen was given merely in support or explanation of this statement.

Grammar in Context

WRITING EXERCISE
Possible Responses:

1. Within 25 years, Shih Huang Ti became the emperor of China.
2. China was ruled by an emperor after 221 B.C.
3. For 30 years, peasants labored on the wall.
4. The emperor's tomb was surrounded by walls after his death.
5. A peasant discovered the tomb in 1974.

Author Activity

Amazing Burials Students might wish to compare the different ways Ch'in Shih Huang Ti and others tried to protect their graves from robbery.

Daniel Cohen

Though Cohen has written about many different subjects, there are some subjects he says he can't or won't write about, including mathematics and disciplining children. But that still leaves him plenty of room, and as he says, he's "turned out books on an alarming number of subjects."

Grammar in Context: Using Adverb Phrases for Sentence Variety

In "The First Emperor," Daniel Cohen uses an **adverb phrase** to introduce the following sentence:

> **At the time,** the land was divided up among a number of small states, all constantly warring with one another.

The words in red form an **adverb phrase**, a prepositional phrase that tells how or when something happened. An adverb phrase always begins with a preposition (in this case the word *at*) and always includes an object (in this case the word *time*). Adverb phrases modify verbs, adjectives, or other adverbs. Writers often use an adverb phrase to begin a sentence.

Apply To Your Writing Adverb phrases can help your readers follow the chronological order or sequence of events that you are describing. Phrases that begin with prepositions such as *after, before, during, in,* and *within* are especially helpful in showing chronological order.

Punctuation Tip: If an adverb phrase is at the beginning of a sentence, a comma separates the phrase from the rest of the sentence.

WRITING EXERCISE Vary each sentence by changing the position of the adverb phrase.

Example: *Original* During the third century B.C., Shih Huang Ti became king of the small state of Ch'in.

Rewritten Shih Huang Ti became king of the small state of Ch'in during the third century B.C.

1. Shih Huang Ti became the emperor of China within 25 years.
2. After 221 B.C., China was ruled by an emperor.
3. Peasants labored on the wall for 30 years.
4. After his death, the emperor's tomb was surrounded by walls.
5. In 1974, a peasant discovered the tomb.

Grammar Handbook Quick Reference: The Sentence and Its Parts, p. R55

". . . eccentric beliefs not only add spice to life, they can stimulate the mind."

Daniel Cohen
born 1936

A Rapid Writer Daniel Cohen has written more than 130 books, most of which are young-adult nonfiction. A Chicago native, Cohen earned a degree in journalism from the University of Illinois. After a decade in the magazine business, he became a freelance writer. His best-known works include *Young and Famous: Sports' Newest Superstars, Phantom Animals,* and *Prophets of Doom.*

Spooky Subjects Research for his popular books on ghost stories and superstitions led Cohen to creep around houses believed to be haunted and to spend "a damp and chilly night in an English churchyard." One of his most popular books is *The Body Snatchers,* a history of grave robbing. About his choice of spooky material, he says, "I don't really 'believe in' most of the subjects I write about, and I don't pretend to." With his wife, Susan Cohen, he has cowritten several popular books for teenagers on subjects ranging from movies to dinosaurs.

AUTHOR ACTIVITY
Amazing Burials Read a chapter from *The Tomb Robbers* to find out about another famous tomb. Share your findings in a report.

736 UNIT FIVE PART 2: VOICES FROM THE PAST

Teaching Options Grammar

ADVERB PHRASES FOR TRANSITIONS
Instruction Remind students that they can show transitions, or how things are related in time, space, or importance, using adverb phrases. Read this sentence aloud: "After his death, the emperor was buried in his tomb." The phrase at the beginning tells when the action of the sentence occurred.

Exercises Ask students to choose the appropriate phrase to provide a transition and complete each sentence.

a. After all
b. Until 1912
c. Over the centuries
d. For decades

_____, China was ruled by an emperor. (b)
_____, laborers worked on his tomb. (d)
_____, everything above ground was stolen. (c)
_____, the tomb has stood for over 2000 years. (a)

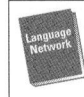 Use **Unit Five Resource Book,** p. 69.
Use **Grammar Transparencies and Copymasters,** p. 107 for more practice.

> Use McDougal Littell's *Language Network,* Chapter 6, for more instruction and practice in using prepositional phrases.

PREPARING to *Read*

Barbara Frietchie

Poem by JOHN GREENLEAF WHITTIER

*"And ever
the stars above
look down . . ."*

Connect to Your Life

Bravest of All Just what is bravery? Is bravery simply a willingness to fight? Consider acts of bravery you have heard about or seen. Then write your own definition of bravery. Give an example with your definition.

Build Background

CONNECT TO HISTORY John Greenleaf Whittier wrote this poem to honor a legendary act of courage. On September 10, 1862, General Robert E. Lee, commander of the Confederate Army of Northern Virginia, and General Thomas J. "Stonewall" Jackson led almost 40,000 soldiers through Frederick, Maryland. They were on their way to Sharpsburg and to defeat in a battle—the battle of Antietam—that would include the bloodiest single day of the war.

One citizen of Frederick was Barbara Frietchie, an elderly widow who was fiercely loyal to the Union. According to legend, as Jackson's troops marched through the town she defiantly waved a Union flag at the Confederate troops.

How did this cartoonist choose to portray Barbara Frietchie? What is included in the picture? What is emphasized?

Focus Your Reading

LITERARY ANALYSIS | POETIC FORM: COUPLET A rhymed pair of lines in a poem is called a **couplet.** Here is a couplet from the poem you are about to read:

> *Bravest of all in Frederick town,*
> *She took up the flag the men hauled down*

"Barbara Frietchie" is a narrative poem—a poem that tells a story—written entirely in couplets.

ACTIVE READING | CLARIFYING When you stop while you are reading to quickly review or figure out what has happened, you are **clarifying.** Clarifying can help you find answers for any questions you might have. Reading aloud can also help you clarify why a story or poem unfolds as it does.

READER'S NOTEBOOK As you read "Barbara Frietchie," you may come across confusing lines or sentences. Sometimes this is because the words were arranged to fit the rhythm of the poem. You may want to pause at the end of every few couplets to clarify what you have just read. Jot down key events in the narrative, using your own words.

LaserLinks: Background for Reading
Historical Connection
Visual Vocabulary
Social Studies Connection

This selection is included in the **Grade 6 InterActive Reader**.

Objectives
1. understand and appreciate **poetry** (Literary Analysis)
2. understand and appreciate the **couplet** as an element of poetic form (Literary Analysis)
3. use **reading aloud** to help with **clarifying** (Active Reading)

Summary
An elderly woman's loyalty proves to be an effective protest to a coming attack during the Civil War. Barbara Frietchie's act of courage is honored in this narrative poem.

Thematic Link
Barbara Frietchie's show of courage serves as a symbol of the power of the individual in American life. Her act of bravery echoes throughout American history as one of many voices from the past that express the freedom that is the best of America.

5-Minute Warm-Up

Daily Language SkillBuilder

Have students **proofread** the display sentences on page 609k and write them correctly. The sentences also appear on Transparency 23 of **Grammar Transparencies and Copymasters.**

LESSON RESOURCES

UNIT FIVE RESOURCE BOOK, pp. 72–73

ASSESSMENT
Formal Assessment, pp. 121–122
Teacher's Guide to Assessment and Portfolio Use
Test Generator

SKILLS TRANSPARENCIES AND COPYMASTERS
Literary Analysis
• Form in Poetry: Rhyme and Meter, TR 17 (for Activity, p. 740)
Reading and Critical Thinking
• Strategies for Reading, TR 1 (for Thinking Through the Literature, p. 740)
Communications
• Giving and Using Feedback to Improve Performance, TR 16 (for Mini Lesson, p. 741)

INTEGRATED TECHNOLOGY
Audio Library
LaserLinks
• Historical Connection; Visual Vocabulary; Social Studies Connection. See **Teacher's SourceBook,** p. 50
Internet: Research Starter

Visit our website:
www.mcdougallittell.com

Literary Analysis

`POETIC FORM: COUPLET`

Ask students to identify and read aloud three couplets. Then have them explain what makes each one a couplet.

Possible Response: Students' answers will vary, but should reflect an understanding of the definition of a couplet— a pair of lines with end rhymes.

Use **Unit Five Resource Book,** p. 73 for more practice. Use **Literary Analysis Transparencies,** p. 17 for more support.

Active Reading `CLARIFYING`

Ask students to clarify the meaning of lines 13–16.

Possible Response: In the morning there were forty Union flags flying. By noon, there were none.

Use **Unit Five Resource Book,** p. 72 for more practice.

Literary Analysis: SOUND DEVICES

Ask students to name some of the sound devices used in this poem.

Possible Response: The poet uses repetition in lines 13 and 14. He also uses alliteration in line 32, in the phrase "snatched the silken scarf," and in line 39, in the phrase "nobler nature."

Reading Skills and Strategies: PARAPHRASE NARRATIVE POETRY

Ask students to use their own words to express the meaning of the poem by paraphrasing every 6 lines as they read.

Possible Response: (for first six lines) On a cool September morning in Frederick, Maryland, when the orchards and fields were full of ripe fruit, . . .

BARBARA FRIETCHIE

BY JOHN GREENLEAF WHITTIER

Up from the meadows rich with corn,
Clear in the cool September morn,

The clustered spires[1] of Frederick stand
Green-walled by the hills of Maryland.

5   Round about them orchards sweep,
Apple and peach tree fruited deep,

 Fair as the garden of the Lord[2]
To the eyes of the famished rebel horde,[3]

On that pleasant morn of the early fall
10 When Lee marched over the mountain-wall;

Over the mountains winding down,
Horse and foot, into Frederick town.

Forty flags with their silver stars,
Forty flags with their crimson bars,

---

1. **spires:** tall, pointed towers.
2. **the garden of the Lord:** the Garden of Eden, described in the opening chapters of the biblical Book of Genesis.
3. **famished rebel horde:** the ragged and hungry Confederate troops moving into Frederick.

Teaching Options

Cross Curricular Link   Social Studies

THE EVOLUTION OF THE AMERICAN FLAG As the nation has changed, so has its flag. The first flag was created by Congress in 1777. It had 13 red and white stripes and 13 white stars in a field of blue. The 13 stripes and stars represented the 13 colonies that originally constituted the U.S. In 1795, after Vermont and Kentucky had joined the Union, Congress adopted a flag of 15 stripes and 15 stars. By 1817, there were 20 states in the Union. It was decided that adding more stripes to the flag would ruin its shape.

Congress voted to return to the original design of 13 stripes and to represent each state with one star. In 1912, President Taft decided that there should be 6 even rows of 8 stars each. Previously, the flag makers determined the placement of the 48 stars. Of course, today there are 50 stars because of the addition of Alaska and Hawaii as states.

There are fascinating stories about the making of our country's early flags. Encourage interested students to research the first flags and report back to the class on their findings.

15 Flapped in the morning wind; the sun
Of noon looked down and saw not one.

2 Up rose old Barbara Frietchie then,
Bowed with her fourscore years and ten;

Bravest of all in Frederick town,
20 She took up the flag the men hauled down;

In her attic window the staff[4] she set,
To show that one heart was loyal yet.

Up the street came the rebel tread,
Stonewall Jackson riding ahead.

25 Under his slouched hat[5] left and right
He glanced; the old flag met his sight.

"Halt!"—the dust-brown ranks stood fast.
"Fire!"—out blazed the rifle-blast.

It shivered[6] the window, pane and sash;
30 It rent[7] the banner with seam and gash.

Quick, as it fell, from the broken staff
Dame Barbara snatched the silken scarf.

She leaned far out on the window-sill,
And shook it forth with a royal will.

35 "Shoot, if you must, this old gray head,
But spare your country's flag," she said.

A shade of sadness, a blush of shame,
Over the face of the leader came;

The nobler nature within him stirred
40 To life at that woman's deed and word;

"Who touches a hair of yon gray head
Dies like a dog! March on!" he said.

All day long through Frederick street
Sounded the tread of marching feet:

45 All day long that free flag tossed
Over the heads of the rebel host.

Ever its torn folds rose and fell
On the loyal winds that loved it well;

And through the hill-gaps sunset light
50 Shone over it with a warm good-night.

Barbara Frietchie's work is o'er,
And the Rebel rides on his raids no more.

Honor to her! and let a tear
Fall, for her sake, on Stonewall's bier.[8]

55 Over Barbara Frietchie's grave,
Flag of Freedom and Union, wave!

Peace and order and beauty draw
Round that symbol of light and law;

And ever the stars above look down
60 On thy stars below in Frederick town!

---

4. **staff**: a pole on which a flag is displayed.
5. **slouched hat**: a soft hat with a wide brim.
6. **shivered**: caused to break into pieces.
7. **rent**: tore or split apart.
8. **bier** (bîr): a coffin and its stand.

BARBARA FRIETCHIE   **739**

Customizing Instruction

Less Proficient Readers
Have students keep these questions in mind as they read:
• Who is Barbara Frietchie?
• In what time period is this poem set?
• Why does Barbara Frietchie put a Union flag in her attic window?
• How does the Confederate leader react when he sees Barbara Frietchie and her flag?

Students Acquiring English
 Explain that the word *rebel* in lines 8 and 52 refers to the Confederate army.
 Tell students that a *score* is 20 years. Then ask them how old Barbara Frietchie is. *(90 years old)*

Use **Spanish Study Guide**, pp. 151–153 for additional support.

Gifted and Talented
Ask students to analyze how the mood of the poem changes from the beginning to the end. Tell them to write down some of the key words that express those moods.

Use **Literary Analysis Transparencies**, p. 26, for additional support.

✓ Assessment Standardized Test Practice

CHOOSING THE BEST SUMMARY For some standardized tests, students will have to choose the best summary of a passage. To give students practice in choosing the best summary, read aloud or write on the chalkboard the following question: Which of the following statements best summarizes "Barbara Frietchie"?

A. During the Civil War, an elderly woman convinces the Confederate leader to turn back.

B. During the Civil War, an elderly woman opposes the Confederate army.

C. An elderly woman shows courage and patriotism by waving a Union flag as the Confederate army approaches.

D. During the Civil War, an elderly woman tells the Confederate leader to shoot her.

Lead students through the process of choosing the best summary. Explain that the best summary should include the most accurate information. A and D both have inaccurate information. B is correct, but does not include the poem's main message. C is the best choice.

GUIDING STUDENT RESPONSE

Connect to the Literature

1. What Do You Think?
Responses will vary. Students may admire the bravery of an unarmed elderly woman who stands up to armed soldiers. They may find her patriotism moving. Others may say that she was foolish to have taken such a risk.

Comprehension Check
• Frietchie challenges Jackson to shoot her instead of the flag.
• It symbolizes light and law.

Think Critically

2. Possible Responses: Whittier might have been sympathetic to the Union, moved by Frietchie's bravery, or impressed by Jackson's fair response.
3. Possible Responses: The Confederate army marched into Frederick, Maryland, tearing down the Union flag. An old woman hung the fallen flag out her window and warned the soldiers to shoot her instead of the flag. The Confederate general was so impressed with her character and loyalty that he let the flag fly all day.

📋 Use **Reading and Critical Thinking Transparencies,** p. 1, for additional support.

4. Responses will vary. Students may say that bravery can mean a willingness to sacrifice for great ideals.
5. Possible Responses: The lines are "'Shoot, if you must, this old gray head,/But spare your country's flag,' she said." These line's show the woman's courage and patriotism— her character, with her own words.

Literary Analysis

Poetic Form: Couplet Students should find several examples of unusual syntax and poetic words, such as: "Over the face of the leader came"; *o'er, yon, thy;* "the staff she set"

📋 Use **Literary Analysis Transparencies,** p. 17, for additional support.

Connect to the Literature

1. What Do You Think? What is your reaction to the character of Barbara Frietchie?

Comprehension Check
• What challenge does Frietchie call out to Jackson?
• What does the speaker say that the American flag symbolizes?

Think Critically

2. In your opinion, why might John Greenleaf Whittier have been inspired to write this narrative poem about Barbara Frietchie?

 THINK ABOUT
   • how Whittier seems to feel about the war
   • Frietchie's age and actions
   • Stonewall Jackson's reaction

3. **ACTIVE READING** **CLARIFYING** Look at the notes you made in your 📖 **READER'S NOTEBOOK.** Briefly retell the sequence of events in the poem.

4. Reread the definition of bravery you wrote before reading this poem. Do Barbara Frietchie's actions fit your definition? Would you revise your definition on the basis of your reading of the poem? Explain.

5. A pair of lines in "Barbara Frietchie" have become famous. Some people can recite these lines from memory, even if they cannot remember one other word from the poem. Which two lines do you think should be famous and why?

Extend Interpretations

6. **Writer's Style** In a group, reread "Barbara Frietchie." How does Whittier reveal the personalities and beliefs of Frietchie and Jackson? Make a chart like the one shown, noting the results of your discussion.

Barbara Frietchie's Personality Traits	Stonewall Jackson's Personality Traits

7. **Connect to Life** A flag is only a piece of fabric. Yet many men and women have acted with courage to protect their national flags. Why do you think flags can be so important to people? Explain.

Literary Analysis

POETIC FORM: COUPLET
"Barbara Frietchie" is divided into pairs of rhymed lines, or **couplets.** Many readers find reading this poem aloud to be fun, because the structure and rhythm allow the reader to move along quickly. Note the brisk pace of this couplet:

Up the street came the rebel tread
Stonewall Jackson riding ahead.

Activity In order to make couplets rhyme, poets may arrange words in a way different from the word order that people generally use in conversation. Or, they may use unusual words, such as *morn* rather than *morning,* to fit the rhyming pattern. Look back through the poem. What examples of these techniques can you find?

REVIEW **SOUND DEVICES**
Sound devices, or the use of words for their sound effects, can convey both meaning and mood. How do sound devices in "Barbara Frietchie" contribute to the feeling of the poem?

Extend Interpretations

6. **Writer's Style** Students' charts will differ, but should include some basic personality traits. Students might say that Barbara Frietchie was brave, loyal, and committed to the Union. They might say that Stonewall Jackson was compassionate, wise, sensitive, and a strong leader.

7. **Connect to Life** Students may say that flags are valued not because they are decorated pieces of fabric but because they are symbols of a country's distinct identity. Flags are held high when diplomats from different countries convene, when athletes compete at the Olympics, and when school children begin the day by reciting the "Pledge of Allegiance." A flag is a source of pride and a symbol that is treated with respect, because it represents values that people cherish, such as liberty and justice.

Choices & CHALLENGES

Writing Options

1. Frietchie Interview Imagine that the Civil War has just ended. You have been sent to interview Barbara Frietchie. What would your first five questions be? Place them in your **Working Portfolio.**

2. Rhymed Couplets Write several rhymed couplets that might be carved on Barbara Frietchie's gravestone. Try to capture the spirit of this brave woman so that all who see her grave marker would have some idea what she was like.

Activities & Explorations

1. Choral Reading With a group of classmates, develop and present a choral reading of "Barbara Frietchie" for the rest of the class or for another class in your school.
~ SPEAKING AND LISTENING

2. Dramatic Dialogue Imagine that Barbara Frietchie and Stonewall Jackson have survived the Civil War and meet again. With another student, create a dialogue between the two and present it to your class.
~ PERFORMING

Inquiry & Research

Comparison Flags Barbara Frietchie waved a Union flag out her window at the approaching troops. How does the U.S. flag of the early 1860s compare with the flag of today? Research how the flag has changed. Present your findings in a series of drawings of the flag at various times.

LaserLinks: Background for Reading
Social Studies Connection

More Online: Research Starter
www.mcdougallittell.com

". . . duty hath no place for fear."

John Greenleaf Whittier
1807–1892

A Poet with a Passion The son of Quaker farmers, John Greenleaf Whittier was born in Haverhill, Massachusetts. At 14, he began to write poetry. However, Whittier found the greatest meaning in his life through the abolitionist cause, a movement of people who demanded freedom for slaves. He worked tirelessly as an abolitionist, speaking publicly and publishing his writings on the subject.

Riches of Many Kinds Whittier's first book was published in 1831. In 1846 he published a collection of antislavery poems, *Voices of Freedom.* After the Civil War, he turned to writing poetry about his youth, his family, and the New England countryside, as in his best-known work, *Snow-Bound.* When Whittier died at 85, he was a famous and well-loved poet as well as a wealthy one. He left money to the Hampton Institute, a school in Virginia for African Americans and Native Americans.

AUTHOR ACTIVITY

Voicing Values Whittier often wrote poems about moral issues or about heroes he admired. Find one of these poems. What do you think it reveals about Whittier's character?

 Speaking and Listening

STORYTELLING

Prepare All poems use words in a special way to get their ideas across. Narrative poems also tell a story. "Barbara Frietchie" is a narrative poem. Have students rewrite the poem as a story, then give it as an oral presentation. They might wish to imagine that they witnessed the event as a resident of Frederick. They may also choose to tell it as a newspaper story (or even a radio or television news report), or in some other format.

Present Students should make sure that their dramatic interpretations use effective rate, volume, pitch, and tone for the audience and for the setting. As they listen to each other's interpretations, students should evaluate them on these same criteria.

 Use **Communications Transparencies and Copymasters,** p. 16, for additional support.

Writing Options

1. **Frietchie Interview** Students' responses will vary but should reflect their understanding of Barbara Frietchie's position. Students might ask her why she risked putting out her flag, how she reacted to Stonewall Jackson's response, or what life is like in Maryland now that the war is over, for example.

2. **Rhymed Couplets** Students' couplets should capture Frietchie's boldness and bravery. They should contain brief descriptions of Frietchie's act so that readers unfamiliar with her will gain an understanding of what she did.

Activities & Explorations

1. **Choral Reading** As groups prepare their reading, encourage them to make notes to remind themselves of which words to stress, which phrases to read with particular enthusiasm, and which to read more quietly, so as to express sadness.

2. **Dramatic Dialogue** Tell students to think about the formal way in which these two would probably have conversed. Also remind students that certain words that are in common use today were not used in the nineteenth century.

 Use **Writing Transparencies,** p. 24, for additional support.

Inquiry & Research

Comparison Flags Suggest that students research not only the various designs but also the reasons behind the design changes. Encourage students to make a presentation in which they explain the evolution of the flag.

Author Activity

Voicing Values Choices of poems will vary, but many will reflect the author's commitment to the abolition of slavery.

John Greenleaf Whittier

In addition to being a poet, Whittier was also a journalist and a leading abolitionist. As such, he endorsed the candidacy of Abraham Lincoln.

Objectives

- understand the differences between denotation and connotation of words
- use reference materials such as a dictionary or thesaurus to determine connotations of words.
- identify relation of word meanings in connotations

EXERCISE

Possible Responses:

1. Cats snoop in places they do not belong.
   Cats like to investigate their surroundings carefully.
2. I admire her unique style of dress.
   Her odd clothing makes her stand out like a sore thumb.
3. Because Malik is so assertive, he is a good salesperson.
   I think that salespeople are a bit too pushy when they call our home.
4. His fussy rules make us feel nervous and trapped.
   We admire his careful way of organizing the class.
5. Her reckless behavior is dangerous.
   Everyone is in awe of her daring feats.

Use **Vocabulary Transparencies and Copymasters,** p. 12, for additional support.

Just the Right Word

Good writers choose just the right word to communicate specific meaning. Untermeyer could have chosen any of the following words to describe the crowded theaters. Why did he instead choose *rocked*?

moved
made some kind of motion

stirred
began to move from a resting position

burst
broke free, or broke open

> The streets were always lively with shining chariots and bright red trappings; the open-air theaters rocked with laughing crowds; sham battles and athletic sports were free for the asking in the great stadium.
>
> —Louis Untermeyer, "The Dog of Pompeii"

In this passage, **rocked** implies strong, rhythmic, dramatic motion.

Strategies for Building Vocabulary

A word's dictionary meaning or definition is called its **denotation.** The images and feelings you connect to a word give it finer shades of meaning, called **connotation.** Connotative meaning stretches beyond a word's most basic, dictionary definition. In fact, it is possible for two synonyms to have different connotations. The strategies below should help you understand the connotations of words.

❶ Look for Positive or Negative Connotations
Writers use the connotations of words to communicate positive or negative feelings. Read the passage below, noticing how the word *obsessed* is used.

> As he grew older, Shih Huang Ti became obsessed with the prospect of his own death. He had survived several assassination attempts and was terrified of another. He traveled constantly between his 270 different palaces, so that no one could ever be sure where he was going to be.
>
> —Daniel Cohen,"The First Emperor"

The word *obsessed* refers to someone who is concerned with a single idea or feeling to the

point of being irrational. Although the words *concerned* or *involved* have similar denotations, they do not have the same negative connotation that *obsessed* does. *Obsessed* gives the best impression of the dark quality of the emperor's situation.

❷ Think About Connotations When You Write
Always consider the connotations of the words you use in your own writing. Think about images and feelings connected to certain words. Some examples are listed in the chart below.

Positive Connotations	Negative Connotations
thrifty	cheap
young	immature
slim	scrawny

EXERCISE The words in the following pairs have similar denotations but different connotations. Think about how they differ, using a dictionary if necessary. Then write a sentence using each word. Make sure your sentence reveals the word's connotation.

1. snoop / investigate
2. unique / odd
3. assertive / pushy
4. fussy / careful
5. reckless / daring

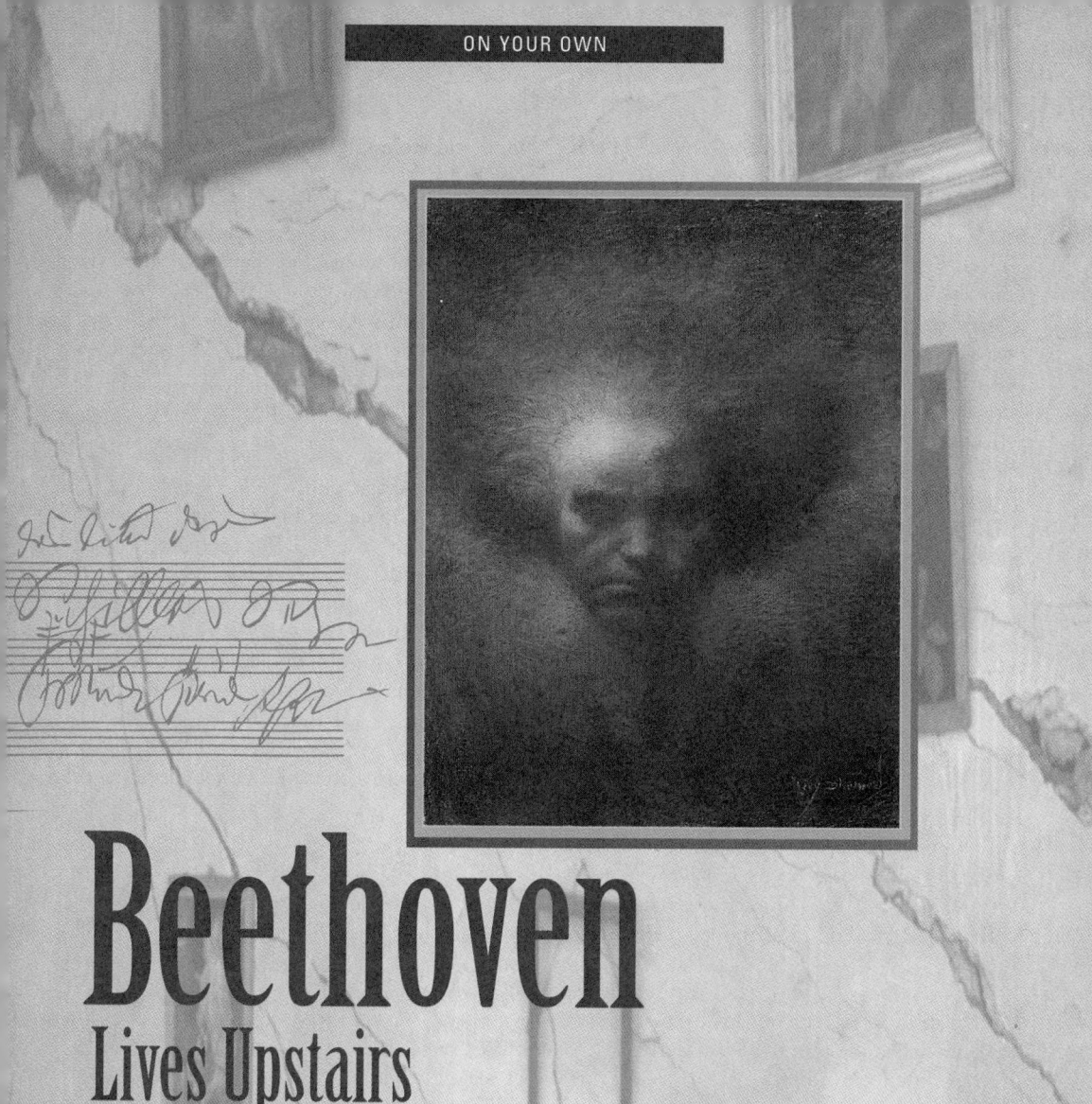

Beethoven
Lives Upstairs

BY BARBARA NICHOL

On Thursday, March 29, 1827, the people of Vienna flooded into the streets. They came to pay their respects to Ludwig van Beethoven, the great composer, who had died three days earlier.

743

You can use this selection to achieve one or more of the following objectives:

Possible Objectives
- enjoy silent sustained reading (Option One)
- read and analyze literature with a group (Option Two)
- use the Reader's Notebook to formulate questions about literature (Option Three)
- write in response to literature (Option Three)

Summary
This story, set in Austria in the 1820s, is a series of letters written between a young boy, Christoph, who lives in Vienna and his uncle, a music student who lives in Salzburg. In the letters, Christoph tells his uncle of the strange gentleman who has rented a room in the boy's home. This gentleman's name is Ludwig van Beethoven. According to Christoph's early letters, Mr. Beethoven is a serious disruption to the household, and Christoph thinks that he may be mad. The uncle replies to the boy's letters with information about the famous Mr. Beethoven. As the boy begins to know Mr. Beethoven, he understands that it is Beethoven's deafness which makes him create so much noise upstairs. Christoph begins to appreciate the genius of the strange house guest. When Beethoven's famous Ninth Symphony is ready to be performed, Christoph informs his uncle that he and his mother are invited to be in the audience. In the letter that follows the performance, Christoph reports the outstanding success of the symphony, and his sympathy and appreciation for the composer are evident.

Reading the Selection

Option One
Silent Sustained Reading

You might set aside time each week for independent reading. During this time, you and all of your students would read for enjoyment. "Beethoven Lives Upstairs" will appeal to many students and can be read independently in about thirty minutes. If you want to encourage students to read for pleasure, you might forego any assignments related to this selection. Should you want to make assignments, Options Two and Three offer suggestions.

Option Two
Shared Reading Groups

You may assign students to groups or allow them to choose their own. Students can read this selection together, alternately reading sections aloud, or they can read independently and meet to cooperate in a project that portrays some element of the story.

Possible Projects

- Students can use the information from the story to create a portrait of Beethoven as he sat on the floor with his piano.
- Using elements from the story, students can create a short play based on the possible interaction of the young boy Christoph and Beethoven after the performance of the Ninth Symphony. They can focus on Christoph's appreciation of Beethoven's talent and his change of feeling for his strange neighbor. They can perform this play for the rest of the class.
- Students can create a setting for the performance of the play, choosing one of the locations described in the story.

At three o'clock in the afternoon nine priests blessed the coffin, and the funeral procession left Mr. Beethoven's house for the church. So dense were the crowds that the one-block journey took an hour and a half.

I wasn't in Vienna on that famous day. I was a student of music in Salzburg at the time. But if you had looked carefully, you might have spotted in the crowd a little boy with a serious face. He is Christoph, my nephew, and there was a time when he came to know Mr. Beethoven quite well.

It was not a happy time in Christoph's life. He was only ten years old, and his father had recently died.

The first of Christoph's letters arrived at my door in the autumn of 1822. I was surprised that he had written. I had not seen my nephew for some years. . . .

7 September 1822

Dear Uncle,

I hope you will remember me. It is Christoph, your nephew, who writes. As to the reasons, I will not keep you in suspense. I write, Uncle, because something terrible has happened. A madman has moved into our house.

Do you remember that when Father died, Mother decided to rent out his office upstairs? Well, she has done it, and Ludwig van Beethoven has moved in.

Every morning at dawn Mr. Beethoven begins to make his dreadful noise upstairs. Loud poundings and howlings come through the floor. They are like the sounds of an injured beast. All morning Mr. Beethoven carries on this way. After lunch he storms into the street. He comes home, sometimes long after the house is quiet for the night, tracking mud and stamping his way up the stairs above our heads.

Mother says I mustn't blame him. He's deaf and can't hear the noise he makes. But he wakes up the twins, and they start their crying. They cry all day.

Uncle, I must make this one request. I beg you to tell my mother to send Mr. Beethoven away.

Your nephew, Christoph

10 October 1822

My dear Christoph,

I arrived home last night to find your letter on the table in the hall. Do I remember you? Of course I do!

I should tell you that I have received a letter from your mother as well. As you know, she is concerned about you and wants you to be happy. She assures me that Mr. Beethoven is peculiar perhaps, but certainly not mad.

Christoph, Mr. Beethoven will settle in soon, I'm sure. I know that life will be more peaceful before long.

Your uncle, Karl

Having answered my nephew's letter, I left Salzburg for some weeks on matters related to my studies. In truth, I expected no further messages. The three letters that follow arrived in my absence.

22 October 1822

Dear Uncle,

I hope you will forgive my troubling you, but I am sure that you will want to hear this news. Our family is now the laughingstock of Vienna.

I opened the door this morning to find a crowd in front of our house. They were looking up at Mr. Beethoven's window and laughing, so I looked up too. There was

Mr. Beethoven, staring at a sheet of music. And Uncle, he had no clothes on at all! It was a dreadful sight!

You should see him setting out for the afternoon. He hums to himself. He growls out tunes. He waves his arms. His pockets bulge with papers and pencils. On the street the children run and call him names.

Mr. Beethoven is so famous that sometimes people stop outside our house, hoping they will see him. But if anyone asks, I say he has moved away.

Your nephew, Christoph

A madman has moved into our house.

29 October 1822

Dear Uncle,

I have now seen with my own eyes that Mr. Beethoven is mad. I will tell you the story in the hope that you will do something at last.

Last night, when I was getting ready for bed, I happened to look up. There were beads of water collecting on the ceiling above my head.

As usual, Mother was busy with the twins, so I climbed the stairs and crept along the hall to Mr. Beethoven's room. I looked in. He was standing there with no shirt on. He had a jug of water in his hands. He was pouring the water over his head, right there in the middle of the room, and all this time stamping his feet like he was marching or listening to a song.

You should see my father's study! Do you remember how tidy he was? Well, now there are papers lying everywhere—on the floor, on the chairs, on the bed that isn't made. There are dirty dishes stacked up and clothing crumpled on the floor. And another thing, he has been writing on the wall with a pencil!

I said nothing to Mr. Beethoven, of course. Luckily, he did not see me, and I ran back down the stairs.

Uncle, if you are thinking of coming to our aid, there could be no better time than now.

Christoph

5 November 1822

Dear Uncle,

Another week has passed, but life is no calmer here.

I've been thinking. If Mr. Beethoven were to leave, surely we could find someone nice to live upstairs. The rooms are large, and Father's patients always talked about the view of the river. Father used to carry me down to the riverbank on his shoulders, even down the steep part right behind the house.

I think that of all the places in the house, I like the outside best. I can be alone there and get away from all the noise inside. But on this day even the stray dog outside was making his pitiful voice heard.

Yours truly, Christoph

22 November 1822

My dear Christoph,

Today I have returned home from a visit away to find three of your letters waiting. Christoph, I will admit that Mr. Beethoven does not seem to be an easy guest.

Perhaps I can help, though, by saying that as strange as Mr. Beethoven seems, there are reasons for the way he acts.

Option Three
Reader's Notebook

- Ask students what impression they initially get of Beethoven and to explain how their perceptions of him as a character change by the end of the story.
- Ask students to read the selection, pausing at the end of the letter dated 10 March, 1823, on page 748. At that point, ask students to predict what they think is going to happen during the rest of the story. Have them write their predictions in their Reader's Notebook. Have them also write any questions they have so far about the story or the characters.
At the end of the story, students can return to their predictions and questions. Ask them to note if their predictions were accurate and if their questions were answered. They may want to write down any additional questions they have about the story or the characters.
- Ask students to write a note from Christoph to an ailing Mr. Beethoven, explaining how knowing Beethoven impacted his childhood and changed his life.

Possible Activities

Independent Activities

- Have gifted students skim over the story, noting details, facts, and descriptions about the character of Christoph. Ask them to write in their Reader's Notebook their analysis of the ways in which his character develops throughout the selection. Remind them to support their responses with evidence from the selection.

- Have students review the Learning the Language of Literature and Active Reader pages, pp. 697–699. Ask them what elements of historical fiction they noticed while reading this selection.

Discussion Activities

- Use the questions formulated by the students in their Reader's Notebooks as the start of a discussion about this story.

- Ask students what role they think the dog has in the story and to explain why they think the author included the details about the dog.

Assessment Opportunities

- You can assess student comprehension of the story by evaluating the questions students formulate in their Reader's Notebook.

- You can use any of the discussion questions as essay questions.

- You can have students turn any one of their Reader's Notebook entries into an essay.

They say he is working on a symphony. And so, all day long, he is hearing his music in his head. He doesn't think, perhaps, how very strange he sometimes seems to us.

Tomorrow I am leaving Salzburg again and traveling with friends to Bonn, the city where Mr. Beethoven was born. I know I will find something to tell you about and I will be sure to write on my return.

Uncle Karl

10 December 1822

Dear Uncle,

It has now been a full three months since Mr. Beethoven moved in, but our household has not yet become like any sort of ordinary place.

Mr. Beethoven has a friend named Mr. Schindler who visits almost every day. He always says, "Poor Mr. Beethoven. He is a lonely man."

You know that Mr. Beethoven is deaf. When he has visitors, they write what they want to say in a book. He reads their message and answers them out loud. He has a low and fuzzy voice.

Mr. Beethoven's eyes are weak as well. When he works too long by candlelight, his eyes begin to ache. He sometimes sits alone, with a cloth wrapped around his head to keep out the light. He sits, not seeing and not hearing, in his chair.

Uncle, there is no hour of the day when I forget that Mr. Beethoven is in the house.

Your nephew, Christoph

© Joseph Daniel Fiedler.

I returned to Salzburg in late January of 1823.

22 January 1823

Dear Christoph,

I have this very day returned from the place where Mr. Beethoven was born. It seems his family is well remembered there.

They say Mr. Beethoven's grandfather was a musician, in charge of all the music at the palace. And Mr. Beethoven's father was a musician, too. But Christoph, this father was an unhappy man who took to drink. Mr. Beethoven was not a happy child.

People who lived near their house remember hearing music coming from the attic late at night. Sometimes Mr. Beethoven's father would

746 UNIT FIVE   PART 2: VOICES FROM THE PAST

come home long after dark and get the young boy out of bed. He would make him practice his piano until dawn.

The little Beethoven would play all night, tired and cold, his face awash with tears. Finally, as the sun came up, he would go to bed to the sound of morning bells.

I will send this letter right away, in the hope that you will answer soon.

Affectionately, Uncle

4 February 1823

Dear Uncle,

This afternoon a messenger arrived, bearing a note for Mr. Beethoven.

The messenger said to me, "This is from Prince Karl Lichnowsky. But the prince says that if Mr. Beethoven's door is closed, he is not to be disturbed."

Mr. Beethoven must be a terrible man if even a prince is afraid of him.

Your nephew,
Christoph

15 February 1823

Dear Christoph,

I've been thinking of your story about the prince. Christoph, I don't think the prince is afraid of Mr. Beethoven. I believe he is showing him respect. In Vienna, music is so loved that even a prince will tread carefully around a composer.

Alas, Mr. Beethoven has not returned their kindness. He has not been gentle with the fine people of Vienna, and they have done everything they can to please him. Mr. Beethoven has always had rough manners. He turns down their invitations, dresses carelessly to visit, and arrives late for their dinners.

He sits, not seeing and not hearing, in his chair.

Sometimes he is very angry if he is asked to play his music. There is one famous story of a grand lady who got down on her knees one evening to beg Mr. Beethoven to play. He refused.

And there is another tale about a prince who teased Mr. Beethoven for not playing at dinner. Mr. Beethoven flew into a rage. "There are many princes," he said, "but there is only one Beethoven."

My belief, Christoph, is that a prince has more to fear from Mr. Beethoven than has a little boy.

Affectionately, Uncle

26 February 1823

Dear Uncle,

No news today but this—do you remember I once told you about a stray dog who was whining on the street? He is a small and spotted dog, and I have found a way to make him stop his crying.

Today he seemed quite pleased to share my sugar cake from lunch.

Christoph

2 March 1823

Dear Christoph,

I write again so soon because I have been making inquiries on your behalf.

I spoke today with a man who once worked for Mr. Beethoven, copying out music for the players. He told me that Mr. Beethoven never stays in one home very long. He moves often— as often as three times a year.

Sometimes Mr. Beethoven wants a sunnier home, sometimes shadier. Sometimes he says he cannot live on the ground floor; then he cannot live on the top. And I hear he has been asked to leave from time to time as well.

He has a restless nature, so perhaps before too long you will have your wish and quieter people will be living upstairs.

But in the meantime, tell me . . . is it true, as I have also heard, that Mr. Beethoven has three pianos in his room?

Your uncle

10 March 1823

Dear Uncle,

No, it is not true that Mr. Beethoven has three pianos. He has four! And you should see them! To begin with, some of his pianos have no legs. He takes the legs off to move them and so that he can play them when he is sitting on the floor. That way he can feel his playing through the floorboards, which he must do because, of course, he cannot hear.

But it's surprising that his pianos can be played at all. Many of the strings are broken and curled up. They look like birds' nests made of wire. And the pianos are stained inside from the times he's knocked the inkwell with his sleeve.

And Mr. Beethoven has all sorts of bells on his desk, and four ear trumpets to help him hear, and something called a metronome as well. It's a little box with a stick on it. The stick goes back and forth and back and forth and tells musicians how fast they should play.

Mr. Beethoven has a name for me. He calls me "the little gatekeeper" because I am always sitting outside on the step.

Yours truly,
Christoph
Gatekeeper

When he laughs, he sounds like a lion.

2 April 1823

Dear Christoph,

Your letter about Mr. Beethoven's piano has reminded me that there was a time when Mr. Beethoven was more famous for his playing than his composing.

When Mr. Beethoven first lived in Vienna, he would sit down with orchestras to play his music, without a single note written out. It was all in his head.

And the music he played! His music was so beautiful that sometimes people who were listening would start to cry. But Mr. Beethoven would laugh at them and say, "Composers do not cry. Composers are made of fire."

Now that Mr. Beethoven is deaf, of course, he plays the piano with the bumps and crashes you hear upstairs all day.

And I have another story for you, a story people tell about his deafness. One afternoon Mr. Beethoven was out walking in the woods with a friend. A shepherd was playing a flute nearby. Mr. Beethoven's friend said, "Listen!" and stopped to hear the flute. But Mr. Beethoven heard nothing. And so he knew, that day, that he was going deaf.

When Mr. Beethoven was still a young man, he began to hear humming and buzzing in his ears. At first he couldn't hear high notes. Then he couldn't hear soft voices. How frightening it must have been for him, Christoph, and how alone that man who lives upstairs must feel.

To hear Mr. Beethoven's story convinces me that I am the most fortunate man alive.

Your uncle

21 April 1823

Dear Uncle,

Do you remember my telling you that Mr. Beethoven leaves each afternoon for a walk? Did you wonder where he goes? Well, now I know, and I will tell you the story.

Mother sometimes says that instead of just staying on the front steps it would be nice if I'd spend some time inside. I used to believe she meant it until this morning.

I thought of something to play with the twins. I rolled up a bit of cardboard like an ear trumpet and put one end in little Teresa's ear. I said, "GOOD MORNING, BABY!" very loudly, and she started to scream. Mother said it hurt her. So I went outside again and sat in my usual place on the step.

Then Mr. Schindler came downstairs. He said to me, "The master needs new pencils," and off I went to the shop.

When I came back, Mr. Schindler was gone. No one was upstairs but Mr. Beethoven, and he was writing at his desk. I stamped my feet on the floor to get his attention and when he didn't notice I stamped harder until at last I was stamping as hard as I could. Then suddenly he turned around and saw me. When he laughs, he sounds like a lion.

So today I went along with him on his walk. At times Mr. Beethoven forgot that I was with him. He would hum and sometimes wave his arms. He took out his papers and made some little notes.

Beethoven's Room at the Time of His Death (1827), Johann Nepomuk Hoechle. Historisches Museum der Stadt, Vienna, Austria/Bridgeman Art Library.

We walked outside Vienna into the tall woods and then past the woods and into the fields. Uncle, if you were to come to visit me, I would show you today.

Christoph

In July of 1823 the following note arrived, unfinished and unsigned. Christoph was preoccupied, I suspect, by the pleasures of summertime and was too busy for letter writing. The note was sent to me by his mother, included in a letter of her own.

30 June 1823

Dear Uncle,

Spring has come and gone, and now it is summer. The house is quiet because tonight Mr. Beethoven has gone to Baden, where he will spend the hottest months. He will finish his symphony and then he will come back.

Tonight as I write you it is evening, but I cannot sleep with the sun still shining through the shutters. From my room I can hear Mother playing piano as she used to when I was small.

I have been sitting here thinking about something Mr. Schindler said. He said, "Mr. Beethoven works so hard because he believes that music can change the world."

In the autumn of 1823 Mr. Beethoven returned to Vienna from his summer lodgings.

29 October 1823

Dear Uncle,

Mr. Beethoven has come home, and so our house is in an uproar again. Someone has

*Oratorio Performance at the
Drury Lane Theatre*
(part two of a triptych, 1814)
John Nixon/Private
Collection/Bridgeman Art Library

given him another piano, and there was a lot of trouble getting it up the stairs.

And then last night he had a party. A lot of people went in and out very late, and the more cheerful they became upstairs, the noisier it was for us.

Finally, it was impossible to sleep. I could hear two ladies singing. I had seen them earlier, laughing on the stairs. They are called sopranos because they are singers who can sing very high.

Mr. Beethoven has a housekeeper. She says that when the sopranos come up the stairs, Mr. Beethoven rushes like a schoolboy to change his coat. And he won't let her make the coffee for them. It must be perfect, with exactly sixty beans for every cup. He counts them himself.

Uncle, I have asked Mother if you can come to visit. She said she would be delighted if you would. She thinks you would enjoy the goings-on.

Christoph

4 January 1824

Dear Christoph,

How glad I was to receive your letter. I hope you will forgive my very late reply. Did you know that your mother has written to me as well? She tells me there's a steady stream of great musicians up and down your stairs.

Since Mr. Beethoven is writing his Ninth Symphony in your very house, perhaps you will be interested in the things I have heard. According to the stories, Mr. Beethoven has felt that he is not appreciated in Vienna. He almost agreed to perform his new symphony in Berlin! I'm happy to say, though, that so many people begged Mr. Beethoven to change his mind that, luckily, he did.

And there is other news: they say the orchestra members are complaining about their parts. The bass players say their instruments aren't nimble enough for Mr. Beethoven's quick notes. The sopranos say their notes are just too high. All over Vienna the musicians are struggling with their tasks.

His symphony will put to music the poem "Ode to Joy."

I hear as well that because Mr. Beethoven is deaf, he will lead the orchestra with another conductor—one who can hear—conducting alongside him.

Amid these great events, little gatekeeper, how is life at home? Do your twin sisters still torment you with their terrible shouts? Perhaps before too long I shall hear them for myself.

Uncle Karl

27 March 1824

Dear Uncle,

I know this will come as a surprise, but this time I write you with good news.

I was standing on the upstairs landing today when my favorite soprano came by to get tickets for the concert. At least she is now my favorite.

She had something to ask of Mr. Beethoven and she wrote her request in his book. Then she wrote another request, handed him the book, and winked at me.

He read her words and said, "Certainly. The boy and his mother will have tickets as well."

And so Mother and I will be going to the Ninth Symphony. I wrote "thank you" as neatly as I could in his book.

As for the twins, Uncle, of course they still torment me. It is what they were put on earth to do.

Now I have a new name for my sisters. I call them the sopranos.

Now I have a new name for my sisters. I call them "the sopranos." It makes my mother laugh.

Yours truly, Christoph

20 April 1824

Dear Uncle,

I know now that all of us have been quite happy of late. And the way I know it is that in the past few days our happiness has vanished once again. With the symphony just two weeks away, Mr. Beethoven's moods are fierce.

Caroline, his housekeeper, is going to leave to marry the baker next door. She told Mr. Beethoven today, and he became very angry. He picked up an egg and threw it at her.

Then Mr. Schindler came rushing down the stairs like a scalded cat. He had told Mr. Beethoven that his new coat won't be ready for the concert in time. He tried to talk to Mr. Beethoven about another coat but, as Mr. Schindler said, "The master is in no mood for details."

And I have not helped matters. Today, when I was in his room, I disturbed some of his papers as I was passing by his desk. They fluttered to the floor. I am afraid these papers had been ordered in some very special way because Mr. Beethoven said, "Now I must do work again that I have already done."

Uncle, just when life was getting better, I have ruined things again.

Your nephew

28 *April 1824*

My dearest Christoph,

How shall I console you? Perhaps by telling you that Mr. Beethoven is famous for his temper and that his moods are not your fault.

Imagine how frustrating his life must be. Imagine how lonely to hear no voices. Imagine hearing no birds sing, no wind in the trees, no pealing of bells. Imagine: he hears no music played, not even his own!

So Mr. Beethoven has a great temper. How could he not? But if you listen to his music, you will hear that his heart is great as well, too great to be angry for long at an innocent boy.

You write me that, for the moment, your happiness has vanished. I can give you my promise, Christoph, that unhappiness has a way of vanishing as well.

Your uncle and friend, Karl

The unsigned and undated note below was written in May of 1824, on the eve of the first performance of the Ninth Symphony. It arrived tucked into the letter that follows it.

Dear Uncle,

Mr. Beethoven has forgotten the incident with the papers. He squeezed my shoulder in a friendly way when he passed me in the hall this afternoon.

Now the house is quiet, and I am alone. The concert is tomorrow night, and so, of course, I cannot sleep. I think of Mr. Beethoven alone upstairs. I have not heard him stir for quite some time. I wonder what he's thinking about. I wonder if he's awake tonight like me.

Perhaps he is hearing something beautiful in his head.

Perhaps he is hearing something beautiful in his head.

7 *May 1824*

Dear Uncle,

Tonight I have been to the Ninth Symphony. It is very late. I have already tried to sleep, but it seems I cannot do so before I describe this night to you.

The concert looked as I expected. There was Mr. Beethoven on the stage, waving his arms as I have seen him do so many times upstairs. And there were the singers. I had seen them often too, tramping up and down our halls. And there were the musicians scowling at their charts. These sights were so familiar.

It was the music, Uncle, that took me by surprise.

And when the music ended, the audience was on its feet. Everyone was standing and cheering and clapping and waving scarves and crying and trying to make Mr. Beethoven hear them.

But he couldn't hear us and he didn't know that we were cheering until one of the sopranos took his sleeve and turned him to face the crowd. Four times the audience finished their clapping and then began to clap and cheer again. Up on the stage Mr. Beethoven bowed and bowed.

As the carriage took us home, I could hear the music in my head. But my thoughts kept turning back to Mr. Beethoven himself.

He has so many troubles, how can he have a heart so full of joy?

I cannot describe the music, Uncle. I can only tell you what the music made me think.

Uncle, how difficult Mr. Beethoven's life must be. To feel so much inside, even so much joy, must be almost more than he can bear.

Christoph

In June of 1824 I finally paid a visit to Vienna, to the home of my sister, her twin girls, and Christoph. It was Christoph, of course, who took the most delight in explaining the many eccentricities of the genius up the stairs. This letter, the final portion of which is now missing, is the last in which my nephew mentions Mr. Beethoven. It arrived at my home in Salzburg almost a year after my visit to Vienna.

31 March 1825

Dear Uncle,

As you know, Mr. Beethoven moved away soon after your visit. But I have seen him again and thought you might like to hear about it.

It was on the street. I saw him rushing by, humming to himself as always. I ran up and caught him by the sleeve. He looked confused at first, but then he recognized me. He said, "It's the little gatekeeper," and took my hands in his.

I took his book and asked if he was well. He had hoped his health would be better living away from the river. He told me his health has not improved. I wrote in his book that when I grow up I'm going to be a doctor like my father and then I will make him better.

He asked about Mother and the twins, and he was glad to hear that Mother is teaching piano again. And then I told him that we miss him. He squeezed my hands and looked down at the ground.

And as for other news, the twins have finally stopped their screaming. I know, however, that our good luck will not hold. I have seen them exchanging looks in their carriage and can see that they are hatching some new plan.

But Uncle! Best of all! Mother has agreed to let me keep the spotted dog.

I have named him Metronome, because of his wagging tail. ❖

"I liked the experience of making [fiction] believable."

Barbara Nichol
born 1954

Hardworking Humorist A comedy writer for television and radio in Toronto, Barbara Nichol is known for her "mockumentary" projects. These include the award-winning television special *The Home for Blind Women* and radio's *The Lying Down*, about a fictional disease that causes people to appear dead but awaken after burial.

Nichol and her two sisters all have had successful media careers. "I think there was a feeling in our family that you have to get out there and roll up your sleeves," she says.

Creative Pursuits Nichol's best-selling first book, *Beethoven Lives Upstairs,* made its debut in audio form but soon gained fame on page and video. Her second book, *Dippers,* caused a stir when it came out on April Fool's Day in 1997. This fantasy about winged, doglike beasts who infest Cabbagetown, Toronto in 1912 has caused some readers to ask, "Is it real?"—high praise for this inventive writer. Recently, Nichol published a book of poems about dogs and their feelings.

Objectives

- create a Multimedia Presentation
- use a written text as a model for writing
- refine a presentation by varying the types of materials
- use consistent form

Introducing the Workshop

Multimedia Presentation Discuss with students multimedia presentations that they have participated in or experienced as members of the audience. Have them think about what types of sounds and visuals these presentations used, and how effective these tools were in creating interest and activity.

Basics in a Box
Presenting the Guidelines and Standards To better understand the assignment, students can refer to the Guidelines and Standards for a successful multimedia presentation. You may also want to share with them the complete guidelines and standards, which describe several levels of proficiency.

Use McDougal Littell's *Language Network,* Chapter 29, for more instruction on essential communication skills.

Power Presentation

To engage students visually, use **Power Presentation 2,** Multimedia Presentation.

Using text, pictures, and sounds to inform . . .

From Reading to Presenting Wouldn't it have been thrilling to find Tutankhamen's tomb or to help uncover the buried city of Pompeii? Archaeological discoveries can teach us a lot about our history and the people who lived before us. One exciting way to bring this information to an audience is to create a **multimedia presentation** that combines sound and visuals with text. Professors, businesspeople, and others use multimedia presentations with audiences of all kinds.

For Your Portfolio

WRITING PROMPT Create a multimedia presentation about a topic in history or any other topic that interests you.

Purpose: To inform and entertain
Audience: Classmates, family, friends

Basics in a Box

GUIDELINES AND STANDARDS MULTIMEDIA PRESENTATION

Content

A successful multimedia presentation should

- capture the audience's attention with a strong beginning
- clearly and logically present information
- use media appropriate to the content
- use media from different sources
- end by summarizing the topic and the points made

Delivery

An effective presenter should

- have good posture and maintain eye contact with the audience
- speak so that the audience can hear and understand
- use gestures and body language to get the point across
- use visual aids effectively to help the audience understand the topic

---

754   UNIT FIVE   PART 2: VOICES FROM THE PAST

LESSON RESOURCES

USING PRINT RESOURCES
Unit Five Resource Book
- Planning and Drafting, p. 75
- Practicing and Delivering, p. 76
- Peer Response Guide, pp. 77–78
- Refining Your Performance, p. 79
- Rubric for Evaluation, p. 80
Writing Transparencies
- Writing Process Transparencies, TR 1–TR 4

- Writing Structure Transparencies Organizing Your Writing, TR 11
- Writing Style Transparencies Varying Sentence Openers and Closers, TR 18
- Writing Template Transparencies Multimedia Presentation, TR 39
Communications Transparencies
- Giving and Using Feedback to Improve Performance, TR 16

Grammar Transparencies and Copymasters
- Punctuating, Choosing, and Incorporating Quotations, CM 128
- Consistent Form, CM 137

INTEGRATED TECHNOLOGY
LaserLinks
Writing Springboards
See **Teacher's SourceBook** p. 56 for bar codes.

Writing Coach CD-ROM
Visit our website: www.mcdougallittell.com

Analyzing a Multimedia Presentation

SPEAKING OPPORTUNITY See the Communication Handbook, p. R100 for speaking and presenting tips.

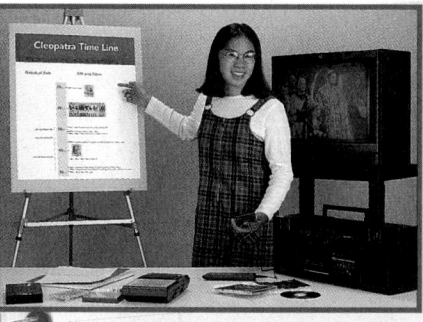

<show first visual: clip of Cleopatra movie>

Cleopatra—The Queen, Queen of the Nile, Queen of Kings, New Goddess, Daughter of the Sun-God—these titles only begin to describe the woman who was the last in a long line of Greek royalty to rule Egypt.

<show second visual: map of Egypt>

Cleopatra was not Egyptian, but she spent her life trying to keep peace within Egypt and trying to stop Egypt from becoming part of the Roman Republic. Although some of her ancestors expanded Egypt's borders and wealth, Egypt was in a terrible state by the time she came to power.

<show third visual: time line of Cleopatra>

Born around 70 B.C., Cleopatra was in her late teens when her father, the king, died. She reigned from 51 B.C. to her death in 30 B.C. During that time, she shared the throne with two brothers and her son, one after the other. However, Cleopatra was the one in control. Her strength and intelligence protected Egypt from the Romans for 20 years.

<show fourth visual: picture of Julius Caesar; play cued audiotape of Shakespeare's *Julius Caesar*>

To keep her country safe, she made friends with Roman rulers such as Julius Caesar. He became Cleopatra's ally and helped her regain her throne after a rebellion led by her brother. Then the Roman leader Mark Antony joined forces with Cleopatra. She would eventually marry him. It was Mark Antony who continued to help her keep Egypt independent. Mark Antony, however, lost power in Rome. A man named Octavian then rose to power. He wanted to conquer Egypt. He did not fall for Cleopatra's charm and he took over Egypt in 30 B.C.

Many people don't think of Cleopatra as an important ruler. However, historians say that she was able to do what many of her male ancestors could not. She won the loyalty of Egyptians and gave Egypt peace and independence for 20 years.

<play cued audiotape of quotation from Shakespeare's play>

Map of Ancient Egypt

GUIDELINES
IN ACTION

1 Captures audience attention with interesting video clip
Other Option:
• Begin with a question.

2 Script includes notes about when to include media elements.

3 Visuals help the audience understand the background of the topic.

4 Effectively combines media elements to reinforce the information

5 Details develop and support the main idea.

6 The conclusion reinforces main idea.

7 Leaves audience with a memorable quote

COMMUNICATION WORKSHOP **755**

Teaching the Lesson

Analyzing the Model
"Cleopatra Presentation"

The student model is the written text for a multimedia presentation on Cleopatra. Notes in the text indicate where the student intends to use visuals and sound effects to enhance and expand the oral presentation. Have students think of a presentation or book report they have given in the past and to consider how they could make it into a multimedia presentation. Then point out the key elements in the student model that correspond to the elements mentioned in the Guidelines in Action.

1. Ask students to think of alternative ways to open the presentation.
   Possible Response: They might begin with a question for the audience or with a quote about Cleopatra from an historian or from literature.

2. Tell students that these reminders to yourself can help you feel well-organized and, therefore, less nervous.

3. Ask students to analyze the benefits of having a map of Egypt included in the presentation.
   Possible Response: It enables the audience to see where Egypt is; it could help the audience to see Egypt's proximity to the Roman Empire.

4. Point out that the student author uses visuals or sound to reinforce all new information that is discussed.

5. Point out that the use of visuals and sound builds on the facts and details in the presentation.

6. Ask students what effect the conclusion has on the audience.
   Possible Response: The paraphrasing of historians lends the conclusion credibility; it reinforces the main idea of the presentation with a statement of fact.

7. Ask why the student might choose to end the presentation this way.
   Possible Response: This would allow the presentation to end on a dramatic note as well as with a kind of epitaph.

Planning Your Presentation
Choosing a Subject

If after reading the Idea Bank students have difficulty choosing a subject for their multimedia presentations, suggest they try the following:

• Think of a hobby or sport that you are interested in. Trace its origins and its development into what it is today.

• Research your family history and prepare a multimedia presentation on the story of your family and how they came to be in America.

Planning the Multimedia Presentation

1. Suggest that, if possible, students talk to an expert on their subject.

2. Encourage students to include unusual or little-known facts about their subject to make it more interesting.

3. Have students talk their subject over with a partner who can help decide what elements need more or less explanation.

4. Suggest that students construct a graph or chart to help them organize the material in a logical manner.

5. Encourage students to brainstorm possible uses for media in their presentations, and then pursue the ideas that seem most available and most effective.

IDEABank

1. Your Working Portfolio

Look for ideas in the **Writing Options** that you completed earlier in this unit.

• **Photo Essay**, p. 687

• **Archaeological Catalog,** p. 726

• **Frietchie Interview,** p. 741

2. Be Inventive

Think about inventions that affect your life today. Choose one that you think is important and trace the history of its creation.

3. Go Global

Choose a culture or country that interests you. Dig into the history of the people or place and choose an event, a person, or an era as the topic of your presentation.

Have a question?

See the **Communications Handbook.**

Using Visuals, p. R95

Creating a Multimedia Presentation, p. R97

Creating Your Multimedia Presentation

❶ Planning Your Presentation

Brainstorm a list of historical figures that fascinate you. **Interview** your relatives to see what important historical events they remember or have witnessed. See the **Idea Bank** in the margin for more suggestions. After you have chosen your topic, follow the steps below.

Steps for Planning Your Multimedia Presentation

▶ **1. Get to know your subject.** Do some general research about your topic by reading an encyclopedia article, searching the Internet, or finding information in a history book.

▶ **2. Narrow your focus.** Ask, What will my audience find most interesting? What is most important about my topic? Once you've decided what part of your subject to focus on, find more facts and details. Check other sources to make sure your facts are correct.

▶ **3. Think about your audience.** How much background information will the audience need to understand your topic? What do they already know about it? How will you capture their interest in the beginning?

▶ **4. Organize your information.** What are some ways you can group the information? In what order should you present it? You might use chronological order, or you might use order of importance.

▶ **5. Decide which media to use in your presentation.** What types of resources are available? Which will help your audience remember the information? Consider the following:

• **Audiotapes and compact discs** add memorable sound effects, such as music and voices.

• **Charts, time lines, posters, slides, and graphs** give the audience a clear way to understand information and to see a visual representation of the ideas you are presenting.

• **Videos** provide both sound and visual effects.

• **Computer programs** can create effective visual aids such as graphs, charts, and drawings. You can also project a slide show, or even project text and graphics, from a computer.

❷ Developing Your Presentation

Once you have gathered your facts and other information, begin putting your media elements into your presentation.

Steps for Developing Your Multimedia Presentation

▶ **1. Write your script.** Include all of the facts you wish to present. Choose the best order for your details. Note where to show visuals or include other media. Write out an explanation for each element if necessary.

▶ **2. Create a strong introduction and conclusion.** Capture your audience's attention in the beginning with a question, an anecdote, or a quotation. You can also begin with music or a powerful image. Reinforce your main idea in your conclusion.

▶ **3. Gather or create your media elements.** Prepare your media elements and find the equipment that you will need. Make sure that charts, time lines, and other visuals are large enough to see from the back of the room and that audiotapes or videos are loud enough.

▶ **4. Look over your media choices.** Be sure that you have chosen the best media for the kind of information you want to give. Lists, charts, and graphs are good for organizing a lot of facts; slides and videos can show powerful images.

❸ Practicing and Presenting

Practice your presentation several times. You should be familiar with your script and feel comfortable handling the media elements.

- **Look at your audience often** during your presentation.
- **Speak loudly and slowly** so that your audience understands what you are saying.
- **Include gestures** to emphasize important points.
- **Work on showing your media elements. Practice with the equipment.**

After rehearsing on your own, invite some friends and family to view your presentation. Use their comments to help you improve your program.

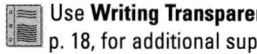

TECHTool

Use a computer with graphics software to help you create a time line. Add images to show important events for some of the years listed. If you need help, see your school's technology adviser.

Ask Your Peer Reviewers

- What did you learn from my presentation?
- What parts of my presentation did you find most interesting?
- What information was confusing? Why?
- Which media elements added the most to the presentation? Which ones seemed unnecessary?

Developing the Presentation

1. Suggest that students keep the language in their written texts as natural as possible, as the text will be listened to, not read, by the audience.
2. Encourage students to be creative in their introductions and conclusions.
3. Encourage students to look into all kinds of media resources for their presentations, and not to eliminate any ideas until they have explored them.
4. Have students consider the effect that they want their presentations to have. Ask them to look critically at the media choices they have made to make sure they achieve this effect.

📖 Use **Writing Transparencies,** p. 18, for additional support.

Practicing and Presenting

Suggest that students become familiar enough with their material that they don't have to read it or recite it from memory. Encourage students to use their written text as a prompt and not rely on it completely for information.

Ask Your Peer Reviewer

Suggest that students ask a classmate to view a preliminary run-through of the presentation and give suggestions on ways to improve it. Remind students to use the peer reviewer's feedback when refining their presentations.

📖 Use **Communications Transparencies and Copymasters,** p. 16, for additional support.

Refining the Presentation
VARYING THE TYPES OF MATERIALS

Review the changes made in the sample script with students. To help students practice varying the types of materials they use in their presentations, ask volunteers to share portions of their presentations with the class. Have the rest of the class suggest other media choices that would create more variety in the presentation.

Editing and Proofreading
CONSISTENT FORM

Remind students that consistency in the way information is presented helps the audience stay focused on the topic and helps them to understand the material more fully. Have the students explain the changes in the sample. For more practice, see the Grammar Mini Lesson at the bottom of the next page.

Reflecting

As they write their reflections, have students consider what they will be more aware of the next time they are part of the audience for a multimedia presentation.

Option
Managing the Paper Load

If students do their initial drafts on a computer, you may wish to consider typing your comments right into their drafts. Students will find typed comments easier to read.

Need revising help?

Review the **Rubric**, p. 754

Consider **peer reviewer** comments

Check **Revision Guidelines**, p. R23

SPELLING From Writing

As you revise your work, look back at the words you misspelled and determine why you made the errors you did. For additional help, refer to the strategies and generalizations in the **Spelling Handbook** on page R86.

Publishing IDEAS

- Dress up as a figure from history. Give your presentation from this figure's point of view.

- Working with your technology adviser or teacher, put your presentation on the computer. Then, with your classmates, set up a tour through history in which the programs are arranged to run chronologically.

More Online: Publishing Options
www.mcdougallittell.com

❹ Refining Your Presentation
TARGET SKILL ▶ VARYING THE TYPES OF MATERIALS

To keep your audience interested, use visuals and audio material to support your main points and to create a balance between your speaking and your presenting.

> ⟨show fourth visual: picture of Julius Caesar; play cued
> To keep her country safe, she made friends with
> audiotape of Shakespeare's Julius Caesar⟩
> Roman rulers such as Julius Caesar. He became
>
> Cleopatra's ally and helped her to regain her throne after
>
> a rebellion led by her brother.

❺ Editing and Proofreading
TARGET SKILL ▶ CONSISTENT FORM When you create a visual, it is very important to present the information consistently. Things like using different formats, changing the order in which dates are presented, and having inconsistent punctuation will confuse the audience. Before you use your visuals, hang them up and look at them from a distance. Ask yourself, Can I read the words? Do I understand the information being presented?

> | 51 B.C. | Cleopatra gains the throne |
> | | Caesar gives Cleopatra Cyprus in 47 B.C. |
> | in 46 B.C. | Cleopatra's arrives arrival in Rome |
> | 44 B.C. | Caesar is assassinated |

❻ Reflecting
FOR YOUR WORKING PORTFOLIO What did you learn about your topic from doing this multimedia presentation? Which parts of your presentation did you like the most? What would you do differently for your next multimedia presentation? Attach your answers to your script. Save your script in your **Working Portfolio.**

Assessment Practice Revising & Editing

Read this passage from the first draft of a student report. The underlined sections may include the following kinds of errors:

- **errors with conjunctions**
- **comma errors**
- **spelling errors**
- **capitalization errors**

For each underlined section, choose the revision that most improves the writing.

> The Anglo-Saxon culture <u>Ruled England until A.D. 1066.</u> Poems
> ⁽¹⁾
> from that time period describe the life of the Anglo-Saxons. <u>Some people
> thought, the poets</u> had made up details about the way of life. Then in
> ⁽²⁾
> 1939 a farmer <u>plowed his field but found clues</u> that hinted at something
> ⁽³⁾
> exciting buried in the ground. When archaeologists completed <u>they're</u>
> ⁽⁴⁾
> work they found the remains of a huge ship containing many treasures
> that were more than 1,300 years old. It was probably the burial ship of
> a king because the center of the ship had <u>many valuable objects: a
> sword, a scepter, a harp,</u> gold buckles, silver drinking cups, and a
> ⁽⁵⁾
> helmet. This ship proved that the <u>storys</u> told by the poets truly
> ⁽⁶⁾
> described the Anglo-Saxon culture.

1. A. ruled England until A.D. 1066
   B. ruled England until a.d. 1066.
   C. ruled england until a.d. 1066.
   D. Correct as is

2. A. Some people, thought the poets,
   B. Some, people thought the poets
   C. Some people thought the poets
   D. Correct as is

3. A. plowed his field and found clues
   B. plowed his field then found clues
   C. plowed his field or found clues
   D. Correct as is

4. A. there
   B. there're
   C. their
   D. Correct as is

5. A. many valuable objects a sword, a scepter, a harp,
   B. many valuable objects; a sword, a scepter, a harp,
   C. many valuable objects. A sword, a scepter, a harp,
   D. Correct as is

6. A. story's
   B. stories
   C. storyes
   D. Correct as is

Need extra help?

See the **Grammar Handbook.**

Correcting Capitalization, p. R73

Correcting Punctuation, p. R76

 Grammar

CONSISTENT FORM For use with Editing and Proofreading, p. 758. Tell students that inconsistencies in a visual will distract the audience from the main idea of the presentation. Remind them that visuals should illustrate the information clearly and uniformly, and should help the audience better understand the information being presented.
Practice Have students find the inconsistencies in form in the following visual and suggest ways to make the visual more uniform and understandable.

GODS AND GODDESSES OF ANCIENT EGYPT
Amon—considered the king of gods
Horus: god of the sky
The goddess of the underworld is Isis, and Osiris is the god of the underworld
Re (Ray)—considered one of the more powerful gods, he is the god of the sun
god of storms, disorder, and warfare—Seth
(Possible response: Make each listing consistent with "Horus: god of the sky")

 Use **Grammar Transparencies and Copymasters,** p. 137, for additional support.

Objectives

- reflect on unit themes
- review literary analysis skills used in the unit
- paraphrase and summarize text to recall, inform, or organize ideas
- recognize how style, tone, and mood contribute to the effect of the text
- assess and build portfolios

Reflecting on the Theme

OPTION 1

A successful response will

- compare and contrast the younger character with the older character
- display an understanding of the character and her/his voice
- support responses by referring to relevant aspects of text
- discuss reasons for opinions in brief written form

OPTION 2

A successful response will

- creatively illustrate the uniqueness of the culture
- show an understanding of the culture and the text through the chosen quotes
- use multiple sources, including electronic texts, experts, and print resources, to locate information relevant to research

OPTION 3

A successful response will

- demonstrate effective communication skills while providing information
- clarify and support spoken ideas with evidence, elaborations, and examples
- illustrate an understanding of the character or person under discussion and the ways in which that character or person developed

Self Assessment

In order to help students organize their ideas, have them create a chart that lists the ways people in this unit made their mark. Suggest that students then look at this list and make a connection based on their own life experiences.

Making Your Mark

By reading the selections in this unit, you have seen that there are many ways to make your mark. A person might develop a particular talent, give an extra effort, or just see where their interests lead. There are as many ways to leave an impression as there are people in the world. Use the following options to reflect on what you've learned.

Reflecting on the Theme

OPTION 1

Predicting Outcomes What impact can early experiences have on a person's future? Imagine that ten years have passed in the lives of Lenore in *Words on a Page*, the narrator in "Crow Call," and James in "The Scribe." Draft a brief description of each character's new situation. Share opinions about how their experiences might have affected the way each found their voice.

OPTION 2

Remembering the Past In her "Newbery Acceptance Speech," Lois Lowry spoke of the character Jonas discovering that "his own past goes back further than he had ever known." What do you think people can gain from learning about the far past? Think about the ancient cultures you read about in this unit. Choose one and make a poster that celebrates it. Include quotes from the selection, drawings of artifacts, and facts you find surprising.

OPTION 3

Comparing Qualities What qualities do you think make it possible for a person to make his or her mark? Make a list of the strongest qualities shown by different characters and real people in the selections in this unit. Use the list to evaluate four of these characters or real people. In your opinion, which one had the greatest impact on his or her world? Consider each one's situation. Which one made the biggest breakthrough? Discuss your choices with a partner.

Self ASSESSMENT

READER'S NOTEBOOK

After reading the selections in Unit Five, what have you learned about the many ways people can make their marks? Which of these ways might you like to pursue? Write a paragraph explaining your response.

REVIEWING YOUR PERSONAL WORDList

Vocabulary Review the new words you learned in this unit. If necessary, use a dictionary to check the meaning of each word.

Spelling Review your list of spelling words. If you're not sure of the correct spelling, use a dictionary or refer to the **Spelling Handbook** on page R86.

Reviewing Literary Concepts

Reviewing Literary Concepts

OPTION 1

Looking at Symbols As you know, objects and images are sometimes used in literature to symbolize things—such as ideas or feelings—that cannot be seen. Copy this diagram and work with a partner to identify a symbol in each of the selections listed. Discuss what you think each symbol stands for.

Use of Symbols

Words on a Page	"How to Paint the Portrait of a Bird"	"Barbara Frietchie"

OPTION 2

Thinking About Voice You have learned that a writer's voice is his or her style of writing. Voice involves such elements as sentence length,

Selection	Description of Voice	Example of Voice

word choice, use of dialogue, tone, and choice of subject matter. Look through the selections in this unit to find examples of three or four different voices. Make a chart like the one shown, and use it to record your examples. Then, with a few classmates, discuss what makes the voices unique.

Building Your Portfolio

- **Writing Options** Several of the Writing Options in this unit asked you to create accounts of events in the selections. Choose the account that makes you most proud. Write a cover note describing what you like about your work. Then add your account and note to your **Presentation Portfolio**.

- **Writing Workshops** In one Writing Workshop, you wrote an opinion statement. In another, you created a multimedia report. Review these two pieces. Which one better shows your strengths? Write a note explaining your choice and place it with the piece in your **Presentation Portfolio**.

- **Additional Activities** Think back to the assignments you completed for **Activities & Explorations** and **Inquiry & Research.** Keep a record in your portfolio of assignments you particularly enjoyed, found helpful, or would like to explore further.

Self ASSESSMENT

READER'S NOTEBOOK

Copy the following list of literary terms introduced or reviewed in this unit. Put a check mark next to each one you do not fully understand. Look at the **Glossary of Literary and Reading Terms** (p. R6) to clarify the meanings of the terms you marked.

theme
personal essay
onomatopoeia
symbol
voice
historical fiction
conflict
informative
  nonfiction

primary
  source
secondary
  source
tone
couplet
sound
  devices

Self ASSESSMENT

Compare the recent additions to your portfolio with earlier pieces. How has your writing improved? Write down your three strongest improvements as a writer and reader.

Setting GOALS

By now you have completed a number of research-based projects. In doing them, what did you discover to be your greatest strength? Write a note describing how that strength can help you with future research projects.

Reviewing Literary Concepts

OPTION 1

Students should choose the symbol that they feel is most significant for each story. Ask for volunteers to share their ideas with the rest of the class.

OPTION 2

Photocopy the Unit Five Resource Book, page 81, to provide students with a ready-made, full-depth chart for analyzing voice.

Building Your Portfolio

Students should evaluate the items in their Working Portfolios and choose pieces that represent their highest quality work for their Presentation Portfolios.

For more information on using Portfolios, use *Teacher's Guide to Assessment and Portfolio Use*, page 53.

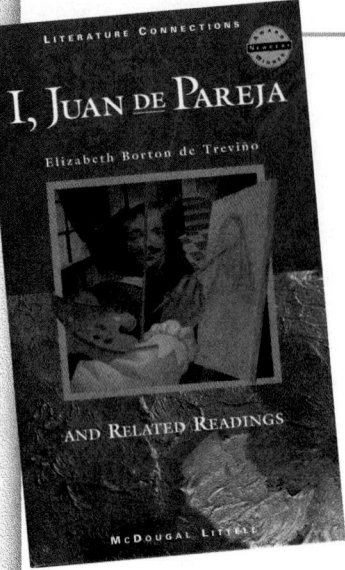

LITERATURE CONNECTIONS
I, Juan de Pareja

BY ELIZABETH BORTON DE TREVIÑO

This Newbery Award–winning historical novel, set in 17th-century Spain, is based on the life of a young black slave inherited by master painter Diego Velázquez. Juan de Pareja begins secretly indulging his own love of painting, an activity forbidden to slaves.

These thematically related readings are provided along with *I, Juan de Pareja*:

**How to Paint the
Portrait of a Bird**
BY JACQUES PRÉVERT

Mi Maestro
BY ANA CASTILLO

The Magical Horse
BY LAURENCE YEP

from **The American Eye**
BY JAN GREENBERG AND
SANDRA JORDAN

The Jade Stone
BY CARYN YACOWITZ AND
AARON SHEPARD

A Work of Art
BY MARGARET MAHY

To Look at Any Thing
BY JOHN MOFFITT

Aunt Zurletha
BY RUBY DEE

And Even *More* . . .

The Witch of Blackbird Pond

BY ELIZABETH GEORGE SPEARE

This historical novel is about a young girl's rebellion against her surroundings. The choices she must make when a woman she knows is accused of witchcraft lead her to challenge prevailing beliefs. This book is available as part of the Literature Connections series published by McDougal Littell.

Books
The African Mask
BY JANET E. RUPERT
Around the year 1000, an African girl discovers her unique talents.

Talking with Artists, Volume III
BY PAT CUMMINGS
Conversations with artists about their work and how they found their artistic "voices"

Bill Peet: An Autobiography
BY BILL PEET
The author's difficult childhood and his love of drawing helped him develop a career as an animator, writer, and illustrator.

Across Five Aprils

By Irene Hunt

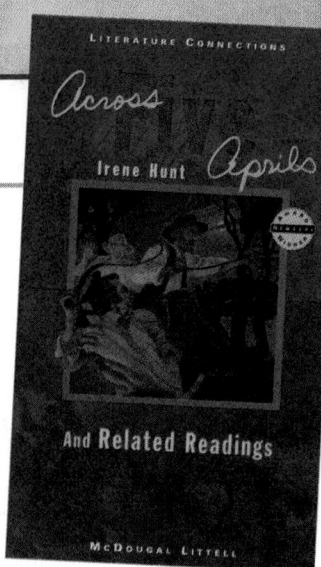

A family is divided by the Civil War when the three oldest boys go off to battle and the youngest, Jethro Creighton, is left to run the farm. Over five years, Jethro grows up with the fears, sorrows, and horrors of war as experienced from the home front. This historical novel is a Newbery Honor Book.

These thematically related readings are provided along with *Across Five Aprils*:

from **The Boys' War**
By Jim Murphy

The Mysterious Mr. Lincoln
By Russell Freedman

The Gettysburg Address
By Abraham Lincoln

The Drummer Boy of Shiloh
By Ray Bradbury

Around the Campfire
By Andrew Hudgins

The Huts at Esquimaux
By Norman Dubie

The Sniper
By Liam O'Flaherty

from **Voices from the Battlefield**
By Milton Meltzer

Crow and Weasel
By Barry Lopez
Two young men of the Northern Plains journey to find their own stories.

Shadow Spinner
By Susan Fletcher
An orphan girl uses storytelling to save the sultan's wife.

Mummies and Their Mysteries
By Charlotte Wilcox
Mummies around the world

Stones, Bones and Petroglyphs
By Susan Goodman, Michael Doolittle
"Digging into Southwest Archaeology"

The Roman News
By Andrew Langley, Philip De Souza
Life in ancient Rome, presented in newspaper form

Other Media

The Multimedia Workshop
Test your creativity.
Davidson & Associates
(CD-ROM)

In the Shadow of Vesuvius
Herculaneum and Pompeii
National Geographic
(VIDEOCASSETTE)

Exploring Ancient Cities
Explore Pompeii, Crete, Petra, and Teotihuacan.
Sumeria/Scientific American
(CD-ROM)

EXTEND YOUR READING   **763**

North America, Year 1000, Time Capsule

OVERVIEW

In *Words on a Page,* Lenore's father, Baba, fears that modern education will erase the traditions of his people. The Ojibway share with many North American first people a struggle to preserve cultures altered and diminished by European influx. In the year 1000 A.D. Europeans had not yet begun regular contact with the Americas. There were no horses on the North American continent. And none of the transplanted crops, such as apples, had arrived here. Of course, no one spoke European languages such as English and Spanish. However many of the foods we now eat, and the words that are now part of everyday English were present here. The word *moose* for example, comes from the Anishnabe word pronounced *mooz.*

Research Questions

● What was life like in the different regions of North America in 1000 A.D.?

● How do archaeologists and history keepers know about earlier time periods?

Investigation The class will act as a team to produce a time capsule that could have been created and buried in the year 1000 A.D. in one region of North America. They might choose the Northern Canadian taiga, where the Ojibway lived during that time, or they might choose a region local to their own school, and learn about a civilization or nation that lived in the area at that time. Alternatively, you might wish to have small groups research different locations and people. Each group's time capsule will include some writing—a traditional myth or legend from early history, some crafted item(s) or illustrations reflecting and crafted clothing illustrations picturing year 1000 technology.

Wrap-up Students should plan to bury the capsule with a ceremony to which other students, teachers, and members of the community are invited. If appropriate, the burial can be accompanied by traditional music and a dedication to the people it represents. The exact burial spot will also be recorded mathematically using a grid.

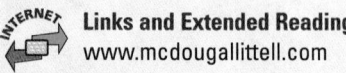

Links and Extended Reading
www.mcdougallittell.com

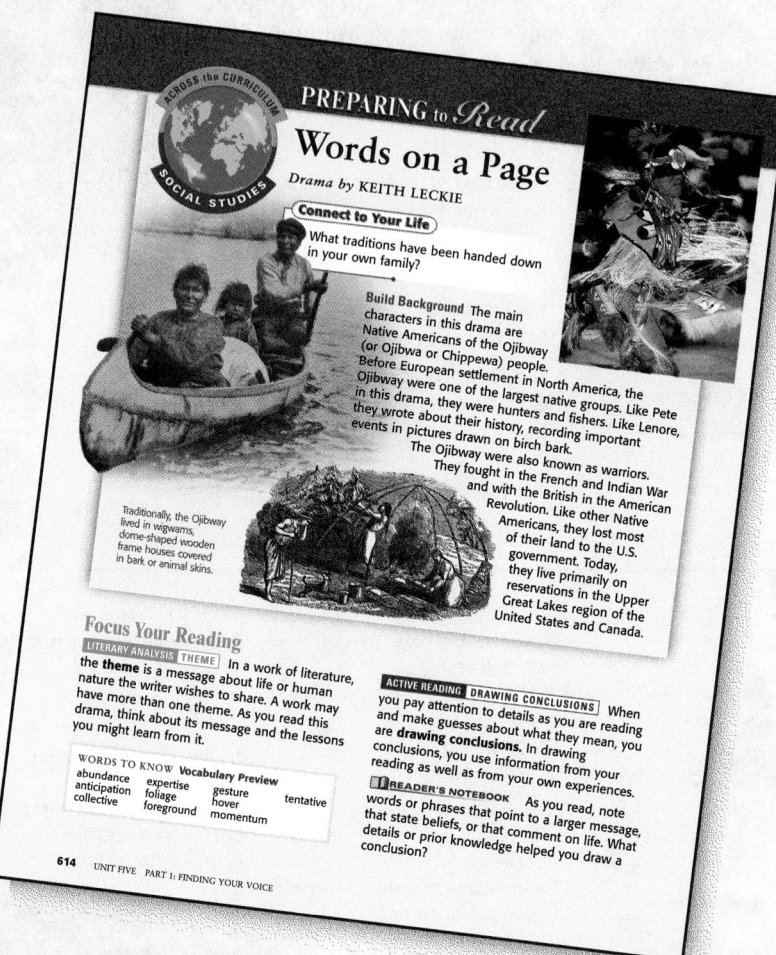

OBJECTIVES

❏ research and retell legends of ancient North America

❏ research and record Native American origins of English words, as well as the meanings of some words and phrases in Native American languages

❏ learn about and report on early clothing, crafts, and other technologies of North America

❏ create a coordinate grid that shows the exact burial spot for a time capsule

Team Teaching Assignments

CONNECT TO **LANGUAGE ARTS** Anishinabe, or the Ojibway language, is rich in oral tradition. There is a vast repertoire of Ojibway stories available for research. One small group of students should research the language. Another group should read some Ojibway stories. Students will find the Ojibway had words for many familiar phrases, for numbers, as well as for the animals around them. For the time capsule, have students create an Anishinabe/English phrase book. Another group can compile a bibliography, and short synopsis, of some Ojibwan tales or legends. If possible, pairs of students could tape record some of the stories, and place the cassette in the capsule. Note that **each** activity can be adapted to a different Native nation. *(2–3 class periods)*

> **YOU WILL NEED:**
> - Web access (optional)
> - tape recorder (optional)
> - books of Native American legends
> - notebook

CONNECT TO **SOCIAL STUDIES** The word "Ojibway" means "puckered up" and refers to the Ojibway style of moccasin. The Ojibway made most of their clothing from buckskin. Have a small group of students research Ojibway clothing—the fabric and design. Students should create pictures of the everyday wear of the Ojibway. An alternative project would be to have a small group of students research and make an article of clothing in this style—perhaps moccassins or leggings or an example of beadwork. If possible, have students caption their pictures or crafted artifact, using both the Anishinabe and English languages. Alternatively the same activity can be adapted to a more local Native American culture. *(3–4 class periods)*

> **YOU WILL NEED:**
> - Web access (optional)
> - reference books
> - sewing materials (optional)

CONNECT TO **SCIENCE** The Ojibway favored woodland areas near lakes. They ate different kinds of berries and nuts as well as meat and fish. They also gathered wild rice, and celebrations of a "wild rice gathering" every year still take place. They were knowledgeable of herbs and medicinal plants. The Ojibway lived in houses built on pole frames in wigwam shape and made of birchbark and cattail mats. They were skilled fishers. Have students research the Ojibway way of life and create illustrations—preferably captioned in both Anishinabe and English—entitled "A Day in the Life of the Ojibway Year 1000" Possible topics might include; housing; plants; hunting; food; rice and berry gathering. Then have a group of students construct and decorate a "capsule" such as a large box or tube. They should place their assignments in the capsule after they have been displayed or presented in the classroom. The same activity can be adapted to a more local Native culture. *(3–4 class periods)*

> **YOU WILL NEED:**
> - Web access (optional)
> - reference books
> - poster paper

CONNECT TO **MATHEMATICS** Have students create a coordinate grid that shows the exact burial spot for the time capsule. First, clear a spot around the school or in another permissionable location. Have pairs of students conduct a survey of the spot for burial, staking it into an archaeological grid, using popsicle sticks and twine. They should then use graph paper to create a coordinatae grid with numbers running up each axis, based on the numbers of sticks along each side of the site. After a burial ceremony, students should mark their grids with an appropriate graph and label for the capsule's exact spot. An alternate activity would be to have a pair of students create a diagram with clues to the burial spot, such as: begin here; turn 90 degrees left; go one meter straight ahead, and so on. *(2–3 class periods)*

> **YOU WILL NEED:**
> - graph paper
> - rulers
> - popsicle sticks
> - twine
> - a small plot of earth to dig in

ACROSS the CURRICULUM

Ancient Egyptian Burial Chamber

OVERVIEW

The burial customs of ancient Egypt have long been a source of fascination. For millennia, the sandy banks of the Nile— "the long river between the deserts"—preserved these ancient wonders. Egypt's majestic pyramids, hidden tombs, mysterious mummies, and buried treasures of gilded objects both fantastic and familiar have not only tantalized the imagination but provided invaluable information about this most ancient of cultures. The following project might serve as part of a larger unit on Ancient Egypt.

Research Questions

• What can be found in the tombs of ancient Egypt?

• Who has been buried there?

• What have archaeologists and historians learned from examining the tombs?

Investigation The class will work as a team to produce a display of information about ancient Egyptian tombs. If possible, this should be housed in a sort of chamber, so that students might simulate the experience of stepping into one of the small rooms that typically housed objects in a tomb. Large appliance boxes might be used; sheets might be draped over a frame; freestanding chalkboards might be used to fence in a corner and topped with a posterboard roof. Ideally, the chamber would be dim enough so that a flashlight could be used during visits. The inside of the chamber should feature depictions and explanations of tomb objects. Also on display should be a map of pyramids and tombs along the Nile, an explanation of mummification, and a time line representing the span of kingdoms and dynasties.

Wrap-up Students will assemble the chamber and decorate it with hieroglyphics. They may wish to invite other classes to investigate the chamber. If possible, have students watch videotapes that show footage of the Nile Valley and explore its pyramids and tombs.

Links and Extended Reading
www.mcdougallittell.com

**LaserLinks: Background
Historical Connection
Art Gallery**

OBJECTIVES

❑ represent and understand the significance of tomb objects

❑ map the pyramids and tombs along the Nile

❑ explain the process of mummification

❑ create a time line that spans the dynasties of ancient Egypt

Team Teaching Assignments

CONNECT TO LANGUAGE ARTS Egyptian tombs were piled high with everything the deceased pharaoh and his family might need in the afterlife—furniture, dishes, headrests, jewelry, cosmetics, linens, food, games, and writing instruments—as well as statues that represented such essential figures as servants and soldiers. Of course, items specific to burial, such as sarcophagi and canopic jars, were of particular importance. Students should be given some time to browse books with pictures of these many objects. Each student should make a picture of a specific object and write a paragraph explaining its significance. If space permits, some students may wish to represent their object with sculpture rather than illustration. These representations will be displayed inside the chamber, taped or pinned to its walls or arranged on shelving. *(3–4 class periods)*

YOU WILL NEED:
- Web access (optional)
- reference books
- paper
- colored pens and pencils

CONNECT TO SOCIAL STUDIES Although the three pyramids of Giza, near Cairo, are by far the most recognizable of these ancient monuments, many more pyramids—as well as tombs, temples, and palaces—once dotted the banks of the Nile. Students should make a large map that represents the Nile Valley. They should accurately note the locations of the pyramid groupings of the Old Kingdom pharaohs. Next, they should note the locations of the rock tombs of the New Kingdom. They may wish to use triangles to represent pyramids and another symbol to represent tombs; these should be clearly indicated in a key. In addition, students might wish to note the locations of the Sphinx, the Colossi of Memnon, and other well-known sites and to make symbols for these on the map. The map might be hung near the chamber. *(2–4 class periods)*

YOU WILL NEED:
- atlases and encyclopedias
- colored pencils or markers
- posterboard

CONNECT TO SCIENCE No aspect of ancient Egypt haunts the imagination like mummies. How are the bodies preserved? What is inside of them? How much fabric was needed to wrap each one? What happened to the brain? Fortunately, scientific research can offer answers to these questions and more. Working in small groups, students should research how the ancient Egyptians embalmed and buried their dead. The class might be divided into four teams to reasearch the following: beliefs and rituals surrounding death; preservation of the body; mummy cases; and animal mummies (millions of animals were bred for the purpose of mummification). Each group should create a poster containing important facts about its subject, as well as diagrams and illustrations. Next, each group should present the information verbally to the class, using the poster as a visual aid. Afterward, the posters might be hung on the outside of the chamber. *(3–4 class periods)*

YOU WILL NEED:
- Web access (optional)
- reference books
- posterboard
- colored pens and pencils

CONNECT TO MATHEMATICS For about 3,000 years, the land of Egypt was ruled by kings who, around 1400 B.C., became known as pharaohs. This span is usually divided into thirty-one dynasties. It also includes the three kingdoms of ancient Egypt: the Old Kingdom, when pyramids were first built; the Middle Kingdom, a great.reunification that brought further building of pyramids; and the New Kingdom, when the empire expanded and pharaohs were interred at the Valley of the Kings. Students should create a time line that stretches from the earliest Egyptian dynasty (c. 3100 B.C.) until the land was conquered by Alexander the Great in 332 B.C. Students might label all the dynasties or simply indicate the three kingdoms as well as famous pharaohs associated with each. The time line could run along the outside of the chamber or simply hang on a bulletin board. *(3–4 class periods)*

YOU WILL NEED:
- reference books
- rulers
- pens or pencils
- paper

Unit Overview

In Unit Six, "Across Cultures," students will explore folk tales, fables, myths, and legends from around the world. The selections in Unit Six are grouped in "links" that correspond thematically to the previous units. The selections may be read separately, or each grouping of "links" may be read with the selections of the corresponding thematic unit.

Links to Unit One: Tests of Courage
- The Boy Who Flew
- Arachne
- Ceres and Proserpina

Links to Unit Two: Growth and Change
- The Disobedient Child
- The Bamboo Beads

Links to Unit Three: A Sense of Fairness
- In the Land of Small Dragon
- King Thrushbeard

Links to Unit Four: Wondrous Worlds
- Why Monkeys Live in Trees
- The Legend of the Hummingbird
- The Living Kuan-yin

Links to Unit Five: Making Your Mark
- The Frog Who Wanted to Be a Singer
- Where the Girl Rescued Her Brother

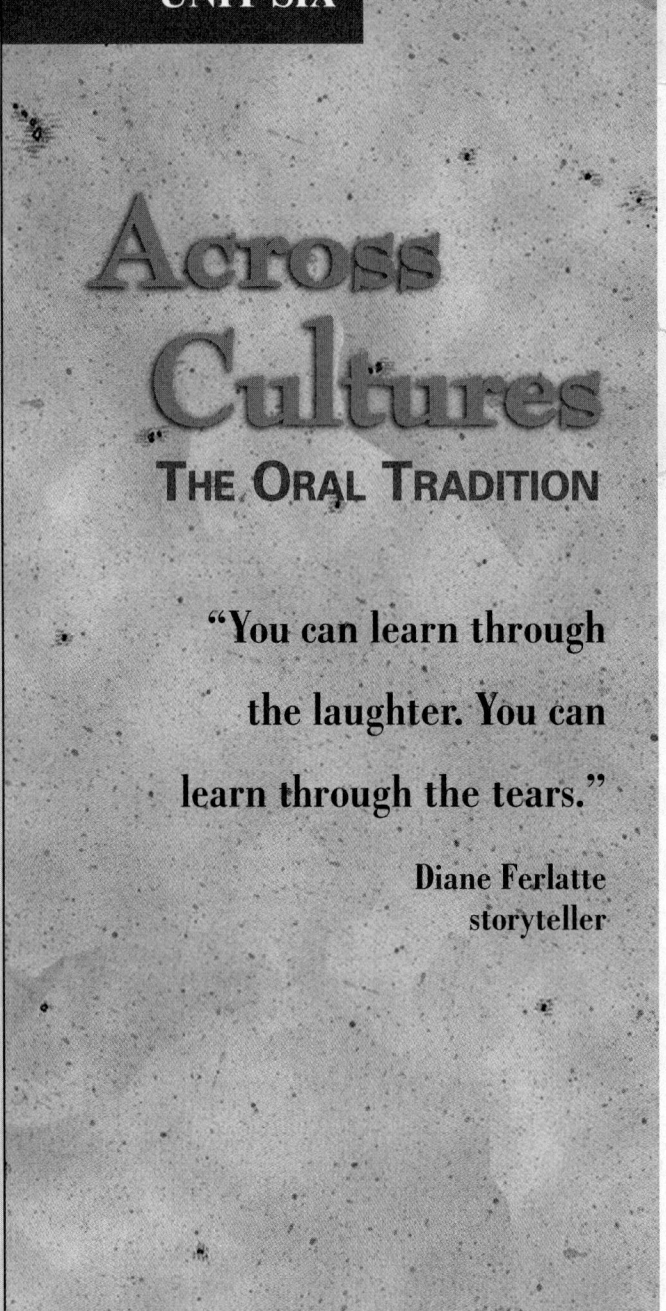

UNIT SIX

Across Cultures
THE ORAL TRADITION

"You can learn through the laughter. You can learn through the tears."

Diane Ferlatte
storyteller

764

Diane Ferlatte lives in California, where she keeps the ancient traditions of her African ancestors alive through storytelling.

Teaching Options

765

Discovering the Oral Tradition

Have students read the quotation on page 764 by storyteller Diane Ferlatte, whose photograph appears on page 765. Then ask the following discussion questions:

1. What do you think Diane Ferlatte means by "the laughter" and "the tears"?

   Possible Response: She means the happiness and sorrow that come into everybody's life.

2. What might a storyteller learn through the laughter and tears?

   Possible Responses: She might learn how to tell a story that moves people; she might learn how to be in touch with and express her own joys and sorrows.

3. What stories have you read or seen in movies or television shows that made you laugh or cry?

Introducing Storytelling

Use the following activity to help students experience how a story takes shape and changes as it is passed around. Divide the class into four or five groups. Have the first group make up or relate a true story about a childhood experience to tell the second group. Groups may wish to appoint one person as storyteller or take turns telling parts of the story. Have the second group tell the story to the third group and so on until all groups have heard it. Have the last group tell the story to the whole class.

Then have students compare and contrast the story that the last group told and the story that other groups told or heard. Challenge students to make a generalization about what happens to a story as it is passed along orally.

Possible Responses: The words change. Details may be added or subtracted. They may become exaggerated. Sometimes the meaning changes, too.

Mini Lesson **Speaking and Listening**

STORYTELLING IN THE CLASSROOM

You might wish to modify the classroom to establish an atmosphere that is conducive to storytelling. You may:

• dim the lights
• lower the window shades
• have students sit in a circle on the floor
• provide a box of props for students to use as they tell stories.

Students can help create an atmosphere for storytelling by being attentive listeners. Consider having them sit quietly for a moment before beginning a story. Some students might try listening with their eyes closed or try helping the storyteller by adding sound effects.

Features and Selections	Literary Analysis	Reading and Critical Thinking	Writing Opportunities	
Across Cultures: The Oral Tradition **Storytellers Past and Present** **Keeping the Past Alive**				
Links to Unit 1		Comparing Texts, 787 Informal Assessment, 775, 780 Standardized Test Practice, 785		
Links to Unit 2		Comparing Texts, 801	Self Assessment, 793	
Links to Unit 3		Comparing Texts, 819 Standardized Test Practice, 812 Comparing a Video with a Story, 815 Informal Assessment, 817	Write Proverbs, 819	
Writing Workshop: Research **Report** **Assessment Practice**		Analyzing a Student Model, 821	Writing Your Research Report, 823	
Links to Unit 4		Comparing Texts, 843 Standardized Test Practice, 833	Write a "Why" Story, 843	
Links to Unit 5		Comparing Texts, 857 Informal Assessment, 854		

Writing Workshop: Comparison-
  and-Contrast Essay
 	
Assessment Practice
		Analyzing a Student Model, 859	Writing Your Comparison-and-
			  Contrast Essay, 861	

Building Your Portfolio **Across Cultures: The Oral Tradition**		Studying Heroes, 864 Self Assessment, 864	Building your Portfolio, 864	

LEGEND   DLS – Daily Language SkillBuilder   Green type – Teacher's Edition

Speaking and Listening Viewing and Representing	Inquiry and Research	Grammar, Usage, and Mechanics	Vocabulary	
Storytelling in the Classroom, 765 Listening to a Story, 766 Storytelling, 767				
Create a Picture Book, 786 Present a Tableau, 787 Art Appreciation, 773, 776 Drama Performance, 774, 783 Investigative Reporting, 779	Map the Wonders of Ancient Greece, 786 Research Flight, 786	Pronoun and Antecedent Agreement, 782	Meaning Clues, 787 Prefix ob-, 777 Capitalization of Proper Names, 781	
Present a Puppet Show, 800 Create a Market Display, 800 Paint a Mural, 801 Viewing and Representing, 790 Art Appreciation, 797 Critical Viewing, 792 Dialect, 794	Investigate Bamboo, 800 Map Hurricanes, 801 Explore Music, 801	Verb Forms, 791	Analogies, 801 Compound Words and Contractions, 798	
Choral Reading, 805 Interviews, 808 Storytelling, 813	Research Life in the Middle Ages, 819	Using Italics, 806 Contractions and Possessive Pronouns, 816	Meaning Clues, 819 Context Clues, 819 The Suffix –ance, 810	
Picturing Text Structure, 822		Focusing Your Report, 826 Compound Subjects, 826 Revising and Editing, 827 Avoiding Double Negatives, 827		
Dramatize a Tale, 842 Art Appreciation, 830 Viewing and Representing, 834, 839 Choral Reading, 837	Celebrate Festivals, 842 Map Ancient Trade Routes, 842 Learn About Money, 843 Find the Trickster, 843	Subject Pronouns, 836 Subject-Verb Agreement, 841	Meaning Clues, 843 The Prefix ex-, 831	
Hold a Storytelling Festival, 856 Make a "Why Story" Bulletin Board, 857 Illustrate Quill Decoration, 857 Art Appreciation, 846, 851 Rhythm and Blues, 850	Research the Horse, 856 Explore Rhythm and Blues, 856 Map Native American Territories, 857	Predicate Adjectives, 848	Example Clues, 857 Acrostic, 857 Suffixes –ible and –able, 852	
Picturing Text Structure, 860		Elaborating with Examples and Other Details, 862 Comparing with Adjectives, 862 Revising and Editing, 863 Subject-Verb Agreement, 863		

To introduce the theme of this unit, use Fine Art Transparencies T34–36 in the Communications Transparencies and Copymasters.

	Unit Resource Book	Assessment	Integrated Technology and Media	Additional Support — Literary Analysis Transparencies
Links to Unit 1 *pp. 770–787*	• Summaries p. 4 • Active Reading p. 5 • Literary Analysis p. 6 • Words to Know p. 7 • Grammar p. 8 • Spelling p. 9 • Selection Quiz p. 10	• Selection Test, Formal Assessment pp. 125–126 ⊙ Test Generator	◯ Audio Library ▬ Video: Literature in Performance, Video Resource Book, pp. 31–38 ⟿ Research Starter www.mcdougallittell.com	• Fables/Myths/Tall Tales T30 • Greek/Roman Gods Chart T31
Links to Unit 2 *pp. 788–801*	• Summaries p. 11 • Active Reading p. 12 • Literary Analysis p. 13 • Words to Know p. 14 • Grammar p. 15 • Spelling p. 16 • Selection Quiz p. 17	• Selection Test, Formal Assessment pp. 127–128 ⊙ Test Generator	◯ Audio Library ⟿ Research Starter www.mcdougallittell.com	• Setting T6
Links to Unit 3 *pp. 802–819*	• Summaries p. 18 • Active Reading p. 19 • Literary Analysis p. 20 • Words to Know p. 21 • Grammar p. 22 • Spelling p. 23 • Selection Quiz p. 24	• Selection Test, Formal Assessment pp. 129–130 ⊙ Test Generator	◯ Audio Library ⟿ Research Starter www.mcdougallittell.com	• Characterization T4

Writing Workshop: Research Report

Unit Six Resource Book
• Prewriting p. 25
• Drafting and Elaboration p. 26
• Peer Response Guide pp. 27–28
• Revising, Editing, and Proofreading p. 29
• Student Models pp. 31–32
• Rubric for Evaluation p. 33

⊙ **Writing Coach**

Writing Transparencies T1–4, T7, T12, T39, T41, T53, T54, T56

Reading and Critical Thinking Transparencies T37

Grammar Transparencies and Copymasters C98

	Unit Resource Book	Assessment	Integrated Technology and Media	Additional Support — Literary Analysis Transparencies
Links to Unit 4 *pp. 828–843*	• Summaries p. 34 • Active Reading p. 35 • Literary Analysis p. 36 • Words to Know p. 37 • Grammar p. 38 • Spelling p. 39 • Selection Quiz p. 40	• Selection Test, Formal Assessment pp. 131–132 ⊙ Test Generator	◯ Audio Library	• Characterization T4
Links to Unit 5 *pp. 844–857*	• Summaries p. 41 • Active Reading p. 42 • Literary Analysis p. 43 • Words to Know p. 44 • Grammar p. 45 • Spelling p. 46 • Selection Quiz p. 47	• Selection Test, Formal Assessment pp. 133–134 ⊙ Test Generator	◯ Audio Library ⊙ LaserLinks, Teacher's SourceBook, p. 53	

Writing Workshop: Comparison-and-Contrast Essay

Unit Six Resource Book
• Prewriting p. 48
• Drafting and Elaboration p. 49
• Peer Response Guide pp. 50–51
• Revising, Editing, and Proofreading p. 52
• Student Models pp. 53–55
• Rubric for Evaluation p. 56

⊙ **Writing Coach**

Writing Transparencies T1–4, T13, T28, T29

Reading and Critical Thinking Transparencies T35

Unit Assessment
• Unit Test, Formal Assessment pp. 135–136
⊙ Test Generator
• Unit Six Integrated Test, Integrated Assessment pp. 13–18

Unit Technology
⟿ ClassZone www.mcdougallittell.com
⊙ Electronic Teacher Tools

Reading and Critical Thinking Transparencies	Grammar Transparencies and Copymasters	Vocabulary Transparencies and Copymasters	Writing Transparencies	Communications Transparencies and Copymasters
• Summarizing (Story Map) T13 • Compare and Constrast T17 • 5Ws and How Question Frame T45	• Daily Language SkillBuilder T24 • Pronoun and Antecedent Agreement C73		• Locating Information in the Library T41 • Using the Catalog T42	• Dramatic Reading T12
• Summarizing (Story Map) T13	• Daily Language SkillBuilder T24 • Verb Forms C81		• Locating Information Using the Internet T47–48	• Evaluation Matrix: Film/Video T7 • Giving and Using Feedback to Improve Performance, T16
• Compare and Constrast T17	• Daily Language SkillBuilder T25 • Using Italics C131 • Contractions and Possessive Pronouns C75		• Locating Information Using Print Resources T45	• Interviewing T9 • Dramatic Reading T12

STUDENTS ACQUIRING ENGLISH

The **Spanish Study Guide**, pp. 154–165, includes language support for the following pages:
• Family and Community Involvement (per unit)

• Selection Summaries and Vocabulary
• Active Reading
• Literary Analysis

Reading and Critical Thinking Transparencies	Grammar Transparencies and Copymasters	Vocabulary Transparencies and Copymasters	Writing Transparencies	Communications Transparencies and Copymasters
• Connecting T2	• Daily Language SkillBuilder T25 • Subject Pronouns C71 • Subject-Verb Agreement C114			• Dramatic Reading T12 • Storyboard Templates T37, T38
• Predicting T7 • Making Inferences T10	• Daily Language SkillBuilder T26 • Predicate Adjectives C87		• Focusing the Report T12 • Comparison-and-Constrast Essay (by Feature) T29	• Appreciative Listening T2

STUDENTS ACQUIRING ENGLISH

The **Spanish Study Guide**, pp. 166–171, includes language support for the following pages:
• Family and Community Involvement (per unit)

• Selection Summaries and Vocabulary
• Active Reading
• Literary Analysis

Selection	SkillBuilder Sentences	Suggested Answers
Links to Unit One	1. Daedalus and Icarus wants to learn how to fly. 2. The gods looks down on people and meddles in their lives.	1. Daedalus and Icarus **want** to learn how to fly. 2. The gods **look** down on people and **meddle** in their lives.
Links to Unit Two	1. Papa Bois did'nt tell anyone who he was. 2. She cant' figure out where those beads came from.	1. Papa Bois **didn't** tell anyone who he was. 2. She **can't** figure out where those beads came from.
Links to Unit Three	1. The Princess didn't want to marry king thrushbeard. 2. This story took place a long time ago in germany, a Country in europe.	1. The **princess** didn't want to marry **King Thrushbeard**. 2. This story took place a long time ago in **Germany**, a **country** in **Europe**.
Links to Unit Four	1. King Gorilla was mean to the animals and tried to play a joke on their. 2. A nasty old King Gorilla was him!	1. King Gorilla was mean to the animals and tried to play a joke on **them**. 2. A nasty old King Gorilla was **he**!
Links to Unit Five	1. Frog had the most deepest voice of all the animals. 2. The show on Friday night was interestinger than usual.	1. Frog had the **deepest** voice of all the animals. 2. The show on Friday night was **more interesting** than usual.

Grammar Focus by Unit	Unit One	Unit Two	Unit Three	Unit Four	Unit Five	Unit Six
	The Sentence and Its Parts	Nouns, Pronouns, and Verbs	Modifiers	Phrases	Compound and Complex Sentences	Review

The Language of Literature offers several options for integrating grammar instruction and literature.

- Each unit has a specific grammar focus. The grammar focus for this unit is highlighted on the planning chart. Categories of grammar skills for this unit are shown in red.
- The Pupil's Edition includes instructive features entitled *Grammar in Context*. The instruction in these features arises from the selections and relates to the grammar focus for each unit.
- The Writing Workshops in the Pupil's Edition include grammar tips that help the students produce error-free drafts.
- Mini Lessons in the Teacher's Edition complement the instruction in the *Grammar in Context* features. Additional Mini Lessons relate to the grammar focus for each unit as well as to the literature.
- Daily Language SkillBuilders in the Teacher's Edition provide students with ongoing proofreading practice and reinforce punctuation, spelling, grammar and usage, and capitalization.
- Grammar Copymasters and Transparencies, which may be used independently or in conjunction with the Mini Lessons in the Teacher's Edition, present grammar in a traditional, systematic sequence.

PE instruction shown in black
TE Mini Lessons shown in green

THE SENTENCE AND ITS PARTS

Compound Subjects
Writing Workshop, p. 826

PRONOUNS
Pronoun and Antecedent Agreement
Links to Unit One, p. 782
Contractions and Possessive Pronouns
Links to Unit Three, p. 816
Subject Pronouns
Links to Unit Four, p. 836

VERBS
Verb Forms
Links to Unit Two, p. 791

ADJECTIVES AND ADVERBS
Avoiding Double Negatives
Assessment Practice, p. 827
Predicate Adjectives
Links to Unit Five, p. 848

Comparing with Adjectives
Writing Workshop, p. 862

SUBJECT-VERB AGREEMENT
Subject-Verb Agreement
Links to Unit Four, p. 841
Assessment Practice, p. 863

PUNCTUATION
Using Italics
Links to Unit Three, p. 806

OVERVIEW

Students plan a program of stories to be told during a storytelling festival.

Project at a glance The selections in Unit Six emphasize how storytelling acts as a means of preserving cultural heritage and passes on oral histories and traditions. For this project, students will work in small groups to plan a Storytelling Festival, in which each member of the group will tell a story which relates to a theme or culture assigned to the group. Groups will collaborate on the selection of stories as well as the props and/or costumes, rehearsing together so others can help with the interpretation of the story and characterization for the narrator. The stories will be told either in a festival or in front of the class.

SCHEDULING

Individual stories should take about five minutes. You may want to schedule the presentations over the course of 2–3 class periods, or at the end of the unit depending on your purposes.

PROJECT OBJECTIVES

- To demonstrate the speaking and listening skills introduced in the activity
- To learn about the importance and use of folklore and storytelling
- To work collaboratively with a small group to prepare a program of stories
- To develop storytelling skills by recognizing what keeps an audience interested
- To develop listening and speaking skills by participating in a storytelling festival

SUGGESTED GROUP SIZE

5–6 students per group

Storytelling Festival

 ## Getting Started

If you are going to create an actual festival with an invited audience, reserve a date in the auditorium or other appropriate room, as well as some rehearsal time for the groups. If you plan to decorate, start gathering sheets for backdrops that groups can paint. Decide if you will get costumes or if they will be the responsibility of individual groups. Invite not only other students but administrators and families as well.

If you are using your classroom as a stage, consider arranging the audience's seats in a large semicircle, in order to give the storyteller adequate room to move around and, perhaps, to interact with the audience.

If you would like to invite a storyteller to talk to the class, now is the time to locate one and schedule a time. You should also make available different types of books about the cultures students will be focusing on.

You might want to record the storytellers on video to preserve the performances for other classes and for your own review. Arrange for a school media person or volunteer parent to assist with the taping.

Writing Workshop Connection

As a springboard, students may use the Writing Workshop assignments **Research Report**, p. 820, and **Comparison-and-Contrast Essay**, p. 858.

 ## Directing the Project

Preparing Divide students into groups. Tell students that they will be working cooperatively to plan and present a program of stories. Each group member will tell a story. Stories should be no longer than five minutes, so group members may have to edit their stories for length:

▶ Select a culture or theme for each group. Have students research the culture before creating their presentation. Groups will decide together which stories will be told and should help one another edit down stories. At this time, explain exactly what you expect in the way of props, costumes, and setting. You might also review with students the Speaking and Listening Skills on the next page.

▶ When groups have finalized their list of stories, meet with them to check for coherency in theme or culture. As groups work to edit the stories, meet again to offer suggestions and help them decide which elements of each story are necessary and which are expendable. Stress that the oral tradition entails personal interpretation each time the tale is retold, so students can add their own touches as long as the basic story and lesson remain intact. Tell students there is no one "correct" interpretation. Encourage them to imagine how they would feel if they were the actual characters in the situations they are depicting.

▶ You should discuss what makes a story interesting to an audience. You might point out that the character of the narrator has a great deal of influence on how the audience responds to the story.

▶ Students should be aware of the guidelines for working in a group, found on page R106 in the Communication Handbook.

Practicing Groups should determine the order in which they would like to tell the stories. They should rehearse as a group, relying on one another to help with interpretation and to give suggestions. Tell students that giving and receiving feedback during the rehearsal stage is crucial. Refer to the tips in the Feedback Center.

▶ Remind students that there is a time limit. If each story is five minutes, give them a cumulative amount of time for the entire group.

Presenting Before the performances, have students focus on the strategies listed in the Communication Handbook on page R102. Share with them this quotation by storyteller Brenda Wong Aoki: ". . . I sculpt a story until I get to the emotional truth, the human truth. It is this truth that makes a bridge of understanding between peoples." Tell them that one of their primary goals is to communicate this truth both verbally and nonverbally.

▶ If you are able to videotape the storytelling, you can share the performance by circulating the tapes around school.

Teaching the Speaking and Listening Skills

The student is expected to:

Identify how language use—for instance, labels (terms) and sayings (idioms)—reflects regions and cultures

Teaching Suggestions: Have students explore and discuss the culture from which their story originates. If they are unfamiliar with the culture, have them research the country of origin and relevant points that might affect language, such as history, climate, and so on. Then you might have them read through the story and pick out language that reflects this culture. For example, the speaker in the story "The Bamboo Beads" uses the idiom "When I was in my bare feet still" to mean "When I was a child." This reflects the warm climate of the islands of Trinidad and Tobago, and the fact that in the speaker's day, many young children did not wear shoes.

Compare oral traditions across regions and cultures

Teaching Suggestions: After students have a solid basis of understanding about the culture they are focusing on, ask them to discuss the key points of the culture's oral tradition. One way to do this might be to ask, "What values of the society are revealed through the stories?" You may want to bring the class together and create a chart on the board comparing the various cultures they are studying. Ask students to hypothesize:

- why the values and traditions of these cultures may be different.
- what factors may have influenced these differences.
- how they might have changed over time. For example, the Greek myth "Arachne" illustrates how treating others fairly and with kindness was important to the ancient Greeks.

Analyze oral interpretations of literature for effects on the listener

Teaching Suggestions: Discuss with students how nonverbal gestures, body language, and tone of voice affect the message. Encourage them to imagine how they would feel if they were making the same gestures and facial expressions. Have students rehearse their stories for one another and provide feedback as to how well the interpretation is working. You may want to have students fill out a brief evaluation sheet to be discussed at the end of each presentation.

Feedback Center

Students can use the following guidelines when giving and receiving feedback during this project:

Giving Feedback

▶ Ask questions concerning content, purpose, and point of view.

▶ Provide feedback about the interpretation (for instance, the overall impact on the listener).

▶ Comment on the verbal delivery (pitch, pace, volume) and its impact on the listener.

▶ Comment on the nonverbal delivery (body language, including facial expressions and gestures) and its impact on the listener.

Receiving Feedback

▶ Listen to constructive criticism with an open mind.

▶ Use audience feedback in order to modify the presentation to clarify meaning or organization.

3 ▶ Assessing the Project

The following rubric can be used for group or individual assessment.

3 Full Accomplishment

Students followed directions and performed successful oral interpretations that demonstrated an understanding of the content and cultural backdrop of their stories. Students used appropriate body language and tone to enhance the stories, and the audience easily followed their presentations.

2 Substantial Accomplishment

Students selected, edited, and performed oral interpretations for an audience, but the selections were unrelated or not easily followed by the audience. The presentations may have lacked a strong delivery and appropriate body language. Some of the Speaking and Listening Skills were demonstrated.

1 Little Accomplishment

Students did not fully complete the project to the point of performing, or the performance did not fulfill the requirements of the assignment.

STORYTELLERS PAST AND PRESENT

Objectives
Through an article and a diagram, students discover the past influences that shaped a modern-day storyteller and her views about why the oral tradition endures.
- To understand and appreciate the richness of oral storytelling
- To apply and practice skills learned in previous selections

Reading and Analyzing

Reading Skills and Strategies: MAKE JUDGMENTS

Have students assess Diane Ferlatte's statement that "the best way to learn about a people and a culture is to know their stories." Then invite volunteers to give examples from their experience of how knowing someone else's life story can make a difference in a personal relationship.

Possible Response: Knowing something about how my parents grew up helped me better understand their values.

Reading Skills and Strategies: MAKE INFERENCES

Ask students to study the figure of the Xhosa Storyteller by Hubert Shuptrine and to think about why contemporary storytellers might wear traditional dress.

Possible Response: They probably feel more authentic when they are dressed this way and think their listeners will pay more attention to what they say.

DIANE FERLATTE

A Present-Day Storyteller Speaks

Diane Ferlatte performs stories from the African-American tradition. Like storytellers from ancient times, she uses gestures, props, and facial expressions to engage listeners in the drama of the story.

When I was 10, my parents moved to California, looking for work. Every summer they drove me back to New Orleans. I would complain, "Why won't you take me back to Disneyland?" But my parents knew what they were doing. They took me back to my roots. They took me back to Grandpa and Grandma, to homemade biscuits, singing on the porch, and stories when there was no TV or video. I heard many stories at my grandparents' home. Sitting on the big porch in a swing, that's what we'd do. The old folks would always be talking about family, about fishing, about true stories, about ghost stories, or about something that happened at church. As a little kid, I heard lots of stuff. If I had known I was going to be a storyteller, I sure would have listened more carefully.

My stories come from anywhere and everywhere. Most of the African stories I tell are from West Africa. In the old days, stories served to pass along information. That was part of the job of the *griots* (grē-ōz′) who kept alive the oral tradition of a village or family. They could tell you about your whole family line—where your mother came from, who your father was, what they did. It's important to keep alive the history of where you come from and what you are about.

Stories also told about people's adventures, their fears, their hopes.

Mini Lesson Speaking and Listening

LISTENING TO A STORY Remind students that to enjoy the performance of a storyteller, they must listen carefully. Review with them these elements of being a good listener:
- Don't whisper or talk while the story is being told.
- Watch the storyteller as you listen to him or her. This will keep your attention on the story.
- Don't interrupt if you hear something you don't understand. Wait to see if the next part of the story makes it clear.
- Keep in mind any questions that arise as you listen. After the story has finished, ask your questions.

Application Have students watch the performance of "The Cow-Tail Switch," shown on the accompanying laser disc and videotape. Afterwards, have them write brief summaries of the story.

An Ancient Storyteller
For over 500 years the Xhosa (kō'sä) people have lived and shared their stories in southern Africa.

Stories were a way of answering questions. That's where a lot of our "why" and "how" stories come from—how the lion got his roar, for example. People were curious. In African cultures, storytelling is not pure narration, or speaking. There is also music and dance and singing and religion connected with storytelling. All the arts are connected.

Stories come from the conditions in which people live. When the Africans came here as slaves, they weren't allowed to speak their own language, to play their drums, even to learn to read or write. But they could still tell their stories. The oral tradition was very strong in the world of the slaves because that was all they had. A lot of African-American stories have humor in them too. Life was so brutal for the slaves they had to laugh to keep from crying.

That's the power of communication, of the oral tradition. Once you hear somebody else's problem, it makes you think, "I'm not alone in this. Somebody else is going through the same thing." When you hear a story, you can see more of a common thread that goes through all of us. With so many cultures in this country today, we need to talk to each other. And the best way to learn about a people and a culture is to know their stories.

 Literature in Performance

 LaserLinks: Background for Reading
Storyteller

An *umnqwazi* (ŏŏm-ən-kwä'zē), a headdress made of many pieces of cloth, was worn by Xhosa women.

A Xhosa storyteller might begin with a phrase that means "Now for a tale."

The hands are nearly as important as the voice in the telling of a tale, or *ntsomi* (ən-tsō'mē). Hands act out major actions, express emotions, and stress ideas.

STORYTELLERS **767**

STORYTELLER
"The Cow Tail Switch," performed here by professional storyteller Diane Ferlatte, is a typical West African folk tale. It is a story that is closely tied to the culture and ancestry of Africa. "Stories come out from the folk," says Ferlatte. "The stories reflect the world in which the people live—their struggles and the conditions of their lives." Ferlatte explains, "The theme of this story shows how important ancestors are in the African culture." She adds, "This story tells us about where Africans come from."

"I tell this story because it has a good message," Ferlatte says. "You are not dead until you are forgotten. Understanding yourself and your family comes from knowing the stories in your life, from your family's stories. The stories you tell come out of who you are and where you're from."

 Mini Lesson **Speaking and Listening**

STORYTELLING Point out that different families have their stories, too. You may wish to provide students with an example of a "family folk tale"—a story that is told over and over again in one's own family.

Application Have students work in small groups. Have each group member tell a story either from his or her home culture or family. Then have the group identify the stories' similarities and differences. If time permits, call on one volunteer from each group to summarize group members' stories for the class.

Objectives
- To understand the history of oral traditions around the world
- To understand and appreciate types of literature in the oral tradition

Reading and Analyzing

Reading Skills and Strategies:
CHRONOLOGICAL ORDER

Point out to students that a time line allows students to see a sequence of events in a visual way. Explain that this time line shows the places where stories in this unit originated and historic events that occurred there.

Ask which event took place first, the reign of the First Emperor or the first Olympic Games in Greece.

Answer: the first Olympic Games

Reading Skills and Strategies:
MAKE INFERENCES

Direct students' attention to the pictures of the Sphinx and the Great Wall. Ask what such structures might tell about the rulers who had them built.

Possible Response: They were very powerful, commanding a huge force to do this work.

Literary Analysis: ORAL TRADITION

Ask students to review the box diagram on page 768 and compare and contrast the four kinds of literature. What are their similarities and differences?

Possible Response: Students may point out the different purposes, characters, or settings in the types. They should be able to point out as similarities the "Common Elements" that all four types share.

KEEPING THE PAST ALIVE

For nearly as long as words have been spoken, there have been tellers of stories and listeners eager to hear them. When they told stories well, they inspired others to retell them. From generation to generation, stories were passed within families, villages, and cultures. The tellers and listeners were taking part in what came to be called the **oral tradition**. The types of stories in the oral tradition appear in the chart below.

The stories of the oral tradition are a major part of folklore. Folklore brings the past to life for tellers, listeners, and readers of today. Like thread connecting pieces of cloth, folklore connects people's lives across time and place. The time line at the right presents important events of the past in cultures around the world. The legendary tales in this unit reflect those cultures. By reading them, you can discover for yourself how the oral tradition links people and keeps the past alive.

MYTHS
- attempt to answer basic questions about the world
- are considered truthful by their originators

FOLK TALES
- are told primarily for entertainment
- feature humans or humanlike animals

COMMON ELEMENTS
- keep the past alive
- teach lessons about human behavior
- reveal the values of the society

FABLES
- are short tales that illustrate morals
- often have characters that are animals

ORAL HISTORY
- is based on real events
- is considered factual by the teller
- passes along information

AFRICA

2600–2100 B.C. *First Egyptian pyramid and Great Sphinx of Giza built.*

THE AMERICAS

2750–2000 B.C. *Farmers begin to settle in region between modern-day Mexico and Nicaragua.*

Teaching Options

Cross Curricular Link History

THE GREAT PYRAMID The Great Pyramid, resting place of King Khufu, is one of the wonders of architecture. It was originally 480 feet high (146 meters), yet it was built without cranes, pulleys, or lifting tackle.

How did the ancient Egyptians manage to build such a huge structure without these machines?

Even today, architects remain unsure of how they did it.

The Great Pyramid is located in Giza, near the modern city of Cairo, Egypt.

GREECE/ROME

. . .

700s B.C. *First recorded Olympic Games in Greece; Founding of Rome*

ASIA

. . .

215 B.C. *Reign of Ch'in Shih Huang Ti (The First Emperor); Construction of Great Wall begins*

EUROPE

. . .

50 B.C. *German tribes practice agriculture and have contact with the Roman Empire.*

CARIBBEAN

. . .

A.D. 1492 *Carib Indians on various Caribbean islands have first contact with Europeans after the arrival of Christopher Columbus.*

Cross Curricular Link   History

THE ROMAN EMPIRE The area controlled by Rome extended so far that Julius Caesar and Tacitus both describe encounters with Germanic and Celtic tribes. The Romans controlled southern and western Europe during the second century B.C. to the fifth century A.D. Around 50 B.C., Julius Caesar conquered tribes west of the Rhine River in Gaul, an area that is modern-day France. The Romans then tried to extend their rule north of the Elbe River in what is modern Germany, but they failed.

The Romans built thousands of miles of roads in order to connect their growing empire. These roads allowed them to trade with people in distant lands and to exchange ideas with other cultures. The roads were so well constructed that portions of them remain to this day.

OVERVIEW

Objectives

1. To understand and appreciate three myths
2. To understand and appreciate the values and customs of ancient Greece and Rome
3. To extend understanding of the myths through a variety of multimodal and cross-curricular activities

Reading Pathways

- Select one or several students to read each story aloud to the entire class or to small groups of students. Assign this reading in advance so that students have time to become familiar with the story—the characters, vocabulary, conflicts, and so on. Have the audience listen carefully to the stories without following along in their texts.
- Read the stories aloud to the class, pausing at key points to discuss how elements of the story inform students about the customs, values, or beliefs of ancient Greece and Rome.
- After students have read the stories once, they can reread them to identify structural elements such as main character, minor characters, conflict, setting, and plot. Then have students identify similarities and differences between these stories and the selections in Unit One.

5-Minute Warm-Up

Daily Language SkillBuilder

Have students **proofread** the display sentences on page 765e and write them correctly. The sentences also appear on Transparency 24 of **Grammar Transparencies and Copymasters.**

ACROSS CULTURES

LINKS TO UNIT ONE

Tests of Courage

The selections in Unit One describe challenges that force people to find their inner courage. Some of these challenges come from relationships with people, and others are found in struggles with forces of nature. In each of the tales that follow, a mythical character responds to a challenge—and must face the consequences.

ANCIENT ROME

The Story of Ceres and Proserpina

retold by Mary Pope Osborne

The ancient Romans had the same gods and goddesses as the ancient Greeks, but called them by different names. Ceres (sîr′ēz) is the Roman name for Demeter dĭ-mēt′ər), goddess of the harvest. Her daughter is Proserpina (prō-sûr′pə-nə), the Roman name for Persephone, goddess of the dead and of the fertility of the earth. Pluto, Proserpina's husband, is called Hades (hā′dēz) in Greek mythology. In this **myth** Pluto kidnaps Proserpina, and Ceres seeks her daughter's return.

MAJOR GREEK AND ROMAN DEITIES		
	Greek Name	Roman Name
Goddess of love	Aphrodite	Venus
God of medicine and music	Apollo	Apollo
Goddess of wisdom, war, and the arts	Athena	Minerva
God of the underworld	Hades	Pluto
Goddess of marriage and women	Hera (wife of Zeus)	Juno (wife of Jupiter)
God of the sea	Poseidon	Neptune
Ruler of the gods, god of the sky	Zeus	Jupiter

LESSON RESOURCES

UNIT SIX RESOURCE BOOK, pp. 4–10

ASSESSMENT
Formal Assessment, pp. 125–126
Teacher's Guide to Assessment and Portfolio Use
Test Generator

SKILLS TRANSPARENCIES AND COPYMASTERS
Literary Analysis
- Greek/Roman Gods Chart, TR 31 (for Multicultural Link, p. 781)

Reading and Critical Thinking
- 5Ws and How Question Frame, TR 45 (for Mini Lesson, p. 779)

Grammar
- Pronoun and Antecedent Agreement, CM 73 (for Mini Lesson, p. 782)

Communications
- Dramatic Reading, TR 12 (for Mini Lessons, pp. 774, 783)

INTEGRATED TECHNOLOGY
Audio Library
Video: Literature in Performance
- Icarus. See **Video Resource Book,** pp. 31–38
Internet: Research Starter

Visit our website:
www.mcdougallittell.com

The Boy Who Flew

retold by Anne Rockwell

Many Greek **myths** focus on individuals who suffer for their prideful or disobedient behavior. The ancient Greeks placed a great deal of importance on showing respect for human rulers as well as for gods and goddesses. Set mainly on the island of Crete in the Aegean (ĭ-jē'ən) Sea, "The Boy Who Flew" retells the Greek myth of Daedalus (dĕd'l-əs) and Icarus (ĭk'ər-əs). Daedalus was a brilliant inventor who disobeyed the rulers of Crete; his son, Icarus, disobeyed him. Both suffered for their actions.

Arachne

retold by Olivia E. Coolidge

In ancient Greece, the rule of the gods and goddesses was not to be questioned. Many Greek **myths** are about characters who do not stay within limits set by the gods or who ignore their warnings. In this myth a weaver, Arachne (ə-răk'nē), pits herself against Athena (ə-thē'nə), the goddess of wisdom and of all crafts, particularly weaving.

AS YOU READ . . .

Make note of what lessons about human behavior the myths teach.

Keep track of characters' choices and the consequences that follow.

Find out what mysteries of nature are explained.

TEACHING THE LITERATURE

Customizing Instruction

Less Proficient Readers
Have students keep these questions in mind as they read each story.
- Who are the main characters in the story you are reading?
- How would you describe the main character's problem, or conflict?
- What is the resolution to the problem?

Students Acquiring English
Tell students that all three of the stories contain names of Greek and Roman gods and goddesses. Tell students to pay close attention to the footnotes, which give pronunciations and in some cases, brief descriptions of the gods and goddesses.

Use **Spanish Study Guide,** pp. 157–159 for additional support.

Gifted and Talented
Encourage students to learn more about Greek and Roman mythology. Suggest that they read other myths and write a summary of one of the ones they like best.

Summary

In "The Boy Who Flew," Daedalus, a brilliant inventor is called upon to create a structure to confine the Minotaur, a monster with a bull's head and a man's body. When Daedalus defies King Minos and has the Minotaur murdered, Daedalus and his son, Icarus, become prisoners on the island of Crete. Their effort to escape by means of flight results in Icarus's death when he flies too near the sun, and his wax wings melt.

Reading and Analyzing

Literary Analysis: DISTINGUISH LITERARY FORMS: MYTH

Ask students to describe some of the features that make "The Boy Who Flew" a myth.

Possible Response: This story is a myth because it is set in ancient Greece, some of the characters, such as the Minotaur, are not realistic.

Use **Unit Six Resource Book**, p. 6 for more practice. Use **Literary Analysis Transparencies**, p. 30, for additional support.

Active Reading: SUMMARIZE

A Students are expected to paraphrase and summarize text. Ask students to tell what has happened up to this point since Daedalus came to Crete.

Possible Response: Daedalus built a maze to contain the Minotaur, but upon learning that the monster killed 12 youths a year, he helped to kill the Minotaur. King Minos imprisoned Daedalus and his son.

Use **Unit Six Resource Book**, p. 5, for more practice. Use **Reading and Critical Thinking Transparencies**, p. 13, for additional support.

THE BOY WHO Flew

by Anne Rockwell

ONE of Athene's[1] pupils was a man called Daedalus.[2] Even though he was mortal, he was almost as remarkable an inventor and craftsman as the god Hephaestus.[3] He became famous throughout the world.

In the island kingdom of Crete, there was a monster that belonged to King Minos[4] and Queen Pasiphae.[5] This monster had the head of a bull and the body of a man. It was cruel and dangerous, and it was called the Minotaur.[6] Worse yet, it was the child of the queen. King Minos asked Daedalus to come to his kingdom and build something that would imprison the Minotaur within the palace walls.

Daedalus came to Crete, bringing his young son, Icarus,[7] with him. Inside the palace walls, he built a marvelous maze. This maze had such complicated passageways that the monster could not find its way out.

But Daedalus soon discovered that, each year, the Minotaur needed to kill twelve youths and maidens from the city of Athens. Each year, twelve fine young men and women from

---

1. **Athene** (ə-thē'nē): the Greek goddess of wisdom, also known as Athena.
2. **Daedalus** (dĕd'l-əs).
3. **Hephaestus** (hĭ-fĕs'təs): the Greek god of fire and metalworking.
4. **Minos** (mī'nəs).
5. **Pasiphae** (pə-sĭf'ə-ē').
6. **Minotaur** (mĭn'ə-tôr').
7. **Icarus** (ĭk'ər-əs).

WORDS TO KNOW   **maze** (māz) *n.* a confusing network of winding paths or passageways

772

Teaching Options

Athens were sent to Crete to die in the maze. Daedalus did not want his work to be used for murder, so he helped one of the young men who came to die to save himself and his companions and to kill the Minotaur.

Queen Pasiphae was very angry because, as its mother, she loved the Minotaur, terrible as it had been. Her husband, in order to soothe her, decided to punish Daedalus. He made Daedalus and his son prisoners.

No captain of any ship that sailed to Crete dared take them away because the king had

Minotaur (1958), Pablo Picasso. Mayor Gallery, London UK/Bridgeman Art Library Copyright © 2001 Estate of Pablo Picasso/Artists Rights Society (ARS), New York.

decreed that the inventor and his son could never leave the island. They lived in an <u>isolated</u> tower, where Daedalus had a simple workshop. They had only the seagulls for company. How Daedalus <u>yearned</u> to show Icarus the world beyond their island prison!

One day as Daedalus was watching the gulls <u>wheeling</u> and circling above the surf, he had

WORDS TO KNOW	**isolated** (ī′sə-lā′tĭd) *adj.* away from others; lonely **isolate** *v.*
	yearn (yûrn) *v.* to desire strongly
	wheeling (hwē′lĭng) *adj.* flying in curves or circles **wheel** *v.*

773

Mini Lesson · Viewing and Representing

Minotaur
by Pablo Picasso

ART APPRECIATION Pablo Picasso (1881–1973) is considered by many to have been one of the 20th century's most creative and most prolific artists. Picasso, originally from Spain, produced thousands of paintings, sculptures, drawings, and ceramics. Although his earlier works show things in a realistic way, Picasso is best known for his many works of Cubist art. Cubist art breaks down its subject matter into fragments, sometimes presenting parts from various angles, or perspectives.

Instruction Point out some of the facial features of the creature depicted in *Minotaur*. Ask students to consider how Picasso succeeds in creating the look of a monstrous and imposing creature while also conveying a sense of the minotaur's monstrous and imposing confinement.

Possible Response: This painting is not a realistic depiction of a bull. You can tell from the horns, the large nostrils, and the big teeth that this is a monstrous and frightening sort of bull. The composition pushes toward the center and many of the lines suggest a maze.

Ask students to tell whether they had predicted that Icarus would disregard his father's warning.

Possible Response: I had a feeling that Icarus might get carried away with himself and try to fly too high, especially when he started to swoop and soar like a gull.

Reading Skills and Strategies:
MAKE INFERENCES

Ask students to make an inference about the message of this myth.

Possible Response: I think that the message of "The Boy Who Flew" is that young people should heed the advice of their elders, because older people have more experience and wisdom. Even though young people have more physical energy, they don't always have the knowledge and experience needed to make good decisions.

Daedalus and Icarus (15th c.) Private Collection/Bridgeman Art Library.

an inspiration. He shouted down to his son, who was gathering shells on the lonely beach, "Minos may rule the sea, but he does not rule the air!"

Daedalus had observed how the gulls' wings were shaped, and how they worked. No mortal had ever before figured out how a bird could fly, but Daedalus thought he understood.

He and Icarus began to collect all the gull feathers they could find along the beach. They gathered the large, stiff ones and the tiny, light, downy ones that floated in the breeze. They saved the wax that honeybees made. Then Daedalus made wings of the seagull feathers and the beeswax for himself and Icarus. He worked long and patiently, and Icarus helped him,

always doing what his father told him to do.

After they had made two pairs of long, curved wings, Daedalus made two harnesses[8] of leather. He showed Icarus how to place the wings on his shoulders. Then he showed him how to run along the beach until he caught the wind and, like a seagull, flew up into the air.

Father and son practiced together until, one day, Daedalus decided it was time for them to leave the island. As they rose into the air and headed away from their island prison toward the sea, Daedalus called out to Icarus, "Follow me! Do not fly too low, or you will lose the air

---

8. **harnesses:** arrangements of straps (for attaching the wings to their bodies).

Teaching Options

 Mini Lesson **Speaking and Listening**

DRAMA PERFORMANCE Tell students that one way to visualize the events in a story is by acting them out. Although there is not a lot of dialogue on these two pages, students can write a dialogue based on the narrative.

Prepare Tell students to spend some time rereading this part of the story. Then have them write a scene based on the events that happen on these two pages. Suggest that the scene include a narrator, Daedalus, and Icarus.

Present Give students time to rehearse the dialogue. Let students take turns reading the dialogue aloud.

Tell the class to listen carefully and provide constructive feedback when each group is finished with its reading.

📖 Use **Communications Transparencies and Copymasters**, p. 12, for additional support.

and sink into the waves. But do not fly too high, or the heat from the sun will melt the beeswax."

"Yes, Father," shouted Icarus above the sea noises and the wailing of the seagulls who flew beside him.

Higher and higher they flew. At last, Daedalus said, "We will stay at this level all the way. Remember what I told you— follow me!"

As they flew by, fishermen dropped their nets in wonder and farmers stopped at their plows. They thought they were seeing two gods in flight, for surely only gods could fly.

Icarus began to feel more and more sure of himself. He flew upward, then downward. He swooped and soared like a gull, laughing joyously as he did so. He cried out, "Look at me, Father!" and soared upward.

Daedalus beckoned him down, but Icarus thought, He is old and timid while I am young and strong. Surely I can fly a little better than he. Suddenly the boy disappeared into a cloud and flew up and up and up, higher and higher.

Too late, he saw feathers begin to fall from his wings. As the hot sun melted the wax, more and more feathers dropped away. Frantically, the boy flapped his arms in the air, but he could not fly without the wings. Instead, he dropped down and down until he fell into the sea and drowned.

Daedalus flew up in search of his son, calling as he went, "Icarus! Come down to me!"

Then he saw the telltale feathers drifting past him, and he heard the distant splash as Icarus fell into the sea. The old man cried as he continued on his journey, but he flew to freedom. He never made wings for anyone again. ❖

Students Acquiring English

1 Help students understand the meaning of the word *beckoned* by explaining that Daedalus is very worried about Icarus. He is urging him to come down, because he knows what will happen if Icarus flies too close to the sun.

2 Define the word *telltale* by telling students that the flying feathers "tell a tale" about what happened to Icarus. They are evidence of his tragic end.

Less Proficient Readers

Ask students to explain why Icarus doesn't listen to his father's warning.

Possible Response: Icarus thinks that because he is younger and stronger, he can fly higher. (Ironically, it is the inexperience of youth that brings about Icarus's death.)

". . . I acquired a love for stories about the Greek gods and goddesses that lasted all my life."

Anne Rockwell
born 1934

A Love of Reading Anne Rockwell has been creating books for more than 30 years. Trained as an artist, she originally worked in an advertising agency. After starting a family, she wanted to write for children in order to share her love of reading. She began her writing career with retellings of folk tales from different cultures. More recently, she has focused on picture books and informative nonfiction for young children.

Writing and Illustrating Rockwell has written and illustrated more than 70 books and has collaborated with other authors and illustrators on many more. Where do all her ideas come from? "I get ideas walking on the beach with my dog," she says, "or traveling in a country where the language is unfamiliar." She keeps a sketchbook to record ideas for stories and illustrations, and she finds classical music very inspiring. "The Boy Who Flew" comes from her book *The Robber Baby: Stories from the Greek Myths.*

THE BOY WHO FLEW   **775**

 Assessment Informal Assessment

PARAPHRASE THE STORY You can informally assess students' understanding of the selection by having them paraphrase the story. Students should be able to clearly retell the plot of the story in a few paragraphs. Let them reread the story, then have them close their books and retell the story in their own words.

RUBRIC

3 Full Accomplishment Response reflects a full understanding of the events in the story and of the characters of Daedalus and Icarus.

2 Substantial Accomplishment Response shows a general grasp of the events but only a partial understanding of Daedalus or Icarus.

1 Little or Partial Accomplishment Response shows little understanding of the events or of the main characters.

SUMMARY

The Greek maiden Arachne boasts that her weaving is as beautiful as that of the goddess Athena. When an old woman warns Arachne to take back her claim, Arachne refuses. The old woman reveals herself to be Athena. The two women then have a weaving contest. Although they are equally skilled, Athena is quicker. Her cloth shows mortals challenging the gods and suffering, but Arachne pays no attention. Her weaving shows the gods' crimes. Athena is insulted, and she rips the cloth in two and hits Arachne. In the end, Athena turns Arachne into a spider as a reminder to all Greeks not to compete with the gods.

Reading and Analyzing

Literary Analysis: SETTING

Ask students to describe the setting of the story.

Possible Response: The setting is ancient Greece, inside a modest cottage in a small town.

Literary Analysis: FORESHADOWING

Ask students to think about how the beginning of the story may foreshadow events to come.

Possible Response: Everything sounds a little too perfect. The description of Arachne as such a gifted weaver makes the reader think that something bad is going to happen to her.

ARACHNE

Illustration by Arvis Stewart, from *The Macmillan Book of Greek Gods and Heroes* by Alice Low. Copyright © 1985 Macmillan Publishing Company, reprinted with the permission of Simon & Schuster Books for Young Readers, an imprint of Simon & Schuster Children's Publishing Division.

RETOLD BY OLIVIA E. COOLIDGE

Teaching Options

 Viewing and Representing

Illustration
by Arvis Stewart

ART APPRECIATION Direct students to the illustration on page 776, explaining that Arvis Stewart creates many illustrations for books, such as the one this is taken from.
Instruction Ask students to identify the rectangular structure in the background. Then ask them to describe what is being made.

Possible Response: The thing in the background is a loom. It is used to weave cloth. It looks like a cloth of many different colors is being woven.
Ask students to identify the characters in the illustration.
Possible Response: The large figure of a woman is probably Arachne, but I'm not sure about the others. Maybe if I read on, I'll figure out who they are.

Arachne[1] was a maiden who became famous throughout Greece, though she was neither wellborn[2] nor beautiful and came from no great city. She lived in an <u>obscure</u> little village, and her father was a humble dyer of wool. In this he was very skillful, producing many varied shades, while above all he was famous for the clear, bright scarlet which is made from shellfish and which was the most glorious of all the colors used in ancient Greece. Even more skillful than her father was Arachne. It was her task to spin the fleecy wool into a fine, soft thread and to weave it into cloth on the high-standing loom[3]

within the cottage. Arachne was small and pale from much working. Her eyes were light and her hair was a dusty brown, yet she was quick and graceful, and her fingers, roughened as they were, went so fast that it was hard to follow their flickering movements. So soft and even was her thread, so fine her cloth, so gorgeous her embroidery, that soon her products were known all over Greece. No one had ever seen the like of them before.

---

1. **Arachne** (ə-răk′nē).
2. **wellborn:** of a high social class.
3. **high-standing loom:** a tall frame used to hold threads in a vertical position as other threads are woven through horizontally.

> WORDS
> TO
> KNOW
>   **obscure** (ŏb-skyo͝or′) *adj.* not well-known or important

777

Mini Lesson **Spelling**

PREFIX *OB-*
Instruction Explain to students that the prefix *ob-* means "against" or "in the way of." The spelling of the prefix depends on the root to which it is joined.

Application Write on the chalkboard the examples below. Have students use one of the words from the box to replace each underlined word or phrase in the following paragraph. Answers are in parentheses.

Arachne was a famous weaver who lived in a <u>small</u> and <u>little-known</u> *(obscure)* village. She <u>complained</u> *(objected)* when people <u>criticized</u>

(opposed) her. One day as Arachne was <u>busy</u> *(occupied)* at her loom, the goddess Athena decided to teach her a lesson.

ob + jected = objected
ob + scure = obscure
oc + cupied = occupied
op + posed = opposed

 Use **Unit Six Resource Book**, p. 9.

Active Reading

A EVALUATE Possible Responses:
Arachne's pride is justified because she is the best weaver anyone has ever seen; her pride is excessive because her talent as a weaver is god-given.

Reading Skills and Strategies:
MAKE JUDGMENTS

Ask students to judge Arachne's character and to tell whether or not they like her, and why.

Possible Responses: She isn't very likeable because she is vain, proud, and rude; she is highly skilled at weaving and therefore is justified in her impatience with others.

Active Reading

B PREDICT Possible Response: It seems that a goddess would have to win the contest over a mortal.

last Arachne's fame became so great that people used to come from far and wide to watch her working. Even the graceful nymphs[4] would steal in from stream or forest and peep shyly through the dark doorway, watching in wonder the white arms of Arachne as she stood at the loom and threw the shuttle[5] from hand to hand between the hanging threads or drew out the long wool, fine as a hair, from the distaff[6] as she sat spinning. "Surely Athena herself must have taught her," people would murmur to one another. "Who else could know the secret of such marvelous skill?"

ACTIVE READING

EVALUATE What do you think of Arachne's pride?

Arachne was used to being wondered at, and she was immensely proud of the skill that had brought so many to look on her. Praise was all she lived for, and it displeased her greatly that people should think anyone, even a goddess, could teach her anything. Therefore, when she heard them murmur, she would stop her work and turn round indignantly to say, "With my own ten fingers I gained this skill, and by hard practice from early morning till night. I never had time to stand looking as you people do while another maiden worked. Nor if I had, would I give Athena credit because the girl was more

skillful than I. As for Athena's weaving, how could there be finer cloth or more beautiful embroidery than mine? If Athena herself were to come down and compete with me, she could do no better than I."

One day when Arachne turned round with such words, an old woman answered her, a grey old woman, bent and very poor, who stood leaning on a staff and peering at Arachne amid the crowd of onlookers.

"Reckless girl," she said, "how dare you claim to be equal to the immortal gods themselves? I am an old woman and have seen much. Take my advice and ask pardon of Athena for your words. Rest content with your fame of being the best spinner and weaver that mortal eyes have ever beheld."

"Stupid old woman," said Arachne indignantly, "who gave you a right to speak in this way to me? It is easy to see that you were never good for anything in your day, or you would not come here in poverty and rags to gaze at my skill. If Athena resents my words, let her answer them herself. I have challenged

"STUPID OLD WOMAN," SAID ARACHNE INDIGNANTLY, "WHO GAVE YOU A RIGHT TO SPEAK IN THIS WAY TO ME?"

---

4. **nymphs** (nĭmfs): in Greek mythology, minor goddesses of nature.
5. **shuttle:** a piece of wood holding the thread that is to be woven horizontally through the vertical threads on a loom.
6. **distaff:** a short rod for holding wool that is to be spun into thread.

WORDS
TO
KNOW

indignantly (ĭn-dĭg′nənt-lē) *adv.* in a way that is angry, because of an insult or an attack on one's self-respect
immortal (ĭ-môr′tl) *adj.* living or lasting forever

 Multicultural Link

Greek Mythology

Greek mythology is the collection of stories told about the gods, goddesses, and legendary humans worshiped or revered by the ancient Greeks. Twelve chief gods and goddesses lived on Mount Olympus, and there were many lesser ones. Zeus ruled the sky and was ruler of all the Olympians. Poseidon ruled the seas and rivers, while Hades oversaw the underworld. The Romans worshiped many of the same deities but called them by different names.

Athena was one of the most important goddesses. She sprang fully grown from the forehead of Zeus and was his favorite child. Athena's major temple, the Parthenon, was in Athens. According to legend, the temple became hers when she won a contest with Poseidon by giving the Athenians the olive tree.

Use **Literary Analysis Transparencies**, p. 31, for additional support.

MAJOR GREEK AND ROMAN DEITIES		
	Greek Name	**Roman Name**
Goddess of love	Aphrodite	Venus
God of medicine and music	Apollo	Apollo
Goddess of wisdom, war, and the arts	Athena	Minerva
God of the underworld	Hades	Pluto
Goddess of marriage and women	Hera (wife of Zeus)	Juno (wife of Jupiter)
God of the sea	Poseidon	Neptune
Ruler of the gods, god of the sky	Zeus	Jupiter

her to a contest, but she, of course, will not come. It is easy for the gods to avoid matching their skill with that of men."

At these words the old woman threw down her staff and stood <u>erect</u>. The wondering onlookers saw her grow tall and fair and stand clad in long robes of dazzling white. They were terribly afraid as they realized that they stood in the presence of Athena. Arachne herself flushed red for a moment, for she had never really believed that the goddess would hear her. Before the group that was gathered there she would not give in; so pressing her pale lips together in <u>obstinacy</u> and pride, she led the goddess to one of the great looms and set herself before the other. Without a word both began to thread the long woolen strands that hung from the rollers and between which the shuttle would move back and forth. Many skeins[7] lay heaped beside them to use, bleached white, and gold, and scarlet, and other shades, varied as the rainbow. Arachne had never thought of giving credit for her success to her father's skill in dyeing, though in actual truth the colors were as remarkable as the cloth itself.

oon there was no sound in the room but the breathing of the onlookers, the whirring of the shuttles, and the creaking of the wooden frames as each pressed the thread up into place or tightened the pegs by which the whole was held straight. The excited crowd in the doorway began to see that the skill of both in truth was very nearly equal but that, however the cloth might turn out, the goddess was the quicker of the two. A pattern

of many pictures was growing on her loom. There was a border of twined branches of the olive, Athena's favorite tree, while in the middle, figures began to appear. As they looked at the glowing colors, the spectators realized that Athena was weaving into her pattern a last warning to Arachne. The central figure was the goddess herself, competing with Poseidon[8] for possession of the city of Athens; but in the four corners were mortals who had tried to strive with gods and pictures of the awful <u>fate</u> that had overtaken them. The goddess ended a little before Arachne and stood back from her marvelous work to see what the maiden was doing.

ACTIVE READING

PREDICT How do you think the weaving contest will end?

Never before had Arachne been matched against anyone whose skill was equal, or even nearly equal, to her own. As she stole glances from time to time at Athena and saw the goddess working swiftly, calmly, and always a little faster than herself, she became angry instead of frightened, and an evil thought came into her head. Thus, as Athena stepped back a pace to watch Arachne finishing her work, she saw that the maiden had taken for her design a pattern of scenes which showed evil or unworthy actions of the gods, how they had deceived fair maidens, resorted to trickery, and appeared on earth from time to time in the form of poor and humble people. When the goddess saw this insult glowing in bright colors on Arachne's loom, she did not wait while the cloth was judged but stepped

---

7. **skeins** (skānz): rolls of thread or yarn.
8. **Poseidon** (pō-sīd'n): in Greek mythology, the god of the sea.

WORDS **erect** (ĭ-rĕkt') *adj.* firmly straight in posture; not bending or slumping
TO **obstinacy** (ŏb'stə-nə-sē) *n.* unreasonable stubbornness
KNOW **fate** (fāt) *n.* a final outcome that cannot be avoided

779

Ask students to summarize the ending of the story.

Possible Response: In the end, Arachne is so humiliated by Athena's actions that she attempts to end her life by hanging herself. Athena intervenes and transforms Arachne into a small spider. Athena's action serves as a warning to other humans not to challenge the gods.

Reading Skills and Strategies:
MAKE INFERENCES

Have students infer from this myth what the ancient Greeks thought about human pride.

Possible Response: The ancient Greeks believed that human pride was a fault that could cause terrible things to happen.

---

forward, her grey eyes blazing with anger, and tore Arachne's work across. Then she struck Arachne across the face. Arachne stood there a moment, struggling with anger, fear, and pride. "I will not live under this insult," she cried, and seizing a rope from the wall, she made a noose and would have hanged herself.

The goddess touched the rope and touched the maiden. "Live on, wicked girl," she said. "Live on and spin, both you and your descendants. When men look at you, they may remember that it is not wise to strive with Athena." At that the body of Arachne shriveled up; and her legs grew tiny, spindly, and <u>distorted</u>. There before the eyes of the spectators hung a little dusty brown spider on a slender thread.

All spiders descend from Arachne, and as the Greeks watched them spinning their thread wonderfully fine, they remembered the contest with Athena and thought that it was not right for even the best of men to claim equality with the gods. ❖

"The more facts I have to work with, the freer I am. . . ."

Olivia E. Coolidge
born 1908

Across the Atlantic Olivia E. Coolidge grew up in England, where her father was a journalist and historian. After completing her studies at Oxford University, Coolidge came to the United States and taught English for several years.

Careful Researcher Coolidge has written a number of biographies for young people in which she needed to carefully separate facts from opinions. As Coolidge says, "Facts are the bricks with which a biographer builds. . . . The more facts I have to work with, the freer I am to design my own book." Coolidge carefully researches her subjects and then forms her own opinions.

Ancient to Modern Coolidge's first book was *Greek Myths,* which she wrote using ancient Greek sources. Since then she has written of other ancient legends, and of daily life in ancient cultures. More recently, her biographical accounts, such as *Gandhi* (1971), have won her awards and a wide readership.

WORDS
TO
KNOW

780

distorted (dĭ-stôr'tĭd) *adj.* twisted out of shape **distort** *v.*

Teaching Options

 Assessment **Informal Assessment**

RETELL THE STORY You can informally assess students' understanding of the selection by having them retell the story from Arachne's point of view. Remind students to use the proper pronouns to reflect the first-person point of view. Suggest that students include comments that would accurately reveal Arachne's feelings about her encounter with Athena.

RUBRIC

3 Full Accomplishment Response reflects a full understanding of the events of the story and the character of Arachne.

2 Substantial Accomplishment Response shows a partial understanding of the events but may not fully reflect the character of Arachne.

1 Little or Partial Accomplishment Response shows little understanding of the story and of Arachne's character.

THE STORY OF
CERES ᴬᴺᴰ PROSERPINA
retold by MARY POPE OSBORNE

Bourrasque (Gust of Wind), Levy Dhurmer, Private Collection/Bulloz.

ne day Proserpina, the young maiden of spring, was picking wildflowers with her mother, Ceres, the goddess of grain. Entering the cool moist woods, Proserpina filled her basket with lilies and violets. But when she spied the white petals of the narcissus flower, she strayed far from her mother.

THE STORY OF CERES AND PROSERPINA   **781**

SUMMARY

While picking flowers one day, Proserpina, the maiden of spring, is kidnapped by Pluto, the god of the underworld. Ceres, Proserpina's mother and the goddess of grain, discovers that Proserpina has been taken by Pluto. Ceres transforms herself into an old woman and is taken in by a family of princesses. While there, Ceres decides to turn the family's baby boy into a god. When the boy's mother realizes who Ceres is, she builds a temple in her honor in exchange for learning the secret rites to make the corn grow. Even after the temple is built, Ceres' sadness continues, causing everything on earth to stop growing. Ceres agrees to make the earth fertile again if her daughter is returned. In the end, Proserpina spends each fall and winter in the underworld with Pluto and returns to earth every spring and summer.

Customizing Instruction

Less Proficient Readers
Have students keep these questions in mind as they read.
• Who are the characters in the story?
• What is the setting of the story?
• What is the main problem in the story?

Students Acquiring English
Tell students to pay close attention to the footnotes. They supply pronunciations of names as well as definitions of some of the unfamiliar words.

Gifted and Talented
Encourage students to research some of the gods mentioned in this story—Ceres, Hecate, Helios, Pluto, Jupiter, and Mercury.

 Use **Literary Analysis Transparencies,** p. 31, for additional support.

Mini Lesson **Spelling**

CAPITALIZATION OF PROPER NAMES

Instruction Point out that in this opening passage, the names Proserpina and Ceres are capitalized. Tell students that proper names, including the names of people, cities, towns, states, countries, and public buildings are always capitalized.

Exercises: In the sentences that follow, have students capitalize the proper nouns.

1. pluto needed permission from his brother, jupiter, to kidnap proserpina.

2. The sun god, helios, told ceres that her daughter was with pluto.

3. When she learned that proserpina was with pluto, ceres thrust her fist toward mount olympus.

4. In ancient greece, ordinary people were expected to show complete respect for the gods.

5. The author who retold the story of ceres and proserpina is named mary pope osborne.

© Copyright Jo Whaley/Swanstock.

Just as Proserpina picked a beautiful narcissus, the earth began to rumble. Suddenly the ground cracked open, splitting fern beds and ripping flowers and trees from their roots. Then out of the dark depths sprang Pluto, god of the underworld.[1]

Standing up in his black chariot,[2] Pluto ferociously drove his stallions toward Proserpina. The maiden screamed for her mother, but Ceres was far away and could not save her.

Pluto grabbed Proserpina and drove his chariot back into the earth. Then the ground closed up again, leaving not even a seam.

When the mountains echoed with Proserpina's screams, her mother rushed into the woods, but it was too late—her daughter had disappeared.

Beside herself with grief, Ceres began searching for her kidnapped daughter in every land. For nine days the goddess did not rest, but carried two torches through the cold nights, searching for Proserpina.

On the tenth day, Hecate,[3] goddess of the dark of the moon, came to Ceres. Holding up a lantern, the shrouded[4] goddess said, "I also heard your daughter's screams, but I didn't see

her. Let us fly to Helios,[5] the sun god, and ask him what happened."

Ceres and Hecate flew to Helios, the sun god; and weeping, Ceres asked Helios if he'd seen her daughter while he was shining down upon the woods.

"I pity you, Ceres," said Helios, "for I know what it is to lose a child. But I know the truth. Pluto wanted Proserpina for his wife, so he asked his brother, Jupiter, to give him

---

1. **underworld:** the world of the dead, believed by the Greeks and Romans to be located underground.
2. **chariot** (chăr′ē-ət): a horse-drawn two-wheeled vehicle used in ancient times.
3. **Hecate** (hĕk′ə-tē).
4. **shrouded:** hidden by wrappings; veiled.
5. **Helios** (hē′lē-ŏs′).

 Mini Lesson **Grammar**

PRONOUN AND ANTECEDENT AGREEMENT
Instruction Tell students that a pronoun must agree with its antecedent in number and gender. The antecedent is the word the pronoun stands for.

Exercises Ask students to complete each sentence below with the correct pronoun.

1. Ceres was grief-stricken because *(her)* daughter had been kidnapped.
2. The princesses felt sorry for Ceres so they brought *(her)* to *(their)* house.
3. Ceres was upset that the boy would die one day so *(she)* decided to make *(him)* into a god so that *(he)* would live forever.
4. After Ceres caused living things to stop growing, Jupiter summoned the gods to speak to *(her)*.
5. Proserpina remembered *(her)* mother with fondness.

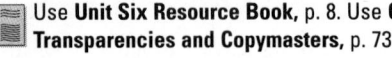 Use **Unit Six Resource Book,** p. 8. Use **Grammar Transparencies and Copymasters,** p. 73.

 Use McDougal Littell's **Language Network,** Chapter 3, for more practice in pronoun and antecedent agreement.

In Greek and Roman mythology, the pomegranate—a fruit containing many seeds—is a symbol of the underworld.

permission to kidnap her. Jupiter gave his consent, and now your daughter <u>reigns</u> over the land of the dead with Pluto."

Ceres screamed in rage and thrust her fist toward Mount Olympus, cursing Jupiter for aiding in the kidnapping of his own daughter. Then she returned to earth, disguised as an old woman, and began wandering from town to town.

ne day as she rested by a well, Ceres watched four princesses gathering water. Remembering her own daughter, she began to weep.

"Where are you from, old woman?" one princess asked.

"I was kidnapped by pirates, and I escaped," said Ceres. "Now I know not where I am."

Feeling pity for her, the princesses brought Ceres home to their palace. At the palace, their mother, the queen, took an immediate liking to Ceres when she noticed how good she was with her baby son the prince. When she asked Ceres if she would live with them and be his nurse, the goddess gladly consented.

Ceres grew deeply fond of the child. The thought that he would someday grow old and die was too much for her to bear. So she decided to change him from a mortal to a god. Every night, when everyone else was asleep, she poured a magic liquid on the body of the baby prince and held him in a fire. Soon the prince began to look like a god; everyone was amazed at his beauty and strength. The queen, disturbed by the changes in her child, hid in the nursery and watched Ceres and the boy. And when she saw Ceres place the child into the fire, she screamed for help.

"Stupid woman!" shouted Ceres, snatching the baby from the fire. "I was going to make your son a god! He would have lived forever! Now he'll be a mere mortal and die like the rest of you!"

The king and queen then realized that the boy's nurse was Ceres, the powerful goddess of grain, and they were terrified.

WORDS TO KNOW **reign** (rān) *v.* to rule as a king or queen

783

Customizing Instruction

Less Proficient Readers

Use the following questions to discuss what happens after Ceres realizes that Proserpina is missing.

1. How does Ceres discover what happened to Proserpina?
   Possible Response: Ceres and Hecate fly to Helios, the sun god. Helios tells them that Pluto kidnapped Proserpina and took her to the underworld.

2. What does Ceres do after learning that her daughter is living with Pluto in the underworld?
   Possible Response: Ceres returns to earth, disguised as an old woman, and moves in with a king and queen and their four daughters and infant son.

3. Why does Ceres decide to turn the baby boy into a god?
   Possible Response: She becomes attached to the baby and realizes that he is mortal and will die one day. She thinks that if she transforms him into a god, she will never have to mourn for him the way she has mourned for Proserpina.

Mini Lesson ## Speaking and Listening

DRAMA PERFORMANCE

Prepare Explain that writing and performing a play helps to get inside of the characters' minds and really understand their thoughts and actions. Tell students that they are going to dramatize "The Story of Ceres and Proserpina."

Divide the class into small groups. Have each group write a scene based on one part of the story. Tell students not to limit themselves to the dialogue from this story. They should feel free to write additional dialogue to tell the story.

Present Give groups time to rehearse their scene. Then have the groups perform their scenes in sequential order. Afterward, encourage students to discuss how acting out their scenes helped them better understand the myth.

Use **Communications Transparencies and Copymasters**, p. 12, for additional support.

Literary Analysis: SETTING

Ask students to describe the setting of the underworld.

Possible Response: The underworld is a grim, dark place. It is smoky and filled with creepy ghosts. It is devoid of color—everything looks gray and old.

Reading Skills and Strategies: PREDICT

Have students make predictions about whether Proserpina will return to earth.

Possible Responses: I don't think Proserpina will return, because she has gotten used to living in the underworld; I think Proserpina will go back, because even though she's grown accustomed to life in the underworld, she still misses her mother.

Literary Analysis: CHARACTER

Ask students to describe the character of Proserpina.

Possible Response: I think Proserpina is brave, because she chooses to leave Pluto, who is a powerful god. She is devoted to her mother, and even though she hasn't seen her mother in a long time, she remembers how much she loved her.

"I will only forgive you," said Ceres, "if you build a great temple in my honor. Then I will teach your people the secret rites[6] to help the corn grow."

At dawn the king ordered a great temple be built for the goddess. But after the temple was completed, Ceres did not reveal the secret rites. Instead she sat by herself all day, grieving for her kidnapped daughter. She was in such deep mourning that everything on earth stopped growing. It was a terrible year—there was no food, and people and animals began to starve.

Jupiter grew worried—if Ceres caused the people on earth to die, there would be no more gifts and offerings for him. Finally he sent gods from Mount Olympus to speak with her.

The gods came to Ceres and offered her gifts and pleaded with her to make the earth <u>fertile</u> again.

1 "I never will," she said, "not unless my daughter is returned safely to me."

Jupiter had no choice but to bid his son, Mercury, the messenger god, to return Proserpina to her mother.

2 Wandering the underworld, Mercury passed through dark smoky caverns filled with ghosts and phantoms, until he came to the misty throne room of Pluto and Proserpina. Though the maiden was still frightened, she had grown accustomed to her new home and had almost forgotten her life on earth.

"Your brother, Jupiter, has ordered you to return Proserpina to her mother," Mercury told Pluto. "Otherwise, Ceres will destroy the earth."

Pluto knew he could not disobey Jupiter, but he didn't want his wife to leave forever, so he said, "She can go. But first, we must be alone."

When Mercury left, Pluto spoke softly to Proserpina: "If you stay, you'll be queen of the underworld, and the dead will give you great honors."

As Proserpina stared into the eyes of the king of the dead, she dimly remembered the joy of her mother's love. She remembered wildflowers in the woods and open sunlit meadows. "I would rather return," she whispered.

Pluto sighed, then said, "All right, go. But before you leave, eat this small seed of the pomegranate[7] fruit. It is the food of the underworld—it will bring you good luck."

Proserpina ate the tiny seed. Then Pluto's black chariot carried her and Mercury away. The two stallions burst through the dry ground of earth—then galloped over the <u>barren</u> countryside to the temple where Ceres mourned for her daughter.

When Ceres saw her daughter coming, she ran down the hillside, and Proserpina sprang from the chariot into her mother's arms. All day the two talked excitedly of what had

---

6. **rites:** religious ceremonies.
7. **pomegranate** (pŏm′grăn´ĭt).

WORDS
TO
KNOW

fertile (fûr′tl) *adj.* rich in vegetation; fruitful
barren (băr′ən) *adj.* lacking vegetation

784

Cross Curricular Link **Science**

THE POMEGRANATE Because of its many seeds, the pomegranate has long been a symbol of fertility. Its large scarlet leaves and spherical shape have also made it a symbol of beauty. For these reasons, there are many references to pomegranates in both literature and art.

The pomegranate grows wild in Iran and other neighboring countries. It is cultivated in the tropics and subtropics. In Iran and Jamaica, the juice from the pomegranate is used in soups, sauces, and jellies.

It takes work to eat a pomegranate. You must pull apart the various chambers and either pick the seeds out, one at a time, or bite into it one section at a time. Despite the effort it takes to eat a pomegranate, many people enjoy this sweet, juicy fruit.

happened during their separation, but when Proserpina told Ceres about eating the pomegranate seed, the goddess hid her face and moaned in anguish.

"What have I done?" cried Proserpina.

"You have eaten the sacred food of the underworld," said Ceres. "Now you must return for half of every year to live with Pluto, your husband."

And this is how the seasons began—for when fall and winter come, the earth grows cold and barren because Proserpina lives in the underworld with Pluto, and her mother mourns. But when her daughter comes back to her, Ceres, goddess of grain, turns the world to spring and summer: The corn grows, and everything flowers again. ❖

"... I've been able to channel so many different interests into books. ..."

Mary Pope Osborne
born 1949

A Nomadic Life Mary Pope Osborne's experiences have provided her with a wealth of material. Her father was in the military, so the family moved often. She found it difficult to settle in one place for long, even as an adult. After studying drama and religion at the University of North Carolina, she traveled extensively in Asia and lived in a cave on the Greek island of Crete. She worked as a window dresser and a travel agent before becoming a full-time writer.

Travels with Books Many of Osborne's books transport readers to different places and times. Along with retellings of ancient myths and legends, she has written the Magic Tree House series of books. In these stories, a tree house is filled with books that involve two young readers in adventures with dinosaurs, knights, and other historical creatures and characters. Osborne has won many awards and honors for her writing. Her books *American Tall Tales* and *Mermaid Tales from Around the World* have been recognized by the National Council for the Social Studies/Children's Book Council.

✓**Assessment** **Standardized Test Practice**

DESCRIBE SETTING Sometimes on standardized tests, students are asked to recognize story setting by choosing the sentence that best describes where and/or when a story takes place. Help them practice the skill by posing the following question:
Which choice below best describes the setting of "The Story of Ceres and Proserpina"?

A. When fall and winter come, the earth grows cold and barren because Proserpina lives in the underworld with Pluto, and her mother mourns.

B. Entering the cool, moist woods, Proserpina filled her basket with lilies and violets.

C. In ancient Greece, Ceres lived with her daughter Proserpina on the surface of the earth.

D. Ceres thrust her fist toward Mount Olympus, cursing Jupiter for aiding in the kidnapping.

Discuss the options with students. A explains why there is fall and winter, but does not tell where or when the story takes place. B points out one detail of the setting (the woods) but is not general enough. D tells of an event in the story. The best answer is C, because it tells where and when the story takes place.

Literature Connection

Create a Picture Book Tell students to write a simple text to go along with their pictures. Remind them that their audience is younger students, so the vocabulary should be easy. Suggest that students read their book to younger brothers, sisters, and friends to make sure that what they have written is appropriate.

RUBRIC

3 Full Accomplishment Students' picture books accurately reflect myths' content. Books use suitable pictures and words for younger children.

2 Substantial Accomplishment Students' picture books for the most part reflect myths' content. Pictures and words are generally suitable for younger children.

1 Little or Partial Accomplishment Students' picture books do not accurately reflect myths' content. Pictures and words are too difficult for younger children.

Social Studies Connection

Map the Wonders of Ancient Greece Encourage students to spend some time in a library conducting their research. Direct individual students to focus on particular topics, such as the role of the city-state, the prominence of Athens, the military might of Sparta, the Trojan War, the birth of democracy, the role of men or women, and everyday life in ancient Greece. Tell students to refer not only to history books but also to art books for their information.

RUBRIC

3 Full Accomplishment Students' maps show a good understanding of the culture and present it in a clear and attractive manner.

2 Substantial Accomplishment Students' maps show a good understanding of the culture. Presentation is moderately clear and attractive.

1 Little or Partial Accomplishment Students' maps do not show a clear understanding of the culture. Presentation is confusing and executed poorly.

Interdisciplinary Projects

LITERATURE CONNECTION

Create a Picture Book Working with a few classmates, make a picture-book version of one of the myths you've read to share with younger students. Consider these suggestions:

Step 1: Images Create a series of pictures that retell the story. Include settings, key characters, and main events. Make your own drawings or use photographs, pictures from magazines, or computer "clip art."

Step 2: Binding Lay out your book so that pages can be sewn or stapled at the spine. If possible, include an action feature, such as pop-up scenery or a mechanism that allows a character to move.

Step 3: Cover Design a cover that will make readers want to open your book. Include a summary and author information.

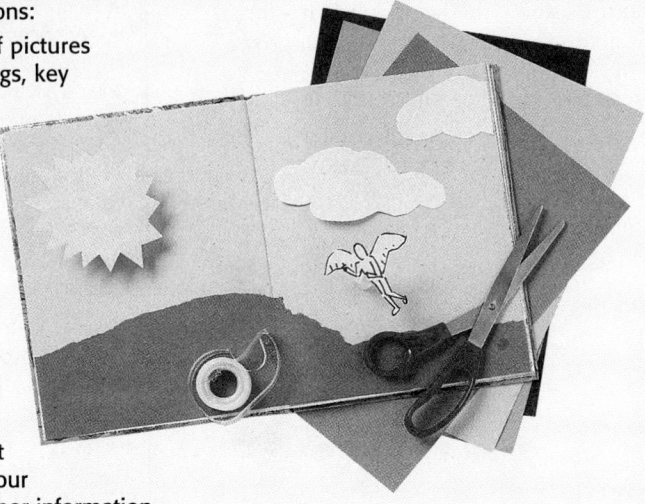

SOCIAL STUDIES CONNECTION

Map the Wonders of Ancient Greece The people of ancient Greece made significant contributions to world civilization, leaving a legacy of literature, art, architecture, and artifacts. With your classmates, create a large map of Greece and Crete. Research the cultures of ancient Crete (roughly 2000–1200 B.C.) and ancient Greece (roughly 1200–300 B.C.). Make sketches of important buildings, objects, people, and events to surround the map. Where appropriate, use yarn to connect sketches to places. Provide captions giving information and dates.

SCIENCE CONNECTION

Research Flight From watching birds fly, Daedalus got the idea for building wings that could help humans fly. Use an encyclopedia and books about flight to research what makes flight possible. Create a display that presents a basic explanation of the physics of bird flight and several modes of human flight (planes, helicopters, dirigibles, and so on).

786 UNIT SIX THE ORAL TRADITION

Science Connection
Research Flight

Students will enjoy learning about the evolution of human flight. You might ask students to find out whether the first airplanes were patterned after bird flight or whether they are based on different principles.

RUBRIC

3 Full Accomplishment Students' displays are clear, complete, and attractively presented.

2 Substantial Accomplishment Students' displays are generally clear, give an adequate amount of information, and are relatively well presented.

1 Little or Partial Accomplishment Students' displays are unclear, give little information, and are poorly presented.

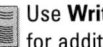 Use **Writing Transparencies,** pp. 41, 42, for additional support.

Across Cultures

Present a Tableau Design a tableau (tăb′lō)— a stop-action scene—of the major gods and goddesses of Greek and Roman mythology. View three versions of the Icarus myth and discuss how the interpretations vary. Try to make your own scene as original and unique as you can, while retaining the identity of the figures. For each god or goddess, create a costume and a prop. Have each group member represent one character and have classmates try to identify the figures portrayed. You may wish to photograph your tableau, or present it to other audiences, using a narrator to introduce each figure.

 More Online: Research Starter
www.mcdougallittell.com

 Literature in Performance

COMPARING TEXTS **Compare Myths**

Look in collections of myths and tales from several cultures. Find stories that teach similar lessons or explain the origins of similar things. For example, there are many stories in the oral tradition about the creation of the world, the origin of the seasons, and the reasons why animals behave the ways they do. Using a chart like the one shown, compare the stories you find.

Stories that explain _____		
Title		
Culture		
Explanation		

Vocabulary in Action

EXERCISE: MEANING CLUES On your paper, write the Word to Know that goes with each boldfaced clue below.

1. Would he ever find his way out of the **winding passageways?**

2. I **desperately want** to show Icarus the world beyond Crete.

3. Alone in his remote tower, Daedalus felt **cut off from the others.**

4. We watched the seagulls **spinning and diving** like dancers.

5. Arachne came from a **small, faraway** village.

6. She was **angry and insulted** by the idea that anyone could be as fine a weaver.

7. As a goddess, Athena will **live forever.**

8. When the old woman **stood straight,** I saw that she was the goddess herself.

9. Filled with **foolish stubbornness,** Arachne challenged Athena to a contest.

10. The mortal **could not avoid** his terrible end.

11. Her body grew **twisted and misshapen** as she turned into a spider.

12. Ceres begged the gods to make the land **rich and fruitful** again.

13. During the long, cold months, Proserpina **rules over** the dead.

14. The kidnapping caused Ceres **great pain.**

15. While Proserpina is in the underworld, the earth is **dry and lifeless.**

WORDS TO KNOW	anguish	erect	immortal	maze	reign
	barren	fate	indignantly	obscure	wheeling
	distorted	fertile	isolated	obstinacy	yearn

Across Cultures
Present a Tableau Tell students participating in the tableau to prepare a short monologue that reveals something about the god or goddess they are portraying. Students should be ready to recite their monologues if the audience can't identify their characters.

As preparation for reciting their monologues, students can watch the two versions of Icarus, presented on the videotape. They may wish to compare aspects of the presentations and to discuss what they liked or disliked about each.

 Use **Literary Analysis Transparencies,** p. 31, for additional support.

COMPARING TEXTS
Compare Myths As students are comparing the myths, suggest that they think about the similarities and differences between myths that teach similar lessons. Encourage them to consider possible reasons for the differences. Tell them to consider how the differences might reflect the differences between the cultures.

Use **Reading and Critical Thinking Transparencies,** p. 17, for additional support. Use **Unit Six Resource Book,** p. 10, for assessment.

Vocabulary in Action
1. maze
2. yearn
3. isolated
4. wheeling
5. obscure
6. indignantly
7. immortal
8. erect
9. obstinacy

10. fate
11. distorted
12. fertile
13. reign
14. anguish
15. barren

 Use **Unit Six Resource Book,** p. 7 for additional support.

Objectives

1. To understand and appreciate a fable and a folk tale that explore a period of growth and change in a young person's life
2. To appreciate the folklore and cultures of Trinidad and Tobago and Guatemala
3. To extend understanding of the selections through a variety of multimodal and cross-curricular activities

Reading Pathways

- Select one or several students to read each story aloud to the entire class or to small groups of students. Assign this reading in advance so that the readers can incorporate into their presentations some of the techniques used by professional storytellers. Have the audience listen carefully to the stories without following along in their texts.

- Read the stories aloud to the class, pausing at key points to discuss how elements of the stories inform students about the folklore and cultures of Trinidad and Tobago or Guatemala. Have students compare these cultures to their own.

- After students have read the stories once, have them read them again to identify structural elements such as main characters, minor characters, conflict, setting, and plot. Then have students identify similarities and differences between these stories and the selections in Unit Two. Students can compare the way the young characters in "Aaron's Gift" and "The Bamboo Beads" grow and change as a result of the stories their older relatives tell.

LINKS TO UNIT TWO

Growth and Change

What does it mean to belong? How do our home and heritage affect the way we grow? These and other questions are raised in the selections in Unit Two. Many folk tales have also explored these issues. Both of the folk tales you are about to read describe periods of growth and change in the lives of young people.

TRINIDAD AND TOBAGO

The Bamboo Beads

retold by Lynn Joseph

This **folk tale** comes from Trinidad and Tobago, a country made up of two islands off the coast of Venezuela. The islands were first inhabited by native Caribbean peoples. Over the years, the islands were claimed by Spain, Great Britain, and the Netherlands. Many French people also settled there to run sugar-cane farms, and Africans were brought as slaves to work on these plantations. After slavery was abolished, plantations employed workers from India.

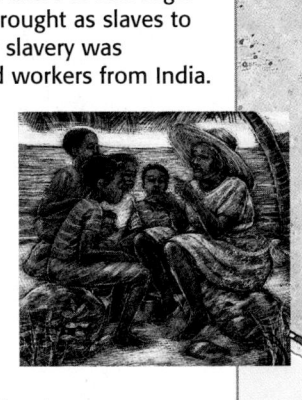

By the time Trinidad and Tobago achieved independence in 1962, it was a country with a diverse heritage. Although English is the official language, the influences of many languages can be heard.

GUATEMALA

TRINIDAD AND TOBAGO

This tale features Papa Bois (pä-pä-bwä'), one of the islands' popular folklore characters. His duty is to protect trees and woodland animals, which include the scarlet ibis, the iguana, and many poisonous snakes.

788 UNIT SIX THE ORAL TRADITION

LESSON RESOURCES

UNIT SIX RESOURCE BOOK, pp. 11–17

ASSESSMENT
Formal Assessment, pp. 127–128

Teacher's Guide to Assessment and Portfolio Use

Test Generator

SKILLS TRANSPARENCIES AND COPYMASTERS
Grammar
- Verb Forms, CM 81 (for Mini Lesson, p. 791)

Communications
- Evaluation Matrix: Film/Video, p. 7 (for Mini Lesson, p. 792)

INTEGRATED TECHNOLOGY
Audio Library
Internet: Research Starter

Visit our website:
www.mcdougallittell.com

The Disobedient Child

retold by Victor Montejo (mōn-tä′hō)

Guatemala is one of the seven countries that form Central America, the narrow land bridge that connects North and South America. One of the first civilizations in the Americas, the Mayan Empire, thrived in Central America from about A.D. 250 to 900. Mayan cities occupied the Yucatán Peninsula, southern Mexico, Honduras, and Belize, as well as Guatemala.

Today, about half of Guatemala's population is descended from the Maya. Many Guatemalans speak Mayan languages and follow traditional ways of life. Ancient Mayan culture is reflected in this Guatemalan **fable** about a boy who ignores warnings. The boy seems unwilling to listen until he is put to the test by someone with supernatural powers.

AS YOU READ . . .

See how the values of family and community are portrayed in different cultures.

Find out which elements of nature and which imagined forces are feared.

See how consequences of characters' choices unfold.

Customizing Instruction

Less Proficient Readers
In both of these stories, the main characters' actions have a strong bearing on what happens to them. Ask students to read these stories paying special attention to what the main character does and what results from this action.

Students Acquiring English
Encourage students to first read each story without stopping to look up unfamiliar words, inferring their meanings from context whenever possible. After they have read the story through, they can reread and look up the words they did not understand.

Use **Spanish Study Guide,** pp. 160–162 for additional support.

Gifted and Talented
Ask students to pay particular attention to the character in each story who has special powers, and to consider how each story would change without such a character.

Summary

This Guatemalan fable tells of a disobedient boy who runs away from home. He takes shelter with an old man, who asks him to cook 13 beans in a pot. When the boy disobeys, the old man next forbids him to open a little door in the house. The boy opens the door, finding three capes and three jars, one of which he opens. When huge clouds spring out of the jar, the boy puts on one of the capes. He is then turned into thunder and lifted into the stormy sky. Hearing the thunder, the old man rushes home, rescues the boy, and restores the sky. The old man then reveals that he is Qich Mam, a powerful rain spirit. The boy feels guilty and promises Qich Mam never again to disobey his parents.

Reading and Analyzing

Literary Analysis: SETTING

Ask students where this story is set.

Possible Response: It is set in a lonely little house in the Guatemalan woods.

 Use **Unit Six Resource Book**, p. 13 for more practice. Use **Literary Analysis Transparencies**, p. 6, for additional support.

Active Reading: STORY MAPPING

Ask students to use a story map like the one shown to represent the story. What parts can they fill in at this point?

Setting: little house in the woods	Characters: boy and old man
Problem: boy is disobedient	
Events:	
Resolution:	

Use **Unit Six Resource Book**, p. 12 for more practice. Use **Reading and Critical Thinking Transparencies**, p. 13, for additional support.

Teaching Options

Effigy vessel (about A.D. 1000–1250), unknown Mayan artist. Ceramic, painted red, blue, and white, 31.7 cm in height, Museo Nacional de Antropología, Mexico. Photo Copyright © Stuart Rome.

Mini Lesson — Viewing and Representing

Effigy Vessel
by an unknown Mayan artist

This hand-painted ceramic pot was made about A.D. 1000–1250.

Instruction Tell students that an effigy vessel is a pot with a human or animal form. This vessel was found in a cave near Chichén Itzá in Mexico and was probably used in Mayan cave rituals. For the ancient Mayas, caves were the source of rain and fertility and embodied the mysteries of life and death.

Application Ask students to describe the expression on the vessel's face.

Possible Response: Students may say the face appears determined, serious, or even angry.
Ask how they can relate the face to the fable of the disobedient boy.

Possible Response: It may relate to the jars in the story, or anger directed at the child.

THE DISOBEDIENT CHILD

RETOLD BY VICTOR MONTEJO

In old times in *Xaqla'* Jacaltenango[1] there was a very disobedient child who often disappointed his parents. No matter how hard they tried to teach him, he never changed.

One afternoon the boy ran away from home, looking for someone who would <u>tolerate</u> his mischief. Walking through the woods he discovered a lonely little house and ran up to it. On the porch of the straw-covered house sat an old man, smoking peacefully. The boy stood before him without saying hello or any other word of greeting.

When the old man noticed the boy's presence, he stopped smoking and asked him, "Where do you want to go, boy?"

"I am looking for someone who can give me something to eat," the boy answered.

The wise old man, who already knew the boy's story, said, "No one will love you if you continue being so bad."

The boy did not respond except to laugh.

---

1. *Xaqla'* Jacaltenango (chäk-lä' häk´äl-tĕ-nän´gô): town in the mountains of Guatemala.

WORDS
TO
KNOW   **tolerate** (tŏl´ə-rāt´) *v.* to put up with

 Mini Lesson ## Grammar

VERB FORMS Remind students to employ standard English usage in writing.
Instruction Explain that a verb can become a different part of speech in certain circumstances. For instance, you can add *-ing* to a verb and use the new word as a noun. This is a *gerund.* Share the following example.
<u>Exploring</u> in caves can be dangerous.
You can add *-ing* to a verb and use it as an adjective, as well. That is a *present participle.* A *past participle* is formed by adding *-d* or *-ed.* The <u>exploring</u> boy gets in trouble. <u>Worried</u>, the old man returns.

Finally, you can put *to* before a verb and get an *infinitive,* which can function as a noun, adjective, or adverb.
I had <u>to explore</u>. It's time <u>to explore</u>. Do you dare <u>to explore</u>?
Exercises Have students underline the verb acting as another part of speech in the following sentences and write what part of speech the word is.
1. Hurrying, the boy threw the cape on. *(Hurrying, adjective)*
2. The man brought the terrified boy back to his home. *(terrified, adjective)*

3. Obeying his parents is what the boy will do from now on. *(Obeying, noun)*
4. To learn more, read the story. *(To learn, adverb)*

Use **Unit Six Resource Book,** p. 15.
Use **Grammar Transparencies and Copymasters,** p. 81.

Use McDougal Littell's *Language Network,* Chapter 4, for more practice in verb forms.

Reading Skills and Strategies:
QUESTION

 A Students can answer different types
and levels of questions such as open-
ended, literal, and interpretive. Ask students to interpret why they think the
old man offers to let the boy stay with
him.
Possible Responses: The old man
takes in the disobedient child because
he wants to teach him a lesson. The
old man has some magical powers, as
shown by the knowledge of the boy's
story. The old man is lonely and wants
the boy's company, despite the boy's
disobedient nature.

Reading Skills and Strategies:
MONITOR

B Students can monitor their own
comprehension and make modifica-
tions when understanding breaks
down, such as by rereading a portion
aloud, using reference aids, searching
for clues, and asking questions. Discuss
the questions or comments students
have about the old man's actions at
this point. You may wish to model
thinking through the story by saying
something like the following: "I wonder
what the old man is up to. Why does
he give the boy this strange warning?
How could it possibly matter whether
the boy puts 13—or 10 or 11 or even
20—beans into the pot? I think the old
man is testing the boy to see if the boy
will obey his instructions."

Active Reading: STORY MAPPING

Have students continue filling in the
story maps they began earlier.

A Then the old man smiled and said, "You can stay with me. We will eat together."

The boy accepted his offer and stayed in the old man's house. On the following day before going to work, the old man told the boy: "You should stay in the house, and the only duty **B** you will have is to put the beans to cook during the afternoon. But listen well. You should only throw thirteen beans in the pot and no more. Do you understand?"

The boy nodded that he understood the directions very well. Later, when the time arrived to cook the beans, the boy put the clay pot on the fire and threw in thirteen beans as he had been directed. But once he had done that, he began to think that thirteen beans weren't very many for such a big pot. So, disobeying his orders, he threw in several more little fistfuls.

When the beans began to boil over the fire, the pot started to fill up, and it filled up until it overflowed. Very surprised, the boy quickly took an empty pot and divided the beans between the two pots. But the beans over-flowed the new pot, too. Beans were pouring out of both pots.

When the old man returned home, he found piles of beans, and the two clay pots lay broken on the floor.

"Why did you disobey my orders and cook more than I told you to?" the old man asked angrily.

1 The boy hung his head and said nothing. The old man then gave him instructions for the next day. "Tomorrow you will again cook the beans as I have told you. What's more, I forbid you to open that little door over there. Do you understand?"

The boy indicated that he understood very well.

The next day the old man left the house after warning the boy to take care to do exactly what he had been told. During the afternoon the boy put the beans on the fire to cook. Then he was filled with curiosity. What was behind the little door he had been forbidden to open?

Without any fear, the boy opened the door and discovered in the room three enormous covered water jars. Then he found three capes inside a large trunk. There was one green cape, one yellow cape and one red cape. Not satisfied with these discoveries, the boy took the top off the first water jar to see what it contained.

Immediately the water jar began to <u>emit</u> great clouds that quickly hid the sky. Frightened and shivering with cold, the boy opened the trunk and put on the red cape. At that instant a clap of thunder exploded in the house. The boy was turned into thunder and lifted to the sky, where he unleashed a great storm.

When the old man heard the thunder, he guessed that something extraordinary had happened at home, and he hurried in that direction. There he discovered that the forbidden door was open and the top was

> **IMMEDIATELY THE WATER JAR BEGAN TO EMIT GREAT CLOUDS THAT QUICKLY HID THE SKY.**

WORDS
TO
KNOW

forbid (fôr-bĭd') *v.* to command someone not to do something
emit (ĭ-mĭt') *v.* to send out; give forth, usually with force

792

 Mini Lesson ## Speaking and Listening

CRITICAL VIEWING Remind students that they can learn by comparing oral traditions across regions and cultures.
Instruction Mention that critical viewing some-times involves comparing and contrasting what they know already and what is shown in a movie, television production, or dramatic performance.
Application Invite students to learn more about some of the best-known fables—those reputedly written by the Greek slave Aesop—by viewing

some on video. After students watch one or more videos, invite them to compare and contrast the versions of Aesop's fables and to critique them. Then they might compare one Aesop's fable to the Guatemalan folk tale they are reading. Students can work in small groups to create a chart showing how Aesop's fables compare with "The Disobedient Child."

Use **Communications Transparencies and Copymasters,** p. 7, for additional support.

off the jar of clouds, from which churning mists still rose toward the sky. The old man covered the jar and then approached the trunk with the capes. The red cape, the cape of storms, was missing. Quickly the old man put on the green cape and regained control over the sky, calming the great storm. Little by little the storm subsided, and soon the man returned to the house, carrying the unconscious boy in his arms.

A little while later the old man uncapped the same jar, and the clouds which had blackened the sky returned to their resting place, leaving the heavens bright and blue again. When he had done this, the old man capped the jar again and put away the red and green capes.

Through all of this the boy remained stunned and soaked with the rains until the kind old man restored his spirit and brought him back to normal. When the boy was alert again and his fear had left, the old man said, "Your disobedience has almost killed you. You were lucky that I heard the storm and came to help. Otherwise you would have been lost forever among the clouds."

The boy was quiet and the old man continued.

"I am Qich Mam,[2] the first father of all people and founder of *Xaqla'*, he who controls the rain, and waters the community's fields when they are dry. Understand, then, that I wish you no harm and I forgive what you have done. Promise me that in the future you will not disobey your parents."

The boy smiled happily and answered, "I promise, Qich Mam, I promise." Qich Mam patted him gently and said, "Then return to your home and be useful to your parents and to your people."

From that time on the boy behaved differently. He was very grateful for the kindness of the old man who held the secret of the clouds, the rains, the wind and the storms in his hands. ❖

---

2. **Qich Mam** (kĕch´ mäm´): a thunder spirit of the Mayan people.

"I want to . . . preserve the history of the Mayan oral tradition."

Victor Montejo
born 1951

Far from Home Victor Montejo was born and raised in Guatemala and later taught primary school in Jacaltenango, the setting of "The Disobedient Child." Unfortunately, because of the political climate in Guatemala, Montejo was forced to flee to the United States in 1982.

Success in the States Since then, he has published a number of stories, fables, and poems and has worked as a writer-in-residence at Bucknell University in Pennsylvania. He has also done doctoral work in anthropology at the University of Connecticut. "The Disobedient Child" is from Montejo's book *The Bird Who Cleans the World.*

793

Summary

The Trinidadian narrator of this tale listens as her great-aunt explains the origin of a string of beads she wears. Tantie describes how, as a young girl at the market, she gave bread to a ragged old man with hooves instead of feet. In return he gave her a piece of string, which she wore as a necklace. There-after, colorful bamboo beads began to turn up everywhere, and Tantie added each one to her necklace. Tantie's mother understood that they had come from the forest spirit Papa Bois. When Tantie encountered Papa Bois again at the market, she learned that the beads represented the number of children she would have someday—who turned out actually to be her grandnieces and grandnephews. After telling this story, Tantie entrusts the necklace to her grandniece—the narrator.

Reading and Analyzing

Literary Analysis: SIMILE

A Tell students that it is useful to identify literary terms across a variety of literary forms. Remind them that a simile is a comparison using *like* or *as*. Ask students to identify the two similes that appear in this passage.

Answer: Her mother's flowers were "red as the evening sun," "the moon was round and white as my Sunday hat."

The Bamboo Beads

by Lynn Joseph

Illustration Copyright © 1991 Brian Pinkney. From *A Wave in Her Pocket* by Lynn Joseph, reprinted by permission of Clarion Books/Houghton Mifflin Co. All rights reserved.

794   UNIT SIX   THE ORAL TRADITION

Teaching Options

 Mini Lesson ## Speaking and Listening

DIALECT Students can identify how language use reflects regions and cultures.

Instruction Explain that a dialect is the language spoken by a group of people from a specific region. It might differ from the standard language in the way it is pronounced, its grammar, or its vocabulary. The characters in "The Bamboo Beads" speak an island dialect.

Application Invite volunteers to select and read aloud from the story a passage featuring a Trinidad dialect. To help students get a better sense of this dialect, play vocal music from Trinidad or other West Indian islands. Discuss the ways in which this dialect differs from the English they are familiar with. Ask whether there are any sayings that are unfamiliar to them.

Possible Response: Students may note use of *de, yuh,* or *chile,* they may notice that a verb is omitted ("This de same string, Tantie?"), or they may be unfamiliar with an expression like "when I was in my bare feet still," to refer to being a child.

Last year during the planting season, I helped Mama plant seeds on our hill. "One seed for each of my brothers and sisters," she said, and she covered up seven seeds with dark dirt. Mama's family lives on the other side of the island, so we hardly ever see them.

Each day I watched Mama water the dark mounds of dirt and weed around them. Soon, flowers grew up. They were red as the evening sun. But one day the floods came and swept them to the sea.

"Poor Mama," I said.

"They'll grow again," she replied.

She looked at her gardening gloves hanging on a nail. "If they don't grow back, we'll plant some more." And she smiled.

That night the moon was round and white as my Sunday hat. I told Daddy how Mama's flowers had drowned in the flood rains. He said, "Did I ever show you how *I* count my brothers and sisters?"

"No," I answered.

Then Daddy showed me the fisherman stars. "They point fishermen to the way home," he said. "There are eight of them. I named one each for my brothers and sisters."

"How do you know which is which?" I asked.

Daddy pointed again to the bright stars. "Well, there's Rupert and Hazel, Anthony and Derek, Peter, Janet, and Neil."

"You forgot Auntie Sonia," I said.

Daddy smiled and pointed to a tiny star. "That one's her."

I nodded my head as Daddy moved his finger around, although I couldn't tell which star was who.

After that, Daddy and I looked for the fisherman stars each night. Some nights when the sea breezes blew dark clouds in the sky, we couldn't see them. But Daddy would say, "They'll come back." And he'd smile.

"I wish I had brothers and sisters to plant flowers for or to count stars on," I told Mama and Daddy one day. "I'm tired of having only myself."

"What about all your cousins?" asked Mama.

"You can count them on something," said Daddy.

"What can I count them on?" I wondered.

"Maybe Tantie can help find you something," said Mama. "She's the one who keeps track of all yuh."

So, the next time Tantie came to visit, I said, "Tantie, Mama said you keep track of me and my cousins."

"That's right, chile," said Tantie. "And is plenty of all yuh to keep track of, too."

"I know," I said, "but how you do it? I want something that I can name after each one of my cousins. Something I can count them on. Like Mama has flowers and Daddy has his fisherman stars."

Well, Tantie looked me in the eye for a long time. Then from underneath the neck of her dress she pulled out a brown string full of bright, colorful beads.

"Tantie, where you get those pretty beads from?" I asked.

"These, my dear, is a story by itself, and if you have de time to listen, I'll tell it to you."

I nodded and sat down on the porch swing next to Tantie. As Tantie told her story, I kept trying to push the swing with my foot. But

A Students can analyze characters, including their traits, motivations, conflicts, points of view, relationships and changes they undergo. Although the reader does not realize it at this point in the narrative, this initial meeting between the old man and Tantie is an important one. Have students describe what they learn about Tantie's character from her behavior in this passage.

Possible Response: Tantie doesn't stare at the man's unusual feet and she gives him food. These acts show that she is kind, generous, and thoughtful.

Reading Skills and Strategies: PREDICT

B Have students predict where the beads have come from. Which clues and details in the story help them make their predictions?

Possible Response: Students may predict that the beads are from the poor man, since he gave Tantie the string.

Tantie was too heavy. The swing sat quiet. The only sound was Tantie's voice.

"A long, long time ago," she began, "when I was in my bare feet still, I went to market with a basket of bread and red-currant buns to sell. Market day was de busiest time. There was plenty to see as I set up my little stall and tucked cloths around de bread and buns so de flies wouldn't get them.

"I hadn't sold one thing yet when an old man came up. His clothes were ragged and he didn't have on no shoes. His feet didn't look like no ordinary feet. They looked like cow hooves. I didn't stare, though, because it rude to do that.

"He asked for a piece of bread. Well, I remember Mama telling me that morning to get good prices for de bread, but I was sure Mama hadn't meant from this man too. So, I cut off a hunk of bread, wrapped it in brown paper, and handed it to him. He looked so hungry that I reached for a bun and gave him that too. De man smiled and bowed his head at me. Then he went his way.

"After that I was busy selling bread. De buns went even faster. By afternoon, I had sold them all. Then I saw de old man coming over again. He didn't look so ragged anymore. His hair was combed and he had on a new shirt.

"'I'm sorry,' I said. 'No more bread left.'

"He didn't answer. Instead he handed me something. It was a piece of brown string. It looked like an ordinary old string, but I didn't tell him that.

"'Thank you for de bread, child,' he said. Then he shuffled off and was gone.

"I looked at de string for a while. I could use it to tie up my bread cloths, I thought. Or I could use it as a hair ribbon. But I decided I would put de string around my neck and wear it like a necklace."

"This de same string, Tantie?" I asked, fingering Tantie's bead necklace.

"De very same," she answered.

"Well, that evening, Mama was so proud I had sold all de bread that she gave me a treat. It was a small blue bamboo bead. It was de exact color of Mama's best blue head scarf.

"'Where you get this bead, Mama?' I asked.

"'Found it in de yard,' she replied.

"I wondered how it got there, but it didn't matter. I pulled out my brown string and untied it. Then I slipped de blue bead on and tied it around my neck again. It looked like a real necklace now that it had Mama's bead on it."

> Then I slipped de blue bead on and tied it around my neck again.

"Is this your mama's bead?" I asked, touching a bright blue bead on Tantie's string.

"Yes, that's it, chile," said Tantie.

"And it shines more now than de day I got it.

"Two days later, Daddy found a smooth black bead down by de sea. He brought it home in his pocket.

"'I thought you might like this,' he said, and handed it to me. It sparkled like a black sun. I untied my necklace and slipped it on next to de blue bead. Now my string was beautiful with Mama's and Daddy's bamboo beads on it.

"During de next few days, Mama and Daddy and I kept finding shiny bamboo beads

---

Teaching Options

Multicultural Link   Trinidad Languages

The official language of Trinidad is English, but islanders also speak French, Spanish, and Hindi. This mixture of languages reflects Trinidad's history as a colonized island. Christopher Columbus claimed Trinidad for Spain in 1498. The island was at that time inhabited by the Arawak and Carib tribes. Haitian planters of French ancestry settled in Trinidad and established a profitable sugar cane industry using African slave labor. The British gained possession of the island in 1802. Trinidad, along with the nearby island Tobago, gained independence in 1962. The Trinidad English that Tantie speaks here is a reflection of these many influences. For instance, her name derives from the French word for aunt, *tante*. *Bois* is the French word for woods, a fitting name for the wood spirit Papa Bois. Words from native Caribbean languages have also been incorporated into the English language. *Hurricane, tobacco, canoe,* and *hammock* all come from words originating in native Caribbean languages.

in de strangest places. I found a red one under de bed. Mama found a green one in de garden, and Daddy found a yellow one in his shoe. Mama and Daddy didn't think nothing of it, but as I added each new bead to my necklace, I got a strange, trembly feeling.

"De next week when I took Mama's bread and currant buns to market, I saw de old man who had given me my string. His clothes were still ragged and he clumped around on his hooves.

"'Hello, mister,' I said when he came over. I wrapped up a chunk of bread and two buns this time and gave them to him. He smiled and shuffled off.

"Again my day of selling flew by. Before lunchtime I had sold everything. Mama hugged me hard when I got home. But then she sat down at de kitchen table and looked serious.

"'What's wrong?' I asked.

"'Look,' she said, pointing to a bowl on the table. I looked inside and there were de most beautiful, shiny bamboo beads I'd ever seen. Lots and lots of them. I put my hand in and touched de smooth wood.

"'Where they come from?' I asked.

"'Don't know,' said Mama. 'They were here when I turned around from de sink this morning. I thought you might know something about them, since you're collecting beads.'

"'No,' I said. 'I don't know about these.'

"Then Mama said, 'Let me see that string of beads around your neck, girl.'

"I showed it to Mama. She looked and looked at de beads and tugged on de string until I thought she'd break it. Then she looked at me and said, 'You've met Papa Bois.'[1]

"'Papa who?'

"'Papa Bois,' she <u>murmured</u>. 'He lives in de

---

1. **Papa Bois** (pä-pä-bwä') *French:* Father Forest.

WORDS TO KNOW	**murmur** (mûr'mər) *v.* to speak so quietly that the words are difficult to make out

797

Customizing Instruction

Students Acquiring English
1 Point out that Tantie pronounces "the" as *de*.
2 You may want to point out that single quotation marks are used when quoting direct speech in already quoted material.

Less Proficient Readers
3 Have students explain what happens after Tantie gives bread to a mysterious old man.
Possible Response: The man gives Tantie a string, which she wears as a necklace. Beads pop up all over the place. Tantie strings the beads on her necklace.

Set a Purpose Have students read to find out what the 33 beads that Tantie acquires represent.

Gifted and Talented
Invite students to find out about Pan, the Greek god of woods, fields, and fertility. How was he like Papa Bois?
Possible Response: He was part man and part animal. Also, he could instill fear in others.
Challenge students to find an English word derived from the name Pan.
Answer: panic

Mini Lesson: Viewing and Representing

Illustration by Brian Pinkney
ART APPRECIATION This illustration, done especially for "The Bamboo Beads," uses a scratchboard technique.
Instruction To create a scratchboard drawing, a specially prepared surface is covered with black ink. The artist then uses a fine, sharp instrument to scratch the delicate lines of the drawing.
Application Ask students if this illustration matches their ideas about how the characters look and act. Why or why not?

Possible Response: Answers will vary but should be supported by details from the story.
Application Ask students to choose a scene from the story to illustrate. To make a scratchboard-like drawing, they can color a heavy white paper completely with black crayon, then use a sharp instrument—such as the end of a compass—to scratch the drawing.

Students can recognize the distinguishing features of various genres. Remind students that a folk tale is a story that is handed down, usually by word of mouth, among the people of a region. Like fables, folk tales often teach lessons. Ask students to describe the characteristics of this story that make it a folk tale.

Possible Response: It is being told aloud to another character, it comes from the region of Trinidad, it is about ordinary people, it contains a supernatural being, and it seems to be teaching the value of kindness.

---

forest and protects de trees and forest animals from hunters. He spends his time <u>whittling</u> bamboo beads from fallen bamboo shoots. He's de only one who could make these beads. They're priceless.'

"Mama looked at me and gave me back de necklace. 'Have you met an old man without any feet?' she asked.

"I immediately thought of de old man from de market. 'Yes, Mama, I met him last week at de market. An old man in ragged clothes and no feet. He had cow hooves instead.'

"Mama closed her eyes and nodded her head. 'That's Papa Bois,' she said. 'He can be dangerous. Once he meets someone, he keeps track of them by counting their sins, their blessings, even their teeth, on his whittled beads. You never know with Papa Bois just what he's counting for you. The last time Papa Bois gave someone beads, the beads represented de number of days he had left to live. These beads on de table must be for you. He's counting something for you.'"

"'What?' I whispered, almost too frightened to speak.

"'We won't know till he's ready to say. Were you kind or mean to him?'

"'I gave him some bread to eat because he looked hungry,' I said.

"'Good,' said Mama, and she pulled me into her arms. 'That was very kind. Now you might as well put de beads on de string and wait until Papa Bois comes back and tells you what he's counting.'

"I put de pretty beads on de string. I didn't think they would all fit, but no matter how many I put on, de string never filled up. When

every bead was on, I counted thirty-three beads. Then I tied it around my neck once more. It wasn't any heavier than when I wore de string empty.

"As de days passed, Mama, Daddy, and I kept our eyes open for Papa Bois. We thought he might come by any time. I wondered over and over what Papa Bois could be counting on my beads."

"Were you scared, Tantie?" I interrupted.

"A little," she answered. "But I knew I had been kind to Papa Bois, and that was all that mattered.

"De next time I went to market for Mama, she wanted to come with me. I told her Papa Bois might not come to our stall if she was there.

"At the stall I laid de bread and buns out nicely and covered them with cloths. I saw de old man shuffling up to my table.

"'*Bonjour, vieux Papa*,'[2] I said. Mama had told me that to say hello in French was de polite way to greet Papa Bois. She also said not to look at his feet no matter what.

"'*Bonjour*,' said de old man.

"'Would you like some bread?' I asked. Papa Bois nodded.

"As I cut him a chunk of bread, I said, 'Thank you for de pretty necklace.'

"'It's for you to wear always,' he said. 'Until you find someone who should wear it instead.'

"*That was de last time I ever see Papa Bois.*"

---

2. *Bonjour, vieux Papa* (bôn-zhoor′ vyœ′ pä-pä′) *French:* Hello, old Father.

WORDS TO KNOW   **whittling** (hwĭt′lĭng) *adj.* carving by shaving away bits of wood with a knife **whittle** *v.*

Mini Lesson Spelling

COMPOUND WORDS AND CONTRACTIONS

Instruction Tell students that when two or more words are connected with no changes, the resulting word is called a compound word. Words joined by a hyphen are another kind of compound word. When two words are joined and one or more letters are omitted, the result is a contraction. An apostrophe takes the place of the missing letter(s).

Application Have students combine the word parts that follow to form compound words and contractions used in the selection.

1. fisher + man *(fisherman)*
2. I + am *(I'm)*
3. some + thing *(something)*
4. you + are *(you're)*
5. my + self *(myself)*
6. neck + lace *(necklace)*
7. do + not *(don't)*
8. thirty + three *(thirty-three)*
9. grand + nieces *(grandnieces)*
10. what + is *(what's)*

Ask students to look for more compound words and contractions in their writing and reading.

Use **Unit Six Resource Book**, p. 16

"Papa Bois's eyes looked kind in his wrinkled face. I decided I go ask him what de beads were for.

"'De beads,' he answered, 'are for all de little children you'll one day have.'

"'Thirty-three children?' I asked.

"'Yes, they'll be yours, but they won't be yours,' he said mysteriously. But then he smiled a big smile.

"'All right,' I said, and I handed him de bread and buns.

"That was de last time I ever see Papa Bois. Mama said he only comes out of his forest when he's lonely for human company. Otherwise his friends are de deer, de squirrels, and de trees. The first person he meets when he leaves his forest early in de morning is de one who counts. If that person stares at his feet or laughs at him—watch out!"

"But Tantie, what happen to de thirty-three children?" I asked.

"You're one of them," she said. "Ever since your oldest cousin Jarise was born, I been de one helping to take care of all yuh. I have thirty grandnieces and nephews now. That mean three more to come. And all yuh are my children, just like Papa Bois said."

Tantie reached up and unhooked her bamboo bead necklace. Then she laid it in my hands.

"Oh," I said, looking at Tantie's necklace again. "I'd like to be de red bead."

Tantie took the necklace out of my hands and put it around my neck. She tied the string. The necklace felt cool and smooth against my skin.

"I wish I had a mirror," I said.

"It looking beautiful," said Tantie. "And it for you now. You can count your cousins on them beads."

"You're giving this to me, Tantie?" I asked, not believing what I had heard.

"Papa Bois said I go find someone who should wear it."

"Thank you," I said. I ran my fingers over the bamboo smoothness of the beads and admired the pretty colors.

"And since you wear Papa Bois's beads, you can start helping me tell these stories," said Tantie. "I been doing de work alone for too long."

Tantie reached over and adjusted the bead string on my neck.

I looked down at the shiny red bead that was me and smiled and smiled. ❖

"... I've never forgotten the smells, sounds, and foods of my island."

Lynn Joseph

My Beautiful Island Lynn Joseph recalls: "When I was a little girl in Trinidad, I could not imagine anywhere else but my beautiful island, with its tall coconut trees, sandy beaches, and happy sounds of steel-band music. I've lived in many other places since then, but I've never forgotten the smells, sounds, and foods of my island." Joseph moved to the United States with her family and graduated from the University of Colorado. She currently lives in New York City. Joseph says she remembers listening to stories like "The Bamboo Beads" when she was growing up. Joseph is best known for her books of poetry *Coconut Kind of Day: Island Poems* and *A Wave in Her Pocket.* She recently published a well-received biography of Bessie Coleman, *Fly, Bessie, Fly.*

Literature Connection

Present a Puppet Show Have students work in "puppet troupes" of five or six students each. Explain that puppet shows should contain as much action as possible and that students' scripts should have a clear beginning, middle, and end. Scripts may be loose and flexible, allowing students to improvise, or they may clearly dictate dialogue and stage business. Either way, a script should not be considered final until the play has had some run-throughs.

The type of puppets students choose may depend on available time and materials.

RUBRIC

3 Full Accomplishment Students' puppet shows accurately reflect the plot, characters, and setting of the chosen selection. Performances are well-rehearsed, show imagination, and are entertaining.

2 Substantial Accomplishment Students' puppet shows reasonably correspond with the plot, characters, and setting of the chosen selection. Performances are fairly smooth and moderately entertaining.

1 Little or Partial Accomplishment Students' puppet shows do not accurately reflect the plot, characters, and/or setting of the chosen selection. Performances are clumsy or incomplete.

Social Studies Connection

Create a Market Display Set aside a portion of the room for the display, and assist students in locating any needed display tables or easels.

Use **Communications Transparencies and Copymasters**, p. 16, for additional support.

RUBRIC

3 Full Accomplishment Students display well-made, appropriate foods and crafts in an organized manner.

2 Substantial Accomplishment Foods and crafts are appropriate, but could be more carefully made or better arrayed.

1 Little or Partial Accomplishment Students have not researched appropriate items. They are not well-made or well-displayed.

Interdisciplinary Projects

LITERATURE CONNECTION

Present a Puppet Show Develop a puppet show based on one of the stories you have just read. Form teams to adapt the story into a script, make and costume puppets, design a set, build a stage, and perform the show. These suggestions may help:

Step 1: Script Identify the characters to be included. List main events and write dialogue that will convey the story. Or, write a script for a narrator. Either way, write stage directions for the puppeteers.

Step 2: Stage Make the stage as simple or as complex as time allows. Three possible arrangements are shown here.

Step 3: Puppets Research techniques in puppet making. Choose to construct paper-bag, sock, glove, fabric, or stick puppets.

Step 4: Performance Present your puppet show as part of an arts program at school, or perform it for a class of younger students.

Three simple puppet-show stages you can make.

SOCIAL STUDIES CONNECTION

Create a Market Display Outdoor markets like the one described in "The Bamboo Beads" are common both in Trinidad and Tobago and in Guatemala. Some people earn their livelihood by selling at market goods they have made or grown themselves. Working in a group, choose either Guatemala or Trinidad and Tobago. Learn about crafts, crops, and other typical products from the country, and create a "market day" display. Each student in the group should contribute an item representing a market good. As an example, for Guatemala you might paint a clay pot, make a festival mask, and fashion a belt out of fabric or paper. If possible, include foods for classmates to sample.

SCIENCE CONNECTION

Investigate Bamboo The beads that Papa Bois gave Tantie were whittled from bamboo, a type of huge, woody grass that grows in the Eastern and Western Hemispheres. Research the bamboo plant and its uses in Asian, Caribbean, and other cultures. Then, as a class, combine your research on a large chart similar to the one shown. On the chart, list and illustrate some of the products derived from bamboo.

Uses of Bamboo		
Country	Products	Other Uses

Science Connection

Investigate Bamboo For their research, students can use an on-line or print encyclopedia or a specialized book on grasses of the world. Students can do a subject search in a library catalog to locate the latter.

RUBRIC

3 Full Accomplishment Charts reflect solid research and synthesis of information. Students clearly and imaginatively use words and pictures to show the uses of bamboo.

2 Substantial Accomplishment Charts reflect solid research but little synthesis of information. Students' use of words and pictures varies in clarity and lacks imagination.

1 Little or Partial Accomplishment Charts reflect inadequate research and use of unsynthesized information. Students' use of words and pictures is ineffective.

Across Cultures

Compare Tales
Characters similar to Papa Bois can be found in the tales of other cultures. Look in folklore collections and other resources to find stories about real or mythical figures known for their affection for animals, as well as for their wisdom. Compare the tales and make illustrations of the characters to display in class.

Map Hurricanes Guatemala and Trinidad are subject to hurricanes, tropical storms that are even more devastating than the one unleashed in "The Disobedient Child." The word *hurricane* comes from the name of the Carib god of evil, Juracán. Find out more about the hurricanes that affect these countries. Use a map to chart the typical formation and movement of hurricanes in the Caribbean.

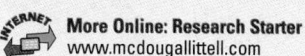 **More Online: Research Starter**
www.mcdougallittell.com

Explore Music Lynn Joseph, the author of "The Bamboo Beads," enjoys the calypso steel-band music of Trinidad. Guatemala is famous for *marimba* music and dances that portray events from history and legend. Research music and dance in one of these countries, and create a multimedia presentation to share what you learn.

Paint a Mural Modern-day Guatemalan artists often draw inspiration from their Mayan heritage. One popular art form is the political mural, a large painting illustrating an idea or a slogan such as "Education brings freedom." Some murals represent events from history and folklore. Often they are painted on the walls of buildings. Find some examples of Guatemalan mural art, and then paint a small version of your own mural in Guatemalan style.

Vocabulary in Action

EXERCISE A: ANALOGIES An analogy compares one pair of words to another. Each pair of words has a similar relationship; for example, *narrow* is to *wide* as *coarse* is to *silky*. To complete the analogies, determine the relationship between the first pair of words. Then decide which Word to Know completes the second pair in a similar way.

1. GREET : WELCOME :: spew : _____
2. SCATTER : GATHER :: reject : _____
3. GROW : SHRINK :: encourage : _____
4. STITCHING : SEWING :: carving : _____
5. RUN : TIPTOE :: shout : _____

EXERCISE B Using the Words to Know, write a folk tale that offers imaginative explanations for a fact of nature. For example, you might explain why a cactus is spiny.

Long ago, the desert was cool and wet. You could hear . . .

WORDS TO KNOW	emit	forbid	murmur	tolerate	whittling

OVERVIEW

Objectives
- To understand and appreciate two folk tales that illustrate a lesson in justice
- To appreciate the folklore and cultural history of Germany and Vietnam
- To extend understanding of the selection through a variety of multimodal and cross-curricular activities

Reading Pathways
- Select one or several students to read each story aloud to the entire class or to small groups of students. Assign this reading in advance so that the readers can incorporate into their presentations some of the techniques used by professional storytellers. Have the audience listen carefully to the stories without following along in their texts.
- Read the stories aloud to the class, pausing at key points to discuss how elements of the stories inform students about the folklore and cultures of Vietnam and Germany. Have students compare these cultures to their own.
- After students have read the stories once, have them read them again to identify structural elements such as main characters, minor characters, conflict, setting, and plot. Then have students identify similarities and differences between these stories and the selections in the Unit 3. Students can compare the treatment received by the king's daughter in "King Thrushbeard" with that of Selo in "Cricket in the Road."

5-Minute Warm-Up

Daily Language SkillBuilder

Have students **proofread** the display sentences on page 765e and write them correctly. The sentences also appear on Transparency 25 of **Grammar Transparencies and Copymasters.**

LINKS TO UNIT THREE
A Sense of Fairness

Do two wrongs make a right? How can you resolve an injustice? What is just and what is unjust? These questions are raised in the selections in Unit Three. Folk tales from many different cultures have also explored these issues. Each of the tales you are about to read illustrates a lesson in justice.

GERMANY

King Thrushbeard

retold by the Brothers Grimm

This tale was recorded by the famous Brothers Grimm, whose stories are still told to children today. In the early 1800s, the brothers collected and wrote down stories that had been told in Germany for generations. Their **fairy tales** include "Cinderella," "The Frog Prince," "Rumpelstiltskin," "Hansel and Gretel," and "Snow White." In this lesser-known story, a princess who finds fault with almost everyone learns a lesson about pride.

The story takes place in medieval Germany, in the days of nobles, knights, and peasants. Although those days are long gone, many German castles from this period of history still stand. Some are open to visitors as museums. Like the Grimms' fairy tales, they help people remember and learn from the past.

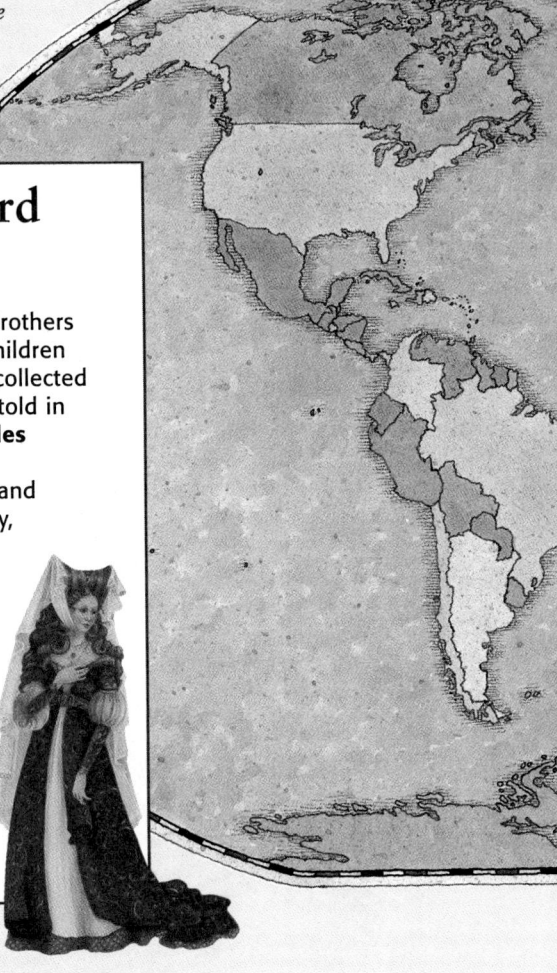

802 UNIT SIX   THE ORAL TRADITION

LESSON RESOURCES

UNIT SIX RESOURCE BOOK,
pp. 18–24

ASSESSMENT
Formal Assessment,
pp. 129–130
Teacher's Guide to Assessment and Portfolio Use
Test Generator

SKILLS TRANSPARENCIES AND COPYMASTERS
Grammar
- Using Italics, CM 131 (for Mini Lesson, p. 806)
- Contractions and Possessive Pronouns, CM 75 (for Mini Lesson, p. 816)

Communications
- Dramatic Reading, TR 12 (for Mini Lesson, p. 805)
- Interviewing, TR 9 (for Mini Lesson, p. 808)

INTEGRATED TECHNOLOGY
Audio Library
Internet: Research Starter

Visit our website:
www.mcdougallittell.com

AS YOU READ . . .

Think about similar stories you may have read in the folklore of other cultures.

Identify traits that vary from one culture to another.

Think about why certain values endure.

Students Acquiring English
If you or members of the class read the story aloud, students might find it helpful to follow along in their texts, to enable them to connect spoken and written language.

Use **Spanish Study Guide,** pp. 163–165 for additional support.

Less Proficient Readers
As students read each story, pause to ask questions to confirm that students are keeping track of critical events in the story. If students cannot answer questions posed, ask more basic questions until students can answer correctly. Then review the story from that point on.

Gifted and Talented
Challenge students to consider questions such as the following as they read.
- What purpose have folk tales served?
- Do they still serve that purpose today?
- Are there any modern folk tales?
- Do these two tales offer lessons we are still in need of learning?

GERMANY

VIETNAM

VIETNAM

In the Land of Small Dragon

told by Dang Manh Kha (dăng'-män'kä) to Ann Nolan Clark

Different versions of the same story may appear in many cultures. Usually these stories focus on values that the cultures hold in common. For example, many versions of the Cinderella story can be found, from Canada to Africa to Japan. This **Cinderella tale** told in verse comes from Vietnam, a country in Southeast Asia.

Vietnam was governed for long periods by China and then by France. Yet the Vietnamese have retained much of their own folklore and cultural identity. Today Vietnam is an independent nation. This version of the Cinderella story includes a jealous stepmother, a fairy godmother, and a magical fish.

LINKS TO UNIT THREE **803**

Summary

In a Vietnamese folk tale similar to "Cinderella," the beautiful T'âm is mistreated by her jealous stepmother and her stepsister, Cám. When the girls' father holds a fishing contest to see who will be his Number One Daughter, Cám cheats T'âm out of the title by stealing all but one of her fish. T'âm feels sorry for her little remaining fish and becomes its friend and caretaker—until Cám eats it. A fairy tells the grieving T'âm to bury her fish's bones; later she digs them up and discovers in their place a silk dress and two jeweled shoes. After she loses one shoe in a rice paddy, a bird carries it to the emperor's garden. There the emperor's son picks it up and proclaims that its owner will be his wife. Although Cám's mother does her best to keep T'âm from going with her stepsister to the palace, T'âm does go. The prince easily slips the shoe onto T'âm's foot and declares that she will be his wife.

Reading and Analyzing

Active Reading:
USING TEXT ORGANIZERS

Students can represent text information in different ways such as in outlines, time lines, or graphic organizers. Invite them to use a family tree to help them identify relationships among characters. Have students copy the family tree into their Reader's Notebooks and refer to it as they follow the emerging family conflict in the story.

Use **Unit Six Resource Book**, p. 19 for more practice.

Teaching Options

804   UNIT SIX   THE ORAL TRADITION

Multicultural Link   **Years of the Chinese Calendar**

The Chinese assign an animal, real or mythical, to each year. There are 12 different animals in the cycle, which is sometimes referred to as the Chinese Zodiac. Like a person's astrological sign, a person's birth year is believed to give the person certain characteristics. For example, people born in the Year of the Rooster (or Chicken, as it is called in the story) are supposed to be loners who are less adventurous than they appear to be. They are supposed to be most compatible with people born in the year of the Dragon, Snake, or Ox. The cycle of animals is as follows:

2000	Dragon	2006	Dog
2001	Snake	2007	Pig
2002	Horse	2008	Rat
2003	Sheep	2009	Ox
2004	Monkey	2010	Tiger
2005	Rooster	2011	Rabbit

Students can count backward (1999 was also year of the Rabbit) to find their own birth year.

In the LAND of SMALL DRAGON

As told by

Dang Manh Kha
to **Ann Nolan Clark**

1

Man cannot know the whole world,
But can know his own small part.

In the Land of Small Dragon,
In the Year of the Chicken,[1]
In a Village of No-Name,
In the bend of the river,
There were many small houses
Tied together by walkways.
Mulberry and apricot,
Pear tree and flowering vine
Dropped their delicate blossoms
On a carpet of new grass.

---

1. **Year of the Chicken:** the name of a year in the old Chinese calendar; commonly called Year of the Rooster. Every year in the Chinese calendar has 1 of 12 animal names. For example, 1911 was a Year of the Pig, which next occurred 12 years later, in 1923.

Mini Lesson **Speaking and Listening**

CHORAL READING Students can listen to proficient, fluent models of oral reading, including selections from classic and contemporary works, and present dramatic interpretations of experiences, stories, poems, or plays to communicate.

Prepare Tell students that a choral reading can make a story sound like music. In a choral reading, groups of readers act as a choir, reading aloud in the same rhythm and volume.

Divide students into small groups for a choral reading. Assign each group a portion of the selection. If class size permits, you might assign five

narrator groups—one for each of the five sections—plus one group for each character, and one group to read all of the italicized portions. Have each group choose a conductor, or leader.

Present Allow groups to practice reading aloud their assignment as a chorus. Then have groups combine their parts in a class choral reading. You may wish to invite families or other classes to attend the choral reading.

📖 Use **Communications Transparencies and Copymasters,** p. 12, for additional support.

A Students can analyze characters, including their traits, motivations, conflicts, points of view, relationships and changes they undergo, as they read. Ask students to interpret the italicized words. How do they apply to Cám?

Possible Response: If a person is bad inside, it shows on his or her face. Cám's ugly face reflects her mean spirit.

 Use **Literary Analysis Transparencies,** p. 4, for additional support.

Reading Skills and Strategies: ANALYZE

B Have students identify the things in this passage that come in twos and ones. Ask students what the narrator communicates by giving Cám's mother a single-minded purpose and a heart with a single door.

Possible Response: The narrator communicates disharmony. If Cám's mother could find room in her mind and heart for two daughters, all would be well.

Literary Analysis: POINT OF VIEW

Remind students that point of view refers to how a writer tells a story. Ask what point of view this story is told from.

Answer: third-person point of view Ask how students can tell.

Possible Response: The narrator is outside the story and uses third-person pronouns such as *he, she,* and *they.*

In a Village of No-Name
Lived a man and two daughters.
Tâm[2] was the elder daughter;
Her mother died at her birth.

A jewel box of gold and jade
Holds only jewels of great price.

Tâm's face was a golden moon,
Her eyes dark as a storm cloud,
Her feet delicate flowers
Stepping lightly on the wind.
No envy lived in her heart,
Nor bitterness in her tears.
Cám[3] was the younger daughter,
Child of Number Two Wife.
Cám's face was long and ugly,
Scowling and discontented,
Frowning in deep displeasure.
<u>Indolent</u>, slow and idle,
Her heart was filled with hatred
For her beautiful sister.

A *An evil heart keeps records*
On the face of its owner.

The father loved both daughters,
One not more than the other.
He did not permit his heart
To call one name more dearly.

He lived his days in justice,
Standing strong against the wind.

B
1
Father had a little land,
A house made of mats and clay,
A grove of mulberry trees
Enclosed by growing bamboo,
A garden and rice paddy,[4]

Two great water buffalo,[5]
A well for drinking water,
And twin fish ponds for the fish.
Cám's mother, Number Two Wife,
Cared only for her own child.
Her mind had only one thought:
What would give pleasure to Cám.

Her heart had only one door
And only Cám could enter.

Number Two Wife was jealous
of Tâm, the elder daughter,
Who was beautiful and good,
So the mother planned revenge
On the good, beautiful child.
To Cám she gave everything,
But nothing but work to Tâm.
Tâm carried water buckets,
Hanging from her bamboo pole.
Tâm carried forest fagots[6]
To burn in the kitchen fire.
Tâm transplanted young rice plants
From seed bed to rice paddy.
Tâm flailed[7] the rice on a rock,
Then she winnowed and gleaned it.[8]
Tâm's body ached with tiredness,

---

2. **Tâm** (täm).

3. **Cám** (cäm).

4. **rice paddy:** flooded field used for growing rice.

5. **water buffalo:** slow, powerful, oxlike animals used for pulling loads.

6. **fagots** (făg′əts): bundles of sticks or twigs; also spelled *faggots.*

7. **flailed:** beat out grain from its husk, or dry outer casing.

8. **winnowed and gleaned it:** separated out the useless parts of the rice and collected the remaining good parts.

WORDS
TO
KNOW   **indolent** (ĭn′də-lənt) *adj.* lazy

806

Teaching Options

 Grammar

USING ITALICS

Instruction Tell students that characters in italic type slant to the right. Point out the use of italics in the proverbs in this story. Here, italics are used to separate those sections and to call attention to them. Explain that there are other reasons to use italics and that these are some of them. Display the following chart on the chalkboard:

Using Italics	
Use:	**Example:**
Words used as words	How do you pronounce *indolent?*
Book and play titles	*The Fun of It; Words on a Page*
Names of ships, spacecraft, and aircraft	*Titanic*
Words from other languages	*Bonjour, vieux Papa*

Her heart was heavy and sad.
She said, "Wise Father, listen!
I am your elder daughter;
Therefore why may I not be
Number One Daughter, also?
A Number One Daughter works,
But she works with dignity.
If I were your Number One
The honor would ease my pain.
As it is, I am a slave,
Without honor or dignity."
Waiting for wisdom to come,
Father was slow to give answer.
"Both of my daughters share my heart.
I cannot choose between them.

2 One of you must earn the right
To be my Number One child."

A man's worth is what he does,
Not what he says he can do.

3 "Go, Daughters, to the fish pond;
Take your fish baskets with you.
Fish until night moon-mist comes.
Bring your fish catch back to me.
She who brings a full basket
Is my Number One Daughter.
Your work, not my heart, decides
Your place in your father's house."
T'âm listened to her father
And was quick to obey him.
With her basket, she waded
In the mud of the fish pond.
With quick-moving, graceful hands
She caught the quick-darting fish.
Slowly the long hours went by.
Slowly her fish basket filled.
Cám sat on the high, dry bank
Trying to think of some plan,

Illustration Copyright © 1982 Vo-Dinh Mai. From *The Brocaded Slipper and Other Vietnamese Tales* by Lynette Dyer Vuong. Reprinted by permission of HarperCollins Publishers.

Customizing Instruction

Multiple Learning Styles
Visual Learners

1 Invite students to draw a picture of Father's land, using details from the story.

Students Acquiring English

2 Invite students from Vietnamese backgrounds to share their understanding of family traditions. Ask them to compare their experiences with T'âm's desired relationship with her father.

Less Proficient Readers
Help students review the tale thus far by asking the following questions:
- Which sister works hard? Which does no work?
  Answer: T'âm works hard; Cám does nothing.
- Who makes T'âm work hard?
  Answer: her stepmother
- What does T'âm want from her father?
  Answer: to be Number One Daughter

Set a Purpose Have students read to find out how a dead fish brings beauty into T'âm's life.

Students Acquiring English

3 Remind students that there are many words in English that can be used as nouns, verbs, and adjectives, and that the context usually makes clear what meaning is intended. Point out that the word *fish* is used in each of these three ways throughout this section and invite students to identify each type of use.

Exercises Ask students to underline the portion(s) of each sentence that should be in italics.

1. If Cám had owned a ship, its name might have been Ship of Number One Daughter. *(Ship of Number One Daughter)*
2. This story comes from a book called The Brocaded Slipper and Other Vietnamese Tales. *(The Brocaded Slipper and Other Vietnamese Tales)*
3. Does curt mean the same thing as rude? *(curt, rude)*
4. T'âm wore jeweled hai and a silken dress. *(hai)*
5. If the emperor had owned a plane, its name might have been Emperor's Wings. *(Emperor's Wings)*

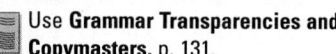 Use **Grammar Transparencies and Copymasters**, p. 131.

 Use McDougal Littell's *Language Network,* Chapter 9, for more practice in punctuation.

A Remind students to offer observations, make connections, react, speculate, interpret, and raise questions in response to texts. Discuss questions or comments students have as the devious Cám addresses T´âm. You may wish to model your own process of thinking:

I wonder what Cám is up to. I don't trust her. If she is so concerned about Father, why doesn't she sing to him herself?

Active Reading: USING TEXT ORGANIZERS

Remind students that they can remember and review a selection by classifying its various elements, including genre, setting, and theme, in a graphic organizer.

Have students classify or identify various elements of the story by completing a graphic organizer such as the one shown.

Genre	folk tale
Theme	the need to belong
Conflict	person vs. person: T´âm vs. her stepmother and stepsister
Setting	a small village in Vietnam
Main Characters	T´âm, her stepmother, Cám, Father

Her basket empty of fish,
But her mind full of cunning.
"I, wade in that mud?" she thought.
"There must be some better way."
At last she knew what to do
To be Number One Daughter.
"T´âm," she called, "elder sister,
Our father needs a bright flower,
A flower to gladden his heart.
Get it for him, dear sister."
T´âm, the good, gentle sister,
Set her fish basket aside
And ran into the forest
To pick the night-blooming flowers.
Cám crept to T´âm's fish basket,
Emptied it into her own.

"Little fish,

dear little fish,

I will put you

in the well."

Now her fish basket was full.
T´âm's held only one small fish.
Quickly Cám ran to Father,
Calling, "See my full basket!"
T´âm ran back to the fish pond
With an armload of bright flowers.
"Cám," she called, "what has happened?
What has happened to my fish?"
Slowly T´âm went to Father
Bringing him the flowers and fish.
Father looked at both baskets.

Speaking slowly, he told them,
"The test was a full basket,
Not flowers and one small fish.
Take your fish, Elder Daughter.
It is much too small to eat.
Cám has earned the right to be
Honorable Number One."

1

2

T´âm looked at the little fish.
Her heart was filled with pity
At its loneliness and fright.
"Little fish, dear little fish,
I will put you in the well."
At night T´âm brought her rice bowl,
Sharing her food with the fish—
Talked to the thin fish, saying,
"Little fish, come eat with me"—
Stayed at the well at nighttime
With the stars for company.
The fish grew big and trustful.
It grew fat and not afraid.
It knew T´âm's voice and answered,
Swimming to her outstretched hand.
Cám sat in the dark shadows,
Her heart full of jealousy,
Her mind full of wicked thoughts.
Sweetly she called, "T´âm, sister.
Our father is overtired.
Come sing him a pretty song
That will bring sweet dreams to him."
Quickly T´âm ran to her father,
Singing him a nightbird song.
Cám was hiding near the well,
Watching, waiting and watching.
When she heard T´âm's pretty song
She crept closer to the fish,
Whispering, "Dear little fish,
Come to me! Come eat with me."

A

Mini Lesson — Speaking and Listening

INTERVIEWS Students can demonstrate effective communication skills that reflect such demands as interviewing, reporting, requesting, and providing information.

Prepare Tell students that before an interview, the interviewer should contact the potential interviewee, learn all he or she can about the subject, prepare questions, and organize supplies. The person being interviewed should think about questions that are likely to be asked and prepare answers, especially to tough questions. At the actual interview, he or she should answer as fully as possible, but not offer more information than he or she is asked for.

Present Select students to portray the stepmother, Cám and Father. Have other students act as journalists, interviewing the characters about their roles in creating a household in which a member was ill-treated. After the interviews, discuss as a class what information interviewers elicited about the characters and how the characters handled uncomfortable questions.

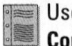 Use **Communications Transparencies and Copymasters**, p. 9, for additional support.

The fish came, and greedy Cám
Touched it, caught it and ate it!
T´âm returned. Her fish was gone.
"Little fish, dear little fish,
Come to me! Come eat with me!"
Bitterly she cried for it.

The stars looked down in pity;
The clouds shed teardrops of rain.

3

T´âm's tears falling in the well
Made the water rise higher.
And from it rose Nang Tien,
A lovely cloud-dressed fairy.
Her voice was a silver bell
Ringing clear in the moonlight.
"My child, why are you crying?"
"My dear little fish is gone!
He does not come when I call."
"Ask Red Rooster to help you.
His hens will find Little Fish."
Soon the hens came in a line
Sadly bringing the fish bones.
T´âm cried, holding the fish bones.
"Your dear fish will not forget.
Place his bones in a clay pot
Safe beneath your sleeping mat.
Those we love never leave us.
Cherished bones keep love alive."
In her treasured clay pot, T´âm
Made a bed of flower petals
For the bones of Little Fish
And put him away with love.
But she did not forget him;
When the moon was full again,
T´âm, so lonely for her fish,
Dug up the buried clay pot.
T´âm found, instead of fish bones,

A silken dress and two jeweled *hai.*[9]
Her Nang Tien spoke again.
"Your dear little fish loves you.
Clothe yourself in the garments
His love has given you."
T´âm put on the small jeweled *hai.*
They fit like a velvet skin
Made of moonlight and stardust
And the love of Little Fish.
T´âm heard music in her heart
That sent her small feet dancing,
Flitting like two butterflies,
Skimming like two flying birds,
Dancing by the twin fish ponds,
Dancing in the rice paddy.
But the mud in the rice paddy
Kept one jeweled *hai* for its own.
Night Wind brought the *hai* to T´âm.
"What is yours I bring to you."
Water in the well bubbled,
"I will wash your *hai* for you."
Water buffalo came by.
"Dry your *hai* on my sharp horn."
A blackbird flew by singing,
"I know where this *hai* belongs.
In a garden far away
I will take this *hai* for you."

4

What is to be must happen
As day follows after night.

In the Emperor's garden,
Sweet with perfume of roses,
The Emperor's son, the Prince,
Walked alone in the moonlight.
A bird, black against the moon,

---

9. *hai* (hī): shoes.

Flew along the garden path,
Dropping a star in its flight.
"Look! A star!" exclaimed the Prince.
Carefully he picked it up
And found it was the small jeweled *hai*.
"Only a beautiful maid
Can wear this beautiful *hai*."
The Prince whispered to his heart,
And his heart answered, "Find her."

In truth, beauty seeks goodness:
What is beautiful is good.

The Prince went to his father:
"A bird dropped this at my feet.
Surely it must come as truth,
Good and fair the maid it fits.
Sire,[10] if it is your pleasure
I would take this maid for wife."
The Great Emperor was pleased
With the wishes of his son.
He called his servants to him,
His drummers and his crier,[11]
Proclaiming a Festival
To find one who owned the *hai*.
In the Village of No-Name
The Emperor's subjects heard—
They heard the Royal Command.
There was praise and rejoicing.
They were pleased the Royal Son
Would wed one of their daughters.

5
Father's house was filled with clothes,
Embroidered *áo-dài*[12] and *hai*
Of heavy silks and rich colors.
Father went outside to sit.

Cám and her mother whispered
Their hopes, their dreams and their plans.
Cám, Number One Daughter, asked,
"Mother, will the Prince choose me?"
Mother said, "Of course he will.
You will be the fairest there!
When you curtsy to the Prince
His heart will go out to you."
T'âm, Daughter Number Two, said,
"May I go with you and Cám?"
Cám's mother answered <u>curtly</u>,
"Yes, if you have done this task:
Separating rice and husks
From one basket into two."

"Stay at home, you Number Two!"

T'âm knew Cám's mother had mixed
The cleaned rice with rice unhusked.
She looked at the big basket

---

10. **Sire:** title of respect for a superior, in this case, an emperor.

11. **crier:** person who makes public announcements in the streets of a village or town.

12. **embroidered *áo-dài*** (ou'dĭ): robes decorated with fancy needlework.

WORDS
TO
KNOW

curtly (kûrt'lē) *adv.* in a way that uses so few words it is either rude or almost rude

810

Mini Lesson **Spelling**

THE SUFFIX -ANCE
Instruction Tell students that the suffix *-ance* is commonly added to words to form nouns or adjectives. Write on the chalkboard *repent + ance*. Ask, *Did Cám show signs of repentance?* Discuss the meaning of *repentance*. Next, demonstrate that when *-ance* is added to words that end with silent *e*, the final *e* is dropped: *endure + ance = endurance*.

Application Have students combine the word parts below to form nouns and adjectives that end in the suffix *-ance*. Tell them to use at least

three of the words in a short paragraph about "In The Land of Small Dragon."

1. disturb + ance
2. annoy + ance
3. accept + ance
4. allow + ance
5. insure + ance
6. assist + ance
7. guide + ance
8. acquaint + ance
9. perform + ance
10. avoid + ance

Ask students to take note of other words that fit this pattern in their reading and writing.

 Use **Unit Six Resource Book,** p. 23.

Full to brim with rice and husks.
Separating the cleaned rice
From that of rice unhusked
Would take all harvest moon time,
When the Festival would end.
A cloud passed over the moon.
Whirring wings outsung the wind.
B A flock of blackbirds lighted
On the pile of leaves and grain.
Picking the grain from the leaves,
They dropped clean rice at T'âm's feet.
T'âm could almost not believe
That the endless task was done.
T'âm, the elder daughter, said,
"May I go? May I go, too,
Now that all my work is done?"
Cám taunted, "How could you go?
You have nothing fit to wear."
"If I had a dress to wear
Could I go to the Palace?"
"If wishes were dresses, yes,
But wishes are not dresses."
When Mother left she said,
"Our dear Cám is ravishing.
Stay at home, you Number Two!
Cám will be the one to wed."
T'âm dug up the big clay pot.
The dress and one *hai* were there—
As soft as misty moon clouds,
Delicate as rose perfume.
T'âm washed her face in the well,
Combed her hair by the fish pond.
She smoothed down the silken dress,
Tied one *hai* unto her belt
And, though her feet were bare,
Hurried, scurried, ran and ran.
She ran to the Festival
In the King's Royal Garden.
At the Palace gates the guards

Bowed before her, very low.
Pretty girls stood in a line
With their mothers standing near;
One by one they tried to fit
A foot into a small, jeweled *hai*.
Cám stood beside her mother,
By the gilded[13] throne-room door.
Her face was dark and angry
Like a brooding monsoon[14] wind.
Cám, wiping her tears away,
Sobbed and whimpered and complained,
"My small foot fits his old shoe—
Everything but my big toe."
T'âm stood shyly by the door
Looking in great wonderment
While trumpeters and drummers
Made music for her entrance.
People looked at gentle T'âm.
Everyone was whispering,
"Oh! She is so beautiful!
She must be a Princess fair
From some distant foreign land."
Then the Prince looked up and saw
A lady walking toward him.
Stepping from his Royal Throne,
He quickly went to meet her,
And taking her hand led her
To His Majesty the King.
What is to be must happen
As day happens after night.

Real beauty mirrors goodness.
What is one is the other.

---

13. **gilded:** covered with a thin layer of gold.
14. **monsoon:** in south Asia, a wind that begins the rainy season.

WORDS TO KNOW **ravishing** (răv'ĭ-shĭng) *adj.* unusually beautiful; delightfully pleasing

811

Customizing Instruction

Multiple Learning Styles
Auditory Learners

1 Invite students to dramatize the role of the Great Emperor's drummers and crier.

Less Proficient Readers
Have students describe the sequence of events through which T'âm escapes her stepmother's clutches.
Possible Response: A raven carries one of T'âm's *hai* to the Prince. With the Great Emperor's approval, the Prince decides that the owner of the *hai* will be his wife.
Set a Purpose Ask students to read on to find out what happens to T'âm.
Possible Response: Her foot slips into the *hai*, proving that she is the owner. T'âm is deemed Wife Number One.

Gifted and Talented
Ask students to finish reading the story and write a brief essay in response to its final lines. Ask them if they believe a person's fate or destiny is set at birth and cannot be changed. Remind students to support their opinions with examples, either from the story or from their own experiences.
Possible Response: Students may agree or disagree, but should back up their response with examples.

Literary Analysis: RHYTHM

Remind students that rhythm is the pattern of stressed and unstressed syllables in a piece of writing, such as a poem or a folk tale. A selection can have a regular or an irregular rhythm. Call on students to read aloud different sections of "In the Land of Small Dragon." Have listeners describe the effect of the line breaks on the rhythm. Then read aloud to students one section of the tale, heeding end punctuation but ignoring line breaks. Ask students to compare and contrast the readings.

"We will

have a

Wedding

feast."

Kneeling, the Prince placed the *hai*
On T'âm's dainty little foot.
T'âm untied the *hai* she wore
And slid her bare foot in it.

Beauty is not painted on.
It is the spirit showing.

The Prince spoke to his father.
"I would take this maid for wife."
His Royal Highness nodded.
"We will have a Wedding feast."
All the birds in all the trees
Sang a song of happiness:
"T'âm, the Number Two Daughter,
Is to be Wife Number One."

What is written in the stars
Cannot be changed or altered.

*"Man cannot know the
whole world, but can
know his own small part."*

Dang Manh Kha

Teacher and Storyteller Dang Manh Kha was born in Vietnam. After attending St. John's University in Minnesota, he taught school in El Paso, Texas, for four years. In 1975 he worked for the Southeast Asian Resettlement Program to aid Vietnamese refugees. Dang Manh Kha now lives in Tucson, Arizona.

*"All of my books are based
upon actual experiences. . . ."*

Ann Nolan Clark
1896–1995

Teacher and Writer Born in New Mexico, Ann Nolan Clark served for many years as a teacher and writer for the Bureau of Indian Affairs and the U.S. Department of Education in Latin America. Clark wrote numerous books about children in various countries, including *Secret of the Andes,* set in Peru, which won the Newbery Medal in 1953.

Writing from Experience Clark once said, "All of my books are based upon actual experiences, knowing the people and places I write about, having been there." She spent her final years near Tucson, Arizona. Her other works include *In My Mother's House, To Stand Against the Wind, Little Navajo Bluebird, Santiago,* and *Tia Maria's Garden.*

Teaching Options

 Assessment Standardized Test Practice

RECOGNIZE PERSUASIVE DEVICES Standardized tests will sometimes ask questions to see if students can recognize when they are being persuaded to think or feel a certain way. Work through the process of deciding which of the following passages from the story is meant to persuade, rather than to inform or entertain.

A. He lived his days in justice, standing strong against the wind.

B. T'âm, sister. Our father is overtired. Come sing him a pretty song that will bring sweet dreams to him.

C. A flock of blackbirds lighted on the pile of leaves and grain.

D. We will have a Wedding feast.

A is not persuasive; it is a poetic description of a just person, and is meant to inform and to entertain. In B, Cám is trying to convince T'âm to sing (so she can eat T'âm's fish). You can see the use of appeal and of flattery in the words *pretty* and *sweet,* so B is the correct answer. C and D are statements of fact and are informative, not persuasive, so both are incorrect.

King Thrushbeard

retold by
The Brothers Grimm

Copyright © Joyce Patti.

Summary

A furious king swears to make his overly particular daughter marry the first beggar who comes to his door. Thus, she winds up marrying a poor minstrel and living with him in extreme poverty. To make ends meet, she unsuccessfully tries weaving baskets, spinning, and selling pots. Finally, she gets a job as kitchen maid in another king's palace. At the wedding feast of the king's eldest son, she fills her pockets with scraps of food. Suddenly the king's son appears and asks her to dance. To her horror, he is King Thrushbeard—the rejected suitor whose chin she compared to a thrush's beak. She runs away in humiliation but is stopped by Thrushbeard, who explains that he masqueraded as her minstrel husband out of love and to teach her humility. Her lesson well learned, the king's daughter and Thrushbeard celebrate their wedding.

Customizing Instruction

Students Acquiring English

Explain that this story contains figurative language, in which the words mean more than their literal meanings. Encourage students to point out phrases they don't understand and ask for clarification.

Less Proficient Readers

Set a Purpose Tell students that this story is a folk tale with a king's daughter for a main character. Ask them what kinds of plot elements they would expect to find in such a story. As students read the beginning of the tale, they should note how the king's daughter treats her suitors and what this reveals about her character.

(Mini Lesson) Speaking and Listening

STORYTELLING Students should understand that it is important to adapt spoken language such as word choice, diction, and usage to the audience, purpose, and occasion. Tell students that when they are thinking about a young audience, they should pay particular attention to their word choice. They may also wish to simplify the plot.

Prepare Have students work in groups of three or four. Tell students to imagine that their group will be presenting "King Thrushbeard" to young children. Have groups decide how they would revise the story to interest this age group. Ask them what storytelling techniques they might use most effectively. Have a recorder for each group keep track of group decisions.

Present Ask each group to present and compare their plans.

You may wish to extend this activity by having groups perform a revised version of "King Thrushbeard" for a first- or second-grade audience.

Students can draw inferences such as conclusions or generalizations and support them with text evidence and experience. Ask students to predict what will happen in the story, based on what they know about folk tales.

Possible Response: The proud, vain king's daughter will learn a lesson about humility and love.

Literary Analysis:
FIGURATIVE LANGUAGE

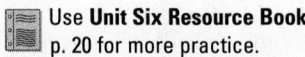 Remind students that figurative language extends the meaning of words beyond their dictionary meaning. Similes are comparisons using *like* or *as,* and metaphors are comparisons without signal words. Ask students to identify metaphors and similes in this passage.

Possible Response: metaphors: one suitor was "a wine barrel," one "a turkey," one "green wood"; similes: "as pale as death," "a chin like a thrush's bill"

Use **Unit Six Resource Book,** p. 20 for more practice.

Literary Analysis: HUMOR

B Help students see the irony in the beggar's comment. Have them contrast the king's daughter's opinion of herself with her husband's opinion. Ask students why the situation is humorous.

Possible Response: The king's daughter is sure of her worth because she is beautiful. Now, however, her beauty is valueless, and she can't even cook or clean. It is ironic for a beggar to find marrying royalty a bad bargain.

A king had a daughter who was unequaled for beauty, but she was so proud and thought so much of herself that no suitor[1] was good enough for her. She rejected one after another and to make matters worse poked fun at them. Once the king gave a great feast and invited all the marriageable young men from far and near. They were all lined up in the order of their rank: first came the kings, then the dukes, princes, counts, and barons, and last of all the knights. The king's daughter was led down the line, but to each suitor she had some objection. One was too fat and she called him a "wine barrel." The next was too tall: "Tall and skinny, that's a ninny." The third was short: "Short and thick won't do the trick." The fourth was too pale: "As pale as death." The fifth too red: "A turkey." The sixth wasn't straight enough: "Green wood, dried behind the stove." She found some fault with every one of them, but she made the most fun of a kindly king who was standing at the head of the line, and whose chin was slightly crooked. "Heavens above!" she cried. "He's got a chin like a thrush's bill!" And from then on he was known as Thrushbeard.

When the old king saw that his daughter did nothing but make fun of people and rejected all the suitors who had come to the feast, he flew into a rage and swore to make her marry the first beggar who came to his door. A few days later a wandering minstrel[2] came and sang under the window in the hope of earning a few coins. When the king heard him, he said: "Send him up." The minstrel appeared in his ragged, dirty clothes, sang for the king and his daughter, and asked for a gift when he had finished. The king said: "Your singing has pleased me so well that I'll give you my daughter for your wife." The princess was horrified, but the king said: "I swore I'd give you to the first beggar who came by, and I'm going to abide by my oath."

All her pleading was in vain; the priest was called, and she was married to the minstrel then and there. After the ceremony the king said: "Now that you're a beggar woman, I can't have you living in my palace. You can just go away with your husband."

The beggar took her by the hand and led her out of the palace, and she had to go with him on foot. They came to a large forest, and she asked:

"Who does that lovely forest belong to?"
"That forest belongs to King
 Thrushbeard.
If you'd taken him, you could call it
 your own."
"Alas, poor me, if I'd only known,
If only I'd taken King Thrushbeard!"

Next they came to a meadow, and she asked:

"Who does that lovely green meadow
 belong to?"
"That meadow belongs to King
 Thrushbeard.
If you'd taken him, you could call it
 your own."
"Alas, poor me, if I'd only known,

---

1. **suitor:** a man seeking to marry a woman.
2. **minstrel** (mĭn′strəl): traveling poet or singer.

Teaching Options

Cross Curricular Link Social Studies

MINSTRELS Though the minstrel in this story never performs to earn his keep, this was certainly not true of real minstrels, who lived in Europe between the 12th and 17th centuries. They were wandering entertainers, especially musicians, who went from place to place, stopping when there was a chance of being paid to perform. Because much of their music was improvised, and since most of them could not write their music down, little of it survives, but the quality of the best of it was probably quite high. Over time, minstrel guilds developed. This brought minstrels further into the mainstream of town life. The guilds saw to it that people found apprenticeships to learn their craft and helped trained minstrels find work. The distinction that existed between musicians who played sacred (religious) music and who could read music, and minstrels, who played secular, improvised music and could not read music, began breaking down in the 1500s. The rise in written compositions and decline of improvisation was the beginning of the end for minstrels. They continued to exist, but slowly vanished as a distinct part of the musical scene.

If only I'd taken King Thrushbeard!"

Then they passed through a big city, and she asked:

> "Who does this beautiful city belong to?"
> "This city belongs to King Thrushbeard.
> If you'd taken him, you could call it
>   your own."
> "Alas, poor me, if only I'd known,
> If only I'd taken King Thrushbeard!"

"You give me a pain," said the minstrel, "always wishing for another husband. I suppose I'm not good enough for you!" At last they came to a tiny little house, and she said:

> "Heavens, this shack is a disgrace!
> Who could own such a wretched place?"

> "If you want
> something done,
> you'll have to
> do it for yourself."

The minstrel answered, "It's my house and yours, where we shall live together." The king's daughter had to bend down to get through the low doorway. "Where are the servants?" she asked. "Servants, my foot!" answered the beggar. "If you want something done, you'll have to do it for yourself. And now make a fire and put on water for my supper because I'm dead tired." But the king's daughter didn't know the first thing about fires or cooking, and the beggar had to help her

or he wouldn't have had any supper at all. When they had eaten what little there was, they went to bed. But bright and early the next morning he made her get up and clean the house.

They worried along for a few days, but then their provisions were gone, and the man said: "Wife, we can't go on like this, eating and drinking and earning nothing. You'll have to weave baskets." He went out and cut willow withes[3] and brought them home. She began to weave but the hard withes bruised her tender hands. "I see that won't do," said the man. "Try spinning; maybe you'll be better at it." She sat down and tried to spin, but the hard thread soon cut her soft fingers and drew blood. "Well, well!" said the man. "You're no good for any work. I've made a bad bargain. But now I think I'll buy up some earthenware pots and dishes. All you'll have to do is sit in the marketplace and sell them." **B**

"Goodness gracious!" she thought. "If somebody from my father's kingdom goes to the marketplace and sees me sitting there selling pots, how they'll laugh at me!" But there was no help for it; she had to give in or they would have starved.

The first day, all went well: people were glad to buy her wares because she was beautiful; they paid whatever she asked, and some didn't even trouble to take the pots they had paid for. The two of them lived on the proceeds as long as the stock held out, and then the husband

_____

3. **withes** (wĭths): tough, bendable twigs.

KING THRUSHBEARD **815**

Mini Lesson **Speaking and Listening**

COMPARING A VIDEO WITH A STORY Students can compare and contrast print, visual, and electronic media such as film with a written story.
Prepare Tell students that when they watch a video, it is doing the visualizing for them. Ask how they have to visualize when they read a story.
Possible Response: They need to use their imaginations and written descriptions.
There are many different video versions of Grimm's fairy tales. One excellent series, put together by actress/producer Shelley Duvall, is *Faerie Tale Theatre* (Playhouse Video).

Present Invite students to watch a video of one or more well-known Grimm's fairy tales which they have also read. Ask them to describe how the version they watched was similar to or different from the way they had visualized it. Then discuss how people today might find aspects of these stories strange. For instance, ask if they think members of royalty would be able to disguise themselves as beggars.

Reading and Analyzing

Literary Analysis: CHARACTER

 A Ask students how they think the princess has changed.

Possible Response: She has lost her pride and arrogance, as shown by the fact that she now gratefully accepts the leftover food. She has learned a lesson in humility.

Literary Analysis: SENSORY DETAILS

B Remind students that sensory details appeal to a reader's sense of touch, taste, smell, sight, and hearing. Ask students to note the senses to which this description of the King's celebration appeals.

Possible Response: touch—putting scraps in a jar;—taste and smell—succulent dishes; sight—lit candles, courtiers' dress, the King's son's clothing and jewelry

Literary Analysis CONFLICT

Students should analyze characters, including their traits, motivations, conflicts, points of view, relationships and changes they undergo when reading. Remind students that plots are usually built around a conflict—a problem or struggle between two or more opposing forces. Conflicts can range from a life-or-death struggle to a disagreement between friends, and can be internal or external. Have students identify the main conflict in this story.

Possible Response: The conflict is an internal one as the king's daughter deals with the consequences of her own pride and arrogance.

---

bought up a fresh supply of crockery. She took a place at the edge of the market, set out her wares around her and offered them for sale. All of a sudden a drunken hussar[4] came galloping through, upset her pots and smashed them all into a thousand **1** pieces. She began to cry; she was worried sick. "Oh!" she wailed. "What will become of me? What will my husband say!" She ran home and told him what had happened. "What did you expect?" he said. "Setting out earthenware pots at the edge of the market! But stop crying. I can see you're no good for any sensible work. Today I was at our king's palace. I asked if they could use a kitchen maid, and they said they'd take you. They'll give you your meals."

A So the king's daughter became a kitchen maid and had to help the cook and do the most disagreeable work. She carried little jars in both her pockets, to take home the leftovers they gave her, and that's what she and her husband lived on.

I t so happened that the marriage of the king's eldest son was about to be celebrated. The poor woman went upstairs and stood in the doorway of the great hall, looking on. When the candles were lit and the courtiers[5] began coming in, each more magnificent than the last, and everything

was so bright and full of splendor, she was sad at heart. She thought of her miserable life and cursed the pride and arrogance that had brought her so low and made her so poor.

<u>Succulent</u> dishes were being carried in and out, and the smell drifted over to her. Now and then a servant tossed her a few scraps, and she put them into her little jars to take home.

B

"I can see you're no good for any sensible work."

And then the king's son appeared; he was dressed in silk and velvet and had gold chains around his neck. When he saw the beautiful woman in the doorway, he took her by the hand and asked her to dance with him, but she refused. She was terrified, for she saw it was King Thrushbeard, who had courted her and whom she had laughed at and rejected. She tried to resist, but he drew her into the hall. Then the string that kept her pockets in place snapped, the jars fell to the floor, the soup

---

4. **hussar** (hǝ-zär′): a cavalry soldier—that is, a soldier who fights on horseback.

5. **courtiers** (kôr′tē-ǝrz): attendants at a royal palace.

WORDS TO KNOW

succulent (sŭk′yǝ-lǝnt) *adj.* tasty; delicious

816

Teaching Options

 Mini Lesson Grammar

CONTRACTIONS AND POSSESSIVE PRONOUNS

Instruction Tell students that possessive pronouns never use apostrophes. Contractions always use apostrophes. A possessive pronoun shows possession. A contraction is two words that have been put together, with one or more letters omitted. Write these examples on the chalkboard.

The shack looked like its roof would blow off.
The minstrel said, "It's my house and yours."

Point out that the first sentence can be restated as, "The roof of the shack looked

like it would blow off." *Its* shows possession. The second sentence can be rephrased, "It is my house and yours." *It* and *is* have been combined to form a contraction.

Exercises Have students choose the correct word, then write *contraction* or *pronoun*.

1. "(You're, Your) the worst cook I ever saw," the minstrel said. *(You're, contraction)*

2. "(It's, Its) because I'm so beautiful—I don't need to cook," she replied. *(It's, contraction)*

3. "I don't think (you're, your) looks are anything much," he retorted. *(your, pronoun)*

4. "If this hovel had (it's, its) own electricity, I could at least blow-dry my hair," she yelled. *(its, pronoun)*

5. The royal couple lived (their, they're) lives happily ever after. *(their, pronoun)*

Use **Unit Six Resource Book**, p. 22.
Use **Grammar Transparencies and Copymasters**, p. 75.

Use McDougal Littell's **Language Network**, Chapter 3, for more practice in possessive pronouns.

spilled and the scraps came tumbling out. The courtiers all began to laugh and jeer, and she would sooner have been a hundred fathoms[6] under the earth. She bounded through the door and tried to escape, but on the stairs a man caught her and brought her back, and when she looked at him, she saw it was King Thrushbeard again. He spoke kindly to her and said: "Don't be afraid. I am the minstrel you've been living with in that wretched shack; I disguised myself for love of you, and I was also the hussar who rode in and smashed your crockery. I did all that to humble your pride and punish you for the <u>insolent</u> way you laughed at me." Then she wept bitterly and said: "I've been very wicked and I'm not

worthy to be your wife." But he said: "Don't cry; the hard days are over; now we shall celebrate our wedding." The maids came and dressed her magnificently, her father arrived with his whole court and congratulated her on her marriage to King Thrushbeard, and it was then that the feast became really joyful. I wish you and I had been there. ❖

---

6. **fathoms** (făth′əmz): units of measurement, each equal to six feet.

"Up to the very end, we worked in two rooms next to each other, . . ."

Jakob and Wilhelm Grimm
1785–1863   1786–1859

A Passion for the Past The brothers Grimm, born in Hanau, Germany, trained to be lawyers. However, an early exposure to old German romantic poems eventually led them to become interested in the language and literature of the German past. Jakob wrote, "It is high time that these old traditions were collected and rescued before they perish like dew in the hot sun."

A Team Effort Happier collecting local folk tales than practicing law, the brothers began a search for folk tales, particularly ones passed along orally to children, that was to become their lifelong commitment. They were always very close; according to Jakob, "Up to the very end, we worked in two rooms next to each other, always under one roof." *Grimm's Fairy Tales* has remained popular to this day.

WORDS TO KNOW   **insolent** (ĭn′sə-lənt) *adj.* rude

817

Literature Connection

Design a Game As students develop the game, one student should serve as recorder to write down the steps. The recorder should read the steps back to the group so that they can make sure the game actually works.

RUBRIC

3 Full Accomplishment The instruction manual clearly explains the rules of the game; the game's design enhances its appeal and strengthens its connection to one of the tales; the game draws significantly and accurately on one of the stories.

2 Substantial Accomplishment The instruction manual explains the rules of the game relatively clearly; the game's design is adequate to strengthen its connection to one of the tales; the game draws on the story in a general way.

1 Little or Partial Accomplishment The instruction manual is unclear, the game's design haphazard, and its connection with one of the tales vague.

Social Studies Connection

Update a Folk Tale If students need help with the chart, ask them more direct questions such as, What is T'âm's strongest character trait? or What event was the climax of "King Thrushbeard"?

RUBRIC

3 Full Accomplishment Entries are clear and accurate; new story retains basic theme and has been updated in imaginative yet believable manner.

2 Substantial Accomplishment Entries are complete but not entirely clear; new story retains basic theme but update could be more imaginative.

1 Little or Partial Accomplishment Entries are incomplete or inaccurate; new story does not retain important elements and does not reflect student's culture.

Interdisciplinary Projects

LITERATURE CONNECTION

Design a Game Working in a small group, design a board game or a computer game based on one of the tales you've just read or another story from folklore. Use these steps to guide you.

Step 1: Rules Decide on an appropriate age level for the game. Then determine the goal of the game. For example, the goal might be to get Cinderella to the palace to attend the ball. Decide which characters will be involved, and brainstorm rules of the game. Write a brief instruction manual.

Step 2: Design Draw sample computer screens or a sample gameboard to show how the game will look. A sample gameboard is shown here.

Step 3: Game Play Share your game in the classroom. Write a summary of the rules to exhibit with the game.

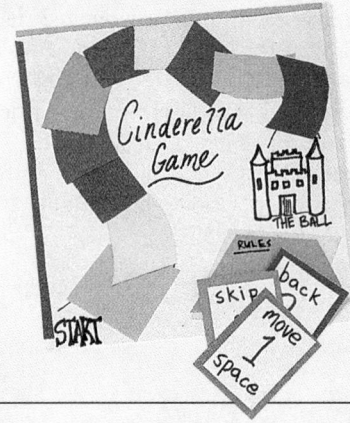

SOCIAL STUDIES CONNECTION

Update a Folk Tale Often, similar folk tales appear in different cultures, each version flavored with details that reflect the setting. Reread one of these tales to find details that reflect the culture of long-ago Vietnam or of medieval Germany. Record your findings in a chart like the one shown. Think about how those details might be different if the story were set in your culture today, and record your ideas. Then write your own version of the story, reflecting the new setting.

Details of Culture	In (name of tale)	In My Community
Valued Possessions		
Valued Traits		
Important Social Events		

SCIENCE CONNECTION

Investigate Rice In the tale "In the Land of Small Dragon," T'âm's work includes growing and harvesting rice. Make a poster about the importance of rice across cultures. How is it grown? What nutritional value does it have?

What are the different types of rice? Make part of your poster a map of the world. Identify countries where rice is a key food or crop. Illustrate your poster with drawings or magazine pictures and display it in the classroom.

818 UNIT SIX   THE ORAL TRADITION

Science Connection

Investigate Rice Students should be able to find the information in an encyclopedia and almanac. They might wish to visit different ethnic grocery stores or look in the international section of a food store to see the different kinds of rice available.

 Use **Writing Transparencies,** p. 45, for additional support.

RUBRIC

3 Full Accomplishment Poster reflects solid research and synthesis of information, answers questions posed, and includes useful map.

2 Substantial Accomplishment Poster reflects solid research but little synthesis of information, doesn't answer all questions, or map is not entirely clear.

1 Little or Partial Accomplishment Poster reflects inadequate research and use of unsythesized information. Answers and/or map are missing.

Across Cultures

COMPARING TEXTS **Compare Versions** Find versions of the Cinderella tale from as many cultures as you can. Compare "In the Land of Small Dragon" (page 804) with Cinderella-like tales from other cultures, such as China, Egypt, Germany, and Native American groups. Get together with classmates and take turns sharing your findings. Arrange a display of any picture-book versions you find.

 More Online: Research Starter
www.mcdougallittell.com

COMPARING TEXTS **Find Similar Stories** Many cultures have stories in which a person disguises himself or herself in order to "test" someone, as King Thrushbeard does. Look in collections of folk tales and fairy tales to find more stories with this theme. Make an illustration of each tale to display in the classroom, and compare the tales in a class discussion.

Research Life in the Middle Ages The king's daughter in "King Thrushbeard" learns to be kinder by spending some time as a peasant. Working with a partner, research how society was structured in Germany or another part of Europe during the Middle Ages. Also look for information about how nobles and peasants lived. Then draw the typical housing that each of these social groups lived in. For each home, write a paragraph or more describing a typical day in the life of someone who lived there. Present your work to the class.

Write Proverbs Proverbs, such as those found in "In the Land of Small Dragon," are old and familiar sayings that express a basic truth. Write at least two proverbs that express truths illustrated in "King Thrushbeard" or "In the Land of Small Dragon." With your classmates, make a bulletin board of these proverbs.

Across Cultures
COMPARING TEXTS

Compare Versions Students can use a school or public library to find Cinderella-like tales from other cultures. Effective displays will enable viewers to compare the tales easily.

 Use **Reading and Critical Thinking Transparencies,** p. 17, for additional support.

Find Similar Stories During the class discussion, students might want to make a list on the chalkboard of all the different reasons they have found for people to be tested. See if students can sort the reasons into different groups.

Research Life in the Middle Ages Students might wish to end their reports by comparing and contrasting life at that time with life in the present.

Write Proverbs Additional proverbs for students to consult as models can be found in *Poor Richard's Almanac* by Benjamin Franklin. Remind students before they begin writing that their proverbs should relate directly to the tales.

Use **Unit Six Resource Book,** p. 24, for assessment.

Vocabulary in Action

EXERCISE A: MEANING CLUES Write the Word to Know that is most closely related to the scene described in each sentence below.

1. The princess smashed the knight's gift and said she hated his cloak.
2. Her mouth watered when she saw the fresh, ripe strawberries and moist chocolate cake.
3. Cám lounged on the riverbank like a lizard on a sunny rock.
4. Barely glancing at T'âm, Cám responded with only a few quick words.
5. The guests could not take their eyes from the beautiful girl with the long black hair.

EXERCISE B: CONTEXT CLUES Write the Word to Know that best completes each made-up book title.

1. Easy Ways to Prepare _____ Meals
2. How to Stand Up to _____ People
3. _____ No More: Ways to an Active Lifestyle
4. The Glamorous Career of a _____ Movie Star
5. Speak _____ to Stop Bad Dog Behavior Today

WORDS TO KNOW	curtly	indolent	insolent	ravishing	succulent

Vocabulary in Action

Exercise A
1. insolent
2. succulent
3. indolent
4. curtly
5. ravishing

Exercise B
1. succulent
2. insolent
3. indolent
4. ravishing
5. curtly

 Use **Unit Six Resource Book,** p. 21.

Objectives
- write a research report
- use a written text as a model for writing
- revise a draft to focus on one topic
- use compound subjects correctly

Introducing the Workshop

Research Report Tell students that a research report is an informational piece that explores one topic in detail. Discuss with students any research reports they may have read for science or social studies class. Have them think about what kinds of topics are usually written about in research reports. Lead the class in brainstorming a list of topics that might be appropriate for a research report.

Basics in a Box
Using the Graphic The elements that make up a research report—introduction, body, conclusion, and works cited list—are shown in the graphic. These elements are combined to form a cohesive report. Help students to understand the term *thesis* as a statement made about a topic. Point out that the graphic contains the elements that students will be asked to include when they draft their report.

Presenting the Rubric To help students better understand the assignment, review the Standards for Writing a Successful Research Report. You may also want to share with them the complete rubric, which describes several levels of proficiency.

 Use McDougal Littell's *Language Network*, Chapters 10–17, for more instruction on essential writing skills.

 Power Presentation

To engage students visually, use **Power Presentation 1**, Research Report.

Writing Workshop — Research Report

Sharing Information . . .

From Reading to Writing Do the places you read about in myths and legends exist? One way to find the answer is to write a **research report**. This will help you learn to organize and share information from a variety of sources, including reference books, the Internet, and materials from certain organizations. When you set out to write a research report, you embark on a mystery and you are the detective.

For Your Portfolio

WRITING PROMPT Write a research report on a topic that interests you.

Purpose: To learn about the subject and share information with others
Audience: Your classmates, your teacher, or anyone who shares your interest in the topic

---

Basics in a Box

Research Report at a Glance

Introduction presents the thesis statement → **Body** presents facts and details that support the thesis statement → **Conclusion** restates the thesis → **Works Cited** lists the sources of information

Research

RUBRIC STANDARDS FOR WRITING

A successful research report should
- include a strong introduction with a clear thesis statement
- use evidence from primary or secondary sources to develop and support ideas
- credit sources of information
- follow a logical pattern of organization, using transitions between ideas
- use information from more than one source
- summarize ideas in the conclusion
- include a correctly formatted Works Cited list at the end of the report

---

LESSON RESOURCES

USING PRINT RESOURCES
Unit Six Resource Book
- Prewriting, p. 25
- Drafting and Elaboration, p. 26
- Peer Response Guide, pp. 27–28
- Revising, Editing, and Proofreading, p. 29
- Student Models, pp. 30–32
- Rubric for Evaluation, p. 33
Writing Transparencies
- Writing Process Transparencies, TR 1–TR 4

- Writing Structure Transparencies:
  Topic Sentences and Thesis Statements, TR 7; Focusing the Report, TR 12
- Writing Template Transparency: Research Report, TR 37
Reading and Critical Thinking Transparencies
- Spider Map/Mind Map, TR 37

Grammar Transparencies and Copymasters
- Avoiding Double Negatives, CM 98 (for Mini Lesson, p. 827)
INTEGRATED TECHNOLOGY
LaserLinks
Writing Springboards
See **Teacher's SourceBook** p. 56 for bar codes.

Writing Coach CD-ROM
Visit our website:
www.mcdougallittell.com

Analyzing a Student Model

SPEAKING OPPORTUNITY

See the Communication Handbook, p. R100 for speaking and presenting tips.

Katherine Helming
English, Grade 6
Mrs. Ruby
April 11

Perseus: Not Just Any Old Star

Have you ever looked up into the northern sky at night and seen the constellation Perseus? A constellation is a group of stars that form a design. Perseus was a hero of Greek mythology, famous for cutting off the head of the terrible Medusa. His character traits of courage, strength, kindness, compassion, and wisdom were important to the Greek people.

The story of Perseus dates back to the mid-400s B.C. in Athens. In Greek myth, Perseus was the son of Zeus, father of the gods, and Danaë, a mortal woman (D'Aulaire 115). Danaë's father, King Acrisius, had been warned that her son would bring him death (Felson-Rubin 295). Acrisius sent them both out to sea. Luckily, they were rescued.

Perseus grew up to be a strong athlete. He could jump higher, run faster, and use a sword better than all others in the kingdom. To the Greeks these traits were important. The Greeks held games (the Olympics!) in which athletes competed against each other. The Greeks believed their efforts pleased the gods (Paul 754, 760). It is easy to see why the Greeks valued Perseus.

Courage and wisdom were other qualities that the Greek people admired. Perseus first showed courage when he agreed to kill Medusa— "a snake-haired monster called a Gorgon whose horrible face turned all who looked at her to stone" (Felson-Rubin 295). Perseus was determined to succeed.

During his travels he met three sisters who told him that he would need both wisdom and strength to accomplish his task. He would also need a magic helmet, winged sandals, a sword, and a shield. The sisters gave him the helmet and sandals that would make him fly. The god Hermes and the goddess Athena gave him the sword and shield and told him where Medusa lived. Clever Perseus looked only at Medusa's reflection in his shield as he hovered above her and chopped off her head (Burn 63).

RUBRIC IN ACTION

❶ Uses a question to catch readers' attention
Another option:
• Begin with a quotation.

❷ States the subject and focus of the report (thesis statement)

❸ Supports main ideas of the report with details paraphrased from more than one source

❹ Uses transitions between ideas and follows a logical pattern of organization

Teaching the Lesson

Analyzing the Model
"Perseus: Not Just Any Old Star"
This research report recounts the story of Perseus from Greek mythology, for whom a constellation was named. Point out the Rubric in Action and discuss its use. Help students to see that the underlined sections correspond to the elements mentioned in the Rubric in Action. Ask students to read the report with a partner, discussing the Rubric in Action elements as they read.

1 Ask students to think about what kind of quotation might open this report. How would they go about selecting an appropriate quotation for their research report?
   Possible Response: The quotation should be powerful and explicit so that the reader is drawn into the report right away. To select a good quotation, you should read carefully through the sources you have collected, looking for something intriguing.

2 Remind students that a thesis statement should clearly state the focus of the report. Ask them to suggest an alternative thesis statement.
   Possible Response: Perseus was an important figure in Greek mythology, performing many heroic acts in his lifetime.

3 Ask students to identify the sources quoted in this section. Help them to see how different sources of information can be used to weave together a coherent report.
   Answer: D'Aulaire and Felson-Rubin and Paul (both writing for) the World Book Encyclopedia are the sources quoted in this section.

4 Ask students to describe how this transition sentence helps the report flow smoothly and easily into the next paragraph.
   Possible Response: In the thesis statement, several character traits are mentioned. The paragraphs that follow it discuss some of those traits. This transition sentence lets the reader know that more of the traits will be discussed in the next section.

5 Ask students what the number next to the name in parentheses represents.
Answer: the page number on which the quote can be found in the source material

Explain to students that a research report would need to continue on for several more paragraphs in order to be complete. Remind them that an important part of a research report is a strong conclusion that restates the thesis. Ask students how they might word a concluding statement for this research topic.
Possible Response: It is easy to see why such a noble hero was so important to the Greek people.

Works Cited: Ask students to look at the list of works cited and to decide which word in each entry was used for alphabetizing the list.
Possible Response: All the resources are alphabetized by the first letter in the first listed author's last name, even if the articles are in an encyclopedia.

Perseus needed compassion and strength in his next adventure. One day he found a beautiful girl chained to a rock. She explained that in her land there was a fierce sea monster. The monster had eaten many people and would stop only if she gave up her life. Perseus' heart filled with compassion for the girl (Burn 65).

Her name was Andromeda, the daughter of the king. The king told Perseus that if he could save Andromeda, he could have her hand in marriage (Burn 65). As the sea monster came toward Andromeda, Perseus jumped on its back. After a struggle, turned it to stone by showing it Medusa's head. Perseus and Andromeda were married that very night.

Though Perseus did not know it, the greatest test of his wisdom, strength, and compassion was upon him. Perseus returned home with Andromeda and found Danaë. Together they traveled to her native kingdom, Argos (D'Aulaire 120). On the way, Danaë told Perseus the story of his grandfather, King Acrisius. When they met, Acrisius could tell that Perseus was kind and would never try to harm him. Acrisius called all the people of the kingdom to come and listen to Perseus' adventures. He offered Perseus a discus and asked him to show the people how far he could throw it. When Perseus threw it, it hit the king.

5 Credits source of each fact or quotation

Works Cited

Burn, Lucilla. Greek Myths. Austin: U of Texas P, 1990.

D'Aulaire, Ingri, and Edgar Parin D'Aulaire. Ingri and Edgar Parin
   D'Aulaire's Book of Greek Myths. Garden City: Doubleday, 1962.

Felson-Rubin, Nancy. "Perseus." The World Book Encyclopedia. 1990 ed.

Hunter, James. "Perseus." The Encyclopedia Mythica. Ed. M. F. Lindemans.
   22 Mar. 1999. <http://www.pantheon.org/mythica/articles/p/perseus.html>.

Paul, C. Robert, Jr. "Olympic Games." The World Book Encyclopedia. 1990 ed.

Works Cited
The writer
• Includes a list of the works used as sources for the report.
• Arranges sources alphabetically by the authors' last names or the first words of the titles.

Mini Lesson ## Viewing and Representing

PICTURING TEXT STRUCTURE
Instruction One way to structure a good research report is to have students identify the focus or thesis of the report, then think of the main ideas of the focus. Finally, students list the details that support each main idea. In other words, each detail supports each main idea, and the main ideas taken together form the thesis statement. Discuss the sample graphic at the right with students.

Activity Have students analyze the organization of the student model by constructing a similar concept web.

Use **Reading and Critical Thinking Transparencies,** p. 37, for additional support.
Use **Writing Transparencies,** p. 7, for additional support.

Main idea — detail

Topic, Concept, or Theme (thesis statement)

Writing Your Research Report

❶ Prewriting and Exploring

As a general rule, the most successful man in life is the man who has the best information.
—Benjamin Disraeli, 19th-century British prime minister

To find a topic that interests you, **list** the countries mentioned in the Unit Six selections. **Write down** traditions or beliefs that the stories deal with. **Name** characters about whom you would like to know more. See the **Idea Bank** in the margin for more suggestions. After choosing your subject, follow the steps below.

Planning Your Research Report

▶ **1. Find a focus.** You can't cover everything about your topic in one report. To find your focus, create a web diagram of ideas. You may also skim through the table of contents in a book on the subject. Reading a general encyclopedia article about your topic can also help you choose one aspect to focus on.

▶ **2. Identify your audience.** How much background information will your readers need to know about your subject? What information will be most useful or interesting to them?

▶ **3. Set a purpose.** Think about why you are writing this report. Try to write your purpose in one sentence. Later, you will use this sentence to help you write your **thesis statement**. This is the sentence that states the subject and purpose of your report. A clear purpose will guide you in your research.

❷ Researching

Researching is the stage where you find facts about your topic. First read a few general articles. Then make a list of questions you want answered. Let your search for answers guide your research.

Remember there are two types of sources—primary and secondary. **Primary sources** provide firsthand information. They include letters, diaries, journals, and historical documents. **Secondary sources** provide explanations and comments on other sources. Encyclopedias, newspapers, magazines, and textbooks are examples of secondary sources. These resources provide different types of information.

IDEABank

1. Your Working Portfolio
Look for ideas in the **Interdisciplinary Projects** you completed earlier in this unit.
• **Research Flight**, p. 786
• **Map Hurricanes**, p. 801
• **Research Life in the Middle Ages**, p. 819

2. Current Events
Watch the news or read a newspaper to find a country that interests you. Research current events in that country. Your report might also explore that country's history.

3. Get in the Know
Ask friends or relatives to list subjects about which they have some knowledge. Choose a subject that you'd like to know more about.

Need help with your report?
See the **Writing Handbook**, pp. R41–R45.

Guiding Student Writing

Prewriting and Exploring

Choosing a Subject
If after reading the Idea Bank students have difficulty choosing a subject for their research report, suggest they try the following:
• Go back to the brainstormed lists of possible topics from the beginning of the lesson.
• Think about the topics they are currently studying in social studies and science.
• Talk with a partner about possible topics on their list.

Planning Your Research Report
1. Students may want to share their topic with a partner and brainstorm ideas about a focus for that topic. The most common error for students is to select a topic that is too big for one report. Encourage students to help their partners think about how to narrow the subject into one strong focus.
2. Remind students that depending on who will be reading the report, specific background information will have to be provided. Encourage them to identify an audience prior to moving on to the next step.
3. Have students do this task individually. It should reflect their personal reasons for writing this research report. Stress the idea that having one strong sentence—rather than a paragraph of explanation that wanders around the topic—will make it easier for them later.

Researching
It may be helpful for students to spend a class period in the library gathering their resources. A place to start is with the examples listed in this section under primary and secondary sources. A librarian or media specialist could be of benefit during this first source-gathering session.

After students have had a chance to look at the sources selected, they may need additional trips to the library as their topic becomes more focused.

Use **Writing Transparencies**, p. 41, for additional support.

Evaluate Your Sources

Encourage students to use the questions included in this section to evaluate each of their potential sources. Remind them that it is okay to not use every source they find initially and to keep looking if their questions are not being answered. Engage the support of your school librarian again for helping students in identifying reliable and current source material.

 Use **Writing Transparencies,** p. 53, for additional support.

Make Source Cards

Ask a student to volunteer to help you model a source card. Have the student provide you with the information needed as you create a large class model. This will give students a visual reminder of how to complete their own source cards. Remind them to number the source cards as they complete them.

Take Notes

Remind students that they should not copy any material directly from a source unless it is a short excerpt to be used as direct quotation. In such cases they should include quotation marks in their notes. Review summarizing and paraphrasing as necessary. Use another large class model card to demonstrate how to take information from a source and paraphrase it for a note card. Tell students to number the note card with the source card number and page number, as this will be important should they need to look up this information later.

RESEARCHTip

Check the list of sources at the end of books or articles and investigate some of the sources that the author of your source used.

INTERNETTip

Ask your librarian to help you carefully choose keywords to do an Internet search.

Need help organizing your note cards?

See the **Writing Handbook,** p. R42.

You may want to explore the computerized card catalog in your local library to help you locate sources. To see if a **book** contains the information you need, look at its table of contents. **Periodicals, newspapers,** and **magazines** can be found by using your library's periodical index, which lists magazine articles by subject. This source may also be on-line in your library. The **Internet** is also a source of many types of information.

Evaluate Your Sources

Remember, you cannot believe everything you read. Checking several sources to see if the facts are the same will help you decide if a source is reliable. Especially when using the Internet, ask these questions.

• **What are the qualifications of the author?** Is the author from a respected institution? Is he or she a professional? Does the author have a bias that affects the way the information is presented?

• **Is the information up-to-date and accurate?** Use the most recent information you can find.

Make Source Cards

Using index cards, create source cards for the sources that you use. Write the relevant information for each source on a separate index card, and number each card. The cards will help you to create your Works Cited list. Follow the format shown on the right.

Take Notes

Use index cards to record information. Write the main idea of each note at the top of the card, along with the number that you assigned the source on the source card. Write just one piece of information on each card.

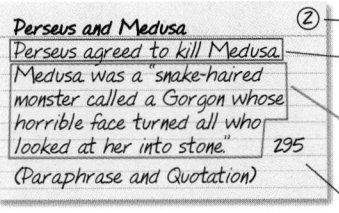

Source Number

Paraphrase. Restate ideas in your own words to avoid plagiarism, which is using someone else's original words without giving credit to the author.

Quotation. Write the quote exactly as it appears in the source. Use quotation marks to show where it begins and ends.

Page Number

Organize Your Material

Now group the cards by similar main points. Think about the order of ideas. You might choose a **chronological, cause-and-effect, comparison-and-contrast,** or **problem-solution** pattern of organization. Once you write down your main headings, think about **subheadings,** specific points to cover.

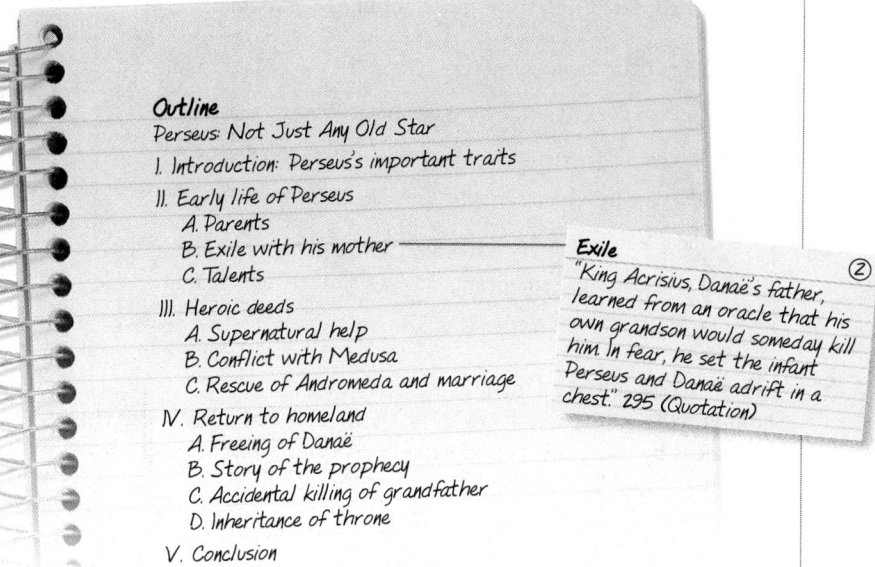

Outline
Perseus: Not Just Any Old Star
I. Introduction: Perseus's important traits
II. Early life of Perseus
   A. Parents
   B. Exile with his mother
   C. Talents
III. Heroic deeds
   A. Supernatural help
   B. Conflict with Medusa
   C. Rescue of Andromeda and marriage
IV. Return to homeland
   A. Freeing of Danaë
   B. Story of the prophecy
   C. Accidental killing of grandfather
   D. Inheritance of throne
V. Conclusion

Exile   ②
"King Acrisius, Danaë's father, learned from an oracle that his own grandson would someday kill him. In fear, he set the infant Perseus and Danaë adrift in a chest." 295 (Quotation)

❸ Drafting

Using your outline as your guide, begin to write your first draft.

- In your **introduction,** capture the attention of your readers with a quotation, an anecdote, or an explanation of why the subject interests you. State the topic and purpose of your report in one sentence if you can. This is your **thesis statement.**

- The **body** of your report presents the main ideas, supporting facts, and the other details that you discovered in your research. However, this doesn't mean that you should only restate facts or retell events. You will need to make inferences and draw conclusions based on the information you have uncovered.

- **Conclude** by summarizing the focus of your report and what you've learned.

DRAFTINGTip

Begin a new body paragraph for each new subheading in your outline.

Ask Your Peer Reader: EVALUATING

- Did you understand my topic?
- Were any parts confusing?
- Where do I need more facts and examples?

Organize Your Material

It may be helpful to students to review the organization methods listed here. Providing them with graphic organizers of each method would also help. Encourage students to select an organizational method that matches the content of their report.

After selecting the organization format, model the outlining process as shown on this page. Again, making a large outline for the model will provide students with a mental and physical image of the process they need to follow as they organize and outline their own reports.

Use **Writing Transparencies,** p. 54, for additional support.

Drafting

Tell students that they may want to refer back to the Standards for Writing a Successful Research Report on page 820 as they begin their first draft. A quick reminder of the rubric will focus students' writing on the key elements.

Ask Your Peer Reader

Asking a peer reviewer to read the draft of the research report will focus on some of the key elements. Encourage peer readers to read critically and to take notes for the writer. As students conference about each report, remind them to be respectful of the author's work, yet constructive in their suggestions for revisions.

Revising
FOCUSING YOUR REPORT

Remind students that their peer reader may have suggestions about what to eliminate in order to keep the report focused on one topic. Ask students to reread their reports and to carefully reconsider each sentence.

 Use **Writing Transparencies,** p. 12, for additional support.

Editing and Proofreading
COMPOUND SUBJECTS

Tell students that using compound subjects in some of their sentences can make their writing smoother. Ask them to think about which short or choppy sentences could be rewritten with compound subjects to make a new, smoother sentence. Ask for student volunteers to share cases from their own writing, and model how to create a new sentence.

Making a Works Cited List

Tell students to take their source cards and highlight the key word by which they will alphabetize. Then they can sort the cards into alphabetical order by the highlighted words. It is then an easy step to copy the information from the source cards into a Works Cited List.

 Use **Writing Transparencies,** p. 56, for additional support.

Reflecting

Encourage students to be specific as they identify the part of the research process they learned the most from. Ask them to think about why this part helped them. Have them list several other topics they may wish to research at another time.

Option
Teaching Tip

Research reports can have a tendency to become dry and boring. Help students to choose engaging topics, use interesting words and descriptions, and have fun with language and information throughout their report.

Need revising help?

Review the **Rubric,** p. 820.

Consider **peer reader** comments.

Check **Revision Guidelines,** p. R23.

Questioning compound subjects?

See the **Grammar Handbook,** p. R60.

SPELLING
From Writing

As you revise your work, look back at the words you misspelled and determine why you made the errors you did. For additional help, refer to the strategies and generalizations in the **Spelling Handbook** on page R86.

Publishing
IDEAS

- Create a multimedia presentation that presents the most important ideas about your topic. Use visual aids to make your report more interesting.
- Find students who chose topics related to yours. Combine your reports into a booklet that gives in-depth information about the topic.

More Online:
Publishing Options
www.mcdougallittell.com

---

❹ Revising

TARGET SKILL ▶ FOCUSING YOUR REPORT Your researching process will sometimes lead you to information on other subjects connected to your topic. Because you can't include everything in one report, however, you need to keep your focus on one topic. Always ask yourself whether a fact, an example, or a detail develops the main idea you have chosen. Check your report for unrelated details.

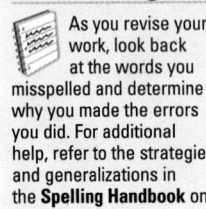

In Greek mythology, Perseus was the son of Zeus, father of the gods, and Danaë, a mortal woman. ~~Zeus had many children that were half god and half mortal. Another famous Greek hero Hercules also had Zeus as his father.~~ (D'Aulaire 115). Danaë's father, King Acrisius, had been warned that her son would bring him death.

❺ Editing and Proofreading

TARGET SKILL ▶ COMPOUND SUBJECTS Get rid of short, choppy sentences by using compound subjects. A **compound subject** whose parts are joined by *and* takes a plural verb.

and Zeus were
Athena ~~was~~ about to ask him to fly over the mountains until he came to the sea.

❻ Making a Works Cited List

When you have finished revising your report, make an alphabetical list of the sources that you used. See page R45 in the **Writing Handbook** for the correct format.

❼ Reflecting

FOR YOUR WORKING PORTFOLIO What did you learn about the research process from writing your report? What other topics would you like to research? Attach your answers to your finished report. Save your research report in your **Working Portfolio.**

Assessment Practice Revising & Editing

Read this passage from the first draft of a research report. The underlined sections may include the following kinds of errors:

- **capitalization errors**
- **verb tense errors**
- **lack of subject-verb agreement**
- **double negatives**

For each underlined section, choose the revision that most improves the writing.

> The gods Odin in Norse mythology and Zeus in Greek mythology
> (1)
> is very different from each other. Odin does not never eat with the other
> (2)   (3)
> gods and goddesses. He sits quietly, thinking about the advice of his two
>
> ravens, whose names are Thought and Memory. Odin is willing to
>   (4)
> pursue wisdom even if he has to suffer. He go to the Well of Wisdom.
>   (5)
> Mimir the wise tells him that he has to give up one of his eyes to gain
>
> the knowledge. Odin hardly doesn't mind at all.
>   (6)

1. **A.** The Gods Odin in norse mythology and Zeus in Greek
    B. The gods Odin in Norse mythology and zeus in Greek
    C. The gods Odin in norse mythology and Zeus in greek
    D. Correct as is

2. **A.** are very different
    B. is very differently
    C. are being very different
    D. Correct as is

3. **A.** Odin never eats
    B. Odin don't ever eat
    C. Odin does hardly not eat
    D. Correct as is

4. **A.** Odin was willing
    B. Odin would have been willing
    C. Odin will be willing
    D. Correct as is

5. **A.** He is gone to the Well of Wisdom.
    B. He goes to the Well of Wisdom.
    C. He is going to the Well of Wisdom.
    D. Correct as is

6. **A.** Odin hardly minds at all.
    B. Odin barely doesn't mind at all.
    C. Odin doesn't scarcely mind.
    D. Correct as is

Need extra help?

See the **Grammar Handbook.**
Using Verbs Correctly, p. R68
Using Modifiers Effectively, p. R70
Correcting Capitalization, p. R73

Assessment Practice
Ask students to read the entire passage prior to correcting the errors. Demonstrate how students can eliminate incorrect choices for the first question.

The words Norse and Greek are both proper adjectives and should be capitalized. Therefore A and C are not correct choices. In choice B, the name Zeus is not capitalized. The sentence is correct as it is, so D is the correct answer.

Answers:
1. D; **2.** A; **3.** A, **4.** D, **5.** B, **6.** A

 Grammar

AVOIDING DOUBLE NEGATIVES

Instruction Remind students to avoid double negatives. Negatives are words that mean "no", like *not, never, nothing,* and contractions ending in *-n't.* Explain that when two negatives are used together, they cancel each other out and change the meaning of the sentence.

Application Ask students to tell which items in the Assessment Practice above use double negatives (3 and 6), to identify the negatives used, and to suggest various ways in which the sentences could be corrected.

Exercises Ask students to write the correct word from parentheses to complete each sentence.

1. Perseus (<u>was</u>, wasn't) no lazy Greek hero.
2. He (<u>could,</u> couldn't) find nobody to fight the sea monster.
3. There wasn't (<u>anyone</u>, no one) to save the king's daughter.
4. The king said it wasn't his fault (<u>any</u>, no) longer.
5. Perseus (<u>never</u>, ever) did realize he was considered a brave and wise man.

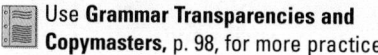 Use **Grammar Transparencies and Copymasters,** p. 98, for more practice.

 Use McDougal Littell's *Language Network,* Chapter 5, for more practice in avoiding double negatives.

Objectives

- To understand and appreciate three folk tales from different cultures that explore the mysteries of nature through oral language tradition
- To appreciate the cultures of China, Puerto Rico, and West Africa
- To extend understanding of the stories through a variety of multimodal and cross-curricular activities

Reading Pathways

- Select one or several students to read each story aloud to the entire class or to small groups of students. Assign this reading in advance so readers can incorporate into their presentations some of the techniques used by professional storytellers. Have the audience listen carefully to the tales without following along in their texts.
- Read the stories aloud to the class, pausing at key points to discuss how elements of each tale inform students about the customs, values, or beliefs of people in Puerto Rico, China, and West Africa. Have students record their responses and observations in their notebooks.
- After students have read the stories once, they can read them again to identify structural elements such as main characters, minor characters, conflict, setting, and plot. Then have students identify similarities and differences between these tales and selections in Unit 4. For example, students might compare and contrast the relationships between Taroo and Alida in "The Legend of the Hummingbird" with the relationship between Sandy and Lob in "Lob's Girl."

Daily Language SkillBuilder

Have students **proofread** the display sentences on page 765e and write them correctly. The sentences also appear on Transparency 25 of **Grammar Transparencies and Copymasters.**

ACROSS CULTURES

PREPARING to *Read*

LINKS TO UNIT FOUR

Wondrous Worlds

The selections in Unit Four demonstrate the wonder that is to be found in the natural world—and in the imagination. The oral tradition often combines these two worlds within a "long ago and far away" setting, as seen in these tales from different cultures.

PUERTO RICO

PUERTO RICO

The Legend of the Hummingbird

retold by Pura Belpré (pōō′rä bĕl-prä′)

Puerto Rico, an island in the Caribbean Sea, is a commonwealth of the United States. Although the U.S. Congress is responsible for the overall government of Puerto Rico, the local Puerto Rican governance generally makes its own decisions. The folklore of Puerto Rico reflects a mixture of cultures, with strong roots in Spain, West Africa, and Asia as well as native Caribbean cultures such as the Taino. Set in a world where people become animals and animals behave in decidedly human ways, this **legend** explains the origin and habits of the hummingbird. Many species of hummingbird thrive on the islands of the Caribbean.

828   UNIT SIX   THE ORAL TRADITION

LESSON RESOURCES

UNIT SIX RESOURCE BOOK, pp. 34–40

ASSESSMENT
Formal Assessment, pp. 131–132
Teachers' Guide to Assessment and Portfolio Use
Test Generator

SKILLS TRANSPARENCIES AND COPYMASTERS
Grammar
- Subject Pronouns, CM 71 (for Mini Lesson, p. 836)
- Subject-Verb Agreement, CM 114 (for Mini Lesson, p. 841)

Communications
- Dramatic Reading, TR 12 (for Mini Lesson, p. 837)

INTEGRATED TECHNOLOGY
Audio Library

Visit our website:
www.mcdougallittell.com

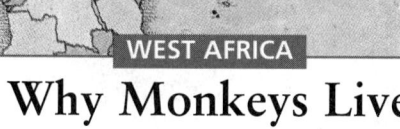

CHINA

The Living Kuan-yin

retold by Carol Kendall and Yao-wen Li (you'wən'lē)

China is bounded on every side by mountains, desert, or ocean. These geographical features have helped to preserve a civilization that dates back nearly 4,000 years. Buddhism, one of the world's major religions, arrived in China before A.D. 100. Kuan-yin (gwän' yĭn') is the Buddhist deity of mercy, who works to save people from their faults and failures. In this **legend,** a man named Chin Po-wan journeys to see Kuan-yin. People ask him for help along the way, and Po-wan's generosity gets him into trouble.

WEST AFRICA

Why Monkeys Live in Trees

retold by Julius Lester

The continent of Africa is home to a rich variety of cultures, each with a wealth of folklore. Many traditional West African tales feature animal characters. This folk tale recounts Monkey's attempt to outwit other animals, and, typical of a **"trickster tale,"** the trickster's cleverness only lands him in trouble. The story also attempts to explain why monkeys behave the way they do. Stories that answer the question *why?* are called **"pourquoi tales."**

AS YOU READ . . .

See how mysteries of nature are explained in various cultures.

Notice which human traits are seen as weaknesses and which are admired.

Notice common images, themes, and other literary elements of the oral tradition across cultures.

Customizing Instruction

Less Proficient Readers
Tell students that folk tales can teach us about various cultures. In these three tales, they will learn something about the cultures of Puerto Rico, China, and West Africa.

Set a Purpose Ask students to think about what they learn about the cultures of Puerto Rico, China, and West Africa as they read the three folk tales.

Students Acquiring English
Ask students to share any stories or tales from their own cultures that have similar characters or situations to those in the folk tales here. Ask them to think about how they first heard the story and to tell what it teaches about their culture.

Use **Spanish Study Guide,** pp. 166–168 for additional support.

Gifted and Talented
Ask students to think about the geography of the places in these tales. As they read each story, have them locate the country and region on a map. Encourage students to discuss the climate, resources, and land forms found there and to speculate about what those factors tell them about the culture of each place.

Multiple Learning Styles
Interpersonal Learners
Have students meet in small groups at the conclusion of each story to discuss and summarize the story. Ask them to share any personal connections they made as they read.

Summary

In this African folk tale, King Gorilla promises a pot of gold to whoever can eat a mound of black dust. Only Monkey succeeds. His winning strategy, it seems, is to swallow a mouthful of the black dust, which is really pepper, rest in some tall grass, and then repeat the process. Leopard, astonished by Monkey's success, climbs onto a tree limb to get a better view. What he sees—a hundred identical monkeys hiding in the tall grass—angers him so much that he jumps into the grass to punish their trickery just as Monkey wins the pot of gold. The only way the monkeys can escape is to climb to the top of the tallest trees, where they still live today.

Reading and Analyzing

Literary Analysis: CHARACTERIZATION

A Ask students to name Leopard's main character trait. Ask what the beginning of the folk tale reveals about Leopard.

Possible Response: The folk tale's opening says that gazing at his own reflection is Leopard's favorite activity. This suggests that Leopard is vain.

Use **Unit Six Resource Book,** p. 36 for more practice.
Use **Literary Analysis Transparencies,** p. 4, for additional support.

Reading Skills and Strategies: PREDICT

B Ask students to predict what kind of contest they think King Gorilla will have.

Possible Responses: Students may predict that the contest will involve running, jumping, climbing trees, or eating fruit.

Exotic Landscape (1910), Henri Rousseau. Oil on canvas, 51¼" × 64". The Norton Simon Foundation, Pasadena, California.

Teaching Options

Mini Lesson ● Viewing and Representing

Exotic Landscape
by Henri Rousseau

ART APPRECIATION
Rousseau (1844–1910), today celebrated as a pioneer in modern art, was unappreciated during his lifetime and was buried in a pauper's grave.

Instruction Rousseau's paintings combine the brilliant colors and decorative patterns of the Impressionists with precise detail and highly polished surfaces of his own devising. In addition to subjects from French middle class life, such as weddings and patriotic celebrations, Rousseau painted realistic figures in fantastical settings.

Application What aspects of this painting look realistic? What aspects do not? How does the painting relate to this selection?

Possible Responses: The trees, grass, and monkeys look realistic. The painting relates to the selection because it is about monkeys living in trees, and both things are pictured here.

Why Monkeys Live in TREES

retold by Julius Lester

One day Leopard was looking at his reflection in a pool of water. Looking at himself was Leopard's favorite thing in the world to do. Leopard gazed, wanting to be sure that every hair was straight and that all his spots were where they were supposed to be. This took many hours of looking at his reflection, which Leopard did not mind at all.

Finally he was satisfied that nothing was disturbing his handsomeness, and he turned away from the pool of water. At that exact moment, one of Leopard's children ran up to him.

"Daddy! Daddy! Are you going to be in the contest?"

"What contest?" Leopard wanted to know. If it was a beauty contest, of course he was going to be in it.

"I don't know. Crow the Messenger just flew by. She said that King Gorilla said there was going to be a contest."

Mini Lesson Spelling

THE PREFIX *EX-* Tell students that the prefix *ex-* means "out" or "beyond." It is added to word roots to make new words.
Instruction Write the following examples on the board and discuss how their meanings relate to "out" or "beyond."
extend (to open or straighten out)
extra (beyond what is normal or expected)
Encourage students to think about the meanings of these *ex-* words as they use them in their writing.

Application Have students add the prefix *ex-* to each of these word parts or roots and to use each one in a sentence.

1. pense *(expense)*
2. pert *(expert)*
3. perience *(experience)*
4. cuse *(excuse)*
5. tent *(extent)*
6. periment *(experiment)*
7. terior *(exterior)*
8. tinguish *(extinguish)*
9. clamation *(exclamation)*
10. ternal *(external)*

 Use **Unit Six Resource Book,** p. 39.

Active Reading: CONNECTING

Ask students to think about "The Walrus and The Carpenter" and to recall the trick these characters played on the oysters. How was that similar to or different from the trick in "Why Monkeys Live in Trees"?

Possible Response: The walrus and carpenter tricked the oysters so they could eat them. King Gorilla tricked the animals, and the monkeys tried to trick King Gorilla, but he found them out.

📖 Use **Unit Six Resource Book,** p. 35 for more practice.
Use **Reading and Critical Thinking Transparencies,** p. 2, for additional support.

Reading Skills and Strategies: CLARIFY

A Ask students what else is explained in this folk tale other than why monkeys live in trees.
Answer: why chickens have no ears

Reading Skills and Strategies: EVALUATE

Have students evaluate the attitudes of the animals who are happy because they still have a chance to win the gold, despite having seen the effects of the dust on Hippopotamus. Ask students what effect the thought of the gold is having on the animals.
Possible Response: The gold is making the animals greedy.

Literary Analysis: CHARACTERIZATION

B Ask students to think about how the monkeys are described in this section. What have we learned about the character of the monkeys?
Possible Responses: Because the monkeys are clever and smart, they are able to outwit the other animals.

Without another word, Leopard set off. He went north-by-northeast, made a right turn at the mulberry bush and traveled east-by-south-by-west until he came to a hole in the ground. He went around in a circle five times and headed north-by-somersault until he came to a big clearing in the middle of the jungle, and that's where King Gorilla was.

King Gorilla sat at one end of the clearing on his throne. Opposite him, at the other side of the clearing, all the animals sat in a semicircle. In the middle, between King Gorilla and the animals, was a huge mound of what looked like black dust.

Leopard looked around with calm dignity. Then he strode regally[1] over to his friend, Lion.

"What's that?" he asked, pointing to the mound of black dust.

1 "Don't know," Lion replied. "King Gorilla said he will give a pot of gold to whoever can eat it in one day. I can eat it in an hour."

Leopard laughed. "I'll eat it in a half hour."

It was Hippopotamus's turn to laugh. "As big as my mouth is, I'll eat that mound in one gulp."

The time came for the contest. King Gorilla had the animals pick numbers to see who would go in what order. To everybody's dismay, Hippopotamus drew Number 1.

Hippopotamus walked over to the mound of black dust. It was bigger than he had thought. It was much too big to eat in one gulp. Nonetheless, Hippopotamus opened his mouth as wide as he could, and that was very wide indeed, and took a mouthful of the black dust.

He started chewing. Suddenly he leaped straight into the air and screamed. He

Hippopotamus **roared** and Hippopotamus bellowed. Then he started **sneezing** and **crying,** . . .

screamed so loudly that it knocked the ears off the chickens, and that's why to this day chickens don't have ears.

A

Hippopotamus screamed and Hippopotamus yelled. Hippopotamus roared and Hippopotamus bellowed. Then he started sneezing and crying, and tears rolled down his face like he was standing in the shower. Hippopotamus ran to the river and drank as much water as he could, and that was very much, indeed, to cool his mouth and tongue and throat.

The animals didn't understand what had happened to Hippopotamus, but they didn't care. They were happy because they still had a chance to win the pot of gold. Of course, if they had known that the mound of black dust was really a mound of black pepper, maybe they wouldn't have wanted the gold.

Nobody was more happy than Leopard because he had drawn Number 2. He walked up to the black mound and sniffed at it.

"AAAAAAAAACHOOOOOOO!" Leopard didn't like that, but then he remembered the pot of gold. He opened his mouth wide, took a mouthful and started chewing and swallowing.

2

Leopard leaped straight into the air, did a back double flip and screamed. He yelled and he roared and he bellowed and, finally, he started sneezing and crying, tears rolling down

---

1. **strode regally:** walked in a grand manner, like a king or queen.

832 UNIT SIX   THE ORAL TRADITION

Multicultural Link   **African Animals**

The jungles and deserts of Africa are rich with animal life. Hippopotamus, leopard, lion, monkey, and gorilla—all of which we meet in this story—are just a few of them. There are also rhinoceros, elephant, zebra, antelope, cheetah, gazelle, hyena, and many more. Large numbers of tourists go on safari to observe and photograph these beautiful animals in their natural habitats.

One particularly interesting animal is the rhino. There are five species of rhinoceros in the world. Two of them live in Africa, the black rhino and the white rhino. Despite their names, both are gray!

The white rhino's name comes from the Afrikaans word describing its mouth, *weit,* which means "wide." The white rhino has a mouth that measures two feet across. It's a grass eater and needs that mouth for "mowing" the grass down. The black rhino has a smaller, triangular-shaped mouth, which it uses for feeding from trees and shrubs. It is probably called "black" because it wallows in the dark local soil and becomes covered with mud, as well as to differentiate it from the white rhino.

his face like a waterfall. Leopard ran to the river and washed out his mouth and throat and tongue.

Lion was next, and the same thing happened to him as it did to all the animals. Finally only Monkey remained.

Monkey approached King Gorilla. "I know I can eat all of whatever that is, but after each mouthful, I'll need to lie down in the tall grasses and rest."

King Gorilla said that was okay.

Monkey went to the mound, took a tiny bit of pepper on his tongue, swallowed, and went into the tall grasses. A few minutes later, Monkey came out, took a little more, swallowed it, and went into the tall grasses.

Soon the pile was almost gone. The animals were astonished to see Monkey doing what they had not been able to do. Leopard couldn't believe it either. He climbed a tree and stretched out on a sturdy limb to get a better view. From his limb high in the tree Leopard could see into the tall grasses where Monkey went to rest. Wait a minute! Leopard thought something was suddenly wrong with his eyes because he thought he saw a hundred monkeys hiding in the tall grasses.

He rubbed his eyes and looked another look. There wasn't anything wrong with his eyes. There were a hundred monkeys in the tall grasses, and they all looked alike!

Just then, there was the sound of loud applause. King Gorilla announced that Monkey had won the contest and the pot of gold.

Leopard growled a growl so scary that even King Gorilla was frightened. Leopard wasn't thinking about anybody except the monkeys. He took a long and beautiful leap from the tree right smack into the middle of the tall grasses where the monkeys were hiding.

The monkeys ran in all directions. When the other animals saw monkeys running from the grasses, they realized that the monkeys had tricked them, and started chasing them. Even King Gorilla joined in the chase. He wanted his gold back.

The only way the monkeys could escape was to climb to the very tops of the tallest trees where no one else, not even Leopard, could climb.

And that's why monkeys live in trees to this very day. ❖

"I have found writing for children of all ages more rewarding than writing for adults, . . ."

Julius Lester
born 1939

Fascinated by Folklore Julius Lester connects his interest in folklore to his father, who was a minister and a good storyteller. Lester says, "As a child, I loved it when my father got together with other ministers on a summer evening,

because I knew that I would be treated to stories for as long as I was allowed to stay up, which was never long enough."

It's an Honor Lester's work has received numerous awards, including a 1969 Newbery Honor award for *To Be a Slave.* "Why Monkeys Live in Trees" is from the book *How Many Spots Does a Leopard Have?*, which contains tales that reflect both African and Jewish story traditions. Lester currently divides his time between writing and serving as a professor at the University of Massachusetts.

✓ **Assessment Standardized Test Practice**

CAUSE-AND-EFFECT RELATIONSHIPS In some standardized tests, students are asked to identify causes and/or effects of related events in a passage they have read. Write the following question on the board or read it aloud:
What event caused the animals in this story to attempt to eat a large pile of black dust?
A. The animals discussed how long it would take to eat the dust.
B. The animals liked eating pepper.
C. King Gorilla offered a pot of gold to whoever could eat all the black dust.
D. The animals decided to have a contest.

Guide students through the process of selecting the correct answer. A is a true statement, but is not the event that caused the animals to attempt to eat the dust. B is not a true statement; in fact the animals did not even know that the black dust was pepper. D is not true. Although there was a contest in this story, the animals did not decide to have it themselves: King Gorilla did. C is the correct answer.

Summary

This Puerto Rican legend explains how the hummingbird came to be. Alida, the daughter of an Indian chief, falls in love with Taroo, a young man from an enemy tribe. The young lovers meet secretly at a pool surrounded by pomarosa trees. When Alida's father learns of their meetings, he arranges for her to marry someone else. Alida begs the god Yukiyú to spare her from marrying a man she doesn't love, so the god turns her into a delicate red flower. Taroo, knowing nothing of Alida's fate, waits for her by the pool until the moon tells him what has happened. Taroo begs Yukiyú to help him find Alida, and the god responds by turning Taroo into a hummingbird. Ever since, the hummingbird flies from flower to flower looking for his lost love.

Reading and Analyzing

Active Reading: CONNECTING

Ask students to think about hummingbirds. Have them share what they know about hummingbirds with a partner.

Active Reading: SET A PURPOSE

Ask students to read to find out what the legend of the hummingbird is and to connect the ideas in the story to what they just talked about.

Reading Skills and Strategies: VISUALIZE

After students have read the opening on page 835, ask them to close their eyes and listen as you read it to them. Ask them to visualize the scene that is described there. Have them share with the class what things they see in the scene, and what it reminds them of.

Hummingbirds in Thistle (1955), Walter Anderson. Watercolor. Walter Anderson Museum of Art, Ocean Springs, Mississippi, courtesy of the family of Walter Anderson.

Teaching Options

Mini Lesson Viewing and Representing

Hummingbirds in Thistle
by Walter Anderson

Walter Anderson made hundreds of wood block prints and thousands of watercolors. He also illustrated fairy tales and classics. Anderson is best known for his depictions of the flora and fauna of the Gulf Coast, which he captured in lush watercolors.

Instruction Ask students to brainstorm everything they know about how hummingbirds move.

Application Ask students the following questions: How many hummingbirds can you find in the picture? What are the hummingbirds doing? How does the artist convey the hummingbirds' rapid wing movement?

Possible Responses: There are at least six hummingbirds in the picture. It appears that they are drinking the nectar from flowers. The movement of their wings is shown through a series of soft, blended lines which, taken together, simulate movement.

The Legend of the Hummingbird

retold by Pura Belpré

Between the towns of Cayey and Cidra,[1] far up in the hills, there was once a small pool fed by a waterfall that tumbled down the side of the mountain. The pool was surrounded by pomarosa trees,[2] and the Indians used to call it Pomarosa Pool. It was the favorite place of Alida, the daughter of an Indian chief, a man of power and wealth among the people of the hills.

1

---

1. **Cayey** (kä-yä′) . . . **Cidra** (sē′drä): towns in Puerto Rico.
2. **pomarosa** (pô-mä-rô′sä) **trees:** trees, found in the West Indies, that bear an applelike fruit; also spelled *poma rosa*.

Ask students to list the character traits of both Alida and Taroo. Ask them to compare the two lists and to think about what it was that drew the two to each other and helped form their friendship.

Possible Responses: Alida was lonely and fond of nature. Taroo also liked the outdoors, and he was honest, lonely, and courageous. They were probably drawn together because they were both lonely and liked to be outside with nature.

Active Reading: CONNECTING

Ask students whether they have ever been in a situation like Alida's, in which their parents forbade them to be friends with someone they liked. Ask how this made them feel. Ask how they handled the situation with their parents and their friend and what they think Alida might do in this situation.

Possible Responses: Students should share personal memories, prompted by this section of the story. Alida probably felt upset, sad, and angry. She might not listen to her father and try to see Taroo anyway.

Reading Skills and Strategies: IDENTIFY CAUSE-AND-EFFECT RELATIONSHIPS

Ask students to describe what events caused Taroo to be turned into a small, many-colored bird.

Answer: Taroo fell in love with Alida, but Alida was forbidden to see Taroo. Alida asked the god Yukiyú for help, and he changed her into a delicate red flower. Taroo missed her desperately, the moon told Taroo what had happened, and Taroo asked Yukiyú to help him find Alida.

One day, when Alida had come to the pool to rest after a long walk, a young Indian came there to pick some fruit from the trees. Alida was surprised, for he was not of her tribe. Yet he said he was no stranger to the pool. This was where he had first seen Alida, and he had often returned since then to pick fruit, hoping to see her again.

And the great god Yukiyú took pity on her and changed her into a delicate red flower.

He told her about himself to make her feel at home. He confessed, with honesty and frankness, that he was a member of the dreaded Carib[3] tribe that had so often attacked the island of Boriquen.[4] As a young boy, he had been left behind after one of those raids, and he had stayed on the island ever since.

Alida listened closely to his story, and the two became friends. They met again in the days that followed, and their friendship grew stronger. Alida admired the young man's courage in living among his enemies. She learned to call him by his Carib name, Taroo, and he called her Alida, just as her own people did. Before long, their friendship had turned into love.

Their meetings by the pool were always brief. Alida was afraid their secret might be discovered, and careful though she was, there came a day when someone saw them and told her father. Alida was forbidden to visit the Pomarosa Pool, and to put an end to her romance with the stranger, her father decided to marry her to a man of his own choosing. Preparations for the wedding started at once.

Alida was torn with grief, and one evening she cried out to her god: "O *Yukiyú*,[5] help me! Kill me or do what you will with me, but do not let me marry this man whom I do not love!"

And the great god Yukiyú took pity on her and changed her into a delicate red flower.

Meanwhile Taroo, knowing nothing of Alida's sorrow, still waited for her by the Pomarosa Pool. Day after day he waited. Sometimes he stayed there until a mantle[6] of stars was spread across the sky.

One night the moon took pity on him. "Taroo," she called from her place high above the stars. "O Taroo, wait no longer for Alida! Your secret was made known, and Alida was to be married to a man of her father's choosing. In her grief she called to her god, Yukiyú; he heard her plea for help and changed her into a red flower."

"Ahee, ahee!" cried Taroo. "O moon, what is the name of the red flower?"

---

3. **Carib** (kăr′ĭb): a Native American people of the West Indies.
4. **Boriquen** (bô-rē′kĕn): an early name for Puerto Rico.
5. *Yukiyú* (yōō-kē-yōō′).
6. **mantle:** covering.

 Mini Lesson **Grammar**

SUBJECT PRONOUNS Remind students that a pronoun can take the place of a noun. Subject pronouns (*I, you, he, she, it, we,* and *they*) are used as subjects of verbs or after linking verbs.

Instruction Use the following examples to demonstrate the use of subject pronouns:

Subject: <u>It</u> was Alida's favorite place.

After Linking Verbs: The red flower was <u>she</u>.

Application Have students rewrite the sentences, choosing the correct pronoun forms.

1. (<u>She</u>, Her) and (<u>he</u>, him) were changed into a red flower and hummingbird.

2. Yukiyú rescued Alida from a loveless marriage. A compassionate god is (<u>he</u>, him).

3. (<u>We</u>, Us) students enjoyed "The Legend of the Hummingbird."

 Use **Grammar Transparencies and Copymasters**, p. 71.

 Use McDougal Littell's **Language Network**, Chapter 3, for more instruction and practice in using subject pronouns.

"Only Yukiyú knows that," the moon replied.

Then Taroo called out: "O Yukiyú, god of my Alida, help me too! Help me to find her!"

And just as the great god had heard Alida's plea, he listened now to Taroo and decided to help him. There by the Pomarosa Pool, before the moon and the silent stars, the great god changed Taroo into a small many-colored bird.

"Fly, *Colibrí*,[7] and find your love among the flowers," he said.

Off went the Colibrí, flying swiftly, and as he flew, his wings made a sweet humming sound.

In the morning the Indians saw a new bird darting about among the flowers, swift as an arrow and brilliant as a jewel. They heard the humming of its wings, and in amazement they saw it hover in the air over every blossom, kissing the petals of the flowers with its long slender bill. They liked the new bird with the music in its wings, and they called it Hummingbird.

Ever since then the little many-colored bird has hovered over every flower he finds, but returns most often to the flowers that are red. He is still looking, always looking, for the one red flower that will be his lost Alida. He has not found her yet. ❖

---

7. *Colibrí* (kô-lē-brē′).

"My vivid imagination . . . kept scenes that impressed me as a child very alive."

Pura Belpré
1899–1982

Filling a Need Pura Belpré, author and puppeteer-storyteller, was born in Puerto Rico and came to the United States in the 1920s. Beginning in 1921, she worked in the New York Public Library as that library's first Hispanic librarian. Belpré realized there were no books of folklore from Puerto Rico on the shelves. She set about expanding the library's Puerto Rican folklore programs.

Honored Storyteller Belpré grew up in a family of storytellers and was fluent in Spanish, English, and French. She incorporated her Spanish ancestry into her puppet shows as well as her books to provide young people with a way of learning more about Puerto Rican culture. Her other works include *Juan Bobo and the Queen's Necklace: A Puerto Rican Folk Tale*, and *Once in Puerto Rico*. In 1978 Belpré was honored for her distinguished contribution in Spanish literature by the Bay Area Bilingual Education League and the University of San Francisco.

 Mini Lesson **Speaking and Listening**

CHORAL READING Tell students that a choral reading can make a story sound like music. In a choral reading, groups of readers act as a choir, reading aloud in the same rhythm and loudness or softness.

Prepare Divide students into small groups for a choral reading. Assign each group a portion of the selection (narrator's passages; words of Alida, Taroo, the moon, and so on). Have each group choose a conductor.

Present Allow groups to practice reading aloud their assignment as a chorus. Then have groups combine their parts in a class choral reading and practice several times together. You may wish to invite families or other classes to attend the final choral reading.

 Use **Communications Transparencies and Copymasters**, p. 12, for additional support.

Summary

Chin Po-wan begins life as a wealthy person, but he gives all his money away to the needy. He undertakes a journey to ask the Living Kuan-yin, a goddess who allows each visitor to ask her three questions, why his fortune has run out. On the way, a snake helps Po-wan cross a river, an innkeeper feeds him a delightful meal, and a rich man lets him sleep in his beautiful home. Each requests that Po-wan ask the Living Kuan-yin a question for him. When Po-wan reaches the Living Kuan-yin, he asks their three questions instead of his own. The goddess tells him the answers. When Po-wan delivers the messages, he becomes a wealthy man again.

Reading and Analyzing

Reading Skills and Strategies: EVALUATE

Have students give possible answers to Po-wan's question, "Why am I so poor?"

Possible Response: You have overestimated the money you inherited—no one has a "never-ending" supply.

Reading Skills and Strategies: CLARIFY

Ask what has happened to Po-wan.

Possible Response: Po-wan has given away his fortune to needy, hungry people and become needy himself.

Literary Analysis: FORESHADOWING

A Ask students to think about the line "he had but one of his own to ask" and remind them that authors often foreshadow future events. Ask them to think about what else might happen in the story related to this line.

Possible Response: Po-wan will meet more people who want him to ask questions, and he won't get to ask his own question.

Teaching Options

THE LIVING KUAN-YIN

RETOLD BY
CAROL KENDALL AND YAO-WEN LI

Even though the family name of Chin means "gold," it does not signify that everyone of that name is rich. Long ago, in the province of Chekiang,[1] however, there was a certain wealthy Chin family of whom it was popularly said that its fortune was as great as its name. It seemed quite fitting, then, when a son was born to the family, that he should be called Po-wan, "Million," for he was certain to be worth a million pieces of gold when he came of age.

With such a happy circumstance of names, Po-wan himself never doubted that he would have a never-ending supply of money chinking through his fingers, and he spent it accordingly —not on himself, but on any unfortunate who came to his attention. He had a deep sense of <u>compassion</u> for anyone in distress of body or spirit: a poor man had only to hold out his hand, and Po-wan poured gold into it; if a <u>destitute</u> widow and her brood of starvelings[2] but lifted sorrowful eyes to his, he provided them with food and lodging and friendship for the rest of their days.

In such wise did he live that even a million gold pieces were not enough to support him.

His resources so dwindled that finally he scarcely had enough food for himself, his clothes flapped threadbare[3] on his wasted frame, and the cold seeped into his bone marrow[4] for lack of a fire. Still he gave away the little money that came to him.

One day, as he scraped out half of his bowl of rice for a beggar even hungrier than he, he began to ponder on his destitute state.

"Why am I so poor?" he wondered. "I have never spent <u>extravagantly</u>. I have never, from the day of my birth, done an evil deed. Why, then, am I, whose very name is A Million Pieces of Gold, no longer able to find even a copper[5] to give this unfortunate creature, and have only a bowl of rice to share with him?"

He thought long about his situation and at last determined to go without delay to the South Sea. Therein, it was told, dwelt the all-merciful goddess, the Living Kuan-yin, who could tell the

---

1. **province of Chekiang** (chŭ'kyäng'): a region on the eastern coast of China.
2. **brood of starvelings** (stärv'lĭngz): starving children.
3. **threadbare:** so worn down that the threads show.
4. **marrow:** the soft tissue that fills the middle of most bones.
5. **copper:** a coin of little value.

WORDS TO KNOW

compassion (kəm-păsh'ən) *n.* sympathy for the suffering of others; pity
destitute (dĕs'tĭ-tōōt') *adj.* living in complete poverty; extremely poor
extravagantly (ĭk-străv'ə-gənt-lē) *adv.* excessively; too much

past and future. He would put his question to her, and she would tell him the answer.

Soon he had left his home country behind and traveled for many weeks in unfamiliar lands. One day he found his way barred by a wide and furiously flowing river. As he stood first on one foot and then on the other, wondering how he could possibly get across, he heard a commanding voice calling from the top of an overhanging cliff.

"Chin Po-wan!" the voice said. "If you are going to the South Sea, please ask the Living Kuan-yin a question for me!"

"Yes, yes, of course," Po-wan agreed at once, for he had never in his life refused a request made of him. In any case, the Living Kuan-yin permitted each person who approached her three questions, and he had but one of his own to ask.

Craning his head towards the voice coming from above, he suddenly began to tremble, for the speaker was a gigantic snake with a body as large as a temple column. Po-wan was glad he had agreed so readily to the request.

"Ask her, then," said the snake, "why I am not yet a dragon, even though I have practiced self-denial[6] for more than one thousand years."

"That I will do, and gl-gladly," stammered Po-wan, hoping that the snake would continue to practice self-denial just a bit longer. "But, your . . . your Snakery . . . or your Serpentry, perhaps I should say . . . that is . . . you see, don't you . . . first I must cross this raging river, and I know not how."

"That is no problem at all," said the snake. "I shall carry you across, of course."

Bodhisattva Guanyin (Song Dynasty, 960–1279), unknown Chinese artist. Wood, 30" × 36" × 64", Eugene Fuller Memorial Collection, Seattle (Washington) Art Museum. Photo by Paul Macapia.

"Of course," Po-wan echoed weakly. Overcoming his fear and his reluctance to touch the slippery-slithery scales, Chin Po-wan climbed onto the snake's back and rode across quite safely. Politely, and just a bit hurriedly, he thanked the self-denying serpent and bade him good-bye. Then he continued on his way to the South Sea.

By noon he was very hungry. Fortunately, a nearby inn offered meals at a price he could afford. While waiting for his bowl of rice, he chatted with the innkeeper and told him of the

---

6. **self-denial:** the giving up of desires or pleasures.

 Viewing and Representing

Bodhisattva Guanyin (Seated Kuan-yin)

This 64-inch high wooden statue by an unknown artist is a particularly fine example of the artistry of the Sung Dynasty (960–1279). The statue represents the goddess Kuan-yin sitting before a rocky grotto and watching the reflection of the moon in the water.

Instruction Ask students to study the statue and think about what they've read so far about Kuan-yin. Ask them what impressions of the goddess the statue conveys. Do they think she will be willing to help Po-wan with his question?

Possible Response: She looks very wise and kind. I think she will tell Po-wan the answers to his question.

Application Ask students to think of three questions that they would ask the Living Kuan-yin if they had the opportunity today. Allow students time to role-play with a partner, one student asking three questions, and the other playing the role of the Living Kuan-yin and answering the questions. Allow students time to switch roles.

Reading Skills and Strategies:
QUESTION

A Have students think about Po-wan's journey so far and what he has encountered. Ask them to create a list of questions they have about the events surrounding the journey.

Set a Purpose Ask students to read to find out if any of their questions are answered.

Reading Skills and Strategies:
PREDICT

B Ask students which question they think Po-wan will leave out and to tell why they think so.

Literary Analysis: THEME

Ask students what they think the theme of this story, or its message about life, is.
Possible Response: Generosity and kindness will always be rewarded.

Snake of the Cliff, which the innkeeper knew well and respected, for the serpent always denied bandits the crossing of the river. <u>Inadvertently</u>, during the exchange of stories, Po-wan revealed the purpose of his journey.

"Why, then," cried the innkeeper, "let me prevail upon your generosity to ask a word for me." He laid an appealing hand on Po-wan's ragged sleeve. "I have a beautiful daughter," he said, "wonderfully <u>amiable</u> and pleasing of disposition. But although she is in her twentieth year, she has never in all her life uttered a single word. I should be very much obliged if you would ask the Living Kuan-yin why she is unable to speak."

Po-wan, much moved by the innkeeper's plea for his mute daughter, of course promised to do so. For after all, the Living Kuan-yin allowed each person three questions, and he had but one of his own to ask.

Nightfall found him far from any inn, but there were houses in the neighborhood, and he asked for lodging at the largest. The owner, a man obviously of great wealth, was pleased to offer him a bed in a fine chamber but first begged him to partake of a hot meal and good drink. Po-wan ate well, slept soundly, and, much refreshed, was about to depart the following morning when his good host, having learned that Po-wan was journeying to the South Sea, asked if he would be kind enough to put a question for him to the Living Kuan-yin.

"For twenty years," he said, "from the time this house was built, my garden has been cultivated with the utmost care; yet in all those years, not one tree, not one small plant, has bloomed or borne fruit, and because of this, no bird comes to sing, nor bee to gather nectar. I don't like to put you to a bother, Chin Po-wan, but as you are going to the South Sea

anyway, perhaps you would not mind seeking out the Living Kuan-yin and asking her why the plants in my garden don't bloom."

"I shall be delighted to put the question to her," said Po-wan. For after all, the Living Kuan-yin allowed each person three questions, and he had but . . .

Traveling onward, Po-wan examined the quandary[7] in which he found himself. The Living Kuan-yin allowed but three questions, and he had somehow, without quite knowing how, accumulated four questions. One of them would have to go unasked, but which? If he left out his own question, his whole journey would have been in vain.[8] If, on the other hand, he left out the question of the snake, or the innkeeper, or the kind host, he would break his promise and betray their faith in him.

"A promise should never be made if it cannot be kept," he told himself. "I made the promises and therefore I must keep them. Besides, the journey will not be in vain, for at least some of these problems will be solved by the Living Kuan-yin. Furthermore, assisting others must certainly be counted as a good deed, and the more good deeds abroad in the land, the better for everyone, including me."

At last he came into the presence of the Living Kuan-yin.

First, he asked the serpent's question: "Why is the Snake of the Cliff not yet a dragon, although he has practiced self-denial for more than one thousand years?"

And the Living Kuan-yin answered: "On his head are seven bright pearls. If he removes six of them, he can become a dragon."

---

7. **quandary** (kwŏn′də-rē): confusing situation.
8. **in vain:** useless.

WORDS
TO
KNOW

inadvertently (ĭn′əd-vûr′tnt-lē) *adv.* by mistake or without meaning to; not deliberately
amiable (ā′mē-ə-bəl) *adj.* good-natured and likable

840

Teaching Options

Multicultural Link   **Folk Tales**

Many cultures have folk tales, like this one, in which a hero is rewarded for his or her unselfishness. Folk tales are a part of the oral tradition and share the characteristics shown on the word web.
Application Have students copy the web shown. Then have them add to their web details about this tale's characters, lessons, and the values it reveals to their webs.

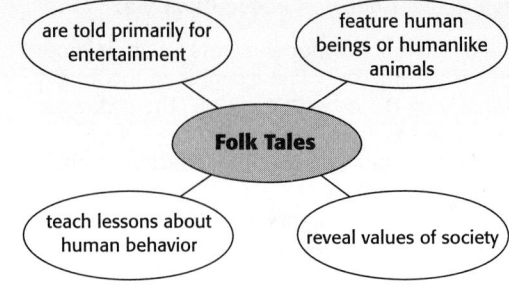

Next, Po-wan asked the innkeeper's question: "Why is the innkeeper's daughter unable to speak, although she is in the twentieth year of her life?"

And the Living Kuan-yin answered: "It is her fate to remain mute until she sees the man destined[9] to be her husband."

Last, Po-wan asked the kind host's question: "Why are there never blossoms in the rich man's garden, although it has been carefully cultivated for twenty years?"

And the Living Kuan-yin answered: "Buried in the garden are seven big jars filled with silver and gold. The flowers will bloom if the owner will rid himself of half the treasure."

Then Chin Po-wan thanked the Living Kuan-yin and bade her good-bye.

On his return journey, he stopped first at the rich man's house to give him the Living Kuan-yin's answer. In gratitude the rich man gave him half the buried treasure.

Next, Po-wan went to the inn. As he approached, the innkeeper's daughter saw him from the window and called out, "Chin Po-wan! Back already! What did the Living Kuan-yin say?"

Upon hearing his daughter speak at long last, the joyful innkeeper gave her in marriage to Chin Po-wan.

Lastly, Po-wan went to the cliffs by the furiously flowing river to tell the snake what the Living Kuan-yin had said. The grateful snake immediately gave him six of the bright pearls and promptly turned into a magnificent dragon, the remaining pearl in his forehead lighting the headland[10] like a great beacon.[11]

And so it was that Chin Po-wan, that generous and good man, was once more worth a million pieces of gold. ❖

---

9. **destined** (dĕs′tĭnd): determined beforehand, as by fate.
10. **headland:** a point of land reaching out into the water.
11. **beacon:** a light for signaling or guiding.

"My life and writing have always been inextricably entangled."

Carol Kendall
born 1917

Born Climber Carol Kendall says the things she likes to do best are writing, reading, studying Chinese, and "climbing to the tops of things." Kendall is best known for *The Gammage Cup*, a 1960 Newbery Honor Book, which was adapted as an animated film for television in 1987. Kendall now lives in Lawrence, Kansas, where she met Yao-Wen Li.

"It just happened, and I found myself a writer."

Yao-wen Li
born 1924

True "Brillance" "The Living Kuan-yin" is from *Sweet and Sour,* a collection of Chinese folk tales that Yao-wen Li coauthored with Carol Kendall. Born and raised in Canton, China, Li has lived in the United States since 1947. A return visit to China in 1973 inspired Li (whose first name means "literary brilliance") to begin collecting traditional Chinese tales.

THE LIVING KUAN-YIN **841**

 Mini Lesson ## Grammar

SUBJECT-VERB AGREEMENT Remind students that a verb must agree in number with its subject. A subject and verb agree in number when they are both singular or both plural.

Instruction Singular verbs in the present tense usually end in *-s* or *-es.* Plural verbs in the present tense do not usually end in *-s.*

Singular: The family name of Chin *means* "gold."

Plural: Many family names *mean* the occupation of an ancestor.

Application Have students write the verb in parentheses that agrees with the subject.

1. The fortune of the Chin family (<u>was</u>/were) as great as its name.
2. Unfortunate people in Po-wan's province (<u>ask</u>/asks) him for help.
3. His compassionate feelings (<u>cause</u>/causes) him to (<u>give</u>/gives) away too much money.

Use **Unit Six Resource Book**, p. 38.
Use **Grammar Transparencies and Copymasters**, p. 114.

 Use McDougal Littell's *Language Network,* Chapter 7, for more practice in subject-verb agreement.

Literature Connection

Dramatize a Tale As students divide the tasks of preparing the storyboard and drafting the script, they should also assign someone the job of editor to review the storyboard for accuracy and continuity. The editor should also review the script to make sure it follows the storyboard before the actors begin to learn their lines.

RUBRIC

3 Full Accomplishment The dramatization grows out of the storyboard. Both depict significant scenes. Dialogue is meaningful and true to character.

2 Substantial Accomplishment The relationship between the storyboard and dramatization is sometimes unclear. Scenes are well played but not always significant enough to merit treatment. Dialogue, while entertaining, shows lapses in understanding of character.

1 Little or Partial Accomplishment Storyboard and dramatization do not reflect careful thought or preparation. The tale would not be intelligible to an audience member who had not heard it already.

 Use **Communications Transparencies and Copymasters,** pp. 37, 38, for additional support.

Social Studies Connection

Celebrate Festivals Prepare index cards with titles of stories in the links to Unit 4. Have each student choose a card from the bag to find the culture he or she will research, putting cards back in the bag until everyone has chosen a title. Students who have picked the same culture might work together on the research and on painting their portion of the class mural.

RUBRIC

3 Full Accomplishment Students' mural paintings and captions show careful research and imagination.

2 Substantial Accomplishment Students' mural paintings and captions are accurate.

1 Little or Partial Accomplishment Students' mural paintings are not accurate. Captions, if any, are poorly written.

Interdisciplinary Projects

LITERATURE CONNECTION

Dramatize a Tale Dramatize and perform one of the tales you have just read. Form teams to carry out the following tasks: creating a storyboard; writing the script; and working as costumers, set designers, actors, and technical crew. Use the following steps as a guide.

Step 1: Storyboard Design and make a storyboard, a series of drawings that illustrate the tale's events. Use the storyboard to determine which events from the tale to include and what they will look like. Include props, costumes, and sound effects.

Step 2: Script Write a script for a narrator and dialogue for the characters.

Step 3: Performance Rehearse and perform your dramatization with lighting and sound effects. If equipment is available, videotape or photograph the performance to share with another class or with parents.

A storyboard shows how the action of a tale unfolds.

SOCIAL STUDIES CONNECTION

Celebrate Festivals Celebrations, festivals, and feasts are important in both ancient and modern cultures. The ancient Greeks, for example, held celebrations such as the Olympic Games, which honored Zeus. In Chinese communities around the world, the Lunar New Year is celebrated with traditional festivities, including dragon dances.

Assign groups to identify and research modern-day festivals of the cultures represented in the links to Unit Four. Then, as a class, combine your research and create a large mural that illustrates these celebrations. Include captions that explain the festivals.

SOCIAL STUDIES CONNECTION

Map Ancient Trade Routes Throughout history, traders have carried goods, ideas, and stories between cultures. Trade in spices, including pepper, flourished between ancient Egypt and the ancient African kingdoms of Kush and Punt. Spices continued to be important trade goods for centuries. In the 13th and 14th centuries, the

great Silk Road enabled traders to bring silks from far eastern China to Europe. Many other goods were traded by sea. Research these ancient trade routes. Make a map showing each route you learn about. Label and date the route, and provide a key giving further information.

Social Studies Connection

Map Ancient Trade Routes Students can research their maps in a print or online encyclopedia, a historical atlas, or a book on ancient African history. Encourage students to consult a school or local librarian.

RUBRIC

3 Full Accomplishment Maps correctly identify trade routes and effectively use arrows, lines, and captions to show the routes and dates of each. The map key is thorough, and symbols are clear and used consistently.

2 Substantial Accomplishment Maps correctly identify trade routes, but arrows, lines, and captions are not used consistently or accurately. The map key is mostly clear but not consistent.

1 Little or Partial Accomplishment Maps contain inaccurate information and are difficult to read. No map key is provided.

Across Cultures

COMPARING TEXTS **Compare Tales**
Po-wan can only ask the Living Kuan-yin three questions. The number three frequently appears in folk tales and fairy tales. What other stories can you recall or find that involve three questions or wishes? In a small-group discussion, compare and contrast those stories with "The Living Kuan-yin." Then present some of the stories to the class.

Learn About Money In "The Living Kuan-yin," Chin Po-wan's name predicts the million pieces of gold that will be his. Throughout history, money has taken various forms. The ancient Roman army paid its soldiers partly in salt. Seashells were once used as currency in the South Pacific. Research forms of money in the cultures represented in Unit Four. Create a poster to share what you learn.

Write a "Why" Story Look in folk tale collections to find more stories that explain animal appearance or behavior; read examples from several cultures. (Rudyard Kipling's *Just So Stories* is a good place to start, or read "The Frog Who Wanted to Be a Singer" on page 846.) Then write your own story that tells how an animal acquired a certain characteristic.

Find the Trickster Almost every culture has trickster tales that have been passed from one generation to the next through the oral tradition. Find out more about tricksters in world folklore. Then create a "Wanted" poster for your favorite trickster. Include an illustration, a description of the suspect, the charges against him or her, and any reward offered.

Vocabulary in Action

EXERCISE A: MEANING CLUES Answer the following questions.

1. Would a person show **compassion** through kindness, through quick thinking, or through strong opinions?

2. Might someone become **destitute** after winning the lottery, after getting a different job, or after losing a home to fire?

3. At a party, would you expect an **amiable** person to insult the host, to make new friends, or to knock over furniture?

4. Would someone who spends **extravagantly** be most likely to say "I only buy things on sale," "Who cares how much it costs!" or "That's too expensive"?

5. If someone stepped on your foot **inadvertently**, would you say that person had been careless, cruel, or childish?

EXERCISE B With a partner, act out each of the Words to Know. Have the rest of the class try to guess the words.

OVERVIEW

Objectives

- To understand and appreciate a folk tale
- To understand and appreciate an oral history
- To understand and appreciate the values and customs of historical and contemporary America

Reading Pathways

- Select one or several students to read each story aloud to the entire class or to small groups of students. Assign this reading in advance so the readers can incorporate into their presentations some of the techniques used by professional storytellers. Have the audience listen carefully to the stories without following along in their texts.
- Read the stories aloud to the class, pausing at key points to discuss how elements of the story inform students about the purpose of a "pourquoi" tale or the history of the Cheyenne people.
- After students have read the stories once, they can read them again to identify structural elements such as main character, minor characters, conflict, setting, and plot. Then have students identify similarities and differences between these two stories and the stories in Unit 5.

5-Minute Warm-Up

Daily Language SkillBuilder

Have students **proofread** the display sentences on page 765e and write them correctly. The sentences also appear on Transparency 26 of **Grammar Transparencies and Copymasters.**

LINKS TO UNIT FIVE

Making Your Mark

The selections you read in Unit Five are about characters and historical figures who find ways to express themselves. In so doing, they leave their imprints, or marks, on the world. Likewise, each tale you're about to read contains a message about the impact that one person can have on his or her community.

UNITED STATES

The Frog Who Wanted to Be a Singer

by Linda Goss

There is a folklore tradition, stretching across all cultures, that uses storytelling to explain how things came to be. "The Frog Who Wanted to Be a Singer" is another example of a "why story" or a **"pourquoi tale."**

Many traditional pourquoi tales have animals as main characters. This contemporary American **folk tale,** which takes place "in the days when the animals talked and walked upon the earth," was inspired by traditional African tales. The story offers one explanation of the way a certain type of music was first created. In it, Frog encounters some serious challenges as he pursues his dream of being a singer.

LESSON RESOURCES

UNIT SIX RESOURCE BOOK, pp. 41–47

ASSESSMENT
Formal Assessment, pp. 133–134
Teacher's Guide to Assessment and Portfolio Use
Test Generator

SKILLS TRANSPARENCIES AND COPYMASTERS
- Predicate Adjectives, CM 87 (for Mini Lesson, p. 848)

Communications
- Appreciative Listening, TR 2 (for Mini Lesson, p. 850)

INTEGRATED TECHNOLOGY
Audio Library
LaserLinks
- Science Connection. See **Teacher's SourceBook,** p. 53

Visit our website:
www.mcdougallittell.com

Where the Girl Rescued Her Brother

retold by Joseph Bruchac (broo'chäk')

This selection is an **oral history**—an account of an event that actually happened, handed down by word of mouth. The Cheyenne (shī-ĕn') are Native Americans whose homeland in the 19th century was the Great Plains, the grassland stretching through the central United States. With the Indian Removal Act of 1830, the U.S. government established land west of the Mississippi River as a reservation for Native Americans.

Western settlement increased in the 1850s, however, and the government began to make treaties with Plains tribes to restrict them to smaller areas. Settlers claimed more and more land. The government changed the terms of some treaties without permission or made treaties with Native Americans who did not represent their tribes. Soon, fighting broke out between Native Americans and government troops. This oral history tells of one such battle, in which a young Cheyenne woman makes her mark.

 LaserLinks: Background for Reading
Science Connection

AS YOU READ . . .

See how the values and customs of the cultures are presented.

Discover what lessons about human behavior are taught.

Think about the conflicts that arise.

LINKS TO UNIT FIVE **845**

Summary

A frog desperately wants to sing, but all the animals in the forest insist that only birds can sing. This frog doesn't give up easily, though. He convinces the fox, who organizes the Friday night concert series, to give him a chance. When Friday night arrives, the frog tentatively approaches the microphone. The audience makes fun of him and pelts him with fruit, but he is not discouraged. The frog stands up to the sly fox and makes his way back on stage. The other animals find that they can't resist the frog's singing, and soon they are all dancing. The frog is the originator of a new style of music, rhythm and blues.

Reading and Analyzing

Literary Analysis: FANTASY

Students should be able to recognize the distinguishing features of genres, including fantasy. Ask students to tell whether this story is fantastic or realistic and explain what details tell them this.

Possible Response: This story is fantasy, because animals don't really talk and frogs can't sing.

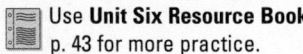 Use **Unit Six Resource Book,** p. 43 for more practice.

Reading Skills and Strategies: PREDICT

Have students make predictions about the story. Ask them whether they think the frog's goal will be met and how he might go about accomplishing it.

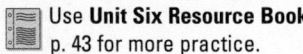 Use **Reading and Critical Thinking Transparencies,** p. 7, for additional support.

The FROG Who Wanted to Be a...

Pine Barren Tree Frog, Andy Warhol, (1928–1987), Endangered Species Series, 1983. One from a portfolio of ten screenprints and colophon, 38" × 38", Printed on Lenox Museum Board. Copyright © 2001 The Andy Warhol Foundation for the Visual Arts/ARS, New York

846

Teaching Options

Mini Lesson — Viewing and Representing

Pine Barren Tree Frog
by Andy Warhol

ART APPRECIATION The late Andy Warhol made several series of prints. He made prints of celebrities, including Marilyn Monroe, Jacqueline Kennedy Onassis, and Mao Tse-tung. Warhol is perhaps best known for his contributions to Pop Art, a style in which everyday consumer items, such as soup cans, are used as subject matter for art.
Instruction Point out the use of primary colors.

Ask students what effect is produced by the colors of the frog and the background.
Possible Response: The bright colors make the frog stand out against the dark blue background. The frog looks vibrant and alive, as though he might jump out of the picture.
Application Tell students to read the caption and discuss why Warhol chose to represent this particular kind of frog.
Possible Response: Warhol chose the pine barren tree frog because he wanted to call attention to its endangered status.

SINGER

by Linda Goss

Well, friends, I got a question for you. Have you ever been frustrated? That's right. I said *frustrated*. Tell the truth now. Everybody in this room should be screaming, "Yeah, I've been frustrated," because you know you have, at least once in your lives. And some of us here are frustrated every single day.

How do you tell when you are frustrated? Do you feel angry? Do you feel depressed? Are you full of anxiety? Are you tense? Are you nervous? Confused? Sometimes you can't stop eating. Sometimes you don't want to eat at all. Sometimes you can't sleep. And sometimes you don't want to wake up. *You are frustrated!*

Well, friends, let's go back. Back to the forest. Back to the motherland. Back to the days when the animals talked and walked upon the earth, as folks do now.

Let's examine a little creature who is feeling mighty bad, mighty sad, mighty mad, and mighty frustrated. We call him the frog. There's nothing wrong in being a frog. But this particular frog feels that he has talent. You see, he wants to be a singer. And there's nothing wrong in wanting to be a singer except that in this particular forest where this particular frog lives, frogs don't sing. Only the birds are allowed to sing. The birds are considered the most beautiful singers in the forest.

So, for a while, the frog is cool. He's quiet. He stays to himself and practices on his lily pad, jumping up and down, singing to himself.

But one day all of this frustration begins to swell inside him. He becomes so swollen that frustration bubbles start popping from his mouth, his ears, his nose, even from his eyes, and he says to himself (in a froglike voice): "You know, I'm tired of feeling this way. I'm tired of holding all this inside me. I've got talent. I want to be a singer."

The little frog decides to share his <u>ambitions</u> with his parents. His parents are somewhat worried about his desires, but since he is their son, they encourage him and say: "Son, we're behind you one hundred percent. If that's what you want to be, then go right ahead. You'll make us very proud."

This makes the frog feel better. It gives him some confidence, so much so that he decides to share the good news with his friends. He jumps over to the other side of the pond and says, "Fellows, I want to share something with you."

"Good!" they reply. "You got some flies we can eat."

"No, not flies. I got talent. I want to be a singer."

"Fool, are you crazy?" says one friend. "Frogs don't sing in this place. You'd better keep your big mouth shut."

They laugh at the frog, so he jumps back over to his lily pad.

WORDS TO KNOW	**ambition** (ăm-bĭsh′ən) *n.* a goal that is strongly desired

847

Customizing Instruction

Students Acquiring English
1 Explain the word *anxiety* by telling students that this noun describes a feeling that people sometimes have when they are nervous. Help them use the context of the paragraph about frustration to figure out its meaning.

Less Proficient Readers
Use the following questions to discuss the frog's dilemma.

• Why is the frog frustrated?
Possible Response: The frog is frustrated because he really wants to sing, but in his forest, only birds are allowed to sing.

• What do the frog's parents think about his goal?
Possible Response: They say that they will support his efforts to become a singer.

• What happens when the frog shares his excitement with his friends?
Possible Response: His friends aren't interested, and one friend tells him to keep his mouth shut.

Literary Analysis: TONE

Ask students to take a close look at the language of this story. Tell them to think about how the author uses particular words and phrases to set the tone. Then ask them to describe the tone.

Possible Response: The author sets the tone by using certain phrases such as, ". . . the frog is cool," the frog is going to "do his thing," and "Boo, you jive turkey." The slang gives the story a conversational feel. It's easy to imagine hearing the story told out loud.

Literary Analysis: CHARACTER

Ask students to use adjectives to describe the frog's character. Then have them characterize the fox.

Possible Response: Frog is determined, confident, persistent, and fairminded. The fox is deceptive, dishonest, and untrustworthy.

Literary Analysis: FANTASY

Describe a scene from these two pages that could only take place in a fantasy.

Possible Response: Only in a fantasy could there be a concert with foxes, lions, elephants, and other animals in the audience.

He rocks back and forth, meditating and <u>contemplating</u> his situation, and begins to realize that perhaps he should go and talk with the birds. They seem reasonable enough; maybe they will allow him to join their singing group.

He gathers up his confidence, jumps over to their tree house, and knocks on their trunk. The head bird flies to the window, looks down on the frog's head, and says: "Oh, it's the frog. How may we help you?"

"Can I come up? I got something to ask you," says the frog.

"Very well, Frog. Do jump up."

Frog enters the tree house, and hundreds of birds begin fluttering around him.

"Come on in, Frog. Why don't you sit over there in the corner," says the head bird. Frog sits down but he feels a little shy. He begins to chew on his tongue.

"Frog, how may we help you?"

"Uh, well, uh, you see," says Frog, "I would like to become a part of your group."

"That's wonderful," says the head bird.

"Yes, wonderful," echo the other birds.

"Frog, you may help us carry our worms," said the head bird.

"That's not what I had in mind," says Frog.

"Well, what do you have in mind?"

Frog begins to stutter: "I-I-I-I-I want to-to-to sing wi-wi-with your group."

"What! You must be joking, of course. An ugly green frog who is full of warts sing with us delicate creatures. You would cause us great embarrassment."

"B-b-but . . ." Frog tries to plead his case, but the head bird becomes angry.

"Out! Out! Out of our house you go." He kicks the frog from the house. Frog rolls like a ball down the jungle path.

When he returns home, he feels very sad. The frog wants to cry but doesn't, even though he aches deep inside his gut. He wants to give up, but he doesn't. Instead he practices and practices and practices and practices.

Then he begins to think again and realizes that even though the birds sing every Friday night at the Big Time Weekly Concert, they don't control it. The fox is in charge. The frog jumps over to the fox's place and knocks on his cave.

"Brother Fox, Brother Fox, it's me, Frog. I want to talk to you."

The fox is a fast talker and a busy worker, and really doesn't want to be bothered with the frog.

"Quick, quick, quick, what do you want?" says the fox.

"I want to be in the concert this Friday night."

"Quick, quick, what do you want to do?"

"I want to sing," says the frog.

"Sing? Get out of here, quick, quick, quick!"

"Please, Brother Fox. Please give me a chance."

"Hmmm," says the fox, shifting his eyes. "Uh, you know something, Froggie? Maybe I could use you. Why don't you show up Friday, at eight o'clock sharp, OK?"

"You mean I can do it?"

"That's what I said. Now, get out of here. Quick, quick, quick!"

Oh, the frog is happy. He is going to "do his thing." He is going to present himself to the world.

Meanwhile, the fox goes around to the animals in the forest and tells them about the frog's plans. Each animal promises to be there and give the frog a "little present" for his singing debut.

And so Monday rolls around, Tuesday rolls around, Wednesday rolls around, Thursday

---

WORDS TO KNOW

contemplating (kŏn′təm-plā′tĭng) *adj.* considering carefully; pondering
contemplate *v.*

848

Teaching Options

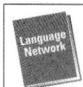 **Mini Lesson** **Grammar**

PREDICATE ADJECTIVES

Instruction Tell students that a predicate adjective is an adjective that modifies the subject of a verb. A predicate adjective follows a linking verb, such as *be, become, seem, grow, appear, look, feel, smell, taste, remain, sound,* and *stay.*

Exercises Have students underline the predicate adjective or adjectives in each of the sentences below.

1. The frog appeared to be <u>calm</u> and <u>cool</u> at the start of the story.
2. The head bird seemed <u>eager</u> to have the frog carry worms for the birds.
3. The fox was <u>willing</u> to give the frog a turn on stage.
4. The frog grew <u>angry</u> after being pelted by flying fruits.
5. The frog was quite <u>pleased</u> at the end.

Use **Unit Six Resource Book,** p. 45.
Use **Grammar Transparencies and Copymasters,** p. 87.

Use McDougal Littell's ***Language Network,*** Chapter 5, for more instruction and practice in predicate adjectives.

rolls around, and it is Friday. The frog is so excited, he bathes all day. He combs his little green hair, parts it in the middle, and slicks down the sides. He scrubs his little green fingers and his little green toes. He looks at his little reflection in the pond, smiles, and says, "Um, um, um, I am *beauuuutiful!* And I am going to 'do my thing' tonight." And soon it is seven o'clock, and then it is seven thirty, and then it is seven forty-five, and there is the frog trembling, holding on to the edge of the curtain.

He looks out at the audience and sees all the animals gathering in their seats. The frog is scared, so scared that his legs won't stop trembling and his eyes won't stop twitching. Brother Fox strolls out onstage and the show begins.

"Thank you, thank you, thank you. Ladies and gentlemen, we have a wonderful show for you tonight. Presenting, for your entertainment, the frog who thinks he's a singer. Come on, let's clap. Come on out here, Frog, come on, come on. Let's give him a big hand." The animals clap and roar with laughter. The frog jumps out and slowly goes up to the microphone.

"For-for-for-for my first number, I-I-I-I—"

Now, before that frog can put the period at the end of that sentence, the elephant stands up, pulls down a pineapple, and throws it right at the frog's head.

"Ow!" cries the frog. And the lion pulls down a banana, throws it, and hits that frog right in the mouth. "Oh," gulps the frog. Other animals join in the act of throwing things at the frog. Some of them shout and yell at him, "Boo! Boo! Get off the stage. You stink! You're ugly. We don't want to hear a frog sing. Boo, you jive turkey!"

The poor little frog has to leap off the stage and run for his life. He hides underneath the stage. Brother Fox rushes back on the stage.

"OK, OK, OK, calm down—just trying out our comic routine. We have some real talent for your enjoyment. Presenting the birds, who really can sing. Let's hear it for the birds." The audience claps loudly. The birds fly onto the stage, their heads held up high. Their wings slowly strike a stiff, <u>hypnotic</u> pose as if they are statues. Their stage presence demands great respect from the audience. They chirp, tweet, and whistle, causing the audience to fall into a soft, peaceful nod.

Everyone is resting quietly except the frog, who is tired of being pushed around. The frog is tired of feeling frustrated. He leaps over the fox. He grabs him, shakes him, puts his hands around the fox's throat, and says, "You tricked me. You tried to make a fool out of me."

"Leave me alone," says the fox. "If you want to go back out there and make a fool of yourself, go right ahead."

"Hmph," says the frog. "That's just what I'm going to do."

Now that little green frog hippity-hops back onto the stage. He is shaking but determined to sing his song.

"I don't care if you are asleep. I'm gonna wake you up. I came here to sing a song tonight, and that's what I'm going to do."

In the style of what we call boogie-woogie, the frog begins to "do his thing":

WORDS TO KNOW

hypnotic (hĭp-nŏt'ĭk) *adj.* trance-inducing **hypnotize** *v.*

849

Customizing Instruction

Less Proficient Readers

1 Point out that a "little present" is in quotation marks. Tell students that this is a clue that there is another meaning to "little present," or that maybe the author is using the word *present* in an ironic way.

Multicultural Link Boogie-Woogie

Tell students that "boogie-woogie" is a style of piano that was later adapted for band performance. While the left hand plays repeated patterns of blues chords, the right hand plays syncopated melodies. In order to play boogie-woogie, a pianist's hands must play independently of each other.

The term "boogie-woogie" was first used in the late 1920s, and it may have originally been used to describe a dance that was accompanied by this lively piano music.

Boogie-woogie was most popular during the Swing Era of the 1930s and 1940s. Musicians like Tommy Dorsey, Count Basie, and the Andrews Sisters all played boogie-woogie.

Bring in some recordings of boogie-woogie music. Ask students to listen to the music and then discuss how it makes them feel. Can they understand how this music affected the animals in the frog's audience?

Literary Analysis: AUTHOR'S PURPOSE

Ask students why they think Linda Goss wrote this story and whether they think she succeeds at her purpose.

Possible Responses: She wrote this story to entertain readers, and she succeeds, because this story is funny—not a serious explanation of the birth of rhythm and blues; She may have wanted to inspire readers to "go for" their dreams.

Literary Analysis: UNCONVENTIONAL TEXT

Lead a discussion about the "wavy" text that describes the frog's singing on pages 849–850. Ask students why they think the words are styled this way. Then ask them whether they like this technique, and why or why not.

Possible Response: The wavy words give you a feeling for the rhythm of the music that the frog is playing. Printed this way, the words make the page look lively and fun.

The frog bops his head about as though it were a jazzy saxophone. His fingers move as though they were playing a funky bass fiddle.

The elephant opens one eye. He roars "Uuumphf!" He jumps from his seat. He flings his hips from side to side, doing a dance we now call the "bump." The lion is the next animal to jump up from his seat. He shouts: "I love it! I love it!" He shakes his body thisaway and thataway and every whichaway, doing a dance we now call the "twist." Soon the snakes are boogalooing and the giraffes are doing the jerk. The hyenas do the "slop" and

the fox does the "mashed potato." The birds also want to join in: "We want to do Dooba Dooba, too." They chirp and sway through the trees.

The whole forest is rocking. The joint is jumping. The animals are snapping their fingers. They are *dancing*, doing something that they have never done before.

The fox runs back on the stage, grabs the mike, and shouts: "Wow, Frog, you are a genius. You have given us something new."

From then on, the frog is allowed to sing every Friday night at the Big Time Weekly Concert.

And, as my granddaddy used to say, that is how Rhythm and Blues was born.

"I have always been a talker."

Linda Goss
born 1942

A Storyteller's Beginnings Linda Goss was born in Alcoa, Tennessee. When asked how she became a storyteller, she has said, "I have always been a talker. When I was in the first grade, my teacher wrote on my report card, 'Linda talks too much.' As I grew older, I decided

to put my talking to good use." She attended Howard University, where she studied drama.

Doing Her Own Thing When Goss was young, few people considered storytelling to be a possible career. She worked as a teacher and then decided to become a full-time professional storyteller, despite the difficulties. "Frog needed to do his own thing, and so do I," she says.

Career Success With her husband, Clay Goss, Goss has edited two collections of African-American stories and written two children's books. She is the official storyteller of Philadelphia, where she now resides.

Mini Lesson ## Speaking and Listening

RHYTHM AND BLUES

Prepare Explain that rhythm and blues is a kind of music that combines elements of blues and jazz. Rhythm and blues, also known as R & B, was developed by African Americans and is characterized by a strong backbeat and repeated variations on instrumental phrases. Most authorities agree that it is a precursor to rock and roll. Bring in some examples of rhythm and blues recordings. Tell students to listen for some of the instruments mentioned in the story, such as the saxophone, bass, and fiddle.

Present Lead a discussion about this kind of music. Ask students whether they have ever heard this kind of music before, and if so, where. Have students think about whether this type of music sounds difficult to play. Students who play instruments might enjoy sharing with the class any knowledge they have about playing R&B. Then discuss how this kind of music makes them feel.

 Use **Communications Transparencies and Copymasters**, p. 2, for additional support.

WHERE THE GIRL RESCUED HER BROTHER

>>> retold by **Joseph Bruchac**

I t was the moon when
the chokecherries were ripe.
A young woman rode out of
a Cheyenne camp with her
husband and her brother.
The young woman's name
was Buffalo Calf Road Woman.

Cheyenne Young Woman,
Edward S. Curtis. Plate #64 from
"The North American Indians."
Philadelphia Museum of Art:
Funds from the American
Museum of Photography.

Summary
Buffalo Calf Road Woman, together with her husband, who is a Cheyenne chief, and her brother ride with a group of Cheyenne to meet their allies, the Lakota. The Native Americans are on their way to engage the white men in battle. Their goal is to drive the whites off Native American lands. During the fierce battle, Buffalo Calf Road Woman sees that her brother is unhorsed and fighting for his life. She rides into the fray on her pony and carries her brother to safety. Both Native Americans and whites pause to cheer her bravery. Her act of courage inspires the Native American warriors to victory.

Customizing Instruction

Students Acquiring English
Tell students that *chokecherries* are a fruit from a shrub or small tree in the rose family. The fruit is dark red or almost black and has a strong flavor.

Discuss the name "Buffalo Calf Road Woman." Ask students whether they are familiar with other Native American names. If students can't think of any names, mention Sitting Bull, a Sioux leader who led his people to victory over General Custer at the Battle of the Little Bighorn in 1876. Lead a discussion about the significance of Native American names.

Mini Lesson **Viewing and Representing**

Cheyenne Young Woman,
Edward S. Curtis

ART APPRECIATION Edward Curtis was a portrait photographer based in Seattle, who devoted himself to documenting Native Americans.
Instruction Between 1907 and 1937, Edward Curtis produced twenty volumes of text and twenty volumes of portraits under the title *The North American Indian.* President Theodore Roosevelt wrote the foreword to the series.

Curtis felt that it was important to record the customs of Native Americans before their traditions disappeared. Because of his feeling that some of these tribes were dying out or would soon become modernized, Curtis sometimes had his subjects pose in the dress of their ancestors so that future generations would have a record of their elders.
Application Ask students to write a paragraph describing the portrait. Encourage them to tell what they know and feel about this woman from studying the photograph.

Active Reading: MAKING INFERENCES

Discuss the passage in which Buffalo Calf Road Woman recalls the incident with the grizzly bear. Ask students to make an inference about why the author includes this anecdote.

Possible Responses: The author probably includes the story about the grizzly bear to illustrate the bravery and intelligence of the women who belong to the Society of Quilters. The author wanted to show that the women could handle threatening situations in a gentle, firm, and highly effective manner.

Use **Unit Six Resource Book,** p. 42 for more practice.
Use **Reading and Critical Thinking Transparencies,** p. 10, for additional support.

Reading Skills and Strategies: ANALYZE

Ask students to analyze the traditions of the Cheyenne warriors, telling what their customs reveal about the Cheyenne attitude toward themselves and toward war.

Possible Response: The Cheyenne warriors have great self-respect. Their custom of wearing fine clothes, raising their headdresses, and painting designs on their ponies are all signs that they take war very seriously. They take great pains to prepare themselves, both mentally and physically, for the battle ahead.

Her husband, Black Coyote, was one of the chiefs of the Cheyenne, the people of the plains who call themselves Tsis-tsis-tas, meaning simply "The People." Buffalo Calf Road Woman's brother, Comes-in-Sight, was also one of the Cheyenne chiefs, and it was well-known how close he was to his sister.

Like many of the other young women of the Cheyenne, Buffalo Calf Road Woman was respected for her honorable nature. Although it was the men who most often went to war to defend the people—as they were doing on this day—women would accompany their husbands when they went to battle. If a man held an important position among the Cheyenne, such as the keeper of the Sacred Arrows, then his wife, too, would have to be of the highest moral character, for she shared the weight of his responsibility.

Buffalo Calf Road Woman was well aware of this, and as she rode by her husband she did so with pride. She knew that today they were on their way to meet their old <u>allies</u>, the Lakota.[1] They were going out to try to drive back the *veho,* the spider people who were trying to claim all the lands of the Native peoples.

1 The Cheyenne had been worried about the *veho,* the white people, for a long time. They had given them that name because, like the black widow spider, they were very beautiful but it was dangerous to get close to them. And unlike the Cheyenne, they seemed to follow a practice of making promises and not keeping them. Although their soldier chief Custer had promised to be friendly with the Cheyenne, now he and the others had come into their lands to make war upon them.

Early Moonlight, Little Horn, Montana, Joseph Henry Sharp. Watercolor on paper. Stark Museum of Art, Orange, Texas.

Buffalo Calf Road Woman wore a robe embroidered with porcupine quills. The clothing of her brother and her husband, Black Coyote, was also beautifully decorated with those quills, which had been flattened, dyed in different colors, folded, and sewed on in patterns. Buffalo Calf Road Woman was proud that she belonged to the Society of Quilters. As with the men's societies, only a few women—those of the best character— could join. Like the men, the women had to be

---

1. **Lakota** (lə-kō′tə).

WORDS
TO
KNOW

ally (ă-lī′) *n.* a person, group, or nation that works with another to achieve shared goals

852

 Mini Lesson ## Spelling

SUFFIXES –*IBLE* AND –*ABLE*

Instruction Explain that the suffixes -*ible* and -*able* mean "capable or worthy of an action" or "inclined to a specific state or action." They sound very similar, but -*ible* is more commonly used with roots rather than with whole words. Point out the word *honorable* on page 852, and ask students what it means.

Exercises Have students add the suffix -*ible* or -*able* to the underlined root in each sentence and tell what the word means.

1. Edward Curtis was a <u>cap</u> *(able)* photographer.

2. I think that the members of the Society of Quilters are <u>admir</u> *(able)* for their bravery.

3. Buffalo Calf Road Woman was <u>respons</u> *(ible)* for sharing the weight of her husband's high position.

4. Buffalo Calf Road Woman's act of bravery is <u>remark</u> *(able)*.

5. Some people think that war is <u>incomprehens</u> *(ible)*.

 Use **Unit Six Resource Book,** p. 46.

strong, honorable, and brave. Buffalo Calf Road Woman had grown up hearing stories of how Cheyenne women would defend their families when the men were away. The women of the Cheyenne were brave, and those in the Society of Quilters were the bravest of all.

Buffalo Calf Road Woman smiled as she remembered one day when the women of the Society of Quilters showed such bravery. It was during the Moon of Falling Leaves. A big hunt had been planned. The men who acted as scouts had gone out and located the great buffalo herd. They had seen, too, that there were no human enemies anywhere near their camp. So almost none of the men remained behind.

n that day, when all the men were away, a great grizzly bear came into the camp. Such things seldom happened, but this bear was one that had been wounded in the leg by a white fur-trapper's bullet. It could no longer hunt as it had before, and hunger brought it to the Cheyenne camp, where it smelled food cooking.

When the huge bear came walking into the camp, almost everyone scattered. Some women grabbed their little children. Old people shut the door flaps of their tepees, and the boys ran to find their bows and arrows. Only a group of seven women who had been working on the embroidery of an elk-skin robe did not run. They were members of the Society of Quilters, and Buffalo Calf Road Woman was among them. The seven women put down their work, picked up the weapons they had close to hand, and stood to face the grizzly bear.

Now of all of the animals of the plains, the only one fierce enough and powerful enough to attack a human was the grizzly. But confronted by that determined group of women, the grizzly bear stopped in its tracks. It had come to steal food, not fight. The head of the Society of Quilters stepped forward a pace and spoke to the bear.

"Grandfather," she said, her voice low and firm, "we do not wish to harm you, but we will protect our camp. Go back to your own home."

The grizzly shook its head and then turned and walked out of the camp. The women stood and watched it as it went down through the cottonwoods and was lost from sight along the bend of the stream.

Buffalo Calf Road Woman turned her mind away from her memories. They were close to Rosebud Creek. The scouts had told them that a great number of the *veho* soldiers would be there and that the Gray Fox, General George Crook, was in command. The Cheyenne had joined up now with the Oglala,[2] led by Crazy Horse. The Lakota people were always friends to the Cheyenne, but this man, Crazy Horse, was the best friend of all. Some even said that he was one of their chiefs, too, as well as being a war leader of his Oglala.

There were Crow and Shoshone scouts with Crook, and the *veho* had many cannons. The Lakota and the Cheyenne were outnumbered by the two thousand men in Crook's command. But they were prepared to fight. They had put on their finest clothes, for no man should risk his life without being dressed well enough so that if he died, the enemy would know a great warrior had fallen. Some of the men raised their headdresses three times, calling out their names and the deeds they had done. Those headdresses of eagle feathers were thought to give magical protection to a warrior. Other men busied themselves painting designs on their war ponies.

Now they could hear Crook's army approaching. The rumble of the horses' hooves echoed down the valley, and there was the

---

2. **Oglala** (ō-glä′lə).

853

Customizing Instruction

Less Proficient Readers

1 Ask students to explain why the Cheyenne refer to the white people as the "spider people."

Possible Response: The Cheyenne call white people "the spider people" because they think that, like a black widow spider, the white people are beautiful but dangerous.

2 Have students identify the season during which the Moon of Falling Leaves takes place. How did they figure this out?

Possible Response: The Moon of Falling Leaves takes place in the autumn, because that's when leaves fall.

Multicultural Link **Native American Beliefs**

Although there are many different Native American tribes, each with its own traditions and history, most tribes share some common beliefs. For example, most Native Americans believe in a unity among the earth's people, animals, and other living things. They believe that each living thing contains a spirit and that any two living things can make spiritual contact.

Native American buffalo hunters gave thanks to the buffalo for giving its life so that people could eat and live. This reverence for life is one of the reasons why Native Americans used every part of the buffalo—nothing went to waste after the buffalo had given its life.

Literary Analysis: SETTING

Ask students to describe the setting of this part of the story.

Possible Response: This part of the story takes place at Rosebud Creek, the site of a battle between the Cheyenne people and the white soldiers. The Lakota tribe is helping the Cheyenne in their fight against the white people, who are getting help from members of the Crow and the Shoshone tribes.

Reading Skills and Strategies: SUMMARIZE

Have students summarize the reason why this battle is taking place.

Possible Response: This battle is taking place because the white people are trying to claim the land of the native peoples.

Reading Skills and Strategies: ANALYZE

Ask students why they think this story about Buffalo Calf Road Woman has particular significance to the Cheyenne people.

Possible Response: This story is probably important to the Cheyenne people because it is an impressive example of the strength and bravery not only of Buffalo Calf Road Woman but also of the Cheyenne people as a whole.

The Battle of the Rosebud, which the Cheyenne call "Where the Girl Rescued Her Brother," was fought on June 17, 1876, on the banks of the Rosebud Creek in southeastern Montana.

sound of trumpets. War ponies reared up and stomped their feet. Many of the Cheyenne men found it hard to put on the last of their paint as their hands shook from the excitement of the coming battle.

Crazy Horse <u>vaulted</u> onto his horse and held up one arm. "*Hoka Hey,*" he cried. "It is a good day to die."

Buffalo Calf Road Woman watched from a hill as the two lines of men—the blue soldiers to one side, and the Lakota and Cheyenne to the other—raced toward each other. The battle began. It was not a quick fight or an easy one. There were brave men on both sides. Two Moons, Little Hawk, Yellow Eagle, Sitting Bull, and Crazy Horse were only a few of the great warriors who fought for the Cheyenne and the Lakota. And Crook, the Gray Fox general of the whites, was known to be a tough fighter and a worthy enemy.

Buffalo Calf Road Woman's husband, Black Coyote, and her brother, Comes-in-Sight, were in the thick of the fight. The odds in the battle were almost even. Although the whites had more soldiers and guns, the Lakota and the Cheyenne were better shots and better

horsemen. Had it not been for the Crow and Shoshone scouts helping Crook, the white soldiers might have broken quickly from the ferocity of the attack.

From one side to the other, groups of men attacked and retreated as the guns cracked, cannons boomed, and smoke filled the air. The war shouts of the Lakota and the Cheyenne were almost as loud as the rumble of the guns. The sun moved across the sky as the fight went on, hour after hour, while the confusion of battle swirled below.

Then Buffalo Calf Road Woman saw something that horrified her. Her brother had been drawn off to one side, surrounded by Crow scouts. He tried to ride free of them, but his pony went down, struck by a rifle bullet and killed. Now he was on foot, still fighting. The Crow warriors were trying to get close, to count coup[3] on him. It was more of an honor to touch a living enemy, so they were not firing

---

3. **count coup** (ko͞o): to touch an enemy in battle with a rod called a coup stick, considered an act of bravery by some Native American peoples.

WORDS
TO   **vault** (vôlt) *v.* to jump or to leap with the use of the hands
KNOW

854

✓ **Assessment** **Informal Assessment**

RETELL THE STORY You can informally assess students' understanding of the story by having them retell it in their own words. Students should be able to retell the events of the story clearly, accurately, and in the correct sequence. Their retellings should also show insight into the character of Buffalo Calf Road Woman.

RUBRIC

3 Full Accomplishment Response reflects a full understanding of story events and of the character of Buffalo Calf Road Woman, and retells events in the correct sequence.

2 Substantial Accomplishment Response shows a general understanding of story events and sequence but does not fully grasp the character of Buffalo Calf Road Woman.

1 Little or Partial Accomplishment Response shows little understanding of story events or sequence, or of the character of Buffalo Calf Road Woman.

their rifles at him. And he was able to keep them away with his bow and arrows. But it was clear that soon he would be out of ammunition and would fall to the enemy.

Buffalo Calf Road Woman waited no longer. She dug her heels into her pony's sides and galloped down the hill. Her head low, her braids streaming behind her, she rode into the heart of the fight. Some men moved aside as they saw her coming, for there was a determined look in her eyes. She made the long howling cry that Cheyenne women used to urge on the warriors. This time, however, she was the one going into the fight. Her voice was as strong as an eagle's. Her horse scattered the ponies of the Crow scouts who were closing in on her brother, Comes-in-Sight. She held out a hand; her brother grabbed it and vaulted onto the pony behind her. Then she wheeled, ducking the arrows of the Crow scouts, and heading back up the hill.

That was when it happened. For a moment, it seemed as if all the shooting stopped. The Cheyenne and the Lakota, and even the *veho* soldiers, lowered their guns to watch this act of great bravery. A shout went up, not from one side but from both, as Buffalo Calf Road Woman reached the safety of the hilltop again, her brother safe behind her on her horse. White men and Indians cheered her.

So it was that Buffalo Calf Road Woman performed the act for which the people would always remember her. Inspired by her courage, the Cheyenne and Lakota drove back the Gray Fox—Crook made a strategic withdrawal.[4]

"Even the *veho* general was impressed," said the Cheyenne people. "He saw that if our women were that brave, he would stand no chance against us in battle."

So it is that to this day, the Cheyenne and the Lakota people do not refer to the fight as the Battle of the Rosebud. Instead, they honor Buffalo Calf Road Woman by calling the fight Where the Girl Rescued Her Brother. ❖

---

4. **strategic withdrawal:** retreat.

"Have pride in what you are and recognize that we as human beings make ourselves."

Joseph Bruchac
born 1942

Sharing the "Good Paths" The poet, novelist, and storyteller Joseph Bruchac began hearing Native American legends as a small child. A descendant of Abenaki Native Americans, Bruchac says he likes to share stories from Native American traditions because "they have messages, sometimes very subtle, which can help show young people the good paths to follow." Born in the Adirondack Mountains, Bruchac has also drawn upon the legends of those mountains for his stories.

Award-Winning Author Before becoming a writer and a scholar, Joseph Bruchac taught English and literature in Ghana, West Africa, and creative writing and African-American literature at Skidmore College in New York. The author of more than 60 books, Bruchac has received numerous awards for his writing, including a fellowship from the National Endowment for the Arts and a Rockefeller Foundation Humanities Fellowship. "Where the Girl Rescued Her Brother" appears in Bruchac's collection *The Girl Who Married the Moon: Tales from Native North America.*

Interdisciplinary Projects

LITERATURE CONNECTION

Hold a Storytelling Festival Work with your classmates to present a storytelling festival for other classes in your grade or for a group of younger students. First, decide which stories from Unit Six and which other tales from world folklore to include in the festival. Then form groups to carry out the following steps.

Step 1: Rehearsals Rehearse each story in front of friends. Practice using gestures and tones of voice that make the stories come alive.

Step 2: Advertisements Create flyers to advertise the festival. Create and distribute invitations containing the date, time, and location. Produce illustrated programs to hand out at the festival.

Step 3: Props and Costumes Locate or construct appropriate props, and provide costumes for the storytellers.

Step 4: Performance Borrow the school's equipment or equipment loaned by the community. Make an audio or video recording of the performance, or take photographs of the festival.

The class might also wish to locate videotapes of professional storytellers for viewing in a separate area during the festival.

HISTORY CONNECTION

Research the Horse Find out more about the importance of the horse to Native Americans of the Plains, such as the Cheyenne and the Lakota Sioux. Where did horses in North America come from? What were they used for? How did horses change the Native American ways of life? Write and illustrate an encyclopedia entry on this topic that could go in a reference book on Native American history.

 LaserLinks: Background for Reading Science Connection

MUSIC CONNECTION

Explore Rhythm and Blues "The Frog Who Wanted to Be a Singer" tells the story of the invention of rhythm and blues music. Design a multimedia presentation for your class on rhythm and blues. First, read about this type of music in an encyclopedia or reference book about popular music. Find out how and where this type of music first developed. How has it influenced other types of popular music? Then listen to recordings of rhythm and blues. In your presentation, include audio recordings, photographs, and other primary sources.

 More Online: Research Starter www.mcdougallittell.com

856 UNIT SIX THE ORAL TRADITION

Across Cultures

COMPARING TEXTS **Compare Characters**
In what way or ways are Frog and Buffalo Calf Road Woman similar? Write a paragraph describing the qualities these characters have in common. Explain how each character demonstrates these qualities.

Make a "Why Story" Bulletin Board "The Frog Who Wanted to Be a Singer" is inspired by traditional African "why stories." Find and read examples of "why stories" from African and other cultures. Take notes on what explanations the tales offer for why animals look or behave in certain ways. Combine the information you gather with that of your classmates. Together, create a "why story" bulletin board. Make drawings or find pictures of animals. Write captions summarizing how each animal got to be the way it is, according to the "why stories" you

read. Label each explanation with the culture from which it comes.

Map Native American Territories Research in what areas of North America the Plains tribes originally lived. Then draw a map of the United States showing these territories and the movement of these Native American groups as they were forced farther West or onto reservations by European-American expansion. Use color-coding and a key to identify the tribes and time periods represented on your map.

Illustrate Quill Decoration Embroidery with porcupine quills is a traditional Native American craft. Look in books of Native American art for examples of quill decoration. What do the designs represent? Make drawings of them to share with the class.

Vocabulary in Action

EXERCISE A: EXAMPLE CLUES Write the Word to Know suggested by each of the following sentences.

1. More than anything, the little frog wanted to be a singer.
2. He sat quietly on a lily pad and thought about his plan.
3. The beautiful song made the audience feel as though they were in a trance.
4. With a sudden leap, Buffalo Calf Road Woman was on the pony's back.
5. The Cheyenne and the Lakota have been on good terms for a long time.

EXERCISE B: ACROSTIC An acrostic is a list of words whose first letters form a word or message when read from top to bottom. Complete an acrostic for each of the Words to Know, using words from or about the stories. An example has been done for you.

> **A**migo, I
> **L**end my
> **L**ife to
> **Y**ou

WORDS TO KNOW	ally	ambition	contemplating	hypnotic	vault

Across Cultures
COMPARING TEXTS
Compare Characters Remind students of the title of Unit 5, "Making Your Mark." Suggest that they consider how the qualities shown by Frog and Buffalo Calf Road Woman allowed them to leave their marks on their communities.

 Use **Writing Transparencies**, p.29, for additional support.

Make a "Why Story" Bulletin Board
Encourage students to give a brief oral presentation about the "why story" that they read. Tell them to use the visuals that they contributed to the bulletin board as well as the notes that they took while reading.

Map Native American Territories
Suggest that students also include key battles and government acts that caused tribes to resettle. When students finish their maps, exhibit them around the classroom for everyone to see.

Illustrate Quill Decoration Invite students to create their own version of traditional quill decoration. Tell them to think of an object that they could substitute for quills. Then have them make their own design patterned after or inspired by one that they found while doing their research.

 Use Selection Quiz, **Unit Six Resource Book**, p.47.

Vocabulary in Action
Exercise A
1. ambition
2. contemplating
3. hypnotic
4. vault
5. ally
Exercise B
Accept acrostics that use words related to the selections.

 Use **Unit Six Resource Book**, p. 44.

Objectives

- write a Comparison-and-Contrast essay
- use a written text as a model for writing
- revise a draft to elaborate
- make comparisons using adjectives

Introducing the Workshop

Comparison-and-Contrast Essay Help students to see that any two subjects can be compared in a comparison-and-contrast essay—it might be two people, two things, or two events. Lead a class discussion to brainstorm possible subjects for comparisons. Choosing two subjects which are too similar or too different does not lend itself well to a comparison essay.

Basics in a Box

Using the Graphic The elements of a comparison-and-contrast essay are shown in the graphic. Students should note that the introduction and conclusion are particularly important because they make the reader aware of the importance of the essay. The introduction sets up the reason for the comparison, and the conclusion explains what new understanding can come from the comparison. Point out the Venn diagram that forms the body of the essay, and remind students of other times they have used this format.

Presenting the Rubric To help students better understand the assignment, review the Standards for Writing a Successful Comparison-and-Contrast Essay. You may also want to share with them the complete rubric, which describes several levels of proficiency.

Use McDougal Littell's **Language Network**, Chapters 10–17, for more instruction on essential writing skills.

Power Presentation

To engage students visually, use **Power Presentation 2**, Comparison-and-Contrast Essay.

Writing Workshop
Comparison-and-Contrast Essay

Pointing out similarities and differences . . .

From Reading to Writing When you read the myths about Icarus and Arachne, you might think that the characters are completely different. Icarus flies; Arachne weaves. However, they share an important similarity. They both have too much pride, which leads to their destruction. Writing a **comparison-and-contrast essay** helps you examine how two things are similar and different and can deepen your understanding of both subjects.

For Your Portfolio

WRITING PROMPT Write a comparison-and-contrast essay about two subjects that interest you.

Purpose: To inform, explain, or clarify
Audience: Anyone interested in your subjects

Basics in a Box

Comparison-and-Contrast Essay at a Glance

RUBRIC STANDARDS FOR WRITING

A successful comparison-and-contrast essay should

- introduce the subjects being compared
- state a clear purpose for the comparison
- include both similarities and differences and support each statement with examples and details
- follow a clear organizational pattern
- include transitional words and phrases to make similarities and differences clear
- summarize the comparison in the conclusion

LESSON SUPPORT

USING PRINT RESOURCES
Unit Six Resource Book
- Prewriting, p. 48
- Drafting and Elaborating, p. 49
- Peer Response Guide, pp. 50–51
- Revising, Editing, and Proofreading, p. 52
- Student Models, pp. 53–55
- Rubric for Evaluation, p. 56

Reading and Critical Thinking Transparencies
- Venn diagram, TR 35 (for Mini Lesson, p. 860)

Writing Transparencies and Copymasters
- Writing Process Transparencies, TR 1–TR 4
- Writing Structure Transparencies: Elaboration, TR 13
- Writing Template Transparencies: Comparison-and-Contrast Essay (by Subject), TR 28; Comparison-and-Contrast Esssay (by Feature), TR 29

GRAMMAR
- Subject-Verb Agreement, CM 115 (for Mini Lesson, p. 863)

INTEGRATED TECHNOLOGY
LaserLinks
Writing Springboards
See **Teacher's SourceBook** p. 56 for bar codes.

Writing Coach CD-ROM

Visit our website:
www.mcdougallittell.com

Analyzing a Student Model

See the Communication Handbook, p. R100 for speaking and presenting tips.

SPEAKING OPPORTUNITY

Yoshio Adachi
St. Walter's School

My Two Countries

I am lucky because I am only ten and I have lived in two countries—Japan and the United States. When I first moved to the United States, I was very shocked at how different it is from my homeland. Japan is one of the oldest empires in the world. It is a small country, located on a chain of islands in the Pacific Ocean. Much of the land is crowded with people. The United States, however, is a young country and is the fourth largest country in the world. As a result, it is quieter, even in cities. The two countries also share similarities and differences—in the areas of transportation and shopping. Comparing these features can help us to understand each country better.

First of all, both countries have public transportation. In Japan, most people don't have cars. Therefore, public transportation, such as subways and trains, must be convenient. There are 12 different subway lines with over 125 train stations in Tokyo alone. People also ride bicycles or walk to stores or to work. In contrast, most Americans have their own cars. They would rather drive than wait for a train or a bus. Even though many Americans do use public transportation, it is not as convenient as it is in Japan. The distance between the stations and American homes makes it more difficult.

There are also similarities and differences in what is called "rush hour." In both Japan and the United States, rush hour is hectic. In Japan, most people ride the train to work. The train gets crowded quickly, and many people must stand. Most subway and train companies hire people called "pushers" who work only during the rush hour. The pusher's job is to push people into the train so the doors will close. When the train stops at a station and the doors open, slowly the crowd of people surges forward. The pusher pushes the rest of the people onto the train before the doors close. In contrast, the American rush hour is mostly a problem for people driving cars. Usually there is only one person in a car and the cars clog the streets. Many Americans try to find shortcuts that will help them get to work faster. Both Japanese and Americans are often frustrated by the start of their work day.

RUBRIC
IN ACTION

❶ States the subjects being compared

❷ Uses a feature-by-feature organization

Other option:
- Use a subject-by-subject organization.

❸ Specific facts support points of comparison and show the writer's knowledge of the subject.

❹ Detailed examples explain differences.

❺ Transitions signal differences and unify the paragraph.

Teaching the Lesson

Analyzing the Model
"My Two Countries"

In this essay, the writer compares her native country of Japan to the United States, where she currently lives. The essay focuses on two main areas—transportation and shopping. She offers the reader a closer look at these two elements in terms of their similarities and differences.

Have students read the model and discuss what makes it a successful comparison-and-contrast essay. Then discuss the Rubric in Action. Point out key sections of the model that correspond to the elements mentioned in the Rubric in Action.

1 Ask why it is important to state here the subjects being compared.
  Possible Response: The reader will know exactly what the essay is about and can activate any prior knowledge about the subjects.

2 Discuss how a subject-by-subject organization would differ from a feature-by-feature organization.
  Possible Response: Instead of analyzing all aspects of transportation, then going on to shopping, a subject-by-subject organization would first tell about Japan, discussing features, and then talk about the United States covering the same features.

3 Have students discuss how the author knew these specific facts and how they will gather facts for their own essays.
  Possible Response: The author has lived in both countries, and she may have talked to experts or read a book to gather specific facts. Students should indicate that those would be good strategies for them to use as well.

4 Ask students to summarize one of the differences stated in this section.
  Possible Response: Most people in Japan get to work by using public transportation. In the United States, most people drive cars.

5 Ask students to suggest other key words that could signal a transition.
  Possible Responses: However; Not all; In the United States

6 Ask students to identify the sentence that summarizes the significant differences between the two countries.

Answer: The differences in transportation and shopping help to make each culture unique.

7 Ask students what the student writer has learned from living in two countries.

Possible Responses: The writer has learned that people are similar, no matter where you go.

Differences in transportation lead to differences in shopping styles. Both Japanese and American people buy most of their groceries in stores. However, the Japanese shop for food items at individual stores. There are many small shops, which usually sell just one thing. There are fish stores, butchers, or bakeries. Many of these small shops are open in the front and are just a few feet from the street. Every day, Japanese people shop for their supper. The shop owners call out to invite people to buy. Taking public transportation doesn't let people "stock up" as Americans do with their big cars. In the United States, many Americans shop just once a week. Storing food in large refrigerators and freezers allows them to plan ahead for a week or more.

Another way to shop in Japan is by vending machine. Vending machines are very popular because it's easy for people taking public transportation to use them. There is probably one on every street corner. Similar to the United States, the vending machines in Japan hold drinks. Soda and tea are common, but some machines have soup. Iced coffee and tea are Japanese favorites. In contrast, there are fewer vending machines in the United States. There are also fewer drink choices in the machines that do exist.

The differences in transportation and shopping help to make each culture unique. But these are not the only things. Japan is a very traditional society that has worked hard to take care of the large number of people living in such a small place. The United States is a very young country with plenty of space. However, having lived in both places, one thing I have learned is that people are people wherever you go. The language and styles may be different, but the people are the same. The friends I have made in the United States are very much like my friends in Japan—loyal, smart, and willing to help me learn more about the beauty of a country.

6 The conclusion summarizes significant differences.

7 The writer shows the importance of the comparison.

Mini Lesson Viewing and Representing

PICTURING TEXT STRUCTURE

Instruction One way to structure a good comparison-and-contrast essay is to have students complete a Venn diagram showing the unique features of each subject and the things the subjects have in common.

Activity Have students analyze the organization of the student model by constructing a Venn diagram to illustrate how the writer organized the essay, such as in the sample shown here.

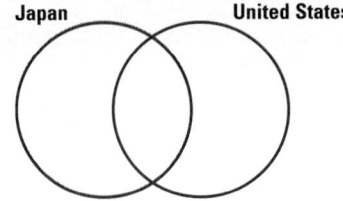

Use **Reading and Critical Thinking Transparencies**, p. 35, for additional support.

Writing Your Comparison-and-Contrast Essay

❶ Prewriting

People compare things for different reasons. **List** stories or characters you want to better understand. See the **Idea Bank** in the margin for more suggestions. After you have selected your two subjects, follow the steps below.

Planning Your Comparison-and-Contrast Essay

▶ **1. Decide on your purpose.** Why do you want to compare and contrast your two subjects? Do you want to understand something better? Do you want to make a decision?

▶ **2. Look at key features of your subjects.** Which do you want to focus on? Which comparisons will help you?

▶ **3. Generate similarities and differences.** Use a Venn diagram or a chart to come up with similarities and differences.

Feature	Similar	Different
population	both have large populations	in Japan, more crowded because less land
transportation	both have public transportation	fewer Japanese own cars

▶ **4. Plan your organization.** Choose one of two methods. You might discuss all of the features of subject A first. Then follow with subject B. This is the **subject-by-subject** method. The second way is the **feature-by-feature** approach. Look at one feature of subject A, then subject B, the next feature of subject A, then subject B, and so on.

Subject by Subject	Feature by Feature
Subject A	Feature 1
feature 1	subject A
feature 2	subject B
Subject B	Feature 2
feature 1	subject A
feature 2	subject B

❷ Drafting

Once you know what features you will be comparing, you can begin to draft your essay. Use **transitions** to link your ideas and to signal which features are similar and which are different. **Begin a new paragraph** for each subject, if using the subject-by-subject approach, or for each feature, if using the feature-by-feature method.

Ask Your Peer Reader: EVALUATING

- Was my reason for comparison clear?
- Did I support my statements with facts and examples?
- Is my organization consistent?

IDEABank

1. Your Working Portfolio 📄
Look for ideas in the **Interdisciplinary Projects** that you completed earlier in this unit.

Compare Myths, p. 787
Compare Versions, p.819
Compare Tales, p. 843
Compare Characters, p. 857

2. Inventions
Set out to compare products new and old, such as CDs with records, or videos with filmstrips. Ask family members for help in getting ideas for writing your comparison.

3. Favorite Activities
Compare and contrast features of two of your favorite hobbies or sports or other activities.

Have a question?

See the **Writing Handbook.**
Transitions, p. R28
Elaboration, p. R29
Compare and Contrast, p. R35

Guiding Student Writing

Prewriting

Choosing two subjects to compare

If after reading the Idea Bank students have difficulty choosing subjects for their comparison-and-contrast essay, suggest they try the following:

- go back to the brainstormed lists of subjects from the beginning of the lesson
- think about people, places, and things in their own lives that interest them
- share ideas with a partner

Planning Your Comparison-and-Contrast Essay

1. Tell students that their essay will be more meaningful if they have a reason for comparing and contrasting two subjects. Help them to think about what those reasons might be.

2. Ask students to brainstorm some of the similarities and differences. Then have them focus in on a couple that will help them achieve their chosen purpose. This will make each student's essay easier to write because it will be more focused.

3. Ask students to work individually to complete a Venn diagram or chart listing the similarities and differences for the features they have decided on. Remind them to keep it simple and focused on their purpose.

4. Remind them of the student sample and the discussion held earlier concerning feature-by-feature and subject-by-subject organizational methods. Use the graphic to help students think about which method may be best for their essay.

Drafting

Once students have completed their Venn diagram or chart and decided on the organization pattern, they should be ready to write their first draft.

Revising
ELABORATING WITH EXAMPLES AND OTHER DETAILS

Look at the two examples given, and help students to see how much more powerful the sentences with examples and details are. Ask for a volunteer to share a sentence from his or her essay. Model how to elaborate using examples and details. Ask students to work with a partner to elaborate in their own essays.

Editing and Proofreading
COMPARING WITH ADJECTIVES

Ask students to read through their own essays looking for comparative and superlative forms of adjectives. Have them check to see if they've used the forms correctly and to edit as necessary.

Reflecting

Encourage students to be specific in reflecting about their essay writing. Ask them to describe what they learned in detail and to suggest other subjects they would like to explore.

Option
Teaching Tip

It is sometimes difficult for students to compare and contrast subjects in a meaningful way. It may be helpful for you to think about authentic purposes for writing comparison-and-contrast essays and to include these suggestions early in the essay writing process. For example, if students choose to compare two books, the purpose might be to provide classmates with information about the books so that they could choose one of them for a particular class assignment.

Need revising help?

Review the **Rubric**, p. 858

Consider **peer reader** comments

Check **Revision Guidelines**, p. R23

SPELLING
From Writing

As you revise your work, look back at the words you misspelled and determine why you made the errors you did. For additional help, refer to the strategies and generalizations in the **Spelling Handbook** on page R86.

Unclear about comparatives and superlatives?

See the **Grammar Handbook**, p. R70

Publishing
IDEAS

- Make a chart to show the differences and similarities between your subjects, and present your essay as a speech.
- Print out your essay on the computer and insert diagrams and illustrations to help emphasize important points. Hang your essay on the bulletin board.

More Online:
Publishing Options
www.mcdougallittell.com

---

❸ Revising
TARGET SKILL ▶ ELABORATING WITH EXAMPLES AND OTHER DETAILS When making comparisons, you must provide examples and other details to support your statements. Giving one example may save several sentences of explanation and allow your reader to visualize what you are saying. For example, instead of simply saying that one movie was better than another, you might describe the reaction of the audience: *Everyone yawned through the first movie.*

> In Japan, most people don't have cars. Therefore, public transportation, such as subways and trains, must be convenient.∧ *There are 12 different subway lines with over 125 train stations in Tokyo alone.*

❹ Editing and Proofreading
TARGET SKILL ▶ COMPARING WITH ADJECTIVES Adjectives such as *fast, faster,* and *fastest* are used to signal a comparison. The comparative form of the adjective is usually created by adding –*er*. If you are comparing more than two items, use the superlative form by adding –*est* to the adjective. Some adjectives have irregular comparative or superlative forms, while some show degrees of comparison when the word *less, least, more,* or *most* is placed before them.

> As a result, it is ~~more quiet~~ *quieter*, even in cities.

❺ Reflecting
FOR YOUR WORKING PORTFOLIO What did you learn about your subjects by comparing them? What other subjects would you like to compare and contrast? Attach your answers to your finished essay. Save your comparison-and-contrast essay in your **Working Portfolio.**

Assessment Practice Revising & Editing

Read this passage from the first draft of a comparison-and-contrast essay. The underlined sections may include the following kinds of errors:

- **unclear pronoun referents**
- **lack of subject-verb agreement**
- **incorrect plural nouns**
- **errors in comparative and superlative forms: adjectives**

For each underlined section, choose the revision that most improves the writing.

> There are many differences between the book and the movie version of *Father, Dancing*. The book has stronger characters whose <u>personalities</u> are fully developed. The director of the movie must have thought ⁽¹⁾ that having big-name actors would make up for a lack of character development. The plot of the book is also <u>best</u> than the one in the movie, ₍₂₎ because <u>some scenes they leave out are important</u>. On the other hand, ₍₃₎ the movie has flashy special effects. However, <u>effects has less meaning</u> ₍₄₎ than plot. In my opinion, the <u>book is</u> more interesting than the movie, ₍₅₎ even though the movie was <u>the more expensive</u> production in the history ₍₆₎ of Hollywood.

1. **A.** personalities'
   B. personalitys
   C. personality's
   D. Correct as is

2. **A.** better
   B. more good
   C. most good
   D. Correct as is

3. **A.** some scenes the movie leaves out are important.
   B. some scenes the book leaves out are important.
   C. some scenes we leave out are important.
   D. Correct as is

4. **A.** effects had less meaning
   B. effects has had less meaning
   C. effects have less meaning
   D. Correct as is

5. **A.** book are
   B. book were
   C. books were
   D. Correct as is

6. **A.** the expensivest
   B. the most expensive
   C. the expensiver
   D. Correct as is

Need extra help?

See the **Grammar Handbook.**

Making Subjects and Verbs Agree, p. R60

Using Nouns and Pronouns, p. R63

Using Modifiers Effectively, p. R70

WRITING WORKSHOP **863**

Ask students to read the entire passage prior to correcting the errors. Then demonstrate how students can eliminate incorrect choices for the first question.

An apostrophe is used to show possession or in a contraction. There is no possession in this sentence, and there are no contractions, so no apostrophe is needed. Therefore A and C are incorrect. When making a word plural that ends in *y*, the *y* is changed to *i* and *-es* is added. Therefore, B is incorrect. The correct response is D.

Answers:
1. D, 2. A, 3. A, 4. C, 5. D, 6. B

 Grammar

SUBJECT-VERB AGREEMENT
Instruction Remind students that the subject and verb in every sentence must agree in number. A subject and verb agree in number when they are both singular or both plural. Singular verbs usually end in *s* or *es*. Singular nouns do not usually end in *s* or *es*. Display the following examples:
In Japan, <u>workers</u> <u>ride</u> the train to their jobs.

In the United States, my <u>father</u> <u>drives</u> his car to work.
Make sure students understand that *workers* and *ride* are both plural, and that *father* and *drives* are both singular.
Application Ask students to write five sentences summarizing what they learned from writing their comparison-and-contrast essays. Ask them to underline the subject and verb in

each sentence and to check for subject-verb agreement.

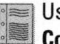 Use **Grammar Transparencies and Copymasters**, p. 115, for more practice.

 Use McDougal Littell's *Language Network*, Chapter 7, for more practice in subject-verb agreement.

WRITING WORKSHOP **863**

Objectives
- reflect on and assess student understanding of the unit
- assess and build portfolios

Reflecting on the Theme

OPTION 1

A successful response will
- identify at least five heroic characters from the folk tales in this unit.
- include a web showing the qualities and actions of the most heroic character.
- present a brief essay explaining why the student chose the character he or she did.

OPTION 2

A successful response will
- identify themes evident in the folk tales in this unit.
- explore one lesson from the unit and explain why the student thinks it stands out the most.

Building Your Portfolio

Literature Connections
Students should evaluate the pieces in their Working Portfolios and choose one that represents their highest quality work for their Presentation Portfolios. As students write the note to attach to the item, remind them to respond to the literature that inspired the writing and express their reasons for selecting this piece.

Setting Goals
Students may wish to look back through the unit to help them identify the authors and cultures they want to learn more about.

Across Cultures: The Oral Tradition

In this unit, you discovered that tales from the past explore universal themes. Across cultures and generations, these stories continue to delight, inspire, and teach readers and listeners. To show what you have learned, complete one or more of the following options.

Reflecting on Theme

OPTION 1

Studying Heroes With a partner, identify at least five characters who act as heroes in the folklore you have read. Then choose the character who you think displays the most heroic qualities. Make a web like the one shown. On one side, list this character's heroic traits. On the other side of the web, list the actions taken by the character that demonstrate these qualities. Use your web to help you write a brief essay explaining why you chose the character you did.

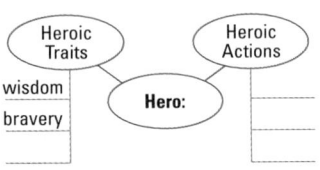

OPTION 2

Self Assessment Use the **Table of Contents** for Unit Six on pages 768–769 to recall what themes are present in the folklore you've read. What one lesson in the tales stands out the most? Why? Respond in your ▢ READER'S NOTEBOOK.

◁ Building Your Portfolio

- **Literature Connections** Select an example of your work for a Literature Connection that you would like to talk about. Perhaps you wrote a script based on a tale, wrote an instruction manual for a board game, or designed a book jacket. In a note, comment on what you enjoyed about creating the work. Explain how the literature you read inspired you. Add the example and the note to your **Presentation Portfolio.** ◁

- **Setting Goals** As you completed the activities in this unit, you probably found certain selections that you really liked. Which author's work would you like to find out more about? Which cultures are you curious about? Which would you like to continue to explore? Write your goals for further reading and research in your ▢ READER'S NOTEBOOK.

Introduction to Mythology

The gods and goddesses, warriors, and heroes of world mythology appear and reappear in literature and films. Here are their origins—presented by scholars and storytellers, from Bullfinch to San Souci. This volume begins with Greek and Roman myths, and travels the globe. Maps, diagrams, and time lines add context. Part of the *NexText* series from McDougal Littell, the book comes with online activities at **www.nextext.com**.

Other Collections

Cinderella
COLLECTED BY JUDY SIERRA
Cinderella in many different cultures
(*Links to* **In the Land of Small Dragon**)

Moon Was Tired of Walking on Air
RETOLD BY NATALIA M. BELTING
Origin myths of South America
(*Links to* **The Disobedient Child**)

Fairy Tales from the Brothers Grimm
COLLECTED BY NEIL PHILLIP
An illustrated edition of these classic tales
(*Links to* **King Thrushbeard**)

The Girl Who Married the Moon
TOLD BY JOSEPH BRUCHAC & GAYLE ROSS
Legends of Native American heroines
(*Links to* **Where the Girl Rescued Her Brother**)

A Ring of Tricksters
RETOLD BY VIRGINIA HAMILTON
Tales of wit and cunning
(*Links to* **Why Monkeys Live in Trees** and **The Frog Who Wanted to Be a Singer**)

Informative Nonfiction

Trinidad and Tobago
BY PATTI UROSEVICH
(*Links to* **The Bamboo Beads**)

The Puerto Ricans
BY JEROME J. ALIOTTA
(*Links to* **The Legend of Hummingbird**)

Ancient China
BY BRIAN WILLIAMS
(*Links to* **The Living Kuan-yin**)

Be a Friend: The Story of African American Music in Song, Words, and Pictures
BY LEOTHA STANLEY
(*Links to* **The Frog Who Wanted to Be a Singer**)

The Cheyennes
BY VIRGINIA DRIVING HAWK SNEVE
(*Links to* **Where the Girl Rescued Her Brother**)

Other Media

American Fairy Tales
From Rip Van Winkle to the Rootabaga Stories
Audio Bookshelf (AUDIOCASSETTE)

Jim Henson's The Storyteller
A storyteller recounts legendary tales.
Jim Henson Productions (VIDEO SERIES)

Legends of the Americas
Illustrated legends of the Maya, Aztec, and Inca
Troll Associates (CD-ROM)

Just So Stories
Kipling's pourquoi tales
Blackstone Audio Books (AUDIOCASSETTE)

My Land Sings: Stories from the Rio Grande
RETOLD BY RUDOLFO ANAYA
Folk tales of the Southwestern United States

Student *Resource Bank*

Words to Know: Access Guide

insolent, 817
instinct, 270
intact, 721
intricate, 732
intrusion, 277
invisible, 29
isolated, 773

J

jalopy, 266

L

laden, 279
lagoon, 126
leisurely, 530
lethargy, 44
listlessly, 583
loftily, 577
luminous, 471

M

magnification, 467
maneuver, 158
mannequin, 670
mantle, 836
margin, 139
marred, 670
marvel, 160
mascot, 252
maze, 772
melancholy, 452
menace, 169
menial, 105
merge, 118
modest, 679
momentum, 620
mope, 423

mortification, 682
mourn, 549
murmur, 798

N

naive, 637
nonchalantly, 577
novelty, 168

O

obnoxious, 679
obscure, 777
obsess, 40
obstinacy, 779
oxygen, 118

P

palatial, 223
pantomime, 539
peal, 334
peer, 679
penetrate, 484
perish, 535
persist, 384
petty, 544
phosphorus, 130
pious, 278
poised, 672
pompous, 278
ponder, 73
practical, 670
predator, 167
premise, 375
preservation, 733
prey, 383
procedure, 374
proclaim, 731

profile, 420
prop, 405
proposition, 106
prosper, 374
pummel, 62

Q

quest, 550
quiver, 405

R

ravishing, 811
reef, 126
regain, 484
reign, 782
relentless, 405
remotely, 224
repentance, 384
reproduction, 732
resentful, 105
reservation, 375
resilient, 214
restore, 710
retort, 56
reveal, 384
ricocheted, 158
rival, 55
rivet, 458
ruddy, 670
rummaging, 169

S

sanitation, 637
savor, 214
scavenging, 167
scornful, 576
seasoned, 156

sector, 576
sentiment, 384
sentinel, 723
shrine, 704
shunned, 224
smirk, 405
smugly, 59
sonar, 468
spectator, 156
splendor, 486
stalemate, 42
stamina, 102
status, 369
stereotype, 221
stoop, 251
straddle, 60
subside, 673
succeed, 383
succulent, 816
sudden, 29
sufficient, 139
surpass, 731
surplus, 266
surveyor, 106
suspicion, 59
swoop, 420
systematically, 720

T

taboo, 224
tangible, 383
tedious, 722
tenement, 223
tentative, 616
terrorist, 421
thatched, 483
thrashing, 250
threaten, 117
tinder, 116

Pronunciation Key

Symbol	Examples	Symbol	Examples	Symbol	Examples
ă	at, gas	m	man, seem	v	van, save
ā	ape, day	n	night, mitten	w	web, twice
ä	father, barn	ng	sing, anger	y	yard, lawyer
âr	fair, dare	ŏ	odd, not	z	zoo, reason
b	bell, table	ō	open, road, grow	zh	treasure, garage
ch	chin, lunch	ô	awful, bought, horse	ə	awake, even, pencil,
d	dig, bored	oi	coin, boy		pilot, focus
ĕ	egg, ten	oŏ	look, full	ər	perform, letter
ē	evil, see, meal	ōō	root, glue, through		
f	fall, laugh, phrase	ou	out, cow		**Sounds in Foreign Words**
g	gold, big	p	pig, cap	KH	*German* ich, auch;
h	hit, inhale	r	rose, star		*Scottish* loch
hw	white, everywhere	s	sit, face	N	*French* entre, bon, fin
ĭ	inch, fit	sh	she, mash	œ	*French* feu, cœur;
ī	idle, my, tried	t	tap, hopped		*German* schön
îr	dear, here	th	thing, with	ü	*French* utile, rue;
j	jar, gem, badge	*th*	then, other		*German* grün
k	keep, cat, luck	ŭ	up, nut		
l	load, rattle	ûr	fur, earn, bird, worm		

Stress Marks

′ This mark indicates that the preceding syllable receives the primary stress. For example, in the word *language,* the first syllable is stressed: lăng′gwĭj.

′ This mark is used only in words in which more than one syllable is stressed. It indicates that the preceding syllable is stressed, but somewhat more weakly than the syllable receiving the primary stress. In the word *literature,* for example, the first syllable receives the primary stress, and the last syllable receives a weaker stress: lĭt′ər-ə-chŏŏr′.

Adapted from *The American Heritage Dictionary of the English Language, Third Edition;* Copyright © 1992 by Houghton Mifflin Company. Used with the permission of Houghton Mifflin Company.

Glossary of Literary and Reading Terms

Act An act is a major unit of action in a play. *The Phantom Tollbooth,* for example, has two acts. An act may be divided into smaller sections, called scenes.

See page 319.
See also **Scene.**

Alliteration Alliteration is a repetition of consonant sounds at the beginning of words. Poets and songwriters use alliteration for emphasis or to add a musical quality. Notice the repetition of the *r* sound in the following lines:

> We rush into a rain
> That rattles double glass.
>
> —Theodore Roethke, from "Night Journey"

See page 191.

Allusion An allusion is a reference to a famous person, place, event, or work of literature. In *The Story of My Life,* Helen Keller makes an allusion to the Hebrew Bible when she says that learning about words made the world blossom for her "like Aaron's rod, with flowers."

Analogy An analogy is a point-by-point comparison between two different things in order to clarify the less familiar of the two. In "Abd al-Rahman Ibrahima," the author uses an analogy in writing about African history:

> . . . The Africans came from many countries, and from many cultures. Like the Native Americans, they established their territories based on centuries of tradition.
>
> —Walter Dean Myers, from "Abd al-Rahman Ibrahima"

Analyzing Analyzing is the process of breaking something down into its elements so that they can be examined individually. In analyzing a poem, for example, one might consider such elements as form, sound, figurative language, imagery, speaker, word choice, and theme.

Anecdote An anecdote is a short, entertaining account of a person or an event. Anecdotes are often included in larger works to amuse readers or to make a point. In "Chinatown," Laurence Yep tells an anecdote about a kickball game to illustrate his feeling of being "shunned and invisible. . . ."

See page 161.

Audience The audience of a piece of writing is the particular group of readers that the writer is addressing. A writer considers his or her audience when deciding on a subject, a purpose for writing, and the tone and style in which to write.

See page 416.

Author's perspective An author's perspective refers to an author's beliefs and attitudes. These beliefs may be influenced by such factors as the author's political views, religion, upbringing, and education. In "Bringing the Prairie Home," the author reveals her attachment to the very soil of the prairie, where she grew up.

> The Earth is like a character who has secrets; the Earth holds important clues to who we are, who we've been; who we will be.
>
> —Patricia MacLachlan, from "Bringing the Prairie Home"

See pages 161–162, 363, 684.

Author's purpose An author's purpose is his or her reason for creating a particular work. The purpose may be to entertain, to inform, to express an opinion, or to persuade readers to do or believe something. An author may have more than one purpose for writing, but usually one is most important.

See pages 142, 409, 424, 611, 676.

Autobiography An autobiography is the true story of a person's life, told by that person. Because autobiographies tell about real people and events, they are a form of nonfiction. Autobiographies are usually told from the first-person point of view. Helen Keller's *The Story of My Life* is an autobiography. The excerpts from *Looking Back* are considered memoir, a specific type of autobiography. A memoir relates the author's personal experiences and may be less formal in tone. Journals and diaries are other types of autobiographical writing.

See pages 97, 142, 170, 362–363, 385.

Ballad A ballad is a poem that tells a story and is meant to be sung or recited. "Barbara Frietchie" is an example of a ballad.

Biographer Anyone writing or having written a biography, or life story, of another person.

See also **Biography.**

Biography A biography is the true story of a person's life, written by another person. Because biographies tell about real people and events, they are a form of nonfiction. Biographies are usually told from the third-person point of view. "Matthew Henson at the Top of the World" is an example of biography.

See pages 97, 111, 362–363, 378.

Cast of characters In the script of a play, a cast of characters lists all the characters. It is usually found at the beginning, and the characters are usually listed in the order they appear.

See pages 319, 324.

Cause and effect Two events are related as cause and effect if one brings about—or causes—the other. The event that happens first is the cause; the one that follows from it is the effect. Writers sometimes signal cause-and-effect relationships with words and phrases such as *because, therefore, since, so that,* and *in order that.* This sentence from *Woodsong* deals with a cause and its effect: "Because we feed processed meat to the dogs, there is always the smell of meat over the kennel."

See pages 76, 446, 459, 674.

Character Each person, animal, or imaginary creature in a work of literature is a character. The most important characters are called main characters. Less important characters are called minor characters. In "The School Play," Robert is the main character, and Belinda and the others are minor characters. In good stories, characters have traits, motivations, and relationships that the reader cares about. Often, the main character will undergo a change as the plot unfolds.

See pages 23, 31, 45, 243–244, 319, 698.
See also **Characterization.**

Character development Characters that undergo change during a story are said to have character development. A character that changes significantly is called a dynamic character; one that changes only a little or not at all is static. Main characters often develop the most. For example, in "President Cleveland, Where Are You?" Jerry changes from acting selfishly to acting on behalf of others. Armand begins and remains a responsible role model.

Characterization The way a writer creates and develops characters' personalities is known as characterization. A writer can develop a character in four basic ways.

1. By describing the character physically
2. By presenting the character's thoughts, speech, and actions
3. By presenting the thoughts, speech, and actions of other characters
4. By directly commenting on the character's nature

See pages 245, 257, 661.
See also **Character.**

Chronological order Chronological order is the order in which events happen in time. In some stories and articles, events are related in chronological order. Other stories jump forward and backward in time.

See pages 121, 364, 378.

Cinderella tale A Cinderella tale is a version of the Cinderella story, often containing elements such as a mistreated stepchild, and a rags-to-riches plot. Cinderella tales are found in folklore all over the world. "In the Land of Small Dragon" is an example of a Cinderella tale from Vietnam.

Clarifying Clarifying is the process of stopping while reading to quickly review what has been read and to check for understanding. Clarifying helps readers keep track of events, characters, and their significance or meaning.

See pages 4, 385, 740.

Climax In a story or play, the climax, or turning point, is the point of greatest interest. At the climax, the outcome of the story becomes clear. The climax of "Tuesday of the Other June" occurs when June T. says *No* to the Other June with such strength that the astonished bully leaves her alone.

See pages 22, 319, 443, 488.
See also **Plot.**

Comedy A comedy is a dramatic work that is light and often humorous. Usually it ends happily with a peaceful resolution of the main conflict. *The Phantom Tollbooth* is an example of a comedy.

See also **Drama.**

Comparison To point out what two or more things have in common is to make a comparison. Writers use comparisons to make ideas and details clearer to readers. In "Eleven," for example, the process of growing older is compared to little wooden dolls that fit together, one inside another.

See also **Metaphor; Simile.**

Conclusion Drawing conclusions means paying attention to details in a literary work and putting these details together to create a larger meaning. Readers draw conclusions by using information from the literature and from their own experiences.

See pages 163, 613, 633.

Concrete poetry In a concrete poem, the arrangement of the poem's words on the page reflects the poem's subject. Note how the lines in Frank Asch's poem "Saguaro" resemble a saguaro cactus.

See page 19.

Conflict Conflict is a struggle between opposing forces. Almost every story is built around a conflict faced by the main character. An external conflict is a struggle between a character and an outside force, such as society, nature, or another character. In *Woodsong,* Gary Paulsen faces an external conflict with a bear. An internal conflict is a struggle within a character's mind. It may occur when the character has to make decision or to deal with opposing feelings. Jerry's uncertainty in "President Cleveland, Where Are You?" about how to spend his money is an internal conflict.

See pages 22, 132, 319, 445.
See also **Plot.**

Connecting When readers relate the content of a literary work to what they already know or have experienced, they are connecting. Connecting helps readers identify with the experiences of the characters. For example, when they read Sandra Cisneros's story "Eleven," readers may remember times when they felt embarrassed or falsely accused.

See pages 4, 31, 281, 346.

Connotation Connotation refers to the ideas and feelings associated with a word, in contrast to the word's denotation, or dictionary definition. For example, the word *mother*, in addition to its basic meaning ("a female parent"), has a connotation of love, warmth, and security.

See page 742.

Context clues Unfamiliar words are often surrounded by words or phrases—called context—that help readers understand their meaning. A context clue may be a definition, a synonym, an example, a comparison or contrast, or any expression that enables readers to infer the word's meaning.

See page 79.

Contrast To contrast is to point out differences between things. Note how the narrator of "The All-American Slurp" contrasts Chinese and American eating habits:

> In fact we didn't use individual plates at all but picked up food from the platters in the middle of the table and brought it directly to our rice bowls.
>
> —Lensey Namioka,
> from "The All-American Slurp"

Couplet A couplet is a rhymed pair of lines in a poem. The poem "Barbara Frietchie" consists entirely of couplets.

See page 740.

Deductive reasoning In nonfiction, the structure of a text may be organized using deductive reasoning. Deductive reasoning is the process of logical reasoning from principles to specific instances; reasoning from whole to part. A text that is organized deductively begins with a generalization and advances with facts and evidence to a conclusion.

See also **Inductive reasoning; Structure.**

Denotation A word's denotation is its dictionary definition.

See page 742.
See also **Connotation.**

Description Description is the process by which a writer uses words to create a picture of a scene, an event, or a character. To create descriptions, writers choose details carefully—usually details that appeal to readers' senses of sight, sound, smell, touch, and taste. Note the details in this passage from "Tuesday of the Other June" about the main character's new home:

> We went into the house, down a dim, cool hall. In our new apartment, the wooden floors clicked under our shoes, and my mother showed me everything. Her voice echoed in the empty rooms.
>
> —Norma Fox Mazer,
> from "Tuesday of the Other June"

See page 272.

Dialect A dialect is the particular use of language spoken in a definite place by a distinct group of people. Writers use dialect to establish setting and to develop characters.

Dialogue The words that characters speak aloud are called dialogue. Dialogue moves a plot forward and reveals the personalities of the characters. In a play, dialogue is the main way the writer tells the story. The dialogue in fiction is usually set off with quotation marks. No quotation marks are used for the dialogue in plays.

See pages 320, 337.

Diction See **Word Choice.**

Drama A drama, or play, is a form of literature meant to be performed before an audience. Dramas for stage are also called theater. In a drama, the story is presented through the dialogue and the actions of the characters. The written form of a drama is known as a script. A script usually includes dialogue, a cast of characters, and stage directions that give specific instructions about performing the play. Two important kinds of drama are comedy and tragedy. A comedy is light and humorous; a tragedy ends in disaster—most often death—for the main character and often for other important characters as well.

See pages 317–320, 321.
See also **Act; Cast of Characters; Comedy; Dialogue; Playwright; Prop; Scene; Script; Stage directions; Tragedy.**

Drawing conclusions See **Conclusion.**

Dynamic character A character in a literary work that changes significantly during the course of events is called a dynamic character.

See also, **Character development.**

Epic poetry An epic poem is a long narrative poem about the adventures of a hero. Epic poetry addresses universal concerns such as good and evil, life and death, and other serious subjects.

Essay An essay is a short work of nonfiction that deals with a single subject. The purpose of an essay may be to express ideas or feelings, to analyze a topic, to inform, to entertain, or to persuade. "All I Really Need to Know I Learned in Kindergarten" is an example of a personal essay, in which Robert Fulghum expresses his ideas by reflecting on incidents in his own life.

See pages 98, 473, 640.

Evaluating Evaluating is the process of judging the quality of something or someone. In evaluating a literary work, you might focus on the elements found in that type of work—for example, the plot, setting, characters, and theme of a work of fiction. You can also evaluate a work by comparing and contrasting it with similar works.

See pages 4, 216.

Exaggeration An overstating of an idea is called exaggeration. Avi uses exaggeration in "Scout's Honor" when he says a character who tripped "took off like an F-36 fighter plane."

Exposition In fiction, the plot normally begins with exposition. In the early part of the story, the exposition sets the tone, establishes the setting, introduces the characters, and gives the reader important background information. In "All Summer in a Day," the exposition leads up to the time when Margot tells her classmates about her memories of the sun.

See also **Plot.**

External conflict See **Conflict.**

Fable A fable is a brief story that teaches a lesson about life. In many fables, the characters are animals that act and speak like human beings. A fable often ends with a moral—a statement that summarizes its lesson. "The Wolf and the House Dog" is an example of a fable.

See also **Moral.**

Fact and opinion A fact is a statement that can be proved, such as "Mars is the fourth planet from the sun." An opinion, in contrast, is a statement that expresses a person's feelings, such as "Mars is the most beautiful planet." Opinions cannot be proved.

See pages 227, 699, 711.

Falling action In the plot of a story, the falling action occurs after the climax. Sometimes called the resolution, during the falling action conflicts are resolved and any loose ends are tied up. In "Ghost of the Lagoon," the falling action begins after Mako throws his spear into Tupa's side.

See pages 22, 443, 488.
See also Climax; Plot.

Fantasy Literature that contains at least one fantastic or unreal element is called fantasy. The setting of a work of fantasy might be a totally imaginary world, or it might be a realistic place where very unusual or impossible things happen. *The Phantom Tollbooth* is a work of fantasy.

See pages 507–510, 552, 561.

Fiction A narrative story that uses made-up or untrue characters or events is called fiction. In some works of fiction, the entire story is made up; in others, the story is based in part on real people or events. Fiction includes both short stories and novels. A short story can usually be read in one sitting. Novels are longer and tend to be more complex.

See pages 21–24, 25.
See also Character; Historical fiction; Novel; Plot; Realistic fiction; Science fiction; Setting; Short story; Theme.

Figurative Language In figurative language, words are used to express more than their dictionary meaning. Figurative language conveys vivid images. In this passage from "The Circuit," note how the figurative language helps create a picture of working in the fields:

> The sun kept beating down. The buzzing insects, the wet sweat, and the hot dry dust made the afternoon seem to last forever. Finally the mountains around the valley reached out and swallowed the sun.
>
> —Francisco Jiménez, from "The Circuit"

See pages 192, 198, 216, 648.
See also Metaphor; Personification; Simile.

First-person point of view See *Point of View.*

Flashback A flashback is a conversation, an episode, or an event that happened before the beginning of the story. Often a flashback interrupts the chronological flow of a story to give the reader information to help in understanding a character's situation. "Crow Call" has a flashback that tells how the narrator got her shirt:

> My father had bought the shirt for me. In town to buy groceries, he had noticed my hesitating in front of Kronenberg's window. . . .
>
> —Lois Lowry, from "Crow Call"

Folklore The traditions, customs, and stories that are passed down within a culture are known as its folklore. Folklore includes various types of literature, such as legends, folk tales, myths, and fables.

See also Fable; Folk Tale; Legend; Myth.

Folk tale A folk tale is a simple story that has been passed down from generation to generation by word of mouth. Folk tales are usually about people, animals, or occurrences in nature and are usually set in times long past. They may include fantastical elements, like the talking animals in "Why Monkeys Live in Trees."

Foreshadowing A hint about an event that will occur later in a story is called foreshadowing. In "Lob's Girl," a stormy night foreshadows the car accident that puts Sandy in a coma.

See page 459.

Form The form of a poem is the shape the words and lines make on the page. Form is determined by the length and placement of the lines and how the lines are grouped as stanzas. "Analysis of Baseball" contains very short lines set in long stanzas. A poet may use the form of a poem to emphasize the poem's meaning. In concrete poetry, for example, the poem's shape reflects its subject.

See page 190.
See also **Genre.**

Free Verse Poetry without regular patterns of rhyme or rhythm is called free verse. Free verse can sometimes sound like conversation. Note the natural flow of the following example of free verse:

> When the bird comes
> if it comes
> observe the deepest silence
> wait for the bird to enter the cage
>
> —Jacques Prévert,
> from "How to Paint the Portrait of a Bird"

See pages 190, 198.

Generalization A generalization is a statement about a whole group. Generalizations may be untrue if they are too broad or not based on fact. For example, the statement "All Americans slurp" is a generalization. The word *all* makes the generalization untrue.

See page 473.

Genre Literature is normally divided into four main categories, or genres: fiction, nonfiction, poetry, and drama.

Haiku Haiku is a traditional form of Japanese poetry. A haiku normally has three lines and describes a single moment, feeling, or thing. In a traditional haiku, the first and third lines contain five syllables each, and the second line contains seven syllables.

See page 207.

Historical fiction Historical fiction is fiction that is set in the past. It may contain references to actual people and significant events in history. This description from the short story "The Dog of Pompeii" is true to historical fact:

> The earthquake of twelve years ago had brought down all the old structures, and since the citizens of Pompeii were ambitious to rival Naples and even Rome, they had seized the opportunity to rebuild the whole town.
>
> —Louis Untermeyer, from "The Dog of Pompeii"

See pages 697–698, 711.

Humor The quality that makes something funny is called humor. Writers create humor using exaggeration, word play, sarcasm, witty dialogue, unlikely comparisons, and other devices. In "Scout's Honor," the narrator describes the subway system map as looking "like a noodle factory hit by a bomb."

See pages 409, 424.

Idiom An idiom is an expression that has meaning different from the meaning of its individual words. For example, "go to the dogs" is an idiom meaning "fall into ruin."

Imagery Words that appeal to readers' senses are referred to as imagery. Writers usually try to describe places, characters, and events in ways that help readers imagine how they look, feel, smell, sound, and taste. In *Words on a Page*, Lenore uses imagery in the essay she reads to her class.

> And there was the beaver and the loon and the hawk circling above the treetops. And below the trout and the sturgeon slipped silently through the black water. . . . She felt the morning sun on her face and the gentle rocking of the canoe and smiled because she knew that here would always be her home.
>
> Keith Leckie, from *Words on a Page*

See pages 192, 415.

Inductive reasoning In nonfiction, the structure of a text may be organized using inductive reasoning. Inductive reasoning is the process of determining principles by logic or observation; reasoning from specific parts to whole situations. A text that is organized inductively begins with examples of specific cases. It advances by drawing logical conclusions and ends with a statement of a logical generalization.

See also **Deductive reasoning; Structure.**

Inference An inference is a logical statement based on evidence. Good readers make inferences, or draw conclusions, as they read—trying to figure out more than the words say. The evidence may be facts the writer provides, or it may be experiences from a reader's own life. For example, readers of "Chinatown" can make inferences about why the narrator felt disgraceful for not excelling at sports.

See pages 198, 272, 395, 661.

Informative nonfiction Informative nonfiction is writing that provides factual information about real people, places, and events. "Summer of Fire" is an example of informative nonfiction. Newspaper and magazine articles, pamphlets, history and science textbooks, and encyclopedia articles are other examples of informative nonfiction.

See pages 99, 121, 725.

Internal conflict See **Conflict.**

Interview An interview is a meeting, or virtual meeting, in which one person asks another about personal matters, professional matters, or both. Interviews may be tape-recorded, filmed, or recorded in writing. The author study for Lois Lowry includes an interview with her.

See page 99.

Irony Irony is a contrast between what is expected and what actually exists or happens. For example, readers of "The Fun They Had" may find it unexpected and ironic that the main character in the story, which is set in the year 2157, longs for the good old days when children went to school together in classrooms and passed in their homework to a teacher. The following description contains irony:

> She was thinking about the old schools they had when her grandfather's grandfather was a little boy. All the kids from the neighborhood came, laughing and shouting in the schoolyard, sitting together in the schoolroom, going home together at the end of the day. They learned the same things so they could help one another on the homework and talk about it.
>
> And the teachers were people. . . .
>
> —Isaac Asimov, from "The Fun They Had"

Legend A legend is a story that is handed down from the past and may tell about something that really happened or someone who really lived. Legends often mix fact and fiction. "The Legend of the Hummingbird" is a legend from Puerto Rico.

Limerick A limerick is a short, humorous poem usually composed of five lines. It has a rhyme scheme created by two rhyming couplets followed by a final line that rhymes with the first couplet. This rhyme scheme is known as *a-a-b-b-a.* A limerick typically has a sing-song rhythm. In some limericks, the second couplet is collapsed into one long, internally rhyming, line.

See page 566.

Literary nonfiction See **Nonfiction.**

Lyric poetry Lyric poetry is poetry that presents the thoughts and feelings of a single speaker. "I'm Nobody! Who Are You?" by Emily Dickinson is an example of lyric poetry.

Main character See **Character.**

Main idea A main idea is a central idea that a writer wishes to express. It may be the central idea of an entire work or the thought expressed in the topic sentence of a paragraph. (A topic sentence may be found at the beginning, middle, or end of a paragraph.) A writer may need to use several paragraphs to develop a main idea. Usually, the main idea is rather general, and details give specific information that support it.

See pages 100, 111, 640.

Memoir See **Autobiography.**

Metaphor A metaphor is a comparison of two things that have some quality in common. Unlike a simile, a metaphor does not contain a word such as *like, as, than,* or *resembles.* Lois Lowry uses a metaphor in "Crow Call" when she describes "the ribbon of road through the farm lands."

See page 191.
See also Simile.

Meter In poetry, meter is the pattern of accented and unaccented syllables. The meter in a line of poetry creates its rhythm. Not all poems have regular meter.

See also Rhythm.

Minor character See **Character.**

Monitoring When readers pay attention to their comprehension as they are reading, they are monitoring. Monitoring, or checking your comprehension, helps readers clearly understand the meaning of what they are reading.

See pages 4, 409.

Mood A mood is a feeling that a literary work conveys to readers. Writers carefully choose words and phrases to create moods. A mood is an emotion such as sadness, excitement, or anger. In "Ghost of the Lagoon," Armstrong Sperry creates a mood of excitement and tension as Mako prepares to meet Tupa.

See page 246.
See also Tone.

Moral A moral is a lesson taught in a literary work such as a fable. At the end of a fable, a moral is often stated directly.

Motivation A character's motivation is the reason why he or she acts, feels, or thinks in a certain way. For example, the narrator in "Scout's Honor" is motivated by a desire to prove that he is tough. A character may have a number of motivations for his or her actions. Understanding these motivations helps readers to get to know the character.

Myth A myth is a traditional story about the origins or workings of the world. Some myths explain how certain things came into being. Others explain elements of nature or social customs. The characters in myths are often superhuman beings. The events may be unlikely or realistic. Because myths have been handed down from one generation to the next for a long time, their original authors are unknown. "Arachne" is an example of a Greek myth.

See pages 768, 770.

Narrative Writing that tells a story is called a narrative. The events in a narrative may be real or imagined. Narratives that deal with real events include autobiographies and biographies. Fictional narratives include myths, short stories, and novels. A narrative may also be in the form of a poem.

Narrative poetry Narrative poetry is poetry that tells a story. Like other stories, a narrative poem contains a setting, characters, and a plot. It may also contain such elements of poetry as rhyme, rhythm, imagery, and figurative language. "The Walrus and the Carpenter" is an example of a narrative poem.

See pages 346, 561, 740.

Narrator A narrator is the teller of a story. Sometimes a story's narrator is a character who takes part in the action; in other cases, the narrator is an outside voice. In "The Scribe," for example, the narrator is James, the main character. "The School Play," in contrast, is narrated by an outsider's voice.

See page 319.
See also Point of view.

Nonfiction Writing that tells about real people, places, and events is called nonfiction. There are two main types of nonfiction. Literary nonfiction reads much like fiction, except that the characters, setting, and plot are real rather than imaginary. Its purpose is usually to entertain or express opinions or feelings. Literary nonfiction includes autobiographies, biographies, and essays. Informative nonfiction provides factual information. Its main purpose is to inform or explain.

See pages 96–99, 100.
See also **Autobiography; Biography; Essay; Informative nonfiction.**

Novel A novel is a work of fiction that is longer and more complex than a short story. In a novel, the setting, the plot, and the characters are developed in detail. Minor characters are developed more fully than in a short story, and have changes, relationships, and motivations of their own.

See page 21.

Onomatopoeia Onomatopoeia is the use of words whose sound suggests their meaning. The words *bang* and *hiss* are examples of onomatopoeia. The onomatopoeic words in "Analysis of Baseball" include *thuds, pow,* and *thwack.*

See pages 191, 647.

Opinion See **Fact and opinion.**

Oral history An oral history is an account of an historical event as told by someone who was there at the time. Oral histories are often handed down from generation to generation by word of mouth. "Where the Girl Rescued Her Brother" is an oral history from the Cheyenne tradition.

Paraphrasing Restating information using your own words is called paraphrasing. Paraphrasing can help you understand and remember what you read. Paraphrasing can also help you in writing research reports. By paraphrasing the information you read, you can avoid plagiarism—the use of another's words as your own.

See page 49.

Personal essay See **Essay.**

Personification The giving of human qualities to an animal, object, or idea is known as personification. In "You Sing," trees are personified when they are said to "speak with their green tongue."

See pages 192, 346, 648.

Perspective See **Author's perspective; Point of view.**

Play See **Drama.**

Playwright The author of a drama for the stage is called a playwright.

Plot The series of events in a story is called the story's plot. A plot usually centers around a conflict—a problem faced by the main character. In a typical plot, the action that the characters take to solve the problem builds, or rises, toward a **climax,** an important event or decision that becomes the turning point of the story. At that point, or shortly afterward, the action falls. The problem may be solved or changed and the story ends.

See pages 22, 45, 76, 132, 319, 443–445.

Poetic form See **Form.**

Poetry Poetry is a type of literature in which ideas, images, and feelings are expressed in few words. Most poetry is written in lines, which may be grouped in stanzas. Poets carefully select words for their sounds and meanings, combining the words in imaginative ways to present feelings, pictures, experiences, and themes vividly. In poetry, the images appeal to readers' senses, as do elements of sound, such as alliteration, rhythm, and rhyme.

See pages 189–192, 193.

Point of view Every story is told from a particular point of view, or perspective. Usually, a story is told from either the first-person or the third-person point of view. In a story told from the first-person point of view, the narrator is a character in the story and uses pronouns such as *I, me,* and *we.* "Eleven" is told by the story's main character, from the first-person point of view. A story told from the third-person point of view has a narrator who is outside the story and uses pronouns such as *he, she,* and *they.* "Aaron's Gift" is told by a narrator who is not a character in the story. It is told from the third-person point of view.

See pages 281, 362.
See also **Author's perspective; Narrator.**

Predicting Using what you already know to make a logical statement about what might happen in the future is called predicting. Good readers gather information as they read. They combine that information with their own knowledge and experience to predict what might happen next.

See pages 4, 132, 247, 257, 272, 337.

Primary source The information that writers of nonfiction present comes from various kinds of sources. A primary source conveys direct, firsthand knowledge. "My First Dive with the Dolphins" is a primary source, because it is an account of Don C. Reed's own personal experience. Primary sources include diaries, letters, interview tapes, memoirs, journals, photographs, and other authentic artifacts.

See pages 227, 261, 363, 378.
See also **Secondary source.**

Prop The word *prop,* an abbreviation of *property,* refers to any physical object that is used in a drama or play. These stage directions from *The Phantom Tollbooth* describe the props in one scene:

(They find themselves in a very unique room, in which all the walls, tables, chairs, desks, cabinets and blackboards are labeled to show their heights, widths, depths and distances to and from each other. To one side is a gigantic notepad on an artist's easel, and from hooks and strings hang a collection of rulers, measures, weights and tapes, and all other measuring devices.)

—Norton Juster and Susan Nanus, from *The Phantom Tollbooth*

See also **Stage directions.**

Prose Prose is the ordinary form of spoken and written language—that is, it is language that lacks the special features of poetry.

Purpose See *Author's purpose; Setting a purpose.*

Quest In literature, a journey or adventure that a character goes on to achieve a specific goal is called a quest. In *The Phantom Tollbooth,* Milo's adventure in the lands beyond turns into a quest when he sets out to rescue the princesses.

Questioning The process of asking questions while reading is called questioning. Good readers ask questions in an effort to understand characters and events. They then look for answers to their questions.

See pages 4, 170.

Radio play A radio play is a drama that is written specifically to be broadcast over the radio. Because the audience cannot see a radio play, sound effects are used to help listeners imagine the setting and action. The stage directions in the play's script indicate the sound effects. *Damon and Pythias* is an example of a radio play.

Realistic fiction Realistic fiction is imaginative writing set in the real, modern world. The characters act like real people who use ordinary human abilities to cope with problems and conflicts typical of modern life. "Tuesday of the Other June" is an example of realistic fiction.

See also **Fiction.**

Repetition Repetition is the use of a sound, word, or phrase more than once. Writers use repetition to bring certain ideas, sounds, or feelings to readers' attention. For example, in the poem "Chang McTang McQuarter Cat," the speaker repeats the phrase "one part" frequently as he presents the qualities of the cat.

See pages 191, 287, 395, 479.
See also **Alliteration; Rhyme.**

Resolution See *Plot; Falling action.*

Rhyme Rhyme is a repetition of sounds at the ends of words. In poetry, rhyme that occurs within a line is called **internal rhyme.** Rhyme that occurs at the end of lines is called **end rhyme.** Note both the internal rhymes and the end rhyme in these lines from "The Walrus and the Carpenter":

> "A pleasant <u>walk</u>, a pleasant <u>talk</u>
>   Along the briny <u>beach</u>:
> We cannot do with <u>more</u> than <u>four</u>,
>   To give a hand to <u>each</u>."
>
> —Lewis Carroll,
> from "The Walrus and the Carpenter"

See pages 191, 287, 479.

Rhyme scheme The pattern of rhymes in a poem is called the poem's rhyme scheme. A rhyme scheme can be described by using a different letter of the alphabet to represent each rhyming sound. Note the rhyme scheme of the first four lines of "The Quarrel." This scheme is called *a-b-a-b.*

> I quarreled with my brother,   *a*
> I don't know what about,   *b*
> One thing led to another   *a*
> And somehow we fell out.   *b*
>
> —Eleanor Farjeon, from "The Quarrel"

Rhythm The rhythm of a line of poetry is the pattern of stressed and unstressed syllables in the line. When a rhythm is repeated throughout a poem, the poem is said to have a regular beat. Note the regular rhythm in the following lines.

> Chang McTang McQuarter Cat
> Is one part this and twenty that.
>
> —John Ciardi,
> from "Chang McTang McQuarter Cat"

See pages 191, 287, 479.
See also **Meter.**

Rising action Rising action refers to the events in a story that move the plot forward. Rising action involves conflicts and complications, and usually builds toward a climax, or turning point.

See pages 22, 443.
See also **Plot.**

Sarcasm Humor that uses words to express something opposite to their literal meaning is called sarcasm. Judith Viorst uses sarcasm in "The Southpaw." For example, when Janet writes to Richard, "Congratulations on your unbroken record," she is being sarcastic. Though Janet sounds as if she is being friendly, she is really teasing Richard, whose "unbroken record" is a series of losses.

Scanning Scanning is the process of searching through writing for a particular fact or piece of information. When readers scan, they sweep their eyes across a page looking for key words that could lead them to the information they want.

Scene In a play, a scene is a section that presents events taking place in a single setting. A new scene begins whenever the story calls for a change in time or place.

See page 319.

Scenery The painted backdrop and other structures used to create the setting for a drama are called scenery.

Science fiction Science fiction is fiction that is based on real or possible scientific developments. Although much science fiction is set in the future, the problems that the characters face may be similar to real problems that people face today. "The Fun They Had," a story about school in the 22nd century, is an example of science fiction.

See pages 216, 507–510.

Script The text of a play, motion picture, radio broadcast, or prepared speech is called a script.

Secondary source A secondary source is one that conveys indirect, secondhand knowledge. "Matthew Henson at the Top of the World" is a secondary source, because the information it contains comes from Jim Haskins's reading and research. Secondary sources include most articles and reports, biographies, textbooks, and other informative nonfiction.

See pages 227, 261, 363, 378.
See also **Primary source.**

Sensory details Words and phrases that help readers see, hear, taste, smell, and feel what a writer is describing are called sensory details. Note the sensory details in this excerpt from "Summer of Fire":

> Boulders exploded in the heat. Sheets of flame leapt forward. Gigantic clouds of smoke ringed the horizon . . . [Snow] sifted through blackened forests and dusted herds of bison and elk.
>
> —Patricia Lauber, from "Summer of Fire"

See pages 207, 385, 648.
See also **Description; Imagery.**

Sequence The order in which events occur or ideas are presented is called a sequence. In a narrative, events are usually presented in chronological order—the order in which they happened. A writer may use clue words and phrases—such as *then, until, after a while,* and *finally*—to help readers understand the sequence of events.

See pages 45, 444.

Setting The setting of a story, poem, or play is the time and place of the action. The time may be past, present, or future. The place may be real or imaginary. In some stories, including many fables, settings may not be clearly defined. In other stories, however, settings play an important part. For example, the desert setting of "Nadia the Willful" plays an important part in the story's action and helps to create its mood.

See pages 24, 64, 243, 246, 272, 508, 509, 579, 585.

Setting a purpose The process of establishing specific reasons to read a work is called setting a purpose. Readers often come to a work with a purpose in mind, such as reading for entertainment, for information, or to analyze or evaluate a piece of writing. Readers can look at a work's title, headings and subheadings, and illustrations to preview the work. Previewing may also guide their purposes for reading.

See page 579.

Short story A short story is a work of fiction that can generally be read in one sitting. Like other works of fiction, short stories contain characters, plots, settings, and themes. The plot of a short story usually involves one main conflict.

See page 21.
See also **Fiction.**

Simile A simile is a comparison of two things that have some quality in common. Unlike a metaphor, a simile contains a word such as *like, as, resembles,* or *than.* Note the simile in this sentence from "The Bamboo Beads": "That night the moon was round and white as my Sunday hat."

See pages 192, 424.
See also **Metaphor.**

Skimming Skimming is the process of reading quickly to get the general idea of a work. It involves titles, headings, graphics, words in special print, and the first sentence of each paragraph.

See page 725.

Sound devices See **Alliteration; Onomatopoeia; Repetition; Rhyme; Rhythm.**

Source See **Primary source; Secondary source.**

Speaker In a poem, the speaker is the voice that talks to the reader—like the narrator in a work of fiction. The speaker is not always the poet, but the speaker may express the feelings of the poet.

See pages 192, 395.

Speech A speech is a prepared talk given in public. Lois Lowry's "Newbery Acceptance Speech" for *The Giver* is an example of a speech.

Stage A stage is the level and raised platform on which entertainers usually perform.

See page 318.

Stage directions In the script of a play, the instructions to the performers, director, and stage crew are called stage directions. They usually appear in italic type and within parentheses. Stage directions provide suggestions about such things as scenery, lighting, music, and sound effects. They may also tell performers how to move and how to speak their lines. Note the stage directions in this passage from *Damon and Pythias:*

> **Damon** *(calm and firm).* I have faith in my friend. I know he will return.
> **King** *(mocking).* We shall see!
> *(Sound: Iron door shut and locked.)*
>
> —Fan Kissen, from *Damon and Pythias*

See pages 318, 330.

Stanza A group of lines within a poem is called a stanza. Stanzas are somewhat like paragraphs in stories. "The Walrus and the Carpenter," for example, contains 18 stanzas.

See page 190.

Static character In fiction, drama, or literary nonfiction, characters who undergo little or no change during the course of the story are referred to as static characters.

See also **Character development; Dynamic character.**

Stereotype In literature, simplistic characters defined by a single trait are called stereotypes, or clichés. Such characters do not usually demonstrate the complexities of real people. Familiar stereotypes in popular fiction include the absent-minded professor, the hard-boiled private eye, and the mustache-twirling villain. The proud, beautiful princess in fairy tales such as "King Thrushbeard" is another example:

> A king had a daughter who was unequaled for beauty, but she thought so much of herself that no suitor was good enough for her. She rejected one after another . . .
>
> —The Brothers Grimm, from "King Thrushbeard"

Story-mapping Creating an outline of the events that take place in a story is called story-mapping. A story map may also identify characters and setting, and the plot's conflict, resolution, and theme. Story-mapping can help you understand what you read.

See pages 330, 488.

Structure The structure of a literary work is the way in which it is put together. In poetry, structure involves the arrangement of words, lines, and stanzas, to produce a desired effect. In fiction, structure involves the arrangement of such elements as sentences, paragraphs, and events. Chapters are a basic unit of structure in novels, as are acts in plays. In nonfiction, the structure of a piece may be chronological or spatial order, cause and effect, comparison and contrast. Or ideas may be presented using inductive or deductive reasoning. Recognizing a text's structure can help in finding the most important ideas as well as the supporting facts and details.

Style A style is a particular way of writing. It involves *how* something is said rather than *what* is said. Word choice, sentence length, tone, imagery, and use of dialogue contribute to a writer's style.

See pages 172, 426, 686.

Subject The subject of a literary work is its focus or topic. In a biography, for example, the subject is the person whose life story is being told. Subject differs from theme in that theme is a deeper meaning, usually inferred by the reader, where the subject is the main situation or set of facts described by the text.

Summarizing Summarizing is telling the main ideas of a piece of writing briefly, in one's own words. When you summarize, you condense a writer's ideas into precise statements, leaving out unimportant details. A summary may include direct quotations, important details, and statements about an underlying theme or message.

See page 341.

Surprise ending An unexpected plot twist at the end of a story is called a surprise ending. The surprise may be a sudden turn in the action, or a piece of information that gives a different perspective to the entire story. "Lob's Girl" has a surprise ending when, in the final scene, it is revealed that Lob may have been in two places at once.

Suspense Suspense is a feeling of growing tension and excitement that makes a reader curious about the outcome of a story or an event within a story. In "Ghost of the Lagoon," suspense is created as Mako sets out into Tupa's territory.

Symbol A symbol is a person, a place, or an object that stands for something other than itself. In literature, objects and images may be used to symbolize things that cannot actually be seen, such as ideas or feelings. In "Flowers and Freckle Cream," for example, the tiger lily Elizabeth receives from her grandfather may symbolize the beauty he sees in her freckled appearance.

See page 674.

Table of contents In most nonfiction books or in books arranged by chapter, or section, the book's contents are listed at the front in a table of contents. The table of contents gives the title of each section and the page number on which it starts. It can be used, like an outline, to get an overview of the material covered. Or it may be used to look for a specific topic covered in one section.

Tall tale A tall tale is a humorously exaggerated story about impossible events, often relating the superhuman abilities of the main character. The tales about folk heroes such as Paul Bunyan and Davy Crockett are typical tall tales.

Teleplay A play written for television is called a teleplay, or television script. In a teleplay, the stage directions usually include camera instructions. *Words on a Page* is an example of a teleplay.

Text organizers Text organizers include headings, tables of contents, and graphic elements such as charts, tables, time lines, boxes, bullets, and captions.

See page 146.

Theme A theme is a message about life or human nature that is conveyed by a work of literature. Sometimes themes are stated directly, but often readers must figure them out. Any lessons learned by the main character of a story can be clues to a theme. For example, a theme of "The Scribe" might be that helping people ultimately helps you.

See pages 24, 76, 346, 510, 611–612, 633.

Thesaurus A thesaurus is a reference tool used by writers to find the precise word to convey a certain meaning and tone. A thesaurus lists words and their synonyms, often including antonyms and other closely related words.

Third-person point of view See *Point of view.*

Title The title of a piece of writing is the name that is attached to it. A title often refers to an important aspect of the work. For example, the title of "Aaron's Gift" refers to the special importance of Aaron's effort to give a gift to his grandmother.

Tone The tone of a work conveys the writer's attitude toward his or her subject. A work may have one tone throughout, such as humorous, serious, or impatient. Sometimes, however, the tone may change several times in the course of a work. For example, the tone of Don C. Reed's essay "My First Dive with the Dolphins" varies from humorous to serious.

See pages 363, 409, 734.
See also **Mood.**

Topic sentence See *Main idea.*

Tragedy A tragedy is a dramatic work that presents the downfall of a dignified character or characters who are involved in historically or socially significant events. The events in a tragic plot are set in motion by a decision that is often an error in judgment. Succeeding events are linked in a cause-and-effect relationship and lead inevitably to a disastrous conclusion, usually death.

Trickster tale A folk tale that features a playful character who plays pranks on or seeks to outwit other characters is called a trickster tale. This type of tale is found in the folklore of cultures around the world. "Why Monkeys Live in Trees" is an example of a trickster tale.

Turning point See *Climax.*

Visualizing The process of forming a mental picture based on a written description is called visualizing. Readers use details of sight, sound, touch, taste, and feeling to visualize the characters, settings, and events in works of literature. Mentally picturing writers' descriptions makes reading more enjoyable and memorable.

See pages 4, 64, 511, 561

Voice A writer's unique way of writing is called voice. Voice is shaped by the choice of words, the way they are put together, and the details and thoughts the writer chooses to write about.

See page 684.

Word choice Word choice, also called diction, is the process by which writers carefully select words to give precision and impact to their writing.

See page 479.

❶ The Writing Process

The writing process consists of four stages:
- *prewriting*
- *drafting*
- *revising and editing*
- *publishing and reflecting*

As the graphic to the right shows, these stages are not numbered. The steps do not have to be followed rigidly. Rather, they represent a cycle. You may return to any stage of the process at any point during your writing, even after completion. Writers use peer response, or feedback from readers, during any or all of the stages.

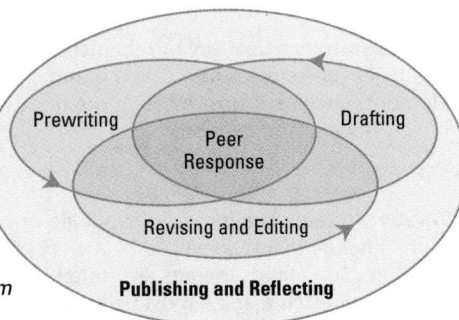

Prewriting   Drafting

Peer
Response

Revising and Editing

Publishing and Reflecting

---

❶❶ Prewriting

In the prewriting stage, you explore your ideas and discover what you want to write about.

Finding Ideas for Writing
Try one or more of the following techniques to help you find a writing topic.

Personal Techniques

- Practice imaging, or trying to remember mainly sensory details about a subject—its look, sound, feel, taste, and smell.

- Complete a knowledge inventory to discover what you already know about a subject.

- Browse through magazines, newspapers, and on-line bulletin boards for ideas.

- Start a clip file of articles that you want to save for future reference. Be sure to label each clip with source information.

Sharing Techniques

- With a group, brainstorm a topic. Try to come up with as many ideas as you can without stopping to critique or examine them.

- Interview someone who knows a great deal about your topic.

Writing Techniques

- After freewriting on a topic, try looping, or choosing your best idea for more freewriting. Repeat the loop at least once.

- Make a list to help you organize ideas, examine them, or identify areas for further research.

Graphic Techniques

- Create a pro-and-con chart to compare the positive and negative aspects of an idea or a course of action.

- Use a cluster map or tree diagram to explore subordinate ideas that relate to your general topic or central idea.

LINK TO LITERATURE Some of the best ideas for writing can come from your own experiences. Isaac Bashevis Singer, author of "Zlateh the Goat," on page 481, says, "I prefer to write about the world which I knew, which I know, best. . . . I write about the things where I grew up, and where I feel completely at home."

Determining Your Purpose
Your purpose for writing may be to express yourself, to entertain, to describe, to explain, to analyze, or to persuade. To clarify your purpose, ask questions like these:

- Why did I choose to write about my topic?
- What aspects of the topic mean the most to me?
- What do I want others to think or feel after they read my writing?

Identifying Your Audience

Knowing who will read your writing can help you focus your topic and choose relevant details. As you think about your readers, ask yourself questions like these:

- What does my audience already know about my topic?
- What will they be most interested in?
- What language is most appropriate for this audience?

Drafting

In the drafting stage, you put your ideas on paper and allow them to develop and change as you write.

Two broad approaches in this stage are discovery drafting and planned drafting.

Discovery drafting is a good approach when you are not quite sure what you think about your subject. You just plunge into your draft and let your feelings and ideas lead you where they will. After finishing a discovery draft, you may decide to start another draft, do more prewriting, or revise your first draft.

Planned drafting may work better for research reports, critical reviews, and other kinds of formal writing. Try making a writing plan or a scratch outline before you begin drafting. Then, as you write, you can fill in the details.

LINK TO LITERATURE Some writers plan and outline. Others write in a great flurry, without much previous planning, as ideas occur to them; of course, the ideas have been developing within them before they begin to write. Walter Dean Myers, who wrote "Abd al-Rahman Ibrahima," on page 365, had to gather many notes about his subject's life before he could begin to write Ibrahima's biography.

Revision Guidelines

The changes you make in your writing during this stage usually fall into three categories: revising for content, revising for structure, and proofreading to correct mistakes in mechanics.

Use the questions that follow to assess problems and determine what changes would improve your work.

Revising for Content

- Does my writing have a main idea or central focus? Is my thesis clear?
- Have I incorporated adequate detail? Where might I include a telling detail, revealing statistic, or vivid example?
- Is any material unnecessary, irrelevant, or confusing?

Revising for Structure

- Is my writing unified? Do all ideas and supporting details pertain to my main idea or advance my thesis?
- Is my writing clear and coherent? Is the flow of sentences and paragraphs smooth and logical?
- Do I need to add transitional words, phrases, or sentences to make the relationships among ideas clearer?
- Are my sentences well constructed? What sentences might I combine to improve the grace and rhythm of my writing?

WRITING TIP Be sure to consider the needs of your audience as you answer the questions under Revising for Content and Revising for Structure. For example, before you can determine whether any of your material is unnecessary or irrelevant, you need to identify what your audience already knows.

Proofreading to Correct Mistakes in Grammar, Usage, and Mechanics

When you are satisfied with your revision, proofread your paper, looking for mistakes in grammar, usage, and mechanics. You may want to do this several times, looking for different types of mistakes each time. The following checklist may help.

Sentence Structure and Agreement
- Are there any run-on sentences or sentence fragments?
- Do all verbs agree with their subjects?
- Do all pronouns agree with their antecedents?
- Are verb tenses correct and consistent?

Forms of Words
- Do adverbs and adjectives modify the appropriate words?
- Are all forms of *be* and other irregular verbs used correctly?
- Are pronouns used correctly?
- Are comparative and superlative forms of adjectives correct?

Capitalization, Punctuation, and Spelling
- Is any punctuation mark missing or not needed?
- Are all words spelled correctly?
- Are all proper nouns and all proper adjectives capitalized?

WRITING TIP For help identifying and correcting problems that are listed in the Proofreading Checklist, see the Grammar Handbook, pages R54–R79. You might wish to mark changes on your paper by using the proofreading symbols shown in the chart below.

Proofreading Symbols

∧	Add letters or words.	/	Make a capital letter lowercase.
⊙	Add a period.	¶	Begin a new paragraph.
≡	Capitalize a letter.	ℐ	Delete letters or words.
⌒	Close up a space.	∿	Switch the positions of letters or words.
⋏	Add a comma.		

1.4 Publishing and Reflecting

Always consider sharing your finished writing with an audience. Reflecting on your writing is another good way to bring closure to a project.

Creative Publishing Ideas

Following are some ideas for publishing and sharing your writing.

- Post your writing on an electronic bulletin board or send it to others via email.
- Create a multimedia presentation and share it with classmates.
- Publish your writing in a school newspaper or literary magazine.
- Present your work orally in a report, a speech, a reading, or a dramatic performance.
- Submit your writing to a local newspaper or a magazine that publishes student writing.
- Form a writing exchange group with other students.

WRITING TIP You might work with other students to publish an anthology of class writing. Then exchange your anthology with another class or another school. Reading the work of other student writers will help you get ideas for new writing projects and find ways to improve your work.

Reflecting on Your Writing

Think about your writing process and whether you would like to add what you have written to your portfolio. You might attach a note in which you answer questions like these:

- What did I learn about myself and my subject through this writing project?
- Which parts of the writing process did I most and least enjoy?
- As I wrote, what was my biggest problem? How did I solve it?
- What did I learn about my own process that I can use the next time I write?

1.5 Using Peer Response

Peer response consists of the suggestions and comments your peers or classmates make about your writing.

You can ask a peer reader for help at any point in the writing process. For example, your peers can help you brainstorm a topic, narrow your focus, notice confusing words or passages, or think of a structure for your writing.

Questions for Your Peer Readers

You can help your peer readers provide you with the most useful feedback by following these guidelines:

- Tell readers where you are in the writing process. Are you still trying out ideas, or have you completed a draft?

- Ask pointed but open-ended questions that will help you get specific information about your writing. Questions that require more than yes-or-no answers are more likely to give you information you can use.

- Give your readers plenty of time to respond thoughtfully to your writing.

- Encourage your readers to be honest when they respond to your work. It's OK if you don't agree with them—you always get to decide which changes to make.

Tips for Being a Peer Reader

Follow these guidelines when you respond to someone else's work:

- Respect the writer's feelings.

- Make sure you understand what kind of feedback the writer is looking for, and then respond accordingly.

- Use "I" statements, such as "I like . . . ," "I think . . . ," or "It would help me if . . . ." Remember that your impressions and opinions are your own. They won't be the same as everyone's.

WRITING TIP Writers are better able to absorb criticism of their work if they first receive positive feedback. When you act as a peer reader, try to start your review by telling something you like about the piece. The chart below explains different peer response techniques to use when you are ready to share your work.

Peer Response Techniques

Sharing Use this when you are just exploring ideas or when you want to celebrate the completion of a piece of writing.

- *Will you please read or listen to my writing without criticizing or making suggestions afterward?*

Summarizing Use this when you want to know if your main idea or goals are clear.

- *What do you think I'm saying? What's my main idea or message?*

Replying Use this strategy when you want to make your writing richer by adding new ideas.

- *What are your ideas about my topic? What do you think about what I have said in my piece?*

Responding to Specific Features Use this when you want a quick overview of the strengths and weaknesses of your writing.

- *Are the ideas supported with enough examples? Did I persuade you? Is the organization clear enough for you to follow the ideas?*

Telling Use this to find out which parts of your writing are affecting readers the way you want and which parts are confusing.

- *What did you think or feel as you read my words? Would you show me which passage you were reading when you had that response?*

---

❷ Building Blocks of Good Writing

Whatever your purpose in writing, you need to capture your readers' interest, organize your ideas well, and present your thoughts clearly. Giving special attention to particular parts of a story or an essay can make your writing more enjoyable and more effective.

2.1 Introductions

When you flip through a magazine trying to decide which articles to read, the opening paragraph is often critical. If it does not grab your attention, you are likely to turn the page.

Kinds of Introductions

Here are some introduction techniques that can capture a reader's interest.

- Make a surprising statement
- Provide a description
- Pose a question
- Relate an anecdote
- Address the reader directly
- Begin with a thesis statement

Make a Surprising Statement Beginning with a startling statement or an interesting fact can capture your reader's curiosity about the subject, as in the model below.

> MODEL
> A male Kodiak bear may weigh 1,500 pounds, measure ten feet long, and run 35 miles an hour. Protected within Alaska's Kodiak National Wildlife Refuge, nearly 3,000 of these bears share 100-mile-long Kodiak Island, where they feast on fish, berries, and whale and seal carcasses.

Provide a Description A vivid description sets a mood and brings a scene to life for your reader. Here, details about running on a track set the tone for a narrative about a foot race.

> MODEL
> In the pale morning light, the shadowy track was still. Rounding the curve, the athlete locked her eyes on the single floodlight at the far end of the track, her every muscle straining toward it.

Pose a Question Beginning with a question can make your reader want to read on to find out the answer. The following introduction asks a question about the importance of a particular person to a sport.

> MODEL
> Why does Danielle Del Ferraro hold a special place in the history of the Soap Box Derby? Since the Derby began in 1934, she has been the only participant ever to win twice. Her success is also noteworthy because girls were not allowed to enter the gravity-powered car race until 1970.

Relate an Anecdote Beginning with a brief anecdote, or story, can hook readers. The anecdote below introduces a firsthand account of an important family event.

> MODEL
> Dressed in my best clothes, I rushed outside, late for my sister's wedding. I waited impatiently for the light to change at the corner. Then, from out of nowhere came an out-of-control in-line skater. The result was a head-on collision.

Address the Reader Directly Speaking directly to readers establishes a friendly, informal tone and involves them in your topic.

> MODEL
> Find out how you can get in shape and have fun at the same time. Come to a free demonstration of Fit for Life on Friday night at 7:00 P.M.

Begin with a Thesis Statement A thesis statement expressing a paper's main idea may be woven into both the beginning and the end of nonfiction writing. The following is a thesis statement that introduces a response to literature.

> MODEL
> In "The Circuit," Francisco Jiménez shows how migrant farmwork affects the children of families that work in the fields.

WRITING TIP You may want to try more than one kind of introduction and then decide which is the most effective.

2.2 Paragraphs

A paragraph is made up of sentences that work together to develop an idea or accomplish a purpose. Whether or not it contains a topic sentence stating the main idea, a good paragraph must have unity and coherence.

Unity
A paragraph has unity when all the sentences support and develop the main idea. Use the following techniques to create unity.

Write a Topic Sentence A topic sentence states the main ideas of the paragraph; all other sentences in the paragraph provide supporting details. A topic sentence is often the first sentence in a paragraph. However, it may also appear later in the paragraph or at the end, to summarize or reinforce the main idea.

> MODEL
> The most important rule for a beginning photographer is this: check before you click. Is the film loaded? Is your subject well lighted or will you need a flash? Have you framed your picture carefully? Are you holding the camera still? Checking the basics will go a long way toward making your snapshots memorable.

Relate All Sentences to an Implied Main Idea A paragraph can be unified without a topic sentence as long as every sentence supports the implied, or unstated, main idea.

> MODEL
> The chef carefully poured in the mixture of freshly sliced apples, sugar, flour, and cinnamon. Then she floured her hands again before adding strips of pastry in crisscrosses across the top. She dotted some butter all along the top. Finally she placed the masterpiece in the oven.

Coherence
A paragraph is coherent when all its sentences are related to one another and flow logically from one to the next. The following techniques will help you achieve coherence in paragraphs.

- Present your ideas in the most logical order.
- Use pronouns, synonyms, and repeated words to connect ideas.
- Use transitional devices to show the relationships among ideas.

> MODEL
> Most scientists believe that all of the earth's land once formed one super continent. About 200 million years ago, this supercontinent began to break into two large masses of land. Since that time the plates on which continents rest have continued to move.

2.3 Transitions

Transitions are words and phrases that show the connections between details. Clear transitions help show how your ideas relate to each other.

Kinds of Transitions

Transitions can help readers understand several kinds of relationships:

• Time or sequence
• Spatial relationships
• Degree of importance
• Compare and contrast
• Cause and effect

Time or Sequence Some transitions help to clarify the sequence of events over time. When you are telling a story or describing a process, you can connect ideas with such transitional words as *first, second, always, then, next, later, soon, before, finally, after, earlier, afterward,* and *tomorrow.*

> MODEL
> During the Revolutionary War, many of the colonists who remained loyal to the British monarchy lost their houses and land by force. After the war, between 80,000 and 100,000 of these Loyalists went to England or emigrated elsewhere.

Spatial Relationships Transitional words and phrases such as *in front, behind, next to, along, nearest, lowest, above, below, underneath, on the left,* and *in the middle* can help readers visualize a scene.

> MODEL
> As I waited, I stared at the bleachers across the rink. My family was lined up in the front row. Behind this group and to the right were friends from school, and next to my friends were three of my teachers.

Degree of Importance Transitional words such as *mainly, strongest, weakest, first, second, most important, least important, worst,* and *best* may be used to rank ideas or to show degree of importance.

> MODEL
> Why do I read mysteries? Mainly because I enjoy suspense. Second, I like meeting characters who are different from anybody I know in real life. Least important, but still a reason, is that I enjoy reading about interesting places.

WRITING TIP When you begin a sentence with a transition such as *most important, therefore, nevertheless, still,* or *instead,* set off the transition with a comma.

Compare and Contrast Words and phrases such as *similarly, likewise, also, like, as, neither . . . nor,* and *either . . . or* show similarity between details. *However, by contrast, yet, but, unlike, instead, whereas,* and *while* show difference.

> MODEL
> Matthew Henson was not recognized as the codiscoverer of the North Pole until 1944, although he and Robert Peary had reached it on April 6, 1909. By contrast, the achievement of Roald Amundsen's team, which made it to the South Pole in December 1911, was recognized almost immediately.

Cause and Effect When you are writing about a cause-and-effect relationship, use transitional words and phrases such as *since, because, thus, therefore, so, due to, for this reason,* and *as a result* to help clarify that relationship.

> MODEL
> Because a tree fell across the electric wires Monday night, we lost our electricity for four hours.

Conclusions

A conclusion should leave readers with a strong final impression. Try any of these approaches.

Kinds of Conclusions

Here are some effective methods for bringing your writing to a conclusion:

- Restate your thesis
- Ask a question
- Make a recommendation
- Make a prediction
- Summarize your information

Restate Your Thesis A good way to conclude an essay is by restating your thesis, or main idea, in different words. The conclusion below restates the thesis introduced on page R27.

> MODEL
> **As these examples from "The Circuit" show, Francisco Jiménez succeeds in making the reader understand the effects of the migrant farmworker's way of life on children.**

Ask a Question Try asking a question that sums up what you have said and gives readers something new to think about. The question below concludes a persuasive essay on the need for bike lanes in the writer's community.

> MODEL
> **More and more people are biking to school and to work and are riding for exercise. Doesn't it make sense to create safe bike lanes throughout our city?**

Make a Recommendation When you are persuading your audience to take a position on an issue, you can conclude by recommending a specific course of action.

> MODEL
> **You can make your research easier by taking advantage of the Internet. Develop a list of key words that will help you narrow your search.**

Make a Prediction Readers are concerned about matters that may affect them and therefore are moved by a conclusion that predicts the future.

> MODEL
> **If landowners continue to drain wetlands, we will see a tremendous decline in the number and variety of wildlife.**

Summarize Your Information Summarizing reinforces the writer's main ideas, leaving a strong, lasting impression.

> MODEL
> **At 64, Denise St. Aubyn Hubbard sailed alone across the Atlantic. Bill Pinkney was in his 50s when he sailed around the world by himself. And Tristan Jones, in his 60s and having lost a leg, sailed solo from California to Thailand. Don't ever think that courage belongs only to the young.**

 ## Elaboration

Elaboration is the process of developing a writing idea by providing supporting details. Choose details that are appropriate to the purpose and form of your writing.

Facts and Statistics A fact is a statement that can be verified, while a statistic is a fact stated in numbers. Make sure the facts and statistics you supply are from a reliable, up-to-date source. As in the model below, the facts and statistics you use should strongly support the statements you make.

MODEL
Women have aided the United States' military efforts for more than a century. Since the 1860s, more than 11 million women have served in or assisted the armed forces. Today approximately 200,000 women are on active duty.

Sensory Details Details that show how something looks, sounds, tastes, smells, or feels can enliven a description.

MODEL
Anna Hawk got off her bike and sat beside the muddy road. The rain on her poncho made the only sound, and nothing on the prairie moved. Anna took a sip of warm, sweet cocoa from her thermos bottle.

Incidents From our earliest years, we are interested in hearing stories. One way to illustrate a point powerfully is to relate an incident or tell a story.

MODEL
Some of our most valuable sources of historical knowledge come from tragic events. The eruption of the volcano Vesuvius in A.D. 79 was a nightmare for the people of Pompeii. About 2,000 inhabitants died, and their homes were buried under tons of volcanic ash.

Examples An example can help make an abstract or a complex idea concrete or can provide evidence to clarify a point.

MODEL
Throughout history, people have used observations of nature to predict the weather. For example, you may have heard that "red skies at night are a sailor's delight."

Quotations Choose quotations that clearly support your points and be sure that you copy each quotation word for word. Remember always to credit the source.

MODEL
The use of dialect in fiction makes the characters and setting seem more real to the reader. In "The Bamboo Beads," the character speaks a dialect of English found in Trinidad and Tobago. Dialogue such as "I put de pretty beads on de string," helps readers hear in their minds just how Tantie sounds.

2.6 Using Language Effectively

Effective use of language can help readers to recognize the significance of an issue, to visualize a scene, or to understand a character. The specific words and phrases that you use have everything to do with how effectively you communicate meaning. Keep these particular points in mind.

Specific Nouns Nouns are specific when they refer to individual or particular things. If you refer to a city, you are being general. If you refer to London, you are being specific. Specific nouns help readers identify the who, what, and where of your message.

Specific Verbs Verbs are the most powerful words in sentences. They convey the action, the movement, and sometimes the drama of thoughts and observations. Verbs such as *trudged, skipped,* and *sauntered* provide a more vivid picture of the action than the verb *walked.*

Specific Modifiers Use modifiers sparingly, but when you use them, make them count. Is the building big or towering? Are your poodle's paws small or toylike? Once again, it is the more specific word that carries the greater impact.

③ Descriptive Writing

Descriptive writing allows you to paint word pictures about anything and everything in the world, from events of global importance to the most personal feelings. It is an essential part of almost every piece of writing, including essays, poems, letters, field notes, newspaper reports, and videos.

RUBRIC **STANDARDS FOR WRITING**

A successful description should

- have a clear focus and sense of purpose
- use sensory details and precise words to create a vivid image, establish a mood, or express emotion
- present details in a logical order

---

③.1 Key Techniques

Consider Your Goals What do you want to accomplish in writing your description? Do you want to show why something is important to you? Do you want to make a person or scene more memorable? Do you want to explain an event?

Identify Your Audience Who will read your description? How familiar are they with your subject? What background information will they need? Which details will they find most interesting?

Think Figuratively What figures of speech might help make your description vivid and interesting? What simile or metaphor comes to mind? What imaginative comparisons can you make? What living thing does an inanimate object remind you of?

MODEL
The sun burned in the sky like a bare light bulb. When I squinted, it looked as if butterflies were dancing on the desert's horizon, though I knew it was really only currents of heat rising from the sand. The plain water in the canteen that I held to my lips tasted sweeter than any soda I could remember.

Gather Sensory Details Which sights, smells, tastes, sounds, and textures make your subject come alive? Which details stick in your mind when you observe or recall your subject? Which senses does it most strongly affect?

MODEL
Andrew slumped against the wall outside the gym. His calves ached more than his stomach, empty and tense. In his mind, he replayed the last minutes of the game—tasting sweat, hearing cheers, feeling the seams of the basketball under his fingers—but he couldn't visualize missing the shot.

You might want to use a chart like the one shown here to collect sensory details about your subject.

Sights	Sounds	Textures	Smells	Tastes

Create a Mood What feelings do you want to evoke in your readers? Do you want to soothe them with comforting images? Do you want to build tension with ominous details? Do you want to evoke sadness or joy?

MODEL
The Condors were one run ahead. Just one more strike by the Cranes' batter would end the game. The crowd stood. Orange and white streamers waved desperately on one side of the stadium while blue and gold ones mimicked them on the other side. One more strike—just one. The pitcher wound up. The batter poised. Here came the ball.

3.2 Options for Organization

Spatial Order Choose one of these options to show the spatial order of a scene.

EXAMPLE 1

Top
↓
Bottom

EXAMPLE 2

Left → Right

EXAMPLE 3

Outside
Inside

EXAMPLE 4

Far
↑
Near

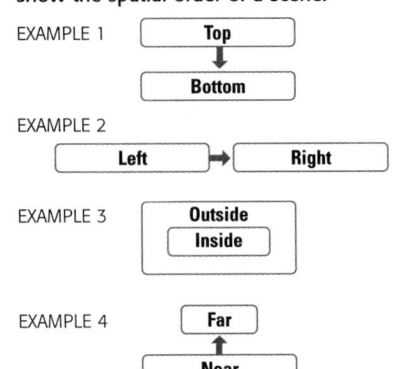

MODEL
Arthur and Chantal came to the bicycle race to cheer for their friends. As the first group of cyclists approached the finish line, Arthur and Chantal cheered wildly when they saw their friend Lindsay leading the pack. Another friend, Charles, was just behind her. Far off in the distance, they could just make out their friend Georgia's red bike.

WRITING TIP Use transitions that help the reader picture the relationship among the objects you describe. Some useful transitions for showing spatial relationships are *behind, below, here, in the distance, on the left, over,* and *on top.*

Order of Impression Order of impression is how you notice details.

What first catches your attention
↓
What you notice next
↓
What you see after that
↓
What you focus on last

MODEL
Mike descended the stairs slowly, so we saw his shoes first—polished to a gleaming black so that they looked almost like patent leather. Then, the satin stripe on each trouser leg told us he was dressed for a formal event. Finally, we saw the white bow tie, just below the grin.

WRITING TIP Use transitions that help readers understand the order of the impressions you are describing. Some useful transitions are *after, next, during, first, before, finally,* and *then.*

Order of Importance (Climactic Order) You might want to use order of importance as the organizing structure for your description.

Least important
↓
More important
↓
Most important

MODEL
Most impressionist paintings were created outdoors. The paintings feature bright colors and loose brushwork. The painters used these techniques to portray the effects of sunlight on objects. The goal of the impressionists was to capture their immediate "impression" of a brief moment in time.

WRITING TIP Use transitions that help the reader understand the order of importance that you attach to the elements of your description. Some useful transitions are *first, second, mainly, more important, most important,* and *more to the point.*

4 Narrative Writing

Narrative writing tells a story. A story from your imagination is a fictional narrative. A true story about actual events is a nonfictional narrative. Narrative writing can be found in short stories, novels, news articles, and biographies.

RUBRIC STANDARDS FOR WRITING

A successful narrative should

- include descriptive details and dialogue to develop the characters, setting, and plot
- have a clear beginning, middle, and end
- have a logical organization with clues and transitions to help the reader understand the order of events
- maintain a consistent tone and point of view
- use language that is appropriate for the audience
- demonstrate the significance of events or ideas

4.1 Key Techniques

Identify the Main Events What are the most important events in your narrative? Is each event part of the chain of events needed to tell the story? In a fictional narrative, this series of events is the story's plot.

MODEL

Event 1 — Danielle receives a gift—a horse to train—from Aunt Jessica.

Event 2 — Danielle and the horse do not get along. The horse seems to be unable to learn anything.

Event 3 — Danielle accepts that the horse is proud and spirited and that she may never train him.

Event 4 — Danielle adjusts her training methods, and the horse begins to respond to her.

Describe the Setting When do the events occur? Where do they take place? How can you use setting to create mood and to set the stage for the characters and their actions?

MODEL

At first, Danielle just sat on the weathered split-rail fence and watched the horse canter. When the sun shone hot on her back, she slid off the fence and walked toward him through the overgrown pasture.

Depict Characters Vividly What do your characters look like? What do they think and say? How do they act? What vivid details can show readers what the characters are like?

MODEL

Danielle let her long blond hair fall around her face to hide the tears in her eyes, and forced herself to smile.

WRITING TIP Dialogue is an effective way of developing characters in a narrative. Choose words that express your characters' personalities and show how the characters feel about one another and about the events in the plot.

MODEL

"I know he's not your favorite horse, but he needs training," said Aunt Jessica.

Danielle tried to keep disappointment out of her voice as she replied, "Thanks, Aunt Jessica. I know I can train him like you taught me."

"You can do anything you set your mind to," Aunt Jessica said.

4.2 Options for Organization

Option 1: Chronological Order One way to organize a piece of narrative writing is to arrange the events in chronological order, as shown below.

	MODEL
Introduction *characters and setting*	**Aunt Jessica gives Danielle her first horse to train.**
Event 1	**He's a horse Danielle doesn't like; he's stubborn, and when Danielle tries to train him, nothing happens.**
Event 2	**Danielle sees the horse running in the field; he looks proud and independent.**
End *perhaps show the significance of the events*	**Aunt Jessica asks Danielle if she would like a different horse to train. Danielle says she wants to keep the horse she has. Aunt Jessica smiles warmly at her.**

Option 2: Focus on Character You may prefer to focus on characters, especially if a change in character—the way someone thinks, feels, or behaves—is important to the outcome of the story.

Introduce the main character.

↓

Describe the conflict the main character faces.

↓

Relate the events and the changes the character goes through as a result of the conflict.

↓

Present the final change or new understanding.

Option 3: Focus on Conflict When the telling of a fictional narrative focuses on a central conflict, the story's plot may follow the model shown below.

	MODEL
Describe the main characters and setting.	**Danielle lives on the Kansas prairie near her Aunt Jessica, who raises horses. Danielle excels at everything she does and is a little spoiled; she looks up to her aunt, who is quiet and thoughtful.**
Present the conflict.	**When Danielle asks for a horse to train, Jessica deliberately gives her a horse that will be hard to train.**
Relate the events that make the conflict complex and cause the characters to change.	**• Danielle is hurt that her aunt has given her a horse she dislikes.** **• Danielle wants to train the horse quickly so that she can ride him in a competition.** **• Danielle and Aunt Jessica have always been very close.**
Present the resolution or outcome of the conflict.	**By dealing with the challenge of training a difficult horse, Danielle becomes more mature. She and her aunt are brought closer together.**

Explanatory Writing

Explanatory writing informs and explains. For example, you can use it to give instructions for cooking spaghetti, to discuss the origins of the universe, or to compare two pieces of literature.

5.1 Types of Explanatory Writing

LINK TO LITERATURE Explanatory writing techniques provide tools for exploring the issues presented by or in literature. The examples presented in sections 5.1 and 5.2 use explanatory writing techniques to examine Elizabeth Ellis's narrative "Flowers and Freckle Cream" (page 231).

There are many types of explanatory writing. Think about your topic and select the type that presents the information most clearly.

Compare and Contrast How are two or more subjects alike? How are they different?

> MODEL
> **The narrator and her grandfather have different ideas about beauty.**

Cause and Effect How does one event cause something else to happen? Why do certain conditions exist? What are the results of an action or a condition?

> MODEL
> **Because she wears freckle remover in the sun, the narrator's freckles grow darker.**

Analysis/Classification How does something work? How can it be defined? What are its parts? How can it be classified into categories?

> MODEL
> **Unlike the narrator, I believe beauty is made up of a good appearance, self-confidence, and character.**

Problem-Solution How can you identify and state a problem? How would you analyze the problem and its causes? How can it be solved?

> MODEL
> **Some people, like the narrator, wish they could look like someone else. The best solution is learning to appreciate your appearance as it is.**

5.2 Compare and Contrast

Compare-and-contrast writing examines the similarities and differences between two or more subjects. You might, for example, compare and contrast two short stories, the main characters in a novel, or two movies.

RUBRIC STANDARDS FOR WRITING

Successful compare-and-contrast writing should

- clearly identify the subjects that are being compared and contrasted
- include specific, relevant details
- follow a clear plan of organization dealing with the same features of both subjects under discussion
- use language and details appropriate to the audience
- use transitional words and phrases to clarify similarities and differences

Options for Organization

Compare-and-contrast writing can be organized in different ways. The examples that follow demonstrate feature-by-feature organization and subject-by-subject organization.

Option 1: Feature-by-Feature Organization

MODEL

Feature 1 **I. The characters' standards of beauty**

    Subject A. The narrator's standard of beauty is based on her cousin's appearance.

    Subject B. The grandfather thinks beauty can take many forms.

Feature 2 **II. The characters' ideas about attaining beauty**

    Subject A. The narrator thinks she will be beautiful if she loses her freckles.

    Subject B. The grandfather thinks the narrator is already beautiful.

Option 2: Subject-by-Subject Organization

MODEL

Subject A **I. The narrator**

    Feature 1. The narrator's standard of beauty is based on her cousin's appearance.

    Feature 2. The narrator thinks she will be beautiful if she loses her freckles.

II. The grandfather

Subject B   **Feature 1.** The grandfather thinks beauty can take many forms.

    Feature 2. The grandfather thinks the narrator is already beautiful.

WRITING TIP Remember your purpose for comparing and contrasting your subjects, and support your purpose with expressive language and specific details.

5.3 Cause and Effect

Cause-and-effect writing explains why something happened, why certain conditions exist, or what resulted from an action or a condition.

RUBRIC STANDARDS FOR WRITING

Successful cause-and-effect writing should

- clearly state the cause-and-effect relationship
- show clear connections between causes and effects
- present causes and effects in a logical order and use transitions effectively
- use facts, examples, and other details to illustrate each cause and effect
- use language and details appropriate to the audience

Options for Organization

Your organization will depend on your topic and purpose for writing.

Option 1: Effect-to-Cause Organization

- To explain the causes of an event, such as the closing of a factory, you might first state the effect and then examine its causes.

Option 2: Cause-to-Effect Organization

- To explain the effects of an event, such as the passage of a law, you might first state the cause and then explain the effects.

Option 3: Cause-and-Effect Chain Organization

• Sometimes you'll want to describe a chain of cause-and-effect relationships to explore a topic, such as the disappearance of tropical rain forests or the development of home computers.

 Problem-Solution

Problem-solution writing clearly states a problem, analyzes the problem, and proposes a solution to the problem. It can be used to identify and solve a conflict between characters, analyze a chemistry experiment, or explain why the home team keeps losing.

RUBRIC STANDARDS FOR WRITING

Successful problem-solution writing should

• identify the problem and help the reader understand the issues involved

• analyze the causes and effects of the problem

• integrate quotations, facts, and statistics into the text

• explore possible solutions to the problem and recommend the best one(s)

• use language, tone, and details appropriate to the audience

---

Options for Organization

Your organization will depend on the goal of your problem-solution piece, your intended audience, and the specific problem you choose to address. The organizational methods that follow are effective for different kinds of problem-solution writing.

Option 1: Simple Problem-Solution

Option 2: Deciding Between Solutions

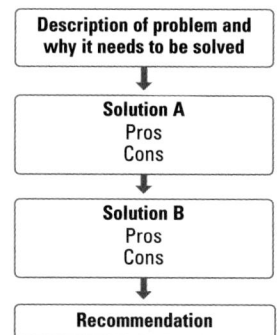

WRITING TIP Have a classmate read and respond to your problem-solution writing. Ask your peer reader: Is the problem clearly stated? Is the organization easy to follow? Do the proposed solutions seem logical?

 Analysis/Classification

In writing an analysis or classification, you explain how something works, how it is defined, or what its parts are. The details you include will depend upon the kind of analysis you write.

Process Analysis What are the major steps or stages in a process? What background information is needed to understand each step? You might use process analysis to explain how to program a VCR.

Definition Analysis What are the most important characteristics of a subject? To define a rain forest, you might include such characteristics as rainfall, vegetation, and animal life.

Parts Analysis What are the parts, groups, or types that make up a subject? Parts analysis could be used to explain the parts of the human brain.

Classification How can one or more items be classified into categories? For example, you might use classification to explain how honey bees may be drones, workers, or queens.

RUBRIC **STANDARDS FOR WRITING**

A successful analysis should

- hook readers with a strong introduction
- clearly state the subject and its parts
- use a specific organizing structure to provide a logical flow of information
- show connections among facts and ideas through transitional words and phrases
- use language and details appropriate for the audience

Options for Organization

Organize your details in a logical order.

Option 1: Process Analysis A process analysis is usually organized chronologically, with steps or stages in the order they occur.

MODEL

Introduction →
Background →
Explain steps →

Insect metamorphosis

Many insects grow through a four-step life cycle.

Step 1: Egg
Step 2: Larva
Step 3: Pupa
Step 4: Adult

Option 2: Definition Analysis You can organize the details in a definition or parts analysis in order of importance or impression.

MODEL

Introduce term →
General definition →
Explain features →

What is an insect?

An insect is a small animal with a skeleton on the outside of its body, three body segments, and three pairs of legs.

Feature 1: exoskeleton
Feature 2: body segments
Feature 3: pairs of legs

Option 3: Parts Analysis The following parts analysis describes the parts of an insect's body.

MODEL

Introduce subject →
Explain parts →

An insect's body is divided into three main parts.

Part 1: Head includes eyes, mouth, and antennae.

Part 2: Thorax has the legs and wings attached to it.

Part 3: Abdomen contains organs for digesting food, eliminating waste, and reproducing.

Option 4: Classification The following model groups things based on characteristics.

MODEL

One way that scientists classify insects is by dividing them into species that are social and those that are not. Most insects are nonsocial. They meet one another only to reproduce. The female lays her eggs near a food source and then leaves them. Social insects, on the other hand, live in organized communities and depend on one another. Social insects have specific roles within their communities. Examples of social insects include termites, ants, many bees, and some wasps.

⑥ Persuasive Writing

Persuasive writing allows you to use the power of language to inform and influence others. It can take many forms, including speeches, newspaper editorials, billboards, advertisements, and critical reviews.

RUBRIC STANDARDS FOR WRITING

Successful persuasive writing should

- state the issue and the writer's position
- give opinions and support them with facts or reasons
- have a reasonable and respectful tone
- answer opposing views
- use sound logic and effective language
- conclude by summing up reasons or calling for action

6.1 Key Techniques

Clarify Your Position What do you believe about the issue? How can you express your opinion most clearly?

MODEL
Our city should create bike lanes on all major streets to increase safety.

Know Your Audience Who will read your writing? What do they already know and believe about the issue? What objections to your position might they have? What additional information might they need? What tone and approach would be most effective?

MODEL
The popularity of bike riding for fun and exercise has greatly increased over the last five years. Unfortunately, there has also been an increase in injuries during this period. I believe the creation of bike lanes is necessary for public safety.

Support Your Opinion Why do you feel the way you do about the issue? What facts, statistics, examples, quotations, anecdotes, or opinions of authorities support your view? What reasons will convince your readers? What evidence can answer their objections?

MODEL
According to the National Safe Kids Campaign, in 1997 more than 350,000 children ages 14 and under were treated in hospital emergency rooms for bicycle-related injuries.

Begin and End with a Bang How can you hook your readers and make a lasting impression? What memorable quotation, anecdote, or statistic will catch their attention at the beginning or stick in their minds at the end? What strong summary or call to action can you conclude with?

BEGINNING
Whether you are a bicyclist, a driver, or even a pedestrian, chances are you've been put in a dangerous situation because bikes must use the same lanes as cars.
CONCLUSION
Please help improve safety for everyone in our community by supporting the creation of bike lanes on all major streets.

6.2 Options for Organization

In a two-sided persuasive essay, you want to show the weaknesses of other opinions as you explain the strengths of your own.

The example below demonstrates one method of organizing your persuasive essay to convince your audience.

Option 1: Reasons for Your Opinion

> MODEL
> **Our city should create bike lanes on all major streets to encourage safety.**
>
> **Reason 1**   **Bicycle accidents often result in serious injuries.**
>
> **Reason 2**   **Bicycle lanes would separate bike traffic from car traffic, making travel safer for everyone.**
>
> **Reason 3**   **Safe bike paths would encourage people to ride bicycles for recreation and transportation.**

WRITING TIP Starting a persuasive piece with a question, a surprising fact, or an anecdote will capture your readers' interest and make them want to keep reading.

The ending of a persuasive piece is often the part that sticks in a reader's mind. Your conclusion might summarize the two sides of an issue or call for some action.

Depending on the purpose and form of your writing, you may want to show the weaknesses of other opinions as you explain the strength of your own. Two options for organizing writing that includes more than just your side of the issue are shown below.

Option 2: Why Your Opinion Is Stronger

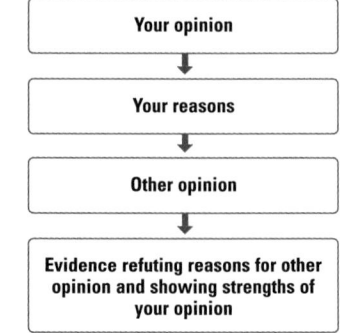

Option 3: Why Another Opinion Is Weaker

⑦ Research Report Writing

In research report writing, you can find answers to questions about a topic in which you're interested. Your writing organizes information from various sources and presents it to your readers as a unified and coherent whole.

RUBRIC STANDARDS FOR WRITING

An effective research report should

- clearly state the purpose of the report in a thesis statement
- use evidence and details from a variety of sources to support the thesis
- contain only accurate and relevant information
- document sources correctly
- develop the topic logically and include appropriate transitions
- include a properly formatted Works Cited list

⑦.① Key Techniques

Develop Relevant, Interesting, and Researchable Questions Asking thoughtful questions is an ongoing part of the research process. You might begin with a list of basic questions that are relevant to your topic. These would focus on getting basic facts that answer the questions *who, what, where, when, how,* and *why* about your topic. If you were researching dragons in world folklore, you might develop a set of questions similar to these.

> MODEL
> **What cultures have dragons in their folklore?**
>
> **How are stories of dragons around the world similar and different?**

As you become more familiar with your topic, think of questions that might provide an interesting perspective that makes readers think.

> MODEL
> **What do dragons symbolize in different cultures?**

Check that your questions are researchable. Ask questions that will uncover facts, statistics, case studies, and other documentable evidence.

Clarify Your Thesis A thesis statement is one or two sentences clearly stating the main idea that you will develop in your report. A thesis may also indicate the organizational pattern you will follow and reflect your tone and point of view.

> MODEL
> **Folk tales and myths about dragons exist in cultures all over the world, but dragons symbolize good in some cultures and bad in others.**

Document Your Sources You need to document, or credit, the sources where you find your evidence. In the example below, the writer paraphrases and documents a passage from David Passes's book about dragons.

> MODEL
> **In Mordiford, England, people tell the legend of a wyvern, a two-legged dragon with wings. The wyvern terrorized the village until a prisoner named Garstone gave his life saving the community from the fire-breathing monster (Passes 30–31).**

Support Your Ideas You should support your ideas with relevant evidence—facts, anecdotes, and statistics—from reliable sources. In the example below, the writer supports the idea that dragon images still exist in cultures today.

MODEL
During the Chinese New Year, the elaborate dragon dance is used in the celebrations to drive away bad luck and bring people good luck for the coming year.

7.2 Finding and Evaluating Sources

Begin your research by looking for information about your topic in books, magazines, newspapers, and computer databases. In addition to using your library's card or computer catalog, look up your subject in indexes, such as the *Readers' Guide to Periodical Literature* or the *New York Times Index*. The bibliographies in books you find during your research may also lead to additional sources. The following checklist will help you evaluate the reliability of the sources you find.

Checklist for Evaluating Your Sources	
Authoritative	Someone who has written several books or articles on your subject or whose work has been published in a well-respected newspaper or journal may be considered an authority.
Up-to-date	Check the publication date to see if the source reflects the most current research on your subject.
Respected	In general, tabloid newspapers and popular-interest magazines are not reliable sources. If you have questions about whether you are using a respected source, ask your librarian.

WRITING TIP Your reading can inspire ideas for research topics. The title of the story "In the Land of Small Dragon," on page 804, might lead you to explore the importance of dragons in Vietnamese traditions as well as in other cultures.

7.3 Making Source Cards

For each source you find, record the bibliographic information on a separate index card. You will need this information to give credit to the sources in your paper. The samples below show how to make source cards for encyclopedia entries, magazine articles, and books. You will use the source number on each card to identify the notes you take during your research.

Encyclopedia Article

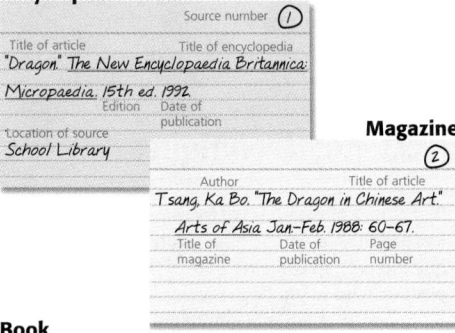

Source number ①
Title of article   Title of encyclopedia
"Dragon." *The New Encyclopaedia Britannica:*
Micropaedia. 15th ed. 1992.
            Edition   Date of publication
Location of source
School Library

Magazine

②
    Author   Title of article
Tsang, Ka Bo. "The Dragon in Chinese Art."
Arts of Asia Jan.-Feb. 1988: 60–67.
Title of   Date of   Page
magazine   publication   number

Book

③
    Author   Title
Passes, David. *Dragons: Truth, Myth, and Legend.* New York: Artists and Writers Guild, 1993.
        City of publication/Publisher
Location of source   Library call number
Public Library   398.2 PAS 1993 4356

7.4 Taking Notes

As you find material that suits the purpose of your report, record each piece of information on a separate note card. You will probably use all three of the note-taking methods listed below.

Paraphrase Restate the passage in your own words. Start by finding the main idea and rewriting it in your own words. Then find and list the details that support the idea. As you restate the passage, try to use simpler language. Remember to note the source of the passage.

Summarize, or rephrase the passage in fewer words. Restate only the main ideas, using your own words. Leave out details. As a final step, check to make sure that your summary is accurate and that it does not include unnecessary information.

Quote Copy the original text word for word if you think the author's own words best clarify a particular point. Use quotation marks to signal the beginning and the end of the quotation.

For more details on making source cards and taking notes, see the Research Report Workshop on pages 820–827.

Main idea
Dragons as war emblems   Source number ①

Norse warriors of Northern Europe
decorated their shields with dragons and
displayed carved heads of dragons on the
prows of their sailing ships.
Type of note
(paraphrase)

7.5 Writing a Thesis Statement

A thesis statement in a research report defines the main idea, or overall purpose, of your report. A clear one-sentence answer to your main question will result in a good thesis statement.

Question How are stories of dragons around the world similar and different?

Thesis Statement Folk tales and myths about dragons exist in cultures all over the world, but dragons symbolize good in some cultures and bad in others.

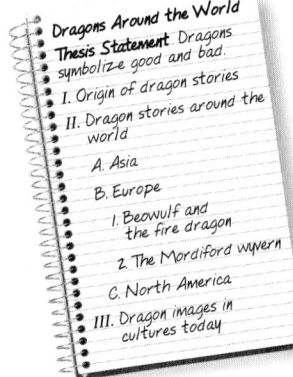

Dragons Around the World
Thesis Statement Dragons
symbolize good and bad.
I. Origin of dragon stories
II. Dragon stories around the world
  A. Asia
  B. Europe
    1. Beowulf and the fire dragon
    2. The Mordiford wyvern
  C. North America
III. Dragon images in cultures today

7.6 Making an Outline

To organize your report, group your note cards according to their main ideas and arrange them in a logical order. With your notes, make a topic outline, beginning with a shortened version of your thesis statement. Key ideas are listed after Roman numerals, and subpoints are listed after uppercase letters and Arabic numerals.

7.7 Documenting Your Sources

When you quote one of your sources or write in your own words information you have found in a source, you need to credit that source. You can do this by using parenthetical documentation. Electronic sources, such as CD-ROMs and Web sites, must be credited just as you would credit print sources.

USING TABLES OF CONTENTS Some students may not realize that the quickest way of finding information in a reference or nonfiction book is with the table of contents. Point out that a table of contents lists the chapters and sections of a book, giving the page numbers on which each begins. Sometimes a brief chapter summary or bulleted list of main ideas appears with each entry.

Locating Information on a Topic In any research that students perform it will be helpful to scan tables of contents. For example, ask students to suppose they have begun researching ways in which horses were important to the Sioux. Ask students: Through use of a library catalog, you have found 30 books about horses and 30 books on the Sioux; how will you know which books contain information on your topic? If they narrow their catalog searches, they might miss some books. Instead they need to go to the library shelves and begin to check the books' tables of contents. If a table of contents has interesting headings, it might even suggest a new or revised research question.

Organizing Information As students compile research reports they might wish to organize them into sections with topic headings. This is also useful with group projects that combine the focused reports of several students under one broader topic. A table of contents for such a project should list the title and author(s) of each section with the page number on which it begins. You might ask students to save their outlines as they draft their research reports and to consider using their outline headings as section or chapter headings.

Guidelines for Parenthetical Documentation

Work by One Author	Put the author's last name and, if appropriate, the page reference in parentheses: **(Passes 19)**. If you mention the author's name in the sentence, put only the page reference in parentheses: **(19)**. For electronic sources, which usually have no page numbers, give the author's name in parentheses unless the name is already included in the text. **(Frieb)**
Work by Two or Three Authors	Put the last names of the authors and the page reference in parentheses: **(Guise, Gushwa, and Donnelly 99)**.
Work by More Than Three Authors	Give the first author's last name followed by et al. and the page reference: **(Park et al. 233)**.
Work with No Author Given	Give the title or a shortened version and, if appropriate, the page reference: **("Dragon")**. Electronic sources usually have no page numbers. No page number is necessary for documentation of an encyclopedia article.
One of Two or More Works by Same Author	Give the author's last name, the title or a shortened version, and the page reference: **(Guccione, "On Dragons' Wings" 71)**.

WRITING TIP Presenting someone else's writing or ideas as your own is plagiarism. To avoid plagiarism, you need to credit sources as noted above. However, if a piece of information is common knowledge—available in several sources—you do not need to credit the source. To see an example of parenthetical documentation, see the essay on page 821.

7.8 Creating a Works Cited Page

At the end of your research report, you need to include a Works Cited page. All the sources that you have cited in your report should be listed alphabetically by the authors' last names. If no author is given for a work, use the editor's last name or the title of the work. Note the guidelines for spacing and punctuation on the model page. Works Cited entries for electronic sources require slightly more information than those for print sources.

Internet Sources A Works Cited entry for an Internet source includes the same information as one for a print source. It also includes the date you accessed the information and the electronic address of the information. Some of the information about the source may be unavailable. Include as much as you can.

CD-ROMs A Works Cited entry for a CD-ROM includes the publication medium (CD-ROM), the company that distributes it, and the date of publication. Some of this information may not be available. Include as much as you can.

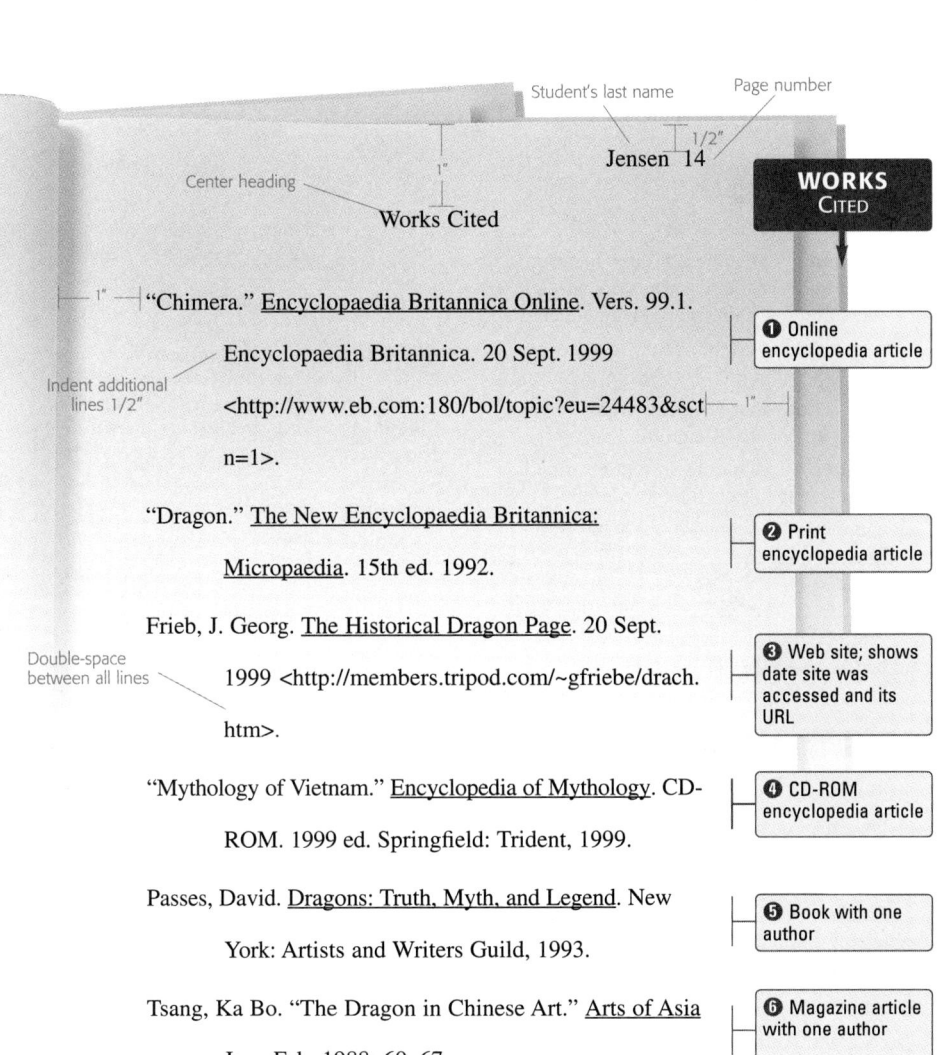

Student's last name Page number

Jensen 14   1/2"

Center heading

Works Cited

WORKS CITED

1"   "Chimera." <u>Encyclopaedia Britannica Online</u>. Vers. 99.1.

Encyclopaedia Britannica. 20 Sept. 1999

Indent additional
lines 1/2"
<http://www.eb.com:180/bol/topic?eu=24483&sct   1"

n=1>.

❶ Online
encyclopedia article

"Dragon." <u>The New Encyclopaedia Britannica:</u>

<u>Micropaedia</u>. 15th ed. 1992.

❷ Print
encyclopedia article

Frieb, J. Georg. <u>The Historical Dragon Page</u>. 20 Sept.

Double-space
between all lines
1999 <http://members.tripod.com/~gfriebe/drach.

htm>.

❸ Web site; shows
date site was
accessed and its
URL

"Mythology of Vietnam." <u>Encyclopedia of Mythology</u>. CD-

ROM. 1999 ed. Springfield: Trident, 1999.

❹ CD-ROM
encyclopedia article

Passes, David. <u>Dragons: Truth, Myth, and Legend</u>. New

York: Artists and Writers Guild, 1993.

❺ Book with one
author

Tsang, Ka Bo. "The Dragon in Chinese Art." <u>Arts of Asia</u>

Jan.–Feb. 1988: 60–67.

❻ Magazine article
with one author

⑧ Model Bank

8.1 Friendly Letter

BASICS IN A BOX

A successful friendly letter should

❶ begin with a heading that contains your street address, town or city, state and ZIP code, and the date you write the letter

❷ have a salutation that begins with a capital letter and is followed by a comma

❸ have a body that is written in an informal, conversational tone

❹ have a closing that begins with a capital letter and is followed by a comma

❺ end with your signature under the closing

Model 1: Friendly Letter

> 309 Mayo Street ❶
> Tallahassee, Florida 33333
> July 29, 2000
>
> Dear Tova, ❷
>
> It was great to get your postcard. I can't believe you are in Alaska! How are you doing?
>
> Last night my mom and I made pizza. We used peppers, sausage, and asparagus to make a cat face. It was really fun, but I would rather be where you are. We don't have so many mosquitoes here, but we don't have glaciers or horseback riding nearby, either. I can't wait until you get back. ❸
>
> Write again and tell me everything!
>
> Love, ❹
> Carlendra ❺

8.2 Friendly Email

BASICS IN A BOX

A successful friendly email should

❶ have the recipient's exact email address in the "To:" line

❷ state the subject of the email in the "Subject" line

❸ have a body that is written in an informal, conversational tone

❹ close with your name

❺ end with your exact email address after your name

Tips on "Netiquette"
- Always end with your name and email address.
- Always include a subject heading.
- Take as much care with spelling and punctuation as you would in a letter.
- Don't write in all capitals or it will look as if you are shouting.

Model 2: Friendly Email

> To: cmitchell@speedy.net ❶
> cc:
> bcc:
> Subject: Hungry in Alaska ❷
>
> I'm sorry I didn't write back sooner. I have been very busy having the best time ever! This place is awesome. Alaska is beautiful and the people here are really nice. I have been canoeing three times, horseback riding once, and I have plans to go rock climbing. My parents are way into hiking, so we're going up a glacier tomorrow. I wish you could visit. I miss you and I miss having pizza. Can you believe, my parents ate reindeer sausage? (yuck!) ❸
>
> See you in ten days!
> :-)
>
> Tova Goodman ❹
> tovagood@root.net ❺

Book Review

A successful book review should

❶ have an introduction that gives the title, author, and some information about the book

❷ summarize the work without giving away the ending

❸ explain why you admire or dislike the work

❹ if the work is fiction, discuss the plot, setting, characters, and theme

❺ support your reactions with details from the work

❻ conclude with a strong statement of your opinion or a recommendation

---

Model 3: Book Review

Lyddie: A Book with Heart

Reviewed by Nadette Wallis

Can you imagine leaving your family to go to work somewhere you've never been? In Katherine Paterson's book *Lyddie*, that's exactly what happens. In the 1840s, a Vermont farm girl named Lyddie leaves home for a factory job in the big city of Lowell, Massachusetts. This amazing book not only holds you in suspense, it tells you what life was really like in the first American factories. ❶ ❷ ❸

I admire Lyddie because she is a tough but caring person. She faces a bear who crashes into her family cottage on the farm. She even pushes a stagecoach out of the mud while three men just stand there. But Lyddie also shows she cares about her friends and family—and strangers too. ❹

She shows the most courage at the factory, where every day is hard. The factory has tall, cracking ceilings, dusty windows, and deafening noises. The workers feel powerless to improve this life, but later Lyddie surprises everyone with her bold actions. Throughout the book, Lyddie cares about other people, like when she helps the runaway slave rather than collecting a reward. My favorite part is when she stands up for her friend Brigid against Mr. Marsden, the overseer, and dumps a full bucket over his head. ❺

What will happen when she gets her boss angry? As you can tell, this book is full of taking chances and facing danger. Lyddie doesn't want to leave home, but in her adventures she becomes a hero. I recommend *Lyddie* to anyone who would like to read a fast-paced novel about a girl who never lets life get her down. ❻

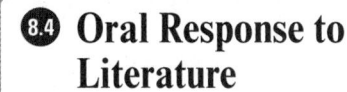

8.4 Oral Response to Literature

BASICS IN A BOX

Content

A successful oral response to literature should:

❶ give the author and the title of the work

❷ clearly express a personal reaction and a judgment about the writing

❸ tell enough about the work for readers to understand the response

❹ contain reasons for the response

❺ draw an overall conclusion

Delivery

An effective speaker should:

• express enthusiam and confidence

• stand with good but relaxed posture

• speak in a loud, clear voice

• make eye contact with the audience

• use expressive gestures and body language

Model 4: Oral Response to Literature

Responding to "The Circuit"   (intro)

by Vanessa Ramirez

When I read and reread "The Circuit" by Francisco ❶
Jiménez, I didn't understand why it made me feel sad, ❷
but then I realized at the end that it reminded me of
when I was small, when I first started school.

In the story a boy named Panchito can't go to school
because he has to work in the fields to help his family. ❸
When he finally goes to school in November, he forgets
how to speak in English.

(body 1)

Panchito says that when he entered the school office, he heard a voice say, "May I help you?" Then he says, "I had not heard English for months. For a few seconds I remained speechless." I put myself in Panchito's place when I read this, because I had already experienced it before. When I first started school, I spoke only Spanish, but my parents spoke for me. So that was a great relief. ❹

The reason I say it was a great relief is because in my situation my parents spoke for me in order to enroll me

(body 2)

and in his situation Panchito had to speak for himself to enroll in school. This part of the story hit my heart. ❹

When people are used to talking in one language, it is very hard when they realize they're being told something in another language. It must be sad because they don't understand, or maybe they do, but they are embarrassed because they don't know how to speak the other language well. That's how Panchito felt when he went to enroll in school and when the teacher asked him to read in class.

(conclusion)

I liked writing about this story because as I was writing, I was imagining that I was there in the story and because it kind of has to do with what happened to me. I think that my response shows that Francisco Jiménez is a good writer. His writing is very realistic, and he really made me feel what Panchito was going through. ❺

8.5 Classification Essay

BASICS IN A BOX

A successful classification essay should:
1. introduce topic and reason for classifying
2. clearly present two or more main categories or aspects of the topic
3. provide one or more main ideas about each category
4. use details to help develop main ideas
5. show the bigger picture in a clear conclusion

Model 5: Classification Essay

The Basics of a Smashing Soccer Team

by Tianna Reyes

① A soccer team sometimes looks disorganized to people who don't play. It's just eleven players running around the field doing whatever they want, right? Wrong! People don't realize the huge amount of planning and strategy involved. **②** A soccer team can be broken down into three main parts, the offense, the midfield players, and the defense.

The offense is an extremely important part of the team. There are usually three players on offense—the right wing, the left wing, and the center forward. **③** The job of the offense is to score goals! Usually they do this by getting the ball from their midfielders and shooting the ball towards the goal. These players must be fast and good at shooting.

③ Midfield players are part offense and part defense. These three players are like a bridge between the offense and defense. They are responsible for passing the ball up the field to the offense players so they can try to score goals. Because they play farther back on the field they see more of the game than the offense does. So midfielders help their offense players see the weak spots in the opponent's defense. Midfield players also help their team's defense to keep the other team from scoring goals. These players do the most running, so they have to have endurance. Good passing skills are also very important for midfielders.

Classification Essay at a Glance

Introduction
- states reason for classifying
- establishes categories

Body
- presents main ideas for each category
- develops main ideas with details

Conclusion
- shows importance of classification

The defense is key, in more ways than one. The defense is the team's "security system." They are there to keep the opposing team from getting the ball and especially from scoring goals. These players are usually four, plus the goalie. They try to take the ball from the other offense and give it back to their own team's offense. "Goalie" is a special defensive position. This player blocks kicks. A good goalie keeps the other team from scoring. She or he is the team's last line of defense. When the ball is shot at the goal, the goalkeeper must do everything he or she can to keep it out of there. Defensive players must be quick and fierce. They must also be sneaky at stealing the ball.

❸

❹

Now you know a soccer team is not just a bunch of people who are good at running and kicking. A soccer team is a group of individuals who have many talents. They are placed in positions that are best for their skills, and they must work together in an overall strategy.

❺

8.6 Persuasive Essay

BASICS IN A BOX

A successful persuasive essay should:

❶ open with a dramatic statement of the issue and your opinion

❷ address the audience you are trying to persuade

❸ provide facts, examples, and reasons to support your opinion

❹ answer opposing views

❺ show clear reasoning

❻ include strategies such as frequent summaries to help readers remember your message

❼ end with a strong position statement or call to action

Model 6: Persuasive Essay

Preserve the Past for the Future

by Brendan Keough

How will we know what it was like to live without electricity or highways? What was it like to watch the first American walk on the moon? The only ones who know the answers are those who lived through these times. But since we pay very little attention to old people, whole chapters of history are being erased. We can stop this great loss by taking the time to interview older relatives.

Hearing people you actually know tell their stories makes history a lot more interesting. Writing down these stories means that others can learn from them, too. Think about how quickly the world changed in the 20th century. When your grandfather or grandmother was a little kid, television hadn't even been invented yet. Your own parents may not have grown up with VCRs, CDs, PCs, or MP3s. What did they do for fun? What were their biggest worries? How was life different for them?

Most of the kids I know don't want to hear their parents talk about "When I was your age. . ." But, if you don't get started recording your family history right now, you'll probably wish you had. My parents are sad that they didn't write down the stories their grandparents told.

Persuasive Essay at a Glance

Introduction
- presents the issue dramatically

Body
- addresses target audience
- gives evidence: facts, examples, reasons

Conclusion
- summary and call to action

And, because they didn't record those stories I never got to hear them. —⑤

Some kids our age probably think that old people's stories are boring. I used to think that, but then when I interviewed my great-uncle, Milton, I found out that he lived a pretty exciting life. For example, he was a well-digger, which is a job I had never heard of before. Even during the Great Depression, when most people lost their jobs and money, he always had work. Later, technology advanced so machines could do his job much faster and cheaper. When everyone else was back working and earning money, he was out of work. Luckily he had nine grown-up kids to help him pull through. —③

I believe that learning about people's lives from the past can help you set goals for your own life. When you hear about how hard your grandparents had to work or what people went through in wars and in the Depression, it really can change the way you look at life's little everyday problems. Don't wait until it's too late! Talk to your relatives and older friends now, and help to preserve the past for the future. —⑥ ⑦

Grammar Handbook

❶ Quick Reference: Parts of Speech

Part of Speech	Definition	Examples
Noun	Names a person, place, thing, idea, quality, or action.	Icarus, Greece, boat, freedom, joy, sailing
Pronoun	Takes the place of a noun or another pronoun.	
Personal	Refers to the one speaking, spoken to, or spoken about.	I, me, my, mine, we, us, our, ours, you, your, yours, she, he, it, her, him, hers, his, its, they, them, their, theirs
Reflexive	Follows a verb or preposition and refers to a preceding noun or pronoun.	myself, yourself, herself, himself, itself, ourselves, yourselves, themselves
Intensive	Emphasizes a noun or another pronoun.	(Same as reflexives)
Demonstrative	Points to specific persons or things.	this, that, these, those
Interrogative	Signals questions.	who, whom, whose, which, what
Indefinite	Refers to person(s) or thing(s) not specifically mentioned.	both, all, most, many, anyone, everybody, several, none, some
Relative	Introduces subordinate clauses and relates them to words in the main clause.	who, whom, whose, which, that
Verb	Expresses action, condition, or state of being.	
Action	Tells what the subject does or did, physically or mentally.	run, reaches, listened, consider, decides, dreamt
Linking	Connects subjects to that which identifies or describes them.	am, is, are, was, were, sound, taste, appear, feel, become, remain, seem
Auxiliary	Precedes and introduces main verbs.	be, have, do, can, could, will, would, may, might
Adjective	Modifies nouns or pronouns.	**strong** women, **two** poems, **lucky** me
Adverb	Modifies verbs, adjectives, or other adverbs.	walked **out**, **really** funny, **far away**
Preposition	Relates one word to another (following) word.	at, by, for, from, in, of, on, to, with
Conjunction	Joins words or word groups.	
Coordinating	Joins words or word groups used the same way.	and, but, or, for, so, yet, nor
Correlative	Joins words or word groups used the same way and used in pairs.	both . . . and, either . . . or, neither . . . nor
Subordinating	Joins word groups not used the same way.	although, after, as, before, because, when, if, unless
Interjection	Expresses emotion.	wow, ouch, hurrah

❷ Quick Reference: The Sentence and Its Parts

The diagrams that follow will give you a brief review of the essentials of the sentence—subjects and predicates—and of some of its parts.

Milo's **car** **stalled** in the Doldrums.

The **complete subject** includes all the words that identify the person, place, thing, or idea that the sentence is about.

The **complete predicate** includes all the words that tell or ask something about the subject.

car

stalled

The **simple subject** tells exactly whom or what the sentence is about. It may be one word or a group of words, but it does not include modifiers.

The **simple predicate**, or **verb**, tells what the subject does or is. It may be one word or several, but it does not include modifiers.

At school, an understanding teacher **had given** Panchito English lessons.

A **prepositional phrase** consists of a preposition, its object, and any modifiers of the object. In this phrase, *at* is the preposition and *school* is its object.

The **subject** tells who or what the sentence is about.

Verbs often have more than one part. They may be made up of a **main verb**, like *given,* and one or more **auxiliary,** or **helping verbs,** like *had.*

A **direct object** is a word or group of words that tells who or what receives the action of the verb in the sentence.

An **indirect object** is a word or group of words that tells *to whom* or *for whom* or *to what* or *for what* about the verb. A sentence can have an indirect object only if it has a direct object. The indirect object always comes before the direct object in a sentence.

❸ Quick Reference: Punctuation

Punctuation	Function	Examples
End Marks period, question mark, exclamation point	to end sentences	We can start now. When would you like to leave? What a fantastic hit!
	initials and other abbreviations	Mr. Gary Soto, J. K. Rowling, McDougal Littell Inc., P.M., A.D., lbs., oz., Blvd., Dr.
	items in outlines	I. Volcanoes 　A. Central-vent 　　1. Shield
	exception: postal abbreviations	NE (Nebraska), NV (Nevada)
Commas	before a conjunction in a compound sentence	I have never disliked poetry, but now I really love it.
	items in a series	She is brave, loyal, and kind. The slow, easy route is best.
	words of address	Maria, how can I help you? You must do something, soldier.
	parenthetical expressions	Well, what if we can't? Hard workers, as you know, don't quit. I'm not a quitter, believe me.
	introductory phrases and clauses	In the beginning of the day, I feel fresh. While she was out, I was here. Having finished my chores, I went out.
	nonessential phrases and clauses	Ed Pawn, captain of the chess team, won. Ed Pawn, who is the captain, won. The two leading runners, sprinting toward the finish line, ended in a tie.
	in dates and addresses	September 21, 2001. Mail it by May 14, 2000, to Hauptman Company, 321 Market Street, Memphis, Tennessee.
	in letter parts	Dear Jim, Sincerely yours,
	for clarity, or to avoid confusion	By noon, time had run out. What the minister does, does matter. While cooking, Jim burned his hand.
Semicolons	in compound sentences that are not joined by coordinators *and,* etc.	I went to Houston in January; in June I'm going to Seattle. I read science fiction; however, I don't like fantasy stories.
	with items in series that contain commas	We invited my sister, Jan; her friend, Don; my uncle, Jack; and Mary Dodd.
	in compound sentences that contain commas	After I ran out of money, I called my parents; but only my sister was home, unfortunately.

Punctuation	Function	Examples
Colons	to introduce lists	**Correct:** Those we wrote were the following: Dana, John, and Will. **Incorrect:** Those we wrote were: Dana, John, and Will.
	before a long quotation	Abraham Lincoln wrote: "Four score and seven years ago, our fathers brought forth on this continent a new nation. . . ."
	after the salutation of a business letter	To whom it may concern: Dear Leonard Atole:
	with certain numbers	1:28 P.M., Genesis 2:3–5
Dashes	to indicate an abrupt break in thought	I was thinking of my mother—who is arriving tomorrow—just as you walked in.
Parentheses	to enclose less important material	It was so unlike him (John is always on time) that I began to worry. The last World Series game (Did you see it?) was fun.
Hyphens	with a compound adjective before nouns	The not-so-rich taxpayer won't stand for this!
	in compounds with *all-, ex-, self-, -elect*	The ex-firefighter helped rescue him. Our president-elect is self-conscious.
	in compound numbers (to ninety-nine)	Today, I turn twenty-one.
	in fractions used as adjectives	My cup is one-third full.
	between prefixes and words beginning with capital letters	Which pre-Raphaelite painter do you like best? It snowed in mid-October.
	when dividing words at the end of a line	How could you have any reasonable expec-tations of getting a new computer?
Apostrophes	to form possessives of nouns and indefinite pronouns	my friend's book, my friends' book, anyone's guess, somebody else's problem
	for omitted letters in numbers/contractions	don't (omitted *o*); he'd (omitted *woul*) the class of '99 (omitted *19*)
	to form plurals of letters and numbers	I had two A's and no 2's on my report card.
Quotation Marks	to set off a speaker's exact words	Sara said, "I'm finally ready." "I'm ready," Sara said, "finally." Did Sara say, "I'm ready"? Sara said, "I'm ready!"
	for titles of stories, short poems, essays, songs, book chapters	I liked Paulsen's "Older Run" and Roethke's "Night Journey." I like Cole Porter's "You're the Top."
Ellipses	for material omitted from a quotation	"When in the course of human events . . . and to assume among the powers of the earth. . . ."
Italics	for titles of books, plays, magazines, long poems, operas, films, TV series, names of ships	*The House on Mango Street, Hamlet, Newsweek, The Odyssey, Madame Butterfly, Gone with the Wind, Seinfeld, U.S.S. Constitution*

❹ Quick Reference: Capitalization

Category/Rule	Examples
People and Titles	
Names and initials of people	Sandra Cisneros, J. R. R. Tolkien
Titles with names or in place of them	Dr. Rodriguez, Senator Long, the Senator
Deities and members of religious groups	God, Allah, the Lord, Zeus; Baptists, Roman Catholics
Names of ethnic and national groups	Asians, African Americans, Navajos, Armenians
Geographical Names	
Cities, states, countries, continents, planets	Philadelphia, Kansas, Japan, Europe, Jupiter, Pluto
Regions, bodies of water, mountains	the South, Colorado River, the Rockies
Geographic features, parks	Great Basin, Yellowstone National Park
Streets and roads	East Sutton Drive, Kings Highway, 125th Street
Organizations and Events	
Companies, organizations, teams	Boy Scouts of America, St. Louis Cardinals
Buildings, bridges, monuments	Empire State Building, Eads Bridge, Washington Monument
Documents, awards	the Declaration of Independence, Stanley Cup
Special named events	Mardi Gras, World Series
Governmental bodies, historical periods and events	U.S. Senate, House of Representatives, Middle Ages, Vietnam War
Days and months, holidays	Thursday, March, Thanksgiving, Labor Day
Specific cars, boats, trains, planes	Edsel, Mississippi Queen, Orient Express, Concorde
Proper Adjectives	
Adjectives formed from proper nouns	French cooking, Shakespearian theater, Atlantic coast
First Words and the Pronoun _I_	
The first word in a sentence or quotation	They thanked him. Then he said, "Let's go."
Complete sentence in parentheses	(Consult the previous chapter.)
Salutation and closing of letters	Dear Sir or Madam, To all concerned, Very truly yours,
First letters in lines of most poetry and the personal pronoun, _I_	Then am I A happy fly If I live Or if I die.
First, last, and all important words in titles	_The Call of the Wild_, "Life Doesn't Frighten Me"

❺ Writing Complete Sentences

5.1 Sentence Fragments A sentence fragment is a group of words that does not express a complete thought. It may be missing a subject, a predicate, or both. A sentence fragment makes you wonder *What is this about?* or *What happened?*

Missing Subject or Predicate You can correct a sentence fragment by adding the missing subject or predicate to complete the thought.

> **FRAGMENTS:** *Rehearsed their parts for three weeks. Even then some students.*
> **CORRECTED:** *The students rehearsed their parts for three weeks. Even then some students forgot their lines.*

Phrase and Dependent-Clause Fragments When the fragment is a phrase or a dependent (subordinate) clause, you may join the fragment to an existing sentence.

> **EXAMPLE:** *Under normal circumstances, the conflicts neighbors have are easy to ignore; however, these unresolved problems can suddenly become huge when a crisis threatens.*

GRAMMAR PRACTICE

Rewrite this paragraph, correcting the sentence fragments.

1) The play in the story. **2)** Is based on a tragedy of the winter of 1846–1847. **3)** Late in October, George and Jacob Donner. **4)** Led a party through the Sierra Nevada in California. **5)** A terrible snowstorm. **6)** Blocked the pass. **7)** By April almost half of the 82 members of the original party. **8)** Had died of starvation. **9)** Some of the survivors. **10)** Resorted to eating the corpses of those who had died.

5.2 Run-on Sentences A run-on sentence consists of two or more sentences written incorrectly as one. A run-on sentence occurs because the writer either used no end mark or used a comma instead of a period to end the first complete thought. A run-on sentence may confuse readers because it does not show where one thought ends and the next begins.

Forming Separate Sentences One way to correct a run-on sentence is to form two separate sentences. Use a period or other end punctuation after the first sentence, and capitalize the first letter of the next sentence.

> **RUN-ON:** Damon and Pythias *retells an ancient Greek legend this version is in the form of a play.*
> **MAKE TWO SENTENCES:** Damon and Pythias *retells an ancient Greek legend. This version is in the form of a play.*

Forming Compound Sentences You can also correct a run-on sentence by rewriting it to form a compound sentence. One way to do this is by using a comma and a coordinating conjunction.

Never join simple sentences with a comma alone, or a run-on sentence will result. You need a comma followed by a conjunction such as *and, but,* or *or* to hold the sentences together.

> **RUN-ON:** *The king was cruel no one dared to criticize him.*
> **ADD A CONJUNCTION:** *The king was cruel, but no one dared to criticize him.*

You may use a semicolon to join two ideas that are closely related.

In addition, you can correct a run-on sentence by using a semicolon and a conjunctive adverb. Commonly used conjunctive adverbs are *however, therefore, nevertheless,* and *besides.*

> **RUN-ON:** *Damon would have taken Pythias' punishment Pythias returned just in time.*
> **ADD A SEMICOLON AND A CONJUNCTIVE ADVERB:** *Damon would have taken Pythias' punishment; however, Pythias returned just in time.*

Grammar Practice Answers

The play in the story "The School Play" is based on a tragedy of the winter of 1846–1847. Late in October, George and Jacob Donner led a party through the Sierra Nevada in California. A terrible snowstorm blocked the pass. By April almost half of the 82 members of the original party had died of starvation. Some of the survivors resorted to eating the corpses of those who had died.

Grammar Practice Answers 5.2

In *Damon and Pythias,* the friendship of two young men helps them face death. Another story about friends is found in the Bible. David and Jonathan were friends who protected each other and warned each other of danger. David was a musician whose songs soothed Saul, the king of Israel. Jonathan was the son of Saul. He also remained David's closest friend throughout his life. David's brave acts made him a hero, and Saul became jealous of him. On more than one occasion Jonathan warned David of Saul's plots. Saul tried to kill David with a dagger. David had opportunities to kill Saul, but he always refused to do bad things. Such honorable conduct shamed Saul. Jonathan defended David even against his own father.

6.1

1. tells
2. take
3. excites
4. seems
5. thinks
6. wonder
7. dates
8. suggests
9. forms
10. measure

GRAMMAR PRACTICE

Rewrite this paragraph, correcting the run-on sentences.

1) In *Damon and Pythias* the friendship of two young men helps them face death another story about friends is found in the Bible. **2)** David and Jonathan were friends who protected each other they warned each other of danger. **3)** David was a musician his songs soothed Saul, the king of Israel. **4)** Jonathan was the son of Saul he remained David's closest friend throughout his life. **5)** David's brave acts made him a hero Saul became jealous of him. **6)** On more than one occasion Jonathan warned David of Saul's plots Saul tried to kill David with a dagger. **7)** David had opportunities to kill Saul he always refused to do bad things. **8)** Such honorable conduct shamed Saul Jonathan defended David even against his own father.

❻ Making Subjects and Verbs Agree

6.1 *Simple and Compound Subjects* A verb must agree in number with its subject. When a word refers to more than one thing, it is plural.

Agreement with Simple Subjects Use a singular verb with a singular subject.

When the subject is a singular noun, you use the singular form of the verb. The present-tense singular form of a regular verb usually ends in *-s* or *-es*.

> **INCORRECT**: *"Tutankhamen" tell of a famous archaeological discovery.*
> **CORRECT**: *"Tutankhamen" tells of a famous archaeological discovery.*

USAGE TIP To find the subject of a sentence, first find the verb. Then ask *who* or *what* performs the action of the verb. Say the subject and the verb together to see if they agree.

Use a plural verb with a plural subject.

> **INCORRECT**: *Two determined men looks for the tomb of Pharaoh Tutankhamen.*
> **CORRECT**: *Two determined men look for the tomb of Pharaoh Tutankhamen.*

Agreement with Compound Subjects
Use a plural verb with a compound subject whose parts are joined by *and,* regardless of the number of each part.

> **INCORRECT**: *Carter and Carnarvon exclaims when they find "wonderful things."*
> **CORRECT**: *Carter and Carnarvon exclaim when they find "wonderful things."*

When the parts of a compound subject are joined by *or* or *nor,* make the verb agree in number with the part that is closer to it.

Usually *or* and *nor* appear with their correlatives *either* and *neither.*

> **EXAMPLE**: *Neither Carnarvon nor the Egyptians know where to look for the rich tomb. A frequent problem for archaeologists is that grave robbers or time causes great damage.*

GRAMMAR PRACTICE

Write the correct form of the verb given in parentheses.

1. "Tutankhamen" (tell, tells) of a great archaeological discovery in Egypt.

2. Many wonderful discoveries also (take, takes) place in our part of the world.

3. A recent discovery (excite, excites) archaeologists in Mexico.

4. The city (seems, seem) to have been abandoned suddenly about A.D. 1000.

5. One archaeologist (think, thinks) that this city hit its peak in the Classic Period, from A.D. 300 to A.D. 600.

6. Sarah Goodman and other archaeologists (wonder, wonders) what brought about such growth.

7. Several smaller settlements (date, dates) from about that time.

---

8. Research (suggest, suggests) that El Pital was a center of trade and culture.

9. Earth or stone (form, forms) more than a hundred dwellings, ball courts, temples, and long platforms.

10. Some buildings (measure, measures) 130 feet in height.

6.2 *Pronoun Subjects* When a pronoun is used as a subject, the verb must agree with it in number.

Agreement with Personal Pronouns
When the subject is a singular personal pronoun, use a singular verb. When the subject is a plural personal pronoun, use a plural verb.

Even though *I* and *you* are singular, they take the plural form of the verb.

INCORRECT: *I believes that "Abd al-Rahman Ibrahima" is a true story.*
CORRECT: *I believe that "Abd al-Rahman Ibrahima" is a true story.*

When *he, she,* or *it* is the part of the subject closer to the verb in a compound subject containing *or* or *nor,* use a singular verb. When a pronoun is a part of a compound subject containing *and,* use a plural verb.

INCORRECT: *Neither the other captives nor he expect treachery.*
CORRECT: *Neither the other captives nor he expects treachery.*

Agreement with Indefinite Pronouns
When the subject is a singular indefinite pronoun, use the singular form of the verb.

The following are singular indefinite pronouns: *another, either, nobody, anybody, everybody, somebody, no one, anyone, everyone, someone, one, nothing, anything, everything, something, each,* and *neither.*

INCORRECT: *During Ibrahima's time with Dr. Cox, everything go well.*
CORRECT: *During Ibrahima's time with Dr. Cox, everything goes well.*

When the subject is a plural indefinite pronoun *(both, few, many,* or *several),* use the plural form of the verb.

INCORRECT: *Ibrahima learns that many deceives or betrays others.*
CORRECT: *Ibrahima learns that many deceive or betray others.*

The indefinite pronouns *some, all, any, none,* and *most* can be either singular or plural. When the pronoun refers to one thing, use a singular verb.

When the pronoun refers to several things, use a plural verb.

INCORRECT: *Of the captives Ibrahima meets, many dies on the trip, and most suffers on landing.*
CORRECT: *Of the captives Ibrahima meets, many die on the trip, and most suffer on landing.*

GRAMMAR PRACTICE
Write the correct form of the verb given in parentheses.

1. Of the people in the world, many (live, lives) on the huge continent of Africa.

2. Some (appear, appears) in the selection "Abd al-Rahman Ibrahima."

3. Each group (speak, speaks) its own language or dialect.

4. Ibrahima speaks Fulani because he (belong, belongs) to the Fula people.

5. Most Fula (wear, wears) their hair long.

6. They are a pastoral people, so many (raise, raises) livestock.

7. In the selection, we (meet, meets) the Mandingo, enemies of the Fula.

8. They (come, comes) from West Africa and belong to many independent kingdoms.

9. One (trace, traces) its dynasty back 13 centuries with hardly a break.

Grammar Practice Answers

1. live
2. appear
3. speaks
4. belongs
5. wear
6. raise
7. meet
8. come
9. traces

6.3 *Common Agreement Problems*

Several other situations can cause problems in subject-verb agreement.

Agreement with Irregular Verbs Use the singular forms of the irregular verbs *do, be,* and *have* with singular subjects. Use the plural forms of these verbs with plural subjects.

WATCH OUT! Look carefully at words that come before the subject. Remember that the subject may not be the noun or pronoun closest to the verb.

	Do	Be	Have
Singular Subjects	I do you do the dog does it does each doesn't	I am/was you are/were Joe is/was he isn't/wasn't either is/was	I have you have Pat hasn't she has anybody has
Plural Subjects	we do dogs do they do many don't	we are/were boys are/were they are/were both are/were	we have girls have they haven't few have

> **INCORRECT**: *"The All-American Slurp" do a good job of describing manners. The story have examples of Chinese and American mistakes. They is both funny.*
> **CORRECT**: *"The All-American Slurp" does a good job of describing manners. The story has examples of Chinese and American mistakes. They are both funny.*

Interrupting Words Be sure the verb agrees with its subject when a word or words come between them.

Sometimes one or more words come between the subject and the verb. The interrupter does not affect the number of the subject.

> **INCORRECT**: *Many of the girls in the group feels embarrassed. A dip of sour cream and onion flakes cause a problem.*
> **CORRECT**: *Many of the girls in the group feel embarrassed. A dip of sour cream and onion flakes causes a problem.*

Interrupting Phrases Be certain that the verb agrees with its subject when a phrase comes between them.

The subject of a verb is never found in a prepositional phrase, which may follow the subject and come before the verb.

> **INCORRECT**: *The members of the Gleason family offers snacks to the Lins. A cooked vegetable, according to many Chinese people, taste better than a raw one.*
> **CORRECT**: *The members of the Gleason family offer snacks to the Lins. A cooked vegetable, according to many Chinese people, tastes better than a raw one.*

Phrases beginning with *including, as well as, along with,* and *in addition to* are not part of the subject.

> **INCORRECT**: *The Lins learn that celery, as well as radishes and carrots, count as a finger food. Each guest, including the parents and the children, skip the dip.*
> **CORRECT**: *The Lins learn that celery, as well as radishes and carrots, counts as a finger food. Each guest, including the parents and the children, skips the dip.*

The subject of the verb is never found in an appositive, which may follow the subject and come before the verb.

> **INCORRECT**: *Meg, daughter of the Gleasons, struggle to eat a traditional Chinese meal. Pot stickers, a Chinese delicacy, is enjoyed by almost everyone.*
> **CORRECT**: *Meg, daughter of the Gleasons, struggles to eat a traditional Chinese meal. Pot stickers, a Chinese delicacy, are enjoyed by almost everyone.*

Inverted Sentences When the subject comes after the verb, be sure the verb agrees with the subject in number.

A sentence in which the subject follows the verb is called an inverted sentence. Questions are usually in inverted form, as are sentences beginning with *here, there,* and *where. (Where are the reporters? There are two press conferences today.)*

INCORRECT: *From knowing the rules of courtesy come confidence. From breaking them, however, come the most fun and laughter.*

CORRECT: *From knowing the rules of courtesy comes confidence. From breaking them, however, comes the most fun and laughter.*

USAGE TIP To check subject-verb agreement in inverted sentences, place the subject before the verb. For example, to check agreement, change *There are many people* to *Many people are there.*

GRAMMAR PRACTICE

Write the correct form of each verb given in parentheses.

1. The story "The All-American Slurp" (does, do) readers a favor; it helps us not take ourselves too seriously.

2. Most of us, at some time or another, (has, have) wondered about etiquette.

3. What (is, are) the right things to do?

4. Raw food, including things like celery, (was, were) difficult for the Lins.

5. (Does, Do) you handle similar problems in another country as well as the Lins do?

6. The difficulties for a traveler (is, are) often embarrassing.

7. (Is, Are) there a gracious way to deal with a disgusting dish? Here (is, are) some ways.

8. Swallowing fast and telling yourself that it "tastes just like chicken" (is, are) a good way.

9. Some people, to disguise the texture of a food, (slice, slices) the item thinly.

❼ Using Nouns and Pronouns

7.1 *Plural and Possessive Nouns* Nouns refer to people, places, things, and ideas. Nouns are plural when they refer to more than one person, place, thing, or idea. Possessive nouns show who or what owns something.

Plural Nouns Follow these guidelines to form noun plurals.

Nouns	To Form Plural	Examples
Most nouns	add -s	jaw—jaws
Most nouns that end in s, sh, ch, x, or z	add -es	fox—foxes flash—flashes
Most nouns that end in ay, ey, oy, or uy	add -s	delay—delays valley—valleys
Most nouns that end in a consonant and y	change y to i and add -es	cavalry—cavalries casualty—casualties
Most nouns that end in o	add -s	alto—altos arroyo—arroyos soprano—sopranos
Some nouns that end in a consonant and o	add -es	echo—echoes hero—heroes tomato—tomatoes
Most nouns that end in f or fe	change f to v, add -es or -s	sheaf—sheaves knife—knives *but* belief—beliefs

WATCH OUT! The plurals of many musical terms that end in *o* preceded by a consonant are formed by adding *-s*. These nouns include *tempos* and *concertos*.

Grammar Practice Answers

1. does
2. have
3. are
4. was
5. Do
6. are
7. Is, are
8. is
9. slice

Grammar Practice Answers

1. world's
2. family's
3. holidays
4. signs
5. emotions
6. People, messages
7. symphonies, compositions
8. years, extremes
9. songs, melodies, critic's
10. heroes
11. critics, Beethoven's

Some nouns use the same spelling in both singular and plural: *series, fish, sheep, deer.* Some noun plurals use irregular forms that don't follow any rule: *teeth, geese, feet, mice, people, children, women, men.*

> **INCORRECT:** *In "Beethoven Lives Upstairs," Beethoven disrupts the lifes of his neighbors. When writing his symphonys, he plays piano with loud bumps and crashs.*
>
> **CORRECT:** *In "Beethoven Lives Upstairs," Beethoven disrupts the lives of his neighbors. When writing his symphonies, he plays piano with loud bumps and crashes.*

USAGE TIP The dictionary usually lists the plural form of a noun if the plural form is irregular or if there is more than one plural form. Dictionary listings are especially helpful for nouns that end in *o, f,* and *fe.*

Possessive Nouns Follow these guidelines to form possessive nouns.

Nouns	To Form Possessive	Examples
Singular nouns	add apostrophe and -*s*	league—league's
Plural nouns ending in *s*	add apostrophe	fields—fields' brigades—brigades'
Plural nouns not ending in *s*	add apostrophe and -*s*	children—children's oxen—oxen's

> **INCORRECT:** *The sopranos voices echoed throughout Christophs house.*
>
> **CORRECT:** *The sopranos' voices echoed throughout Christoph's house.*

WATCH OUT! Be careful when placing apostrophes in possessive nouns. A misplaced apostrophe changes the meaning. For example, *boy's* refers to possession by one boy, but *boys'* refers to possession by two or more boys.

GRAMMAR PRACTICE

Write the correct form given in parentheses.

1. Many people consider Ludwig van Beethoven the (world's, worlds') greatest composer.

2. His (family's, familys') many musicians included his father and grandfather.

3. Born in Germany, Beethoven, as a young man, settled in Vienna, thereafter leaving only for summer (holidays, holidaies, holiday's).

4. Before he was 30, he began to notice (sign, signs) of deafness.

5. After experiencing a range of (emotions, emotiones), he swore to "seize fate by the throat" and went on to compose groundbreaking works.

6. (People, peoples) wrote (messages, messages') in "conversation books" to communicate with him.

7. His nine (symphonys, symphonies) and many other (composition's, compositions) show great achievement.

8. Particularly in earlier (year, years), his music leaned toward (extreme's, extremes) of piano and forte.

9. His passionate (songs, songs') and simple folk (melodys, melodies) moved many a (critics, critic's) heart.

10. His powerful work and personality made some musicians call him one of the artist (heros, heroes) of modern times.

11. Many music (critics, critic's) of the 19th century found (Beethoven's, Beethovens') music impossible to understand.

7.2 *Pronoun Case* A personal pronoun is a pronoun that can be used in the first, second, or third person. A personal pronoun has three forms: the subject form, the object form, and the possessive form.

Subject Pronouns Use the subject form of a pronoun when it is the subject of a sentence or the subject of a clause. *I, you, he, she, it, we,* and *they* are subject pronouns.

Using the correct pronoun form is seldom a problem when the sentence has just one pronoun. Problems can arise, however, when a noun and a pronoun or two pronouns are used in a compound subject or compound object. To see if you are using the correct pronoun form, read the sentence, using only one pronoun.

> **INCORRECT:** *"The Circuit" tells the story of a boy and his family. The story begins and ends as he and them pack to move yet again.*
> **CORRECT:** *"The Circuit" tells the story of a boy and his family. The story begins and ends as he and they pack to move yet again.*

Use the subject form of a pronoun when it follows a linking verb as a predicate pronoun.

You often hear the object form used in casual conversation as a predicate pronoun. ("It is him.") For this reason, the subject form may sound awkward to you, though it is preferred for more formal writing.

> **INCORRECT:** *The boy is the narrator. It is him who helps the readers feel his joy and pain.*
> **CORRECT:** *The boy is the narrator. It is he who helps the readers feel his joy and pain.*

USAGE TIP To check the form of a predicate pronoun, see if the sentence still makes sense when the subject and the predicate pronoun are reversed. *(It was he. He was it.)*

Object Pronouns Use the object form of a pronoun when it is the object of a sentence, the object of a clause, or the object of a preposition. *Me, you, him, her, it, us,* and *them* are object pronouns.

> **INCORRECT:** *We share with his family and he the frustration of not staying in one place.*
> **CORRECT:** *We share with his family and him the frustration of not staying in one place.*

Possessive Pronouns Never use an apostrophe in a possessive pronoun. *My, mine, your, yours, his, her, hers, its, our, ours, their,* and *theirs* are possessive pronouns.

Writers often confuse the possessive pronouns *its, your,* and *their* with the contractions *it's, you're,* and *they're.* Remember that the pairs are spelled differently and that they have different meanings.

> **INCORRECT:** *They're disappointment at moving again touches us. Its as if we, and not them, come home to find boxes packed. The sad circuit, or cycle, is our's.*
> **CORRECT:** *Their disappointment at moving again touches us. It's as if we, and not they, come home to find boxes packed. The sad circuit, or cycle, is ours.*

GRAMMAR PRACTICE

Write the correct pronoun form given in parentheses.

1) The life of a migrant worker would be hard for you and (I, me). **2)** (Them, They) and other workers must struggle at low-paying jobs just to survive. **3)** (They're, Their) working conditions are sometimes intolerable. **4)** Not only must workers settle for extremely low wages, but (they're, their) often unable to find any jobs for half the year. **5)** When (they, them) do, employers provide poor housing for (they, them). **6)** No sick days, holidays, or other benefits are offered to their families or (them, they). **7)** You and (I, me) might wonder why anyone would settle for such work. **8)** Many workers come from other countries, however, where (its, it's) even harder to make a living. **9)** Black and Hispanic men, women, and children make up most of the migrant work force; poor whites and (they, them) suffer equally. **10)** Some travel with (they're, their) families; others send money home.

Grammar Practice Answers

1. me
2. They
3. Their
4. they're
5. they, them
6. them,
7. I
8. it's
9. they
10. their

7.3 *Pronoun Antecedents* An antecedent is the noun or pronoun to which a personal pronoun refers. The antecedent usually precedes the pronoun.

Pronoun and Antecedent Agreement A pronoun must agree with its antecedent in

NUMBER—*singular or plural*
PERSON—*first, second, or third*
GENDER—*male or female*

Use a singular pronoun to refer to a singular antecedent; use a plural pronoun to refer to a plural antecedent.

Do not allow interrupting words to determine the number of the personal pronoun.

> **INCORRECT**: *In "In the Land of Small Dragon" it is the younger half-sister and the step-mother, not the father, who is unkind to T´âm.*
> **CORRECT**: *In "In the Land of Small Dragon" it is the younger half-sister and the step-mother, not the father, who are unkind to T´âm.*

If the antecedent is a noun that could be either male or female, use *he* or *she (him* or *her, his* or *her)* or reword the sentence to avoid the need for a singular pronoun.

> **INCORRECT**: *A reader may wonder who T´âm is. They might think she is a princess.*
> **CORRECT**: *A reader may wonder who T´âm is. He or she might think T´âm is a princess.*
> **CORRECT**: *Readers may wonder who T´âm is. They might think she is a princess.*

Be sure that the antecedent of a pronoun is clear.

In most cases, do not use a pronoun to refer to an entire idea or clause. Writing is much clearer if the exact reference is repeated.

> **UNCLEAR**: *Both this story and the Cinderella tale end happily, and it is what we hope for.*
> **CLEAR**: *Both this story and the Cinderella tale end happily, and happy endings are what we hope for.*

USAGE TIP To avoid vague pronoun references, do not use *this* or *that* alone to start a sentence. Instead, include a word that clarifies what *this* or *that* refers to—*this experience, this situation, that concept.*

Indefinite Pronouns as Antecedents When a singular indefinite pronoun is the antecedent, use *he* or *she (him* or *her, his* or *her)* or rewrite the sentence to avoid the need for a singular pronoun.

> **INCORRECT**: *Everyone at the festival rejoiced.*
> **CORRECT**: *All who were at the festival rejoiced.*

Indefinite Pronouns

Singular

another	each	everybody	neither	somebody
anybody	either	everyone	nobody	someone
anyone	one	everything	no one	something
anything			nothing	

Plural

both	few	many	several

Singular or Plural

all	any	most	none	some

GRAMMAR PRACTICE

Rewrite this paragraph to make the pronoun reference clear.

1) A tale like "In the Land of Small Dragon" is found in many countries; they remind you of Cinderella. **2)** *Mufaro's Beautiful Daughters* is one of these tales. **3)** In this book Nyasha was loved by everyone, but they usually did not like her sister. **4)** She encouraged the snake to live in her garden, where it was very comfortable. **5)** Manyara was unkind and rude, and people could not help but see it. **6)** One day a messenger arrived, and they said that the king was looking for a bride. **7)** Manyara left on her journey to the king's city before Nyasha, and she was afraid she would be late. **8)** On the way Manyara met an old woman; she reminded her to be helpful to anyone she met. **9)** Instead, she was often rude to them. **10)** Nyasha was kind and courteous, and it was rewarded in the end.

Grammar Practice Answers

1) A tale like "In the Land of Small Dragon" is found in many countries. Such tales remind me of Cinderella. **2)** *Mufaro's Beautiful Daughters* is one of these Cinderella tales. **3)** In this book Nyasha was loved by everyone, but most people did not like her sister. **4)** Nyasha encouraged the snake to live in her garden, where it was very comfortable. **5)** Manyara, the sister, was unkind and rude, and people could not help but see these qualities. **6)** One day a messenger arrived to say that the king was looking for a bride. **7)** Manyara left on her journey to the king's city before Nyasha did. Nyasha was afraid she would be late. **8)** On the way Manyara met an old woman who reminded her to be helpful to anyone she met. **9)** Instead, Manyara was often rude to strangers along her way. **10)** Nyasha was kind and courteous, and she was rewarded for it in the end.

7.4 *Pronoun Usage* The form that a pronoun takes is always determined by its function within its own clause or sentence.

Who and Whom Use *who* or *whoever* as the subject of a clause or sentence.

INCORRECT: *In "The Legend of the Hummingbird," the young girl Alida falls in love with Taroo, whom is from an enemy tribe.*

CORRECT: *In "The Legend of the Hummingbird," the young girl Alida falls in love with Taroo, who is from an enemy tribe.*

Use *whom* as the direct or indirect object of a verb or verbal and as the object of a preposition.

People often use *who* for *whom* when speaking informally. However, in written English the pronouns should be used correctly.

INCORRECT: *First Alida meets a young boy with who she talks and picks fruit. Then she learns that his people, who Alida fears, had abandoned him on her island.*

CORRECT: *First Alida meets a young boy with whom she talks and picks fruit. Then she learns that his people, whom Alida fears, had abandoned him on her island.*

WATCH OUT! Watch for prepositions and verbs that precede the word *who*.
To whom—object of a preposition.
To interview whom—object of the infinitive verb *to interview*.

In trying to determine the correct pronoun form, ignore interrupters that come between the subject and the verb.

INCORRECT: *Whom do you think has the saddest fate?*

CORRECT: *Who do you think has the saddest fate?*

Pronouns in Contractions Do not confuse the contractions *it's, they're, who's,* and *you're* with possessive pronouns that sound the same—*its, their, whose,* and *your*.

INCORRECT: *Its sad when Alida's father arranges for her to marry someone else. Alida and Taroo both beg the god Yukiyú for help with they're tragic situation.*

CORRECT: *It's sad when Alida's father arranges for her to marry someone else. Alida and Taroo both beg the god Yukiyú for help with their tragic situation.*

Pronouns with Nouns Determine the correct form of the pronoun in phrases such as *we girls* and *us boys* by dropping the noun and saying the sentence without the noun that follows the pronoun.

INCORRECT: *I believe a story is best when us readers are kept in suspense.*

CORRECT: *I believe a story is best when we readers are kept in suspense.*

GRAMMAR PRACTICE

Write the correct pronoun given in parentheses.

1. Many people say the hummingbird is (their, they're) favorite bird.

2. This tiny bird can beat (its, it's) wings 60 times a second.

3. People (who, whom) observe a hummingbird's wings in motion see only a blur.

4. The beating of (its, it's) wings causes a humming sound.

5. (Their, They're) tiny feet are almost useless; they must fly to travel only a few inches.

6. The hummingbird can use (its, it's) wings to move in any direction.

7. Because of (their, they're) special skeletal structure, (their, they're) able to fly backward, sideways, or even upside down.

8. (Who, Whom) could not be fascinated by this sight?

9. If (your, you're) interested in attracting hummingbirds, consider making a hummingbird feeder.

10. A hummingbird drinks nectar through (its, it's) hollow tongue.

Grammar Practice Answers

1. their
2. its
3. who
4. its
5. Their
6. its
7. their, they're
8. Who
9. you're
10. its

❽ Using Verbs Correctly

8.1 *Verb Tenses and Forms* Verb tense shows the time of an action or a condition. Writers sometimes cause confusion when they use different verb tenses in describing actions that occur at the same time.

Consistent Use of Tenses When two or more actions occur at the same time or in sequence, use the same verb tense to describe the actions.

> **INCORRECT**: *"Scout's Honor" tells about a camping group that starts in Brooklyn and went into New Jersey. The trip nearly became a disaster.*
> **CORRECT**: *"Scout's Honor" tells about a camping group that starts in Brooklyn and goes into New Jersey. The trip nearly becomes a disaster.*

A shift in tense is necessary when two events occur at different times or out of sequence. The tenses of the verbs should clearly indicate that one action precedes the other.

> **INCORRECT**: *Now that the trip is over, it seems funny. But for a while we are all miserable.*
> **CORRECT**: *Now that the trip is over, it seems funny. But for a while we were all miserable.*

Tense	Verb Form
Present	open/opens
Past	opened
Future	will/shall open
Present perfect	have/has opened
Past perfect	had opened
Future perfect	will/shall have opened

WATCH OUT! In telling a story, be careful not to shift tenses so often that the reader has difficulty keeping the sequence of events straight.

Past Tense and the Past Participle The simple past form of a verb can always stand alone. The past participle of the following irregular verbs should always be used with a helping verb.

Present Tense	Past Tense	Past Participle
be (is/are)	was/were	(have, had) been
begin	began	(have, had) begun
break	broke	(have, had) broken
bring	brought	(have, had) brought
choose	chose	(have, had) chosen
come	came	(have, had) come
do	did	(have, had) done
drink	drank	(have, had) drunk
eat	ate	(have, had) eaten
fall	fell	(have, had) fallen
freeze	froze	(have, had) frozen
give	gave	(have, had) given
go	went	(have, had) gone
lose	lost	(have, had) lost
grow	grew	(have, had) grown

> **INCORRECT**: *They have did a lot to prepare for the trip. For instance, Max have brought a compass.*
> **CORRECT**: *They had done a lot to prepare for the trip. For instance, Max had brought a compass.*

USAGE TIP Some writers use gradual shifts in verb tense (such as from the past to the past participle) to move from the past up through to the present. This can be used to show developments over a period of time as in the example above. When using this technique, be careful to use verb tenses that clearly convey your message.

GRAMMAR PRACTICE

Write the correct verb tense for each sentence.

1) In "Scout's Honor" we (seen, have seen) an attempt to build a campfire. **2)** When I camped

Grammar Practice Answers

1. have seen

with Aunt Zarefa, we (bring, brought) along dry firewood. **3)** She said the first step is to (find, found) a clear area. **4)** We (gather, gathered) fuel such as twigs and sticks. **5)** Then we (build, built) a tepee of twigs over a small pile of tinder. **6)** She asked me to (use, used) sticks to build walls around the tepee. **7)** The next task was to (place, placed) logs around the walls and lean sticks on them. **8)** After I (light, lit) a match and slipped it into the sticks, our campfire blazed. **9)** When I woke up the next day, I saw that Auntie had (use, used) water and dirt to put out the last of the fire.

8.2 *Commonly Confused Verbs* The following verb pairs are easily confused.

Let **and** *Leave* *Let* means "to allow or permit." *Leave* means "to depart" or "to allow something to remain where it is."

> **INCORRECT:** *"Aaron's Gift" leaves the reader imagine what to do about a wounded animal. Should you let it to die?*
>
> **CORRECT:** *"Aaron's Gift" lets the reader imagine what to do about a wounded animal. Should you leave it to die?*

Lie **and** *Lay* *Lie* means "to rest in a flat position." *Lay* means "to put or place."

> **INCORRECT:** *Almost dead, the pigeon laid down. He lied his ruffled feathers close to his body.*
>
> **CORRECT:** *Almost dead, the pigeon lay down. He laid his ruffled feathers close to his body.*

WATCH OUT! If you're uncertain about which verb to use, check to see whether the verb has an object. The verbs *lie*, *sit*, and *rise* never have objects.

Sit **and** *Set* *Sit* means "to be in a seated position." *Set* means "to put or place."

> **INCORRECT:** *Pidge would often set quietly and look at Aaron. Aaron was glad he'd sat out food to help the bird get well.*
>
> **CORRECT:** *Pidge would often sit quietly and look at Aaron. Aaron was glad he'd set out food to help the bird get well.*

Rise **and** *Raise* *Rise* means "to move upward." *Raise* means "to move something upward."

> **INCORRECT:** *Raising up quickly, Pidge escaped. He rose his healed wing and flapped desperately.*
>
> **CORRECT:** *Rising up quickly, Pidge escaped. He raised his healed wing and flapped desperately.*

Learn **and** *Teach* *Learn* means "to gain knowledge or skill." *Teach* means "to help someone learn."

> **INCORRECT:** *Pidge learned Aaron much about standing up for a friend.*
>
> **CORRECT:** *Pidge taught Aaron much about standing up for a friend.*

Here are the principal parts of these troublesome verb pairs.

Present Tense	Past Tense	Past Participle
let	let	(have, had) let
leave	left	(have, had) left
lie	lay	(have, had) lain
lay	laid	(have, had) laid
sit	sat	(have, had) sat
set	set	(have, had) set
rise	rose	(have, had) risen
raise	raised	(have, had) raised
learn	learned	(have, had) learned
teach	taught	(have, had) taught

GRAMMAR PRACTICE

Choose the correct verb from each pair of words given in parentheses.

1. Biologists have (left, let) us know that rock doves are the ancestors of pigeons like the one in "Aaron's Gift."

2. Rock doves like to (sit, set) their nests on cliff ledges, so their descendants thrive in modern cities.

3. People started (raising, rising) rock doves for food around 4500 B.C.

4. (Leave, Let) me tell you that today there are about 285 kinds of pigeons.

Grammar Practice Answers 8.1 (continued)

2. brought
3. find
4. gathered
5. built
6. use
7. place
8. lit
9. used

Grammar Practice Answers 8.2

1. let
2. set
3. raising
4. Let

Grammar Practice Answers 8.2 (continued)

5. lie
6. rise
7. laid
8. teach

9.1

1. proud
2. hardworking
3. quickly
4. stern
5. nervous
6. greatly
7. reluctantly
8. extensive

---

5. Pigeons are active during the day, but do they ever (lay, lie) down to sleep?

6. Some kinds of pigeons weigh as much as three pounds, so they must be strong fliers to (raise, rise) into the air.

7. When we raised pigeons, they usually (lay, laid) two eggs at a time.

8. Biologists (teach, learn) us that some pigeons use the sounds their feathers make during flight to signal each other.

❾ Using Modifiers Effectively

9.1 *Adjective or Adverb?* Use an adjective to modify a noun or a pronoun. Use an adverb to modify a verb, an adjective, or another adverb.

> **INCORRECT:** *In "Oh Broom, Get to Work," the author writes amusing about some especial boring visitors to her home.*
> **CORRECT:** *In "Oh Broom, Get to Work," the author writes amusingly about some especially boring visitors to her home.*

USAGE TIP Always determine first which word is being modified. In the preceding example, where *writes* is the word being modified, the correct choice is an adverb. A verb can only be modified by an adverb.

Use an adjective after a linking verb to describe the subject.

> **INCORRECT:** *Yo Chan and her sister felt unhappily about the many dull visitors. Only one minister seemed entertainingly.*
> **CORRECT:** *Yo Chan and her sister felt unhappy about the many dull visitors. Only one minister seemed entertaining.*

Remember that in addition to forms of the verb *be*, the following are linking verbs: *become, seem, appear, look, sound, feel, taste, grow,* and *smell*.

GRAMMAR PRACTICE

Write the correct modifier in each pair.

1) In "Oh Broom, Get to Work," Yo Chan's parents are (proud, proudly) graduates of a Christian university in Japan. **2)** Christianity was brought there by (hardworkingly, hardworking) missionaries. **3)** The religion spread (quick, quickly) throughout Japan beginning in 1549. **4)** The (stern, sternly) rulers of the nation thought that a Western religion would undermine their power. **5)** In the early 1600s the (nervously, nervous) rulers began to limit the religion. **6)** The number of people practicing Christianity dropped (great, greatly) by 1640. **7)** Missionaries were (reluctant, reluctantly) allowed back into the country in 1873. **8)** After two centuries they found some evidence of Christianity that had survived the (extensive, extensively) persecution.

9.2 *Comparisons and Negatives*

Comparative and Superlative Adjectives
Use the comparative form of an adjective when comparing two things.

Comparative adjectives are formed by adding -*er* to short adjectives (*small, smaller*) or by using the word *more* with longer adjectives (*horrible, more horrible*).

> **INCORRECT:** *"Summer of Fire" is dramaticer than many article I have read. Forest fires are one of the more scary disasters you could encounter.*
> **CORRECT:** *"Summer of Fire" is more dramatic than many articles I have read. Forest fires are one of the scarier disasters you could encounter.*

Use the superlative form when comparing three or more things.

The superlative is formed by adding -*est* to short adjectives (*tall, tallest*) or by using the word *most* with longer adjectives (*interesting, most interesting*).

> **INCORRECT:** *Which fire is threateningest? Which spreads most fast?*
> **CORRECT:** *Which fire is most threatening? Which spreads fastest?*

WATCH OUT! When using the comparative form to compare something with everything else of its kind, do not leave out the word *other. (Kim is shorter than any other member of her family.)*

The comparative and superlative forms of some adjectives are irregular.

Adjective	Comparative	Superlative
good	better	best
well	better	best
bad	worse	worst
ill	worse	worst
little	less or lesser	least
much	more	most
many	more	most
far	farther or further	farthest or furthest

WATCH OUT! Do not use both *-er* and *more.* Do not use both *-est* and *most.* Notice the improvement when *more* and *most* are removed from the following sentence: *The ship was more faster than the most fastest winds.*

When comparing more than two actions, use the superlative form of an adverb, which is formed by adding *-est* or by using the word *most.*

> **INCORRECT:** *Of all the park buildings, the Old Faithful Inn was considered importantest.*
> **CORRECT:** *Of all the park buildings, the Old Faithful Inn was considered most important.*

Comparative and Superlative Adverbs

When comparing two actions, use the comparative form of an adverb, which is formed by adding *-er* or the word *more.*

> **INCORRECT:** *More oftener than not, the fires spread quicklier than fire fighters could control them.*
> **CORRECT:** *More often than not, the fires spread more quickly than fire fighters could control them.*

Double Negatives To avoid double negatives, use only one negative word in a clause.

Besides *not* and *no,* the following are negative words: *never, nobody, none, no one, nothing,* and *nowhere.*

> **INCORRECT:** *No one could hardly believe the fires continued for so long. It seemed they wouldn't never stop.*
> **CORRECT:** *No one could believe the fires continued for so long. It seemed they would never stop.*

GRAMMAR PRACTICE

Rewrite the paragraph, correcting the underlined modifiers.

1) Most of the animals in Yellowstone, including the park's <u>most large</u> mammals, the bison, survived the fire. **2)** The <u>very bigger</u> bison can weigh over 1,800 pounds. **3)** They are also <u>more tall</u> than you—about six feet at the shoulder. **4)** The wild bison in the park wander <u>freer</u> than most bison on ranches. **5)** They usually seem to walk <u>slowlier</u> than other animals. **6)** However, if you get <u>too closer</u> to a bison, you might be suprised at how fast it can move. **7)** In winter, bison use their huge heads to push aside the <u>most heaviest</u> snow and find grass. **8)** They also hang around the <u>more warm</u> areas, near the geysers. **9)** Some visitors say the park bison are the <u>awesomest</u> animals they ever saw in the wild.

9.3 *Special Problems with Modifiers*

The following terms are frequently misused in spoken English, but they should be used correctly, especially in written English.

Them* and *Those *Them* is always a pronoun and never a modifier for a noun. *Those* is a pronoun when it stands alone. It is an adjective when followed by a noun.

> **INCORRECT:** *In "Flowers and Freckle Cream," Elizabeth learns that them freckles of hers aren't so bad after all.*
> **CORRECT:** *In "Flowers and Freckle Cream," Elizabeth learns that those freckles of hers aren't so bad after all.*

Grammar Practice Answers

1) Most of the animals in Yellowstone, including the park's largest mammals, the bison, survived the fire. **2)** The biggest bisons can weigh over 1,800 pounds. **3)** They are also taller than you—about six feet at the shoulder. **4)** The wild bison in the park wander more freely than most bison on ranches. **5)** They usually seem to walk more slowly than other animals. **6)** However, if you get too close to a bison, you might be surprised at how fast it can move. **7)** In winter, bison use their huge heads to push aside the heaviest snow and find grass. **8)** They also hang around the warmer areas, near the geysers. **9)** Some visitors say the park bison are the most awesome animals they ever saw in the wild.

Grammar Practice Answers

1. those
2. badly
3. Fewer
4. those
5. well
6. badly
7. that
8. those
9. little
10. well

Bad and Badly Always use *bad* as an adjective, whether before a noun or after a linking verb. *Badly* should generally be used to modify an action verb.

> **INCORRECT**: *Grandpa saved the day when Elizabeth felt so badly. She acted bad when she refused to tell anyone what was wrong.*
> **CORRECT**: *Grandpa saved the day when Elizabeth felt so bad. She acted badly when she refused to tell anyone what was wrong.*

WATCH OUT! Avoid the use of *here* after *this* or *these*. Similarly, avoid using *there* after *that* or *those*. Notice the improvement when *here* and *there* are removed from the following sentence:

> **INCORRECT**: *I was shocked by this here story. Those there baseball managers really angered me.*

This, That, These, and Those Whether used as adjectives or pronouns, *this* and *these* refer to people and things that are nearby, and *that* and *those* refer to people and things that are farther away.

> **INCORRECT**: *All day long, Elizabeth worked outdoors in this faraway field. When she came home, she had these hateful freckles on her face.*
> **CORRECT**: *All day long, Elizabeth worked outdoors in that faraway field. When she came home, she had those hateful freckles on her face.*

Good and Well *Good* is always an adjective, never an adverb. Use *well* as either an adjective or an adverb, depending on the sentence.

When used as an adjective, *well* usually refers to a person's health. As an adverb, *well* modifies an action verb. In the expression "feeling good," *good* refers to being happy or pleased.

> **INCORRECT**: *Hoeing tobacco under the hot sun, Elizabeth did her work good. She felt well when she saw all her fine work.*
> **CORRECT**: *Hoeing tobacco under the hot sun, Elizabeth did her work well. She felt good when she saw all her fine work.*

Few and Little, Fewer and Less *Few* refers to numbers of things that can be counted; *little* refers to amounts or quantities. *Fewer* is used when comparing numbers of things; *less* is used when comparing amounts or quantities.

> **INCORRECT**: *Because she felt appreciated by Grandpa, having less freckles didn't matter. She decided that the fewer she spent on freckle cream, the better.*
> **CORRECT**: *Because she felt appreciated by Grandpa, having fewer freckles didn't matter. She decided that the less she spent on freckle cream, the better.*

GRAMMAR PRACTICE

Write the modifier from each pair in parentheses that fits the meaning of the sentence.

1. In "Flowers and Freckle Cream" Elizabeth makes one of (them, those) mail-order purchases.

2. In the 1870s big-city department stores decided that mail order was needed (bad, badly) by people on farms.

3. (Less, Fewer) rural people than today could travel to the city to shop.

4. The stores sent (these, those) customers catalogs.

5. Mail-order merchants did (good, well) by serving farm families.

6. When more people moved to the cities, mail-order business did (bad, badly).

7. Later, (this, that) kind of business was advertised in magazines.

8. Later still, (those, these) merchants began sending catalogs to city dwellers.

9. The merchants also sent catalogs to people who had (few, little) time to shop.

10. Today, the Internet works (good, well) to provide another mail-order experience.

⑩ Correcting Capitalization

10.1 *Proper Nouns and Adjectives* A common noun names a whole class of persons, places, things, or ideas. A proper noun names a particular person, place, thing, or idea. A proper adjective is an adjective formed from a proper noun. All proper nouns and proper adjectives are capitalized.

Names and Personal Titles Capitalize the name and title of a person.

Also capitalize the initials and abbreviations of titles that stand for those names. *Thomas Alva Edison, T. A. Edison, Governor James Thompson,* and *Mr. Aaron Copeland* are capitalized correctly.

> **INCORRECT:** *"President Cleveland, Where Are You?" tells about jerry's search for a trading card. Other characters include roger lussier and mr. lemire.*
> **CORRECT:** *"President Cleveland, Where Are You?" tells about Jerry's search for a trading card. Other characters include Roger Lussier and Mr. Lemire.*

Capitalize a word referring to a family relationship when it is used as someone's name *(Uncle Al)* but not when it is used to identify a person *(Jill's uncle)*.

> **INCORRECT:** *Armand, Jerry's Brother, was in charge of buying their Father a gift. Last year, my Sisters and I bought a gift for aunt Marisol.*
> **CORRECT:** *Armand, Jerry's brother, was in charge of buying their father a gift. Last year, my sisters and I bought a gift for Aunt Marisol.*

WATCH OUT! Do not capitalize personal titles used as common nouns. *(We met the mayor.)*

Languages, Nationalities, Religious Terms Capitalize the names of languages and nationalities as well as religious names and terms.

Capitalize languages and nationalities, such as *French, Gaelic, Chinese,* and *Tagalog*. Capitalize religious names and terms, such as *Allah, Jehovah, the Bible,* and *the Koran*.

> **INCORRECT:** *Jerry is part of a french-american family in a small town. His family attends the local catholic church.*
> **CORRECT:** *Jerry is part of a French-American family in a small town. His family attends the local Catholic church.*

School Subjects Capitalize the name of a specific school course (Civics 101, General Science). Do not capitalize a general reference to a school subject (social studies, algebra, art).

> **INCORRECT:** *Jerry's teacher for social studies 2 was amazed at how much he knew about History.*
> **CORRECT:** *Jerry's teacher for Social Studies 2 was amazed at how much he knew about history.*

WATCH OUT! Do not capitalize minor words in a proper noun that is made up of several words *(Field Museum **of** Natural History)*.

Organizations, Institutions Capitalize the important words in the official names of organizations and institutions *(Congress, Duke University)*.

Do not capitalize words that refer to kinds of organizations or institutions *(college, hospital, museum)* or words that refer to specific organizations but are not their official names *(to the museum)*.

> **INCORRECT:** *The smithsonian institution has old trading cards. Maybe the frenchtown historical society or another Library does too.*
> **CORRECT:** *The Smithsonian Institution has old trading cards. Maybe the Frenchtown Historical Society or another library does too.*

Geographical Names, Events, Time Periods Capitalize geographical names, as well as the names of events, historical periods and documents, holidays, and months and days, but *not* the names of seasons or directions.

Grammar Practice Answers

1. This story made me curious about President Cleveland.
2. My uncle took me to the library to find reference books, such as *The Big Book of U.S. Presidents.*
3. I learned that Cleveland was the only president to leave the White House and later return.
4. He was also the only one to get married in the White House.
5. At his marriage to Francis Folsom, thousands of citizens crowded the lawn.
6. Throughout his career, Cleveland was famous for doing what he thought right whether or not it was popular.
7. As president, like he had done as sheriff, then mayor, and then governor in New York state, he focused on reforming government.
8. Between his two terms, Cleveland worked as a lawyer in New York and spent time with his family.
9. Late one autumn night in 1891 the Clevelands welcomed their baby daughter, Ruth, the first of the couple's five children.
10. Many Americans were fascinated by the little girl, and a candy bar was named for her: "Baby Ruth."

INCORRECT: *Stephen Grover Cleveland was born in caldwell, new jersey, on march 18, 1837.*
CORRECT: *Stephen Grover Cleveland was born in Caldwell, New Jersey, on March 18, 1837.*

Names	Examples
Continents	Africa, South America
Bodies of water	Pacific Ocean, Lake Charles, Amazon River
Political units	Maine, Japan, Brasília
Sections of a country	the South, Middle Atlantic States
Public areas	the Loop, Boston Common
Roads and structures	Park Avenue, Hoover Dam, Chrysler Building
Historical events	the War of 1812, the Emancipation Proclamation
Documents	Magna Carta, the Treaty of Paris
Periods of history	the Middle Ages, Reconstruction
Holidays	Arbor Day, New Year's Day
Months and days	May, Sunday
Seasons	summer, autumn
Directions	north, south

10.2 *Titles of Created Works* Titles need to follow certain capitalization rules.

Poems, Stories, Articles Capitalize the first word, the last word, and all other important words in the title of a poem, a story, or an article. Enclose the title in quotation marks.
INCORRECT: *Carl Sandburg's poem primer lesson talks about risks you take when you say harsh things.*
CORRECT: *Carl Sandburg's poem "Primer Lesson" talks about risks you take when you say harsh things.*

Books, Plays, Magazines, Newspapers, Films Capitalize the first word, the last word, and all other important words in the title of a book, play or musical, magazine, newspaper, or film. Underline or italicize the title to set it off.

Within a title, don't capitalize articles, conjunctions, and prepositions of fewer than five letters.
INCORRECT: Primer lesson appeared in Sandburg's book *complete poems.*
CORRECT: "Primer Lesson" appeared in Sandburg's book *Complete Poems.*

GRAMMAR PRACTICE

Correct the capitalization in the sentences below.

1. This story made me curious about president cleveland.
2. My Uncle took me to the Library to find Reference Books, such as *The Big book Of U.S. presidents.*
3. I learned that cleveland was the only president to leave the white house and later return.
4. He was also the only one to get married in the white house.
5. At his marriage to francis folsom, thousands of Citizens crowded the lawn.
6. Throughout his Career, cleveland was famous for doing what he thought Right whether or not it was popular.
7. As President, like he had done as Sheriff, then Mayor, and then Governor in new york state, he focused on reforming Government.
8. Between his two Terms, cleveland worked as a Lawyer in new york and spent time with his Family.
9. Late one Autumn night in 1891 the clevelands welcomed their baby Daughter, ruth, the first of the Couple's five Children.
10. Many americans were fascinated by the little girl, and a Candy Bar was named for her: "baby ruth."

⓫ Phrases and Clauses

11.1 Phrases A phrase is a group of words that does not have a subject and predicate and that functions in a sentence as a single part of speech.

Prepositional Phrases When a phrase consists of a preposition, its object, and any modifiers of the object, it is called a prepositional phrase. Prepositional phrases may function as adjectives or adverbs.

> **EXAMPLE:** Adjective Phrase: *In the excerpt from* The Story of My Life, *Helen Keller tells the story of her awakening to language.*
> **EXAMPLE:** Adverb Phrase: *She had suffered in confused darkness.*

Appositive Phrases An appositive phrase identifies or provides information about a noun or pronoun.

> **EXAMPLE:** *Helen Keller, a young girl, lost her hearing and sight.*

Infinitive Phrases An infinitive phrase consists of an infinitive (*to* + a verb) along with its modifiers and objects.

> **EXAMPLE:** *For many years, Helen tried to express her thoughts and feelings.*

Participial Phrases There are two kinds of participles. The past participle is usually formed by adding *-d* or *-ed* to the present tense. Irregular verbs, however, do not follow this rule. The present participle is formed by adding *-ing* to the present tense of any verb. A participle with its objects and modifiers is called a participial phrase. Participial phrases act as adjectives.

> **EXAMPLE:** *Having read her autobiography, I can better imagine what life was like for her.*

Gerund Phrases A gerund is a verb form ending in *-ing* that functions as a noun. A gerund phrase is a group of words that includes a gerund, its modifiers, and objects.

> **EXAMPLE:** *Learning to communicate became her main goal.*

Identify each underlined phrase as prepositional, appositive, infinitive, participial, or gerund.

1. After reading about Helen Keller, I wanted <u>to find out more about Anne Sullivan.</u>

2. <u>Searching through the library,</u> I came across many biographies about her.

3. During her lifetime, <u>the years between 1866 and 1936,</u> she overcame her own disability and shared her strategies with others.

4. Sullivan, <u>through patience and understanding,</u> helped Helen Keller learn to use words.

5. People <u>reading of her work</u> must have wept real tears for her triumphs.

6. <u>Learning about this amazing teacher</u> was sometimes a painful experience.

11.2 Independent and Dependent (Subordinate) Clauses A clause is a group of words that contains a subject and a verb. There are two kinds of clauses: independent clauses and dependent, or subordinate, clauses. An independent clause can stand alone as a complete sentence. A subordinate clause cannot stand alone and must be attached to an independent clause to form a complex sentence.

> **EXAMPLE:** *Independent clause: I read "Where the Girl Rescued Her Brother."*
> **EXAMPLE:** *Dependent clause: After I had finished dinner*
> **EXAMPLE:** *Complex sentence: After I had finished dinner, I read "Where the Girl Rescued Her Brother."*

Adjective and Adverb Clauses A subordinate clause may be used as an adjective. Adjective clauses are usually introduced by the relative pronouns *who, whom, whose, which,* and *that.* A subordinate clause may also be used as an adverb to modify a verb, adjective, or another adverb.

> **EXAMPLE:** *Adjective clause: Buffalo Calf Road Woman was the name of the girl who saved her brother.*
> **EXAMPLE:** *She rode into battle when she saw that her brother was surrounded.*

Grammar Practice Answers

1. infinitive
2. participial
3. appositive
4. prepositional
5. participial
6. gerund

Grammar Practice Answers

11.2

1. phrase
2. clause
3. clause
4. clause, phrase
5. clause

12.1

"Matthew Henson at the Top of the World" describes the discovery of the North Pole, but the Peary expedition wasn't the first to seek it. The earliest Arctic expedition probably took place in the late 300s B.C.; a Greek explorer said he found an island six days north of Scotland. People didn't believe him; they thought there was nothing but ice that far north. In the late 1500s people wanted a quick way to the Orient; therefore the Englishman Martin Frobisher tried to find a northwest passage through the Arctic. In the 1770s Samuel Hearne was the first European to travel by land to the Arctic Ocean from Hudson Bay, and much exploration followed his journey. In 1926 Richard Byrd and Floyd Bennett made the first flight over the North Pole; the next step was to complete a submarine passage across the pole.

Noun Clauses A noun clause is a dependent (subordinate) clause used as a noun. A noun clause may be a subject, a direct object, an indirect object, a predicate noun, or the object of a preposition.

> **EXAMPLE:** *Buffalo Calf Road Woman proved that a girl can be as brave as a boy.*

GRAMMAR PRACTICE

Identify each underlined group of words as either a phrase or a clause.

1. Some Crow and Shoshone scouts tried <u>to help white soldiers defeat the Cheyenne.</u>

2. Buffalo Calf Road Woman grew worried <u>when her brother's horse was shot.</u>

3. No one imagined <u>what would happen next.</u>

4. The girl, <u>who was very brave,</u> galloped straight <u>into the fight.</u>

5. Everyone knew <u>that this was heroism.</u>

---

⑫ Punctuation

12.1 *Compound Sentences* Punctuation helps organize longer sentences that have several clauses.

Commas in Compound Sentences Use a comma before the conjunction that joins the clauses of a compound sentence.

> **INCORRECT:** *Henson reached the North Pole and he worked hard to make the most of his opportunity.*
> **CORRECT:** *Henson reached the North Pole, and he worked hard to make the most of his opportunity.*

Semicolons in Compound Sentences Use a semicolon between the clauses of a compound sentence when no conjunction is used. Use a semicolon before, and a comma after, a conjunctive adverb that joins the clauses of a compound sentence.

Conjunctive adverbs include *therefore, however, then, nevertheless, consequently,* and *besides.*

> **EXAMPLE:** *He made the dream of his boyhood come true; however, racism interfered with his ambition.*

USAGE TIP Even when clauses are connected by a coordinating conjunction, you should use a semicolon between them if one or both clauses contain a comma.

> **EXAMPLE:** *Matthew's father, unable to support him, sent the boy to live with an uncle; however, soon Matthew's uncle could no longer support him.*

GRAMMAR PRACTICE

Rewrite the paragraph, adding commas and semicolons where necessary.

1) "Matthew Henson at the Top of the World" describes the discovery of the North Pole but the Peary expedition wasn't the first to seek it. **2)** The earliest Arctic expedition probably took place in the late 300s B.C. a Greek explorer said he found an island six days north of Scotland. **3)** People didn't believe him they thought there was nothing but ice that far north. **4)** In the late 1500s people wanted a quick way to the Orient therefore the Englishman Martin Frobisher tried to find a northwest passage through the Arctic. **5)** In the 1770s Samuel Hearne was the first European to travel by land to the Arctic Ocean from Hudson Bay and much exploration followed his journey. **6)** In 1926 Richard Byrd and Floyd Bennett made the first flight over the North Pole the next step was to complete a submarine passage across the pole.

12.2 *Elements Set Off in a Sentence* Most elements that are not essential to a sentence are set off by commas to highlight the main idea of the sentence.

Introductory Words Use a comma to separate an introductory word or phrase from the rest of the sentence.

> **INCORRECT:** *Definitely "The First Emperor" gets me thinking about ancient China.*
> **CORRECT:** *Definitely, "The First Emperor" gets me thinking about ancient China.*

Use a comma to set off more than one introductory prepositional phrase, but not for a single prepositional phrase in most cases.

INCORRECT: *With its images of cruel behavior this article makes me doubt that I could have survived in that world.*

CORRECT: *With its images of cruel behavior, this article makes me doubt that I could have survived in that world.*

Interrupters Use commas to set off a word that interrupts the flow of a sentence.

EXAMPLE: *What, perchance, would make a king of the weakest state want to unite all the neighboring states?*

Use commas to set off a group of words that interrupts the flow of a sentence.

EXAMPLE: *The discovery of the tomb, including the soldiers guarding it, has astonished archaeologists.*

Nouns of Address Use commas to set off a noun in direct address at the beginning of a sentence.

INCORRECT: *If I could talk with Emperor Ch'in, I'd say, "Emperor why put people in danger?"*

CORRECT: *If I could talk with Emperor Ch'in, I'd say, "Emperor, why put people in danger?"*

Use commas to set off a noun in direct address in the middle of a sentence.

INCORRECT: *Then I'd say, "How many people Emperor did you kill?"*

CORRECT: *Then I'd say, "How many people, Emperor, did you kill?"*

Appositives Set off with commas an appositive phrase that is not necessary to the meaning of the sentence.

The following sentence could be understood without the appositive.

INCORRECT: *The emperor a strong-minded person dug his own grave.*

CORRECT: *The emperor, a strong-minded person, dug his own grave.*

Do not set off with commas an appositive phrase that is necessary to the meaning of the sentence.

The following sentence could not be understood without the words set off by commas:

INCORRECT: *Ch'in, the warrior, seems very different from Ch'in, the worried mouse.*

CORRECT: *Ch'in the warrior seems very different from Ch'in the worried mouse.*

For Clarity Use a comma to prevent misreading or misunderstanding.

INCORRECT: *Excavators finally found the tomb that professors had searched for for so long.*

CORRECT: *Excavators finally found the tomb that professors had searched for, for so long.*

GRAMMAR PRACTICE

Rewrite the paragraph. Add or delete commas where necessary.

1) Ch'in Shih Huang Ti "The First Emperor" sounds like a typical emperor. **2)** An emperor rules not just one but several countries by always staying alert to outside threats. **3)** Clearly his country, is the strongest one. **4)** Empires those vast political machines are formed by war. **5)** Once an empire is established however it reduces the number of wars for a while. **6)** In an empire, with strong central control everyone knows who's boss. **7)** Empires can have good effects when for example they force people to exchange languages, art, and technology. **8)** If I could, I'd say to Ch'in, "Tell me Emperor what you accomplished."

12.3 Elements in a Series Commas should be used to separate three or more items in a series and to separate adjectives preceding a noun.

Subjects, Predicates, and Other Elements Use a comma after every item except the last in a series of three or more items.

Subjects or predicates may occur in series.

INCORRECT: *In* The Story of My Life, *Helen Keller learns to fingerspell discovers that everything has a name and finds her world changed as a result.*

CORRECT: *In* The Story of My Life, *Helen Keller learns to fingerspell, discovers that everything has a name, and finds her world changed as a result.*

Grammar Practice Answers

1) Ch'in Shih Huang Ti, "The First Emperor," sounds like a typical emperor. **2)** An emperor rules not just one, but several countries by always staying alert to outside threats. **3, 4)** Clearly, his country is the strongest one. Empires, those vast political machines, are formed by war. **5)** Once an empire is established, however, it reduces the number of wars for a while. **6)** In an empire with strong central control, everyone knows who's boss. **7)** Empires can have good effects when, for example, they force people to exchange languages, art, and technology. **8)** If I could, I'd say to Ch'in, "Tell me, Emperor, what you accomplished."

Predicate adjectives often occur in series.

INCORRECT: *As the selection begins, Helen is silent angry and careless.*
CORRECT: *As the selection begins, Helen is silent, angry, and careless.*

USAGE TIP Note in the example that a comma followed by a conjunction precedes the last element in the series.

Adverbs and prepositional phrases may also occur in series.

INCORRECT: *As Helen learned more words, her teacher developed new teaching plans with speed with creativity and with great success.*
CORRECT: *As Helen learned more words, her teacher developed new teaching plans with speed, with creativity, and with great success.*

Two or More Adjectives In most sentences, use a comma after each adjective except the last of two or more adjectives that precede a noun.

If you can reverse the order of adjectives without changing the meaning or if you can use *and* between them, separate the two adjectives with a comma.

INCORRECT: *Helen's eager young hands caught the flow of dark, blue water.*
CORRECT: *Helen's eager, young hands caught the flow of dark blue water.*

GRAMMAR PRACTICE

Rewrite each sentence, inserting commas where they are needed.

1. *The Story of My Life* was written by Helen Keller, writer activist and speaker.
2. Keller was left blind and deaf by a childhood illness was taught to communicate by her teacher Anne Sullivan and went on to graduate from college with honors.
3. Photographs show Helen Keller meeting with such famous persons as Mark Twain Charlie Chaplin and President Kennedy.
4. Less well-known is Keller's love of dogs, including her shiny pug-nosed Boston terrier.

12.4 **Dates, Addresses, and Letters**
Punctuation in dates, addresses, and letters makes information easy to understand.

Dates Use a comma between the day of the month and the year. If the date falls in the middle of a sentence, use another comma after the year.

INCORRECT: *I went to the game on Monday August 30 1999 a sunny day.*
CORRECT: *I went to the game on Monday, August 30, 1999, a sunny day.*

Addresses Use a comma to separate the city and the state in an address or other location. If the city and state fall in the middle of a sentence, use a comma after the state too.

EXAMPLE: *Janet called Richard the laughingstock of Mapesville, New Jersey.*

Parts of a Letter Use a comma after the greeting and after the closing in a letter.

INCORRECT:
Dear Janet
  Here's the silver horseback riding trophy that you gave me.
    Your former friend
    Richard
CORRECT:
Dear Janet,
  Here's the silver horseback riding trophy that you gave me.
    Your former friend,
    Richard

GRAMMAR PRACTICE

Rewrite the following sentences, correcting the comma errors.

1. After reading "The Southpaw," I sent a postcard to my friend Shinobu in San Francisco California where I used to live.
2. Dear Shinobu

   A girl in a story I read played baseball with a team that used to be all boys. It reminded me of you being the first girl to pitch for the Berkeley Bees!

                    Yours truly
                    Elizabeth

Grammar Practice Answers
12.3

1. The *Story of My Life* was written by Helen Keller, writer, activist, and speaker.
2. Keller was left blind and deaf by a childhood illness, was taught to communicate by her teacher Anne Sullivan, and went on to graduate from college with honors.
3. Photographs show Helen Keller meeting with such famous persons as Mark Twain, Charlie Chaplin, and President Kennedy.
4. Less well-known is Keller's love of dogs, including her shiny, pug-nosed Boston terrier.

12.4

1. After reading "The Southpaw," I sent a postcard to my friend Shinobu in San Francisco, California, where I used to live.
2. Dear Shinobu,
   A girl in a story I read played baseball with a team that used to be all boys. It reminded me of you being the first girl to pitch for the Berkeley Bees!

                    Yours truly,
                    Elizabeth

3. Shinobu said she still remembers that day on June 14 1996 when she first stood on the pitcher's mound.

4. I thought my uncle in Reno Nevada might have some pictures from that day.

5. Dear Uncle Ernesto

　　Remember when you came to visit me and we saw my friend Shinobu pitch? If you still have any of the photos you took, I'd love to see them.

Love always
Elizabeth

12.5 *Quotations* Quotation marks let readers know exactly who said what. They are also used for some titles.

Quotation Marks Use quotation marks at the beginning and the end of direct quotations and to set off titles of short works.

INCORRECT: *The narrator in Crow Call had never gone hunting. She said to her father, What if I don't know what to do?*

CORRECT: *The narrator in "Crow Call" had never gone hunting. She said to her father, "What if I don't know what to do?"*

Capitalize the first word of a direct quotation, especially in a piece of dialogue.

INCORRECT: *The waitress, who questioned whether they really wanted three pieces of pie, said, "you mean two?"*

CORRECT: *The waitress, who questioned whether they really wanted three pieces of pie, said, "You mean two?"*

USAGE TIP If quoted words are from a written source and are not complete sentences, they can begin with a lowercase letter.

EXAMPLE: *Mark Twain said that cauliflower was "nothing but cabbage with a college education."*

End Punctuation Place periods inside quotation marks. Place question marks and exclamation points inside quotation marks if they belong to the quotation; place them outside if they do not belong to the quotation. Place semicolons outside quotation marks.

INCORRECT: *I said to my brother, "I would have been nervous too"!*
　　"Are you saying you're not brave"? he said.
　　I responded, "Not really;" I added that I had enjoyed "Crow Call".

CORRECT: *I said to my brother, "I would have been nervous too!"*
　　"Are you saying you're not brave?" he said.
　　I responded, "Not really"; I added that I had enjoyed "Crow Call."

Use a comma to end a quotation that is a complete sentence but is followed by explanatory words.

EXAMPLE: *"Have a good day," I said to the waitress as we left.*

Divided Quotations Capitalize the first word of the second part of a direct quotation if it begins a new sentence.

INCORRECT: *"I know," he said. "are you scared?"*

CORRECT: *"I know," he said. "Are you scared?"*

USAGE TIP If a capital letter would not be used, then do not use one in the divided quotation.

Do not capitalize the first word of the second part of a divided quotation if it does not begin a new sentence.

EXAMPLE: *"Okay," said my father, "you can do the crow call now."*

GRAMMAR PRACTICE

Rewrite these sentences, correcting punctuation and capitalization.

1. Erik and Ron found a pamphlet called Super-Simple Cherry Pie.

2. Erik said, "to learn more, first I researched how to make a pie crust."

3. Ron noticed that "Cookbooks can be handy."

4. "The trick" Erik said "Is to avoid adding too much water to the dough."

5. Ron said, "Well maybe;" then Erik continued "You also need to flour the rolling pin."

6. "The problem is, we already ate all the cherries" muttered Ron.

Grammar Practice Answers 12.4 (continued)

3. Shinobu said she still remembers that day on June 14, 1996 when she first stood on the pitcher's mound.

4. I thought my uncle in Reno, Nevada, might have some pictures from that day.

5. Dear Uncle Ernesto,
　　Remember when you came to visit me, and we saw my friend Shinobu pitch? If you still have any of the photos you took, I'd love to see them.

Love always,
Elizabeth

12.5

1. Erik and Ron found a pamphlet called "Super-Simple Cherry Pie."

2. Erik said, "To learn more, first I researched how to make a pie crust."

3. Ron noticed that "cookbooks can be handy."

4. "The trick," Erik said, "is to avoid adding too much water to the dough."

5. Ron said, "Well maybe."
Then Erik continued, "You also need to flour the rolling pin."

6. "The problem is we already ate all the cherries," muttered Ron.

Grammar Glossary

This glossary contains various terms you need to understand when you use the Grammar Handbook. Used as a reference source, this glossary will help you explore grammar concepts and the ways they relate to one another.

Abbreviation An abbreviation is a shortened form of a word or word group; it is often made up of initials. (B.C., A.M., Maj.)

Active voice. *See* **Voice.**

Adjective An adjective modifies, or describes, a noun or pronoun. (*happy* camper, she is *small*)

A *predicate adjective* follows a linking verb and describes the subject. (The day seemed *long.*)

A *proper adjective* is formed from a proper noun. (*Jewish* temple, *Alaskan* husky)

The *comparative* form of an adjective compares two things. (*more alert, thicker*)

The *superlative* form of an adjective compares more than two things. (*most abundant, weakest*)

What Adjectives Tell	Examples
How many	*some* writers *much* joy
What kind	*grand* plans *wider* streets
Which one(s)	*these* flowers *that* star

Adjective phrase. *See* **Phrase.**

Adverb An adverb modifies a verb, an adjective, or another adverb. (Clare sang *loudly.*)

The *comparative* form of an adverb compares two actions. (*more generously, faster*)

The *superlative* form of an adverb compares more than two actions. (*most sharply, closest*)

What Adverbs Tell	Examples
How	write *carelessly* eat *quickly*
When	*Soon* I'll be home. I'll see you *later.*
Where	They traveled *far.* Put it *someplace.*

Adverb, conjunctive. *See* **Conjunctive adverb.**

Adverb phrase. *See* **Phrase.**

Agreement Sentence parts that correspond with one another are said to be in agreement.

In *pronoun-antecedent agreement,* a pronoun and the word it refers to are the same in number, gender, and person. (*Bill* mailed *his* application. The *students* ate *their* lunches.)

In *subject-verb agreement,* the subject and verb in a sentence are the same in number. (*A child cries* for help. *They cry* aloud.)

Ambiguous reference An ambiguous reference occurs when a pronoun may refer to more than one word. (Bud asked his brother if *he* had any mail.)

Antecedent An antecedent is the noun or pronoun to which a pronoun refers. (If *Adam* forgets *his* raincoat, *he* will be late for school. *She* learned *her* lesson.)

Appositive An appositive is a noun or phrase that explains one or more words in a sentence. (Cary Grant, *an Englishman,* spent most of his adult life in America.)

An *essential appositive* is needed to make the sense of a sentence complete. (A comic strip inspired the musical *Annie.*)

A *nonessential appositive* is one that adds information to a sentence but is not necessary to its sense. (O. Henry, *a short-story writer,* spent time in prison.)

Article Articles are the special adjectives *a, an,* and *the.* (*the* day, *a* fly)

A *definite article* (the word *the*) is one that refers to a particular thing. (*the* cabin)

An *indefinite article* is used with a noun that is not unique but refers to one of many of its kind. (*a* dish, *an* otter)

Auxiliary verb. *See* **Verb.**

Clause A clause is a group of words that contains a verb and its subject. (*they slept*)

An *adjective clause* is a dependent (subordinate) clause that modifies a noun or pronoun. (Hugh bought the sweater *that he had admired.*)

An *adverb clause* is a dependent (subordinate) clause used to modify a verb, an adjective, or an adverb.

(Ring the bell *when it is time for class to begin.*)

A *noun clause* is a dependent (subordinate) clause that is used as a noun. (*Whatever you say* interests me.)

An *elliptical clause* is a clause from which a word or words have been omitted. (We are not as lucky as *they.*)

An *independent (main) clause* can stand by itself as a sentence. (*the flashlight flickered*)

A *dependent (subordinate) clause* does not express a complete thought and cannot stand by itself. (*while the nation watched*)

Clause	Example
Independent (main)	The hurricane struck
Dependent (subordinate)	while we were preparing to leave.

Collective noun. *See* **Noun.**

Comma splice A comma splice is an error created when two sentences are separated with a comma instead of a correct end mark. (*The band played a medley of show tunes, everyone enjoyed the show.*)

Common noun. *See* **Noun.**

Comparative. *See* **Adjective; Adverb.**

Complement A complement is a word or group of words that completes the meaning of a verb. (The kitten finished the *milk.*) *See also* **Direct object; Indirect object.**

An *objective complement* is a word or a group of words that follows a direct object and renames or describes that object. (The parents of the rescued child declared Gus a *hero.*)

A *subject complement* follows a linking verb and renames or describes the subject. (The coach seemed *anxious.*) *See also* **Noun (predicate noun); Adjective (predicate adjective).**

Complete predicate The complete predicate of a sentence consists of the main verb plus any words that modify or complete the verb's meaning. (The student *produces work of high caliber.*)

Complete subject The complete subject of a sentence consists of the simple subject plus any words that modify or describe the simple subject. (*Students of history* believe that wars can be avoided.)

Clause	Example
Complete subject	The man in the ten-gallon hat
Complete predicate	wore a pair of silver spurs.

Compound sentence part A sentence element that consists of two or more subjects, verbs, objects, or other parts is compound. (*Lou* and *Jay* helped. Laura *makes* and *models* scarves. Jill sings *opera* and *popular music.*)

Conjunction A conjunction is a word that links other words or groups of words.

A *coordinating conjunction* connects related words, groups of words, or sentences. (*and, but, or*)

A *correlative conjunction* is one of a pair of conjunctions that work together to connect sentence parts. (*either . . . or, neither . . . nor, not only . . . but also, whether . . . or, both . . . and*) A *subordinating conjunction* introduces a subordinate clause. (*after,*

although, as, as if, as long as, as though, because, before, if, in order that, since, so that, than, though, till, unless, until, whatever, when, where, while)

Conjunctive adverb A conjunctive adverb joins the clauses of a compound sentence. (*however, therefore, yet*)

Contraction A contraction is formed by joining two words and substituting an apostrophe for a letter or letters left out of one of the words. (*didn't, we've*)

Coordinating conjunction. *See* **Conjunction.**

Correlative conjunction. *See* **Conjunction.**

 D

Dangling modifier A dangling modifier is one that does not clearly modify any word in the sentence. (*Dashing for the train, the barriers got in the way.*)

Demonstrative pronoun. *See* **Pronoun.**

Dependent clause. *See* **Clause.**

Direct object A direct object receives the action of a verb. Direct objects follow transitive verbs. (Jude planned the *party.*)

Direct quotation. *See* **Quotation.**

Divided quotation. *See* **Quotation.**

Double negative A double negative is the incorrect use of two negative words when only one is needed. (*Nobody didn't care.*)

 E

End mark An end mark is one of several punctuation marks that can end a sentence. See the punctuation chart on page R56.

Fragment. *See* **Sentence fragment.**

Future tense. *See* **Verb tense.**

Gender The gender of a personal pronoun indicates whether the person or thing referred to is male, female, or neuter. (My cousin plays the tuba; *he* often performs in school concerts.)

Gerund A gerund is a verbal that ends in *-ing* and functions as a noun. (*Making* pottery takes patience.)

Helping verb. *See* **Verb (auxiliary verb).**

Illogical comparison An illogical comparison is a comparison that does not make sense because words are missing or illogical. (My computer is *newer than Kay*.)

Indefinite pronoun. *See* **Pronoun.**

Indefinite reference Indefinite reference occurs when a pronoun is used without a clear antecedent. (My aunt hugged me in front of my friends, and *it* was embarrassing.)

Independent clause. *See* **Clause.**

Indirect object An indirect object tells to whom or for whom (sometimes to what or for what) something is done. (Arthur wrote *Kerry* a letter.)

Indirect question An indirect question tells what someone asked without using the person's exact words. (*My friend asked me if I could go with her to the dentist.*)

Indirect quotation. *See* **Quotation.**

Infinitive An infinitive is a verbal beginning with *to* that functions as a noun, an adjective, or an adverb. (He wanted *to go* to the play.)

Intensive pronoun. *See* **Pronoun.**

Interjection An interjection is a word or phrase used to express strong feeling. (*Wow! Good grief!*)

Interrogative pronoun. *See* **Pronoun.**

Intransitive verb. *See* **Verb.**

Inverted sentence An inverted sentence is one in which the subject comes after the verb. (*How was the movie? Here come the clowns.*)

Irregular verb. *See* **Verb.**

Linking verb. *See* **Verb.**

Main clause. *See* **Clause.**

Main verb. *See* **Verb.**

Modifier A modifier makes another word more precise. Modifiers most often are adjectives or adverbs; they may also be phrases, verbals, or clauses that function as adjectives or adverbs. (*small* box, smiled *broadly*, house *by the sea*, dog *barking loudly*)

An *essential modifier* is one that is necessary to the meaning of a sentence. (Everybody *who has a free pass* should enter now. None *of the passengers* got on the train.)

A *nonessential modifier* is one that merely adds more information to a sentence that is clear without the addition. (We will use the new dishes, *which are stored in the closet*.)

Noun A noun names a person, a place, a thing, or an idea. *(auditor, shelf, book, goodness)*

An *abstract noun* names an idea, a quality, or a feeling. *(joy)*

A *collective noun* names a group of things. *(class, flock, group)*

A *common noun* is a general name of a person, a place, a thing, or an idea. *(valet, hill, bread, amazement)*

A *compound noun* contains two or more words. *(hometown, pay-as-you-go, screen test)*

A *noun of direct address* is the name of a person being directly spoken to. (*Lee*, do you have the package? No, *Suki*, your letter did not arrive.)

A *possessive noun* shows who or what owns or is associated with something. (*Lil's* ring, a *day's* pay)

A *predicate noun* follows a linking verb and renames the subject. (Karen is a *writer*.)

A *proper noun* names a particular person, place, or thing. *(John Smith, Ohio, Sears Tower, Congress)*

Number A word is singular in number if it refers to just one person, place, thing, idea, or action, and plural in number if it refers to more than one person, place, thing, idea, or action. (The words *he, waiter,* and *is* are singular. The words *they, waiters,* and *are* are plural.)

Object of a preposition The object of a preposition is the noun or pronoun that follows a preposition. (The athletes cycled along the *route*. Jane baked a cake for *her*.)

Object of a verb The object of a verb receives the action of the verb. (Sid told *stories*.)

Participle A participle is often used as part of a verb phrase. (had *written*) It can also be used as a verbal that functions as an adjective. (the *leaping* deer, the medicine *taken* for a fever)

The **present participle** is formed by adding *-ing* to the present form of a verb. (*Walking* rapidly, we reached the general store.)

The **past participle** of a regular verb is formed by adding *-d* or *-ed* to the present form. The past participles of irregular verbs do not follow this pattern. (*Startled*, they ran from the house. *Spun* glass is delicate. A *broken* cup lay there.)

Passive voice. *See* **Voice.**

Past tense. *See* **Verb tense.**

Perfect tenses. *See* **Verb tense.**

Person Person is a means of classifying pronouns.

A **first-person** pronoun refers to the person speaking. (*We* came.)

A **second-person** pronoun refers to the person spoken to. (*You* ask.)

A **third-person** pronoun refers to some other person(s) or thing(s) being spoken of. (*They* played.)

Personal pronoun. *See* **Pronoun.**

Phrase A phrase is a group of related words that does not contain a verb and its subject. (*noticing everything, under a chair*)

An **adjective phrase** modifies a noun or a pronoun. (The label *on the bottle* has faded.)

An **adverb phrase** modifies a verb, an adjective, or an adverb. (Come *to the fair*.)

An **appositive phrase** explains one or more words in a sentence. (Mary, *a champion gymnast,* won gold medals at the Olympics.)

A **gerund phrase** consists of a gerund and its modifiers and complements. (*Fixing the leak* will take only a few minutes.)

An **infinitive phrase** consists of an infinitive, its modifiers, and its complements. (*To prepare for a test,* study in a quiet place.)

A **participial phrase** consists of a participle and its modifiers and complements. (*Straggling to the finish line,* the last runners arrived.)

A **prepositional phrase** consists of a preposition, its object, and the object's modifiers. (The Saint Bernard does rescue work *in the Swiss Alps.*)

A **verb phrase** consists of a main verb and one or more helping verbs. (*might have ordered*)

Possessive A noun or pronoun that is possessive shows ownership or relationship. (*Dan's* story, *my* doctor)

Possessive noun. *See* **Noun.**

Possessive pronoun. *See* **Pronoun.**

Predicate The predicate of a sentence tells what the subject is or does. (The van *runs well even in winter*. The job seems *too complicated*.) *See also* **Complete predicate; Simple predicate.**

Predicate adjective. *See* **Adjective.**

Predicate nominative A predicate nominative is a noun or pronoun that follows a linking verb and renames or explains the subject. (Joan is a computer *operator*. The winner of the prize was *he*.)

Predicate pronoun. *See* **Pronoun.**

Preposition A preposition is a word that relates its object to another part of the sentence or to the sentence as a whole. (Alfredo leaped *onto* the stage.)

Prepositional phrase. *See* **Phrase.**

Present tense. *See* **Verb tense.**

Pronoun A pronoun replaces a noun or another pronoun. Some pronouns allow a writer or speaker to avoid repeating a proper noun. Other pronouns let a writer refer to an unknown or unidentified person or thing.

A **demonstrative pronoun** singles out one or more persons or things. (*This* is the letter.)

An **indefinite pronoun** refers to an unidentified person or thing. (*Everyone* stayed home. Will you hire *anybody?*)

An **intensive pronoun** emphasizes a noun or pronoun. (The teacher *himself* sold tickets.)

An **interrogative pronoun** asks a question. (*What happened to you?*)

A **personal pronoun** shows a distinction of person. (*I* came. *You* see. *He* knows.)

A **possessive pronoun** shows ownership. (*My* spaghetti is always good. Are *your* parents coming to the play?)

A **predicate pronoun** follows a linking verb and renames the subject. (The owners of the store were *they*.)

A **reflexive pronoun** reflects an action back on the subject of the sentence. (Joe helped *himself*.)

A **relative pronoun** relates a

dependent (subordinate clause) to the word it modifies. (The draperies, *which* had been made by hand, were ruined in the fire.)

Pronoun-antecedent agreement. *See* **Agreement.**

Pronoun forms

The *subject form* of a pronoun is used when the pronoun is the subject of a sentence or follows a linking verb as a predicate pronoun. (*She* fell. The star was *she*.)

The *object form* of a pronoun is used when the pronoun is the direct or indirect object of a verb or verbal or the object of a preposition. (We sent *him* the bill. We ordered food for *them*.)

Proper adjective. *See* **Adjective.**

Proper noun. *See* **Noun.**

Punctuation Punctuation clarifies the structure of sentences. See the punctuation chart below.

Quotation A quotation consists of words from another speaker or writer.

A *direct quotation* is the exact words of a speaker or writer. (Martin said, *"The homecoming game has been postponed."*)

A *divided quotation* is a quotation separated by words that identify the speaker. (*"The homecoming game,"* said Martin, *"has been postponed."*)

An *indirect quotation* reports what a person said without giving the exact words. (*Martin said that the homecoming game had been postponed.*)

Reflexive pronoun. *See* **Pronoun.**

Regular verb. *See* **Verb.**

Relative pronoun. *See* **Pronoun.**

Run-on sentence A run-on sentence consists of two or more sentences written incorrectly as one. (*The sunset was beautiful its brilliant colors lasted only a short time.*)

Sentence A sentence expresses a complete thought. The chart at the top of the next page shows the four kinds of sentences.

A *complex sentence* contains one independent (main) clause and one or more dependent (subordinate) clauses. (*Open the windows before you go to bed. If she falls, I'll help her up.*)

A *compound sentence* is made up of two or more independent clauses joined by a conjunction, a colon, or a semicolon. (*The ship finally docked, and the passengers quickly left.*)

A *simple sentence* consists of only one independent clause. (*My friend volunteers at a nursing home.*)

Punctuation	Example	
Apostrophe (')	Shows possession	Lou's garage Alva's script
	Indicates a contraction	I'll help you The baby's tired
Colon (:)	Introduces a list or quotation	three colors: red, green, and yellow
	Divides some compound sentences	This was the problem: we had to find our own way home.
Comma (,)	Separates ideas	The glass broke, and the juice spilled over.
	Separates modifiers	The lively, talented cheerleaders energized the team.
	Separates items in series	We visited London, Rome, and Paris.
Exclamation point (!)	Ends an exclamatory sentence	We had a wonderful time!
Hyphen (-)	Joins parts of some compound words	daughter-in-law, great-grandson
Period (.)	Ends a declarative sentence	Swallows return to Capistrano in spring.
	Indicates most abbreviations	min. qt. Blvd. Gen. Jan.
Question mark (?)	Ends an interrogative sentence	Where are you going?
Semicolon (;)	Divides some compound sentences	Marie is an expert dancer; she teaches a class in tap.
	Separates items in series that contain commas	Jenny visited Syracuse, New York; Athens, Georgia; and Tampa, Florida.

Sentence fragment A sentence fragment is a group of words that is only part of a sentence. (*When he arrived. Merrily yodeling.*)

Kind of Sentence	Example
Declarative (statement)	Our team won.
Exclamatory (strong feeling)	I had a great time!
Imperative (request, command)	Take the next exit.
Interrogative (question)	Who owns the car?

Simple predicate A simple predicate is the verb in the predicate. (John *collects* foreign stamps.)

Simple subject A simple subject is the key noun or pronoun in the subject. (The new *house* is empty.)

Split infinitive A split infinitive occurs when a modifier is placed between the word *to* and the verb in an infinitive. (*to quickly speak*)

Subject The subject is the part of a sentence that tells whom or what the sentence is about. (*Lou* swam.) *See also* **Complete subject; Simple subject.**

Subject-verb agreement. *See* **Agreement.**

Subordinate clause. *See* **Clause.**

Superlative. *See* **Adjective; Adverb.**

Transitive verb. *See* **Verb.**

Unidentified reference An unidentified reference usually occurs when the word *it, they, this, which,* or *that* is used. (In California *they* have good weather most of the time.)

V

Verb A verb expresses an action, a condition, or a state of being.

An ***action verb*** tells what the subject does, has done, or will do. The action may be physical or mental. (Susan *trains* guide dogs.)

An ***auxiliary verb*** is added to a main verb to express tense, add emphasis, or otherwise affect the meaning of the verb. Together the auxiliary and main verb make up a verb phrase. (*will* intend, *could have* gone)

A ***linking verb*** expresses a state of being or connects the subject with a word or words that describe the subject. (The ice *feels* cold.) Linking verbs include *appear, be (am, are, is, was, were, been, being), become, feel, grow, look, remain, seem, smell, sound,* and *taste*.

A ***main verb*** expresses action or state of being; it appears with one or more auxiliary verbs. (will be *staying*)

The ***progressive form*** of a verb shows continuing action. (She *is knitting*.)

The past tense and past participle of a ***regular verb*** are formed by adding *-d* or *-ed*. (*open, opened*) An ***irregular verb*** does not follow this pattern. (*throw, threw, thrown; shrink, shrank, shrunk*)

The action of a ***transitive verb*** is directed toward someone or something, called the object of a verb. (Leo *washed* the windows.) An ***intransitive verb*** has no object. (The leaves *scattered*.)

Verb phrase. *See* **Phrase.**

Verb tense Verb tense shows the time of an action or the time of a state of being.

The ***present tense*** places an action or condition in the present. (Jan *takes* piano lessons.)

The ***past tense*** places an action or condition in the past. (We *came* to the party.)

The ***future tense*** places an action or condition in the future. (You *will understand*.)

The ***present perfect tense*** describes an action in an indefinite past time or an action that began in the past and continues in the present. (*has called, have known*)

The ***past perfect tense*** describes one action that happened before another action in the past. (*had scattered, had mentioned*)

The ***future perfect tense*** describes an event that will be finished before another future action begins. (*will have taught, shall have appeared*)

Verbal A verbal is formed from a verb and acts as another part of speech, such as a noun, an adjective, or an adverb.

Verbal	Example
Gerund (used as a noun)	Lamont enjoys *swimming*.
Infinitive (used as an adjective, an adverb, or a noun)	Everyone wants *to help*.
Participle (used as an adjective)	The leaves *covering the drive* made it slippery.

Voice The voice of a verb depends on whether the subject performs or receives the action of the verb.

In the ***active voice*** the subject of the sentence performs the verb's action. (We *knew* the answer.)

In the ***passive voice*** the subject of the sentence receives the action of the verb. (The team *has been eliminated*.)

Spelling Handbook

Improving Your Spelling

Like hitting a fastball or mastering the backstroke, becoming a spelling whiz takes planning and practice. By following these tips and basic rules, you can become a better speller.

Spelling Tips

1. **Identify your own spelling demons.** Make a list of the words you have misspelled in your writing.

2. **Pronounce words carefully.** Sometimes people misspell words because they say them incorrectly. For example, if you say the word *library* correctly, you will not misspell it *l-i-b-e-r-r-y.*

3. **Make a habit of seeing the letters in a word.** Pay attention to every letter of a new or difficult word. For example, when you come upon a word like *library,* look at each letter to fix the spelling in your mind.

4. **Invent memory devices for problem words.** Here are some examples:

princi**pal** (pal)	The princi**pal** is my **pal.**
tra**ge**dy (age)	Every **age** has its tra**ge**dy.
emba**rrass** (rr, ss)	I turned **r**eally **r**ed and felt **s**o **s**illy.

5. **Proofread what you write.** Reread your work word for word so that you catch incorrectly spelled words.

Steps for Mastering Difficult Words

1. Look at the word and say it one syllable at a time.
2. Look at the letters and say each one.
3. Picture the word in your mind as you write it.
4. Check to see that you have spelled the word correctly. If you misspelled the word, notice what the mistake was and repeat steps 1–3.

One of the best ways to improve your spelling is to learn the following rules.

Words Ending in a Silent e

Before adding a suffix beginning with a vowel to a word ending in a silent e, drop the e (with some exceptions).

love + -able = lovable
improve + -ing = improving

The following words are exceptions:
dye + -ing = dyeing
mile + -age = mileage

When adding a suffix beginning with a consonant to a word ending in a silent e, keep the e (with some exceptions).

hate + -ful = hateful
excite + -ment = excitement

The following words are exceptions:
true + -ly = truly
argue + -ment = argument

Words Ending in y

When adding a suffix to a word that ends in a y preceded by a consonant, change the y to i.

noisy + -ly = noisily
nutty + -est = nuttiest

However, when adding *-ing,* do not change the *y.*

cry + -ing = crying
deny + -ing = denying

When a suffix is added to a word that ends in a y preceded by a vowel, the y usually does not change.

play + -ing = playing
enjoy + -ment = enjoyment

Words Ending in a Consonant

If a one-syllable word ends in one consonant preceded by one vowel, double the final consonant before adding a suffix beginning with a vowel, such as -ing or -ed. (Such a word is sometimes called a 1 + 1 + 1 word.)

sit + -ing = sitting
red + -est = reddest

The rule does not apply to words of one syllable that end in a consonant preceded by two vowels.

meet + -ing = meeting
dream + -er = dreamer

For a word of more than one syllable, double the final consonant when the word ends in one consonant preceded by one vowel and the word is accented on the last syllable.

ad•mit´   be•gin´   pre•fer´

In these examples, note that after the suffix is added, the accent remains on the same syllable.

ad•mit´ + -ed = ad•mit´ted
be•gin´ + -ing = be•gin´ning

In this example, the accent does not remain on the same syllable; thus, the final consonant is not doubled.

pre•fer´ + -able = pref´er•a•ble

The Suffixes -ly and -ness

When adding -ly to a word ending in l, keep both l's. When adding -ness to a word ending in n, keep both n's.

practical + -ly = practically
mean + -ness = meanness

Prefixes

When adding a prefix to a word, do not change the spelling of the base word.

un- + known = unknown
mis- + spell = misspell

Words with the Seed Sound

One English word ends in -sede: *supersede.* Three words end in -ceed: *exceed, proceed,* and *succeed.* All other words ending in the sound *seed* are spelled with -cede.

concede   precede   recede   secede

Words with ie and ei

When choosing between ie and ei, if the sound is long e (ē), you should usually spell the word with ie except after c.

i before e		except after c	
belief	niece	conceit	deceive
shield	field	receive	receipt
yield		ceiling	

Exceptions: *either, neither, weird, leisure, seize*

Using the Right Word

*The following words are commonly misused or misspelled. Some of these words are **homonyms,** or words that have similar sounds but are spelled differently and have different meanings. Study this section to make sure you are using words correctly in your writing. Try using memory devices to help you associate words and meanings.*

accept, except *Accept* means "to agree to" or "to receive willingly." *Except* usually means "not including."

My brother will *accept* the job at the grocery store.

Luis likes every flavor of yogurt *except* lemon.

Spelling Handbook

all ready, already *All ready* means "all are ready" or "completely prepared." *Already* means "previously."

> Janet was all ready to pitch in the big game.

a lot *A lot* is informal. Do not use it in formal writing. *Alot* is always incorrect.

borrow, lend *Borrow* means "to receive on loan." *Lend* means "to give temporarily."

> I *borrowed* my sister's watch.

> Please *lend* me your eraser.

capital, capitol, the Capitol *Capital* means "very serious" or "very important." It also means "seat of government." A *capitol* is a building in which a state legislature meets. *The Capitol* is the building in Washington, D.C., in which the U.S. Congress meets.

> The *capital* of Illinois is the city of Springfield.

> The Illinois *capitol* is a stately building in Springfield.

> The senator arrived at the *Capitol* in time to vote.

desert, dessert *Desert* (dĕz'ərt) means "a dry, sandy, barren region." *Desert* (dĭ-zûrt') means "to abandon." *Dessert* (dĭ-zûrt') is a sweet food, such as pie.

> Tall cactus plants grow in the *desert.*

> The crane would not *desert* his injured mate.

> Jake loves ice cream for *dessert.*

good, well *Good* is always an adjective. *Well* is usually an adverb that modifies an action verb. *Well* can also be an adjective meaning "in good health."

> That dress looks *good* on you.

> Anne performed her skating routine *well.*

> Nikki didn't feel *well* today.

hear, here *Hear* means "to listen to." *Here* means "in this place."

> Every time I *hear* this song, I feel happy.

> The mayor's family has lived *here* for generations.

its, it's *Its* is a possessive pronoun. *It's* is a contraction of *it is* or *it has.*

> The boat lost *its* sail during the storm.

> *It's* nearly midnight.

lay, lie *Lay* is a verb that means "to place." It takes a direct object. *Lie* is a verb that means "to recline" or "to be in a certain place." *Lie* never takes a direct object.

> Don't *lay* your coat on the couch.

> The terrier likes to *lie* under the swing.

> The island *lies* in the path of the hurricane.

lead, led *Lead* can be a noun that means "a heavy metal" or a verb that means "to show the way." *Led* is the past tense form of the verb.

> These pellets contain *lead.*

> Ask the lieutenant to *lead* her troops.

> He *led* a group of explorers out of the jungle.

learn, teach *Learn* means "to gain knowledge." *Teach* means "to instruct."

> In social studies we are *learning* about frontier life.

> He is *teaching* us to use a computer.

like, as, as if *Like* is a preposition. Use *as* or *as if* to introduce a clause.

> He ran the pass pattern *as* he should.

loose, lose *Loose* means "free" or "not fastened." *Lose* means "to mislay or suffer the loss of."

> The rider kept the horse's reins *loose.*

> If you *lose* your book, tell the librarian right away.

of Use *have,* not *of,* in phrases such as could *have,* should *have,* and must *have.*

> We should *have* invited her to our party.

passed, past *Passed* is the past tense of *pass* and means "went by." *Past* is an adjective that means "of a former time." *Past* is also a noun that means "the time gone by."

> A car that was driving too fast *passed* us on the highway.

Past problems at the parade have included littering.

It is important to remember the mistakes of the *past*.

peace, piece *Peace* means "calm" or "quiet." *Piece* means "a section or part."

After two years of war came *peace*.

The statue was carved from a *piece* of jade.

principal, principle *Principal* means "of chief or central importance" or "the head of a school." *Principle* means "basic truth," "standard," or "rule of behavior."

The *principal* export of Brazil is coffee.

The *principal* of our school organized a safety council.

One *principle* of science is that all matter occupies space.

quiet, quite *Quiet* means "free from noise or disturbance." *Quite* means "truly" or "almost completely."

The library is *quiet* in the afternoon.

The aquarium tank is *quite* full.

raise, rise *Raise* means "to lift" or "to cause to go up." It takes a direct object. *Rise* means "to go upward." It does not take a direct object.

Can you *raise* the sail by yourself?

The jury will *rise* when the judge enters the courtroom.

set, sit *Set* means "to place." It takes a direct object. *Sit* means "to occupy a seat or a place." It does not take a direct object.

I *set* the bag of groceries inside the door.

Sit still while we take your picture.

stationary, stationery *Stationary* means "fixed or unmoving." *Stationery* means "fine paper for writing letters."

Robin rode a *stationary* bicycle for exercise when the weather was bad.

Use your best *stationery* when you write to your grandmother.

than, then *Than* is used to introduce the second part of a comparison. *Then* means "next in order."

I like mysteries better *than* science fiction stories.

Jane put the spaghetti on a serving dish and *then* grated cheese over it.

their, there, they're *Their* means "belonging to them." *There* means "in that place." *They're* is a contraction of *they are*.

Our neighbors sold *their* house and moved to a farm.

Please play with the squirt guns over *there*.

My sisters don't swim, but *they're* eager to learn.

to, too, two *To* means "toward" or "in the direction of." *Too* means "also" or "very." *Two* is the number 2.

The surgeon dashed *to* the emergency room.

It was *too* hot to run a race.

Only *two* of the six lifeboats reached shore.

weather, whether *Weather* refers to conditions such as temperature or cloudiness. *Whether* expresses a choice.

The *weather* is perfect for a picnic.

Whether we drive or take the train, we will arrive late.

whose, who's *Whose* is the possessive form of *who*. *Who's* is a contraction of *who is* or *who has*.

Whose wallet is lying under the chair?

Who's been chosen the student of the month?

your, you're *Your* is the possessive form of *you*. *You're* is a contraction of *you are*.

Please bring *your* cameras to the assembly.

You're doing much better this semester than last.

❶ Getting Information Electronically

Electronic resources provide you with a convenient and efficient way to gather information.

⓵ Online Resources

When you use your computer to communicate with another computer or with another person using a computer, you are working "online." Online resources include commercial information services and information available on the Internet.

Commercial Information Services
You can subscribe to various services that offer information, such as the following:

- up-to-date news, weather, and sports reports

- access to encyclopedias, magazines, newspapers, dictionaries, almanacs, and databases (collections of information)

- forums, or ongoing electronic conversations among people interested in a particular topic

Internet
The Internet is a vast network of computers. News services, libraries, universities, researchers, organizations, and government agencies use the Internet to communicate and to distribute information. The Internet includes two key features:

- The **World Wide Web,** which provides information on particular subjects and links to related topics and resources

- **Electronic mail** (email), which makes possible communication among email users worldwide

What You'll Need
- To access online resources, you need a computer with a modem linked to a telephone line. Your school computer lab or resource center may be linked to the Internet or to a commercial information source.

- To use CD-ROMs, you need a computer with a CD-ROM drive.

⓶ Navigating the Web

With access to the World Wide Web, you can find virtually any piece of information once you know how to look for it. Here are some tips to get you started and keep you going.

Choose a Search Engine or a Directory
A **search engine** combs through Web sites looking for your topic. A **directory** allows you to search within a collection of sites, or databases that are grouped by subject, such as *reference, sports,* or *entertainment.*

Enter Key Words
Once you've chosen a starting point, enter the **key word** or words that describe your topic. By using more than one word, you will narrow your search. For example, using the key word "baseball" will find a variety of sites with information on baseball, whereas the key words "Dodgers baseball" will help you find sites with information on the specific team.

Investigate Your Options
Once you receive the results of your search, scan the site listings and their summaries to see which ones look promising. If you click on a site and it's not useful, you can always back up and try again. The sites at

the top of the list usually will be more relevant to your search than those found farther down.

Tips for Getting the Most from Your Searching

- **Note the source** Because anyone can put information on the Web, it's wise to check where the information comes from. For example, sites produced by government agencies or educational institutions tend to be more reliable than the personal Web pages of individuals.

- **Refine your search** If you're not getting the results you want, search again, using more key words or different key words.

- **Explore other avenues** One search engine may produce different results than another, and the same goes for directories.

- **Link around** Many Web sites have links to other sites with related content that you might not find searching on your own.

 CD-ROMs

A CD-ROM (compact disc–read-only memory) stores data that may include text, sound, photographs, and video.

Almost any kind of information can be found on CD-ROMs, which you can use at the library or purchase, including

- encyclopedias, almanacs, and indexes
- other reference books on a variety of subjects
- news reports from newspapers, magazines, television, or radio
- museum art collections
- back issues of magazines
- literature collections

1.4 Library Computer Services

Many libraries offer computerized catalogs and a variety of other electronic databases. A database is a collection of information, stored electronically and arranged for easy retrieval.

Computerized Catalogs

You may search for a book in a library by typing the title, author, subject, or key words into a computer terminal. If you enter the title of a book, the screen will display the kind of information shown below, including the book's call number and whether it is on the shelf or checked out of the library. You may also be able to search the catalogs of other libraries.

Other Electronic Resources

In addition to computerized catalogs, many libraries offer electronic versions of books, and other reference material such as online databases of periodical literature. They may also have a variety of indexes or other data on CD-ROM. Often these resources allow you to search for magazine or newspaper articles on any topic you choose. Ask your librarian for assistance in using these resources.

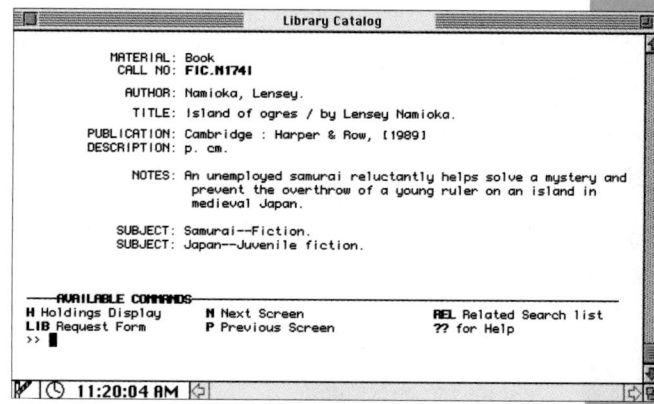

COMMUNICATION HANDBOOK **R91**

2 Word Processing

Word-processing programs allow you to draft, revise, edit, and format your writing and to produce neat, professional-looking papers. They also allow you to share your writing with others.

2.1 Revising and Editing

Improving the quality of your writing becomes easier when you use a word-processing program to revise and edit.

What You'll Need
- Computer
- Word-processing program
- Printer

Revising a Document
Most word-processing programs allow you to make the following kinds of changes:

- add or delete words
- move text from one location in your document to another
- undo a change you have made in the text
- save a document with a new name, allowing you to keep old drafts for reference
- view more than one document at a time, so you can copy text from one document and add it to another

Editing a Document
Many word-processing programs have the following features to help you catch errors and polish your writing:

- The **spell checker** automatically finds misspelled words and suggests possible corrections.
- The **grammar checker** spots possible grammatical errors and suggests ways you might correct them.

- The **thesaurus** suggests synonyms for a word you want to replace.
- The **dictionary** will give you the definitions of words so that you can be sure you have used words correctly.
- The **search and replace** feature searches your whole document and corrects every occurrence of something you want to change, such as a misspelled name.

WRITING TIP Even if you use a spell checker, you should still proofread your draft carefully to make sure you've used the right words. For example, you may have used *there* or *they're* when you meant to use *their.*

2.2 Formatting Your Work

Format is the layout and appearance of your writing on the page. You may choose your formatting options before or after you write.

Formatting Type
You may want to make changes in the typeface, type size, and type style of the words in your document. For each of these, your word-processing program will most likely have several options to choose from.

These options allow you to

- **change the typeface** to create a different look for the words in your document.

Typeface
Geneva
Times
Chicago
Courier

- **change the type size** of the entire document or of just the section headings in the paper.

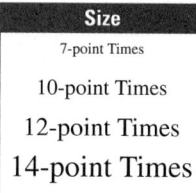

Size
7-point Times
10-point Times
12-point Times
14-point Times

- **change the type style** when necessary; for example, use italics or underlining for the titles of books and magazines.

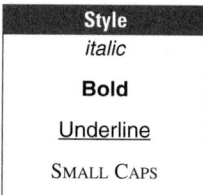

Style
italic
Bold
<u>Underline</u>
SMALL CAPS

WRITING TIP Keep your format simple. Your goal is to create not only an attractive document but also one that is easy to read. Your readers will have difficulty if you change the type formatting frequently.

Formatting Pages

Not only can you change the way individual words look, you can also change the way they are arranged on the page. Some of the formatting decisions you make will depend on how you plan to use a printout of a draft or on the guidelines of an assignment.

- **Set the line spacing,** or the amount of space you need between lines of text. Double spacing is commonly used for final drafts.

- **Set the margins,** or the amount of white space around the edges of your text. A one-inch margin on all sides is commonly used for final drafts.

- **Create a header** for the top of the page or a footer for the bottom if you want to include such information as your name, the date, or the page number on every page.

- **Determine the alignment** of your text. The screen below shows your options.

TECHNOLOGY TIP Some word-processing programs or other software packages provide preset templates, or patterns, for writing outlines, memos, letters, newsletters, or invitations. If you use one of these templates, you will not need to adjust the formatting.

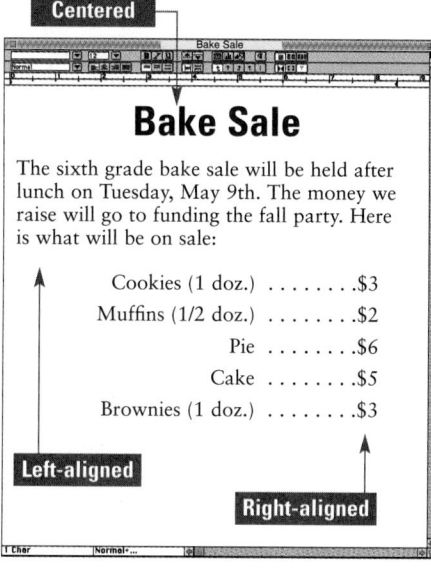

Centered

Bake Sale

The sixth grade bake sale will be held after lunch on Tuesday, May 9th. The money we raise will go to funding the fall party. Here is what will be on sale:

Cookies (1 doz.) $3
Muffins (1/2 doz.) $2
Pie $6
Cake $5
Brownies (1 doz.) $3

Left-aligned

Right-aligned

Working Collaboratively

Computers allow you to share your writing electronically. Send a copy of your work via email or put it in someone's drop box if your computer is linked to other computers on a network. Then use the feedback of your peers to help you improve the quality of your writing.

Peer Editing on a Computer

The writer and the reader can both benefit from the convenience of peer editing "on screen," or at the computer.

- Be sure to save your current draft and then make a copy of it for each of your peer readers.
- You might have your peer readers enter their comments in a different typeface or type style from the one you used for your text, as shown in the example below.
- Ask each of your readers to include his or her initials in the file name.

- If your computer allows you to open more than one file at a time, open each reviewer's file and refer to the files as you revise your draft.

TECHNOLOGY TIP Some word-processing programs, such as the Writing Coach software referred to in this book, allow you to leave notes for your peer readers in the side column or in a separate text box. If you wish, leave those areas blank so that your readers can write comments or questions.

Peer Editing on a Printout

Some peer readers prefer to respond to a draft on paper rather than on the computer.

- Double-space or triple-space your document so that your peer editors can make suggestions between the lines.
- Leave extra-wide margins to give your readers room to note their reactions and questions as they read.
- Print out and photocopy your draft if you want to share it with more than one reader.

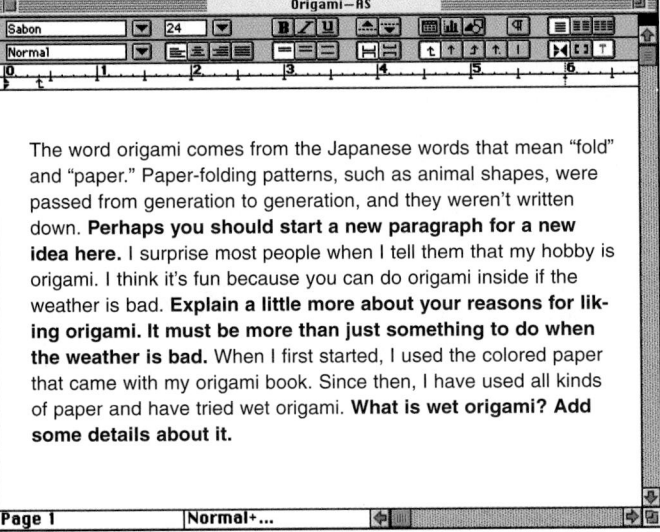

③ Using Visuals

Charts, graphs, diagrams, and pictures often communicate information more effectively than words alone do. Many computer programs allow you to create visuals to use with written text.

③.① When to Use Visuals

Use visuals in your work to illustrate complex concepts and processes or to make a page look more interesting. Although you should not expect a visual to do all the work of written text, combining words and pictures or graphics can increase the understanding and enjoyment of your writing. Many computer programs allow you to create and insert graphs, tables, time lines, diagrams, and flow charts into your document. An art program allows you to create border designs for a title page or to draw an unusual character or setting for narrative or descriptive writing. You may also be able to add clip art, or pre-made pictures, to your document. Clip art can be used to illustrate an idea or concept in your writing or to enliven a page.

What You'll Need
- a graphics program to create visuals
- access to clip-art files from a CD-ROM, a computer disk, or an online service

③.② Kinds of Visuals

The visuals you choose will depend on the type of information you want to present to your readers.

Tables

Tables allow you to arrange facts or numbers into rows and columns so that your reader can compare information more easily. In many word-processing programs, you can create a table by choosing the number of vertical columns and horizontal rows you need and then entering information in each box, as the illustration shows.

TECHNOLOGY TIP A spreadsheet program provides you with a preset table for your statistics and performs any necessary calculations.

Graphs and Charts

You can sometimes use a graph or chart to help communicate complex information in a clear visual image. For example, you could use a line graph to show how a trend changes over time, a bar graph to compare statistics, or a pie chart, like the one below, to compare percentages. You might want to explore ways of displaying data in more than one visual format before deciding which will work best for you.

TECHNOLOGY TIP To help your readers easily understand the different parts of a pie chart or bar graph, use a different color or shade of gray for each section.

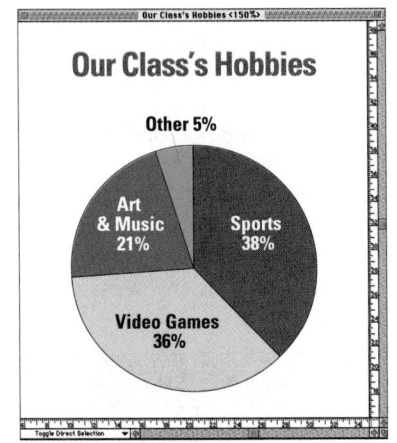

Other Visuals

Art and design programs allow you to create visuals for your writing. Many programs include the following features:

- **drawing tools** that allow you to draw, color, and shade pictures, such as the drawing below

- **clip art** that you can copy or change with drawing tools

- **page borders** that you can use to decorate title pages, invitations, or brochures

- **text options** that allow you to combine words with your illustrations

- **tools for making geometric shapes** in flow charts, time lines, and diagrams that show a process or sequence of events

④ Creating a Multimedia Presentation

A multimedia presentation is a combination of text, sound, and visuals such as photographs, videos, and animation. Your audience reads, hears, and sees your presentation at a computer, following different "paths" you create to lead the user through the information you have gathered.

4.1 Features of Multimedia Programs

To start planning your multimedia presentation, you need to know what options are available to you. You can combine sound, photos, videos, and animation to enhance any text you write about your topic.

What You'll Need
- individual programs to create and edit the text, graphics, sound, and videos you will use
- a multimedia authoring program that allows you to combine these elements and create links between the screens

Sound
Including sound in your presentation can help your audience understand information in your written text. For example, the user may be able to listen and learn from
- the pronunciation of an unfamiliar or foreign word
- a speech
- a recorded news interview
- a musical selection
- a dramatic reading of a work of literature

Photos and Videos
Photographs and live-action videos can make your subject come alive for the user. Here are some examples:
- videotaped news coverage of a historical event
- videos of music, dance, or theater performances
- charts and diagrams
- photos of an artist's work
- photos or video of a geographical setting that is important to the written text

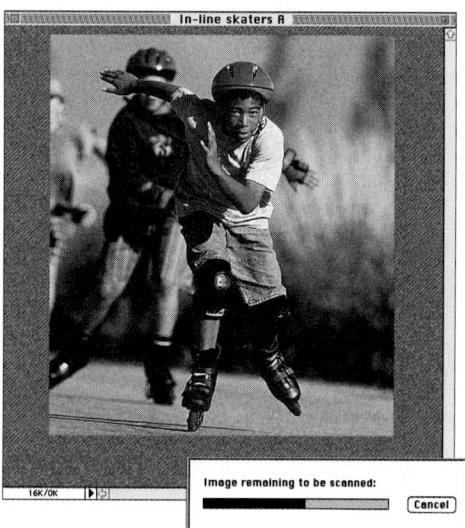

In-line skaters A

16K/OK

Image remaining to be scanned:

Cancel

Animation

Many graphics programs allow you to add animation, or movement, to the visuals in your presentation. Animated figures add to the user's enjoyment and understanding of what you present. You can use animation to illustrate

- what happens in a story
- the steps in a process
- changes in a chart, graph, or diagram
- how your user can explore information in your presentation

TECHNOLOGY TIP You can download photos, sound, and video from Internet sources onto your computer. This process allows you to add elements to your multimedia presentation that would usually require complex editing equipment.

4.2 Planning Your Presentation

To create a multimedia presentation, first choose your topic and decide what you want to include. Then plan how you want your user to move through your presentation.

Imagine that you are creating a multimedia presentation about in-line skating. You know that you want to include the following items:

- photos of in-line skaters
- a text history of how in-line skating was developed
- a diagram of an in-line skate

- text on "how to skate" for beginners
- a video of a skating demonstration
- a glossary of in-line skating terms
- an audio description of safety tips

You can choose one of the following ways to organize your presentation:

- **a step-by-step method** with only one path, or order, in which the user can see and hear the information
- **a branching path** that allows users to make some choices about what they will see and hear, and in what order

A flow chart can help you figure out the path a user can take through your presentation. Each box in the flow chart below represents something about in-line skating for the user to read, see, or hear. The arrows on the flow chart show a branching path the user can follow. When boxes branch in more than one direction, it means that the user can choose which item to see or hear first.

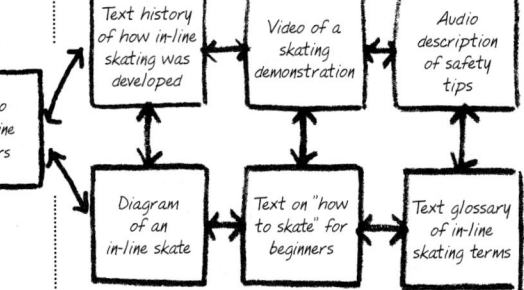

TECHNOLOGY TIP You can find CD-ROMs with videos of things like wildlife, weather, street scenes, and events, and CD-ROMs with recordings of famous speeches, musical selections, and dramatic readings.

4.3 Guiding Your User

Your user will need directions to follow the path you have planned for your multimedia presentation.

Most multimedia authoring programs allow you to create screens that include text or audio directions that guide the user from one part of your presentation to the next. In the example below, the user can choose between several paths, and directions on the screen explain how to make the choice.

If you need help creating your multimedia presentation, ask your school's technology adviser. You may also be able to get help from your classmates or your software manual.

The user clicks on a button to select any of these options.

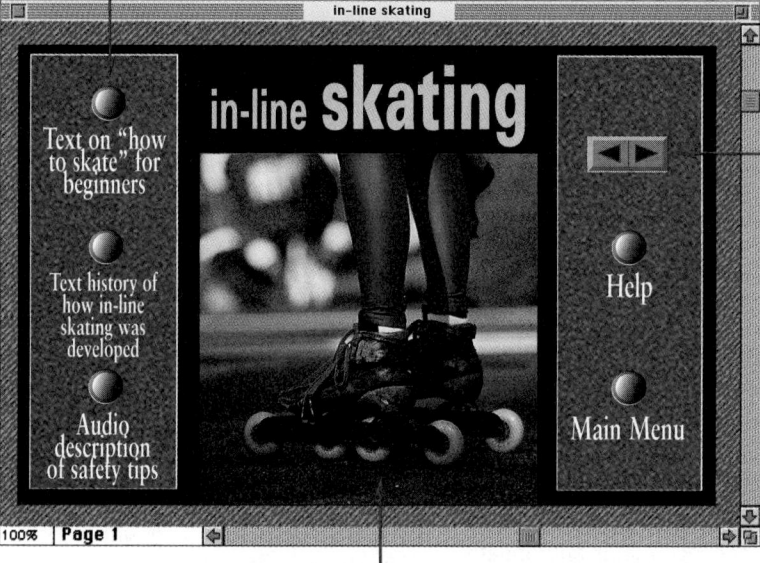

Navigational buttons take the user back and forth, one screen at a time.

This screen shows a video of a skating demonstration.

Speaking and Listening

Good communicators do more than just talk. They use specific techniques to present their ideas effectively, and they are attentive and critical listeners.

5.1 Speaking and Presenting

In school, in business, and in any community, one of the best ways to present information is to deliver it in person—speaking directly to a live audience.

Audience and Purpose

When preparing and presenting a speech, think about your audience's level of knowledge and interest in your subject. Understanding your audience can help you tailor your speech to your audience's interests. Also, keep in mind your purpose for speaking. Are you trying to persuade the audience to do something? Are you presenting the audience with some of your latest research, or perhaps just entertaining the audience by relating some of your own experiences?

Writing Your Speech

If you are writing your speech beforehand, rather than working from notes, use the following guidelines to help you.

- **Create paragraphs** Make sure that your speech is organized into paragraphs, each of which develops a single main idea.

- **Use appropriate language** Make sure that you use language that is appropriate for the audience, purpose, and occasion.

- **Provide evidence** Include facts, statistics, sensory details, and incidents; quote experts to support your ideas. Elaborate to clarify your ideas.

- **Unify your speech** Just as all the sentences in a paragraph should support the main idea of the paragraph, so all the paragraphs in your speech should support the main idea of the speech.

- **Clarify your ideas** Make sure that you show clear relationships between your ideas. Transitions, or connecting words, can help listeners follow your arguments. (See the Writing Handbook page R28, for a list of transitional expressions.)

- **Use aesthetic language** Effective speakers use vivid imagery and sound devices such as onomatopoeia, alliteration, and assonance to help them express their ideas. Onomatopoeia describes words that sound like the thing or action they represent. For example, the word *hiss* sounds very much like the noise of a snake. A speaker might also use a series of words that begin with the same consonant sound to get the audience's attention. This device, which is called alliteration, can be found in a phrase such as "destroy this deadly disease." Finally, assonance allows speakers to emphasize words through the repetition of vowel sounds. The phrase "a campaign of blame" is an example of assonance.

- **Begin your speech** Start with a "hook"—an interesting question or statement to capture people's attention.

- **Finish strong** Restate your main ideas; end your speech with a powerful example or anecdote to reinforce your point.

Prepare/Practice/Present

Confidence is the key to a successful presentation. Use these techniques to help you prepare and present your speech to your class.

Prepare

- **Review your information** Reread your written report and review your background research—you'll feel much more confident during your speech.

- **Organize your notes** Some people prefer to include only a minimum of key points. Others prefer the entire script. Write each main point, or each paragraph, of your speech on a separate index card. Be sure to include your most important evidence and examples. It helps to number your cards.

- **Plan your visual aids** If you are planning on using visual aids, such as slides, posters, charts, graphs, video clips, overhead transparencies, or computer projections, now is the time to design them and decide how to work them into your speech.

Practice

- **Rehearse** Rehearse your speech several times, possibly in front of a practice audience. If you are using visual aids, practice handling them. Adapt your rate of speaking, pitch, and tone of voice to your audience and setting. Your style of performance should express the purpose of your speech. Use the following chart to help your style express your purpose.

Purpose	Pace	Pitch	Tone
to persuade	fast but clear	even	urgent
to inform	plenty of pauses	even	authoritative
to entertain	usually builds to a "punch"	varied to create characters or drama	funny or dramatic

TIP: It might also be helpful to time yourself during rehearsals, to ensure that your speech does not run overtime.

- **Evaluate your performance** When you have finished each rehearsal, evaluate your performance. How did you do? Did you slow down for emphasis, pause to let an important point sink in, or use gestures for emphasis? Make a list of aspects of your presentation that you will try to perfect for your next rehearsal.

Present

- **Begin your speech** In order to break the tension of the opening moments, try to look relaxed and remember to smile!

- **Make eye contact** During your speech, try to make eye contact with audience members. This will not only establish the feeling of personal contact, but will help you determine if the audience understands your speech.

- **Remember to pause** A slight pause after important points will provide emphasis and give your audience time to think about what you are saying.

- **Maintain good posture** Stand up straight and avoid nervous movements that may distract the audience's attention from what you are saying.

- **Use expressive body language** A good speaker captures the attention of an audience through body language as well as through speech. Instead of standing motionless in front of an audience, use your entire body to help express your meaning. Lean forward when you make an important point; move your hands and arms for emphasis. Your body language will show that you really believe in what you are saying.

Oral Interpretation

When you read a poem, a play, or a story aloud, your voice can bring the literature to life.

Oral Reading

An oral reading can be a monologue, during which you assume the voice of a character, the narrator, or the speaker in a poem. Or it may be a dialogue, during which you take on the roles of two or more characters. Reading a poem aloud is another example of an oral reading. Use the following techniques when giving an oral reading.

- **Speak clearly** As you speak, pronounce your words carefully and clearly. Don't mumble.
- **Control your volume** Make sure that you are loud enough to be heard at the back of the room, but do not shout.
- **Pace yourself** Read at a moderate rate, but vary your pace if it seems appropriate to the emotions of the character or to the action you are describing.
- **Vary your voice** Use a different voice for each character. Stress important words or phrases. Use your voice to express different emotions and moods.

Dramatic Reading

When several speakers participate in the reading of a play or other work divided into parts, it is called a dramatic reading. Use the following techniques in your dramatic reading.

- **Prepare** Rehearse your material several times. Become familiar with the humorous and most dramatic parts of your script. Come up with a special voice that fits the personality of your character.

- **Project** As you read your lines, aim your voice toward the very back of the room. This will allow everyone to hear you.
- **Perform** React to the other characters as if you were hearing their lines for the first time. Deliver your own lines with the appropriate emotion. Use your whole body, as well as your hands and face to express your emotions.

 Active Listening for Information

Active listeners listen carefully and think about what they hear—before, during, and after any presentation, whether it's a speech, a class lecture, or even a television program.

Before Listening

Keep an open mind Don't prejudge the speaker. Instead, try to determine the speaker's purpose and main topic. Try to predict what he or she might focus on.

Prepare yourself Review what you already know about the speaker's topic. Then think of some questions you'd like to ask or information you'd like to hear about.

Listen with a purpose Try to match *how* you listen with *why* you're listening.

There are many ways of listening to someone; each way of listening may reflect a different purpose for listening. For example, you would not listen to a friend's joke in the same way that you would listen to a teacher's lesson, because your purpose for listening would be different in each situation. You might listen to a joke for entertainment, while you would listen to a lesson in order to gain information. The following chart will show you how each way of listening reflects a different purpose.

Listening with a Purpose		
Situation	Reason for Listening	How to Listen
Your friend tells a funny story about her pet gerbil.	For enjoyment; to provide your friend with an audience	Maintain eye contact; show you understand; react to the story.
You're listening to a talk and slide show called "Wolves of the Tundra."	For enjoyment; to learn something new	Think about what you already know; listen for ideas that add to your knowledge.
Your mother explains why you can't keep an alligator as a pet.	To understand her point of view; to find opportunities to share your own ideas	Listen carefully; respond positively to valid points; listen for opportunities to state your own reasons.
You and your friends are trying to arrange a trip to a concert.	To solve a problem	Identify goals and problems; listen closely to each other's ideas and build on them.
You are watching a television program about cooking or carpentry.	To follow directions	Listen for words such as *first, second, next,* and *finally;* take notes that you can refer to later.

While Listening
Look for signals of main ideas
- Listen for ideas presented first or last or repeated several times.
- Note statements that begin with phrases such as "My point is . . ." Then listen carefully to what follows.
- Pay attention to ideas presented in a loud voice or with forceful gestures.
- In a multimedia presentation, note the points the speaker has reproduced on a chart or on any other visual aid.
- If the situation permits, ask for clarification of points you do not understand or have questions about.

Block out distractions and focus on the speaker
- Keep your eyes on the speaker.
- Focus your mind if it starts to wander.

Take notes, if appropriate
- Don't worry about writing complete sentences.
- List questions that occur to you as you listen.
- Think about points you would like to explore further.
- Afterward, read over your notes to help you remember what you heard.

Look for relationships between ideas
- Look for comparisons and contrasts. Signal words include: *similarly, but,* and *on the other hand.*
- Pay attention to causes and effects. Signal words include: *because; if . . . , then;* and *as a result.*

After Listening
Ask questions for clarification
- Review any notes that you might have taken.
- Ask for explanations of points that are unclear to you.
- Indicate if you don't agree with something or if you need more information.
- Repeat the speaker's words in your questions, so that you check your understanding as you get answers.

Summarize, paraphrase, and evaluate
- Identify main ideas and details that support them.
- Restate the speaker's ideas in your own words.
- Clarify your reasons for agreeing or disagreeing.

Oral Directions
Active listening to understand oral instructions is a skill that will help you both with your schoolwork and outside of school.

- Listen to understand exactly what you are being asked to do.
- Take notes to refer to as you go about completing the task.
- Ask questions to clarify anything you do not understand.
- Restate the directions in your own words either mentally or in writing.

Critical Listening

As you listen to a speaker's ideas, you will want to analyze, evaluate, and critique those ideas. Use the following critical listening strategies as you listen to a public speaker:

- **Determine the speaker's purpose**
  Identify the speaker's purpose in giving the speech. Is the speaker trying to inform, to persuade, to express thoughts or feelings, or to entertain?
- **Listen for the main idea** Try to figure out the speaker's main message; do not get distracted by details of the speech.
- **Distinguish between fact and opinion**
  Make sure you distinguish between the speaker's opinion and facts that can be verified or proved.

Recognizing Persuasive Devices

An important part of critical listening is the ability to recognize persuasive devices—techniques that the speaker uses to persuade listeners to accept a particular opinion. Persuasive devices often represent faulty reasoning. Here are some persuasive devices that you should learn to recognize.

- **Inaccurate generalization**
  A generalization is a broad statement about a number of people or things, such as "Maps are hard to read." Although some generalizations are true, other generalizations are too broad to be true. The statement, "All teenagers like television" is an example of an inaccurate generalization.
- **Either/or** A writer may try to convince an audience that there are only two choices, or ways of looking at something, when in fact there may be many. The statement "If you don't support the construction of this new road, you are against progress" is an example of either/or reasoning.
- **Bandwagon** A bandwagon statement appeals to people's desires to belong to a group. For example, a statement like "Join the millions of people who have chosen this product" is an example of a bandwagon device.
- **Snob appeal** This technique appeals to people's need to feel superior to other people. A statement like "You deserve the best, so buy this product" relies on snob appeal.

Group Communication

Group communication can help you in school as you work on group or paired assignments; it can also help prepare you for jobs. Participating in group communication requires all of your listening, speaking, and social skills.

Assigned Roles
A group discussion operates most effectively when each member plays a specific role. A chairperson and a recorder can help group participants keep focused.

Role	Responsibilities
Chairperson	• Introduces the topic for discussion • Explains the goal or purpose of the meeting • Participates in the discussion • Keeps the discussion focused • Helps resolve conflict and maintains fairness
Recorder	• Takes notes on discussion • Participates in discussion • Organizes and writes up notes
Participants	• Contribute facts or ideas to discussion • Respond constructively to others' ideas • Reach agreement or vote on final decision

Guidelines for Discussions

Use these techniques to develop your group communication skills.

- **Listen attentively** Listen carefully and respectfully to each member. Pay attention to important ideas and details. Take notes about issues you want to discuss later.

- **Contribute to the discussion** Join in and share your ideas. Don't be afraid if your ideas are new or different. Share reasons for your ideas. Avoid sarcasm and contribute positive and helpful comments.

- **Compare notes** Everything we see and hear is colored by our own experiences, knowledge, and personality. Because of this, it's always a good idea to compare your perception of a spoken message with the perceptions of others.

5.7 Conducting Interviews

Conducting a personal interview can be an effective way to get information.

Preparing for the interview

- Research any information by or about the person you will interview. The background details will help you get to the point during the interview.

- Prepare a list of questions. Think of more questions than you will need. Include some open-ended questions. Arrange your questions in order of significance, from most important to least important.

Participating in the interview

- Work with a partner. You might choose one note taker and one speaker.

- Ask your questions clearly and listen carefully. Give the person that you are interviewing (the interviewee) plenty of time to answer.

- Listen interactively. Be prepared to follow up on a response you find interesting.

- Avoid arguments. Be tactful and polite.

- Take notes even if you have a recording device. This will help in your write-up of the interview. Jot down main ideas or important statements that can be used as quotes.

Following up on the interview

- Summarize your notes while they are still fresh in your mind.

- Send a thank-you note to the interview subject.

  TIP: Remember that as an interviewer, your role is to listen rather than to talk about yourself. Show that you are interested in the person you are interviewing.

Index of Fine Art

Index of Skills

Literary Concepts

Act, 319, R6
Action
    falling, 22, 34, 45, 443, 481, 488, R11
    rising, 22, 34, 45, 481
Aesthetic language, R100. *See also* Figurative language; Sound devices; Word choice.
Alliteration, 191, R6. *See also* Sound devices.
Allusion, R6
Analogy, 348, 379, 675, 801, R6
Analysis, R6
Anecdote, 154, 161, R6
Audience, 416, R6
Author's perspective, 161–162, 363, 611, 684, R6
Author's purpose, 142, 409, 424, 611, 676, R7. *See also* Author's purpose *under* Reading and Critical Thinking Skills.
Author's style. *See* Style.
Autobiography, 97, 100, 135, 142, 165, 170, 362–363, 385, 640, R7
Ballad, R7
Bias, 363, 464, 824. *See also* Author's perspective.
Biographer, 97, 111, R7
Biography, 97, 100, 101, 111, 362–363, 378, R7
Cast of characters, 319, 324, R7
Cause and effect, 76, 446, 459, 674, R7
Character, 23, 31, 45, 183, 243–244, 319, 343, 346, 445, 555, 698, R7
    development of, R7
    main and minor, 23, 26, 31, 45, 124, 244, 319
    and motivation, R14
    in nonfiction, 97
    real and imaginary, 698
    traits, 26, 31
Characterization, 245, 248, 257, 264, 305, 653, 661, R8
Chronological order, 121, 364, 378, R8
Cinderella tale, R8
Clarifying, 4, 385, 740, R8
Climax, 22, 319, 443, 459, 481, 488, R8. *See also* Plot.
Comedy, R8
Comparing literature, 31, 64, 76, 111, 161, 216, 227, 287, 330, 346, 378, 409, 479, 561, 566, 572–573, 633, 648, 684, 711, 734, 801, 819
Comparison, R8. *See also* Metaphor; Simile.
Conclusion, 163, 613, 633, R8. *See also* Conclusions, drawing, *under* Reading and Critical Thinking Skills.
Concrete poetry, 190, R8
Conflict, 22, 45, 124, 132, 319, 445, 459, 481, R8. *See also* Plot.
    internal/external, 124, 132, 445
Connecting, 4, 31, 281, 346, R9
Connotation, 742, R9
Context clues, 79, R9
Contrast, R9

Couplet, 479, 566, 737, 740, R9
Deductive order, 718, 725, R9. *See also* Inductive order; Structure.
Denotation, 742, R9
Description, 264, 272, 473, R9
Details, 101, 111, 409, 555, 561. *See also* Sensory details.
Dialect, R9
Dialogue, 317, 320, 333, 337, 437, R9
Diary, 97, 142
Diction. *See* Word choice.
Drama, 317–320, 321, R10. *See also* Act; Cast of characters; Comedy; Dialogue; Playwright; Prop; Scene; Scenery; Script; Stage directions; Tragedy.
Dynamic character, R10
Elaborating, 201
End rhyme. *See* Rhyme.
Entertaining, 473
Epic poetry, R10
Essay, 98, 465, 473, 640, R10
Evaluating, 4, 216, R10
Exaggeration, R10
Exposition, 22, R10. *See also* Plot.
Expository essay, 98
External conflict. *See* Conflict.
Fable, 768, R10
Fact, 203, 277, 699, 711, R10
Falling action. *See* Action, falling.
Fantasy, 507–510, 512, 552, 555, 561, R11
    elements of, 599
Feature story, 99
Fiction, 21–24, 25, R11. *See also* Fantasy; Historical fiction; Novel; Realistic fiction; Science fiction; Short story.
    character in, 23
    plot in, 22
    setting in, 24
    theme in, 24
    types of, 21, 61
Figurative language, 192, 194, 198, 216, 648, R11
Figure of speech. *See* Idiom; Metaphor; Personification; Simile.
First-person point of view, 142, 275, 281, 362. *See also* Point of view.
Flashback, R11
Folklore, 768, R11. *See also* Fable; Folk tale; Legend; Myth; Tall tale.
Folk tale, 768, R11
Foreshadowing, 447, 459, R11
Form, 190, R11. *See also* Poetry.
Formal essay, 98, 473
Free verse, 190, 191, 198, R12
Futuristic setting, 508
Generalization, 473, R12
Genre, 207, R12. *See also* Drama; Fiction; Nonfiction; Poetry.
Haiku, 205, 207, R12

Reading & Critical Thinking Skills

conflict, climax, resolution, 45, 321, 322, 481, 488

connections, 26

details, 52, 64, 143, 154, 161, 205, 207, 555

events, 34, 114, 121, 148, 321, 322, 365, 366, 444, 459, 474, 481, 488

fact and nonfact, 700

fantasy and science fiction, 599

K-W-L (know, want to know, learned), 114

plot, 45, 321, 322, 444, 459, 481, 488, 553

predictions, 22

problem solving, 653

pros and cons, 459

setting elements, 52, 573, 579, 585

sound devices, 479

stage directions, 330

symbolism, 391, 674, 761

theme, 612

tone, 409

traits, 143, 161, 864

transitions, 114

word choice, 479

Chronological order, 114, 121, 148, 364, 365, 378, 474, R8. *See also* Sequence of events.

Clarifying, 4, 6, 11, 12, 13, 14, 25, 106, 193, 254, 325, 364, 368, 372, 373, 381, 385, 446, 543, 737, R8

Classifying and Categorizing, 64, 143, 161, 205, 207, 257, 321, 322, 444, 459, 479, 481, 488, 555, 573, 579, 585, 661, 700, 726, R38, R50–R51

in writing, 726, R38, R50–R51

Clues, inferences from, 194, 198, 247, 264, 391, 395, 621, 653, 661

Comparing and contrasting, 573, 580, 585, 760, 858–863, R35

characters, 46, 111, 217, 331, 634, 740, 857

cultures, 711, 787, 801, 819, 843, 857, 859–860

in writing, 587, 858–863, R35

myths, 787

play vs. novel, 553

science fiction, 572–587

tales, 843

texts, 31, 64, 76, 111, 161, 216, 227, 287, 330, 346, 378, 409, 479, 561, 566, 633, 648, 684, 711, 734, 801, 819

versions, 143, 217, 527, 537, 553, 562, 634, 787, 819

Complex directions, following, 650–652. *See also* Directions *under* Speaking and Listening.

Comprehension check, 31, 64, 76, 111, 132, 142, 161, 170, 198, 207, 216, 227, 198, 257, 281, 287, 337, 346, 385, 395, 409, 415, 424, 459, 473, 477, 479, 488, 531, 552, 561, 579, 585, 633, 640, 645, 648, 661, 674, 684, 711, 725, 734, 740

Conclusions, drawing, 163, 164, 613, 614, 618, 625, 628, 630, 633, R9. *See also* Inferences, making.

Conflict, distinguishing external and internal, 132, 445, 633, R8

Connecting, 4, 7, 11, 13, 14, 25, 26, 28, 29, 31, 247, 275, 281, 343, 346, 446, 511, 518, 534, 613, 708, R9

Cooperative learning,

in groups, 31, 76, 132, 161, 216, 272, 281, 330,

378, 409, 633, 648, 711, 734

in pairs, 45, 64, 142, 170, 198, 207, 227, 257, 287, 337, 346, 385, 395, 415, 459, 479, 561, 566, 579, 585, 661, 674, 684

Critical thinking, 31, 64, 76, 111, 132, 142, 161, 170, 198, 207, 216, 227, 198, 257, 281, 287, 337, 346, 385, 395, 409, 415, 424, 459, 473, 477, 479, 488, 531, 552, 561, 579, 585, 633, 640, 645, 648, 661, 674, 684, 711, 725, 734, 740

Culture, 766–769, 770–771, 787–788, 801–802, 818–819, 828–829, 842–843, 844–845, 856–857, 864–865

Deductive and inductive logical order, 718, 725, R9, R22

Denotative meanings. *See* Connotation *and* Denotation *under* Vocabulary Skills.

Derivative words, 149, 663

Description clues, 79

Descriptive language, 172, 264, 272, 426, R31–R32

Details, noting, 52, 64, 100, 101, 111, 142, 154, 161, 205, 207, 257, 264, 555, 636, 640. *See also* Charting.

Differences, noting. *See* Comparing and contrasting.

Directions, *See* Complex directions, following.

Distinguishing

fact from nonfact, 700, 704, 705, 711

fact from opinion, 219, 227, 699, R10

Drama, 317–320, R10. *See also* Drama *under* Literary Concepts.

notes for staging, 355–359

strategies for reading, 321

Drawing conclusions. *See* Conclusions, drawing.

Elaboration, 201–204, 434, 862, R29. *See also* Elaboration *under* Writing Skills, Modes, and Formats.

Electronic Texts. *See* Electronic texts *under* Inquiry and Research.

Enjoyment, reading for. 184–185, 306–307, 438–439, 600–601, 762–763, 865. *See also* Setting purposes for reading.

Evaluating, 4, 8, 9,11, 13, 14, 15, 25, 100, 193, 209, 216, 247, 326, 364, 454, 503, 539, 544, 550, 595, 613, 778, 825, R10

Examples. *See* Elaborating.

Extending interpretations, 31, 64, 76, 111, 132, 142, 161, 170, 198, 207, 216, 227, 257, 281, 287, 330, 337, 346, 378, 385, 395, 409, 415, 424, 459, 473, 479, 531, 552, 561, 566, 633, 640, 648, 661, 674, 684, 711, 725, 734, 740, 786, 800, 818, 842, 856

Extending reading, 184–185, 306–307, 438–439, 600–601, 762–763, 865

Fact and opinion. *See* Distinguishing.

Fiction, strategies for reading, 21–25

Focusing reading, 26, 34, 45, 64, 101, 114, 124, 154, 163, 165, 194, 205, 209, 219, 248, 264, 275, 284, 322, 333, 365, 381, 391, 402, 411, 416, 418, 447, 465, 476, 481, 512, 555, 563, 574, 580, 614, 636, 643, 653, 668, 676, 678, 700, 718, 728, 737, 740

Following directions, 650–652

Foreshadowing, 447, 459, R11

Forms
poetic, 189–192, R11
reading instructions for, 21–25, 96–100, 189–193, 316–317
Generalizations, making, 465, 473, R12
Genre, R12. *See also* Drama; Fiction, strategies for reading; Nonfiction, strategies for reading; Poetry.
Graphic organizers, 22, 26, 34, 45, 46, 52, 53, 64, 67, 73, 114, 121, 122, 143, 148, 154, 161, 183, 205, 207, 217, 257, 305, 321, 322, 330, 365, 366, 391, 409, 444, 446, 447, 459, 474, 479, 481, 488, 489, 509, 553, 555, 573, 579, 585, 612, 661, 668, 674, 700, 761, 787, 864. *See also* Charting; Text organizers, using.
Graphic sources of information, using, 145–148, 755–758, R95–R96
Graphs, 347, 641, 662, R96
Greek roots. *See* Roots *under* Vocabulary Skills.
Imagery, understanding, 192, 411, 415, R12
Inferences, making, 194, 198, 264, 391, 395, 621, 653, 661, R13. *See also* Conclusions, drawing; Generalizations, making; Judgments, making; Predicting.
about author's purpose, 100, 135, 142, 418, 424, 611, 676, 677, R7
about characters, 31, 64, 245, 247, 257, 264, 337, 424, 531, 653, 661, 674, R8
about effects of author's perspective, 154, 161, 164, 165, 363, 170, 464, 678, 684, R6
about plot, 45, 132, 247, 248, 333, 337, 443–446, 447, 459
about speaker, 192, 193, 194, 198, 346, 391,395, 740
about symbolism, 193, 194, 198, 668, 674, 761, R20
about theme, 76, 611–613, 614, 633
Information, reading for. *See* Reading for information; Setting purposes for reading.
Interpreting. *See* Extending interpretations; Oral interpretation *under* Speaking and Listening.
Judgments, making, 462–464. *See also* Conclusions, drawing; Evaluating.
Latin roots. *See* Roots *under* Vocabulary Skills.
Listing, 92, 179, 239, 301, 386, 433, 503, 693, 696
Logical progression. 718, 725, R9, R38. *See also* Deductive and inductive logical order; Text structure.
Main ideas and supporting details, identifying, 49, 51, 100, 101, 104, 106, 111, 341–342, 389–390, 588–591, 636, 640, 714–717, 728, 734
Making connections. *See* Connecting.
Making inferences. *See* Inferences, making.
Making predictions. *See* Predicting.
Map reading, 65, 67, 101, 146–147, 165, 173, 264, 365, 402, 447, 715, 718
Monitoring, 4, 402, 409, R14. *See also* Strategies for reading.
Motivation, analyzing, 64, 132, 337, 424, 531, 653, 661, 674, R14. *See also* Character; Characterization.
Narrator, point of view of, 272, 275, 281, 319, 362, 474, 674, R14, R16

Nonfiction, strategies for reading, 101–105. *See also* Note taking; Outlining; Paraphrasing; SQ3R; Summarizing.
Note taking, 51, 588–591, 728, 734. *See also* Reader's Notebook.
Opinions. *See* Distinguishing; Evaluating; Judgments, making.
Order of ideas. *See* Text structure.
Organization. *See* Text structure.
Outlining, 51, 587, 588–591, 824–825
Overgeneralization. *See* Generalizations, making.
Paraphrasing, 49–51, 589, 591
and avoiding plagiarism, 49, 824
Peer response, using, 92, 179, 239, 301, 386, 433, 503, 693, R25
Personal response, 16, 31, 64, 76, 89–94, 111, 132, 142, 161, 170, 198, 207, 216, 227, 257, 281, 287, 330, 337, 346, 378, 385, 395, 409, 415, 424, 459, 473, 479, 531, 552, 561, 566, 633, 640, 648, 661, 674, 684, 711, 725, 734, 740, 786, 800, 818, 842, 856, R48–R49. *See also* Connecting.
Perspectives, different, 45, 161, 170, 216, 227, 363, 385, 424, 474, 661, 674. *See also* Author's perspective; Point of view.
Persuading, 65, 379, 489, 662, R39, R52–R53, R104
Play. *See* Drama.
Plot, 22, 45, 76, 132, 319, 321, 443–445, 481, 488, R16. *See also* Analyzing; Story-mapping.
cause and effect in, 444, 446, 447, 459, R7
climax of, 22, 45, 443, 481, 488, R8
conflict, 22, 45, 122, 132, 142, 481, 488, R8
endings, 459
exposition, 22, 443, R10
falling action in, 22, 45, 443, 481, 488, R11
foreshadowing, 447, 459, R12
in historical fiction, 698, 711
resolution, 22, 45, 443, 481, 488
rising action in, 22, 45, 443, 481, 488, R17
surprise ending, R20
Poetry, 189–192, 193, 236–241, R15
forms, 190, 205, 207, 563, 566, R11
narrative, 343, 346, 561, 740, R14
speaker in, 192, 391, 395, R19
strategies for reading, 189–192, 193
Point of view, 281, 362, R16
changing, 45, 161, 170, 216, 227, 363, 385, 424, 474, 661, 674
first person, 142, 275, 281, 362
third person, 281, 362
Predicting, 4, 12, 14, 25, 123, 132, 247, 248, 250, 255, 257, 333, 337, 455, 522, 528, 543, 549, 760, 779, R16
Prefixes. *See* Prefixes *under* Vocabulary Skills.
Previewing, 25, 100, 193
Print vs. nonprint media, 143, 217, 527, 537, 553, 562, 634
Prior knowledge, activating, 26, 34, 45, 64, 101, 114, 124, 154, 163, 165, 194, 205, 209, 219, 248, 264, 275, 284, 322, 333, 365, 381, 391, 402, 411, 416, 418, 447, 465, 476, 481, 512, 555, 563, 574, 580, 614, 636, 643, 653, 668, 676, 678, 700, 718, 728,

737, 740

Problem solving, 20, 340–342, 361, 386, 430–435, 653

Pronunciation, key to symbols, R5

Purpose. *See* Author's purpose; Setting a purpose for reading.

Questioning, 4, 6, 7, 9, 12, 14, 25, 104, 165, 170, 328, 364, 446, 450, R16

Questions, forming and revising, 388–390. *See also,* SQ3R.

Rate, adjusting. *See* Scanning; Skimming; Monitoring; Reading, aloud.

Reader's Notebook, 16–17, 26, 31, 34, 45, 52, 64, 67, 101, 111, 114, 121, 132, 135, 142, 154, 182–183, 194, 198, 205, 207, 209, 216, 219, 227, 247, 248, 257, 264, 272, 275, 281, 284, 287, 304–305, 322, 330, 337, 343, 346, 365, 378, 381, 385, 391, 395, 402, 409, 411, 415, 418, 424, 436–437, 446, 447, 459, 465, 473, 476, 479, 481, 488, 512, 552, 555, 561, 563, 566, 574, 579, 580, 585, 598–599, 614, 633, 636, 640, 643, 648, 653, 661, 668, 674, 678, 684, 700, 711, 718, 725, 728, 734, 737, 740 760–761, 864

strategies for using, 16–17

Reading

actively, 2–17, 25, 26, 31, 34, 45, 52, 64, 67, 100, 101, 111, 114, 121, 132, 135, 142, 154, 193, 194, 198, 205, 207, 209, 216, 219, 227, 247, 248, 257, 264, 272, 275, 281, 284, 287, 321, 322, 330, 337, 343, 346, 365, 378, 381, 385, 391, 395, 402, 409, 411, 415, 418, 424, 446, 447, 459, 465, 473, 476, 479, 481, 488, 511, 512, 552, 555, 561, 563, 566, 574, 579, 580, 585, 613, 614, 633, 636, 640, 643, 648, 653, 661, 668, 674, 678, 684, 699, 700, 711, 718, 725, 728, 734, 737, 740

aloud, 172, 193, 284, 287, 322, 426, 563, 566, 686, R103–R104

directions, 650–652

drama, strategies for, 317–321

fiction, strategies for, 25

for information, 48–51, 145–148, 201–204, 260–263, 340–342, 388–390, 462–464, 588–591, 651–652, 714–717, 718

model for, 4–15

nonfiction, strategies for, 100

poetry, strategies for, 193

skills and strategies. *See* Active reading.

Realistic detail, 555, 561, 698

Recalling facts, 11, 121, 725. *See also* Comprehension check; Test taking.

Reflecting, 20, 95, 182–183, 188, 242, 304–305, 316, 361, 436–437, 442, 506, 598–599, 610, 696, 760–761, 864

Rereading, 193, 207, 342, 714–717, 728

Root words. *See* Roots *under* Vocabulary Skills.

Scanning, 148, 389, 612, R17

Sensory detail, 205, 207, 281, 385, 415, 473, 480, 643, 648. *See also* Details, noting; Imagery, understanding.

Sequence of events, 34, 45, 148, 364, 444, R18. *See also* Chronological order.

Setting, 52, 64, 132, 183, 243, 246, 272, R18

comparing, 183, 572–587

in historical fiction, 697–698,

and mood, 246

in science fiction, 507–510

visualizing, 52, 64, 193, 411, 511, 512, 520, 524, 533, 537, 548, 552, 555, 561, 623, 706

Setting a purpose for reading, 574, 579, R18

Skimming, 715, 728, R19

Sources, 163, 219, 227, 363, 365,

multiple, 163–164, 260–263

primary, 219, 227, 261, 363, 365, 378, R16

secondary, 219, 227, 261, 363, 365, 378, R18

Specialized language, 473, 568

SQ3R (Survey, Question, Read, Recite, Review), 714–717, 728, 734

Stage direction, 318, 321, 322, 330, 331, 355–360, 511, R19

Story-mapping, 321, 322, 330, 415, 481, 488, R20. *See also* Analyzing; Charting; Summarizing.

Strategies for reading, 4–17. *See also* Active reading, strategies for.

clarifying, 4, 6, 11, 12, 13, 14, 25, 106, 193, 254, 325, 364, 368, 372, 373, 381, 385, 446, 543, 737

connecting, 4, 7, 11, 13, 14, 25, 26, 28, 29, 31, 247, 275, 281, 343, 346, 446, 511, 518, 534, 613, 708, R9

evaluating, 4, 8, 9,11, 13, 14, 15, 25, 100, 193, 209, 216, 247, 326, 364, 454, 503, 539, 544, 550, 595, 613, 778, 825, R10

monitoring, 4, 402, 409, R14

predicting, 4, 12, 14, 25, 123, 132, 247, 248, 250, 255, 257, 333, 337, 455, 522, 528, 543, 549, 760, 779, R16

questioning, 4, 6, 7, 9, 12, 14, 25, 104, 165, 170, 328, 364, 446, 450, R16

visualizing, 4, 25, 52, 64, 193, 411, 511, 512, 520, 524, 533, 537, 548, 552, 555, 561, 623, 706, R21

Strategies for reading types of literature

drama, 321

fiction, 25

informational texts, 48–51, 100, 145–148, 201–204, 260–263, 340–342, 388–390, 462–464, 588–591, 651–652, 714–717, 718

nonfiction, 100

poetry, 193

Style, analyzing, 121, 172, 272, 281, 415, 426, 488, 552, 640, 686, 725, R20

Suffixes. *See* Suffixes *under* Vocabulary Skills.

Summarizing, 258, 340–342, R20

Table of contents, using 824, 864, R20

Test-taking, practice and preparation for, 46, 94, 171, 181, 241, 258, 303, 308–313, 338, 360, 379, 410, 435, 460, 505, 587, 597, 602–607, 641, 675, 695, 735, 759, 801, 827, 863

Text organization, determining. *See* Text structure.

Text organizers, using, 145–148, 864, R21. *See also* Graphs; Map reading; Time lines.

Inquiry and Research

Author activity, 33, 47, 66, 113, 123, 134, 200, 208, 218, 229, 259, 274, 283, 339, 380, 387, 396, 461, 475, 490, 554, 584, 635, 642, 662, 713, 727, 736, 741

Authority of sources, 824, R42, R91

Author study project, 173, 427, 687

Background, building, 26, 34, 52, 67, 101, 114, 124, 135, 154, 165, 194, 205, 209, 219, 248, 264, 275, 284, 296, 322, 333, 343, 365, 381, 391, 402, 411, 418, 447, 465, 476, 481, 512, 555, 563, 574, 580, 614, 636, 643, 653, 668, 678, 700, 718, 728, 737, 770–771, 788–789, 802–803, 828–829, 844–845

Bias, recognizing, 363, 464, 824

Bibliographies, using, 824, R42. *See* Works cited list.

Card catalogs, computerized, R91

Charts, 143, 228, 586, 787, 800, 818, R96

Collaborative learning
    in groups, 31, 76, 132, 161, 216, 272, 281, 330, 378, 409, 633, 648, 711, 734
    in pairs, 45, 64, 142, 170, 198, 207, 227, 257, 287, 337, 346, 385, 395, 415, 459, 479, 561, 566, 579, 585, 661, 674, 684

Computers. *See also* Databases, using; Electronic texts; Software.
    CD-ROM, R91
    computerized card catalogs, 824, R91
    Internet, 112, 173, 228, 474, 634, 687, 712, 756, 824, R90
    Web site, R90–91

Connecting literature to life, 26, 31, 34, 45, 52, 64, 67, 76, 101, 111, 114, 121, 124, 132, 135, 142, 154, 161, 165, 170, 194, 198, 205, 207, 209, 216, 219, 227, 248, 257, 264, 272, 275, 281, 284, 287, 322, 333, 337, 343, 346, 365, 378, 381, 385, 391, 395, 402, 409, 411, 415, 418, 424, 447, 459, 465, 473, 476, 479, 481, 488, 512, 552, 555, 561, 563, 566, 579, 585, 614, 633, 636, 640, 643, 648, 653, 661, 668, 674, 678, 684, 700, 711, 718, 725, 728, 734, 737, 740

Databases, using, 263, R90–91

Dictionaries, using, 149, 289, 491, 663

Documenting sources, R43–44

Electronic texts, 260–263, R90–R91

Fact vs. opinion, 219, 227, 699, R11, R29

Five W's, R41

Graphs, 347, 641, 662, R96

Indexes, using for research, 824, R42, R91

Information
    gathering, 824, R41–42
    reading for, 48–51, 145–148, 201–204, 260–263, 340–342, 388–390, 462–464, 588–591, 651–652, 714–717, 718

Inquiry activities, 32, 33, 46, 47, 51, 65, 66, 77, 112, 113, 122, 123, 133, 134, 143, 148, 199, 200, 204, 208, 217, 218, 228, 229, 258, 259, 263, 273, 274, 282, 283, 288, 331, 338, 339, 342, 347, 379, 380, 386, 387, 390, 396, 460, 461, 464, 474, 475, 480, 489, 490, 553, 554, 562, 567, 584, 586, 591, 634, 635, 641, 642, 649, 652, 662, 712, 713, 717, 726, 727, 735, 736, 741, 786, 787, 800, 801, 818, 819, 842, 843, 856, 857. *See also* Background, building.

Internet, 112, 173, 228, 474, 634, 687, 712, 756, 824

Interviewing, 32, 65, 112, 258, 474, 586, 712, 735, 741, R105

Main idea, 49, 51, 100, 101, 104, 106, 111, 341–342, 389–390, 588–591, 636, 640, 714–717, 728, 734, 824–825

Mass Media,
    Internet, 260–263, R90–R91
    Magazines, 48–51, 145–148, 388–390, 462–464, 588–591
    Newspapers, 201–204, 340–342, 714–717
    Television, 304, 442, 634, 635

Note taking, 51, 588–591, 728, 734, 824, R43. *See also* Organization *under* Writing Skills, Modes, and Formats.

Organizing information, 49, 756, 825, R43
    alphabetically, 826
    chronologically, 121, 148, 364, 365, 380, 474
    numerically, 51, 587, 588–591, 824–825

Outlining, 51, 587, 588–591, 824–825, R43

Paired activities. *See* Collaborative learning.

Primary sources, 219, 227, 258, 261, 362–363, 823

Questions, forming and revising, 388–390, R41. *See also* SQ3R *and* Strategies for reading, questioning *under* Reading and Critical Thinking Skills.

Reading for information, 48–51, 145–148, 201–204, 260–263, 340–342, 388–390, 462–464, 588–591, 651–652, 714–717, 718

Real world link, 48–51, 145–148, 201–204, 260–263, 340–342, 388–390, 462–464, 588–591, 650–652, 714–717

Research activities, 32, 46, 51, 65, 77, 112, 122, 133, 143, 148, 199, 204, 208, 217, 228, 258, 263, 273, 282, 288, 331, 338, 342, 347, 379, 386, 390, 396, 460, 464, 474, 480, 489, 553, 562, 567, 586, 591, 634, 641, 649, 652, 662, 712, 717, 726, 735, 741, 786, 787, 800, 801, 818, 819, 842, 843, 856, 857

Research report, 820–827

Scanning, 148, 389, 612, R17

Searching the Internet, R90–R91

Secondary sources, 219, 227, 261, 362–363, 823

Skimming, 715, 728, R19

Software
    graphics, 756, 757, 758, R95–R96, R98
    multimedia authoring, R97, R99
    word processing R92–R94,

Sources
    evaluating, 824, R42, R91
    finding, 824, R42, R91
    primary and secondary, 219, 227, 258, 261, 362–363, 823

Strategies for inquiry
    main ideas, inferring, 49, R43
    skimming, 715, 728, R19
    summarizing, 258, 340–342, R43

Summarizing, 258, 340–342, R43

Text organizers, using, 145–148, 864.
    graphics, 145–148

Speaking and Listening

Index of Titles and Authors

Page numbers that appear in italics refer to biographical information.

Acknowledgments *(continued)*

Curtis Brown, Ltd.: *Nadia the Willful* by Sue Alexander, first published by Alfred A. Knopf. Copyright © 1983 by Sue Alexander. Reprinted by permission of Curtis Brown, Ltd.

Excerpt from *Nadia the Willful* by Sue Alexander, first published by Alfred A. Knopf. Copyright © 1983 by Sue Alexander. Reprinted by permission of Curtis Brown, Ltd.

Random House: "Life Doesn't Frighten Me," from *And Still I Rise* by Maya Angelou. Copyright © 1978 by Maya Angelou. Reprinted by permission of Random House, Inc.

Excerpt from "Life Doesn't Frighten Me," from *And Still I Rise* by Maya Angelou. Copyright © 1978 by Maya Angelou. Reprinted by permission of Random House, Inc.

Norma Fox Mazer: "Tuesday of the Other June" by Norma Fox Mazer, from *Short Takes,* selected by Elizabeth Segel. Copyright © 1986 by Norma Fox Mazer. Reprinted by permission of Norma Fox Mazer. All rights reserved.

Harcourt Brace & Company: "Primer Lesson," from *Slabs of the Sunburnt West* by Carl Sandburg. Copyright 1922 by Harcourt Brace & Company and renewed 1950 by Carl Sandburg. Reprinted by permission of Harcourt Brace & Company.

"Older Run," from *Puppies, Dogs, and Blue Northers: Reflections on Being Raised by a Pack of Sled Dogs* by Gary Paulsen. Copyright © 1996 by Gary Paulsen. Reprinted by permission of Harcourt Brace & Company.

Walker and Company: "Matthew Henson at the Top of the World," from *Against All Opposition: Black Explorers in America* by Jim Haskins. Copyright © 1992 by Jim Haskins. Reprinted with permission from Walker and Company, 435 Hudson Street, New York, NY 10014, 1-800-289-2553. All rights reserved.

Orchard Books: Excerpt from *Summer of Fire: Yellowstone 1988* by Patricia Lauber. Text copyright © 1991 by Patricia Lauber. Reprinted by permission of the publisher, Orchard Books, New York.

Scott Meredith Literary Agency: "Ghost of the Lagoon" by Armstrong Sperry. Copyright © 1980 by Armstrong Sperry. Reprinted by permission of the author and the author's agents, Scott Meredith Literary Agency, L.P.

Academy Chicago Publishers: Excerpt from *The Fun of It* by Amelia Earhart. Copyright © 1932 by Amelia Earhart Putnam. Reprinted by arrangement with Academy Chicago Publishers.

Viking Penguin: "Daring to Dream," adapted excerpt from *Taking Flight: My Story* by Vicki Van Meter with Dan Gutman. Copyright © 1995 by Vicki Van Meter and Dan Gutman. Used by permission of Viking Penguin, a division of Penguin Putnam Inc.

Times Newspapers: Excerpts from "A Life in the Day of Gary Paulsen" by Caroline Scott, *The Sunday Times,* November 15, 1998. Copyright © Times Newspapers Limited, 1998. Reprinted by permission of Times Newspapers Limited.

Simon & Schuster Books for Young Readers: Excerpt from *Woodsong* by Gary Paulsen. Copyright © 1990 Gary Paulsen. Reprinted with the permission of Simon & Schuster Books for Young Readers, an imprint of Simon & Schuster Children's Publishing Division.

Unit Two

Harcourt Brace & Company: "It Seems I Test People," from *When I Dance* by James Berry. Copyright © 1988 by James Berry. Reprinted by permission of Harcourt Brace & Company.

"Saguaro," from *Cactus Poems* by Frank Asch. Copyright © 1998 by Frank Asch. Reprinted by permission of Harcourt Brace & Company.

HarperCollins Publishers and Kids Can Press: "Growing Pains," from *Hey World, Here I Am!* by Jean Little. Text copyright © 1986 by Jean Little. Used by permission of HarperCollins Publishers and Kids Can Press Ltd., Toronto.

New York Times: Excerpts from "Laureate's Mission Is to Give Voice to a Nation of Poets" by Francis X. Clines, *The New York Times,* national edition, March 17, 1998. Copyright © 1998 by The New York Times Company. Reprinted by permission.

Penguin Books: "Beautiful, seen through holes" by Issa, from *The Penguin Book of Japanese Verse,* translated by Geoffrey Bownas and Anthony Thwaite (Penguin Books, 1964). Translation copyright © Geoffrey Bownas and Anthony Thwaite, 1964. Reproduced by permission of Penguin Books Ltd.

Raymond R. Patterson: "Glory, Glory . . . ," from *26 Ways of Looking at a Black Man and Other Poems* by Raymond R. Patterson. Copyright © 1969 by Raymond R. Patterson. Reprinted by permission of the author.

Don Congdon Associates: "All Summer in a Day" by Ray Bradbury, published in *Magazine of Fantasy and Science Fiction,* March 1954. Copyright © 1954, renewed 1982 by Ray Bradbury. Reprinted by permission of Don Congdon Associates, Inc.

Excerpt from "All Summer in a Day" by Ray Bradbury, published in *Magazine of Fantasy and Science Fiction,* March 1954. Copyright © 1954, renewed 1982 by Ray Bradbury. Reprinted by permission of Don Congdon Associates, Inc.

Scott Treimel New York: "Change," from *River Winding* by Charlotte Zolotow. Copyright © 1970 by Charlotte Zolotow. Reprinted by permission of Scott Treimel New York.

Excerpt from "Change," from *River Winding* by Charlotte Zolotow. Copyright © 1970 by Charlotte Zolotow. Reprinted by permission of Scott Treimel New York.

Simon & Schuster Books for Young Readers: "Chinatown," from *The Lost Garden* by Laurence Yep. Copyright © 1991 Laurence Yep. Reprinted with the permission of Simon & Schuster Books for Young Readers, an imprint of Simon & Schuster Children's Publishing Division.

"Oh Broom, Get to Work," from *The Invisible Thread* by Yoshiko Uchida. Copyright © 1991 Yoshiko Uchida. Reprinted with the permission of Simon & Schuster Books for Young Readers, an imprint of Simon & Schuster Children's Publishing Division.

Elizabeth Ellis: "Flowers and Freckle Cream" by Elizabeth Ellis, from *Best-Loved Stories Told at the National Storytelling Festival,* edited by Jimmy Neil Smith (National Storytelling Press, 1991). Copyright © Elizabeth Ellis. Reprinted by permission of the author.

Arte Público Press: "Same Song," from *Borders* by Pat Mora (Houston: Arte Público Press–University of Houston, 1986). Copyright © 1986 by Pat Mora. Reprinted with permission from the publisher.

HarperCollins Publishers: "Aaron's Gift," from *The Witch of Fourth Street and Other Stories* by Myron Levoy. Text copyright © 1972 by Myron Levoy. Used by permission of HarperCollins Publishers.

Statue of Liberty–Ellis Island Foundation: "Your Family's History Will Come Alive," from www.ellisisland.org, Web site designed and hosted by Vanguard InterActive, Inc. Copyright © 1998 The Statue of Liberty–Ellis Island Foundation, Inc. Reprinted by permission of The Statue of Liberty–Ellis Island Foundation, Inc.

Francisco Jiménez: "The Circuit" by Francisco Jiménez, *Arizona Quarterly,* Autumn 1973. Reprinted by permission of Francisco Jiménez.

BOA Editions: "the 1st," from *Good Woman: Poems and a Memoir, 1969–1980* by Lucille Clifton. Copyright © 1987 by Lucille Clifton. Reprinted with the permission of BOA Editions, Ltd., 260 East Avenue, Rochester, NY 14604.

Brandt & Brandt Literary Agents: "Western Wagons" by Stephen Vincent Benét, from *A Book of Americans* by Rosemary and Stephen Vincent Benét, first published by Holt, Rinehart & Winston, Inc. Copyright © 1937 by Rosemary and Stephen Vincent Benét, copyright renewed © 1964 by Thomas C. Benét, Stephanie B. Mahin, and Rachel Benét Lewis. Reprinted by permission of Brandt & Brandt Literary Agents, Inc.

Doubleday: "Night Journey" by Theodore Roethke, from *The Collected Poems of Theodore Roethke.* Copyright 1940 by Theodore Roethke. Used by permission of Doubleday, a division of Random House, Inc.

Scholastic: "Ta-Na-E-Ka" by Mary Whitebird, *Scholastic Voice,* December 13, 1973. Copyright © 1973 by Scholastic Inc. Reprinted by permission.

Unit Three

Houghton Mifflin Company: *The Legend of Damon and Pythias,* from *The Bag of Fire and Other Plays* by Fan Kissen. Copyright © 1964 by Houghton Mifflin Company, renewed © 1993 by John Kissen Heaslip. Reprinted by permission of Houghton Mifflin Company. All rights reserved.

Excerpts from *The Legend of Damon and Pythias,* from *The Bag of Fire and Other Plays* by Fan Kissen. Copyright © 1964 by Houghton Mifflin Company, renewed © 1993 by John Kissen Heaslip. Reprinted by permission of Houghton Mifflin Company. All rights reserved.

Andre Deutsch Ltd.: "Cricket in the Road," from *Cricket in the Road* by Michael Anthony. Copyright © 1973 by Michael Anthony. Reprinted by permission of Andre Deutsch Ltd., London.

Marian Reiner, Literary Agent: "Mean Song," from *There Is No Rhyme for Silver* by Eve Merriam. Copyright © 1962, 1990 Eve Merriam. Used by permission of Marian Reiner, Literary Agent.

Dallas Morning News: Excerpt from "Young Peer Mediators' Effectiveness Is Hard to Dispute" by Janis Leibs Dworkis, *The Dallas Morning News,* February 4, 1997. Reprinted with permission of the Dallas Morning News.

Harold Ober Associates: "The Quarrel" by Eleanor Farjeon, from *Eleanor Farjeon's Poems for Children,* first published by Lippincott, 1951. Copyright © 1951 by Eleanor Farjeon. Reprinted by permission of Harold Ober Associates Incorporated.

Lescher & Lescher: "The Southpaw" by Judith Viorst, from *Free to Be . . . You and Me,* edited by Christopher Cerf et al. Copyright © 1974 by Judith Viorst. This usage granted by permission of Lescher & Lescher, Ltd.

Literary Estate of May Swenson: "Analysis of Baseball" by May Swenson, from *American Sports Poems* (Orchard Books, 1988). Used with permission of the Literary Estate of May Swenson.

HarperCollins Publishers: "Abd al-Rahman Ibrahima," from *Now Is Your Time!: The African-American Struggle for Freedom* by Walter Dean Myers. Copyright © 1991 by Walter Dean Myers. Used by permission of HarperCollins Publishers.

Excerpts from "Abd al-Rahman Ibrahima," from *Now Is Your Time!: The African-American Struggle for Freedom* by Walter Dean Myers. Copyright © 1991 by Walter Dean Myers. Used by permission of HarperCollins Publishers.

National Geographic Society: Excerpt from "Technology Testers" by Jane R. McGoldrick, *National Geographic World*, March 1996. Reprinted by permission of the National Geographic Society.

F. E. Albi: "Street Corner Flight" by Norma Landa Flores, from *Sighs and Songs of Aztlan*, edited by F. E. Albi and J. G. Nieto. Copyright © 1975 by F. E. Albi and J. G. Nieto. Reprinted by permission of F. E. Albi, editor.

Alfred A. Knopf: "Words Like Freedom," from *Collected Poems* by Langston Hughes. Copyright © 1994 by the Estate of Langston Hughes. Reprinted by permission of Alfred A. Knopf, Inc.

Dell Publishing: "The School Play" by Gary Soto, from *Funny You Should Ask,* edited by David Gale. Copyright © 1992 by Gary Soto. Used by permission of Dell Publishing, a division of Random House, Inc.

Harcourt Brace & Company: "Ode to My Library," from *Neighborhood Odes* by Gary Soto. Copyright © 1992 by Gary Soto. Reprinted by permission of Harcourt Brace & Company.

Gary Soto: Excerpts from "Who Are Your Readers?" by Gary Soto. Text copyright © 1999 by Gary Soto. Used by permission of the author. All rights reserved.

Gary Soto and BookStop Literary Agency: "The Jacket," from *Small Faces: Stories* by Gary Soto. Text copyright © 1986 by Gary Soto. Used with permission of the author and BookStop Literary Agency. All rights reserved.

Unit Four

Random House Children's Books: "Lob's Girl," from *A Whisper in the Night* by Joan Aiken. Copyright © 1984 by Joan Aiken. Used by permission of Random House Children's Books, a division of Random House, Inc.

National Geographic Society: Excerpts from "Animals to the Rescue" by Laura Daily, *National Geographic World,* September 1997. Reprinted by permission of the National Geographic Society.

Little, Brown and Company: "My First Dive with the Dolphins," from *The Dolphins and Me* by Don C. Reed. Text copyright © 1988 by Don C. Reed. Illustrations © 1988 by Pamela & Walter Carroll. By permission of Little, Brown and Company.

"A bugler named Dougal MacDougal," from *Primrose Path* by Ogden Nash. Copyright © 1935 by Ogden Nash. By permission of Little, Brown and Company.

Simon & Schuster Books for Young Readers: "Something Told the Wild Geese," from *Branches Green* by Rachel Field. Copyright © 1934 Macmillan Publishing Company, copyright renewed © 1962 Arthur S. Pederson. Reprinted with the permission of Simon & Schuster Books for Young Readers, an imprint of Simon & Schuster Children's Publishing Division.

Henry Holt and Company: "Questioning Faces" by Robert Frost, from *The Poetry of Robert Frost,* edited by Edward Connery Lathem. Copyright © 1962 by Robert Frost, © 1969 by Henry Holt and Company, Inc. Reprinted by permission of Henry Holt and Company, Inc.

HarperCollins Publishers: "Zlateh the Goat," from *Zlateh the Goat and Other Stories* by Isaac Bashevis Singer. Text copyright © 1966 by Isaac Bashevis Singer. Used by permission of HarperCollins Publishers.

"Chang McTang McQuarter Cat," from *You Read to Me, I'll Read to You* by John Ciardi. Copyright © 1962 by John Ciardi. Used by permission of HarperCollins Publishers.

"Where the Sidewalk Ends," from *Where the Sidewalk Ends* by Shel Silverstein. Copyright © 1974 by Evil Eye Music, Inc. Used by permission of HarperCollins Publishers.

Samuel French, Inc.: *The Phantom Tollbooth* by Susan Nanus and Norton Juster. Copyright © 1977 by Susan Nanus and Norton Juster. Reprinted by permission of Samuel French, Inc. **Caution:** Professionals and amateurs are hereby warned that *The Phantom Tollbooth*, being fully protected under the copyright laws of the United States of America, the British Commonwealth countries, including Canada, and the other countries of the Copyright Union, is subject to a royalty. All rights, including professional, amateur, motion picture, recitation, public reading, radio, television, and cable broadcasting, and the rights of translation into foreign languages, are strictly reserved. Any inquiry regarding the availability of performance rights, or the purchase of individual copies of the authorized acting edition, must be directed to Samuel French, Inc., 45 West 25th Street, New York, NY 10010, with other locations in Hollywood and Toronto, Canada.

Houghton Mifflin Company and HarperCollins Publishers, London: "All That Is Gold," from *The Fellowship of the Ring* by J.R.R. Tolkien. Copyright © 1954, 1965 by J.R.R. Tolkien, copyright © renewed 1982 by Christopher R. Tolkien, Michael H. R. Tolkien, John F. R. Tolkien, and Priscilla M.A.R. Tolkien. Reprinted by permission of Houghton Mifflin Company and HarperCollins Publishers, London. All rights reserved.

Jack Prelutsky: "A silly young fellow named Ben" by Jack Prelutsky. Copyright © 1989 by Jack Prelutsky. Reprinted by permission of the author.

Virginia Hamilton: "Under the Back Porch" by Virginia Hamilton. Copyright © 1992, 1999 by Virginia Hamilton Adoff. Used by permission of the author.

Ralph M. Vicinanza, Ltd.: "The Fun They Had," from *Earth Is Room Enough: Science Fiction Tales of Our Own Planet* by Isaac Asimov. Copyright © 1957 by Isaac Asimov. Published by permission of the Estate of Isaac Asimov, c/o Ralph M. Vicinanza, Ltd.

Bilingual Press: "The Sand Castle," from *Weeping Woman: La Llorona and Other Stories* by Alma Luz Villanueva. Copyright © 1994 by Alma Luz Villanueva. Reprinted by permission of Bilingual Press/Editorial Bilingüe, Arizona State University, Tempe, Arizona.

Time: Excerpt from "Home on an Icy Planet," *Time for Kids*, March 13, 1998. Copyright © 1998 Time Inc. Reprinted by permission.

Matthew Ryan Keenan: Excerpt from "Seolforis" by Matthew Ryan Keenan. Copyright © 1998 by Matthew Ryan Keenan. Reprinted by permission of the author.

Unit Five

Keith Ross Leckie: *Words on a Page* by Keith Ross Leckie. Reprinted by permission of the author. Copyright © 1986 by Keith Ross Leckie.

Dutton Children's Books: "Bringing the Prairie Home" by Patricia MacLachlan, from *The Big Book for Our Planet*, edited by Ann Durell, Jean

Craighead George, and Katherine Paterson. Copyright © 1993 by Dutton Children's Books. Used by permission of Dutton Children's Books, a division of Penguin Putnam Inc.

Villard Books: Excerpt from *All I Really Need to Know I Learned in Kindergarten* by Robert L. Fulghum. Copyright © 1986, 1988 by Robert L. Fulghum. Reprinted by permission of Villard Books, a division of Random House, Inc.

University of Texas Press: "Sonnet 52," from *100 Love Sonnets* by Pablo Neruda, translated by Stephen Tapscott. Copyright © 1959 Pablo Neruda and Fundación Pablo Neruda. Copyright © 1986 by the University of Texas Press. Reprinted by permission of the University of Texas Press.

Agencia Literaria Carmen Balcells: "Soneto 52," from *Cien sonetos de amor* by Pablo Neruda. Copyright © 1959 Pablo Neruda and Fundación Pablo Neruda. Reprinted by permission of Agencia Literaria Carmen Balcells, S.A.

Editions Gallimard and London Management: "How to Paint the Portrait of a Bird" by Jacques Prévert, translated by Paul Dehn. Copyright © Editions Gallimard, 1949. Reprinted by permission of Editions Gallimard and London Management, Ltd., on behalf of the estate of Paul Dehn.

Michael Manning: "Flip Out!," adapted from "Flip Books" by Michael Manning. Copyright © 1986 by Michael Manning. Reprinted by permission of the author.

Jane Dystel Literary Management: "The Scribe," from *Guests in the Promised Land* by Kristin Hunter, published by Avon Books. Copyright © 1968 by Kristin E. Lattany. Reprinted by permission of Jane Dystel Literary Management, Inc.

Harold Ober Associates: "Crow Call" by Lois Lowry, first published in *Redbook Magazine,* December 1975. Copyright © 1975 by Lois Lowry. Reprinted by permission of Harold Ober Associates Incorporated.

American Library Association: Excerpt from Newbery Award acceptance speech by Lois Lowry, June 1994. The Newbery Medal is awarded annually by the Association for Library Service to Children and is a trademark of the American Library Association. Reprinted by permission of the American Library Association.

Houghton Mifflin Company: Text excerpts from *Looking Back: A Book of Memories* by Lois Lowry. Copyright © 1998 by Lois Lowry. Reprinted by permission of Houghton Mifflin Company. All rights reserved.

Professional Publishing Services Company: Excerpts from "The Dog of Pompeii," by Louis Untermeyer, from *The Donkey of God* by Louis Untermeyer. Copyright © 1932 by Louis Untermeyer. Published by arrangement with the Estate of Louis Untermeyer, Norma Anchin Untermeyer, c/o Professional Publishing Services Company. This permission is expressly granted by Laurence S. Untermeyer.

Los Angeles Times: Excerpt from "Remains of House in Oregon May Be Most Ancient in U.S." by Thomas H. Maugh II, *Los Angeles Times,* October 10, 1998. Copyright © 1998 Los Angeles Times. Reprinted by permission.

Random House: Excerpt from *Lost Worlds* by Anne Terry White. Copyright © 1941 by Random House, Inc., copyright renewed 1969 by Anne Terry White. Reprinted by permission of Random House, Inc.

Dudley Randall: "Ancestors," from *After the Killing* by Dudley Randall. Copyright © 1973 by Dudley Randall. Reprinted by permission of the author.

Henry Morrison, Inc.: Excerpt from "The First Emperor," from *The Tomb Robbers* by Daniel Cohen. Copyright © 1980 by Daniel Cohen. Reprinted by permission of the author and his agents, Henry Morrison, Inc.

Orchard Books and Stoddart Publishing Company: *Beethoven Lives Upstairs* by Barbara Nichol, illustrated by Scott Cameron. Text copyright © 1993 by Classical Productions for Children Limited. Reprinted by permission of Orchard Books, New York, and Stoddart Publishing Company Ltd., Don Mills, Ontario, Canada.

Unit Six

Greenwillow Books: "The Boy Who Flew," from *The Robber Baby: Stories from the Greek Myths* by Anne Rockwell. Copyright © 1994 by Anne Rockwell. Reprinted by permission of Greenwillow Books, a division of William Morrow & Company, Inc.

Houghton Mifflin Company: "Arachne," from *Greek Myths* by Olivia E. Coolidge. Copyright © 1949, renewed 1977 by Olivia E. Coolidge. Reprinted by permission of Houghton Mifflin Company. All rights reserved.

Scholastic: "The Story of Ceres and Proserpina," from *Favorite Greek Myths,* retold by Mary Pope Osborne. Copyright © 1989 by Mary Pope Osborne. Reprinted by permission of Scholastic Inc.

"Why Monkeys Live in Trees," from *How Many Spots Does a Leopard Have? and Other Tales* by Julius Lester. Copyright © 1989 by Julius Lester. Reprinted by permission of Scholastic Inc.

Curbstone Press: "The Disobedient Child," from *The Bird Who Cleans the World and Other Mayan Fables* by Victor Montejo, translated by Wallace Kaufman (Curbstone Press, 1991). Copyright © 1991 by Victor Montejo. Translation copyright © 1991 by Wallace Kaufman. Reprinted with permission of Curbstone Press. Distributed by Consortium.

Clarion Books/Houghton Mifflin Company: "The Bamboo Beads," from *A Wave in Her Pocket* by Lynn Joseph. Copyright © 1991 by Lynn Joseph. Reprinted by permission of Clarion Books/Houghton Mifflin Company. All rights reserved.

"The Living Kuan-yin," from *Sweet and Sour: Tales from China,* retold by Carol Kendall and Yao-wen Li. Copyright © 1978 by Carol Kendall and Yao-wen Li. Reprinted by permission of Clarion Books/Houghton Mifflin Company. All rights reserved.

Viking Penguin: *In the Land of Small Dragon* by Dang Manh Kha, as told to Ann Nolan Clark. Copyright © 1979 by Ann Nolan Clark. Used by permission of Viking Penguin, a division of Penguin Putnam Inc.

Doubleday: "King Thrushbeard," from *Grimms' Tales for Young and Old* by Jakob and Wilhelm Grimm, translated by Ralph Manheim. Copyright © 1977 by Ralph Manheim. Used by permission of Doubleday, a division of Random House, Inc.

Frederick Warne Books: "The Legend of the Hummingbird," from *Once in Puerto Rico* by Pura Belpré. Copyright © 1973 by Pura Belpré. Used by permission of Frederick Warne Books, a division of Penguin Putnam Inc.

Linda Goss: "The Frog Who Wanted to Be a Singer" by Linda Goss, from *Talk That Talk: An Anthology of African-American Storytelling,* edited by Linda Goss and Marian E. Barnes. Copyright © 1983 by Linda Goss. Reprinted by permission of the author.

BridgeWater Books: "Where the Girl Rescued Her Brother," from *The Girl Who Married the Moon,* told by Joseph Bruchac and Gayle Ross. Text copyright © 1994 by Joseph Bruchac and Gayle Ross. Reprinted by permission of BridgeWater Books, an imprint of Troll Communications L.L.C.

Art Credits

Cover

Illustration copyright © 1999 Gary Overacre.

Front Matter

ix School Division, Houghton Mifflin Company; **x** Copyright © Reggie Holladay/SIS; **xi** Courtesy of Flannery Literary; **xii** *Spring Fair, Old Westbury Gardens,* David Peikon. Acrylic on canvas, 30" × 40". Copyright © 1998, courtesy of The Mark Humphrey Gallery, Southampton, New York; **xiv** *Pushball*, Pavel Kusnetzov. Copyright © Estate of Paul Kusnetzov/Licensed by VAGA, New York, NY; **xv** Courtesy of Gary Soto; xvi *Party Animals* (1995), Julia Lucich. Pastel over acrylic, 17" × 22"; **xviii** *top* Copyright © Philip & Karen Smith/Tony Stone Images; *bottom* Karen Ahola/Houghton Mifflin Company; **xx–xxi** Photos by Gordon Lewis.

Unit One

2 *top* From the Archives of The Ninety-Nines, Inc.; *center* Detail of *La caravane* [The caravan] (1880), Alexandre-Gabriel Decamps. Musée du Louvre, Paris, Giraudon/Art Resource, New York; *bottom* Copyright © Leland Bobbe/Tony Stone Images; **3** *top* Culver Pictures; *bottom left, Tenement Flats (Family Flats)* (1934), Millard Sheets. National Museum of American Art, Washington, D.C./Art Resource, New York; *bottom right* RMIP/Richard Haynes; **18** *background* Copyright © PhotoDisc; **20** Copyright © PhotoDisc; **21** *left* School Division, Houghton Mifflin Company; *right* From *Hatchet* by Gary Paulsen. Jacket painting by Neil Waldman. Copyright © 1987 Bradbury Press; Reprinted with the permission of Simon & Schuster Books for Young Readers, an imprint of Simon & Schuster Children's Publishing Division; **23** *left to right, Wee Maureen* (1926), Robert Henri. Oil on canvas, 24" × 20". Courtesy of the Museum of American Art of the Pennsylvania Academy of the Fine Arts, Philadelphia, gift of Mrs. Herbert Cameron Morris; *Tahitian Woman and Boy* (1889), Paul Gauguin. Oil on canvas, 37¼" × 24¼". Norton Simon Art Foundation, Pasadena, California, gift of Mr. Norton Simon, 1976; *Bobby* (1939), Jack Humphrey. Collection of John Corey. Copyright © Estate of Jack Humphrey. Used by permission; *Siri* (1970), Andrew Wyeth. Tempera on panel, 30" × 30½". Collection of the Brandywine River Museum, Chadds Ford, Pennsylvania, copyright © 1970 Andrew Wyeth; **24** *Station Platform,* Dong Kingman. Hirshhorn Museum and Sculpture Garden, Smithsonian Institution, gift of Joseph H. Hirshhorn; **25** RMIP/Richard Haynes; **27** Detail of *Cake Window (Seven Cakes)* (1970–1976), Wayne Thiebaud. Courtesy of Allan Stone Gallery, New York; **30** Courtesy of Lois Lowry; **32** Edge Productions; **33** AP/Wide World Photos; **34** Detail of *Whelan's Drug Store,* Berenice Abbott. Photography Collection, Miriam and Ira D. Wallach Division of Art, Prints and Photographs, The New York Public Library, Astor, Lenox and Tilden Foundations; **35** Archive Photos; **36** Courtesy Smoky Mountain Knife Works; **47** Copyright © Richard Howard Photography; **49** Courtesy of Brad Kellogg; **66** Coppelia Kahn; **67** *background* Copyright © Eric A. Wessmann/Stock Boston; *inset right* Copyright © Jose Fuste Raga/ The Stock Market; **68–69** *background* Copyright © Hugh Sitton/Tony Stone Images; **77** School Division, Houghton Mifflin Company; **78** Willy Leon; **88**

George Janoff; **95** *top* Copyright © PhotoDisc; *bottom* Courtesy of Flannery Literary; **96** *left* From *Summer of Fire* by Patricia Lauber. Text copyright © 1991 by Patricia Lauber. Jacket photograph copyright © Erwin and Peggy Bauer. Reprinted by permission of Orchard Books, New York; *right, How to Write a Letter* by Pat Dragisic. Copyright © 1998 Franklin Watts, Inc. Used by permission of Grolier Publishing; **97** *top* Corbis-Bettmann; *bottom, Woodsong* by Gary Paulsen. Copyright © 1991 Puffin Books/Penguin USA; **99** Copyright © Ted Wood; **100** RMIP/Richard Haynes; **101** *background* Copyright © Jamie Bloomquist/Outside Images/PNI; *inset top left* Copyright © Sisse Brimberg/ National Geographic Society Image Collection; *inset bottom left* Copyright © George Holton/Photo Researchers, Inc.; **103** The Bettmann Archive; **105** Victor R. Boswell, Jr. Copyright © National Geographic Society; **109** Culver Pictures; **112** Copyright © Lawrence Migdale; **114** Jim Peaco, Courtesy of Yellowstone National Park; **115, 116–117** Copyright © Ted Wood; **117** *inset* Jim Peaco, Courtesy of Yellowstone National Park; **118–119** Copyright © Ted Wood; **119** *inset* Jim Peaco, Courtesy of Yellowstone National Park; **120** Copyright © Ted Wood; **123** Courtesy of Patricia Lauber; **124** Copyright © Joshua Singer; **133** Detail of *Tahitian Woman and Boy* (1889), Paul Gauguin. Oil on canvas, 37¼" × 24¼". Norton Simon Art Foundation, Pasadena, California, gift of Mr. Norton Simon, 1976; **134** Courtesy of Mrs. Armstrong Sperry; **135** From the Archives of The Ninety-Nines, Inc.; **136–137** Copyright © Albert L. Bresnik; **136** *top left* National Air and Space Museum, Smithsonian Institution, Washington, D.C.; **138** Corbis-Bettmann; **139** From the Archives of The Ninety-Nines, Inc.; **140–141** Copyright © Telegraph Colour Library/FPG International; **141** National Air and Space Museum, Smithsonian Institution, Washington, D.C.; **143** Copyright © Albert L. Bresnik; **144** Corbis-Bettmann; **145** *background* School Division, Houghton Mifflin Company; *bottom right* Copyright © Kevin Foster/Twenty Twenty Photography; **146–148** *background* School Division, Houghton Mifflin Company; **148** Copyright © Kevin Foster/Twenty Twenty Photography; **150** *top, middle, bottom left* Courtesy of Flannery Literary; *bottom right* Copyright © 1997 Michael Tamborrino/FPG International; **151** *top right* Courtesy of Flannery Literary; *center right* From *Dogsong* by Gary Paulsen. Jacket painting by Neil Waldman. Copyright © 1985 Bradbury Press. Reprinted with permission of Simon & Schuster Books for Young Readers, an imprint of Simon & Schuster's Children's Publishing Division; *bottom left* Copyright © 1967 James Pickerell/Black Star; *bottom right* Courtesy of Apple Computer, Inc.; **152–153** Copyright © Jeff Schultz/Leo de Wys, Inc.; **152** *top* Courtesy of Flannery Literary; **153** *top* RMIP/Richard Haynes; **154** Ruth Wright Paulsen; **163, 164, 172** Courtesy of Flannery Literary; **166–167** Sharon Hoogstraten; **173** Copyright © Jack Montgomery/Bruce Coleman, Inc.; **174** *top* Copyright © 1998 Star Tribune/Minneapolis-St. Paul; *bottom left* From *Hatchet* by Gary Paulsen. Jacket painting by Neil Waldman. Copyright © 1987 Bradbury Press; Reprinted with permission of Simon & Schuster for Young Readers, an imprint of Simon & Schuster's Children's Publishing Division; **174–175.** *Bottom right* School Division, Houghton Mifflin Company; *bottom background* Copyright © Jeff Schultz/Leo de Wys, Inc.; **175** *bottom left* Jacket painting copyright © 1989 by John Ward. Reprinted by permission of Orchard Books; *bottom center* From *The Voyage of the Frog* by Gary Paulsen. Copyright © 1989. Used with permission of Dell Publishing, a division of Random House, Inc.; *bottom right* From *Soldier's Heart* by Gary Paulsen. Copyright © 1998 by Gary Paulsen. Used by permission of Random House Children's Books, a division of Random House, Inc.; **182–185** *background* Copyright © PhotoDisc; **184, 185** School Division, Houghton Mifflin Company.

Unit Four

CALIFORNIA

Steve Bass 8th Grade Team Leader, Meadowbrook Middle School, Ponway Unified School District

Cynthia Brickey 8th Grade Academic Block Teacher, Kastner Intermediate School, Clovis Unified School District

Karen Buxton English Department Chairperson, Winston Churchill Middle School, San Juan School District

Sharon Cook Independent Consultant, Fresno Unified School District

Bonnie Garrett Davis Middle School, Compton School District

Sally Jackson Madrona Middle School, Torrance Unified School District

Sharon Kerson Los Angeles Center for Enriched Studies, Los Angeles Unified School District

Gail Kidd Center Middle School, Azusa School District

Corey Lay ESL Department Chairperson, Chester Nimitz Middle School, Los Angeles Unified School District

Myra LeBendig Forshay Learning Center, Los Angeles Unified School District

Dan Manske Elmhurst Middle School, Oakland Unified School District

Joe Olague Language Arts Department Chairperson, Alder Middle School, Fontana School District

Pat Salo 6th Grade Village Leader, Hidden Valley Middle School, Escondido Elementary School District

FLORIDA

Judi Briant English Department Chairperson, Armwood High School, Hillsborough County School District

Beth Johnson Polk County English Supervisor, Polk County School District

Sharon Johnston Learning Resource Specialist, Evans High School, Orange County School District

Eileen Jones English Department Chairperson, Spanish River High School, Palm Beach County School District

Jan McClure Winter Park High School, Orange County School District

Wanza Murray English Department Chairperson (retired), Vero Beach Senior High School, Indian River City School District

Shirley Nichols Language Arts Curriculum Specialist Supervisor, Marion County School District

Debbie Nostro Ocoee Middle School, Orange County School District

Barbara Quinaz Assistant Principal, Horace Mann Middle School, Dade County School District

OHIO

Joseph Bako English Department Chairperson, Carl Shuler Middle School, Cleveland City School District

Deb Delisle Language Arts Department Chairperson, Ballard Brady Middle School, Orange School District